THE BLACK WORKER

VOL. 7

THE BLACK WORKER FROM THE FOUNDING OF THE CIO
TO THE AFL-CIO MERGER, 1936-1955

Other volumes in this series:

The Black Worker
A Documentary History from Colonial Times to the Present

Volume **VII**

The Black Worker from the Founding of the CIO to the AFL-CIO Merger, 1936–1955

Edited by
Philip S. Foner and Ronald L. Lewis

Temple University Press, Philadelphia

Temple University Press, Philadelphia, 19122
© by Temple University. All rights reserved
Published 1983
Printed in the United States of America

Library of Congress Cataloging in Publication Data (Revised)
 Main entry under title:

The Black Worker.

 Includes indexes.

 CONTENTS: vl. 1. The Black worker to 1869.--v. 2. The Black worker during
the era of the National Labor Union --[etc.]--v. 6. The era of post-war prosperity and the Great Depression, 1920-1936.
 1. Afro-Americans--Employment. 2. Afro-Americans--Economic conditions.
3. United States--Race relations. I. Foner, Philip Sheldon, 1910-
II. Lewis, Ronald L., 1940-
HD8081.A44B56   331.6'3'96073   78-2875

ISBN 0-87722-136-7 (v. 1)   AACRI
ISBN 0-87722-197-9 (v. 7)

TABLE OF CONTENTS

PART I

THE CONGRESS OF INDUSTRIAL ORGANIZATION
AND THE BLACK WORKER, 1935-1940

PART II

THE SOUTHERN TENANT FARMERS' UNION

PART III

THE BLACK WORKER DURING WORLD WAR II

PART IV

THE AMERICAN FEDERATION OF LABOR AND THE BLACK WORKER, 1936-1945

PART V

THE POST WAR DECADE, 1945-1955

PREFACE

This is the seventh volume of THE BLACK WORKER: A DOCUMENTARY HISTORY
FROM COLONIAL TIMES TO THE PRESENT, a series which represents the first compilation of original materials to encompass the entire history of Afro-American
labor. As with the preceding volumes, the documents presented are placed in
historical context by introductions and notes. Original spellings have been
retained except where they obscure the intended meaning.

Volume 7 begins with the relations between the Congress of Industrial
Organizations and black workers. In contrast to the American Federation of
Labor, which continued its refusal to attack the color bar erected by union
affiliates, the CIO offered blacks an opportunity to make real strides toward
equality in the labor market. Led by John L. Lewis of the United Mine Workers
of America, one of the historically interracial unions, the CIO organized
America's basic industries by actively recruiting black workers with a corps
of black organizers. Since Negroes played a prominent role in the organization
of steel, auto, tobacco, transit, and other industries, Afro-American leaders
and their organizations came to view the industrial organization, as "Citizen
CIO," and such organizations as the National Association for the Advancement of
Colored People and the National Urban League were won over to the movement.
Support also came from leftist black organizations such as the National Negro
Congress and the National Negro Labor Council. During World War II, the federal
government gave further impetus to the fight against job discrimination by
establishing the Fair Employment Practices Committee to monitor hiring practices.

The editors wish to express their appreciation to those who have
assisted in the compilation of these documents. In particular, we thank the
staffs of the following institutions: American Federation of Labor Archives;
Birmingham Public Library Archives; Chicago Historical Society; Franklin D.
Roosevelt Papers, Hyde Park, New York; Fur and Leather Workers' Union Archives;
Library of Congress; Lincoln University Library, Lincoln University, Pennsyl-
vania; National Archives; Paul Robeson Archives, German Democratic Republic;
Schomburg Collection of the New York Public Library; Tamiment Institute;
University of Delaware Library; U.S. Department of Labor Library; Walter Reuther
Library of Labor and Urban Affairs, Wayne State University. Also, we are grate-
ful to Stephen Brier and to Daniel Leab for permission to reproduce a document
from LABOR HISTORY, and to H. L. Mitchell of the Historic Southern Tenant
Farmers' Union, Montgomery, Alabama, for permission to reproduce materials from
the STFU Papers and for his informative comments on those documents.

We owe a special note of appreciation to the National Association for
the Advancement of Colored People for permission to reprint articles from the
CRISIS. A number of articles from OPPORTUNITY also appear in this volume, and
they are reprinted with permission of the National Urban League. For decades
both organizations have been in the forefront of the struggle for economic
equality, and, without their cooperation, this book would not contain a representative gathering of documents.

There is no adequate phrase which conveys our gratitude to Lila Prieb
for her long labors at the typewriter, to Susan Lewis for copyediting the manu-
script, and to Gail Brittingham for her crucial assistance. We can only
reiterate our sincere appreciation. Finally, we gratefully acknowledge the
material assistance granted to this project by the Black American Studies Program,
and the College of Arts and Science at the University of Delaware.

Philip S. Foner   Ronald L. Lewis
Philadelphia, PA   University of Delaware

PART I

THE CONGRESS OF INDUSTRIAL ORGANIZATIONS
AND THE BLACK WORKER, 1935-1940

Part I

THE CONGRESS OF INDUSTRIAL ORGANIZATIONS AND THE
BLACK WORKER, 1935-1940

    In 1935, President Roosevelt signed into law the National Labor Rela-
tions Act (the Wagner Act). It gave workers the right to vote for the union
of their choice, outlawed certain unfair labor practices used by employers
against unions, and created the National Labor Relations Board with powers of
enforcement. Black leaders tried to have written into the Wagner Act a clause
barring racial discrimination by unions, but American Federation of Labor
spokesmen let it be known that with the clause included in the bill, they
would rather see the entire measure defeated, and the Wagner Act was passed
without the clause.
    The emerging industrial unions of the CIO did not oppose the antidis-
crimination clause, and most of the AFL unions which founded the CIO already
accepted the premise that there should be no racial discrimination in the
labor movement. Therefore, the CIO had a distinct advantage in its rivalry
with the AFL for enlisting black workers in the mass-production industries
where they were concentrated, especially in steel, auto, rubber, and meat-
packing.
    Beginning in 1936, the CIO conducted the most massive organizing cam-
paign in American labor history, and from the beginning the CIO opened its
doors to all workers without regard to race. At first, black community leaders
were suspicious, but it soon became clear that the CIO industrial unions would
be beneficial for black workers, and the initial skepticism of race leaders
soon changed to general support. What was true for the national leadership
did not always prevail at the local level, of course, but as black workers
were organized, local black resistance diminished.
    The impact of this open door policy soon became apparent in the steel
industry. In 1936, the CIO's Steel Workers' Organizing Committee (SWOC) undertook to organize the nation's steel workers, 85,000 of whom were black. The
two key leaders, Philip Murray and William Mitch, were both officials in the
interracial United Mine Workers of America, and they determined to follow the
UMA model of interracialism in steel. Numerous black organizers were put
into the field, and by the eve of World War II the steel industry was under
CIO control. The same course was pursued in other industries. For example,
in the Richmond, Virginia, tobacco factories, the AFL affiliated Tobacco
Workers' International rejected aid to black strikers in 1917. Therefore,
several thousand black tobacco workers were organized into the Tobacco
Stemmers' and Laborers' Industrial Union who then marched en masse into the
CIO fold. Similarly, black seamen on the East Coast had suffered discrimination from the AFL's International Seamen's Union. Therefore, in 1937, when
the CIO's National Maritime Union was formed, it followed a policy of racial
equality, and its black membership soared. Black seaman Ferdinand C. Smith,
who had helped found the NMU, became its first secretary and vice-president.
    Much of the CIO's success resulted from the active participation and
support of black organizations such as the National Negro Congress. Founded
in 1935, the NNC took as its major objective the organization of those
hundreds of thousands of unorganized black workers, and over the next few
years it fashioned an alliance with the CIO. The NNC assisted the CIO in
tobacco, auto, steel, and other industries by contributing volunteer organizers who carried the campaign deep into the black community.
    When the AFL expelled the CIO in March, 1937, the CIO had grown to
thirty-two international unions, and many blacks believed that perhaps a new
day had finally dawned for organized labor.

THE CONGRESS OF INDUSTRIAL ORGANIZATIONS AND BLACK WORKERS

1. UNITY

By Len Zinberg

Bob was a white man and he was pretty sore when he found out that the company had hired a colored helper, and he was boiling when he found out that the colored man was to work on his truck.

He thought: "They sure got a nerve taking on a black boy. And me of all the drivers getting him. They say that black boys are lazy, well this guy had better not pull any lazy stuff over my eyes. I'm no sucker."

Bob had never even spoken to a colored man before; all he knew about the colored race was from the jokes that he had heard in the movies and read in the comics.

The colored man's name was Joe and as he was sitting alongside the white man, he thought:

"Seems like I'm the only colored boy here. I bet these white men will give me the biggest and heaviest boxes to handle. Well, here's one little brown boy that won't take any truck. I want to do my share of the work, but he had better not mess with me!"

And Joe never had much to do with white men before. He had been told to leave white folks alone, not to trust any of them.

Both Work Hard

They didn't say much the first day out. The truck was loaded to the top and they both had to work hard and fast. When they got back to the warehouse, they had to work three hours overtime and they were both tired and mad--mad because they were not getting any overtime pay.

When they had finally checked out and were walking toward the subway, Joe thought: "He split the work fairly. He's as tired as I am. I think I'll say good night to him. But I bet he'll try to give me all the work tomorrow!"

Bob, the white man, said to himself: "That black boy is a good worker. I'll say good night to him. Aw, why the hell should I talk to him?"

At the subway they just looked at each other, hesitated, and went their different ways.

The next day they put in another day of hard work and when they parted at the subway, they both shyly mumbled: "So long."

Get Cut in Pay

On the third day there was a little sign over the time clock and the sign read that, due to business being bad, there would be a 10 per cent cut in all wages, beginning next week. The boss "hoped that the workers would be willing to do their share in keeping the business running."

The other six men that worked on the trucks came over and stood next to Bob as they read the notice. Everybody was mad as the devil. Bob said: "What the ____. This is the second cut we've had in three months!"

Another fellow said: "At this rate we'll be paying them for letting us work here."

Joe said: "Seems kind of funny that they aren't making any money. Here we been working overtime without pay. They must be busy. If this is their slack season, I'd sure hate to be working here when they're busy!"

"We all know they're busy," Bob said. "They're just taking advantage of us because we didn't say anything when they gave us that other cut. I say we ought to strike and not only fight this cut, but demand that we get our full wages back again! After all, even our full wages weren't much."

And the white men and the colored man yelled: "Yes, we'll strike!"
    As they began to make picket signs and form a committee to see the
boss, Bob looked at Joe and thought: "They say that colored boys sometimes
scab." He looked fiercely at Joe and said: "You know, we all have to stick
together, that's the important thing."

Black and White Picket

    "Yeh, we all have to stand together," Joe said, looking him squarely
in the eyes. "It's hard for a white man to find work, but it's a damn sight
harder for a colored man to get work. This strike has to be a success. Nobody had better scab!" And he flexed his mighty muscles.
    "That's right, we had better not catch anyone scabbing," Bob said.
"It's a sure way to land in the hospital," and he smacked his fist against
the palm of his hand.
    Joe and Bob went outside and did picket duty for an hour and then two
other men walked the picket line.
    When the boss heard about the strike, he said to his partner: "I told
you they wouldn't stand for another cut; now what are we going to do? If
those trucks don't move today, we stand to lose fifteen hundred bucks."
    The partner shook his fat head. "Don't get excited. There are ways
of breaking strikes. What's the name of the colored man we hired a couple of
days ago?"
    "Joe. Why?"
    "Well, if we can get one truck moving, that will take the fight out
of the others. I got an idea that maybe we can get Joe to take out a truck.
I'll call him up here."

Boss Offers Joe a Raise

    When Joe heard that the boss wanted to see him, he looked at Bob and
the other men and shrugged his shoulders, and finally said: "I guess I'll
see what he wants anyway."
    The others didn't say anything, but their silence told him plenty.
    When he came into the office, the boss offered him a cigar, and the
partner said:
    "Joe, you know it's kind of hard for colored boys to get work. Now,
the boys say we've treated them unfair, but you know that ain't so. You
know, too, even though I'm a white man, I got to say this: that those white
boys don't give you a square deal.
    "See me, I'm a friend of the colored people. Why, some of my friends
are colored people. What I'm driving at is this: we'll give you a five-
dollar raise in salary and a bonus of fifty dollars if you'll take out one
of the trucks. What do you say?"
    Joe said slowly:
    "Here's what I say: I could use that extra money, but I'm no rat,
see? Those boys treated me fairly. Both of our backs hurt just as much at
the end of the day. You worked the white boys as hard as you did me. It
doesn't make any differenc if your muscles are black or white, it still makes
you tired juggling cases all day.
    "I'm not sure whether the white workers are my friends or not, but I
know that you are not a friend of mine! Working me, and rest of us like
horses." Joe had more to say, but he knew that it was a waste of breath, and
he suddenly turned and walked out of the office.

    "Well," the boss said to the partner, "that certainly was a smart idea
you had. What now? We have to get those trucks moving by tonight."
    "Listen," his partner said, opening the telephone book, "there are
only eight of them. We'll call up one of these strikebreaking detective
agencies and they'll send over a couple of guards who will beat those strikers.
It will be worth the hundred bucks it will cost us."
    "And if that doen't work?"
    "Then we'll settle the strike. But it will work. These strikebreakers
are tough babies, mostly a bunch of thugs and ex-cons."

Home Problems Discussed

Downstairs as Joe and Bob were eating their lunch, Joe told him what happened. "You sure told them off," Bob said. "You know, I bet my wife wouldn't like this idea of striking so much. We need the dough at home. But heck, we have to be men, too."

"I got a wife and two kids," Joe said.

"I've got one kid and one coming," Bob said.

They both looked at each other in surprise. The white man thought: "Why, that poor guy is in the same fix as I am. I bet he has to walk the kid at night and argue with the landlord, just like me. Just like me."

The black man thought:

"The poor devil. His wife will nag him about this. Lord, I bet he has a pile of bills waiting for him at home, too. And will I have to do some quick explaining to my wife!"

Bob said: "It looks like we're right in the same boat. Here, you want some pork sandwiches? The wife gave me too many."

"Pork?" Joe said, smiling, "Say, that's like candy to me. Here, I got a lot of chocolate cake. You want some?"

"There's nothing I like better than to wrap myself around some cake."

Thugs to Break Strike

While they were eating and telling each other what good cooks their wives were, a flashy car drove up in front of the building and three hard-looking men got out. They were big men with noses that were slightly flat and ears that were out of shape. Joe put down his sandwich and said: "Looks like trouble is about to tap us on the shoulder."

"Tap us! Trouble is going to slap us on the shoulder!" Bob said getting to his feet. Joe got up too and they watched one of the thugs walk over and bump into a picket and yell: "Why don't you look where you're walking, you ____!" Then he clipped the picket on the jaw and knocked him down.

Joe and Bob started toward the thug. The thug saw two men, a black man and a white man, running toward him. He saw two fists, a black one and a white one, come sailing through the air, and after that he saw nothing but the stars and the moon and the sun, all going around and around at a great speed. "You got a good punch, Joe," Bob said.

"You're no push-over," Joe said, smiling. Bob pointed to where some of the other men were battling with the thugs. "Come on, pal, let's go over and knock off a few more of these yeggs. It's great for your appetite!"

Joe said: "Buddy, I'm on my way! I like my yeggs scrambled, how about you?"

They both laughed and then they shook hands. As they were running toward the fight, the white man said: "You know, you're a square guy."

"You're kind of regular yourself," the black man said.

THE END

Baltimore Afro-American, January 16, 1937.

2. ALABAMA MINE STRIKE FIRM AS ARBITRATION HANGS FIRE

By Beth McHenry

Bessemer, Ala., June 13.- While union officials talk over plans for a strike settlement with the mediation board of state and federal representatives, the 2,500 striking ore miners continue determined against any settlement with the Tennessee Company which will compromise their demands for continuance of the hourly wage rate and no layoffs.

The ore miners under the leadership of the Mine, Mill, and Smelter Union struck the T.C.I. (U.S. Steel) mines here June 1 when the company levied a new plan of work providing for tonnage rate wages, mass layoff,

speed up and longer hours. The Tennessee Company officials called it an
"incentive plan" to make the men work harder so that the company's orders will
increase and the men can earn more money. It provides for the layoff of 500
miners in the seven live mines which stretch chain fashion along the ridge of
Red Mountain here.

Ambush shooting along the roads leading to Muscoda, Wenonah and Ishkooda
mines has been identified by Newcomb Barco, federal mediator, as the work of
private detective agencies and mercenary thugs, bent on creating an atmosphere of terror in order to sell their "protective" services to the company.

Miners Shot

Richard Holt, Negro union miner is in a serious condition at the T.C.I.
Fairfield Hospital. Holt was shot at Muscoda mine on the evening of the first
day of the strike. Since the beginning of the strike eight persons have been
shot along the mine ridge. Five of these were company deputies. The union
men shot in self-defense when company thugs opened fire.

Pete Casey, Negro union miner, was severely beaten by company cops
along the road leading to Wenonah mine on the night of June 3. Casey was
stopped in the road by three men in a car who said they were police. Searching
the miner, they located a union card in his pocket. They then jumped on him,
kicking and beating him unmercifully.

Company thugs and provocateurs have penetrated the mine workers'
villages, attempting to destroy the strike by acts of violence. McDuff men
have been seen in the neighborhood of the mines. The McDuff National Detective
Agency was one of the most active forces in the breaking of the last ore
strike back in the spring of 1934. McDuff, who was transferred from the police
department to the private detective office by the Tennessee Coal Iron and
Railroad Company and Republic Steel, took a prominent part in the preparation
and carrying out of 23 bombing frameups against members of the Smelters Union.

The mines have been shut down since the first day of the strike.
T.C.I officials have issued statements to the effect that the closing down was
a move on the part of the company to protect its "loyal workers." Because of
the scarcity of loyal workers, union miners state that the company's reason
for shutting down is because there are not enough scabs in Bessemer to operate
any part of the mines.

The strikebreaking program of the company, built up over a period of
two years, fostered the setting up and growth of the "Brotherhood," or
company union.

Daily Worker, June 4, 1936.

3.   'BLACK WORKER' LAUDS THOMAS AS CHAMPION OF NEGRO CAUSE

High tribute to Norman Thomas as a champion of the cause of the Negro
people was paid the Socialist candidate for President in a laudatory article
in the current issue of the "Black Worker," official organ of the Brotherhood
of Sleeping Car Porters. The Brotherhood which recently received an international charter from the American Federation of Labor, is a militant union
whose fight against the railroad magnates has attracted world-wide attention.[1]

The "Black Worker" said:

"As chairman of the Emergency Committee for Strikers Relief, Norman
Thomas has played one of the most effective roles of any citizen in public
life in helping the workers and their families in strikes. He has gone to
the aid of distressed workers' families in all parts of the country, in all
types of industries, without ever asking the question as to what is their race,
religion, nationality or politics.

"He can be found not only on the platform proclaiming the cause of the
exploited and oppressed strikers but also on the picket line too, and, taking
his turn before the courts for alleged infraction of the city ordinances
because he refused to desert the strikers.

"There is unquestionably no white man in America who is more courageous

and honest in championing the cause of the Negro people than Norman
Thomas."

Socialist Call, September 19, 1936.

4. LABOR LEAGUE

Chicago.-- A. Philip Randolph, national president of the Brotherhood
of Sleeping Car Porters and famous Negro unionist, has accepted the chairman-
ship of the Labor League for Thomas and Nelson. [2]
Randolph was one of the founders of the Brotherhood and led in the
fight against the Pullman Company, one of the most ruthless corporations in
the country. Under his leadership, the porters have raised their living
standards.
Speaking of the Socialist candidate, Randolph said:
"As chairman of the Emergency Committee for Strikers' Relief, Norman
Thomas has played one of the most effective roles of any citizen in public
life in helping the workers and their families in strikes. He has gone to
the aid of distressed workers' families in all parts of the country.
"There is unquestionably no white man in America who is more courageous
and honest in championing the cause of the Negro people than Norman Thomas."
Members of the national organizing committee of the Labor League
include George Baldanzie, vice president of the United Textile Workers; George
W. Bookuff, Amalgamated Assn. of Iron, Steel and Tin Workers; Eugene Cooney,
president Local 1135 Int'l. Assn. of Machinists; Frank Crosswaith, Chairman
Negro Labor Committee; Franz Daniel, Amalgamated Clothing Workers.
Jerome Davis, president American Federation of Teachers; Murray Gross,
Int'l. Ladies' Garment Workers' Union, Howard A. Kester, Southern Tenant
Farmers' Union; Leo Krzycki, Steel Workers' Organizing Committee; David
Lasser, president Workers' Alliance of America ; John C. Lawson, president
Quarry Workers' International.
Edward Levinson, American Newspaper Guild; James W. Miller, Brotherhood
of Locomotive Engineers; H. L. Mitchell, secretary, Southern Tenant Farmers'
Union; Alan Strachan, United Automobile Workers; and B. J. Widick, Editor,
"Rubber Worker." [3]
Headquarters for the Labor League, for Thomas and Nelson, are located
in room 721, 549 Randolph St., Chicago, Ill.

Socialist Call, October 10, 1936.

5. COLORED LABOR

Finds C. I. O. Free From Race Discrimination

From The Afro-American, Baltimore, Md.

Discussing the conflict between the American Federation of Labor and
the Committee for Industrial Organization, Victor H. Daniel, former president
of Cardinal Gibbons Institute, lauded the latter as the real opportunity for
colored workers in the labor union movement.
Mr. Daniel, who was guest speaker before the International Union of
Operating Engineers, spoke on "The Significance of the Conflict Between the
American Federation of Labor and the Committee for Industrial Organization."
"An impartial survey," Mr. Daniel said, "will show that the American
Federation of Labor has failed repeatedly to accord to colored labor the protection which its constitution promises. It is interesting to note that in
1886, when the American Federation of Labor was in its swaddling clothes, it
was rather anxious for the support that it could get from colored labor.

"Here in Baltimore, a colored delegate from Buffalo to an American Federation of Labor convention was carried on the shoulders of white men around the hall in which the meeting was held after he had made a speech in which he prophesied that colored labor would support the infant organization."

In pointing out the policy of the Committee for Industrial Organization, even in the South, Mr. Daniel stated that a district president of its largest local in Alabama is a colored man.

"It is particularly significant in this case," he said, "because after all it is what stand any American institution is willing to take toward the colored citizen in the South that will have to serve as its badge of sincerity towards him.

"Out on the west coast, colored workers are fully integrated in all the unions under jurisdiction of the Committee for Industrial Organization. The same thing is true here in Baltimore."

In describing the basic differences between the American Federation of Labor, headed by William Green, and the Committee for Industrial Organization, headed by John L. Lewis, Mr. Daniel stated that there were other vital reasons why we should be aligned with the Committee for Industrial Organization.[4]

"The Committee for Industrial Organization stands for the development of the various crafts into one big union—that is, along vertical lines and one union for industry. The American Federation of Labor stands, with but few exceptions, for organization by crafts—that is, along horizontal lines."

"Both Messrs. Green and Lewis," the speaker said, "rose from the mining ranks, and this fact is a splendid tribute to American democracy. But the difference between the leaders is that while Mr. Green stands for the old order which depends upon conciliatory tactics, Mr. Lewis stands for definite changes to the new order created by mechanization, technological improvements and mass production.

"He sees that this order means the passing of the skilled worker and wants to prepare the American workman for the titanic struggle that is upon him.

"Regardless of the outcome of the present conflict, I think that labor can learn a very definite lesson from it. Mr. Lewis and those standing with him are determined to work for superior advantages for the men and women who must labor for a living. Colored labor must do likewise.

"Colored labor should concern itself with the quality and quantity of preparation that young men and women are receiving in school. Further, it must seek and find the way to open new channels in the industrial field for them."

United Mine Workers Journal, January 1, 1937.

6. C.I.O. AUTO UNION WILL NOT TOLERATE
NEGRO DISCRIMINATION, MARTIN SAYS

President of Growing Union Assails Jim Crow
In Letter to Roy Wilkins of N.A.A.C.P.—
Spikes Ford-Inspired Rumors

By Ben Davis, Jr.[5]

Discrimination against Negro members in the United Automobile Workers Union, an affiliate of the C.I.O., will definitely not be tolerated, according to Homer Martin, general president of the union.

The statement was made in a letter addressed to Roy Wilkins, assistant secretary of the National Association for the Advancement of Colored People.

The letter, made public here yesterday, was in answer to an inquiry of Wilkins in connection with rumors that separate Jim Crow locals of the union were being organized in the Ford auto plant and Negro workers had been omitted from the seniority rules at the Chrysler factory.

"The U.A.W.A. is very emphatic and pronounced in its attitude on the matter of color lines," Martin declared.

"We stand for the full protection of the Negro worker by the union in every way. We also do not believe in, nor will we stand for, the establishment of separate Negro locals."

NO FOUNDATION

"With direct reference to the two instances where the color line seems to have been raised in the U.A.W.A., let me say that in the Chrysler Corporation seniority applies to all employees regardless of race, color or creed, and the rumor that Ford Negro employees have been called together in separate groups seems to be entirely without foundation," the letter continued.

Earlier, Wilkins explained to the Daily Worker that rumors of discrimination against Negro workers by the C.I.O. affiliate had been brought to him by a "prominent person" during his recent visit to Detroit.

He immediately directed a letter to Pres. Martin, later learning that the source of his information had been in the pay of the multi-millionaire Ford Company.

Almost simultaneously with this rumor reaching Wilkins, there appeared in the Chicago Defender, nationally circulated Negro newspaper, an article boosting Henry Ford as the "friend of the Negro people" and urging Negroes to "back Ford in his anti-labor war on the U.A.W.A. The article which appeared in the April 3, issue of the Defender was signed by V. Bertram Marion, and syndicated in about 110 Negro newspapers.

RAPPED BY LABOR GROUP

The Negro Labor Assembly of Harlem representing 40,000 organized Negro workers two weeks ago denounced the article as "an attempt to make strike-breakers and scabs of Negroes and to divide them from their white fellow workers."

Martin's letter spiking these groundless Ford-inspired rumors against the C.I.O. affiliate, went on to say further:

"There has not been a single instance where Negro workers have not been welcomed into the local unions and given full protection. In addition to that the Negro worker is always welcome into the membership meeting without being segregated. I have made many pronouncements on this matter clarifying the constitution which states 'that the membership of the union is open to workers regardless of race, color, creed or political affiliation.'

FIGHT FOR NEGRO

"In one instance, at least one of our local unions threatened to go on strike when one Negro worker had his wage rate lowered. The management acceded to the threat of the local union and this Negro brother was restored to his former rate of pay.

"The U.A.W.A., along with the Committee for Industrial Organization is very anxious to collaborate in erasing in the minds of the workers of this country the prejudice arising from race distinction. Our program comprehends the elimination of prejudice as well as discrimination and proposes to protect the Negro workers with the full strentgh of our union.

"I hope this statement will clarify this situation as regards the U.A.W.A. and I shall be glad to look personally into any reported discrimination.

"With you, looking forward to a new day for all workers regardless of race, color or creed."

Daily Worker, May 1, 1937.

7. INTERVIEW WITH HENRY JOHNSON, 1937 [6]

I've seen a lot of things, I've roamed all over this country--done just about everything from picking cotton to organizing for the C.I.O. I make friends in a town and when I leave--that's a closed book. I never write back. My wife's got a yearning for New York but it doesn't mean a thing to me.

I was born in Siblo, Texas. Never heard of the place? No, it's not on the map. It's a delta in the Brazzos Bottom between [the] Colorado and Brazzos Rivers, 35 miles from the Gulf and 75 miles from the Louisiana state line. . . . My folks were farmers. They had 11 children, eight boys and three girls. I was the ninth. We had our own farm and raised cotton and corn but we never made enough to pay our debts. Every winter my father and four or five of my brothers had to go to town to do plastering and brick laying to make money and pay off our debts.

Right after the Civil War, the slogan among white folks coming into the South was "A double team of mules, a league of land and a nigger wench." There was a large family of Insulls that lived in Missouri. They came to Missouri from England by way of New England. The men folks left their families in Missouri and came down into Texas where they got themselves Negro concubines. My grandfather was a child out of one [of] those unions. He hated the Insulls so much that he changed his name to Johnson. There are still plenty of Negro Insulls around Port Arthur. I've got grand uncles living yet who go by the name of Insull. Between the Insulls and their in-laws, the Howards, all the Negroes are kin to each other. There are very few whites in this area. This the the "black delta" of Texas where they never take the census. Just as in the Mississippi delta, nobody knows how many Negroes are there.

The Insulls sent many of their bastered [sic] children and grand children to school. If Insull Negroes from the farms got in trouble in the towns, the [white] Insulls would see that they got home safely; nobody could lynch an Insull "nigger" but an Insull. Arrest laws were very lax. A murder charge where one Negro had killed another would be vacated if the murderer didn't show up in "Corporation" (city) limits inside 2 years. I've heard many a man turn down a ride to town because "I done kilt dat man, I can't go to 'Corporation' till next yeah."

We had to leave Siblo and go to San Antonio when I was nine years old. My brother went to a small town to buy something and a white man kicked our dog. My brother hit him and he beat my brother with an axe handle. Then papa went to town and beat the white man up and stomped his teeth out in the road.

After papa came home, our only white neighbor came over. He and my father were strong friends. They grew up together and worked in the oil fields, logging camps, and I.W.W. together. Our two families helped each other pick cotton and harvest the crops. My father and his white friend used to ride down to the Mexican border at Laredo, Texas where the Mexicans worked for 25¢ a day and 50¢ was good money. They used to herd wild horses and cows and brand them with the buyer's brand as they sold them. They would jump across the Rio Grande River for 50¢ a head. Papa and this white man would drive their herds 65 and 70 miles to the cities and sell them to the farmers and share-croppers for fifteen to twenty dollars a head on the installment plan. Whatever they got as down payment, say, anywhere from two and a half to five dollars usually closed the deal. The law never bothered them about getting cattle and selling them this way. In Texas any man who had 25 or so head of his won could go in another man's herd and put his brand on all unbranded horses and cows and nothing could be done about it.

I know down South [Papa] was called a "bad nigger!" That was because he was very militant and a member of the I.W.W. He was always in trouble in the sawmills and logging camps. But he was an expert with a revolver and the white folks were scared of him. He liked to show off too. He'd go to little towns on Sundays and fellows would throw up six tomato cans and he'd shoot holes in all six before they fell. He used to say, "If a man shot me six times through the heart, I'd kill him before I fell." He would have, too. He had a good education and even taught at Wiley but they kicked him out because he was an atheist. His relatives sent him to Prairie View College.

Well this white man [the neighbor] came to tell my father that they
were planning to lynch him. Papa gave all my brothers a gun and decided to
barricade himself in the house and fight it out. Papa was hotheaded and mama
always did the thinking. She and this white man persuaded him to leave. We
started to go to this white neighbor's house. Then we knew they would look
for us there so we lit across the fields. We went to a pond in some woods back
of our house and got in up to our noses. It was dark by this time. The mob
came and shot into the house until it burned down while all 13 of us watched
from the pond. We stayed in the pond for eight hours. Then our neighbor came
and loaded us on his wagon and drove 15 miles through the bottoms to the mainline railroad at Columbus. We couldn't go to Sardine Switch, which was five
miles from Siblo because the train didn't come there but once a week. That
was on Fridays and it stayed over night and left on Saturday. He [the white
neighbor] sent us to San Antonio on the train.

Two weeks later his own brother-in-law killed him when they found out
he had helped us get away. We didn't hear from Siblo for a long time and it
was about a year before we knew that he had been killed.

I've been on my own since I was 13. By that time I was going around
with my father on bricklaying and plastering jobs. We belonged to the union--
Oh' we didn't go to meetings--the man just came around and collected our dues.
I was getting $1.15 an hour and papa was getting $1.70. About eight years
later when I was working for Henry Ford, a foreman found my old union card and
I was fired after being on the job only six months. Then I did plastering
there in Detroit and worked as a general mechanic at an auto sales company.
Off and on while I was in New York I did plastering. That's when I got a
chance to go back to school. I was in a Seventh Day Adventist school there.

I went as far as the 11th grade. When I went to New York I finished
high school, that was in 1927. I traveled around all out in the east with a
quartet that we first organized in Huntsville. We had a quartet and an orchestra then and entertained at meetings and sang once over the radio in Chattanooga. We sang over the radio in New York too, over station WCJU on the
opening night. I was singing bass then--I don't sing anything now.

I've been in two race riots. They were hell! One was in Oklahoma City.
I had gone there from Huntsville. Didn't stay long though. In both cases the
incident which strated the rioting was trivial, but conditions were so bad and
the tension so great that it was like touching a match to a powder keg. In
Oklahoma City, things were real bad. The Negroes were very poorly paid.
Everything was bought on the installment plan. All kinds of collectors came
to the Negro homes, the "rug man," "curtain man," "bedspread man," "insurance
man," etc. These, of course, were all white. If a customer was unable to pay
one of his installments when it was due, he was threatened and told "You'd
better have that money by Friday," or something like that. If there was no
money forthcoming on Friday, the collector might, and often did, pick up a
broom or mop handle and beat the housewife. Nothing could be done--there was
no one to protest to.

The Negroes lived on the east side of the railroad tracks, the whites
on the west side. One day a Negro who worked for a white family had an argument with a white man about parking space for his "white folk's buggy." They
fought--the Negro was lynched and the mob headed for "niggertown." The Negroes
barricaded themselves in their shacks and fought off the mob with stones,
sticks, pots, pans, bottles, kettles, etc. It was hard for the white snipers
to get close enough to shoot anybody. If a brave mobster did come close, somebody would come down the back steps, slip up behind him and "open his neck"
with a razor. The whites set fire to some of the shacks which belonged to the
Union Pacific Railway Co. About 75 of them burned down in almost no time.
The Negroes were desperate by now and decided to die fighting, if necessary.
They crossed the tracks with all sorts of arms--axes, guns, sticks, stones,
etc. They gained the offensive against the whites and as they went they broke
into hardware stores and stocked themselves with guns and ammunition. They
took delight in smashing plate glass show-windows--they set fire to business
buildings and homes. The Negroes had control and then the state troops came.
More Negroes were killed then than during the rioting. The soldiers were
ruthless--they shot every Negro they saw no matter which way he was running.
I saw a soldier stop a colored woman and demand to know where she was going.
When she answered, "that's my business," he knocked her down and beat her
senseless with the butt of his rifle. The spirit of the Negroes was completely

broken. Men who had, an hour before, been in the thickest of the fight were
cowarded down and shrinking and whimpering in corners and under houses like
dogs that have been whipped. Many Negroes moved to California and other
western states. At this time I left and went to Detroit.

In the Houston riot, the situation was much the same--great tension
between the races--the Negroes living under a terrible strain. It was a
common thing for Negroes to be short-changed on the street cars. One either
had the exact fare or said nothing when he was short-changed. On this particular day, a colored woman who had been short-changed argued with the conductor. When she got off the car, he struck here on the head with an iron crank
or lever. A Negro soldier, one of those stationed just on the outskirts of
the city (this was during or right after the War), intervened. The whites on
the car rushed him and he ran back to the barracks.

I was going across a street in the evening when I saw a group of white
men armed with clubs. One of them yelled "There's a nigger!" and they started
towards me. I got out in the middle of the street. It was simply paved with
loose stones. I began throwing these and running back toward the colored
section of the city. I finally got away from this gang and met hordes of
Negroes and soldiers (colored) coming to fight the whites. They built barricades in the streets. The soldiers directed the fighting. When the rioting
was finally quieted down, the first papers off the press stated that at least
a hundred people had been killed and many wounded. These papers disappeared
from the newsstands, and the later editions said 19 were killed and 100 injured. I know that there were more than 100 killed and hundreds wounded.
That was my first knowledge of the freedom of the press to distort and falsify
the news. A reign of terror set in. Negroes were picked up indiscriminately
and beaten brutally. I caught a train and left. Now if a Houston Negro wants
to try on a hat before he buys it, he goes to Dallas to shop.

Yes, I traveled around a lot. I guess I'm like my father--an adventurer.
After a year of college I did some plastering for a year. Then in 1930
I went back to City College in New York and finished in 1934. Off and on from
1932 to 1934 I was an organizer for I.W.O. I had been down in Baltimore, Norfolk and Richmond organizing longshoremen. I got married in 1934. I met my
wife through her brother who went to school with me at City College. She'd
been to school at an American Missionary College at Berrien Springs, Michigan.

I came to Chicago late in 1934 and organized for I.W.O. for 13 months.
In 1936 I started organizing for C.I.O. in steel--now here I am packing.

This version of the Works Progress Administration interview is from Stephen
Brier (ed.), "Labor, Politics, and Race: A Black Worker's Life," 23 (Summer
1982):416-21. Reprinted with permission of *Labor History* and Stephen Brier.

8. NEGRO, WHITE WORKERS JOIN IN VA. STRIKE

CIO Union Unites All Workers in Demand for More Pay

By Alexander Wright

NORFOLK, Va. Aug. 19.--The Workers of the M.F.G. Co., members of the
Veneer Box and Barrel Workers Union, CIO, began their strike as a sitdown,
the first of its kind in this city, with complete solidarity between the Negro
and white workers.

Now in its fifth day, the strike has kept the plant closed despite the
arrest of 72 strikers.

The sitdown was started by the Negro workers but was soon joined by all the white workers in the plant. In the first attempt to break the solidarity of the workers the company called upon police who arrested 72, all Negroes. The white workers, however, refused to be driven back to work and walked out of the plant 100 per cent.

The arrest developed still greater solidarity among the workers. A Negro member of an A.F. of L. union gave a property bond to bail out the CIO members. A white business man put up the remainder of the needed bail. At the police court still more unity was displayed next morning when a Negro and white lawyer appeared to defend the strikers.

MARCH TOGETHER

But the greatest example of unity was when the white workers followed the Negroes to court and back to the hall where 16 joined the union and took cards to canvass all the remaining white strikers for union membership.

The strike committee is composed of white and Negro workers. Mrs. Lena Jarvis, a Negro, is chairman of the strike committee. Although 80 per cent of the workers are men, she was elected unanimously.

The factory is one of the worst slave mills in Norfolk. It has been operating for over 40 years at wages as low as 15 to 20 cents an hour for skilled labor and at 20 and 22 and one half cents for machine operators. There are no toilets or washrooms, no safety devices and no regular hours. The workers are prepared to stay out for six months, they say, if their demands aren't granted.

A unity meeting is scheduled for Monday in support of the strikers. There will be representatives of the Non-Partisan Voters League, Socialist Party, Communist Party and trade unions to form a citizens committee in support of the strikers.

There is a probability that the strike will spread to three other southern cities.

Daily Worker, August 20, 1937.

9. LOOSE TALK ABOUT LABOR

There has been a lot of loose talk about the "menace" of militant labor organization in the past year.

Significantly enough, much of the talk about this "menace" has come from those who stand to lose something from the increasing power of those who toil.

There are far too many Negroes mouthing the same jargon, which is obviously culled from the headlines and editorials of the reactionary daily newspapers.

The worker has no power, no security save that which he gains through organization. As an individual he is helpless against great aggregations of corporate wealth.

The most effective weapon these workers' organizations have is the right to strike, hence the reactionary hue and cry for outlawing strikes and "regulating" labor unions.

It is admittedly annoying and inconvenient to employers and the general public when thousands of men stop work.

On the other hand, it has all along been much more annoying and inconvenient to the workers to have plants shut down or move away and leave workers to shift for themselves as best they can.

It is a simple matter to appraise the cost of a strike; it is not so easy to appraise the cost of a lockout, a factory closing or a factory flight to another part of the country.

Workers who lose their jobs through these lockouts, closings and flight have wives, children and dependents whose support is suddenly shut off. The general public has to support them on relief until they can find other work, if any.

Recently much has been made over the breaking of a few windows and the overturning of a few automobiles, and the losses in wages to striking workers, but very little has been said about the gains to the successfully striking workers in increased wages, decreased work periods, seniority rights, abrogation of the "right" of employers to fire (starve) workers without explanation, and the acquirement of new safeguards to health and human happiness.

Many middle-class Negroes have viewed the efforts to organize Negro labor with almost much alarm as the employers of Negro labor. Yet in steel, automobiles, coal mining and a dozen other industries where Negroes are largely employed, recent labor organization drives have increased the purchasing power of these Negroes by millions of dollars.

Hundreds of humble Negro workers are today organizers and officials of labor unions and sit on the committees which bargain with employers for a higher standard of living and more human conditions of work.

These Negroes have attained new dignity and importance, and their association as equals with white labor has advanced race relations farther than anything that has happened in recent years.

Yet there are those who would scare Negro labor into opposing labor organization with white labor and bolster their fears with loose talk.

There must come a larger realization on the part of Negro leaders and educated folk that a revolution is taking place in American life; that Labor is on the road to rule, and that the day of unrestricted individualism on the part of employers is ended.

To advise Negro labor avoid the responsibility and opportunity which is now in its grasp is little short of criminal.

Pittsburgh Courier, August 28, 1937.

10.   CIO DRIVES BRING HOPEFUL DAWN FOR NEGRO LABOR

By Ben Davis, Jr.

In the great organizational drives of the CIO is the dawn of a new hopeful day for the Negro worker.

Jim-Crowed, segregated, discriminated against and barred from countless labor unions by the reactionary leaders of the A.F. of L., the Negro worker has been made the worst victim of the anti-labor policies of the reactionary capitalists.

Precisely what the industrial barons, assisted by the labor-splitting William Green and his cohorts, did not wish is taking place: The CIO is bringing Negro workers into the organized labor movement on a basis of full equality with all other workers, regardless of race, creed or color.

Since 95 per cent of the Negro people are workers, any movement which raises labor's standard of living, at the same time bursting the discriminatory chains which have long shackled Negro workers, strikes at the whole super-structure of political, social and economic inequality forced upon an entire race.

No one realizes this more clearly than the Negro's bitterest enemies, who are in white heat against the CIO. A most efficient test of what is good for the Negro people is what these enemies don't like.

Certainly, the reactionaries of the South--the would-be lynchers of the Scottsboro boys, the murderers of the croppers--fit like a glove into this category.[7]

Ku Klux Stooge Raves

Witness the ravings in Congress of Rep. E. E. Cox, Ku Klux Klan stooge from Georgia, who frothed at the mouth in the House last June 30, "warning John L. Lewis and his Communistic cohorts that carpet-bag expedition into the Southland under the red banner of Soviet Russia . . . would be tolerated."[8]

This "southern gentleman's" tirade was of course in protection of the wealthy textile magnates against the CIO's Textile Workers Organizing Committee. But he truly revealed his hand when, waxing hot and, with his "southern chivalry" aflame, he exclaimed:

"CIO organizers were now in the South preaching social, political and economic equality to the Negro population."

This, Mr. Cox, explained, would "corrupt our colored citizens." In other words, any effort of the Negro people to avail themselves of their constitutional rights--or even of their right to organize into labor unions under the Wagner Act--is to "corrupt our colored citizens."

Confession of Reactionary

No clearer confession of its own reaction has come from the Southern ruling class since the arch-reactionary Mr. Justice Van Devanter, in his swan-song dissent from the Supreme Court, declared that Angelo Herndon's "crime" was that he appealed to Southern Negroes "by picturing their condition as an unhappy one resulting from asserted wrongs on the part of white landlords and employers."

The idea is not only to inflict worse lynch-oppression upon the Negro people but also to twist the United States constitution so that the Negro's plight becomes legal and unshakably "American." And shades of Hitler, Mussolini and Hearst, don't let Negro and white workers be organized into the same unions on a footing of equality--for such labor organizers will be sent to hades--via rope and faggot--along with 5,000 Negroes lynched since the Civil War!

Such was the expressed opinion of Hiram W. Evans, Imperial Wizard (Buzzard) of the Ku Klux Klan, blood brother of Henry Ford's Black Legion, who declared on July 11, in Atlanta, Ga. :

"The CIO is infested with Communists and the Klan will ride to wipe out Communism."

Proud of Enemies

But all those who fight against the reactionaries drive toward freedom are today labeled as "Communists" including: workers who seek the right to organize and collectively bargain; Negroes who fight "too" militantly against lynching and discrimination; those who support an anti-fascist national Farmer-Labor Party. Even the middle-of-the-roader Roosevelt is today labeled a Communist by the fascist forces in the country.[9]

The CIO and the forces of progress in general can well be proud of such enemies as Congressman Cox, the Ku Klux Klan, as well as other such foes of democracy as the Henry Fords, the Memorial-Day-Massacre Girdlers, and the Hearsts. But the very hatred of the CIO by these breeders of murder, violence and hooded terrorist gangs, serves as an unerring weather-vane to the Negro people that their own best interests lies unmistakably on the other side of the fence. It lies side by side with the CIO and progressive movements growing in the country today, in defense and extension of the fundamental rights of labor--in defense and extension of the Negro's constitutional right to a new and square deal in the economic life of the nation.[10]

Organization Into the CIO

The CIO is a non-political organization and its program does not expressly call for the "political, social and economic equality for the Negro people." This is the province of a political organization and ONLY the Communist Party maintains and fights for such a program.

But the organization of Negro and white workers on an equal plane into the CIO is the rock-bottom basis of the whole struggle for the political and social and economic equality of the entire Negro people.

The CIO in its powerful organizational campaigns seeks the legal and American right of workers--wage and salary earners irrespective of race, sex, color or creed--to bargain collectively and to earn a decent living under human working conditions.

In the words of John L. Lewis, CIO chairman, made public on July 7:

"Labor now demands its rightful heritage. It holds in contempt those
who would restrict human privileges. It demands the right to organize and
bargain collectively. It demands legislative enactments, making realistic
the principles of industrial democracy. . . . The CIO stands as a bulwark
for democracy.
     "Labor no longer signifies 'the man with the hoe.' It does signify
the great masses of wage and salary earners--all those who toil for a live-
lihood--regardless of sex, race, color or previous condition of servitude.
Labor to us extends from unskilled industrial and agricultural workers
throughout the so-called white-collar groups, including technicians, teachers,
professional men and women, newspaper employees and others."

Aid Negro Working Man

     With the objectives of the CIO to raise the living standards of the
33,000,000 American workers--including the rank and file of the A. F. of L.--
such an aim must inevitably aid the Negro workers who are the most exploited
and discriminated against of all workers.
     More and more large sections of the white workers in the progressive
labor movement are recognizing that they can better their own conditions only
by unity with the Negro workers on a basis of full equality. Likewise, the
Negro workers throughout the vicious system of oppression against them--which
manifests itself fundamentally in job-organization--can be effectively fought
only through the closest unity between Negro and white working people.
     The CIO is the cornerstone of this growing progressive movement for
unity and full equality between Negro and white workers. There are no
principles which are more fundamental and deeper in the traditions of American
democracy.
     The fact that the CIO is called a "Communist" organization reveals the
fascist character of the Girdlers, the Hearsts, the Herald Tribunes, and other
such reactionary forces which are out to destroy everything progressive in
American life.
     To be labeled "Communist" is not a discredit to the CIO. Rather it is
a credit to the Communist Party whose early pioneering in the American Labor
movement for industrial unionism and for full equality of the Negro workers,
paved the way for the great surge of progress which the CIO today represents.

Daily Worker, September 5, 1937.

11. UNION AGREEMENT RESULTS IN HIGHER WAGES FOR WORKERS

     DETROIT, Sept. 9.--Negro workers who constitute 70 per cent of the
foundry workers, led by Luke M. Fennell, played an important part in the successful development of the Union at the Budd Wheel Company.
     Since the coming of the U.A.W., the wages and conditions of all workers
have improved considerably. After a victorious strike three months ago, the
company agreed to discontinue the piece work system within 90 days. The
piece work system always acted as a method of speed up. "Much of our work was
lost because a great deal of our production was classified as scrap of which
we received no pay," said Mr. Fennel. Today all the workers enjoy seniority
rights that enable them to be hired and laid off in accordance with their
seniority. Throughout the shop steward system, all of the grievances of the
workers are dealt with and adjusted. Follow me through this little problem
in arithmetic and compare the wages before and after Union came 18 months ago:
     Minimum wage per hour: 55¢, after: 75¢.
     Maximum wage per hour: 75¢, after: $1.15.
     Average wage per hour: 62¢, after: 90¢.
     Average weekly wage, $25, after: $38.
     This problem proves beyond all doubt that we have benefited tremen-
dously from the Union.
     "The Union Negotiating Committee was forced to take a firm stand on
behalf of the workers in the three days of negotiating with the company

officials," says Mr. Fennell.

Personnel Director, Mr. Heidt, was surprised and rather annoyed to see
Mr. Fennell, a Negro, on the Negotiating Committee of the Union. Mr. Heidt
stated that he did the poor Negro workers a favor by hiring them in his factory and now they are not satisfied.

Pittsburgh Courier, September 11, 1937.

12. A YEAR OF THE CIO

A year ago the Committee for Industrial Organization began organizing
the workers in the steel industry, something that had previously never been
successfully accomplished.

CIO Leader John L. Lewis, now announces that 500,000 workers in steel
have been organized by the Steel Workers Organizing Committee.

In every organized plant this has meant increased pay, shorter hours,
seniority rights and industrial democracy, and of particular interest to us
is the fact that these advantages have come to thousands of Negro steel workers
from Birmingham to Pittsburgh and points between.

The unionization of all the big automobile companies by the CIO affiliated Automobile Workers Union has done the same thing for thousands of
Negro workers who help produce the country's automobiles.

In many other directions this new, virile labor organization, with its
practical and sensible philosophy and policy of absolute democracy and no
discrimination based on color, creed or nationality, has reached out and
organized colored and white workers together.

It has set a healthful example to organized labor in America and done
more than any single agency in the history of the country's labor movement to
eliminate the biracialism which has so slowed the emancipation of the workers
from industrial feudalism.

In the complaints about violence which occurred here and there in a
year of hectic organization, many of our people have lost sight of the fact
that in this year hundreds of Negro workers have been privileged to rise to
positions of leadership and help negotiate contracts for wages and hours
with some of the mightiest corporations in America.

Perhaps never before have colored people played so important a part in
shaping the course of basic affairs in the United States. They have previously
worked, but had nothing to say about what they should get for that work or
how they should work to get it. Thanks to the organizational drive in labor,
all that has been changed, and Negroes are sitting down with white workers
and employers negotiating and signing contracts involving millions of dollars.

The effect of this drive is already apparent on race relations in many
parts of the country. It has been demonstrated to white labor that if it will
meet Negro labor half way the loyalty of the latter can be always counted
upon. Suspicion and race hatred have been allayed.

In the face of the success of the CIO, the A.F. of L. unions have in
many instances abandoned their traditional attitude of indifference to Negro
labor which frequently bordered on hostility, and are often as eager to
eliminate every trace of color discrimination as the CIO organizations.

All this has been accomplished in a single short year, during which
the strength of organized labor has doubled, millions of extra dollars have
gone into pay envelopes and millions less hours have been worked to earn it.

Steel workers, automobile workers, mine workers, laundry workers,
garment workers, electrical workers, ship workers, dock workers, chauffeurs,
construction workers and numerous others, among all of which Negroes are
numbered, have benefitted from the magic of organization.

The success of this drive vindicates the position taken by the "rebel"
unions that broke from the traditional A.F. of L. policy and began the
organization of industrial unions.

The wisdom of the Negro workers who joined this stand for better working conditions and industrial democracy is to be commended.

The immediate task, now that Negroes are organized is to broaden their
participation in the administration of the unions.

Pittsburgh Courier, September 18, 1937.

13.   SELLING OUT THE WORKERS

By A. J. Allen

Will the leadership of a working population seize the opportunity of
forming an alliance with progressive industrial unionism as represented by
the C.I.O.? The writer hopes so, but seems to have his doubts.

One of the most important qualities of effective minority group
leadership is opportunism. This ability to take advantage of opportunities
as they present themselves, properly used, can ofttimes more than compensate
for numerical or material weakness. And minorities have a right to expect
such opportunism in intelligent leaders.

Especially is this ability at a premium in a period of swift and unprecedented change such as this through which we are now passing. Old creeds
and customs are crumbling, party lines are dissolving, social and economic
stratification that has stood for scores of years is breaking up before our
eyes and new alliances are being formed.

Earning a livelihood has always been fundamental in any reasoned consideration of the American Negro's problems. Sociologists and economists
have for years told the Negro that since his is predominantly a race of workers, his interests are those of the working class. This means, primarily,
alignment with organized labor, with the trade union movement.

Yet however valid the theory, union color lines prevented such alignment from taking place and the Negro was forced by economic necessity to
allow the employer to play him as a scab and a cheaper worker against white
labor.

However, since 1935 there has arisen a group of unions in the mass
production industries which welcome Negro membership. Whether this welcome is
extended because of an enlightened sense of brotherly love or because of a
realization of the Negro's strong position in these industries, is neither
here nor there. The thing that does matter is that in the industrial form of
unionism common ground has been found on which black and white labor, long
pitted against each other, can unite.

Here is a chance, if there ever was one, for Negro leadership to take
opportunity by the forelock and effect a unity of forces which, more than any
other single move, would make secure the position of the Negro breadwinner in
the American economy.

Said James Weldon Johnson in 1934, "Organized labor holds the main gate
of our industrial and economic corral; and on the day that it throws open
that gate in realization of the truth that the cause of the white worker and
the cause of the black worker are one, there will be a crack in the wall of
racial discrimination that will be heard around the world."[11]

Leaders Standing Pat

But our leaders are standing pat. And Negro labor for the most part is
standing pat. Those few black workers who have cast their lot with the C.I.O.
have done so largely without the benefit of Negro clergy or Negro editorial
sanction. What could have been an Exodus from Egypt has thus far turned out
to be a fizzle.

Negro leadership in many places is doing worse than standing pat. In
trying to stand up so straight it has leaned over backwards into a morass of
extreme conservatism.

During the Little Steel Strike of last spring, investigators found
Ohio employers using Negro churches as recruiting stations for strike breakers.

Not only did Detroiters protest the appearance of union officials on
the public programs of the N.A.A.C.P. national conference, but they even refused

audience to the president of Howard university because he had made what were
reputed to be liberal statements. The objection to Dr. Mordecai W. Johnson
was that he had on a previous visit dared allude to a fact known by every
high school student of economics, "Labor finds its strength through organization." The hue and cry was that because of this speech several Negroes
lost their jobs. But, according to the news releases, these unfortunates
could not be located.

It is interesting to speculate as to the "why" of this phenomenon of
reactionary leaders of a proletarian population. Ten years ago it might
have been blamed on allegiance to the Republican party, but today that
allegiance, together with its object, has pretty well gone by the board.

Ignorance to Blame

Some claim the employers control everything in most communities and
this by necessity would include Negro leadership. But in many cases it is
probably nearer the truth to say that is the fear of employer control rather
than its actual exercise that keeps the local leader jumping through the hoop.

Other answers could be attempted, but to many none would seem to be
more convincing than Samuel Johnson's classic response to an old lady's query
as to why he had made such an obvious error: "Ignorance, Madame, pure ignorance!"[12]

It is no doubt true that in some instances a policy of watchful waiting
may be superior to vociferous pronouncements, for cool headed calculations
often net more than headlong attack. But there should be no power on earth
strong enough to make a man take up arms against a movement for the best
interests of his people.

And then, there's another angle to it. If white labor is forced to
fight alone in its battle for better working conditions and a higher standard
of living, is it likely that the Negro will be invited to share rewards he
did not help to earn? There used to be a story about a little red hen who,
after trying futilely to get the other barnyard animals to help her prepare a
meal, spread the table and asked, "Now, who will eat this meal?" To say her
listeners were very willing would be understatement. But her curt comeback
was, "Oh, no you won't. I will!" And she did!

The American race problem has brought us many anomalies. But it may
be some time before it equals the Negro leader, supported by workingmen's
dollars, leading a working population, and yet enunciating a philosophy which
would do credit to the original economic royalist or the most eloquent spokesman for America's "sixty sinister families."

The Crisis, 45 (March, 1938): 80.

14. COMMITTEE ATTACKS IRT NEGRO DISCRIMINATION

New York Co-ordinating Committee for Employment to Launch Drive to End IRT Job
System Tonight at St. Marks Church

Negro men with college degrees clean the toilets of the I.R.T. because
it is the only job the I.R.T. will give them. They grow old on the job sweeping the platforms and running the elevators.[13]

Negro men with college degrees are never promoted to office positions.
Some of them take exams in engineering; they pass but they never get jobs to
drive the trains. The I.R.T. has decreed that driving trains is a white man's
job.

When the regular employee in the change booths goes to lunch the Negro
porter very often takes his place. But it is always only temporary. Giving
change in an I.R.T. subway station is a job denied to Negroes.

Demand Employment

For years the Negro people have groaned under the lash of Negro dis-crimination by the I.R.T. Now they demand a hearing, and swift adjustment of the wrongs committed against them.

More than half a million Negroes in Harlem will make themselves heard by the management of the I.R.T. this week on the matter of job discrimination. Through the Greater New York Co-ordinating Committee for Employment they will demand of the I.R.T. that Negroes be given employment in all capacities without discrimination.

If the I.R.T. refuses to erase its policy of Negro discrimination picket lines will be thrown around its main offices and in front of all subway entrances in Harlem. In a release to the Daily Worker last night, the Com-mittee for Employment said that Michael Quill, City Councilman and president of the Transport Workers' Union, has pledged his union's full support to the campaign for jobs for Negroes in the I.R.T. without discrimination.[14]

Mass Meeting Tonight

The Rev. A. Clayton Powell is chairman of the Committee for Employment which won an unprecedented victory over the Edison Gas and Electric Company two weeks ago, when the company agreed to give white collar jobs to Negroes.[15]

The Committee for Employment will hold a mass meeting tonight 8:00 P.M. at St. Marks Church, 139th Street and Edgecombe Avenue, to review its work in fighting Negro discrimination and to launch its campaign against the I.R.T.

Among the speakers at tonight's meeting are included: Borough Presi-dent Stanley M. Isaacs; City Councilman Michael Quill; Vito Marcantonio, presi-dent of the International Labor defense; Rev. Lloyd Imes; the Honorable Thomas Dyett, delegate at large to the State Constitutional Convention, and Walter White, president of the National Association for the Advancement of Colored People.[16]

Manhattan Borough President **Stanley** M. Isaacs is actively cooperating with the Committee for Employment and is now engaged in negotiations with the New York Telephone Co. in the interest of wiping out Negro discrimination by the company.

Supported By 294 Groups

The Committee for Employment is supported by 294 organizations, trade unions included, with a total membership of 155,000 persons, Negro and white. Other officials of the Committee are: A. Philip Randolph, president of the Brotherhood of Sleeping Car Porters, Rev. Lloyd Imes, Mrs. Elizabeth Ross Haynes, social worker, and A. Johnson.

The New York Council of the National Negro Congress is a co-sponsor of the Committee for Employment.

As a means of financial income the Committee has sponsored a Grand Carnival and Barbecue Dinner to be held on May 30, Decoration Day, at Brandt's Farm on the Sawmill River Road. The publicity Department of the Committee for Employment is at 2357 Seventh Avenue.

Daily Worker, May 16, 1938.

15. WE WIN THE RIGHT TO FIGHT FOR JOBS

By John A. Davis

Recently the New Negro Alliance of Washington, D.C., won in the United States Supreme Court a victory of far-reaching importance to the maintenance of civil rights, to the broadening of democracy, to the enlightment of the economic and social system, and to the protection of all minorities, both racial and economic; it legally obtained for the Negro the right to picket those business establishments which refused to employ colored workers.[17]

The decision handed down by the court freed the Alliance to continue
its use of "consumer pressure" to acquire employment for Negroes. But more
than that, it paved the way for action of a similar nature by groups all over
the country. As a result, by-where-you-can-work movements now are being
planned or prosecuted in many cities throughout the country where the Negro
population is large enough, and socially intelligent enough, to support them.

In its case against the Sanitary Grocery Store of Washington, the
Alliance, through its chief counsel, Belford Vance Lawson, contended, and the
Court agreed, that the picketing of stores largely supported by Negroes for
the purpose of obtaining jobs for colored workers constituted a "labor dispute" within the meaning of the Norris-LaGuardia Act, and that under the Act
the Federal courts cannot issue injunctions restraining peaceful picketing.
In accepting this point of view, the Court pointed out that the Act defines
a "labor dispute" as including any controversy concerning the terms or conditions of employment, regardless of whether or not the disputants stand in
the proximate relation of employer and employee. It denied that the case was
out of the scope of the Act because the dispute was racial, on the grounds
that the Act does not concern itself with the background or motives of the
dispute. It ruled that "race discrimination by an employer may reasonably be
deemed more unfair and less excusable than discrimination against workers on
grounds of union affiliation." [18]

Since the case was a labor dispute within the meaning of the Act, and
since the picketing was peaceful as required in the Act, the highest court
ordered the District Court to reverse the decree by which it granted an injunction restraining the Alliance from picketing the Sanitary Grocery Company.
In this decision it definitely denied the older philosophy expressed in the
dissenting opinion of Mr. Justice McReynolds, which would prevent social
legislation from abridging the absolute freedom of individual economic action
for the sake of social justice. In doing so it signalized the economic broaden-
ing-down of democracy; it took a step toward loosening the rigid economic
bindings of social fascism; and it contributed to the maintenance of civil
rights so important to the social order if economic justice is to be achieved
by any means.

The New Negro Alliance was organized in the summer of 1933, preceding
similar organizations in Philadelphia, New York, Richmond, Cincinnati, and
Pittsburgh. At the outset it was principally interested in such general
problems as obtaining civil rights, setting up racial co-operatives, securing
employment for Negroes in the District of Columbia government, and securing
jobs in private industry through the use of consumer pressure.

This breadth of purpose resulted to a large extent from the irritation
which the younger Negro felt from the general passivity and complete lack of
militancy among the organizations already existing in Washington--most of them
dominated by older and well-established Negroes. To the younger generation
the citizens' associations in Washington, which were the only advisory units
recognized by the municipal government, seemed to be completely dormant. They
were unattended by more than a few of the outstanding citizens, and suffered
from addle-brained, timid leadership. The local N.A.A.C.P. at the time was a
fashionable organization, completely dominated by the respectable, the well-off,
and the stuffed-shirt residents of the city, and beyond this the general
atmosphere of the entire Negro population appeared to be socially lethargic
and completely smug. The public school teacher and the government employee--
who together form the educated, the responsible, the well-to-do of Washington
Negro society--had hardly been disturbed by the depression beyond the short-
lived Economy Act.

To the task of bringing social consciousness to these groups and to the
general Negro petty bourgeoisie, which was only gradually becoming aware of
the dire economic plight of its clients, the Alliance dedicated itself. At
first it attempted to be concerned with the whole problem of civil and social
betterment, but as time went on it began to concentrate more and more upon
the work of securing jobs for Negroes in businesses largely supported by
Negro consumers.

In this work the Alliance was for a short while surprisingly successful.
Before long it had many of Washington's leading school teachers, administrators,
lawyers, and doctors carrying picket signs, a thing previously unheard of in
"respectable," "family-conscious" Washington. Within the first half year of
its operation the Alliance prosecuted a successful campaign against the local

A. & P. Stores, the High Ice Cream Company, and several other establishments, securing jobs for Negro workers carrying an annual payroll of approximately $50,000.

Early in 1934 its program met a setback. A court injunction restraining it from picketing the Kaufman Department Store a business built and largely maintained upon Negro trade, was issued. Later in the spring a similar injunction kept it from further picketing the High Ice Cream Stores, and in the summer the Sanitary Grocery Company (a chain like the A. & P.) obtained a third injunction.

Legally deprived of its most effective weapon, the Alliance for a time was bogged down. But the group kept up its work and through heroic efforts maintained its morale and spirit through four long years of legal fights, until its battle finally was won.

The organization, however, was far from inactive during the four years it was restrained from using the picket. It sponsored a Civil Rights Bill for the District of Columbia which has been introduced into Congress, and it made some attempt at sponsoring co-operative enterprises. The methods of education and house-to-house canvass were used to initiate boycotts as a means of procuring jobs, and employers were made to see the advertising value of hiring Negroes.

For the Alliance, and for all minority groups, both racial and economic, the decision of the Supreme Court was a substantial victory. Already the organization has recommenced its work with renewed vigor, and the rapid strides that it made in 1933-34 are again possible. The Kaufman Department Store has recently hired Negro clerks and new drives are now being prosecuted against the Peoples Drug Store Company and the Sanitary Grocery Company.

The work of the Alliance is considered especially significant because of its level-headed and careful development of the theory of consumer pressure as a minority tactic. It has gone further in completely rationalizing this technique than any other similar Negro organization of recent years. Fortunately situated in Washington, the Alliance has had the advantage of being influenced by two important forces, each of which has clarified its aims and purposes so that in its activities it has been able to avoid the blundering of rabid chauvinism into which so many other buy-where-you-can-work movements have fallen.

The first of these forces was the Division of Social Sciences at Howard University, and especially its Professor Abram L. Harris. The second was the recent establishment of liberally-led and socially intelligent government employee labor unions, which have at last made it clear to the Washington Negro that the white race is not all rich or prejudiced, and that economic security is the problem of the white worker and petty bourgeoisie as well as that of the Negro. [19]

In setting up the program of the Alliance, the founders first of all took into careful consideration the many plans of action that the Negro race heretofore has followed in its approach to a solution of its problems. As a minority group, they felt that all of these to large degree had failed because they had missed a basic economic significance in the social position of the Negro in America.

There was, first of all, the Booker T. Washington approach, which sought to develop the Negro as a semi-skilled and skilled worker. The members of the Alliance felt that this program had come entirely too late historically, for even as Booker T. Washington and others had founded industrial schools to train the Negro, the American labor movement had been taking steps to exclude him from the craft and industrial occupations. The members of the Alliance granted that some kind of sound economic foundation for the newly-freed Negro had been necessary, and that the semi-skilled and unskilled occupations had offered the best opportunities for his economic advancement. But they maintained that such a program was, and still is, economically impossible. They saw unmistakable signs of the failure of the program in the increased emphasis on academic and professional training for Negroes, even in those institutions which were founded to carry out agricultural and industrial education. [20]

A second approach was that proposed by Dr. W. E. B. DuBois, which first gained popularity as a reaction to the less ambitious Booker T. Washington program, with its inherent limitation of the Negro to the lower type of social achievement. DuBois's idea was the development of the "better Tenth" of the race. He insisted that the Negro should attempt to assimilate the best of the

Western and American culture, and advocated the training of at least ten per
cent of the race in things academic and professional. By such training, he
averred, not only would the race receive through those trained the services
necessary to its improvement, but at the same time white America would be
afforded a demonstration of the ability of the Negro to assimilate and command even the finest of culture. This approach was at one time especially
popular with the Negro petty bourgeoisie, just appearing in the Eastern sea-
board cities, who were particularly interested in obtaining civil rights as
their social standing improved.[21]

An off-shoot from this approach was the theory proposed by Dr. Alain
Leroy Locke, who looked forward to a peculiar and special contribution to
American culture by the Negro. By this approach the Negro not only would
master Western civilization, but at the same time would produce his own negroid
contribution for the great stream of American culture. Dr. Locke and the
followers of his philosophy believed that racial prejudice soon would disappear before the altars of truth, art, and intellectual achievement.[22]

The members of the Alliance realized that the American Negro had long
fulfilled the hopes and expectations of both these theories, for students and
scholars of the Negro race not only had mastered their fields brilliantly but
had contributed to their development. And yet, they realized, the white race
still was not willing to accept the Negro, either as an American capable of
mastering the entire civilization and culture, or as a significant contributor.
Socially and economically, they knew, the Negro remained an oppressed minority.

Faced with these facts, the Alliance took the position that minority
oppression is basically economic and that therefore there could hardly be a
cultural remedy. It saw proof of its contention in the oppression of the
Chinese people, who long before the coming of the Western powers to the Orient
had a meaningful and rich culture. It decided that the essence of a minority
position rests not so much upon the inability to produce culturally, but upon
the capitalistic necessity of labor differentials, increased profit, and the
rest that goes with economic exploitation, and it felt that it was no longer
essentially desirable to stress the cultural differences of the Negro, nor
his peculiar racial characteristics which are now hardly extant.

The third approach of Negro leaders to the economic problem had been
the struggle for civil rights. Such a struggle, the Alliance felt, could
never be successful by itself. It is an old principle that the law is only
that which the people will respect as such. The fate of the 18th Amendment
makes this quite clear in another field; and the fate of the 13th, 14th, and
15th Amendments, together with the Civil Rights laws, proves the truth of this
statement for the Negro. Driven on by economic and social factors, the great
majority of Americans can hardly be expected to honor the law, so far as the
Negro is concerned, simply because it is the law.

However, the Alliance did not underestimate the importance of the civil
rights approach as a minority tactic. In a manner of speaking, the law, if
properly influenced by the idealism of the jurist and the scholar, will often
lift the community above its determining factors. Temporarily at least, the
idealistic scholar and jurist can build an idealogical super-structure in the
law which can check-mate the anti-social forces of unbridled self-interest,
profit-seeking, and racial exploitation. Much can be achieved through the
civil rights approach also in pushing over old restrictions and taboos which
may remain in the law long after the popular will has moved on to an enlightened position.

In fact, it was realized that the Alliance's approach could not succeed in its application of consumer pressure without a corresponding civil
rights struggle as a means of protection. The Alliance merely maintained
that, alone, a fight for civil rights was far from complete as a minority
tactic.

The civil rights struggle was also a part of the program of Dr. W. E.
B. DuBois, as expressed through the N.A.A.C.P. But Dr. DuBois attacked the
Alliance and similar movements because of his early distaste for anything that
smacked of segregation. His contention was that such organizations accept
segregation, and even hope to solidify it, by giving it an economic basis.
In short, his position was that white America would more or less gladly give
the Negro jobs in Negro-supported businesses in order to segregate him more
adequately.

At that time Dr. DuBois still looked forward to a social life without segregation, in which full freedom of economic opportunity also would develop. His attitude has since changed.

On this point the Alliance took the position that segretation in a city like Washington is a fact and that its disappearance at any early date is hardly probable because of the lethargy of the Negro, the prejudice of the white man, the law, the pressure of real estate values, and similar socio-economic factors. Even in northern cities, where segregation theoretically does not exist, these social and economic factors bring it about. If segrega-tion is to exist, then, the Alliance felt that it should not be coupled with racial exploitation--the best jobs even in the Negro areas going to members of other races.

Such a situation as that which exists in Philadelphia, for instance, excited the organization's reformist zeal. In this city there is no segrega-tion in the public school system--theoretically! No Negro teachers, however, are appointed above the graded schools, and in schools where as high as eighty per cent of the student body is Negro, the teachers are all white. To have Negro teachers over white children is hardly possible with the existing racial attitudes in Philadelphia. The Alliance felt it is better to have outright segregated schools, which already exist in fact, and to procure the resulting jobs, than to feebly struggle against tremendous odds for the appointment of Negro teachers over white students. Its opinion was backed by observation of the high type of intellectual and cultural achievement that segregated schools had made possible in Washington through the stimulus provided by the avail-ability of excellent occupational opportunities. Is it not better to have Washington's segregated schools than to continue to foster the lethargic attitude of Philadelphia's young Negroes, who seldom even go to college since the occupational opportunities available to them are so limited? If grievous psychological factors develop from segregated schools, Washington's high intellectual development shows it to be relatively a less important factor than the job opportunities afforded.

The next major approach to racial economic salvation was also Booker T. Washington's. Dr. Washington, with characteristic feeling for the strenthening of the Negro's economic basis, was a strong advocate of building Negro business. Present-day proponents of this school, largely incipient Negro business men hoping to become capitalists, point out that the race is made up for the most part of unskilled industrial workers, agricultural workers, laborers, and professional persons. To fill in the occupational scheme, they say, it is absolutely necessary to build Negro business to provide opportunities for Negro youth. They hasten to recite the rise of many foreign-born Americans from shoe-string peddlers to department-store owners.

With this shoe-string school of thought the Alliance could not agree. History showed that the Negro was hardly emerging from slavery when American business was coming of age in the form of the modern corporation. Thus the Negro missed, or rather never had, the opportunity to get in at the start, and now, try as he will, he is unable to build anything but small businesses. Even here he faces the competition of chain methods of distribution which he has not yet found a way to overcome.

Without capital, individually or collectively, and with no business tradition, the Alliance saw the Negro as almost totally incapable of competing with highly organized and capitalized American business. It appeared from the record that Negro business was entirely incapable of surviving except in the fields of insurance and undertaking, where white corporations did not care to compete; in the first instance because the mortality rate was too high and in the second because of social prejudice. In banking, it was recognized that the Negro had made some small success, but it still seemed that in the final analysis the business ended up in the larger white banks which the Negro banks had to use for clearing, deposit, credit, and other purposes. And so the Alliance decided that it would not concern itself with attempting to aid in the erection of a Negro capitalist class. It took the attitude that only through consumers' co-operatives, which had proved capable of competing in the capitalistic system in the Scandinavian countries, Ireland, England, the West Coast of Africa, and the United States, could any business progress be made within the race.

On the positive side, the Alliance decided to concern itself with filling out the occupational structure of the race in accordance with the limiting conditions of the existing economic and social pattern. In surveying its field, it found that the Negro is occupationally all hands and feet, largely feet. He is generally either an unskilled industrial worker, a laborer, a farmer or agricultural worker, or a professional. Comparatively few Negroes are engaged in the skilled trades or hold business or clerical positions. According to the 1930 Census, 32.2 per cent of America's native white men and 67.1 per cent of its native white women were employed in general clerical capacities, while only 8.5 per cent of the colored men and 3.5 per cent of the colored women were employed in this manner. The Alliance therefore decided that its primary aim must be to forcefully increase, by the use of consumer pressure, the number of Negroes employed in clerical capacities, business positions, and generally in the higher occupational levels.

As its chief weapon it decided upon the consumer's boycott, undoubtedly the most powerful force which the Negro has yet discovered as a minority technique, believing that since the basis for minority persecution is chiefly economic, the remedy should likewise be economic. As outstanding world examples of the efficacy of the boycott it studied the Indian boycotts and the Chinese boycott against Japan. It believed that in its case retaliatory force would not be used as it was in China's; the Negro and the Indian have the advantage of dealing with democratic countries while the Chinese face a fascist Japan which emerged from feudalism no earlier than the nineteenth century.

The Alliance saw special power in the boycott because of the nature of modern capitalism. Since the modern corporation is organized to carry on mass production on a marginal basis, it is especially vulnerable to consumer action, for in order to destroy profit it is merely necessary to destroy sales to a point where marginal profit disappears. Thus the basic aim of the organization became placement of Negroes in clerical positions in distribution units; but a secondary aim was semi-skilled, skilled, and professional placements in factories and other points of production.

In the four years that the Alliance has carried on its work, its ablest critic has been Dr. Abram Harris of Howard University. It was Dr. Harris who brought labor consciousness to the organization at a time when it was foolishly racial and chauvinistic. He pointed out that the result of such a movement as was at first visualized was inevitably and finally the antagonism of the white worker, with whom the Negro must sooner or later ally in the general evolution in America toward greater social justice. His criticsm appeared at a time when the CIO first loomed on the national horizon and liberal government employee trade unions first came to Washington.

From the outset, the Alliance never asked for outright displacements of white workers, but for employment of Negroes during the course of normal labor turnover. It soon began to become active in the new labor renaissance in governmental Washington, insisting that the Negro be organized with equal opportunity for all occupations. The CIO met the question squarely, guaranteeing that the Negro would get the same jobs as went to members of other races; although it could not, as a labor union, admit the wholesale displacement of its members. In short, it was wholly in accord with the gradual turnover idea. It organized the Negro clerical workers for whom the Alliance had secured jobs, as well as a large number of Negro government cafeteria employees. The Alliance became integrated into the general movement for social justice for all workers.

In his book, *The Negro As Capitalist,* Dr. Harris made several criticisms of buy-where-you-can-work movements. With some of these criticisms the Alliance has never agreed; with others it has felt that they do not apply in its case. [23]

Dr. Harris objected to such movements, first of all, because he felt that economic retaliation on the part of whites employing Negroes would mean the loss of more jobs than could be gained. The Alliance disagreed with his position, feeling that it was essentially a type of defeatism. One might just as well say that Socialist and worker movements for social justice should all cease at once, for their impending success inevitably results in fascism and the complete suppression of workers as in Germany, Italy, and Spain. But the fact that this not always the case is apparent in France, England, and the United States; it all depends upon the techniques employed and the complete historical, political, social, and economic situation.

The same danger of retaliation is true of all forms of tactics where ultimate power does not reside in the hands of the agitating group. The

Negro can do nothing through buy-where-you-can-work movements without the
sympathy of liberal elements and of labor. Rabid racialism must be avoided
at all costs, and movements in Chicago and New York have been none too suc-
cesful in doing this.

Dr. Harris insisted, in the second place, that buy-where-you-can-work
programs must result in the absolute displacement of white workers regardless
of the use of the method of placing Negroes only when normal labor turnover
affords an opportunity. The Alliance felt that in taking such a stand he
assumed the complete poverty of capitalism as far as any future expansion is
concerned, and that he intimated that there is little rotating employment resulting from shifts and types of production which would afford opportunity
for the frictionless placement of Negroes. Through its program the Alliance
has shown that, far from causing a general displacement of white workers and
thereby alienating their support, the buy-where-you-can-work program can be
carried out in close cooperation with even the most advanced elements of the
labor movement.

Dr. Harris stated that buy-where-you-can-work programs are generally
anti-Semitic because in their mere activism they strike at the neighborhood
Jewish storekeeper. But the Alliance has always felt that it has been notably
free of anti-Semitism. Certainly anti-Semitism has never been expressed in
any of its publicity. Only one Jewish concern, the Kaufman Department Store,
has ever been picketed, and then in the regular course of a city-wide campaign.
Neighborhood Jewish stores which employ only members of the operator's family
have never been approached.

The Alliance approach resulted from a feeling that the great modern
corporation structure was a huge collective instrument with which individual
members of the race could not compete. This was true for two reasons, namely,
lack of capital and lack of opportunity to partake of the drive to trustification which got under way even as the Negro emerged from savagery. Con-
sciously or unconsciously this corporation economy has afforded none of the
higher occupational opportunities for Negroes. Hence the Alliance felt that
the only way occupations could be secured was by a collective consumer attack.
The Alliance held that when any consumer movement attacked neighborhood family
businesses, it in effect denied the principle of freedom of economic enterprise, on which the very survival of the Negro depends, and substantially
took a position of demanding that all black dollars go into black hands. Such
a consumer movement is in essence the same as that of German Fascism, which
demands racial autarchy.

The Alliance felt that all consumer movements must admit the principle
of fair individual economic enterprise or suffer disastrous retaliation, for
the other position basically accepted two separate economies, one white and
one black, which if adopted by other races would completely crush the Negro.
The aim of the Alliance was to better integrate the Negro into the economy
which exists and whose corporate nature has excluded him, not further to
separate black and white economy. The Alliance took the position that if
Harlem Negroes were disturbed about individual Jewish businesses, the only fair
and safe approach would be to establish competing Negro businesses.

Traditionally only the most intimate and best relationships have
existed between the Jewish neighborhood storekeeper and the Negro. The German
persecution has given the Jew a new sympathy for the Negro and the Negro a
new understanding of the Jewish situation. The philanthropy of the Jew in
Negro education has made him undoubtedly one of the outstanding and most
appreciated friends of the Negro. In view of these facts, however, it is
important that all buy-where-you-can-work movements mark well the fear and
criticism of Dr. Harris.

Social understanding saved the Alliance from anti-Semitism. Even when
there was some talk of anti-Semitism at, as Dr. Harris put it, "that greatest
institution for the higher education of Negroes," the Alliance was forceful in
its criticism of such an attitude. The organization, furthermore, never
sought to apply any principle of racial employment to the higher education of
the Negro. Such a principle would be unsound, both from considerations of
endowment, excellence of faculty, and psychological balance in education. The
Alliance is only concerned with insisting upon some kind of employment for the
young products of the many Negro institutions of higher learning.

In general summary, Dr. Harris was apparently of the opinion that the
buy-where-you-can-work movement must necessarily be in essence minority fascism.

He felt that it applies a principle of racial economic self-sufficiency to a minority situation, exposes the race to the possibility of retaliation, and "becomes a spiritual ally of German Fascism." In short, he believed that a minority could hope to gain little but further persecution when it attempted to close the free interplay of the economic system by a program which is in the slightest concerned with racial self-sufficiency, or rather, racial well-being.

This argument assumed that the economy is, or was, open to the Negro and that for the Negro, social fascism does not already exist. The Alliance felt that through the effective shutting off of all opportunities, social fascism did already exist for the Negro. What can be lost by way of economic opportunities when 70 per cent of the Negro population is on relief in some urban centers, and when the Negro is unfairly denied employment in the very businesses which are supported by his consumer power (or relief consumer power)? The Alliance believed that, characteristic of many capitalistic, democratic institutions, social fascism exists for the Negro; and it believed that to some extent through the exercise of the freedom, civil and economic rights guaranteed under a democratic system of government, this condition could be alleviated. It knew that labor unions had made headway against similar social fascist situations.

Comparisons are odious, and historical comparisons at present are at best highly problematical and subject to numerous qualifications. But the Alliance has always emphatically denied any essential similarity between its program and that of German Fascism, for while the latter is concerned with complete racial self-sufficiency, racial chauvinism and supremacy, the former is merely concerned with equal economic opportunities under a system which professes liberalism and enlightened economic individualism. To say that some buy-where-you-can-work groups appeal to racial chauvinism in their propaganda is beside the point. The Communist Party does the same thing in its appeal to the Negro in this country, yet it hardly looks forward to a racial chauvinistic state.

Buy-where-you-can-work movements rest, or rather should rest, entirely upon that concept of liberal democratic government which limits individual economic enterprise by principles of social justice and equal opportunity. If Dr. Harris means to imply that any deviation of a minority group in a liberal democratic system from the complete individualistic system must necessarily result in the opposite or completely collectivistic racial system, both on their part and the part of the majority race, and that there is no such thing as individualism modified by social justice, then he places himself close to the most reactionary of the theories of individualism. In fact, he finds himself in company with such conservative persons as Mr. Justice McReynolds and Mr. Justice Butler.

The former, in dissenting from the majority opinion in the recent case won by the Alliance in the United States Supreme Court, stated, "Under the tortured meaning now attributed to the words 'labor dispute,' no employer . . . who prefers helpers of one color or class can find adequate safeguard against intolerable violations of his freedom if members of some other class, religion, race, or color demand that he give them precedence. . . . The ultimate result of the view now approved to the very people whom the petitioners claim to represent, it may be, is prefigured by the grievous plight of minorities in the land where the law has become a mere political instrument." The Alliance denies that such must be the case and believes there is a middle ground.

The Alliance, however, is not ungrateful to Dr. Harris for his criticism. It is especially thankful for his admonitions on the irrelevances of racialism, for his caution on the dangers of racial chauvinism, for his more basic analysis of the Negro's underprivileged position as that of the worker, and for his clear demonstration that the Negro must look to the new labor movement for real and lasting economic and social advancement.

However, it stands firm in its belief that it is on the right track. It intends, now that its program has been sanctioned by the nation's highest court, to carry on that program with redoubled vigor. It hopes that other groups in other cities will follow in its footsteps, profit through its victories and benefit by its mistakes. For only thus can a start be made in the tremendous task of securing for Negroes their rightful share of jobs in business and in industry.

Opportunity, 16 (August, 1938): 230-37.

16. NEGROES URGED FOR WAGE-HOUR BOARDS

NEW YORK CITY--Appointment of colored people to the national and local administrative boards which will be set up to administer the Federal wages and hours bill was urged upon Administrator Elmer F. Andrews, administrator of the law, by the National Association for the Advancement of Colored People.

In a letter addressed to Andrews, William Pickens, director of branches for the association, said:

"If these colored workers are to be included, for the sake of the entire program, some special attention will have to be given to the local administration of that law in the ex-slave states."

Asserting that "wages and hours discrimination," against colored workers will, in the final analysis, stop effective operation of the law, Pickens said that the only effective guarantee against discrimination is "that colored men should be members of the local committees which administer this law."

"We should start," he advised the administrator, "by setting them a good example; by putting Negroes in positions in the national administration of this law. Then we should require that local administration include Negro workers on the basis of their percentage of the whole number of workers."[24]

United Mine Workers' Journal, October 15, 1938.

17. THE CIO CONVENTION AND THE NEGRO PEOPLE

By Alan Max

We have seen a sharp contrast between the decisions on labor unity, world peace and other questions as railroaded through the A.F. of L. convention by the ruling clique and the way these same matters were handled at the CIO convention.

On the vital issue of the Negro people, however, the position of the A.F. of L. convention was more progressive than it had ever been before. It gave the CIO a real mark to shoot at.

Not that Matthew Woll and John P. Frey, who tried to shut the door to labor unity and fired blast after blast against the New Deal, had a change of heart on the Negro question. The improved stand taken by the convention on several Negro questions, was due to the rapid awakening in recent years by the membership, to the resolutions and speeches of the delegates from the Hotel and Restaurant Workers and the Teachers Unions, and, above all, to the splendid floor fight waged by the outstanding Negro leader, A. Philip Randolph of the Sleeping Car Porters. These factors grudging recognition of the rights of the Negroes from the top leadership.[25]

Condemning Negro Bias

Previous A.F. of L. conventions had flatly rejected a demand for wiping out the color bar still existing in many international unions. This time, however, the convention went on record condemning this discrimination, although it took no practical steps to end it. The convention also asked the Executive Council to look into measures that might come up from time to time to end the Southern poll taxes, whereby many white workers and practically all Negroes in the South are disfranchised.[26]

The CIO convention not only matched the position of the A.F. of L., but went way beyond it. As Earl Browder declared at the recent meeting of the National Committee of the Communist Party, the "Pittsburgh gathering of the CIO, by its energetic actions and future plans for organizing the Negro workers on the basis of complete equality, finally closed the old and shameful chapter of labor's indifference to this question."[27]

It did this not only with the actual decisions adopted, but also by the entire spirit of the convention. This was evidence by the rising ovation given the speeches of the Negro delegates like Henry Johnson, assistant

national director of the Packinghouse Organizing Committee, and the way the
delegates chose to act on the Negro questions, not by the formal "aye", but by
a rising vote.

At the outset, the convention set down its foot against any discrimination when it declared in its constitution that its firm aim was:

Regardless of Color

"To bring about the effective organization of the working men and
women of America regardless of race, creed, color, or nationality and to
unite them for common action into labor unions for their mutual aid and
protection."

It was in the following resolution, however, adopted with a rising ovation, that the CIO dedicated itself to an "uncompromising" struggle against
Negro discrimination in every phase of life:

WHEREAS, Employers constantly seek to split one group of workers from
another, and thus to deprive them of their full economic strength, by arousing
prejudices based on race, creed, color or nationality, and one of the most
frequent weapons used by employers to accomplish this end is to create false
conflicts between Negro and white workers; now therefore be it

RESOLVED, That the CIO hereby pledges itself to uncompromising opposition to any form of discrimination, whether political or economic, based
upon race, color, creed or nationality.

The convention discussed the Negro question mainly in connection with
its decision to launch a broad organizing campaign in the South. The convention went on record to sponsor and support legislation to abolish the
Southern poll taxes. It called for the enactment of legislation to remedy
the frightful conditions described in the report on Economic Conditions in
the South prepared by the President's National Emergency Council. It sent
greetings to the Southern Conference for Human Welfare which was to open a
week later in Birmingham (and which turned out to be a breath-taking success
in welding Southern whites and Negroes together for progress in the South!)

Paper Lauds Position

The unhesitating position taken by the CIO convention with regard to
the Negro workers, had a tremendous and immediate effect among the Negro
people. The Pittsburgh Courier, for example, one of the most influential
Negro papers in the country, declared that "there has been no convention in
the history of this nation which was more important to the broad mass of
Negroes and which has taken more significant action in respect to that mass
than that of the CIO."

"One of the features of this convention," the Courier continued, "was
the manner in which it attacked the problem of the Negro as problems belonging
in common to the working class. Its action was all the more significant when
one notes that this attack was led by whites. Southern whites at that. It
was not necessary to pack the convention with Negro delegates for the Negro
to get a hearing. Nor was it necessary for the Negro delegates to restrict
their activities to the special interests of their people. The Negro delegates were kept busy along the entire firing line. It was easy to perceive
that Negro and white delegates were looking beyond race."

The progressive position taken on the Negro question by the A.F. of L.
convention and, more especially, by the CIO, shows how the workers in both
organizations are making a clean break with the false prejudice that had been
forced upon them in the past years. It gives new promise of greater unity in
the future of all workers, Negro and white, working shoulder to shoulder for
the welfare of all.

Daily Worker, December 9, 1938.

18. UNION HELPED HER

The Negro Champion
169 West 133rd Street
New York City

Dear Friends:

     I read your paper and I notice that you ask for workers' correspondence.
I will therefore relate something that happened to me in the dress
makers' strike we are now having.
     I am seventeen years old and went to high school. When I left school
I could not get anything to do, so a friend took me down to her factory and I
got a job as an examiner on dresses.
     The boss offered me $15 a week and promised to raise me when I got ex-
perienced. Of course I did not know how much they were paying examiners and
as I was out of work and needed money badly I took the job. . . . Then one day
some men came into the factory and told us to come down stairs and go to union
headquarters. I didn't know what it was all about but the presser told me to
come along. When the boss saw that all the workers in the factory were walking
out, he came to me and pulled my hat off of my head and told me that I had
nothing to do with the others as they were all white and it was their affair.
But I refused to listen to the boss and went along with the other workers.
Most of them were union members and the others agreed to join the union. When
they learned that I was getting only $15 a week they told me that I should be
getting $26 a week instead. They began to make arrangements with the boss and
he agreed to everything except to pay me $26 a week. So the workers all said
that they would not go back to work unless he agreed to pay me. Then he began
to find fault with my work, but the workers struck out and finally he was forced
to agree to all our demands and we are now back in the shop working under union
conditions and I am a member of the new Needle Trades Industrial Union.

                                         Yours truly,

                                         Nellie Hall

Negro Champion, February 25, 1939.

19. WALTER HARDIN--A LEADER IN NEGROES' FIGHT FOR JUSTICE

By Swanson C. Shields

     DETROIT, June 24--Kidnapped and flogged, clubbed on the picket line,
threatened with "bodily violence" a score of times and victim of other anti-
labor uprisings . . .
     That may read like a page from a fiction thriller but to Walter T.
Hardin, outstanding Negro CIO leader in Michigan, it's all in a day's work.[28]
     Despite the blackjacks, the horsehide whip and other foul weapons
turned on Hardin by the union haters, the veteran Negro leader has not been
silenced. Today he stands out as one of the gamest fighters for labor's cause
in Michigan, his name an inspiration to both his colored and white brothers.
     His courage in refusing to be bullied by vigilante mobs symbolizes the
driving spirit of the CIO in this state.
     Always a staunch supporter of industrial unionism, Hardin early de-
serted Homer Martin when the latter started his "union busting" tactics.
Hardin had been an appointee of Martin. One of the first steps of the new
UAW-CIO president Fred Thomas, when he took office was to appoint Hardin
General Negro Organizer.[29]
     Wheeling into action his first day back on the firing line, Hardin
launched a vigorous drive among the more than 15,000 Negro automobile workers
in Michigan.

AFL MISTREATED NEGROES

Martin's decision to leave the CIO and re-enter the AFL spelled his defeat among the Negro workers, Hardin reports.

"The overwhelming majority of Negro unionists are solidly behind the
CIO today, because the CIO has given a new spirit of racial equality to the
colored race" he points out.

"The Negro was never given democratic rights in the AFL. Green, Wolf
and their crowd discriminated against the Negroes so notoriously that Jim-
Crowism became as widespread in the AFL as below the Dixie Line."

Smiling, Hardin added:

"For Martin to invite the Negroes into the AFL is tantamount for Hoover
or Girdler to ask the support of the CIO in 1940."[30]

In Bondage At Ford

What about Ford?

"Negro Ford workers, like their white brothers, are crying for unionsm.
They have been held in bondage by Ford terrorism for many years but today they
are throwing away the yoke of Fordism and want to enjoy the protection offered
by the CIO."

Kidnapped In '31

Hardin had his first baptism in anti-labor violence in 1931 when he
was kidnapped, taken to a desolate park outside Pontiac, undressed and then
brutally whipped and forced to stagger 10 miles back into the city without
shoes or stockings--in freezing weather.

His crime: Fighting starvation among Pontiac's unemployed.

Two In Asylum

Two other labor leaders, kidnapped and flogged along with Hardin were
clubbed so viciously and their vital organs crushed so violently that they
went insane shortly afterwards. Today they are inmates in a State asylum, a
living testimonial of the industrial terror that once stalked Michigan.

But the highlight of this story is that the perpetrators of the bloody
crime were never brought to justice. They were identified but a sympathetic
judge gave them only words of praise. Among the vigilantes was the personnel
director of a big auto plant here and the owner of a large foundry--both of
them outspoken labor foes.

But Hardin's greatest thrill came when he personally watched the two
"industrial floggers" sign UAW-CIO contracts two years ago.

CIO News, June 26, 1939.

20. JOHN L. LEWIS ON THE POLL TAX

Speaking February 10 in Washington to the American Youth Congress,
John L. Lewis, chairman of the Congress of Industrial Organizations, president
of the United Mine Workers, pioneer non-jim crow union, said:

"The Congress of Industrial Organization . . . stands for the preservation of civil liberties. It asks that that protection and those liberties
be accorded every citizen born under this flag, regardless of his color or
his creed or his geographical location.

"You know, we have a brand spanking new Supreme Court, 1940 model.
And I am in favor of giving that Supreme Court one particular job right away
so that we can find out whether or not we really have as good a Supreme Court
as some of us believe.

"There are these eight southern states that deprive Americans without
money of the right to vote. They levy poll taxes against the poor, Negroes

and whites, and they cannot vote in elections unless they pay their poll tax, and in addition to that if through a period of years they have been so poor that they could not either pay it or vote, whenever the time comes for them to pay up if they have any money, they have to pay for all the defaulted years in order to vote.

"There isn't any politician in this country, there isn't any lawyer or a Congressman or a sociologist or ordinary citizen who does not understand that those laws and those poll taxes are levied against the people of those States in order to impair their constitutional rights as native Americans to vote in the political elections. All right.

"I think that is just about as cowardly a practice as any politician could ever devise to take away from a free-born American inalienable rights granted under the Constitution and supposed to be protected under the flag.

"I am in favor of the President and the Attorney General of the United States instructing the Civil Liberties Bureau of the Department of Justice to bring in the Federal courts of this country a judicial proceeding and carry it to the Supreme Court of the United States, a judicial proceeding to attack and strike down those damnable provisions inflicted upon the citizenship of those southern states in the iniquitous poll taxes.

"While we are talking about civil liberties in this country, and the Attorney General of the United States talked about them to you from this platform last night, let him exercise the wits of those hundreds of lawyers that his department employs, by putting them to work upon a judicial procedure that is designed to restore to Americans in the southern states just the right to vote, and when that is done, why, then we can take time out to see who the people of those states would like to vote for in some election."

The Crisis, 47 (March, 1940): 81.

21.   COLORED PEOPLE TO HEAR PRES. LEWIS ON JUNE 18

PHILADELPHIA, June 15--CIO Pres. John L. Lewis will address the 31st annual conference of the Natl. Association for Advancement of Colored People here on Tuesday, June 18.

The meeting, which is the national get-together of the organization, will be held at the Tindley Temple, Broad and Fitzwater Streets. Lewis is scheduled to speak at 8:30 P.M.

Other speakers will include Arthur B. Spingarn, head of the Association, a nationally-known liberal leader.

Pres. Lewis' address will be the third in recent months that he has delivered to progressive pro-labor organizations. In February he spoke at the convention of the American Youth Congress, and a month later he appeared at the National Negro Congress meeting in Washington.

CIO News, June 17, 1940.

22.   LEWIS TELLS NEGRO GROUP:
U.S. MUST AVOID WAR
SOLVE OWN PROBLEMS

Following are excerpts from the speech delivered by CIO Pres. John L. Lewis to the 31st annual conference of the National Association for the Advancement of Colored People, in Philadelphia on June 18:

I appreciate very deeply the honor of your invitation to appear before the Thirty-First Conference of the National Association for the Advancement of Colored People. Your Association has, since it was first conceived by public-spirited citizens in 1909, fought a courageous fight for the rights of American citizens. Fundamentally, labor's fight is the same as yours--to obtain for American citizens those rights which are their heritage.

The problems of the Negro people are the problems of all American wage earners, but they are the problems in an aggravated form.

Unemployment, still the first bane of our land, rests with unequal heaviness upon the Negroes. When the census of unemployment was made in 1937, it showed that 15.7 per cent of the white working force was totally unemployed, while at the same time over 23 per cent of the Negro working force was totally out of work. We know that kind of a disproportion exists today.

The National Resources Committee has shown in cold facts what we already know, that the income of the Negro families falls far below the common level; for example, one of the studies showed that in Southern rural towns 91 per cent of the yearly incomes of Negroes was below one thousand dollars ($1,000), while only 45 per cent of the white population was under that level. In the large Northern cities 42 per cent of the Negro incomes was below one thousand dollars ($1,000), while only 18 per cent of the white incomes was below that figure. This income disproportion is reflected in the housing and medical care which the Negroes can get.

Negroes' Problems

The needs of no group in the nation are greater than those of the Negro people.

Their incomes as a group are the lowest.

Their living conditions are the poorest.

Their unemployment is the highest.

The discrimination against them is the worst.

Most of the Negroes are wage earners and their salvation lies in the same measure as does that of labor as a whole.

Two great essential rights guarantee the advance of labor and of the Negro in a democracy. The first is the right to organize into unions as workers. The second is the right of political expression free and unhampered.

Equal economic opportunity will come to the Negro workers only when they are organized industrially, side by side with all other workers.

CIO Principles

In the CIO all workers have equality of opportunity. There is no discrimination in wage rates between any of the workers. They have equal rights to all others within the organization, and they must be paid equal wages for doing equal work. The United Mine Workers brought that principle home to the thousands of Negro mine workers in the South, when in 1933 it established equal rights for white and Negro workers in the Southern mines.

Many Negroes are leaders of CIO unions and stand high up in the ranks of the leaders of organized labor. They lead not unions of Negroes alone, but unions of all workers, no matter what their color.

Equal economic opportunity for Negroes under organized labor is the first step toward their rightful place in the sun for the Negro people.

The right to vote establishes the rightful place of every group in our nation. That is why the Negroes as well as the millions of other Southern workers must be released from the shackles of the poll tax, so that they can exercise their franchise.

A Sound Program

The CIO's program offers to Negroes, as well as to the other people of the nation the basis for a sound program.

1. The CIO is the instrument through which the fight of the workers for the right to bargain collectively is being carried on.

2. The CIO is fighting for the end of the poll tax which destroys the right to vote.

3. The CIO demands the passage of the anti-lynching bill.

4. The CIO calls for the end of unemployment, for adequate security and decent housing and free and equal education.

Clearly the CIO program, and that of the welfare of the Negro people, are to all intents and purposes, practically the same. The way to attain

such a program is by common action, and that common action labor freely offers
to those who would cooperate with it to the same ends.

Unemployment

In the United States, there are 11,259,000 unemployed.
This is substantially the same number as were unemployed on March 4th,
1933. It is unfortunate for the nation that nothing has been done in seven
years to correct this situation. It is tragically unfortunate for those
millions who have borne the brunt of the human suffering which these figures
suggest.
Government figures recently released reveal that 19 million American
families are compelled to subsist on a monthly income of $26.00. Government
figures further reveal that under-consumption threatens the health and physical
standards of the population. One half of all the people in the United States
have incomes which enable them to spend for food requirements only ten cents
per meal per person.
Those who love to fuminate against the menace of Fifth Columns and
Trojan Horses should thus stop to consider that the most menacing condition in
American national life is the inadequate diet and the empty stomachs of one-
half of the population.
Increased national income and employment for all Americans is a fundamental and imperative problem, which the major political parties and the Government must face. It is truly tragic that the current Administration in power,
after seven years of experimentation, has made no substantial contribution
toward the abatement of this problem. It is equally tragic that the political
party in power, and its spokesmen, have even now no suggestion to offer for
national unemployment, except that possible involvement in a European war may
relieve them from the responsibilities of unsolved domestic problems.

No War!

Involvement or intervention in the European war is repugnant to every
healthy-minded American. The American electorate is anxious to demonstrate
this fact in the political election of 1940. The major political party that
permits war, or potential war profiteers, or professional politicians, with
an aggressive military complex, to dominate or write its platform will find
itself hopelessly beaten by the votes of an outraged electorate in November.
All of the labor and liberal organizations, with which I am identified
stand unalterably for the adequate defense of the nation and its democratic
institutions, and against involvement in the European war and against those
who advocate such involvement.

No Recovery

A great depression came on the world in 1929. That depression arose
fundamentally from the financial collapse of Europe, which was inevitable as
the aftermath of the losses and inflations of the World War.
The economists all agree that recovery from that world-wide depression
began in the United States and in every other democratic country in the spring
of 1932. The other democratic countries in the world went straight on out of
that depression from 1932. They had recovered employment for their people,
most of them in the year 1934, and practically all of them by 1935.
The United States alone went backward after the election of Franklin D.
Roosevelt, and under his policies it has stayed depressed in the United States
ever since. We have never recovered our national income within ten billions
per annum. And with our growth of population at the normal rate of progress,
it should be 30 billions greater today than it now is. If it were 30 billions
greater we would have no unemployment.
In Great Britain they not only recovered their pre-depression national
income by 1935, but they marched ahead to 25% above it, while we sweated along
20% below.
Mr. Roosevelt made depression and unemployment a chronic fact in American
life. It was a slogan of the 1932 presidential election that Herbert Hoover
was responsible for that depression. As a simple matter of justice, let me say
here and now that the workers of the United States realize that he had nothing
whatever to do with it. It was laid on his doorstep when he came to the White

House. It is only the self-seeking politicians that blame Mr. Hoover. The
policies he pursued, in cooperation with other nations, had a powerful effect
in the start at recovery in 1932. The New Deal did not fulfill their promises
or complete their undertakings. It was their policies and their weaknesses
which have kept this country in depression for seven more years.

The Future

        It is time for all Americans to take stock of the problems which face
them today. When the European war ends, and the populations of the warring
countries return to the peacetime production of essential commodities, our own
country will face terrific economic repercussions. It is time for the major
political parties to appraise the situation and keep faith with the American
people, by enunciating policies and selecting candidates equal to the task before them. Otherwise, every American will pay the price of our national
failure--a price that may well be beyond their ability to pay.

CIO News, June 24, 1940.

23. THE LABOR READER: THE NEGRO AND THE CIO

By C. W. Fowler

        One of the annual events at American Federation of Labor conventions
just as regular as the re-election of Bill Green and other extinct volcanoes
to the AFL leadership, is a pious resolution of discrimination against Negro
workers. Annually the resolution is passed, with favorable comment, and
annually ignored. AFL unions, having voted for the resolution, go home to
continue what they have always practiced--with honorable exceptions--the rule
of exclusion and Jim Crow against Negro workers.
        It took the advent of the CIO to change this age-old custom just as it
took the CIO to bring organization to the masses of industrial workers in the
United States. There is no discrimination in CIO unions. The constitution
of the CIO expressly forbids it, all CIO affiliates have consistently refused
to practice it, just as an industrial union refused to discriminate against
a worker because of skill or occupation, so it cannot discriminate against
a worker because of race--and remain an industrial union.
        The CIO doesn't need any pious resolutions on discrimination to remind
it of certain basic facts, ably stated in the introduction to "Black Workers
and the News Unions," a new study of Horace R. Cayton and George S. Mitchell.[31]
The CIO has been aware from the beginning, as the authors say, that:

PROFITS IN PREJUDICE

        "The employer class has found racial prejudice a profitable thing, for
since the Negro has not been drawn into a working class organization, he has
been available for the exercise of the 'divide and rule' policy in connection
with labor disputes. During a strike, the employer could import from another
region Negroes who felt no solidarity with his employes and who were well
beyond the control of the local public opinion which supported the strikers.
        "Another advantage for the employers was the adoption of a lower wage
scale which the Negro accepted because of the difficulty in obtaining other
employment. As a rule a prerequisite to employment was that Negroes would not
demand the wage and working conditions granted the white workers."
        This advantage is something, as the authors point out, that anti-union
employers have never hesitated to use, as long as the labor movement allowed
them to. Negro workers were brought in to break strikes in the north as early
as 1875, when they first came into the steel industry. Thirty thousand of them
were imported as strikebreakers in 1919, as before in the great Homestead walkout of 1890.

UNION MEN TODAY

The same technique was used in other basic industries. In the packing industry, now organized like steel by the CIO, Negroes were imported to break the back of organizing effort after the first world war and in sporadic outbursts before. The employers succeeded then, to the point of provoking disastrous race riots.

They are not succeeding now, as the overwhelming success of the CIO Packinghouse Workers union shows. Here again, as in other CIO organizing drives. Negro workers take their full place in the membership and in the leadership of the new industrial union. The packing industry has a high percentage of Negro workers, and the percentage of Negro leaders, from the Assistant National Director to local officials, is equally high.

This is the way the CIO organizes industrial workers, not, as Cayton and Mitchell point out, in the way the AFL and some other organizations have attempted to organize, by discrimination and Jim Crow.

CIO News, December 4, 1940.

24. NEGROES SHOULD JOIN THE CIO, SAYS PAUL ROBESON [32]

I know about the situation at Ford's and I'll be glad to tell you what I think about it. Most Negroes think of me as a football player and song star. They do not know that before I could get through college, I worked as a bricklayer, on an ice wagon and as a waiter in a restaurant.

My first contact with the labor movement came while I was living in England, because of the problems affecting Negroes. The British Labour Party was intensely interested in problems affecting the Negro workers.

I gained the favor of the labor movement and decided I must do something about the problem of the Negro, their special problem and those that face all workers, white and colored. I came to certain conclusions while watching the movement there.

I am against separate unions for Negro workers. All should belong to the same organization. I am glad that is the policy that has been accepted by the CIO.

Coming back to this country, it seemed to me that the simple right to organize into a Union was a common fact and should be accepted. I was amazed that such a right should be questioned here in the U.S. It is astounding that a man like Ford and a large industry like Ford Motor Company have been able to operate in a democracy and not have to deal with the movement. . . .

The Negro problem cannot be solved by a few of us getting to be doctors and lawyers. The best way my race can win justice is by sticking together in progressive labor unions. It would be unpardonable for Negro workers to fail to join the CIO. I don't see how that can be argued. Insofar as the AFL is concerned, A. Philip Randolph, President of the Brotherhood of Sleeping Car Porters, a Negro, had difficulty getting the floor at the AFL Convention just to present the demands of Negro workers for full rights.

There is no reason in the world why Negroes should not join the CIO. If they fail to do so, they classify themselves as scab labor Negroes and cannot be a part of the American Democracy except through labor unions. A democracy cannot exist without labor unions.

In the United States today there is a terrific effort going on to take away the all too few rights of labor. If that happens, the Negroes, who have the fewest rights, will suffer most.

Remarks during campaign to organize Ford Motor Company--*Ford Facts,* December 20, 1940, *CIO News,* December 23, 1940.

25. THE CIO AND THE NEGRO WORKER

The CIO's Stand

The objects of the organization are:
"To bring about the effective organization of the working men and women of America regardless of race, creed, color or nationality, and to unite them for common action into labor unions for their mutual aid and protection."

From the Constitution of the Congress of Industrial Organizations.

WHEREAS, The history of organized labor in the United States is replete with instances in which reactionary employing interests have sought to divide the workers by playing on the prejudices and special interests of whites against Negroes, or the reverse; and
One of the great contributions which the CIO has made to the strength of organized labor in the United States has been to break down the barriers which have existed in the past between Negro and white workers in labor organizations; now, therefore, be it
RESOLVED, That the CIO reaffirms the position which it has consistently maintained from the beginning in opposition to any and all forms of discrimination between one worker and another based upon considerations of race, creed. color, or nationality, and pledges itself to work with vigor toward the elimination of outworn prejudices of this kind wherever they may be found in American life; and
That the CIO condemns the policies of many employers of discriminating in their hiring and other employment conditions against Negroes, which constitutes a direct attack against our nation's policy to build democracy in our fight against Hitlerism.
Resolution of the fourth convention of the CIO held in Detroit, Mich., November, 1941.

The CIO and the Negro Worker

The CIO is an organization of all American workers united as its constitution and its leaders declare, "regardless of race, creed, color or nationality" for the purpose of improving the living and working standards of all Americans and for the purpose of maintaining and expanding democracy and freedom.
Today the CIO stands with every other American and with liberty-loving people everywhere against the murderous attack of Hitler, Japan and their Axis puppets; determined to defend the right of all people to live and to work out their own destiny in freedom.
The CIO has always recognized that all people--"regardless of race, creed, color or nationality"--must stand together to defeat common enemies and achieve common aims. Hatred and disunity between peoples is the greatest weapon Hitler has found in his bloody march to conquest, just as it has always been the greatest weapon of the exploiter and the anti-labor politician.
The resistance of the nations fighting Hitler and the Axis depends on how well they stand together fighting as one. The resistance of our own people to Hitler and his Japanese allies depends on how well we stand together in our own country--Negro and white, Jew and Gentile, native and foreigner born.
The CIO was founded in 1935 on the strength of a principle--the principle. that all workers deserve equal consideration, the principle that all workers must unite on common terms to get it.
The principle is not only democratic, it is also a matter of common sense. For many generations anti-labor employers were able to keep American workers apart on racial and religious prejudices. As a result, they were able to exploit them much more easily, on the well-known policy of divide and misrule.

Discrimination Out

The men who founded the CIO in 1935 knew this, and they determined to build an organization that would rob the exploiters of the weapon of disunity. The unions they headed were industrial unions, where every worker had an equal voice, where every worker got equal consideration.

They had a long history of rejecting all forms of discrimination in their own ranks, where Negro workers were active side by side with their white fellow-members.

What is more, they were strong unions, because they were not split up into tiny groups that fought with each other rather than fighting for their common interest.

The new organization, the CIO, determined to keep out every form of discrimination that had held the labor movement back before. It had to keep out racial discrimination just as it had to keep out craft discrimination. The modern labor movement realized from experience that you could no more exclude workers because of the color of their skin than you could exclude them because of differences in their occupations--if you wanted a strong labor movement.

How well this principle has worked is seen in the fact that there were fewer than 125,000 Negroes in the labor movement before the CIO. Today, after six years, there are more than 500,000--most of them in the CIO.

The CIO is the strongest force in American labor today because its unions have consistently refused to let racial or religious or nationalist disunity weaken them. That is one basic reason why the CIO has organized more than five million American workers, why it has won billions of dollars in wage raises, why it has been able to serve the people of America more than any other organization in the nation.

And it is a basic reason why the CIO today is a great force for victory, why the five million men and women of the CIO are able to give so much to their nation and to our allies in the war for freedom from fascist slavery.

The men and women of the CIO are at work today in the arsenal of democracy, turning out the tanks and guns, planes and ships the United Nations need to crush Hitlerism. They are the soldiers of production, the people who stand beside the machines that are digging Hitler's grave.

The CIO is organized in the basic industries of America, in coal and steel, in machine building, in aircraft, in shipbuilding, in electrical industry, in oil, in aluminum, in copper and other vital metals, in textiles, in packing, in the maritime trades, in the thousand and one industries working to arm our nation and the nations with us.

Equal Voice

In every one of these unions, Negro workers take their place as members with the same democratic rights, with the same voice as all other members.

The Steel Workers Organizing Committee has contracts covering more than 600,000 workers. Negro workers in the SWOC have equal voice with all others. The United Automobile Workers of America has contracts covering over 700,000 workers. Negro members have equal voice in the UAW-CIO with all members. In all these unions, Negro members can and do take official positions, are elected to places of leadership by their fellow members.

A Negro trade union leader, Mr. Willard S. Townsend, president of the United Transport Service Employes, CIO, is a member of the top CIO Executive Board which is the highest CIO policy making body between conventions. Other Negro union leaders are members of important CIO committees. [33]

All of the unions of the CIO have won benefits for their members. The CIO has raised and maintained the standard of living for many millions beyond its own membership.

Between 1940 and 1941, the CIO added one and a quarter billion dollars to the annual payroll of America workers. This has meant more food, more clothing, more shelter for millions of the American people. It has meant a better chance for the kids, an easier job for the wife who has to stretch the paycheck to meet the cost of living. And just as important, it means better health and higher morale for American workers--health and morale, we desperately need to defeat Hitler and Japan.

The CIO policy of higher wages does not stop with gains already won. Today rising living costs make wage increases more than ever necessary. The CIO is pressing its drive for wage increases in every industry where workers are organized in CIO unions.

In every case, the CIO makes sure that Negro workers receive the same benefits. In every union, the Negro worker and his family have the same chance to win a better life that the white worker has.

In every union auxiliary Negro women and white women unite for this same end.

This has reached not only the basic mass-production industries. The CIO has organized thousands of Negro and white workers in agriculture, bringing hope to the most savagely exploited people in our country. It has organized thousands of Negro and white workers in the packing industry, where Negro workers have been special victims of exploitation. It has organized Negro along with white workers in the government, in the white collar and professional fields, in transport, in maritime, in construction--everywhere the CIO has gone.

Southern Drive

The CIO has brought new hope to the underpaid and sweated workers of the South. Many thousands of Southern workers, Negro and white alike, have come under the protection of the CIO. Today the CIO is carrying on a major drive to bring economic freedom and social decency to millions more.

The CIO fights for the right of Southern workers to live and to work for a better way of life just as it has fought and won for millions of workers in other parts of the country.

This is not done out of goodness of heart alone. The CIO is not a charity organization. The CIO has organized Negro and white workers alike because that is the only way strong, industrial labor unions can be built. For a union to practice discrimination is to hand over half its strength to the employer, who uses it to weaken and divide the workers.

For the same reason, the CIO leads in uniting all the people for the defeat of Hitler, of Japan and the junior partner in murder, fascist Italy. Unity of all the people of America for victory is not just idealism. It is hard common sense, for all of us will be slaves if the Axis wins, and all of us are needed to keep our country free.

What the CIO Stands For

The CIO stands for a better life for all workers, for higher wages, for security, for the right to live and the right to work as free men and women. To this end, the CIO has organized powerful industrial unions where men and women unite to achieve common ends. The CIO intends to keep these unions of the people strong, to defend them against attack from any source.

For this reason, the CIO carries on vigorous campaigns for social laws that will help the people better their lives. It fights to keep the good laws we have, to make them stronger, and to win new ones where they are needed.

The CIO has fought for five years to defend the Wagner Act, because it helps protect the right to organize and bargain collectively. The CIO fights to defend the wage-hour act, because it helps protect the workers from the sweatshop. The CIO fights to improve social security, to get more aid for the unemployed, to guard the workers against sickness and old age. The CIO fights for more housing for workers, for a national health program, for fair taxation, for price control to prevent the disaster of inflation.

The CIO has carried on a long campaign to end the poll tax that robs millions of workers and farmers, Negro and white alike, of the basic right of all Americans. The CIO fights constantly for effective measures against lynching, this worst of all stains on America. The CIO fights constantly against discrimination on the job, to bring the skill and strength of millions of Negro and other workers to the aid of the victory program.

These campaigns will be fought by the CIO until every issue is won. The CIO does not lie back on its record. It keeps on fighting, and will keep on fighting, until democracy is secure, until every American has the rights guaranteed by our Constitution and our Declaration of Independence.

The War of Production

Today the CIO is in the lead in the battle for production that must be
won to save our nation. Through the Industry Council Plan of President Philip
Murray, through the various detailed plans offered by the CIO unions, the CIO
has charted the blueprints for out-producing the Axis. These plans are freely
offered to the nation. They would let loose the productive forces that our
country needs to keep us free.[34]
    Basic to all these plans is the full participation of the men and women
of labor in the victory program. Full participation means that all workers,
Negro and white, of any creed or origin, must be brought into the national
war effort. None can be left out, because we can afford to lose the strength
and skill of none.
    This is why the CIO fights discrimination against Negro workers on arms
production jobs. Excluding 10 million people, or any part of them, from our
arms factories is an aid to Hitler. It robs the nation of production soldiers
just when we need them most.
    The Fair Employment Practices Committee set up by the government was
created as a result of CIO's campaign against discrimination and of CIO demands
for all-out production. President Philip Murray of the CIO is a leading member
of this committee. The unions of the CIO cooperate with it in reporting cases
of discrimination. They want not only to see justice done to the Negro workers,
they want also to see that our nation gets every ounce of production for the
war.
    The Negro people of America have made great contributions to the nation's
wealth and strength. Their sweat and toil have been freely spent for hundreds
of years. Today, the CIO wants to bring the strength and patriotism of the
Negro people to bear on the greatest task of all our history--the task of
wiping out the modern form of slavery created by Hitler.

A People's Movement

    The CIO is a people's movement, for security, for jobs, for civil rights
and freedom. It speaks for all the working men and women of America, Negro
and white. It does not ask questions of race or color or creed or origin.
The CIO fights to bring the benefits of industrial organization to all working
people. The CIO does this job in the only way it can be done--by organizing
all the workers, excluding none, discriminating against none.
    The CIO is the strongest force for progress in America today. The CIO
leads in the victory program, because the CIO unites all the people in the war
for freedom.
    Hitler makes slaves of all the people he conquers, beginning with
minority groups. The CIO has freed millions of workers from economic bondage--
including those from minority groups.
    The CIO, as President Philip Murray said, "is in this war for the sole
purpose of winning it." Winning the war calls for the highest national unity.
It calls for the united effort of every man and woman in America, Negro and
white, Gentile and Jew, native and foreign born.
    The CIO is organizing for freedom over tyranny in every form in which
it is expressed. The CIO organizes for victory over fascism and exploitation.
    Negro workers, join the CIO union in your industry. The CIO welcomes
you. It gives you strength to win justice and fair play. The CIO unites you
with your fellow workers of all races and all creeds in the common struggle
for freedom, for democracy, for a better life.

Civil Liberties

    Be It Resolved, That in the present national and world crisis, the CIO,
in the interests of victory over our Axis foes, renews its pledge to carry on
the fight for the preservation of civil rights, calls upon the Department of
Justice and State governments to prosecute to the fullest extent those responsible for lynchings, calls upon Congress to enact legislation making
lynching a Federal offense, and calls upon all agencies of our Federal and
State government to join in crushing any and all anti-democractic efforts to
deny our basic human and civil rights.

Discrimination

Whereas, Discrimination against workers because of race, religion or
country of origin is an evil characteristic of our fascist enemies. We of the
democracies are fighting fascism at home and abroad by welding all races, all
religions and all peoples into a united body of warriors for democracy. Any
discriminatory practices within our own ranks, against Negroes or other groups,
directly aids the enemy by creating division, dissension and confusion. Such
discrimination practiced in employment policies hampers production by depriving the nation of the use of available skills and manpower.

Be It Resolved, That the CIO now reiterates its firm opposition to any
form of racial or religious discrimination and renews its pledge, as a war-time
duty, to carry on the fight for protection in law and in fact of the rights of
every racial and religious group to participate fully in our social, political
and industrial life.

Resolution of the 5th convention of the CIO, held in Boston, Mass.,
November, 1942.

Pamphlet published by the CIO (Washington, D.C., 1942), 11 pp.

STEEL WORKERS' ORGANIZING COMMITTEE

26. NEGROES BACK C.I.O. STEEL DRIVE
GIVE MANDATE IN FIGHT FOR UNITY

By Ben Davis, Jr.

The nation-wide drive to organize steel workers into the Amalgamated
Association of Iron, Steel and Tin Workers, has set a precedent in rallying
support from all sections of the Negro people.

This is not a coincidence. For years Negro workers supported by white
progressives have beat upon the doors of the reactionary American Federation
of Labor executive council, clamoring for admission into the organized trade
union movement on a basis of equality with all other workers. The council
in turn has contemptuously sought to perpetuate conditions of jim-crowism and
discrimination in the labor movement of which only the capitalist open-shoppers
could be proud.

Back C.I.O.

Of the more than 100,000 Negro workers in the organized labor movement,
the overwhelming majority are without doubt active sympathizers with the C.I.O.
drive.

At the Tampa A.F. of L. convention the International Brotherhood of
Sleeping Car Porters, headed by A. Philip Randolph, outstanding Negro leader,
was among the progressive unions which voted against the suspension of the
C.I.O. unions and opposed the splitting policies of the Green-Woll-Hutcheson
clique. This and countless other examples prove that the Negro workers are
among the most progressive and valuable members of the organized labor movement. [35]

Following the lead of the Negro workers and the progressive movement as
a whole, other stratas of the Negro population have endorsed the C.I.O. drive.

The ball started rolling when the historic National Negro Congress representing indirectly a million Negroes, last year endorsed the C.I.O. in a
sweeping resolution.

Since that time branches of the Congress throughout the country have
been active arousing popular support among the Negro people for the steel

drive. John P. Davis, young national executive-secretary of the Congress, has just ended a transcontinental tour after which he reported that the Congress resolution was being "brought to life in Baltimore, New York, Chicago, Los Angeles, Pittsburgh and other urban centers." Davis spoke to hundreds of Negro and white steel workers.

Role of Negro Press

Councils of the National Negro Congress in a dozen cities have become the center of activities for Negroes of widely different political views to mobilize support for the steel campaign.
The National Negro Bar Association, and the National Negro Medical Association, two of the most influential organizations among the Negro people, went on record in support of the C.I.O. early last summer. Scarcely a dissenting voice has been heard from among the 300 odd Negro newspapers which, almost unanimously, have urged their readers to rally behind the C.I.O.
Leading among the Negro newspapers which have endorsed the drive are the New York Amsterdam News, the Baltimore Afro-American, the Crisis, official organ of the National Association for the Advancement of Colored People.

Mandate Against Oppression

Prominent Negroes who have endorsed the drive are: Lester Granger, Workers Bureau of the National Urban League, William N. Jones, Baltimore Afro-American; the Rev. A. Clayton Powell, Jr., pastor of Abyssinia Baptist Church; and others from every corner of America.[36]
After all, besides being pinched by national oppression themselves, Negro leaders are bound to hear the militant rumblings among the Negro masses.
The large support to the Steel Workers Organizing Committee, headed by Phillip Murray, vice-president of the C.I.O., is a mandate from the Negro people for the breaking down of the discriminatory policies long-enforced by the A.F. of L. craft union dynasty.

Step to Strong Unity

Ninety-nine per cent of the Negro population are workers who have been hamstrung, jim-crowed, segregated and denied the right to decent wages and trade union conditions because such A.F. of L. officials as Green, Frey, Wharton, would rather protect the reactionary employers than the Negro and white workers.[37]
The triumph of the C.I.O. steel drive means a powerful step toward a strong united trade union movement purged of countless color-bars against Negro workers. Thus the fight for the full equality of Negro workers in the trade unions is the fight of the whole labor movement. It means breaking the back of the steel and auto trust drives to make scabs of Negro workers--a policy fostered by reactionary members of the A.F. of L. council.

Foster on Drive

Forward and significant strides have been made by the Steel Workers Organizing Committee in uniting Negro and white workers on a firm footing of equality.
The possibilities of further extending this healthy trend have been outlined excellently by William Z. Foster, great leader of the magnificent 1919 steel strike. In his recent pamphlet, "Organizing Methods in the Steel Industry," page 17, Foster wrote:
"It is absolutely essential that the large number of Negroes in the steel industry be organized. For this, special Negro organizers are imperative. Special demands for Negroes must be formulated and widely popularized. Prominent Negro speakers, including those of the National Negro Congress, should be brought into the steel districts to address meetings.
"When necessary, special meetings of Negro steel workers should be called. The Negroes should become members of the regular local Amalgamated Association unions with full rights. Close attention should be paid to bringing them into responsible official posts in the unions and in the organizing crew. There should also be immediately developed an active

campaign against the prevalent jim-crow practices in the steel towns and steel
industry. Local organizations of Negroes should be enlisted in support of the
campaign."[38]
    These words serve as a beacon light not only for organizing thousands
of Negro steel workers with full and equal trade union rights, but also for
making the steel drive one of the biggest triumphs in the history of the
American labor movement.

Daily Worker, January 9, 1937.

27. NEGRO LEADERS TO ISSUE CALL TO 100,000 IN INDUSTRY

John P. Davis, James W. Ford and Howard Davis[39]
Speak at Conference in Pittsburgh--Negro
Congress Pledges Its Support

By Adam Lapin

PITTSBURGH, Pa., Jan. 10--Far flung plans to speed the organization of
Negro steel workers were mapped here on Saturday by a conference of Negro
civic and fraternal leaders together with Negro organizers on the staff of the
Steel Workers Organizing Committee.
    The group of Negro leaders unanimously resolved to call a broad national
conference with representation from every conceivable Negro organization for
the purpose of putting the entire Negro community behind a last minute spurt
to complete the S.W.O.C. drive.
    Tentative plans are that the conference will be held around Feb. 22,
Lincoln's birthday, in Pittsburgh.

To Call 100,000

Saturday's meeting was attended by 16 Negro leaders, many of whom had
come from long distances and was convened by a number of Negro S.W.O.C. organizers.
    Active in the work of the meeting were John P. Davis, secretary of the
National Negro Congress, Howard Davis, of the Workers Alliance of Pittsburgh,
William E. Hill, industrial secretary of the Pittsburgh Urban League, James W.
Ford, outstanding Negro Communist leader, Sam Peterson, negro I.W.O. organizer,
J. Washington of the American Woodmen and other community and fraternal
leaders.
    Negro S.W.O.C. organizers and volunteers who were active in calling the
meeting, and placed their problems before it included Ben Careathers, A. W.
McPhearson, Henry Johnson, of Chicago, B. D. Amis of the Philadelphia Negro
congress and volunteer S.W.O.C. organizer, Joseph Howard, Birmingham organizer
and Henry Jackson, C.I.O. youth organizer.[40]
    The meeting decided to prepare a pamphlet urging the Negro steel workers
to join the union, and to issue 100,000 calls to the proposed conference. A
special committee was set up to carry on the work of the meeting and to discuss
further plans with Philip Murray, S.W.O.C. chairman.
    To the consternation of the business executives, Murray declared accord-
ing to Hill, that the S.W.O.C. was organizing Negro and white workers into the
same lodges in Birmingham, was experiencing no trouble, and intended to pursue
this policy nationally.
    Others who cited the support they had received from S.W.O.C. organizers
in making special efforts to reach Negro workers were Amis of Philadelphia,
Johnson of Chicago, and Davis of the Negro Congress.

Fraternal Groups Aid

Organized support from fraternal organizations, churches, ministers
and other Negro groups was considered essential to winning the support of the
masses of Negro workers in the outstanding steel centers.

Johnson made the main report to the meeting. He stated that one out
of every five steel workers were Negroes. He cited various forms of discrimination including lower wage rates and consistent refusal to promote
Negro workers in proportion to their ability and skill.
     As a result, he pointed out, Negro workers are not only more poorly
paid than the average white workers, but are also engaged in the most hazardous
and undesirable types of work.
     This discrimination is an "ace in the hole for the steel bosses,"
Johnson said, stating that Negro workers were made glowing promises of advancement during strikes in an effort to enlist them as scabs.
     Citing his own experiences in the Chicago area, Johnson showed that all
barriers between Negro and white workers were broken down as soon as masses
of Negro workers were recruited as active members of the Union.
     He proposed the convening of a national conference to speed the mass
recruiting of Negro workers.

Negro Congress To Aid

John P. Davis brought the conference the full support of the National
Negro Congress and assured the leaders present that the Negro congress would
support all of their plans.
     He said that the local councils of the Congress were giving their
fullest support to the steel drive and estimated that approximately 200,000
leaflets were issued and distributed by the Congress to Negro steel workers.
     One of the points emphasized by organizers active in the field was the
need for a more effective and larger apparatus with which to help organize
the Negro workers.
     This point was stressed by Howard, the Birmingham organizer, who felt
that the work in that strategic steel area was being handicapped by a lack
of a sufficient number of trained organizers.
     In many places, organizers said, they are overcoming this deficiency
by organizing volunteer crews of Negro organizers.

Ford Urges Speed

Ford placed great stress on the need for speeding up the tempo of the
drive among Negro workers.
     He said that the steel drive was important to the entire Negro people,
and that its success would immeasurably aid the organization of Negro workers
in other industries.
     He cited the writings of William Z. Foster, leader of the great 1919
steel strike, as explaining the importance of the Negro workers in any successful effort to unionize steel.
     The committee set up to continue the work of the meeting consisted
of Ben Careathers, A. W. McPhearson, Henry Johnson, John P. Davis, William E
Hill, B. D. Amis and Joseph Howard.

Daily Worker, January 11, 1937.

28. NEGRO AND WHITE STICK--STEEL LOCKOUT FAILS

Pittsburgh Federal Metals Plant Forced to Con-
cede Union Recognition, Pay Increases for All
Hands and Other Gains After Mill Organizes

PITTSBURGH, Pa., Jan. 18--"Before we put our heads together we had
nothing, is that right?"
     A deep, rumbling "that's right" came from the throats of 150 triumphant
Negro and white workers of the Federal Metals plant gathered in the crowded
Butler Street headquarters of the S.W.O.C. on Saturday.
     "You didn't want to be pushed around, is that right?"

And again "that's right" traveled from the lips of 150 workers around the smoke-filled room.

"You didn't want a company union, did you?"

This time it was a sharp, angry "no" that answered the question of President Mike Gorham of newly formed Lodge 1154 of the Amalgamated Assn. of Iron, Steel and Tin Workers.

The tough, lithe president of the lodge was explaining to the membership the concessions that had been wrung from Manager A. S. Simon after he had tried to fool the union men and then lock them out from the plant for three days.

Gorham read off the gains made by the union one by one, and asked for the opinions of the men which came in a mass chorus of approval.

Then the union members voted on the agreement, unanimously resolving to return to work under vastly improved conditions.

Federal Metals is just a small smelting and refining plant in Pittsburgh employing some 250 workers, almost half of them Negroes. But weakness here might have retarded the union drive in the great steel mills of the city.

Negro, White Solidarity

And the strength shown by the union, on the other hand, has its significance far out of proportion to the size of the plant.

Not only did the workers force the management to abandon the lockout, but they demonstrated in practice that solidarity of Negro and white which will be of such decisive importance to the steel workers.

Negro and white were packed close together in the union headquarters. Before the meeting began they were chatting together, talking over problems of strategy, their arms around each other.

Walter Clark, a Negro, was chairman of the meeting and is one of the Lodge leaders. He is affectionately called Clarkey.

John Detchman, S.W.O.C. organizer, told the Daily Worker in glowing terms of the fine union spirit and discipline displayed by the Negro workers.

When 200 of the 250 workers in the plant had been organized, a committee was sent to the management asking for a union agreement. Mr. Simon seemed to agree readily to all of the demands. He promised to recognize a shop committee.

The next morning 19 workers were fired, including some of the members of the committee.

That evening the workers were discussing strike action. But when they arrived at the plant the next morning, they found that they were locked out.

Simon was trying to outsmart the union and break the spirit of the men.

Strategy Fails

A lack of materials was the reason given for the lockout, although men inside the mill had seen enough material for several days' work.

However the stratagem failed. The men did not come pleading for mercy. They stuck together, and indicated that they could keep the plant shut down indefinitely.

The next time a committee met with Mr. Simon he was willing to listen to reason. He not only gave up the lockout but agreed to the following conditions:

1. Recognition of a union committee.
2. Seniority rights.
3. Increases of 12 per cent and in some cases 12-1/2 per cent for all men instead of the originally offered 10 per cent.
4. Time and a half for overtime.
5. Full pay for the three days they were locked out.
6. A work week beginning on Monday instead of on Sunday as in the past.

Daily Worker, January 12, 1937.

29.   NEGRO GROUPS IN STEEL DRIVE TO HOLD PARLEY IN FEBRUARY

Campaign Is Hailed by Press as
Major Issue for Negro People

PITTSBURGH, PA., Jan. 28--Added support for the Negro conference of
Negro organizations in Pittsburgh in February to rally support for the steel
drive was announced here today.

Among the Negro leaders who have declared their full support of the
conference are William N. Jones, an editor of the Baltimore Afro-American,
Lester Granger, secretary of the Workers Councils of the Urban League, Wayne
L. Hopkins, secretary of the Armstrong Association, and Edward Lewis, Baltimore Urban League leader.[41]

Negro S.W.O.C. organizers working for the conference commented on the
fact that leading Negro newspapers have taken a favorable position on the
steel drive and the C.I.O.

They cited the editorial remarks of the Cleveland Eagle to the effect
that present C.I.O. efforts to organize Negro and white workers together in a
powerful steel union "may develop into the most important event in Negro
history since Lincoln's Emancipation Declaration."

Many outstanding Negro leaders and organizations have already declared
their support of the conference which will have the aim of rallying the entire
Negro community behind the steel drive in an effort to speed up recruiting of
the Negro workers in the steel industry.

Daily Worker, January 29, 1937.

30.   NEGRO AMERICA ACTS TO BUILD STEEL UNION

Delegates from Many Groups Map Campaign to
Bring Organization Drive to People--
Workers and Professionals United

By Adam Lapin

PITTSBURGH, Pa., Feb. 7--Negro America made an historic decision here
on Saturday which will not only hasten the great drive to unionize steel, but
may leave its imprint on the future development of the labor movement in the
United States.

Distinguished representatives of the Negro church, business men, leading
professionals, delegates from women's clubs joined together at the Elk's Rest
with Negro men of steel, horny-handed, plain-spoken workers, in a solemn
resolve to unionize the Negro steel workers as a decisive step toward the
economic emancipation of their people.

The significance of the conference was clearly indicated in a stirring
impassioned keynote address by Philip Murray, chairman of the Steel Workers
Committee.

"There is no industry where there is greater discrimination against the
Negro than in steel," he charged.

He described the great union drives now sweeping the country as spelling
economic freedom for the Negro people, and pledged in the name of the 15 international unions and the more than 1,500,000 workers in the Committee for
Industrial Organization complete equality for the Negro worker in the shop and
in the union hall.

As Murray came to the end of his appeal to build the steel union, spell-
bound attention turned to applause, to stamping of feet and finally to a
rising vote of thanks.

Present at this gathering of 165 delegates representing 100,000 Negroes
in every walk of life were many of the outstanding leaders of the Negro people
in the United States.

There were present and active in the proceedings, A. Philip Randolph,

leading Negro trade unionist and president of the Brotherhood of Sleeping Car
Porters; T. Arnold Hill, National Industrial Secretary of the Urban League;
James W. Ford, the distinguished Negro Communist, and John P. Davis, secretary
of the National Negro Congress.

There were present such outstanding church leaders as Bishop W. J.
Walls of Chicago, Dr. J. C. Austin, pastor of the Pilgrim Baptist Church in
the same city, and Rev. T. J. King of Pittsburgh. [42]

Workers In Spotlight

There were present doctors, lawyers, business men, and women's leaders
such as Mrs. Nanny Reed, president of the Illinois Association of Women's
Clubs.

But dominating the entire conference, occupying the center of attention at all times were Negro steel workers who had come from the mills of
Youngstown, Gary, South Chicago and Pittsburgh, as well as Negro S.W.O.C.
organizers such as Henry Johnson of Chicago and Ben Careathers of Pittsburgh.

It was an important and frequently repeated fact that many of the
steel workers present are presidents and officers of lodges of the Amalgamated
Association, that many of them had been elected by a predominantly white
membership, and that the expenses of many of them had been paid for by white
workers.

This gathering, one of the most representative of Negro leaders that
had ever been held, had a profound unity of purpose: unionization of the
Negro steel workers.

Concrete Steps Taken

It was pointed out both by A. Philip Randolph and T. Arnold Hill that
this would be but one step toward the unionization of the entire Negro working
class, as well as toward making the Negro people an integral part of the
American labor movement.

The resolutions adopted by the conference were noteworthy for their
specific nature for their very definite recommendations for immediate action
to speed the steel among Negro workers.

Among the steps decided on were:

To set up a continuation committee to carry on the work of the conference.

To set up committees in every community to help the steel drive.

To bring back the message of the conference throughout the country and
everywhere to urge workers to join the union.

To arrange mass meetings for this purpose.

To have special Sundays arranged in the churches where workers will be
urged to join the union.

To set up women's auxiliaries.

To issue the resolutions of the conference in pamphlet form for wide
distribution.

Prepared in less than a month, the conference had been called by a
group of Negro leaders and S.W.O.C. organizers who met in Pittsburgh at a
preliminary meeting a few weeks ago.

It was fitting for the conference to be opened by Ben Careathers,
S.W.O.C. organizer who had called the first meeting together and was in charge
of preparations in Pittsburgh.

The chairman, William Hill, of the Pittsburgh Urban League, was also
one of the small group of initiators. Elected as vice-president was Mrs.
Nanny Reed, and as secretary, Maude White, Cleveland Negro Congress leader.

Chairman of the resolutions committee was Dr. Charles Wesley Burton,
head of the Negro Congress in Chicago.

Following the election of officers and a brief opening service, Philip
Murray delivered what was in many respects the outstanding address of the
conference.

"I regard your conference," he said, "as perhaps the most important
conference of its kind that has been held since the beginning of this campaign
to organize steel."

He blamed the failure of previous drives to organize steel on the division of workers into 28 or 29 separate craft unions, and rapped craft union

leaders for their discrimination against Negroes.

"Many of these craft unions," Murray declared, "deny a colored worker the right to belong to their organization."

"No Discrimination"

"The Committee for Industrial Organization is committed to the formation of a different type of organization, which will bring in every worker in that industry which shall see that there shall be no discrimination regardless of race, color or creed."

Citing the record of the United Mine Workers which had resolutely refused to yield to the demands of Southern coal operators for lower wages for Negro workers, he said, "We relegated to the scrap heap these Southern traditions."

He promised full equality to the Negro workers in the new steel union which had already, he said, reached a membership of almost 168,000.

Robert L. Vann pledged the full support of the Pittsburgh Courier to the steel drive and declared that it would expose in its pages those Negroes who betrayed the best interests of their people by supporting the bosses.[43]

T. Arnold Hill praised the CIO unions for their excellent record in guaranteeing equality of Negroes.[44]

He emphasized that the drive to unionize Negro steel workers must be "an opening wedge" in a drive to unionize the Negro workers of the nation and declared: "I think I can speak for the National Urban League and say that it is 100 per cent for unionization."

Ovation For Ford

After relating the experiences of the Pullman porters in building their union and, in the process, destroying a powerful company union, A. Philip Randolph said:

"It is my hope that you here will go out and engage in the business of contacting the steel worker himself. I hope that this conference is a turning point in the history of our group."

A tremendous ovation was given to James W. Ford, who called for unity within the ranks of labor and urged that the fight for equal rights for Negroes not be abandoned within the American Federation of Labor.

Declaring that "hope of our people rests on the steel workers," he pledged to the conference the full support of the Communist Party.

Not only was cooperation to the unionization drive promised by the leading preachers who addressed the conference, but they urged that they be considered as participants in the work ahead, and not merely as spectators.

"I wish to be regarded as one of you," Dr. Austin declared, stating that the Negroes must now unite their ranks in the great fight ahead for economic freedom.

"If there are honest and necessary battles to be fought, we want to fight too," said Rev. T. J. King.

Bishop Walls said that the workers themselves should demand that their ministers should support them.

Daily Worker, February 8, 1937.

31.   NEGROES PLEDGE AID TO STEEL DRIVE
TO ORGANIZE 90,000 NEGRO WORKERS IN CIO

By Ben Careathers
(Negro S.W.O.C. Organizer)

Pittsburgh

At the National Conference of Negro Organizations, held in Pittsburgh, Pennsylvania, Feb. 6, 1937, there were present 186 delegates representing 110 organizations with a total membership of over 100,000 Negro people, who pledged their full support to the organizing of the tens of thousands of Negro steel workers together with their white brothers into a strong industrial union.

A complete cross-section of the Negro population was represented at the

Conference. Many outstanding individuals from every steel locality in the country were present; bishops, ministers, lawyers, doctors, publishers, civic and social leaders. There were present outstanding trade union leaders. A very prominent feature of the Conference was the presence of a number of steel workers from various lodges of the Amalgamated Association.

Philip Murray, Chairman of the Steel Workers' Organizing Committee, who made the keynote address, received a large ovation when he stated that "the Committee for Industrial Organization, now campaigning in the mass production industries, is dedicated to the proposition that there shall be no discrimination under any circumstances, regardless of creed, color or nationalities, in its unions."

Addressed by Many Leaders

The Conference was addressed by many of these outstanding individuals and steel workers themselves.

The following resolutions, part, were adopted. One pointed out that "approximately 90,000 Negroes were employed in the steel industries and that the steel magnates have always practiced a deliberate policy of discrimination against them and went on record condemning this policy of discrimination as well as recognizing that the efforts of the Steel Workers' Organizing Committee is in the best interests of the Negro steel workers. Another resolution proposed the carrying out of the following program:

1. The immediate setting up of committees in every Negro community to help the organizers.

2. Organization of mass meetings in all cities to hear reports of the Conference.

3. The use of pulpits, press and radio to urge all Negro steel workers to join the union.

4. A selected Sunday to be set aside for talks in all churches in support of the steel union drive.

5. Special activities to recruit young Negroes into the union.

Organizers in the field are already reporting achievements in organizing Negro steel workers as a result of the Conference.

Daily Worker, February 28, 1937.

32. CHANCE FOR NEGRO WORKER

PITTSBURGH, Pa.--Negro workers are "doomed to economic degradation unless they seek the protection of a great industrial union," Philip Murray, chairman of the Steel Workers' Organizing Committee, told 300 negro delegates attending a national conference here.

The conference was called to align negro fraternal organizations behind John L. Lewis' drive to unionize the steel industry.

Murray said that a study of wages in the steel industry revealed cases of colored workers being paid from fifteen to twenty-five cents an hour less for the same kind of work the whites perform.

United Mine Workers Journal, May 15, 1937.

33. RESOLUTIONS PASSED BY THE STEEL WORKERS
ORGANIZING COMMITTEE CONVENTION, 1937

At the Combustion Engineering Company in Chattanooga, the company refused to negotiate with the SWOC. Petition was filed with the regional Labor Board demanding an election. Intervening petitions were filed by several A.F. of L.

organizations, including the Molders, Boiler Makers and Machinists. A hearing was held in Chattanooga in August, 1937. No decision has been made as yet by the National Labor Relations Board.

We are also demanding an election to be held at the Pullman-Standard Car Manufacturing Company, Bessemer, Alabama. A number of charges have been filed against various companies charging violation of the National Labor Relations Act.

We encountered many obstacles, some peculiar to the South. The same opposition to unionism that was found elsewhere was very evident in our section. Some workers, because of bitter past experience, questioned our ability to organize. Others felt that by opposing the organization their chances for personal advancement would be increased. A number of cities passed ordinances prohibiting mixed meetings (white and black meeting together). Some meetings were broken up by the so-called law enforcement officers and general misleading propaganda was used to discourage white workers meeting with Negro workers.

State laws were used against us in many instances, especially the old antiquated anti-picketing law. We refrained from calling strikes but in many of the foundries and fabricating plants strikes were forced upon our membership.

Many subterfuges were used by the employers, some insisting on the employes putting up a bond to guarantee the enforcement of the contract, others refusing to meet and bargain colectively, and still others insisting on making verbal contacts and refusing to put contracts in writing. In these various local strike situations, as a rule, we handled them by voluntary contributions from the CIO local organizations, thanks to the membership of the United Mine Workers of America local unions who usually contributed liberally. . . .

RESOLUTION R-20

Federal Anti-Lynching Legislation

Whereas, Labor has an important stake in the maintenance of law and order and in the use of firm measures by the government to prevent self-appointed groups from taking the law into their own hands for any purpose whatsoever; and

Whereas, In many instances over a period of years, at localities scattered throughout the United States, such self-appointed groups have assumed the power of the government and even now continue to do so, displacing the established local authorities, frequently with the tacit approval of the latter, thus making it apparent that the highest governmental authority must have power to step in to prevent the practice of lynching where local authorities fail; now, therefore, be it

Resolved, That this convention endorses the principles of Federal Anti-Lynching legislation designed to protect all persons whatever their creed, class, or race, and in whatsoever locality, against the indifference of local public officials to lawless mob action and against the connivance of such officials in such action and providing penalties of a nature to completely eradicate the shameful scourge of lynching from our national life. [45]

Resolution No. 450, submitted by Lodge 1024, deals with the same subject. The committee recommends the adoption of Resolution R-20. The recommendation of the committee was unanimously adopted.

RESOLUTION R-27

Unity of Negro and White Workers

Whereas, The employers constantly strive to deprive the workers of their full economic strength and seek all means to split one group of workers from another, and the most frequent weapon used by the employers to accomplish this end is to create false conflicts between Negro and white workers; and

Whereas, The workers of this country will obtain their powerful labor organizations only when they have united within such labor organizations all workers regardless of their race, creed, color or nationality; and

Whereas, The Negro workers, because of the fact that we have not as yet brought them into powerful labor organizations throughout the country, have,

not received any economic or political justice nor enjoyed the benefit of any
constitutional or civil liberties in this country, as indicated in the most
flagrant and outstanding miscarriage of justice perpetrated in the convictions
of the Scottsboro boys, which cases were twice reversed by the Supreme Court
of the United States and, on the third occasion, the Supreme Court refused to
grant a hearing or review for such cases; now, therefore, be it

Resolved, That this convention specifically condemn the actions of the
courts in connection with the Scottsboro cases and urge the Governor of the
State of Alabama to issue a pardon to the convicted defendants; and be it
further

Resolved, That this convention wholeheartedly and completely endorse the
policy of organizing into powerful industrial labor organizations in this
country all workers regardless of race, creed, color or nationality.

Your committee recommends the adoption of this resolution.

A motion was made and seconded to adopt the committee's report.

The subject matter of the resolution was discussed by Delegates Lowrey,
Lodge 1109, and Favorito Lodge, 187, after which the motion to adopt the
committee's report was carried.

First Wage and Policy Convention of the Steel Workers Organizing Committee,
Pittsburgh, December 14-16, 1937, pp. 61, 110-11, 118.

34. BLOOD FOR THE CAUSE

The battle between labor and the independent companies finds the Negro
workers on the firing line, giving and taking. A Negro organizer for the CIO
has been beaten up and driven out of the town of Monroe, Mich. Steel, which
has the worst labor record of any great American industry, is conducting open
warfare against labor. The massacre of unarmed pickets by Chicago police
during the Memorial Day weekend, gives an accurate picture of the fifty-years-
ago ideas of the independent steel magnates and the stupidity and servility of
of city administrations in providing police to shoot down its own citizens
who do not happen to own factories and mills. The activities of the "vigilantes" at Monroe are one with the Chicago police, the only difference being,
perhaps, that the Monroe crew was paid directly by the Republic Steel Company.

In this struggle of labor to organize and win the right of collective
bargaining it is fitting that the Negro workers be represented in the front
line trenches. There are 960,000 of them in industry, mostly in the unskilled
and unorganized classifications. They have everything to gain and nothing to
lose by affiliation with the CIO and if they fight now, side by side with
their white fellow workers, when the time comes to divide up the benefits they
can demand their share.

The Crisis, 44 (July, 1937): 209.

35.
SCHUYLER VISITS STEEL CENTERS IN OHIO AND PENNSYLVANIA;
FINDS RACE WORKERS LOYAL TO COMPANIES; MAKING BIG MONEY

By George S. Schuyler[46]

YOUNGSTOWN, O., July 22--Race feeling, already tense, is likely to grow
more bitter in Johnstown, Youngstown, Warren, Canton and Massillon, where the
CIO is battling against the Republic Steel Co., the Bethlehem Steel Co., the
Youngstown Sheet and Tube Co., and subsidiary plants.

In these centers Negro labor, a vital factor in the basic and fabricating
plants, has turned a deaf ear to the entreaties of embattled white labor and
elected to remain loyal to the companies.

Here, striking white workers, mostly of alien extraction, have watched with growing bitterness their black fellow workers flaunting appeals of CIO organizers and either staying in struck plants or trooping back at the first opportunity to make big money. They have warned that they will not forget that black labor deserted them in the crisis. Jeering of white pickets, clashes at mill gates, and flaunting of new "scab cars" by suddenly enriched black workers augurs ill for future race relations in these communities.

Discrimination and segregation which have followed migrating Southern black labor to these centers in increasing volume during the past two decades will surely grow as a result of the tense situation, and remain to plague all Negroes long after the issues involved in the strike have been settled.

Johnstown Jittery!

I found Johnstown, Pa., with a bad case of jitters. There had been beatings and bombings, and clashes between white and Negro workers. Mounted constabulary patrolled the ominously quiet streets, special officers guarded the reservoirs, and mill yards bristled with company police.

Johnstown's 2,800 Negroes were justifiably nervous. Out of 400 Negroes employed in the Bethlehem Company's Cambria plant, only a half dozen had joined the white workers on strike. Unionists declared that many Negroes recently from the South had been imported as strikebreakers or induced by the company through their relatives to come up and work in the struck plant.

At the big mass meeting addressed by Governor Earle on July 4, there were only 400 Negroes present as against 20,000 white workers. And those 400 Negroes were militant members of the United Mine Workers Union from out of town. They were shocked and puzzled by the failure of their black fellow workers in the steel mills to attend.

Their amazement was not without foundation, Johnstown, to say the least, is unrepossessing. The mean, tawdry, dun-colored rookeries in which the workers are forced to dwell are in marked contrast to the vivid green of the steep hills that hem in the town. For eight miles along the tortuous Conemaugh Valley, the rusty mills sprawl like some puffing, Mesazoic monster stuffed with the blood and bones and hopes of men, women and children.

The company supplies mean, weather-beaten houses at $8 a month. When the men are not working they are permitted to remain in these rookeries and supplied with wood, coal, and food, but they must pay fancy prices later, deducted from their pay envelopes. Both the Cambria plant and the Lorain Steel Co., have the familiar pension plans and sick relief, and other such forms of welfare but the condition of the workers is far from being one to inspire such loyalty as they have shown.

Many of the Negro workers have been employed in the mills from 12 to 15 years. They have systematically been given the most miserable and exhausting jobs with smallest pay and no promotion, the last to be hired and the first to be fired.

Negroes Skeptical!

Why, then have not the Negroes joined the white strikers? Manifestly, they are "in the middle." The Slavs and others of alien extraction who are the backbone of the strike have never helped the local Negroes in their struggle for equal citizenship rights. Nor have they ever insisted the Negroes be given a wider variety of employment in the mills. Their attitude has been almost identical with that of the American whites, and Negroes recall that twice the Ku Klux elements have sought to banish them from the community.

Race relations were showing a marked improvement just prior to the strike, thanks to the leadership of such men as Rev. E. E. Swanston. The first Negro policeman in the town's history was appointed last month. About 20 eating places now serve Negroes where 10 years ago they would have been refused. Two colored playground attendants have been appointed and at one time there were 15 WPA Negro teachers. Many of the classes started with mixed attendance. Last January, a local forum held a symposium on the "Nature of Race Hatred" in which Rev. Swanston, a Jewish rabbi and a Catholic priest, discussed the question before more than 1,000 people. The same Rev. Swanston serves along with

the Mayor, Chief of Police and 22 other prominent white citizens as one of the
Committee of Governors of the Civic Welfare Citizens Council where he speaks
for the Negro group.

The workers of foreign extraction who are the backbone of the CIO strike,
do not therefore, have as much claim on the Negroes' allegiance as the white
American middle class backed by the mill bosses. And since the latter have
enlisted the aid of the merchants, clerks, lawyers and professional folk who
make up this middle class in a poorly disguised vigilance committee with the
power of the police behind them, the Negroes largely feel that they are pur-
suing the wisest course. If the strike succeeded, they felt that the
company would never again employ Negroes, and there is no other employment to
be had in this one-industry town. If the strike failed, however, they would
be more solid with the powerful steel company and be given better jobs.

The Union Viewpoint!

The viewpoint of the Negro unionist was given by Houston Underwood, a
striking wheel roller who has worked for Bethlehem Steel Company since 1919.
He is a member of the Steel Workers Organizing Committee and a local organizer.
Negroes are opposed to him because of his union activities. A well-educated
man with a fine gift of expression, he strikes one as the finest type of labor
unionist.

"The CIO is more sympathetic to Negro labor than any previous union
that has sought to organize the mills," he said. "It has guaranteed no color
discrimination and has so far lived up to that guarantee. I have been treated
splendidly by all classes of white workers during this strike, despite the
bitter feeling against my people who have stayed with the company. I have
done organizing work among both white and colored, but have had little success
with my people.

"Just before the strike I was third-term employee representative for the
wheel plant where there are only six Negroes in a total of 300 workers. Two
years ago I was representative of the Franklin Open Hearth where there were
897 men, 13 being colored. I am the only colored man to serve here as employee representative.

"I feel that my interests lie with the working class. Only by identify-
ing ourselves with our white fellow workers in crises of employment in the
mills when the strikes are over."

Mr. Underwood ran for Director of the Poor for Cambria on the Democratic
ticket in 1935. He received 928 votes to 1,000 votes for the winner.

Many whites have gone back to the mills along with the Negroes, although
not in so great proportion. This fact will be overlooked by the striking
workers, doubtless, and only the fact that the Negroes remained solidly with
the steel company in this struggle will be long remembered.

What that will mean to the Negro's future in Johnstown, only time will
tell.

"Timid and Distrustful!"

The picture is not greatly different in Youngstown, Ohio, where Negroes
are 10 per cent of the 179,000 population. Here the mills were closed for
a month by the strike and the more than 5,000 Negroes employed by the Youngstown Sheet and Tube, the Republic and the Carnegie mills were thrown out with
the rest.

At the union headquarters opposite the Republic plant considerable bitterness was expressed by labor officials against the Negroes.

"About 2 per cent of the colored workers have joined up with us," said
Joe Gallegher, a white organizer. "They have more to gain by unionization
than by scabbing. Solidarity with the white workers will eliminate discrim-
ination against the colored workers. But they don't seem to understand that.
They have flocked back to the mills. When the gates were first opened few
went back. One morning 80 men returned to work and 50 of them were colored.
Now the proportion of white and black returning is about the same, but the
Negroes going back started the stampede.

A Mr. Lynch, another official, spoke up. "They distrust us and they are timid," he charged. "We have had four Negro organizers here but they have been able to make no headway. The companies sent men around telling Negroes they would have a better break after the strike if they remained loyal, so they remained loyal."

"We had Ernest Rice McKinney here as organizer," continued Gallegher, the white organizer, who boasted of 15 years experience in the steel mills. "He is a man of great intelligence and unusual ability. We also had Curly Jackson, another colored organizer, in the Republic plant. Neither could prevail upon their people to join with us in this effort."
Said Lynch again, "We asked the colored workers to prove to the white workers that they could be trusted, and they were the first to go back. We tried to organize colored meetings but that was a flop. Nobody came out."

Organizer Gallegher pointed out that the Negroes had always been given the lowest-paid and most exhausting work in the mills, none had been made foreman, and while the highest paid Negroes were employed by the Youngstown Sheet and Tube Co., only a few attained an annual wage in excess of $2,000 yearly. The Negroes are naive enough to believe that the companies are going to ultimately oust the foreigners and give their jobs to colored men.

Shortcomings Of The CIO

Attorney William Howard, president of the Youngstown Branch of the N.A.A.C.P., a former steel worker, declared that few Negroes had been active as pickets but that the city had put on 30 Negro special police out of the 125 appointed. The sheriff, however, had appointed no Negroes as deputies.

Attorney Howard pointed out that in the 1921 steel strike the scabbing of Negroes had tended to prejudice the whites against them when conditions in the mills again became normal. Whereas the Negro workers had been given good jobs during that strike, as soon as it was settled, the old conditions soon prevailed with Negroes holding only the lowest paid jobs.

It is significant that there is no ill-feeling among white strikers against the Negroes who have gone out with them. I noticed them eating together at strike headquarters and generally fraternizing. It is quite likely that the adherence of these colored workers somewhat tempers the ill-feeling engendered by the defection of the majority of the Negroes.
Attorney Howard criticized the CIO for not enlisting the aid of him and other leading Negroes in staging meetings. The union officials, he held, had not used the services of Negroes who were familiar with, understood and had the confidence of the colored steel workers. Had this been done, he asserts, the Negro workers would have attended the strike meetings and joined the union in larger numbers. In their ignorance, the CIO officials placed dependence in any Negro who declared his loyalty to the union, and many such Negroes were wholly incompetent to do the job expected of them.
Indicative of the attitude of the ordinary Negro steel worker, was the viewpoint of a young Negro high school graduate, whom I met on a street corner near the union headquarters. This young man, a fellow in his early twenties who boasted a knowledge of economics, was violently opposed to the CIO. He declared that John L. Lewis, head of the drive, had no right to collect a fee of $1 a month from the workers. The Negroes, he held, did not need the unions, were getting along all right, and that furthermore, the steel companies were not making as much money as had been reported. He expressed the opinion that most of the steel workers would be poor, anyway, regardless of the union.
Another Negro, Bill Houston, who works in the Sharon (Pa.) Steel mills, said that when the vote for union affiliation was taken in the mill, 1,700 voted for the union, while 700, mostly Negroes, voted against it.

Youngstown Contradiction

In Youngstown, there is the contradiction of most Negro steel workers being violently opposed to unionization while the Negro truckdrivers and building service employees enthusiastically support it. Truckdrivers Union No. 377, of

which a Negro, Samuel Palm, is business agent, pulled a sympathetic strike
with the CIO, although the union is affiliated with the A.F. of L.

A Negro, Carl B. Howard, is president of the carmen's local at the Erie
roundhouse, while another Negro, A. C. King, is secretary-treasurer of bus
repairmen's union. The president of the building service employees local
No. 109 is William Johnson, who has done much to make Negroes union-conscious
in the community. His secretary is a white girl. There are many Negro shop
stewards.

Garbage men who were getting from $4 to $7 a week are now reported to be
getting $25 weekly.
Hotel men have gained an 8-hour day and vacation of one week with pay as
a result of unionization, while bellhops have been jumped from $18 to $22.50
a week.

Negro workers in one hotel sought to get a jim-crow union and the white
workers vigorously opposed such a move, declaring it unnecessary.
Youngstown's Negro community shows considerable progress. There are
nine physicians and three dentists; five undertakers, nine lawyers, one of them
being a city prosecutor. There are eight Negro policemen and one Negro
policewoman, 14 letter carriers and one lively newspaper, "The Review."

"Bolshevik Movement"

A Negro steel worker in Warren, Ohio, where the Republic Steel Co. employs
upwards of 400 Negro workers, said of the CIO: "It's a Bolshevik movement.
Whether the CIO wins or not, the colored man is at the same place."

The Warren plant was the only one of the Republic group that never
stopped operating. Of the 400 Negro workers, only about six joined the union.
The others never left their jobs but stayed in, many earning from $300 to
$500 during the first 30 days of the strike. Of the 6,000 workers normally
employed, around 2,500 stayed in. Some of the Negro workers even crawled
through the swamps to work in the mills.

Warren is a town of 45,000 population with a Negro total of 3,000. There
are no Negro organizers, but one came from the United Mine Workers. He made
little headway among the Negro workers.
Before the Wagner Act was adopted, there was an employee representation
plan but no Negro representatives. Negroes are barred from the hot mills.
The white population consists largely of Irish-Americans, Welsh, Slavs
and Italians. In all there are some 20 nationalities and those of alien extraction have been the backbone of the strike.
Fifty per cent of the life of Warren depends upon the steel mills. As a
consequence, the storekeeping middle-class and professional people were
violently opposed to the strike. Perhaps with the backing of the steel
bosses, a John Q. Public League of vigilants has crystallized into a CIO
opposition, and it has been freely stated that if the National Guard had not
come into the city, the vigilants were to be deputized by the sheriff and
sent against the strikers with rifles.

The Negro point of view in Warren is a reflection of the views expressed
by this League and by the local press. The Negro ministers are solidly
opposed to the CIO and 90 per cent of the Negroes of the town are against it.

John M. Ragland, executive secretary of the Warren Urban League, expressed
the view that the initial violence of the CIO drive turned the public against
it. A dozen Negroes, including two colored women, were beaten up by the
strikers. The company police, who are quite numerous, also did more than their
share of beating of strikers and pickets.
Times had been getting better at the time the strike was called. More
than 30 per cent of the people own their homes, pay had been raised and the
salaries of Negro steel workers had averaged around $1,500 the previous year.
Some few received as high as $2,000 and $2,500. It was natural that they
should oppose any cessation of work.

The CIO men, according to one Negro worker interviewed, "Threatened Negro workers telling them that if they didn't join now they would be sorry later. They also stood around calling the Negroes 'Black Bastards' because they refused to desert the mills."

On the other hand, Negro workers drawing temporarily high pay have purchased expensive automobiles (for which they often have no garages) and jested openly about owning "scab cars." At the same time the whites have become impoverished and many forced to move from their homes. This has done much to increase the race prejudice.

Feeling Is Running High

Dan B. Gutelius, Director of Public Service, who has charge of the police, told me that he had experienced difficulty in maintaining law and order because he had but 32 officers. "I am trying to maintain law and order," he declared; "trying to preserve peace and safety. I don't believe conditions as they exist should be . . . It all might develop into a racial situation. Feeling is running high not only between Negroes and whites but between Americans and foreign born. I have tried as near as possible to preserve peace and do everything to prevent rioting."

Warren is definitely a jim-crow town. There is jim-crow in the theatres, restaurants, luncheonettes and swimming pools. There is only one Negro policeman. One colored steel striker, named Watkins, has been indicted with 11 whites on a charge of bombing. Director Gutelius complained that while several Negroes had been beaten by white strikers, they invariably failed to report these outrages.

To the casual observer it seems evident that race relations in Warren will become more strained as a result of the Negro worker's attitude. In the meantime, however, the Negroes are making big money and having a "ball."

Negroes Aid Bosses In Canton

In Canton, the picture is much the same. With the exception of a half dozen, all Negroes stayed in the mills. In many instances they forced their way into the mills with guns. A Negro organizer from Pennsylvania, who stayed around town four weeks was unable to make any headway.

A CIO meeting was called near the Negro section on July 9. Nobody came except four Negro steel workers.

Prior to the strike the mills hired from 35 to 40 Negroes daily including many young colored collegians. Wages were raised to $6 a day and since then there have been other raises. The workers are getting time and a half for overtime, something that has never happened before. Following the example of the Republic Steel Co., the Timken Roller Bearing Co., increased Negro employment from 10 to 400.

Some Negroes came to town seeking work declaring that down South they had been working for 35 cents a day. They were hired.

Loyal colored workers who spurned unionization have been making from $14 to $28 a day. One Negro made $1,000 for 36 days work.

As the whites left the mills the Negroes moved in. Many of the whites stayed in because they feared to come out. Numbers of these men were attacked physically by the strikers but singularly enough few of the Negroes were beaten. This may have been due to the fact that Negroes were ready to fight. Many of them carried guns back and forth to work after the company got permits from the city for them to do so. Nevertheless, there has been some violence visited upon Negro workers. One man was stripped of his clothes by the whites and the garments burned. The white strikers have threatened to "make it hot" for the Negroes when the troops are removed.

The 2,000 Negro steel workers contend that they don't want any checkoff for union dues and that adherence to the union will get them no better jobs.

But during the emergency they HAVE got better jobs. They are working in mills which never before hired colored workers. For the first time they are running machines, having been instructed eight weeks before the strike.

The mill has put on 50 Negro special police, and of the three Negro city police, two have been appointed since the strike.

Negro truckdrivers refused to join the CIO union and the building service union made a drive only in those hotels employing solid white staffs.

The Town Is Booming

Negro Canton has not seen such prosperity in a long time. From the looks of the miserable housing one might conclude that prosperity is greatly needed. Most of the big money, however, is going for new automobiles. The workers continue to live like cattle.

From Cleveland, Toledo, Detroit and Chicago, pimps, gamblers and "Stables" of loose women have descended upon the town to garner the pickings. At "The Jam Session," a greasy Greek joint on Cherry street, where a three-piece orchestra nightly "goes to town," rough steel workers and fancy girls in gay prints guzzle liquor and do the "Suzy Q."
At Johnny Parks' Commodore, an interracial gathering place, every night "the cats are leaping" and "Pitching a fog," while orchestra and "scat men" make whoopee for the crowd.

A few miles away at Massillon, Ohio, where the Union Drawn Steel and Central Steel Companies employ over 200 Negroes, not more than 10 joined the union. Some of these went on to the picket line with the whites but the overwhelming majority remained loyal to the bosses.

"They didn't see where the CIO would benefit them" said one worker, "because they wouldn't get any better jobs."

They are making from $10 to $12 a shift working on the pickler, but the work is terrible on their health. This is the worst place in the mill. The fumes get into their lungs and many have died. The company will not hire whites for such a job. The acid vapor even eats out the roof. . . . Negroes also work on the bar shears and are making now from $135 to $140 every two weeks.
Most of the money is being spent for new cars which usually have no garage and sit in the back yards surrounded by high weeds. There are few home owners.
The customs of the old South prevail in Massillon. Many of the Negroes are migrants from Dixie. When they first started coming 20 years ago, Massillon was a good place for Negroes. But the newcomers were rough and belligerent. Today they are barred from all good hotels and restaurants. Even the mill restaurant segregates Negroes to one or two tables. There is not even a saloon where they can get a drink. The Negroes are so backward that for a period of a year there was not even a Negro barber shop in the town.

Race feeling has become more intense as a result of the Negroes remaining at work. While there have been no race clashes, white strikers have not refrained from calling Negroes "Black Bastards," and other names.

Such is the picture in these small steel cities. Surprisingly enough the attitude of the majority of Negro steel workers in Chicago, Gary and Cleveland is much different. There the solidarity of white and black labor has advanced race relations at least 10 years.

Pittsburgh Courier, July 24, 1937.

36. NEGRO WORKERS LEAD IN GREAT LAKES STEEL DRIVE

By George S. Schuyler

CLEVELAND, OHIO, July 29--The enthusiasm with which the black steel
workers in the Great Lakes area have aligned themselves with their white
fellow workers in the great drive to organize the steel industry belies the
oft-repeated charge that Negroes are not susceptible to unionization appeals
and are inclined to strike-breaking activities.
The depressing picture, from the labor viewpoint, presented by Negro steel
workers in Johnstown, Warren, Canton and Massillon who elected to remain almost
100 per cent loyal to the companies, is offset to marked degree by the unanimity
with which they have joined the union drive in Chicago, Gary and Cleveland,
where there are some 15,000 employed in basic steel and 35,000 in fabricating
plants.
In Pittsburgh where the steel companies signed with the Steel Workers
Organizing Committee without a struggle, I visited the spacious offices of the
SWOC on the 36th floor of the Grant Building and interviewed Secretary-Treasurer
McDonald. He informed me that there are 15 full-time Negro organizers throughout the country on the payroll.[47]
"We find," he said, "that the colored men join the union pretty much as
the white boys do. Many of our lodges have colored officers. I cannot praise
too highly the loyalty of the Negro workers to the union and their solidarity
with the white workers in this struggle."
A visit to the great Pittsburgh offices which resemble those of some
great corporation reveals that this is a different kind of union drive from
that to which America is accustomed. The drive is being headed by educated
men, many of them college graduates, who understand well the part race prejudice
and color discrimination has played in retarding the organization of Negro
workers in the past and who do not intend that this sort of thing shall creep
into this latest effort.

Great Meeting of Negro Organizers

It was in Pittsburgh where a great conference of Negro steel organizers
and leaders was held just prior to the launching of the organization drive.
Outstanding Negroes in all walks of life, including the editor of the Pittsburgh Courier, Mr. Robert L. Vann, attended the conference which discussed
ways and means of getting Negro workers aligned with this new effort to increase the influence and dignity of Negro labor by encouraging solidarity
with white labor. Among those who took a prominent part in the conference
were the officers of the Pittsburgh Urban League.
Mr. Moss, the executive secretary of the Pittsburgh Urban League, informed
me that "While he cannot make any blanket statement about the reaction of the
Negroes to the drive, I can say that the Pittsburgh workers have played a
prominent part in the drive. This is the more remarkable because the Negroes'
past experience with the A.F. of L. has not been a happy one. More education,
of course, is needed. Collective bargaining is still much of a theory to Negroes.
To sell it to them is hard work. One thing that has helped in Pittsburgh has
been the fact that this is a union town and that the Negroes have been treated
fairly through the years by the United Mine Workers of America which is playing
so prominent a part in this steel drive. There has been a marked extension of
unions such as this one which have always been fair to Negroes and those unions
are now more militant than ever."
Mr. Moss pointed out that the most interesting development in Pennsylvania
has been the McGinnis Labor Law, the strongest ever written to protect labor.
It was framed to conform to the national Wagner labor act. Representative
Homer Brown and other interested persons worked out an amendment which was
adopted after some dickering and which outlawed any discrimination because of
color. Under this measure unions which discriminate against Negroes are
outlawed.
"The awakening of labor as a whole to its plight," Mr. Moss believes,
"cannot help but aid the Negro."
Nevertheless many of the A.F. of L. unions still bar Negroes. In the
strike of the Teamsters' Union, for example, Negroes are losing jobs because
of inability to join the union, according to Mr. Moss.

From the Urban League official, I learned that 40,000 of the 83,000 Negroes in the county are on relief. The percentage has jumped from 18 per cent of the total at the height of the depression to 28 per cent at present, with some 4,000 Negro families on direct relief.

There is a feeling among some informed persons that the CIO is growing too fast and is not prepared to take advantage fully of its great opportunity. Some criticism was expressed because there were not four or five Negro organizers of the CIO in the county. White organizers, some held, are not capable of winning over the Negro workers like Negro organizers. This was also the opinion expressed by many persons in Johnstown, Warren, Canton, Youngstown and Massillon where the CIO has failed to win the Negro workers.

Meantime, while the great Jones & Laughlin Steel Company, which hires nearly 8,000 workers, has signed with the S.W.O.C. it is using insidious methods designed to undermine the union. It is making contributions to certain Negro churches and using the ministers of these churches as employment agents, it is charged. These preachers give a note to a prospective worker whereupon the applicant is hired. They try not to give any notes to CIO Negroes if they can help it.

Of more than passing interest was the viewpoint of one Pittsburgh Negro steel worker employed by the Jones & Laughlin Company whom I interviewed on Wylie avenue. He said there were 380 Negroes employed in the particular mill in which he is employed. The company foremen, he charged, were prejudiced against Negroes and restricted them to menial tasks wherever possible. Wages of pushermen and door jack men had recently been raised by the company. Nevertheless he felt that there was no chance of advancement in the mill for Negroes. Most of them favor the union to which they all now belong but many are getting shaky because they have paid their union dues and don't know whether or not the present contract with the union will be renewed. He asserted that there was a colored union organizer in the field and a Negro representative on the union executive committee, but then added: "I don't think much of the union myself. I've never seen a union mean anything to a Negro yet."

This is a viewpoint that the union is trying desperately to combat.

Militant Chicago Steel Workers

In the Chicago area most of the organizational activity centered around the Republic Steel Company in South Chicago plant, the East Chicago plant of the Youngstown Sheet and Tube Company and the Inland Steel Company's plant at Indiana Harbor. There and in Gary where the steel mills precipitately signed with the S.W.O.C. the Negroes are nearly 100 per cent with the CIO.

According to Henry Johnson, the giant deep-voiced college-trained Negro, who is the ace CIO organizer of the area, the Negroes have shown up wonderfully well. He asserted that 85 per cent of the Negroes came out of the Republic's plant while all of them left the Youngstown Steel's plant, and very few went back.

In Gary where there are 8,000 Negroes employed in the big steel mills, nearly 7,000 are dues-paying members, while at Indiana Harbor there are 5,000 dues-paying members.

Negroes are extremely active in the Inland's plant and serving on all committees. In Gary Negroes predominate on the union's executive board. The general council has a white president and a Negro secretary. This, it is asserted, is making for marked improvement in race relations. At the Youngstown's plant, there are three or four Negro officers directing union affairs along with their white fellow officers.

At Gary, Stanley Cotton, a Negro, is vice president of the tin mill Lodge No. 1066. Walter Mackrell, a Negro, is inside guard for the union, while a white worker is outside guard. Theodore Vaughn, a Negro, is a union secretary, although formerly employee representative under the old company union plan. He joined the S.W.O.C. and became an ace organizer. He vigorously fought the yellow dog contract and his was the only mill that repudiated it. He represented his mill at the Pittsburgh conference with the company to ratify the contract with the union.

These men were the first volunteer organizers and the first to organize their departments and to hold departmental meetings.

In Gary there have been six cases of seniority for Negroes and four of them were won. These men went from semi-skilled to skilled work under the provisions of the contract signed by the mill with the union and passed upon by the union grievance committee of whites and Negroes.

In the Youngstown plant the case of a Negro electrician was similarly taken up by the grievance committee for seniority rating. The fight was won and the Negro got his rating, but then turned around and deserted to the company.

Companies Used Anti-Negro Propaganda

It is charged that the companies have used anti-Negro propaganda extensively in an effort to hamper the union drive. They pointed out to white men that the seniority provision would put black men over white men. Singularly enough this propaganda did not succeed.

Despite the supposed or pretended love of the companies for the Negro workers, it is noticeable that they continue the discrimination against them in the more skilled work of the mills. Many have no Negro rollers or electricians, first helpers or second helpers, although there are Negroes eminently qualified for these positions. Seniority provisions, according to union officials, will ultimately knock out this discrimination against colored men.

Another example of company appreciation of the loyalty of misguided workers is offered by the Republic's South Chicago plant where the Memorial Day massacre took place. The skilled workers were the first to walk out. Many of the unskilled workers, thinking to improve their position, stayed in. When they discovered that there was to be little improvement, they turned to sabotage and ruined much steel. This was accomplished by spitting on the hot steel and making defects known as birds eyes which causes the steel to be rejected.

During the strike this plant is alleged to have taken a day's wages out of each two weeks pay for police protection for the men who worked.

I visited the plant and found it continuously picketed by about a dozen striking workers at the gate. Among them were two Negro workers. Despite the boasts of the company that operation is normal, informed union men claimed that less than 400 of the normal 2,400 workers are working.

On the day of the massacre when 10 workers including a Negro, Lee Tisdale, were murdered by the Chicago police, two Negro and one white picket stayed on the line continuously for 36 hours. With from 700 to 1,000 policemen about, this required courage of a high order. Of the 400 Negroes normally employed in the plant, more than 300 are on strike.

Negroes Strong in Small Plants

While the general public has heard mostly about the larger steel companies, there are in this area scores of small companies, usually fabricating concerns. From George McCray, young Negro CIO educational director, and from the aforementioned Henry Johnson, I learned something of the part played by Negroes in organizing these mills.

At the Valley Mould and Iron Corporation plant, there are a dozen Negroes doing skilled work out of a total of 250 workers. Joe Cook, a Negro is president of the union, and is not only the elected, but the moral and spiritual leader. This union, Local No. 1029, has two Negro officers.

Some idea of the attitude of the white unionists out here may be gleaned from the following incident. The Ku Klux Klan threatened to run Cook out of town. Immediately the union came and escorted him to the picket line. Not only that but they made the bartender in a saloon serve him although no Negro had ever been served there before.

The vice president of the Tin Mill Lodge at the Youngstown plant is Jesse Reese. In the eyes of Negro and white workers he is the hero of the strike. At one time he stayed for 72 hours on the picket line. He is extremely popular.

Sometimes Negroes constitute from 75 to 80 per cent of the workers in the small mills. Organizers have found these mills easier to organize than the big ones. As a result of unionization the wage scale for women in these mills has jumped from 14¢ and 24¢ an hour to 35¢, while that for men has gone from 50¢ to $1.10 per hour. The women's maximum pay is now 47¢ an hour.

The Wilson & Bennett Company, manufacturers of can containers, has a total of 1,100 workers, of whom 700 are Negroes. In the spring these people

organized themselves and went on a sitdown strike because their wages only
ranged from $13 to $22 a week. It was the only successful sit down strike in
the area.

The workers hung out a sign "Go Get the CIO." The organizers saw the
sign but could not go to organize them because the plant was surrounded by
police.

A Negro woman organizer, undaunted, slipped through the police lines,
scaled a 15-foot fence, got inside the plant and signed up everybody. This
woman was Miss Eleanor Rye. Other ace Negro organizers, although voluntary,
were the Misses Fanny Brown and Ola Bell Francis.

The president of the union now is George Sanford, a Negro. So also, are
the financial secretary and the treasurer members.

At the American Car and Foundry Company there are 200 Negroes and about
600 whites. The entire group went on a sitdown strike and very shortly the
company signed a contract with the union.

CIO Fortunate In Organizers

The CIO has been fortunate in getting the Negro organizers it has, and
this accounts in no small measure for the success of its drive in this area.
Many of them are former Socialists or Communists and possess some idealism.
Many are identified with the National Negro Congress or the Garvey movement.

One of the most successful Negro organizers is Leonidas McDonald, formerly a member of the Universal Negro Improvement Association.

He and Henry Johnson have been followed alike by black and white workers.
They didn't just go to the numerous suburban communities and talk to the
workers, but actually lived in the communities, visiting each family in turn.

They explained the function of the shop stewards of whom many are Negroes.
They told them this was a great chance to fight segregation and lynching, that
mobs were recruited from the white masses; that the new union's policy of no
discrimination would better race relations.

In one Negro-hating community Henry Johnson was threatened by the prejudiced whites who were intent on running him out. Nevertheless he remained
with a bodyguard of four Italian workers.

It is generally felt that the CIO needs more competent Negro organizers
and a better educational set-up among colored people. It seems to be in sad
need of a training school like Brookwood College at Katanah, N.Y., where
educated young men and women could be schooled in labor philosophy and tactics.
Considering this shortcoming the accomplishments of the union in this area is
the more surprising.[48]

A. L. Foster, executive secretary of the Chicago Urban League, confessed
that he was "pleasantly surprised to see the way Negroes have become a very
definite part of the labor movement. Previously they were opposed to the
unions because of the bad record of the A.F. of L. in ducking the race issue.
Negroes should take full advantage of the present labor disturbance to further
their economic interests.

Mr. Nicholas Fontecchio, field organizer for the S.W.O.C., in the Great
Lakes area, declared that "I am very favorably impressed with the loyalty of
the Negro workers. They're all right."

Negro Leaders Cooperated

Perhaps some of the success of the drive in this area should be attributed to the advanced position taken by the intelligent Negro leaders. In
most places the Negro middle class seems to know nothing and care less about
these momentous labor questions. Here in this area they faced the issue.
Mr. Foster believes that the Chicago Council of Negro Organizations had paved
the way for a more enlightened sentiment.

Henry Johnson of the CIO spoke enthusiastically of the cooperation of
enlightened Negro ministers like Bishop Walls and Rev. Nicholson of the C.M.E.
connection and the N.A.A.C.P. who invited several CIO organizers to hold
programs and place exhibits in his church.

Strangely enough, of the Negro newspapers in the area only the Chicago
Bee is not employer conscious, according to the Negro union officials and
organizers.

Steel has not been the only union activity in Chicago that has involved
Negroes.

The Red Caps have organized an international union of which a Negro is president. At the Northwestern station alone it is said that 30 per cent of these workers are college graduates. If these men's schooling has meant anything at all, they should form the nucleus of a more enlightened corps of Negro organizers for Labor.

The International Ladies' Garment Workers' Union, noted for its fairness to Negro labor, has a colored girl, Miss Redmond, as organizer. She is heading the drive to organize five shops brought to Chicago's South Side to exploit the cheap labor supply. A strike is now on at the factory of Sopkins & Co., where 400 colored girls make dresses. The union is now picketing the Urban League offices because it declares that the industrial secretary has been or is a tool of Sopkins and has played a prominent part in misleading the Negro workers. Whether or not this is true, the pickets continue their march in front of the Urban League offices.

The Household Employes union has 150 Negro women and is said to be growing rapidly under the leadership of its president, Miss Neva Ryan, a colored woman.

The president of the Upholsters' Union local is a colored woman, Miss Katherine Williams, who organized and led the 115 colored girls who comprise the union. It is affiliated with the A.F. of L. There are also unions of Negro barbers and beauticians.

Some 8,000 black and white workers are organized in the Meat Packers union where Negroes assume a prominent role. In the meat industry Negro workers even applied to the union offices for cards before the organizers ever reached them. Negroes are in both the A.F. of L. Amalgamated Association of Meat Cutters and Butcher Workers who are the more skilled and in the new Packing House Workers Industrial Union, a CIO adjunct.

While conditions are by no means utopian in the Chicago-Gary area and while there is certainly much room for improvement in the relations between the unions and the Negro workers, so much progress has been and is being made that it cannot help but favorably influence race relations, to say nothing of improving the economic status of the Negroes.

Cleveland Steel Workers Solidly Union

In Cleveland Negro steel workers have joined the strike almost 100 per cent. George M. Washington, Industrial Secretary of the Negro Welfare Association said, "The percentage that did not join the strike is so small as to be negligible."

There are about 4,000 Negroes in the various steel mills. The National Malleable & Steel Casting Company has 47 per cent Negro workers. The others work for the Otis Steel Company, the Upson Nut, Corrigan-McKinney, Truscon and the Youngstown Steel and Tube. The National Malleable and the Otis companies have signed with the union.

The National Malleable conducts jim crow social activities and has contrived to keep 400 of its 600 Negro employes in debt through salary advances.

"Outsiders have been used to reopen these plants," said one educated Negro informant. "The union men are standing fast. I attended a meeting of 600 Negro strikers who pledged themselves not to go back. Only seven of them have gone back."

Negro pickets are in the line and in considerable numbers although I found the National Guard limiting picketing. There has been a Negro organizer, James Hart, in town since November.

Negroes are fully participating in the administration of the steel union locals, and there is at least one Negro on each committee.

At the time when newspapers throughout the country were saying the struck Republic Steel plants in Cleveland were in full operation, these plants were practically idle as a visit to them convinced me. At the big Corrigan & McKinney plant (Republic) there were less than 250 workers, an insufficient number to operate such a mill. Out of the 400 original Negro workers, only about 20 were working. None of the struck plants sounded as if they were doing much work. All around them at intervals of 200 or 300 feet were little camps of pickets. Among whom I saw considerable number of Negroes.

According to William Donald, chairman of the CIO Relief Committee, Negro pickets are the best for loyalty and steadfastness. He expressed the belief that "the relief offices of the city are discriminating against the strikers." He charged that some strikers had been refused relief orders.

An old steel worker, he scoffed at the claim that the mills were in full operation. "Normally they roll from 30 to 41 tons per hour," he said. "Now they are only rolling 34 tons in twelve hours."

The union relief offices were a beehive. Food was stacked high and there was much activity in the big kitchen. At the counters and tables white and black workers were sitting together eating and conversing, a perfect picture of labor solidarity and social equality.

Mr. Conners, head of the Negro Welfare Association, was not as enthusiastic as some Cleveland Negroes about the new labor drive. "The attitude of the labor unions has been such that suspicion has been created," he said. "Negroes think these new unions are the same old white men who have been keeping them down. They are getting better jobs in the steel mills than ever before." He scored the A.F. of L. craft unions for discriminating against Negroes and criticized Negro leadership for not helping the Negroes consolidate the gains they have made because of loyalty to the corporations.

Negroes, according to Mr. Conners, have a natural sympathy with the employers because they regard them as better than the white workers who never contribute to Negro schools or churches. He felt that Negroes should proceed with caution because the steel companies, after all, have always given colored men SOME jobs.

I visited General Organizer Max J. Damisch in the S.W.O.C. suite of offices in downtown Cleveland. He was most affable and a very likeable man of middle age, somewhat corpulent, with keen but kindly eyes and a shock of pure white hair. He is an official of the United Mine Workers.

Of the Negro worker he held "It is hard to get him into the union but once in there is no better unionist in America. I understand his hesitancy very well because I have worked with Negro labor all my life. The Negro worker has been terribly discriminated against. He has been made to do the dirty work which paid little while the good work he couldn't get.

"Color discrimination should not be. It is a curse to the Negro and to the labor movement. I have every confidence that the Negro worker is as good as any other, and better than some. He is very loyal to his union."

Mr. Damisch expressed satisfaction with the response of Negro steel workers in Cleveland to the steel organizing drive.

Informed Negroes know that the local background is chiefly responsible for the difference between the response of Cleveland Negro steel workers and those in Youngstown, Warren, Canton and Massillon. Cleveland has always been a strong union town with a great liberal tradition. Its newspapers are not openly company organs, as in smaller cities, because there are numerous industries and businesses. It has also been a Socialist and Communist stronghold, and some of the best organizers have seemingly come from the radical ranks.

A Visit to Buffalo

A visit to Buffalo, a notorious open shop city completed my survey of the Great Lakes steel area. There seems to be very little union activity there affecting its 13,563 Negroes. The two steel mills, Bethlehem and Republic, are located in Lackawanna, an ugly suburban collection of rookeries which is as wide open to all forms of vice as an Alaskan gold rush town.

About 10 per cent of the 3,500 employes of Republic are Negroes. Bethlehem's plant, which has signed with the union, has 1,200 Negroes out of 4,000 employes. The president of one of the steel locals at Lackawanna is a Negro. There is said to be a fairly good Negro job distribution in the two plants.

An example of how these corporations exploit their workers was Bethlehem's refusal to accept relief rentals for its houses. Then when the men were taken back to work with returning prosperity, Bethlehem took these vast accumulations of back rent out of their pay. In addition they have boosted the rents of their unsightly rookeries by about 15 per cent.

The CIO sent a Negro organizer into the area but he was lazy and dishonest, and they soon caught up with him and fired him.

Like many of the smaller cities, Negro Buffalo suffers from a lack of enlightened Negro leadership. Here as elsewhere too many supposedly educated Negroes are callous and indifferent where they are not plainly ignorant of the immense issues involved. As a rule these people know practically nothing of the momentous occurrences affecting the Negro workers on whose backs they live, and what they do know is gleaned largely from the newspapers which, as

in the smaller cities, are anti-union. To talk to some of these Negroes about
strikes and labor issues is like talking to an official of the Merchants and
Manufacturers Association.

Pittsburgh Courier, July 31, 1937.

37. VIRGINIA AND MARYLAND NEGROES FLOCK TO UNIONS

By George S. Schuyler

Negro labor in the notoriously non-union States of Virginia and Maryland
are surprising doubting Thomases by flocking into the labor unions. These
exploited workers, considered sub-human by the white and Negro upper classes
that live parasitically off their labor, have astonished everyone by their
response to the new labor drive.

With the exception of Newport News, which is owned and dominated by the
Newport News Shipbuilding Company, the picture is a favorable one from the
viewpoint of organized labor.

Norfolk has always boasted of strong unions of longshoremen led by the
militant George W. Millner, brown and bulky Vice President of the International
Longshoremen's Union.

I interviewed the forceful Mr. Millner in the large two-story brick
building owned by Local 1248 of the ILA and found him bubbling over with
enthusiasm and optimism.

There are approximately 8,000 Negroes working on and around the docks in
Norfolk. Of this number 5,000 are unionized and 90 per cent of them are
colored men. At this time of the year work is a little slow. It is mostly
casual and dependent upon the amount of cargo available.

White Unions Under Negro

The number of longshoremen's locals has jumped during the current labor
drive fron nine to twenty. Since June 1 the membership has increased 100
per cent. Five of these locals under Millner's leadership are white. All the
others are composed of Negroes and headed by Negroes. The entire area for a
radius of 35 miles is controlled by this Negro vice president of this important
A.F. of L. union.

"My idea," he told me, "is to organize the whole darn town."

"We've been trying for a year, he continued, "to get through recognition
for all the men in the various industries in this town. We have just got
through an agreement with the City, Tidewater, Southgate, and other terminals."

Increased Wage Scale

"We found men working for 25 and 30 cents an hour, with no overtime, and
working Sundays and holidays. They worked from 7 o'clock in the morning
until 9 or 10 o'clock at night. We got through a wage scale of 40 cents an
hour straight time and 60 cents an hour for overtime with a 9-hour day. We
got a guarantee of four hours work at 40 cents an hour for day work and 60
cents an hour for night work.

"At the same time we put thru an agreement covering checkers who were
getting $14 a week. These men are mostly high school boys who also act as
foremen. They are now getting a $25 weekly minimum wage throughout, based on
a 9-hour day, with a week's vacation with pay and reasonable sick leave with
pay if able to produce a doctor's certificate proving that illness occurred in
line of duty. These men never received overtime before."

Co-operating With CIO

This A.F. of L. group is not bothering its head about jurisdiction. It
is felt that the important thing is to get the men organized in some kind of
union to enable them to bargain collectively.

When the CIO through the newly organized National Maritime Union, sent its organizers into the field, Millner says he immediately had a conference with them and promised to cooperate with them. The CIO group is now trying to organize the teamsters but many of the teamsters have joined A.F. of L. groups.

"In this drive," Millner asserted, we are taking in the marine freight handlers, the railroad freight handlers, the coastwise longshoremen, the lumber handler, the salt handlers and the veneer plant workers." A large number of these workers are skilled men.

Organization of proceeding space in two plants of box and shook makers totaling 600, and Burlap and Bagging Company which employs 1,000 workers on night and day shifts, the 300 workers in the junk yards, the large number of employes of the fertilizer plant, the 200 fruit and banana handlers and the 1,000 freight handlers.

Has Made Agreements

Agreements have been made with the Old Bay Line, the Chesapeake Steamship line, the Baltimore, Norfolk and Carolina Line and the Thomas E. Cole Lumber Company. Negotiations are now in progress with the veneer plants, with two non-union stevedore companies employing 400 men, and with the Standard Fruit and S. S. Co. Organizers have also been asked to address the large number of men, women and children employed in the Richmond Cedar Works. It should be emphasized that the larger proportion of these workers are Negroes and they are eagerly yielding to organization.

Plans are afoot to organize the 300 workers in the dock builders and pile drivers group, the 500 men in the fertilizer plants and the 500 more in coal and lumber yards and sand and gravel industry.

No efforts have yet been made to contact the large number of workers employed by Du Pont at his Hopewell plant.

In Richmond a new organization of coastwise longshoremen has been set up and their pay boosted to 40 and 60 cents an hour.

A drive is in progress among the caulkers in the shipyards, the structural iron workers, the bakery employes and the teamsters.

The Sage of Junius Vines

Illustrative of the new kind of leadership being developed by Negroes in the labor movement, is Junius Vines, a former chauffeur for the manager of the Tidewater Terminal.

Because of his union activities Vines lost his job. He promptly became a volunteer organizer and has built an organization of 700 members. "He went out and got everybody," said one enthusiastic laborite. "He got the teamsters together and away from the CIO."

Not satisfied with organizing Negroes, Vines started signing up the white locomotive engineers and electricians, the carpenters and the blacksmiths at the Army Base, which is now 100 per cent organized, according to the A.F. of L. officials.

In addition to Millner and Vines, other Negroes prominent in the Norfolk labor drive are W. G. Anderson, business representative of the local I.L.A., Hugh Brown, W. J. Hundley and David Austin.

Some Negro officials were bitter in their criticism of the Brotherhood of Railroad Freight Handlers, Clerks and Teamsters, which still continues the old policy of discrimination against Negro workers. They have no outlet for expression and no voice in administration although they pay dues like the rest. They assert that it is this sort of thing which gives the A.F. of L. a bad reputation among Negroes and hamper efforts to organize them.

The Finkelstein Factory

Another dark spot in the Norfolk labor front is the Finkelstein clothing factory, one of the plants from the North which moved South to escape decent wage standards. Many colored men and women are employed there. An effort was made a year ago to organize these workers but the effort failed. Some of the workers lost their jobs as a result of this effort.

A tobacco factory employing colored women in considerable numbers at low wages has also been able to stave off organization.

The colored cleaners and dyers have a small organization which is said not to have made much headway, and colored draymen and expressmen with a similar organization complain that they are being replaced with whites.

In view of the local feeling against whites and Negroes being in the same organizations of any kind, the success so far attending the labor drive, which would be considered modest elsewhere, is remarkable in Norfolk.

I heard considerable criticism of the so-called leading Negroes because of their alleged indifference to the struggles of the black workers. "They don't give a damn about how the workers make it," said one unionist. "All our support comes from what they call the riffraff, the Negro who has little or no education but a whole lot of loyalty and common sense."

The story is told about one Negro physician who had been secured to handle compensation cases arising from injuries sustained by workers in the ships and on the docks. This man refused to serve the workers when called, complaining that they were "filthy dirty," as if a workingman sweating in the bowels of a ship or hustling cotton bales along the dock was supposed to be clean.

It is indeed striking to a stranger to find the "respectable" Negroes so blandly uninformed about the conditions and problems of the Negro workers upon whom they must always depend for their living.

Newport News Jittery

The recent invasion of Newport News by the CIO has got the town jittery with almost everybody afraid to even talk about labor conditions there. The town depends absolutely upon the shipbuilding company which seems to dominate public opinion. The newspapers, the chamber of commerce, the railroads and the shipyards are united in a solid phalanx against organization of the thousands of black and white workers employed in this basic industry.

There are some 3,000 Negro workers in the shipyards. Most of them ARE only laborers, skilled work being restricted to whites with a few exceptions. The Negroes that have skilled work are used by the company as bellwethers to keep the bulk of underpaid black workers from unionization.

The union drive has just started and has made but little headway. Whether or not it will be successful is problematical.

More success has attended the efforts to organize the large number of Negro women employed in the city's laundries. But here too, the result has been little better than negligible.

Tobacco Workers Triumph

One of the most unusual stories in the saga of black labor is the speed and completeness with which a handful of militant young college-trained Negroes organized the workers in Richmond's tobacco factories.

Among these militants are Attorneys J. T. Hewin, Jr. and J. Byron Hopkins, Jr., Charles B. Case, Leslie Smith, Rev. C. C. Queen, Milton Richmond, Wiley A. Hall, Urban League secretary and Columbus Austin, CIO organizer.

Their efforts are largely the outcome of the Southern Negro Youth Congress held in Richmond in February of this year. They have had the co-operation of Dr. Tinsley, Local N.A.A.C.P. head and Editor Norrell of the Richmond Planet who continues in the footsteps of the late lamented John Mitchell. [49]

During the recent drive among the tobacco workers, of whom most are colored, nearly 4,000 have been organized. Most of these Negro workers are stemmers or doing semi-skilled and unskilled work. There have been three strikes and all of them have been won. One strike lasted a month. The two others lasted only a week. Each factory has been organized into a local affiliated with the CIO.

Increase $200,000 Yearly

It is said to take ten years to learn how to stem tobacco efficiently. The average is from 15 to 17 pounds a day but expert workers sometimes stem 30 or more pounds. The best stemmer in the city is a Negro woman, totally blind, who has 25 years of experience.

Before the union drive, women working 48 and 58 hours a week received about $5 for their labor. The wages have now been boosted 50 to 100 per cent. The organizers estimate that the increases won total of $200,000 annually.

The men in the tobacco industry were getting 25 cents an hour before unionization. They are now getting 35 and 40 cents an hour.

Didn't Wait for the CIO

These young Negroes did not wait for the CIO to come along before they began organizing the tobacco workers. They knew the plight of the laborers and went about doing the only thing that could help them better their living conditions.

With the exception of Rev. Queen, no Richmond Negro preacher offered his church for organization meetings. They all seemed to be indifferent, although they get their money from these same tobacco workers. Mr. Hall of the Urban League also permitted use of his premises for meetings of the embattled workers.

This group of militants was also aware of the plight of the Negro fishermen and so promptly began organizing them under the auspices of the Fishery Workers' Organizing Committee, CIO.

There are 2,300 Negro fishermen in the Reedville-Kilmarnock area. Nearly 2,000 of them have been organized since the drive began. Most of them have been getting less than $1 a day for years. Among those unusually active in the organization were Chas. B. Case, a Negro insurance man, and Milton Richmond, director of the Negro Forum Council.

The Fishing companies are not taking unionization lying down. They have refused to recognize the union. They are staging a house-to-house canvass in an effort to discourage unionization. But the workers are sticking by their guns. The CIO is citing the companies under the Wagner Labor Law for their coercion.

Driving On Other Fronts, Too

The labor drive is not stopping at the tobacco and fishing workers. At present the laundry workers are being organized by a CIO group. The A.F. of L. was working among them but the workers felt that they were not getting results so they turned to the new outfit.

It is significant that the white and black employes of the Manchester Board and Paper Company, which is one of three factories of its kind, are co-operating 100 per cent. The Negro organizers say there has been no difficulty in getting the two groups to work together in the unions they have organized.

Teamsters of the city are being organized by the A.F. of L., with white workers in one local and Negro workers in another. Most of the teamsters are colored.

Plans are afoot by the CIO to organize hotel employes, janitors, domestic workers, and Negro office workers.

Negro Railroad Firemen

The A.F. of L. groups here come in for the usual criticism leveled against them elsewhere. It is asserted that they hold separate meetings for each racial group in a union while the CIO holds mixed meetings. CIO men declare that the A.F. of L. never got busy organizing Negro workers until the CIO came along and launched its activities.

In Richmond there is an organization of Negro railroad firemen and also one of coal passers. It is said that the local Negro longshoremen, about 112 in number, are drifting toward the CIO Maritime Union, but I was unable to confirm this. They are said to have recently won an increase of 7 cents an hour.

Mr. Wiley A. Hall, the executive secretary of the Richmond Urban League feels that "this drive is the most significant thing that has happened to Negroes since Emancipation. The welfare of the workers depends upon labor organization."

Dr. Tinsley, president of the N.A.A.C.P., declared that "Negroes can eat and pay rent a little better because of the recent labor union activity."

Won Spurs On Picket Line

CIO men spoke proudly of how the Negroes had won their spurs on the picket line during the tobacco strike. Some of them remained on the picket line for 24 hours in their zeal to win a living wage agreement.

There were two unions in the tobacco industry in Richmond, the old A.F. of L. Tobacco Workers' of America and the new CIO Tobacco Stemmers and Laborers Union. Most of the Negro workers, being semi-skilled or unskilled, belong to the latter organization.

A campaign has been on for some time to get more Negroes to qualify for the franchise in Richmond. That such a step is urgently needed is evidenced by the fact that of the 3,304 city employes, only 281 are Negroes and 273 of them are school teachers. Street cleaners, garbage men and other public servants are all whites. This condition is attributed to the fact that only 1,600 dark Richmonders can vote and less than 1,000 do.

The young militants who successfully engineered the tobacco workers strike have high hopes that the new spirit manifested by Negro labor here will find expression along political and social as well as economic lines.

Baltimore Sixty Percent Organized

For one year Arthur Murphy, militant and earnest young Negro organizer for the Steel Workers' Organizing Committee has been laboring among the 6,000 black steel workers who labor for the Bethlehem Steel Company at its Sparrows Point, Md. plant in the Baltimore suburbs.

"We have no complaint to make about the progress of our work," he said, pointing out that more than 4,000 of the 6,500 black workers have joined the new steel union, while 13,000 of the 19,000 white workers were aligned with the S.W.O.C.

It would indeed seem that the S.W.O.C. has no need to worry about its progress in Baltimore, but a great deal to feel proud about, considering the fact that Baltimore is a notorious jim-crow non-union town.

There is one general steel lodge. In this Negroes serve on all committees along with the whites, and also on the executive committee.

A Negro, Bedford Livingstone, is third vice president and another Negro, Clarence Stewart, is assistant secretary.

There are also some Negroes serving on the trustee board of the local.

It is traditional at this plant that Negroes do only the hardest and most laborous work, and they are terrorized by the foremen, especially since the recent union activities. Many have been fired because of their work for organization but the union has rallied behind them and got them back on the job.

Get New Opportunities

Before the coming of the union, Negroes working in the tin mills worked only on the opening floor, in the bar yard and the grease house. Since the union came in with its insistence on equal rights, one Negro has been put in the hot mill. Negotiations are now in progress for the working of Negroes on the furnaces and in the hot mills where the pay is from $10 to $15 a day.

In the pipe mill Negroes were doing only the heaviest and least paid work before the union came on the scene. The highly paid work on the testing and grinding machines was barred to them. The union has succeeded not only in getting some Negroes on those machines but on threading machines as well.

In the plate mill some Negroes who were getting only $3 a day six months ago are now drawing down as much as $22.

Company Propaganda

In order to wreck the union, the company, it is said, has spread the rumor that if the CIO is successful the whites will lose their jobs to the Negroes. Unmindful of this propaganda the white workers have continued to join the union.

The real test of strength will come in a very short time when the election is held to determine who will represent the toilers in the Sparrows Point plant. The S.W.O.C. is making a strenuous effort to organize the plant 100 per cent with a good prospect of doing so, acording to its organizers.

Negroes Strike 100 Percent

Not content with organizing the Bethlehem Steel Co. plant, the CIO has turned its attention also to copper works, sugar refineries, molding plants, etc.

At the plant of the Standard Sanitary Company, there are 260 Negro workers out of a total group of 672. There was a strike under CIO auspices which lasted ten days. Every single Negro worker joined the strike, and won an agreement with the company. The local is known as Columbus Lodge No. 1492, and although Negroes constitute less than half the number of employes in the plant, they have half the officers in the union. The strike was pulled a month ago.

At the plant of the Wisekettle Co., which makes bathtubs and oil stoves, there are 300 workers of whom 125 are Negroes. Two weeks ago there was a spontaneous strike. Young Organizer Murphy went out to the plant, organized the workers and called off the strike. The new union, Lodge No. 1910, meets with the company officials next week to sign an agreement. The vice president and the recording secretary of this union are Negroes. Colored men also serve as trustees of the organization.

Negroes On Every Committee

The Easton Rolling Mill has 800 employes of whom 300 are colored. These men are organized into Lodge No. 1245. Negroes are on every committee. The contract between the union and the company was negotiated by one Negro, Harry Dennis, and two white workers.

There is one lodge of chemical workers in Baltimore. This has 200 Negro members and the officers of the union are evenly divided between white and colored.

A contract has been negotiated with the sugar refineries. At a plant which employs 1,500 men, the majority of whom are colored, a Negro named Gilmore is vice president of the lodge.

Lodges have been organized at the Devere Cooper Works and the Baltimore Brass and Copper Co. Here too, Negroes take a prominent part in the administration of the unions, serving on all committees.

Release Negro Pickets

The stirring activities in connection with the organization of the employees of the Philipps Canning Co. at nearby Cambridge, Md., illustrate the new solidarity between colored and white labor which is manifesting itself in so many places where only racial antipathy is normally expected.

This plant employs 3,000 workers, the majority of whom are said to be Negroes. They were getting from 18¢ to 22¢ an hour. The workers got together and called a strike.

Six white and six colored workers marched to the company offices and submitted a set of demands. These were rejected. Immediately the plant was closed. The workers picketed it day and night.

When Negro workers were arrested for picketing, the white workers
marched in a body to the jail and freed them.

An A.F. of L. organizer then entered the picture and settled the strike.
After considerable dilly-dallying, the company got tough, rejected the union
and blacklisted all those known to be active in it.

CIO Negotiates Contract

The CIO then got busy, reorganized the strike and signed 460 of the
workers. At the next meeting 1,100 were signed up. A committee of white and
black workers met with the Philipps' management, and is now negotiating a
contract. The CIO has filed charges of intimidation against the company with
the National Labor Relations Board.

The CIO IS RELATIVELY NEW TO BALTIMORE. It has not been as active in as
many directions here as in some other cities I have visited. Here is a drive
on by the CIO. United Hotel and Restaurant Workers which has already increased wages from 30 per cent to 50 per cent in the eight restaurants it
has organized, according to M. E. Pappas, the organizer.

Considerable difficulty has been experienced in getting Negroes to join
this union. It is said that many have refused to join because they believe
the CIO to be "Communistic."
One Negro, Jesse Smith, is serving as organizer.
Considering Baltimore's background, it seems remarkable that the drive
has been so successful with so little inter-racial friction.
Some optimists feel that we are on the threshold of a new day in race
relations as a result of the fight of Negro and white labor side by side for
a higher standard of living.

Pittsburgh Courier, August 7, 1937.

38.   SCHUYLER FINDS PHILADELPHIA NEGROES ARE
RALLYING TO "NEW DEAL" CALL

By George S. Schuyler

PHILADELPHIA, Aug. 12--Negro workers of this city are living up to the
tradition of intelligent militancy established over a century ago WHEN THE
FIRST CONFERENCES of free Negroes were held. This may be "Sleep Town" in
common parlance but the activities of Negro workers belie this nickname.
Accompanied by Donald W. Wyatt, industrial secretary of the Armstrong
Association, I visited the CIO headquarters on North Broad street to find out
just what part Negro labor is playing in the drive now on to organize the
workers of this metropolis.
An old 4-story building with stone facade and ornate entrance, the place
is a beehive of activity with clerks busy and telephone bells jangling. One
gets the impression of money, skill and brains in this important nerve center
of the CIO. The young white men who are directing things are not the type
commonly associated with labor unions. Here is none of the indifference
toward Negro investigation commonly experienced in the past. Everyone is
courteous, helpful and understanding.

Negro President of Teachers Union

From a young white man, George Steele, organizer of the Credit Salesmen
and Outside Collectors Local of the United Retail Employes Union, A CIO
affiliate, who is also a member of the organizing staff and educational committee of the local CIO I learned something of the manifold activities going
on in the busy headquarters.
He gave me a sidelight on the militant attitude of Philadelphia Negroes.
When a strike was recently declared on an installment house whose patrons
were largely Negroes, the striking collectors asked them not to go pay their

installments until the company had signed with the unions. "The colored
people gave us 100 per cent cooperation," Mr. Steele declared.

The contagion of the union drive in this city has so spread that even
the boy bootblacks have formed a union, demanding a 10-cent shine. A large
number of Negro bootblacks have joined and a colored boy is president. While
it is more like a club than a union, it is an indication of the attitude
prevailing in the city.

The Association of Educational and Recreational Workers' Local No. 474
of the American Federation of Teachers has a president, Mr. Charles Hunt, a
colored man.

The station cleaners, chiefly Negro, has as organizer a colored man,
Townsend Johnson.

Negroes in United Auto Workers

From Frank Hellman, president of Local No. 344 of the United Auto Workers,
I learned that a big membership drive had been in progress for three months.
There are a large number of Negro workers in the industry employed in the
various agencies as washers, laborers and dealers. Negro workers, I learned,
were easily organized. Some Negroes are on the executive committee of the
union, which is local No. 258.

The United Bedding and Glider Workers' Union has organized some 20 firms
in the present drive, and its membership includes a considerable number of
Negro workers. According to a woman official, no difficulty has been experienced in getting Negroes into the union.

From George Nott, president and organizer of the local union of the
United Mine Workers which is organizing the Philadelphia Gas Works, I learned
that a considerable number of Negroes are employed in the gas works. While
Negroes were at first reluctant to be organized, little difficulty is now
being experienced in doing so. One Negro is trustee of a station and another
is trustee-at-large. Both serve on the executive committee of the union.
Approximately 500 Negroes are employed in this industry in gas and coke plants.

"The Negroes," said Mr. Nott, "are very faithful and militant union
members. They make good organizers and prove their sincerity."

The CIO lost the election in the Philadelphia Gas Works and this is
attributed to the fact that the company used anti-Negro propaganda, telling
the white workers that it was the union policy to put Negro workers over
white workers.

Food Workers "Proud" of Negro Members

In the office of the United Food Workers' Independent Union Local No.
107, David Blitman, one of the business agents, told me of the result of the
nine-week drive in the industry. He declared that of the 300 organized in
the union, 65 per cent are working under the closed shop, and 30 per cent of
these members are Negroes. This union covers all the handling of food except
in bakeries.

"We have experienced no difficulty at all in organizing the Negroes in
the industry," he declared. "They are as fine a bunch of fellows as
imaginable. They have given us 100 per cent cooperation."

Of the 14 members on the executive board of the union, seven are colored
workers. Two Negroes are shop chairmen and one is slated to become a paid
organizer.

"We are proud of our Negro members," declared Blitman. "They are the
first to join as soon as we start organizing a store. They have a fine
spirit. They are most interested to know what it is all about."

This union has succeeded in reducing working hours from 52 and 55 hours
a week to 45 hours, and whereas wages ranged from $6 to $15 a week, the minimum is now said to be $22.

Negroes Dominate Among Cleaners and Dyers

Mr. Daniel Elkins, young president of the Cleaning and Dying Workers'
Industrial Union, a CIO affiliate, was even more enthusiastic about the result
of the drive among Negro workers in the industry.

Of the 2,500 workers in the trade, he declared that from 70 to 80 per
cent are colored. Of the 600 members of the union 500 are Negroes. An
organizing drive has now been in progress for two months. The two largest
shops and three of the smaller ones of the total of 29 have signed contracts
with the union.

Mr. Elkins was very frank about the problems of the union as they pertain
to colored workers. "We must prove to our people in the trade," he said,
"that we are sincere and above board. Of our executive board of fifteen, 10
are colored workers. The vice-president is a Negro and so is the chairman
in the largest shop, the United Tailors' Association. So also is the shop
committee of five in this plant.

"We are putting four full time organizers in the field," said Mr. Elkins,
"and two of them are colored men. This is the third union to enter the field
in this city in the past five years. The two previous unions were affiliated
with the A.F. of L. The organization was killed by the mistakes of the
leadership which was weak and undemocratic. As a result we are hampered by
a perfectly justifiable watching and waiting policy on the part of the workers.
We are not collecting dues or initiation fees from anyone until we get a
closed shop. Our union is run democratically. Every position is an elected
position, and we tolerate no discrimination against Negro workers."

Negro Shop Chairman Negotiates

"James Shorter (Negro), shop chairman in the North Cleaning Plant and
chairman of our organizing committee," said Elkins, "actually made negotiations for affiliation with the CIO. He organized his own shop of 90 people
in three weeks time. Indeed, Negroes initiated this whole organization. Mr.
Shorter, who is also a musician, is a member of Local No. 274, American
Federation of Musicians, of which he is the business agent. When he had
difficulties with the white union he fought for a separate charter. Joseph
H. McCommer (Negro) our vice-president kept together the remnants of the
former A.F. of L. union and used it as a nucleus of our present organization."

"We have brought hours down," he continued, "from 55 to 75 hours a week,
to 44 hours a week. When the industry is organized, we will boost the wages.
We are calling for a sharing of work and a living wage. The union scale will
represent an increase of from 15 to 25 per cent."

Negroes Strong in Meat Cutters Union

The Amalgamated Meat Cutters and Butcher Workingmen of North America,
Local No. 195, A.F. of L., has been conducting an organization drive for over
two months. Because of past discrimination against colored workers, organizers report a certain joining, but claim that it is being overcome.

Of the 2,300 workers in the local industry, comprising of 19 different
nationalities, about 30 per cent are Negroes. A colored man, Dewey Bucannon,
is vice president. William Banks is shop steward at Duffy Bros., and Samuel
Elliott at the Consolidated Dressed Beef Company. All are trustees of the
union. The Negroes in the industry are both laborers and craftsmen.

George Rooney, organizer of the Transport Workers' Union, a CIO affiliate, declared that "It is taking a considerable effort to persuade Negro
workers to go along with us. The response has been slow. However, we have
succeeded to a certain extent in breaking down the terrific fear of the union.
There is a very definite need of a union. While our principal effort is
organizing the Philadelphia Rapid Transit, we are taking in all transportation.
The cab drivers are being organized by the A.F. of L."

This union has just started its drive and no local has as yet been set up.
So far as Negroes are concerned, they are mostly porters in the subway system
and laborers.

Most Hodcarriers Are Negroes

Of the 3,500 hodcarriers and building laborers in Philadelphia in Local
No. 332 of the International Hod Carriers and Building Laborers Union, approximately 75 per cent are colored. The union has four business agents of whom two
are Negroes. One of these Negro business agents is Harry Murray, said to be
a former A.F. of L. organizer.
Half of the members of the chemical workers are Negroes.
Of the 200 members of the Building Service Employes International Union,
Local No. 125, A.F. of L., 100 are Negroes. This includes the president,
vice president, treasurer and recording secretary.

In the International Brotherhood of Teamsters, Chauffeurs, Stablemen
and Helpers of America, Local 107, the Negro membership has risen from 50 in
1933 to over 500 at present. Negroes are trustees and members of the
executive board of the union.
Of the 600 members of Pennsylvania State Employes Association, Local
No. 6, 70 are Negroes. The union is affiliated with the CIO.
Almost 80 per cent of the members of the laundry workers union is colored.

Drives are in progress among the tobacco workers, the woodworkers and the
hotel and restaurant workers, all of these groups having a large Negro representation. Indeed, aside from the CIO activities, of the 50 A.F. of L. unions
organized since the NRA, half of them have Negro membership.

CIO Makes A.F. of L. Wake Up

All in all it is evident that Negroes are responding as well to the
union drive as the white workers. This is the more remarkable since widespread discrimination against them in the past has engendered a feeling of
skepticism about labor organization. They have been tricked in the past and
accordingly are wary.
This is said to be especially true in the building trades where in the
past there has been marked discrimination against Negro craftsmen. Often Negro
artisans have been sent to the worst jobs and then only after white artisans had
been placed. Difficulty has been experienced by Negro craftsmen in getting on
PWA projects. Many Negro plasterers failed for this reason to pay their dues
and were dropped from the union.
At the same time there has been, until recently the usual feeling on the
part of white workers that Negroes could not be trusted and would desert in
the first struggle.
But there is general agreement that the coming of the CIO has made a
difference. It has made the A.F. of L. outfits wake up and do the organizing
work that should have been done long ago.
Competition, it seems, is not only the life of trade, but also the life
of the labor movement.

Among the strongest and oldest unions in Philadelphia are those of the
coastwise and deepwater longshoremen. They have always been among the most
militant in the United States, and a large proportion of them are Negroes,
with Negro officers and business agents.

If any proof were needed of the essential oneness of humanity and the
equality of black and white, it is demonstrated by the manner in which the
black workers of Philadelphia have organized in unions to improve their
standard of living and increase their economic power.

Chester Negro Workers "Play Possum"

As a visitor enters Chester, a large suburb of Philadelphia, a big sign
announces that "What Chester Makes, Makes Chester." It is true that Chester
makes a whole lot of things.
First there is the Sun Shipbuilding Company, several fabricating steel
mills, the Congoleum company, the Logood mill, the General and Sun Oil
companies, and the Chester Tube and Pipe Company.

All of these companies employ Negroes to a considerable extent, but while the spirit of unionism is present, the Negroes are rather scary and choose to play possum.

Rev. Barbour severely scored the "better" Negroes for their reactionism and slave psychology. "They do not lift a finger," he said, "to protect the masses of their people. They have the utmost contempt for the masses."

He charged that the city's liquor interests "are fighting labor by plying the workers with drink. They have dropped the price of liquor for that purpose."

Of the 20 college Negroes employed in the town's plants, he charged that not one had lifted a finger to help the labor drive, while he pays his own railroad fare to go to organize labor. Only he and Rev. H. W. Watson have opened their churches for union meetings.

"Need a Good Negro Organizer"

"We need a good Negro organizer who can speak the language of these people," he declared. "We can't get a prominent Negro to make a talk. Only the common, ordinary Negro supports union activity."

Chester is a town dominated by oil and shipbuilding people. There are a large number of Negroes on relief and the WPA has recently laid off lots of them to shift for themselves.

There is a big undercover fight going between the CIO and the A.F. of L., the politicians are trying to chisel in on the labor unrest and the company propagandists and the newspapers are playing up the old Communist scare to discourage labor organization.

Several Negro leaders are tacitly opposed to the union drive. One of them told me that the shipbuilding company "pays good wages" and that the Congoleum company pays from $24 to $40 a week. One Negro technician, Curtis Holmes, is employed in the laboratory department and there are said to be many Negro foremen in the plant. The Viscose Co., world's largest producers of rayon, has a Negro foreman and employs many colored workers.

"Many Negroes," declared a colored saloon keeper, "have drawn from $40 to $50 a week right through the depression while white men were eating out of swill cans."

"Good Time" Town

Chester is known throughout the state as a "good time" town where the sky is the limit and joy is unconfined. It is "wide open" with the underworld, an extensive area known as Bethel Court, openly taunting every form of vice. It is said that the large floating population makes this necessary, but recently efforts were made to curb the growing power of this vicious area, without avail.

The town has five Negro policemen, a Negro magistrate, Casper H. Green; 61 Negro school teachers; city janitors and laborers; a Negro member of the school board, Louis Hunt, and Dr. W. E. Smith on the staff of the local hospital.

Some of the Negroes are said to be buying homes, but the majority are not reported to be following this example.

It is interesting to note that Henry Ford, a reputedly great friend of the Negroes, employs not a single Negro at his assembly plant in Chester where some 4,000 workers are kept busy.

Trenton Negroes Organized in Rubber

Approximately half of Trenton's 9,000 Negroes are recipients of relief or employed on relief jobs. Those who are employed are chiefly in rubber with a small minority in the pottery and wire plants. The chief drive has been in rubber.

At the Puritan Rubber Company which employs a total working force of 150, about 20 Negroes have jobs. The plant is 100 per cent organized with Negroes on almost every committee of the union. One Negro worker, Thomas Kelly, is a member of the union's executive committee, along with another colored man.

A three-week strike was staged and the Negro workers went out 100 per cent. Wages now run from 30 to 60 cents an hour and the workers have won seniority rights.

Mr. Kelly is a modeler at the Puritan plant where he has been working for eleven years. Previously he was shipping clerk. Nevertheless he struck along with the rest for better working conditions and more power to the workers.

Head Compound Man a Negro

At the plant of the Acme Rubber Company, which employs the largest number of colored workers, they number 125 of the total union membership of 500.

From George Shepard, a Negro who has worked for this company for 11 years, I learned that a Negro, Mose Johnson, is secretary of the local of the Rubber Workers' Union, and that all the Negroes except the latest hired, are members of the union. Most of them are semi-skilled workers. Two Negro workers are on shop committees.

As a result of the union drive, these workers have won seniority rights, annual vacations with a week's pay, and minimum of 50 cents an hour for men and 42 cents an hour for women. Some Negro workers get $35 a week.

A small number of Negroes are employed at the other rubber plants, while in the three wire mills at least 40 per cent of the employes are Negroes. There is a union in all these plants and Negroes boast of proportionate membership in it.

All Quiet On the DuPont Front

There is almost no activity on the labor front in Wilmington, capital of the DuPont barony, where Negroes constitute more than 16 per cent of the population.

From Attorney Louis H. Redding, an alert and informed Negro barrister, I learned that Negroes are chiefly engaged in leather work, trucking, domestic work, building trades, railroad repair shops, steel mills and the Pennsylvania railroad. Most of them are unorganized, this being a notorious non-union town, the beneficiary of much of the DuPont paternalism through the years.[50]

In the spring there was a strike of the truck drivers. The Negroes went out with the whites but eventually the strike was lost.

Another strike was pulled on the automobile repair shops where Negroes are employed mainly as laborers although some are mechanics in the smaller shops. The strike at one time assumed serious proportions and Negroes were prominent in the picket lines.

A few Negroes are employed at the mill of Joseph Bancroft and Sons, textile manufacturers, but mainly as laborers and janitors. Wages are low and paternalism the order of the day.

It is considered a great gain that some sort of organization has been perfected in the industries where strikes were pulled. Whites and Negroes cooperated and marched together in labor demonstrations.

But as one man said, "You can sum up by saying that these people here are not organization minded."

Negroes Head Camden Hod Carriers

Aside from being on relief, Camden, N.J. Negroes, totalling 10,000 are chiefly employed in the Campbell Soup plant as packers and porters. In a strike pulled two years ago, many of the Negroes went out and helped picket the plant. They are now serving on shop committees and as officers of the union. But informed persons declare that this is an "inside" union.

Most of the remaining employed Negroes are domestic workers, porters, in the coke works, as building laborers, in the gas works and at the Victor phonograph plant where they are chiefly laborers. The Victor plant is organized but has an "inside" union. Many canny Negro workers are said to have joined both unions just to play safe.

It is in Local 222 of the International Hodcarriers and Building Laborers Union that the Negroes play the largest role as union men.

The president of the local is Joseph Huggins, Jr., a Negro, while his father, Joseph Huggins, Sr., is recording secretary. A highly intelligent Negro, Charles Mimms, is business agent, and also vice president of the district Council comprising 12 or 14 local unions.

Of the 538 members of the local, 75 per cent are Negroes. All the men in the union are working.

As an evidence of what Negro organizers can accomplish in getting Negroes signed up in a union, Mr. Mimms, who hails originally from Birmingham, points to the fact that last January when he was elected to his job, there were only about 80 members in the union. All the rest have been brought in by him in the past seven months.

The teamsters' union has a large number of Negro members as the result of its drive.

Taylor and White, dyers, which employs 25 per cent Negroes, had a two-week strike in June. All demands were won.

All in all the great Philadelphia district where nearly a half million Negroes live, compares more than favorably with other sections of the country so far as the organization of Negro workers is concerned. Indeed, it is much better than most sections.

Where the Negroes have not joined the unions, the same thing is largely true of the whites. And the Negroes, at least, have some justification for their hesitancy in view of the unsavory record of the more reactionary unions of the A.F. of L.

The coming of the new, energetic CIO has been a powerful stimulant to labor organization. Whatever the outcome of its effort, its influence will long be felt in the labor movement.

Pittsburgh Courier, August 14, 1937.

39. HARLEM BOASTS 42,000 NEGRO LABOR UNIONISTS

By George S. Schuyler

NEW YORK, Aug. 19--Here in the world's greatest industrial shipping and mercantile center, Negro workers have been so influenced by the deep currents of liberal and radical thought through the years that the necessity for labor organization is no longer questioned as it is in many other colored communities.

Union membership is taken as a matter of course and scores of thousands of Negro workers carry a union card. In Harlem alone, according to Frank Crosswaith, head of the Negro Labor Committee and a general organizer for the International Ladies Garment Workers' Union, there are 42,000 organized Negro workers. And perhaps no more than three-fifths of the Negroes in New York City reside in Harlem.

The current drives of the unions affiliated with the Committee for Industrial Organization and some affiliated with the older American Federation of Labor are bringing in hundreds of new Negro unionists weekly. On a dozen different fronts black and white workers are marching together toward industrial democracy.

Ladies Garment Workers Lead

The highly enlightened International Ladies Garment Workers' Union, with its educated and far-sighted leadership, claims the largest Negro membership in the metropolis. Of its 255,00 total membership, over 10,000 are Negroes, and 7,000 of these are in New York City.

The I.L.G.W.U. has a definite policy of encouraging its Negro members to participate fully in all its activities: organizational, administrative, cultural and recreational.

One of its ace general organizers is Frank Crosswaith, veteran laborite

and Socialist of 20 years experience. One of the business agents of giant
Local No. 22 is Miss Edith Ransom, a colored woman. Of the 28 or 30 members
of the various executive boards of the New York locals, six are colored.
Another colored woman, Miss Winifred Gittens, is chairman of the finance committee of Local No. 25, and also secretary of the Negro Labor Committee, whose
directors are representatives of the various labor groups in the metropolis.

100% Increase In Membership

In the big membership drive still going on, the I.L.G.W.U. has increased
its membership 100 per cent, and the Negro increase has been proportionate.
Today the union is about the third largest in America.

One source of its great strength is the protection, security and cultural
and recreational facilities offered its members, regardless of color. All
members have the advantages of sick and death benefits. The union maintains a
health center and clinic open to all members and which specializes in diseases
of the industry.

It goes in for extensive educational work in classes and forums in
various sections of the city, including Harlem, and it gives annual scholarships to selected members for study at the labor colleges at Brookwood and
Bryn Mawr. There is always at least one colored girl among those selected.

The union even holds classes in Negro history and the history of the
Negro in the trade union movement. It maintains Naturalization Bureaus to
train alien members (some of whom are Negroes) for citizenship.

Its physical activities include baseball, football, swimming, dancing,
hikes and excursions. In addition, there are summer camps, concerts, plays,
mass meetings with outstanding speakers, and educational trips to the numerous
museums throughout the city.

And all these activities are free to all members of the union. Regardless of color or creed, they all agitate, study, strike, dance, hike and
swim together.

From $12 to $60 a Week

At the Harlem Labor Center on 125th street, the nerve center of labor
organization and administration in the Harlem area and headquarters of the
Negro Labor Committee, Mr. Crosswaith told something of what membership in the
I.L.G.W.U. has meant to colored women.

"As a rule," he said, "the Negro worker received the lowest wage in the
shop before the union came in. But a basic principle of the I.L.G.W.U. is
equal pay for Negro work, so immediately you see the advantage of the Negro
worker.

"Another advantage is protection on the job. After five days employment
in a shop a worker has 'citizenship rights' there. This means that if there
is a shortage of work in the shop, it must be equally divided among the
workers and none laid off.

"The average wage for colored girls was $11 or $12 a week in the open
shops. Few ever received more than that. Today we have some Negro girls
who are earning as high as $60 a week. This is due solely to the closed
shop enforced by the I.L.G.W.U."

Mr. Crosswaith declared, in answer to a question concerning Negro activities within the union, that "Negro delegates are in attendance at every
convention. They all have their expenses paid and suffer no loss of wages.
They participate fully in the deliberations at these conventions."

Send Atlanta Girl to Bryn Mawr

At the union's international headquarters at 3 W. 16th street, Mark Starr,
I.L.G.W.U. Educational Director, told me something of the manner in which
Negro members are integrated into the union's educational and recreational
activities. In the union newspaper he pointed to several group photographs in
which Negroes appeared and told of the union's insistence that there be no
suggestion of separation of races in any activities.

"That's Barbara Shell," he said, indicating an attractive brown girl in
a group of a half dozen tennis players photographed on the campus at Bryn
Mawr. "She comes from Local No. 122 in Atlanta, Ga. The local there was

recently organized by Frank Crosswaith, and we have already sent Miss Shell to the labor college at Bryn Mawr. Indeed, our colored members are partic- ipating in all our summer institutes.

"Our chorus contains a number of colored girls. We have just released a record, 'The Song of the CIO,' rendered by them. It will be sung everywhere in the labor world."

Mr. Starr told of the response of the Negro workers to unionization in Atlanta and Chicago. "We are at present engaged in organizing Negro and white workers together in the same local in Houston, Texas," he declared.

Answers Questions About CIO

The record of the I.L.G.W.U. with Negro labor is significant because it answers in part the question often asked by Negroes. "Will the CIO be any different from the A.F. of L.?"

The I.L.G.W.U., the Amalgamated Clothing Workers and the United Mine Workers are chief among the ten unions that launched the CIO and were read out of the A.F. of L. for so doing. President Dubinsky of the I.L.G.W.U., Presi- dent Hillman of the A.C.W.A., and President Lewis of the United Mine Workers are the brains of the CIO and the directing heads of its activities. They have created the CIO and the directing heads of its activities. They have created the CIO in the likeness of their unions. And their unions are the most enlightened in America in according justice and fair play to Negro members. Everywhere the CIO unions seem to be trying to follow the example set by the I.L.G.W.U., the model for organized American labor. These men are labor statesmen, not labor skates, and they seem to envision a new America in which race prejudice and color discrimination will be at a minimum. It is noteworthy that every CIO union's constitution specifically prohibits discrimination based on color.

Union Gets Negro Pharmacists Jobs

One of the major drives being directed from the Harlem Labor Center is that of the United Retail Drug Store Employes Union No. 199, which recently went over from the A.F. of L. to the CIO.

Prior to this drive most of the Negro pharmacists in New York with licenses were red caps at the various railroad stations. Out of 101 drug stores in the Harlem area, two gave employment to two Negro pharmacists with licenses.

Today, as a result of the unionization drive, 27 licensed Negro pharma- cists are employed in the drug stores of the area. There are about 80 colored members in the local and two of them sit on the executive committee.

Grocery Clerks Pay Boosted 100%

Another union that has quit the A.F. of L. and joined its rival is the Retail, Dairy, Grocery and Fruit Employes Union No. 336. It has a total membership of 10,000, of whom about 250 are colored. According to George Snipe, Negro organizer, 200 of these Negro members have been organized in the last 75 days. There are several on the executive committee despite the small percentage of Negroes in the union.

Six weeks ago the local signed an agreement with the Harlem Grocery Store Owners Association involving $250,000 in increased wages.

Prior to the current drive, the practice of the store owners was to hire youngsters in school or just out of school and pay them $5 or $7 a week. In some cases they toiled as long as 79 hours a week. The union jumped in and boosted the pay to $75 a week minimum with a 54-hour week.

Commenting on the current drive, an officer said: "The Negroes have proved to be the most valuable union members. They have joined with facility. Today it is practically easy to talk labor unionism with the Negro."

Janitors-Elevator Men Unionized

Next to the I.L.G.W.U. in point of Negro membership is the Building Ser- vice Employes Union, affiliated with the A.F. of L. Of its 30,000 members, more than 4,000 are colored. The union has a half dozen Negro business agents and several Negroes on its executive board. Thomas Young, a colored man, is

first vice president of the union. Mr. Young is also vice chairman of the
Labor Committee. The union maintains an office in the Harlem Labor Center.
    This union embraces janitors, elevator operators, superintendents, por-
ters and other employes of office and residential buildings.
    At one time Negroes had a monopoly on this kind of work in New York City.
There are still more Negroes than whites in the industry.
    In the past the union suffered from racketeering. For years it never had
more than 200 members. When Mr. Crosswaith was made organizer in 1924, he
alarmed the officials by bringing in 500 Negro elevator operators in 90 days.
Fearing they would lose control of the union, the white officials fired him.
Today the union has a more enlightened leadership and its Negro members are
too numerous and militant for anything to be put over on them. Moreover,
they are helping to direct the union's policy.

200 Negroes in Painters' Union

    It has been the traditional policy of the skilled workers to exclude
Negroes from their unions either by constitutional provision or subterfuge.
This has been the case in practically every city in America.
    It was the more surprising, then, to learn that there were 200 Negro
members of District Council No. 9 of the Painters' Union, and that is also a
member of the Negro Labor Committee.
    Negro membership in the last two or three months has increased 80 per
cent.
    "There has been a very decided change in the attitude of white workers
toward the colored workers," said one official. "Today they seem to be
recognizing the Negroes as equals in the army of labor."
    Another A.F. of L. union making tremendous strides in the organization
of Negro workers is Cafeteria Workers' Union No. 302, with offices at 260 W.
39th street. I was unable to learn the proportion of Negroes in the membership but was given to understand that it is quite large. Mr. Manning Johnson,
a Negro, is one of the organizers.

Soft Drink Workers Lift Pay 80%

    Equally vigorous in its drive is Soft Drink Workers Union No. 368, A.F.
of L. It claims to be 100 per cent organized. It is a new union but is
definitely going places. The Negro workers were getting almost no wages. Today the average wage is up 80 per cent. The union has a Negro on its executive
board, although Negroes are considerably in the minority. There are about 50
Negro members. In this instance, too, the Negro Labor Committee was instrumental in launching the drive.
    Drives are being instituted by the International Barbers Union No. 110,
and an effort has been started to organize the funeral chauffeurs of the
Harlem area.
    The Association of Works Progress Relief Agencies of the American Feder-
ation of State, County and Municipal Employes has a Negro, William Gaulden,
as organizer and member of its Executive Board. The Union has a large number
of Negro members.

Laundry Workers 65% Negroes

    One of the most powerful unions in this area is the United Laundry Work-
ers. It has a membership of 15,000 of whom about 65 per cent are Negroes.
There are about 50,000 workers in the industry in New York City, 65 per cent
of them colored.
    The union has recently gone over to the CIO and is associated with the
Amalgamated Clothing Workers of America. Prior to this shift it was doing
practically nothing except collect dues. Radicals jumped in, started a drive
for members on June 16, and since that date it has grown from 2,500 to 15,000
members.
    The Negro Labor Committee loaned the union a clever young Negro, Noah
Walter, as organizer. Walter is now first assistant manager of the union
with complete control of the Organization and Complaint Department.
    In addition to Mr. Walter, there are four full time Negro organizers,
two women and two men. There are two Negro members on the executive board
of 13, and of the 30 members of the unit trade councils, 15 are colored.

Negro Workers Responded 100%

"The Negro workers responded 100 per cent to the organization call," Mr.
Walter declared.   "They didn't even wait for the union to call them in some
instances.   They wrote in for the CIO to come and organize them.
    "We find Negro and white workers getting along harmoniously.   Indeed,
Negro workers are often shop chairmen in laundries employing mostly whites.
The bosses have been respectful to these shop chairmen."   Before the laundries
were organized, women workers got from $6 to $12 for 48 hours, and men workers
received from $12 to $16 for 55 to 70 hours work.
    The union scale for women is $15.75 to $25 for 45 hours, with time-and-a
half for overtime, legal holidays with pay, a week's vacation with pay, a
week's sick leave with pay, and protection from being fired without just cause.
    The union scale for men ranges from $20 to $65 for 48 hours, with the
same benefits.   "We have Negro washers getting $55 a week," boasted Mr. Walter,
"and drivers getting from $35 to $65 according to the type of laundry in which
they are employed."

Unanimously Quit A.F. of L.

    The union withdrew from the A.F. of L. by unanimous vote.   Officials
say this was because it had never given its support to any organization drive.
Many workers dropped out of the union because of its racketeering officials
who were later tried and ousted.   The union did not hold a convention for
20 years.
    Under the old regime the policy was to never organize Negroes if possible.
It thus fanned race prejudice and often threw out duly accredited members.
While Negro members were in the majority, they were not represented among
either the paid or unpaid leadership.
    The CIO came along with its policy of organizing everybody and democratic
administration, It won easily.
    The union's biggest fight has been against the company unions but is
about to close two contracts with employers, each covering more than 10,000
workers.

A.F. of L. Aids Bosses

    Union officials charge that the A.F. of L. union has been helping the
employers fight the union.   At one time it is alleged that A.F. of L. officials
called a meeting and supplied the union men with whisky and the union women
with ice cream.   CIO members took the floor and stampeded the whole group out
of the hall and into the nearby CIO office.
    Union officials now claim to have eliminated all gangsters from the
local.
    The Chinese laundry workers are seeking an autonomous union allied with
the CIO union.   They "have shown a great deal of self reliance" one union man
declared.

Workers Showing New Spirit

    Union officials related two or three incidents that show the new spirit
of the workers.   One big laundry called a company union meeting for 6 o'clock.
The union promptly got out a leaflet against it.   About 175 workers attended
the meeting called by the legitimate union and in 24 hours every worker in
the laundry had signed up.
    Another plant had only 15 workers organized out of 450 employes.   The
boss fired a Negro girl.   The union warned him to rehire her.   He refused.
The whole shop stopped work and everybody joined the union.   The boss recognized the union and rehired the Negro girl he had fired.
    One of New York's largest laundries laid off 35 workers and refused to
rehire them.   The workers threatened to tie up the plant.   The boss then
agreed to take back those he had laid off.   He signed a contract with the
union, agreeing not to lay off anybody but to spread the work around.   It was
customary for this laundry to lay off 50 workers during the dummer.

Negro Shipbuilders Out 100%

A journey of nearly an hour on the subway took me from midtown Manhattan to the busy headquarters of the Industrial Union of Marine and Shipbuilding Workers of America at 54th street and 3rd avenue in Brooklyn and hard by the waterfront.

Here war was in progress. A strike marred by violence had tied up all the shipyards in the vicinity since June 14. Around the old three-story brick building grim shirt-sleeved white men loitered, eyeing everyone suspiciously.

Challenged at the door, I managed to get in to see Charles George, a representative of the union's national office.

From him I learned that of the total of 15,000 workers in the union, over 1,000 are Negroes. "They have come out 100 per cent with us" he declared. "The Negro shop stewards are among the best we have."

He reported a large number of Negroes in Local No. 16 at Kearney, N.J., and was quite enthusiastic about the manner in which the Negroes had picketed the struck plants. He asserted that his was the only organization in this industry to hold mixed, racial meetings in Mobile, Ala., and Newport News, Va.

Dept. Store Employes Join Up

From James Webster, Negro organizer of the Department Store Employes Union Local No. 1250, I learned that the three-month membership drive has increased membership approximately 100 per cent. Every union committee has a Negro member, there are two Negroes on the executive board and two white and eight Negroes are on the section-action committee. He reported a "fair response" from Negro workers but bitterly scored the raising of the race issue by certain employers aided and abetted by a "race racketeer" who has been terrorizing the district for his won personal gain. Out of the 6,000 members in the union, there are less than 50 Negroes.

Mr. Webster is typical of a new type of Negro leader in the labor movement. Most of them have had college training or its equivalent. Webster, hailing originally from Stamford, Conn., is a graduate of Hampton and has studied at Columbia U. Edward Summers, second vice president of the Department Store Employees Union, has attended Howard University. Noah Walter of the Laundry Workers Union comes from Brooklyn, N.Y., and is a graduate of Bluefield (W.Va.) State Teachers College and the Rand School of Social Science.

"A Lot of Work To Be Done"

No survey of the New York labor picture would be complete without visiting T. Arnold Hill, veteran Industrial Secretary of the National Urban League and an authority on the labor movement as it relates to Negroes. Mr. Hill has recently completed a tour of the country.

"There is a lot of work yet to be done among Negroes," he declared as we sat in the spacious Urban League offices high above the bustle of Broadway. "The SWOC must make a more definite campaign in the larger centers to bring Negroes into the union. It must show in the plants more evidence of equality and better distribution of jobs. This would encourage more Negroes to join the union.

"The Negro does not realize today that he does not lose his job because of union activities.

"I think the CIO might go in a little deeper for Negro members than it has. It has not yet exerted itself sufficiently to meet Negroes' criticism.

New Negro Attitude 'Encouraging'

"It is very encouraging," he went on, "to see the increasing understanding that Negroes have of the necessity for labor organization. While there is room for great improvement we do have a nucleus in various centers of the country upon which we should be able to construct a healthy growth.

"In industries where Negroes constitute a semi-skilled group, their one chance of advancement is to join industrial unions. Craft unions do not provide for organization of laborers and unskilled workers. For this reason Negroes should identify themselves with the CIO.

"However," he added, "the CIO has been shortsighted because it has failed to utilize the existing channels of information to reach the Negroes.

It should call in one or more persons to advise and consult as to ways and means of getting more Negro workers.
So far as the National Urban League is concerned, we are wholeheartedly in favor of Negro organization and are in many directions working to bring this about."

Pittsburgh Courier, August 21, 1937.

40. DETROIT AWAITING FORD CRISIS[51]

By George S. Schuyler

DETROIT, Mich., Sept.2--Black Detroit is in uproar and confusion as the zero hour looms for the showdown fight between the Ford Motor Company and the United Automobile Workers of America.
Sides are being taken violently. Most of the preachers and professional men are against the U.A.W. and openly in favor of the Ford Motor Company. Dependent upon the masses for their livelihood, they fear that if the Ford Negroes espouse the union cause they will ultimately lose their jobs which would be a major disaster for Detroit.
There are from 16,000 to 18,000 Negroes working for the company and getting a minimum of $6 a day. About 400 more are in the Chrysler plant and considered equally well paid. But at the Ford Company the Negroes have been given skilled work in practically all departments. There are some skilled workers at Chrysler but the diversity of employment there does not at all compare with that given Negroes at Ford's. Negroes are also employed at the Brigg and Detroit Steel Products companies. Graham Brothers is said to be the only large plant at which Negroes are not employed.

Own 3000 Automobiles

Those who side with Ford and the "inside" union known as The Ford Brotherhood, which the Negro workers are said to be dragooned into joining, point with pride to the prosperity which has come to the Negroes working at Ford's.
They say that a large number of Negroes have been able because of the good wages to purchase homes and that more than 3000 own automobiles.
As a result of the example set by Ford, they say, Negroes have been getting into factories in the Detroit district in larger numbers than ever before. They are ready to almost fight any stranger who comes in town and says a good word for the U.A.W.A.
The workers themselves are keeping quiet. The professional folk claim that few have joined the U.A.W.A. but union advocates say that at least two-thirds of the Ford Negro workers have joined. Many for safety sake belong to both the Ford Brotherhood and the U.A.W.A. until it is definitely settled who will represent the workers in collective bargaining under the provisions of the Wagner Labor Relations Act.

Ford Spy System Active

Union sympathizers present another side of the picture. They point first to the fact that the extensive Ford spy system allegedly headed by gunmen, thugs and ex-convicts supervises the men as in a penitentiary. That all sorts of threats are being made to prevent them from joining the auto workers union.
They claim that in the Ford plant segregation is rife as it is also at the other plants; that all restaurants and wash rooms are racially separate although there is no law in Michigan forcing segregation of the races.
They point to conditions in the Ford foundry which is almost exclusively run by Negroes. Here the Negro death rate is said to be appalling with the stay of the average Negro worker very short before his health is impaired.
They point also to the fact that at present the workers have no security in their jobs and can be fired at a moment's notice for any reason whatsoever or none at all.

Ford Workers Turning to Union

While union officials refused to give any figures on membership of Ford workers in the union because of the impending struggle, they assert that despite the Ford pay system and the attitude of the Negro preachers and professional men, the attitude of Ford's Negro workers toward the U.A.W.A. has undergone a marked change in the past two months.

Two months ago their attitude was one of contempt and ridicule. Today they are willing to receive the union propaganda "literature" and a large number are signing up. This is especially said to be true since the Ford Brotherhood, the "inside" union was organized. The workers argue that since they must apparently join some union, they would rather belong to the U.A.W.A. They are also beginning to understand that under the provisions of the Wagner Act they cannot be discharged for union membership, as Negro leaders have been telling them.

Union leaders assert that the attitude of the Negro leaders, many of whom they charge with having received Ford money, is based entirely upon the experience of Negro workers with the old craft unions and not with the new industrial unions that have sprung up all over the country and are following a policy of no discrimination because of color.

Crane Operator Heads Union Drive

Heading the drive of the union for Negro membership in Detroit is young organizer Paul Silas Kirk, a graduate of Talladega, Ala. High school who has been in Detroit since 1929 and with the U.A.W.A. since 1936. He was formerly a crane operator with the Michigan Steel Casting Co. which produces auto parts.

This plant was first organized by calling small meetings. Then large meetings were held and demands were made on the company. Company stool pigeons "snitched" and the men were locked out. The union struck and was finally granted a contract.

According to Kirk the U.A.W.A. has 200,000 members in the Detroit area of whom 7,500 are Negroes. Of the 34 locals of the union, 18 have Negro membership.

Chief Negotiator a Negro

At the Michigan Steel Foundry Negroes constitute about 50 per cent of the 500 workers. Two of the union's departmental committees are headed by Negroes, Clarence Jones and Jack Harrison. The Corresponding Secretary is a Negro. The union's chief negotiator with the management is a Negro, Samuel Lawson.

At the Cadillac Motor Company where 5,000 are employed there are 350 Negroes. The union has 65 per cent of these workers.

The Chief Shop Steward there is a Negro, Baker Wall. He was the Assistant Chairman of the Strike Committee and was largely instrumental in bringing the Negroes into the union. There are in all 25 Negro shop stewards in the plants.

At the Dodge Motor Company's plant which employs 70,000 more than 75 per cent are in the union. Of the 1,500 Negroes, 65 per cent are in the union.

Curtis Davis, a Negro, is chief shop steward in the foundry department and Jesse Wilson is chief shop steward in the cleaning department. Wilson is also Chairman of the union's Welfare Committee.

Negro On Executive Board

At the Chrysler plant where 10,000 workers are employed, 85 per cent are in the union. Samuel Fanroy, a Negro, is chief shop steward of the Sanding Department, a member of the Executive Board of the local and also a member of the U.A.W.A. District Council. There are, in all, ten Negro shop stewards in the Chrysler plant.

At the Chevrolet Auto company's plant 98 per cent of the 60,000 workers are members of the union. Of the 700 Negro workers better than 98 per cent are union men. It is said that the Chevrolet plant has the most progressive and intelligent group of Negroes as reflected in their militancy and their participation in the administration of the union.

At the Murray Body Co. plant some 80,000 workers are employed of whom 78 per cent are in the union. Half of the 900 Negroes are union men. Three of the chief shop stewards are colored men.

Of the 7,000 men employed by the Bohen Aluminum company which makes auto parts, 95 per cent are in the union, while 50 per cent of the 800 Negro workers are union men. The chief shop stewards in plants Nos. 2 and 3, are Negroes, Messrs. Hodges Mason and Herman Bonds.

Wages Boosted 40 Per Cent

Union officials point to many gains as a result of union organization. Before the coming of the union, Negroes' wages averaged 45¢ and 50¢ an hour. They now average 75¢ an hour.

In the past Negroes were laid off when the employers saw fit. Now if a white worker starts after a Negro worker he is laid off first.

These officials assert that union membership has laid the foundation for the Negro worker to realize equality in the performance of any work for which he is fitted.

In Dodge's Dept. 82, a Negro applied for the job of cone setter. The white workers objected to a colored man having such a skilled job and he did not get it. After the union came, the same man applied for the same job again. He got the job and it is one of the highest paid in the department. His wages are about $1.25 an hour.

Race Relations Improve

Considerable improvement in race relations has been noted as a result of the policy of the U.A.W.A. in this regard. At the Chevrolet plant, for example where most of the whites are Southerners, a picnic was arranged by the union for August 21 at Paris Park.

When the question of interracial attendance was raised, there was a revolt on the part of the racial reactionaries, but after several meetings the union went on record against any discrimination. Negro members were placed on the Picnic Committee and colored union members were given tickets to sell.

After the election of delegates to the recent convention it was discovered that no Negroes had been elected. The vote was reconsidered, more delegates were called for and several additional ones, all Negroes, were unanimously elected. I was told that a Negro would surely be elected to the executive board, the governing body of the international union at the convention. The U.A.W.A. recognizes that the Negroes are the key to the Ford organization drive and every effort is being made to give them the fullest representation.

Negroes in Union Upstate

Accompanied by Walter T. Hardin, Negro, Field Organizer for the U.A.W.A. outside the Detroit area, I journeyed by automobile 100 miles north of Detroit to Saginaw, stopping at several places by the way.

Hardin is an experienced labor organizer who was in the 1919 steel strike and in 1930 was a leader in the unemployed movement when there were 750,000 jobless in the state. On November 12, 1931, he was grabbed by the Black Legion because of his activities in behalf of the unemployed, severely beaten and left by the roadside. Another leader in the jobless movement was beaten crazy by these hooded ruffians. In 1936 Hardin joined the U.A.W.A. in the Pontiac district.

The response of the Negro workers outside the Detroit area to the union drive has been very good. In Fostoria most of the Negroes are in the union and dominate the locals. In Rochester, Mich., where there are 100 Negroes in a union membership of 580, the local has colored leadership. In New Haven, Mich., where a foundry does jobbing for Chrysler, Negroes constitute 400 of the 700 union membership. There, too, they dominate the local. In Grand Rapids there is a malleable iron foundry with 500 workers including 35 Negroes. The president of the local is a Negro, Henry Shed.

Negro Vice-President in Saginaw

At Saginaw I visited the home of a quiet-spoken, thoughtful dark man, Boss McKnight, who is highly regarded by everyone. He has worked for the Gray Iron Foundry, a Chevrolet subsidiary, for many years. Of the 4,700 employees only 630 are Negroes, 75 per cent of whom are in the union, Local 461. McKnight took an active part in forming the union and was unanimously elected its vice president.

At Pontiac I had the pleasure of meeting Oscar Noble, an upstanding young Negro who holds the highly responsible union office of Chairman of the Bargaining Board at the Pontiac Motor Company. William Banks, also colored, is a member of an interdepartmental bargining board. There are 14,000 workers in this plant of whom less than 500 are colored. Incidentally, the Pontiac local of the U.A.W.A. is one of the largest in the State. The company here used the most drastic efforts to keep Negroes out of the union educational and recreational activities, but failed.

Union Boosts Pay in Flint

In Flint, Mich., 80 per cent of the Negroes employed by the Buick Co., in its foundries are union men. A Negro, Henry Clark, is part-time organizer and one Negro is a shop committeeman.

A few Negroes are employed in the Chevrolet plant and during the sit-down strike, a number of them stayed in with the whites. These Negroes are mostly porters. The Fisher Body plant employs Negroes only as kitchen help. There is much Negro unemployment in the city.

While one professional man informed me that "All the Negro workers are skeptical as hell about the union" and that a quiet effort was on foot to ease foreigners and Negroes out of the union, he pointed out that the union had made quite an effort to get Negro members. Large meetings were held in Negro neighborhoods and well attended. Some Flint Negroes participated in the historic Monroe, Mich., demonstration and played a significant part there.

I learned that the Flint strike was accelerated by the speed-up system in the plants. With the coming of the union the men are working more slowly and this is better for their health.

In the Buick Foundries Nos. 70 and 71, working conditions are terrible on the health. There, as in the Ford foundries in Detroit, Negroes die like flies from Type No. 3 pneumonia as a result of coming out of the terrific heat into the cold.

The union has boosted the wage of these Negroes from 45¢ an hour to 80¢ and 95¢ an hour, and the pay day is now weekly instead of fortnightly. The men are paid $15 a week during the compulsory seasonal layoff and have secured seniority rights.

Negroes High in Cleaners Union

Back in Detroit, I had a conference with Hyman Schneider, general organizer of the Amalgamated Clothing Workers of America, who organized Cleaners and Dyers Local No. 124. Of the total of 1,700 members, 30 per cent are Negroes. The union has signed up the entire 69 shops in the city since last February.

Out of 15 members on the strike committee, six were Negroes. The Negroes are reported to have picketed exceptionally well. At the largest plant in Detroit, a Negro has been elected shop steward.

There are three Negroes on the executive board of the local, Ed. Curry, a colored man, is vice president and another colored man, William Bradley, is recording secretary.

From J. Cross, representative of the International Bakery and Confectionary Workers Union, Local 326, I learned that the membership had jumped from 20 in February to 2,000 at present of whom 10 per cent are Negroes.

Two of the five union members who comprised the committee that negotiated the contract with the Ward Baking Company were Negroes. While Negroes are usually porters in the trade, many are serving as shop stewards representing the men in their relations with the company.

"Once the union is explained to the Negroes" declared Mr. Cross, they give it good support."

As a result of the union drive, men in the organized plants do not work over ten hours on Saturday and Sunday as formerly, have a 40-hour instead of a 60-hour week, and the minimum wage has been boosted from 40¢ to 55¢ an hour throughout the city. They also now enjoy seniority rights and a week's vacation with pay.

Out of a total of 5,000 members of United Dairy Workers No. 83 only 20 are Negroes, but they are enjoying the benefits of closed shop agreements which the 23 companies doing 80 per cent of the volume of business have signed.

5000 Negroes In Steel Unions

In February 1937 there was not a single local of the Amalgamated Association of Iron, Steel and Tin Workers in the Detroit area. Today there are 5,000 Negro union members alone in steel. This is about one-third of all the Negroes employed in steel and scrap iron business.

"We have been able to sign contracts with all concerns in this area without resorting to the strike" declared Charles Kiser, Detroit district director for the United Mine Workers, "I have never met a finer bunch of colored people in union activity in the entire country than there is here in this area."

From Leonidas McDonald, stalwart Negro S.W.O.C. field organizer, who has a desk at the headquarters, I learned that there are numerous Negro committee members. One lodge has a colored president and financial secretary. Another lodge numbering 125 members has only eight Negroes and yet two of them were elected officials.

"In no case," asserted Mr. Kiser, "have we negotiated a contract without the Negro's participation in the deliberations."

Negro Business Agent

From Ed. Thal, secretary of the Building Trades Council, I learned that the Sanitary Workers have a Negro business agent and have boosted their pay to 75¢ an hour. There are a large number of Negroes in the union. In the building laborers union, the majority are colored men. Negroes are represented also in the lathers, plasterers, bricklayers and cement finishers unions.

There are around 800 Negro rubber workers in the area and a majority of them are organized.

Leonidas McDonald said that some Negroes in the steel industry in the area are now getting $40 a week regularly, a considerable increase over the prevailing wage before the union came in. Mr. McDonald is something of a hero in the labor world in this area because of his fine organizational work in the Chicago district and also because he went to Monroe, Mich., at the height of the disturbance there to organize, was set upon by company thugs and vigilantes aided by the police and severely beaten. He was knocked unconscious, revived and knocked unconscious again and again. Rushed to the hospital he was given a private room. Soon white workers and their wives from miles around came to his bedside with tears in their eyes and loudly expressing their sorrow.

Race Prejudice Broken Down

Mr. McDonald said that "Race prejudice is practically down in the labor movement in Detroit."

Supporting this view, Walter Hardin, the U.A.W.A. Negro field organizer pointed out that he had negotiated contracts for the men in shops where no Negroes are working at all. As an outstanding example of the new attitude he cited the case of the local of the Romeo Foundry situated between La Peer and Rochester, Mich. The plant has 13 Negroes and 365 whites working in it. At first a white delegate was elected to represent the local at the U.A.W.A. convention. This action was later overruled and a Negro was elected delegate because the white man was a pattern maker while the Negro was a laborer. The men in explaining the switch said they wanted somebody to represent them who understood the bad conditions in the plant rather than a worker who had a comparatively easy job.

Pittsburgh Courier, September 4, 1937.

41. UNION DRIVE SLOWS IN BORDER CITIES: LEADERS HOSTILE

By George S. Schuyler

ST. LOUIS, Mo., Sept. 9--The current unionization drive has so far touched Indianapolis, Louisville and St. Louis only lightly. The Steel Workers Organizing Committee has been active for many months in Indianapolis and St. Louis, but CIO offices have only recently been established in those cities and Louisville and the general drive is only in its initial stages.

This is due in part to the CIO strategy of concentrating major organizational efforts in the great industrial centers, in part to the face that these border cities are notoriously non-union communities where low wages and long hours are the rule, and in part to the Southern tradition of segregation and discrimination which hangs heavily in the atmosphere of all of them and has been so instrumental in perpetuating industrial peonage.

Thus the labor conditions in these border cities reflect the instability, insecurity and uncertainty of this social and economic No-Man's-Land.

The newspapers are mostly opposed to the new union drive and busily working the Communist scare against the CIO. The Negro professional class, with a few notable exceptions, reflects the views of the editorial writers of the daily press. The Negro workers are, in the main, scary and hesitant. Nevertheless, from the point of view of the laborites, the gloomy picture is illuminated by a few bright spots that give some promise of better things to come. Here and there Negro labor is displaying a new spirit, a new solidarity, a new pioneering enterprise that strengthens the view that the working masses are beginning to think fundamentally about the basic problems of food, clothing and shelter.

Colored Woman On Committee

At the CIO headquarters in Indianapolis, Joseph D. Persily, the regional director, told me something of their progress in the two months the office had been open.

The Wadley Poultry Company, with 200 workers, of whom 35 per cent are Negroes, is completely organized, the local being affiliated with the United Cannery and Agricultural Workers of America. One of the five members of the negotiating committee which arranged the contract with the company is a colored woman. Mr. Persily, a young white man with the new labor viewpoint, assured me that "Our policy is to bring out Negro leadership wherever possible."

Negroes constitute 25 per cent of the 200 workers in the Piel Bros. Starch Company, which is 100 per cent organized. There, it is said, a number of Negroes have blossomed out as leaders. The plant is at present completely closed down. Two of the seven members of the union's negotiating committee are Negroes.

Public Workers Organized

One of the guiding spirits in the organization of the United Municipal Employes is Mr. Robert Obelton, a Negro. There are 200 Negroes out of the 1,100 members. Colored members are said to be very active, and two of them are on the union's negotiating committee. The Negroes played a prominent part in a recent demonstration against the decision of the city council to cut wages.

At the plant of the Century Biscuit Company, where 10 per cent of the employes are colored, the most important and influential member of the union next to the president is a Negro named Shirley, who is on the negotiating committee. He is a former coal miner. The union, now on strike, is the United Bakery Workers No. 86.

Half of the members of the United Ice and Fuel Workers Union No. 87 are Negroes, and some are serving as officers.

This is also true of United Grain Workers No. 88, which covers the different plants in the city.

The local of the Hod Carriers and Building Laborers has a two in one Negro membership, and practically all of the officers from the president down are colored.

Non-Union Men Laid Off

Of the total of 4,000 workers employed in the meat packing plants of the Kingan, Armours, Swift and smaller companies, about 35 per cent are colored. The main plant is Kingan, where the A.F. of L. union has obtained a contract, but the CIO union is contesting it before the National Labor Relations Board. It is, or should be, of interest to Negro workers to know that as a result of Negro workers having shunned the union, over 40 per cent of the 800 men recently laid off in the industry were Negroes.

At the Indianapolis Glove Company, which employs 300 colored women, the leading spirit for unionization is a Miss Louise Dawson, who has been responsible for the little bit of success obtained in organization there. Although these 300 Negro girls are getting much less than 300 whites in the company's other plant, they are refusing to join the union and are positively hostile to all efforts to improve their workingclass status.

Negro Steel Workers Scary

Harvey James of Huntington, W. Va., and Local 6006, District 17, United Mine Workers of America, is an experienced labor unionist, a worthy representative of that fine type of honest, upstanding Negro workman supplying so much of the new militant leadership among the masses. I had a long talk with him in the fine offices of the Steel Workers Organizing Committee in the Amalgamated Clothing Workers building on West Ninth street. He is at present Field Representative of the SWOC, trying to organize the Negro workers in the various steel fabricating plants in Indianapolis.

It has been a hard fight to organize these Negroes. At the plant of the National Malleable & Steel Company, 50 per cent of the 866 workers are colored and only about 125 have joined the SWOC drive. The plant has a company-fostered union, which is using the usual pressure on the workers to keep them out of the legitimate union. Most of the Negroes are as frightened as rabbits, although it is said they are favorably inclined. No contract has as yet been secured.

Negroes Stay In Boss's Union

At the foundry of the Link Belt Company, 400 of the 900 workers are colored. They have almost all remained in the company-fostered union. At the Dodge plant of this same company, where Negroes are 35 per cent of the 800 workers, the majority of the whites have joined the new steel union, but only 40 Negro workers have done so. A contract is now being negotiated between the union and the company.

At the Switzer Cummings Company, where there are only 23 colored out of a total of 800 workers, only 4 Negroes have joined the overwhelming majority in the union.

It is illuminating that while segregation is not the law of Indiana, the colored workers at National Malleable are segregated in the washrooms as if they were in Mississippi. Most of the Negroes are reported to be in debt to the company, which uses the old loan shark method of keeping the workers enslaved and thus docile. Many of them are so deep in debt that they draw practically nothing for their killing labor. The colored women workers are terrorized by the white woman who hires them and she threatens to fire anyone who joins a union. Colored women get 40 cents an hour in this plant, while white women get 48 cents an hour. Men get 50 to 65 cents.

Henry Ford, whom certain Negro leaders in Detroit think is in love with Negroes, has one of his assembly plants in Indianapolis. Not a single Negro is employed there.

Preachers Cold-Water Union

"All we have met from the Negro preachers," said a union official, "is discouragement. They don't seem to care anything about the low wages and bad working conditions their people suffer, nor the feudal conditions under which the people here live. We have been assisted by Dr. Cable, the Negro city councilman and Secretary F. E. DeFrantz of the Y.M.C.A., but by no one else." The attitude of the rest of the leading Negroes allegedly runs from

indifference to hostility. They quote the local N.A.A.C.P. head as saying,
"I have come to the conclusion Negroes had better stay out of the union."
   Nevertheless, the union organizers are optimistic, "I believe we'll be
successful in getting the Negro here lined up," Mr. James stated. He pointed
out that since last Labor Day the CIO had signed up 12,000 members in Indianapolis and environs, and that there was evidence of a definite change taking
place in the attitude of the Negro workers.

Louisville Remains Dormant

   Most of the Negroes in Louisville are employed in the tobacco industry,
in domestic service, building construction for the various railroads and
miscellaneous pursuits. It is a typical border anti-CIO town, where union
labor has never had much of a foothold.
   There is one colored A.F. of L. tobacco local of which a Negro, William
Brown, is president. Some idea of labor conditions in the tobacco industry
may be gleaned from the fact that stemmers range from $7 to $10 a week with
the first figure the most prevalent. But this is better than the $5 a week
average paid for domestic service.
   I went to the CIO office in the Starks Building at Fourth and Walnut,
where I talked with Peter Campbell, a former A.F. of L. official, who is now
regional director of the CIO. The office has just recently opened and he had
little to tell me. Moreover, he was the first big CIO official I've met who
seemed to be completely steeped in the traditions of the old South so far as
Negroes are concerned.

Construction Workers Alert

   Hod Carriers' and Building Laborers' Local No. 86 has all Negro officers
and George Dougherty is president. There are 200 members and in recent months
it has grown 100 per cent. It has managed to boost wages from 75 cents to
87½ cents an hour, according to Mr. Dougherty.
   Building and Construction Laborers No. 576 is a mixed union with 2,300
members of whom better than 50 per cent are colored. The secretary is
Charles J. Newton, a Negro. These workers, allegedly less skilled than the
hod-carriers, are now getting 50 cents an hour. They were getting 35 cents
and 40 cents before unionization.
   Both these locals belong to the A.F. of L. There are three Negroes on
the Louisville District Council. There are about a half dozen Negro carpenters
belonging to the local union.
   The only work of the CIO so far has been the organization of a local of
the Iron, Steel and Tin Workers' Union. There are said to be 100 Negro members of this school.

Stirrings in St. Louis

   Labor is marching forward on many fronts in St. Louis. But owing to the
Southern traditions that hang like a miasmic pall over the metropolis that
sprawls from the Mississippi to the Missouri rivers, and to the previous dominance of reactionary A.F. of L. officials, labor is not marching forward very
fast. Nevertheless, all things considered, much progress is being made in
organizing steel, furniture, electrical manufacturing and automobiles. Of
the 900,000 population of the city, Urban League officials estimate there are
110,000 Negroes, 40 per cent of whom are from Mississippi and Arkansas. Just
like the whites, they have brought the Dixie mores along with them. They are
slow to heed the appeals of labor organizers, having obtained what they consider a favorable position in steel plants by scabbing years ago. Then, too,
they have noted the manner in which the A.F. of L. building trades in the
past have driven the ablest Negro mechanics out of the city or out of their
trades. As one intelligent Negro said: "It is a crime the way the building
trades choke off the Negro artisans."
   Just two Negro preachers out of the hundreds in the city have taken any
favorable interest whatever in the strengthening of Negro labor through
unionization. The Negro educated (?) class as a whole is lying low, indifferent or outspokenly anti-union. By comparison, the Urban League is radical
in its labor interests and activities. One reason advanced for the indifference

or hostility of most of the Negro preachers to organized labor is that they are constantly begging small sums (or large ones if they can get them) from various business concerns and so feel indebted to them.

Negro S.W.O.C. Organizer

There are 25,000 steel workers in and around St. Louis and the S.W.O.C. started in August, 1936, to organize them. There are a large number of Negroes in the industry and realizing this, the S.W.O.C. early sent George Edmonds, a veteran Negro organizer, into St. Louis. He considers the area very complete and difficult, and different from any other place in the country. The Negro workers he holds, play a most important industrial part. [52]

There are 26 locals of the S.W.O.C., and Negroes are active members in all of them. All have Negroes as officers when they can get them, but many Negro members, it is asserted, are too timorous to serve in positions of responsibility and reluctant to even attend meetings.

The largest lodge is that at the American Car Foundry, where Negroes are 50 per cent of the 1,700 workers. At the Scullins Steel Company, 60 per cent of the 1,400 workers are colored, and great difficulty has been experienced in organizing them because of the diversity of work offered them and the fear of unions instilled by the company's propagandists.

There are 2,000 Negroes at the Granite City Casting Company, where a total of 3,800 workers are employed. The S.W.O.C. is now struggling to become sole bargaining agent. There has been no great rush of Negroes to join the union.

Negro Vice-President

At the Missouri Rolling Mill, Negroes constitute half of the 600 workers. The plant is 85 per cent organized, and a colored man is vice-president of the union.

The Sheffield Steel Company recently signed a contract with the union. Five hundred of its 700 workers are Negroes, and there are a number of colored members serving as union officials. They are on all committees.

Most of the other steel plants are small fabricating concerns which do not employ many Negroes.

About 400 of the 4,000 auto workers in the city are colored. At the time of the strikes, no effort was made to organize them and only 15 Negroes joined. Negroes were openly used as scabs during the strikes. The union, it is said, has now changed its policy.

The situation in the laundry industry also reveals how the Southern white attitude works to the detriment of labor in this border city. The A.F. of L. is directing the current drive to organize the 100 laundries in the city. Negroes constitute the majority of the workers, and yet there is not a single Negro organizer or official in the union. Moreover, the laundry drivers in the Truck Drivers' Union will not support the inside laundry workers. As a result, only 42 laundries have been organized and the bulk of Negro laundry workers are not joining the union. Of course, some of this is due to sheer inertia more than anything else, inertia and fear.

Hotel Employees Organized

The Hotel and Restaurant Employees' Association has 3,000 members of whom well over 600 are colored. It is an A.F. of L. outfit. While there are some Negroes on committees, there are no Negro officials or organizers. The Negro maids, who have a virtual monopoly in the city's hotels, were wise enough to get through a clause safeguarding their position.

Of the 500 Negroes in the Local No. 603 Teamsters' Union, most of them are moving van men. There are, however, about 20 Negro milkwagon drivers traveling routes for big dairy companies. There are no Negro officials or organizers in the union. One intelligent Negro member said, "Just dumb Irish Catholics run the outfit."

The Amalgamated Association of Street and Electric Railway Employees has about 50 Negro members, all car cleaners. It is said that Negroes are being gradually squeezed out of this work.

There are reported to be many Negroes in the A.F. of L. Cleaners' and Dyers' Union.

T.W.O.C. Action "Phenomenal"

The Textile Workers' Organizing Committee has been very active in St.
Louis, but there are few Negroes in the industry. In one plant, the Burkhardt
Manufacturing Company, they are credited by observers with having done a
"phenomoneal thing." This company manufactures auto seat covers and employs
300 workers, half of them Negroes. Race relations were very bad there. The
T.W.O.C. organized the plant, the officials of the local are equally divided
between the races and race relations have improved greatly. When the company
recently fired a Negro checker, the whole working force, white and black,
pulled a 90-minute strike of protest, which led to the man's reinstatement, it
is said.

The workers in garages and auto agencies have been organized by the CIO
and there are about 100 Negroes in the union. The A.F. of L. has the repair
shops.

Longshoremen Boost Wages

The International Longshoremen's Association has two locals, No. 1400
in St. Louis, of which Frank Hargraves is president, and No. 1401 in E. St.
Louis, of which Jones is president. The membership of the two locals is
entirely Negro and numbers around 250. Mr. Hargraves is special organizer
for the I.L.A.

These workers were formerly getting about 25¢ an hour and often had to
borrow from the commissary, to say nothing of enduring "lay time." They
pulled several successful strikes and today they are getting 50¢ an hour.

There are two rival unions of shoe workers, A.F. of L. and CIO. One
factory has about 100 colored workers, but Negroes in the industry are mostly
janitors and laborers. Few are as yet in either union.

The A.F. of L. tobacco workers union has about 50 per cent Negroes. There
are a large number of Negro women in this industry but they are said to be
indifferent to labor organization.

A drive is on to organize city and government employees in whose ranks
there are many Negroes including 500 employed by the Board of Education. But
as elsewhere this type of Negro seems timorous and ultra-conservative as a
result of his "education."

Negro Heads Building Service Group

The Building Service Employees Union is headed by Mr. Messingale, a
colored man. A drive is in progress to organize the many Negro elevator
operators, porters and maids in department stores. A union official declared
that "The Negro is becoming more labor conscious and tends to react favorably."
This union, which is 50 per cent colored, is credited with having more contact
with Negroes than any other in the city.

It is interesting to note that the Negro beauticians are trying to set up
a separate (Jim Crow) union. It is equally significant that the strong local
branch of the Brotherhood of Sleeping Car Porters refused to pay an assessment to fight the CIO.

I met W. Sentner, national representative of the United Electrical and
Radio Workers of America, a CIO affiliate, which covers the plants manufacturing electrical and radio equipment. He reported 6,600 workers in the industry
in St. Louis and 5,600 are in the union. Of this number approximately 400
are Negroes. The current drive got well under way in March, 1937.

Negroes Strike 100 Per Cent

When the workers struck at the Emerson Electric Co. on March 8, the 46
Negroes in the plant went out 100 per cent with the other workers. They are
all in the union. Very few Negroes are in production, being mostly porters
and dip room laborers. During the strike one Negro was on the negotiating
committee of 11 members.

The Wagner Electric Co. has 3,110 employes, 10 per cent colored. A Negro
member was recently elected to the executive committee of 17, and one is on
the negotiating committee.

At the Century Electrical Co., a Negro, Lawrence Young, is one of the
seven members of the union's negotiating committee, although only four of the
50 Negroes in the plant are members of the union. Young has spoken over the
radio more time for the union than any other member.

Meat packing is an important industry in this city and while many workers
are oganized the CIO is preparing to launch a determined drive to get all of
them.

The Hod Carriers and Building Laborers group is almost exclusively colored,
but aside from that Negroes are virtually barred from the building trades. By
some necromancy a Negro was recently permitted to join the plasterers' union
and everybody viewed it as a nine-day wonder.

After a long struggle with the reactionary A.F. of L. motion picture projectors union during which time Negro projectors were getting from $8.00 to
$18.00 weekly, the 20 Negro operators were finally admitted to the union.
They now earn from $32.00 to $55.00 a week.

Negro Workers Council Active

Many of the more enlightened Negroes of St. Louis like Sidney Williams,
Industrial Secretary of the Urban League, and Arnold Walker, also of the league,
have realized the necessity of labor education and the significance of the
current labor drive, and have sought through the St. Louis Negro Labor committee to inform and guide the bewildered Negro workers. The committee has
done excellent work in this direction. It is directed by a board of 15. The
president is the well-known E. J. Bradley, 3rd vice president of the Brotherhood of Sleeping Car Porters.

At CIO headquarters in the Title & Guarantee Building, I talked with
Bert Taventer, regional director, who claimed 40,000 CIO members in the St.
Louis district. As to the Negro's reaction to the current labor drive, Mr.
Taventer said, "We have found that they have been very reticent in coming out.
We understand that that is because they have been bulldozed in the past.
When we get them in the movement and they find that we don't discriminate be-
cause of race or creed, they become enthusiastic supporters of the union.
They make it a religion."

Concerning the objection of some of the St. Louis white workers to
associating with Negroes in the union halls, he said "Race has undoubtedly
interfered with the organization work here. But our position is that if
Negroes are good enough to work in the industry, then they are good enough to
meet with for the common good."

Mr. Taventer there reflected the spirit prevalent in all of the many CIO
offices I have visited.

Pittsburgh Courier, September 11, 1937.

42.

INDUSTRIAL SOUTH SHAKY: MEMPHIS A.F. OF L. SEES 'HAND WRITING ON WALL;'
RACE MEN ON BARGAINING BOARD IN BIRMINGHAM;
MANY NEGROES OFFICERS IN DIXIE STEEL UNIONS

By George S. Schuyler

ATLANTA, Sept. 11--The almost hysterical vehemence with which the Southern
press denounces the "Communistic" CIO, is a barometer of the rising fear of
labor unionism and its more enlightened attitude toward union labor in Memphis,
Birmingham and Atlanta. The Southern employers who have waxed sleek and fat
off the proceeds of quasi-slave labor and lured numerous sweat shops from
Northern industrial centers with the bait of colonial wage standards, grow
jittery as both A.F. of L. and CIO invite the Negro to march with them toward
industrial democracy. They know only too well that leveling up the wages of
black and white workers, long fooled into fighting each other, marks the beginning of the end of the halcyon days of industrial feudalism in the land
that still worships Lee. Already the Negroes they see, are restive.

Memphis A.F. of L. Sees Handwriting

It is obvious that the Memphis A.F. of L. has seen the "Mene, Mene, Tekel Upharsin" of the new labor deal on the industrial wall, and is heeding the handwriting. With the town serving as a "refuge" for CIO organizers working to emancipate the wage slaves in Mississippi and with a CIO office scheduled to open this month with Attorney Robert Tillman of Mississippi in charge, the A.F. of L. hears the hound of competition baying on the heath and is tossing the burden of Negrophobia overboard.

When Frank Hargrave, International Longshoremen's Association organizer, from St. Louis, visited the town about six weeks ago, organized a strike of the low-paid Negro stevedores who defied efforts of the bosses to prevent picketing, the A.F. of L. Memphis Trade and Labor Council came to the mens' assistance and aided them in negotiations with the employers.

The men won their rights to organize, went back to work, their local No. 27 became affiliated with the Council and they now meet regularly in the Labor Temple where all the city's organized workers meet.

Negotiations are now going on with reference to wages and hours.

Being young to the labor movement, most of these men are lacking in labor education and are said not to be paying dues or attending meetings as they should, but labor officials are optimistic about the future of this union.

Negroes "More Susceptible"

Up historic Beale Avenue, immortalized in the affable George W. Lee's "Beale Street: Where the Blues Began," I strolled early one morning to the imposing, castle-like Labor Temple on the corner of Lauderdale. There I interviewed President Ley G. Loring of the Memphis Trades and Labor Council who was most courteous and obliging.[53]

He declared that "In the last six months there have been more Negro workers susceptible to labor organization than ever before. They are beginning to feel the need of organization and we are beginning to feel the necessity of organizing them. We are just now getting an international organizer from the A.F. of L. to start our campaign."

He boasted of the plans to celebrate the biggest labor day in the history of the South when Negro and white workers would parade together to demonstrate the new solidarity of labor in Memphis.

Negroes Head Unions

Mr. Edw. Smith, a veteran Negro laborite, is president and business agent of Local No. 52, International Hod Carriers and Building Laborers Union which has a membership of 200. This union now has a minimum wage of 62½¢ an hour for an 8-hour day. A year ago the minimum scale was 50¢ an hour.

Back in 1934, the whites didn't pay much attention to this union. "They are much more cordial now than ever before," declared Mr. Smith. "Race relations have unquestionably improved in the labor movement here." At one time, not far back, whites were accustomed to use the epithet "nigger" in union meetings. Mr. Smith and others protested against this practice and it has ended. This labor leader feels that "history is being made" in Memphis. There are two locals of the longshoremen with a total membership of 300. All officers from president down are Negroes.

Local No. 427 of the International Ladies Garment Workers Union is composed of some 20-odd colored girls who are pressers in a clothing factory.

Some "Mixed" Unions

There has as yet been no organization drive among building service employes or laundry workers. Local No. 521 of the cement finishers has 25 Negroes in a total of 60 members. There are about 25 Negroes in the 150 members of the bricklayers union, while 12 of the 50 organized plasterers are colored. There are two locals of carpenters, one is colored with about 30 members and the other whites with about 400.

The Coopers Union has 175 Negroes out of a total of 250 while the Firemen and Oilers group is entirely Negro with a Negro president.

The bricklayers meet separately according to "race."

While a few Negro steamfitters have been taken into the union, it is charged that Negro painters have been given the runaround.

The Switchmens Union is mixed but Negroes predominate. Among the structural iron workers, there are a few Negroes as helpers, so-called. Efforts are being made to organize the Virginia Bridge and Iron Works where some Negroes are employed.

Last year a federal labor union was established at the American Finishing Co. with 500 members, of whom 250 are colored.

Concerning the painters, I learned that efforts were being made to organize a separate Negro local. Some Negroes want it but some do not. The whites are similarly divided.

Of the 16,000-odd organized workers in Memphis, more than 3,000 are Negroes.

Opposes Firestone Training Negroes

Indicative of the attitude which labor must overcome in Memphis, is the story told me about Firestone's tire plant where both white and colored are employed. The company opened schools for members of both groups to prepare them for upper bracket jobs according to the story. When this news came to the attention of the Chamber of Commerce, a committee was delegated to take up the question with the company and voice the strenuous objection of the Chamber to Negroes being prepared for or assigned to upper bracket jobs.

At the McCollum & Robinson Mop Factory, the white workers refused to work in the same department with Negroes. When the white went on strike, the Negroes stayed in, joined the company union and refused to have anything to do with the labor union.

Such incidents reveal the distance that has yet to be traveled in Memphis. But there is no doubt that such attitudes are not so general as before and do not today represent the viewpoint of organized labor in the city. Quite likely they will almost disappear when the CIO begins to supply the competition which elsewhere has been like a breath of fresh air to the labor movement. Meantime, Memphis Negro workers are slowly awakening.

Negroes On Bargaining Boards In Birmingham

There is, of course, little of the NEW labor drive in Memphis as yet. Conditions in Atlanta are almost identical, so much so that it is scarcely necessary to dwell at length on them. There as in Memphis, Negroes dominate the building labor and are in a mixed plasterers union. Painters, bricklayers and carpenters, however, are in separate unions. Recently Frank R. Crosswaith, brilliant general organizer of the International Ladies Garments Workers Union, organized Local No. 207 in Atlanta, which has 300 Negro girls in it. Aside from this, the labor picture in Atlanta varies little from that in Memphis. But CIO organizers are now at work in the city and ere long it is probable a great deal will be heard from the capital of Georgia.

In contrast to Memphis and Atlanta, there has been much new labor activity in Birmingham, the Pittsburgh of the South. Not only have Negro workers joined the unions in great numbers but they have met with bosses' representatives to negotiate contracts.

Many Negro Officers In Steel Unions

At the headquarters of the Steel Workers Organizing Committee in the Steiner Building, I interviewed Thomas Pate, the field director, whom I found quite cordial and co-operative. Of the 32 steel lodges in the district, all except one have Negro members. In many of the lodges, Negroes predominate and several have Negro officers, among them a number of vice-presidents. In a number of lodges, I learned Negroes could have all of the offices from president down, but seemed to prefer to elect white men to the leading offices. Among the Negro organizers employed by the S.W.O.C., in the Birmingham district are Ed. Cox, A. G. Johnston, Rev. Alonzo Walker and James J. Israel. Mr. Pate told me the Negroes on the whole had responded as good as whites and sometimes better.

The S.W.O.C. has signed contracts with the Tennessee Coal and Iron Company a subsidiary of U.S. Steel, of whose 10,000 workers, 55 per cent are Negroes.

Approximately 40 per cent of the Negroes are in the union. It has also signed
contracts with the Woodward Iron Co., and the Continental Gin Co., Unit Stove
Co., McWain Pipe Shop, Birmingham Stove and Range Co., Virginia Bridge Co.,
and various scrap iron firms.

Labor Organization Lifts Wages

At the Continental Company the 340 Negroes are almost all union men.
After a five-week strike they won raises of 11 cents an hour.

The Ensley SWOC Lodge, of which a Negro minister, the Rev. W. M. Hall,
is vice-president, has a totaled membership of 1800 of whom half are Negroes.
Union activities have boosted the wages from $2.68 a day to $3.60 a day.

The McWain Pipe Shop, with 400 workers, mostly Negroes, organized a lodge
even before the SWOC came. Efforts to force them into the A.F. of L. failed.
Jesse Gill, a core maker of eight years' experience, said there were 275
Negroes and 100 whites in the McWain plant. The lodge has a colored vice-
president and secretary, Mr. Gill told me the treatment of the men had vastly
improved and the wages are much better as a result of the union. They used
to work from dawn to dusk and were constantly cussed out by the foreman.
That has been ended. Common labor which formerly received 30 cents an hour is
now getting 40 cents.

Stage Five-Week Strike and Win

There are 450 employees at the plant of the Birmingham Stove and Range
Company. Most of them are Negroes and all but two are in the union. Last
winter they staged a five-week strike. Other lodges in the district sent
food and money to help out, but singularly enough no white striker was given
anything. It was explained that the whites had been getting better wages than
the Negroes and consequently were in less need than their colored fellow
workers. That seems to be a new high in solidarity.

Mr. Pate showed me some of the pay envelopes the men had received prior
to the strike; 50 hours, $7.94; 60 hours, $8.86; 30 hours, $4.55; 27 hours,
$3.02; 54 hours, $6.98. Other weekly salaries were: $10.93, $11.51 and $11.76
for a six-day, 54-hour week.

The strike won the men a general 20 per cent increase.

Mr. Pate deplored the fact that there were Negro moulders in the city
getting $25 a week who should be getting the union scale of $8 a day, but who
refused to join the union.

At the Virginia Bridge Company, with 349 workers, of whom only a seventh
are members of the union, the few Negroes have been slow to join as, it would
seem, have the whites.

Scrap Iron Workers Cut Hours

There are ten scrap iron yards in Birmingham and environs employing a
total of some 400 men, mostly Negroes. Before the union came along they were
getting $1.50 for a ten-hour day. Now they are getting $2 for an eight-hour
day. In addition to winning recognition of their union, they have won
seniority rights. Most significant of all, their contract calls for no cussing out of Negroes by their bosses. That alone would seem to be worth the
union fee and dues.

At the Unit Stove plant, Negroes number 175 out of the 250 employees.
All of them are in the union. Prior to the organization of the lodge, the
minimum pay was 25 cents an hour. It is now 30 cents an hour, with 15 per
cent bonus every three months.

"Welfare" Thwarts Unionization

At two of the plants where extensive "welfare" is furnished the workers,
the SWOC has made no headway. These plants are the Stockham Pipe and Fittings
Company, which hires 1300 men, mostly Negroes who get half of what white men
get elsewhere, and the American Cast Iron Pipe Company of whose 1000 workers,
650 are Negroes.

Several Negro workers said the Negro welfare worker at the Stockham plant
is more reactionary than his brother Congressman Mitchell of Illinois, which is
certainly a grave charge. He has long been a bitter opponent of unions.[54]

The ACIPCO is one of the country's outstanding examples of "employes ownership," with welfare features difficult to find elsewhere. While all the facilities are strictly segregated, they appeared to be identical and adequate. A $100,000 dispensary has recently been completed with a staff of the finest physicians and dentists . . . (white, of course), obtainable in the city. Free hospitalization is given not only to employees, but to their families. There are three colored nurses, each supplied with a personal Ford touring car.

There is a well-stocked company store allegedly "cooperative" where the best quality goods are said to be sold to workers at lowest cost. All clerks are white, I noticed.

There are 53 company-owned houses renting from $9 to $15 monthly, and the company has a real estate agent to arrange home buying on terms for the workers.

"Welfare" But No Democracy

One is justified in dwelling somewhat at length on this company because it is unique. The plant was left by its founder to the workers in it, and every worker is a stockholder, and an equal one under the so-called Eagan plan. Almost all are industrial veterans, a large number having been working there for fifteen or twenty years. New men are on probation for six months until found "desirable" to receive benefits. Each man is insured for $500.

This is an apparently democratic arrangement, something new in American industry, until you examine it carefully. There are, as I have said, 650 Negroes out of 1,000 employees, yet the Negro workers, even though employed there for 25 years have no say whatever in the administration of the business built up by their brain and brawn.

There are three boards in the company. Two are white; the Board of Management, which is the highest, and the Board of Operatives, and one, the Colored Auxiliary. The Board of Operatives cooperates with the Board of Management in admiministering affairs, but the colored board is only advisory, and the colored officers would not seem to possess any real power.

Thus, 350 whites with the higher paid jobs, run the plant, while 650 Negroes have no voice whatever. Which probably isn't strange in Alabama.

With a minimum pay of 42 cents and a maximum of 58 cents an hour, it cannot be said that the Negro workers are growing rich under the Eagan plan, but they seem satisfied and have spurned all overtures of the SWOC organizers. The majority of the supervisory jobs are held by white men. Negroes are not employed in the moulding and machine shops, but are everywhere else except, of course, in the administrative offices. The mimeographing office, however, is run by Negroes.

Negro Workers Picket Lumber Company

At the CIO office on the seventh floor of the National Bank Building (reached via jim-crow elevator) N. B. Swick, field representative, boasted that the Alabama CIO leads the U.S. in activities. He told of the four-week strike of 37 Negro workers at the Grayson Lumber Company, and the manner in which they daily picketed the plant. He said, "They stacked up 1000 per cent." It was the same, he reported, in the American Bakeries strike.

In nine out of ten cases, he said, a Negro is the vice-president of the union, and there are always several Negro officers. The CIO seems determined, according to its officials, to eliminate every possible trace of color discrimination. This is admittedly difficult when the vicious Alabama laws do not permit mixed racial meetings.

American Bakeries workers are 60 per cent Negro, Martin Biscuit, 85 per cent; Grayson Lumber, 98 per cent, and Nehi Bottling, 65 per cent. These figures indicate the importance of Negro labor in Birmingham.

Saw Mill Workers Respond 100 Per Cent

There are a number of saw mill and timber workers in and around the city and 75 per cent of them are Negroes. These men have responded 100 per cent to the union call and several Negroes are serving as officers of the union. The workers were formerly getting 14, 15 and 16 cents an hour, but a minimum base pay of 38 cents an hour has been established, regardless of color or race.

The United Agri. and Cannery workers recently held a convention at Johnstown, Ala. About 35 of the 50 delegates from 16 locals were Negroes.

United Soft Drink and Bottling Workers' Local No. 220 has a majority of Negro workers. The vice-president and most of the committeemen are Negroes.

A CIO official said: "These local unions here are really functioning."

There are some Negroes in the unionized skilled crafts, but not very many. Here as elsewhere, the old spirit of race reactionism is said to dominate the thinking of craft union officials. No particular advances have been made in that direction. The United Mine Workers, with its large Negro membership, Negro officers and organizers, is flourishing.

"Most Negroes Want CIO"

According to young James J. Israel, who has been doing organizing work for the SWOC among Negroes for 9½ months, "The majority of the Negroes really want the CIO."

H. D. Coke, managing editor of the Birmingham World, who has done much to enlighten Negro workers, thinks "The CIO drive is teaching the Negroes in industry the value and necessity of cooperation and mass action. Its weakness here lies in the lack of trained organizers. I believe they shipped A. Q. Johnson away from here to Chattanooga recently, mainly because he insisted upon the same wage scale for whites and Negroes."

In this connection, Mr. Coke cited the strike at the H. W. Smith foundry, which was finally settled after 45 days. The Negroes got a 5-cent increase while the whites got a 15-cent increase on hourly pay. Organizer Johnson, a Negro, protested against this and was promptly transferred.

Mr. Coke feels that the CIO has been lax in organization, and has failed to touch many plants as yet. "It needs a little more zip and life," he asserted.

A Revolution Has Taken Place

After traveling 6,000 miles, visiting 35 cities in eleven states since July 4, I am convinced that a revolution has taken place the effects of which are bound to be far-reaching, not only in labor relations, but in race relations. For the first time in fifty years, Negroes have been invited to join with white workers on a plane of equality for better working conditions for both, and, in the main, they have responded admirably, considering some of their unfortunate experiences with reactionary unions in the past.

A year ago there were three million organized workers. Today there are over seven million. In every part of the country, Negroes have not only flocked to the unions, but, what is more important, they are sitting around the conference table with white workers and bosses, negotiating working and wage agreements involving millions of dollars. We are on the way to getting a new and important leadership concerned with the basic and fundamental things of life rather than the froth. This the Negro group needs badly.

Inasmuch as the group having the majority of the workers in a plant can legally represent, ALL the workers under the provisions of the Wagner Act, Negroes who refuse to join unions will find themselves represented, without any voice whatever, by the white workers. It is far better then, for them to join the union now so they WILL have some voice. Those that are looking to employers to mother them along will be cruelly disillusioned because the employers dare not now do the things they did just little more than a year ago. The Wagner Act forbids it.

New Labor Drive Spells Freedom

The CIO drive, and, to a much lesser extent, the A.F. of L. drive, points to a new freedom for Negro workers. Almost every one of the hundreds of new unions has paragraphs in its constitution guaranteeing no color discrimination or racial segregation in the administration of its affairs. They are leaning over backwards to get Negroes to attend meetings and assume office. This is a great opportunity for Negroes to improve race relations fundamentally and they should avail themselves of it more than they have.

Both the CIO and the A.F. of L. need to hire more trained Negro organizers and spend more money for educational work among Negroes. Both have

lamentably failed to produce union literature adapted to organization work
among Negroes and have criminally neglected to use the vast machinery of the
Negro press which is read weekly by one quarter of the colored people in
America. They must realize the danger to labor of an indifferent, ignorant
or hostile Negro upper class and take immediate steps to counteract it by
presenting the facts concerning the number of unionized Negroes, the number
of Negro organizers and officials, the part Negroes are playing in negotiating
contracts, news about interracial union gatherings, and generally do about a
hundred times more than they have done to woo the indifferent or antagonistic
Negro worker to their standards.

Negroes Key to Industrial Democracy

Both the CIO and the A.F. of L. must realize that the Negro worker in
America is the key to industrial democracy. When he achieves a free labor
status, all other workers will be emancipated. This is truer today than ever
before because technological advance has completely undermined the exclusive-
ness of the skilled white workers who previously excluded or discriminated
against Negro labor. Today, almost all the industrial processes can be performed by what was known years ago as unskilled labor, thanks to invention
and industrial rationalization. This strengthens the position of the Negro
worker, mainly "unskilled."

Many of the more intelligent labor officials realize this, especially
those who guide the destinies of the CIO. But all white workers must be
brought to clearly understand the changes that have taken place and what is
their significance socially, economically and racially.

Now that the drive is well under way and tens of thousands of Negroes
have joined it, the CIO and A.F. of L. must solidify the position of labor by
sincerely striving to break down industrial segregation in mills and factories. They strive to keep all obstacles from the path of the smart Negro who
aspires to rise above the station of laborer or helper. This they can and
must do if they expect to hold the Negro.

Need Negro Labor

Both the CIO and the A.F. of L. should immediately hire a competent
Negro familiar with labor problems and with the peculiar problems of Negroes
to advise them on race relations, educational work, publicity, and every
means of cementing the bond between white and colored workers and eliminating
any shadow of discrimination from the labor movement once and for all. Such
an advisor should work as assiduously among white workers as among colored,
and arrange to have a capable speaker at all union conventions, picnics and
other gatherings, and generally to do all the things that are now crying to
be done with nobody doing them.

Marvelous progress has been made in this new labor drive. Much greater
progress can be made if the two major labor groups will not take the Negro
for granted and will not forget that the 1937 Negro is no fool.

Pittsburgh Courier, September 18, 1937.

43.   THE NEGRO IN "LITTLE STEEL"

By Romare Bearden [55]

The vastness of American industrial enterprise is impressively realized
in her steel areas. There is the tremendous steel province centering about
Gary. Another is in the South with Birmingham as its heart. The last great
district sprawls about Pittsburgh, extending eastward to Bethlehem, south
through Wierton and Huntington, and west along Ohio's Mahoning Valley.

With over a half million men employed in steel, it is natural that
attempts would have been made to organize them. However, until recently the
larger corporations have vigorously counteracted all attempts to bring the
workers into the unions. In this the corporations were under the domination

of men like Gary, Schwab and Carnegie. Gary openly stated that U.S. Steel
would have no dealings with unions. [56]

Beginning with the Homestead strike of 1892, some of the bloodiest and
most bitter industrial conflicts have occurred in the steel areas. Therefore,
when John L. Lewis signed a contract on behalf of the CIO with Big Steel in
March of 1936, he had smashed through a veritable fortress of reaction and
intrenched capital. With the recognition of the CIO by the U.S. Steel Company
and its subsidiaries, or what is commonly termed Big Steel, the CIO had organized 70 per cent of the steel industry. In accomplishing this, Lewis had the
backing of such powerful unions as The Amalgamated Clothing Workers, his own
United Mine Workers, and the newly organized United Auto Workers. All of
these unions contributed to an organization fund for the Steel drive. It has
been variously estimated that Lewis spent upwards of $75,000 a month in union-
izing the steel workers. His success in organizing the steel workers, as well
as other mass production industries, can be attributed mainly to his policy
of industrial unionism. Previously, most of the organization done in steel
was among the skilled workers who were brought together in different crafts of
the trade. Machinists, electricians, millwrights, all had their own unions.
Little attempt was made to bring together the thousands of unskilled laborers
who comprised the bulk of the steel industry. There was little rapprochement
between the skilled and unskilled workmen. They could never join the positive
and united action. This was one of the causes of the failure of the great
steel strike of 1919 when Foster tried to bring all the workers together.
However, Lewis, with this resuscitated plan of industrial unionism, has organized everyone who works in the plants into one large federation. Especially is
the industrial union advisable at this time, because with the increasing technological advances in the industry the skilled workman is being pinched harder
and harder.

When Big Steel saw how well-knit their workmen were, they were forced
to give in to the CIO's demand for union recognition, increased wages, an
eight-hour day, and time and a half for overtime. Big steel did not want a
halt in its production. The steel industry has been on the upgrade since
1936. The American market has been good, and there has been a stream of
foreign orders largely for the purpose of rearmament.

Flush with their initial success in Big Steel, the CIO rushed into the
organization of the big independent mills. The six largest of these include
nearly all the other men employed in steel. These companies are known as
Little Steel, and include, The Youngstown Sheet and Tube, Jones & Laughlin,
Republic Steel, the Bethlehem Steel Co., Weir's National Steel Co., and
Inland Steel. The workers at these companies went out on strike--with the
exception of those employed at the Jones & Laughlin Mill (they signed a
CIO agreement) and the workers at the Weirton National. But whereas Big
Steel has met the union demands, Little Steel has fought the CIO with a
ruthlessness for which the CIO was hardly prepared. The strikers were
intimidated and beaten by company thugs, aeroplanes were used to fly food to
the men who remained in the Republic Mill, vigilantes and other flag-waving
organizations were formed in the Little Steel towns, back-to-work movements
were initiated, and all this was accompanied by furious anti-CIO propaganda.

The strikes were broken to the extent that the mills have started
working again. This does not mean that there is no hope for the CIO in Little
Steel. The mills have been crippled. When a mill is shut down and the fires
are allowed to cool, the insides of the furnaces often have to be ripped out
and relined. The gauges in the rolling mills have to be reset, necessitating
a large waste of steel. Higher wages are paid to the strike-breakers who are
less efficient than the regular men. It is alleged that huge sums have been
appropriated to bribe town officials and to pay the salaries of the Babbitts
who headed the anti-union citizens' Committees. The profits at Girdler's
Republic Mill were less by over $5,000,000 in the second quarter of 1937 than
in the first quarter. Therefore, if the CIO can plug certain apparent weak
spots in its setup, the chances are that Little Steel will be fully organized.
Although most of the strikers have gradually gone back to the mills, a number
are still in favor of unionism. But when the strikes began to drag out and
the pay-checks were really missed, the men grew restless. They wilted under
the pressure from home, the grocer, and the installment man. Couple this with
the well-organized propaganda against the CIO and it is understandable why

they were taken in by the back-to-work movements. If the CIO has the patience
to continue working in the areas, will undertake to educate the men, and
develop leaders from their numbers, Little Steel will be forced to recognize
the union. Little Steel has become the Verdun in the conflict between labor
and capital in the steel industry, and a victory for labor will be as vital
as that battle was to the Allied forces.

II

With an understanding of the nature of the struggles in steel, we can
turn our attention to the Negro worker. Previously, the Negro steel worker
had been denied entrance to the unions. He was employed in the menial jobs,
and the old Amalgamated was not interested in him or in any unskilled workman.
But with the coming of the CIO and the active policy of industrial unionism,
an earnest effort has been made to get the colored workers into the union.
When Big Steel signed the CIO contract, most of the colored workers in U.S.
Steel joined the union. However, they waited at first to see which way the
cat jumped. At the Jones and Laughlin Mill the colored men were hesitant about
wearing their union buttons until the agreement was actually signed. It is
difficult to get accurate figures, but roughly 75,000 Negroes are employed
in the steel industry. They have migrated to the steel areas from the South,
have little education, and a great deal of their life centers around the church.
In the larger cities they live in narrow, ancient, cobble-stoned alleyways,
flanked on both sides with densely packed houses. In the smaller towns their
houses cluster wearily along the railroad tracks or around the hulking mills.
In talking with many of the Negro steel men in the Pittsburgh area, the
writer found a variance of opinions concerning the CIO. Most of the objections
were unfounded and came out of a lack of understanding of the principles and
operation of the union. However, a few of these adverse opinions might be
stated. One man who was a chipper at the Allegheny Steel Co. said that when
the company recognized the CIO his wages were raised from $.83 an hour to
$1.03 an hour. A chipper is a man who works with an automatic hammer and
drill and cuts out the imperfections in the steel. The man contended that
the company has started "scarfing" a lot of its steel, which is a mechanical
method that accomplished the same results as "chipping." He feels that there
will be less work in the future for the chippers. A number of the Negro
workers denounced the fact that the more skilled men in some of the larger
plants did not allow the Negro men to rest in certain shanties or use the best
lavatories and showers, which they reserved for themselves. This, in spite
of the fact that the companies had placed these conveniences in the mills for
all the workers and did not intend any Jim Crowism. The men feel this is hardly
fair treatment from fellow union workers. The more ambitious colored workers
are angered because they are given the worst jobs with little chance for
advancement. They want to work as electricians, millwrights, crane operators,
and machinists. In answer to the objection that they might not be qualified
for these jobs, they say that promising white workers are apprenticed to the
skilled men until they can learn the craft. These Negro workers feel that the
union should fight for the same opportunities for the colored men.
The writer talked with some of the white workers in the Pittsburgh district
to learn their feelings towards the Negro workers and found that out of the
struggles there is slowly growing a kindredship between the two groups. John
Dutchman, a CIO director in the Lawrenceville section of Pittsburgh told of
how at the beginning of the drive he had to meet with a few colored workers
in their homes at night, with the shades down. Later he spoke at their
churches and organizations. Gradually he was able to break down their antipathy toward the union. Dutchman said: "It is difficult to organize the
Negro workers, but once they are in the union they become good union men."

III

In the Little Steel areas the Negro workers have been reluctant to join
with the CIO. Here in these small towns the colored worker is in a position
analagous to Mohammed's coffin--"suspended between heaven and earth." On one
hand he is faced with the disrespect of organized labor if he refuses to join
its ranks. And if he sides wholly with labor he must face the wrath of his
employers and the fascist-minded vigilante groups. The whole pattern and
background of his life tend to make him faithful to the employer. He is

isolated in his social life. He is under the influence of inept and backward leaders. He thinks in terms of his stomach and pocket-book and does not
understand the broader issues of the labor struggle. His feelings are typi-
fied in an experience the writer had with a colored steel worker in Warren.
After a talk with the man on the street, the writer was invited home for
dinner. The man said he had gone back to the mills after the back-to-work
movement had started. "You know," he said, "a man can't stand to see his
kids go hungry." He was definitely interested in the CIO and listened closely
during the meal to an explanation of the workings of the CIO and of industrial
unionism. Finally he stopped chewing his food, and "Son," he said, "what you
say sounds pretty good. But what I go by is this. Here on my plate I got one
chop. If I join the CIO can I get two chops?"

In Warren, Ohio, a town typical of the smaller steel communities, there
is a real bitterness between the white and colored workers. A few instances
might suffice. The writer went to the base headquarters of the CIO set up
for the strike at Girdler's Republic Mill in Warren. There the writer interviewed one of Clint Thomas' assistants. This man formerly worked in the mill.
He was discouraged over the actions of the Negro workers during the strike.
He said that about 2,000 men were still out on strike and only ten of these
were Negroes. In reply to the query of whether attempts had been made to
organize the Negro men, the writer was informed that a colored organizer had
been brought to the area and had tried unsuccessfully to get the Negro workers
into the union. The colored workers had been promised that they would receive
the same treatment in their particular job classifications as the whites. He
said, "We feel here that the Negro worker has his place," and named several
of the ugly jobs usually given to the colored men. Then continuing, he said,
"I wouldn't care to work alongside of a Negro, or have a Negro as my foreman."

Afterwards the writer talked to several of the white workers in front
of the headquarters. All of them trenchantly denounced the Negro. In fact,
quite a few colored men had been beaten. While talking to a group of the
strikers, two colored men, dressed in mill clothes and carrying their lunch-
buckets, passed on the opposite side of the street. One of the strikers, a
tall, hard-featured fellow, drew a knife, held it up to the group and said
in a long Southern drawl, "I bet if I stick one of them black bastards with
this, he'll howl."

These feelings, harsh as they are, arise naturally from the conditions
of the strike. The strikers hate all scabs, and here the Negroes are considered scabs. Possibly the CIO leadership could have affected a better
understanding between these workers by a thorough educational program. As it
was, it was easy for the colored workers in Warren to sense the hostile attitude towards them, even when they were first approached to join the union.
Even the Negro men who stuck with the CIO seldom come to the headquarters
except to get their supply of groceries from the commissary. The CIO cannot
get the full support of the Negro workers in Little Steel by a "middle of the
road" course. Instead, the Negro worker must be made to feel that he is
welcomed as a significant part of the labor movement.

IV

The colored workers in the Pennsylvania Iron & Steel Company at Tarentum,
Pa., can be offered as evidence that the Negro worker will seek the union
when opportunities for advancement are not denied him. When fully staffed,
the company employs about 350 men, of whom nearly 250 are colored. Every
man in the plant belongs to and enthusiastically supports the CIO. The
president of the Local is a Negro, Hunter Howell. By their own ruling the
local requires their dues to be paid a month in advance of the CIO requirement.
Not only must a man belong to the CIO in order to work in the mill, but his
dues must be paid up.

The mill is one of the few old "puddling mills" that are still operated.
Most of these mills have been replaced by those mills using the blast and
open-hearth furnaces. The major principles in the operation of the plant are
not difficult for the layman to understand. Pig iron billets are heated in
small furnaces by crews of two or three men under the charge of one man who
is called a puddler. The iron is constantly turned by the men, who work before
the withering heat of the furnaces with long iron rods. The white hot iron
is worked until it is roughly the shape of a large ball. When the puddler

feels that the iron is sufficiently heated, it is taken out of the furnaces
with a big clamp. Then it is rushed along a stationary cable, dripping hot
iron and slag all the while, until it is pushed into the rollers. The rollers
are a series of cylinders in constant motion. When the iron strikes the
rollers it is pressed out like biscuit dough. After its trip through the
rollers, the iron is passed out into the yard in the desired shape. In this
case, strips averaging eighteen feet in length, six inches in width, and half
an inch in thickness were the result. When the strips are cooled they are
sent to the finishing mill. Here the iron is reheated to rid it of imperfections and sent through another set of rollers. But, at this point, the
iron is finished in long, round strips to be cut into bolt forms.

The company's chief product is a bolt used in the linings of engines
called the "Lewis Staybolt." In the trade it is considered one of the finest
products of its kind. This is very significant when it is considered that
colored workers in the mill are employed in skilled capacities. There are
colored rollers, puddlers, and millwrights. Joe Langston, the head roller,
is a Negro.

The writer interviewed Mr. W. A. Hicks, the president of the mill, and
his superintendent, Mr. John Davis. Mr. Hicks was well satisfied with his
colored workers and found them equally efficient as the white workers. Mr.
Hicks said that he did not practice racial discrimination in the mill, and
that the colored workers could advance according to their abilities. When
white workers applied for jobs they were not considered if they did not care
to work with colored men.

In the plant, as well as on the outside, there is a fine relationship
between the workers. They live near each other. Their children play together
in a large ballfield back of the mill. The writer took some pictures of
Howell, the president of the local, in the mill yard. After snapping several
pictures, one of the white workmen came over and asked the writer to take his
picture with Howell. When the picture was completed, the white worker said,
"I wanted you to take my picture with Howell because he's my best friend in
the mill. And if I'm not his friend he hasn't a friend in this mill."

And finally, the picture of American life is changing. Along with his
white brothers the Negro steel worker is being tested in the mighty cauldron
of American life. The Negro leaders, as well as the leaders of labor, must
spend time and patience in considering his problems. His own leaders from
out of the ranks must be developed. The outworn patterns of his thinking
must be recreated. If this is done, the Negro steel-worker will be moulded
into a powerful unit in the ranks of organized labor.

Opportunity, 15(December, 1937): 362-65, 380.

44. NEGRO WOMEN IN STEEL

By Mollie V. Lewis

"Perhaps you are a Negro woman, driven to the worst part of town but
paying the same high rent," writes Jenny Elizabeth Johnstone in her challenging little pamphlet *Women in Steel.* "You are strong. There is nothing new
in suffering to you," she continues. "Your man is driven even harder than
the white workers, but your man gets lower pay--hired the last and fired the
first."

I know these women of the steel towns of which Miss Johnstone writes--
these women living dreary lives under the domination of powerful and imperson-
al corporations. I have been one of them. The conditions under which they
live, the excessive rents demanded for cramped and inadequate shelter, the
uncertainty of employment for their men folk and the disruptive inconvenience
of the mill shift all combine to make life a hard and uneven road for them.
It is because of such conditions, faced by the women of every mill worker's
family, that the Steel Workers' Organizing Committee, of the Committee for
Industrial Organization, has sponsored the formation of women's auxiliaries
in the campaign for the unionization of the industry.

Last summer I revisited Gary, that hard and unbeautiful metropolis of
steel upon the banks of Lake Michigan. In the mills which line the lake
shore, furnaces were going full blast, twenty-four hours a day. Steel was
pouring from them in molten streams. Thousands of men of both races and many
nationalities, sweaty and grimy, were tending the furnaces and conducting the
ore through its processes to the finished product.

Something new had come into the lives of these men. Thousands of them
had joined the union. For the first time it was possible for them openly to
be union men in the mills of the United States Steel Corporation. For the
first time this vast corporation for which they worked had recognized their
union and entered into an agreement with it.

Only a few miles distant, however, in Indiana Harbor and South Chicago,
Little Steel had taken a bitter stand against the union and against the spirit
of the New Deal and had engaged in a costly fight which was climaxed by the
Memorial Day Massacre. The strike was now over and the men were returning to
work without the recognition which had been negotiated with Big Steel.

Hand in hand with the campaign to organize the mill workers went the
drive to bring the women folk of these men into active participation in the
labor movement. The agency for organizing the women was the Women's Auxiliary
of the Amalgamated Association of Iron, Steel and Tin Workers of North America.
The objectives of the campaign were to organize the women "to lend aid to the
union in all possible ways," to help them to maintain the morale of the steel
workers, to educate them in the principles of trade unionism, and to weld them
into a force for social betterment.

Bringing Races Together

In the matter of race relations, Gary and the adjacent steel towns are by
no means utopian. From time to time bitter racial animosities have flared,
not only between Negroes and whites, but also between native citizens and the
foreign born. In addition many of the foreign born brought with them to this
country nationalistic enmities rooted in Old World conflicts. To induce the
women of such diverse groups to join the same organization, even for their own
benefit, has been no easy task.

In Gary I talked with Mrs. Minneola Ingersoll who was in charge of the
organization of women's auxiliaries in the Chicago-Calumet district. Mrs.
Ingersoll is a young southern white woman and a graduate of the University of
Alabama. Together we visited the homes of members of the auxiliary of both
races and various nationalities.

"Our policy in the auxiliary, as in the union," Mrs. Ingersoll said, "is
to organize all regardless of their race, color, creed or nationality. When
it comes to exploitation, the mill owners draw no color line. They exploit
the native white workers just as they do the Mexican, Polish and Negro workers."

In Indiana Harbor where Inland Steel had forced its workers into a long
and bitter strike rather than grant their demand for recognition, a number of
Negro women had been drawn into the auxiliary. In Gary, however, Negro women
seemed more reluctant to join and the campaign had been less successful among
them. Along with the women of other groups, Negro women were represented on
the picket lines of the struck plants.

During the strike they cooperated with others behind the lines in the
preparation and serving of hot meals to the strikers. They were members of
the various committees which sought contributions of money and food to keep
the strike going.

Negroes Aided in Strike

In her pamphlet, Miss Johnstone calls attention to "the swiftness with
which Negro women have taken the leadership in our chapters. There is not one
auxiliary where the staying power of these courageous women has not carried the
organization over some critical period, especially in the first days of unseen
and unsung organizing drudgery before the body took form. They were undaunted
and gave great moral strength with their persistence."

The organizing of white and Negro women in the same units has naturally
had its by-product in the field of race relations. While the auxiliaries have
by no means eliminated racial barriers in a district where jim crowism flour-
ishes, they have for the first time made it possible for the women of both
races to get to know one another on friendly terms.

While the municipal government of Gary continues to keep the children apart in a system of separate schools, their parents are getting together in the union and in the auxiliary. And after school hours, the children meet jointly in a junior lodge under guidance of an instructor. It is noteworthy that the only public eating place in Gary where both races may be freely served is a cooperative restaurant large patronized by members of the union and auxiliary.

These, it may be true, are of minor importance. But they represent steps toward inter-racial cooperation on a mass basis. When the black and white workers and members of their families are convinced that their basic economic interests are the same, they may be expected to make common cause for the advancement of these interests. Women of both races have, for traditional reasons, been inclined to be more stand-offish than men when it comes to organizing in a common body. The efforts of the auxiliary to bring the women together may ultimately prove to be a significant factor in overcoming racial barriers which still retard the advance of the labor movement in this country.

The Crisis, 45 (February, 1938): 54.

45. NOEL R. BEDDOW TO MR. CHARLES E. FELL, NOVEMBER 29, 1938 [57]

Dear Sir:

The criticism of the Southern Conference for Human Welfare by Mrs. Sharp's committee and the Real Estate Board just goes beyond anything heretofore known in the South. According to these so-called great Democrats it is a crime even to confer with negroes or union labor or, indeed, anyone or anything that may in any way call attention to conditions in the South that are so bad that they smell to high Heaven.

In fact, according to these high lights, intellectual monstrosities, exalted brain trusters, there is nothing wrong anywhere in the South. The Southern workers are so contented, the share cropper's life is a bed of roses, their life is one of supreme bliss and would continue to be so if it were not for Reds and Communists who have inveigled and persuaded them into conferring in Birmingham. So it is that Dr. Graham, Dr. Nixon, Dr. Mason and Mrs. Louise Charlton, Congressman Patrick, in fact any and everybody who does not subscribe to their cruel philosophy of hunger, destitution, misery and crime are Reds and Communists and have sinister motives when they confer with these alleged happy, but truly unhappy people.[58]

Can you beat it? Can you even approximate the ostrich-like attitude of these would-be saviors and, finally, what sinister influence prompts this spasmodic outburst?

According to these high lights, only Real Estate Boards can confer, only bankers in Houston can confer, only industrialists in Nashville can confer, only Liberty Leaguers in Washington can confer. No sinister motives there. Oh no! No investigation as to who called the conference or who paid the bills, but when suffering masses represented by college presidents, life long labor leaders and understanding leaders of the Negro race confer, then and only then do sinister influences raise their unholy heads? Oh yeah? [59]

So the Dies Committee has been invited to investigate those sponsoring the conference. Labor welcomes this if the Dies Committee will come in, without bias and prejudice, and conduct a thorough and complete investigation, without the interference or assistance of Mrs. Sharp's committee, the Real Estate Board or the Better Birmingham Committee because if they interfere or participate, the time and money would be worse than wasted if the true facts are to be known.[60]

Communism--apparently those who mouth the word with such freedom and ease do not know the difference between Communism and rheumatism. They know they have an ache or pain somewhere so they yell, Communism. Certainly Labor is not in favor of Communism. Communism means the end of liberty, freedom, organizations whether in churches, lodges or labor. Of course Labor is not Communistic. It could not be communistic and believe in God, a democratic form of government, and Labor does believe in God, a democratic form of govern-

ment, liberty, the marriage vows, free speech and peaceful public assembly.
No, Labor is not communistic. It is merely seeking those rights guaranteed it
under the self-same Constitution that business resorts to so frequently to
set aside legitimate legislation passed by those seeking the benefits guaranteed them by this Constitution under which we all live but which is often
interpreted so unjustly.

Equality--the only equality labor is seeking in the South is the equality
of wages and working conditions. The Negro worker certainly is not seeking
any social equality. He has his churches, his schools, his teachers and if
he is a true, upright and honest Negro, he should be an honor to himself and
his race. There is no question of social equality in labor organizations.
Workers meet in the same hall, the white man sitting on one side and the
colored man sitting on the other to discuss their mutual problems of bread
and meat. When these discussions are ended they depart to their humble homes
in order to secure much needed rest that they might enter the mills and
factories to make another day. So, again, these Liberty Leaguers and their
cohorts who are crying race equality are wrong. There is no race equality
even among their own organizations.

                                          Very truly yours,

                                          Noel R. Beddow

Philip Taft Research Notes, Birmingham Public Library Archives, Birmingham,
Alabama.

               46. RESOLUTIONS PASSED BY THE STEEL WORKERS
                    ORGANIZING COMMITTEE CONVENTION, 1940

                          RESOLUTION No. 38

                   Federal Anti-Lynching Legislation

A resolution on this subject was presented by Lodge No. 1531.
Your committee recommends the adoption of the following substitute
resolution:
Whereas, (1) A bill was introduced at the last session of Congress intended to eliminate lynching and pave the way for extending the benefits of
the New Deal and democracy to millions of Negro workers and underprivileged
white workers; and
(2) Such anti-lynching legislation passed by Congress would help the
free organization of labor; now, therefore, be it
Resolved, (1) That this convention endorses the principle of Federal anti-
lynching legislation; and
(2) That the Executive Officers of the SWOC be instructed to work for the
passage of an Anti-Lynching Bill in the present session of Congress.
A motion was made and seconded to adopt the substitute resolution offered
by the committee.
Delegate Spillers, Lodge 1014: I fully agree with this resolution. I
also would like to ask, Mr. Chairman, that a copy of this resolution and also
the resolution dealing with poll tax in the South be sent to our Senators and
Congressmen, especially Senator Barkley, of the state of Kentucky, and also
that gigantic Senator from the state of Texas, Mr. Martin Dies.
Delegate Cotten, Lodge 1066: I would like to make this recommendation
to the Steel Workers Organizing Committee Executive Board, that all friendly
Negro organizations they can reach and have contact with be furnished with
a copy of this resolution, so that they may see the position the Steel Workers Organizing Committee has taken upon the question of lynching.
Chairman Murray: I might say for the information of the delegates that
the officers of the organization, upon the passage of this part of the committee's report, intend to forward a copy of your action to each member of the
Federal Congress, in both the Upper and Lower houses.

We will also be pleased to send it to all other organizations throughout the country who are interested in the promotion of this cause and the passage of this legislation. That is our purpose, of course.

Delegate Wilson, Lodge 1961: I do not look upon that bill solely as a race bill. The thugs paid by the bigger companies throughout the United States ride up and down the streets slugging workers throughout this whole CIO drive. I think it is a good resolution, and we ought to go back and work and send telegrams, just like we did on this other resolution.

The motion to adopt Resolution No. 38 was carried by unanimous vote. . . .

RESOLUTION NO. 42

Unity of Negro and White Workers

The committee recommends the adoption of the following substitute resolution:

Whereas, Employers constantly seek to split one group of workers from another and thus to deprive them of their full economic strength, by arousing prejudices based on race, creed, color or nationality, and one of the most frequent weapons used by employers to accomplish this end is to create false conflicts between Negro and white workers; now, therefore, be it

Resolved, That the SWOC hereby pledges itself to uncompromising opposition to any form of discrimination, whether political or economic, based upon race, color, creed or nationality.

A motion was made and seconded to adopt the substitute offered by the committee.

Chairman Murray: That is one of the age-old fundamentals of this organization, that there be no discrimination exercised against any individual, regardless of race, creed, color or nationality--a mightyfine structure upon which to build a great union.

Delegate Balint, Lodge 1666: I believe there should be a statement made in the resolution concerning political discrimination in the South.

Director Mitch: Several resolutions have been passed dealing primarily with problems that affect all of us, but particularly the South. This one question is more acute in the South than in any other part of our nation. The question of Negro and white workers meeting together and considering their common problems has been one of the real obstacles thrown in the way of organized labor in the South.

We have met that situation and I can say for the colored workers that I think generally they understand that our organization is trying to provide equal rights for them economically, and they have adhered accordingly. We know that city ordinances have been passed in practically all of the industrial sections prohibiting the colored workers and white workers from meeting in the same hall. Our meetings have been broken up, particularly in Gadsden, Alabama, where the Republic Steel Corporation is in control and associated with other industries who have carried out the program of busting the organization of the workers.

I refer particularly to the Goodyear Tire and Rubber Company. In every instance where arrests have been made they refuse to prosecute. They simply let them out on their own recognizance, and on appearance before the court, the matter is dismissed. We have no opportunity to test the constitutionality of these various ordinances, and hence they are only used for the purpose for which they were enacted, and that is to intimidate the workers, to prevent them from meeting for the purpose of perfecting their organization.

It has affected us in many ways. The various state laws, antiquated state laws that were put on the books at a time when organized labor did not know what was going on, are still on the statute books, all of the anti-laws and all of the weak laws. For instance, the Workmen's Compensation Laws in the various Southern states are particularly weak compared with any of the other industrial states of the nation. The unemployment compensation law in the South is particularly weak, and in Alabama our own law was recently amended, where the interpretation of a labor dispute was written into the law, and it will forever prohibit anyone from drawing unemployment compensation if they even think about stopping work.

This question has been a real one as far as my activities in the South have been concerned, but I may say to you that as a general rule we have

overcome most of the real opposition, because the workers do meet together
and consider their common problems. They have organizations wherein some
of them are not permitted to meet, and some of them are not even permitted
membership.

The American Federation of Labor, with its high officials, met in the
city of Atlanta recently, and there they made a pronouncement that they were
again going to organize the South. They make that statement periodically, but
the big thing they tried to emphasize that they were going to do, was that
they were appealing to the colored workers, and I say to you frankly, when I
was President of the Alabama State Federation of Labor, twenty-one Negroes
came to my office and wanted me to take up the matter of getting a charter
for them, because they had been deprived of membership in the regular carpenters' union in that city. I sent in the charter fee and all the necessary
information to the Carpenters' headquarters at Indianapolis, and they replied
acknowledging receipt of the charter fee and all other information and said
that the matter would be handled in due form. About a month later they
received a letter returning the charter fee and saying that an investigation
had been made, and under the circumstances they felt it was inadvisable to
issue the charter as requested.

The point is that many labor organizations, particularly those affiliated
with the American Federation of Labor, will not permit Negroes to hold membership. The Negro workers understand that. They also understand that when
Bill Green and some of his associates make an appeal to the Negro workers
to join the American Federation of Labor, when they were asked why it was
that the A.F. of L. did not make provision to take care of the membership of
the colored workers, they were unable to reply, because Bill Green would then
have to say the same thing he usually says--"I have no authority." This is
what he said when I went over the heads of the representatives of the Carpenters' Union to him, at the request of the Negro carpenters in Birmingham
who wanted to organize.

There is a great deal that could be said about the antiquated laws and the
denial of the right of franchise not only to the Negroes but to the white
workers as well, because of the cumulative poll tax laws in the state of Alabama. Thousands of eligible age who would have the right to vote in other
states are deprived of that right in Alabama, because of the accumulation in
poll tax that has gone on for years, and they cannot get enough money ahead
to pay their poll tax. Less than 20 per cent of the voters of eligible age
do vote in Alabama, and that is typical of the other Southern states.

This problem is a real problem in the South. We had hoped that this convention would be meeting in Birmingham, but because of some circumstances
that arose we thought it was advisable not to hold the convention in Birmingham.

This is one of the problems that we had in our minds because of some of
the things that came up recently. I know you all have these problems to a
certain degree, but it means so much to us in the South. I say to you frankly
we are overcoming these problems, we are overcoming this traditional prejudice that has grown up and has continued ever since the civil war between
the states. Thank God, as far as labor organizations are concerned the Negroes
know where they belong, they are really coming into the various CIO organizations. They want to come in and we want them in, because they are doing
everything possible to elevate their race.

Delegate Prebeg, Lodge 1014: This is the foundation of the resolution
which we had in our policy before. This is something like the constitution of
our United States, the constitution which gives to all American citizens in the
United States a country that was built of all kinds of nations. This resolution
covers all the laborers, regardless of creed or color or nationality, and this
is the very foundation we must put in force when we go home, we must do this
through our lodges and spread this news among all the workers. If we want a
100 per cent labor organization, from the stewards in our lodges to the chairman and directors of the Executive Board, if we want them to enforce and believe what they preach, we will succeed and have a 100 per cent Union in the
United States.

Delegate Wilson, Lodge 1961: I just want to say a few words and tell the
brothers how we have overcome the race situation in our little plant. I am
elected a delegate here out of my plant for the majority of the members. We
have whites and Negroes, and we do not know what color each one is outside

of our plant. When a brother is sick, regardless of race, creed or color, if
he is financially disabled we meet him.

Gentlemen, I want to say that I was elected by the solid vote of our local
union, not by the majority.

The colored man sought to win his freedom, and you can easily draw the
colored man into our organization, where they all belong. In the South you
have a problem, but that problem consists of a little bit more than the Negro
membership. You have to offer them jobs on your committees and instruct
them how to handle them. In some sections the Negro has been dominated so
long that he is bound to be unfamiliar with the way of doing things. So the
officers will encourage those boys by elevating a few of them to stewardships
and jobs of that kind, and you will find your job much easier.

Delegate Walker, Lodge 1102: In respect to the representative from
Alabama, I heard him make the statement that the Negro knows his place. I
am not going to raise any question about that, unless he is willing to voluntarily advance the answer, but we as Negroes hear that so much, that the
Negro knows his place. I don't say this as a matter of insinuation or insult,
because I believe he is all right, at least I am advancing that thought, anyway.

But we want to clear up these things. We don't want to have these things
happen in the CIO, infringements and intimidations. We frequently hear the
remark yet, even among the reactionary forces, that the Negro knows his place.
Here is one thing that we want to understand and we want to advance this
information to every CIO member here, be he black or white, male or female,
regardless of who they are, even to their religious denominations, that so far
as the Negro's place is concerned he is just like anybody else, he is a man
created in this world by God, and God has placed us here as human beings,
irrespective of nationality, race, creed or color.

I thought once I was going to be elected a delegate to the Alabama convention. I didn't want to go very much because I knew where it was going to
be held, but when the Lodge said they were going to elect me down there I
said that was all right. I said, "If the CIO sits in Alabama and you send me
as a delegate I am going, because I am a man and expect to take my place as a
man wherever I go."

As for the Negro's intelligence, certainly we haven't had the chance in
the United States of America for educational advancement that the white people
had had, but we do have just as intelligent Negroes in the United States as
there are anywhere in the world.

Getting back to the resolution, the resolution refers to any form of discrimination, whether political or economic, and that resolution should be
couched in these words, "His full rights," regardless of what they are. If
this country goes into war are you going to segregate the Negro from his white
brother? You didn't do it in France.

I say, let the CIO take their stand and let the white and Negro brothers
from the South fight this out as best they can, but we up here, let's give
them their full rights.

Director Mitch: I don't know, but it seems to me that the delegate who
just spoke certainly did not understand what I said. After I explained that
the American Federation of Labor would not take Negroes into membership
and said that the CIO wants them as members, I then said that the Negroes
recognized their place and were coming into the CIO. That is what I meant,
that they felt their place was in the CIO.

As far as doing something for the Negro is concerned, I think I can answer
that, or the Negroes of Alabama can answer it as to what the CIO, through the
United Mine Workers and the Steel Workers particularly have done for the Negro
in the South.

Not to take up any further time on it, let me say the misconstruction
has always been that the Negro is advocating social equality. We know that is
a lie put out for the purpose of further dividing our forces. We know all the
Negro wants is economic and industrial equality.

Delegate Brown, Lodge 2110: Mr. Chairman, I had not intended to say
anything on this, in view of the fact that I was out on committee work and was
busy during the time the resolution was read. I came in in time to get on the
tail end, and I want to say that this racial prejudice not only exists in
Alabama, but it also exists in the East, in the West, in the North, and in the
South, throughout the length and breadth of the United States of America, and
we cannot solve our vexing problems except we take the bull by the horns.

I happen to occupy the position as presiding officer in my local Lodge, vice-president and delegate to this convention, and I have the same problems that are in Alabama in Jersey now. I hear it said, "I would join the organization, but you have a Negro presiding officer there." They stay out, they haven't backbone enough to come into the organization, because of the blackness of my skin they stay out, and I say it is because of ignorance and superstition that they look with suspicion upon the Negro.

God made all men to dwell upon the face of the whole earth. I don't believe any intelligent Negro is seeking social equality, but I am here to tell you I want all the educational and industrial and political equality I can get, and if you give the Negro an opportunity he will do as the white man has done. He will prove that he is equal to any other man that lives. I tell you I am willing to live for the CIO and I am willing to fight and die for those principles.

Executive Director Beddow, Southern Region: Mr. Chairman and delegates, I had not intended to say anything on this most important resolution, but my good friend and colleague, William Mitch, from the state of Indiana, stated in his talk that in the South as in the North and the East and the West the Negro knows his place. He does, and he is a poor man of any race if he does not know his place. He knows that he is working side by side with the white man in the mills, and even though God Almighty made him black as charcoal, if he is a good, honest American citizen, he ought to be proud that he is a Negro.[61]

The Negro knows his place in our organization, and I am telling you now that in the Deep South it is side by side of me and Bill Mitch in Alabama and Tennessee and Georgia.

You heard the quartette sing here. They came from Bessemer, Alabama, only twelve miles from the city of Birmingham. The president of that organization is a man whom God Almighty chose to make black, and he is proud of it. He sits over there now, and so I repeat what Brother Bill Mitch said--the Negro, the white man, the Indians, the Chinamen, any man who comes into this organization knows his place, and it is to take the rightful place that he can and does acquire in the organization.

We have been fighting the workingmen's battles in the South. Brother Mitch told you people that in Gadsden, just a few nights ago--that is Tom Girdler's place--and I am going to confess something now, I used to be a little bit wild, but I am living a better life because Tom Girdler can't go to Heaven and I'm not going to Hell with him. There is no room for both of us down there. It would indeed be a hell of place if we both got down there.

We went to Gadsden. We have a Lodge started in Gadsden, and the police in Gadsden raided that Lodge and arrested twenty-nine men. Why? Because there were three colored men in it. Brother Will Watts, one of the organizers, called me up and he was so nervous that his heart sounded like a jackass kicking a tin can, even over the telephone. He said, "Mr. Beddow, what are you going to do about it?" I said, "Sign their bonds, and if you haven't got it, put it up in some way and I will get them out, I will be there tomorrow." I went over to Gadsden the next morning and sat down with George Rains, the city attorney, and I said, "Will you accommodate me?" He said, "In what way?" I said, "Convict one of these men. I want to show you how lousy your laws are in Alabama. I want to take it to the Supreme Court of the United States, and we will advertise Gadsden to the world for what it is."

We went up to the hearing and we took a stenographer. She sat by the judge and he was so nervous he could not even conduct his case properly. Mr. Cowherd and I were acting as attorneys. The judge said, "We are going to call on one of the cases and let them represent all of them." I said, "Oh, no, you're not, we are going to try them one at a time." He said, "If we acquit one of them will it be all right?" I said, "Yes."

To make a long story short, they acquitted one of these men and we left the police court. I made the announcement that we were going to hold a meeting, and we took sixty black men and white men and we held a meeting.

We still believe in God Almighty in the South, and whenever you kneel down in prayer and pray, "Our Father, which are in heaven," you don't say the black man's Father or the white man's Father--he is the Father of us all.

I make these remarks in amplification of what Brother Bill Mitch said. The black man knows his place. There is only one place for him in the United States, and that is in the CIO where we can help him and take them on to where they ought to be.

Delegate Freeman, Lodge 2176: I would like to back up what Brother
Beddow said. It is another hell hole, it is another Harlan County, Kentucky.
I was one of the twenty-nine men arrested in that place and we have some good
colored men in our organization, as good as there are anywhere. If every man
in all the locals all over the country would work as hard as the organizers,
it wouldn't take so long to get this CIO organization everywhere. The CIO
has done more for the country in the last three or four years than the
American Federation of Labor has done for it in the last sixty years. I am
awfully proud of it.

A motion to close debate was carried.

The motion to adopt substitute Resolution No. 42 was carried by unanimous
rising vote.

Proceedings of the Second International Wage and Policy Convention of the
Steel Workers Organizing Committee, Chicago, May 14-17, 1940, pp. 182, 184-89.

47. STEEL DRIVE MOVES COLORED PEOPLE INTO ACTION!

All throughout the towns of Penna. wherever there are steel mills, the
population is in motion to unionize the steel industry under the leadership of
the Steel Workers Organizing Committee (SWOC). Never before was the opportunity
as great for the colored people to join the union which insures for Industrial
Organization (CIO) which is determined to march forward to organize the unorganized in the mass production industries. Contrary to the old time-worn
policy of some labor leaders, the CIO firmly takes the stand to organize all
the workers regardless of race, creed and color.

What does this mean to the colored people? This organization drive means
the securing of better wages, shorter hours, better conditions on the job and
for the home. It means the elimination of those barriers which formerly
spelled discrimination to the colored worker in steel. It means more adequate
education for our children and higher living standards.

IN THE UNION THERE IS STRENGTH!

To achieve this, we colored workers must join hands with our white
brothers and sisters, marching shoulder to shoulder, to abolish company
unionism and to establish an organization of our own which shall deliver us
from the clutches of the steel barons.

The Labor Committee of the National Negro Congress pledges its full
support in this drive to organize the steel industry. We urge all organizations of the colored people, churches, lodges, fraternal orders, civic groups
and so forth, to support this drive. We appeal to all colored workers in the
steel mills to join the union. Only a powerful trade union movement can give
us better economic security and liberate us from the shackles of company
union slavery.

Visit the SWOC headquarters and get literature. Invite SWOC speakers to
your meetings and organizations to further explain the great importance of
organizing the steel industry.

Issued By The Labor Committee
National Negro Congress
Philadelphia Area
1605 Catherine St.--YWCA.

Flier in possession of the Editors.

48. THE STORY OF BEN CAREATHERS

By Phillip Bonosky

When Ben Careathers boarded a bus to take him to Ambridge, a town near
Aliquippa, one morning in '36, he was not traveling blind nor really alone;
the way led like a living chain from comrade to comrade. For in the Negro
section of Ambridge, call Plan 11, there was a man waiting for him; it was
at his door that Ben knocked and entered that evening.

They waited inside until darkness arrived. The area was saturated with
spies and deputies, company stool pigeons; eyes and ears bought and paid for.
Darkness was the other, third comrade they were waiting for; and when it
arrived, they went with it the long way round into Aliquippa--city under
siege. Again, hand led him to hand, workingman's hand; a door opened, and a
comrade pressed him in.

The day before he had met in the SWOC office in Pittsburgh with Philip
Murray and Clint Golden, in charge of organizing steel in Pittsburgh. Murray
had looked keenly at him and asked him one direct question: "Will your
politics interfere with organizing the workers?"

Those hands that had reached out through the darkness to take him were
his politics. The blunt, smog-stained hills surrounding Pittsburgh and
looking down on the booming mills whose fire consumed the sky--this too, was
in his politics. The men rushing from those dark mills, as though from prison,
coughing up bitter smoke--these were his politics most of all!

What he had learned in struggle had brought him to Communism; and if his
life meant anything at all, it meant, it *had* to mean one thing above all this
moment, as he sat in the kitchen of a Negro comrade's house, pondering his
next step; those steel-workers sleeping now in beds for fear and distrust
were waiting for him. They could not know that he was there, in this kitchen,
listening to the tin clock; still they were waiting.

Dawn was gray. Smog hovered over the town like a dark lid. He could
taste it, that bituminous sweet taste, with bitter steel mixed; he could feel
that jagged, stained air go down into his lungs. He coughed to clear his
throat, feeling his lungs good and solid.

He made his way to a corner saloon, which swept him in with its malty
breath of beer. Negro workers were lined up along the damp bar; few were
drinking. Money was scarce in this year of the depression.

He took up the traditional stance at the bar, one foot raised on the
brass rail, the spittoon within easy range, and ordered a bottle of Iron City
beer. He poured himself a foaming glass, drank, examining the men over the
yellow rim.

They were steel workers, and their talk was steel talk--his talk. Those
faces were the faces of his memories, of his everyday struggle, his own face,
in fact, reflected like an endless mirror down the bar.

The man he picked out to open up a conversation with was a youngish worker
whose face had given him what he wanted. "Have a drink?" he said, nodding to
the bottle. The other turned to look at him; their eyes met steadily for a
moment, and he made a half-salute and poured himself a glass.

Ben watched it go down, and then asked casually, "How are things here?"
"Tough."

Ben chewed on this. "Suppose a guy wanted to get a job here?" he said.
"How'd he go about getting one?"

"Get a job?" The other shook his head. "They ain't hiring. But if they
were hiring, *you* couldn't get nothing but open hearth or blast furnace. . . ."

Ben understood what he meant by *you*, so he nodded slowly.

"But, look here, come over and talk to my friends," the other said.
"They'll give you the real low-down." And he took Ben down to the other end
of the bar. Then, before he could do anything about, the one thing happened
that he had been in a sweat about; somebody recognized him!

"Why, Ben Careathers!" the voice boomed out in the deputy-crawling town.
"What are you doing down here? I'll be damned!"

"You sure you know me?" Ben asked.

Know you! Why, weren't you fighting for those Scottsboro boys? I
heard you speak for them!"

For once he wished he hadn't been so public! He took a look at every face in the crowd. His friend was reintroducing him to the others. "This man's a real fighter, man!"

He shook hands all around, and when the silence developed and he felt their eyes on him, he took a breath and said: "Well, friends, I'll give the story to you straight. I'm here from the Steel Workers Organizing Committee of the CIO. I'm trying to set up a union in this town."

His friend broke into laughter. "Man," he cried, "why didn't you say so at first?"

Ben smiled. But his friend continued studying him, puzzling something out, his face in a frown. Finally he said: "I just want to ask you one thing." Ben invited him to ask. "Tell me straight now; is the Communist Party conducting this drive?"

"No," Ben said slowly, "not exactly. It's interested in organizing steelworkers in the CIO though."

"But the Communist Party says it's Okay?"

"Oh, yes," Ben replied.

"Then I'll join! he cried, slapping down his flat hand on the bar. "Otherwise, I wouldn't have confidence in it. If the Party says so, I know it's going to be all right. The Amalgamated is Jim Crow; but now I swear the CIO isn't going to have any 'for whites only.'"

Scottsboro had led to Aliquippa; struggle was a phoenix constantly renewing itself, endlessly reborn.

Like good news he was taken from house to house, and he talked to groups of four and five, behind closed windows, drawn blinds, locked doors; whites came, too; and slowly Aliquippa, surrounded by terror, itself became surrounded by workers. . . .

Two weeks after the first discussion in the SWOC office, Ben walked into Clint Golden's office and poured out a pile of application cards on his desk.

Golden looked startled.

"Where'd you get these?" he cried.

"You and Murray sent me to Aliquippa, didn't you? That's where I got them."

"And the initiation fees?"

Ben made another green pile.

"Wait a minute," Golden cried. "I got to get Phil to see this!"

In a moment he was back with Murray, pointing to the piles on his desk. "Ben," he directed, "just tell Phil how you did it!"

He tried to tell Phil Murray "how he did it," but Murray never fully understood.

The fact that he was a Communist was key. Murray tacitly conceded this by appointing men like Gus Hall, Ben Careathers and other Communists on his organizing staff. Murray had asked Ben whether being a Communist would interfere with his organizing the workers. Ben could have told him that being a Communist interfered with nothing whatsoever except capitalism, starvation, disunity, the open shop in the steel industry.

It had started far earlier than two weeks ago, or even months ago when John L. Lewis was thrown out of the A.F. of L. and launched the CIO, and the Party had mobilized its membership as an army of "volunteer organizers," of which Ben had been one, bringing hundreds of workers into the CIO. It had started in a log cabin outside of Chattanooga, Tennessee, when a Negro youth of fourteen had run away from starvation on a sharecropper's patch and struck out on his own. It had started perhaps when Ed Johnson was lynched for "rape," and his body twirled from a rope tied to the Tennessee River bridge, while thousands stood on the bank and gaped.

Part of the beginning lay in his struggle to obtain for himself the elementary tools of learning, literacy. At eighteen he couldn't read or write. Somehow the sovereign state of Tennessee had overlooked the Careathers' share-cropping patch, and left it unsullied by learning. It was not provided in the scheme of things for Negro children to become scientists, writers, musicians, artists.

He followed Bill Holt, a fifteen-year-old Negro high school student, who worked in the same shop with him, around the shop copying down the numbers he marked on furniture. Numbers weren't so hard, and he could get away with it; but one day he received a letter from his sweetheart, Lela, and he stood there helplessly staring down at the mysterious words. Finally he picked out a word at random and asked Bill Holt to tell what it was, pretending it was too "big"

for him. The whole letter was too "big" for him, actually, and he turned it
over at last to Holt who read it to him, and then tactfully suggested that Ben
take lessons from him so that he could learn to read "better." So he studied
his ABC's!

But once he had learned to read, he began to read the print off the paper.
He read now with a hunger that only the starved know. He read on his way to
work; on the streetcar coming back home; he read as he ate, and read as he ran.
He resented the time wasted in sleep, and propped himself up to the light at
night, with the book swaying in his hand, until he collapsed out of sheer exhaustion. He read Carter Woodson and W. E. B. Du Bois, Benjamin Brawley, Kelly
Miller. He joined Toussaint L'Ouverture in his struggle for Haitian freedom
against Napoleon, as P. G. Steward described in his book. . . .

All the time he was seeking for the answer to the question which life
posed in such gigantic terms with which every Negro in one way or another
grappled all his life long. For a Negro there could be no peace, no sunny
acceptance of things as-they-are no matter how stubborn one shut one's eyes.

This was no overnight revelation.

He had been working as an upholsterer for Mister Balfour (*Mister* Balfour;
but Mister Balfour's boy called *his* father, Spencer) 66 hours a week for $7.50.

Balfour's assistant, Jim, said to him one day: "Ben, take these chairs
to the corner of Fourteenth and Elm."

"Put the number down," Ben said.

"Just take them over to Fourteenth and Elm," he repeated.

Ben picked the heavy chairs up and lugged them to Fourteenth and Elm,
thinking there must be only one building there; but there were three and a
vacant lot. He brought the chairs back.

"Jim," he said, "I can't find the place. Where is it *exactly?*"

Jim called over another man.

"Covey," he said, "tell Ben here where I want these chairs delivered."

"Fourteenth and Elm," Covey replied.

"On the corner?" Ben asked. Or fourteenth or on Elm?"

"Ben," Jim said, "this man told you, and I told you. You can hear, can't
you? I say it's on Fourteenth and Elm, and what I say I mean!"

That was it; all the advice about being cautious in a white man's world
flew out of his head; he grabbed a chair. "I say to hell with you! And what
I say I mean!"

They turned green now with panic, and yelled for the boss, who came run-
ing. When he heard the story, he turned on Jim and the other and said:
"Look, now, don't bother Ben--he's a good worker, but he's cracked. Let him
alone!"

This "benevolence" cost him $7 or $8 a week compared to what the white
workers got; Mr. Balfour knew a gold mine when he saw one. But this "tolerance"
was priced too high, and Ben Careathers went on strike--a strike of one--and
returned to work when he was promised another dollar a week.   When, by degrees,
he finally achieved the dizzy height of $9 a week, he had reached the limit,
no more sky.

All this was behind the story of "how he did it;" but there was more.

He came North just before World War I, looking for higher wages.

He was in Pittsburgh during the war years, working as a janitor, as a
"helper" in the Pittsburgh Railways Company, trying to save enough money to
set up an upholsterer's shop of his own. The war to "save the world for
democracy" failed to stir his pulses. But it did open up jobs, including jobs
for Negroes. It also raised the whole question of the meaning of war itself.
One day, as Ben hurried home from work, he was accosted by a Negro man selling
pamphlets. He took one of the pamphlets thrust into his hands, cast a casual
glance at it, and said "this is socialistic, isn't it?"

"Yes," the Negro man replied, "It's socialistic. Do you know about
socialism?"

"No, Ben answered, "and I don't want to know."

The other man looked at him for a moment. "You know," he said, "anybody
who knows all about it, and doesn't want it--well, I can understand that.
But if you don't know, and don't *want* to know--then you're a fool!"

Ben walked on, but the man's voice had stung him! He turned abruptly
back and said: "Give me one of those!"--determined to read it and show up who
the real fool was! It was so easy to cry, "Down with this! Down with that!"
--he had done that himself, cursing the evils of the world, and not one Jericho
had fallen! But *how*, in what sensible realistic way could the common people

hope to win their freedom? He had never found the answer, and didn't expect
to find it now.

But he opened the pages and read, and continued to read, and read on
through to the end, whispering finally almost in spite of himself: "Jesus
Christmas! This sounds like what I want!"

The address of the Socialist Party was published on the back, and he
found his way there quickly, and spent the evening listening to the speeches,
talking, discussing, reading more literature, including Bellamy's *Looking
Backward*.

Then one day he joined.

They were all brothers--Negro and white; there was no discrimination here,
the only place in which he had ever found this to be so! He was happy, jubilant, so happy and jubilant that he invited all his friends to the dance the
Socialist Party was holding in Moose Temple. His dreams were really coming
alive now, the smothering lid of oppression was lifting a bit!

The proceedings had hardly begun when two of the SP leaders took him
aside (how many times had he been so taken aside?) and, with deep embarrass-
ment, they explained to him: "Ben, we're having trouble. We in the Socialist
Party believe in full equality, of course; but the hall owner has been objecting
to Negroes here and threatens to close the hall."

They didn't have to say any more. He went out of there, burning with
anger; he felt that a hope, a profound dream, lay dead. "It went to my heart,"
he said, recalling that early incident. He was through. From now on, he would
devote himself to his shop (which he had succeeded in establishing) and to
that alone. Except that he could continue to find in books what life did not
have. That door need never close!

Three years slipped by, and one day, Bill Scarville, the same comrade who
had sold him his first socialist pamphlet, turned up at his door with a copy
of a newspaper and tales of a new workingman's party. The paper was called
Voices of Labor, and was put out by the Communist Party (the first time Ben
had heard the name); and it transpired that Bill, too, had left the Socialist
Party and helped found the Communist Party.

So what about the Communist Party? Grand words--but deeds? True, it was
born in struggle against the policies of the Socialist Party, which was all to
the good; but words, like birds, flew away when you tried to catch them.

They talked and debated and argued; Ben was tougher now, harder to convince. When the *Worker* came out as a weekly, he subscribed to it; no harm in
that; but he kept his mind unreconciled. His brother, who had also come North,
had joined the new Party, and also spent hours arguing with Ben. Ben put up
every argument he could think of, except the deepest one of all; the wound that
the SP had dealt him had never healed. Socialism equaled --or did it?--brother-
hood, but it was they, those who had called him "comrade" who had also asked
him to "understand" chauvinism.

But one day, in 1928, he was persuaded to go down to the Lyceum to listen
to a "real porch-climber" speak. The man's name--William Z. Foster--was quite
familiar to Pittsburghers; he had led the famous 1919 steel strike. Ben
listened, and the language of the man was instinct with struggle, with echoes
of mines and mills, of railroads and factories, this man, knew work and men
who worked!

When he was asked, then, to sign a card that brought him into the Communist Party, he did not refuse. . . .

But for the next two years he did little, attended few meetings. His
family was growing; he was busy at the work he knew so well. The revolutionary tides of the world tugged him only weakly. The country was riding a
boom, and nothing seemed more common than money.

In 1929 the smiling face of "prosperity" split wide open, and the sickness that had been growing like a cancer showed itself to the world. . . .

On March 6, 1930, Ben Careathers took a bundle of leaflets under his
arm and went downtown to hand them out to the unemployed workers. This leaflet had been issued by the Communist Party, and called for nationwide demonstrations against hunger and unemployment. Thousands came out on the streets
in Pittsburgh that day, and the police came with them. Ben was arrested,
taken to jail, and fined $10.

There was no turning back now, no arguments, no waiting-and-seeing.
Political struggle was to be his bread from now on. The depression forced
him to sell his shop, plunged him into the middle of the unemployed movement.

He was soon leading the demonstration of hungry at the Penn Station Courthouse to force recognition of the Unemployed Councils. He was in Chicago at
the first convention of the Unemployed Councils to set up a national organization. People were starving on a state "food-basket" grant of 90 cents a
week; and they fought bitterly to raise this to $1.50 a week! In cash, not
in baskets--and they won.

The way he threw himself into the struggle, passionately but without
losing his common sense, his easy-going ways, his courage or resourcefulness,
convinced the Party that he was equipped for a responsible post, and he became full-time secretary of the Allegheny Unemployed Councils. Then came the
Scottsboro case, and he fought to free the Alabama-framed. He went down into
the hills of West Virginia to set up soup kitchens for the striking miners
during the '31 strike. He marched to Washington, heading a Pennsylvania
contingent on the National Hunger March in 1932. That same year he first
met Steve Nelson who was leading, as he was leading, a state hunger march
group to Harrisburg.

He fought evictions--lugging the furniture back into the house from the
street where the Sheriff had dumped it. He fought for jobs for Negroes. He
helped eliminate the coal-and-iron police in Pennsylvania. He went to the
Soviet Union for three months and saw with his own eyes that land where the
workers ruled, and this sealed forever his conviction, profound as it then
was, that he had indeed found the right road, the inevitable road for his
people and for all American workers.

He was down in the books of the Mellons and Rockefellers and Morgans a
hundred times. Their police knew his face, his name, his voice. When, in
1940, he ran for lieutenant-governor of the state on the Communist ticket,
they pounced on this brazen act and intimidated dozens of workers who had
signed petitions to put Careathers on the ballot--and then indicted him, along
with 30-odd other Communist leaders of Western Pennsylvania, for "fraud" in
gathering petitions. They sent him and the others, among whom was Lloyd L.
Brown, to the jail which Brown was to describe in his novel *Iron City*. [62]

The war interrupted all this. Ben found a new situation when he came
out. The mills were booming day and night producing steel for the armies.
He threw himself into the struggle to convince the Negro workers that this
anti-Axis war was their war, too; and to do this he led the fight for upgrading
and hiring Negroes, breaking through Jim-Crow barriers at the huge Dravo Shipyards that built invasion barges for D-Day. And when the war ended, he
continued to fight for these objectives, even though this was no longer "popular" . . . in fact, seditious.

Now, the iron fist of U.S. imperialism showed itself openly. To Ben, it
was no surprise, that fist had never, even under the best circumstances, been
quite absent. Western Pennsylvania is the very heart of industrial America.
Here, the vast billionaire interests are anchored.

Ben reflected in himself that deep, almost folk wisdom, of the miners
and steel workers of this region, who know what they want . . . let the fine
words fall where they may! Western Pennsylvania has been *ruled* with an iron
fist always. The workers have learned both how to endure--to keep alive,
healthy, cheerful; and how, when the moment comes, to *strike*. Lightweights
cannot survive here. Workers will go about their business, in their own way,
living in the ways that the oppressed learn to live, moving slowly, or not
at all, exasperating the middle class theorists of social change.

They will not butt their heads pointlessly against iron walls, nor will
they, overwhelmed by oppression, turn over and die. . . .

They are wrong . . . those who meet Ben Careathers, misled by his calm
expression, his quick laugh, the radiance of his face. He is profoundly
typical of Pittsburgh! Those eyes, which have seen everything, are glowing
with hope! There is not a shred of illusion in the man--and not a trace of
pessimism. He is modest, but no intellectual from any Harvard, Yale or what-
have-you could outwit him or negate his knowledge. He is mild and gentle,
but like iron.

Misleading, as the prosecutor learned the day Ben took the stand to testify
for Steve Nelson during Nelson's first trial. The prosecutor knew how to
"handle" Negroes, he came up to Ben, and wagged his finger at him.

"Get back--*back!*" Ben snapped. The prosecutor was so startled he jumped
back four feet--and stayed there! In jail, he acts as though he is free and
the jailers are in jail. In court, he acts as though he were judging . . .

and the judge feels it, and struggles to convince the man that he should play the role assigned to him by the state!

On trial, he forgets that his life is in jeopardy, and demands the right to appear to testify in favor of FEPC! A man under indictment, nevertheless, he shows up in the midst of his enemies and denounces them and demands that a law be passed protecting the Negro people from discrimination in employment. His voice is free, and men who can slap him into jail any moment have to listen to him, and be persuaded. . . . For Ben's voice is the voice of the Negro and white workers of Pittsburgh, and try as they might--malign him as they do-- when he speaks, the enemies of the workers know that the oppressed speak through him. How to chain that voice too!

On August 17, 1951, they arrested him, along with Steve Nelson, Bill Albertson, Irving Weissman, James Dolsen, on the charge of conspiring to advocate and teach the violent overthrow of the United States government. Obviously, a man fighting for FEPC was conspiring overthrow!

They knew he was sick. They knew because the court-appointed doctor knew it, and knew he was very sick,but stated that he could continue the trial, nevertheless. Struggle had not left him untouched, tuberculosis, the disease of the oppressed, had taken hold of him. With almost open delight that its victim was also physically helpless, the court ordered Ben to leave the hospital and appear before it--even at the price of his life!

He walked--a 62-year-old man--slowly to the lectern in the courthouse so close to Mellon's great banks, Rockefeller's huge power, Morgan's gigantic mills and mines.

"My name," he said in a low, clear voice, "is Benjamin Lowell Careathers." He began to cough. The court watched him struggle to regain his strength. "I was born in the South. My life has been an open book. . . . My father was born a slave about 100 years ago. My mother died when I was very young. My father was left with nine small children to care for. I was the third of the nine, and it fell to my lot to look after the smaller ones and to work on the farm. In the winter months, after harvest, my father would chop wood and dig ditches for the white landlords. He took the older children to work with him and--"

The judge listened to the stool-pigeons and perjurers malign this man's life, cutting it to fit the pattern of "conspiracy." He was not interested in the halting story which this sick man was struggling to bring out. "This personal history," he interrupted, "is out of order." And so he dismissed with a wave a whole life's struggle . . . this story . . . the way the rulers dismiss the history as well as the lives of the people they oppress!

When I interviewed Ben Careathers in Pittsburgh, he told me in his soft voice: "I'm convinced that capitalism is responsible for the crimes I've seen in my life. If I don't live to see socialism--I want my children to. We tell a story in my family. My father's father was a slave--but, slave though he was, he never let his master whip his child. . . ."

He coughed cruelly for a moment, and then said: "My party--the Communist Party--is dearer to me than my life. It means what it says. Nothing will cause me to flinch--no matter what happens. For we'll win out in the end."

"We'll win out in the end. . . ."

And the tearing cough took possession of him and I sat still as he struggled with lungs that already were bleeding.

"They want to kill you!" I said, turning from those eyes full of courage and a belief so profound that it was his strength took with me, as though he had so much to give!

But to *you* . . . fight for this man! Yes, they want to lynch him "legally," and only the voice, the aroused voice of humanity can save him.

Masses and Mainstream, 6 (July, 1953): 34-44.

TOBACCO WORKERS

49. NEGRO-WHITE PICKETS MARCH IN RICHMOND

RICHMOND, Va., Aug. 7.--In one of the first solidarity actions of the
kind, more than 200 white clothing workers, members of the Amalgamated Clothing Workers of America, marched in a mass picket line Thursday around the
plant of the Export Leaf Tobacco Co. (Brown and Williamson) where 200 Negro
tobacco workers have been on strike since Monday.

Both groups of workers are relatively new to unionism--the clothing
workers having been organized, 800 strong, last year after the passage of the
Wagner Act. About the same time an organizational drive by the Southern Negro
Youth Congress brought about 3,000 Negro tobacco stemmers and laborers into a
union which later affiliated with the CIO.

The policy of Southern employers is to keep Negro and white labor
completely divided, either into separate branches of industry, or separate
departments, if working in the same plant. The same division has been maintained in the A.F. of L., where the policy of refusing to organize Negro
workers has been rigidly followed, with only an exceptional instance where
Jim Crow locals were set up.

But with the coming of the CIO, unity of Negro and white is now developing.
This mass demonstration of white workers, met joyfully by singing and clapping
Negro pickets, was the first experience of its kind for all who participated.

Earlier the ACWU local had voted to donate $50 for the strike.

Pays Wages $4 to $6 a Week

The strike is going strong, with union leaders maintaining a 24 hour
picket line, and appealing for support to the whole community. Last night a
15 minute broadcast was made over station WRTD by Dr. James E. Jackson, Jr.,
educational director of the union.

Among the other leaders of the strike are C. Columbus Alston, the Southern Negro Youth Congress leader, Francis Grandison, business agent, and
Edward E. Strong, Southern Negro Youth Congress general secretary.

The Export Leaf Tobacco Company is a subsidiary of Brown and Williamson
Tobacco Co., makers of Wings, Kool, and Raleigh brands. These brands carry
a union label issued by the International Tobacco Workers Union, A.F. of L.,
which has completely ignored the Negro workers employed on the preparation
and stemming of tobacco before it is ready for the cigarette machines. It is
well known that the white workers have little benefit from the union either
since their wages are generally lower than decent living standards require.
The union is run autocratically by E. Lewis Evans, who has refused to hold a
convention for the last 30 years, and has taken over all offices (president,
secretary and treasurer) for himself.

Daily Worker, August 8, 1938.

50. VICTORY OF NEGRO TOBACCO WORKERS JOLTS BOURBONISM

Wage Increases and Other Benefits Won In
Richmond Strike Where White and Negro
Pickets Marched Together

RICHMOND, Va., Aug. 21--The victory of 300 exploited Negro tobacco
workers in a strike against the powerful British-American Tobacco Co. in
which the workers' CIO union won wage increases and other benefits, struck a
vital blow to Southern Bourbonism.

The workers were engaged in the stemming and cleaning process of the
tobacco industry, the most grueling and unsanitary in the trade. The victory

concluded a three-weeks' strike.

Francis Grandison, business agent, and James Jackson, Jr., educational director, young Southern Negro leaders, led the Tobacco Stemmers and Laborers Local Industrial Union, CIO, to a successful fight against the combine.

Settlement of the strike, which was supported by the white workers in Richmond, was made on the basis of minimum demands presented by the union to Thomas B. Morton, Virginia Commissioner of Labor, who was attempting to mediate the dispute. The company capitulated on all but one of the many stipulations, and signed yesterday the contract drawn up by the union embodying these demands.

Wage Increases

The provisions pay increases for tobacco stemmers of from 1 to 2 cents a pound, on various grades of tobacco, averaging about $1.25 a week; 2½ cents per hour for men and women wage workers or about $1 a week, with time and a half for overtime; 26 cents a day increase in expense account on out of town hauls for chauffeurs; and special increases for firemen. Workers were previously paid as low as $4 to $6 a week at a time when the holding company of Export Leaf was paying over 21 per cent dividends.

The company will also check off union dues from wages upon written order of the worker; furnish the union with seniority lists to be used as a guide in priority of reemployment; furnish space on its bulletin board for union announcements; continue the grievance setup contained in the old contract, make any health improvements considered necessary; and provide 7 holidays with pay, 3 days vacation with pay for employers who have worked for the company 30 weeks or more, and a week's vacation for some workers on a merit basis.

Blow To Bourbons

The strike was epoch-making in many respects, chiefly in the blow it dealt the Southern Bourbons and their British and Wall Street financial allies in their most important industry, tobacco--the fortress of low wages, exploitation, race differentials, and the open shop. It represented equally striking a marked advance for Negro workers through their first venture in unionism in the South, and pointed up a brilliant set of rising young Negro leaders in the South who are the founders and directors of the union.

The struggle was won through unprecedented solidarity all down the line, illustrated by a picket line that massed at least 200 workers daily, and by a determination that twice voted to refuse minor concessions from the company even when the strikers were threatened with eviction and other hardships. Interracial solidarity, too, was demonstrated during the strike two weeks ago when 200 white Southerners from the Amalamated Clothing Workers marched en masses to the plant and strengthened the Negro picket line by their numbers and rousing enthusiasm. Support from other unions came in the form of contribution to the strike fund from other tobacco locals, the ILGWU, the Agricultural and Cannery Workers, the Newspaper Guild, locals of the American Federation of Teachers, the Amalgamated Clothing Workers, and others.

The victory of the union was especially significant in that Export Leaf is, along with Brown & Williamson Tobacco Co., a part of the giant industrial octopus of British-American Tobacco Co., which controls 100 subsidiaries in all parts of the world from Nazi Germany to New Zealand, and is controlled in turn by the Imperial Tobacco Co., English tobacco trust, and by the Duke family and other stockholders of the old American Tobacco Co.

"This does not represent, however, a climax, but a beginning," James Jackson, educational director, declared, "With this as a beginning, plans are being laid and a committee set up to launch an organizing drive throughout the tobacco industry in the Piedmont area of Virginia, North Carolina, and Kentucky. A start has already been made at Export Leaf and other factories in Southside Virginia by C. Columbus Alston, aggressive young Negro founder and representative of the Tobacco Locals, where workers in many plants are restless. The new Tobacco Workers Organizing Committee is also girding to force the tobacco trusts to abide by the Wage and Hours Law.

Funds to be used for these purposes will be received by Francis Grandison,

CIO Hall, 1201 W. Broad St., Richmond, Virginia, it was announced.

Daily Worker, August 22, 1938.

51. A NEW DEAL FOR TOBACCO WORKERS

By Augusta V. Jackson

Newly organized unions of Negro tobacco stemmers and laborers have won
four strikes, an eight hour day, wage increases totaling $300,000, and
brought about collective bargaining with managers who used to fire Negroes
for just walking into the office.

One of the most remarkable but little heralded advances in race and labor
relations has been brought about by three young CIO organizers among the Negro
tobacco workers in Richmond, Va.
"Evangels of John L. Lewis" was the title mockingly hurled at two young
labor organizers by the derisive and hostile press of the "open shop" town
in Eastern Virginia into which they ventured. Though famed for its tobacco
industries, the town was a sleepy place never rent by labor struggles or
disturbed by race friction. The status quo on the labor and the racial
fronts was maintained, as it is in many places of the South, by means of an
unobtrusive but complete suppression of all opposition by the political industrial combine that ruled the town. The toiling, illiterate, leaderless
Negroes had no conception of struggle. The wealthy, paternal factory owners
could not vision the possibility of discontent among their workers. They were
to be suddenly shaken when the advent of the CIO into the South substituted
the terms of written labor contracts for the vague "master and man" relationships that employers sought to maintain with their workers. The hostility
of the press was just an indication of the opposition that was to face the CIO
in forming labor unions among the thousands of hitherto unorganized Negro
stemmers and laborers in the tobacco factories.
I had already come into contact with the tobacco workers the night before
a strike meeting held in the basement of a church. Three hundred men and women,
tired and worn looking, and dressed in the pathetic and incongruous Sunday-
best of underpaid workers, had clapped and shouted approbation of the speaker
who had described the huddled conditions under which they worked. He had
spoken of the leaking roof at the factory, the damp, poisonous atmosphere,
the dim lighting. Each charge was greeted in the crowd of workers by loud
choruses of affirmation which became more hushed, but none the less emphatic
as he told how women had no dressing rooms except the shelter afforded behind
kegs and barrels in the factory—how in some instances they had to endure the
personal insults of foremen. There had been tremendous applause as he finished
his speech with a call for a New Deal in the South. Obviously the speaker was
not a tobacco worker; many of them still could not read or write. Virginia,
I remember having been told, is one of the six states having the lowest per
capita expenditure for public school education, and one of the eight states
with the lowest percentage of literacy.

A Union Meeting

The experience of that night remains vividly in my mind. They sang
spirituals and union songs all through the meeting. For one who has lived in
sophisticated city circles these old songs evoked a stirring comparison
between our slave forefathers who wrought these songs in the struggle with
their misery and these men and women who must still fight wage slavery. They
sang with a fervor I have seldom heard in the churches. Strains of "There's
a Bright Star Somewhere" and "Everytime I Feel the Spirit" mingled with the
Union song,
                    "Mr. Alston is our leader
                    We shall not be moved."
and with talk of higher wages, closed shop, and vacations with pay. Except

for this, the rapture and earnestness of the gathering was hardly distinguish-
able from that of a prayer meeting. The same confidence that God was with them
and would see them through, that there was a great day of victory coming prevailed. At the end a quiet little woman, a licensed preacher, she told me
later, and a thirty-year veteran of the tobacco factories got up to pray. She
asked God for the righteous victory of His servants; thanked Him for Mr. Alston,
the Moses sent to guide them through the wilderness, and for Mr. Grandison,
the Joshua who would lead them into battle. Then among the echoed Amens of
her fellow workers the strike meeting had adjourned.

The strike vote had been unanimously taken. I had witnessed the first
step. Tomorrow I would meet the "evangels;" I would visit factories and talk
with strikers.

Access to the factory was difficult. I had left behind the "Wall Street"
of Richmond and the rich shopping district. Here were dilapidated old houses
and numerous factories crowding down to the waterfront. A pungent, sweetish
odor was noticeable in the air becoming stronger and sickening as one approached
the James. At this point the river was much narrowed and filled with mud
flats; a dense cloud of smoke hung over it and choked the air. The tobacco
stemmery clung wearily to one bank. Through the small dark windows of the
red pile one could glimpse workers huddled around a table in the dark interior.

A whistle sounded for lunch, and the crowd poured out of a side door. It
was hard to recognize them as the men and women of the night before. I had
thought them poorly dressed then when they were in their Sunday-best. Now
they appeared in their everyday clothes--clothing worn to the last thread of
usefulness, frayed coats, torn dress, and broken hulls of shoes through which
the bare feet showed. Old and young, there was very little difference in
appearance or in dress. Here and there a daub of powder or a pair of earrings
betrayed its owner as some young girl, still in her teens perhaps, who only at
a second glance seemed any more youthful than the older women around her.

Francis Grandison, the "Joshua" of the night before was pointed out to me.
I hastened to meet him, eager to find what sort of personalities were behind
this stirring on the lowest levels of Southern industrial life. He talked
freely of the tobacco industry, the workers, of himself.

Much attention has been paid in recent years to the Negro in tenant-farm-
ing and in sharecropping where millions of them are the victims of drudgery
and poverty. Little, however, has been written and little known of the hundreds
of thousands exploited by the tobacco industry. The Piedmont area has grown
rich from the billions of cigarettes manufactured here each year. In the city
of Richmond, twenty billion were produced last year. Few industries are as
lucrative as tobacco, even in depression years. Few industries the world over
can cite profits comparable to those of the "Big Four" of tobacco; the makers
of Lucky Strikes (The American Tobacco Company), of Camels (R. J. Reynolds),
of Chesterfields (Liggett and Myers), and Old Gold (P. Lorillard). More than
any other industry tobacco employs a high percentage of Negro workers who are,
on an average, the lowest paid of any workers in the major industries of this
country. When we think of tobacco, we usually think of the agricultural
workers who farm it, and of the manufacture of cigars and cigarettes. Before
the tobacco leaf can be used for smoking, however, it must go through a processing. Here, in this rehandling, Negroes are employed almost exclusively as
stemmers and as laborers. The average wage paid them last year was a little
over six dollars a week--and in many factories hours have no top!

The Tobacco Stemmers' and Laborers' Industrial Union has become the medium
through which these workers voice their desire for higher wages, a shorter
working week, and for more tolerable working conditions. I had a chance to
see some of the pay envelopes in a Richmond factory--$4.45, $6.84, $5.00--
each a full week's wage for people who had families to feed.

Spontaneous Strike

As low as these wages are, they represent increases of from 33% to 50%
over the wages paid before the coming of the Union. The story of the building
of the seven functioning locals now in Richmond can be given here only in outline. In the spring of 1937, the great impetus given by the CIO to unionization within the basic industries had repercussions as far south as Richmond
where three hundred tobacco stemmers in the Carrington and Michaux plant undertook a spontaneous strike. At the time no unions had been organized any-

where among the tobacco stemmeries, and the workers were totally unacquainted
with the methods of collective bargaining. Prior to the strike they had not
even submitted their demands to the management. The walkout had been entirely
an undirected protest on the part of the workers against wages of three dollars
a week. Once the step was taken, they were uncertain where to turn.

For twenty-four hours they looked about for aid, first having their case
rejected as hopeless by American Federation of Labor officials, but at last
obtaining counsel from the leaders of the Southern Negro Youth Congress and
from a hastily formed Citizens' Committee. Within forty-eight hours negotiations were being carried on which brought the stemmers a satisfactory
percentage of wage increases, an eight-hour day, a forty-hour week, and recognition of their representatives as bargaining agents for the group. On the
heels of the Carrington and Michaux settlement, another walkout of four
hundred stemmers occurred at the I. N. Vaughn factory. At this time a bargaining apparatus had already been established, and again a contract hoisting
wages and reducing hours was signed.

The most signal victory of the year was at the Tobacco By-Products
Company, a chemical plant employing about two hundred Negro workers. Here the
struggle centered not so much around higher wages, for Tobacco By-Products
employees were better paid than the stemmers, as around job classification.
Most of the employees classified as "helpers" and "laborers" were in reality
engaged in such skilled capacities as machine operating and tending. A two
weeks' strike was successfully terminated with recognition of the skilled
workers and with consequent wage increases, with the granting of vacations
with pay, a forty-hour week, and guarantees of just compensation for overtime
work.

First Strike Since 1905

This dramatic struggle of Negro laborers for a subsistence wage becomes
more remarkable as we examine labor history. According to press reports the
Carrington-Michaux and the I. N. Vaughn strikes were the first in the tobacco
industry since 1905, and the first strike of any kind in Richmond since 1922.
In eighteen months time the Tobacco Stemmers' and Laborers' Industrial Union
has negotiated contracts for its locals on eight occasions. Four strikes
have been successfully conducted. The eight-hour day now prevails in the
unionized factories where formerly the working day was seldom shorter than
nine and often as long as fourteen hours. A total of approximately $300,000
in wage increases has been added to the purchasing power of the tobacco workers.
There are guarantees of increased pay for overtime and for holiday work. The
successes of the tobacco unions have stirred other ranks in the Richmond Community, and now among the under salaried teachers (some of whom earn less
than certain classes of tobacco workers) there is the nucleus of a chapter of
the American Federation of Teachers. Lastly, but not the least consideration,
is the fact that for the first time an organizational drive that is here to
stay, and that will reach and move the thousands of Negro stemmers and laborers
has penetrated the tobacco industry in one of its major strongholds.

The organization of the factories was a labor not easily done. For decades it was traditionally held that Negroes could not be organized into unions,
that they were scabs and strikebreakers. Even among the members themselves
there had been murmurs, "our people don't ever all pull together." Yet in the
Richmond Tobacco Unions, they have pulled together successfully, to their own
credit and to the credit of their young leaders.

Young Leadership

These young men have come into the labor movement through various paths,
each for a different reason. Francis Grandison, who acts as business agent
for the unions, it challenged, confesses that he is twenty-one, but cautious
that those few years cover a multitude of experiences. At fifteen or sixteen
he found himself cut adrift from his home where he had spent a sheltered boy-
hood, reading everything he could get his hands on from fiction to philosophy.
In search of work, curious about the world, he wandered over the eastern coast,
seeing life at its worst in the crowded flophouses of depression years, working
at odd jobs as waiter and busboy, always making friends among older associates
with whom he would talk, trying to probe the things he saw. He worked for

a while in the CCC camps; he found a place as clerk where he stayed and began to save money. He was settling to a steady life in the North. Then one day he revisited his old home, and was persuaded to stay. He was still very young; he returned to school, but his years of hard experiences, his long education in human misery unfitted him for this carefree environment. He was becoming bored and cynical. At that time the tobacco workers of Richmond had appealed to the public to help them organize. He feels that here among these people, in the fight against wage slavery, he has found a purpose to fill what was otherwise an empty life.

The others, C. Columbus Alston, who was responsible for organizing the Tobacco Union, and James E. Jackson, Jr., their educational director, are about twenty-three. Alston learned his first trade while he was still in his early teens. At sixteen he was on a job in the auto plants of Detroit, a member of the youth committee of the A.F. of L. United Workers Union, later participating in the first big strike in the auto industry. When he found employment at his own trade he was one of a handful of Negro coopers in the city. He was made secretary of Detroit's all-white Cooper's International Union, and made their delegate to the Central Trades and Labor Council where he was the youngest member.

He had just entered his twenties when John L. Lewis and the CIO launched the movement for industrial organization in the mass production industries and began to bring the message of labor unionization to the hitherto neglected workers of the South. Alston's experience in the Ford plants had convinced him how inadequate the craft unions were to represent the needs of thousands of workers in the auto industry. As a Negro he knew how rarely his people were accepted into the aristocratic ranks of the craft unions. His experience made him valuable to either section of the labor movement. He decided to transfer from the American Federation of Labor to the CIO, from Detroit to the South.

James Jackson, the third of the union leaders, university trained, brilliant, serious, tenacious, has not been a worker as have the others. His early years were spent studying, questioning, attempting to initiate reforms. He has never been satisfied with the clichés extant about the needs of the Negro and the problems of the South. What he learned in college and in the university only made him more than before aware of the need for widespread social and economic readjustments in the South. Wherever he lived or studied, there was soon a study group or a nucleus of liberal thought forming about him. By profession he is a pharmacist. Most of his spare time is spent with the unions, or in speaking and writing for their cause. Like his young associates, he makes no mention of personal ambitions. Their aim is to see the whole tobacco industry unionized; until then they will not cease their efforts, and now there is no end in sight.

These young men are known to thousands of the working population of Richmond. They are personally loved by the three thousand members of the Tobacco Unions, and respected by the general citizenry. The recent strike of the Negro tobacco stemmers and laborers successfully carried through at the Export Leaf Tobacco Company placed these personalities involved, however, was the revelation brought about by the strike of the vast significance of a labor movement among Negroes in the South.

Wage Increase Won

Briefly, the strike began in August when workers of the Export Leaf Company, two hundred men and women who had been living on the margin of neces- sity, at weekly wages of five and six dollars, presented a new contract to their management. They had been organized just the year before, and they had already negotiated for shorter hours and better working conditions. For months they had eagerly followed press reports on Wages and Hours Bill, and had voted to incorporate in their next contract the ten dollar minimum wage provided by the law.

As yet the management of the Export Leaf Company had had no labor trouble involving a stoppage of work. The concern is a part of Brown and Williamson Company and a subsidiary of the powerful British American tobacco trust, with branches both here and abroad. Despite the fact that the Export Leaf Company's stemmers were among the lowest paid in the city, the management undoubtedly counted on its strength to discourage strikes. The victory at the Export Leaf

Company was the hardest won in the short history of Richmond's Tobacco Unions.
The company threatened to close its doors, and ship its tobacco elsewhere, and
frightened city officials offered to intervene to end the walkout. On the
other hand, public opinion was behind the strikers, and their fellow unions
helped to contribute to their support both morally and financially. During
the eighteen days of the strike food was distributed to the families of the
strikers through the union, and pressing debts and rent problems were skill-
fully managed by the union leadership. It was impossible to break the morale
of the strikers. When a settlement was made the demands of the union were
met. A minimum wage of twenty-five cents an hour for women and thirty-five
cents an hour for men was established; vacations with pay and seniority rights
were granted, and a "check off" system under which the management check off
monthly dues from the wages of union employees and pays the total collection
to the financial secretary of the union. In the absence of a closed shop
agreement, the "check off" system is invaluable to the life of a Union.

At approximately the same time, while these workers rejoiced that President Roosevelt was behind them, the Tobacco Association of the United States,
a convention of tobacco executives assembled. Instead of the usual conference
on internal conditions in the industry, the important problem for consideration
was means of securing exemption in tobacco rehandling from the new minimum
wage scales. With an appeal to public sentiment on the grounds that the
industry hires older workers whom other industries would discharge, and with
a threat that they may displace thousands of laborers by introducing machinery,
the tobacco magnates have publicized their plans for a war against the ten
dollar minimum.

Over 20,000 Negroes families depend for existence upon work in the tobacco
industry. Much is in the balance in this conflict for the welfare of the race
in the tobacco areas. The building of the unions brings a hope of ending the
long existent exploitation of Negro workers in the tobacco industry. But the
manufacturers have indicated that they are prepared for a fight to maintain
the fabulous profits of the world's largest tobacco industries. Is it possible
that, through the combine of powerful magnates, the vast industries of the South
will remain unchanged in this era of labor unionization and of labor legislation?

Public Support Needed

The answer must come from the people of the South themselves, not only
the tobacco workers, but also the white and Negro citizens of each industrial
community. These workers have been silent for decades; they fill the slums
of their cities; many are illiterate; few are voters. A drive for unionization among them will need the strength of public opinion behind it, for the
press of industrial cities is not theirs but the manufacturers. In Richmond
the tobacco workers are trying to prepare themselves. They look to the Union
for the fraternization and education they have missed all their lives. They
have asked for elementary classes at night; their interest has extended to
citizenship rights, and they want to be ready to register and vote. The
Richmond community, too, has undergone a great lesson in cooperation. During
the strike of the Export Leaf Tobacco Company, the community, though unused
to strikes and somewhat timorous of them gave generously to support the strikers.
The churches of Richmond were foremost in volunteering assistance, and making
appeals for the workers in their Sunday services. Even white Richmond was
friendly, and for the first time in the state's history, white union members
from a clothing factory, three hundred strong, picketed with the Negro strikers.

This process of re-education is perhaps too new to make deepseated changes,
but its effects are visible everywhere. Managers of the factories survey the
new situation somewhat perplexedly. They have been won only gradually to bargain in good faith with the representatives of their workers. For years they
have not considered the workers in their employ as men like themselves. Now
they face these men and women across the conference table to discuss conditions of employment with them. One factory owner was overheard saying after
such a conference, "Times certainly have changed; I remember when I used to
fire a nigger for just walking into my office."

There is every evidence that the next few months will see even greater
changes. The strike at the Richmond factory of the Export Leaf Tobacco Company,
a gigantic concern with branches throughout the Piedmont area, emphasized the

need for unionization in the entire tobacco industry. The CIO, accordingly, has recently established a Tobacco Workers Organizing Committee under the leadership of Richmond's union leaders, James E. Jackson, Jr., Francis Grandison, and C. Columbus Alston. Their objective is the complete organization of every factory of the tobacco industry in Virginia, North Carolina, Kentucky, and Eastern Tennessee. The situation described in Richmond will be met in dozens of other communities during the drive. The drive will require time, money, organizing genius, and tenacity. For the organization of Negro workers in the heart of the South will be a difficult task. If we are to hold, however, any hope of seeing a regenerated South, this must be one of the paths to it.

The Crisis, 45 (October, 1938): 322-24, 330.

52. THE MAKING OF MAMMA HARRIS

She was a scrawny hardbitten little woman and she greeted me with that politely blank stare which Negroes often reserve for hostile whites or prying members of their own race.

I had been directed to her tenement in Richmond's ramshackle Negro section by another woman, a gray-haired old grandmother whose gnarled hands had been stemming tobacco for five decades.

"The white folks down at union headquarters is all right," she had said, "and we love 'em--especially Mr. Marks. But if you want to know about us stemmers and the rumpus we raised, you better go see Mamma Harris. She's Missus CIO in Richmond."

The blank look softened on the thin dark face when I mentioned this.

"Must've been Sister Jones," she said, still standing near the door. "They all call me Mamma though. Even if I ain't but forty-nine and most of 'em old enough to be my grandmammy."

I edged toward a rocking chair on the other side of the bed.

"I'm a CIO man myself," I remarked. "Newspaper Guild. Our local boys just fixed up The Times-Dispatch this morning."

She yelled so suddenly that I almost missed the rocker.

"Bennie!" she called toward the kitchen, "you hear that, Bennie? CIO's done organized The Dispatch. Moved right in this morning. What I tell you? We gonna make this a union town yet!"

A hulking overalled Negro appeared in the kitchen doorway. His booming bass voice heightened his startling resemblance to Paul Robeson.

"Dispatch?" he thundered. "God Amighty, we do come on."

Mrs. Harris nodded in my direction.

"He's a CIO man from up New York. Wants to know about our rumpus out at Export. He's a Guilder too, just like the white 'uns."

Benny limped toward the other chair.

"They give us hell," he said, "but we give it right back to 'em. And it was we'uns who come out on top. The cops was salty. Wouldn't even let us set down and rest. But I told the women, I told 'em 'Sit down' and they did. Right in front of the cops too. Didn't I, Louise?"

Mrs. Harris nodded energetically from her perch on the bed.

"You dead did. And they didn't do nothing neither. They 'fraid of the women. You can outtalk the men. But us women don't take no tea for the fever."

Bennie boomed agreement. "There was five hundred of the women on the picket line and twenty of us mens. But we sure give 'em hell. I talked right up to them cops, didn't I, Louise? Didn't I?"

Finally Mrs. Harris got around to the beginning.

"I wasn't no regular stemmer at first," she cried, "but I been bringing a shift somewhere or other since I was eight. I was took out of school then and give a job minding chillun. By the time I was ten I was cooking for a family of six. And I been scuffling ever since.

"But I don't work in no factory till eight years ago. Then I went out to Export. Well, it took me just one day to find out that preachers don't know nothing about hell. They ain't worked in no tobacco factory."

Bennie was smiling to himself and gazing at the ceiling.

"Them cops beat up them strikers something awful out at Vaughn's he said. "They even kicked the women around. But they didn't do it to us, huh, Louise?" We stood right up to 'em."

Mrs. Harris waved aside the interruption.

"Then there was this scab," she went on, "only he ain't no scab then, cause we don't have no union. We ain't even heerd of no union nowhere then, But I knew something was bound to happen. Even a dog couldn't keep on like we was. You know what I make then? Two dollars and eighty cents a week. Five dollars was a too bad week."

"I put in eighty-two and half hours one week," Bennie said, "and they only give me $18.25. I think about this one day when one of them cops . . ."

Mrs. Harris shushed him.

"Now this scab—only he ain't no scab then—he rides me from the minute I get to Export. He's in solid with the man and he always brag he's the ringtail monkey in this circus. He's a stemmer like the rest of us but he stools for the white folks.

"There's two hundred of us on our floor alone and they only give us four and a half and five cents a pound. We don't get paid for the tobacco leaf, you know. You only get paid for the stems. And some of them stems is so puny they look like horse hair."

Bennie was chuckling softly to himself but a glance from Mrs. Harris held the cops at bay for the moment.

"And as if everything else wasn't bad enough, there was this scab. We's cramped up on them benches from kin to can't, and he's always snooping around to see nobody don't pull the stem out the center instead of pulling the leaf down both sides separate. This dusts just eats your lungs right out you. You start dying the day you go in."

She coughed automatically and continued.

"Well, I keep this up for six long years. And this scab is riding me ever' single day. He's always riding everybody and snitching on them what don't take it. He jump me one day about singing and I ain't got no voice nohow. But I like a song and I gotta do something to ease my mind or else I go crazy.

"But he jump me this morning and tell me to shut up. Well, that's my cup. Six years is six years, but this once is too often. So I'm all over him like gravy over rice. I give him a tongue-lashing what curled every nap on his head."

For a moment she had the same beaming look which Bennie displayed when he spoke of the cops.

"I sass him deaf, dumb and blind, and he takes it. But all the time he's looking at me kinder queer. And all at once he says 'You mighty salty all of a sudden; you must be joining up with this union foolishness going on around here.'

"You coulda knocked me over with a Export stem. I ain't even heard of nothing about no union. But as soon as he cuts out, I start asking around. And bless my soul if they ain't been organizing for a whole full week. And I ain't heerd a peep."

"I ain't heerd nothing neither then," Bennie put in, "and I been there fifteen years."

Mrs. Harris caught another breath.

"Well, I don't only go to the next meeting downtown, but I carries sixty of the girls from our floor. They remember how I sass this scab and they're all with me. We plopped right down in the first row of the gallery. And when they asked for volunteers to organize Export, I can't get to my feet quick enough."

"I come in right after," Bennie remarked.

"And it ain't no time," Mrs. Harris continued, "before we got seven hundred out of the thousand what works in Export. The man is going crazy mad and the scab is snooping overtime. But they can't fire us. The boom time is on and the warehouse is loaded to the gills."

She paused dramatically.

"And then on the first of August, 1938, we let 'em have it. We called our strike and closed up Export tight as a bass drum."

Bennie couldn't be shushed this time.

"The cops swooped down like ducks on a June bug," he said, "but we was

ready for 'em. I was picket captain and there was five hundred on the line.
And all five hundred was black and evil."

Mrs. Harris was beaming again.

"Then this scab came up with a couple hundred others and tried to break
our line," she recalled, "but we wasn't giving a crip a crutch or a dog a bone.
I made for that head scab personal--but the cops wouldn't let me at 'im."

"I stayed on the line for twenty-four hours running," Bennie chuckled,
"and I didn't take a inch from none of them cops."

"And we wasn't by ourselves neither," Mrs. Harris went on. "The preachers,"
Dr. Jackson, the Southern Aid Society and all the other union people help us.
GWU and them garment ladies give us a hundred dollars right off the bat. Mal-
gamate sent fifty. The ship folks down in Norfolk come through, and your
white Guild boys give ten dollars too."

"It was them white garment ladies what sent the cops," Bennie cut in.
"They come out five hundred strong and parade around the factory. They got
signs saying 'GWU Supports Export Tobacco Workers.'

"Them cops jump salty as hell. 'White women,' they say, 'white women out
here parading for niggers.' But they don't do nothing. Because we ain't taking no stuff from nobody."

"We was out eighteen days," Mrs. Harris said, "and the boss was losing
money hand over fist. But you know how much we spend in them eighteen days?
Over seven hundred dollars."

Her awed tones made it sound like seven thousand.

"But it was worth it. We win out and go back getting ten, eleven and
twelve cents a pound. And better still we can wear our union buttons right out
open. We might even have got them scabs fired if we wanted, but we didn't
want to keep nobody out of work."

Bennie stopped smiling for the first time.

"We might be better off if we did," he said soberly. "I bet we do next
time."

Mrs. Harris explained.

"They been sniping away at us ever since we win. They give the scabs all
the breaks and lay off us union people first whenever they can. They give all
the overtime to the scabs and even let 'em get away with stripping the stem
down the center. But we ain't licked yet. We still got two hundred members
left and we still got union conditions."

Her face brightened again.

"And we fixed that old scab--even if he is been there nineteen years. We
moved him off our floor completely, and he ain't allowed to ride nobody.

"We got a good set of people downtown now and we're reorganizing right
along. By the time our new contract comes up in June, we'll probably have the
whole thousand."

"And if we strike again, and them cops jump salty,"--Bennie began.

And this time Mamma Harris let him pursue the subject to his heart's
content.

                                                            TED POSTON

The New Republic, 103 (November 4, 1940): 624-26.

53. SOUND ADVICE FROM AN OLD COLORED BROTHER ON UNIONS

By James E. Jackson, Jr.

An old man with a sparkle in his eyes and a young fellow about twenty-
three were earnestly engaged in heated conversation in the back row of a
meeting of Local Union No. 31 of the Tobacco Stemmers and Workers Industrial
Union. Columbus Alston, negro Committee for Industrial Organization organizer
had just spoken. Workers in the audience were now filling the aisles of the
Leigh Street M.E. Church, where the meeting was being held, slowly filing up
to the secretary's table, paying their initiation fee and signing membership
cards.

Unobserved, I took a seat in front of the old man and listened intently.

"So your jes'gonna be workin' wid us a li'l while, Jim. You say you are going in business fo' yo'self an' soon get rich. An you gon' give yo' money to solve de problem of de po' after you become rich? Well, tis very brave of you to think like dat, Jim, but I'se afraid you ain't bein' very realistic.

"Lissen to me boy, de cards has all been shuffled and dealt long befo' we got into de game. Dere ain't no new gold mines to be found, Jim. You cain't start no new business widout big money; you cain't get dis cap'til 'cept by borrowin' it from men's who own it, and dese men ain't goin' len' it to you to use against them, or to invest and make money for you'self that they could be making. Now, Jim, we done tried it befo'--dat is, yo' people has. 'Member Anthony Overtone? Why, he was the greatest pretender to a rich man our whole people could boast of, an' along come the depression (when de big fellows took all from de smaller big fellows)--an'--shoo!--our fondes' hopes of escape into de ranks of de bosses jes' went kerplunk. No, Jim, Mr. Alston done said 95 per cent of our people are wage workers. The five per cent business men can't grow because they ain't no more room in de house of Morgan to let 'em in.

"We is a po' people, Jim, we's a race of workers. De one thing we own is our labor--and dat ain't enough. We got to organize; we got to jine wid millions of whites in a fix jes' like us; we got to unite our labor in one mighty union--our only economic weapon, our one hope for freedom and equality. I done thought about dis thing for a long time, Jim. An' now it's here. All we gotta do is jine and study an' learn all dey says. 'Cause we's buildin' somethin,' Jim, bigger'n me an' you an' any of us. One day dis south gonna be a fittin place fo' a mans young 'uns to grow in. 'Tis gon' be beautiful an' healthy an' free an' kind, Jim, an' we's on our way. Yassah, an' we's helpin to make it wid our own hands. Go on, Jim. Sign up boy; dey's a new day, and a new day's a comin soon."

United Mine Workers Journal, April 15, 1938.

BLACK SEAMAN

54. NEGRO, WHITE STAND SOLID IN DOCK STRIKE

Maritime Union Backs 8,000 Longshoremen
In Southern Ports

JACKSONVILLE, Fla., Oct. 18--Eight thousand striking longshoremen continued to bottle up nine ports from Wilmington, N.C., to Tampa, Fla., today in one of the biggest walkouts in recent years.

Initiated by rank-and-file firm today despite efforts of shipping lines, merchant and representatives of Joseph P. Ryan, reactionary union head, to effect a "truce."

The longshoremen are demanding recognition, higher wages, and eight-hour day and time and a half for overtime for its members, many of them Negroes, in the ports of Wilmington, Charleston, S.C., Savannah and Brunswick, Ga., and Jacksonville, Miami, Ft. Pierce, Port Everglades and Tampa, Fla.

Will Stay Out For Pact

A contract between the International Longshoremen's Association and the shippers expired Sept. 30 and the walkout began last Saturday following the breakdown of negotiations.

V. E. Townsend, Southern representative of the union, conferred tonight with business spokesmen, who attempted to have a "truce" called "which would permit handling of cargo to be resumed" during negotiations.

Local rank-and-file leaders declared vehemently that they would oppose any such move, and that the strikers would remain out until the shippers grant the demands.

Strikebreakers were being used to work two Clyde-Mallory ships in Miami, and an official of the line said all of its sailings out of New York and Miami for Charleston, Jacksonville, Key West and Tampa had been "cancelled until further notice."

Both white and Negro dock workers stood shoulder to shoulder in these deep-South ports, ready to defy either the police, shipping lines or sell-out maneuvers of the Ryan machine from its New York City headquarters.

Meanwhile the National Maritime Union, organization of 47,000 unlicensed seamen on the Atlantic and Gulf coasts, also with main offices in New York, pledged its support to the 8,000 rank and file longshoremen now on strike in six southern ports for wage increases and overtime pay.

Joseph Curran, general organizer for the N.M.U., announced that the seamen in the struck ports had agreed to move no ships, loaded or unloaded by strikebreakers.[63]

This action, he pointed out is in line with union policy since the rank and file seceded from the International Seamen's Union last spring and set up its own union.

"We are now following the general policy adopted by the principal CIO unions," Curran said. "With the rise of industrial unionism, the desire of rank and file trade unionists to cooperate with one another in winning their demands can now be fulfilled.

"In the event that scabs are put aboard the ship to handle cargo, the crews will, in all likelihood, refuse to work with them.

"Of course, if the company wishes to move a ship to another port, we have no alternative but to take her out--providing, that the lines are not released by scabs.

"However, if the seamen move a ship to another port, we will be sure that a telegram is sent ahead to the destination notifying the longshoremen there the reason for the move.

"In a case of that kind, undoubtedly the striking longshoremen will call upon their fellow longshoremen in the next port to refuse to load or unload the ship."

Daily Worker, October 19, 1937.

55.   LABOR GAINS ON THE COAST:

A report on the integration of Negro workers
into the maritime unions of the Pacific
Coast states.

By Ford Bellson

San Francisco is the metropolis of the West, and towers over the two other large urban centers of the Pacific Coast, Los Angeles and Seattle. The rapid growth of San Francisco has been stimulated by the industrial and commercial economy that has become the life of the city by "The Golden Gate."

The people of San Francisco have profited with the growing business developments of the shipping industry that now thrives at the "western gateway" to America. Perhaps nowhere in America are wages as high as they are here, and it is the boast that the working conditions are the best in the country. This situation, however, cannot be attributed so much to the wealth of the city or to the interests that control its capital, as to the strong trade union movement among San Francisco's workers. This movement has not been easily and peacefully established, but is the result of a long struggle among the mass of workers, who have waged a vigilant battle to mature their organizations into powerful weapons for their own protection. Negroes, although they constitute but a small portion of the State's population, have played an important role in the development of this trade union unity. They are enlisted in every large A.F. of L. Union that does not maintain jim crow practices,

They have taken a prominent role in the formation and guidance of the unions, occupying many positions of trust and responsibility, and governing the employment of many thousands of workers, both Negro and white.

Among the Negroes who occupy such positions at present are Lem Greer, Joe White and C. Richardson, officers of the Executive Committee and the Board of Trustees of the mighty International Longshoremen's and Warehousemen's Union, Locals 1-10; and Reveals Cayton, business agent of The Marine Cooks' and Stewards' Union, and a trustee of the Marine Federation; Alex Forbes, business agent of The Musicians' Union; Pat Slater, a member of the executive board of the Building Trades Laborers' Union; and Alex Waters, a dispatcher in the hiring hall of the International Longshoremen's and Warehousemen's Union.

The present encouraging status of the Negro in the San Francisco trade union movement has come as a result of militant activity for equality for Negro workers on the part of both Negro and white trade unionists. The effectiveness of this struggle was clearly evidenced in the recent successful fight for checkerboard (Negro and white) crews on all ships that sail out of the port. This activity was initiated by the Marine Cooks' and Stewards' Union, and had the backing of most of the other union groups.

The whole question of equality of employment opportunities for Negroes on ships touching the West Coast came up during the general strike of 1934. Prior to that time only a few Negro seamen were affiliated with the Marine Cooks' and Stewards' Union. The majority of those that were organized at all were associated with the Colored Marine Benevolent Association. This organization was controlled by the Pacific Steamship Company, now known as the Dollar Lines. The conditions under which the men worked and the manner in which they were exploited were almost beyond belief. They were constantly harassed, and penalized for the slightest offense. There was no means of redress for grievances. They worked from 16 to 18 hours a day, and sometimes longer. Various forms of "kickbacks" cut into their meager pay. In order to keep their jobs, they were practically forced to gamble away portions of their salaries. "Cuts" from such games were palmed off to the individuals in control of the organization and others who possessed an "in" with petty officials. Another form of kickback took the form of forced drinking; the workers were coerced into buying a certain amount of the bad liquor that was sold to them on shipboard each payday, at exorbitant prices. Negro workers who rebelled against these conditions were threatened with the loss of their jobs. and from time to time a "bad Negro" would be discharged as an example to the others.

In 1934, during the strike of seamen on the Pacific Coast, about 500 Negro workers joined the picket lines just when the shipping companies were trying to get them to sign up as "scabs." As a reward for their help in winning the strike, they were later taken en masse into the Marine Cooks' and Stewards' Union. Their new affiliation not only guaranteed them better conditions of work, but gave them definite assurance that they would always have racial representation in the counsels of the union, with a minimum of two official positions at all times. The two positions now held are as business agents for the union's offices in the ports of Seattle and San Francisco.

With the enrolling of Negroes in the Marine Cooks' and Stewards' Union, several lines tried to take punitive action against the Negro union members, hoping thereby to demoralize the racial unity. Some refused to hire Negroes in any capacity. The union elected a committee of five, two of whom were Negroes, to study this problem. The committee made the following recommendations:

(1)   That equal shipping rights be established regardless of race to all members of the Marine Cooks and Stewards on *all ships*, and

(2)   That seniority rights be established; the oldest membership card to receive the first job *regardless of race and regardless of the ship*.

As a result of this stand, "checkerboard crews" were literally forced upon the ship operators. And today on all freighters and steamschooners, as well as on the American President Lines, Negroes are being placed as members of the crews.

The contracts of 1934, won by the striking seamen, bettered the conditions of all seamen, but the effect of the contracts was felt more by the Negro workers than by the white ones. They had gained protection by a strong union, in which were Negro representatives to handle any cases of discrimination that might take place either on the ships or in the hiring halls. Their working hours had been cut to nine a day, and they had established a grievance committee to prevent the subtle forms of exploitation under which they had previously suffered.

In 1936, the contracts were opened for negotiation instead of being renewed as in 1935. This resulted in a new maritime strike. By this time the Negro workers were deeply entrenched in the union. They took an active part in protecting their rights as workers, and enlisted the help of the entire Negro community in the struggle.

The strike was caused by the desire of the workers to maintain the system of hiring men through the union's hiring halls, rather than placing their employment security in the hands of the shipping concerns. They also wanted an eight-hour day, both for men aboard ships and for longshoremen; and cash payment for overtime worked at sea, instead of time off in port.

The first point was of particular importance to Negro workers, for the union-controlled hiring halls preserved the seniority rights of all seamen and longshoremen regardless of race, and prevented discrimination against Negro workers. The eight hundred Negro seamen and longshoremen employed on the Pacific Coast struck along with all the white unionists. They were on the picket lines as rank and filers, and also occupied leading positions of trust on the strike committees that guided the actions of the unions during the crisis. Fifteen Negroes were on the longshoremen's strike committee. Negroes also served on the strike committees of the Marine Cooks' and Stewards' Union, the Miscellaneous Workers' Union and the Bargemen's Union. The Joint Strike Committee, which controlled the action and decisions of all the smaller committees, included three Negroes, Joe White, Reveals Cayton and George Novelle.

The attitude of the maritime unions to the Negro worker was clearly shown during this strike by the positions of leadership accorded Negro workers. Since 1934, when the Maritime Cooks' and Stewards' Union had opened its doors, the others had followed suit. The Negro had been accepted in nearly all the maritime unions, had been assured of equal protection as a worker, and had functioned in various official capacities in the various union groups. An encouraging outgrowth of this situation has been a strong trade union movement, one that recognizes the need for unity among all workers, in other fields of work. This movement still has a long way to go, but each month brings new victories against Labor Jim Crow on the West Coast, the latest being in the Painters' Union of the A.F. of L., where a Negro was admitted recently after many months of agitation and the restrictive racial term "white" was erased from the constitution and by-laws of the local.

Opportunity, 17 (May, 1939): 142-43.

56.   SHOULD THE "FORGOTTEN MEN OF THE SEA" STAY ASHORE?

By Robert C. Francis

In an enlightening and interesting article in the April *Opportunity,* Mr. S. A. Haynes, of the Philadelphia Tribune, tells us of the plight of Negro seamen in many of the seaports of the world. We must concur with Mr. Haynes in most of his analysis and, as he has indicated, the majority of these ex-seamen who "are now eking out a miserable existence as underpaid longshoremen and habitues of the waterfront" . . . "constitute an integral part of the world's social and economic order." It is true that there is injustice in the black seamen's "ostracism from the high seas," but whether or not the matter is worthy of challenge is highly problematical. The discussion of this problem gives rise to some fundamental and worthwhile questions which involve the future outlook for seagoing persons. It is a questionable fact that the sea as a calling now offers the opportunity for the ex-sailor that is presented even by the most menial jobs ashore. The condition of the seamen is slowly being improved and the outcome of the Geneva Maritime Conference of last year may, at some later date, find them on a basis more comparable to that of other workers. The credit for much of this must go to "The Old Man of the Sea," Andrew Faruseth, President of the International Seamen's Union, who has been fighting the battle since the days of "crimping" and "shanghaing ." Yet the working conditions with which sailors are forced

to contend, are still abominable and this is conclusively demonstrated by the
fact that labor turn-over on American ships is in the neighborhood of 25 or
30 per cent. Those who have followed the history of the Morro Castle disaster,
realize that such things occur as a result of "hiring inexperienced men at low
wages." In the ranks of the white longshoremen of the country, one may find
more and better sailors than those who are now in our Merchant Marine and
passenger service for the reason that they have become disgusted with the
virtual slavery that exists while aboard ship.[64]

Today, ships are operated by crews who learned their seamanship like
Gilbert and Sullivan's "Admiral of the Queen's Navee,"--"Post Card Sailors,"
--the "old Salts" call them. They go to sea with a new suitcase and buy post-
cards at each port to send to their friends back home. Many of them are irresponsible boys in quest of adventure, or older individuals of like degree.[65]

Mr. Haynes says: "Three decades ago, when ocean travel was not the
lucrative enterprise it is now; when the great clippers and sailing vessels
of the seven seas were at the height of their glory; when ocean liners were
yet in swaddling bands, and cargo contracts, smuggling and contraband were
the chief sources of revenue; steamship companies in Europe, the Americas and
Africa took pleasure in signing on Negro crews--the Negro seaman was a welcome
guest at shipping offices and in all ports of commerce and trade;" but, as a
poet has said, "Earth will not see such ships as those again." He might have
added: "Neither will it see such sailors."

An interesting observation is that the decline in the use of Negro seamen
is parallel with the decline in the use of the sailing vessel. There is here
an implicit tribute to the Negro seaman. Notice the fact that with the decrease in the amount of skill, courage and physical ability occasioned by the
ascendancy of the steam-vessel, there has been a decrease in the demand for
the black sailor. In the days of wooden ships and iron men, the Negro seaman
was to be seen in any seaport, but in these days of wooden men and iron ships,
the demand for the easier, less hazardous jobs has so increased that the
colored man is forced out by competition. Surely it is a compliment to the
Negro that when the going was hard, he was in demand, but as it became easier,
he was replaced by others.

The black seaman did not quit the sea for the same reason old tars of
other races have. As Mr. Haynes so aptly shows, he was forced to become a
"landlubber," while less experienced and less capable workers were given the
jobs. Had economic pressure not motivated the change, he would probably have
continued to "go down to the sea in ships" because it is harder for him to find
decent work ashore.

The question is: Has he gained or lost? In the first place, it must be
recalled that no group has been more affected by progress than has the sea-
faring class. The seaman who was once the original "Jack-of-all-trades" is
now merely a sea-going laborer. In the days of the sailing vessel, it had
been necessary to go aloft in a storm and repair rigging or do a number of
other most dangerous tasks. A sailor could mend a pair of shoes or do a multitude of similar things in a facile manner. Today, however, cleaning and
scrubbing consume most of his time and his other duties are not much more involved. That is the reason the result is sometimes disastrous when an emergency does arise on a ship in mid-ocean. The greater percentage of present-
day sailors are not sailors--they are workers on board ships. This is not
true of some foreign countries which still train sailors in the old-time way.
Sailors are still more subject to the whims of their superiors than are any
other laboring group because of the very nature of work on shipboard. If
they are abused by their superiors, they cannot quit until they get in port,
and that hinges upon the articles under which they have been signed on. A
Negro in a crew now has a more difficult time than formerly because it was
skill and ability that made him respected by his shipmates; while now, he is
just another laborer--and a black one at that. Of course, we realize it presents the oppressed seamen of other races with the opportunity to feel superior to someone else.

In view of the foregoing, it were probably the better part of valor for
the black man to stay away from marine occupations.

Another entirely different aspect of the whole question is the relationship of the sailor to the family unit. The position of the families of
steadily employed laborers in our industrial system is none too secure. Very
few of them make enough to support a group of five on a health and decency
standard.

The average sailor has never made sufficient wages to support any kind of a family. This is the main reason why many of them do not marry. Hence, it might be for his improvement that the Negro has forsaken the sea. In the case of those sailors who have taken upon themselves the responsibility of a family, many of these families are forced to supplement their income in other ways. Much the same thing is true of the families of seamen as is true of those of longshoremen. The "wife toiling at underpaid employment to keep her home, but finally losing strength and hope, and letting her family drift to improvidence and misery; and the children ill-nourished and ill-cared for, driven into blind alley employment and forming as they grow up, a new generation of casuals."

Beyond the inadequate income is the truism that a sailor is not a good husband. He is not, because he must, of necessity, spend most of his time away from home. The man may have all of the attributes that are necessary for the successful carrying out of the role of husband, but the fact that he is absent so much means that companionship is lacking. One of the most necessary elements for successful family life is companionship. A seaman is really a stranger to his family. Indeed, there are grounds for arguing that they (the seamen), should not marry. This being the case, one may wonder if the Negro seaman has lost so much in being barred from the sea. Mayhap this is an example of discrimination that will be to the advantage of the race.

Most of the romance and beauty left the sea when the famous Clippers were replaced by steamships. No modern vessels can compare in grandeur with such famous vessels as the "Sovereign of the Seas," or the greatest Clipper of them all, "The Northern Light." The Negro left the sea at the time when the Clippers left--he took a conspicuous role in the days of glory and daring. During these early days, there were Negro skippers in charge of well-known sailing vessels. An example of this is the case of Captain Shorey, who was in command of one of the best-known whalers that sailed out of San Francisco Bay. He shipped an entire Negro crew. Today, what chance does a black man have to get into a cabin, except to clean it? All things considered, is it not better that we look away from the sea?

A bit more of subjective observation may be excused at this time. These comments were written because of a definite interest aroused by Mr. Haynes's article. The above analysis comes as a result of conclusions occasioned by some study of seamen in the United States generally and those of the Pacific Coast in particular.

It is hoped that these observations will be provocative of further discussion which may prove to be instructive. Seamen, like longshoremen, have not been subjected to economic and sociological discussions as have other groups of workingmen. There is a definite need for such study because it is as the result thereof that the conditions of laborers are improved. (For instance, it was Upton Sinclair's book, "The Jungle," that caused the government investigation of the Packing Industry which resulted in the Pure Food and Meat Inspection Acts of 1906, and gave status to the workers in that industry). But until such a change is forced on the ship-operators, it would be well for the Negro to stay on land "and never go to sea."[66]

Opportunity, 14 (July, 1936): 211-12.

57. NEGRO AND WHITE UNITY WON BOSTON SHIP STRIKE

Eastern Steamship Lines Victory Marks Growth
of Rank and File Movement Among Seamen--
Grange's Threats Ignored by Crews

By J. Lambert

BOSTON, April 17.--A major victory was won here last week by the crews of the Eastern Steamship Line when they tied up three passenger ships, the Arcadia, the New York and the Boston, to force the ship owners to grant their demands. Their demands were a ten-dollar increase and overtime pay and double time for Sundays and holidays. Previous to the strike, the rank and file had organized,

for the first time in the history of this company, a joint meeting of five
ships crews to advise the union officials of their demands. The officials
showed plainly by their reactionary tone that they were against the interests
of the seamen. They tried to convince the seamen that through peaceable
negotiations their cause could be won.

The members of the Eastern Steamship crews, who for the past twenty years
had been heralded as the backbone of the reactionary clique at the head of the
union, saw a new light. For the first time since the infamous betrayal in
1921, the talk of strike began to develop. It gained momentum as facts of
the strikebreaking activity of the officialdom were laid before them. Rank
and file leaders aboard the ships worked out plans for action; meetings were
held and spokesmen elected to carry forward plans for strike. A meeting of
the three ships' rank and file leaders decided that the crew of the S.S.
Arcadia should start the strike when they would be asked to sign an agreement.
The steamer New York, lying at the dock, was directed to follow.

Rank and File Leadership

On Thursday afternoon the ship owners and reactionary union leaders were
dumbfounded when, instead of signing the old agreement, the sailors and the
engine room crews on the Arcadia declared a strike and piled off. Ten minutes
later the crew of the New York followed, and they were followed by the Negro
stewards department of the two ships, consisting of 400 men.

Telegrams were sent the S.S. Boston and other ships. The owners were
forced to cancel both sailings. Four hundred passengers were already aboard.

When the S.S. Boston docked on Friday morning, all the reactionary
officials in the union were aboard to prevent a walk-out. Starting with attacks on the rank and file leaders, calling them "Moscow agents," they ordered
that the elected spokesmen of the crew be fired in an attempt to break the
strike, but this action only urged the crew to act with more decisiveness.
They walked off to a man. The Negro stewards department, consisting of 200
went ashore with wild enthusiasm.

Officials' Plans Defeated

The first move of the reactionary leaders of the union was to try to
divide the men up into their respective crafts, to try to reach separate
agreements. This was defeated when every man to a thousand strong piled up in
one union hall, demanding a joint settlement for all men, Negro and white.

Dave Grange, vice-president of the International Seamen's Union, tried
sob stories to get the men to call off the strike. He immediately changed his
tactics when rank and file leaders jumped on the platform and called for
election of a real negotiations committee. Grange, seeing that he could not
break the unity of the men, suddenly became very militant, but this did not
fool the seamen, especially the Negro stewards department who were over 600
strong.

Four times Grange and the other reactionary leaders went to the ship
owners and came back to the seamen with concessions, but the men stood solid
for the original demands. They cried and bullied the seamen and had their
gangsters beat up the militants, and tried to stampede the seamen into joining
the attack by calling the militants "Communist agitators." The seamen were
not to be foiled by these tactics.

They drove the gangsters out and told Grange they would drive him out if
he started any more of his mud slinging and red-baiting.

Finally, a settlement was reached for the stewards department, but they
refused to go back to work until the demands of the seamen and engine room
crews had also been settled. The officials and the ship owners were licked
to a frazzle with this show of unity of Negro and white. After three hours
they were forced to agree to all the demands put forward by that much-heralded
section of seamen called the backbone of the reactionary clique of the head
of the union.

The whole strike was settled in 24 hours with the greatest increases yet
won by the seamen on the East Coast. The men are jubilant over their great
victory and realize it was not only a victory over the ship owners, but also a
victory over their reactionary leaders in the union, who have misled them for

so many years. They are not stopping with this victory, but are pushing
forward for a rank and file union and for an East Coast Federation!

Daily Worker, April 18, 1936.

58. HARLEM RALLY TO SUPPORT SHIP STRIKE

Outstanding Leaders of Negro People to Talk at Mass Meeting

        Joe Curran, leader of the seamen's strike strategy committee, the Rev.
William Lloyd Imes and Thyra Edwards, outstanding Negroes, will head the list
of speakers at a mass meeting in support of the striking seamen Jan. 14, in
Harlem.
        The meeting, scheduled under the auspices of the Harlem Citizens Com-
mittee to Aid the Striking Seamen, will take place in St. James Presbyterian
Church 141st Street and Edgecombe Avenue at 8 P.M.
        Other speakers will be: Frank R. Crosswaith, chairman of the Negro Labor
Committee, and Lester Granger of the Urban League, vice-chairman of the
Citizens Committee.
        Lodie Biggs, secretary of the Citizens Committee said yesterday that
the meeting was for the purpose of "increasing support of the Negro people
for the thousands of Negro and white seamen fighting for a decent living.
        Officers of the Committee are Benjamin McLaurin, Brotherhood of Sleeping
Car Porters, chairman; the Rev. A. Clayton Powell, treasurer; Ben Davis, Jr.,
Daily Worker editorial staff, publicity.
        Among the members are: Dr. Arnold Donawa, D.D.S.; James Baker, National
Negro Congress; Ted Poston, Negro newspaper man; Manning Johnson, Cafeteria
Union, Local 302; Frank R. Crosswaith; Lillian Gaskins, member of the Inter-
national Ladies Garment Workers Union; the Rev. David N. Licorish; Ashley
Totten, Brotherhood of Sleeping Car Porters; Cecil Marquez, M.D.; and Dr.
William Lloyd Imes, pastor of St. James Presbyterian Church. [67]

Daily Worker, January 5, 1937.

59. HARLEM GROUP RALLY TO AID SHIP STRIKERS

Citizens Committee to Hear Speakers on Thursday Night

        The Harlem Citizens Committee to Aid the Striking Seamen, beginning today,
will enter an intensive campaign preparatory to its meeting Thursday evening,
Lodie Biggs, Negro bacteriologist and secretary of the Committee, stated
yesterday.
        The meeting will take place at the St. James Presbyterian Church, 141st
St., and St. Nicholas Ave., at 8 P.M. Among the speakers are the Rev. Wm.
Lloyd Imes, pastor of the church; Vito Marcantonio, progressive labor attorney
and former Congressman; Joseph Curran, leader of the Seamen's Strike Strategy
Committee and others.
        Miss Biggs said that 200 additional Harlem leaders, representative of all
phases of the community's life, would be asked to endorse the meeting.
        She announced also that the Greater New York Federation of the National
Negro Congress had officially endorsed the rally. James H. Baker, Jr., and
Thyra Edwards, prominent leaders of the Congress, have been invited to address the meeting.
        Lester Granger, of the National Urban League and vice-chairman of the
Committee, is now writing a popular folder on the five seamen who died of
pneumonia due to exposure on the picket line. Several thousand of these are
to be distributed in Harlem early this week.

Fifty-three Harlem churches have been circularized by the Committee requesting a special collection for the Seaman Jan. 16. Heading this phase of
the work is the Rev. David N. Licorish, young Harlem pastor.
The week's activities of the Harlem Committee will be climaxed with full
cooperation with the downtown Seamen's Aid committee which holds a city wide
tag day on Jan. 16-18.

Daily Worker, January 12, 1937.

60. NEGRO'S STAKE IN SEA STRIKE PARLEY'S TOPIC

Unions to Meet in Two-Day Conference on Friday, Saturday

The city's most progressive unions and organizations will meet in an
unusually important two-day conference, sponsored by the Greater New York
Federation of the National Negro Congress, Friday and Saturday, Feb. 5 and 6,
at the Harlem Y.M.C.A., 180 West 135th St.
The attention of the gathered delegates will be centered upon, "The
Stake of the Negro in the Maritime Strike." The Eastern and Gulf seamen's
strike was concluded over a week ago, and was the first real united front of
Negro and white workers in the maritime industry in the East.
Among the sponsors of the conference are:
James H. Baker, Jr., chairman, Greater New York Federation of the National
Negro Congress, and leader in the Brotherhood of Sleeping Car Porters; Miss
Louise Cothran, National Youth Administration; Henry K. Craft, secretary,
Harlem branch Y.M.C.A., Thyra Edwards, National Chairman, Women's Section,
National Negro Congress, James W. Ford, outstanding leader of the Communist
Party; Lester Granger, Workers Bureau, National Urban League; T. Arnold Hill,
industrial secretary, National Urban League; Local 149, Household Mechanics
Union; Benjamin A. McLauren, Brotherhood of Sleeping Car Porters; Cyril
Phillips, Committee on Aid to Ethiopia; William Pickens, National Association
for Advancement of Colored People; Philip Randolph, national president,
Brotherhood of Sleeping Car Porters; Miss Lucille Spence, of the Teachers
Union; Ashley T. Totten, national secretary, Sleeping Car Porters; Upper
Harlem Council of the Progressive Womens Councils; Max Yergan, national
secretary, Y.M.C.A. Work in Africa.[68]
All progressive organizations and trade unions have been asked to send
delegates.

Daily Worker, February 4, 1937.

61. PROTECTING THE NEGRO SEAMAN

By Ferdinand C. Smith[69]

The constitution of the National Maritime Union guarantees to all its
members equal rights, privileges and opportunities, regardless of color,
creed or political belief. The Constitution of the United States contains
similar guarantees. Both make fine reading for comfortable liberals--but the
proof of the pudding is in the eating. Negroes and other minority groups have
recently found the winters long and tough, with pudding at a distinct premium.
The seamen wrote their equal rights policy in their constitution not
simply because they were a group of impassioned liberals. Bitter experience
had taught them a lesson--that the broadest unity and cooperation is necessary
to win any kind of struggle, whether it be a war, an election, or a decent
standard of working and living conditions.
Under the old A.F. of L. Maritime labor setup, in which trade-unionists
were organized by crafts into white and colored locals, the International
Seamen's Union had for years waged a losing struggle against the pressure of

change. The working conditions of the seamen were taking the same nosedive
as the stockmarket. The seamen were divided, demoralized; but the dues col-
lectors--as the International Seamen's Union officials were known--went on
collecting their tribute. They did little to draw the seamen together under
a constructive program; in fact, they apparently aided and abetted disunity,
playing one type of seamen, and one race, against another.

The New Deal came along and other workers enjoyed its fruits, but the
seamen remained on the toboggan slide. By 1936, maritime workers on the East
Coast were pretty well fed up with the labor fakers who professed to speak in
their name on the one hand and sold them down the river to the lowest bidder
on the other. They revolted, and after a series of strikes, were successful
in giving their officials the "bum's rush." In May, 1937, a new union was
formed--the National Maritime Union--and a new constitution was written for
the seamen.

Their experience with disunity in the International Seamen's Union, and
their strikes--in which Negroes played a recognized role--convinced the seamen that only a united organization of vast scope could hope to gain their
objectives. Under the ISU setup, the sailors, firemen, and stewards--the
three departments on a ship--had been placed in separate and distinct unions.
When one of these unions took action to win improvements, it could never be
sure that the others would support it. The National Maritime Union decided
not to make this fatal mistake. It organized ships industrially, taking in
all the crew except the licensed officers and engineers. In two and half
years this progressive industrial policy has proved itself dozens of times.

The International Seamen's Union had avoided a knotty problem by dividing
white and Negro workers. They had kept white seamen and Negro seamen segregated on different ships. More and more of the ships formerly manned by
Negroes had been laid up or their crews replaced by white ones, but that had
never seemed to bother the ISU officialdom.

The National Maritime Union met the problem of racial prejudice head on.
It wrote into its constitution a provision that all members must be shipped
through Union halls in a rotary system. When a seaman leaves a ship for any
reason, he must register on the shipping list at the Union hall in whatever
port he may be. He gets a number and is put on the bottom of the list. As
jobs are called, the men on the top of the list, those who registered earlier,
have the choice of accepting or refusing the job. Gradually those ahead receive employment until finally the man who was on the bottom of the list rises
to the top and gets first choice for a job in his rating.

This rotary system must be adhered to strictly in order to be effective.
Any discrimination is therefore strictly forbidden.

This sounds fine on paper, but in practice the new system had to buck a
century of prejudice instilled into the minds of workers by those forces which
profit when labor is divided. Certain white crews wouldn't accept a Negro
shipmate. "We don't object to being in the same union with him; he's a good
guy and a good union man, but we don't want him on our ship," they would say.
Sometimes the same thing would happen on a ship manned by white sailors and
firemen and Negro stewards, if the hall sent a Negro sailor or fireman as a
replacement.

Such incidents soon began to throw the rotary shipping system out of gear.
Most Negro members of the Union recognized that the problem was one that
couldn't be solved overnight, especially by a union whose membership constituted the merest fraction of the population of the country. However, as
in all groups and organizations, there is always a small clique ready to
create disunity, either for personal or pecuniary reasons. In the National
Maritime Union, on several occasions, this clique, using a few self-seeking
Negroes, was able to raise dissension on several occasions on the question
of this or that case of discrimination.

The problem of discrimination had become complicated by increasing un-
employment among Negro members through no fault of the Union or their own.
As Joseph Curran, President of the NMU, in his report to the Second Biennial
Convention of the Union last summer, pointed out: "Since the formation of the
National Maritime Union in May, 1937, at least 1,000 Negro members of this
Union have lost jobs . . . in Atlantic Coast steamship and tanker companies.
How many jobs have been lost by them on Gulf (of Mexico) ships has not been
estimated. . . ."

These jobs, he added, had apparently been permanently lost and when

compared with the number of Negro members in the NMU--roughly 5,000--it was
obvious that the problem was a serious one.

Contributary causes of this unemployment were: ships were laid up,
companies employing Negro seamen were going out of business; the transfer
of ships from a company employing Negroes to one which did not; changes in
the classification of ships in a given trade; and the refusal of certain ships'
crews to accept Negro replacements for jobs.

With unusual energy the new union met the problem. By now it has pretty
well solved it. First of all the group of disrupters, paid labor spies and
shipowner stooges, who had been plaguing the Union since its inception, were
either expelled for just cause or rendered harmless. This clique had kept the
membership in a turmoil for a long time and was behind much of the prejudice
against Negroes. When they went, most of the prejudice went with them.

Secondly, educational efforts among the members were redoubled. The problem was discussed at numerous meetings and proposals and counter-proposals
were submitted. Committees were elected to deal especially with the problem.
The entire membership finally realized that something had to be done.

Something was done. It was decided that Negro members were to remain
aboard ships which they manned entirely, and no other but Negro replacements
were to be sent to them. Strong measures were taken to adhere to the rotary
system of shipping, and where companies allowed the hiring of Negroes, such
members were sent to the ships. Unless objections of the crew were overpower-
ing, they had to accept Negro shipmates. In many instances the iron fist
didn't have to be used because, through education, white crews lost much of
their prejudice.

A further policy of the new union is to place Negro crews on new and laid-
up tonnage put into operation again. The Union has also been successful in
putting Negro stewards aboard several round-the-world liners. When the Neutrality Act put a curb on shipping to North European ports, many seamen, including
Negroes, were thrown out of work. The Union succeeded in getting some of them
work-relief jobs.

Within the National Maritime Union, at present, the Negro is entitled to
all the benefits of membership, such as protection of wage, working and living
conditions; he votes; he voices his opinion at meetings and in the union's
paper--the *Pilot*--and he holds office.

In the port of New York alone, seven Negroes are officers of the union,
one is National Secretary; a second heads the Stewards' Department. There are
two Negro organizers, one in the New England area and another in the Middle
Atlantic area.

In two years the new union has boosted wages 36 per cent and improved
conditions on the ships accordingly. Negro members got these benefits along
with their white shipmates; there is only one scale and it holds for all members
of the Union.

Negro delegates go aboard ships manned by white crews and help settle their
complaints against company officials. Negro officials have had the unique
privilege of serving on negotiating committees representing the entire union.

When the European war broke out, certain companies which served the North
Atlantic routes chartered ships from other companies to cash in on the rush
of American tourists and expatriates to get home. Some of these ships were
manned, up to 60 per cent, by Negro crews sent out from the Union hall.

The last traces of prejudice in the minds of the Union's membership are
being burned out under the powerful light of education. The program of education has taught Negroes as well as white seamen. It has shown them that their
destiny is linked up with all other workers, that their problem is not separate
and apart from the broader problems of society, that they must fight patiently
and intelligently side by side with other workers, and not behind them, to win
a future of dignity and freedom.

The National Maritime Union is just one sector in this struggle, but it is
a leading and shining one. It hasn't yet completely won its own particular
fight. But with the National Maritime Union to help them, the prospects for
Negro employment in the maritime industry at respectable wages and conditions
can be made bright, if all the Negro seamen get together in one organization
and pull together in a common cause. The European war has cleared the decks of
American ships of many aliens. The Maritime Commission is building many new
ships. The union is agitating for the establishment of new American trade
routes and for the government to take over those abandoned by warring nations.

All this combined will make room for more jobs, including work for Negroes in
the industry.

Opportunity, 18 (April, 1940): 112-14.

62. SPEECH AT NATIONAL MARITIME UNION CONVENTION

(Brother Paul Robeson arrives and is greeted with a tremendous ovation).

THE CHAIR: At this time we will suspend the regular order of business.
A privilege that we have long been waiting for has been accorded us now.
Everybody here has been waiting since the Convention opened for this moment.
I particularly am glad to be able to present our guest because we come from
the same town in New Jersey. We grew up together in the same town.
So it is a great honor for me to be able to present to you a man, who is
not only one of the greatest singers in the world today, but a man who is also
known as one of the greatest fighters for civil liberties, democracy and trade
unions throughout the country as well as throughout the world. (Applause)
And one who has never failed to give of his time and his great voice in the
cause of democracy and civil liberties.
I give you at this time Brother Paul Robeson.
(The delegates rose to their feet and thunderously applauded and cheered
Mr. Robeson. It was some time before the demonstration ceased).

Joe Curran and fellows and brothers: I needn't say how happy I am to be
here, because I am here, I don't come as a singer of importance or anything
like that. I come today because I feel very close to the maritime unions. I
remember coming on a ship with Mr. Brown from abroad after the war began. I
remember stepping on an American ship and after being on board a couple of hours
a delegation came up to me and said: "Paul, we know who you are, and anything
we can do for you we shall surely do." I remember later singing for them below
and having a great time.
I know the whole background of your Union, and I would like you to know
that among the colored people of this country your Union stands among the
foremost for giving complete equality and for the advancement of the colored
people. I just want to tell you. (Applause).
I remember when I was going through school--I had a brother I lived with
out in Westfield, N.J.--he went to sea and I went to sing, (laughter) while working my way through school. I used to go down to the docks. My brother worked
on the Fall River Line. And then I learned how to sling hash in one of the
hotels.
I come as one who has worked very hard in the early part of his life, and
I still work very hard for the things in which I believe. I don't feel a
stranger; I know Joe and Ferdy Smith, and one of my best friends is here.
Revels Cayton from out in San Francisco. But more than personal friendship,
I know that we are all one in the things for which we stand. Here at home, of
course, for complete rights for labor, for complete equality for the colored
people of this country, and for a right to a better life for every worker in
this land of ours. (Applause) Further than that, I know that we spread out
and we stand not alone, but we stand for mankind wherever it may suffer and
wherever it may be oppressed. (Applause)
I have had the opportunity to work with refugees from Austria, Germany,
for the Spanish people and for the Chinese people, and I saw very clearly how
all of our problems come together, no matter whether we may be black or white
or yellow. As long as we are struggling for a better life we have one cause,
and I don't know about you, but I feel awfully happy today and awfully optimistic now that fascism has come to grips with a power that will show it no
quarter. (Applause)
I have been in the Soviet Union and I know that the people of the Soviet
Union know who they are fighting, why they are fighting and for what they have
to fight. I know that this Union with its militant background, will come to a
decision to urge the government to give the Soviet Union all aid possible in
its fight against fascism, for the Soviet Union is standing four-square for

the cause and the rights of all the oppressed peoples of the world.

This is my first time among you. And whenever your next convention comes--I see by the papers it may be in 1943--I will be back again. (Extended applause)

(Mr. Robeson then sang the following songs requested by the audience). Bill of Rights, Water Boy, Joe Hill, Fatherland, Old Man River, Jim Crow, It Ain't Necessarily So, Spring Song, Song to Joe, Ballad for Americans.

THE CHAIR: I know he would like to sing all day. He sings because he loves to sing, but we have to be sure that a voice like his must be saved so that all can hear him. So though we would like to hear more, we must think of preserving his voice.

I would recommend that we give consideration to extending to Paul Robeson for the work he has done in all fields of endeavor, an honorary membership in the National Maritime Union. (Extended applause)

M/S/C To extend to Paul Robeson honorary membership in the Maritime Union.

(The Convention again rose amid a demonstration of applause as Paul Robeson left the hall).

Proceedings of the Third National Convention of the National Maritime Union of America, Cleveland, Ohio, July 7-14, 1941, pp. 56-57.

THE NATIONAL NEGRO CONGRESS

63. MARTEL WILL ADDRESS NATIONAL NEGRO CONGRESS

Detroit Labor Leader to Speak as Official Representative of Lewis--Chicago A.F. of L.
Donates Radio Time--Funds Needed

By Milton Howard

CHICAGO, Ill., Feb. 6.--Powerful and influential trade union leaders of Detroit and Chicago yesterday joined in support of the National Negro Congress which will open its historic three-day sessions here on Feb. 14 at the Eighth Regiment Armory, 34 South Giles Street.

Frank X. Martel, president of the Wayne County (Detroit) Central Labor Council, wired to John P. Davis, executive secretary, his acceptance of an invitation to address the opening sessions, and John Fitzpatrick, president of the Chicago Federation of Labor, pledged to send an official speaker from the Federation.

The acceptance by Martel is given added importance by the fact that he will come to the National Negro Congress as the official representative of the Committee for Industrial Organization of the American Federation of Labor, the group of powerful trade unions fighting for industrial unionism, and also as the personal representative of John L. Lewis, president of the United Mine Workers of America.

Preparations for the Congress which will bring together more than 1,000 Negro delegates and sympathetic observers from all parts of the country, are proceeding rapidly. The committee announced today the following schedule: Sessions on Saturday, Feb. 15, 10:30 A.M., 2:30 P.M. and 7:00 P.M., for Sunday, Feb. 16, 2:30 P.M. and 7:00 P.M., Monday Feb. 17, 10:30 A.M., 2:30 P.M., and 7:00 P.M.

A dance and ball has been arranged for Saturday evening, February 15, at the Armory with Tiny Parham's Cotton Club orchestra providing the music.

John P. Davis and Charles W. Burton were given radio time over the Chicago Federation of Labor Station WCFL.
Many local unions have already pledged to send delegates.

Funds Needed

Mr. Davis emphasized today the urgent need for funds. "We have the responsibility and the honor of having to pay for the scores of poverty-stricken sharecroppers who will come to Chicago from the plantations and the Cotton Belt," he said, "These brave people are practically penniless. They are facing all kinds of obstacles in their efforts to come with their message from the deep South. In addition, we have large expenses for rent, office help, printing, etc. I appeal to every friend of the Negro people to come to our aid with contributions right now. Every dollar will help some sharecropper to reach this great national congress of his people, a congress that affects the welfare also of the entire country. Please send your contribution to the Negro National Congress, 4401 South Park, Chicago, Ill., care of John P. Davis."

Daily Worker, February 7, 1936.

64. RANDOLPH SAYS HOPE OF NEGRO PEOPLE
LIES IN UNITY WITH LABOR

The National Negro Congress held in Chicago on February 14-16, and which brought together more than 900 delegates representing hundreds of organizations of Negro people and their friends built a living monument to the great Negro Abolitionist, Frederick Douglass.
Perhaps the outstanding factor together with the energetic and capable work of John P. Davis, influencing the success of the Congress was the participation of A. Philip Randolph, President of the Brotherhood of Sleeping Car Porters. The speech of Brother Randolph gave a clear line for the Congress to follow. His words on the united front, trade unions and the Labor Party represented a new change within the ranks of the Negro people, viz, first, the maturing of the Negro working class, its willingness and readiness to fight determinedly against oppression; and secondly the realization on its part of its power, force and leadership in the Negro liberation movement. We are printing in an abridged form the speech of Brother Randolph.

Greetings and felicitations upon this great Congress. Though absent in the flesh, I am with you in the spirit, in the spirit of the deathless courage of the 18th and 19th century black rebels and martyrs for human justice in the spirit of Frederick Douglass and Nat Turner, of Gabriel and Denmark Vesey, of Harriet Tubman and Sojourner Truth.[70]

Economic Plight

With the economic affliction of nation-wide joblessness stand the liquidation of the farmers, the small shop owners, the middle class, the poor sharecrop and tenant farmers and farm laborers, the foreclosure of hundreds of thousands of mortgages upon the homes of the workers and the lower strata of the middle class, with no prospects of permanent rehabilitation by the hectic, sketchy, patchy, and makeshift capitalist program.
But economic insecurity, though baffling, is not the only challenge to the American workers, black and white and the middle classes. There is also political and civil insecurity. Even the most credulous can sense an existing grave danger to our democratic institutions and constitutional liberties.
This danger is fascism--Fascism which seeks the complete abrogation of all civil and political liberties in the manner and method of Nazi Germany and Fascist Italy. It is a menace to America.
And war is the twin evil sister of Fascism. Its coming is not now improbable. It is a danger.

"National Negro Congress"

But this congress is called to attempt to meet the problems of blacks, they are a hated, maligned tenth of the population. While this is true, it is also true that the problems of the Negro peoples are the problems of the workers, for practically 99 per cent of the Negro peoples win their bread by selling their labor power in the labor market from day to day. They cannot escape the dangers and penalties of the depression, war or Fascism.

However, our contemporary history is a witness to the stark fact that black America is a victim of both class and race prejudice and oppression. Because Negroes are black, they are hated, maligned and spat upon; lynched, mobbed, and murdered. Because Negroes are workers, they are brow-beaten, bullied, intimidated, robbed, exploited, jailed and shot down.

No Union Card

Thus, voteless in 13 states; politically disregarded and discounted in the others; victims of the lynch terror in Dixie, with a Scottsboro frame-up of notorious memory; faced with the label of the white man's job and the white man's union; unequal before the law; jim-crowed in schools and colleges throughout the nation; segregated in the slums and ghettos of the urban centers; landless peons of a merciless white landlordism; hunted down, harassed and hounded as vagrants in the southern cities, the Negro peoples face a hard, deceptive and brutal capitalist order, despite its preachments of Christian love and brotherhood.

War Brings Change

What has brought us to this, is the insistent question? The answer in brief lies in the World War, the sharpening and deepening of capitalist exploitation of the workers of hand and brain, the acceleration of a technological revolution creating a standing army of unemployed, the ripening and maturing of monopoly capitalism thru trustification rationalization and the rapid march of financial imperialism, and the intensification of racial and religious hatreds, together with increasingly blatant and provocative nationalism.

But the war itself was the effect of a deeper cause and that cause was the profit system which provides and permits the enrichment of the few at the expense of the many, allowing two per cent of the people to own ninety per cent of the wealth of these United States, a condition not much different in other capitalist countries, and also makes for the robbery and oppression of the darker, and weaker colonial peoples of the world.

"Of the Remedies"

But the diagnosis of the causes of social problems such as wars, economic depressions and Fascism is only designed to enable the victims to seek and find a remedy. Before dealing with some of the remedies, however, let me speak briefly of what are not remedies:

First, the New Deal is no remedy. It does not seek to change the profit system. It does not place human rights above property rights, but gives the business interests the support of the state. It is no insurance against the coming of Fascism or the prevention of war or a recurrent depression, though it be more liberal than the Republican Tories.

Second, the restoration of Republican rule is no solution. It was during the rule of the Grand Old Party under which the depression came. Negroes have watched themselves disfranchised and lynched under both regimes, Republican and Democratic.

Third, the Townsend Plan is no panacea. While an adequate old age pension should be fought for, a pension far greater than that offered by the New Deal Security legislation, the Townsend Plan is well nigh impossible of execution, and if executed would not achieve its aim. [71]

Back to Remedies

But back to remedies. At the top of the list of remedies I wish to

suggest the struggle of the workers against exploitation of the employers.
Next, the struggle of the workers against Fascism and for the preservation of
democratic institutions, the arena in which alone their economic power may be
built.
    Third, the struggle to build powerful Negro civil rights organizations.
Fourth, the struggle against war which wrecks the organizations of the workers,
and stifles and suppresses freedom of speech, the press and assembly. Fifth,
the struggle to strengthen the forces of the exploited sharecrop and tenant
farmers. Sixth, the struggle to build mass consumers' movements to protect
the housewives against price manipulation.

Instrumentalities for Action

    But the struggle to apply the aforementioned remedies can only be
achieved through definite social, economic and political instrumentalities.
Thus the fight against the economic exploitation of the workers can only be
effectively carried on through industrial and craft unions, with the emphasis
on the former.
    The industrial union is important in this stage of economic development
because modern business has changed in structure and assumed the form of giant
trust and holding companies, with which the craft union can no longer effectively grapple.
    Moreover, the craft union invariably has a color bar against the Negro
worker, but the industrial union in structure renders race discrimination
less possible, since it embraces all the workers included in the industry,
regardless of race, creed, color or craft, skilled or unskilled.

Must Fight Color Bar

    Thus, this congress should seek to broaden and intensify the movement to
draw Negro workers into labor organizations and break down the color bar in
the trade unions that now have it.
    The next instrumentality which the workers must build and employ for their
protection against economic exploitation, war and fascism, is an independent
working class political party. It should take the form of a farmer-labor
political organization. This is indispensable in view of the bankruptcy in
principles, courage and vision of the old line parties, Republican and
Democratic.
    They are the political committees of Wall Street and are constructed to
serve the profit making agencies.
    The fight for civil and political rights of the Negro peoples can effec-
tively be carried on if only those organizations that are pushing the struggles
are broadened and built with a wider mass base. Those organizations that are
serving on the civil rights front effectively for the Negro are the National
Association for the Advancement of Colored People, and the International Labor
Defense.
    It needs to be definitely understood, however, that the fight in the
courts for civil and political rights cannot be effective except when backed
by a broad, nationwide, of not international mass protest through demonstrations in the form of parades, mass meetings and publicity.

United Front

    But the fight for civil and political liberties for the Negro peoples,
while it has been brilliantly waged by the N.A.A.C.P. and the I.L.D., the
gravity and complexity of the problems of civil and political liberties, accentuated and widened by the evil of fascist trends in America, demands that
new tactics and strategy be employed to meet the situation.
    The maneuvering and disposing of the forces of Negro peoples and their
sympathetic allies against their enemies can only be effectively worked out
through the tactics and strategy of the united front. The task of overcoming
the enemies of democratic institutions and constitutional liberties is too
big for any single organization. It requires the united and formal integrating and coordinating of the various Negro organizations, church, fraternal,
civil, trade union, farmer, professional, college and whatnot, into the framework of a united front, together with the white groups of workers, lovers of

liberty and those whose liberties are similarly menaced for a common attack
upon the forces of reaction, backed by the embattled masses of black and white
workers.

Mass Action

The united front strategy and tactics should be executed through methods
of mass demonstration, such as parades, picketing, boycotting, mass protests,
the mass distribution of propaganda literature, as well as legal action.

The united front does not provide an excuse for weakness or timidity or
reliance by any one organization upon the others who comprise it, but, on the
contrary, it affords an opportunity for the contribution of strength by each
organization to the common pool of organizational power for a common attack
or a common defense against the enemy. Thus the Negro peoples should not
place their problems for solution down at the feet of their white sympathetic
allies, which has been and is the common fashion of the old school Negro
leadership, for, in the final analysis, the salvation of the Negro, like the
workers, must come from within.

Clear Issues

The power and effectiveness of the united front will be developed by
waging the struggles around definite, vital and immediate issues of life and
living.

These issues should be obvious, clear and simple, such as prevention of
stoppage of relief, cuts in relief allotments, lay-offs, of relief workers,
of workers in any industry, discrimination in the giving of relief, exorbitant rents, evictions, rent increases, police brutality, denial of free assembly, freedom of the press, freedom of speech to unpopular groups, denial
of civil rights to Negroes, such as the right to be served in hotels and
restaurants, to have access to public utilities and forms of transportation,
such as the Pullman car.

Wage struggles around war upon Ethiopia by the fascist dictator Mussolini,
strikes and lockouts of black and white workers, the amendment to the federal
Constitution of the adoption of social legislation such as the Retirement
Pension Act for railroad workers, fight for the freedom of Angelo Herndon,
the Scottsboro boys, the Wagner-Costigan anti-lynching bill,the violations of
the Wagner Labor Disputes bill, etc., American Liberty League, William Randolph
Hearst and the Ku Klux Klan, and supporting the movement of John L. Lewis for
industrial unionism.[72]

Such is the task of Negro peoples. This task comes as a sharp and decisive challenge at a time when new atrocities and nameless terrorism are
directed against black America and when the workers, black and white, are
being goaded by oppression and intimidation, to resort to general strikes
such as took place in San Francisco and in Pekin, Ill., as well as national
strikes such as the textile workers, the miners, and the workers' revolts in
Minnesota and Toledo.

To meet this task, the Negro people, pressed with their backs against
the wall, must face the future with heads erect, hearts undaunted and undis-
mayed, ready and willing and determined to pay the price in struggle, sacrifices and suffering that freedom, justice and peace shall share and enjoy a
more abundant life.

Forward to complete economic, political and social equality for Negro
peoples. Forward to the abolition of this sinister system of jim-crowism in
these United States! The united front points the way. More power to the
National Negro Congress! The future belongs to the people!

Daily Worker, March 1, 1936.

65. NEGRO CONGRESS MUST STRENGTHEN ITS TRADE UNION BASE

By Ben Davis, Jr.

The militant program of the National Negro Congress puts another nail in
the coffin of the capitalist theory that Negroes are "naturally docile." It
showed that the Negro people are ready to struggle against the monopoly of
wealth, which has brought them the grossest misery, poverty and oppression;
secondly, they are ready to struggle jointly with all their allies against
lynching, jim-crowism and for their national rights. Frederick Douglass, the
great Negro abolitionist, would have been proud of this history-making gathering!
     Nor did the delegates at the Congress fail to see the necessity of
carrying out this program. They set up a permanent organization--a federation
of organizations--comprising a national council, a small, readily assembled
executive committee, and 15 regional heads for every section of the country.
Represented among these individuals are Republicans, Democrats, Communists,
Socialists, Church folk, trade unionists, sharecroppers and virtually every
type of organization active among the Negro people.
     Recognizing the pressure of this newly formed weapon for Negro libera-
tion, the sedate and aloof "Nation" begrudgingly yielded the following comment
in its March 11, issue: "The National Negro Congress at Chicago . . . presented
a united front against a reactionary world."

Hair Splitting

     But the "Nation" did not stop there. It makes a profoundly insignificant
and hair-splitting criticism--from the left! It uses the trick of quoting out
of context to attack the resolutions adopted by the business and church sections.
     It snatches from the church program the following:
     "We still feel that the Negro church is the most potent agency to be used
in the further progress and advancement of our people," (Emphasis ours).

Omits Vital Proposals

     It thus entirely omits the proposals of the resolution which commit the
churches to devoting every fifth Sunday to the Congress; to working unitedly
with non-Christian groups; to urging ministers to preach "social and economic
as well as spiritual gospel." Nor does it consider the fact that the church
division supports the program of the Congress in every other field.
     Would that the "Nation" used its influences among white church people to
commit them even as far along this road!
     Here is how the "Nation" deletes the resolution pertaining to business:

     "Whereas the development of sound and thriving Negro business is most
indispensable to the general elevation of the Negro's social and economic
security, therefore, be it resolved, that all Negroes consider it their inescapable duty to support Negro business."

Neglects Union Issue

     Again the "Nation" "forgets" to mention the proposals of the resolution
which include: the establishment of producers and consumers cooperatives;
that Negro business and employers employ only union labor. Unable to see the
Negro people as an oppressed nation, the Nation does not understand that the
fight against segregation, jim-crowism, and oppression includes the struggle
for Negroes to set up and maintain their businesses free from imperialist
discrimination.
     The Nation pooh-poohs the idea of union labor in Negro business as a
"pious wish," conveniently ignoring the Amsterdam News strike and the fact
that its success opened the way for unionization in thousands of Negro
businesses.

The united front or federated character of the Congress leaves each
organization free to do its work independently. The Communist Party, as always, will continue--yes, strengthen--its independent activity among Negro
people in and out of the Congress, constantly clarifying them on such issues
as the church and Negro business.

Congress Weaknesses

Notwithstanding the excellent beginning made by the Congress, there were
certain serious weaknesses which should be corrected before the next Congress
convenes in Philadelphia in May, 1937.
The most glaring weakness was the absence of sufficient representation
from the South--where eight million Negroes are subject to the most barbarous
lynch oppression. Only fifteen delegates come from extreme southern states.
More delegates should have come from the Southern church and uplift groups
and economic as well as social and religious activities. Three fourths of the
delegates came from four states--Illinois, New York, Indiana and Pennsylvania.
In the South the Congress must have its deepest roots--among the sharecroppers,
poor farmers, and the disfranchised Negro population.

Trade Unions

The trade union representation from 80 unions--most of which were af-
filiated to the A.F. of L.--was weak though the group as a whole was very
advanced.
Such unions as the International Ladies Garment Workers, the United Mine
Workers of America, and the Amalgamated Clothing Workers should have had large
Negro delegations. Clearly the trade unions must form the solid base of the
Congress.
It remains to be seen whether Frank Crosswaith, prominent Negro Socialist
and head of the Harlem Labor Committee, will continue to sabotage the Congress
as he did before it met, or whether he will conform with the growing senti-
ment for this powerful new weapon for Negro rights.

Barred From Unions

In view of the number of Negro churches--where the bulk of the Negro
people are organized and women's organizations, these delegations were also
too small. It is in the hundreds of small churches throughout the country
that Negro workers barred from trade unions by discriminatory policies of the
A.F. of L. leadership congregate.
The next Congress must represent an even larger cross-section of the
Negro people--but with a decidedly firmer trade union base.
The enthusiastic reception given the addresses of James W. Ford, and A.
Philip Randolph is a mandate for further efforts to popularize the Farmer-
Labor Party among the Negro people.
In the final article, we shall deal with the democratic procedures of
the Congress, and the immediate tasks before it.

Daily Worker, March 16, 1936.

66. UNION DRIVE TO ORGANIZE NEGRO WORKERS IS ASKED

National Negro Congress Labor Committee
Promised Full Support of Cleveland
Metal Trades Council

CLEVELAND, Ohio, April 16.--A request to organize the Negro workers of
Cleveland into trade unions was favorably received by the Metal Trades Council
at its last meeting, Monday.
A delegation of four, representing the Negro Labor Committee of the National
Negro Congress and Local 610 of the Paint and Varnish Makers' Union, was

accorded a good reception by the Metal Trades Council when it appeared before
the meeting. Their spokesman, Miss Maude White of Federal Teachers' Union
Local 448, made the following requests of the Metal Trades Council:
   Endorsement of the Philip Randolph resolution urging the unionization of
Negro workers;
   Inclusion of the organization of Negroes in the present organizational
drive conducted by the Metal Trades Council;
   A public statement of their stand on the organization of Negroes, to be
released through both the white and Negro press.

Officials Act

   Following the presentation of Miss White, delegates at the Metal Trades
Council rose to speak in favor of the proposals.
   Joel Faith, international vice-president of the Moulders' Union, urged
strong support to the organization of Negro workers into the trade unions.

Steel Union Pledged

   George Haas, secretary of the Moulders' Union, spoke in similar vein. J.
Casey of the Amalgamated Association of Iron, Steel and Tin Workers promised
the assistance of his union to this aim. He stated, that their union was
taking in Negroes and would continue to do so in the future.
   Ray Bomby of Local 18946 of the Laborers' Union also stated that their
union was accepting Negroes.
   James McWeeney, president of the Metal Trades Council, asserted he would
do everything he could to help the organization of Negro workers.

Congress Active

   The Negro Labor Committee of the National Negro Congress is energetically
promoting the trade unionization of the Negro workers. It has received the
endorsement of Painters' District Council, which had sent out the following
letter to all labor unions in the city:

   "To all District Councils and Local Unions:

   "Painters' District Council takes this means of affirming our policy of
accepting membership of all qualified mechanics in our respective trades, black
or white, without discrimination. We urge all trade unions to do likewise as
the true spirit of unionism would then be carried out.

                           Fraternally yours,

                           (Sgd.) CHARLES COLVIN,
                           District Council Secretary"

   The Labor Committee of the National Negro Congress is planning to visit
every local union in the city to secure endorsement of the Randolph resolution and promote the trade unionization of Negroes.
   A conference of all organizations interested in economic and social
justice for Negroes will take place this Sunday at 2:30 in the afternoon at
Bethany Baptist Church, Seventy-first and Kinsman Streets, to hear the reports
of the National Negro Congress.

Daily Worker, April 17, 1936.

67. THE NATIONAL NEGRO CONGRESS: AN INTERPRETATION

By Lester B. Granger

   It is a paradoxical fact that the National Negro Congress held in Chicago
last February provided a powerful impetus toward national racial unity, while

at the same time it has stirred up more bitter controversy than any gathering
of Negroes since the days of Marcus Garvey's "provisional presidential in-
cumbency."[73]

It was not the first time in recent years that a truly national meeting
had been attempted. The Equal Rights Congress at Washington during war days,
the Negro Labor Congress of 1925, and the more recent "Sanhedrin" were all attempts to produce a racial gathering from all parts of the country to take
counsel on racial problems. Because of previous failures the National Negro
Congress was opposed by many sincere persons who felt that this latest
ambitious attempt was foredoomed likewise to failure.[74]

Not all opposition came from those who feared its failure, for there were
many individuals who saw in the possible success of this movement a future
crippling of national organizations already serving the economic and social
welfare of Negroes. Still others suspected undue radical influence in the
Congress leadership, while in the same breath suspicions were openly voiced
that it was a gigantic anti-New Deal effort financed by the Republican Party
or the Liberty League.

Now that the Congress has been held and is over, some of these criticisms
are lost, while others have been magnified and intensified. A prelate of the
Negro church participated until the closing moments of the final session, then
stamped out in high dudgeon, denouncing the entire Congress as atheistic. A
Republican national committeeman protested throughout the Congress that it had
been sold out to the Democratic Party, and later went back to Washington
branding the meeting as Communistic. Various Walter Winchells and Lippmans
of the Negro press failed to attend, but deplored the entire proceeding as
"pitifully futile" or as "a remarkable waste of time and money." Meanwhile
the Congress delegates went back to five hundred and fifty-one organizations
to report on what actually took place in Chicago. Increased racial unity will
grow out of the public's reception of these reports, even though that unity
grows amid acrimonious dispute.[75]

It is unfortunate that practically all criticism has been aimed at an
assumed malign influence in the Congress leadership, or at presumed secret
ambitions on the part of its promoters. Almost no critics have analyzed the
actual program of the Congress, or enumerated its many virtues, or specifically
pointed out its weaknesses--which there were many. This article is an attempt,
not to answer the critics of the Congress, but to interpret its real significance and to point out its possible usefulness to the people in whose service it was called--five million wage earners and heads of Negro families.

To understand the meeting itself, one must know its background. The
Congress grew out of a conference on the "Economic Condition Among Negroes"
held at Washington, D.C., in May, 1935, under the combined sponsorship of the
Joint Committee on National Recovery and Howard University's Department of
Political Economy. That conference produced disturbing evidence showing that
depression and "recovery" trends are forcing Negroes into an even lower
economic and social position than they now occupy. Immediate action was indicated as imperatively needed to combat these trends, but it was also recognized that such action must be preceded by a wide education of Negroes in
the techniques of group action.

A small meeting after the Conference made plans for calling a national
congress to initiate this education and to plan action. Here was the birth
of the National Negro Congress, under the organizing genius of John P. Davis,
a meeting to include all types of Negro organizations and to devise a platform
which would unite them on a program of fundamental issues involving their
economic, social and civil security. It was to be a Congress which would cut
across political lines and philosophies; it was to be a realistic gathering
dealing with bread-and-butter problems; it was to be an interracial meeting
giving whites as well as Negroes a chance to help attack a problem which is
the problem of all America.

With this background, it was to be expected that the Congress would produce a stranger assortment of delegates and a varied conglomeration of
political and economic philosophies. Negroes in every walk of life were
there--ministers, labor leaders, business men--mechanics, farmers, musicians,
--housewives, missionaries, social workers. Many whites were present--trade
unionists, church leaders, and lookers-on drawn by curiosity. There were
representatives of New Deal departments and agencies; old line Republican
wheel horses and ambitious young Democrats exchanged arguments; Communists

held heated altercations with proponents of the Forty-Ninth State Movement, and Garveyites signed the registration books immediately after Baha'ists.[76]

The Congress produced an amazing attendance past even the most optimistic expectations of its promoters. In the middle of the worst winter in fifty years, the delegates traveled through sub-zero weather by train, bus and auto, paying their own way or financed by poverty-stricken club treasuries. Nevertheless, 800 delegates proffered credentials from 551 organizations in 28 states, including California, Florida and Massachusetts. On the opening night five thousand men and women jammed the drill hall and balconies of the Eighth Armory, filled the standing space, and remained from eight in the evening until past midnight. They came back next day at nine and left at midnight. On the closing day they sat from early afternoon until nearly midnight, scarcely leaving their chairs, intent on the reports of committees and the final speeches.

Here, it seems to this writer, is the inner significance of the Congress-- a significance which has been missed by its critics. Such a gathering, such enthusiasm, such sustained interest are indicative of a deep-rooted and nation-wide dissatisfaction of Negroes that rapidly mounts into a flaming resentment. It is idle to attempt its dismissal as "a Communist gathering." All the Communists in America and Russia could not have inveigled the great majority of those delegates into that trip last winter unless something far deeper than inspired propaganda were driving them. As a matter of fact, delegates were plentiful from the very states where radical parties are weakest.

The Congress was significant, moreover, of the growing importance of labor leadership and of the power of the labor movement. Delegates were present from 80 trade unions, as opposed to only 18 professional and educational groups. The trade union section was the most largely attended and hotly discussed--so much so that it starved the attendance at other important sections. A powerful youth group was present, articulate and aggressive. The church militant was represented on platform and discussion floor, expounding the new social gospel of justice for the underdog.

Criticism of the mechanical operation of the Congress can be most easily justified, for here was evident the committee's lack of promotional funds and the haste of its last-minute preparations. Difficulties were further increased by the armory's inadequate convention facilities and the unstable attitudes of its officials, to say nothing of the mutual suspicion with which rival and dissenting groups regarded each other. Then there was the unpardonably stupid threat of local authorities to close the armory on the opening night because of the discovery of Communist delegates. On the other hand, criticism was freely made that the speakers who were scheduled did not sufficiently represent the different points of view among the delegates.

The true test of the Congress, however, lay in the quality of the resolutions adopted and its plans for making these resolutions effective. The resolutions were uniformly of a high order. To be sure, those on the Church were for the most part full of vague generalities, with the exception of an insistence upon an economic and social, as well as a spiritual gospel. Likewise those on Negro business fell into grievous errors of contradiction with resolutions on labor. It is manifestly inconsistent to urge that "all Negroes consider it their inescapable duty to support Negro business by their patronage," without first exacting a pledge that business men will in turn support labor by paying adequate wages, encouraging union organization and following the spirit of other resolutions passed.

Still, these inconsistencies were surprisingly few in view of the intense speed with which the resolutions committee worked during its few hours of existence. Thoroughly sound positions were taken by the Congress for the most part. There can be no quarrel with resolutions that condemn lynching, exploitation of sharecroppers, civil and social discrimination, and the vicious endorsement of racial equality in trade unions, organization of Negro workers into unions and cooperatives, and support of the Urban League and the N.A.A.C.P.

Plans for continuance of the Congress seem at this writing completely sound. The local sponsoring committees that sent delegates to Chicago are to be continued as follow-up groups. It is to be their task to sell to the Negro public the fundamental correctness of the resolutions passed at Chicago, and to encourage organizations to incorporate these resolutions into their programs. Sectional chairmen are appointed; labor, youth and church committees are to be formed; a National Council of seventy-five members will meet in June to follow up the work that remains to be done after Chicago. There is nothing in the

program that implies supplanting or curtailment of any existing organization
that fights the Negro's battles; rather is the race urged to support these
organizations all the more effectively.

Two dangers exist in the future that must be prepared for in the present.
One is the tendency of praiseworthy enthusiasm to grow tired or go off on a
new tangent. There is the possibility that in many instances the original
sponsoring committees may lose their earlier zeal and local racketeers take
over the Congress idea, to the detriment of its program. This has often
happened, for instance, in "Don't Spend Your Money Where You Can't Work"
campaigns. The National Council must be prepared to discover such deviations
from policy and to break itself--the natural desire of any organization to
perpetuate itself. To do its job properly the Congress must extend over at
least a few years and must grow in size and influence. Yet, the older it grows
and the larger it becomes, the more it will be exposed to the danger of
political control and corrupt bureaucracy--evils which are totally absent today. Definite commitments should be made at once, that the Congress will
deal not with political parties but with economic and civil issues, just as
was the case at Chicago. Definite goals should be set, capable of achievement within two or three years, and it should be agreed now that when these
are arrived at, the Congress will close up shop and disband. By taking these
or similar precautions the National Negro Congress, which is already a noteworthy gathering in our racial history, has the opportunity of completing a
really constructive job and cementing its place in the brilliant annals of
racial progress.

Opportunity, 14 (May, 1936): 151-53.

68.   CIO COUNCIL HEADS NAMED IN PHILADELPHIA

Transport, Gas, Food Legislation Drives Are Discussed

PHILADELPHIA, Pa., Sept. 26.--John L. Lewis, chairman of the Committee
on Industrial Organization, yesterday sent "warm greetings" to the forthcoming
Second National Negro Congress and commended Negroes for the able part they
are "playing in the CIO's march to bring a better life to American workers."

The CIO leader's message was contained in a letter to John P. Davis, exe-
cutive secretary of the Congress, at the convention headquarters in the O. V.
Catto's Elk Lodge, 15th and Fitzwater Sts. The three-day sessions of the
Congress will take place Oct. 15-17.

Earlier the CIO had already endorsed the Congress and last Thursday night
the Philadelphia Council of the CIO followed suit after a stirring address by
John P. Davis.

Lewis' Letter

Lewis' letter in full declared:
"Please convey my warm greetings to the delegates of the National Negro
Congress.

"The Negro people have a great role to play, not only in the American
labor movement, but in the American nation itself. The Committee for Industrial
Organization welcomes this Congress of American men and women to weigh the
problems of the Negro people.

"I want to extend the CIO's gratitude, too, for the able part that Negro
men and women are playing in the CIO's march to bring a better life to American workers. I am convinced that the share of the American Negro in our labor
movement will be even greater in the future.

"Sincerely,
Signed: "JOHN L. LEWIS."

Daily Worker, September 27, 1937.

69. NEGRO CONGRESS GETS SUPPORT FROM CIO

Sessions to Open in Philadelphia October 15--
Will Mark Anniversary of John Brown's
Raid--Preparations Are Speeded

PHILADELPHIA, Pa., Sept. 9.--As this city began to hum with preparations
for the second annual convention of the National Negro Congress, John P. Davis,
national secretary of the Congress, announced today that the Committee for
Industrial Organization had endorsed the forthcoming convention. The Congress
will meet here October 15-17.

Davis, who arrived in the city a few days ago to take charge of preliminary work, made the announcement from the local convention headquarters in
the O. V. Catto Elks Lodge Building, South 16th and Fitzwater Streets.

In addition, the young Negro leader stated that Lieutenant-Governor
Thomas J. Kennedy of Pennsylvania and Mayor S. Davis Wilson of Philadelphia
would address the Congress during its three-day session here next month. A.
Philip Randolph, president of the Brotherhood of Sleeping Car Porters and of
the Congress, will also speak. [77]

To Speak For CIO

Lieutenant-Governor Kennedy will be the principal speaker representing
the CIO and Mayor Wilson will address the opening session which will be in
commemoration of the 150th anniversary of the signing of the Constitution.

The first session's program will begin with exercises at Independent Hall,
culminating in a huge mass meeting in Convention Hall which 15,000 people are
expected to attend.

"The Second National Negro Congress will be larger, more representative
and more successful than the first," Davis said today.

"It will carry forward the historic beginnings which were made at the
first Congress held in Chicago in February, 1936. Since the Chicago meeting
the Congress can record many important victories in behalf of Negro rights in
both the social and economic fields," Davis pointed out.

"At the opening session, in connection with the program commemorating
the anniversary of the constitution, we hope to stress particularly the enforcement of the 13th, 14th and 15th Amendments, and also the fight for passage
of the federal anti-lynching bill, sponsored by the National Association for
the Advancement of Colored People," he explained.

Praises Local Group

A call to the Congress, entitled "Negro America Faces a Crisis," has been
sent to hundreds of Negro labor, civic, religious, fraternal and to all "who
are willing to fight for economic and social justice for Negroes," Davis revealed. "And there have been scores of responses supporting the Congress and
promising participation," he stated.

"Just as our first Congress in Chicago met on the anniversary of the
birthday of Frederick Douglass and Abraham Lincoln, so this one will have
equally historic significance.

"The second day of the Congress--October 16--will be historically important because John Brown's raid struck the first blow at chattel slavery on
that same day in 1851," Davis continued.

At the First National Negro Congress held in Chicago in February 1936,
approximately 600 delegates participated representing a half million Negroes.

Additional information on the Second National Negro Congress can be
secured by writing to the Congress, permanent headquarters at 717 Florida Ave.,
N.W., Washington, D.C., or to the convention headquarters.

Daily Worker, September 10, 1937.

70. NEGRO CONGRESS CALLS FOR UNITED LABOR
MOVEMENT IN CLOSING SESSION

Davis Attacks Tories' Use of Klan
Issue in Case of Justice Black

By Ben Davis, Jr.

METROPOLITAN OPERA HOUSE, PHILADELPHIA, Pa., Oct. 18.--A stirring appeal for "one powerful and united labor movement" marked the closing session of the 3-day Second National Negro Congress, which was attended by a predominantly Negro audience of more than 4,500 persons here last night.

The call for a "healing of a breach in the labor movement" came in a series of some 174 resolutions which were adopted unanimously by the Congress' final business session. Other resolutions sharply condemned the curtailment of WPA, stressing the discriminatory firings of Negroes throughout the country, and upheld the Congress' original policy of a united front for Negro rights and against war and fascism, adopted in Chicago last year.

Earlier in the evening John P. Davis, national executive secretary of the Congress, received wild applause when discussing the controversy over the appointment of Supreme Court Justice Hugo L. Black, declared:

"We condemn the deplorable Klan past of Justice Black. But at the same time, we cannot forget that it is the Liberty League and Hearst forces of reaction in the nation which are today backing Klanism, Black Legionism, and lynch terror against the Negro people." [78]

Honor Allen

The final session was "Richard Allen Night"--in honor of the founder of the Negro Methodist Church 107 years ago and the first Negro who organized a Negro Congress. [79]

The group of noted Negro leaders who spoke included: Walter White, secretary of the National Association for the Advancement of Colored People, who made a brilliant plea for enactment of the Federal anti-lynching bill, Vito Marcantonio, president of the International Labor Defense; Dr. Charles Wesley, professor of History at Howard University; Pres. F. D. Patterson of Tuskegee Institute in Alabama; Crystal Bird Fauset, Negro woman leader of Philadelphia; and Charles W. Burton a prominent lawyer of Chicago. [80]

Among the highlights of the convention were: an address by Lieutenant-Governor Thomas J. Kennedy, of Pennsylvania, and secretary-treasurer of the United Mint Workers of America, who spoke as an official representative of the CIO; a speech by James W. Ford, Negro Communist leader; a special youth session; and a symposium on war and fascism.

Hathaway Speaks

The "war and fascism" symposium was featured by an address of "Collective Security" by Clarence Hathaway, editor of the Daily Worker, who received a tremendous ovation after attacking a previous speech by Norman Thomas, Socialist leader. Thomas argued that collective security "might lead to war."

The Congress reelected A. Philip Randolph, Negro labor leader, as president; John P. Davis as executive secretary. Gladys Stoner, young trade union leader, was elected financial secretary, and U. Simpson Tate of Washington, treasurer. Arthur Huff Fauset of Philadelphia, Max Yergan, director of the International Committee on African Affairs, and Rev. William Jernagins, of Washington, D.C., were elected vice presidents. The Congress also set up a national executive committee, and made other changes in its organizational form and structure.

In addition to greetings from President Roosevelt, the Congress received greetings also from Mayor Fiorello La Guardia, candidate for re-election on the American Labor Party ticket in New York. [81]

Discrimination Hit

Lieut. Gov. Kennedy bitterly condemned discrimination in the labor movement against Negroes and went on to declare:

"Since its origin fifty years ago, the UMWA has had an enforced policy
of admitting all workers into its membership without regard to creed, color
or nationality. We must have legislation against discrimination of every
sort--but we must also have powerful organizations to see that this legislation is enforced.

"You're going to get those things that are yours only if you take them.
See that you're organized and united in such Congresses as this to get those
things."

In an impassioned appeal for unity of Negro and white workers, Lieut.
Gov. Kennedy said:

"If the Negro people of this nation are completely organized in industrial
organizations--joining with their white brothers for progress on every front--
the very lessons of unity learned here can be spread into other avenues. This
will aid the solution of other problems which confront Negro people. It will
open the door of opportunity to the Negro in every other walk of life, and
solve other problems which spring from economic sources."

Welcome Ford

One of the most impressive ovations of the convention was given to Ford,
who was greeted with cheers and whistling as he arose to speak. The ovation
soared to greater heights when he finished a masterful address with the stirring and historic words, "John Brown's Body Marches On."

Other addresses set a high point in the growing political development and
solidarity of all sections of the Negro people.

Among them were speeches by Edward E. Strong, outstanding young leader of
the national youth division of the Congress, and leader of the Southern Negro
Youth Conference of Richmond, Va.; Max Yergan, director of the International
Committee on African Affairs, of New York, who blasted to smithereens the
Japanese militarist theory, that "Japan is the friend of the darker peoples
of the earth;" the Rev. Marshall Shepherd, Negro Pennsylvania legislator, who
pointed out the identity of interest between the Negro church and the progressive trade union movement. The session was presided over by Arthur Huff Fauset,
regional vice-president of the Congress, and outstanding Negro author and
leader.

Calls For New John Browns

"John Brown symbolized the unity of Negro and white people against slavery
and reaction of his day. The times call for New John Browns, Abraham Lincolns,
Frederick Douglasses, and Sojourner Truths, and modern abolitionists. Our
people are not lacking in modern figures of this type," Ford stated amidst
resounding applause.

"Thousands of Angelo Herndons are rising among our people. There are
John Browns and many Douglasses. The fighters for Twentieth Century Americanism are growing throughout the land.

The National Negro Congress has set its imprint upon our people and the
country. Under the leadership of A. Philip Randolph, John P. Davis, and
Edward Strong and their collaborators in trade unions, in mills, factories,
in schools and colleges, and among the young people generally, and in the
churches, fraternal organizations, we are marching forward. We are marching
forward with the support of our sympathizers among white workers, intellectuals,
and middle classes," Ford declared.

Hathaway Appeals

In the session on war and fascism, Clarence Hathaway won the day with an
unanswerable appeal for the policy of collective security against war and a
caustic trimming of Norman Thomas who echoed the fascist argument that collective security means war.

Speakers at the symposium included: Dr. Harry P. Ward, chairman of the
American League against War and Fascism; Louise Thompson, Negro woman leader
who reported on the recent Paris conference against Anti-Semitism and racialism, which she attended as a Congress delegate; C. S. Chang, Chinese leader
and outstanding figure in the American Friends of the Chinese people; the

Rev. Wm. Lloyd Imes, New York Negro minister, and chairman of the United Aid
for Peoples of African Descent; Dr. Malaku E. Baven, of the World Ethiopian
Federation, and personal representative of Emperor Haile Selassie to America;
William L. Patterson, who explained the peace policy of the Soviet Union; and
Harris Harwood, chairman.

Norman Thomas's speech was marked by thorough-going condition and a doctrine of abject surrender on the part of the peoples of the world to the
fascist warmakers. "The main danger to the people is not so much fascism, but
capitalism," said Thomas before a conspicuously silent audience.

The Socialist leader asserted--again amidst noticeable silence--that
collective security "might lead to war."

Calmly, cooly, the Daily Worker editor tore Thomas's argument to shreds.
"We face reality," Hathaway began. "There is war and there is fascism.
Concretely our tasks are how to stop them from spreading throughout the world.
All the pretty speeches will not make any difference, unless backed by clear-
headed action. That means that we must use all the forces at our disposal
today to stop these two main evils. Ultimately the decisive anti-war force
is the peace-loving people of the world, but every force against war must be
united now to stop the present reality of growing war and fascism."

Putting the question of immediate action, Hathaway aroused a veritable
storm of applause when he said with rapier-like thrusts:

"We have advocated for years--even as now--the unity of the Socialist and
Communist Parties as a basic force in the fight against war and fascism. We
have advocated and still advocate the unity of the trade union movement. Already the action of the CIO and the A.F. of L. supporting the boycott movement
against Japan show the real potentially effective force which the labor movement can be in an anti-war, anti-fascist movement.

Calls for Boycott

"Mr. Thomas is an opponent of collective security. I am an advocate of
it," Hathaway declared amidst another burst of applause.

The Daily Worker editor called for a boycott against Japanese goods--
and Nazi and Italian fascist products as well. He called for support of the
American League Against War and Fascism as the type of mass organization which
can materially aid in stopping the fascist aggressors, who now "butcher the
Spanish, Ethiopian and Chinese peoples."

Chang, who urged the unity of the Negro people with the people of China
in the fight against Japanese militarism, received a tremendous ovation, be-
speaking the sympathy of the Negro people with the Chinese people.

In a well-reached correction of Dr. Imes, who had urged the theory of the
"darker races" as against the white races, Chang stated:

Cites "Company"

"How can Japan be called the friend of the darker races and at the same
time be the friend of Mussolini, the butcher of the Ethiopian people, and
Hitler, the fascist persecutor of the Spanish and German people. We know
people by the company they keep."

Dr. Ward said any idea of the "isolation" of the United States was a
"myth."

"The United States is already in the present world conflicts up to her
neck," the distinguished religious leader asserted.

Because we can't trust capitalist governments, he said, we must use our
pressure to force them to do what they should. That means that the United
States must be forced to lift the embargo against Spain, and place one against
Hitler and Mussolini, he continued.

Daily Worker, October 19, 1937.

71. NEGRO CONGRESS WILL GIVE WEIGHT
TO UNION DRIVES, RANDOLPH SAYS

A. Philip Randolph is president of the National Negro Congress which will
hold its second national convention in Philadelphia, Oct. 15-17. He is also
International President of the Brotherhood of Sleeping Car Porters, an affil-
iate of the American Federation of Labor, and one of the outstanding labor
leaders of the country.
His article below was written exclusively for the Daily Worker.

By A. Philip Randolph

The Negro people hail the second annual meeting of the National Negro
Congress!
The liberal and progressive people of the country without regard to race
or color, creed or nationality, all hail the Congress. The Second National
Negro Congress comes at a crucial period of transition in the life of the
world and the Negro race. Problems of the gravest import challenge the progressive forces of modern society. All groups are faced with the necessity of
taking decisive action on the significant and vital trends of social forces,
for war is abroad in the world and fascism is rampant.
The Negro is confronted with the task of holding on to the liberties he
already has and fighting to secure those he is entitled to in these United
States in particular, and the world in general. Different from other groups
in the country, the Negro people have never secured the elementary civil and
political rights that come with the establishment of democratic government,
following the overthrow of the slave regime.
While the right to vote, to be voted for, and to have an economic stake
in the country, and to secure an education are the natural rights and privileges that come with the transition from an autocratic slave system to the
creation of a democratic republic, the Negro race has never enjoyed these
rights and privileges, especially in the Southern states. Because he has never
participated in the fruits of a bourgeois revolution which was achieved
partially by the Civil War, Negroes have the problem of completing their incomplete political and civil emancipation.
It is a notorious fact that in the Southern states, grandfather clauses
are invoked against Negroes seeking to exercise the right to vote vouchsafed
them by the Fourteenth Amendment to the Constitution. When grandfather clauses
fail fully to bar Negroes from participating in national, state and municipal
elections, the new device of the "lily white primaries" was invented and
thrown into the balance against them.
But the Negro people are awakening. They are becoming more conscious of
their rights as American citizens. They are also sensing their power. They
are turning their backs on the old Uncle Tom type of leadership which counsels
"let well enough alone." They are courageously beginning to demand their place
in the sun.

New Spirit

This new spirit is expressed in the Second National Negro Congress as it
was expressed in the first. While there are many Negro organizations, such
as the National Association for the Advancement of Colored People which are
ably fighting the battles of the Negro on the civil and political fronts, none
has been able to rally the mass support of the Negro people, upon any vital
and pressing issue. However, without the support of the Negro masses, the
battles of the race cannot be won. The masses possess the power. This is the
supreme job of the Second National Negro Congress.
Now, the tactic and strategy of the National Negro Congress is to stir,
mobilize and rally the masses in the development of a united front. The united
front means the unity of all of the various and varying Negro organizations,
together with liberal and progressive movements among the white population
upon a minimum program. Because of the menace and threat of lynching to black
Americans, all Negro organizations, regardless of their differing philosophies
on religion and politics, are of one mind in their desire to wipe out this
disgrace in America.

The right to vote and to be voted for and the abolition of disfranchise-
ment through grandfather clauses and lily-white primaries, together with en-
forcement of the Fourteenth Amendment is the demand of all Negro people, alike.
Peonage, too, a form of involuntary servitude which is a violation of the
Thirteenth Amendment to the Constitution is also assailed and condemned by
Negro leaders and movements in all camps.[82]

In Labor Unions

The right to work and to join labor organizations that increase the power
of the Negro people to improve their standard of living are, too, an important
objective of the race. Adequate relief and the securing of justice in the
courts provoke no differences of opinion among Negroes so far as their interest
in obtaining these results are concerned.

To the end of fusing and cementing the forces in Negro life together for
the purpose of realizing the aforementioned demands, the Second National Negro
Congress is called. The church, school, fraternity, sorority, fraternal lodge,
home, trade union, social club, art guild, and all of the various agencies
that express Negro thought and action will be embraced in this Congress. Resolutions and proclamations bearing upon the consolidation of the Negro liberation movements will be presented and discussed in the various sections to provide the directive and driving forces in the Negro struggle for emancipation.

Trade union and industrial organization for Negro workers, will occupy
an important place on the agenda. The great drive to organize the mass production industries by CIO has had its appeal for the Negro masses. Hundreds of
thousands of Negro workers are embraced in these industries. They are ready
for organization. They demand it. They are willing to pay the price along
with their white brothers in struggle, suffering and sacrifice, to achieve
labor solidarity to protect and advance their rights. Thus, they are pouring
in large numbers into the CIO unions that are organizing these industries.
They are not only becoming members, but they are playing a significant and
constructive role in the work of organization itself.

Play Big Role

Some of the most aggressive and effective organizers in the Committee for
Industrial Organization are Negro workers. They have done a great job
in the steel mills, in automobile and rubber factories, and throughout the far
flung mass production industries of the country. Participation in this momentous organization struggle is bringing a new prospective to the Negro people.
They are realizing that they constitute an integral part of the working class
of America and that they will rise or fall with this class. They are beginning to see that their hope lies in increasing their bargaining power so as
to raise the price or wage of their labor. They are recognizing that this
cannot be done alone, merely as Negro workers but only as a part of organized
labor.

Thus, in unions, affiliated with the American Federation of Labor or the
Committee for Industrial Organization, Negroes are seeking membership if they
are workers in industries covered by these labor movements.

The National Negro Congress will throw its weight behind the drive to
organize Negro workers in all industries, mass production and otherwise. It
will urge Negro workers to join hands with their white brothers and fight
for trade union solidarity and democracy. It will counsel Negroes to turn
their backs on the company union and participate in the bona fide, trade and
industrial unions of America affiliated with the CIO and A.F. of L. according
as they are in industries that are covered by these two sections of labor.

Fight on Lynching

The brilliant and significant fight waged against lynching through the
effort to enact the Wagner-Gavagan Anti-lynching Bill, by the National Association for the Advancement of Colored People will receive the support of the
Congress.

Negro business enterprises, especially of the co-operative form will also
receive the interest and attention and support of the Congress. The youth
movements among the Negro people will constitute one of the outstanding sections

of the Congress and serve as a powerful force in calling the Congress to the struggle of the Negro in the South to achieve the status of manhood.

Within the period of a few weeks, the Second Congress, whose headquarters are established in Philadelphia, and whose sessions begin Oct. 15 and extend through the 17th under the able and vigorous direction of John P. Davis, national secretary, has caught the imagination and interest of the wide masses of Negro people. It is eminently timely that the Congress makes its second bow to the American public in historic Philadelphia where the Declaration of Independence and the Federal Constitution were framed and adopted. The Negro people through the Congress will assert their right to the Constitution on its hundredth and fiftieth birth year. They will demand that the basic principles of the Constitution be enforced to preserve democratic institutions and traditions in America and to complete their emancipation.

Daily Worker, September 28, 1937.

72.   COMMITTEE FOR INDUSTRIAL ORGANIZATION
1106 Connecticut Avenue, N.W.
Washington, D.C.

September 22, 1937

National Negro Congress
Convention Headquarters
Philadelphia, Pennsylvania

Gentlemen:

Please convey my warm greetings to the delegates of the National Negro Congress.

The Negro people have a great role to play, not only in the American labor movement, but in the American nation itself. The Committee for Industrial Organization welcomes this Congress of American men and women to weigh the problems of the Negro people.

I want to extend the CIO's gratitude, too, for the able part that Negro men and women are playing in the CIO's march to bring a better life to American workers. I am convinced that the share of the American Negro in our labor movement will be even greater in the future.

Sincerely,

(Signed) John L. Lewis

In the letter reproduced above John L. Lewis, Chairman of the Committee for Industrial Organization, pledged the support of the unions affiliated with the committee to the National Negro Congress which opens soon in Philadelphia. In the letter Lewis hailed the militancy of the Negro members of the CIO unions and praised their activities during the recent strikes in the Midwest.

Daily Worker, September 28, 1937.

73.   HARLEM UNIONS BACK NATIONAL NEGRO CONGRESS

Randolph Gives Local Developments His Closest Attention--
Gaulden, Other Leaders Give Time for Organizing Problems

Harlem's leading organizations and trade unions were placing their best
talent at the disposal of the preparatory activities of the local council of
the National Negro Congress, it was learned this morning.

A. Philip Randolph, international president of the Brotherhood of Sleeping
Car Porters and president of the National Negro Congress, is following local
developments with close attention and urging trade unions to participate in
the congress in Philadelphia, Oct. 15, 16, and 17.

Headquarters were opened a few days ago at 189 Lenox Ave., with A. W.
Berry, organizer of the Upper Harlem Section of the Communist Party, in
charge as chairman of the action committee.

Crosswaith a Delegate

William Gaulden, national organizer of the American Federation of State,
County, and Municipal Employes Union, is devoting much of his time in
speaking to trade unions, urging them to take a leading role in the Philadelphia proceedings.

In discussing the situation, Mr. Gaulden stated:

"We are especially pleased over the report that Mr. Frank Crosswaith,
chairman of the Negro Labor Committee, will be a delegate to the Philadelphia
Congress."

It is expected that the Negro Labor Committee will officially endorse
the congress, thereby laying the foundation for a firm trade union base in the
congress proceedings.

Among other Harlem leaders who have donated their services to the local
preparations of the congress are: Gladys Stoner, ERB employe; Rev. A. Clayton
Powell, Jr., pastor of the Abyssinian Baptist Church; and many others whose
names will be announced later.

Unions Responding

The most heartening feature of the congress preparations is the widespread
response of CIO and progressive A.F. of L. unions to John L. Lewis' recent call
read in part:

"The Negro people have a great role to play, not only in the American labor
movement, but in the American nation itself. The Committee for Industrial
Organization welcomes this Congress of American men and women to weigh the problems of the Negro people."

Present indications are that an unprecedentedly large trade union delegation will go to the congress. To facilitate transportation, a special train
has been chartered to leave New York, at the Pennsylvania Station on the afternoon of Friday, Oct. 15, 3:30 P.M. The cost of a round-trip for each delegate
will be $2.80

Daily Worker, October 4, 1937.

74. ROOSEVELT GREETS NEGRO CONGRESS

800 Delegates Attend Sub-Sessions on Trade Unions

By Ben Davis, Jr.

PHILADELPHIA, Oct. 17.--Meeting with the encouragement of a telegram of
"best wishes" from President Roosevelt, the National Negro Congress today
entered the third day of piercing discussions of all phases and walks of Negro
life as they form part of the main current of American progress.

President Roosevelt sent a telegram of greetings to the opening session
of the Congress Friday night, which brought forth deafening applause when read
by John P. Davis, brilliant young national secretary of the Congress.

"I am glad to extend greetings to the Second National Negro Congress,"
the President's telegram read. "It seems to me that participation of delegates

from the United States and foreign countries in a discussion of such pertinent and major issues as housing, education and employment cannot but be significant and productive of tangible results. Please accept my best wishes for the success of your deliberations."

More than 4,000 Negroes packed the Metropolitan Opera House here at the opening session Friday night when A. Philip Randolph, president of the National Negro Congress, sounded a powerful call for unity in the fight for Negro rights and scathingly denounced the "fascist governments who have enveloped large areas of the world in the flames of war."

Davis Speaks

John P. Davis National Secretary of the National Negro Congress, told an audience of more than 3,000 delegates and visitors this afternoon, that one of the "biggest unfinished jobs of the Congress is to clean out jim-crowism against Negro workers in the massive railroad industry." Davis' speech was followed by open discussion from the floor.

Making his annual report before a business session of the congress, Davis evoked repeated applause as he described the "inspiring achievements" of the congress and declared:

"Of course, we have made mistakes--but these have been the mistakes arising out of the growth of our congress. The congress was born more than a year ago out of the united desire of the Negro people for liberation. To that task it is dedicated--and with out combined and united strength, its opportunities for carrying forward the fight for freedom of Black America are today greater than ever before."

Secretary Davis cited the assistance of the congress in the CIO campaigns, declaring that the congress had distributed 250,000 pieces of trade union literature.

"It has also established the southern conference representing 250,000 Negro youth, the gut of the Negro to take his place beside the peace-loving people of the World."

"We hope in the immediate future to aid in the organization of a world congress of Negro people which will register a solid phalanx against fascism, war and to aid the liberation of the peoples of Africa, America and the oppressed everywhere."

Just before Davis spoke the congress passed a resolution condemning a neighborhood restaurant, the Rural, located on Broad St., which discriminated against a Negro delegate, John McNeil. It elected a committee which is to "force a public apology" from the owner and throw a picket line around the store. Chas. Wesley Burton, Negro leader of Chicago was chairman of the business sessions.

Scottsboro Mother Speaks

The keynote of the various sessions, whether they were directly concerned with labor or not, was the organization of the Negro worker in the present surge of organization sweeping the United States.

Throughout the various sessions the words which were most frequently heard were "CIO" and "organize the unorganized."

A note of tragedy crept into the Civil Liberties division yesterday when Mrs. Ada Wright, mother of Andy Wright of the five imprisoned Scottsboro boys, brought the audience to tears with a touching description of how her son Andy is now in danger of losing his right arm due to prison mistreatment.

As she spoke, tears trickled from eyes. Ruby Bates, star Scottsboro defense witness and Olen Montgomery and Roy Wright, two of the freed Scottsboro boys sat in the audience.

Sub Sessions

"We must hasten every bit of help we can give to the Scottsboro Defense Committee, in the fight to free my son and the other boys before they are dead," the world-famous Scottsboro mother stated.

The convention has been divided into the following sub-sessions, covering practically every field of Negro life: Trade unions, cultural, fraternal, church, youth, women, war and fascism, unemployment, civil liberties, housing,

and others. These sub-session discussions, in which the trade union section
played the leading role, have taken place in the morning and afternoons.

Herndon Cheered

Richard Moore, Negro ILD leader, made an eloquent appeal for the Scottsboro Boys, and later introduced a resolution for the freedom of the boys which
was adopted by the session.[83]
In addressing the Civil Liberties session late this afternoon, Angelo
Herndon, receiving a tremendous ovation, said:
"The right to freedom of assembly is still jeopardized by the reactionary
United States Supreme Court which only freed four of the Scottsboro boys and
myself because of the united mass pressure of the Negro people and their white
supporters. Yes, the words of Chief Justice Taney that the 'Negro has no
rights which a white man is bound to respect' is today a cardinal principle of
the Supreme Court with its dictatorial power to thwart the will of the people."

Trade Union Session

The trade union session which is held in the orchestra of the giant hall
and is attended by an average of 800 delegates--mostly Negroes--continues to
occupy the center of the attraction. Meanwhile, the rest of the congress
revolved into encroachments of reaction upon all phases of Negro life.
The Wall Street-Liberty League tories were assailed as the main enemies
of the Negro people in culture, women's, youth, church, and the trade union
sessions alike.
As one Negro artist in the cultural session put it: "We are artists, but
can we continue to be unless we eat, have jobs and a place to live? It seems
to me that our interests lie with all those who have to struggle for the right
to live decently." It appeared certain that the cultural session would pass
a resolution calling for endorsement of H.R. 8239, for a Federal Permanent
Arts bill.

Leading Writers Speak

Rex Ingram, famous Negro actor and screen star, urged the Negro theatre
"to develop plays with social content, expressing the hopes and desires of the
Negro people and how to win them." He suggested plays on such historic Negro
leaders as Frederick Douglass, Harriet Tubman, Sojourner Truth, and great
fighters during the pre-Civil War days who "acted in real life the drama of
the underground railway," which liberated many Negro slaves.[84]
Loren Miller, brilliant young Negro writer and Attorney of Los Angeles,
in addressing the cultural session said:
"The Negro artist must understand the trend of world events so that we
know best how to break down the jim-crow ghetto in which we live."[85]
Among others who addressed the cultural session were Gwendolyn Bennett,
young Negro representative of the Harlem Artists Guild, Dr. Alaine Leroy Locke,
head of the Department of Philosophy of Howard University, and Sterling Brown,
distinguished young Negro poet and author.[86]
Speakers at the trade union session this afternoon included William
Gaulden, prominent Negro leader in the Federation of State, County and
Municipal Employees, Lillian Gaskins, Negro woman member of Local 22, of the
powerful International Ladies' Garment Workers Union, CIO, Henry Johnson,
Negro organizers of the CIO in the steel and packing house workers and execu-
tive secretary of the Chicago Negro Congress, B. D. Amis, Negro CIO organizer
of Philadelphia and A. W. Berry, Negro member of the Central Committee of the
Communist Party.
Columbus Alston, 24-year-old Negro CIO organizer of tobacco workers in
Virginia, received an ovation this morning upon organization of 4,000 Negro
tobacco workers in Richmond.
The congress will close its three-day session here tonight, when the
Resolutions and Presiding Committees will report and national officers are
to be elected.
Other greetings came from: John L. Lewis, CIO leader, the Toledo Ohio
Industrial Council of the CIO, the Marconian Ethiopian Association of Paris,
France, the New York division of the Brotherhood of Sleeping Car Porters,

Ben Gold, president of the Fur Workers Union and Communist leader, the National
Committee of the International Labor Defense, the Connecticut Methodist conference, the Workers Alliance's, federal writers local of New York, and the
Club Obrero Espanol.[87]
Receiving a standing ovation as he rose to speak. Randolph discussed
virtually every major national and international issue as they affect the Negro
people. A spontaneous outburst of cheers and applause interrupted his address when he said: that "the Czar of all Russia was relegated to oblivion
by the new Soviet Union."

Woman Leader Speaks

Preceding Randolph's address, the audience was swept to dramatic heights
by the speech of Dr. Charlotte Hawkins Brown, Negro woman president of Palmer
Memorial Institute of North Carolina.
Her voice marked by a tremulous but unfaltering tone, Mrs. Brown reached
the high point of her address when she said;
"Until this intelligent Negro links up with this ignorant Negro--who must
even be taught what you're talking about--we cannot win freedom. And let me
tell you not all the ignorant Negroes are below the Mason-Dixon line. Our
freedom to eat, live, and even sleep as decent human beings--must be obtained
at a great price. But I say to you in the words of Patrick Henry: 'Give us
liberty or give us death!'"
The audience leaped to its feet and it was several moments before the
Negro woman leader could resume her eloquent speech.
"The constitution was a compromise document," declared Randolph, whose
controlled passion made his delivery all the more impressive, "but the 13th,
14th and 15th amendments were placed there to assure the full rights of
citizenship for the Negro people.
"Victory for the Negro people is not yet complete, for peonage of Black
America--economic, and social, remains.

Daily Worker, October 18, 1937.

75. KENNEDY SPEAKER AT THE NEGRO CONGRESS

PHILADELPHIA.--Three thousand delegates to the second annual convention
of the National Negro Congress, to be held October 15-18 in this city, will
hear Lieutenant-Governor Thomas J. Kennedy of Pennsylvania; Senator Robert M.
LaFollette, Jr.; Mayor S. Davis Wilson, of Philadelphia; and A. Philip Randolph,
president of the Brotherhood of Pullman Porters, as principal speakers.[88]
The convention has been endorsed by John L. Lewis, chairman of the Committee for Industrial Organization.
The delegates, who represent more than 600 Negro workers' organizations,
will hear Lieutenant-Governor Kennedy discuss "The Committee for Industrial
Organization and the Negro People." The congress has been active during the
year and a half of its existence in promoting Committee for Industrial Organization activities among Negro workers in steel, mining, tobacco, maritime and
a number of miscellaneous industries.

United Mine Workers' Journal, October 1, 1937.

76. BROPHY RAPS LYNCHING AT NEGRO PARLEY

WASHINGTON.--Delegates from 20 states and 30 organizations heard John
Brophy, CIO director, denounce lynching as a weapon of anti-labor employers at
the conference of the National Negro Congress on the anti-lynching bill held
this week in Washington.[89]

"The crime of lynching has a definite economic base," Brophy told the delegates. "Unscrupulous elements in the south and elsewhere have used it for generations as a device to split white and Negro workers."

"It is as much a weapon in the arsenal of anti-union terror as clubbing, tear-gassing and other ways of breaking picket lines and destroying union organization," he declared.

"Behind every lynching is the figure of the labor exploiter, the man or the corporation who would deny labor its fundamental rights."

Support Anti-Lynch Bills

Brophy explained that the CIO supported anti-lynch legislation as part of its program for the organization of all workers, regardless of race, nationality or political belief. The AFL, he pointed out, had a long record of discrimination against Negro workers, which was a serious factor in its failure, after 50 years of existence, to organize industrial workers.

Brophy cited the record of the CIO in organizing Negro workers, pointing to the large numbers elected as officers of their local unions, and quoted the stand of the CIO at its Atlantic City conference against lynching and all types of terrorist acts on the part of employers.

Labor's Non-Partisan League promised its full support for the anti-lynching bill, stating that voting records of Senators and Congressmen were being closely watched for their action on this and all similar progressive labor legislation.

CIO News, March 25, 1938.

77. PRES. LEWIS DISCUSSES MAJOR U.S. ISSUES AT NATL. NEGRO CONGRESS

THE CIO NEWS presents in abridged form, the text of CIO Pres. John L. Lewis' speech to the Natl. Negro Congress at Washington on April 26:

I appreciate deeply the honor of being invited to address this assembly of American citizens. The Negro people have a growing importance and place in American life. The great contributions which have been made by Negro leaders to American life to the past and the even greater contributions which will come in the future emphasize the significance of your fine gathering. I am glad to have this opportunity to pay tribute to these accomplishments.

It is fitting indeed that you asked to appear before you a representative of organized labor. Most of the Negro people in this country are wage earners. Many of them are members of the CIO, active and effective in their union membership. They are American workers, and, as such, they have a common stake in the growth and power of organized labor. Within the CIO all American workers have equal rights, as the CIO Constitution says, "regardless of race, creed, color or nationality."

Not Yet a Fact

You know full well, some of you from bitter experience, that these rights are not yet a fact in our nation. You know that the iniquities of the poll tax have held from millions of American citizens their right to cast their vote. In this great capital city today, many of those who are in the forefront of the fight to strike down the rights of labor and the common people are men who have been sent to Washington by a small minority of citizens in their states, men who would not be here in Washington if the citizens whom they are supposed to represent could cast a vote.

I have publicly urged the President and the Attorney General of the United States to instruct the Civil Liberties Bureau of the Department of Justice to bring into the Federal courts of this country a judicial proceeding to attack and strike down the cowardly restraints inflicted upon the citizens of the Southern states by poll tax laws. There has been no reply. Nothing has been done.

Let there be no mistake about it, labor will not rest until the right to
vote becomes the right of every citizen, unhampered by such devices as the
poll tax.

Stop Lynching

Last week the chief of our national police force frightened a hall full
of elderly ladies with immoderate and fantastic stories of plots against our
country by foreign powers. Let him turn his face to cabins where American
people are being lashed by white-robed riders. Let him look to cities, where
American workers who seek their right to organize are cruelly maimed and killed.
Let him seek the dark night trails of lynching parties, who thrust aside the
fundamental principles of American justice.

Let those who are responsible in this country rout out these evils. So
let them use this influence and high office to enact Federal anti-lynching
legislation, so long delayed by the cowardly tactics of those who would knife
it behind the scenes. We will not need to fear the plots of foreign powers
if our people have faith in their government.

Save America First

There are people in this country who want to get us into war. They are
growing bolder. Mark you, soon they will have worked up their courage to talk
about going to war to save Iceland and Borneo. We must not go to war.

If it is our mission to save Western civilization, then let us begin by
saving it right here in our own country. Our responsibility is to preserve
American civilization. We will defend our country--let no one doubt that the
sons of American working men and women will be the first in line should the
integrity of our nation be attacked. We must not send them to die in foreign
fields. There is work to be done at home.

There is an ancient and dishonorable formula well known to the practitioners
of politics, through all the centuries of recorded history, which teaches that
the failure to solve domestic problems can often be obscured by the excitement
of a foreign war. Somehow it is easier to interest the rich and the powerful
in sending other people's sons to Borneo than it is to get them to concern
themselves about providing jobs and education for other people's sons.

Some politicians tire too quickly of wrestling with the knotty questions
which are attendant upon getting full employment and decent security for our
people. They recoil from the necessity of thinking and acting in new ways.
How much easier it is for them to forget these troubles, to mount a reviewing
stand and wave a silk hat while other people's children march off to the sound
of a military band.

The temptation is strong to forget the hard difficulties of unemployment,
of the aged, of ill health, of housing and dream of the rule of saviours of
the world. Only the voice of the American people lifted unceasingly against
war can keep politicians from dreaming these dreams.

The CIO office has a staff which follows very closely the journals of
trade and industry. They tell me that increasingly these papers report that
economic recovery depends upon the outbreak of more deadly, more destructive
war abroad. I do not believe for one minute that the majority of American
business men want to make profit out of war. I know too many who have told me
of their horror of such commerce. Yet our failure to determine upon and to
take domestic measures that will bring internal prosperity leads them more and
more to cast their eyes abroad.

We Cannot Forget

We cannot forget the years between 1914 and 1917, when the economic
powers of this country became persuaded that American prosperity was dependent
upon the European war. We cannot forget that the few in this country enriched
themselves on the basis of foreign debts to our government, debts which were
never repaid and now lie against the account of this United States as a bar to
expenditures for our unemployed, our ill and our aged.

The Way to Stay Out

The best way to stay out of war, the best defense against external or internal attack, so to create within our borders a prosperous happy nation. That is labor's answer to those who want war.

There are almost 12 million unemployed today. But even this startling figure includes only the outside boundaries of the real problem. Unemployment cannot be measured alone by those who are completely out of work, but must also encompass those whose incomes do not provide a livelihood.

Leaders of CIO unions have just been engaged in presenting a series of notable statements to the Temporary National Economic Committees proving that it is now the trend of American industry to throw out upon the streets hundreds of thousands of workers replaced by machines each year. In steel alone within three years the automatic strip mills will have thrown out more than 80,000 workers, leaving ghost towns and gutted homes in once prosperous cities. I could tell the same story in the coal industry, and in the auto industry, in textiles and many others.

Seek Conference

We in labor have cried aloud during the past two years asking that the President of these United States call together in this city a working conference of the nation's leaders in industry, in government in labor and in agriculture. We have asked them to lay before that committee this problem of unemployment and tell them that they must sit about a table until they can agree upon proposals. We are sincere about this proposal. We believe it is an honest and sensible American way to proceed. Yet we have had no reply.

Let me read you a statement: "We believe that unemployment is a national problem, and that it is an inescapable problem of our government to meet it in a national way. . . . where business fails to supply . . . employment, we believe that work at prevailing wages should be provided in cooperation with the state and local governments on useful public projects, to the end that the national wealth may be increased, the skill and energy of the worker may be utilized, his morale maintained, and the unemployed assured the opportunity to earn the necessities of life."

Not Fulfilled

That is taken from the platform of the Democratic Party in 1936. Most of us supported that party, that platform, in 1936. We believe that the party should meet its obligations as set forth in this platform. Yet at no time since 1936 has even this obligation to the unemployed been fulfilled. And right now the provision of work through WPA and PWA for the unemployed is lower than at any time since 1936 and it is going down.

A recent poll in a national magazine of some repute indicated that the American people wanted money first spent for work to end poverty and unemployment. That is a common plank upon which we as American citizens can join.

I know the problems of the men and women who work for a living, and I know only too vividly how great is the terror that lies in their hearts when they think of the day when they are old and can no longer work for their bread. But as yet the best that unemployed old people can hope for is an average of $10 to $15 a month for single people, and $15 to $20 a month for married couples at the age of 65. What a pittance! It cannot be dignified with the name of old age security. The CIO calls upon the government to set up at least a minimum system of old age security to pay $60 a month to all over 60 years of age and $90 a month for each married couple.

Program for Youth

In the same way we speak for a real program to give jobs and education to young people. Out of the 12 million unemployed more than five million must be young people between 16 and 25 years of age, most of whom have never had the chance to lay their hand to work in industry.

It is on the basis of such principles that we of labor call upon other groups of American citizens interested in the common welfare to join in demanding that the political leaders of the nation stand by and deliver or give way to those who can.

It is not sinful to ask for security. Those who cry aloud that security is an unworthy aim have never known insecurity.

Invitation to Join

No group in the population feels more heavily the burden of unemployment and insecurity than the Negro citizens. Among the unemployed and among the low income families the proportion of Negroes is far greater than that of any other group. The denials of civil liberties lie with heavy discrimination upon Negroes. Only when these economic and political evils are wiped out will the Negro people be free of them.

In this same hall in February, I extended an invitation to the American Youth Congress and the millions of young people affiliated with it to make common cause with Labor's Non-Partisan League for the promotion of a just and sensible program for public welfare. To the National Negro Congress and to your affiliates I would extend that same invitation to affiliate with or to reach a working agreement with Labor's Non-Partisan League that our common purposes may better be attained.

CIO News, April 29, 1940.

78. LEWIS INVITES NATL. NEGRO CONGRESS TO JOIN LABOR LEAGUE

By C. W. Fowler

WASHINGTON, April 26.--Labor in America will not rest until unemployment, the threat of war, and the injustice of the poll tax and lynch law are wiped out and all Americans enjoy equal rights, John L. Lewis told a cheering audience today of more than 2,500 at the Natl. Negro Congress here. His speech, which was the main event of the meeting, was broadcast over a national radio hookup of the Natl. Broadcasting Company.

Lewis' speech contained an invitation to Negro organizations to "make common cause with Labor's Non-Partisan League for the promotion of a just and sensible program for public welfare."

Lewis praised the "great contributions made by Negro leaders" and the work of the Natl. Negro Congress, pointing out that many thousands of Negro wage earners are "active and effective" members of the CIO, where they enjoy equal rights with all other workers.

He hit sharply at the Administration and the Dept. of Justice for its failure to do anything about the particular oppressions felt by the Negro workers, in the poll tax and in the teror waged against them by lynchers and "white robed riders." He reminded his hearers that he had called on the President and the Department to outlaw the un-American poll tax and upon Congress to pass the anti-lynch bill, but, "There has been no reply. Nothing has been done."

Scores FBI

He accused Chief G-Man Hoover of frightening "a hall full of elderly ladies with fantastic stories of plots against our country by foreign powers," while ignoring Ku Kluxism and vigilantism. [90]

"Let him turn his face to cabins where American people are being lashed by white-robed riders," he said. "Let him look to cities where American workers who seek their rights are cruelly maimed and killed. Let him seek the dark night trails of lynching parties, who thrust aside the fundamental principles of American justice."

Hits Poll Tax

Lewis was equally sharp in attacking the poll tax used to disfranchise Negro and white workers in eight Southern states, which he described as a means for perpetuating the rule of a handful of Southern Bourbon Congressmen and Senators.

"In this great capital city today, many of those who are in the forefront of the fight to strike down the rights of labor and the common people are men who have been sent to Washington by a small minority of citizens in their states

--men who would not be here if the citizens they are supposed to represent
could cast a vote," he said.

War Monger Bolder

Politicians who want to get us into war are growing bolder, Lewis declared, as they turn away from knotty domestic problems they are unwilling to
solve by the "dishonorable formula of a foreign war. Mark you, they will soon
have worked up their courage to talk about going to war to save Iceland and
Borneo," he warned.
"The best way to stay out of war, and the best defense against external
or internal attack is to create within our borders a prosperous, happy nation.
That is labor's answer to those who want war."

No. 1 Problem

Unemployment is still the "first problem" of all Americans, he declared,
with 12,000,000 out of jobs, yet to date the leaders of Government have refused
to reply to the CIO request for a national conference of government, labor,
business and farm representatives to work out a solution.
"It is not sinful to ask for security," Lewis said, in urging adequate
care for the aged, the unemployed, and the disabled. "Those who cry aloud
that security is an unworthy aim have never known insecurity."

CIO News, April 29, 1940.

79. THE NEGRO CONGRESS--ITS FUTURE

By Lester B. Granger

With A. Philip Randolph refusing to stand for re-election as president of
the National Negro Congress, with the Congress voting to consider affiliation
with Labor's Non-Partisan League, with National Secretary John P. Davis winning
a roar of applause from the delegates with his praise of the Soviet Union,
what is the future of the Congress as an important national organization?
It would take a real political seer to predict the eventual fate of the
Congress, in view of the stormy proceedings that took place on April 27th as
the third biennial Congress met in Washington. On one fact, however, general
agreement will be reached, both by those who read the press accounts and by
those who attended the sessions and managed to maintain an objective viewpoint.
It will be agreed that the meeting marked the passing of the Congress from any
effective role as a coordinating agent serving the Negro population on a
national basis. Instead, it has become a source of arguments among Negroes
similar in bitterness and content to those caused among American liberals by
the Soviet conquest of Finland.
Perhaps the change of role is a good thing, in the interest of defining
more clearly the issues that face American Negroes during these critical days.
Perhaps it was an unrealistic and dangerous plan to set up a national organization that tried to cover the whole front of the Negro's battle for economic
and social emancipation. Certainly there is no reason for undue surprise over
the Washington developments, since the very nature of the organization made
them predictable. Such developments were foreseen at the first Congress four
years ago in Chicago, and many who helped to organize that meeting urged the
adoption of preventive safeguards. This writer, then a national vice president,
pointed out to *Opportunity* in May, 1936, the certainty that one or another of
the political parties would try to gain control of the Congress, becoming the
political tail that wags the organizational dog. It was this writer's belief,
expressed then as now, that a National Negro Congress should not be a permanent
organization, but should be a delegate body convening annually only to formulate and publicize a body of social, economic and political principles which
the average Negro organization could be brought to support.

It would have been surprising if these suggestions had been willingly
adopted by those at the helm of the new organization. Power and prestige
are a heady drink for most of us. Mix these with a dramatic and moving cause,
put them into an organization representing a thousand groups with hundreds of
thousands of individual members--and there are few leaders able to resist the
intoxicating appeal. Thus the dangers of organizational permanency were
laughed off at Chicago as the fears of over-timid souls.

Besides the danger of capture by a political party--or disruption through
political factionalism--there were other threats to a long-time usefulness of
the Congress. One was the difficulty of sticking to its original program.
Set up originally as a coordinating agency, the National Negro Congress was
designed as a rallying point for counsel and exchange of opinion on problems
facing the Negro. It aimed at swinging public support to specific causes,
while educating the American public on matters pertaining to the interests of
Negroes. It was specifically promised that the Congress would not wander all
over the map, would not duplicate efforts of existing organizations, would not
desert its coordinating role for a functional one. This promise, of course,
would have been difficult to keep, with the best of intentions. Public education is a slow and painstaking process, and program coordination is generally
a thankless task. The temptation is always strong for any organization working
in these fields to stray from its appointed path into more dynamic fields of
activity. Especially is this true of a new organization that feels it must
"make a showing" in its bid for public support.

The Congress's empty treasury provided another danger, for salaries must
be paid, traveling expenses provided and literature produced. Both of these
dangers were related, so it was natural that the Congress fell into both at
almost the same time. Less than a year after Chicago the national secretary
appeared in Pittsburgh to endorse in the name of the Congress, the campaign
of the Steel Workers' Organizing Committee to unionize the steel industry.
He also offered the Congress's services to raise $1,000 toward the campaign
fund in the Birmingham area. It was a generous offer, but it gave pause to
many supporters who were even then trying to build local units of the Congress
in their own communities. Not only was the treasury resoundingly empty; but
the endorsement and pledge were both given without consultation with the
national executive committee or the national trade union committee. This oversight was all the more serious in view of the fact that the national secretary
was officially supporting a CIO organization against the A.F. of L., with
several A.F. of L. unions extremely active in the Congress membership. The
chairman of the national trade union committee was himself an officer of an
A.F. of L. union in New York City.

With this early departure from a coordinating function, further deviation
was increasingly easy for the Congress. Major organizations frequently reported that their local or national programs were ignored, blocked or embarrassed by the over-zealous activity of local or national Congress officers.
An example was seen in 1938 when the Congress called an anti-lynching conference
in Washington "to place public support behind the anti-lynching bill." The
conference was called in spite of strong disapproval by the National Association for the Advancement of Colored People, which looked with disfavor upon
an independent anti-lynching program and considered a conference at that
particular time a hindrance to its current lobbying activities.

As organizations with well-established programs began more and more
to regard the Congress as an interloper and nuisance, if not as a rival for
public support in their own spheres of activity, they tended to develop resistance to such interference. Their supporters reflected this resistance
and there was a continuing difficulty in obtaining financial backing for the
program of the Congress. It was sometimes necessary to seek out "angels" to
make up budget deficits. But angels often have dirty faces, and when they drop
something into the treasury they keep tight hold on the strings of influence
attached to their donations. It may have been this fear of hidden controls
that prompted President Randolph's public condemnation of secret gifts to the
Congress and his demand that Secretary Davis make public the sources of support.
Though Mr. Randolph's objections were partly based on opposition to Communist
backing, they would have been equally valid had contributions appeared from
the war chests of Republicans or Democrats. It is a dangerous thing for an
organization like the Congress to accept any contributions from "interested
groups," for it is hard to set a limit on such acceptance. Certainly, if

contributions are to be accepted, Communists have the same right as Socialists or Republicans to bring their "free will offerings."

Mistakes such as those referred to above are to be expected as part of the growing pains of a new organization. Less to be expected and more serious in its effects, was the Congress's action in regarding favorably the bid of John L. Lewis to join forces with Labor's Non-Partisan League.

If the Congress moves into Lewis's political camp, it moves away from that 90 per cent of Negro voters who are either pro-New Deal or committed to the Republican opposition. Few Negroes trust Lewis as a political leader, whatever feeling they may have for his skill, as a labor leader. The political label that the Congress will apply to itself will be far more damaging than the "Red" label which unfriendly critics have attempted to apply ever since it was organized. The Negro community does not excite itself unduly over so-called "communistic influences," but it does take its politics very seriously. Especially will this be true in a Presidential election year. For its influence with the Negro population, it would be better for the Congress to choose the New Deal or the Republican banner. Any choice of political allegiance, however, will be fatal in that the support of political dissenters will immediately be lost.

Thus the Congress finds its future functions may be stripped down to two principal activities: political action in behalf of the Lewis group and a possible third party, and progressive action in the labor movement. It is possible that this stripping down process represents an increase in the usefulness of the Congress. Few rival organizations will oppose a Congress program for increasing the participation of Negroes and decreasing racial discrimination in the trade union movement. There is no more important program operating at this time, in view of the rising strength of the labor movement, the growth of pro-labor legislation and the increase of closed shop agreements in industry. It is a program that can be put across only through the kind of mass organization which the Congress offers; it calls for close cooperation of whites with Negroes. It is a job for which the Congress's machinery is well-suited, provided that radical ideology of any type is kept sternly out of the picture.

Its activities along the political line will be comparatively unimportant, for as long as CIO unions at their national conventions are regularly refusing to follow the Lewis march out of the New Deal camp, the National Negro Congress will have difficulty in persuading any considerable number of Negro voters to go along. And yet, the Washington vote has a certain nuisance value, even after the discounting reckoned above. It has served notice on leaders of both major political parties that a considerable group of Negroes is dissatisfied with both Democratic performances and Republican promises.

The Congress still has a place in the picture of Negro progress—a place that can become larger or smaller according to the way in which Negro organizations represented in its membership do their own thinking and plan their own action. The much advertised Communist influence has been important only because non-Communist groups have been satisfied to do the flag-waving while someone else plans the program. It would be well for the Congress to drop all pretense at coordinating generally the national programs for improvement of the Negro population. It has an important job to do in a specific field, a field in which it can actually function without opposition or repudiation. It would be unfortunate for the Congress, in its present role, to claim spokesmanship for the general Negro population, except in those interest fields wherein the Congress program operates. It would be equally unfortunate, however, for Negro leadership openly to repudiate the Congress. It has a vitally important job to do in the field of labor's education. Until other organizations are ready to move into this field and show at least as much accomplishment as the Congress can point to, their criticism of the Congress's effort is in some wise a criticism of themselves.

In the meantime, A. Philip Randolph deserves the congratulatory thanks of those who have for a long time wished for a clearer definition of the Congress's functions and policies. His courageous and thoughtful speech brought the issues clearly into the open where they could be voted upon and where they could be understood even by persons not in actual attendance. The fact that his position was voted down is not necessarily cause for disappointment. Some of the opposition was no doubt ideologically inspired; some of it may have been the thoughtless enthusiasm of inexperienced delegates swept along in the hysteria of a mass meeting. Some of the opposition, however, was thoughtful enough and honestly arrived at, growing out of some delegates' conviction that the Congress has a job to do in the field of political and labor action. It is to be hoped that the future will see such thoughtful and honest leadership reflected in the Congress's policies and achievements.

Opportunity, 18 (June, 1940): 164-66.

PART II

THE SOUTHERN TENANT FARMERS UNION

THE SOUTHERN TENANT FARMERS UNION

Black agricultural workers also suffered severely during the Depression. When cotton prices plunged the Agricultural Adjustment Act (1933) required that some cotton land be plowed under the create scarcity. In eastern Kansas acute poverty resulted from the increasing mechanization of agriculture, and the effects of the new AAA program, which left many sharecroppers without work or homes. Under the AAA, the government compensated for the financial loss resulting from the plowing under of cotton by sending subsidies to planters. Benefits were to be shared by the landlord and tenant according to their interest in the crop. Since the landlord signed the contract, and the money was sent to him to distribute, however, few tenants ever received their shares.

It was against this background that the Southern Tenant Farmers Union was organized. During the summer of 1934, eleven whites and seven blacks met in a one-room schoolhouse on the Arkansas Delta. Assisted by Harry L. Mitchell (see Vol. VI, note 142), who became executive secretary, and Clay East, both active members of the Socialist Party, the black and white sharecroppers united into one union. An alliance was formed with Commonwealth College, a socialist school in the Ozark Mountains which was training labor leaders. After a year of organization, STFU claimed 10,000 members. As it grew in size and effectiveness, the repressive measures against it grew apace. The union could no longer hold public meetings in the field, and its officers were warned that they would be lynched if they remained in eastern Arkansas. Therefore, STFU headquarters were moved to Memphis for reasons of safety.

Despite the repression, STFU conducted a series of mass struggles over the next several years. Although STFU was interracial, by 1937, over 80 per cent of the membership was black. Many of the local leaders were ministers in black churches. E. B. McKinney, the union's first vice-president, was a black minister. Considerable animosity existed between McKinney and STFU President J. R. Butler. McKinney became the spokesman for disgruntled blacks who believed that they should have a stronger voice in policy-making, while Butler demanded adherence to class-conscious principles. STFU was further weakened by a dispute with the CIO International with which it affiliated--the United Cannery, Agricultural, Packing and Allied Workers of America (UCAPAWA). Mitchell favored independence, while Butler favored a merger, and the dispute diverted the organization's attention from its struggle with the planters.

The most dramatic event of the sharecropper movement occurred in January, 1939, when about 1,700 evicted sharecroppers and their families encamped themselves along Highway 61 in Missouri. For nearly a week black and white families huddled around open fires as travellers passed by to witness the fate of those who were poor and powerless. Reporters from major newspapers, newsreel camera teams, and federal government investigators momentarily brought the nation's attention to rest on these unfortunate Americans. They may have received the nation's sympathies, but the embarrassed governor of Missouri had the encampment declared a health hazard, and even before help could arrive, the campers were forced to evacuate the public highway to freeze and starve out the public's sight.

STFU was able to bring the plight of the sharecropper to the nation's consciousness as never before. Actually, STFU was more of a social movement to end the vicious quasi-serfdom which prevailed in southern agriculture. STFU succeeded in making some influential Americans conscious of the truth behind Karl Marx's dictum: "Labor in the white skin cannot be free as long as labor in the black in branded."

STFU AND BLACK SHARECROPPERS

1. SOUTHERN SHARE-CROPPER

By Marcus B. Christian

He turns and tosses on his bed of moss;
  The moon wheels high into the Southern sky;
  He cannot sleep--production, gain, and loss
  Harass him, while a question and a cry
  Stir through the dim recesses of his soul--
  This slave to one-fourth, one-third, and one-half;
  His sow will litter soon; his mare will foal;
  His woman is with child; his cow, with calf.
  Earth screams at him--beats clenched, insistent hands
  Upon his brains--his labor and his health
  He gives unceasingly to her demands;
  She yields to him, but others grow in wealth.
  What nailed his soul upon the wrack of things--
  That he must slave, while idlers live like kings?

Opportunity, 15 (July, 1937):217.

2. FORMATION OF THE SOUTHERN TENANT FARMERS' UNION

By Howard Kester

     Because of the furor which has been raised in Arkansas and Washington
over the alleged "meddling of socialists and communists," it is well to point
out at the beginning that the Southern Tenant Farmers' Union was an indigenous
movement, springing up out of the very soil which bore the sharecroppers'
bitter grievances. It should be said, furthermore, that the Southern Tenant
Farmers' Union is not, nor ever has been, an adjunct or organ of either the
Socialist Party or the Communist Party. That individual members of these
parties have been prominent in the work of the Southern Tenant Farmers' Union
we do not deny, but to the contrary we affirm and are proud of their achievements. Probably the reason that they were asked to assist the sharecroppers
in the formation of the union was due to the fact that experienced working-
class leaders were the only ones who were not on their backs, and who had the
intelligence, love of human justice and courage to help them.
     Just south of the little town of Tyronza, in Poinsett County, Arkansas,
the Southern Tenant Farmers' Union had its beginning. In the early part of
July, 1934, twenty-seven white and black men, clad in overalls, gathered in a
rickety and dingy little schoolhouse called Sunnyside. The schoolhouse was
old and it had witnessed many strange sights but none so strange as the one
being enacted between its four leaning walls that hot summer night. Dimly
lighted kerosene lamps cast strange shadows upon the faces of the men as they
talked. On rough-hewn benches sat white and colored men discussing their common problems in a spirit of mutual regard and understanding.
     Little time was lost in agreeing that they should form some sort of union
for their mutual protection. Their main problem was to secure for themselves
and their fellow-sharecroppers their share of the benefits granted under the
AAA contracts. The contracts entered into between the landlords and the
Secretary of Agriculture gave the tenant farmers very little and the sharecropper next to nothing but something, and they considered it worth struggling
for anyway. Wholesale violations of the contracts by the planters were
occurring daily. Tenants were not getting their "parity payments"; they were
being made to sign papers making the landlords trustees of the bale tags;

landlords were turning to day labor at starvation wages; the AAA was making things worse. They knew they could not get anything trying to dicker with the landlord individually: he would just "kick them off the place." Most of them had never been in a union and they scarcely knew how to go about organizing one. Anyway, they had to have one and they were sure that they could find someone who would know how and who would help them.

The meeting had not been in progress long when the inevitable question, which always rises when Negro and white men come together to consider joint action, arose. "Are we going to have two unions," someone asked, "one for the whites and one for the colored?" It had been many a day since the ancient walls of the schoolhouse had heard such silence. The men had thought about this before they came together, but now they had to face it and it was not an easy question to answer. A lot depended on their answer, certainly the future of their organization and maybe the future of a whole people. It was time for deep silence and exhaustive thinking. Finally the men began to speak. One man believed that since the churches divided the races that maybe the union should do likewise. He wasn't sure though, for he had noticed that the churches hadn't done very much to help the sharecroppers and that some of the church members were the cause of their suffering. Another observed that it would be dangerous for the white and colored people to mix together in their union and he was sure that the planters wouldn't stand for it. An old man with cotton-white hair overhanging an ebony face rose to his feet. He had been in unions before, he said. In his seventy years of struggle the Negro had built many unions only to have them broken up by the planters and the law. He had been a member of a black man's union at Elaine, Arkansas. He had seen the union with its membership wiped out in the bloody Elaine Massacre in 1919. "We colored people can't organize without you," he said, "and you white folks can't organize without us." Continuing he said, "Aren't we all brothers and ain't God the Father of us all? We live under the same sun, eat the same food, wear the same kind of clothing, work on the same land, raise the same crop for the same landlord who oppresses and cheats us both. For a long time now the white folks and the colored folks have been fighting each other and both of us has been getting whipped all the time. We don't have nothing against one another but we got plenty against the landlord. The same chain that holds my people holds your people too. If we're chained together on the outside we ought to stay chained together in the union. It won't do no good for us to divide because there's where the trouble has been all the time. The landlord is always betwixt us, beatin' us and starvin' us and makin' us fight each other. There ain't but one way for us to get him where he can't help himself and that's for us to get together and stay together." The old man sat down. The men decided that the union would welcome Negro and white sharecroppers, tenant farmers and day laborers alike into its fold.

When this question had been cared for the men turned toward the formation of their new organization. A white sharecropper of great ability, Alvin Nunally, was elected chairman. A Negro minister, C. H. Smith, was chosen vice-chairman. An Englishman with a ready hand for keeping minutes and writing letters was chosen secretary. A holiness preacher was elected chaplain. Some of the men had belonged to lodges and they wanted to introduce all of the secret rigamarole of the fraternal societies into the union. Some of them had formerly ridden with the Ku Klux Klan and they thought it would be a good idea for the union to operate in secret and for the sharecroppers to ride the roads at night punishing dishonest landlords and oppressive managers and riding bosses. One of the men had formerly been a member of the Farmers' Educational and Co-operative Union and advanced the idea that it would be best to have the union made a legal organization and for it to operate in the open. The men agreed that this was the best policy and they turned their minds toward getting it accomplished.

They did not know exactly how to go about having the union made legal. They could not expect any aid from any of the planter-retained lawyers and they did not have any money for fees anyway. Someone suggested that H. L. Mitchell and Clay East might help them. Mitchell was the proprietor of a small dry-cleaning establishment in Tyronza and, next door to him, Clay East ran a filling station. The two men were known throughout the countryside as "square-shooters" who always gave the underdog the benefit of the doubt, and who were, to the amusement of most people, always discussing strange ideas about labor,

politics, economics and most everything else. Mitchell had once been a
sharecropper himself and all of his people were farmers. He knew something
about almost everything. He was known generally as a Socialist but to the
landlords and planters as a "Red." Some months before Mitchell had brought
Norman Thomas down to Tyronza to speak to an overflow audience at the
schoolhouse. After Thomas had visited some of the plantations, he told the
audience gathered in the schoolhouse what he had seen. The planters were
there *en masse* and so were the sharecroppers. The planters writhed in their
seats and the mouths of the sharecroppers stood agape as Thomas denounced the
system of semi-slavery under which they all lived. The planters did not
forget Mitchell for this nor did the sharecroppers.

A committee from the sharecroppers called on Mitchell and East. The two
men told them that while they did not know much about running a union they
would be glad to help all they could. Mitchell subsequently became the
secretary of the union and East its president. Mitchell wrote letters to
people all over the country asking for help and advice. J. R. Butler, an
ex-school teacher, sawmill hand, hill farmer, or as he prefers to be known,
"just an Arkansas Hill Billy," came down to write the first constitution and
to help spread the organization among the cottonfield workers. Ward H.
Rodgers, a young Methodist minister with an eye to social justice, who had
been preaching in the Ozark Mountains, decided to come down and preach to the
sharecroppers and planters. He gave up his churches and soon became Mitchell's
right-hand man.

Each night would witness Mitchell's and East's battered old automobiles
loaded down with sharecroppers going to some outlying church or schoolhouse
to organize a local. Enthusiasm among the sharecroppers ran high and they
talked "union" with the abandon of a backwoods' revivalist. New locals sprang
up everywhere the organizers went. The people were hungry for the "New Gospel
of Unionism."

When the union was first formed the idea of organizing sharecroppers
rather amused the planters. They generally poked fun at the boys who were
scouring over the country in all kinds of weather organizing new locals. One
man was heard to say, "Oh, well, let them try to organize the sharecroppers;
they won't succeed for the sharecroppers are too lazy and shiftless to ever
amount to anything worthwhile." But as the union continued to grow and the
planters saw the Negro and white people getting together they were not quite
so amused as formerly. When a car-load of white and colored sharecroppers
would start off together to a union meeting someone would say, "The Socialists
and the Republicans (meaning the Negroes) have joined hands." It has been
rumored that Mitchell and East had "political ambitions," and that they were
going to run for office in the forthcoming elections. The politicians and
planters could not quite understand though why men who had "political ambitions" would bother with Negroes who had been disenfranchised and could not
vote, and poor white sharecroppers who had not been disenfranchised but were
too poor to pay the poll tax. Gradually the planters got the right idea.
These men were not even mildly interested in the kind of politics for which
Joe Robinson and Hattie Caraway had made Arkansas famous; they were interested
in organizing the sharecroppers to abolish the planters' organized system of
semi-slavery.

On July 26, 1934, the organization was incorporated under the laws of
the state of Arkansas as the Southern Tenant Farmers' Union. The papers were
taken out in White County and a certificate of incorporation received. The
movement rapidly became a sort of sharecroppers' crusade and every day new
applications for membership in the union were received. Men came from all
over the countryside asking for organizers' papers. The union was definitely
on the move. . . .

During the middle of March Mr. Norman Thomas visited Arkansas. After a
long and fruitless interview with the governor, J. Marion Futrell, Thomas
began a tour of the cotton country in which the union had been most active.
Thousands of sharecroppers turned out to see the man about whom they had
heard so much. A union bulletin issued at the close of the tour tells the
story in a graphic manner. It subsequently appeared in scores of papers
throughout the country. "Norman Thomas spoke to thousands of sharecroppers,
some of whom walked seventy miles to hear him. He saw conditions as they are,
stark starvation stalking the most fertile land in all America; a land which

is potentially the richest on earth now holding the poorest paid and most exploited workers in the world. While driving over the plantation roads visiting the people he witnessed one of the thousands of evictions that have recently occurred. He saw a white sharecropper's family, household goods and all, dumped upon the roadside. Upon inquiry it developed that the reason for the eviction of this family was that the father was a union member and that he and his wife had attempted to bring to justice a plantation rider who had violated their fourteen-year old daughter. After drugging and kidnapping the child, this prototype of the old-time slave driver raped her and after two weeks returned her to her father's home. Upon discovering what had happened to their daughter the husband and wife sought to have the fiend arrested. Instead of arresting the rapist, officials arrested the father on a trumped up charge of 'stealing two eggs.' After being released from jail, the father, who was a staunch union member, was brutally beaten. The riding boss, a relative of the plantation owner, still holds his job while the unfortunate family is thrown upon the roadside.

"Although the planting season was getting under way, this man and his family were thrown upon the roadside to starve. Without home, job or work of any sort the mother showed to Mr. Thomas the 'relief' which her husband had just received from the relief authorities at Harrisburg. The food which was to last them--a family of seven--for thirty days consisted of the following items: 8 cans of evaporated milk, 5 tins of processed beef, 1 twenty-four pound sack of flour, 1 twenty-four pound sack of meal, and three pounds of salt pork."

This story is related here because it represents a type of violence inherent in the plantation system of the South and, secondly, because it represents a type of violence used again and again by the planters, their retainers, relief officials and others against those who are active in the Southern Tenant Farmers' Union.

The Union Bulletin closes by relating the now famous "Birdsong incident" which took place on the final day of Thomas' tour of the country. "As Mr. Thomas' party approached the little town of Birdsong, where he had been invited to speak by the officials of the church, it was noted that many new shiny automobiles were parked on the roadside. As some five hundred workers began to assemble in orderly fashion, thirty or forty armed and drunken planters led by a man who later turned out to be the sheriff of Mississippi County, forced their way to the front of the Negro church. As Howard Kester began with the phrase, 'Ladies and Gentlemen,' a chorus of voices broke out, 'There ain't no ladies in the audience and there ain't no gentlemen on the platform.' The gunmen surrounded the speakers and violently jerked Kester from the platform. Mr. Thomas, holding a copy of the Constitution of Arkansas in his hands, called attention to the excellent Bill of Rights contained in the document and asked by whose authority he was being prevented from holding a meeting and if his meeting was not legal. They admitted that his meeting was 'legal all right' but 'There ain't goin' to be no speakin' here. We are citizens of this county and we run it to suit ourselves. We don't need no Gawd-damn Yankee Bastard to tell us what to do with our niggers and we want you to know that this is the best Gawd-damn county on earth.' In spite of their guns, which were carelessly brandished about over the speakers, Mr. Thomas got in a few words before he was struck at from behind and finally jerked from the platform. Jack Herling, secretary of the Strikers' Emergency Relief Committee, was severely knocked on the head by a riding boss. The sheriff, sensing the desire to the mob to 'start something,' came forward and advised Mr. Thomas to leave at once as he could not give protection to him or to the innocent men, women and children who had gathered to hear him speak. He told Mr. Thomas if he didn't go there would be trouble and 'somebody might get hurt.' Mr. Thomas and his party were thrown into their waiting automobile and warned never to return. Several carloads of planters followed the car to the county line."

An Associated Press correspondent from Little Rock arrived on the scene just as the meeting was being broken up. Not knowing exactly what was happening he met some of the men who followed Thomas' car from the churchyard. "My name is --- from the Associated Press," he said offering a friendly hand.

"We don't give a damn what your name is or who you are. Get the hell out of here and don't you write a line."

The whole story as everyone knows was practically scuttled by the
Associated Press from its Memphis office. Freedom of the press is not always
wanted by the press--particularly in Arkansas. . . .

Shortly after Norman Thomas returned to New York he spoke over a coast-
to-coast hook-up of the NBC. He opened his address with these words: "There
is a reign of terror in the cotton country of eastern Arkansas. It will end
either in the establishment of complete and slavish submission of the vilest
exploitation in America or in bloodshed, or in both. . . . The plantation
system involves the most stark serfdom and exploitation that is left in the
Western world."

Howard Kester, *Revolt Among the Sharecroppers* (New York, 1936), pp. 54-59,
79-81, 85.

3. NIGHT RIDERS, WITH GUNS AND PISTOLS BUT JOHN ALLEN, [91] NEGRO SHARECROPPER, FIGHTS FOR HIS HOME AND UNION

By Myra Page

John Allen's powerful frame blocked the cabin doorway.
"Howdy, boss," he said.
The plantation overseer, known as "riding boss," in cotton country,
barely nodded, as the wheels of his car grazed the stoop. "John, I've come
for the last time to tell you to get off."
John Allen's slow gaze traveled from the cotton rows that began right
at his cabin door and ran as far as the eye could reach. He didn't ask the
riding boss why. He knew. The Twist brothers didn't intend to have any
croppers' union on their 20,000-acre plantation, one of the largest in
Eastern Arkansas. But John Allen and many more of the thousand "hands" who
raised cotton for the Twists had built them a union.
"You see, boss," John said quietly, "I've worked on this place going on
fourteen years."
"I know that. But you got notice to go."
"I don't know where to go. I wouldn't know where to look."
"This is your third and last notice to get off." The white man was
losing his temper.
"If you want me to leave, bring an officer of the law and read me off,"
Allen told him. "I won't go before."
"We'll read you off, you dam' nigger!" Then riding boss raised his fist,
"We'll throw you into the St. Francis river."

Night Riders

That Saturday night, he and more of Twists' men came to get John Allen,
but the cropper was being guarded elsewhere on the plantation by union men, so
the night riders rode to no avail that night.
The bright moon scanned the endless mile of cotton, the cabins, outhouses
and wells, then came to rest on the white pillars of the "Big House," as the
croppers called it, standing so graciously among the tall oaks and southern
pines. Here there was music, happiness, far removed from the cotton fields.
All that week John Allen was hidden in friendly cabins while he carried
the union word. Amanthy and their twelve children worked on in the fields
that they had come to feel a part of, and to love as much as they despised the
outright slavery of their common lot.
"John, they'll be the death of you," his wife moaned.
"What is that but death?" he answered. How could a man see the truth,
and not fight for it.

Guns and Pistols

That Sunday came the meeting which the planters had said should never take place. Men and women crept one by one out of their cabins across the fields, and into skiffs on the St. Francis river, where they rowed to Turkey Island to hold their union meeting beyond reach of the planters' men.

Someone though, had played the snitch, for as they lay plans and exposed their wrongs, the banks on each side of the river grew thick with deputy sheriffs and planters' men. Their guns and pistols gleamed in the sun.

When the croppers and their women left Turkey Island, John Allen was left off not on the Twist plantation, but on the far side, adjoining Morris Smith's place. Later, as he made his way to hiding, he was seized by two carloads of men. He fought to keep his union record books from them, but they slugged and bound him. "Now we'll drown you, you black rat." As they dragged him toward the river, two white men who heard his cries came running. John recognized union croppers, a man and his son. They brought help, and John had his first narrow escape for "carrying the word."

Traveling along the swamp and woods, trailed through Parkin, Earle, and other Arkansas towns, sleeping under bridges at night, always avoiding the highways, this 67-year-old cropper walked for three weeks to cover the forty-five miles to Memphis, headquarters of the Southern Tenant Farmers' Union. This was a year ago, this February. John Allen had traveled many tens of miles since then, organizing for the union in Jefferson and other counties, being beaten up, threatened, but quietly going on. He hasn't been able to see his family since that fatal night in February, nor can his family come to him. The Twist brothers are holding them on their plantation, on a charge of debt.

The Union

Hundreds of croppers, both white and colored, are being so held on plantations in the Southern states, quite against the law. The planters keep all accounts, so how can a cropper expect to ever come even? At the same time, hundreds of other croppers and their families are being evicted, either for union membership, or because the planter thinks he can make more out of somebody else.

John Allen knows all these things. He has been growing cotton since a small boy barely able to tote a hoe, cotton that floods Memphis and New Orleans warehouses, making planters rich, but leaving him without so much as a roof over his head or a good cotton shirt to his back. He has seen his own and others' children wasting away from pellagra, "the hungry disease." And in his last years, when hope was nearly gone, he has seen the union come, and swung into it with his whole agonized heart.

I met John Allen at the recent convention of the Southern Tenant Farmers' Union, held in Little Rock, Arkansas, in the Labor Temple. I met many men and women like him, colored and white; I heard them tell, in their soft Southern drawl, of the terrors they have braved and the victories they have won, in building an organization 25,000 strong, which is truly theirs, "a fortress in the time of storm." How common suffering and need has helped them "bridge the chasm bringing to pass a new South. All of us who were born and reared in which once separated us white from black"; how they are willing to stake their lives on the hope, "To the Disinherited Belongs the Future."

Leaders

It is men like John Allen who are the South, who love its fields and rivers, its folklore and songs, and its warmhearted people, but who also know too well the South's wrongs; we who have felt the lash in the Southern owners' boast of "cheap and contented labor," can now feel proud that out of our cotton fields are rising such great, simple leaders of the South's working people as John Allen.

Among those who stood shoulder to shoulder with John Allen singing

                              The union is a-marching
                              We shall not be moved!
                              The union fights evictions
                              We shall not be moved!
were men like Odis Sweeden, son of an Oklahoma Cherokee Indian and a Scotch-
Irish mother (could such a combination ever know defeat!). As a boy he organized his fellow bootblacks to get fifteen cents a day, and he has been at it
for seventeen years since. Tired of picking spinach for a quarter a day, and
paying the Griffin Manufactures a dime transportation out of that; he started
organizing the Oklahoma Indians, Negroes, Mexicans and "Poor Whites," and in
ten short months they tripled their pay, won free transportation and built 75
S.F.T.U. locals with 9,500 members.
     There were fighters like the Walter and Lee Moskops, women and men of
old native "Poor White" stock. Evicted from their shacks by the landlords,
the Lee Moskops are living in a small houseboat, and organizing, being
arrested and bailed out again, and going back to organizing again.
     You can never kill a movement that has spirit like this.
     Walter Moskop told how the first union convention, held only a year ago,
had only a handful present, and all the lunch among them a dime's worth of
crackers and fifteen cents' worth of cheese. "Look at us now," he told the
convention, and they cheered. Twenty-five thousand strong, and in the coming
year, these Southern croppers and farm-laborers promise themselves to organize
twice that number. Over in Alabama there is a brother Sharecroppers'
Union. Together they will organize the entire cotton belt. They have gone on
record in support of a Farmer-Labor Party, a party that will help them win
their civil and economic rights. They stand as one on the demand, "Land to the
Landless" and in their hard daily lives there shines the hope:
     "To the Disinherited Belongs the Future."

Daily Worker, January 12, 1936.

                              4. FRANK WEEMS CASE

                              By Norman Thomas

     There is a Negro named Frank Weems whose name deserves to be made a
symbol like John Brown's in the struggle for emancipation. Mr. Weems was a
leader of the Southern Tenant Farmers' Union near Earle, Arkansas. A meeting
which he led was broken up by violence. He was beaten until he fell to the
ground dead or unconscious. It was to plan for his funeral that the Rev. Claude
Williams and Miss Willie Sue Blagden came into Arkansas at the time of the
whippings which were administered to them. After this whipping called particular attention to this situation the sheriff of the county, the governor of the
state, and as I recall it, Senator Robinson, the great Democratic leader, all
affirmed that Weems was not dead and that he would at the right time be produced. Since then some ten weeks have passed. He either is dead or held
unlawfully in some place of confinement or intimidated so that he dare not show
himself to his nearest and dearest friends. The failure to produce Weems of
itself convicts the Democratic party, one of whose most prominent leaders is
Senator Joe Robinson of Arkansas, of complete insincerity in its professions of
devotion to the cause either of the workers or of the Negro. [92]
     But it will be observed that it is not the Republicans who have taken up
the fight of the sharecroppers. They are responsible for similar acts of
tyranny to workers white and black where they or the economic loyalists who
belong to them are in control. Frank Weems is a symbol not merely of the shame
of the plantation system, but of the shame of capitalism. How can the workers
support the old parties which are accomplices in that shame?
     But let me get back to my main theme. Once we get planned production for
abundance on the basis of social ownership there will be enough and to spare for
all. There will be work for all, leisure for all, security for all. The
jealousy and bitterness of men who now feel that they have to fight for crusts

shall disappear. Socialism gives the economic basis for brotherhood. It up-
holds the ideals of applied brotherhood. It will create the atmosphere which
will end discrimination. . . .

The Crisis, 43 (October 1936):294-95, 315.

5. PLANTERS RAILROAD UNION MEN TO PRISON,
FEBRUARY 21, 1936

Jim Ball, Secretary of the St. Peters Local, Southern Tenant Farmers'
Union, was given a seven year prison sentence yesterday by the Crittendon
County Circuit Court. He was convicted of "Assault with intent to kill" by a
jury picked of planters, and sentenced by a judge who is also a large land-
holder. Jim Ball's crime consisted of trying to preserve order in a peaceful
meeting which was illegally raided and broken up by Deputy Sheriffs and a mob
of planters on the night of January 16th. Jim Ball attempted to take a shot
gun away from Everette Hood, the plantation deputy, who led the raiding party.
After Ball was placed under arrest, Hood and another, so called, officer of the
law returned to the scene and shot two men in the back as they were walking
alongside the road.
In the Court Room yesterday planters were betting that the "damned Union
men" would get the limit 21 years. Defense Attorney Newell Fowler, well known
labor lawyer of Memphis, Tenn., said that no evidence to warrant conviction was
presented.
Simon Bass, John Ligons and Sam Brown, are to be given a similar trial
next week on a charge of Rioting. "Rioting" consists of having reported the
raided meeting to Union Headquarters in Memphis. Local newspapers were given
the news, and on attempting to get a statement from the planters all refused to
talk. These three men will no doubt be given prison sentences similar to
Ball's. This is plantation justice. Sharecroppers are framed up and railroaded
to prison. Criminals who break up peaceable meetings in churches in violation
of all the laws go scot free. No attempt is ever made to punish the guilty
parties.
The Central Defense Committee of the Southern Tenant Farmers' Union appeals
to all our friends thru out America. Help us fight these cases. An appeal to
the Supreme Court must be made. Bonds must be given. Won't you help to save
these innocent men from the Tucker Prison Farm (Arkansas equivalent of a Georgia
Chain Gang). Funds are needed badly. Send all contributions--Howard Kester,
Sec'ty, Central Defense Committee, Southern Tenant Farmers' Union--Box 5215,
Memphis, Tenn.

Southern Tenant Farmers Union Papers, microfilm edition, reel 1.

6. H. L. MITCHELL TO E. B. MCKINNEY,
JULY 31, 1936

Dear McKinney:
Found your letter upon my return to Memphis a few days ago and I believe
that Butler answered the question you raised in part anyway. The statement was
issued by the Executive Council and not by me the first I saw of it was in the
Chicago Tribune, of course they quoted Mitchell etc. but they always do that you
know, but in all papers that I saw it said that the Executive Council at the
Muskogee meeting called it off and I believe you were there and voted for the
statement, if I recall a right made the motion for its adoption. So why should
you and I squabble about something we have already done.
Your letter excited Butler, Kester and others but not me I know you too
well, and how you feel some times and I can't say that I blame you much because

I feel like saying and doing the same damn thing myself--so let's just forget
it all and go to work for the cause which you and I have done more to further
than anyone else.

Want to have a long talk with you sometime soon--you ought to forget the
race lines and think of them really important ones--the class against class--
the solidarity of black and white workers is much more important than what
happens to a white man or a black man. Who cares it has happened before and
will again, we can only do what our resources permit and you know as well as
I do that there is no racial discrimination in the STFU. That is why we are
powerful and feared.

I will certainly see that money is sent you old friend--how finances are
right now I don't know but we will make it the best we can some how--until the
planters get one or both of us. I appreciated your strong statement at Muskogee about standing side by side with me until we both went down together--that
was the kind of man you are that was talking that day, and I am not apt to
forget either.

                              H. L. Mitchell

Southern Tenant Farmers Union Papers, microfilm edition, reel 2.

          7. J. E. CLAYTON TO H. L. MITCHELL,[93]
              DECEMBER 28, 1937

Mr. H. L. Mitchell
Exec. Sec. - STFU
Memphis, Tenn.

Dear Mr. Mitchell:--Your letter received a few minutes ago, and I thank you
for it.

Mr. Mitchell! If there ever was a time that the International needed an
International worker among the colored people in the Southern states, it is
right now. If the International waits, while the A.F. of L. and the Big Capitalists have put on an aggressive campaign to prejudice the great host of colored
workers against the C.I.O., and its affiliates, it will find the host of
colored workers scattered, hence, hard to line up. We should start now lining
them up in our Southern states.

Mr. Mitchell! You don't need a worker for each craft or body of workers
among the colored people, as you have among the whites. My people are an
Emotional, and a Group Conscious People, and 98% of them can be reached in the
churches. If you can arrange to have some Ordained Minister of the Gospel put
on the Field as an International speaker, that Ordained Minister can get into
all of the colored churches with his message, because the colored churches
never debar an Ordained Minister. And when this International organizer goes
into a church to speak, he will find in there the colored workers of all occupations, including the farmers. Therefore, the colored organizer will not have
to go to shops, hotels, laundries, factories, or plantations to seek a chance
to talk to the workers. He can reach all workers in the churches, therefore,
you will not have to have a Regional Organizer for each craft or group of
workers. Have a Live-wire Regional Organizer to travel and speak, and appoint
and direct Local organizers. If you can have this done while you are in
Washington, you will sweep the South when it comes to lining up the colored
workers and farmers.

The International should get one colored Regional Organizer now to push
the work among the colored workers and farmers, before the Enemies of the C.I.O.
scatter them. I find the Enemies of the C.I.O. working here in Chicago to
prejudice the colored people against the C.I.O., and I have done quite a deal of
work here these few days, getting my group to get with the C.I.O.

Mr. Egan told me that he is somewhat handicapped in Houston, in getting
a colored organizer put on, because, he has lost some of his white organizers.

But he said one is badly needed, and said he would have me put on now if he could. He said also that he believes that you can get a colored Regional Organizer put on much quicker than he can. So I hope you will pull every wire you can, while in Washington, to have one put on at once.

Write me at 2312 Gregg St., Houston, Texas.

I will leave here Friday morning for Texas.

I hope you will get the application from Littig before you leave. Either 30, or 31 members had paid in their enrollment fees before I left Littig.

Yours very truly,

J. E. Clayton

Southern Tenant Farmers Union Papers, microfilm edition, reel 5.

8.   J. R. BUTLER TO STFU EXECUTIVE COUNCIL,
JULY 18, 1938

Brethren:

Inclosed with this you will find a bulletin which I have felt it necessary to send to the locals, especially in Arkansas and Missouri. This bulletin refers especially to activities of Vice President, E. B. McKinney.

As some of you know, McKinney has for some time agitated for a separate office set-up for himself for the purpose of allowing him to handle all business of the Union that anyway affects the Negro membership. This virtually means a separation of the Union into two elements with little or no coordination or co-operation between the two parts. This is opposed to the principle on which the Southern Tenant Farmers Union was built and on which it has been maintained. In addition to this disruptive propaganda he has written at least one letter to the UCAPAWA headquarters asking that practically all the locals in Jefferson County, Arkansas be allowed to affiliate direct with the international getting out of the STFU entirely. He has asked some of the locals to assess their membership extra above their regular dues to enable him to get around and spread this poisonous propaganda. There are any number of other charges that could be made against him but which I consider unnecessary to make at this time.

In view of these matters I have taken the liberty to ask the secretary to withhold any further payments of salary or expenses to E. B. McKinney until such time as I can hear from you. I hope that you will reply to this immediately and state whether you approve or disapprove my action in withholding money from McKinney until these matters can be cleared up. Is it your desire that these matters shall be put into form and that McKinney shall be charged with attempting to disrupt the Union? If so it will be necessary to call a special meeting of the Executive Council in order to give him a chance to appear and answer the charges.

If your answer to the above question is "Yes," then, shall I call a special meeting of the Council at an early date even though the Union may not be able to pay all the expenses of such a meeting? This would mean that if we cannot raise enough money to pay the full expense of such meeting that you would each have to dig down in your own pocket for a part of your expenses while attending the meeting.

There is another matter also that should receive your serious consideration the international convention of the UCAPAWA is to be held sometime the latter part of November or first of December. It is very necessary that the Southern Tenant Farmers Union be represented at this convention with a full delegation. That means that it will be necessary to raise money by some means to meet the expenses of the delegates. If a majority of you agree we will take a referendum vote of the membership on the question of making a special assessment of 50 cents per member to be paid on or before Oct. 15th to be divided and used as follows: 12½ cents to the UCAPAWA, 12½ cents to be used to pay the expense of holding a preconvention conference of all our delegates so that there will be no confusion

in our ranks when we get to the main convention, and 25 cents to be held in
trust for each local for the purpose of having the expenses of its delegate to,
at and from the convention. Please say whether you think such a referendum
should go out and whether this plan of division is satisfactory to you.
Please answer on all these matters at once.

Fraternally,

J. R. Butler, Pres.

Southern Tenant Farmers Union Papers, microfilm edition, reel 8.

9. J. R. BUTLER TO CLAUDE WILLIAMS,
AUGUST 22, 1938

Dear Claude,
        The inclosed mimeographed copy of a document that purports to be a report
of Commonwealth College and the Communist Party in charge of same and which I
have no reason to doubt, but on the other hand every reason to believe authentic, should be explanation enough for what follows.
        Ever since the re-organization of Commonwealth College when you became
its Director I have defended you against all charges of Communism and against
all charges of attempting to disrupt the Southern Tenant Farmers Union. I did
those things on the basis of your word of honor (such as it was) to me, assuring me that your whole effort should be directed toward building a Trade Union
school that could and would adapt itself to the needs of and be a help to the
Southern Labor Movement. You assured me that you yourself were not a Communist
and that as a member of the Executive Council of the Southern Tenant Farmers
Union, that your whole effort would be to further the interest of the STFU at
all times and places.
        Now please do not get the idea that I am censuring you or any other per-
son for belonging to the Communist Party. That is your privilege. The thing
that I am censuring you for is that under the guise of friendship you worked
to disrupt the Southern Tenant Farmers Union in its basic principle of being
strictly non-partisan.
        The inclosed report shows conclusively that you have connived and that you
are still attempting to connive with the Community Party to "capture" the
Southern Tenant Farmers Union for the Communist Party.
        Since you have violated every principle of friendship and every principle
of trade unionism I am hereby requesting, in order to save further trouble, that
you prepare and transmit to me at as early a date as possible your resignation
from the Executive Council of the Southern Tenant Farmers Union. I especially
hope that such a document may be in my hands before the next regular session of
the Council on September 10, 1938.
        Since your purpose with regard to the STFU has been as clearly and unmis-
takenly stated, I ask also that you notify Whitfield that you cannot be present
at the mass meeting that he has arranged for you on August 25th at Charleston,
Mo. Also that you ask Lee Hayes, Jim Gow, Arthur Ornits, and Mike Kilian to
remove themselves immediately from the field of the STFU and that they desist
from making or showing any pictures that may in any way purport to represent the
activities of the Southern Tenant Farmers Union or the Southern Labor Movement.
        Inclosed with this communication you will find my resignation, effective
at once, from the non-resident board of Commonwealth College.
        It pains me deeply to have to break the friendship that has existed be-
tween us for so many years, but you know that with me friendship counts for
nothing, individuals count for nothing where the welfare of the Southern Tenant
Farmers Union is concerned. You no doubt are curious to know how the inclosed
document came into my possession and when. You left your coat at my house; my
nephew, Silas Butler, put your coat on and wore it to town. He removed all the
papers that you had in your coat and put them in one of our bookshelves. On

his return he replaced what he thought to be all of your papers in your pocket, but evidently he missed one, for upon my return from the mass meeting yesterday afternoon I went to the bookshelf for a book and found the document.

I know that you will easily see why I now sign myself,

Your one time friend,

J. R. Butler, President
Southern Tenant Farmers Union

Enclosure

A meeting was held last night at Commonwealth College of 20 faculty, Maintenance and Administration workers who are Party members. The total number of Faculty, maintenance and Administration workers at the College is 25.

A visitor to the College, also a Party member, said: "If we think of the United States as a war map on which flags are stuck as the troops move in to new territory, then clearly it is time our Party stuck a flag in at Mena, Arkansas."

A committee was appointed to draw up a report to Party headquarters on the present situation at Commonwealth. This report follows.

1. The situation from a Party standpoint at Commonwealth is known to the District Organizer at St. Louis, with whom the College had been working closely. But we wish to draw the attention of national headquarters to the very great national importance of the College to our Party at the present time.

2. Since the reorganization of the school in August 1937, when a Party member became director of the school (Claude Williams), there has been on the campus complete political unity, an absence of such outside or disturbing elements as previously existed, and a conscientious adherence to the Party program in all the educational and field work. The figures quoted in par. 1 above show the numeric situation in faculty and administration, and it may correctly be said that students who are not members when they arrive almost invariably become members either here or immediately after they leave.

3. Since the reorganization the school, in addition to unifying and strengthening its resident program, has greatly developed its working relationship with the Southern labor and democratic movement.

(a). Claude Williams is a member of the National Exec. Council of the Southern Tenant Farmers Union, has played a decisive part in insisting upon progressive union policies, and has carried the need for a militantly progressive program to thousands of rank-and-file members who have the greatest confidence in him.

(b). The school has not only given resident instruction to members of the STFU but has conducted field classes as well (for example an interracial Institute for preacher members of the union was held at Little Rock from July 27 to August 1).

(c). The school has the full support of the Arkansas State office of the Farmers Educational and Cooperative Union. Two students have been commissioned as organizers and the school has conducted an extensive educational and organizational campaign on behalf of--and financed by--the union.

(d). For several months the school supported two persons to work full time in the labor movement at Fort Smith, the industrial center of this area.

(e). The Commonwealth College Association, governing body of the school, was expanded to include nine leading union officials of this area.

(f). Under direction of the District Organizer the school played a leading part in organizing the Arkansas Conference for Economic and Social Justice, held in Little Rock, July 23rd. Party members who took responsibility for setting up this Conference--the most important step to date in building the Democratic Front in Arkansas--were trained at Commonwealth, used it as their headquarters, and received financial assistance from the school.

4. In Commonwealth College the Party has a unique institution of national value and importance. Commonwealth owns the best and best-maintained labor library in the country, a 320-acre tract in a location enabling it to serve both industrial and agricultural workers. The natural facilities of the plant are used to foster democratic responsibility for maintenance and keep operating costs at a minimum. Students develop labor discipline in their work in farm, laundry, kitchen, etc.

5. The school has been operating under ceaseless financial stress. The ever-broadening scope of the work presents more and more opportunities which could be seized and followed up if money were available. The work is entirely dependent on voluntary donations.

6. A situation has now arisen which offers us an extraordinary opportunity to move into the most important organization in the agricultural South: the STFU. H. L. Mitchell, secretary of the STFU, who has been consistently opposed to the International with which that union is affiliated, to the Party, and to Commonwealth, is on a leave of absence from his office. The President of the union (J. R. Butler) and other members of the Executive Council who are friendly to us have invited us to conduct an intensive program of mass meetings throughout Arkansas and Missouri, beginning August 21st. At these meetings Claude Williams would be the principal speaker and a play which our school has in readiness for the purpose of dramatizing the union's needs could be presented. If this program could be carried out we believe it would place us in a position to capture the union for our line at the next convention. This is an opportunity for establishing a real party base in the STFU.

7. The situation is that we cannot undertake this program in the STFU without immediate financial assistance. We would not make an appeal to the Party if we were not assured of the paramount importance and urgency of carrying out such a program. The Center traveled from east to west coasts soliciting contributions to Commonwealth. Last year he went to the Center for the first time and asked only for an entree to the Hollywood group, which was given, and of which he was most appreciative. It was estimated at the Center that he could raise $3,000 in Hollywood but the net amount collected on the whole Pacific coast was $1,300. The reason for this is simply that most Hollywood progressives who are sympathetic to Commonwealth's present program are Party members and are committed to give all they can spare direct to the Party.

8. Commonwealth is possibly the Party's most strategic position from which to work at this time in the South, where the danger of Fascism is greatest. We do not pretend that it is the only important phase but it is a very important one. We believe the problem of our Party work in the South needs to be approached on a broad basis, that the importance of our Southern work should be carefully appraised and that a sum of money from the National funds should be allocated to it, so that not only Commonwealth but all other Party activities in the South may be assured of a definite income. We recommend to this end the calling of a southwide conference of Party workers in the field. We are convinced that as a result of such a conference the Center would allocate funds for the South where they are so sorely needed.

At the present time, however, we wish to draw special attention to the immediate problem of financing the STFU program above described, which cannot be undertaken unless funds can be raised before the end of next week. The program could be undertaken for $500 and we ask the Center to give most careful study to our request for that sum. Another like opportunity is hardly likely to occur.

Southern Tenant Farmers Union Papers, microfilm edition, reel 8.

10. CLAUDE WILLIAMS' RESPONSE TO J. R. BUTLER,
AUGUST 25, 1938

The document purporting to be a report from Commonwealth College to headquarters of the Communist Party which gave rise to a misunderstanding of the school's program and of my attitude toward the union; between J. R. Butler,

president of the Southern Tenant Farmers' Union and myself as member of the
Executive Council of the STFU and Director of Commonwealth College; and upon
which J. R. Butler based his letter of August 22 to me is not an authentic
statement by the school. It was merely a tentative appraisal of an individual
in class work of the school's program as a possible basis and a suggestion of
a possible source of support and was submitted along with several other individual appraisals for and suggestions of possible sources of potential
support.

     This report does not represent the **strictly** non-factional labor-union
policy of Commonwealth College, is largely fictional in nature and actually
violates importants [?] in its statements.

     It is not my desire nor the desire of the faculty at Commonwealth College
to "move into" or "capture" the Southern Tenant Farmers' Union or any other
union for any political group or party. In all my activities as an Executive
Council member of the STFU it has been my purpose to help build it into an
effective labor union. I have supported it and shall continue to support the
program and policies of the union as adopted in its conventions.

     The above referred to report was not concurred in by myself nor by the
school nor was any such a report submitted to any person or group.

                              Claude Williams

Southern Tenant Farmers Union Papers, microfilm edition, reel 8.

                    11. J. R. BUTLER TO E. B. MCKINNEY,
                              AUGUST 27, 1938

Dear Mr. McKinney:

     With the concurrence of a majority of the members of the Executive Council
of the Southern Tenant Farmers Union I have prepared and hereby present to you
certain specific charges:
     1. Disruption, through letters, speeches, and actions
     2. Non-cooperation. No reports of your activities have been made to
         this office since June 22, 1938.
     3. Insubordination in that you have refused to abide by the rules laid
         down by the Executive Council of which you are a member and which
         rules you helped to formulate and
     4. Conduct unbecoming to a Union member and an officer in that you
         have maliciously and viciously gossiped about the officers of the
         Union.
     You are requested to appear before the Executive Council of the STFU at
its next regular session which has been called for September 16th and 17th,
1938, and answer to the above charges.
     Your failure to appear, unless legal reason for your non-appearance can
be shown, will be taken as an admission of your guilt and will likely result
in your removal from your place as vice-president, from your place as Executive
Council member, and from membership in the Southern Tenant Farmers Union.

                              Sincerely,

                              J. R. Butler, president
                              Southern Tenant Farmers Union

Southern Tenant Farmers Union Papers, microfilm edition, reel 8.

12. E. B. MCKINNEY TO J. R. BUTLER,
AUGUST 31, 1938

Mr. J. R. Butler
President of S.T.F.U.
Memphis, Tenn.

Dear Mr. Butler.--I have your letter of the 27-Aug. together with the list of
specific charges which was recently filed against me by the executive council
of the S.T.F.U.   Of course there may be other charges against me that you
did not specify in the present list; evidently there are others.
    In the recent past there were charges against me, but not of such malig-
nant nature as has been described in these charges, and yet I sought redress
which proved futile, and instead of reparation which I had hoped would have
been the results, it turned out to be a near riot.
    In my opinion, such could not happen in a democratic concern as our
union pretends to be.   It could only happen where there are Dictators who
demand only yes men.
    This will always happen when men pose as infallibles, above reproach, can-
not be upbraided; and their colleagues must serve only as wards.   Their
elections are no more than appointed by them, they must be such as will suit
them, no offence committed but what must first be paraded before the public.
Such action as the latter, is an effort to justify the boss in making contact
upon his subjects.
    In the executive council meeting held at the S.T.F.U. office in June,
it was remarked, that the controversy which adjustment had been attempted with
regards to the Jefferson County troubles would have to abide by the unsatis-
factorily decision to me; or they could just get out.   So the next day of the
meeting I offered up my resignation, which did not interest the body.   Therefore I took for granted that I should go out with them, since I had tried in
vain for reconsideration.
    Knowing as I am almost sure I do, of the perpetration before, and also at
the national convention held in Little Rock in Feb. and the previous decision
of what would be done in that meeting, but of course it did not materialize,
but the contrivance did not cease with that failure.   And the position as vice
president of the S.T.F.U. was not conceded to be.   Rather my opponent, after
being defeated was provided with a created position, in violation of the constitution of the Southern Tenant Farmers Union.   This act in my judgement could
be nothing shorter than a contemptible one, and displays all the collars of a
marred vicious move, directed solely at me.
    For about 44 years, I have labored among my own people, of course I need
not apologize for the crude procedures, most of which, when other people than
the Negro know about it, they will find that it is unique.   But if the import
would be studied instead of being criticized, a better understanding could be
had.
    Now to the Czars of the Southern Tenant Farmers Union.   You may put it
down that I shall not attend the Council on the 16th inst.   And will attempt
to work among my people in the capacity which I worked in before the birth of
the Union, which was supervising over 36 congregations, comprising 4000 people.
Most of whom will stay in, or go out of what ever I think, and impress them
that it is not sound.
    But we stand ready for a treaty with any fair minded concern.   But shall
endeavor to retain race autonomy.

                          Sincerely,

                          E. B. McKinney

Southern Tenant Farmers Union Papers, microfilm edition, reel 8.

13. E. B. MCKINNEY'S PLEDGE OF ALLEGIANCE,
DECEMBER 5, 1938

I the undersigned pledge my allegiance to the Southern Tenant Farmers
Union and agree to abide by the Constitution now in force or which may here
after be adopted by the regular annual convention of the Union.

I withdraw all statements bearing my signature and agree to support
only the program and policies of the Southern Tenant Farmers Union now in
force or which may be adopted by the regular Annual Convention and its coming
sessions.

I believe in the basic principles of the Southern Tenant Farmers Union
and stand only for the organization of Negro and white workers in a united
movement.

E. B. McKinney

In view of the above statement we the undersigned officers and members
of the Southern Tenant Farmers Union agree to recommend that the Annual Convention re-instate E. B. McKinney as a member in good standing in the STFU.

H. L. Mitchell

Blaine Treadway

Southern Tenant Farmers Union Papers, microfilm edition, reel 9.

14. J. E. CLAYTON TO H. L. MITCHELL,
MAY 6, 1939

Mr. H. L. Mitchell
Secy.-Treas., STFU
Memphis, Tenn.

Dear Bro. Mitchell:--I just left Gould, Ark. I saw a number of our Brethren
from out on the South Bend Plantation today, and because they are going to have
a funeral near there tomorrow, I did not go out there to be there tomorrow.
Am on my way back to Texas tonight.

Mr. Mitchell! I have started our campaign this week to get enough buyers
to buy in the fine 12 thousand acre plantation of Ex-Gov. Lowden of Illinois. [94]
We colored have had it leased for 3 years, and we want to get buyers to buy it
in between now and fall. The prices will be from $24 to $27 an acre, and terms
of 1/3 down, and 20 years on the balance at only 4% interest. I'm planning to
sell from 2000 to 3000 acres of the improved lands in 1 acre tracts, the same
to be a cooperative farm. We can get 2 or 3 thousand share croppers and tenants
and day laborers to buy 1 acre each to be worked as a cooperative farm for them.
The price will be $27 an acre, and terms of $9.00 down, and $4.00 per week for
18 weeks, without interest. Now if we could get the poor colored people of the
STFU to buy this 2000 or 3000 acres as a cooperative farm, that would cause
nearly every Negro renter and share-cropper in the South to flock into your
Union. And as there is a very large plantation mansion on the plantation it
could be used for the Union, and you could operate there without being molested.
Write me by return mail and let me know what you think of it. I will close
school on the 22nd of this month, and will have my commencement exercises at
10:00 in the morning. I now write you to be with us. We will have a big free
picnic after the Graduation Exercises, which will be over at noon. Let me know
if you will be with us at our school and Littig on the morning of the 22nd. If
you will, we can talk over everything.

Mr. Egan is working in The Houston Chronicle Printing office in Houston.

Yours truly,

J. E. Clayton
P.O. Box 74
Littig, Texas

P.S.   I want you to be one of our Guest Speakers on Commencement Day.   May I
place you on program?   J.E.C.

Southern Tenant Farmers Union Papers, microfilm edition, reel 9.

15.   J. E. CLAYTON TO J. R. BUTLER,
JUNE 9, 1939

Pres. J. R. Butler
Pres., STFU
Memphis, Tenn.

Dear Bro. Butler:--Your letter of the 5th inst. received, and I thank you for
it, and for sending mine to Bro. Mitchell in New York.
       Bro. Butler! The land policy you have in mind is fine, but it will take
time to convert the masses of the people to that idea.   I had this in mind:
If your organization can put over one worth-while Project that the masses of
poor colored farmers want, that will cause them to flock into your organization
by the thousands, and tens of thousands.   After we get them in, we can then
convert them over to your progressive idea of farm ownership.   But you must get
the masses in your organization before you can change them from their old ideas
to your new and progressive ideas.
       If you and Bro. Mitchell could get some Philanthropist to make us a loan
this summer; that is, make the loan of $75,000.00 to about 250 Honest, Progres-
sive Race Farmers to make the down-payment on that 12 thousand acre fine plantation near Gould, Ark., that would show the Negro farmers of the South that your
organization had done more to help them become independent than any other organization in America; therefore, they would flock into your organization by
the tens of thousands and the STFU would sweep the South in a years time.   And
at the same time, we could add a small profit of about $2 an acre to the price
of the land to go to the STFU, and that would give the STFU over $25,000.00 to
go into its Treasure to operate on.   The 250 farmers could pay the $75,000.00
loan back in the fall, as they will make more than that on the place.   I know
the wire to pull to bring the masses of the Race Farmers into the Union.   Write
me here at once.

Yours truly,

J. E. Clayton

Southern Tenant Farmers Union Papers, microfilm edition, reel 11.

16.   GEORGE MAYBERRY TO H. L. MITCHELL,
NOVEMBER 23, 1939

Mr. H. L. Mitchell
Memphis, Tenn.

       I am writing you these lines to let you know what happened to me.   I went
on Monday the 20th day of November to get the date and place from the County

Agent, and he asked me do I belong to this union, and I told him, Yes sir, and
he asked me would I take his advice it would be better for me to join the Farm
Bureau. I told him that I was a member of that, and he said tht he hadn't got
the date. Then I asked him when I could get it, and he told me about the first
of December, and I told him all right, I would come back, and he asked me for
my name. And on the 22nd, listen to me, in came Mr. C. M. Addam, the County
Clerk to my house and Mr. Anderson Lindy came to my house and hand-cuffed me
and shoved the pistol on me and hand-cuffed me and put me in the car and
carried me away from my house. When I was handcuffed I gave my sign, and Mr.
Lindy hit me in the head two times, and when they got me to the other four men,
then Mr. Leonard Perkins hit me 5 times right in the head and stamped me twice
with his feet, and put me in the car and carried me to Macon River Bridge, and
put me on highway 45, and told me to go to the water mill before I turn out,
and don't come back no more, and gave my family one day to get out of the
county. It is so bad, I want some help. They took my box from my wife and my
membership card and organizer's credentials and going to get after all they
can. They can't have no meeting, and told me they better not hear from me, and
I better not tell you all about it that they would spend money to find me and
kill me, so what am I to do?
        Mr. Anderson Linzy hit me 2 times side the head. Mr. L. Perkins hit me
4 times side the head and stamp me 2 times. Mr. C. V. Adams, the County Clerk,
he got me for these men. Mr. H. Gland, Mr. Chas. Jackson and Mr. Sturd
Addams, these other men I did not know, all from Macon, Miss. And I got one
of my brothers word and he came to me. I was in the woods when he found me,
and he gave me what money he had, and I am trying to get to the train for here,
but I can't get my clothes, but I am coming like I is. Look for me, I am in
the woods and my wife and children all got to get out, and I can't go home.
Please let me hear from me and write the letter to Y. C. Cotton, Macon,
Mississippi, Rt. 3, Box 81 and he will get it to me.

                              G. B. Mayberry, 282

Southern Tenant Farmers Union Papers, microfilm edition, reel 13.

                    17.   AFFIDAVIT OF GEORGE MAYBERRY,
                              NOVEMBER 29, 1939

STATE OF TENNESSEE
COUNTY OF SHELBY

        Personally appeared before me, the undersigned notary public, of and for
the state and county aforesaid, George Mayberry, who makes oath in due form of
law as follows:
        That he is a resident of Noxubee County, Mississippi, and has farmed near
the town of Macon for 39 years. That during these years he has never been involved in any difficulties with the law-enforcing officers and has never been
imprisoned.
        That on the 20th day of November he went to the office of the County Agent
of Noxibee County, Mr. C. W. Gary, and asked for information as to the date of
the election of the County Committee of the County Conservation Association.
Mr. Gary told him that he did not know the date, and told him to come back a
month later. Mr. Gary then asked him if he believed in the Southern Tenant
Farmers' Union, and he replied that he did. Mr. Gary then advised him to join
the Farm Bureau, stating that he would get more out of it than he would from
the Southern Tenant Farmers' Union. He replied that he was already a member,
and Mr. Gary advised him to return to the office a month later for the information he wanted.
        That on the 22nd day of November, while he was cutting fire wood near his
home at about Eight O'clock in the morning, three men, C. V. Adams, the Chancery
Clerk; Anderson Linzy and Leon Perkins came to his home and had his wife send to
the woods for him. When he got to the house Mr. Adams told him to get in the

car and go with them down to the store where Mr. H. G. Land wanted to talk with
him about some land. That when he did not respond immediately to this order
Mr. Linsy and Mr. Perkins drew their pistols, and Mr. Linsy put hand-cuffs on
him. After having been forced to enter the car, these men drove about a
quarter of a mile from the house where they met a second car containing four
men, H. G. Land, Chess Jackson, Steward Adams and Henderson Tinzy. The affi-
ant was then dragged from the car by Leon Perkins and jerked to the ground.
Perkins then stamped twice on his head. When he had arisen Mr. Perkins again
struck him on the side of the head and knocked him down, commenting that he
should kill him and throw him in the creek. Linzy then hit him twice. After
the beating, they then put him back in the car and drove about eight miles to
Highway #45, where they stopped, took off the handcuffs and put him out of the
car, ordering him to go south and to never come back. Mr. C. V. Adams then
told him that he would give his family 24 hours to leave the community, and
if they had not left in that time he would kill them.

That he remained in hiding until Tuesday morning, November 28th, when he
came to Memphis, Tenn.

IN WITNESS THEREOF, the aforenamed George Mayberry has affixed his hand
and seal at Memphis, Tennessee, this the 29th day of Nov. 1939.

George Mayberry (Sr.)

SWORN TO AND SUBSCRIBED before me

this 29 day of Nov. 1939
Notary Public

Southern Tenant Farmers Union Papers, microfilm edition, reel 13.

18. LETTERS FROM A SHARECROPPER

*The incidents related in these letters are true, but the towns are
fictitous and the author must remain anonymous.*

Mt. Sterling, Miss., Feb. 5.

Mr. Cary Stevens,

Dear Sir:

A few days ago when me and brother Ed. Jackson was up at Union headquarters we talked with two NAACP lawyers who was down here to argue a case
about Negroes going to school to study medicine. We didn't know that this
kind of case could be brought into court. The lawyers made us feel mighty
good when they told us that a lot of folks is interested in the way we is getting along down here. You see we got a union down here what both colored folks
and white folks belongs to, we has been going on for about two years. Me and
brother Jackson was set off the plantation in Arkansas where we made crops four
years and we come here to make a crop this season. When we was setting out on
the road this winter our organizers brought us some tents and some can goods.
That was all that kept us alive. Our folks was beat awful. Some of them died.
The NAACP lawyers give us your name and told us to write to you. We needs
help. Please write us a kind word.

Yours truly,

Phillip Wills.

Philadelphia, Pennsylvania, Feb. 13.

Mr. Phillip Wills,

Dear Sir:
   I was indeed glad to receive your letter telling me about your union. It
is quite a treat to me to receive a letter from someone in the Delta country
who belongs to the Union, and who is actually working to build a better society.
Yes, it is true that I am interested in the work you are doing. At a meeting of
the local Committee to Aid Agricultural Workers a woman told how she was flogged when she started to the funeral of a slain sharecropper. She told horrible
tales of hunger, poor housing, and brutality on the part of some of the planters.
Can these things be true?
   It is my opinion that your burdens are my burdens, and that as long as
you are oppressed I am too, although I might suffer a little less than you do.
This is my last year in college. The month of June will see me on the way to
your part of the country. Please send me more news, and some suggestions as
to how I can help you. Regards to Mr. Jackson.

Yours sincerely,

Cary Stevens.

Mt. Sterling, Miss., March 6.

Dear Mr. Stevens:
   I read your letter to our local meeting. They was overjoyed to hear that
you was coming down here. We don't have contack with very many college people.
Some of them has helped us organize but they had to quit cause they would of
lost they jobs. Most of the educated folks thinks they is better than us.
This makes it very hard. It rained something terrible last week. Brother
Jacksons house leaked so bad till he had to move the bed to keep it from being
soaked. His wife had another take of pellagacy. Me and brother Jackson has
been quite worried lately. A white lawyer what was working with us was found
dead in his wrecked auto. One of the vice presidents wants to split the Union
and have one for colored and one for white. We has been treated very bad by
white folks, but in the Union we go down the line together. We thinks that the
NAACP might give us some advice, but we don't have none here. Please tell us
what you think about having two unions.

Yours truly,

Phillip Wills.

Philadelphia, Pa., April 2.

Dear Mr. Wills:
   It was very sad to learn of the death of the lawyer. The Committee for the
Aid of Agricultural Workers received notice of the "accident" several days ago.
We mourn your loss, for he was a brave man whom all of us respected. Keep
courage. There is no gain without pain, says a Spanish proverb.
   I gave your letter to one of the NAACP lawyers. Although he was not, at
that time, in position to speak for the entire organization, he said that the
Association would in no way support a split in the Union. My own idea is that
whether the sharecropper be black or white, the problem is the same. This being
true, you must do everything in your power to prevent having two unions. One
race cannot rise without the other.
   With best wishes, I remain

Yours sincerely,

Cary Stevens.

Mt. Sterling, Miss., April 29.

Dear Mr. Stevens:
Thanks very much for giving us your thoughts about having two unions.
Most of us feels that it is better for us all to go along together. We is
working very hard. Brother Jackson is been walking all over the country with
a white member of our local trying to get people to join the union. They goes
most times at night cause this work is very dangerous. Our local owns a car
but we don't have no money to buy gas and oil. The car was give to us by
somebody up north. Is you really coming down here soon?

Yours truly,

Phillip Wills.

Philadelphia, Penn., May 7.

Dear Mr. Wills:
Final examinations begin within the next few weeks. I am confident of
being graduated, although one never knows until the event has actually taken
place. I hope to leave here soon after commencement exercises. Please excuse
such a short letter.

Sincerely,

Cary Stevens.

Mt. Sterling, Miss., June 2.

Dear Friend:
Brother Jackson was killed last week. One day he had an argument his
plantation boss beat him something terrible while another white man held a gun
on him. He was setting on the porch with his wife in the evening when he seen
some men coming to the house on horses. His wife told brother Jackson to run
and hide in the woods. He couldn't run very fast cause he was sore and the
boss rode up and shot him in the back. The union had his funeral and he wore
his badge to his grave. It was all very sad but we still has hopes. Here is a
piece I tore out of the paper.

"NEGRO KILLED RESISTING OFFICER"

"May 14--Ed. Jackson, a huge Negro, was killed today while resisting a
deputy sheriff. An attempt was made to arrest Jackson on a charge of disorderly
conduct. A struggle took place, and the officer had to shoot in self defense."

Your friend,

Phillip Wills.

The Crisis, 46 (November 1939):335.

19. FARMER'S MEMORY SINGS 'RAGGEDY' TUNE

"Raggedy, raggedy are we
Just as raggedy as raggedy can be
We don't get nothin' for our labor
So raggedy, raggedy are we."

by William Thomas

John L. Handcox wrote that song for the Southern Tenant Farmers Union more than 40 years ago--but he remembers it like it was yesterday.
"It was written for rough, tough, raggedy times," said Handcox, 78, who sang some of his songs yesterday during the 48th anniversary celebration of the union's founding in Historical First Baptist Church Beale Street.
Handcox, a one-time sharecropper from Brinkley, Ark., was among the more than 150 former union members who met for a two-day get-together designed to pay tribute to the union's beginnings.
"I used to write both poems and folksongs," said Handcox, who now lives in San Diego. "I don't write songs, anymore. But if I wrote a song today it would be about hard times. I could write one about modern conditions if I wanted to. They don't exactly compare to the '30s, but they're still hard. A lot of folks are out of work."
Handcox, a lean, white-bearded black man, said people worked harder during the Great Depression--but they didn't know anything about high prices.
"The highest-paid hand was 75 cents. He worked from can to can't. That's from the time you can see till the time you can't. They used to ring the bell at 5 a.m., and you had to get down to the barn and harness the mule by lantern light."
A pair of runaway mules killed Handcox' father when he was a boy.
"I had an older brother, but he didn't have no get-up," Handcox said. "So I had to take over and help raise the rest of the kids. There were 10 of us at the time. It was rough and tough. Our land was too poor to farm. So we rented land on the thirds and fourths--a third of the cotton, a fourth of the corn."
Handcox wrote a song about it: "The poor man raises all the rich man can eat, and then gets tramped down under the rich man's feet."
Handcox said things are a little better now, but only because of the government's help.
"If it wasn't for social security, it would be pitiful," he said. "The social security it not enough to live on, but it's enough to exist. I'm one of the fortunate poor because I've always had enough to eat. My stomach was never in danger of collapsing. It will do that, you know, if you don't get something between your front and your back."

The Commercial Appeal (Memphis), April 17, 1982.

20. KING COTTON

by John Handcox

The planters celebrated King Cotton in Memphis, May fifteen.
It was the largest gathering you most ever seen.
People came from far and near -- to celebrate King Cotton
Whom the planters love so dear.
Thousands of flags were hung in the street,
But they left thousands of sharecroppers on their farms with nothing to eat.
Why do they celebrate Cotton? Here, I'll make it clear,
Because they cheat, beat and take it away from labor every year.

Cotton is King, and will always be,
Until labor in the South is set free.
The money spent for decorations and flags,
Would sure have helped poor sharecroppers who are hungry and in rags.
Oh! King Cotton, today you have millions of slaves
And have caused many poor workers to be in lonesome graves.
When Cotton is King of any nation,
It means wealth to the planter -- to the laborer starvation.

[1936]

Southern Tenant Farmers Union Papers, microfilm edition, reel 3.

21.   STRIKE IN ARKANSAS

By John Handcox

The day labor called a strike the eighteenth day of May,
For they cannot live on what the planters pay.
They asked the people in Memphis not to go out on the truck,
But the picketeers found that jail was their luck.
The Union having many friends and good support had to pay
A ten dollar fine to the unjust Memphis Court.

In Earl, Arkansas they threw so many in jail,
That anyone would class such arrest as "wholesale."
Some planters have forced the labor into the field with gun,
And are driving them like convicts from sun to sun.
The planter is using pistols and whipping labor across the head,
Telling them "If you don't get in my field, I kill you dead."

The Planter say to ask for a dollar and a half a day is unfair,
They never mention high prices the labor have to pay him for what he eat and wear.
Everybody knows the Union isn't asking for enough,
If we remember how the planter sell his beans and stuff.
They're riding around cussing and raising sand,
When it's known they sold the 25¢ size baking powder for 50¢ a can.

They arrested Mr. Gilmartin, a New York guest,
Who was investigating the people who were in distress.
On May twenty-second, the most terrible thing happen you ever could record.
Peacher attacked Miss Evelyn Smith and Mrs. Clay East,
Told them to leave there at once for they were disturbing the peace.
They went out to take a picture of Union people he had in stockade,
Only wanting to seek some way to give the Union people aid.
Peacher took their Kodak, and tore up their film,
Saying, "You'd better leave Arkansas, or you be hung to a limb."
The planter saw in Arkansas is raising Cain,
They have no respect for person--woman or man.

If you go through Arkansas, you better drive fast,
How the labor is being treated, you better not ask.
I warn you to carry enough money to give bail,
For if planter law find you in sympathy with labor, they put you in jail.
It make no difference, whether white or black,
If you not in the ring, you all look alak.

[1936]

Southern Tenant Farmers Union Papers, microfilm edition, reel 3.

THE MISSOURI ROADSIDE DEMONSTRATION OF 1939

22.   TEN MILLION SHARECROPPERS

By Mildred G. Freed

*Eviction day draws near for the sharecroppers on the plantations of the
South.   This account of the plight of 96 families is a fair picture of the
predicament of the others.*

New Year's day to some ten million sharecroppers is the day the "boss-man" hands them their eviction notices.

Last January 10, last day of grace after eviction notices had been served, 100 miles of highway along Route 61 in "Swamp-East" Missouri were covered with sharecroppers, white and Negro.

With sticks of furniture piled up beside the fence, with women and children sleeping through sleet and through snow, almost 2,000 homeless sharecroppers huddled beside the ice-bound highway.

Two thousand evicted sharecroppers with nowhere to go.

Highway 61 is one of the most travelled highways in the country. People going east and west, people going north and south saw these shelterless families and stopped to talk to them. Newspapermen came down and asked questions. Photographers flashed bulbs in their faces as they slept.

But local planters weren't pleased with this highlighting of their sins. They angrily called for an "impartial investigation." They got it. The F.B.I. proved that the leader of the demonstration was a man who had been a share-cropper for 35 years--Rev. Owen H. Whitfield. (The planters, still dissatisfied, I was told, then began to yell for a Dies' investigation).

These sharecroppers suffered the sleet and the snow because they were determined to show the country just what sort of conditions surrounded them. They were convinced that once the American people were aware of their plight something would be done about it.

Something was.

One night the State Health Doctor came out to these people living beside the frozen roadside, poked around their teeth and declared, "These people are a serious menace to public health--they must be removed."

Highway patrolmen and vigilante committees snapped into action. Thirty-two families were dumped into an old two-room abandoned building; twenty-three families, white and Negro, were piled on top of the Mississippi levee; twenty-five families were crowded into an unused church. A few weeks later the owners of these buildings instituted proceedings against these "tresspassers"!

96 Families Still Live There

Today on the banks of the Little Black River, on their 93-acre tract of barren land in Butler county, live 96 white and Negro families--the nucleus of the roadside demonstration. (This land was bought for them by a group of sympathizers in St. Louis in conjunction with UCAPAWA, the C.I.O. Union to which these sharecroppers belong).

They live in barrel-stave huts and rag tents. The occasional army tent--there are several ex-servicemen in the group--looks very spic and span in contrast to the dreary mud-chinked "homes" of the others.

Although there are over 50 log-cabins built on the partially-clear timberland, only the odd one has a roof. I inquired about this and a tall gaunt man replied, "We's hopin' gonna be some way t'git nails an' roofin befo' the cold comes. Cain't seem t'git nails without money nohow."

Food at the camp is obtained from relief. "Relief" consists of four pounds of corn grit (chicken feed looks more appetizing): four pounds of meal and two pounds of beans. This has to last a family, often as large as ten, for a whole month.

Meals are eaten twice a day on a homemade table by the side of the tent. I sat on a chair that was a wooden frame with a few stray wires that kept me from falling through. Drum barrels added to the number of chairs. The children ate standing up--digging their bare toes into the dust.

In the center of the table was a plateful of soupy corn grit; a sorry-looking mess of crumpled beans; a pasty concoction of meal and water is baked in the wood-burning stove and called "bread." One bite and sickly smell of the dough cooked without salt or grease upset my stomach so that I had to smoke innumerable cigarettes to keep from insulting my hosts in a manner beyond my control.

Naturally this shockingly ill-balanced diet leads to bad health. Most of the children at the camp have rashes. Mothers, with the inevitable exhaustion of sharecroppers' wives, feed their children at the breast for two or three years--they have nothing else to feed them. Noon is lunchtime in New York, but just another hour in the sharecropper camp.

There was a young married woman at the camp who had been feverishly ill
ever since she had come to the camp three months ago. She was suffering from
her third miscarriage within the year.

"Why don't you get a doctor to see her?" I asked with the naive confidence
of the North.

"Private doctor he won' come 'cause we ain't got no money and county
doctor he said he ain't never gonna help us." (Later I heard from a local
newspaperman in Poplar Bluff that the county doctor is a brother of a large
landowner in Mississippi county, where the roadsiders staged their demonstration. He said he'd "be damned" if he'd ever help the camp in any way. Camp
delegations to see him proved fruitless).

The patient was deliriously ill. Her husband went to Poplar Bluff (15
miles) for a doctor who agreed to come for $5.

The worried crowd gathered outside the rag tent made way for the doctor.
Inside, the tent was completely filled with two large beds and a battered trunk.
A few women sat on one bed. The patient tossed feverishly in the other. At
the foot of her bed her husband sat, silent.

The doctor was brief. "What you need, young lady," said he in a professional manner, "is a light diet of milk, eggs, orange juice,--umm, perhaps a
little corn flakes."

"But she ain't got nuthin but corn grit, doctor," said the husband.

The doctor left a few fever pills, took his $5 and hurried off.

For the next ten days or so the patient received a few basic food stuffs.
Her fever dropped and by the time I left the camp I thought she was completely
cured. But her tiny store of food was soon exhausted. A week later she died.

The Red Cross

"Have you asked the Red Cross to help?" I asked.

"Red Cross they said they cain't help 'cause this is a man-made disaster."

"Isn't war a man-made disaster?" I couldn't help interjecting.

"When I said that they kicked me out."

And the phrase "man-made disaster" applies here--as it does to war. These
sharecroppers are a part of what President Roosevelt called "our economic problem
No. 1." Congress passed a parity bill to help them. Under the Cotton Crop Control, planters can only grow a certain amount of cotton. The government pays
them per acre for the land that lays idle. The law also says the sharecropper--
who works for a percentage of the amount of cotton he picks, sometimes as little
as three-eighths--should get the same per cent of the government parity payment.

But too often he doesn't. Many planters, hard-up themselves, figured out
the following "economical" plan.

They evicted their sharecroppers, whom they had to feed all year on
credit (sharecroppers work to pay the landlord back for the food eaten between
cotton seasons. Of a group of 2,000 families surveyed in Alabama, 61.7% broke
even; 26% "went in the hole"; and 9.4% made a profit of from $70 to $90 a year).

The planters then keep the government payments and during the cotton season, they re-hire their former sharecroppers as day laborers. Planters find
this system much cheaper because they only pay the day laborer from 40¢ to $1 a
day--with wife and children picking too. Out of this amount the day laborer
has to pay rent and buy food, usually at the planter's store. In between seasons these homeless families have no money and nowhere to go.

The fight against becoming day laborers led these evicted sharecroppers
to "sit down" in the State highways last January. These same conditions, and
the increase in the use of tractors, according to government estimates, will
make an additional 40,000 sharecroppers homeless each year.

"Forty acres and a mule" is the American conception of what is needed to
adequately support a family. On these 93 acres of the camp live 96 families
with nowhere to go.

Leader Whitfield

Rev. Owen H. Whitfield, the leader of last year's roadside demonstration
is a thin, light-skinned man with Indian features. When anyone asks his
nationality he laughs:

"Y'see its this-a-way," he'll begin. "On m'mother's side, m'gran-mother, she were Creole Indian; m'gran'father, he were white man. But on m'father's side, m'gran'mother, she were Indian 'nuther tribe, an m'gran'father, he were African. And so," (this always tickles him) "I ain't sure what nationality I is exactly but I know its American."

The mother of ten children, Mrs. Whitfield is a charming, youthful-looking woman sincerely interested in helping her people.

Born in a drab sharecropper's cabin, their earliest recollections are of the cotton patch where they struggled along behind their parents picking cotton.

The Whitfield family found their first security on the LaForge Project. But, says Rev. Whitfield, "If'n I were in the Garden of Eden an I heard a lil baby cryin on the other side o that door, I couldn't be happy less'n I got that baby in too."

And so when almost 2,000 sharecroppers were evicted last January, he left his home to lead his people "an show the country what condition they's in."

Today he is a District President of UCAPAWA. "I believes in this here union," he will tell you, "as bein th'only way t'raise the people up out'n their slavery." And that sentiment is echoed by the whole camp.

"But what would you like to see done for the 500 people at the camp?" I asked.

"I'd like t'see them put back on the land on a gov'ment project," Whitfield answered, "like the LaForge Project."

The LaForge Project is a self-liquidating one under the Farm Security Administration. It consists of 100 sharecropper families, white and Negro, who would otherwise have had to go on relief. The government furnished their homes and tools on long term payments, and they farm the land cooperatively, although each family has its own little home it will eventually own.

Everything is under government supervision. The men are taught to care for the soil. The women are taught to preserve fruits, fish, etc. Children are sent to schools to make up for their too-often neglected backgrounds.

The F.S.A. has more than a dozen such rehabilitation projects already started in the South. Some are farmed cooperatively; others are based on individual ownership. Some start with sharecroppers who advance to the renter's class and, if they make good, eventually own their land.

Travelling through the drab sharecropper areas in the South, the white paint, the new methods of subsistence farming which replace the soil-depleting one-crop system of the cotton states, all prove that the self-liquidating projects of the F.S.A. offer America the hope of adjusting this tremendous economic problem of the South.

As one of the sharecroppers at the camp puts it, "Seems like there's enough land in this here country fer everybody t'live comfortable. All we want is t'be able t'use the gov'ment's idle land t'raise food so's we could keep the children from starvin."

A new year is coming.

What hope can the new year bring to the thousands of sharecroppers who again face eviction this January? I received a letter from Rev. Owen H. Whitfield written from the field Nov. 14, 1939:

> "Our people on farms are getting eviction notices by the hundreds. Those who are not evicted outright must accept day labor at starvation wages or get out without written notices. And you can see what this means. It means we will be faced with another exodus with no place to go. . . ."

The Crisis, 46 (December 1939):367-68.

23. TELEGRAM FROM H. L. MITCHELL TO
MRS. FRANKLIN ROOSEVELT, JANUARY 18, 1939

Mrs. Franklin D. Roosevelt:

Remembering your concern for the welfare of evicted sharecroppers farm laborers encamped on Missouri Highways last Thursday may I urge that you use

your influence to have tents supplied for 159 families located at Homeless
Junction near New Madrid and 23 families on River Levee near Dorena over 600
men women and children without shelter despite stories that all are being
cared for by government agencies. A number of expectant mothers many small
children in open weather little food or firewood, drinking water supply from
open ditches, highway camps were broken up by state police on pretext health
protection. Landowners had these people moved from highways to back roads
out of public sight emergency still exists with problem unsolved. May I again
urge your help.

H. L. Mitchell

Franklin D. Roosevelt Papers, Hyde Park, New York.

24. MR. HERBERT LITTLE, NYA REPRESENTATIVE CALLED
MR. AUBREY WILLIAMS FROM MISSOURI, 1/15/39

Mr. Little:	I have 16 of these case histories. I shortened them somewhat but they will take about two minutes each to dictate - it means about 30 or 35 minutes.
Mr. Williams:	In general, what is the situation?
Mr. Little:	That the State Police, plus the Sheriff with some armed citizens, have broken up most of these camps. We saw them break up two. They are taking these folks and their effects away to an isolated place in the country in State Highway Department trucks. I interviewed 16 of these fellows with the help of the State staff and got pretty adequate answers as to where they contended they were from, what they were there for, and how they got there - and they are, most of the 16 I talked to in the space of two or three hours in the early morning, nearly all residents of Missouri, with the exception of maybe one-third who came from Arkansas a year ago or two years ago. There were none from Mississippi and only one from the tip of Kentucky. Fifteen of them were Negroes and one, White.
Mr. Williams:	Most of them are Negroes?
Mr. Little:	About 90-95% of the whole group are Negroes.
Mr. Williams:	Were they sharecroppers or laborers?
Mr. Little:	About two-thirds were sharecroppers at some stage, although some had been kicked down to day laborers. Maybe, one-fourth were day laborers and two or three of them tenant farmers.
Mr. Williams:	How many are there out there where you are?
Mr. Little:	We went up about 20-25 miles of highway and there were four camps along the road. One camp had 250, another 60 or 70.
Mr. Williams:	Are they going to break up those camps?
Mr. Little:	Yes, they have already done it today. They moved them away starting about 10 o'clock on trucks to an isolated place down the country.
Mr. Williams:	What have they there?
Mr. Little:	Forty acres and no provision for keeping them, according to what the Sheriff told me.
Mr. Williams:	They are just going to dump them on the ground?
Mr. Little:	That is the impression the Sheriff gave me.
Mr. Williams:	Is that in Missouri or Arkansas?
Mr. Little:	Missouri, about 50 or 60 miles from Arkansas.
Mr. Williams:	What do they think they will do down there?
Mr. Little:	I don't know. My impression is they will probably starve or go back to day laboring jobs mostly.
Mr. Williams:	Is that near a town or is it in a town?
Mr. Little:	No, it is ten miles off the main highway on a farm-to-market road.
Mr. Williams:	Of course, there is nothing to compel them to stay there.

Mr. Little:	They have plenty of shotguns – these citizens that the Sheriff brought around – when they took them away from their present camps.
Mr. Williams:	They are not going to establish an armed camp?
Mr. Little:	I don't know. That is up to the Sheriff. It was a little bit like Harlan County, with a few differences.
Mr. Williams:	Have you that stuff so you could put it in envelopes and air mail it to me so I could get it in the morning.
Mr. Little:	We are 170 miles from St. Louis, but the boys can drive it in about 5 hours. In addition to these 16 cases, I have a 2000-word description, which I dictated while the Sheriff and the men were preparing to tear down their shanties, being transcribed now and it will take another hour. I have already transcribed and organized these case histories and, if you say so, I will send them both and catch the 11 o'clock plane here tonight which ought to get to your desk in Washington not later than 10 or 11 o'clock in the morning.
Mr. Williams:	I think that is the thing to do and I would like for you to stay on – go on down there and see where they are putting them and get the whole view of the thing. Be careful, though, that nobody finds out you are there.
Mr. Little:	The State Police tried to arrest one of the NYA boys that came along with me and I told them who I was – that I was making a study.
Mr. Williams:	I mean the papers.
Mr. Little:	I am avoiding any newspaper people and I don't think the State Police will do anything about it.
Mr. Williams:	I would keep on getting these case histories – go way down there.
Mr. Little:	I have the typical ones. I can get more, but I think we pretty well covered what we can get.
Mr. Williams:	I understood there were 1700 families all-told involved.
Mr. Little:	No, I think about 1600 or 1700 persons.
Mr. Williams:	I see – only about 300-400 families.
Mr. Little:	That would be my guess from what I saw and what I heard about the ones the Sheriff had evicted.
Mr. Williams:	You think probably 350 are Negroes.
Mr. Little:	90% or more.
Mr. Williams:	Would it be too dangerous for you to get back in there where they are taking them and see what they are doing to them?
Mr. Little:	Not at all, the Highway Police have been very decent to me.
Mr. Williams:	I would like for you to do that. I would like to have an eye witness description of where they are taking them and the conditions under which they are being placed.
Mr. Little:	I will try.
Mr. Williams:	I understand the thing goes South clear to the Arkansas line.
Mr. Little:	I think in the next County down – I will have to go and see – they are trying to get most of them to go back to day laboring on the farm or plantation. I don't know for sure.
Mr. Williams:	I think this is grand. Send those boys on up to St. Louis with that stuff, get it on the plane by Special Delivery marked "PERSONAL" and mark it so that it gets here to me at 723 Washington Building.
Mr. Little:	Yes sir.

Franklin D. Roosevelt Papers, Hyde Park, New York.

25. SAMPLE CASE HISTORIES COMPILED BY
HERBERT LITTLE FROM THE ROADSIDE DEMONSTRATORS IN JANUARY 1939

WILLIE SCOTT

Husband ill with flu, staying with neighbor.

Age 42

Two children, one 16, one 24 years.
Both children living here with parents.

Previous address, Portageville, Mo. Route #1, 1¼ mi. from camp.

Lately tenant for Murray Phillips, Sikeston, Mo. Farmed "all my life," in
    Arkansas and Mo.

Tenant previously at Ristine, Mo. near New Madrid on Hall Hunter's Farm.
    Never owned a farm.

No cash on hand, small amount of bread and fruit from Surplus Commodity.

No relatives in a position to help.

No member of family receiving W.P.A., relief, old age pension or other public
    assistance.

Says she was evicted, being given notice the Friday before Christmas and
    joined this camp on January 10, 1939.

Does not wish to stay longer on "this farm." "Any place for a farm that would
    make a living." She has her own stock on Murray Phillip's farm including
    three head of mules.

A sort of leader at the largest camp. Known among the other campers as "the
    writing woman."

O. J. JULIN

Married

Age 45

Seven children from 9 to 21 years old. Six of the children and his wife were
    at the camp and the oldest boy is taking care of his grandfather at
    Wardell, Mo.

Previous address, Marston, Mo.

Lately tenant, for one year, for Walter Richardson, Marston, Mo.

Previously rented farm from Central States Life Insurance Co., near Marston
    for one year, preceded by renting from B. Brinkman, Wardell, Mo. for one
    year. Prior to this, he sharecropped for Brinkman whom he described as
    a member of the Legislature. Never owned a farm.

Had one penny, food to last a week and "some" clothes.

No relatives to help although his oldest brother, works some.

Father receives old age pension, apparently about $10.00 a month, and Julin
    obtained a rehabilitation loan in 1936 to buy farm equipment.

His tenant house burned in July and the owner did not rebuild. Julin and
    family lived in a tent through the cotton picking season. He says
    he had written as well as verbal notice from Richardson to move. He
    Left January 10 and moved to the roadside camp.

He wants to farm "any good place" where there is good land.

DAVE WILKINS

Married

Age 48

Three children, 5, 8 and 12 yrs. age. All at camp with wife.

Previous address, Cathron, Mo. since last October, when he came here from
    Arkansas.

Lately day laborer for J. C. Mathis, Cathron.

Share cropped "all my days" except for 1934, when he rented a farm in Arkansas. Never owned a farm.

No cash, a little flour, two cups of lard, work clothing and a grimy overcoat.

No relatives in a position to help.

A sister in Arkansas is farming but unable to help him.

No public assistance received.

He stayed on the Mathis farm after the cotton picking season, but his money went and he sold his pig and chickens to come to the Highway to live.

He desires to continue farm work "anywhere except Arkansas."

JIMMIE HAMILTON

Married

Age 27

One 8 yr. old child at camp with wife.

Previous address, Bragg City, Mo., 49 miles away, also Cathron, Mo.

Lately Share cropper for J. C. Mathis in Cathron.

Share cropper previously two years fro Dr. Victor, Bragg City, Mo. and Willis Weaver, the latter a Negro. He never owned a farm.

No money, some Surplus Commodity food, overalls and a light top-coat.

No relatives who can help.

No public assistance.

Says he quarreled with Weaver over the amount of money due on his 1937 crop. Says Mathis told him two weeks ago he could not use him. Without telling him to move, Mathis said he would use no share croppers in future.

He desires to continue farming.

ROBERT HAYNES

Married

Age 42

Has seven children. Wife and children in camp.

Previous address Cathron, Mo.

Lately employed at Cathron, Mo., by P. M. Barton as day laborer at $1.00 a day. Worked for Mr. Barton three years.

Previously worked two and one-half miles East of Portageville for George Worth. Worked as day laborer at 75¢ a day. Never owned a farm.

Has 20¢. Also has 24 pounds of flour, 15 pounds of lard and some beans. Has one suit of work clothes, and one good suit.

Has one cousin in camp. No other relatives with the exception of wife and children.

Has never made application for WPA employment and no aid received.

Says he left his last job on January 6 because he could not support his family on $1.00 a day.

Wants to "work on farm for the Government if possible." Does not want to work for land owners, says they are unfair.

Note: This fellow has two wounds on his forehead, and one on his right cheek which, he says, were inflicted by the sheriff's deputy on Sunday,

January 15. He said that one of the sheriff's deputies hit him in the
face with a gun, and another hit him on the forehead with a cane,
cutting his face.

CORNELIUS MCCANLEY

Married

Age 52

Fifteen children born, eleven living. Nine children and wife in camp. One
son in St. Louis, married and unemployed.

Route #1, Mathews, Mo.

Lately employed at Mathews, Mo., by Billy McGee, farmer. Worked as share
cropper.

Previously had worked for fourteen years on a farm East of Noxall, Mo., owned
by Elon Proffer. Has a small farm in Arkansas which he purchased in
1912. This is a five acre farm, and he says he could not support his
family on such a small farm.

Has $10.00 in cash. Has a month's supply of some foods, and will have to buy
other foods within the next few days. Has two pairs of overalls and one
"Sunday suit."

Has a brother working on the LaForge Cooperative Farm. No other relatives,
except wife and children. Brother has sixteen children.

Has not applied for WPA employment. Received one check from the Government
in the amount of $100.00 about a month or so ago. Says, "I never read
the check to see the reading on it, but I think it was a loan on cotton."
After paying doctor bills and buying clothing he has $10.00 of this money
left.

"Left the last job because I was told I was not needed anymore." Says the
landlord's son was put to work in his place.

Wants farm job "any place in Missouri out of the bottoms." Would like to be a
share cropper, also have a warm, dry place to stay.

ROBERT HILL

Widower

Age 50

One child in Pennsylvania.

Previous address two miles East of Essex, Mo.

Lately employed at Essex, Mo., by George Bunch, farmer, as a day laborer, for
which he received only his board and shelter. Worked on this farm six
months.

Came to this section of Missouri, from Washington, D.C., July, 1932, and has
been employed as a day laborer wherever he could find work. Is an ex-
service man having participated in the World War.

No cash. "I does not have even a piece of bread, will have to eat with
friends." Has poor suit of work clothes only.

Has no relatives, other than the son in Pennsylvania, and from whom he has not
heard from since 1932.

Has never made application for WPA employment. Received a bonus of about
$100.00 on June 15, 1936, which he has since spent for food and clothing.

Left last job because "I was not going to work for nothing." After seeing
"evicted share croppers" on the highway he decided to stay with them.
Never was given a notice of eviction.

Wants farm job on "Government farm."

SAM BROWN

Married

Age 74

Three children born, one living in Arkansas, the others are dead. Wife is ill and has gone to the home of a son, by a previous marriage.

Previous address Buckley, Missouri.

Last employment was at Morehouse, MO., where he was a share cropper on the farm of Willie Martin.

Previously was a renter for three years at Morehouse, Mo. Prior to moving to Morehouse he was a share cropper at Frisco, Mo., for Joe Snyder.

No cash. Says, "Food is getting pretty scarce." Has a day's supply, which was purchased with his "pension money." Has two suits of overalls.

Has no relatives other than wife and stepson. Stepson is a share cropper.

Is not eligible for WPA as he draws an old age pension of ten dollars a month.

Was notified by written order, along with other share croppers, that he would be evicted, and went to the highway camp on January 10.

Wants a place to call home.

MANUEL JENKINS

Married

Age 45

Has three children. Wife and children in camp.

Previous address Cathron, Mo.

Lately employed at Cathron, Mo., by P. M. Barton as day laborer at $1.00 per day. He worked on this farm three years.

Prior to being employed by Mr. Barton he lived at Marston, Mo., and was employed by Fred Copeland as a share cropper. Previous to this job he worked at Burney, Mo., for Howard Moore, as a share cropper. Never owned a farm.

No cash. A supply of food for one or two days. This food was received from surplus commodities. Only clothes this man has are the ones he is wearing. He has a very fair overcoat.

Has one brother in Arkansas who is a day laborer. He is unable to help this man.

Has not asked for relief, nor made application for WPA employment.

Left the farm on which he was employed because he was unable to care for his family on the wages paid by Mr. Barton. Was not notified to leave the farm.

Wants farm job. Desires to be a share cropper.

JAMES DUPRIEST

Married

Age 40

Four children and wife in camp.

Previous address Mathews, Missouri.

Lately employed on Alvin Earl's place as day laborer at $1.00 per day.

During the year 1937 worked in Bragg City, Missouri, also worked as share cropper on the farm of Willis Weaver (colored) at Bragg City.

No cash. Has enough food to last 1½ or 2 days. This food he purchased with
money from the sale of cotton. He has also received a small supply of
commodities from the Surplus Commodities. He has one dress suit, and
the clothes he was wearing.

Has an uncle, with three boys, working on WPA. This uncle is unable to
assist him.

Has applied for work on WPA but has not anything further regarding this application.

This man states, "The boss man had to move and I had no place to live." He
later stated that the man, on whose place he lived, desired to replace
him with an uncle, and this uncle wished to live in the house occupied
by James DuPriest.

Wants farm job. "Any good farm where I will be allowed to work." He prefers
to be a share cropper.

Franklin D. Roosevelt Papers, Hyde Park, New York.

26. MEMORANDUM FROM HERBERT LITTLE TO
AUBREY WILLIAMS, JANUARY 16, 1939

SUBJECT: Eyewitness account of dispersal of roadside camps of farmers by
Sheriff in New Madrid County near Sikeston, Missouri, Sunday,
January 15, 1939.

W. M. Tanner, part time organizer for the Southern Tenant Farmers Union,
came from Memphis by bus January 15 and met me at Sikeston, Missouri. He said
he and another organizer on a tour of inspection of the roadside camps had
been met here the day before by the State Police and escorted out of the state.
Tanner is an Arkansas man, a member of the Executive Board of the S.F.T.U.
and lives near Cotton Plant, Ark. He gave me the names of William R. Fisher
(white), Doreeno, Missouri, and Rev. J. W. Moore and Willie Scott of Portageville, Missouri, both colored, as leaders of two of the remaining camps.
We drove Tanner to the New Madrid bus station, choosing not to have him
along when we started to interview the campers in view of the possible difficulty with the State Police. He said he and Mr. Butler, official of the
S.F.T.U. on their trip here January 14 had advised the campers to accept accommodations offered to them by farm owners and leave the Highway if the accommodations were liveable. Mr. Tanner told of one farmer who offered the
head of a family of nine a wage of $0.50 a day. Tanner said he did not know
how the concentration of the workers had started.
At the largest camp 20 miles south of Sikeston, we witnessed the attempted
evacuation by the Sheriff and armed local citizens of more than 200 negroes.
There were about twenty five men in the sheriff's posse, no state police were
present.
Sheriff K. F. Stanley said the negroes were demonstrating and trying to
get another Farm Security Settlement, that they could all get houses and jobs
at $1.00 a day had they stayed on the farm. Sheriff Stanley invited us to
watch. He claimed the negroes were armed. His men forced all the Negro men
across the Highway while some of them made a careful search of all the thirty
or forty make-shift tents occupied by the negroes on the other side. The
citizens carried shot guns. One of our party saw a negro struck in the face
by one of the citizens. Another negro was put in handcuffs. Sheriff Stanley
announced to us it was his intention to move these and the demonstrators from
the other camps in New Madrid County to a forty acre plot about eighteen miles
away, nines miles off the main road on a farm-to-market road. I asked would
the county provide for the negroes. He said no one would provide for them.
I saw one double barrelled shot gun from one of the negroe's tents. I
also saw another rifle or shot gun wrapped in cloth taken from the same tent.
At least four shot guns were taken from the tents. This happened at approximately 10:00 A.M. Sunday, January 15 after I and three members of the Missouri

N.Y.A. staff has spent nearly two hours taking statements from members of the camp. Seven trucks described as state highway trucks were backed up to move the campers away.

The second largest roadside camp of approximately 50 or 60 people, blacks and whites, was being evacuated by several State Highway Department trucks at 11:00 A.M. No arms were in evidence as we drove by.

The smaller camp of only two tents occupied by whites had not been dispersed at this time. Took a statement from the head of one of the white families at the smaller camp.

One negro at the big camp said cotton planters had imported pickers from Memphis this past season thereby depriving them of work as day laborers. This man also reported that Sheriff Stanley had tried to get them to leave the roadside the previous day. He had told them the planters would take care of them. The workers replied they had no place to return to and declined to leave at that time.

The roadside camps were tattered and make-shift tents totally inadequate for protection against cold weather. The ground was wet from recent rains. Nearly all of the shoes of the campers were worn shapeless and were full of holes. The "Hooverville" of the depression period was the only comparable sight I have seen.

Franklin D. Roosevelt Papers, Hyde Park, New York.

27.   REPORT OF HERBERT LITTLE, DICTATED OVER
THE TELEPHONE, JANUARY 16, 1939

Most of the following comes from Captain Sheppard, in charge of the State Highway Police in this area, in the presence of one of the State Highway Commissioners.

The State Public Health Director visited the camps the day after they were formed on January tenth. He ordered them removed from the major highway. One of these highways is North and South, and the other is transcontinental. The reason was to prevent possible widespread disease. It is agreed that at least 400 families with 1200 persons in them, 90% or more Negroes, were in the camps. They were scattered along 38 miles of U.S. Route 60, East and West, and 70 miles of U.S. 61, North and South, forming a cross with Sikestown as the center. The State Police on January fourteenth, after enlisting the aid of sheriffs of the three counties involved, dispersed most of the East-West highway camps by threat of force. One group, estimated by Highway Commissioner Simpson at 10 or 15 families who would not return to their old homes, was established in what Captain Sheppard called a concentration camp in a school house at Charleston, Missouri. Also on January fourteenth local citizens tried to disperse some large camps at Lelbourn. Leaders of this camp refused to disperse. No state police were present. The Negroes objected because they were to be moved in privately owned trucks. On January fifteenth Sheriff Stanley of New Madrid County, with a group of armed but not uniformed citizens, 25 or more in all, captured this camp and transported it away. Captain Sheppard told me later, Sunday, that the 291 persons in this camp and the 121 in a camp at Mathews, also on Route 61, were all taken to a 40 acre tract provided by the County. They were taken in State Highway Department trucks. These camps, isolated from highways, are to be under the local authorities. Captain Sheppard said highway police jurisdiction ended when the Health Department's orders to move them had been carried out.

Captain Sheppard said he expected the State Health Department to provide one or more physicians to care for the people. He said no one would be allowed in or out of the camp, but later he said he expected those who wanted to leave would be allowed to.

About 25 State Highway Police early Monday cleared out the last camp about one mile from Sikestown and took the 100 or more persons in it to the 40-acre Madrid County tract. There was a WPA investigator there from Louisiana who was present taking pictures and he told me that the State Police offered them the alternative of returning to their former homes. Few, if any, did so.

Captain Sheppard said that from his knowledge of Negroes, he expects the two concentration camps to be dispersed and the occupants to return to their former farms in a few days. He and many others were saying the demonstration really is a strike to obtain a Government Homestead Project for Negroes, like the one at LaForge, a few miles away from Sikestown.

A local Negro preacher, Reverend O. N. Whitfield, with the aid of Southern Tenant Farmers Unions, is said to have organized the protest at a meeting on January eighteenth. The demonstration started on January tenth, Tuesday.

Captain Sheppard also said that one farm owner offered to take back 121 Negroes who left his farm for the camp, but they refused to go.

One newspaper report says the Southern Tenant Farmers Union people promised the sharecroppers a 40-acre farm, a white house, and a dug well on the proposed new project, similar to the facilities on the LaForge project.

Captain Sheppard indicates his officials will permit me to inspect the concentration camps.

On the eviction orders, Captain Sheppard says only one legally served eviction order has been filed with the necessary authorities this year in the three affected counties. He admitted, however, that written notices, and not legally served eviction orders, had been issued to many farmers under the prevailing custom of the farm owners who desire to rearrange their farm personnel.

NOTE: I suggest that you obtain from Mark Childs or Ray Brandt of the Washington Post Dispatch office, a clipping from the editorial page of Sunday's St. Louis Post Dispatch. It is a description by Josephine Johnson, Pulitzer Prize Novelist, describing vividly her visit to the camp and presenting the conflicting versions of the sharecroppers and the land owners.

Franklin D. Roosevelt Papers, Hyde Park, New York.

28. MEMORANDUM FROM AUBREY WILLIAMS TO
PRESIDENT FRANKLIN D. ROOSEVELT, JANUARY 16, 1939

SUBJECT: Missouri Sharecropper Encampment

Following your request for information I sent Herbert Little, former newspaperman, now a member of the staff of the National Youth Administration, to investigate the situation of sharecroppers encamped along two highways in Missouri. I am enclosing material submitted by Mr. Little and call your attention particularly to the individual case histories which he has secured.

In brief the situation is as follows: This is the season when southern landlords either renew or discontinue contracts with their tenants and sharecroppers. This year many landlords failed to renew contracts, preferring, because of the necessity of making AAA payments to sharecroppers, the responsibility for carrying them through the season and the uncertainty of the cotton market to release them and rely on day labor for next year's labor requirements. This has resulted in many virtual evictions of former sharecroppers and tenants throughout the south.

In the area of south eastern Missouri centering around New Madrid County a substantial number of families apparently received written notices to move from their present homes. It appears that these evictions led to a meeting in Sikestown on January eighth, at which local leadership in some way connected with the Southern Tenant Farmers Union is supposed to have urged these evicted families to encamp along two highways forming a cross at Sikestown.

In any case on January tenth a series of encampments began to form along these highways. Approximately 450 families, of whom at least 90% were Negro, were found to be living in tents or improvised shelters with very inadequate food supply in these camps. These groups were composed in part of those persons who had been forced out of their former homes and in part of persons who joined them voluntarily out of profound dissatisfaction with the arrangements under which they were living and working. This has led to confused reports as to whether these people were actually homeless.

It is reported that the group had been led to believe that this demonstration of their need would lead the Farm Security Administration to establish a project for them similar to one operating at LaForge, Missouri, but
Mr. Little found no evidence that they had neither formed a cohesive organization nor presented definite demands to any public agency.

Efforts to disperse these groups by persuasion and threats having proved
ineffective, on January fourteenth, and sixteenth the camps were broken up by
armed citizens under the direction of the State Police and County Sheriffs and
in part by State troopers. The State assumed jurisdiction on the grounds that
these encampments on State Highways constituted a menace to public health.

It is estimated that approximately half of the families actually dispersed.
The other half were moved to what the State Police described as "Concentration
camps," one in a Charleston, Missouri, schoolhouse and the other on a forty
acre tract without shelter or facilities of any kind located ten miles off the
highway. These camps are under county rather than state control. It is believed that individuals in them have been placed under technical arrest
although definite information on this point is not yet available. It was
stated that no one would be permitted to visit them, but that they would be
permitted to leave under certain conditions.

Apparently no relief has been extended these persons other than limited
surplus commodities which have been made available by the local relief to individual families applying at the offices in person. This has proved impossible for most families.

This situation, serious as it is for the individual families and the communities in which they are located, is even more serious as a symptom of the
widespread situation existing throughout the South. It has been conservatively
estimated that at least a quarter of a million families are being forced off
farms in the South this year. Not only does this situation present a serious
unmet relief problem, but the Missouri situation clearly demonstrates that
local communities, faced with a grave economic situation which they are powerless to solve alone, will take measures toward the individuals made most
desperate by that situation which ignores the civil rights and liberties our
government is supposed to guarantee.

As further reports are submitted by Mr. Little, I will send them to you.

Franklin D. Roosevelt Papers, Hyde Park, New York.

29. AUBREY WILLIAMS TO PRESIDENT FRANKLIN D. ROOSEVELT,
JANUARY 19, 1939

Dear Mr. President:

Here is my report summarizing facts and conclusions on major issues involved in the sharecropper demonstration in southeastern Missouri in January
of 1939.

Causes: The primary cause is the feeling of the workers, sharecroppers,
ex-sharecroppers, renters and day laborers all, that their economic condition
is intolerable. They say they had just as well starve and freeze on the
highways, or in their present concentration camps, as in their shacks. Their
cotton picking money and sharecropping payoffs are all gone. After that, all
that most of them have in prospect is 100 days work a year, at $1.00 a day -
some of the farmers pay only seventy-five cents. As far as our man can learn,
there is no credit available to them.

This condition has become increasingly serious in recent years, through
the action of land-owners in switching from sharecropping and renting to
operation of their land by day labor. The principal reason for this is to
enable the land-owner to retain all of the AAA benefit money, which otherwise
would go to the renter or in part to the sharecropper. In addition, many
land-owners are reducing the amount of land given sharecroppers to operate,
apparently in line with acreage reduction. In two cases interviewed, sharecroppers produced "wildcat cotton" and were deprived of any return, the land-
owner explaining that the penalty tax took all the crop money.

Of the 102 family heads interviewed, some spoke of their hope that the government would set them up in cotton growing. The movement as yet has formulated no definite demand for a resettlement project, however. It is quite likely that the hope for such a project is responsible to a considerable extent for their action. Their determination to hold out against returning to their former status is indicated by the fact that about one-half of the 1200 persons on the highways went to the concentration camps off the highways when evacuated by State Highway Police, instead of returning to farm shacks as proposed by the land-owners and the authorities.

Southern Tenant Farmers Union activities may have had some part in organizing the protest, although the persons interviewed in many cases were apparently unacquainted with the organization.

The 102 histories demonstrate the falsity of the charge that the demonstrators were day laborers from Arkansas. Most of them are or have been in recent years, sharecroppers or renters in this section of Missouri.

As to the charge that wholesale eviction orders caused the protest, this is not literally true. State Highway Police said that only one legally-served eviction order (in Mississippi County, Missouri) has been registered with the proper legal authorities. In substance, however, the charge is true. Our investigator was shown at least three notices, couched in legal language, in the concentration camp near Wyatt, Missouri. The 102 personal histories are full of statements, obviously truthful because of the circumstantial details given to the interviewer, that farmowners orally informed these folk that (1) he was switching from sharecropping to day labor basis, (2) that he wanted the house for a larger family, (3) that he would not be wanted next year. There are many variations, nearly all of which gave the worker to believe that there was nothing for him to do at that place.

It seems to me that the mere presence in the vicinity of the LaForge cooperative colony, (Farm Security, 100 homesteads including 80 white and 20 black families) was a large factor in leading the workers to make their demonstration.

Civil Liberties: There appear to have been numerous violations of civil liberties. The action of the State Highway Police in escorting organizers of the Southern Tenant Farmers Union out of the state on January fourteenth is one. The forcible removal of the demonstrators from the public highways, in one instance by Sheriff Stanley of New Madrid County, and in the others by the State Highway Police, in State Highway Department trucks in all instances, is another. This was done under the pretext of the order by the State Public Health Commissioner that they were a menace to public health. In fact, their living conditions in the two concentration camps to which they were moved are as conducive to serious epidemic sickness, if not more so, than in their highway camps. The seizure of the campers' shotguns and a few rifles, necessary to enable them to add rabbits, squirrels, etc. to their diet, is another example. Sheriff Stanley reported this seizure, and our men there witnessed a part of it. One Negro was struck by two men in Sheriff Stanley's posse during the highway evacuation, being clubbed in the face and gashed by blows from a pistol in one man's hand and a can in another's. See Case 45. In addition, there is an apparent guard, or at least a consciousness of compulsion for the demonstrators to remain at the two concentration camps, away from the highways. Several white men were present at the levee camp during most of January seventeenth, and a uniformed State Highway Policeman visited the camp and inquired what was our purpose in interviewing these people, although our man had previously called on Highway Police Captain Sheppard in Sikeston and explained his mission of information gathering. Captain Sheppard was frank in expressing hope and belief that the demonstrators would return to their previous farm existence in a few days. He commented that our man did not appear to be a southerner and might not understand what was necessary in "handling niggers."

Relief Possibilities: These people will not starve for a few weeks, and may continue indefinitely, as a few are getting $10 relief checks from the Farm Security Administration. The Farm Security Administration, however, is understaffed and slow to clear applications. The regional FSA man has informed the regional relief man in Sikeston that he is planning to do something definite soon to prevent difficulties. In addition, surplus commodities are being distributed at relief centers, such as New Madrid, ten or twelve miles away from the levee camp, to those who apply in person. A few of them have old automobiles and trucks. However, their egress for this purpose may be shut off by the unsumpathetic whites in the neighborhood and by the land-owners. One member of the New Madrid County Advisory Committee on Relief has complained against the County Supervisor because of this issuance of food. No inquiry was made as to whether Farm Security Administration has any long range plan to provide for them.

Effect of Interviews: Nearly all those interviewed indicated by their manner a rather child-like confidence that the federal government would act to relieve their condition. Many appeared to feel that giving their name and the other information would place them in a position for early aid.

One other item may be noted: Ryland, the Missouri director of the National Emergency Council, was reported in the Missouri press as having stated, after a visit to the highway camps, that he was investigating "subversive influences" in connection with the demonstration.

Press Attitude: Most of the news and headlines noted, as usual in such circumstances, were based on statements and activities of the authorities and land-owners. The St. Louis Globe-Democrat displayed active bias against the demonstrators in its reports, and the St. Louis Post-Dispatch did a full and complete job of reporting both sides and an accurate report of conditions as seen by our investigator.

Basic remedy: This is a boil that has come to a head, indicating a wide-spread condition in the cotton region. It is probable that nothing less than a great resettlement campaign, involving both housing and land, could material-ly improve living conditions among these folk.

                              Sincerely yours,

                              Aubrey Williams, Administrator
                              National Youth Administration

Franklin D. Roosevelt Papers, Hyde Park, New York.

THE BLACK WORKER DURING WORLD WAR II

THE BLACK WORKER DURING WORLD WAR II

Of the nearly 13 million blacks in the United States, more than 5 million were in the labor force in 1940. But compared with whites, Afro-Americans were disproportionately unemployed, even though the industrial boom which accompanied the defense build-up absorbed all the available white males. Soon employers were crying out for more workers, although the racial ban on blacks remained. By the end of 1941, sociologist Gunnar Myrdal ascertained that the "great bulk of the war plants did not have any Negroes at all among their workers."[95]

Black protests brought little action. Therefore, A. Philip Randolph, president of the Brotherhood of Sleeping Car Porters, organized the March on Washington Movement. Randolph's call for a protest march on the capitol spawned MOWM committees throughout the nation's black communities from New York to San Francisco. The movement could not be ignored, and the nation's key political leaders were unable to quash MOWM. Randolph demanded that President Roosevelt issue an executive order banning racial discrimination in war industries, and the movement leaders would accept nothing less. On June 25, 1941, Roosevelt succumbed and issued Executive Order 8802, which banned racial discrimination, and organized the Fair Employment Practices Committee to see that employers observed the decree.

The FEPC began to function on July 18, 1941. Hampered by a lack of funds, and segregationist politicians, the FEPC had the formidable task of inducing employers and trade unions to admit black workers. In March, 1942, two years after the start of the defense program, the FEPC reported that Negro workers constituted only 2.5 to 3 per cent of all workers in war production. By late 1944, that percentage had grown to over 8 per cent. This impressive gain was achieved despite the harassment of segregationist congressmen, and the recalcitrant opposition of employers and AFL trade unions. For example, in the West Coast shipyards, blacks bitterly complained that many companies would employ them only as laborers , if at all. Part of the reason was demonstrated by the discriminatory policies of such craft unions as the International Brotherhood of Boilermakers, which organized blacks only into Jim Crow auxiliaries, and then tried to force the companies to fire those blacks who protested.

"Hate strikes" occurred in some cities where the FEPC ordered an end to discrimination. Tradition had long ruled that Negroes could be employed only in menial positions by the Philadelphia Transportation Company, and after the FEPC ordered the company to "cease and desist" from practicing discrimination in November, 1943, the company union informed the FEPC that it would ignore the order. A few months later, however, the workers voted in the Transit Workers Union (CIO) as its bargaining agent, and the TWU agreed to employ blacks as operators. When they showed up for work, however, a strike began which led to the intervention of the U.S. Army. By mid-August the Army had withdrawn, the strike was broken, and the blacks continued their instruction for becoming operators.

Perhaps the most important test of the CIO's commitment to equal treatment came in Detroit with the United Automobile Workers' strike to organize the Ford Motor Company in 1941. The UAW recognized that it had to develop a strong relationship with the black community if it were to prevail against the paternalism practiced by Ford. A number of blacks were employed as union organizers, and a committee was formed which included Negro community leaders. In fact, one of the most impressive aspects of the strike was the effort of black leaders, such as Walter White of the NAACP, and John P. Davis of the National Negro Congress, to convince the 17,000 black workers at Ford not to permit themselves to be used as strikebreakers. With such effective organization, Ford capitulated on April 11, 1941, after only eleven days. The victory would have been impossible without support from the black community, and that support would not have been forthcoming if the UAW had not convinced Negroes that the CIO's policy against discrimination was more than rhetoric.

BLACKS AND THE WAR ECONOMY

1. INDUSTRIAL DEMOCRACY

Ordinarily the term "industrial democracy," in the average person's mind, revolves around the rights of workers to organize and to negotiate agreements as to wages, hours and conditions of labor through representatives of their own choosing. This has been the dominant note in the literature and in the programs of those organizations which have for many years sponsored the study of labor history in school and college and initiated activities designed to stimulate labor to greater awareness of its role in industry. The right to work of all men, without regard to race or creed or color, has not been entirely disregarded but it has been subordinated to what has appeared to be the more important phase of the workers' struggle.

The time has now come when such movements for industrial democracy must place the problem of racial discrimination in industry on a parallel plane to other industrial problems. For if men are to be denied the right to work at all because of their race or color or religious predilections, then industrial democracy can never be fully attained and the rights of labor will be forever in jeopardy.

There is a growing feeling on the part of Negro workers that the failure of Negroes to obtain jobs in defense industries is due to tacit collusion between organized labor and management. How much truth there is in this contention we are unable at this time to say. But there has unquestionably been a reluctance on the part of unions--even the CIO unions--to take up the cudgel for the Negro. In too many instances the union leadership has been content to point to the clause in the constitution of the unions which bans discrimination because of race. They fail to note that there has been little energetic action to make this clause live.

This attitude on the part of unions is the very apotheosis of stupidity. For the struggle to gain the historic rights of labor is not conditioned by race. And the allegiance of the stubborn industrialists who oppose organized labor outright, or who seek to emasculate its strength, is not determined by color. The Negro becomes a factor only when white industrialists seek to crush white labor by utilizing the Negro as a scab, and the success of this measure is in every single case dependent on the attitude which organized labor has maintained toward the Negro worker.

Mr. Sidney Hillman, Associate Director General of the Office of Production Management, has recently issued a statement to industries which hold defense contracts requesting the management to refrain from erecting the color bar at this critical time in the nation's history. But if industry, particularly the aircraft industry, has given heed to his request we would be happy to be so informed. Up to the writing of this editorial neither private industry, nor public industry as represented by the various governments engaged in defense preparation, has inaugurated a change in policy. All apparently continue on a course of racial discrimination that is inexcusably unfair and undemocratic, and that will in the end prove to be unwise.[96]

Opportunity, 19 (May, 1941): 130.

2. A WORD FROM OPM

As a result of the pressure that has come from every section of the Negro population, the Office of Production Management in Washington issued on April

11, through its co-director, Sidney Hillman, a statement on Negro labor addressed to manufacturers holding defense contracts. The letter is so important as the first official recognition by the government of the treatment of Negro workers that THE CRISIS reprints it in full:

"To All Holders of Defense Contracts:
"Pursuant to the decision of the Office of Production Management, I wish to advise you as follows:

    "Current reports on the labor market of developments indicated skilled labor stringency in a number of fields vital to defense production. This threatens to become more general within the next three months. Artificial factors, however, are tending to aggravate this increasingly serious situation. In some of these occupations, we are informed there are good workers available who are not being hired solely because of their racial identity.
    "The Office of Production Management expects defense contractors to utilize *all* available local labor resources before resorting to the recruiting of additional labor from outside their local areas. Our programs of training and labor clearance are being established in accordance with such a policy. In many sections of the Nation there are today available labor reserves of Negro workers. Plans for their training and employment in capacities commensurate with their individual skills and aptitudes should be undertaken at once.
    "In many localities, qualified and available Negro workers are either being restricted to unskilled jobs, or barred from defense employment entirely. Because of this situation, Negro workers of skills and aptitudes are in many instances not being included in many of the training programs for defense. Such practices are extremely wasteful of our human resources and prevent a total effort for national defense. They result in unnecessary migration of labor, in high rates of labor turnover, and they increase our present and future housing needs and social problems for defense workers.
    "All holders of defense contracts are urged to examine their employment and training policies at once to determine whether or not these policies make ample provision for the full utilization of available and competent Negro workers. Every available source of labor capable of producing defense materials must be tapped in the present emergency.

                                        "Yours very truly,

                                        "SIDNEY HILLMAN
                                        Associate Director General
                                        Office of Production Management."

    It is the contention of OPM that it does not have the power to *act* in regard to Negro employment; it may only advise. Two big factors determine employment in private industry: the employers themselves and the unions. The time may come, if the situation does not improve (both as to Negro employment and the war) when OPM will have to act on this matter. In the meantime the Negro public and its friends should understand clearly how important it is to continue the fight, and especially to continue to write to Washington. Mr. Hillman stated he had received 3,000 letters on this subject in one week. He should have received 30,000.

The Crisis, 48 (May, 1941): 151.

        3. NEGRO PARTICIPATION IN DEFENSE WORK

    From the very beginning of the present emergency the directors of the defense efforts of the United States were aware that total defense would be impossible without a full utilization of the country's human resources. This was pointed out in an address, made before the First Annual Conference on the Negro in Business, by Sidney Hillman, Associate Director of the Office of

Production Management. The following data are taken from his address.

Training program.--As a first step in solving the problem at issue the National Defense Advisory Commission endeavored to have provision made for the training of Negro workers in order that they might be qualified for employment under the defense program when industrial expansion would require an increased number of workers. Consequently, when the United States Office of Education started its defense training program in the summer of 1940, the Commissioner of Education stated, at the request of the National Defense Commission, that "in the expenditure of Federal funds for vocational training for defense, there should be no discrimination on account of race, creed, or color."

This announcement was implemented when further appropriations were made for training for national defense. Again, in accordance with the plans of the National Defense Advisory Commission, the training legislation provided that--

No trainee under the foregoing appropriations shall be discriminated against because of sex, race, or color; and where separate schools are required by law for separate population groups, to the extent needed for trainees of such groups, equitable provision shall be made for facilities and training of like quality.

Employment policy.--Paralleling this drive for training Negroes for defense work, the Commissioner of Education took up the problem of equitable job opportunities, stating from the outset that "workers should not be discriminated against because of age, sex, race, or color."

Construction work.--At Fort Meade in Maryland, Fort Jackson in South Carolina, Fort Robinson in Arkansas, and in scores of other camp constructions, skilled, semiskilled, and unskilled Negroes were widely employed. Over 2,500 Negro carpenters alone worked on these various projects at $8 to $12 per day, and thousands of brickmasons, roofers, cement finishers, plasterers, power-saw operators, and other skilled and semiskilled Negroes, were and are being employed. At one time during the construction work at Fort Jackson, over 600 Negro carpenters were on the pay roll. The hiring of 300 Negro carpenters during the construction of the United States Army Hospital at New Orleans set a record for that occupation in that community.

In the Ozark Mountains in Missouri, in a locality in which not over 10 Negro families were living, over 150 Negro carpenters were given jobs through the aid of Dr. Robert C. Weaver's office; moreover, approximately 300 Negro bricklayers were placed on a single construction job in Indiana, and tens of thousands of unskilled Negroes obtained employment throughout the United States.

The recent hirings of Negroes in building construction have been duplicated less conspicuously in other fields in which Negro labor had already been trained. For example, the iron and steel industry indicates a greater absorption of skilled and semiskilled Negroes. Establishments in several northern sections have recently been seeking to bring Negro foundry workers from the South; and job opportunities are also increasing in the latter section.

In reporting on the developments in the above-mentioned fields, the speaker said that he did not wish to give the impression that the Office of Production Management is "interested only in advancing the Negro skilled worker in the fields in which he has already gained employment." He stated that the position of the OPM had been recently expressed by him in a communication to all defense contractors, which declared "that every available source of labor capable of producing defense materials must be tapped in the present emergency. And this applies to the important new defense industries as well as to the old established ones."

The Negro in aviation.--The problem of a fair deal in employment for Negroes has already arisen in the aviation industry as in all other industries, and the OPM intends to continue its campaign there. Three significant developments indicate that progress may be looked for in that field. Confronted with a labor shortage, one aircraft factory in California is trying out a Negro unit. An aircraft manufacturer in Ohio is contemplating hiring at least 300 Negroes. In Missouri another employer has pledged himself to use a substantial number of Negroes in his aircraft establishment.

Statement of Committee on Negro Americans in Defense Industries

On May 7, 1941, about 60 representative citizens of the North and South

issued a statement urging that greater numbers of competent Negroes be employed
in defense industries and that opportunities for special industrial training be
made more generally available to them.   In releasing this statement to the
press, Dr. Anson Phelps Stokes, the chairman of the Committee on Negro Americans in National Defense Industries, said: "We wish as independent citizens
to support the recent efforts made with encouraging results through the
Office of Production Management to speed up defense industries. One way of
accomplishing this is by the larger employment of skilled Negro mechanics,
especially in fields where there is a labor shortage. In this way we can help
place our industrial life in this national emergency on a more effective basis.
An 'all-out' defense effort cannot disregard the Negro tenth of our population
which is known for its loyalty."

Monthly Labor Review, 52 (June, 1941): 1388-90.

4. EMPLOYERS, UNIONS AND NEGRO WORKERS

By Thomas A. Webster

     The treatment of this topic is based entirely upon experiences in Greater
Kansas City and the great mid-western region which surrounds the city.
     The fact that Kansas City is a border line center, often termed a northern
city with a southern exposure, may account for the similarity of experiences
that are characteristic of both our southern and northern industrial communities.
     The role of the Negro in the trade union movement in Kansas City is this
in brief: Negro union members are either in distinct Negro locals such as the
Brotherhood of Pullman Porters, and the Hod-Carriers' Union, or in mixed
locals like the International Ladies' Garment Workers' Union and the packing
industry locals, or in separate and auxiliary units of the white parent bodies
such as the Federated Musicians Local.
     Negro carpenters, bricklayers, painters, plumbers, electricians, cement
finishers and sheet metal workers have been barred either by constitutional
provisions, ritual or some other device from union membership in Kansas City.
     Since the social study is the chief tool of a social work agency, the
Kansas City Urban League made a six-months' study of Kansas City Negro workers
as they were affected by trade union organization. The study treated the
Negro worker as a part of the organized labor movement, in the role of a
strike-breaker, and also studied experiences and problems of Negro workers
both within and outside of labor organizations in Kansas City. This study,
"The Negro Worker of Kansas City," served as the basis on which social action
was planned to open union membership to more Negro workers.
     Board and staff members of the Urban League held conferences with the
executive officers of the Labor Council of Kansas City, composed of one hundred representatives from as many locals in the city. An appeal was made to
have those unions which had bars against Negroes to drop them, or to make plans
whereby Negroes would not be eliminated entirely from work where union membership was the first requirement. These attempts met with no success. It was
only after public mass meetings, protests to Congressmen, labor officials and
federal agencies, that union barriers began to break in Kansas City. First,
Negro carpenters hurdled the 30-year bar which would not permit Negro members
to belong to the same local as white members. Since becoming union members,
Negro carpenters have worked on all of the cantonment projects and other
important government construction work where white carpenters had threatened
to walk off if Negroes were hired. Contractors have used them in mixed crews
without any difficulty. Many Negro carpenters have been engaged on private
jobs where whites said they would not have a chance.
     Next came the induction of Negro bricklayers into the white local where
already one Negro has been made a foreman by a contractor in a munition plant
project. Despite the fact that Negro bricklayers are few compared with white
members, three are serving as stewards on jobs with white workers.

Recently seventeen Negro painters have successfully passed an examination
for union membership and probably have received their charter by now. For
thirty-five years the Painters' District Council had barred Negro mechanics
from union membership.

The League has also been holding meetings of Negro cement finishers,
sheet metal workers, electricians, and plumbers. We expect to break the
traditional bars against Negro workers in these crafts. With public and defense housing jobs, as well as other government construction to be started
soon in Greater Kansas City, union membership will mean thousands of additional
dollars to Negro workers.

Contact with employers is a very definite factor in the placement of
workers. In 1929 the Urban League made a comprehensive survey of the industrial status of the Negro in Kansas City. Out of 1,235 industries in 1929,
only 308 employed Negroes in any capacity. Forty-eight per cent of all Negro
workers were employed as porters; of forty-eight plants using mixed crews,
only seventeen offered real promotion for the Negro workers. In none of these
plants had there ever been racial friction, and the labor turnover among Negro
workers was low.

Eleven years later conditions are substantially the same. The Federal
government has sunk over four hundred million dollars in Kansas City plants to
manufacture tents, trunks, engines, radios, clothing, airplanes and scores of
other supplies.

Believing that such a volume of new business for Kansas City industries
would call for additional workers, the League interviewed fifty-four employers
holding defense contracts. The interviews disclosed that only eleven of these
firms employed Negroes, and only four of these plants employed them other than
as janitors, watchmen or common laborers. These were the statements that
employers gave to hundreds of jobless Negroes who expected the new industrial
boom to include them:

"White men won't work with Negroes."

"We would have to build separate locker and toilet facilities."

"The unions never send us Negro workers."

Despite repeated efforts to get Negro workers into these plants, no substantial numbers have gained employment.

Believing that if trained workers were available, color would be less of
a factor when serious shortages occurred, training was sought for Negro workers.
Educational authorities refused to set up classes until employers gave reasonable assurances of employment. Employers claimed they could not promise employment for untrained workers. Negroes were caught in the traditional vicious
circles of buck-passing and run-around.

A conference of city officials, educational directors and employers was
called to discuss plans for employing more Negro workers. Employers using
Negro workers in skilled jobs without friction between them and white workers
were invited. Employers who had flatly refused to consider Negro workers were
also asked to attend. Only those employers who used Negro workers came to the
conference. They were only able to reiterate that they were using Negro
skilled workers, and would use more if production increased. These companies
use Negroes as car builders, car inspectors, machinists' helpers, coach
cleaners, hostlers, welders, moulders, grinders, chippers, boiler builders,
paint sprayers and as punch press and overhead crane operators.

Employers attitudes have limited both refresher and supplementary training
programs for Negro workers. Managers of new industries coming to the city
would often promise unlimited employment to Negroes, only to rescind these
promises later by claiming they might have to conform to community patterns.
In all instances they used as the community pattern those industries that use
Negroes only in the custodial and service occupations. Added to an already
gloomy picture were the malicious statements of several responsible citizens.
It was circulated that the North American Aviation Corporation said through
its Mr. Kindelberger that it would employ only as janitors, and that Negroes
could not be employed because they were petty thieves. They said small,
costly airplane precision parts which could be pocketed easily were to be
manufactured. This plant, it was also rumored, would not use Jews, Orientals,
Germans or Italians. Whoever circulated the rumor overlooked the fact that
the packing and manufacturing industries in Kansas City used Negroes and they
experienced no more theft on the part of Negroes than from white workers.

During the same week this lie was being circulated, two airplane factories in
Wichita, Kansas, issued an order prohibiting workers from bringing their own
tool boxes into the plants. The workers would invariably leave with a micro-
meter or a handful of rivets in the bottom of the tool box.
     These plants did not even employ a Negro janitor and one stated specif-
ically in its application blank, "white workers only need apply."
     On the heels of this a director of records of the Kansas City Police
Department, on hearsay evidence, in a public meeting stated there were
10,000 Communists in Kansas City, of whom 6,000 were Negroes. Although this
statement was later repudiated, irreparable damage was done to already job-
impoverished Negroes. Many employers needed only such a statement as a further
excuse for not using Negroes.
     Believing that the position and policy of the Federal government as one
of the largest employers of workers will influence and determine the policies
of private industrialists, special attention has been given to three major
concerns in Greater Kansas City. These are government-owned plants to be
operated under the supervision of the Federal government. They are the North
American Aircraft Corporation, which will employ at its peak production around
10,000 workers, the Remington Small Arms Plant, to use 8,000 workers, the
majority of whom will be women to tend automatic machines, and the Kansas City
Quartermaster's Depot.
     The Quartermaster's Depot has already employed its personnel of several
hundred workers with civil service status; eighty-one Negro classified laborers are used in storage and distribution work. The Commanding Officer believes
that labor work offers the best promotion in the depot for Negroes because
they all work in the same department; only one Negro is detached from this
department. A clerk in the Finance Department with all white clerks is tolerated because his work is largely outside of the depot, auditing reports in
nearby camps. Negro storekeepers, clerks, packers, guards and shippers have
been told these are "white men's jobs," or this temporary work, while laborers'
jobs are more permanent.
     The bomber plant and the small arms plant have said they will not dis-
criminate against Negro workers in any department, yet to date real consideration is being given only to the employment of Negro custodians, grounds keepers,
laborers, and box makers. Only forty-two Negro trainees have received sheet
metal training for the bomber plant which intends to use 8,000 to 10,000 sheet
metal workers. Conformity with the community pattern is being interpreted to
mean that only Negro custodial and maintenance workers can be used.
     Kansas City, similar to many communities, found hundreds of Negro workers
lacking training and industrial experience essential to defense industries.
Many had been without foresight and felt specialized training was costly and
a waste of effort when immediate employment opportunities offered them no
chance to utilize such skills as they might acquire. Yet there are those who
had gained skilled occupational experience during the last World War or had
migrated to Kansas City from communities that did employ Negro skilled workers.
Hundreds of Negro workers sought refresher and supplementary training classes
when the emergency program started. At first they were offered training on a
car-washing project and a form-building project, neither of which was needed
by defense industries. Negro youth on NYA work-shop projects were being
offered personal grooming and janitorial training.
     Today less than fifty Negro youth have had short intensive training in
aircraft sheet metal work. Less than a score are being given gas welding instruction and a like number instruction in operating multiple needle sewing
machines. Despite the shortage of more than 1,000 operatives in the garment
industries, no Negro women have been accepted. Both the garment industries
unions and the employers say they are needed and will not stand in their way,
but the two forces have not reached an agreement on the actual employment of
these women.
     The public employment office registrations on which labor supply for the
Kansas City region is determined, indicate few Negroes listed with skills
necessary for defense production. During the depression period Negro applicants, despite the fact they could offer skilled occupational experience,
preferred to be classified for jobs which were traditional. Many preferred
steady work as laborers on WPA projects to temporary work as carpenters or
bricklayers. In some instances applicants were encouraged by employment
officials to apply for such work.

Still others who registered for work with employment agencies failed to return or telephone to reactivate their registration after the usual thirty-day period. Still others have been purely negligent in using the public employment service.

Proof of citizenship by the presentation of a birth certificate or equivalent documentary evidence has worked a hardship on Negro trainees. Many were born in communities where registration of Negro births was not available, either because the birth was attended by a mid-wife or Negroes were not born officially as far as vital statistics recordings were concerned.

Hundreds of Negroes who possess skills which can be increased by supplementary training have not sought such training opportunities. Of three hundred and fifty trainees referred by three major industries on the training within industry basis, no Negro workers are included.

The Negro Defense Committee of Kansas City has used personal interviews, bell-ringing and door-knocking as methods to reach trained Negro workers or those who could profit by refresher and supplementary training courses. Plans are being projected to hold a public meeting, with the cooperation of Negro churches, to have Negro skilled workers to list their skills and present this information to officials in charge of labor supply to the Kansas City area.

Despite the President's Executive Order, hundreds of Negro workers still believe nothing will change the status of their employment in Kansas City. The evidence of the gains by bricklayers, carpenters and painters is not enough to give hope to other skilled mechanical workers.

Opportunity, 19 (October, 1941): 295-97.

5. COLORED LABOR FACES A BOTTLENECK

By Joseph S. Himes, Jr.

Absorption of Negro labor by industry in this period of national defense is subject to the operation of the economic law of supply and demand. Both aspects of this process contain serious bottlenecks.

Available indexes show that Negro labor is benefiting from the national defense boom. This quickening of demand for colored workers is evident in spite of the persistence of discriminatory personnel practices and the slow yielding by industry to governmental policy and pressure.

The ranks of colored labor on WPA and relief rolls are being thinned daily by the return to work. The Columbus Chamber of Commerce employment index for August, 1941, was 134.8 and although the rate of Negro employment lags behind this figure, it is measurably above the level of a year ago.

To take a typical month for example, in May, 1941, the Columbus office of the Ohio State Employment Service placed over 1,000 colored applicants. In May, 1940, this office placed only a few more than 1,700 applicants of all races. These 1,000 Negro placements constituted 35 per cent of total placements through the Columbus office in May.

This increased demand is reflected in the experience of a number of Negro employers. Insurance companies, automobile service establishments, and building repair contractors complain about the inability of securing satisfactory workers. Capable men, formerly available to these employers, are being drawn off by the army and the swelling tide of national defense stimulated employment.

Analysis of the employment figures by occupations reveals a significant trend. Encouraging proportions of these workers find production jobs in industries related to national defense. The majority, however, replace white workers in service occupations. They are filling jobs in automobile repair and service shops, filling stations, laundries, office machine repair and service establishments, cleaning and pressing concerns, hotels and restaurants, delivery service and like concerns.

Although defense production jobs are more glamorous and often pay higher wages, these service jobs have some advantages. Even the optimists expect the defense boom to come to an end sometime, and workers will no longer be needed to build fighter planes, machine guns and military uniforms. Meanwhile, the services which are now engaging increasing numbers of colored workers may reasonably be expected to continue. These service jobs, supported by the thick crust of American tradition regarding the place of Negro labor, are relatively permanent, involve some, often considerable, skill and are fairly well paid.

The entry of Negro labor into defense stimulated jobs is hindered by a supply bottleneck. Under the unremitting pressure of government agencies, local organizations and mounting labor shortages, additional industries express a willingness to accept colored workers. The about face of the Curtiss-Wright Corporation in Columbus is a dramatic case in point.

The call is for skilled, technically trained workers with recent experience; machinists, sheet metal workers, engineers, draftsmen, layout men and the like. Information of opportunities for many hundreds of Negro workers in these and similar lines in Ohio today rests on the desks of Urban League offices and the Clearance Department of the Ohio State Employment Service. It is impossible to find colored workers to fill these jobs. Those who are qualified are employed. Those who are available are unqualified, either by virtue of inadequate training or lack of recent industrial experience.

The movement of skilled labor into defense-stimulated employment is caught in this bottleneck of technology and narrowed down to insignificance.

Some colored labor, however, is entering defense production as learner-helpers and trainees. Industry-controlled training programs like those of Curtiss-Wright and publicly supported programs are important inlets for Negro labor into national defense jobs. Available figures indicate that many colored workers in defense employment enter as trainee-learners and replacements of white single-skill workers. Unfortunately, the flow of colored labor into these jobs by this channel is further bottle-necked by the reluctance to seek available technical training.

In view of the shortage of technical and skilled colored workers with recent experience, the industrial practices of *down-processing and up-grading* are developing some opportunities for Negro labor. Down-processing is the practice of breaking highly skilled jobs down into component operations and assigning these to crews of single-skill workers on the assembly-line plan and under the supervision of a highly skilled mechanic who puts the finishing touches on the work as it comes off the line. Workers of limited ability can be taught to perform a single operation with great efficiency and with far less time and cost than it requires to produce an all-round mechanic.

The need in this situation is for men with some mechanical aptitude, limited ambition and psychological equipment capable of standing the monotony of the work. The casting and machining of metal parts once performed by moulders and machinists, is now down-processed in some shops to an assembly-line operation. This practice is employed by the Curtiss-Wright Corporation in the manufacture of fighter planes in the Columbus plant.

Young Negro workers, with some training and no experience, find an opportunity to enter production industries under this system. As a matter of fact, the volume of Negro placements in production industries in this area is due in part to the application of this processing technique.

Employed on single-skill jobs colored workers have an opportunity for promotions and pay increases as they improve in skill and efficiency by the practice of up-grading. The importance of this process is indicated by the instances of the up-grading of alert Negro workers in Columbus industries. Moreover, for instance, the capable worker who passes up through all jobs on the machine assembly line may expect to become a first-rate all-round machinist with current industrial experience.

The movement of colored workers into defense production industries, however, is retarded by their reluctance, particularly young workers, to seek technical training. Current reports show that this situation is general. A recent bulletin from the Industrial Relations Department of the National Urban League contains the following figures. In Cincinnati only 21 Negroes were included in 700 trainees enrolled in Federal defense courses. In Pittsburgh the corresponding figures were 25 Negroes out of a total defense training enrollment of 825; and in New York, 268 out of a total of 10,000. In Cincinnati 200 of the total of 4,000 youths enrolled in vocational high schools were colored; and in Pittsburgh 135 Negro youths were found among the 5,234 in vocational high schools.

As is evidenced by placement figures, the integration of colored labor into national defense production is measurably retarded by this reluctance to

seek necessary training. Furthermore, the indifference of employed workers
to in-service training reduces their opportunity of being up-graded and tends
to hold them in marginal jobs. Finally, the failure of Negro workers to
achieve progressively increasing industrial competence and usefulness will
probably limit their chances of retaining this newly gained foothold after
the defense bubble bursts.

The present configuration of labor supply for defense production has
developed two points of entry for Negro workers; namely, as service workers
and as single-skill learner-helpers. However, their reluctance to seek available technical training tends to bottleneck the ready integration of available
Negro workers into defense industries and threatens to create a problem of the
first magnitude for Negroes in industrial communities.

Opportunity, 19 (November, 1941): 329-30.

6. LABOR UNION SUPPORTS DEMAND OF NEGRO MEMBERS

White Members Picket Company When Violence Flares
Between Strikers and Non-Strikers
Demands Higher Pay

SHREVEPORT, La., Dec. 18--(By B. Everett Moore for ANP)--A strike on the
part of Negro employees at a local wholesale grain distributing company has
caused many unusual incidents which should bear watching. Under orders from
the local AFL office, Negro employees at the company demanded an increase of
10 cents per hour. Their demand was refused by the company and 26 Negro
truck drivers and helpers refused to work.

Trouble burst upon the scene when non-union workers attempted to defy
the striking procedure and go to work. Following a series of fights and
attacks, 26 Negro strikers were arrested and hailed into city court on charges
of threatening the lives of non-strikers. After a reprimand by the city judge,
they promised that there would be no more trouble, however, to make their
promises hold good, each striker was put under a $100 peace bond, in effect
pending good behavior.

Whites Take Over Picket Duty

The strikers apparently agreed to also cease their picketing because they
are no longer part of the picket lines. Instead (and this is extremely unusual)
the local AFL office has placed white pickets on the grounds to protest the
company's unfairness to its Negro employees by refusing to give an increase in
pay of 10 cents per hour to grant seniority rights to veteran employees.

Today there is irony in the scene created by the local white union which
is backing its Negro members to the extent of engaging white pickets to alleviate the dangers which Negro workers would be subjected to if put in the
picket lines.

The strike is one of the most demonstrative on the part of Negroes in
this section. They are determined in their demands to force the company to
accede to their desires and for once the union stands staunch behind them.

Pittsburgh Courier, December 20, 1941.

7. "U.S. NAVY YARDS INCREASE RACE
WORKERS A HUNDRED-FOLD"--WEAVER

Survey Shows Heavy Increase in Skilled Jobs and
Decrease of Laborers--Stress Need for Youth
to Get Training

WASHINGTON, D.C., Dec. 18--Negro civilian employment in United States
Navy Yards increased by more than one hundred per cent during the year ending
Sept. 30, 1941, Dr. Robert C. Weaver, chief of Negro employment and training
branch of the Labor Division of OPM announced this week.

According to the findings of a survey made public by Dr. Weaver, a total
of 13,401 Negro technical, skilled, semi-skilled and unskilled workers were
employed in United States Navy Yards on Sept. 30, 1940. During the same period,
the percentage of Negro workers in these yards increased from 6.03 per cent to
8.03 per cent of the total employment figures.

Urges Youths to Obtain Training

Dr. Weaver revealed the Navy Yard employment figures in urging Negro youths
to enroll in national defense training classes as a means of obtaining skilled
employment.

"Navy Yards throughout the country," he said, "are hiring thousands of
defense training graduates as helpers in various skilled categories. These
trainees, who are chosen without regard to race, creed, color or national
origin, are given credit for six months experience and are hired at starting
wages of $4.72 to $5.12 a day. These youths are then upgraded as rapidly as
possible into skilled mechanics."

The greatest increase in Negro employment was in two southern navy yards,
the survey indicated. The Charleston Navy Yard at Charleston, S.C., increased
its number of Negro employees from 453 to 1,802 during the one year period,
with the percentage to the total number of employees rising from 9.5 per cent
to 17.7 per cent.

A Decrease in Unskilled Class

At the same time, Negro employment in the Norfolk Navy Yard at Portsmouth,
Va., increased from 2,111 in September, 1940, to 5,426 on Sept. 30, 1941.
Officials at the Norfolk Navy Yard stated in November that their Negro employees
now exceed 6,000 and comprise more than 23 per cent of total employment.

An analysis of the occupational distribution of Negro workers in the
United States Navy Yards revealed an increase in clerical and technical workers
from 118 to 205; skilled workers, 1,003 to 1,830; helpers and classified
laborers, 4,153 to 10,822 and apprentices, 103 to 205. Negro common laborers
decreased from 557 to 350 during the twelve-month period.

Pittsburgh Courier, December 20, 1941.

8. CREW REFUSES TO SAIL SHIP UNLESS COLORED MEN HIRED

NEW YORK, Jan. 29--As further proof of the solidarity and comradeship
which distinguishes its membership from that of any other labor union, the
National Maritime Union disclosed last week that a crew of white seamen had
refused to sail on the S.S. Mormacport, a cargo ship built by the government
for the Moore-McCormack Lines, when officials of the line refused to hire
four able-bodied seamen who were Negroes.

In order to obtain a crew, the line finally yielded its position and took
on a mixed crew which included the four rejected Negro seamen--Jacob Green,
Zuvendee Wyllis, Allan David and Harry Jones, all of whom have seen from 15 to
20 years service at sea.

Line Official Denies Blame

It took the intervention of President Roosevelt three weeks ago to force
the United States Lines to rescind its rejection of twelve Negro seamen who
had been assigned to the S.S. Kungsholm by the National Maritime Union. As in
the case of the Mormacport, white seamen were willing to sail as members of
the mixed crew but line officials would not allow it.

Although the NMU has accused the Moore-McCormack Lines of discrimination, Robert C. Lee, executive vice-president of the shipping firm, has entered an emphatic denial. "It's a lie, he said, "and I'm perfectly willing to be quoted.   The NMU informed us that there was a shortage of seamen and asked us if we would take colored men.

"I said all right, but there must not be any checkerboard. I have no color line. We'll take an all-white crew or an all-colored crew, but we won't quarter them together. We'll take colored men provided the whites don't object. That's positively the only basis I'd accept." Mr. Lee admitted that the whites had not objected in the case of the Mormacport. "It seems that they are Comies," he said.

Pittsburgh Courier, January 31, 1942.

9. THE WHITE HOUSE

Washington

January 14, 1942

Mr. Joseph Curran, President
National Maritime Union
346 West 17th Street
New York, N.Y.

My dear Mr. Curran:

I am informed that the discrimination against colored seamen, referred to in your telegram of January 2nd, was eliminated by the action of the United States Maritime Commission on the day it occurred.

It is the policy of the Government of the United States to encourage full participation in the National Defense program by all citizens, regardless of race, creed, color, or national origin, in the firm belief that the democratic way of life within the nation can be defended successfully only with the help and support of all groups within its borders.

The policy was stated in my Executive Order signed on June 25, 1941. The order instructed all parties making contracts with the Government of the United States to include in all defense contracts thereafter a provision obligating the contractor not to discriminate against any worker because of race, creed, color or national origin.

Questions of race, creed and color have no place in determining who are to man our ships. The sole qualifications for a worker in the maritime industry, as well as in any other industry, should be his loyalty and his professional or technical ability and training.

Sincerely yours,

Franklin D. Roosevelt

Pittsburgh Courier, January 31, 1942.

10. PHILADELPHIA'S EMPLOYERS, UNIONS AND NEGRO WORKERS

By Charles A. Shorter

Philadelphia is a city which has achieved an enviable eminence in industry.

Its manufacturing, according to the Ninth Industrial Directory of Pennsylvania
(1937), consisted of 5,537 establishments with a total personnel of 292,691
employees.

The introduction of the National Defense Program into the city has caused
a large expansion in both the physical facilities and personnel of its industries.
The city ranks among the top flight industrial areas in the country, and as a
consequence has received several billion dollars in defense contract awards.

Negro workers first made their entree into Philadelphia industries in the
year 1915, when as a result of a labor shortage they were given their first
opportunity. Since that time, notwithstanding the unfavorable consequences
of the depression years, the Negro has been able to a degree to maintain the
gains afforded by the first World War. This is evidenced by the fact that in
1935, according to the report of the Bureau of Statistics, Department of
Internal Affairs of Pennsylvania, there were 13,181 Negroes employed in the
eleven major divisions of industry in the city.

Likewise, with respect to the unions, Negroes in the pre-defense days
held membership. Their status today in the organized labor movement in Philadelphia may be divided into three classifications. There are locals which
have mixed memberships, a typical example being the construction unions, both
skilled and unskilled. In the International Hod Carriers' Building and Common
Laborers' Union, the Negro membership is placed in the thousands. Negroes
hold membership in the following construction unions: painters, lathers (wood-
wire), bricklayers, cement finishers, plasterers and carpenters. There are
not any in the electrical and plumbers unions, although the unions have made
the commitment that qualified Negroes will be accepted into membership. In
the garment industry unions, International Ladies' Garment Workers' Union and
the Amalgamated Clothing Workers' Union of America, is found a mixed membership. There are other unions in the city which have a membership which is
totally colored, and still others where Negroes are not accepted. A typical
case of the latter being International Association of Machinists. Unions in
Philadelphia have good and bad classifications with respect to Negro workers,
and in many instances they have operated to restrict Negro employment.

This review shows briefly the status of Negroes with respect to industry
in Philadelphia before the introduction of the National Defense Program. It
also reveals that in making an effort to have Negroes integrated into the many
factories and plants of the city in connection with defense, those dealing with
this problem did have an entering wedge.

Since the inception of the defense program, an examination of the status
of Negroes with regard to finding employment in the industries holding contracts discloses that there are three major barriers which must be overcome
before a statement can be made that a satisfactory condition exists. The first
is the inclusion of qualified Negroes in the intraining programs of the city's
plants. On this matter there is evidence that employers have completely succumbed to the virus of race prejudice. A similar state of condition also
exists in connection with the up-grading of qualified Negro workers who are
already employed in industry. Likewise there is need for a more widespread
use of Negroes or increase in numbers of such workers in many of the plants.
This latter condition, however, is not as unfavorable as the other two.

Concerning Negroes and the training within industry it may be said that
the non-inclusion of them in such a program has been sufficient to create
consternation within their ranks; many have assumed a defeatist attitude in
their job-seeking efforts. This is evidenced by the fact that of the 3,500
Negroes who enrolled for defense training within the past year, the mortality
has been high, only 3 or 4 per cent have been listed as completing the training course. This is important in light of the fact that many of the defense
employers have done their recruiting in the schools. Also in connection with
defense training, a study of the type of courses in which Negroes are enrolled
shows very clearly that in many instances they are too concentrated in too
few important courses. For example, it has been estimated that 70 per cent of
the defense contract awards in Philadelphia have been for ship construction
and naval equipment. In examining Negro enrollment in training courses allied
to these fields one finds only a small percentage of such trainees. Only a
few have taken such courses as ship-fitting, marine pipe fitting and ship
mold loft. There has been on the other hand a large Negro enrollment in the
automotive courses such as auto-maintenance. In connection with this matter
of guidance into the proper courses of defense training, the members of the

staff of the Armstrong Association, an affiliate of the National Urban League,
in conferring with prospective enrollees, have always tried to channel them
into the courses where there is the greatest need for such trained workers,
before sending them to places of registration.

Contacts with employers in an effort to have the integration of Negro
trainees into their intraining programs have brought varying responses. Some
of the more commonly given ones are: "We would very readily accept Negro
trainees, we have no policy against them, but our employees will not accept
them as co-workers;" "No bar against the use of Negro workers, but there seems
to be evidence that Negroes and whites don't get along so very well together;"
"We do not have any Negro trainees, because our work is highly technical--we
select the best minds among the trainees enrolled in the defense courses and
employ them in our intraining programs." To offset this first listed reason
we bring to the attention of the employer the many cases where Negroes and
whites are working as co-workers. On the second, we refer to the voluminous
testimony given by other employers as to the harmonious relationship existing
among their Negro and white employees. In connection with the third reason
set forth by employers as to the non-inclusion of Negro trainees, we cite the
many instances where, according to defense training instructors, Negroes have
rated among the best in the classes. There is some evidence that our responses
have had their effect, a case in point being Edward G. Budd Company where the
commitment was given that Negroes would be included in this program. But, on
a whole, the inclusion of Negroes in the training program matter is unfavorable.

In reference to the second major barrier to be overcome, the lack of upgrading Negro workers, employers usually say, "it can't be done" and refer to
long established competitive feeling which has existed between black and white
workers. A summation of this condition may be stated thus: In comparison
with white workers assuming competence as normal, Negroes are not promoted in
accordance with abilities and length of service in the preponderance of Philadelphia's defense industries. Of course this statement must be qualified with
the remark that there are exceptions.

Another unfavorable situation which exists in many of the local defense
industries is the scarcity of Negro workers found in some of the plants. There
are a number of such firms in which the Negro personnel represents only one
per cent of the total. Employers of these firms when approached point with a
great deal of pride to the fact that they have Negroes in their employ. There
is little evidence that they know or have given consideration to the fact that
there are 251,000 Negroes in the city representing approximately 13 per cent
of the total population. With such firms it may be likewise brought out that
in most instances the few Negroes employed are serving only in menial work
capacities and have nothing whatever to do with the various production operations.

Some of the most frequently given reasons by employers for the non-
employment of qualified Negro workers or the limited inclusion of such workers
are: "My employees are not willing to accept Negroes as co-workers;" "Our
work is highly technical, we haven't found any Negroes qualified;" "My
employees will not use the same toilet facilities which are available to
Negroes;" "Negroes and whites don't get along so well as workers;" "The
union never sends us any Negroes;" "Our jobs are handed from generation to
generation by the white persons in our plant." The most overworked of these
reasons is the first. In Philadelphia, however, although defense employers
have fortified themselves with the aforementioned arguments or excuses and have
in many instances taken a rather determined stand with respect to Negro workers,
favorable changes have been brought about. There have been very definite gains
made in the defense industries by Negro workers. Gains from the standpoint
of increase in their personnel, the number of elevations to skilled positions
and also in the number of factories and plants using Negroes for the first time.
A review of this situation and specific instances where gains have been evidenced is more important in stimulating the morale among Negroes than the
negative side of the matter is in building a spirit of defeatism. It is our
feeling that if we are to induce the group to train and prepare successfully,
we must be able to show progress.

While one finds many unfavorable instances in the employment conditions
among Negroes in Philadelphia, a close examination brings out that they are
not preeminently as bad as the average layman thinks. In the three governmental agencies, which have a vital part in defense work, the Philadelphia Navy

Yard, Frankford Arsenal, and the Quartermaster's Depot, there are approximately 3,168 Negroes employed. This figure represents a little over 6 per cent of the total. At the Philadelphia Navy Yard there are 1,768 Negro workers. While the weighty majority fall under the occupational grouping of classified laborer, it is interesting to note that Negroes are found in 36 other work classifications at the Yard. Some of the jobs held are: ship-fitters, coppersmiths, boatbuilders, machinists, sheetmetal workers, apprentices, electricians, assistant chemist, boiler-makers, pipefitters, welders, drillers, shipwrights, painters, sewers (female), and clerks. The Quartermaster's Depot affords the greatest opportunity for Negro female workers. This agency has hundreds of Negro power-machine operators, and also has Negro workers as checkers, under-mimeograph operators, and employed in various other occupations. The Frankford Arsenal has a number of Negro workers; an examination, however, reveals that while there are Negroes working in skilled capacities in the agency, it also discloses that a great majority are serving in unskilled jobs. The Marine Depot has a sizeable number of Negro workers. All of the jobs which Negroes have received in connection with these governmental agencies have been through Civil Service. And in connection with the latter it may be added that there is evidence in Philadelphia that there would be a larger number of Negroes employed with these agencies if there wasn't so much power vested in the authority of the appointing officers.

The year 1941 has witnessed qualified Negro workers being introduced into factories where in previous years they weren't even accepted as applicants. Perhaps the most outstanding instance of the kind was the introduction of five Negro workers into the Edward G. Budd Manufacturing Company, in July. Recent contact with this company revealed that the number of Negro workers had increased to 50 and that Negroes had been integrated into several classifications of work. They are employed as shear-operators, workers on assembling lines, truckers (inside), garage workers and elevator operators. The Cramp Shipbuilding Company, which had its second beginning last year, has at the present time 107 Negroes employed in the following capacities: chippers, general helpers, riveters, drillers, laborers, riveter-helpers, driller-helpers, and janitors. Likewise, Negroes, since the beginning of the defense program, have been introduced the first time as workers into the S. L. Allen Company, the Bendix Aviation Corporation, the Kellet Autogiro and the Electric Storage Battery Company.

Perhaps the greatest gains afforded Negro workers of Philadelphia during the past year have been in such plants and factories where they were already established. Figures have been gathered recently by our office which indicate specific gains for Negro workers in defense plants. Some of these are: The General Steel Casting Corporation (Eddystone,Pa.), in September, 1940, had 170 Negroes in its employ; today has 383, an increase of some 125 per cent. Dodge Steel Company increased its Negro personnel from 70 to 100 in number, a 42 per cent increase. The Philadelphia Navy Yard in February, 1941 had 1,400 Negro workers; this figure has been increased by 368, representing a 26 per cent increase. Baldwin Locomotive Works (Eddystone,Pa.), in 1940 had 85 Negro employees; today the company has 135, an increase of 58 per cent. The Keystone Coat and Apron Company during the past year has increased its Negro personnel from 75 persons as of September, 1940 to 200 in October, 1941, a 166 per cent increase. The Frankford Arsenal last year had 284 Negro employees; today this agency has 500, an increase of 76 per cent. There are numerous other Philadelphia companies which may be placed on this list, and while the aforementioned has been given as evidence in bringing out the favorable side of the matter of defense work and Negroes, it must be kept in mind that there are still many inequalities. To briefly summarize the situation, it may be said that Philadelphia is a city which does not fully practice unlimited discrimination. There have been gains made by Negroes in defense industries and also in those industries which have been indirectly affected by the national preparedness program.

Efforts made by the Armstrong Association to have qualified Negro workers fully integrated into the defense program have been constant, varied and numerous. Contacts have been made individually with defense employers in an effort to sell them on the use of Negro labor and likewise with non-defense employer groups. As a result of our contact with the Metal Manufacturers' Association, a statement requesting the full utilization of Negro labor was placed in the monthly bulletin of the organization. This publication has a

mailing list of several hundred of the metal firms. Copies of "I Can Run Your
Machines," published by the National Urban League, along with lists of qualified available Negro workers, have been placed in the possession of a number
of local employers.

Since so many employment opportunities are predicated upon either joining
or the approval of organized employee groups, union contacts have been made
by the staff of the Armstrong Association in an effort to enhance work opportunities for Negroes. Influential Negro and white groups, through our efforts,
have been influenced and induced to take a stand on the matter of job discrimination against qualified Negroes. Advice, counsel and information on the
defense program have been given to the hundreds of Negroes who have come into
our offices. We have directed the attention of Negro workers to Civil Service
examinations and to possible sources of private employment. In this effort
we have sent out special notices to the list of applicants which we have on
file.

In the all important matter of training the Armstrong Association has
conducted an extensive educational program along the line of encouraging and
inducing Negroes to go in for training. We have rendered an invaluable service to a large number of persons who had no understanding as to the first
step to take to get a job or better the one which they had already. Many have
been directed to sources of registration for defense training.

To reiterate a statement previously made, the status of the Negro in
Philadelphia with respect to the National Defense Program has both its favorable and unfavorable aspects. Favorable developments have been of a nature
and degree as to afford real encouragement of the possibility of greater progress; the unfavorable do not suggest that they cannot, through proper efforts,
be modified for the better.

Opportunity, 20 (January, 1942): 4-7.

11. NEGRO LABOR IN MIAMI

By Judge Henderson

Labor in Miami and its vicinity known as the Greater Miami Area, has
improved considerably and fairly satisfactorily, in the last five years
considering what it was in years previous, and yet it is far from what it should
be.

We speak of semi and unskilled labor which constitutes the major part of
our populace.

This so-called improvement, is in living and working conditions. It was
brought about by men who had vision to see that individually nothing could be
done to better the living and working conditions, and they set out to preach
the importance of uniting for a common cause. The International Longshoremen's Association was organized in 1892 in Detroit, Mich., and is a chain
organization that extends throughout the United States and Canada.

In 1936 Miami became a link in that great chain. Prior to 1936, the
basic rate of pay for longshoremen was 35 cents per hour. Since the organization came into being, the wages and working conditions have improved 75%.

The Longshoremen's Association is very essential to National Defense, as
our country depends largely upon the flow of commerce. We recognize that
ability makes the man, and not wealth. We recognize no nationality, color or
creed, for the good of our association, and pledge ourselves to carry out
the principles of our organization.

The Int'l. Hod Carriers Building and Common Laborers Union of America,
Local 864, was organized one year later than the Longshoremen's local, receiving its charter April 1, 1937. Previous to the formation of this organization, the living was low and working conditions poor.

This organization caters principally to common labor in the building and
construction field, and while the field is white with harvest, the laborers
are few, speaking from an organization standpoint.

With approximately 3,000 to 3,500 laborers engaged in this class of work, only about 15 or 17 per cent enjoy the privileges and benefits of the organization, which has brought a definite improvement in working conditions, even to those outside of the fold.

The large percentage of those not organized is due to more than one reason. They believe that too many ventures have been tried and failed along this line, causing fear on their part. Another is that the employers intimidate the employees if they organize, by threatening loss of their jobs, and give a small raise in pay as a sop to keep them satisfied. There are other frivolous reasons too weak to stand up. The small number of members in this organization, now enjoy a 50 per cent increase in wages and working conditions, which was 35 cents to 40 cents per hour before the Union was organized, and is now 62-1/2 cents per hour. Of course the non-union men as formerly stated, receive all the benefits of the union. Now see what it would mean if all were organized. Organized labor keeps up the standard of living.

There is also the Red Cap Organization, which unquestionably has benefitted 75 per cent in wages and working conditions since organization.

The Freight Handlers Union can also claim a substantial improvement in their conditions by 50 per cent.

The Tile Setters and Terrazo Helpers Union has been organized for four years and receives recognition from employers, enjoying the fruits of its efforts in every way.

The Barbers themselves have their organization, which functions 100 per cent without opposition.

The Butchers are putting on an organizing effort to better their working conditions and living standards. All the above organizations are AFL affiliates.

Definite and substantial benefits have been received by the organization as a whole. Organization has brought about a closer collaboration between employer and employee.

Organized labor does not intend to be unfair to the employer. Employer and employee do not always see eye to eye. Sometimes they fight like soldiers for what they believe and think is right, but at the end they settle like gentlemen.

The aforesaid organizations have the same administration now as when organized. To all wage earners, the only solution to fair wages and working conditions is organization.

The Crisis, 49 (March, 1942): 95.

12. EMPLOYMENT SURVEY SHOWS DISCRIMINATORY PRACTICES
WIDESPREAD--NATIONAL UNITY THREATENED

By Emmett J. Scott[97]

WASHINGTON, D.C., March 5--As national mobilization of man power proceeds, it becomes increasingly evident that a labor shortage in the United States is in the offing--forecast to occur between July 1, 1942 and July 1, 1943.

The conversion of industry to war productuon will call for a schedule of 10,000,000 additional war productional workers and an additional 2,000,000 men for contingents of the Army, Navy and Marine Corps.

This startling revelation gives some notion of America's colossal war preparation now underway, calling for 4,200,000 in uniform, and 15,000,000 others to be employed in turning out the implements of war by December of this year.

Coincident with the release of this information comes a survey-study of employment prospects for Negroes in armament industries just published by the Reports and Analysis Division of the Bureau of Employment Security of the Social Security Board.

Summary of Findings

A summary of its findings indicates that Negroes were not considered for

employment in 51 per cent of 282,245 openings that occurred in selected
establishments in defense industries during the period September 1941-February
1942.

Questioning of employers by Employment Service interviewers revealed that
the degree of exclusion is even greater at the higher skill levels. At all
skill levels there are occupations with heavy defense labor requirements in
which most employers expect to continue to exclude Negroes.

Considerable differences in employer responses among the various industries and in various states were noted, it is stated. The least exclusion
was reported by employers in the shipbuilding industry. (During the last
World War record for driving of rivets was broken by a singing colored crew
in an American shipyard--at Norfolk, Va.).

This is a depressing state of affairs after the struggles made during the
past eight months to focus attention on the exclusion of Negroes from defense
industries. The right of this group to participate fully in the defense
program has been buttressed by an Executive Order from the White House.
Government defense contracts which forbid discrimination against Negroes have
been issued. Enlightened public opinion has expressed itself. Still the
practice continues.

Pertinent Inquiries

The Bureau of Employment Security interviewers requested employers in
communities where Negroes are considered a significant minority group in the
labor force to respond to these inquiries.

1. Whether they can employ Negroes in those occupations in which openings
would occur?

2. Whether, if Negroes are not employed, they will employ them in the
future?

Responding employers indicated that they do not and will not employ
Negroes in more than half of the 282,245 jobs that were filled. They reported,
however, that they would give consideration to Negroes in 30 per cent of the
openings in categories from which Negroes have heretofore been barred. The
remaining 19 per cent of the hires are to be made by employers who had Negroes
working for them in occupations in which they are hiring.

Sadly, the Bureau relates, the evidence of relaxation of discriminatory
practices is open to the criticism that employers' responses may have been
biased by a desire to appear cooperative with the government's plea for an end
to Negro discrimination in defense hiring. In actual practice the prospects
for Negro employment may be even poorer than are indicated by the study.

Pittsburgh Courier, March 7, 1942.

13. GOVERNOR OPPOSES EQUALITY IN PLANT

ATLANTA, Ga., Mar. 19--Negro workers in Georgia who have any hope of
getting a job in the giant aircraft plant now being built on the outskirts of
Atlanta, will not receive the same pay as white workers if Governor Eugene
Talmadge has his way. This was revealed last week when the Governor addressed
a luncheon meeting at the Capital Club where the plant construction was discussed.[98]

Giving evidence of his race hatred, Talmadge let loose all the venom and
vitrolic abuse he has become noted for. "The Negro here in Georgia is not
used to being paid the same wages as the white workers," he told the diners.
"The Negro in the South is paid low wages because of their low standard of
living and their low average of intelligence and it would be unwise for any
northern industrialist to venture here in Georgia, build a giant enterprise
like this bomber plant, and raise the wages of the skilled Negro worker to
that of the skilled white worker."

"This is White Man's War"

The Georgia dictator even went so far as to call upon the members of the

Cobb and Fulton counties Chamber of Commerce to sponsor a bill providing for
them to have jurisdiction over all salaries on public jobs and Negro wages.

Continuing the GeorgiaFeuhrer stormed, "This is a white man's war against
the yellow man doggism and this war can be won without the Negroes help. The
Negro has never done anything to help develop America so why should he be
given a chance to enjoy the fruits like the white man or be given an even break.

Raps Air Cadets

"One of the worse things that the government did was to permit the
training of Negroes to become U.S. Army flying cadets. The state of Georgia
never has granted a Negro a pilot license and never will as long as I am the
chief executive," he concluded.

The Bell Aircraft Corporation of Buffalo, N.Y. announces it will build a
giant bomber plant 17 miles from Atlanta at a total cost of $30,000,000 and
would employ 42,000 people working on three shifts daily. The plant will be
located between Marietta and Smyrna, the scene of mob violence in 1939 when
white mobsters brutally beat and forced Negroes to leave their homes.

Pittsburgh Courier, March 21, 1942.

14.   NEGROES OFFER PLAN TO NELSON FOR TRAINING 50,000 WORKERS

WASHINGTON, D.C., April 11--Suggested plans for training 50,000 Negroes
for jobs in war industries were discussed this week with Production Chief
Donald Nelson and were to be forwarded to the White House for further consideration.

Earl Dickerson, Chicago Negro alderman and a member of the President's
Fair Employment Practices Committee, and Sec. Ferdinand Smith of the CIO
National Maritime union presented the four-point proposal.[99]

Its main suggestions as given to Nelson:

1. "That you, as War Production director, publicly announce that the
War Production Board will take immediate steps to use Negro labor throughout
the nation in the war production program.

To Avert Shortages

2. "That as a first step to carry out this announced policy, the War
Production Board take effective measures to train fifty thousand Negro workers
in the next three months; and allocate these trainees throughout the country
where serious shortages exist or will exist within the near future.

3. "That a national production conference on the subject of Negro manpower be called within the next thirty days by you, which will include representatives of labor, management, government and representative Negro organizations for the purpose of working out detailed plans for full utilization of
Negro manpower for winning the war. From such a conference will develop similar
area production conferences.

4. "That you recommend to the President, Negro representation on the War
Manpower Board."

First Conference

Presentation of the plan to Nelson marked the first time that Negro leaders have conferred with the War Production Chief, and advanced a plan for
utilizing Negro manpower for all-out war production.

Both Dickerson and Smith were high in their praise of what they described
as Nelson's "frank and direct approach to the production plan."

They said he expressed a keen interest in every phase of the plan, and
indicated that he will take it up with the War Production Board, when the
board meets at the White House this week.

CIO News, April 13, 1942.

15.
LABOR LEADER WARNS OF WORKER SHORTAGE IN BARRING NEGROES

LOS ANGELES, May 14--"Our message to the Negro community is that just as 'business as usual' and 'trade unionism as usual' are out for the duration of the war, so must 'race prejudice as usual' be thrown into the ash can and kept there."

Thus does Revels Cayton, dynamic and hard-hitting Negro who is vice-president of the California CIO Industrial Union Council, sum up the new job he is working on in Southern California.[100]

For eight years Cayton has been a top-ranking leader in the California labor movement, putting in three years as business agent for the Marine Cooks and Stewards and three more as secretary-treasurer of the Maritime Federation of the Pacific.

Heads Setup on Minorities

After the Maritime Federation was dissolved to become a part of the CIO, Cayton made a trip to Australia with a convoy. Upon his return, the State CIO Council assigned him to direct its efforts in airing the involvement of workers from minority groups in the war production effort.

"America must produce enough tanks, guns, airplanes and other weapons of war to enable democracy's fighting men on the far-flung battlefields of the world to smash and destroy the race-hating Fascist hordes," Cayton says.

"But this is no small job,and if the Herculean task is to be accomplished the productive energy of every man and woman must be utilized."

War Work Bottleneck

"Yet in this hour of crisis more than 13,000,000 black hands lie idle because of a bottleneck of discrimination which plays right into the hands of Hitler and must be broken if we are to win."

A key problem in the scrap to break jim-crowism in employment is that of training Negroes for war industry work, Cayton points out.

Further, Cayton says that "our investigation shows that there is widespread discrimination in the referring of Negroes and Mexicans to defense training classes offered by the United States Employment Service."

Submits Program

As a first step toward getting necessary job training for Negroes and Mexicans, the Los Angeles CIO Industrial Union Council has submitted a program to the Los Angeles Board of Education, Cayton says continuing:

"We first recommended that classes in aircraft and sheet metal work be opened at Jefferson High School and that the existing classes in machine shop at that school be expanded.

"We also ask that other classes in shipfitting, pipefitting, etc., be set up in the Negro district immediately.

"Our third demand is that all forms of discrimination be immediately abolished throughout the training program, and fourth, we ask that Negro teachers, advisors, supervisors, field workers, file clerks stenographers, etc., be hired and placed in the defense training setup.

"Our fifth and last demand is that defense classes be opened for women.

"We think that this is very important because, as bad as the discrimination has been against Negro men workers, it has been even worse against women.

"Since it is estimated that 30 per cent of the workers in Southern California defense industries will be women before the war is won, this point takes on special significance."

Labor Shortage is Acute

While Negroes and members of other minority groups are being excluded from the training programs, the Southern California employment situation becomes more acute daily, according to Cayton.

"A responsible government official told me that before long we will face
the possibility of a real shortage of manpower in this section," Cayton says.
"In view of this situation, the crime that is being committed by those who
are responsible for the exclusion of these thousands of minority people from war
industry begins to take on a most treacherous character."

Pittsburgh Courier, May 16, 1942.

16. LABOR AT THE CROSSROADS

The half million organized colored workers undoubtedly read with alarm the
warning given by Wayne Lyman Morse, so-called public member of the War Labor
Board, at its meeting last week, that the laws against treason will be applied
to anyone in a labor organization who tries to bring about work stoppage over
jurisdictional disputes.

Nor were they reassured when three days later Rober D. Lapham and Cyrus
Ching, industry members of the WLB called upon Labor to live up to its no-
strike vow and appoint an arbiter in a specific jurisdictional dispute on pain
of government intervention.

These are straws in the wind and they indicate in which direction the
wind is blowing.

Labor today seems to be at the crossroads, faced with the momentous
problem of deciding whether or not it will accept government dictation and
control.

There is a war in progress with the earth as the stake, and Labor wants
to win that war in order to preserve its nation, its independence of action
and its very identity.

On the other hand, Labor is reluctant to surrender its independence of
action for fear it may never get it back, being frankly skeptical of the self-
sacrificing patriotism and good intentions of many of the erstwhile lawyers
who are heading the managerial revolution in Washington.

Labor realizes that it is only a short step from considering a jurisdictional strike treasonable to considering ANY strike treasonable; the reasons
for outlawing the one being as cogent as the reasons for outlawing the other,
so far as the central authority is concerned.

It is chiefly a matter of opinion, and things being as they are, Labor
has a good idea what and whose opinion will prevail.

There is a widespread feeling in the ranks of organized labor that once
the right to strike is surrendered, it will eventually lose all the advantages
and privileges gained by a century of sacrifice.

This is not, of course, a racial problem specifically, but it nevertheless
concerns a half million colored workers, three-fifths of whom have entered the
ranks of organized Labor since 1937 and profited by increased wages, shorter
hours and vacations with pay.

Undoubtedly Labor would be more willing to relinquish its prerogatives
if the vast war production effort were being more largely directed by its
elected officials with industrialists and managers subordinated to them rather
than the other way around.

The slowly gathering drive for a ceiling on wages, ostensibly to halt
inflation, does nothing to weaken Labor's apprehension.

Pittsburgh Courier, August 1, 1942.

17. RESOLUTION TO HIRE NEGRO BEER DRIVER-HELPERS KILLED

NEW ORLEANS, La., Sept. 3--On Thursday, of last week, seven members of
the executive board of the Beer Drivers' Local Union, No. 215, met at the New
Orleans Urban League to discuss plans for re-employing Negro helpers on

brewery trucks in this area. The committee was headed by A. M. Tolivar and
J. G. Muhs, president and secretary of the union, respectively.

On August 6, a result of the action of the union, seven Negro youth, who
had been working as helpers on beer trucks, were fired and the members of the
union employing these boys were fined five dollars each. Moreover, heavier
penalties were promised those who did not comply with the union's wishes.

Resolution For Hiring Killed

As a result of contacts made by Clarence A. Laws, executive secretary of
the league, the matter was again introduced at the meeting of the union on
August 20. A resolution which would have permitted the drivers to hire
Negroes if they desired was killed by a vote of 42 to 35.

Negroes Buy Much Beer--But Not Hired

Said Mr. Laws after the meeting, "I sincerely believe that the members
of the executive board of the Beer Drivers' Union appreciate the unfairness
of barring Negroes solely on the basis of color and that they will reconsider
the matter favorably at their next regular meeting. I do not know what action
Negroes will take if Negro youth are not rehired. In the meantime I want it
clearly understood that the Urban League is for or against any brewery. We
know that some hire more Negroes than others and we appreciate this fact. At
the same time we are cognizant of the fact that none of the breweries are
hiring Negroes in proportion to their consumption of beer."

The Urban League secretary also stated that a letter was received from
the Jackson Brewing company during the past week in which it was stated
that the company is "very decidedly against the action taken by Local Union
215."

Pittsburgh Courier, September 5, 1942.

18. PROGRESS REPORT, WAR MANPOWER COMMISSION, MARCH, 1943

The most effective approach to the utilization of Negro labor has been to
select certain industries, firms and occupations in which there are shortages
and press for the use of Negroes in these areas. An illustration is offered
in the shipbuilding industry. Due to custom and union opposition, Negroes
were generally excluded from welding, electrical work and machine shop prior
to 1941. Starting first in government navy yards and extending the activity
to private yards in tight labor markets, an effort was made to break down
this occupational limitation. Progress has been made. U.S. Navy Yards in
general hire colored welders, electricians and machinists. Private yards on
the West Coast, in the Middle Atlantic States, and in New England now utilize
Negro welders on a large scale and offer employment to Negroes in skilled
occupations. Little has been accomplished in private yards in the South. The
employment of Negroes in a large number of occupations by the Sun Shipbuilding
and Dry Dock Company in Chester, Pennsylvania and the use of thousands of
Negroes by the Kaiser yards on the West Coast illustrate developments in this
field. As of March 16, 1943, the Richmond shipyards of the Kaiser Corporation
reported 6,100 Negro employees. Of these, 905 were female. The breakdown
as to classifications of Negro workers was as follows:

Boilermakers	2,033
Shipfitters	801
Shipwrights	749
Joiners	169
Painters	159
Stage riggers	101
Sheet metal	87
Warehousemen	19
Laborers	1,994

Employment of Negroes in the aircraft industry was effected by the same
approach. Here there was a problem of opening new jobs to Negroes and gaining
acceptance for Negro women. Starting on the West Coast, a definite program
was initiated to deal with these problems. By 1943, most of the aircraft
assembly plants outside the South were accepting Negro men and women on production jobs. It cannot be reiterated too often that numerical employment
for Negroes is intimately related to opening new types of jobs to them. The
unemployed Negroes on the labor market cannot all be absorbed in unskilled
and service jobs. Certainly there can be no successful approach to the problem
of shifting colored workers now in non-essential pursuits to vital war production unless new types of jobs are opened to Negroes.

War Manpower Commission Records, RG 211, Series 11t, Box 793, National
Archives.

19. OCCUPATIONAL STATUS OF NEGRO RAILROAD EMPLOYEES

The Negro employees of the Pennsylvania Railroad are in 74 different
occupations, many of which require skilled and semiskilled workers. The
16,155 Negroes employed by the company, as of September 28, 1942, represent
a gain of more than 6,000 persons over its normal number of Negro workers.
According to the National Association of Negroes in American Industry, as
reported in Service (Tuskegee Institute, Ala.) for January 1943, the railroad
is thus the largest single industrial employer of that racial group.
These Negro employees are scattered through the eastern, central, and
western regions, the New York zone, the Long Island Railroad (a subsidiary),
the system's general offices, and its Altoona works. The eastern region, which
includes Philadelphia but excludes the New York zone, had a total of 5,437
Negro workmen, the central region 2,340, and the western region 2,408. The
New York zone, exclusive of the Long Island Railroad with its 548 Negro workers,
employed 2,063 of that race. The repair shops at Altoona hired 18 Negro
workmen, and the dining-car department employed 3,208. In the general offices
of the company there were 133 Negroes.
Of the total number of colored employees, 154 were women, whose occupations
ranged from marine stewardesses to coach cleaners, and included elevator operators, matrons, crossing watchwomen, and locomotive preparers.
Male Negro workers were listed in the mechanically skilled and semiskilled
classes as well as the unskilled. Those employed in the skilled and semi-
skilled classes, it is stated, had more than doubled during recent years,
beginning well before the outbreak of war. Among the workers in these classes
were 37 marine firemen, 65 tallymen, 14 machinists and 72 machinists' helpers,
151 oilers and 12 stationary engineers and firemen.
Indicative of the railroad's tendency to upgrade Negro workers, it is
said, is the fact that they are represented in such skilled occupations as
electricians, painters, welders, masons and masons' helpers, blacksmith's
helpers, cranemen, and tractor, turntable, and stoker operators. In the main-
tenance-of-way department, 12 Negro track foremen headed units with 17 assistants, and 19 in the group acted as machine operators.
Negro freight truckers and station baggagemen, numbering 2,012 and 317,
respectively, were engaged in handling the system's freight and baggage. The
greatest number in this group were in the eastern region (1,197), and in the
western and the central division and the New York zone (784).
The dining-car department employed Negroes in the following occupations:
549 chefs and cooks; 2,598 waiters and other food attendants; and 61 attached
to trains in various capacities. Altogether, 621 Negroes were station porters,
with 14 acting as captains. More than half (approximately 350) of the station
porters were in the New York zone and 194 were in the Philadelphia area.

Monthly Labor Review, 56 (March, 1943): 484-85.

20. BEG WOMEN TO TAKE WAR JOBS YET DENY THEM TO NEGROES

By Eleanor Fowler
Secretary-Treasurer, CIO Women's Auxiliaries

Labor Day, 1943, will see more women at work than ever before in our
country's history. Two million new women workers will be needed in industry
before the end of the year. The War Manpower Commission and the Office of
War Information are planning a nation-wide campaign to induce women over 18,
with no children under 14, to take jobs.
At the Executive Board of the Congress of Women's Auxiliaries last week-
end in Cleveland we discussed this need for women workers. Each member of the
Board--and they all come from big industrial centers--cited instances in which
Negro women had been denied jobs in the face of labor shortages.
Two of our Board members had had personal experiences. They had stood
in line at an employment office where women were being hired, had been told,
when their turns came, that no more help was needed, and had seen white women
coming after them hired for the jobs.
There's a new bomber plant in Cleveland. Over 60% of the employees are
scheduled to be women--and they're talking of bringing women workers in from
other areas. But Negro women who want jobs in Cleveland are still waiting.

Negroes Turned Away

In Indianapolis the papers carry urgent ads for women workers in war
industry, and Negro women applying for those jobs are turned away.
The auxiliary executive board realized that this situation is undermining
the morale of the Negro citizens of our nation. Negro men give their lives to
win the war against Hitlerism on the battle front. It is utterly unfair that
their wives and sisters should be denied the opportunity to work for Victory
on the production front.
Our Board voted to call the matter to the attention of the President of
the United States and to ask him to force employers to observe the official
policy of our government banning racial discrimination in war industry.

Other Discrimination Too

Discrimination because of color is not the only discrimination we must
fight. Many older women--the very ones who have "no children under 14"--are
being denied jobs too. Employers set up all sorts of age, height and weight
requirements by which they limit the women they will employ.
Women with young children who must have jobs--wives of servicemen, for
instance, whose government allowance is utterly inadequate--are denied employment, too.
Our auxiliary board voted to urge the War Manpower Commission to conduct
a national registration of women in those areas where labor shortages exist
or are developing. Such a registration would give the local manpower authorities a real picture of the available labor supply which they do not have
at present.
A firm policy of requiring employment of all available local labor before
workers are imported must then be instituted to help break down the discriminations now hampering our war production.

CIO News, May 31, 1943.

21.
DEVELOPMENTS IN THE EMPLOYMENT OF NEGROES IN WAR INDUSTRIES
WAR MANPOWER REPORT
OCTOBER 16, 1943

<u>Summary</u>
Although there has been an increase in the total employment of Negroes

in practically every branch of war production, there is a serious time-lag both in the wider use of Negroes among many of the smaller individual firms and in the occupational upgrading of Negroes in all firms. This concentration of Negroes in a relatively few large firms, together with slow occupational progress generally, has had the effect of restricting the use of Negro workers as a means of meeting immediate labor needs.

The degree to which Negroes are effectively employed varies widely among specific plants, areas, and industries. In the shortage areas of the South, Negroes are concentrated in those establishments and occupations where heavy unskilled work is to be performed. In the South, also with few exceptions, no steps are being taken in the direction of upgrading Negroes to new occupations nor is there any hiring of Negroes to meet the demand of establishments seeking workers for skilled jobs.

In the acute labor shortage areas of the North where war industries are much more diversified than in the South, the utilization of Negroes has progressed much further, but Negro employment is concentrated with respect to occupations, establishments, and industries. There is very little indication of an increase in diversified employment of Negroes to meet shortages generally in the tight labor market areas.

Although current placement developments outside the South show slight improvement in the placement of Negroes in skilled war jobs as compared with unskilled and service occupations, discriminatory job specifications are still a formidable barrier in many plants and occupations.

The successful recruitment of Negroes for war work is now fundmentally a problem of the removal of discriminatory barriers against the employment of Negroes in many smaller individual establishments and against the general use of Negroes in all occupations for which they can qualify. This problem is now being accentuated by the efforts of Negroes to transfer from non-essential to essential war occupations in accordance with Selective Service policies.

Trends in employment and placement of Negro workers

Employer reports indicate a slow but continued upward trend in the general level of employment of Negroes. As shown in the table below, Negro workers in July 1943 represented 7.3 per cent of total employment in those major war establishments reporting nonwhite employment. In July 1942, a year ago, Negroes constituted 5.8 per cent of total employment in such establishments.

Nonwhites Employed in War Industry Establishments,

July 1942--July 1943

	Month	Total employment in establishments reporting nonwhites	Per cent nonwhite of total
	July	11,993,874	5.8
1942	September	12,153,755	5.7
	November	13,148,356	6.0
1943	January	13,375,000	6.4
	March	13,954,463	6.7
	May	14,262,614	7.0
	July	14,157,099	7.3

Placements of nonwhite persons by the Employment Offices increased by about 20 per cent between July 1942 and July 1943, but the proportion of nonwhite to total placements declined slightly (from 18.2 per cent to 15.9 per cent) chiefly as a result of the reduced emphasis on filling service jobs, in which Negro placements formerly predominated. Only very small advances have been made in the placement of Negroes in skilled and semiskilled occupations. During the second quarter of 1945 Negro placements were 3.2 per cent of all placements in skilled jobs as compared to 2.7 per cent in the same quarter of 1942; placements in semiskilled occupations were 7.6 per cent in 1943 and 7.3 per cent in 1942. Out of every hundred placements of nonwhites, 6 were in skilled and semiskilled jobs in the second quarter of 1942, while a year later the number had risen only to 10.

Variation in the extent of Negro employment

Although the long-run employment trend of Negroes has shown some progress, the real problem is to get employers to hire locally available and qualified Negroes to meet all types of labor needs. A current illustration of this difficulty now prevails in the textile mills in Spartanburg, South Carolina. There, employers are refusing to hire locally available Negroes and at the same time are insisting that the Government provide additional housing facilities to house in-migrant white workers. This situation and many other similar situations have not been met because the practice has been not to employ Negroes where serious opposition has appeared. Hence, the employment of Negroes in war industries has scattered and varied as between areas, industries, and plants.

There is a large variation from one industry to another in the extent of utilization of Negroes. For example, in May 1943, Negroes represented approximately 43.2 per cent of total employment in tobacco manufactures, 21.8 per cent in lumber and timber basic products, 17.2 per cent in contract construction, at the same time, Negroes constituted only 2.7 per cent in textile mill products, and 4.0 per cent in transportation and other public utilities.

Within a given industry there is a large variation from one geographical area to another in the extent of employment of Negroes. For example, in May the proportion of Negroes employed in aircraft establishments ranged from 2.3 per cent in the Buffalo-Niagara Falls area to 10.4 per cent in Detroit; and in shipbuilding establishments from 12.7 per cent in Savannah to 25.1 per cent in Charleston. While geographical variations cannot be adequately interpreted without an analysis of variations in supply, it is known that an important part of the variation is due to differences in employer, labor and community attitudes and practices. The importance of variation in employer attitudes and practices is evidenced by the variation between plants in the same industry in the same locality.

The result of this pattern of extreme variability in the utilization of Negroes is that unnecessary shortages are allowed to develop and persist in occupations for which Negro workers are available. For example, the Office of War Information reports that in some cities transport vehicles are lying idle due to lack of people to run them. Out of 227 local transportation companies--representing 80 per cent of total employment in the industry--only eight employ Negro operators.

Developments in areas of acute labor shortage

Precise data for comparing changes in the overall employment of Negroes in acute labor market areas are lacking. However, employer reports in those establishments reporting nonwhite employment indicate an increase in the use of Negroes in the tight labor market areas. In the field of unskilled occupations, there is wide use of available Negroes in all areas of acute labor shortage. Indications are, however, that there has been but little increase in the use of Negroes in skilled occupations. This is especially pronounced in Southern labor market areas.

The employment of Negroes in acute labor shortage areas of the South.

In the tight labor market areas throught the States of Alabama, Florida, Georgia, Mississippi, and Texas, Negroes are principally used as unskilled labor in ship and boat building and in Government establishments.

In none of these tight labor markets in the South has there developed a trend toward upgrading Negroes to new occupations, with the possible exception of one shipyard, which has recently set up a segregated unit for Negroes following a race riot there.

There is some indication that wider employment opportunities will eventually be made available to Negro women in the Charleston area. A new attitude in this connection was shown when a number of construction contractors placed Negro women on building jobs. The work was found generally unsuitable for women, but it made dramatic the large potential supply of Negro women available in the area for production work.

Employment of Negroes in acute labor market areas of the North

At the very beginning of both the defense and the war program there appeared throughout the North and Far West scattered instances where larger war establishments consented to use Negroes at all levels of skill. In some cases this development was purely voluntary on the part of the employer and in other instances it was the result of negotiations through the Negro Employment and Training Branch of the Office of Production Management.

The wide use of Negroes in these establishments and some of the other larger establishments which later adopted the same policy toward Negroes tends to weigh the overall figures on Negro employment in many acute labor market areas, and obscures the more basic problem of the limited employment of Negroes in a large number of smaller individual firms scattered throughout the tight labor market areas. Examples of this situation are especially notable in the Buffalo-Niagara Falls area. In this area there are two firms in the professional and scientific instruments industry which have more than 3,000 employees and only 8 Negroes. Likewise, in the communications equipment industries, there are two firms employing more than 3,000 employees with only 18 Negroes. In this area, out of a total of 80 firms representing the important war industries, 45 per cent of the 9,490 Negroes employed in May were in 5 firms in the blast furnaces, steel works and rolling mills industry.

In the Akron area during the month of May there were only 6 Negroes in 9 firms employing more than 2,000 workers. Five firms in iron and steel products industry in the Dayton, Springfield area employed half of the 2,277 Negroes in approximately 50 firms with a total employment of 41,750 workers. There are many other tight labor market areas in the North, such as the Evansville area and the Gary-Hammond-E. Chicago area, where Negroes are chiefly concentrated in a relatively few individual firms.

Even in those areas in which Negroes are employed extensively, the industrial distribution of the Negro workers tends to show a considerable concentration. In Baltimore, for example, slightly more than half of the 22,478 Negroes employed in reporting establishments were in ship and boat-building and repairing, while approximately 40 per cent of total employment was in this industry. Similarly, in the Detroit area 64 per cent of the Negroes in reporting establishments were employed in aircraft and parts while approximately 58 per cent of total employment was in the industry.

In none of the tight labor markets of the North does there appear a significant use of skilled Negro workers in war industry as a whole. In the Detroit area it is reported by the Employment Service that in May 1943 only 6.7 per cent were in skilled classifications as compared with 20.5 per cent for all employees. Available data on individual firms indicate considerably less use of skilled Negroes in other tight areas.

Employment of Negro Women

Among war industries, establishments in aircraft, communications equipment, electrical equipment, shipbuilding, and small arms ammunition are the principal employers of women. Available data indicate that the employment of Negro women is limited to a small number of firms in a few industries. For example, a recent survey of selected war industries in the Baltimore area reveals that 75.5 per cent of the 2,249 Negro women employed were working in only four establishments. In the Detroit area the Employment Service reports considerable opposition to the employment of Negro women in even the unskilled grades.

Reports of discriminatory hiring specifications

Of 685 reports of discriminatory specifications submitted to Fair Employment Practice Committee between January and June 1943, 486 or 71 per cent were submitted from Region V. This particular concentration of discriminatory job orders is largely due to the incidence of discrimination against Negroes in the Detroit area. An analysis of 242 reports from the Detroit area indicates that approximately one-third of the discriminatory job orders came from firms

in the ordnance industry, followed by nearly 25 per cent from the machinery
industry (except electrical) and 23 per cent from the aircraft industries.
There were relatively few reports of discrimination in forms engaged in automobile and automobile manufacturing, iron and steel, and nonferrous metals and
products. Throughout the East North Central states, excepting Wisconsin, the
largest proportion of discriminatory job specifications have been reported on
firms in the machinery industries.

An analysis of reports of discriminatory specifications indicates a wide
range of occupations. In the Detroit area the most frequent reports of discrimination in the aircraft industry involved unskilled jobs such as machinist
helper and break-in machine operators. Similarly, in the machinery and ordnance industries in Detroit the most frequently involved occupations were
break-in machine operators and machine cleaners. The occurrence of discriminatory specifications in unskilled occupations leading to skilled machine jobs
is primarily a restriction upon the entry of Negroes into skilled work involving machine tools and electrical machinery.

War Manpower Commission Records, RG 211, Series 115, Box 793, National Archives.

22. WHITE AND NEGRO AMERICANS MUST UNITE FOR VICTORY

It is our Responsibility to Defeat Race Prejudice
and Intolerance, Hitler's Fifth Column

Statement by the Executive Board

DISTRICT COUNCIL NO. 8
UNITED ELECTRICAL, RADIO & MACHINE WORKERS OF AMERICA, CIO

The recent outbreaks of racial strife in major war production centers call
for sober thought by all our members.

Look at the results of the Detroit "race riot," instigated and organized
by Hitler's volunteer Fifth Column in America:

34 dead--more than 700 injured--three million man-hours of work lost--a
terrific drop in production, already too low for our urgent war needs--an
example, unmatched in years, of disunity, disregard of the war, disregard of
the democracy for which we are fighting.

The Detroit "riot"--a planned attack upon the Negro population--did not
just happen. It was the worst of a series of "race riots," attacks upon Mexicans in Los Angeles, upon Negroes in Beaumont, Texas; Newark, N.J., Mobile,
Alabama; all major war production centers.

Civic leaders in Detroit, including R. J. Thomas, president of the United
Automobile Workers of America, largest union in the world, and the Rev. Benjamin Rush, president of the Detroit Council of Churches, have pointed out that
outbreak was worked up by the Ku Klux Klan and allied Fascist groups. These,
the Klan, the Black Legion, the Gerald L. K. Smiths, and Charles Coughlins,
are the people who seek to defeat democracy at home, to establish Hitlerism
over American workers. To achieve their ends, they serve as the Axis' Fifth
Column in our country. [101]

Stabbing our Soldiers in the Back

The reason for these outbreaks at this particular time is clear.

American and British armies are moving to the invasion of Europe, which
must bring about the final defeat of Nazi Germany and free the world. Hitler's
Italian ally is crumbling. Hitler's back is to the wall. His agents and
American friends are making a last desperate attempt to prevent this invasion
by disrupting our war effort at home. If they cannot block the invasion, they
hope to weaken it by continuing attacks on our home front.

Hitler's friends are stabbing our fighting boys in the back--by inciting
strikes--by fighting against price control so the people will be demoralized

by skyrocketing prices—by organizing attacks in Congress on important war
services—by inciting racial strife.

Hitler's Fifth Column is inciting race riots in the great war production
centers of the country, where the greatest damage can be done to war production
and to the unity of the American people. It works by preying upon the intolerance, the un-American prejudices of some people who still put their personal
hates above their patriotism and their belief in democracy.

It works by spreading rumors and starting trouble around minor disputes
between people of different color. Days before the Detroit riots, word was
spread among the whites that they would be attacked by Negroes, word was spread
among the Negroes that they would be attacked by whites.

Victory is Threatened

Hitler looks at the work of his agents and their dupes—and he laughs.
He looks at Detroit, Newark, Los Angeles, Mobile, Beaumont, and crows:

"These people can't beat me. They're too busy fighting among themselves."

And let those who cockily think the war is won, that we cannot lose—let
them take heed. Given much more of the kind of attacks on unity that we had
in Detroit, our offensive can be stopped—preventing that complete victory over
the Axis which *we must have* to guarantee democracy abroad *and at home.*

Hitler looks hopefully to other cities—to San Francisco, New York, Pittsburgh, yes, to St. Louis, to Evansville—any war center where workers may fall
prey to un-American race hatreds—where a minor street car dispute may flare
into a Detroit riot.

American workers must furnish the answer to the Fifth Column—in a determination not to be misled by Fascist agents and sentiments, in a recognition
of the contribution which all American workers are making to the war.

A prominent Southerner, Dr. Frank Graham, public member of the War Labor
Board and President of the University of North Carolina, in a recent board
opinion abolishing wage differences between white and Negro laborers, declared
that racial or religious discrimination "is in line with the Nazi program."[102]

The Brotherhood of Man

Said Dr. Graham:
"The Negro is necessary for winning the war, and, at the same time, is a
test of our sincerity in the cause for which we are fighting.

"Whether as vigorous fighting men or for production of food and munitions,
America needs the Negro; the Negro needs the equal opportunity to work and
fight.

"More hundreds of millions of colored people are involved in the outcome
of this war than the combined populations of the Axis powers. Under Hitler and
his Master Race, their movement is backward to slavery and despair. In America,
the colored people have the freedom to struggle for freedom. With the victory
of the democracies, the human destiny is toward freedom, hope, equality of
opportunity and the gradual fulfillment for all people of the noblest aspirations of the brothers of men and the sons of God, without regard to color or
creed, religion or race, in the world neighborhood of human brotherhood."

This union, the UE-CIO, has a special opportunity and a special responsibility in the present situation, because it takes seriously the democracy
for all, regardless of race or creed, demanded by the Constitution of the
United States of America.

The UE, along with the whole CIO, fights for equal job opportunities for
all, for unity of all American workers.

We Have a Job To Do

It is the job of our members to achieve that unity. If they are unwilling
or unable to rid themselves of race dislikes, it is their job to put their
patriotism and their union first. They must check their prejudices in favor of
a united effort to work and fight for victory.

We must permit no one, whether he be a stooge for an unscrupulous employer,
or a conscious or unconscious Fascist, to split our ranks. Disunity, racial

and religious intolerance, will be used to endanger our job conditions. It will
bring defeat to American workers. Unity will bring better working conditions,
victory over the enemies of democracy at home and abroad.

It is our job to fight vicious rumors and slanders. It is our job to
avoid careless or unpleasant remarks about persons of another race, to avoid
disputes. It is the job of officers and stewards to exercise their leadership
by giving an example of mutual understanding, by exerting a firm hand on any
member, white or Negro, who may start trouble.

Our officers and stewards will have the full backing of their union. This
union will not tolerate anyone starting trouble or behaving irresponsibly. Any
one, white or Negro, found responsible for creating dissension within our ranks,
will be dealt with vigorously.

We rely upon the union spirit, upon the patriotism of our members, to set
an example for the whole community--to insure that the Shame of Detroit shall
not happen here.

We call upon our members to lead in unity for victory.

Flier in possession of the editors.

23. NEGRO WOMEN WAR WORKERS

For America at War

BEHIND THE NOISE--the hammer, the thunder, the drive--that typifies
America at war is a group of women. Negro women, who have pooled their
strength with that of all other Americans in an effort to achieve a common
goal--Victory. Carrying their full share of the Nation's wartime load, they
are at work in every section of the country. In the steel mills and the
foundries, in the aircraft plants and the shipyards. Negro women are helping
to make the weapons of war. Not only are they working in war plants but their
services in laundries and restaurants, on railroads and farms, and in countless
other essential civilian industries have helped to make it possible for America
to become the arsenal of the United Nations. Negro women's wartime performance
has proved that, given the training, they can succeed in any type of work
that women can do.

Trail Blazers for Uncle Sam on the Production Front

Shipyards

More than one precedent was broken when in 1942 women mechanics were hired
at the Brooklyn Navy Yard for the first time in 141 years. It was a red-letter
day for women when the doors of the navy yard swung open. For Negro women
especially it was a triumphant day, for a Negro girl received a grade of 99,
the highest rating of any of the 6,000 women who took the civil-service examination for navy-yard jobs. She and another Negro girl who also showed special
aptitude for work with precision instruments were assigned to the instrument
division, where binoculars, telescopes, and range finders are reconditioned.
Of the first 125 women hired at the Brooklyn Navy Yard about 12 were Negro.
At a second eastern navy yard, highly qualified Negro girls were among the
first women hired in 1942. Since the work is skilled and strenuous, every
new employee is required to pass rigid aptitude and physical tests.

In the Washington D.C. Navy Yard, Negro women are employed in the cart-
ridge-case shop as well as in other shops. Some several hundred Negro women--
most of whom are married and are mothers--are working there. They are operating punch and blanking presses as well as lathes and tapping machines in the
manufacture of cartridge cases.

In the summer of 1943 about 2,000 women were employed in the Washington
Navy Yard. Women were hired for naval ordnance jobs only if they had had
100 hours of training in machine-shop practice. In paying tribute to the
splendid contribution of Negro women, an official of the navy yard said:

"Negro women have played an important role in the production of ordnance materials during the present war. In the production of cartridge cases they are responsible for keeping production at a high peak. Both the output and morale in the shop reflect the cooperative spirit in which women have been accepted. Negro women have demonstrated their ability to adapt themselves to a field of endeavor that was foreign to them as well as to other women in the yard."

Negro women also were working on fuze-loading at the Bellevue (Md.) Naval Magazine. Behind steel barricades they measured and loaded pom-pom mix, lead azide, TNT, tetryl, and fulminate of mercury. The various loading operations are strung along differently grouped assembly lines. On one line, for example, women loaded tetryl lead-ins for bomb fuzes, or delay elements containing small cells of black powder, or mercury fulminate and lead azide for detonators. In small steel booths others received an element through a hole in the wall, put in the measured miligrams of powder, and passed it cautiously through an opposite hole to the next booth for another twist, tap, or turn.

Aircraft

In aircraft plants also there are many Negro women pioneers. More than 2 years ago Negro women were working on production, including machine operation assembly, and inspection, in at least 15 major aircraft plants on the west coast, the east coast, and in the Middle West. Many of them had received their job training from NYA or other free Government training classes. One of the first aircraft plants to hire Negro girls in mechanical jobs was the airplane engine division of the Philadelphia Navy Yard.

Electrical equipment and machinery

Another of the large woman-employing industries in which Negro women have been at work for several years is the manufacture of electrical machinery and equipment. From the personnel director of one of the leading electrical manufacturing companies this report came to the Women's Bureau early in the war: "We have on our rolls at the present time approximately 2,000 Negro women, the majority of whom have been added in the last 6 to 9 months. They are engaged in 45 separate and distinct occupational classifications covering a rather wide range of skills. Included among their assignments are bench hands on various kinds of partial and final assemblies, cable formers, clerks, inspectors, many kinds of machine operators, solderers, stock selectors, electrical testers, and wiremen."

"One of the best men in the shop," according to the foreman, was a Negro girl in the electrical repair department of the overhaul and repair shops of a large eastern airline field.

Ordnance

In little more than a year after Pearl Harbor, Negro women were assigned to many of the more difficult technical laboratory jobs at the Army Proving Ground at Aberdeen, Md., where all types of guns, tanks, and other fighting equipment are tested. The girls employed in the ballistics laboratory were college graduates, and all had a thorough background of higher mathematics. Only two years of college were required, however, in the star gaging section, where they tested bores and curvatures of guns. According to a War Department personnel specialist, the Negro girls in the Aberdeen laboratories "proved very satisfactory."

Early in the present armament program, Negroes comprised at least 350 of the women employed at an Ohio ordnance plant. One of the Negro women who came in as a warehouse worker was put in charge of a crew of women packers, both white and Negro, and later was made a counselor.

Another midwestern ordnance plant employed 700 Negro women soon after the war began. They worked in a variety of jobs, and included supervisors, stenographers, machine operators, nurses, photograph technicians, draftsmen, machine adjusters, movemen, janitors, and matrons.

In a survey made by the National Metal Trades Association in 1943, 62 plants were found that employed women. Of these plants 19 employed Negro

women, most of whom were in janitor service. However, one plant reported a
total of 1,200 Negro women distributed among all the departments where women
were at work. Other plants reported successful employment of Negro women in
such occupations as work in a foundry, operation of machine tools including
turret lathes, all types of winding operations, inspection, a variety of bench
work, assembly, painting, electrical work, riveting, flame cutting, and welding.

Steel mills--Foundries

     Negro women were employed in most of the 41 steel mills surveyed by the
Women's Bureau in 1943. Areas visited by Women's Bureau agents included
Pittsburgh-Youngstown, Buffalo, Chicago-Gary, and West Virginia, and one mill
each in Colorado, Sparrows Point (Md.), and Bethlehem (Pa.). While women
were working in most divisions of the steel industry, their proportion was
small, about 8 per cent covering all races. In some of the mills, however,
women were found in almost every department. There were women working at
the ore docks, in the storage yards for raw materials, on the coal and ore
trestles, in the coke plants, the blast furnaces, the steel furnaces, the
rolling mills, and the finishing mills that were doing fabricating on shells,
guns, and regular products such as nails, spikes, and bolts.
     The majority of the Negro women, like the white women, worked at labor
jobs. The proportion of Negro women in the masonry and outside-labor gangs
was large. Where women were employed in the sintering plants they were chiefly
Negroes, and were reported as moving as much dirt and material as men. Jobs
around a sintering plant are all dirty and chiefly of a labor grade; everything
around such a plant is covered with iron dust. The sintering plant salvages
ore dust and blast-furnace flue dust by mixing it with water and spreading
it on moving conveyors that carry it under gas flames for baking into clinkery
masses known as sinters, which are charged back to the furnace. Considerable
numbers of women in these plants worked on dumping the cars of ore and dust,
inspecting along the sides of the conveyor to remove lumps of slag and foreign
matter, shoveling up spills along the conveyor lines, screening coal and
dust, carrying tests to the laboratory, etc.
     Plants on the Great Lakes receive most of their ore supply by boat. At
one of these plants women were working at the ore docks. Though the boats
are unloaded by electric ore bridge cranes that scoop up 15 to 20 tons in
each bucket load and empty a boat in a few hours, it is necessary for labor
gangs to go down into the bottoms of the boats and sweep and shovel up the
leavings of ore into piles for removal by special hoists, as the grab-buckets
cannot clean up around the sides and edges. To do this work a crew of women,
chiefly Negro, and with a woman gang leader, went from boat to boat as needed.
When there were no boats ready for cleaning, they worked around the docks and
stock yards as a part of the general clean-up gang. The ore, coal, and lime-
stone are heavy to handle, even when a small shovel is used.
     In two of the steel mills visited by the Bureau, a Negro woman was
employed as panman. The job of the panman is to mix the fire clay, shoveling
the materials into a mixing mill, for sealing the casting hole of the blast
furnace. The work is carried on in a blast-furnace shed. Mud mixing is not
a full-time job and is incidental to other labor.
     Another unusual job held by a Negro woman was that of operating a steel-
burning machine. This intricate machine, 25 feet long and 6 feet high, cuts
parts for 6 different kinds of antiaircraft guns from huge plates of steel.
The acetylene torches cut two parts at a time and must be set and guided with
precision. The operator must have a dozen or more controls set exactly right.
     In the Buffalo area Negro women were breaking into many jobs tradition-
ally closed to women in the steel industry. In one large plant in this area
Negro women made up about one-third of the total number of women employed.
     Review of the situation in the steel mills, however, indicates quite
general acceptance of the position that women's employment in steel is only
for the duration of the war, and that men returning from the armed services
will take over the jobs on the basis of seniority and priority rights in the
industry.
     Negro women were employed in 8 of the 13 foundries visited by Women's
Bureau representatives in the latter half of 1943. A few of the foundries
produced small as well as large castings. In the foundry itself, excluding

other departments, the 13 establishments surveyed reported the proportion of
women (race not stated) as 16 per cent (3,631) of the workers. In one mid-
western foundry 50 per cent of the women were Negro, and in one steel-castings
corporation such per cent was 67.

Women were found in occupations ranging from the shoveling and mixing of
sand and other unskilled types of labor to fairly skilled work in the fine
finishing of molds. A few foundries indicated that they might keep women
after the war in some of these jobs, individual foundries stating that women
may be retained in jobs at which they excelled. Included in the list of jobs
mentioned were clerical work, drafting, laboratory work, sand testing, operation of the heat-treat furnaces, and the making of small cores. Many foundries
were convinced that women were better than men at the making of small cores.
No large numbers of women, however, seemed likely to remain in foundry work
after the war, even if they wished to do so. In a predominantly male industry
they would have little opportunity to acquire the higher skills or advance up
the job-progression ladder. The heavy nature of much of the work in itself
would prevent that.

Arsenal of the United Nations--Detroit

The Bureau of the Census reports that the number of nonwhite women employed
in the Detroit-Willow Run Area rose from 14,451 in March 1940 to 46,750 in June
1944. Fewer than 30 Negro women were employed in war plants in this area in
July 1942, but by November 1943 about 14,000 were so employed. Early in 1944,
7 to 8 per cent of the workers in the entire State of Michigan were Negroes,
and it was estimated that almost 6 per cent of them were women.

Negro women in the Detroit area early in 1944 were working as machine
operators, assemblers, inspectors, stenographers, interviewers, sweepers,
material handlers, and at various other jobs in all types of work where women
can be used. The first woman hired as a detailer by a small engineering company was a Negro woman trained in engineering. A company that for some time
resisted taking Negro women employed two as inspectors in the middle of
December 1943; a few months later it had 47 Negro women inspectors and machine
operators.

In one Detroit company Negro women made up 10 to 12 per cent of the 1,000
women employed. Another that used a large number of women had about 25 to 30
per cent Negro women; they were in every department and worked at almost every
skill. In this company, management and the union backed the rights of its
Negro workers--men and women--for advancement on a basis of seniority and
skill.

A foundry that employed some 250 women had about 12 per cent Negro women.
Women applicants were interviewed and hired on a basis of qualifications
and ability to adjust to other workers without regard to creed or color.

Though a company had been violating War Manpower Commission regulations
on discriminatory newspaper advertising, it was persuaded to withdraw the
advertisement and cooperate with the WMC and the union in introducing Negro
women workers. As a result, in 1944 the proportions of Negro women in this
company's two plants were 20 per cent and 35 per cent.

A company that had hired about 1,500 Negro women reported that they made
up from 8 to approximately 25 per cent of the women in its various plants.
Another company opened certain departments to women in one of its plants. At
the beginning it hired one Negro in every two women employed. In 1944, of
approximately 8,000 women in this plant, around 75 per cent were Negro, and
the company was pleased with their production performance.

Essential Civilian Industries

Service Jobs

The foregoing pages report a few of the recorded instances typical of
great numbers of Negro women who with loyalty and skill have forwarded the
massive war production program of their country. Even at its maximum, however,
that record would register but a small share of the support coming to the war
economy through the labor of Negro women workers. Customary work positions
and previous experience easily account for their presence in great numbers in

essential civilian jobs in laundry, food, and restaurant establishments, in
hotels and lodging houses, and in other service industries. Doubtless many
of the women so employed do not even realize that they are doing war work,
work which affects directly the country's war production.

Said the president of a large west coast aircraft corporation late in
1943: *We think every worker we can place in a laundry is worth three new
workers in our own plants.* A company survey had revealed that in these plants
most absenteeism was caused not by hangovers but by a lack of such community
services as laundries and restaurants. Bomber production was being affected
because workers in these plants could not get their washing done, nor buy their
meals in restaurants. "The result was," said the president, "that we had to
start an advertising campaign to urge unemployed people to take jobs in
laundries and restaurants so our own people could stay on their jobs."

Canneries

Large numbers of Negro women were working in New Jersey and New York
canneries visited by Women's Bureau representatives in the summer and fall of
1943. Much work in the fields also was being done by them. Products handled
by the canneries ranged from soup to coffee and from baby food to army rations.

Cannery labor was secured from many sources--housewives, students, soldiers,
sailors, migratory workers taken north in trucks from Florida, Kentucky, Tennessee, West Virginia, and other Southern States in numbers far exceeding
those of previous years, Jamaicans and Bahamians. Women were used in a wide
range of jobs in the preparation of fruits and vegetables. Their jobs included the more usual ones of sorting, peeling, trimming, feeding machines,
on the can line as well as jobs new to women in those particular plants; jobs
involving the control of retorts and of pulping, extracting, evaporating, and
scalding equipment. Some women were doing heavy labor such as unloading cars,
handling cases weighing from 15 to 42 pounds, handling bushel baskets filled
with produce. Others were employed as general laborers feeding cans, salvag-
ing cans, shaking sacks, and as conveyor and belt attendants. As maintenance
and miscellaneous workers women were employed as janitors, elevator operators,
truckers, directors of shed and yard traffic, and to clean and grease machines.

Housing provided for migratory workers ranged from tent colonies to a
trailer camp and a converted summer hotel. In three of the camps in which
Negro families were living in tents it was stated that new housing had been
planned for them and was to be built by the Federal Public Housing Authority.
Nearly 150 Negro women were living in the barracks built originally for a CCC
camp. At a Farm Security Administration camp, 100 Negro families were living
in tents but gradually were being provided with other accommodations. At
another camp occupied by Negro families, the housing consisted of a combination
of frame houses built during World War I, of new prefabricated houses, and of
tents. One company built a one-story dormitory on cannery property for 250
women, both white and Negro.

Transportation

Filling jobs from "baggage smasher" to trackworker, Negro women railroad
employees have done their share to keep the Nation's war wheels turning. The
work of these women is invaluable, since the railroads are one of the country's
major war arteries, transporting the armed forces and carrying to them food,
clothing, and weapons, and at the same time supplying civilians with the essentials of everyday living. Negro women have filled a variety of jobs, ranging
from the unskilled, such as cleaning and janitor work, to the semiskilled. A
few have held highly skilled jobs. Neither Negro nor white women, however,
have found their way as yet into many skilled jobs in transportation, which
long has been considered a man's industry.

A railroad survey made by Women's Bureau representatives revealed that
one large railroad system employed over 4,500 Negro women in 1943; in fact,
Negroes made up 21 per cent of all women employed by this road. The largest
groups worked as section and extra gang men (1,138); laborers (1,019); coach
cleaners (967); and callers, loaders, and truckers (546). This railroad was
also employing Negro women as dining-car waitresses and as coach-lunch waitresses. A Negro woman was head waitress on one of the diners. Other Negro

women worked in the railroad's commissary kitchen and as station elevator
operators. A Negro woman was forewoman of a gang of 38 coach cleaners at one
of the yards.
    The Bureau found 400 Negro women working for one western railroad system,
making up over 13 per cent of the total of their sex employed. The largest
groups of these women were general laborers (148), section and extra gang men
(114), and coach cleaners (83). Another western railroad had 48 Negro women as
coach cleaners in one of its yards.
    One of the most unusual railroad jobs for a woman was held by a Negro
woman in Georgia. Probably the first woman train announcer in the United
States, she started her railroad career 25 years ago by doing odd jobs, icing
and watering the trains, cleaning up the station's carpenter shop. Her job as
caller started accidentally when the stationmaster asked her not to let anyone
miss a train. She got copies of all schedules and began to memorize them.
Today her voice is a station essential.
    Various street-transportation companies have hired Negro women as car and
bus cleaners and as helpers in shops. In several large municipalities they
have acted as car or bus operators and conductors. For example, New York
City's first woman streetcar operator was a Negro woman.
    The intercity bus industry has employed Negro women in various sections
of the country, chiefly as cleaners and maids. One company employed Negro
women at filling stations, servicing trucks. This company not only states
that their work has been satisfactory, but stresses their stability and says
they have presented no special problem in absenteeism or labor turn-over.
    The inland waterways, including the Great Lakes, have employed Negro
women as cooks, waitresses, maids, and stewardesses. A few women have done
overhaul and repair work for the air lines.

In the Line of Duty

    In the performance of their work many Negro women achieve unusual in-
dividual distinction. An outstanding example of such a woman is an Arkansas
arsenal worker. A munitions laborer in the production division, she twice
rescued fellow workers from burning to death when fire broke out in the plant's
incendiary section. For this heroism she became the first woman to receive
War Department's highest civilian award for exceptional service. The Award
of Emblem for Exceptional Civilian Service, the civilian equivalent of the
Distinguished Service Medal, was presented to her. The citation accompanying
the award praised her for "exceptional conduct in performance of outstanding
service beyond the call of duty."
    Among the Negro women who have shown exceptional skill in their war-plant
jobs is a worker who became champion arc welder and one of two winners in the
Negro Freedom Rally's competition for "Miss Negro Victory Worker of 1944."
One of seven Negro girls in a New York war plant, she admits it was no easy
task to surpass her fellow workers and thereby win the national merit award
that was given her and the co-winner, a Negro girl from Detroit. After the
presentation of the award in Madison Square Garden, both girls were taken to
New York City Hall to receive Mayor LaGuardia's congratulations.
    In speaking of her award, the champion arc welder said: "When you
work in a war plant--and maybe this is my own personal feeling--you talk very
little while you work but you do a lot of thinking. And with the roar of
machinery you sort of get a message which seems to say to you that this job must
be well done, because the stake in getting it out is perhaps the life of some
boy fighting on the beachheads. That's what I keep thinking."
    Also in the "champ" class are two Negro women riveters, who set a record
of 104 rivets in 120 seconds. Workers in a west coast aircraft plant, these
women were giving more than full measure of their strength and skill. They
worked as a team on bomb-bay doors for the PV-1 Ventura bomber, among the
first American planes consistently to bomb the Japanese homeland of Paramo-
shiri, northernmost bastion of the Nippon home defenses.
    Among the Negro women workers serving in leadership positions in their
unions was an Illinois gun-plant employee who was elected shop steward early
in the war by a department composed of 5 Negro women and 90 white women. In
a New York plant making cloth and leather war goods, 6 of the 14 union shop
chairladies were Negro. They were elected by the 1,000 men and women members,
half of whom were white and half Negro. Another Negro woman early in 1945

was the only woman on the general executive board of a union of transport and service workers, and president of the local to which she belonged. A Negro woman, educational director of a local union of garment workers, was one of the four representatives of American women workers to visit Great Britain early in 1945 in an exchange designed to bring about a better understanding between the two countries. The four women were selected by their respective unions and arrangements for their trip were made by the Office of Labor Production of the War Production Board and the Office of War Information.

Recognition came to another Negro woman war worker when she entered a national magazine contest on "What My Job Means to Me" and won first place plus a $50 war bond. In her essay she said in part:

"I am an inspector in a war plant. For 8 hours a day, 6 days a week, I stand in line with 5 other girls performing a routine operation that is part of our production schedule. We inspect wooden boxes that are to hold various kinds of munitions, and that range in size from 8 inches to 6 feet. When we approve them they are ready to be packed with shells, bombs, fuses, parachutes, and other headaches for Hitler and Hirohito. Did I say my job isn't exciting or complicated? I take that back. It may be a simple matter to inspect one box or a dozen, but it's different when you are handling them by the hundreds. The 6 of us in my crew sometimes inspect as many as fourteen or fifteen hundred boxes during one shift. That means 250 apiece—an average of one every 2 minutes, regardless of size.

"Of course the work is hard and sometimes dangerous, but Victory in this war isn't going to come the easy way. . . ."

Women in Uniform

Negro nurses, 1944

By 1944 the number of graduate Negro nurses was estimated at 8,000. Besides those serving in such official public health agencies as the American Red Cross and the Army Nurse Corps, Negro nurses were employed by the War Food Administration and the Veterans' Administration. Three hundred Negro nurses were in the Army Nurse Corps, some of whom went overseas. In March 1945 the first Negro nurse was commissioned by the Navy Reserve Nurse Corps.

United States Cadet Nurse Corps

In June 1943 the acute military and civilian need for nurses was responsible for a significant forward step in nursing education which has greatly aided Negro women seeking such training. This was the passage of the Bolton Act, establishing a United States Cadet Nurse Corps, which operates under the Public Health Service.

Under the provisions of this act, Federal aid is made available for students to take an accelerated nursing course ranging from 24 to 30 months. Federal funds may be used for maintenance for the first 9 months for all students who join the Cadet Nurse Corps. During this period students are known as precadet nurses and are given concentrated instruction and supervision. The act also provides scholarships and a monthly allowance for all students of the Corps. Scholarships cover tuition and all other fees charged by the school and include the cost of books and the school uniform.

In return for advantages received through the Corps, Cadet Nurses must promise that, health permitting, they will remain in essential nursing for the duration of the war. The choice of which essential service is theirs. They are not required to pledge themselves to military service. Almost 2,000 young Negro women have joined the Cadet Nurse Corps. They represent all but about 600 of the total number enrolled in all schools of nursing admitting Negroes. Of these student nurses, 1,600 are studying in 20 all-Negro schools; the rest are enrolled in schools having both white and Negro students. At the end of one year of the Corps' existence, it was reported that 33 schools of nursing of a possible 55 that admit Negro students have qualified under the Federal program. Five collegiate schools are operating now to prepare young Negro women for administrative, supervisory, and educational positions in the nursing field.

The effect of Federal aid on Negro nursing enrollments is clearly indicated at Freedman's Hospital in Washington, D.C. Freedman's, a Negro school of nursing, had an enrollment of 77 student nurses in 1939 and 78 in 1942, but in 1943, the year the Bolton Act was passed, the enrollment went to 116 and in 1944 jumped to 166.

Directors of schools of nursing admitting Negroes see the Corps as accomplishing a twofold service: it is enabling young women who finish high school to enter a professional field, and it is enabling schools of nursing to set higher scholastic standards.

Another progressive step was that taken by Sydenham Hospital in New York City when it announced in December 1943 that it would admit any qualified Negro into the ranks of its internes, resident physicians, surgeons, and nurses, and that Negroes also would be represented on its board of trustees. Thus, Sydenham has become the first voluntary hospital in the United States to function on a completely interracial basis. The reorganization of the hospital was carried through by an interracial committee organized by the New York Urban League. Among those commenting favorably on Sydenham's action was the Medical Society of the County of New York, which passed a resolution urging the acceptance of a similar policy by all voluntary hospitals.

Women's Army Corps

Of the first 436 to become officers in the WAAC (Now WAC), 36 were Negroes. By January 1945 there were 120 Negro officers and 3,900 enlisted Negro WACS. In the course of their service, many WACS are being given new training. In some cases this covers work not previously done by women. Negro WACS are competently filling jobs ranging from pharmacist to graphotype-machine operator.

"I just had to sell my share in the drug store and get into a uniform before I could feel right, said the only Negro WAC on duty at the Station Hospital at Fort Dix, N.J., who qualifies for her job as a pharmacist. Now a sergeant, in civilian life she was co-owner for 4 years of a city drug store and secretary of a druggists' association.

Thousands of letters and parcels, incorrectly addressed, never would reach the soldiers for whom they are intended if it were not for the job Negro WACS are doing in the post office at Camp Breckinridge, Ky. These "detectives" of the post locator department deal with wrong spelling, incomplete addresses, poor handwriting, and whatever else comes up to interfere with speedy delivery of soldiers' mail.

Using a spray gun to paint names, numbers, and insignia on various types of Army vehicles is one of the jobs of a Negro sergeant and a private serving in the Ordnance branch at the Automotive General Maintenance Shop at Camp Breckinridge. Other Negro WACS in this camp are assigned such jobs as cleaning and inspecting spark plugs for Army motor vehicles, painting jeeps, staff cars, and trucks. One Negro WAC operates a graphotype machine to produce the metal identification plates, commonly referred to as "dog tags."

Servicing trucks is the job of a Negro WAC at Fort Huachuca, Ariz. Another Negro WAC operated a mimeograph machine at the station hospital, while other WACS at Fort Huachuca have served in such varied capacities as switchboard operator, office worker, cook. The first Negro WAC unit to be sent overseas arrived in England in February 1945. It is serving as a postal battalion for the European theater. A total of 24 officers and 677 enlisted women are in the unit.

Women's Naval Reserve

On October 19, 1944, the Navy Department announced that Negro women would be accepted in the Women's Reserve, U.S. Naval Reserve. The Navy's statement is quoted here:

The President today approved a plan submitted by the Navy Department providing for the acceptance of Negro women in the Women's Reserve of the Navy. The plan calls for the immediate commissioning of a limited number of especially qualified Negro women to serve as administrative officers. They will assist in the subsequent planning and supervision of the program for Negro women which will be administered as an integral part of the Women's Reserve. Enlistment of Negro women will be undertaken as soon as these plans have been completed . . . Officer candidates and enlisted women will be trained at existing schools for the training of WAVES. The number to be enlisted will be determined by the needs of the service.

American Red Cross

Some 200 Negroes, the majority of them women, were in Red Cross overseas work late in 1944. They were in every theater of war--in Great Britain, Italy, France, North Africa, South Pacific, Australia, and the India-Burma-China theater. Bending their varied talents toward the single vital objective of backing up America's fighting men, these women have shelved their peacetime activities for the duration. They were appointed as assistant club directors, staff assistants, assistant program directors, and personal-service directors at overseas military stations.

In this country by the middle of 1944 the Home Service Division of the Red Cross was employing Negro women as case workers and in clerical jobs in a great many cities of the United States. In Chicago alone more than 100 Negro women were so employed. Among the other cities where Negro women were on the Red Cross home-service pay rolls are Savannah, Birmingham, New Orleans, Dallas, St. Louis, Louisville, Columbus, Cleveland, Evansville, New York City, Brooklyn, and Washington. Negro women have worked in the Home Service Division both at the District of Columbia Chapter and at National Headquarters of the Red Cross, in the latter only since late in 1944. Some dozen were employed there as stenographers, and as junior and senior correspondents.

STATUS IN 1940 AND IN 1944

In 1940

Generally speaking, women who have jobs or who are looking for work must earn their own living or help in the support of their families. This is especially true of Negro women. The income of the Negro family is much lower than that of the white and the woman's earnings are very much needed. According to a study made by the National Resources Committee, the median income of white families in the rural South in 1935-36 was more than twice as high as that of Negro families, the median for white families being $1,100 and that for Negro families $480. In the urban South white incomes were three times as high, on the average, as Negro incomes; white families' incomes had a median of $1,570, while that for Negroes was $525. In 3 large north-central cities the median income of white families was almost 60 per cent higher than that of Negro families, the median for white families being $1,720 and that for Negro families $1,095.

In 1940 nearly 2 in every 5 Negro women, in contrast to 2 in every 8 white women, were in the labor force. A little over 1-1/2 million (1,542,273) Negro women, of a total of 4,785,233 Negro women 14 years old and over, were employed in 1940; 60,168 were on public emergency work and 178,521 were experienced workers seeking jobs.

Over a million Negro women, constituting 70 per cent of all Negro women employed in 1940, were in the service occupations, according to the census for that year. An enormous number of these women--about 918,000--were employed in private families, and some 98,000 were cooks, waitresses, and other such service workers elsewhere than in private homes. The remaining 60,000 workers in service trades were in miscellaneous personal-service occupations, such as beauticians (14,800), boarding-house and lodging-house keepers (13,600), charwomen and janitors (12,400), practical nurses (11,000), housekeepers and hostesses (3,000), and elevator operators (3,300).

Agriculture employed the next largest number of Negro women. About 245,000 were agricultural workers in 1940, of whom some 128,000 were unpaid family workers. Over 70,000 were paid farm laborers and foremen. More than 46,000 were farmers and farm managers.

Practically 66,000 Negro women were engaged in professional and semi-professional work, teachers accounting for 50,000 of this number. In addition, some 900 were college presidents, professors, and instructors, while 95 were artists and art teachers. The nearly 6,700 trained nurses and student nurses ranked next in this classification, and the 1,960 musicians and music teachers ranked third. Almost 1,700 were social and welfare workers. More than 120 were dentists, pharmacists, osteopaths, or veterinarians, and 129 were physicians and surgeons. Nearly 200 were actresses and over 100 were authors, editors, and reporters. Thirty-nine were lawyers and judges. Four hundred were librarians.

Practically 11,000 Negro women were proprietors, managers, and officials
in lines other than farming; more than 4,800 of these were in eating and
drinking places and more than 3,900 in other trade enterprises.

Sales and kindred workers in general numbered 7,600; agents, brokers, etc.,
accounted for 1,300, saleswomen 5,300, and canvassers, news venders, and the
like the remaining 1,000 and more.

Clerical and kindred workers were an important group, numbering more than
13,000. Stenographers, typists, and secretaries aggregated 4,100; bookkeepers,
accountants, and cashiers 2,100; and clerks not specified 6,500. Only 92 were
reported as operators of office machines, and only 267 were telephone and
telegraph operators.

Operatives and kindred workers numbered more than 96,000 of the Negro
women reported. Not far from 36,000 were in manufacturing, the chief groups
being 11,300 in apparel and other fabricated textile products, 11,000 in
tobacco manufactures, and 5,600 in food and related products. About 7,200
were reported as in nonmanufacturing industries and services. Also in the
operatives' total were the 11,300 dressmakers and seamstresses not in factories,
the 39,300 laundry operatives not in private families, and 2,800 other women.

Government service employed approximately 8,300 Negro women. Of this
number, not far from 1,000 were in the Postal Service; 218 were in national
defense, and over 7,000 were classified on as "Government."

Changes, 1940 to 1944

The employment of Negroes in civilian jobs increased by almost a million
between April 1940 and April 1944. Six hundred thousand of this increase was
in women's employment. During this 4-year period the employment of Negro women
rose from 1.5 million to 2.1 million. Their employment increased by 40 per cent,
in contrast to a 51 per cent gain for white women.

	Negro		White	
	1940	1944	1940	1944
Per cent employed women were of--				
All women of their racial group 14 and over...	32.2	40.2	21.0	30.8
All employed women 14 and over	13.8	12.5	85.9	87.5
All employed persons of their racial group				
14 and over.................................	34.4	39.6	23.6	32.1
All employed persons 14 and over.............	3.4	4.1	21.2	28.8

Most dominant changes in Negro employment during the 4 years were a marked
movement from the farms to the factories, especially to those making war
munitions, and a substantial amount of upgrading, but there was little change
in the proportions occupied in unskilled jobs.

Slightly over 7 in every 10 employed Negro women were in some service
activity in April 1940. The great majority of these (918,000) were domestic
employees. After 4 years there was only a slight decrease in the proportion
in the services, though a significant internal shift had taken place. While
the proportion of domestic employees showed a marked decrease, those occupied
in such personal services as beautician, cook, waitress, etc., showed a
corresponding increase. The actual number of Negro domestic workers increased
slightly between 1940 and 1944, the number in these occupations rising by
about 50,000, but this addition was not sufficient to offset the decline of
400,000 among white domestic employees.

As before stated, for both Negro women and men the most definite occupational shift was from the farm to the factory. The proportion of Negro
women on farms was cut in half in the 4 years. In April 1940, 16 per cent
of all Negro women in the labor force were on the farms; 4 years later only
8 per cent remained, and the number employed on farms had decreased by about
30 per cent.

While the total number of Negro women employed had increased by about a
third, the number employed as craftsmen and foremen and as factory operatives
almost quadrupled.

For both Negro women and men the greatest gain in employment opportunities
came in skilled and semiskilled factory operations which few had performed
before the war. Consequently, for a great many Negro workers this is the first
opportunity to demonstrate their ability to perform basic factory operations in

such capacities. Negro women's employment increased not only in the munitions
factories but in food, clothing, textiles, leather, and all other manufacturing.
The greatest increase was in the metals, chemicals, and rubber group. Fewer
than 3,000 Negro women were employed in this group in April 1940; 4 years later
50 times as many were so employed.

In the other major occupational groups the percentage increases were
large, but the numbers involved were not sufficient to have much effect on the
occupational distribution of Negro women. The number working as proprietors,
managers, or officials trebled. Those working as saleswomen almost doubled,
while those engaged as clerical workers rose to a number five times as great
as before.

The proportion of Negro women in the professional and semiprofessional
fields decreased slightly, but there was a small increase in numbers.

There was a notable increase in Negro employment in Government service
(Federal, State, county, municipal). In April 1944 about 200,000 Negroes
were employed in this field in contrast to fewer than 60,000 in the same month
of 1940.

The 1940 major occupation groups are not comparable with those for preceding decades because of the changes in occupational classifications. However, there has been developed a classification on the basis of social-economic
groups, which permits tracing broad occupational levels. Social-economic
groupings are not the same as the major occupation groups used elsewhere in
this report. Though titles may show similarity, for a specific social-economic
group some occupations are omitted and others added, as compared with the
occupation group it resembles. The 1940 data include the employed, the experienced seeking work, and those on public emergency work; the distribution
in the various social-economic groups has been estimated. For the decades
before 1940, figures are for "gainful workers."

Negro Women War Workers, Bulletin 205 (Washington, D.C.: Women's Bureau,
U.S. Department of Labor, 1945), pp. 1-19.

24. WOMEN IN WAR INDUSTRIES BREAK ALL PRECEDENT
IN LEARNING INTRICATE JOBS

Before the War, the Sign "Men Only" Was Hung on Many Jobs . . .
Now the Women of the Nation Have Taken Down That Sign

WASHINGTON--Mrs. Rosalie Ivy, an energetic young woman, works in mud, but
she's neither a pottery maker nor a maker of mud pies. She is a "Pan Man" in
a giant Gary, Ind., steel mill, and mixes a special mud used to seal the
casting hole through which molten iron flows from a blast furnace. In the
entire steel industry few women, or men either, are "Pan Men," for this is a
rare job.

Mrs. Ivy belongs to that growing list of Negro women war workers who have
replaced men in jobs for the first time. The Women's Bureau of the U.S.
Department of Labor recently compiled a list of some of the odd jobs held by
such women.

Among those listed in this group is Evelyn Samuels, who went to work at
the Brooklyn Navy Yard last year when they hired women mechanics for the first
time in 141 years. In the Civil Service examinations given for Navy Yard jobs
Miss Samuels received 99, the highest rating of any of the 6,000 women tested.
Doris Wilson, Hunter college student and Brooklyn resident, was another high
ranking applicant in the same examination. Both Miss Samuels and Miss Wilson
were assigned to the instrument division, where binoculars, telescopes and
range finders are reconditioned.

First Woman Chipper

Sarah T. Francis, formerly a presser in a laundry, is not only the first
woman in the country to be employed as chipper and caulker, but the first in
the history of shipbuilding. She is working at the Todd Shipyards in Hoboken,
New Jersey.

Mrs. Susie T. Glover of Georgia holds a unique job for a woman. She was probably the first woman train announcer in the United States. Mrs. Glover started her railroad career 25 years ago doing odd jobs, icing and watering the train, cleaning up the station's carpenter shop, etc. Her job as caller started accidentally when the stationmaster asked her not to let anybody miss a train. She got copies of all schedules and began memorizing them. Today her voice is part of the essential station noises.

At the Bartlett-Hayward plant in Baltimore, Md., a woman runs a steel-burning machine. It is an intricate machine, 25 feet long and 6 feet high, which cuts huge pieces of steel for use in six different kinds of anti-air-craft guns. The acetylene torches which cut two parts at a time must be set and guided with precision. The operation must have a dozen or more controls set exactly right.

One of the most unusual jobs held by a colored woman in war industries is that assigned to Ethel Maxwell Williams, of St. Paul, Minn. Mrs. Williams is assistant to Cecil E. Newman, director of Negro personnel for the Twin Cities Ordnance plant at New Brighton, Minn. Her work includes labor relations, personnel adjustment, race relations and related spheres of administrative activity. Last spring this plant was employing more than 17,000 workers, 700 of whom were colored. They work at a variety of jobs and include supervisors, stenographers, machine operators, nurses, photograph technicians, draftsmen, machine adjustors, janitors and matrons.

"MEN ONLY" PRE-WAR THEME

The pre-war theme song of the aircraft industry was "men only." Shortly before Pearl Harbor some 4,000 women were employed in the entire aircraft industry, and most of them were in sewing jobs. By September of 1943, however, the tune had changed; more than 240,000 women were at work in the industry in air frame, engine, and propeller plants. Another 4,000 were employed on gliders.

Negro women are now to be found in every one of the key war industries. They are sharing, sometimes in small measure, the wartime advances being made by all women. Today, because of the critical lack of manpower, age-old pre-judices are beginning to crumble. Into the entering wedge have gone women of many nationalities.

The need for women war workers is still acute, and there is still the need and opportunity for women in civilian jobs to transfer to war work.

Pittsburgh Courier, February 8, 1944.

25. MONTY WARD BIAS BARED

Chicago, Mar. 4--Montgomery Ward, billion dollar mail order house, is being accused of "flagrant discrimination against minority groups" by Local 20, United Retail, Wholesale & Dept. Store Employees. The charge was made to the Chicago Council on Religious and Racial Equality.

"The only jobs open to Negroes in the Chicago properties of Montgomery Ward," declares the memorandum, "are those of porter, bus boy, bus girl, elevator operator and matron. The bulk of mail order house, retail store and warehouse jobs are therefore closed to Negro workers.

"Although Ward's runs large advertisements in the 'Help Wanted' sections of the newspapers every day, scores of Negroes have been turned away from the employment office and refused employment."

CIO News, March 6, 1944.

THE MARCH ON WASHINGTON MOVEMENT

26. WHY SHOULD WE MARCH?

by A. Philip Randolph

Though I have found no Negroes who want to see the United Nations lose
this war, I have found many who, before the war ends, want to see the stuffing
knocked out of white supremacy and of empire over subject peoples. American
Negroes, involved as we are in the general issues of the conflict, are confronted not with a choice but with the challenge both to win democracy for
ourselves at home and to help win the war for democracy the world over.

There is no escape from the horns of this dilemma. There ought not to be
escape. For if the war for democracy is not won abroad, the fight for democracy cannot be won at home. If this war cannot be won for the white peoples,
it will not be won for the darker races.

Conversely, if freedom and equality are not vouchsafed the peoples of
color, the war for democracy will not be won. Unless this double-barreled
thesis is accepted and applied, the darker races will never wholeheartedly fight
for the victory of the United Nations. That is why those familiar with the
thinking of the American Negro have sensed his lack of enthusiasm, whether
among the educated or uneducated, rich or poor, professional or non-professional,
religious or secular, rural or urban, north, south, east or west.

That is why questions are being raised by Negroes in church, labor union
and fraternal society; in poolroom, barbership, schoolroom, hospital, hairdressing parlor; on college campus, railroad, and bus. One can hear such
questions asked as these: What have Negroes to fight for? What's the
difference between Hitler and that "cracker" Talmadge of Georgia? Why has a
man got to be Jim-Crowed to die for democracy? If you haven't got democracy
yourself, how can you carry it to somebody else?[103]

What are the reasons for this state of mind? The answer is: discrimination,
segregation, Jim Crow. Witness the navy, the army, the air corps; and also
government services at Washington. In many parts of the South, Negroes in Uncle
Sam's uniform are being put upon, mobbed, sometimes even shot down by civilian
and military police, and on occasion lynched. Vested political interests in
race prejudice are so deeply entrenched that to them winning the war against
Hitler is secondary to preventing Negroes from winning democracy for themselves.
This is worth many divisions to Hitler and Hirohito. While labor, business,
and farm are subjected to ceilings and floors and not allowed to carry on as
usual, these interests trade in the dangerous business of race hate as usual.

When the defense program began and billions of the taxpayers' money were
appropriated for guns, ships, tanks and bombs, Negroes presented themselves
for work only to be given the cold shoulder. North as well as South, and
despite their qualifications, Negroes were denied skilled employment. Not
until their wrath and indignation took the form of a proposed protest march on
Washington, scheduled for July 1, 1941, did things begin to move in the form
of defense jobs for Negroes. The march was postponed by the timely issuance
(June 25, 1941) of the famous Executive Order No. 8802 by President Roosevelt.
But this order and the President's Committee on Fair Employment Practice,
established thereunder, have as yet only scratched the surface by way of
eliminating discriminations on account of race or color in war industry. Both
management and labor unions in too many places and in too many ways are still
drawing the color line.

It is to meet this situation squarely with direct action that the March
on Washington Movement launched its present program of protest mass meetings.
Twenty thousand were in attendance at Madison Square Garden, June 16; sixteen
thousand in the Coliseum in Chicago, June 26; nine thousand in the City
Auditorium of St. Louis, August 14. Meetings of such magnitude were unprecedented among Negroes. The vast throngs were drawn from all walks and levels
of Negro life--businessmen, teachers, laundry workers, Pullman porters, waiters,

and red caps; preachers, crapshooters, and social workers; jitterbugs, and
Ph.D.'s. They came and sat in silence, thinking, applauding only when they
considered the truth was told, when they felt strongly that something was
going to be done about it.

The March on Washington Movement is essentially a movement of the people.
It is all Negro and pro-Negro, but not for that reason anti-white or anti-
semitic, or anti-Catholic, or anti-foreign, or anti-labor. Its major weapon
is the non-violent demonstration of Negro mass power. Negro leadership has
united back of its drive for jobs and justice. "Whether Negroes should march
on Washington, and if so, when?" will be the focus of a forthcoming national
conference. For the plan of a protest march has not been abandoned. Its
purpose would be to demonstrate that American Negroes are in deadly earnest,
and all out for their full rights. No power on earth can cause them today to
abandon their fight to wipe out every vestige of second class citizenship and
the dual standards that plague them.

A community is democratic only when the humblest and weakest person can
enjoy the highest civil, economic, and social rights that the biggest and most
powerful possess. To trample on these rights of both Negroes and poor whites
is such a commonplace in the South that it takes readily to anti-social, anti-
labor, anti-Semitic and anti-Catholic propaganda. It was because of laxness
in enforcing the Weimar constitution in republican Germany that Nazism made
headway. Oppression of the Negroes in the United States, like suppression of
the Jews in Germany, may open the way for a fascist dictatorship.

By fighting for their rights now, American Negroes are helping to make
America a moral and spiritual arsenal of democracy. Their fight against the
poll tax, against lynch law, segregation, and Jim Crow, their fight for economic, political, and social equality, thus becomes part of the global war for
freedom.

PROGRAM OF THE MARCH ON WASHINGTON MOVEMENT

1. We demand, in the interest of national unity, the abrogation of every
law which makes a distinction in treatment between citizens based on religion,
creed, color, or national origin. This means an end to Jim Crow in education,
in housing, in transportation and in every other social, economic, and political
privilege; and especially, we demand, in the capital of the nation, an end to
all segregation in public places and in public institutions.
2. We demand legislation to enforce the Fifth and Fourteenth Amendments
guaranteeing that no person shall be deprived of life, liberty or property
without due process of law, so that the full weight of the national government
may be used for the protection of life and thereby may end the disgrace of
lynching.
3. We demand the enforcement of the Fourteenth and Fifteenth Amendments
and the enactment of the Pepper Poll Tax bill so that all barriers in the
exercise of the suffrage are eliminated. [104]
4. We demand the abolition of segregation and discrimination in the army,
navy, marine corps, air corps, and all other branches of national defense.
5. We demand an end to discrimination in jobs and job training. Further,
we demand that the F.E.P.C. be made a permanent administrative agency of the
U.S. Government and that it be given power to enforce its decisions based on
its findings.
6. We demand that federal funds be withheld from any agency which
practices discrimination in the use of such funds.
7. We demand colored and minority group representation on all administrative agencies so that these groups may have recognition of their democratic
right to participate in formulating policies.
8. We demand representation for the colored and minority racial groups
on all missions, political and technical, which will be sent to the peace
conference so that the interests of all people everywhere may be fully recognized and justly provided for in the post-war settlement.

Survey Graphic, 31 (November, 1942): 488-89.

27. MEMO TO ALL N.A.A.C.P. BRANCHES, MAY 12, 1941

An eloquent appeal to Negro America to march on the Nation's capital
for jobs and an equal share in national defense work was issued to the press
of the nation last week. Fifty thousand are expected to participate.

The March on Washington is scheduled for July 1st, and is one of the most
militant actions ever planned by Negroes of this country and should be the
largest mass movement in their history. It is vitally important to the future
well-being of the race that the March be a success.

The call for marchers to organize was signed by Walter White, Reverend
William Lloyd Imes of St. James Presbyterian Church, N.Y.; Lester Granger of
the National Urban League, Frank Crosswaith, labor leader; Dr. Rayford Logan,
Howard University professor; Henry K. Craft, head of the Harlem Y.M.C.A;
Richard Parrish, youth group leader; Layle Lane, vice-president of the
Brotherhood of Sleeping Car Porters, who conceived the idea.[105]

The Association stresses the importance of the cooperation of all Branches
with local March committees in organizing marchers, distributing March buttons,
which sell for ten cents, and disseminating publicity.

Find out if there is a local March committee in your community, and give
it the support of the entire membership. Further instructions and information
can be obtained from the local committee or from the office of the steering
committee, at 217 W. 125th Street, New York City, c/o Brotherhood of Sleeping
Car Porters. If there is no local March committee in your community, write
to the national committee at the above address, informing them of this fact.

The success of this March on Washington may mean a job for you and thousands of other colored Americans. The time to act is now!

National Association for the Advancement of Colored People Papers, Group 2,
Library of Congress.

28. CALL TO THE MARCH

July 1, 1941

We call upon you to fight for jobs in National Defense.

We call upon you to struggle for the integration of Negroes in the armed
forces, such as the Air Corps, Navy, Army and Marine Corps of the Nation.

We call upon you to demonstrate for the abolition of Jim-Crowism in all
Government departments and defense employment.

This is an hour of crisis. It is a crisis of democracy. It is a crisis
of minority groups. It is a crisis of Negro Americans.

What is this crisis?

To American Negroes, it is the denial of jobs in Government defense projects. It is racial discrimination in Government departments. It is widespread Jim-Crowism in the armed forces of the Nation.

While billions of the taxpayers' money are being spent for war weapons,
Negro workers are being turned away from the gates of factories, mines and
mills--being flatly told, "NOTHING DOING." Some employers refuse to give
Negroes jobs when they are without "union cards," and some unions refuse Negro
workers union cards when they are "without jobs."

What shall we do?

What a dilemma!

What a runaround!

What a disgrace!

What a blow below the belt!

'Though dark, doubtful and discouraging, all is not lost, all is not
hopeless. 'Though battered and bruised, we are not beaten, broken or bewildered.

Verily, the Negroes' deepest disappointments and direst defeats, their
tragic trials and outrageous oppressions in these dreadful days of destruction
and disaster to democracy and freedom, and the rights of minority peoples, and
the dignity and independence of the human spirit, is the Negroes' greatest

opportunity to rise to the highest heights of struggle for freedom and justice in Government, in industry, in labor unions, education, social service, religion and culture.

With faith and confidence of the Negro people in their own power for self-liberation, Negroes can break down the barriers of discrimination against employment in National Defense. Negroes can kill the deadly serpent of race hatred in the Army, Navy, Air and Marine Corps, and smash through to blast the Government, business and labor-union red tape to win the right to equal opportunity in vocational training and re-training in defense employment.

Most important and vital to all, Negroes, by the mobilization and coordination of their mass power, can cause PRESIDENT ROOSEVELT TO ISSUE AN EXECUTIVE ORDER ABOLISHING DISCRIMINATIONS IN ALL GOVERNMENT DEPARTMENTS, ARMY, NAVY, AIR CORPS AND NATIONAL DEFENSE JOBS.

Of course, the task is not easy. In very truth, it is big, tremendous and difficult.

It will cost money.

It will require sacrifice.

It will tax the Negroes' courage, determination and will to struggle. But we can, must and will triumph.

The Negroes' stake in national defense is big. It consists of jobs, thousands of jobs. It may represent millions, yes, hundreds of millions of dollars in wages. It consists of new industrial opportunities and hope. This is worth fighting for.

But to win our stakes, it will require an "all-out," bold and total effort and demonstration of colossal proportions.

Negroes can build a mammoth machine of mass action with a terrific and tremendous driving and striking power that can shatter and crush the evil fortress of race prejudice and hate, if they will only resolve to do so and never stop, until victory comes.

Dear fellow Negro Americans, be not dismayed in these terrible times. You possess power, great power. Our problem is to harness and hitch it up for action on the broadest, daring and most gigantic scale.

In this period of power politics, nothing counts but pressure, more pressure, and still more pressure, through the tactic and strategy of broad, organized, aggressive mass action behind the vital and important issues of the Negro. To this end, we propose that ten thousand NEGROES MARCH ON WASHINGTON FOR JOBS IN NATIONAL DEFENSE AND EQUAL INTEGRATION IN THE FIGHTING FORCES OF THE UNITED STATES.

An "all-out" thundering march on Washington, ending in a monster and huge demonstration at Lincoln's Monument will shake up white America.

It will shake up official Washington.

It will give encouragement to our white friends to fight all the harder by our side, with us, for our righteous cause.

It will gain respect for the Negro people.

It will create a new sense of self-respect among Negroes.

But what of national unity?

We believe in national unity which recognizes equal opportunity of black and white citizens to jobs in national defense and the armed forces, and in all other institutions and endeavors in America. We condemn all dictatorships, Fascist, Nazi and Communist. We are loyal, patriotic Americans, all.

But, if American democracy will not defend its defenders; if American democracy will not protect its protectors; if American democracy will not give jobs to its toilers because of race or color; if American democracy will not insure equality of opportunity, freedom and justice to its citizens, black and white, it is a hollow mockery and belies the principles for which it is supposed to stand.

To the hard, difficult and trying problem of securing equal participation in national defense, we summon all Negro Americans to march on Washington. We summon Negro Americans to form committees in various cities to recruit and register marchers and raise funds through the sale of buttons and other legitimate means for the expenses of marchers to Washington by buses, train, private automobiles, trucks, and on foot.

The Black Worker, May 1941.

29.
WAR DEMANDS NEW METHODS FOR SOLUTION OF THE NEGRO QUESTION

How shall we solve this problem of discrimination against one section of
our American people? Can we postpone the solution of this question until
after the war is over? Would it be correct for the Negro people to allow
themselves to be sidetracked from the war issue and concentrate only on their
own domestic problem?

The Negro people know the record of the Communist Party as the defender
of Negro rights. We Communists did not hesitate to organize and struggle for
the Scottsboro boys, for Angelo Herndon, WPA and relief during those depression years. The Communist Party need not profess its friendship for the Negro
people--it is a part of the Negro people, as well as of all Americans. That
is why we say frankly: today we cannot organize our demands in the same way
as in those former years.

We must find a solution to this problem within our national unity and
not outside of it. We can solve this problem only through unity of Negro
and white workers.

March on Arms Plant is Ill-Advised

We have received a copy of the leaflet issued by the St. Louis unit of
the March on Washington Committee, which calls for a march on the small arms
plant this Saturday, to protest against discrimination and firing of 150
Negro workers. While we fully agree with the demands expressed in the leaflet,
we cannot support the demonstration nor the method in which the committee is
proceeding to remedy the situation.

Here is the reason why we cannot support it:

1. Our country is involved in a just war against Hitler and his Axis
partners who are the enemy of the Negro people, just as much as of other
Americans. Therefore, we must seek solutions to our grievances in ways that
will not affect the war effort. Demonstration at the war plant certainly
is a most ill-advised procedure which, however well intended, might be turned
into a provocation against the best interests of both Negro and white workers.

2. The March is to include only Negro workers. This a cardinal mistake,
which can only play into the hands of the appeasers and enemies of our
country. The firing of 150 Negro workers is not the concern of the Negro
people alone, but the concern of all Americans--we must unite and not split
at this grave hour of our history.

3. We feel that the correct approach would be for the labor movement,
Negro and white, to undertake the fight through established channels and, if
that failed, a joint action of labor unions and Negro organizations would
strengthen unity and would guarantee victory.

4. We cannot agree with the slogan, "Winning Democracy for the Negro
is Winning the War for Democracy." This is a misleading slogan which can
only serve to divide and divert. A proper slogan would be "Winning victory
over Hitler's Axis includes winning democracy for the Negro."

End Discrimination Through United Effort
of the Labor Movement, Negro and White

Instead of sectional movements, which can only tend to weaken our national unity, we firmly believe that these just grievances of the Negro people can
be solved through the united effort of the Negro and white workers. We propose the following immediate action:

1. Demand that Mayor Becker immediately convene a Conference of
Employers, Labor and Negro Representatives to end discrimination against the
Negro citizens.

2. Immediate calling of a public hearing at which to take testimonials
of all cases of discrimination and name employers and companies which have
failed to give proper employment to the Negro workers. Exposure at these
hearings of those officials and leaders and organizations which continue to
violate President Roosevelt's executive order, and demanding that the government take over the plant which still continues to Pursue Anti-Government
policies.

3. Immediate establishment of Joint Negro and White Fair Employment
Committee in the State and in the City.

4. Immediate Federal Investigation of the charges of discrimination at
Small Arms, TNT, and other plants having government contracts.

FOR UNITY OF ALL AMERICANS, NEGRO AND WHITE.

FOR FULL ENFORCEMENT OF PRESIDENT ROOSEVELT'S EXECUTIVE ORDER AGAINST
DISCRIMINATION.

FOR NATIONAL UNITY AND VICTORY OVER HITLER'S AXIS IN 1942.

> State Committee, Communist Party of
> Missouri
> 1041 North Grand

Flier in possession of the editors.

30. NATIONAL MARCH ON WASHINGTON MOVEMENT POLICIES AND DIRECTIVES

Local Units--March On Washington Movement

Part I

The March On Washington Movement - That it is.

The Movement originated out of the protests, grievances and injustices
that beset the Negro people and the mass cry for deliverance. It grew out of
a threatened March On Washington called by A. Philip Randolph, its founder
and philosopher, to break down discrimination in the army, navy and air corp,
in the government and in defense industries, and which resulted in the establishment of the Fair Employment Practice Committee - Executive Order #8802.
A series of mass meetings and conferences and the resolutions growing
out of them indicated the need for a type of permanent organization that would
have as its objective the following:

1. To develop mass power through a mass organization with an active
   program, aggressive, bold and challenging in spirit but non-violent
   in character.

2. To crystallize the mass consciousness of grievances and injustices
   against Negroes and project it into a Cause for which Negroes themselves will gladly and willingly suffer and sacrifice.

3. To re-educate white America on the question of equality for Negroes.

4. To enlist the support of liberal and Christian white America in
   an all-out struggle for unadulterated democracy at home as well as
   abroad.

5. To operate by means of mass maneuvers and demonstrations.

The March On Washington Movement is All-Negro but not Anti-White nor
Anti-American.

Part II

Now the Movement is organized.

Our Movement should be well knit together. It must have moral and
spiritual vision, understanding and wisdom. We advise against rash judgment
and misguided action. Our aim is to think through on issues and plan and
discipline well our action so that none of our energies are dissipated

or lost. We take no responsibility for provocateurs either locally or nationally. Persons acting in our name must be organized and disciplined by duly
constituted authorities recognized by our National Office to execute policies.
    Our job is actually to organize millions of Negroes and build them into
block systems with captains so that they may be summoned to action over night
and thrown into non-violent physical motion. Our forces must be marshalled
with Block Captains to provide immediate and constant contact. Our Block
Captains must hold periodic meetings for their blocks to develop initiative
and the capacity to make decisions and move in relation to directions from the
Central Organization of the Division and from the National Office.

Part III

The Job of the Division of Local Unit

    Our divisions must serve as Negro Mass Parliaments where the entire com-
munity may debate the day to day issues as police brutality, high rents, jobs
in public utilities, discrimination and segregation--Jim Crow laws and patterns,
utilization of Negro manpower in defense and in government and other questions
and make judgments and take action in the interest of the community.
    These divisions should hold meetings twice a month. In them every Negro
should be made to feel his importance as a factor in the liberation movement.
We must have every Negro realize his leadership ability, the educated and the
uneducated, the poor and the wealthy. In the March On Washington Movement the
highest is as low as the lowest and the lowest as high as the highest. Numbers
in mass formation is our key, directed of course by the collective intelligence
of the people.

The Education Program

    Our education program must be developed around the struggle of the Negro
masses. We must develop mass plans to secure mass registration of the people
for the primaries and elections. Through this program the masses can be given
a practical and pragmatic view of the mechanics and functioning of our government and the significance of mass political pressure.
    Plans should be mapped and strategy studied by the various divisions to
fight for Negro integration in the public utilities and safeguard and police
the Fair Employment Practices Committee. Workers Education should be carried
on to inform workers about the trade union and social legislation. Public
affairs education should be integrated in our bulletins and in our regular
meetings.
    Vigorous campaigns and giant public protest meetings should continue in
order to develop Cause Consciousness and to give moral and spiritual strength
to our Movement and the Negro masses.

The Mass Action Program

    The day-to-day exercise of our Civil Rights is a constant challenge.
Negroes have the moral obligation to demand the right to enjoy and make use
of their civil and political privileges. The fight to break down Jim Crow
barriers in every city should be carefully and paintakingly organized. By
fighting non-violently but directly for these civil rights the Negro masses
should be disciplined in struggle. Court battles may ensue but this will
give the Negro masses a sense of their importance and value as citizens and
as fighters in the Negro liberation movement and in the cause for democracy
as a whole.

Part IV

Division of Authority

    Until the May Conference and the proposed Constitution is amended and
adopted, central authority is vested in the National Director, who is our
philosopher and founder.
    The National Office has been temporarily established in the Hotel
Theresa Building, 2084 Seventh Avenue, New York City and Miss E. Pauline Myers

is the General Organizer of the Movement. Her term of office shall be for a term not longer than that of the appointing Director, but she may be reappointed by the continuing or succeeding Director.

Her duties are to supervise, direct and administer a program of membership on a national scale. She shall collaborate with National Officers and the National Committee. She shall develop policies and procedures, prepare standardized forms to be used in membership campaigns, plan, coordinate and execute membership campaigns on a national scale, establish and maintain a close working relationship with the Regional, State and Divisional Organizers, issuing to them from time to time as needs require directive procedures and policies relating to membership activities, prepare and submit to the National Director reports concerning the program of membership and progress in the accomplishment of this program.

Local units are members of State Organizations, which in turn are members of Regional Organizations. The Detroit Conference designates five geographical areas and the National Director has the power to appoint five Regional Directors. Each Regional Director has the power to appoint one Regional Organizer--the said organizer shall be responsible for the execution of policies and procedures and plans for membership as established by the National Executive Secretary so as to conform to a National pattern. She shall submit to the Regional Director and the National Executive Secretary periodic reports on the development and progress of membership within his region.

The State organizer shall have the authority of directing and coordinating the membership activities of the various divisions subject to his supervision; plan and conduct a program pointing toward the organization of new city divisions.

In city divisions employing Executive Secretaries this secretary shall serve as Division Organizer. The responsibility shall be to organize and develop by districts and by blocks the membership of the particular division; plot and lay out districts of not more than ten square blocks to which he may appoint and assign District organizers. Organize and advise the standing committees on Education techniques, mass action strategy, finance and membership activities. Act in an advisory capacity to district organizers in matters relating to organizational work. Allocate to district organizers literature and material for distribution among block organizers. See that block organizers hold regular meetings among themselves and within their blocks. He should submit regular reports to the division director or president and the State organizer on the progress of the division's activity.

Policies and directives governing local units will be handed down directly from the National office.

Part V

Relationship to Other organizations

The March on Washington Movement is not and is not intended to be a rival organization to any established organization already functioning to advance the interest of the Negro. It seeks only to demonstrate the techniques of militant mass pressure in the field of minority problems where other techniques have broken down.

The fundamental policy of the MOWM should be to cooperate with other agencies in a multiple attack on the problem. It should seek to advance overlapping of function and organization by seeking continuous discussion with other organizations to affect a division of labor and the best utilization of community organizational resources. For example, where established recognized agencies are handling a specific situation, like the NAACP and the Urban League, the MOWM should not seek to supercede their activities or techniques in any way which will adversely affect the ultimate solution of the common problem. Once other agencies seek support, the MOWM should then use its facilities to attain the desired ends. Where problems arise, such as legal cases, job placement, etc., which can be handled efficiently by agencies already in the field the MOWM will refer such cases to the proper agencies.

The March On Washington Movement would do well to concentrate on limited objectives within a given area and a given time than to dissipate its energies in sporadic attacks on many varied problems.

Undated leaflet in the Fur and Leather Workers' Union Archives.

31. MARCH ON WASHINGTON MOVEMENT

Press Release, August 17, 1942

Reports from chapters of the March on Washington Movement and from individuals all over the country indicate that the Negro is genuinely alarmed
over the prospect of the transfer of the Fair Employment Practice Committee
by President Roosevelt to the War Man Power Commission of which Paul McNutt
is chairman. As soon as the proposed change was announced, A. Philip
Randolph, our National Director, and Lawrence M. Ervin, President of the New
York Division, dispatched telegrams of protest to the White House.

Yesterday, Eardlie John, Chairman of the Fair Employment Practice Committee of the New York Division of the March on Washington Movement, wrote
to the President outlining the reasons for the objection to the change.

August 16, 1942

The President of the United States
The White House
Washington, D.C.

My dear Mr. President:

If the proposed transfer of the Fair Employment Practice Committee to
the War Man Power Commission is consummated, the spiritual progress of our
country would be set back at least a quarter of a century.

When you issued Executive Order #8802, the morale of the Negro, which
had struck a new low, was materially heightened. Although it was but a crumb
that fell from the rich man's table, we were grateful to you. In each Negro
American's heart welled the hope that at long last the Great Humanitarian had
looked our way and maybe would look again. Maybe we were wrong! Maybe justice
and right and decency to one's fellow-men would be triumphant!

On December 7th the Negro American was, without exception, fighting mad
because a foreign power had dared to attack our country. We only wished to
get within rifle and hand range of the enemy.

We have always been in the vanguard of the fight for freedom from Boston
Commons to Bataan.

We asked only that we be allowed to serve with dignity. Our offer to
serve on a dignified basis was rejected. We were accepted only as an inferior, jim-crowed and humiliated by our own Government. One of the most
important functions of a Government is to set its spiritual level far above
that of the individual so that in the striving of mankind to reach as near
perfection as is humanly possible, the exalted and meek could seek inner
strength and guidance from its Government. If only our Government would
strike out boldly for the right, for justice for all, our country would be
impregnable.

Prior to the appointment of the Fair Employment Practice Committee,
Negroes were on the verge of despair. Everywhere men were talking about
democracy, even in the dark South, but their action belied their words. We
listened attentively to the cruel words, for all said, "All men are created
equal and that in this country all men have equality of opportunity." The
Committee, though working under a budgetary handicap, performed near miracles
within its limited sphere. Whatever success has come to it, came almost
solely because of you, Mr. President. Its effectiveness stems solely from
the dynamic moral force and sanction of your high office, added to the respect
and love of the great majority of the American People for you as a Great
Humanitarian. If the Committee is denuded of this authority, its future
work will be worthless.

The articulation of all America into the war effort is of serious and paramount importance. Without such there can be no unity of purpose. Without such there can be no favorable peace. It is the responsibility of our country to lead the world out of the horror chamber of fear and prejudice and despair to that higher ground of peace and good will to all men. There can be no peace until our country cast off the shackles of discrimination and segregation and lead the world into that higher spiritual leadership for which mankind longs.

The work of the Fair Employment Practice Committee, if it is allowed to remain responsible only to you, will be a driving force in accelerating the democratic process. Men everywhere must see that our country is a democracy in fact for the eyes of all the world are focused upon the United States. Oppressed peoples, not only the Poles and the Danes but the Indians, the Chinese, the Africans and the Negro American look to you for spiritual leadership.

The Man Power Commission, if it is to be effective in immediately mobilizing the productive capacity of our country, must keep clear of controversial issues. Equality of economic opportunity is not controversial, but because the South is determined to use its exaggerated influence to deny the Negro elementary democratic rights, this equality of economic opportunity is thrown into the field of controversy. In these circumstances, the Commission may not contemplate moral punitive action against employer and at the same time ask them to speed up production. The Southern mind would resent Mr. McNutt's Committee to the point of non-cooperation but will obey the edicts of the President's Committee.

If the Fair Employment Practice Committee is transferred to the Man Power Commission, it will undoubtedly be subject to the orders of the regional directors. As is noted above, the chief offenders are Northerners. There is where much work needs to be done. Southern Regional Directors will bend every effort to sabotage the Committee's work. War Man Power Commission will soon have to ask Congress for more funds. Congressmen and Senators from the South who enjoy their abnormal prestige and power from the numerical strength of the Negro while at the same time withholding from him the right of vote, will refuse to appropriate funds for the Commission unless the Fair Employment Practice Committee is killed or hamstrung.

Further, the Chairman of the Man Power Commission is a candidate for the Democratic Nomination for the Presidency in 1944, if you do not chose to run. As such a candidate, he must seek votes in the Democratic Convention from the solid South. The South is committed to the proposition that Negroes shall never be given equality of opportunity. It is too much to ask a human being aspiring to the greatest office on earth to clash violently with the small men of the South. You are the exception. The people have confidence in you and no matter what these small men of the South may think or feel, they can never affect your high place in the history of the world and in the hearts of your countrymen.

In the years to come let history recall that you did more for democracy and for world peace than perhaps any other man. It is upon this issue, the equality of all man, that the peace of the world rests. The Fair Employment Practice Committee is the one active Agency of our Government that is laying the foundation for a lasting peace; and it must have the authority and sanction and prestige of you and your office directly behind it.

Respectfully yours,

EARDLIE JOHN,
Chairman,
Fair Employment Practice
Committee

Copy in the Fur and Leather Workers, Union Archives.

32. ST. LOUIS NEGROES!!

The March on Washington Movement, 10,000 Strong

MARCHES Saturday, 29, 1942
         August

ON

CARTER CARBURETOR COMPANY

(Located at Grand - Spring - Dodier and St. Louis Avenues)

THIS PLANT IS NOW ENGAGED IN WAR CONTRACT PRODUCTION
THIS PLANT EMPLOYS OVER 2,650 WORKERS BUT HAS

NOT ONE NEGRO EMPLOYED !

THIS PLANT IGNORED OUR REQUEST FOR A CONFERENCE HENCE IT

ASKED FOR A MARCH!

AT THE AUDITORIUM MEETING, AUGUST 14, YOU PROMISED TO
HELP WHEN NEEDED . .

NOW IS YOUR CHANCE!

HELP FIGHT   F   JOBS!!
             O   FREEDOM!!
             R   EQUAL OPPORTUNITIES!!
                    FULL CITIZENSHIP!!

THE MARCH FORMS at Tandy Park, Cottage and Pendleton Avenues

SATURDAY, AUG. 29, 2:30 P.M.

BE THERE!!----WE MUST NOT FAIL!!

MARCH ON WASHINGTON COMMITTEE

Flier in possession of the editors.

33. 400 NEGROES IN PROTEST PARADE

March From Tandy Park to Plant of Carter Carburetor

    Some 400 St. Louis Negro men and women yesterday afternoon paraded from
Tandy Park to the Carter Carburetor Corporation plant at 2840 North Spring
avenue in an orderly demonstration against alleged discriminatory labor
policies of the war industry.
    Occasional street corner groups watched without comment as the silent
marchers walked in slow single file the long hot mile from the park to the big
plant.
    The marchers, who paraded for the most part on the sidewalk, were led by a
flag-bearer and T. D. McNeal, St. Louis chairman of the Negro March on Washington Committee. Behind the leaders sauntered the long procession of placard-
bearing demonstrators.

Marchers Carry Signs

    Some of the placards read:

"Barring Negroes from war industries makes Axis propaganda."
Others declared:
"Carter employs 3,000 people, not one Negro; Is that democracy?"
Still others asserted:
"Shut our mouths and stop our marches with jobs, democracy and freedom."

Bystanders Orderly

A large crowd of staring but unopinionated spectators lined the sidewalks at St. Louis and Spring avenues, the southwest corner of the Carter plant. A detachment of motorcycle patrolmen checked traffic as the marchers quietly circled the block-square factory.

After circling the Carter plant, the marchers paraded west on St. Louis avenue to Tandy Park where the procession disbanded.

Although McNeal had predicted about 10,000 Negroes would participate, he expressed himself satisfied with the mass protest.

"All we wish to do," he said, "is to keep our problem before the people of St. Louis. The conscience of the people will do the rest. The purpose of this demonstration was to dramatize the plight of the discriminated Negro, who only asks to be allowed a place in his country's war effort."

Others To Follow

The demonstration at the Carter plant, McNeal said, would be followed by similar mass protests directed at other St. Louis plants which allegedly discriminate against Negro labor.

In addition, he said, a mass prayer meeting sponsored by the March on Washington Committee here will be held the afternoon of September 20 at Memorial Plaza.

"We intend to continue our protests and our demonstrations until Negroes are given an equal share in war work in St. Louis, he declared.

H. H. Weed, general manager of the Carter Corporation, asserted the plant had no established policy barring Negroes from employment.

St. Louis Globe, August 30, 1942.

34.
SPEECH DELIVERED BY DOCTOR LAWRENCE M. ERVIN, EASTERN
REGIONAL DIRECTOR OF THE MARCH ON WASHINGTON MOVEMENT
AT THE "WE ARE AMERICANS, TOO" CONFERENCE, HELD AT THE
METROPOLITAN COMMUNITY CHURCH, CHICAGO, ILL.,
JUNE 30, 1943

Mr. Chairman, Fellow Marchers, Ladies and Gentlemen:

We are assembled here at a time of great racial tension and stress. It is a time when the rapidity of this tension's increase has reached a most dangerous point--in truth, at a time when the tides of democracy are running very low for the Negro people.

It is a time when all of the responsible leaders of our government from the President of the United States, our Commander-in-Chief, to the heads of all of its various bureaus and branches are saying that we are not fighting this war for men to live together as master and slaves, but we are fighting for the spirit of universal brotherhood. At a time when Mr. Sumner Welles, our Assistant Secretary of State, has publicly proclaimed to Negroes that "equality to all men is the democratic promise." At a time when the national press, in bold headlines states that we are fighting for the extension of the democratic way of life to the four corners of the earth. At a time when every radio commentator is filling the air waves with beautiful phrases extolling the virtues of our democracy.

As citizens we ask ourselves, "What is this thing called Democracy?" I will tell you. Democracy has for its meaning and its purpose the long-time interest, welfare, and happiness of all the people, regardless of race, creed, color or national origin. It respects the personality of every

individual; it seeks to develop in him a sense of belongingness. It assumes
that the maximum development of every individual is for the best interest of
all. It encourages and directs him to respect himself and to make the best
of his own natural gifts, to develop his own unique personality for the
benefit of the whole. For we are all of one stupendous whole, whose body
Nature is, and God the Soul. And the soul of democracy rests upon the Equality
Clause, penned by the immortal Thomas Jefferson, when he wrote in the Declaration of Independence that, "We hold these truths to be self-evident, that
all men are created equal; that they are endowed by their Creator with certain inalienable rights, and among these are the Right to Life, Liberty and the
Pursuit of Happiness."

We assemble here knowing that democracy renews its strength by continued
education as to its meaning and its purposes. We, of ths Movement, take
democracy seriously. We know it has developed as a struggle for principles
that has penetrated deeply into the consciousness of all our citizens, and
has established even amongst the lowly, a sense of equality for human dignity
and justice. Some, however, take it for granted that sound economic and
political problems under the shibboleths of so-called democratic principles
will continue automatically to take care of themselves. They close their
eyes to the growing confusion and bitterness, trusting child-like, that
"mother democracy" will somehow make all well again. But we have come to
enlist other men's minds in this crusade of Winning Democracy for the Negro.
We say that nothing can take the place of struggle. We seek to develop a
contagious enthusiasm for this struggle. We demand that Americans, black and
white, come out of their "ivory towers" and carry the fight for freedom of
the Negro people into the market places of the world, Now.

There are those who will say that this is not the time to parade upon
the public platform the indignities that are heaped upon the minority groups
in this democracy. They cry aloud "our national house is on fire--stop
everything and put out the fire."

"Remember you are the minority and minority must bow to the approved
program of the majority." "Win the war," they say--" and your rights can
then be demanded." They say it is better to suffer the indignities of a
Negro hero under a democracy than to live a slave under a Nazi yolk. Again
let me quote the immortal Jefferson on the will of the majority, "Though
the will of the majority is in all cases to prevail, that will to be uplifted
must be reasonable, that the minority possess their equal rights, that equal
laws must protect and to violate would be oppression." I say to you, Ladies
and Gentlemen, that an organization can be critical of its government's
directive actions and yet remain patriotic and loyal. And we say to those
critics who say that our leadership should be silenced during the war, that
we still have in America freedom of assembly and freedom of speech. Thus we
have assembled and we will not be silenced, but we will be heard.

From the day of the legal lynching of Odell Waller by the sovereign State
of Virginia, to the day of the complete emasculation of the President's Committee on Fair Employment Practice, to the hour of the Detroit riots, our
government itself has maintained a rigid pattern of oppression, segregation,
discrimination and jim-crow, against the Negro people.

The failure of this administration to take a moral stand against the
native forces of fascism in this country, while six hundred thousand Negroes
in the uniform of Freedom fight in Bataan, Corregidor, Dutch Guinea, Hawaii,
the Phillippines and Africa--has left us bewildered. Yes, bewildered we are
and passion tossed. Mad, we are, with the cries of a mobbed and mocked and
murdered people. Standing here I hear their cries. They say "show us the
way and point us the path." They know that within their race are cowards,
[line missing] those of us assembled here, "give us a plan of action Now."
A plan that will teach us to respect ourselves. A plan that will make us
stand and face pomp and glory in our pure white robes of simplicity, un-
afraid. A plan that will teach us to walk on our own feet; to work with our
own hands; to speak with our own minds. To rely upon our own strong right
arm. To overcome a system that pits worker against worker, brother against
brother, and father against son; that causes men to crush the weak; that
spits in the face of the fallen; that strikes at those who dare not strike
back, that hates the image that God himself has stamped upon a brother's
soul." Too long, they say, has color in the world and in America, been the
infallible guide to a man's ability and his dessert. They want the instruments

to win this freedom--not the instruments of hate and of violence, but rather
the instruments of Equality, Education, and the Right to Work and become first-
class citizens of our democracy. Lincoln said that this nation cannot remain
half slave and half free. I say that under a democracy we cannot have a first
and second class citizenship. Either the Negroes of America enter into the
pattern of American life on a plan of complete, perfect, and unlimited equality
or they don't enter. I also say that unless the Negro contend and fight for
his democratic rights now during this war he will never get them. And after
the war he will have the status of "untouchables," for we must remember that
one can win a war and still lose one's democratic rights.

Who are the people who deny the Negro his democratic rights? Who believe
that the democratic right of freedom from fear--freedom from want--freedom of
religion--fredom of speech--the right of habeas corpus--the right of trial
by jury--the right of petition and the right of equality before the bars of
justice, are the rights of white people only. Whose boast is it that this is
a white man's government? They are the Rankins and Bilbos of Mississippi.
They are the Talmadges and Coxes of Georgia; the Cotton Ed Smiths of South
Carolina. They are the Ellenders of Louisiana; the Connallys and Sumners of
Texas. They are the Martin Dies'. They are the Dixons and Starnes of Alabama; the Glass's and Smiths of Virginia. They are the Donald Smiths of the
Ku Klux Klan; the Christian Frontiers; the Black Shirts. This host of little
men, who take but who never give; who share but who never spare. These Negro
phobists who strut in the Halls of Congress and make a mockery of democracy.
Who rant and wave the bloody shirt of racial superiority and preach the inflammatory doctrine of Negro domination for political advantage whose every
thought and every action is designed to keep the Negro in his place. No,
this is not a white man's government--rather, it's man's government. Long
before Patrick Henry said "Give me liberty or give me death" a Negro, Crispus
Attucks, had died on Boston Commons to establish this government.[106]

Our forefathers fought, bled and died to outlaw this reactionary doctrine
of superior races; of separate classes, of first families and of segregated
peoples. This nation was conceived and dedicated to the proposition that all
men should have equality of citizenship. This was every Puritan's prayer.
This was every immigrant's hope. This was every free man's desire. This was
every emancipated slave's dream. This was the very epitome of man's effort
toward honest government and universal brotherhood.

The problem of the Negro in this democracy of ours is a problem of prejudice, discrimination, segregation and jim-crowism in all of the social,
economic, political, educational and religious institutions of this country.
But the Negroes are awakening, and they are beginning to question the domination of the so-called master white race. They are rapidly reaching social
maturity. They are defining terms. They know jim-crow to mean a spiritual,
moral and intellectual insult to their very soul, and they are determined to
get rid of this insult. They hold, in spite of the reasoning of the Supreme
Court of our land, that segregation is discrimination, and they will never
submit to it. For we are full men, and as such we expect to be treated.

No, we will never accept a status of second-class citizenship in
America, and we know that the majority of Americans hope for a true democracy
where all men live in peace and good will. However, we know that Negroes
must win this freedom, this equality; and we must win by methods that are new
and revolutionary. Gradualism and appeasement have failed. The powers that
be always give us two bad choices or none at all--either jim-crow or don't
enter; either segregation or don't work. We must take the good choice and
On to Victory. We say to you that the power to win the [illegible] resides
in the masses and if we organize thirteen millions of Negroes and discipline
them to follow leadership and join with our natural allies, which are labor
and other minorities, we will win this struggle of the common man for his
place in the Sun.

Yes, the Common Man. Common as air is common, whose sweetness we never
guess until it is polluted. Common as water is common, without which ship-
wrecked men go mad. Common as God's sky is common--lit by day with infallible
light and starred at night with whirling worlds of beauty. Common as Jesus
Christ himself was common.

Copy in the Fur and Leather Workers' Union Archives.

35.

205 JAM PHONE CO. AT ONCE PAYING BILLS AS PROTEST TO JOB DENIALS

Considerable excitement was caused at the Bell Telephone Building at
10:30 a.m. on Saturday morning, September 18th when 205 members of the March
On Washington's picket committee showed up at one time to pay their telephone
bills en masse. Many of the March On Washington pickets paid their telephone
bills in pennies. This was designed to slow up the process of collection. However, some one had evidently tipped off the telephone company that this
technique would be used and the cashiers had been equipped with individual
money sacks into which such payments were raked subject to later verification.
During the demonstration practically all of the officials of the telephone
company gathered on the mezzanine balcony and watched the irate Negro telephone subscribers show their resentment against the undemocratic employment
policy of the telephone company through this non-violent technique.
T. D. McNeal, Director of the March Movement, after the demonstration
stated that it was a completely successful project in that it again dramatized
this un-American situation and forcibly called to the attention of the telephone
management the fact that Negro citizens here have an abiding determination to
see this fight against the telephone company through no matter how long a time
or what sacrifice might be entailed.

St. Louis Argus, September 24, 1943.

THE FAIR EMPLOYMENT PRACTICES COMMITTEE

36. THE WARTIME UTILIZATION OF MINORITY WORKERS

America is a nation of many different peoples. The white majority itself
is composed of various minorities and when questions of creed or national
origin arise around the issue of job opportunities, the minority status of
the individual concerned becomes a very important question. For example, the
average white American who happens to be a member of the Jehovah's Witnesses
sect finds himself in much the same position as a Negro worker if other white
workers object to his being employed on the same job. A Mexican worker who
can get any job for which he is qualified in the East will face considerable
discrimination in the Southwest. Fully one-third of the total American population belongs to minority groups of one kind or another that fall within
the protective provisions of Executive Order 9346. There was a time in America
when it was quite common for orders to the United States Employment Service
to include the requirement "WXP" (White, Christian, Protestant).
Figures for nonwhite workers will be used chiefly in this chapter because
they constitute the best data available on the employment of minority groups.
For the United States as a whole, Negroes represent about 96 percent of all
nonwhite workers, the remainder including persons of Japanese, Chinese, Filipino,
and Indian origin. In 1940, there were in the United States about 13,000,000
Negroes, 127,000 persons of Japanese, and 78,000 persons of Chinese origin,
46,000 Filipinos, and 362,000 American Indians.
The other principal minority groups consist of approximately 5 million
aliens, 3 million Lat Americans, and 4-1/2 million persons of Jewish ancestry.
Altogether, the national origin minorities, including Germans, Italians,
Canadians and others totaled some 21,000,000 persons.
But of America's minorities, its 13 million Negroes are the main objects
of discrimination and 78 per cent of FEPC's case load is concerned with their
employment problems. . . .

The Depression and Negro Losses in Employment

The economic depression of the thirties gave impetus to the already
established trend of removing Negroes from jobs which had become desirable
either as a result of technical improvement or the raising of wage scales
through unionization. Negroes lost heavily on railroads as firemen and in the
building trades, while continuing their downward trend in employment as boilermakers and machinists. Unemployed whites took over the traditional "Negro
jobs" of waiters, bell-men, porters and truck drivers and, with the loss of
these service jobs, the Negro was literally pushed off the bottom rung of the
occupational ladder.

The depression seriously curtailed occupational gains which Negroes
had made in such industries as iron, steel, meat packing, shipbuilding, and
automobile manufacturing during World War I and the decade thereafter. In
1940, colored workers constituted even a smaller proportion of the workers in
mining, manufacturing, trade, and transportation than they had in 1910. The
greatest relative and absolute loss occurred in manufacturing, a decline from
6.1 per cent of the total in 1910 to 4.9 per cent of the total in 1940.
Despite the lack of employment opportunities in the North, Negro migration
northward out of the South continued during the depression. It was not as
high during the thirties as in the preceding decade, but estimates indicate
that 317,000 Negroes moved from the South to the North betweeen 1930 and 1940.

Negro Workers and World War II

Comparisons between the occupations of whites and Negroes in 1940 reveal
that Negro labor was disproportionately concentrated in unskilled, service,
and agricultural jobs. Agricultural workers and other laborers constituted
62.2 per cent of all employed Negro men but only 28.5 per cent of all employed
white men. Only about 5 per cent of Negro men as compared with approximately
30 per cent of white men were engaged in professional, semiprofessional,
proprietary, managerial, and clerical and sales occupations. Skilled craftsmen represented 15.6 per cent of employed white men but only 4.4 per cent of
employed colored men. Moreover, more than half of the Negro craftsmen were
mechanics or artisans in the construction trades, further indicating the
scarcity of Negro skilled workers in manufacturing industries. Striking
differences also were shown between the occupations of white and colored women.

When the period of defense preparation began in 1940, local white labor
was absorbed and outside white workers were imported into centers of expanding
activity, but the local Negro labor supply was not utilized to any appreciable
degree. Both management and the unions practiced a policy of excluding Negroes
from the new job openings. The Tolan Committee found in 1941 that 9 A.F. of L.
unions and the Railway Brotherhoods still had constitutional provisions barring
Negroes from membership. Numerous other unions discriminated by tacit consent
or by forcing Negroes into auxiliaries. A survey in the fall of 1941 by the
Bureau of Employment Security of the Social Security Board revealed that Negroes
would not be considered by industry for 51 per cent of 282,215 job openings
expected to occur by February 1942. The War Manpower Commission estimated
early in 1942 that nonwhites constituted 2.5 to 3 per cent of employees in war
industries.

Factors which have hindered the participation of Negroes in war industries
include racial discrimination, the occupational characteristics of the Negro
labor force, and the geographic distribution of the Negro labor force in
relation to the geographic distribution of war contracts. Three-fourths of
the Negro population lived in the South in 1940, and two-thirds of the colored
labor force was located in 14 Southern states where only 13.5 per cent of the
nation's war contracts have been awarded.

The major factors which have contributed to the present industrial advancement of the Negro worker have been the tight labor market characteristic
of wartime and the action of the Federal Government in breaking down the
barriers to job opportunities. Pre-employment and in-plant training courses
have prepared colored workers for skilled and semiskilled jobs, thereby making
possible the transition from agricultural and service jobs and the upgrading
from unskilled industrial work. The migration of southern Negroes to urban
areas in the South and from the South to northern and western centers of
production has rearranged the geographic distribution of the colored labor
force.

War Training Programs

The participation of Negroes in war training programs is worthy of special notice. Pre-employment and supplementary training were provided for the following industry groups: aircraft industries, shipbuilding, sheet metal and welding, automobile mechanics, machine shops, electricity and radio, and inspection and foremanship. Non-white trainees participated in training for each of these groups, but have been concentrated most heavily in machine shops, aircraft, and shipbuilding. These were the industries, the latter two being highly marginal, in which Negroes were almost entirely denied employment in the earlier phases of the defense effort.

In the South Negro trainees participated in very much less degree than would be indicated on the basis of their local population ratio, but this was slightly offset numerically by increased participation in other regions. A survey in 1942 indicated that the South with roughly 80 per cent of the Negro population was training about 20 per cent of all Negro participants, while the North with 20 per cent of the Negro population was training about 80 per cent of all Negro participants.

Employment Gains in Defense Industries

The per cent of nonwhite workers in firms reporting to the War Manpower Commission has risen steadily. From less than 3 per cent in early 1942, non-white participation rose to 4.6 per cent in September 1942, 6.4 per cent in January 1943, 7.2 per cent in January 1944, and 8.3 per cent in November 1944. More than a million nonwhite workers are now employed in war industries.

Some idea of the industrial advance of the Negro in specific industries can be obtained by noting the following comparisons between July 1942 and November 1944.

Shipbuilding has been the area of most dramatic increase in nonwhite employment. Nonwhite employment increased from 10,099 in the whole industry in 1940 to 157,874 in 96 shipyards in March 1944. While total employment increased 888.9 per cent, nonwhite employment during the period of wartime growth increased 1,463.2 per cent.

Negroes in the Local Transit Industry

Increased transportation needs at a time of gasoline and rubber shortages have made local transit companies war industries of prime importance. Tra-ditionally both the management and unions of local transit companies have excluded Negroes from platform operations in nearly all major cities of the United States. However, by January 1945, the number of local transit companies hiring Negroes in platform operations had risen to 21 and the number of Negroes in such positions had risen to 3,601. New York and Detroit each had more than one thousand Negroes in platform jobs and San Francisco had 750. In other cities the employment of Negroes as drivers, operators, and conductors signaled their entrance and consolidation of gains in an important occupational field.

Negroes in Government

Improvement has been noted in Government as well as in industry. In March 1944, Negroes formed 19.2 per cent of Federal departmental service (chiefly located in Washington, D.C.). This figure can be compared roughly with that in 1938 when Negroes were only 8.4 per cent of all persons employed by the Federal Government in Washington. According to the 1940 Census, Negroes were 28.2 per cent of the local population. The gain has also been qualitative. Whereas in 1938, 90 per cent of all Negro Federal employment in Washington was custodial, only 10 per cent was clerical, administrative, and fiscal, clerical-mechanical, and professional. Today 40 per cent of Negro workers are custodial and 60 per cent are in the higher-paid and more de-sirable clerical and professional jobs. Thus one-half of all Negro depart-mental workers have been redistributed into higher levels of pay and status. In addition, whereas Negroes were less than 10 per cent of Federal employment throughout the country in 1938, they are today almost 12 per cent. This low figure, in comparison with their representation in departmental service, may be accounted for by the fact that they were only 11.2 per cent of the field service where 90 per cent of all Federal employment is found.

Industry	Nonwhite workers as per cent of all employees	
	July 1942	November 1944
Agricultural machinery and tractors	1.9	5.8
Aircraft...	2.9	6.4
Aluminum and magnesium products.........................	7.1	12.6
Ammunition (except for small arms)......................	5.2	11.0
Blast furnaces, steel works, and rolling mills..........	9.8	12.0
Communication equipment and related products............	.7	4.8
Electrical equipment for industrial use.................	1.0	2.8
Engines and turbines....................................	1.9	2.7
Explosives..	3.3	6.3
Firearms under .60 caliber (small arms).................	.7	4.5
Fireworks and pyrotechnics..............................	0.0	6.9
General industrial machinery............................	1.6	4.7
Guns, howitzers, mortars, and related equipment.........	3.4	7.1
Iron and steel foundry products.........................	18.6	24.8
Metalworking machinery..................................	1.0	1.7
Ordnance accessories, not elsewhere classified..........	1.4	5.9
Plastic materials.......................................	0.0	7.6
Primary smelting and refining of nonferrous metals and alloys..	8.7	8.6
Rolling, drawing, and alloying of nonferrous metals (except aluminum)......................................	4.6	9.9
Scientific instruments..................................	.9	2.6
Shipbuilding..	5.7	12.4
Small arms ammunition...................................	7.2	8.5
Tanks...	2.2	8.6
Tires and inner tubes...................................	3.3	9.8

The present relatively good position of the Negro in the Federal Government is qualified by the fact the most of the heavy employment and good utilization, in terms of skill, has been achieved in temporary war agencies. The overwhelming proportion of Negro employment, 70 per cent, is really industrial and is confined to the Army Service Forces and Navy shore establishments. Only 30 per cent of all Negro Government workers are in classified service. Moreover, 57.7 per cent of those in classified Civil Service jobs were employed in temporary war agencies.

Impact of the War on the Negro Labor Force

Employment of Negroes in civilian jobs increased by almost a million between April 1940 and April 1944, the number of employed men rising from 2.9 to 3.2 million and the number of employed women from 1.5 to 2.1 million. The shift from the farm to the factory was the most outstanding change in the male Negro labor force. The proportion of Negro workers on farms declined from 41 per cent to 28 per cent, or by 13 points, and the proportion in industry increased by the same amount. Moreover, the number of Negro males employed as skilled craftsmen, foremen, and semiskilled operatives doubled from one-half million to one million during the 4-year period. Despite these increases, the proportion of Negroes in unskilled jobs remained the same, or one in five. The employment changes of Negro women followed the same pattern.

The numerical increases made by Negoes in the higher occupations
(skilled, semiskilled, clerical, and sales, proprietors, and professional)
have been offset by the entry into the labor force of a million workers, most
of whom are unskilled workers from the farms or women and men seeking work
for the first time. Thus, the Negro labor force is still made up predominantly
of unskilled and service workers.

Below are tables which show the distribution of total and nonwhite workers
in major industry divisions. Table A covers the entire labor force and table
B shows total and nonwhite employment in manufacturing industries.

TABLE A.--*Labor force pattern, November 1944*
[In thousands of workers]

	Total la-bor force	Nonwhite labor force	Per cent nonwhite
Total labor force.........................	64,110	7,280	11.4
Armed forces...............................	11,900	910	7.6
Civilian labor force.......................	52,210	6,370	12.2
Unemployed...............................	680	151	22.2
Employed.................................	51,530	6,219	12.1
Agriculture............................	8,140	1,783	21.9
Nonagriculture.........................	43,390	4,436	10.2
Mining................................	812	134	16.5
Construction..........................	629	61	9.7
Transportation and public utilities...	3,771	256	6.8
Trade.................................	7,299	540	7.4
Finance, business, personal and miscellaneous services..............	4,315	423	9.8
Domestic service......................	1,730	950	54.9
Federal War Agencies..................	1,611	193	12.0
Other Federal Government..............	838	97	11.6
State and local government............	3.045	100	3.3
Manufacturing (public and private)....	16,020	1,282	8.0
All other.............................	3,320	400	12.0

Current Minority Employment Before VE-Day [107]

The two foregoing tables show the nonwhite labor force pattern which has
been established as the result of the changes that have taken place during the
war. This pattern serves as the basis from which to measure the further changes
that will occur after VE-day and before victory over Japan.

In speaking of the current period of intense war production, former
Director of War Mobilization and Reconversion James F. Byrnes said in his
report of April 1, 1945, "Manpower has become the major limiting factor. There
is no pool of unemployed to draw upon. We have committed our reserves.[108]

"If we are to meet schedules, we must draw on workers in less essential
activities. There is no other way out. We must still concentrate on getting
the right workers into the right jobs and places at the right time."

Utilization of Minority Workers

It is estimated that over 400,000 minority group workers are still available for war industries or for other essential work. Approximately 151,000
nonwhite workers were unemployed in November 1944; and, even though a certain
amount of frictional unemployment is unavoidable, this number could be considerably reduced. Furthermore, minority workers comprise a more than proportionate number of persons now engaged in less essential industries and

TABLE B.--*Labor force pattern in manufacturing industries, November 1944*
[In thousands of workers]

	Total labor force	Nonwhite labor force	Per cent nonwhite
Manufacturing........................	16,020	1,282	8.0
Munitions...........................	9,070	726	8.0
Aircraft...........................	1,670	107	6.4
Shipbuilding......................	1,470	182	12.4
Ordnance and accessories..........	1,590	142	8.9
Communications equipment..........	400	19	4.8
Basic iron and steel..............	530	60	11.4
Basic nonferrous metals...........	210	22	10.6
Rubber............................	230	16	6.8
Other munitions and metallic non-munitions.......................	2,970	178	6.0
All other manufacturing...............	6,950	556	8.0
Lumbering.........................	480	30	6.3
Furniture.........................	400	48	12.0
Stone, clay, and glass............	390	20	5.2
Textiles..........................	1,160	44	3.8
Apparel...........................	930	47	5.1
Leather...........................	330	7	2.1
Food and kindred products.........	1,370	201	14.7
Tobacco manufactures..............	90	33	36.6
Paper and allied products.........	370	31	8.5
Printing and publishing...........	510	23	4.5
Petroleum and coal products.......	200	14	7.1
Other chemicals...................	400	44	11.1
Miscellaneous manufacturing.......	320	14	4.4

NOTE.--Nonwhite employment in lumbering and printing and publishing estimated from available data. All other percentages of nonwhite employment obtained from Summary of ES-270 Reports of the War Manpower Commission, November 1944.

occupations. A considerable pool of such workers might be shifted from the amusement, personal, and domestic service occupations into more essential work. Finally, a great number of these workers are still employed in relatively unproductive agricultural areas, and could be shifted to more productive work.

Perhaps an even more important source of increased labor productivity lies in the upgrading, in accordance with experience and skill, of minority workers now limited to unskilled work in essential industries. A great many cases have come to the Committee's attention in which experienced Negro and Mexican-American workers actually train newly recruited white workers for promotion to more highly skilled jobs denied to themselves. It is by taking action to assure the more effective employment and utilization of minority workers in war production that the Committee can make its principal contribution to solving the current manpower problem.

Minority Employment During "Period I"

The time between victory in Europe, "VE-day," and victory over Japan, "VJ-day" is now being referred to as "Period I." The Director of War Mobilization and Reconversion has outlined the Government's plans for reducing war production and increasing civilian output during that period. The overall release of resources from munitions production in the first quarter following the defeat of Germany is estimated at about 20 per cent, with an additional 5 per cent to be released in the second quarter, and still another 5 per cent in the third quarter.[109]

Conservative estimates for the reduction in Army requirements amount to about 15 to 20 per cent for the first 3 months after VE-day and about 40 per cent before the end of the year following the defeat of Germany. The programs of the Navy and the Maritime Commission, which are now on curtailed production schedules will undergo little further change after VE-day. The ship construction program of the Navy decreases from a quarterly rate of $1,570,000,000 in the first quarter of 1945 to approximately $1,000,000,000 by the first quarter of 1946. The ship-construction program of the Maritime Commission decreases from $970,000,000 in the first quarter of 1945 to $400,000,000 in the fourth quarter of 1945.

The declining schedules in ship construction may be expected to result in the displacement of a considerable portion of the 180,000 nonwhite workers who were employed in that industry in November 1944. A portion of the workers released from ship construction may be absorbed by the increased labor requirements for ship repair work.

There has been some increase in the employment of nonwhite workers even in those munitions industries which have had stationary or declining total employment since November 1943. This may indicate that white workers have greater alternative employment opportunities, and that a larger proportion of white than nonwhite workers have tended to move into jobs which will continue after the end of the war, or else have withdrawn from the labor market. This trend may continue during the current period and may be intensified after VE-day. It will mean that VJ-day will find Negroes heavily concentrated in war industries and their prospects poor for finding work in reconverted plants. Generally, however, minority workers have accumulated less seniority in those war industries which have post-war possibilities, and will be in a more precarious position during the reconversion to peacetime production.

Negro War Migration

Throughout the entire period of defense and war mobilization there has been an extensive movement of people from agricultural regions to industrial areas. They have migrated from the rural South and the states in the interior of the country, to the East and West coasts and the rim of the Great Lakes region. If we assume the same racial composition of population flow since 1940 as before, we may estimate a net migration across state lines of 4,350,000 persons, including 470,000 Negro migrants, between April 1940 and November 1944. If we add to these figures the movement of Negro workers and their families from rural areas and smaller communities to major war production centers, within the same states, we get a total figure for Negro migration which has been estimated at 600,000 through 1943 and 750,000 through 1944.

Three main streams of Negro population flow were developed before 1930 and much of current migration has followed the same course: from Georgia through the Atlantic Coast states to Pennsylvania and New York; from Mississippi and Alabama through Tennessee and Kentucky to Michigan, Ohio, Indiana, and Illinois; and from Louisiana through Arkansas and Missouri to Illinois, Indiana, and Michigan. The new flow which has been gaining in importance since 1940 has been from Louisiana, Texas, Arkansas, Oklahoma, and Missouri to the West coast.

The total population increase between 1940 and 1944 for the 10 congested production areas surveyed by the Bureau of the Census amounted to 1,840,000 including over 205,000 or 11.2 per cent nonwhite migrants. The general movement of Negro migrants has been from southern agricultural areas to the southern cities, and from southern cities and towns to northern and western industrial centers. For example, 37 per cent of the Negro migrants into Mobile, Ala., came from farms, whereas only 14 per cent of the Negroes who migrated to Detroit, Mich., were from rural areas. Again 70 per cent of the Negroes who moved to Charleston, S.C., came from elsewhere in the same State and only 27 per cent from other states. On the other hand, only 15 per cent of the Negroes who migrated to San Francisco came from other parts to California, whereas 85 per cent came from other states.

Historical records and current surveys indicate that between one-half and two-thirds of the minority workers who have migrated into war production centers will remain in these communities after the war. In addition to the general problem of absorbing permanently a large increase in population, the communities to which large numbers of minority workers have migrated will be faced with the necessity of adjusting intergroup relations.

First Report: Fair Employment Practice Committee, July 1943-December 1944 (Washington, D.C., 1945), pp. 85, 88-97.

37. F.E.P.C. ASKS ROOSEVELT TO ENFORCE ORDER

Group Meeting in Chicago Cites Two Coast Machinists' Locals for Barring Race Workers--Hears Buick Aircraft Case

CHICAGO, Jan. 22--The President's Committee on Fair Employment Practices this week cited two locals of the American Federation of Labor Machinists' Association for violation of the Executive Order in barring two colored workers from employment in defense plants. The citation is expected to be the text of the effectiveness of the President's decree.

The committee recommended to President Roosevelt that he summon to Washington the heads of the two locals, together with Harvey W. Browne, international president of the machinists, and require them to take necessary corrective measures at once.[110]

Hears Buick Case

The two locals, No. 751 of Seattle and No. 68 of San Francisco, are charged with violation of the national policy to the detriment of the war effort on the basis of testimony heard at Los Angeles last October. The committee charged that Charles Sullivan of San Mateo, Calif., had been denied the opportunity to work at the Bethlehem shipbuilding plant by Local 68, and that C. L. Bellums of Oakland, Calif., was barred from skilled occupation with the Boeing Aircraft Company in Seattle by Local 751.

The action of the committee was taken Monday at its meeting in Chicago prior to the opening of hearings on discriminations in Illinois industrial defense plants. The first case heard was that of the Buick aircraft engine plant in Melrose Park, which had been charged with violation of the fair labor order.

Members of the committee present for the hearings are David Sarnoff, Milton Webster and Frank Fenton, representing William Green, and John Brophy, representing Philip Murray.[111]

Pittsburgh Courier, January 24, 1942.

38.
10 FIRMS ORDERED TO STOP RACE BIAS OR LOSE CONTRACTS

WASHINGTON, April 18--Ten big firms, all of them working on war orders, were told to stop discriminating against any Negro and Jewish applicants in the most sweeping order issued to date by the President's Committee on Fair Employment Practices.

The order directs the 10 companies, located in Chicago and Milwaukee, to submit monthly reports describing workers newly hired and showing the number of Negro workers included and the jobs to which they are assigned.

The companies were accused in a two-day hearing held by the committee of having refused jobs to Negroes and Jews and of having told employment agencies to send only whites and Gentiles, and of having specified "gentile" or "Protestant" or "white" in ads placed in newspapers. The charges were denied by the 10 firms, but evidence at the hearings substantiated them.

Brophy on Group

The Fair Employment Committee, set up by President Roosevelt some months ago, has representation from organized labor, with John Brophy, director of Industrial Union Councils, representing Pres. Murray and the CIO.

The companies involved are: Stewart-Warner Corp., Buick Aviation of Melrose, Ill., Bearse Mfg. Co., Simpson Mfg. Co., Nordberg Mfg. Co., A. O. Smith Co., Heil Co., Allis-Chalmers Corp. and the Harnischfeger Co.

"The findings and directions will give the committee a continuing jurisdiction over the employment practices of these industries, which hold contracts for war implements and material, as each concern has been asked to file reports with the committee showing the extent to which steps have been taken to bring the company's employment policies and practices into line with the national policy: Dr. Malcolm S. Mac Lean, chairman of the committee explained.

CIO News, April 20, 1942.

39.   THE FEPC: A PARTIAL VICTORY

The effort to completely hamstring the Fair Employment Practice Committee has been defeated owing to the unanimous and extremely vocal disapproval of colored citizens.

Unfortunately, the strenuous effort to have the Committee returned to an independent status has failed.

The FEPC will have a greater personnel and will be able as formerly to conduct investigations and hearings wherever it chooses, but final decisions as to action will be in the hands of War Manpower Commissioner McNutt, which is something less than the independence the Committee originally enjoyed.

Beyond their demand that the Committee not be reduced to complete impotence, colored citizens also wanted to see the work of the committee implemented by a strong Federal law enabling it to punish violators of both the letter and spirit of Executive Order 8802.

So long as there is no such law, the Committee cannot go beyond gathering evidence and warning firms to comply with the Presidential order.

If discriminating companies, industries and agencies do not choose to abide by the President's order beyond small token employment, there is now nothing more the FEPC can do about it.

Hence, the next step of those who want to see the letter and spirit of the President's order carried out, is to fight for the passage of a Federal law setting up drastic penalties for its violation.

The hurdles, obstacles and barriers in the path of the FEPC which almost led to its death, were placed there by reactionary business interests determined to keep American economic enterprise "for whites only" and it was their loud complaints that finally reached the top and brought about the Committee's transfer from an independent to a subordinate status.

It is evident that the plan was to completely sabotage the Committee for why else should Robert Weaver and Will Alexander have been given charge of Negro and minority affairs within the War Manpower Commission when the FEPC had been specifically set up to cover the same or similar ground?[112]

Happily, the FEPC had mass pressure of Negroes behind it and Messrs. Weaver and Alexander did not, and the history of the New Deal has shown its responsiveness to the strongest and most persistent pressure.

If colored citizens present a united front on all questions affecting their welfare as they have in this fight to save the FEPC, a larger measure of success will crown our efforts to make democracy a living reality in the United States.

Pittsburgh Courier, November 7, 1942.

40.   FEPC CRACKS DOWN ON DIXIE SHIPYARD

Ordered to Cease Discriminating Against
Negro Skilled Labor--Union Also Cited

WASHINGTON, D.C. Nov. 19--The President's Committee on Fair Employment
Practice on Tuesday directed the Delta Shipbuilding Corporation at New Orleans
"to cease and desist its discrimination against skilled Negro labor and from
its practice and policy of refusing to employ skilled Negro workers."
      The committee also directed that Local No. 37 of the International
Boilermakers, Shipbuilders, Welders, and Helpers of America likewise, "cease
and desist from its discrimination against Negro workers qualified for skilled
positions or classifications or employment in the Delta shipyards."
      Hearings which brought about these directions were held in Birmingham,
Ala., June 20, 1942.

Had Only Common Laborers

      The formal complaint alleged that investigation by the committee's field
representative disclosed that out of a total employment of 7,000 at the Delta
shipyards, there were only a few hundred Negroes employed as common laborers
or in menial capacities.
      Louis B. Dapremont testified at the hearings that he is a carpenter of
27 years' experience and on June 4, 1942, was referred for work to Delta by
Local 584, Shipbuilders, Carpenters and Joiners' Union.
      He stated that he worked during the next two days but noticed no other
colored mechanics employed. Mr. Dapremont disclosed to the union secretary
and the shipyard employment office that he was a Negro and inquired whether
he had been referred and hired under the impression that he was not a Negro.

Negro Carpenter Told to Quit

      Upon his disclosure, both the union secretary and an employment official
at the shipyard advised him to quit his job, which he did.
      Paul D. Dixon stated he had 22 years' experience in the shipbuilding
trade and was hired by the Boilermakers' Union through Mr. James B. McCollum,
international representative to organize a Negro auxiliary.
      Mr. Dixon organized several thousand Negro mechanics and sought employment
at Delta for himself and his men on March 10, and several subsequent occasions.
He was freely given application forms, on one occasion receiving as high as
200.
      These applications were filled out and filed with the company, but none
of the applicants were hired although many white applicants were employed at
or about the same time.
      At one time, said Mr. Dixon, he was told at the employment office that
the applications meant nothing. At another time the labor manager at Delta
told him to see Mr. McCollum. When he did so, he was reportedly told by Mr.
McCollum, "Keep your mind off Delta because Negroes are not going to work
there . . . because every white man in there would walk out."

Fired for His Pains

      In an effort to remedy conditions, Mr. Dixon wrote letters to the mayor
of New Orleans, the governor of Louisiana, and to the FEPC. For so doing, he
related, he was discharged by Mr. McCollum from his position as organizer.
      Clarence L. Laws, secretary of the New Orleans Urban League, testified
that during the summer of 1941, over a month before the first keel was laid
in Delta, he conferred with John H. Steinman, vice-president of the American
Shipbuilding Company of which Delta is a subsidiary and was informed that
Negroes would be hired on all levels of employment. 300 APPLY! NONE HIRED.
      Following that conference, more than 300 applications were made by Negro
welders, ship carpenters, painters, ship fitters and pipe fitters. None were
hired.
      R. B. Ackerman, vice president of the corporation, testified that "we

are from Cleveland, Ohio, and are not prejudiced. The problem is new to us,
but it is more or less controlled by conditions of the South."

He said further that the company entered into a preferential hiring
agreement with the New Orleans Metal Trades Council in October of 1941, and
under that agreement the company hires all of its workers through the unions
affiliated therewith.

Further explaining the company's policy, Mr. Ackerman said that if the
union under the hiring agreement referred skilled Negro workers to the
company, the latter would hire them but that no such referrals had ever been
made.

Feared Friction, Strikes

Robert Quinn, president of the New Orleans Metal Trades Council, said there
are 23 union members of the council, but denied racial discrimination is the
policy. He admitted, however, that Negro union members had an equal chance
with the whites of being referred to or hired by the company. He asserted
that he believed to hire Negroes in Delta would cause friction and strikes.
His attention was called to Negro and white bricklayers in the same New
Orleans union, who have worked side by side since 1922.

Mr. McCollum also denied the boilermakers discriminated or that Negroes
were organized into an auxiliary local with discriminatory intentions. He
said that he had not sent any boilermakers to Delta because he had none to
send. He denied "firing" Mr. Dixon because of complaints to the FEPC and
others.

Pittsburgh Courier, November 21, 1942.

41. POST MORTEM ON FEPC

In resigning as chief counsel to the President's Committee on Fair Employment Practices after War Manpower Commissioner McNutt had torpedoed the
scheduled hearings into anti-Negro railroad discrimination, Henry Epstein,
former New York State Solicitor General, wrote:

The sudden cancellation of the hearings without warning or opportunity
for discussion by the President's Committee is, in my judgment, an irreparable
blow to your committee's prestige and must result in loss of public confidence
in its effectiveness.

Mr. Epstein is just about 100 per cent right and no amount of weasel
words like "indefinite postponement" can obscure the ugly truth. When the
FEPC sought to get down to rock bottom on this question of discrimination
against Negro labor in a major industry vital to the winning of the war, it
was ruthlessly sidetracked.

This action marks the final triumph of a long and consistent campaign
to make the FEPC completely ineffective, so far as ending discrimination in
war industry is concerned.

The FEPC was handicapped from the first in having no punitive measures
to work with, as in the case of other government agencies aiding the prosecution of the war.

In consequence, the FEPC, when it found rank color discrimination in
existence, could only tap the war contractor on the wrist, figuratively
speaking, and urge him to "Go and sin no more."

It got some co-operation from war contractors outside the Solid South
and Negro workers entered many plants from which they had been previously
barred, but they were largely employed at unskilled tasks, and promotion
in accordance with experience, tenure, aptitude and skill has been dis-
appointingly slow where it has happened at all.

The campaign to scuttle the FEPC got into full swing when it announced
the hearings in Birmingham.

Some Alabama newspapers, aided and abetted by local demagogues, waved the bloody shirt and mobilized the dervishes of racial proscription to battle against any threat to white supremacy.

At the hearings Mark Ethridge, "true to his native land," administered the kiss of death.

After the hearings, the conspiracy to scuttle the committee gained impetus with some never-publicized skullduggery in high places, egged on by Congressional Negrophobes, which resulted in burying the FEPC in the War Manpower Commission where Mr. McNutt owns its body if not its soul.

It is significant that prior to the transfer, Mr. McNutt had already established a Negro setup whose purpose, though suspected, was never clearly defined.

The transfer brought forth such a clamor from liberal circles that everybody in authority yelled "'tain't so" and professions of love for the committee were profuse. The rival jim-crow setup was banished from the WMC payroll.

The FEPC got more money and allegedly more freedom but remained in the shadow of the McNutt veto.

Then came the announcment of the hearings into charges of discrimination against Negroes by the country's railroads and the autocratic, lily-white railroad unions--charges that would have been as easy to prove as the existence of cold weather in Siberia.

This sort of thing was "embarrassing" and "unthinkable" to powerful business and labor czars who have slowly been eliminating Negroes from the few skilled jobs they still hold, and who do not intend to change their anti-Negro policies, war or no war.

So the hearings have been "indefinitely postponed."

When the hearings will be held is anybody's guess, but skeptics profess to believe that it will not be in our time.

The FEPC may continue to function but after this severe blow its future existence will probably be like that of a zombie UNLESS THERE IS A TREMENDOUS AND NATION-WIDE COMPLAINT FROM NEGRO ORGANIZATIONS, CHURCHES, UNIONS AND BUSINESSES, and those white groups eager to see democracy work in the United States.

Pittsburgh Courier, January 23, 1943.

42. MEMBERS ADVISED NOT TO TALK UNTIL AFTER CONFERENCE

FEPC Developments During Week

Walter P. Reuther, vice-president of the UAW-CIO, and member of the Labor-Management Policy Committee of WMC, protested to President Roosevelt and Chairman McNutt against postponement of FEPC hearings on discrimination in the railroad industry.

Powerful National Maritime Union wired Mr. McNutt denouncing the postponement as a "blow to the war against fascism."

Evidencing his resentment at McNutt's action, Harry Epstein, FEPC special counsel, tendered his resignation.

Walter White, NAACP secretary, held Roosevelt's secretary, Marvin McIntyre, partly responsible for suppression of FEPC hearing and called McIntyre "self-appointed President of the Negroes."

A delegation from Detroit, headed by Rev. Charles Hill, conferred with McNutt but received no "encouragement" that the hearing would be held.

George Marshall, president of National Federation for Constitutional Liberties, in a letter to the President expressed "grave concern" over the indefinite postponement.

The National Lawyers Guild called on President Roosevelt to "re-create" FEPC as an independent agency with complete autonomy.

The CIO, through James B. Carey, secretary, leveled a sharp attack on McNutt and charged the postponement was a "serious blow to the war morale of Negro citizens and to all whites who know that racial discrimination is a Hitlerite weapon."

William Green, AFL president, has instructed Boris Shishkin, Federation
representative on FEPC, to voice AFL's opposition to McNutt's action at the
committee meeting this week.[113]

The Socialist Party called upon McNutt to "rescind" his postponement
order.

NAACP branches throughout the country began organizing for mass protest
on the ban on FEPC investigation.

The National Urban League, through President William H. Baldwin, wired
President Roosevelt and Commissioner McNutt that it was "disturbed over apparent trends toward immobilization of the Committee's authority."

Dr. Max Yergan, president of the National Negro Congress, demanded the
restoration of FEPC's power as an independent agency.[114]

A. Philip Randolph, head of the March on Washington Movement and militant leaders of the Porters' Brotherhood, led a delegation of labor and civic
leaders to Washington for a conference with McNutt on Monday.

By E. W. BAKER
(Staff Correspondent)

WASHINGTON, D.C., Jan. 21--War Manpower Boss Paul V. McNutt remained
adamant in the face of the most withering blast of criticism and protests ever
leveled at a government official in one week, and he steadfastly refused to
clarify his order to the Fair Employment Practice Committee, forcing it to
halt a scheduled investigation into discrimination within the railroad industry or to satisfy two delegations as to the reason for its issuance.

With many wild rumors abroad as to the reason for squelching the probe,
members of FEPC, acting on orders from Dr. Malcolm S. MacLean, chairman, have
refused to publicly comment on McNutt's action. The members had no opportunity to discuss the postponement and it came as a complete surprise to them.

Members May Resign

Dr. MacLean has called a meeting of the entire committee for Friday and
it is expected they will thoroughly analyze McNutt's order and the future of
FEPC in being able to enforce Roosevelt's Executive Order 8802.

Members who were polled separately were unanimous in stating the ban on
the committee's probe was a challenge to FEPC's existence and would hamper or
completely make ineffective any further probe against jim crow in the nation's
war industries. It is believed the committee will make a direct appeal to
President Roosevelt following their Friday meeting and if that procedure is
not effective, they are expected to resign in a body.

Labor Leaders Oppose Order

With the strong position taken by both the CIO and the AFL, it is a
certainty their representatives on the committee will make a strong protest
against the suppression of the hearing, which was scheduled for January 25.

William Green, AFL president, has already advised Boris Shishkin, AFL
representative, to register the Federation's opposition to McNutt's order.
Green is believed to feel the railroad hearing should go on as scheduled.

John Brophy, CIO representative, and Milton P. Webster, of the Brotherhood of Sleeping Car Porters, are expected to join Shishkin in demanding
that McNutt rescind his order.

Wendell Willkie Consulted [115]

After consultation with Wendell Willkie in New York last week, a group
of citizens issued a statement saying "The cancellation not only is an irreparable blow to the Negro people, but does the utmost damage to the whole
prosecution of the war." The committee was composed of Ferdinand Smith,
of the National Maritime union; Dr. Max Yergan, of the NNC; Dr. Warren Banner,
National Urban League; Edward Lewis, New York Urban League; Joseph People's
committee, and Rev. A. Clayton Powell, Jr., city councilman.

A. Philip Randolph, militant leader, whose threat to lead a "March" on
Washington forced President Roosevelt to issue the Executive Order, in a
statement, said: "McNutt's action is a slap in the face of/and insult to,
upwards of 20 millions of Negro Americans. It makes them feel that the
President is surrendering to the race-prejudice-mongering political demagogues
of the South. President Roosevelt stated in the famous White House conference
that some agency was needed to which could be presented complaints of discriminations. He established such an agency and charged it with the responsibility of investigating discriminations in war industries. Such is the
function and responsibility of FEPC."
    Walter White, NAACP secretary, strongly urged President Roosevelt to
"restore the Fair Employment Practice Committee to its full independent
status prior to its transfer to the War Manpower Commission."

Pittsburgh Courier, January 23, 1943.

43. WHAT ABOUT THE FEPC?

    The enthusiasm that swept colored America in the summer of 1941 over
Executive Order 8802 and the formation of the Fair Employment Practices Committee is as dead as Montezuma.
    In the first flush of optimism the order was hailed as a second Eman-
cipation Proclamation destined to free colored labor from the shackles of job
discrimination, it being forgotten that the original proclamation of emancipation actually freed nobody.
    The Executive Order was to apply to all new contractors for war produc-
tion and, of course, to the far-flung government agencies.
    True, the Committee possessed no punitive powers and depended entirely
upon moral suasion to enforce the President's order but this serious weakness
was overlooked or minimized at the time.
    It is probable that Congress, which has just abolished with great haste
the $25,000 salary ceiling, would not have passed a law punishing war con-
tractors for jeopardizing national existence by insisting on job jim crow,
but neither the Administration forces nor members of the Opposition introduced
any such law.
    In consequence the FEPC has been passively and actively resisted by its
numerous enemies almost from its birth.
    Passively it has been resisted by calculated failure of numerous war
contractors to hire colored workers at all, to hire them only in certain
positions from which they could not advance, or to hire only a very few in
order to escape the charge of colored discrimination.
    Actively it has been resisted and attacked by certain Southern white
politicians and employers as an effort on the part of the Administration to
saddle social equality upon Dixie, and this attack served as the signal for
rallying Southern reactionism against the more liberal policies of the New
Deal.
    The rest of the country possessed sufficient political power to force the
reactionary minority in the South to end color discrimination on the job in
order to speed victory which is dependent upon industrial production, but, as
usual, it refused to do so.
    It might be added that the Administration has set a rather bad example
by its approval and extension of segregation and color discrimination throughout the armed forces.
    Apparently the Committee itself was not above suspicion of insincerity
after Mark Ethridge lifted the hopes of the reactionary South and dashed those
of colored citizens by his Birmingham speech, and after Dr. Malcolm MacLean,
president of Hampton Institute, another member, was revealed as wholeheartedly
approving suspension of the railroad hearings.
    Even Lawrence Cramer, former governor of the Virgin Islands and the com-
mittee's secretary whose appointment to the job was "plugged" by the NAACP on
the ground of alleged friendliness to colored folk, is accused in the March
issue of Common Sense as having "often said that Negroes are too emotional

about their problems and that whites can be more objective and should therefore administer policy on Negro affairs."

Weak and handicapped as it was from the beginning, the FEPC was rendered
more helpless by transfer to the War Manpower Commission and now seems to be
almost completely impotent.

What gains have been made in the employment and promotion of colored
workers in war industries have been due more to the pressure of production
demands and the shortage of manpower than to the efforts of the FEPC although
its efforts have not been entirely ineffective.

Now the colored people of this country want to know what the Administration proposes to do about the FEPC.

Is it to be given an independent status and real power to compel obedience
to the President's order? Is it to continue its present zombie-like existence?
Or is it to be quietly buried, unhonored and unsung?

Pittsburgh Courier, April 3, 1943.

44. HAAS COMPROMISE BITTERLY SCORED

Opponents See Government Approval of Segregation--Dr. Graham
Issues WLB Ruling Outlawing Race Classifications

By John P. Davis
(Staff Correspondent)

WASHINGTON, June 10--A Sharp struggle over the future of FEPC, which
involved the question of the whole future status of Negro workers in industry,
is developing at rapid pace this week. Before many weeks have passed, it is
likely that this battle will loom as one of the most bitter and significant
actions on the home front.

Here in brief is the FEPC news this week: Monsignor Francis Joseph Haas,
newly selected chairman of the FEPC, sworn in at the White House on May 31,
last week, postponed again--this time indefinitely--the FEPC hearings on discrimination against Negro workers by the Capitol Transit company, which had
already once before been postponed.[116]

Approves Mobile Solution

Reasons given for this action were that the full six-man committee,
created under the new executive order (Executive Order 9346 replacing Executive Order 8802) of President Roosevelt, had not been named and that hearings
would not be held until the committees had been re-organized.

Next Monsignor Haas announced that a solution of the difficulties at the
shipyard of the Alabama Drydock and Shipbuilding company had been approved by
him, by the War Manpower Commission Chairman, Paul V. McNutt, by the Assistant
Secretary of the Navy (Ralph Bard), by the chairman of the U.S. Maritime
Commission (Rear Admiral Emory S. Land).

The announcement stated: "Under the arrangement confirmed by the heads
of the interested agencies. Negroes will be upgraded in all skills necessary
for bare hull construction on ways one through four of the Alabama Drydock
and Shipbuilding company, and these ways will be set aside for bare hull
construction by Negro workers."

Places Okay on Segregation

Back of these actions lies a hidden meaning that is of utmost importance
to all Negro America. The decision in the Alabama case simply means that the
federal government--acting through the War Manpower Commission, the Maritime
Commission, the Navy and the President's Committee on Fair Employment Practice,
itself, has agreed to segregate Negro workers to one section of the shipyard
and has approved their exclusion from all other sections of the shipyard.

The arguments of those who support the solution in the Alabama case are important to examine. Here is a summary of their point of view from an important actor in the whole developing drama:
"The attempt to upgrade Negro workers in the Mobile shipyards led to racial violence with several Negro workers severely beaten and mobbed. The white Southern anti-Roosevelt leaders, who bitterly attacked the Birmingham hearings of the FEPC, will make political capital out of the upgrading of Negro workers if these workers have to work side by side with whites in superior positions. If there is any attempt to insist on upgrading without segregation then there will be nothing but violence, a halt to vital war production and no real benefit to Negro workers. On the other hand, the real meaning of the solution in the Mobile case is that 5,000 Negro workers will be employed in addition to 7,000 now working there; that Negro workers will be rapidly trained and employed at practically all skills on the four segregated all Negro shipways.

Establishes Jim Crow Job Pattern

As Lawrence Cramer, executive secretary of FEPC, stated it to The Courier "The FEPC has in the past refused to decide hypothetically that segregation of Negro from white workers was discrimination referred to in the President's Executive Order. We always take the position that if in a segregated situation any individual can show that by being segregated he is discriminated against, we will take action."
Now that is one side. Here is the other. Opponents of the recent FEPC decision point out that if Negroes are segregated from whites on the job, it will be impossible to prevent discrimination against them; that in fact segregation is discrimination. They point out that the Alabama decision threatens to establish a jim-crow job pattern throughout the country of frightening proportions, that every industry all over the country will seize on the formula of a segregated section or plant for Negro workers, and that after the war the Negro will be driven out of industry completely. They claim that the action of Chairman Haas, acting alone and not even waiting for the selection of the other members of the committee, has destroyed his usefulness to the FEPC. This side declares that it is precisely because there must be all-out war production that the "Haas Compromise"--like the "Missouri Compromise" will settle nothing. [117]

Graham Raps Classification

If the side opposed to the new FEPC chairman had purposely sought a champion for its cause, it could have done no better than it did last week when quite by accident a spokesman for its side fell into its lap. That spokesman was Dr. Frank P. Graham, white Southerner, president of the University of North Carolina, member of the War Labor Board, and the first man sought by President Roosevelt to head the FEPC. In a decision by the National War Labor Board written by him and adopted unanimously, Dr. Graham lashed out bitterly against the classification "colored laborer." The case which arose in Texas concerned the practice of an oil company in paying Negro workers a lower wage than white workers for the same work.
Said Dr. Graham: "In this small but significant case the National War Labor Board abolishes the classifications "colored labor" and white labor" and reclassifies both simply as "laborers" with the same rates of pay for all in that classification without discrimination on account of color.
Dr. Graham pointed out that this decision was in line with the President's Executive Order 8802, "with prophetic Americanism; and with the cause of the United Nations."
Said Dr. Graham:

Praises Loyalty of Negroes

"Economic and political discrimination on account of race or creed is in line with the Nazi program. America, in the days of its infant weakness the haven of heretics and the oppressed of all races, must not in the days of its power become the stronghold of bigots. The world has given America the vigor and variety of its differences. America should protect and enrich its differences for the sake of America and the world. Understanding religious and

racial differences make for a better understanding of other differences and
for an appreciation of the sacredness of human personality, as a basic to
human freedom. The American answer to differences in color and creed is not
a concentration camp but co-operation. The answer to human error is not
terror but light and liberty under the moral law. By this light and liberty,
the Negro has made a contribution in work and faith, song and story, laughter
and struggle which are an enduring part of the spiritual heritage of America.

"There is no more loyal group of our fellow-citizens than the American
Negroes, north and south. In defense of America from attack from without,
they spring to arms in the spirit of Dorie Miller of Texas, the Negro mess boy,
who, when the machine gunner on the Arizona was killed, jumped to his unap-
pointed place and fired the last rounds as the ship was sinking in Pearl
Harbor. [118]

"It is the acknowledged fact that in spite of all the handicaps of
slavery and discrimination, the Negro in America, has compressed more progress
in the shortest time than any race in human history. Slavery gave the Negro
his Chiristianity. Christianity gave the Negro his freedom. This freedom
must give the Negro equal rights to home and health, education and citizenship,
and an equal opportunity to work and fight for our common country.

Dean Morse Notes Agreement

"Whether as vigorous fighting men or for production of food and munitions,
America needs the Negro; the Negro needs the equal opportunity to work and
fight. The Negro is necessary for winning the war, and, at the same time, is
a test of our sincerity in the cause for which we are fighting. More hundreds
of millions of colored people are involved in the outcome of this war than the
combined populations of the Axis Powers. Under Hitler and his Master Race,
their movement is backward to slavery and despair. In America, the colored
people have the freedom to struggle for freedom. With the victory of the
democracies, the human destiny is toward freedom, hope, equality of opportunity and the gradual fulfillment for all peoples of the noblest aspirations
of the brothers of men and the sons of God, without regard to color or creed,
region or race, in the world neighborhood of human brotherhood."

The opinion of Dr. Graham so strongly represented the opinion of the War
Labor Board that Dean Wayne L. Morse, although he had not taken part in the
decision, asked consent to have the record show that he agreed completely
with the opinion of Dr. Graham. [119]

Thus the battle between these two opposing points of view is clearly
developing and on its outcome will depend the whole future of FEPC.

Pittsburgh Courier, June 12, 1943.

45. THE NEW FEPC

It was a year ago this month that the President's Committee on Fair
Employment Practice was transferred to the War Manpower Commission and thus
hamstrung in its activities. Throughout the fall, winter and spring the
committee was engaged in disputes as to its scope and power and no progress
was made on the main business of halting discrimination in employment. Indeed,
the sudden cancellation of the scheduled railroad hearing in January and the
sidetracking of the Capital Transit case suggested that the committee was
about to be dissolved.

But under pressure from many sources, and in the face of an unprecedented
unity of Negro groups, Mr. Roosevelt has issued an amended executive order
creating a new committee with a paid director, Mgr. Francis J. Haas. The
committee has been removed from the jurisdiction of the WMC and has its money
supplied, as it was originally, from the executive funds at the disposal of
the President.

The first action of Mgr. Haas, taken before the full committee had been
named, was a grievous and unfortunate mistake, the condoning of the segregation of workers in the Mobile shipyards case. But since then steps have been

taken which indicate that the committee is to pick up where it left off last
August. The staff has been reorganized and augmented. An FEPC field staff,
responsible to the committee and not to other agencies, is being set up. The
railroad hearing has been re-scheduled. The Detroit hearing will be held.
The Capital Transit case, involving the refusal of the management to employ
Negroes on trolleys and buses, has been re-opened. Positive action has been
taken on the complaint of Negro workers in West Coast shipyards that they have
been forced into a jim crow auxiliary union which gives them no power or protection in collective bargaining.

In short, the FEPC seems to be on its way again, after a year of immobilization. If the events of that year have any meaning it is that the
people who want FEPC to be effective must be constantly on the alert to see
that its enemies do not once more shackle the agency--and its enemies are
numerous and powerful.

The Crisis, 50 (August, 1943): 231.

46. RAILROADS PLEAD GUILTY

Twenty-two major railroads of the country and fourteen railroad unions
have pleaded guilty to charges of deliberate and systematic discrimination
against Negro and Mexican workers. In four days of hearings before the
President's Committee on Fair Employment Practice bald admissions of discriminatory policies were placed in the record by the carriers. The unions
did not deign to appear and deny or affirm their lily-white policies.

The railroads admitted they did not hire Negroes as firemen, enginemen,
trainmen, conductors, or stewards, and that they did not promote Negroes from
certain categories in which they are at present employed. Negro firemen, once
numerous on southern carriers, are being frozen out; none has been hired since
the middle Twenties. Negroes may be porters, waiters, cooks, laborers, and
helpers--nothing else.

There was a great hue and cry when these hearings were summarily cancelled
last January. Pressure finally brought about a reorganization of FEPC and a
re-scheduling of the hearings. The revelations in the record are ample justification for the long fight for, although most Negroes knew of the policies in
effect, they had little idea of the ramifications and the complete shackling of
our people in the railroad industry. Few white people outside of those in
the industry knew the facts.

We are not naive enough to believe that a hearing by a government agency
in itself can change conditions, but it is a step forward in the fight for
economic opportunity to have an official record of the discrimination. We can
go on from here. We can spread the story (and we will have to do it, since
the daily papers, with two exceptions, boycotted the hearings) and we can
mobilize our pressures, political, moral, and economic, to effect a change.

Our fight here and abroad is for democracy. The essence of democracy is
equality of opportunity. We must put down our anger at the arrogance of the
railroads and the miserableness of the railroad unions and get to work on the
problem. We can win.

The Crisis, 50 (October, 1943): 295.

47. CIVIL RIGHTS

The hateful practice of discrimination because of race, religion or
national origin against which we are fighting abroad must be stamped out at
home. Economic, political and civil equality must be guaranteed to every
American, regardless of his race, creed or national origin.

We call for the establishment of a permanent Fair Employment Practices

Committee with adequate appropriations and enforcement powers. We urge legislation to prohibit activities or propaganda directed against any individuals
because of their racial, religious or national origin.
 (a) The immediate passage of the anti-poll tax bill and elimination of
other restrictions on the right to vote;
 (b) Enactment of a genuine soldier vote bill.
 Free, strong and responsible labor organizations are the bulwark of
democracy. Their growth, and the extension of the process of collective
bargaining throughout American industry must be encouraged as an objective of
national policy. The right to join labor unions of their own choosing must
be guaranteed and protected for all wage earners, including federal, state
and local government employees.

CIO News, June 12, 1944.

48. DITCHING THE PERMANENT FEPC

 Congresswoman Mary T. Norton, chairman of the House Labor committee, has
postponed hearings on the creation of a permanent Fair Employment Practices
Committee, and said that "It is our intention to continue hearings when Congress reassembles after the election, report the bill and do everything possible to have it enacted before the expiration of the 78th Congress."[120]
 This sounds very much like the death knell of the permanent FEPC.
 If the bill can be enacted after election, it has a much better chance of
being enacted before election.
 But indications are rather clear that a permanent FEPC will not be
enacted either before or after election.
 The war may soon be over and when peace comes it is very unlikely that
any such effort will be made to force private business to do what war industry
was induced to do.
 If there is no permanent FEPC, Negroes will have to launch a tremendous
campaign before election, and the time seems to be too short.
 At any rate, the bill is now ditched and it will take a herculean effort
to revive it.
 President Roosevelt could lend his powerful support to the measure, but
so far no word has come from him.
 Apparently he would rather risk losing the Negro vote than the support
of the Solid South which is opposed to a FEPC, whether temporary or permanent.
 So far, only the Republicans have promised to enact such a measure.

Pittsburgh Courier, September 16, 1944.

49. OUR STAKE IN A PERMANENT FEPC

By Ina Sugihara

*This article points out the accomplishments and weaknesses of the present
FEPC, an outgrowth of the war emergency, and explains why a permanent agency
is necessary in postwar America.*

 Congress will soon decide whether or not millions of Americans of color,
and of unpopular creeds and backgrounds, will have a chance to earn a living
following this war. The Scanlon-Dawson-LaFollette bills in the House of
Representatives (H.R. 3986) and in the Senate (S. 2048), as they stand now,
are the basis for an effective Fair Employment Practice Commission.
 The 1944 lame duck Congress, after a day and a half of hearings before
the House Labor Committee, chose to act on the measures. A favorable vote
will mean a federal agency fighting job discrimination permanently. The temporary President's Committee on Fair Employment Practice, created June 25, 1941,

by an Executive Order, is slated to go out of existence next June.
The existing FEPC was originally empowered to discourage discrimination in
employment by government agencies and defense plants based on race, creed,
color or national origin. This Committee was organized because Walter White,
A. Philip Randolph, Frank R. Crosswaith, and Layle Lane, representing thousands,
visited the President and threatened a march on Washington if he would not make
such an effort.
The FEPC was later reinforced by Executive Order 9346, issued on May 27,
1943, which gave it additional scope and larger facilities. The Committee's
jurisdiction today extends over any company holding a contract or sub-contract
with the government, in addition to government agencies and war plants. Discrimination on the basis of ancestry was added to the original complaints of
race, creed, color, and national origin. A Presidential statement in January,
1942, included aliens among these.
This means that because of the work of many organizations like the NAACP,
the Workers Defense League, the Brotherhood of Sleeping Car Porters, the March
on Washington Movement, the American Civil Liberties Union, and the Socialist
Party, not only Negroes but Catholics, Jews, Japanese-Americans, Chinese-Ameri-
cans, Mexican-Americans, Jehovah's Witnesses, Seventh-day Adventists, and
refugees are protected from unfair treatment by certain employers.

Protection Temporary

But this protection is a temporary expedient without sufficient power and
scope to remove discrimination in our economy on any large scale. The Committee has only executive powers in a limited field, though it has done well
in that field, and it has met unusually difficult hardships. Only a Permanent
Fair Employment Practice Commission can hope to tackle the most flagrant
practices in our major industries.
The present FEPC has had a harder struggle for existence than perhaps any
other agency. Aside from lacking sufficient funds and personnel, its status
as a committee has been changed often. First it functioned in the Labor
Division of the Office of Production Management; then it was placed under the
War Manpower Commission, where Paul V. McNutt postponed indefinitely the
Railroad Hearings scheduled for February, 1943; now it is an independent agency,
as a result of Executive Order 9346, with funds appropriated by Congress every
June and twelve regional offices which handle complaints and make investigations.
The Committee never had free enough rein or authority necessary to do its
job. It has no power to appeal to the courts and, being a government agency,
it cannot look for cases--the cases must come through complainants or the
United States Employment Service which refers instances of discrimination
against applicants and of employers requesting "Christians," "whites," etc.
Even though members of the Committee or its regional directors may know that
X Company discriminates against Negroes, or Jews, or others, neither the
Washington headquarters nor the regional directors can conduct an investigation
on X Company or make it change its policy unless the USES requests an investigation or someone complains of having been denied a job with the concern
because of his minority status, refused promotion, or given an unfair salary.
As a federal agency the Committee's scope is not complete, for it has no
jurisdiction over the armed forces, nor does it have jurisdiction over all
inter-state Commerce--only over those industries and businesses that are considered war plants or have contracts or sub-contracts with the government.
This leaves out some of our biggest businesses. For example, the Committee
does not touch the major portion of the garment industry not producing clothes
for the armed forces; it cannot work on banks or insurance houses, five-and-
ten-cent stores, movies, department stores or mail-order houses.

Jurisdiction Limited

It has no jurisdiction over intra-state or local commerce. For these do
not have contracts with the government or produce war materials; otherwise,
they would necessarily be inter-state. The existing FEPC cannot handle cases
of discrimination in beauty parlors, small grocery or department stores, local
banks, real estate concerns. It cannot influence state, county, or municipal
agencies, being a federal committee.

When the war is over, the FEPC will have control over even less territory than it has now; for there will be no war plants and very few businesses having contracts with the government. Most of our major industries will still be excluded and the Committee will become even more than now an excuse to appease those who demand full employment.

Moreover, since the Committee is a temporary agency to help the war effort, its examiners cannot go to employers and say, "Look, Bud, this is a democracy. We want it in reality as well as in name. That means that we hire people on the basis of their ability, and not on the basis of color or race. . . ." They must instead point to the economic need of the moment: "We're fighting a war. We need goods for our men and our allies. You're hindering production by not hiring Jews. . . ." This argument will be washed away in peacetime and employers will not have been educated.

But the FEPC, despite its handicaps, has made substantial contributions to the cause of greater justice and equality for all.

One of its most important functions has been to prove to people, some of whom were previously concerned over the welfare of one minority group or another, that the fate of each minority depends upon the extent of justice given all other groups. As stated previously, the Committee handles cases involving a variety of people as covered by Executive Order 9346. In so doing, it eliminates the practice of discrimination as such and makes for better treatment for all, just as inequality crosses group boundaries and becomes a cancer in the lives of all of us.

Of permanent value to future efforts for better race relations are the lessons learned by the Committee from handling actual cases on race discrimination. This is an unprecedented practice, except unofficially on the part of outside private organizations. This experience can be the foundation for any new agency created to destroy inequality in any sphere.

Flagrant Practices Revealed

As an investigating agency its hearings, held throughout the country, have revealed flagrant practices. The railroad hearings, finally held in September, 1943, showed that both carriers and unions had been conniving to squeeze Negroes out of the industry for several decades, that Negroes cannot become engineers on diesel engines, that colored locomotive firemen had been shot out of their cabs, that one road alone needed 1400 skilled and semi-skilled workers in 1943, and that carriers hired new men and women for these jobs while experienced Negroes were being fired and no new ones hired. The findings were referred to the President, who in December, 1943, appointed the Stacey Committee to conduct further investigation and make recommendations. A year has passed and that committee has not yet taken action.

As an administrative agency, the FEPC has done wonders, despite inadequate funds and personnel. It has changed policies of officials who were real Bourbons. One manager insisted that he would not be responsible if "one of those 'coons' (meaning Negroes) gets a piece of red hot iron down his pants or . . . a man (gets) dropped into an acid trough." The FEPC induced this concern to eliminate its segregated toilet and washroom facilities without compromising any of the employer's responsibilities.

The Committee has had personnel managers changed where they and not the company were found to discriminate. In one instance, all Jews referred to a plant as timekeepers were refused jobs, though people had been obtained from other sources and gentiles sent were always hired. Negroes and Jews were employed in production. The fair practice examiner from the regional FEPC office observed after numerous conversations that the company itself did not discriminate. He ordered the person hiring timekeepers to be replaced and directed the company to issue a statement to all its personnel managers, its officials, the union with whom it had a contract, and the U.S. Employment Service that it was hiring persons regardless of race, creed, color, national origin, or ancestry in compliance with Executive Order 9346.

This statement is required of all companies found to discriminate in hiring. If any concern refuses to obey an FEPC order, the Committee refers the case to the procurement officer of the Army, Navy, or Marines, who can cancel the company's contract for war materials. This is the economic, not judicial, enforcement now in effect. Final appeal is to the President.

The FEPC has for the first time challenged the Civil Service Commission's prerogative of appointing one out of the three highest ranking applicants for a position, which eliminated "undesirable" persons on any basis. A regional director recently referred the case of a Negro, who had not been promoted though two people with lower grades had been, to the deputy regional director of the War Manpower Commission, who reprimanded the appointing civil service officer. The man got his post.

Employers cannot go back on promises to their employees if they now produce war materials or have contracts with the government, because of the FEPC. One company tried it. It did not give Negroes the third of three raises promised when they were hired. Three of these complained through the Committee. The fair practice examiner visited company officials and demanded the raises. The company paid it.

Accomplishments of FEPC

Perhaps the most notable accomplishments of the FEPC is its successful handling of cases involving Japanese-Americans through a maze of other government agencies, necessarily and unnecessarily involved, war hysteria, hidden circumstances and personalities, and other factors not found in the usual cases.

In the New York regional office of the Committee one of the fair practice examiners is a "Japanese expert." He is a Negro. He obtained fair treatment for twenty-eight Japanese-American seamen in the Coast Guard who were stranded in New York--their homes are in Hawaii--through a complaint by one of them. The State Department would not issue passports for them to sail on the high seas even though they had all the necessary requirements. The examiner encountered considerable buck-passing between the State and Navy Departments and then convinced the Coast Guard, where the case finally landed that machinery for appeal should be created for the one seaman. This was done and all the men can now appeal a denial of a passport to the district Coast Guard officer, who is actually their superior officer.

All of these contributions of the FEPC will be valuable in forming the basis for any agency we may adopt in the future to fight race discrimination.

But only through a permanent Fair Employment Practice Commission, as outlined in the Scanlon-Dawson-LaFollette bills in the House and in the Senate, authorized by Congress to carry out the law of the land made by that body, can we hope to solve the tremendous problem of eliminating discrimination in employment by big business during postwar dislocation and depression. The argument we now use that people should be hired because we need them for war production will no longer hold; employers will be quick to fire workers since labor supply will exceed demand. Moreover, unrest among workers will cause greater hostility toward minority groups as job competitors. It will be a situation in which the economically strong are likely to "pit race against race, class against class; divide and conquer."

Most of the defects of the present FEPC are corrected in the permanent FEPC bills introduced in the House and the Senate with of course, the exception of that problem of local industries. This can be handled only by state FEPC's, which will be a "must" if we want to end job discrimination on a large scale.

Of course, no government agency can ever completely end discrimination by itself, for we can do that only by ridding ourselves as a nation of fear and prejudice. It can only meet the needs of those who know that they are wronged and who want to do something constructive about it. But the sooner we have an agency battling job inequality, the sooner we insist on the establishment of such an agency, the more quickly will the people learn that discrimination in employment exists and should be abolished. Just as the anti-lynching bill, which has never been passed, has reduced the number of known lynchings, the fight for the FEPC will cause flagrant unfair employment practices to decrease.

The federal bills cover all employers in interstate and foreign commerce hiring more than five persons; this in addition to those holding contracts with the government or performing work indirectly for government purposes. They include labor unions among groups that must not discriminate; i.e., those who have five or more persons employed in concerns affected by the act.

They state: "The right to work and to seek work without discrimination because of race, creed, color, national origin, or ancestry is declared to be an immunity of all citizens of the United States, which shall not be abridged by any State or by an instrumentality or creature of any State."

Perhaps the greatest hope for success by the projected new FEPC is its authority to petition circuit courts of appeals to enforce its orders, as has been done by the National Labor Relations Board. Likewise, persons dissatisfied with the Commission's orders could appeal to the courts. Penalties are provided for employers and unions that do not comply with the Commission's orders.

The present FEPC's personnel, funds, and records would be transferred to the new Commission.

Thus the administrative and investigating ability of the present FEPC combined with the authority inherent in a permanent Fair Employment Practice Commission would make a strong agency to fight job discrimination after this war.

The bills in the House and the Senate are at this writing in the hands of the Labor Committees of both bodies.

These measures would make it possible for the permanent FEPC to change the pattern of discrimination in our major industries. The railroads would not be as dangerous a field for Negroes to work in as they now are and Negroes would not be eliminated from them.

The five-and-ten-cent stores would not be able to flout discrimination in people's faces by hiring no Negroes in stores where the trade is almost completely colored. Of course, cases would have to be brought by complainants against these groups, but the authority would be there for people to use.

If a permanent FEPC is bolstered by effective state FEPC's throughout the country, we will have licked the biggest problem of discrimination that we have had to tackle. Greater unity among workers and consequently stronger bargaining power, better working conditions for all labor, and a breach, that might be enlarged, in the wall of discrimination would be the gains. It would no longer be necessary for members of minority groups to "scab" and lower labor standards in order to earn a living. Strong businessmen who will not maintain fair employment practices unless compelled to do so by law would be beaten.

Backers of New FEPC

The same people who demanded the original FEPC are now campaigning for the new one. They are organized in the Council for a Permanent FEPC with headquarters at 1410 H Street, N.W., Washington, D.C., which prods the labor committees of both houses to report the bills out favorably, obtains promises from representatives and senators, wherever possible, to vote "yes" once the bill is on the floor, and conducts a public relations drive through key people throughout the country to get local support and to educate the electorate.

Fair employment practice is a crucial issue for everyone in planning for a postwar America without race riots, without "Boss Hagueism," without another lost generation. For only by giving people an equal chance to produce and to be useful can we attain an economy of plenty with enough to go around, which alone will prevent stocked warehouses and empty stomachs.

The Crisis, 52 (January, 1945): 14-15, 29.

50. FEPC BILL KILLED

Action on funds for the Fair Employment Practice Committee had come to a full circle stop as The CIO NEWS went to press this week.

Fought by the poll tax Democrats and given only lukewarm support by most Republicans, the appropriation for the present FEPC had gone (July 6) to a point where the whole process of getting it passed in both House and Senate must be begun again.

Briefly, the tangled parliamentary situation was this: the War Agencies bill (in which FEPC funds were included) was sent back to the Senate by determined action of House liberals in raising points of order against it which they did in order to force a vote on FEPC.

Earlier, the Senate had sent the war agencies bill over to the House minus any appropriation for FEPC. This was done on demand of filibuster leaders Bilbo (D., Miss.), and Eastland (D., Miss.). An attempted compromise to give FEPC $250,000 (half its regular appropriation) had failed.

One of the sharpest battles in recent Congressional history has been fought around this issue, with the CIO, the labor and liberal movement generally, and liberal Congressmen ranged against the poll taxers and apathetic Republicans on the other.

Republicans, in fact, have been quietly cheering at the exhibition, in which they simply stand by and watch the poll tax Democrats sabotage an issue of key importance in the next elections.

CIO News, July 9, 1945.

THE FEPC AND DISCRIMINATION AT WEST COAST SHIPYARDS

51. JULIA AND DAISY DOLLARHYDE (SAN JOSE, CALIF.)
TO FRANKLIN D. ROOSEVELT, JANUARY 6, 1943

I am writing in concern with shipyard work, about prejudice. Ten of us Negroes here from San Jose have went up to the Richmond shipyard and have been turned down because of our race. We have been up to the employment agency four times and they still refuse us employment. We would like to know whether or not there is any prejudice in the defense work. Our boys are fighting for this country and we would like to be working to help the war. We've done things such as turning in rubber, metals, and cooking. . . . We would like to be helping more if we can. We see people come from other states every day getting jobs, and us living in the same state and cannot secure work. We would like very much to hear from you in regard to prejudice in shipyards.

Records of the Committee on Fair Employment Practice, Region XII, RG 228, Box 99, National Archives.

52. HERMAN PATTEN (PORTLAND, OREGON) TO PAUL MCNUTT,
WAR MANPOWER COMMISSION, FEBRUARY 11, 1943

Dear Mr. McNutt,

As American born citizen I write to you in regards of discrimination in defense projects. I have been trained for war production and obtained a certificate of training in welding.

I have been denied a chance to work at my skill at the Kaiser's shipyards owing to the fact I am Negro.

There are over two million Negroes in the Armed Forces fighting for the same cause, democracy and we are buying bonds and do everything to help in winning this war. I don't see why we or anyone should be discriminated against because of color. As long as this is to exist in national defense this war is futile and the peace is already lost.

As chairman of the Manpower Commision would you be so kind to inform me where I can work and be more essential in War Production?

Records of the Committee on Fair Employment Practice, Region Xll, RG 228, Box 99, National Archives.

53. RITA QUEIROLO (BERKLEY, CALIF.) TO PAUL MCNUTT,
WAR MANPOWER COMMISSION, JANUARY 5, 1942

Dear Sir:

Thank you for your attention to my letter of Nov. 30th. The President's Committee of Fair Employment Practice wrote and I replied Dec. 28th, filing a form acknowledged by Notary Public. I do so hope action can be taken to dispel the power of Ku Klux Klanism which now manages the shipyards. The waste of manpower is now atricious; the qualification for positions of authority still remains; not the need to know what you're doing, but rather your ability to practice and preach the KKK code.

This is horrible, now, of all times.

And you should know more about the U.S. Employment Service which is, I understand directly under your office.

It, while operating under the State of California, was infamous for its discriminatory mis-classifying registrants.

In my case: I registered with them in Berkeley in 1936, Mrs. Johnson was in charge. Because I had been cashier of a company she referred me to a job as cashier of a cash register, first time I'd ever punched a cash register in my life. From that time—1936—to the present that was the only job the agency offered me.

Mrs. Johnson was soon promoted to a better position in the Oakland office.

Marjorie Walker was put in charge of Berkeley and she continued the wrong classifying.

Altho' I had many years experience in charge of bookkeeping and in managing offices, my card still rates me in the lowest clerical class.

Some friends finally became annoyed over this stupid injustice and, as I was on WPA, went through the Democratic Machine in this district with the result that the local WPA administrator raised the rating slightly higher, then the local official was eased out of office and the position given to a Miss Hally who had always been promoted each time she performed an injust act.

These are the acts which have caused people to believe the New Deal is just a false front for real action, more cruel and undemocratic than the reactionary rulers. If I believed that I shouldn't bother to write to you, only my faith that what we call the New Deal will clean its own house and give the people something more tangible than a fine front to support, prompts these efforts.

While in the slightly higher classification on WPA, I was receptionist in the Re-employment and Training Program.

Women streamed into that office begging to be trained for defense jobs (spring of 1942). Most of them were directed to a Mrs. Jean Differding, who in turn insisted all Negroes must leave WPA to go to work as servants. Today I saw Jean Differding working in your Berkeley office of U.S. Employment Service.

While I was working on the Re-employment Program, Mrs. Marjorie Walker wrote to the head of that Program, Nye Wilson, (Mar. 13, 1942, I believe) that I was not even registered with the employment service—of course I was not only registered but had been calling at that office nearly every month for 6 years. Mrs. Marjorie Walker is still manager of the Berkeley office and I am still rated in the same very low classification.

There is a definite parallel between this contemptuous appraisal of the U.S. Employment Service and the management of Kaiser Shipyards.

I know the former WPA administrator Burr, left his bad treatment of WPA workers and was given a fine job as personnel director for Todd Shipyards.

I know that as fast as timekeepers on WPA failed to allow me to be paid for actual hours worked, the man who had the power to give out jobs from the (U.S.) State Employment office, placed each timekeeper in a comparatively good job.

Your U.S. Employment Service is an excellent pool for distributing manpower if properly directed, but it is useless as long as it is stacked with the same people who have undermined every progressive step the Administration has taken, or tried to take, forward.

Records of the Committee on Fair Employment Practice, RG 228, Box 99, National Archives

54.   RITA QUEIROLO TO PAUL MCNUTT, NOVEMBER 30, 1942

Dear Sir:

Thank you for your honest effort to correct the acts of discrimination against Negroes in the government agency WPA, about which I wrote to you some time ago.

Mr. Lawson's WPA (San Francisco) office replied with their habitual sophism and even lied by disclaiming any knowledge of Chas. Owens. They know him well, their files contain definite charges against him. They dismissed responsibility for the others mentioned saying these were no longer with WPA. Both the California and Washington offices were completely informed all these past years, their condonation of this malfeasance has been observed. Mr. Olson made himself a party to it--no wonder he endured such a landslide out of office.

The facts remain:

(1)   The U.S. government refused to act against such perpetrators.
(2)   These perpetrators have always been advanced to bigger and better positions.
(3)   They are still free to repeat their acts of breaking down Democracy.

Many of them must be active in the policies of the shipyards as the policies are so parallel, using government money to create dissention.

I am at Richmond Yard 3. Not a single colored person is employed in the offices I contact. All persons I know who are advanced to leadermen or other supervisory jobs are mostly from Oklahoma or Texas. They are willing to boss anybody like slaves and they are sure to hate Negroes. Another qualification for advancement is to be anti-labor.

The pay and working conditions are pretty bad for the white collar group. Naturally no one will stay and take it. So, now they misuse the Manpower Act. We received the following memo: It has been agreed between the shipyards in the S.F. Bay Area, the Navy and the U.S. Maritime Comm., that all employees, union or non-union, come under the terms of the freezing act. Therefore, it will be necessary for us to issue termination clearances to all employees-- office, clerical, guards, etc.--that are not covered by union agreements. . ." Nov. 6, 1942, signed D. C. Peacock, Sr.

I do not believe my government intends to hire us out at a wage on which we cannot live, for the benefit of a very few individuals and pay those few a percentage for mistreating and underpaying us--then demand that we stay and take it.

I do not believe the freezing of salaries included those already making too little--yet the head of the Purchase Dept. at my yard said that it did.

As this concerns the Manpower department, maybe you can catch up with these brutes.

Records of the Committee on Fair Employment Practice, RG 228, Box 99, National Archives.

55.   RITA QUEIROLO TO GEORGE M. JOHNSON, WAR MANPOWER COMMISSION, DECEMBER 28, 1942

Sir:

Thank you for your attention to my letter of November 30th.

Most employers of Defense workers, are aware that they have no right to openly discriminate against employees because of race, creed, color or national origin. So, they operate quietly to continue the discrimination.

At this Richmond Yard No. 3, I know of no individual cases in which the management openly says, "You may not have equal pay or hold a position for which you are qualified because of your race or religious belief; or because you believe in Fair Employment Practice." I do know that not one colored

person is employed in any of the many offices I have been in; I know that the
office help is packed with people holding racial prejudices; that the group
of people Kaiser has imported from Oklahoma and Texas and placed in supervising positions, express themselves from time to time, and these expressions
are pure Ku-Klux-Klanism; I know the Negroes and Chinese are kept at menial
jobs and bossed by those who hate them; I know that my religion does not
appease nor tolerate these policies, of Kaiser Co. nor of my government which
rewards these un-Christian and un-American individuals.

I do know that I work side by side, do the same work (except more of it)
with others, and am paid less than the KKK's. My skin happens to be white,
and of course Kaiser doesn't say "We are working you out of classification
and underpaying you because you won't join our KKK."

I do not know if you can do anything about the unfair conditions, but
they certainly exist.

Anyway, I'm enclosing the formal complaint in the hope that some action
may break down the very un-American structure of Defense Industries, the
waste of manpower just because a Defense Plant puts "wasters" in supervisorial
positions and works others out of a classification in which they can contribute
most to Defense.

You may be sure many of us wouldn't be in the yards so long except that
we do want the ships built. But we don't believe we should be wasted while
they are being built.

Records of the Committee on Fair Employment Practices, RG 228, Box 99, National
Archives.

56. FEPC NEWS RELEASE, DECEMBER 14, 1943

The International Brotherhood of Boilermakers and its local lodges in
Portland, Ore., and Los Angeles, Calif., have been directed by the President's
Committee on Fair Employment Practice to eliminate all membership practices
which discriminate against workers because of race or color, Malcolm Ross,
FEPC Chairman, announced today.

At the same time, Mr. Ross revealed, five West Coast shipbuilding companies
have been directed by the Committee to reinstate all Negro workers discharged
because of their refusal to pay dues to Boilermaker auxiliary unions. The companies were also ordered to cease discharging or refusing to hire Negroes
solely because they had failed to obtain clearance from the union.

Firms notified by the Committee included the Oregon Shipbuilding Corporation and the Kaiser Company, Inc., in the Portland-Vancouver area, and the
California Shipbuilding Corporation, Consolidated Steel Corporation (Shipbuilding Division) and the Western Pipe and Steel Corporation in the Los
Angeles area. Both the unions and the companies have been directed to report
to the Committee within 45 days on actions taken toward compliance.

The Committee's findings and directives, signed by all seven members,
resulted from public hearings held in Portland, November 15-16, and Los Angeles,
November 19-20, on charges of discriminatory employment practices in West
Coast shipyards. The hearings followed complaints filed with the Committee
after several hundred Negro shipyard workers had been fired for refusing to
pay dues to Auxiliary Boilermakers' locals. The dismissals were under terms
of a "Master Agreement" between the union and West Coast shipyards under which
all workers under Boilermakers' jurisdiction must become and remain members
of the union before they can work. The Negroes charged that the Auxiliary
locals were discriminatory.

The Committee findings were that the Auxiliaries are created only for
Negro workers and are placed directly under control of the white Subordinate
(regular) Lodge for the area. Auxiliary members, the findings continued,
have no vote or voice in the conduct of the union's affairs and must accept
as their business agent the business agent of the supervising (Subordinate)
Lodge in whose election the Auxiliaries have no part. The supervising Lodge's
grievance Committee also serves the Auxiliary Lodge, with the addition of
one member from the Auxiliary.

Other Committee findings on the Auxiliary question included unfair differences in insurance benefits provided for members by the union and in the age limits for admission to membership.

The International Brotherhood was not represented officially at the hearings. Its contention (through correspondence with FEPC) that the Auxiliary Lodges are not discriminatory drew the Committee's reply that "there is nothing in the written Constitution and By-Laws of the International Brotherhood or the Subordinate Lodge Constitution prohibiting the admission of Negroes into the organization."

The Committee cited records of past conventions of the union which showed the question of admitting Negroes to membership had been considered.

"The by-laws governing Auxiliary Lodges," the Committee said, "represents the results of efforts of the International President and the Executive Council of the union."

The companies, all of whom were represented at the hearings, contended that they were bound by a Master Agreement and that "to look beyond the unions so far as the employment of Negroes is concerned would be 'to interfere with the internal affairs of the unions' and lay themselves liable to violation of the National Labor Relations Act."

In reply the FEPC said: "Reluctance of the Corporation to involve itself in a violation of the National Labor Relations Act is understandable, but will find no basis for its concern in the National Labor Relations Act or in decisions construing it."

The Committee cited an NLRB General Counsel's opinion which states in part: ". . . the enforcement of the provisions of the collective bargaining agreement, once it is made, rests with the parties to the agreement and does not come within the jurisdiction of this Board."

Also cited by the FEPC was the recent NLRB decision in the Bethlehem-Alameda Shipyard Case in which "the Board (NLRB) intimates strongly that an employer who has a closed shop contract with a union which excludes Negroes, far from violating the Act if he ignores the union's request for discharge of a Negro employee, will violate the Act if he gives effect to the request."

"The sincerity of the Companies' motives in this case need not be drawn in question," the Committee declared. ". . . Regardless of the measure of the union's responsibility in this case, the power to hire and fire remains with the Companies, and their obligation to eliminate the obvious and admitted discrimination because of race or color in hiring and firing is primary and fundamental."

The FEPC also pointed out that the companies' production is vital to the war effort; that a critical manpower shortage exists and is being aggravated by rejection of qualified Negro applicants and discharging of others on the basis of provisions in the union agreement.

Records of the Committee on Fair Employment Practice, Files of Cornelius Golightly, RG 228, Box 398, National Archives.

57.
BEFORE THE
PRESIDENT'S COMMITTEE ON FAIR EMPLOYMENT PRACTICE

In Public Hearings Held in Portland, Oregon

November 15 and 16, 1943

SUMMARY, FINDINGS AND DIRECTIVES

Relating to

Kaiser Company, Inc., and the Oregon Shipbuilding Corporation

International Brotherhood of Boiler Makers, Iron
Ship Builders, Welders and Helpers of America,
A.F. of L.

Subordinate Lodge No. 72
Subordinate Lodge No. 401
Auxiliary Lodge No. A-32

Issued by order of the President's Committee on Fair Employment Practice
December 9, 1943

Malcolm Ross [121]
Chairman

John Brophy   Sara Southall
Boris Shishkin   P. B. Young, Sr. [122]
Milton P. Webster   Samuel Zemurray

In this hearing, held in Portland, Oregon, on November 15 and 16, 1943, the Kaiser Company, Inc., and the Oregon Shipbuilding Corporation were represented by their Attorney, Mr. Gordon Johnson and Mr. Edgar F. Kaiser, the General Manager for the shipyards of both Companies in the Portland-Vancouver area.

There was no appearance or representation on behalf of the International Brotherhood of Boiler Makers, Iron Ship Builders, Welders and Helpers of America, or on behalf of Subordinate Lodge 401 of said International Brotherhood. Subordinate Lodge No. 72 was represented by its Attorneys Messrs. Charles W. Robison and Leland Tanner, and its Secretary and Business Agent, Mr. Thomas Ray.

Prior to the hearing, the Committee mailed to the Companies and to the Unions a "Summary of Complaints." In addition to the complaints relating to the central issue in the hearing, the Committee received a number of complaints alleging discriminatory practices on the part of the Companies unrelated to the central issue. These complaints will be dealt with separately. The charges in the "Summary of Complaints" relating to the central issue here involved were as follows:

Numerous Negroes, available and qualified for employment, have been refused employment altogether.

Numerous Negroes sought to join the Union but were denied membership although otherwise qualified, notwithstanding that without membership in the Union it was and is the practice of the Union to request the Companies to discharge such persons; and it is and has been the practice of the Companies to honor such requests.

Numerous Negroes have joined Auxiliary Lodge A-32 under threat of discharge if they failed to do so; notwithstanding said Auxiliary Lodge A-32 does not give to its members rights equal to those of the members of the Subordinate Lodge; and notwithstanding that in many respects the organization and operation of such Auxiliary Lodge constitutes serious discrimination between members of the Union which discrimination is based entirely upon race or color.

1. The Position of the Complainants

Negroes employed in skills under the jurisdiction of the Boilermakers Union, or applicants for such employment, testified that when they attempted to secure or continue such employment they were told by the Companies that they would have to obtain "clearance" from the Boilermakers Union; that when they sought such "clearance," they were told by officials of said Union that because they were Negroes they could not become members of Subordinate Lodges 72 and 401, the regular Boilermakers Locals in the Portland-Vancouver area, and that before they would be "cleared" for employment they would have to become members of Auxiliary Lodge A-32, established solely for Negroes. These Negro workers testified that they refused to join said Auxiliary because of

its discriminatory nature. They testified further that they were, and still
are, willing and ready to join the regular Boilermakers Locals where they will
have rights and privileges as well as obligations, equal to those of their
white fellow workers. There was ample testimony that Negro and white workers
in various kinds of shipyard employment work together harmoniously and without
racial friction. Moreover, there was testimony that in other unions, notably
the Electricians Union and the Laborers Union, both affiliated with the
American Federation of Labor, Negro and white workers in these same shipyards
belong to the same locals and enjoy the same rights and privileges, including
insurance benefits, without any friction.

II. The Position of the Unions

The International Brotherhood, Subordinate Lodges 72 and 401, and
Auxiliary Lodge A-32 were notified of the hearings by registered mail and
requested to send official representatives. Return receipts indicate that
these notices were received in due course.

Neither the International Brotherhood nor its officers appeared at the
hearings. However, the Constitution and By-Laws of the International Brotherhood (which includes the Subordinate Lodge Constitution) and the By-Laws
Governing Auxiliary Lodges, were made a part of the record, together with
other documentary evidence relating to the official position of the International Brotherhood with regard to the admission of Negroes to membership
in the Union. An expert witness carefully analyzed these documents and his
testimony, added to the uncontroverted testimony of complainants, fully
supports the charges set forth in the "Summary of Complaints."

A telegram to the Committee dated August 27, 1943, from Charles J. Mac
Gowan, International Vice President of the Brotherhood, was made a part of the
record. This telegram states:

> "OUR INVESTIGATION DISCLOSES THAT THERE IS NO
> FOUNDATION FOR THE CHARGE THAT THERE HAS BEEN
> ANY DISCRIMINATION ON THE PART OF OUR LOCAL
> UNIONS AGAINST ANY MAN ON ACCOUNT OF RACE CREED
> COLOR OR NATIONAL ORIGIN, AND WE UNEQUIVOCALLY
> DECLARE THAT WE HAVE FULFILLED THE LETTER AND
> SPIRIT OF THE PRESIDENT'S EXECUTIVE ORDER NO. 8802.
> IN OUR TELEPHONE CONVERSATION WITH YOU YESTERDAY
> YOU REPEATEDLY SAID THAT YOU WANTED TO GET THESE
> NEGROES BACK TO WORK. WE HAVE NO SPECIFIC KNOWLEDGE
> OF ANY NEGROES BEING HELD OUT OF WORK BUT NEGROES
> AND WHITES ALIKE CAN RETURN TO WORK IF AND WHEN
> THEY PAY THEIR DUES, AS PROVIDED BY THE CONSTITUTION
> OF THE INTERNATIONAL BROTHERHOOD OF BOILER MAKERS,
> IRON SHIPBUILDERS AND HELPERS OF AMERICA INCLUDING
> THE AUXILIARY CONSTITUTION CONTROLLING THE AUXILIARY
> OF WHICH THEY ARE MEMBERS PROVIDED ALL OF THEM HAVE
> COMPLIED WITH THE REQUIREMENTS OF THE ORGANIZATION,
> AND IF WE LEARN THAT A SINGLE PERSON IS NOT IMME-
> DIATELY PUT BACK TO WORK UNDER THE SAME CONDITIONS
> AS ANY OTHER MEMBERS OF THIS UNION WE WILL RECTIFY
> THE SITUATION AT ONCE."

If this telegram represents the official position of the International
Brotherhood, obviously, it does not meet the issue raised in the complaints.
It assumes the validity of the Auxiliary Lodge arrangement, whereas, the
complainants allege that the establishment and operation of the Auxiliary
Lodge violates the provisions of Executive Order 9346.

Other documentary evidence made a part of the record includes excerpts
from the Report of the Proceedings of the Sixteenth Consolidated Convention
of the International Brotherhood held in 1937 and an Analysis of the
Discriminations Against Negroes in the Boilermakers' Union. This documentary
evidence and supporting testimony reveals that as early as 1908 a ritual of
the Union restricted membership in the Union to white workers and that this
ritual is still operative. It appears however, that there is nothing in

the written Constitution and By-Laws of the International Brotherhood or the
Subordinate Lodge Constitution prohibiting the admission of Negroes to
membership in the organization. It shows further that at the International
Convention of the Brotherhood in 1937, the issue of admitting Negroes to
membership was before the Convention, and that the Executive Council recommended "that this convention authorize the granting of separate charters to
colored workers . . . that the membership of the colored men be confined to
such separate locals; . . . they to enjoy all the rights and benefits provided for under our laws, except that of universal transfer." The reports of
this Convention further show that there was a difference of opinion among the
delegates on the question of admission of Negroes to membership, some delegates taking the position that Negro workers are entitled to equal rights
and privileges without regard to their race. The Convention finally adopted
"the purpose sought in the recommendation of the Executive Council," with
certain important changes, and stricken out were the words "they to enjoy
all rights and benefits provided under our laws." The International President
and the Executive Council were given full authority to work out the details
and the By-Laws Governing Auxiliary Lodges represent the result of their
efforts.

In the document referred to above, entitled An Analysis of the Discriminations Against Negroes, there are set out ten points of contrast between
the rights and privileges accorded Subordinate Lodges and their members and
those accorded Auxiliary Lodges and their members. This Analysis shows that
Auxiliary Lodges, wherein membership is restricted to Negroes, are so constituted under the laws of the Union as effectively to deny to Negroes basic
rights and privileges fundamental to the very concept of union membership, by
virtue of which denial they are deprived of essential union representation
and protection in regard to hire, tenure, and terms of employment.

Subordinate Lodge No. 401, like the International Brotherhood, failed
to appear, but Subordinate Lodge No. 72 was represented. The discriminatory
policies and practices charged, were frankly admitted by representatives of
Local 72. Their position was that Local Lodges of the International Brotherhood of Boilermakers have no choice in the matter but are obligated to follow
the dictates of the International Brotherhood and its officers. Mr. Leland
Tanner, Counsel for Local 72, made the following statement:

"Lodge 72 is an organization that exists by virtue of a charter that
was given by the International. The ritual . . . is a ritual which should
have been referred to the parties responsible for its making. Now we dis-
claim responsibility for the unfortunate situation in which we find ourselves."

. . . . .

"Mr. Ray, and Lodge 72, have been struggling with this problem, and have
attempted to work out a solution within the structure in which we live . . .
for the making of which we are not responsible. We live in that house; we
did not build that house; and we are not the architects of it. Mr. Ray has
attempted to live within the structure, and whatever position, he, or his
counsel may have taken heretofore, has been taken within the confines and
limitations that were imposed upon him by this framework that we term our
International Constitution and our International Ritual. We have not the
power to change either."

Mr. Charles W. Robison, also Counsel for Local 72, stated:

"Let me make it clear to you the structure of the Union, the local Union,
and the relationship between the International and the local. It is contractual. They protect and provide us with a constitution, and they give us
a constitution, which is contractual, by which we protect and provide for our
membership. As I pointed out to you and point out to you now, change that
Constitution by the International. Give us an opportunity and we will change
our procedure. But you can't tie our hands and say 'Make so and so'--with
our hands tied. We can build no further than our blueprint. Let me make
that plain to you now, ladies and gentlemen. Because we are restricted."

Mr. Ray, Secretary and Business Agent of Local 72 submitted for the record a statement of his position "On the matter of opportunity for the Negro." The last two paragraphs of this statement are as follows:

"In a word, Mr. Ray is prepared to sponsor for Negroes in this area, all rights and economic opportunities possible under the International Constitution. Any objections to be made to such program here in Oregon and vicinity are objections that should be addressed to the International and not to Mr. Ray.

"In conclusion, Mr. Ray will proceed as far as the International Brotherhood of Boilermakers will allow him to proceed; namely, to provide and promote to the ends contemplated in the President's Orders and enunciated in the convention of the American Federation of Labor."

III. The Position of the Companies

The case for the Kaiser Company, Inc., and the Oregon Shipbuilding Corporation, consisted of the statement of counsel, the testimony of Mr. Edgar F. Kaiser, General Manager of the two companies, and corroborating documentary evidence.

The Companies admit that they are and have been following the policy and practice of refusing to hire Negroes in skills subject to the jurisdiction of the Boilermakers' Union, unless cleared by Subordinate Lodges 72 and 401, and the policy and practice of discharging Negro employees certified as not in "good standing" by these unions, notwithstanding the Companies have had notice and knowledge that Negroes are not admitted to membership in these Locals, and that failure of Negroes to obtain clearance or certification of "good standing" has been due solely to the insistance of the Union that Negroes accept and maintain discriminatory membership in Auxiliary Lodge A-32.

The Companies further admit that the rejection and discharge of Negroes under these circumstances has resulted in a serious aggravation of the critical manpower shortage in the shipyards. Mr. Kaiser acknowledged that to the extent Negroes have been employed their aid has been of "immense importance." He testified that he could not get all the workers he needed among white persons, and that aside from the unknown number of man-hours lost from Negro workers who might have been employed, the loss of man-hours from Negroes already employed "who got those stop orders and terminated their employment because they didn't wish to join the auxiliary, has been great in itself." Figures submitted by the Companies indicate that since January 1, 1943, "upon order" of the Unions here involved, a total of 345 Negroes were discharged, of whom 217 were rehired within one week (presumably after acceptance of the discriminatory union status)--a net loss of 128 employees.

The Companies, engaged as they are in the production of "Liberty" and "Victory" merchant ships, tankers, and escort aircraft carriers, recognize that they manage a vital war industry and are fully obligated not to discriminate because of race or color by Executive Order 9346 and by the non-discrimination clause which was incorporated in their contract with the United States Maritime Commission.

They avow that their constant intention and purpose has been to comply; that if the Order has been violated the blame is not theirs.

First, the Companies contend that they are bound to follow the aforesaid practices because of the closed-shop provisions of a contract, known as the "Master Agreement," in effect between the major Pacific Coast ship builders and the International Brotherhood.

This contention cannot be accepted. While it is not the province of this Committee to construe the contract for the parties, it is obvious that neither of the parties, consistently with their obligations under Executive Order 9346, can give to any provision of this private agreement a construction on effect which directly results in discrimination because of race or color in violation of the Order.

Secondly, the Companies assert that they have followed the foregoing policies and practices because of advice of counsel; that for them "to look beyond the unions so far as employment of Negroes is concerned" would be "to interfere with the internal affairs of the unions" and lay themselves "liable to violation of the National Labor Relations Act." *

Reluctance of the Companies to involve themselves in a violation of the National Labor Relations Act is understandable. However, they will find no basis for their concern in the National Labor Relations Act or in decisions construing it. The Committee has sought and received from the General Counsel of the National Labor Relations Board, situation presented in this case, stating in part as follows:

"When the Board certified a collective bargaining representative in accordance with the principles stated above, the terms and conditions of employment are matters which are properly left to collective bargaining between the employer and the certified representative. Likewise, the enforcement of the provisions of the collective bargaining agreement, once it is made, rests with the parties to the agreement and does not come within the jurisdiction of this Board." (Emphasis supplied)

* At the hearing it was stated for the Companies that their position in this respect had been supported by advice from officials of the Maritime Commission. Since the hearing, the Committee has received from Mr. Daniel S. Ring, Director Division of Shipyard Labor Relations, United States Maritime Commission, a letter dated December 3, in which Mr. Ring advises that he has communicated directly with the Company representatives involved, and there is apparent agreement that the statement at the hearing was based on a misunderstanding.

In the course of the opinion there is cited the recent decision of the Board in the Bethlehem-Alameda Shipyard Case, No. R-5693, which the Board intimates strongly that an employer who has a closed shop contract with a union which excludes Negroes, far from violating the Act if he ignores the union's request for discharge of a Negro employee, will violate the Act if he gives effect to the request. The Board said:

"We entertain grave doubt whether a union which discriminatorily denies membership to employees on the basis of race may nevertheless bargain as the exclusive representative in an appropriate unit composed in part of members of the excluded race. Such bargaining might have consequences at variance with the purposes of the Act. If such a representative should enter into a contract requiring membership in the union as a condition of employment, the contract, if legal, might have the effect of subjecting those in the excluded group, who are properly part of the bargaining unit, to loss of employment solely on the basis of an arbitrary and discriminatory denial to them of the privilege of union membership. In these circumstances, the validity under the provise of Section 8 (3) of the Act of such a contract would be open to serious question." (Emphasis supplied)

The sincerity of the Companies' motives in this case need not be drawn in question. Their motive in engaging in discrimination in conflict with the Executive Order is entirely irrelevant.

Regardless of the measure of the Union's responsibility in this case, the power to hire and fire remains with the Companies, and their obligation to eliminate the obvious and admitted discrimination because of race or color in hiring and firing is primary and fundamental.

By virtue of the authority conferred upon it by Executive Order 9346 to "make findings of fact and take appropriate steps to obtain elimination of . . . discrimination" forbidden by the Order, the Committee makes the following findings and issues the following directives:

FINDINGS

1. The Committee finds that the Oregon Shipbuilding Corporation, on May 12, 1941, and the Kaiser Company, Incorporated, on April 17, 1942, became parties to an agreement, known as the "Master Agreement," between the major Pacific Coast shipbuilding companies and the Metal Trades Department of the American Federation of Labor, the Pacific Coast District Metal Trades Council, the Portland Metal Trades Council and Affiliated International Unions, Section 2 of which agreement provides in part that the "employer agrees to hire all workmen it may require hereunder . . . through and from the Unions and to continue in its employ . . . only workmen who are members in good standing of the respective Unions signatory hereto."

2. The Committee finds that the International Brotherhood of Boilermakers, Iron Ship Builders, Welders, and Helpers of America (who are parties
to the "Master Agreement"), and Subordinate Lodges 72 and 401 of said International Brotherhood exclude Negroes from membership, and that they establish
as a condition to the employment of Negroes under the quoted provision of
Section 2 of the "Master Agreement" as set forth in Finding No. 1, that Negroes
accept and maintain membership in Auxiliary Lodge A-32 of said International
Brotherhood.

3. The Committee finds that the policies and practices of the Union
involved herein with respect to membership in the aforesaid Auxiliary Lodge
A-32 discriminate against Negroes in regard to hire, tenure, terms of employment and union membership, solely because of race or color in the following
respects:

(a) The establishment, jurisdiction, and proceedings of the
     Auxiliary are supervised by and subject to the approval
     of the "supervising" Local, from which Negroes are excluded.

(b) The Auxiliary Lodge and the members thereof are denied any
     voice or direct representation in the International Convention,
     the supreme and final policy and rule-making body of the
     International Brotherhood; and they are denied any voice or
     vote in the selection of delegates to said International Con-
     vention.

(c) The Auxiliary Lodge and its members are denied any voice or
     vote in the selection of the Business Agent of the "supervising"
     Local, from which Negroes are excluded, although said Business
     Agent is designated to perform the functions of that office for
     the Auxiliary Lodge.

(d) The Auxiliary Lodge and its members are denied any voice or
     vote in the selection of the grievance committee of the "super-
     vising" Local, from which Negroes are excluded, which committee
     is designated to perform the grievance function for said
     Auxiliary and its members, except that the Auxiliary is permit-
     ted to select one member to serve on said grievance committee.

(e) Members of the Auxiliary Lodge are denied the right and oppor-
     tunity to change their classification except with the approval
     of the "supervising" Local, from which Negroes are excluded.

(f) Members of the Auxiliary Lodge are denied the right of universal
     transfer afforded to members of the "supervising" Local, but may
     transfer their membership only to another Auxiliary Lodge.

(g) Members of the Auxiliary Lodge are denied equal opportunities
     to purchase and receive insurance benefits for themselves and
     families, provided by the International Brotherhood for members
     of Subordinate Lodges and their families.

(h) The Auxiliary Lodge is denied the right to receive apprentices,
     and its members are denied the right to be apprentices, although
     these rights are afforded respectively to the "supervising"
     Local and its members.

(i) Members of the Auxiliary Lodge are subject to a penalty for mis-
     conduct (intoxication) not similarly provided for members of
     the "supervising" Local.

(j) Membership in the Auxiliary Lodge is restricted to Negro males
     between the ages of sixteen (16) and sixty (60) years, whereas
     membership in the "supervising" Local is extended to males be-
     tween the ages of sixteen (16) and seventy (70) years.

4. The Committee finds that the Oregon Shipbuilding Corporation and the
Kaiser Company, Inc., have been and are following a policy and practice of
refusing to hire Negroes in skills subject to the jurisdiction of the Boilermakers Union, unless said Negroes are cleared by Subordinate Lodges 72 and 401
of the International Brotherhood of Boilermakers, Iron Ship Builders, Welders
and Helpers of America, and have been and are following a policy and practice
of discharging Negro employees certified as not being in "good standing" by
said Unions, notwithstanding said Companies have notice and knowledge that
Negroes are not admitted to membership in said Unions, and that the failure of
such Negroes to obtain clearance or certification of "good standing" from
such Unions is due solely to insistence of the Union that Negroes accept and
maintain discriminatory membership in Auxiliary Lodge A-32.
5. The Committee finds that the policies and practices of the Oregon
Shipbuilding Corporation and the Kaiser Company, Inc., as set forth in Finding
No. 4, constitute discrimination because of race and color in regard to hire,
tenure, terms of employment and union membership and that these policies and
practices are in violation of Executive Order 9346.
6. The Committee finds that the shipyards here involved are engaged in
production vital to the Nation's war effort; that in these shipyards a critical manpower shortage exists; that the discriminatory practices of the Companies as found above have contributed to and are aggravating this shortage in
that these practices have directly resulted in the refusal of many qualified
Negroes to apply for employment, in the rejection of a large number of qualified
Negro applicants, and in the discharge of large numbers of Negroes, and in that
these practices have been a contributing factor in the impairment of the morale
of those Negroes whose continued employment is at the price of discriminatory
union status, all to the detriment of the prosecution of the war.

DIRECTIVES

1. The Committee directs that the Oregon Shipbuilding Corporation and
the Kaiser Company, Inc., immediately cease the policies and practices found
in Finding No. 4 to be in violation of Executive Order 9346.
2. The Committee directs that until such time as it shall notify the
Companies that the Unions involved herein have eliminated the discriminatory
policies and practices set out in Findings Nos. 2 and 3, said Companies shall
desist from refusing to hire and discharging Negroes who fail to secure clearance from said Unions, where the Companies have notice or knowledge that such
failure is due solely to the insistence of the Union that such Negroes accept
and maintain membership in Auxiliary Lodge A-32.
3. The Committee directs that the Companies offer, upon application, to
employ in line with their qualifications, or to reinstate to their prior status
and classification, as the case may be, all persons who have heretofore been
discriminated against in violation of Executive Order 9346, as found in Findings Nos. 4 and 5.
4. The Committee directs that each of the Companies give formal notice
to the Unions named herein that they will comply fully with their obligations
under Executive Order 9346 not to discriminate against workers, because of
race, creed, color or national origin in regard to hire, tenure, terms or
conditions of employment, and specifically that they will comply with Directives Nos. 1 and 2, and that said Companies furnish the Committee with a copy
of such notice.
5. The Committee directs that the Companies report to the Committee
within forty-five days of the receipt of these directives, the steps taken
to comply therewith.

Records of the Committee on Fair Employment Practice, Files of Cornelius
Golightly, RG 228, Box 398, National Archives.

58. BOILERMAKERS' UNION CLAIMS COMMUNISTS INFLUENCED FEPC

WASHINGTON--(ANP)--Insinuations that the Fair Employment Practice Committee might be communistically influenced and that what Negro shipyard workers on

the West Coast are asking for is but a forerunner to mixed housing, mixed schools and integrated social activity, are contained in the letter of complaint which the Boilermakers' Union (AFL) has filed with the Smith Investigating committee whose chairman, Howard W. Smith (D) of Virginia has announced that a probe would be made of FEPC.

Contents of the letter were obtained over the week-end from a reliable source, and for the first time reveals the arguments which the boilermakers are making in answer to the directives of the FEPC to them to stop discriminating against Negro workers through the medium of jim crow auxiliary lodges.

Meanwhile, in New York, George Marshall, chairman of the National Federation for Constitutional Liberties, in a letter to the speaker of the House, Sam Rayburn, urged that the Smith committee be immediately terminated because of its "irresponsible investigations which disrupt the work of important war agencies."[123]

Monday a week ago, a representative of the committee seized the records of the FEPC in both the boilermakers' and the railroad cases preliminary to undertaking a probe of the anti-discrimination agency. The seizure was made allegedly on the basis of the complaint of the boilermakers.

Pittsburgh Courier, January 15, 1944.

59.   NEGRO STATUS IN THE BOILERMAKERS UNION

By Thurgood Marshall

The status of the Negro in the Boilermakers union recently reached the front page as a result of Judge Churchill's decision that the purpose and effect of the so-called "auxiliary" was to segregate Negroes and persons of no other race and color and that therefore "auxiliaries" are illegal and void. This decision is epoch making, for it is the first one of its type involving the legal status of "auxiliary unions."

At least fifteen unions exclude Negroes from membership by provisions in either their constitution or ritual. Nine international unions bar Negroes from admission to their regular unions and locals, admitting them only to "jim crow" auxiliary bodies. Herbert R. Northrup, in the *Journal of Political Economy*, June, 1943, has summarized the discriminatory tactics used by labor unions against Negroes as follows: (1) Exclusion of Negroes by provision in the ritual; (2) exclusion by provision in the constitution; (3) exclusion by tacit consent; and (4) exclusion by forcing the Negro to join a segregated auxiliary.[124]

The International Brotherhood of Boilermakers, Iron Shipbuilders and Helpers of America, AFL, refuses to admit qualified Negroes to membership in its regular locals. Although union officials claim they exclude Negroes pursuant to provision in the ritual, a careful examination of their ritual reveals no mention whatever of race or color. This makes it clear, therefore, that Negroes are relegated to "jim crow" auxiliary unions as a result of the whims of officers of the International.

Further investigation of the practices of the Boilermakers reveals the adoption of a new constitution at their 1937 convention. According to this constitution, membership in the Boilermakers is open to male citizens "of some civilized country between the ages of 16 and 70 years, working at some branch of the trade at the time of making application." No reference is made to race or color anywhere in the constitution, nor even in the by-laws adopted by the International. They have, however, issued another book labeled "By-Laws Governing Auxiliary Lodges," which purports to have been adopted by the Executive Council of the Boilermakers. These rules profess to restrict membership to "colored male citizens."

A comparison of these two sets of rules shows clearly that the only equality between the auxiliary lodges and the regular lodges is in the amount of dues paid. Though members of an auxiliary, Negroes have to pay the same dues as the white members of the regular lodges. After this, all semblance of equality vanishes.

Other Inequalities

In addition to segregation, there are other glaring inequalities. Insurance policies provide for Negro members about half the benefits they do for white members, and Negro auxiliary lodges are all under the direct control of the white local lodges, designated as "supervising lodges." "Auxiliaries" are also denied the right to have a business agent of their own; the right to have a grievance committee; and the right to promotion on the job without the permission of the supervising local. Membership in auxiliaries is limited to persons under 60 years of age, while white persons are eligible for membership in a local up to 70 years of age. Clinching proof of the ephemeral status is that the International president has the uncontrolled discretion to suspend any auxiliary or any officer or member. He may do this upon a mere whim, since he is answerable to no one. But a local, which consists exclusively of members of the white race, may be suspended by the International president only when he acts in conjunction with the Executive Council, and then only after such a local shall have been proved guilty of violation of the constitution and by-laws. Handicaps are even placed on the right of employment of "auxiliary members" in other cities.

In view of the fact that more and more Negroes are being employed in the shipbuilding industry these discriminatory practices of the Boilermakers union, since they hold a closed-shop contract in most of the shipyards, have become the target of attack by the NAACP and other liberal organizations.

Discriminations against Negroes in the Boilermakers union is the same old story of discrimination tied up with the evil of segregation. And past experience teaches us that with a reduction in the number of contracts for ships, and the consequent reduction in employment, the members of the Negro auxiliary are not going to have the protection of the union, and the old story of the Negro's being "the first to go" will again face us.

During the earlier months of the war emergency, Negroes were excluded from most skilled jobs in shipyards. However, need for workers became so acute that it became necessary to employ Negroes and the Boilermakers, being unable to secure a sufficient number of white workers, had to admit Negroes to these jobs. While the Boilermakers permitted the Negroes to work, they did not intend for them to have full membership in the union. So in order to protect their closed-shop agreements, they began to inaugurate the policy of setting up jim crow auxiliary unions. On the West Coast many Negroes, while paying their dues, including initiation fees, to the regular locals of the Boilermakers, at the same time refused to be relegated to the status of members in auxiliary locals. This situation prevailed for some time.

Complaint Filed

Finally the Portland, Oregon branch of the NAACP, in conjunction with the National Office, filed formal complaints with the FEPC concerning this type of discrimination, and full hearings by the FEPC were held in Portland and Los Angeles in November of 1943. The Boilermakers, however, on November 28, 1943, ordered the Marinship Corporation in San Francisco, Calif., to discharge all non-members, which included all of the Negroes who had refused to join the auxiliary. The Negro workers, then, led by Joseph James, a shipyard worker, secured a temporary injunction in the local federal court preventing the discharge of these men. But the case was dismissed on the ground that no diversity of citizenship was involved nor sufficient federal question to warrant such action in the federal courts. Through their lawyers the Negro workers applied for and secured a second temporary injunction, this time from the local courts. This case is now pending.

While the federal case was pending, FEPC, on December 9, 1943, issued its findings and directives in regard to the Boilermakers union, ordering the union to "take such necessary steps and put in course of execution such required procedures as will effect elimination of the discriminatory policies and practices found to be in conflict with and in violation of Executive Order 9346."

Despite this ruling by FEPC, the Boilermakers have refused to discontinue their discriminatory policies.

Providence Case

In the shipyards in Providence, R.I., the Boilermakers union was anxious to win the election among the workers in order to be designated as the bargaining agent. Preceding the election the Boilermakers had admitted all persons, regardless of race or color, and were more than anxious to sign up Negroes. These Negroes were admitted into the regular union, attended meetings, made motions, voted and were treated as any other members. After the election had been won by the Boilermakers and the closed-shop agreement signed, officers of the International of the Boilermakers attempted to set up an auxiliary, though a majority of the local officers of the union, as well as the Negro members of the local and a majority of white members, were opposed to this move. As a matter of fact a large majority of both Negro and white members had adopted in September, 1943, a resolution to the effect that there should be no distinction as to race in the membership of the local. Yet the International officers continued their efforts to remove Negro members from the local, and it was soon discovered members, after paying their dues as members of the local, were receiving "auxiliary cards." These "auxiliary cards" were ignored by the Negroes and other members of the local and Negroes continued to attend meetings along with others and were ostensibly considered regular members.

When the December election of officers was held, the International made efforts to have men elected who would discriminate against Negroes. In order to insure the election of such men, International representatives challenged all ballots cast by Negro members and refused to permit them to be counted. A case challenging this type of discrimination is now pending in the local Providence court.

On January 13, Judge Churchill handed down his epoch-making decision. He said, among other things "That the purpose and effect of the so-called 'auxiliary" was to segregate Negroes and persons of no other race and color, in a position less favorable in substantial matters than the position enjoyed by other members [white] of Local 308. . . . It is clear beyond doubt that such acts as this election of December 14, 1943, in respect to ballot offered Negro voters, under instructions of the officials of the International, constitute a discrimination based on race and color, and the question is, is this discrimination illegal? . . . I rule that the conduct at the election on December 14, 1943, and that the by-laws and constitution of the so-called 'auxiliary,' in so far as they discriminate between members of the colored race, Negroes, and persons of all other races, as compared with the by-laws and constitution of the Brotherhood, are illegal and void." In concluding his decision, Judge Churchill said: "I rule that colored members of the so-called auxiliary are members of Local 308, and that their dues ought to be kept in Rhode Island."

Negro shipyard workers on the West Coast and in Providence, R.I., have refused to be discriminated against by the Boilermakers and have shown their willingness to fight this un-American practice through legal means. Negro members of the Boilermakers union are anxious to contribute their part toward the war effort by building ships, but at the same time they insist on being accorded their full rights as American citizens while building ships to enable the United Nations to win the war for freedom abroad.

The Crisis, 51 (March, 1944): 77-78.

THE PHILADELPHIA "HATE STRIKE," 1944

60. WASTED MANPOWER

Part I

THE P.T.C. DILEMMA[125]

PTC HALTS JOB BAN . . . PTC BARS COLORED WOMEN. These are the headlines
that have been carried by the local press lately, both colored and white. I
often wonder if our press completely understands the PTC situation, even
though they have carried thousands of lines in their weekly issues on it during
the past year.

When certain newspapers state that they doubt the sincerity of the PTC,
they are certainly justified in their doubt, but to include the union in that
doubt is an injustice done to an organization that is doing its best to bring
about Democracy within a company where it has never existed before.

For the life of me, I do not understand how the press and their editorial
writers expect to see prejudice completely erased from the PTC scene by insisting that a clause be embodied in the contract stating that there shall be
no discrimination in regards to upgrading or employment because of race, creed,
color, or national origin.

Words never have, do not, and never will enforce Democracy. It takes the
workers themselves to bring this about.

In the first place, a contract is an agreement between two parties--the
Union and the Company. Every article and clause in any collective bargaining
contract is mutually agreed upon between the two parties involved. This does
not mean that everything the Union demands for the workers the company will
agree to. During the process of negotiation, there is a constant battle going
on between the negotiating committee and the company officials, the Union
trying to get the most it can for the workers and the company fighting hard to
keep from giving them anything.

The TWU-CIO fought hard for a no-discrimination clause to be put into the
contract, but the Company, which will never give up trying to break the Union,
would not agree to it; and it was only through the TWU-CIO being the bargaining
agent that the notice put out by the WMC ending discrimination against minorities
was allowed to be posted.[126]

If anyone is under the impression that winning a Labor Board election is
the most difficult part of becoming the bargaining agent, they should read up
a little more on collective bargaining. The most trying and difficult period
a union goes through is during the period of contract negotiations.

The Company still encourages the former Company Union stooges to breed
discontent amongst the workers, The AFL, which ran second to the TWU-CIO in the
number of votes cast in the State Labor Board election, is doing everything it
can to disrupt the program of the TWU-CIO; and also there is a group of workers
who have migrated from the South and who are certainly not encouraging better
race relations.

This group represents a small but active minority (their actions are
typical of fascist thinking). With encouragement from the Company stooges and
AFL, these backward elements are continuing to incite racial friction amongst
the employees.

These Fascist-minded workers have spread anti-Negro propaganda and other
types of vicious literature to increase the intensity of the racial situation
that now exists within PTC.

Some of this group, with the stooges and the AFL, have joined the Union
with one purpose in mind--to destroy it, to bore from within, divide and rule
is their program.

Several weeks ago a number of workers went to the Union officials and
asked them if the Union would support them if they should strike in protest
against the upgrading of Negroes. The Union officials state definitely that
they stood and were fighting continually for a policy of no discrimination.

One of the Union Officials told me that six months ago, when they called
meetings in the various car barns and would bring up the race issue, they
would be battling alone for Negroes' rights. The picture has now changed, and
it is to the credit of the TWU-CIO that they now have made white workers
understand the fraternity of interests which exists between them and colored
workers.

In many shops and barns, where Negro-white disputes took place, they were
settled on the basis of this understanding.

Philadelphia Tribune, July 29, 1944.

61. UN-AMERICAN AND INTOLERABLE

The surprise work stoppage by PTC car and bus operators is an outrage
against the people of Philadelphia and this wartime Nation.

By tying up transportation in this vital war production zone the perpetrators of the sneak strike are sabotaging America's war effort.

Whatever the real cause or causes of this walkout, it is inexcusable
and intolerable.

Particularly unpardonable is the PTC work stoppage if it is mainly the
result of racial prejudice.

On July 8 the Philadelphia Transportation Company agreed to accept for
employment all qualified applicants, regardless of race, creed, color or
national origin.

This agreement was in compliance with a ruling of the War Manpower Commission requiring impartial hiring.

It also constituted acceptance by the company of the U.S. Fair Employment Practice Committee's directive to cease discrimination against Negro
employees.

Negroes have a right to work at any tasks for which they are qualified.
PTC has followed not only the required, but the proper, procedure in training
them for jobs on cars.

In whatever degree the PTC walkout is based upon race prejudice it is
wholly indefensible and thoroughly un-American.

To end for all time the vicious creed of race supremacy this Nation today
is fighting the greatest war in history. Our Allies, especially in China and
India, are wondering whether we practice the racial tolerance we preach.

Don't the work-stopping PTC employees believe in America's cause? Don't
they care whether or not Philadelphia's war plants and Navy Yard are slowed
down?

This walkout came only a few hours after the War Manpower Commission
declared the Philadelphia-Camden district a "Group I critical labor market
area" and entered a 48-hour week in all business and industrial establishments.

By stopping work in defiance of a War Manpower Commission order and of
Federal directives to the PTC, the car and bus operators are in effect striking against the United States Government in the midst of war.

If the transport employes wanted to strike for any reason why didn't they
go about it in an orderly manner, with a statement of their intentions and
ample warning to both the PTC and the city's workers?

In putting their work stoppage into effect by stealth they used the most
cowardly of tactics. Why? Were they afraid to come out in the open and make
known their demands?

What will our gallant fighting men on Saipan and Guam, in Normandy,
Brittany and Italy think of America's Home Front when they learn that the workers upon whom they are counting for the tools of victory couldn't get to their
jobs because of sneak strikers who hadn't even the courage to say what they
were striking for?

This walkout already has inconvenienced and exasperated hundreds of thousands of busy Philadelphians. It has slowed output in this, the second
greatest war production center in America. It has incited lawlessness and
ill-feeling.

It represents nothing but insult and injury to millions of Philadelphians.
It is a shameful pullback on America's war effort and offers gratuitous aid
and comfort to Adolf Hitler and the whole gangster crew of the murderous Axis.

This unspeakable walkout must be settled without delay and nothing like
it must happen again.

Philadelphia Inquirer, August 2, 1944.

62. TRANSIT STRIKE LONG THREATENED

By William Mensing

Yesterday's paralyzing tieup of the city's electrical transportation system came as the drastic fulfillment of a threat made seven months ago by the employees of the PTC that they would go on strike if Negroes were elevated to operational positions with the company.

This materialized despite the fact that just one month ago the workers ratified a new contract between the Transport Workers Union, Local 234 (CIO), and the company, calling for no discrimination against minority groups.

Reviewed on Monday

The threat began smoldering again on Monday, however, when eight Negroes --first group of motormen trainees of their race--began a three-week training course on practice tracks at 3rd St. and Wyoming avenue preparatory to taking over regular routes around the end of this month.

From many quarters, as the year began, came opposition to the November directive of the President's Fair Employment Practice Committee that Negro employees be raised on the basis of ability to jobs as motormen, conductors, operators and station trainmen.

Powers Challenged

The P.R.T. Employees Union, then the bargaining agent for the workers, challenged the powers of the FEPC before a Congressional committee in Washington, contending such action was in direct violation of a contract then in force between the union and the company. [127]

The company itself, first on the fence in the dispute, finally announced that it would abide by the FEPC order if a mutual agreement could be worked out with the independent union.

Overhwelming Victory

Then, in March, the T.W.U. which campaigned on the ground that it followed the CIO policy of no discrimination because of race, creed or color--won an overwhelming victory in a State Labor Relations Board election conducted among workers in the transportation and maintenance departments of the company

This, to all appearances, ended the racial question after the defeated P.R.T. Employees Union sought the choice as bargaining agent on the basis of maintaining the status quo with regard to union-management contracts, which excluded employment of Negroes in operational jobs.

Supporting the Fight

Supporting the fight for upgrading of the minority employees were many religious groups, and the National Association for the Advancement of Colored People.

The new contract with the T.W.U. was ratified by more than 2,000 employees on June 30 and the problem appeared to be settled and until the company announced that Negroes would be ready to become operators before the end of August.

Philadelphia Inquirer, August 2, 1944.

63. TEN ARE INJURED IN STREET FIGHTS

At least ten persons were injured, one critically, when fights broke out in scattered sections of the city last night following the Philadelphia Transportation Co. workers' protest strike against the upgrading of Negroes to operational jobs.

Most seriously injured when tension burst into street fighting at 23rd St. and Ridge Ave., was John Young, 39, of 2164 N. Dover Street, beaten unconscious with a brick after he was dragged from an automobile near the intersection.

Four Others Injured

Also injured were his brother-in-law, John Collins, 52, of 2166 N. Dover St., with whom he was riding; Eric Husak, 52, of 1832 W. Hunting Park Ave.; Louise Quigg, 37, of 224 George St., and Harry Miller, 41, of 2802 W. Oxford St.

The victims were treated at Lankenau and Women's Homeopathic hospitals. Mr. Young's condition was critical last night.

Store Window Broken

At the height of the disturbance in this area, during which a brick was thrown through a jewelry store window at 2208 Ridge Ave., more than 100 policemen patrolled the streets in red cars and on foot, warning residents to remain indoors.

Minor disorders were suppressed by police at 45th St. and Woodland Ave.; 40th St. and Lancaster Ave.; 40th St. and Girard Ave.; 63rd and Haverford Ave.; 57th and Larchwood Ave., and in the 3100 block of S. 82nd St.

Coal Spilled

The disturbance at 23rd St., and Ridge Ave., began when a number of youths attending a carnival nearby lowered the tailgate of a passing coal truck, spilling the coal across the intersection.

Mr. Young, driving home from the seashore with his wife and two children, was beaten when he stepped from his car to protest after it was showered with coal.

200 Rounded Up

Nearly 200 youths were rounded up by police and arrested for hearings this morning when disorders spread throughout the neighborhood.

Three others were slightly injured by thrown pieces of coal.

Others injured were Patrolman John O'Donnell, of 1843 W. Albanus St., struck by a milk bottle hurled through the window of his automobile near 11th and Norris Sts., and James Getty, 50, of 1718 N. 26th St., beaten as he walked near 21st and Columbia Ave.

Philadelphia Inquirer, August 2, 1944.

64. ATTEMPT TO OPERATE EL AND SUBWAYS FAILS

By George M. Mawhinney

The first excuse offered by the men and women for the walkout when they failed to appear at work early Tuesday morning was that they were sick.

Following the strikers' meeting, Mr. McMenamin sent a telegram to War Mobilization Chairman Byrnes urging him to take over the transit system and "to settle the matter the way it should be settled--by a vote of the employees," on the up-grading of Negro employees.

The attempt at service resumption met with variations in co-operation from cashiers on the two high speed lines. No attempt was made to resume operation on the Delaware River Bridge Line.

Action in Washington

In the daylight hours that preceded the moves toward reinstating service, official Washington had been a-broil.

Although it was learned on reliable authority that the WLB unanimously, wanted Government seizure, it also became apparent that either of the two agencies which might act in the seizure was reluctant to act.

The Army made it more than apparent that it did not wish to send in troops and a spokesman suggested that possibly the Pennsylvania State Guard might be able to take over.

Later it also became apparent that the Office of Defense Transportation, the logical agency to take over a transportation system, was not anxious to accept the issue. There was no word, at a late hour last night concerning the President's attitude.

The Government's moves came while Philadelphians were plodding through the rain to and from their jobs, finding transportation by the hitch-hike method, or riding in special buses and trucks provided by many large companies.

It came, too, after Philadelphia's magistrates had held hearings on 300 persons accused of street fights or malicious mischief; while taprooms and liquor stores remained closed, and while absenteeism in war plants and other commercial institutions continued as high as 40 per cent, in some cases.

140,000 Absentees

According to an incomplete WMC survey, it was estimated that yesterday 120,000 of Philadelphia's 600,000 war workers were unable to reach their benches, and that an additional 20,000 failed to report to work in Delaware county.

Among the outstanding developments of the second day of the walkout-- staged by nearly 6,000 men and women employees of the transit company in protest over the upgrading of Negro workers to posts of motormen--were these:

1. The protesting employees announced today they would not return to work unless the company returned to its status of July 30. July 31 was the day the company began training Negro operators.

2. The company declared that it must take the viewpoint that the walkout is a strike, although it is unapproved by any union, and in the late afternoon ordered all loitering employees out of its carbarns and locked the barns tightly.

3. Two hundred and fifty shop stewards of Transport Workers Union (CIO), the bargaining agent for the employees, held a meeting and denounced the walkout by an almost unanimous vote. At this meeting, Harry Sacker, general counsel of the union, denied the claim of the strikers that Negro trolley operators would achieve seniority dating back to the time they first were employed by the company in varying capacities.

4. Taxicab business and central city hotel business continued on a boom basis, with occasional reports some independent cab drivers and some smaller hotels were taking advantage of the lack of transportation by making overcharges.

5. At least one of the city's Selective Service Boards cancelled occupational deferments of striking PTC employees and classified them 1-A, and other boards were expected to follow this procedure.

6. Motorists everywhere in the city continued to jam into ration boards to get extra rations of gasoline, which, to a great extent, was used on a share the ride basis.

7. Frank L. McNamee, regional director of the War Manpower Commission, and C. James Fleming, regional director of the President's Fair Employment Practices Commission, made an appeal to all citizens to refrain from "rabble rousing," and the FEPC's division of review and analysis pointed out that Philadelphia is not the only city affected under a WMC directive for using Negro trolley and bus operators. Negroes are employed in such jobs in New York, Detroit, Cleveland, Chicago, San Francisco, Tulsa, Buffalo and Winston-Salem, N.C.

8. The American Friends Service Committee "deplored" the walkout and urged a return to work; the Philadelphia Metropolitan Council for Equal Job Opportunity urged immediate Federal intervention, and the National Association for the Advancement of Colored People posted handbills on telephone poles urging Mayor Samuel and the PTC to "stand pat."

Lead to White House

Developments in Washington, D.C., starting in the morning at an extraordinary session of the War Labor Board and leading by afternoon to the White House, were all aimed at a quick restoration of transportation for Philadelphians.

At the outset, War Labor Board Chairman William H. Davis received a detailed report on the local situation from Sylvester Garrett, WMC regional chairman, and Eli Rock, head of the disputes division of the Philadelphia region.

Presidential Aide

Soon after that report had been received, Jonathan W. Daniels, administrative assistant to President Roosevelt, and Brigadier General Edward S. Greenbaum, executive officer to the Undersecretary of War, joined the conference. As it concluded, Mr. Daniels told reporters that "there is every indication that the case will be referred."

By those words he meant that the Philadelphia walkout would be referred to the President for action.

Army Makes Its Plans

General Greenbaum, at that time, offered no comment, but it was learned later that War Department officials had conferred most of the day in the Pentagon Building, presumably laying plans for troop movement, should it be decided to use the Army in taking over the transport system.

During the morning hours it also was learned that the WMC had recommended to War Mobilization Director Byrnes that the ODT or the War Department assume direction of Philadelphia transit, although on the subject there was no official comment.

Executive Order Prepared

It was not until late in the afternoon that it was learned that an Executive order was being prepared in the White House and had been sent to the President. At that time it was said that a White House announcement was momentarily expected.

Up to that time, it was learned there was no decision whether to use the Army immediately or first to assume direction of the transit system and appeal to the workers to go back to their jobs as employees of Uncle Sam.

War Output Hurt

Meanwhile the War Department reported that the strike had "seriously affected the production of radar, heavy artillery, heavy ammunition, military tracks, bombs and other supplies vitally needed."

The department also announced officially that the important activities affected were those of the Frankford Arsenal, the Quartermaster's Depot, the Philadelphia Ordnance District, the Philadelphia Signal Depot, and the Storage and Issue Agency, which is an Army funnel for front-line materials.

In Washington Walter White, secretary of the National Association for the Advancement of Colored People, announced sending a telegram to the President urging Army intervention "so that war production may be resumed and that workers may be employed irrespective of race or of color."

Steps Toward Solution

Philadelphia continued struggling along on its feet or in whatever transportation vehicles were available as the walkout entered its second day.

But as the day began, city and Government officials were making every effort to find a solution for the situation which has stagnated war production and all other business enterprises in the city.

Conference in Washington

One of the major efforts looking toward some sort of solution was centered in Washington, D.C., where the National War Labor Board pondered the problems involved. In that city a conference was held, attended by Sylvester Garrett,

chairman of the Philadelphia Regional War Labor Board, and Eli Rock, Director
of the board's disputes division.

Before leaving for Washington, Mr. Garrett said he had had a telephone
conversation with William H. Davis, national chairman of the War Labor Board
on Tuesday night, and had informed that official that the transit situation
remained "very serious."

Appeals to Workers

Early today he pointed out that all appeals of Army and Navy officials,
and of other public spirited citizens, to the men and women participating in
the walkout had failed of desirable results. He added, however:

"There will be no slackening of our efforts to bring the men and women
back to work at the earliest possible moment."

Another conference of moment during the early morning hours was one held
in the office of Mayor Samuel. It was attended by the Mayor, Director of
Public Safety James H. Malone, Assistant City Solicitor James F. Ryan, and
John F. Sears, head of the Philadelphia office of the Federal Bureau of
Investigation.

The men and women participating in the walkout, estimated at approximately 6,000 of the PTC's 12,000 employees, held a second mass meeting in the
big "headquarters" carbarn at 10th and Luzerne Sts. It followed a mass meeting
held Tuesday night, at which they reiterated their determination not to return
work while Negro operators of trolley cars are used by the PTC.

At yesterday morning's mass meeting they decided to continue with the
walkout, and thus leave all Philadelphians to get to their places of employment
as best they could.

During the first day of the walkout, according to Regional War Manpower
Chairman McNamee, there was an estimated production loss of 70 per cent on Navy
contracts and 50 per cent on Army contracts.

Yesterday, with the completion of organization of buses, trucks and private
automobiles to carry workers to their places of employment, general production
in war factories was considerably improved.

Although the walkout has been principally to motormen, conductors and some
maintenance men, many other employees of the PTC failed to report to work
yesterday because of transportation difficulties. The company said that the
600 Negroes it has in track repair crews reported for duty.

Union Continues Pleas

The Transport Workers Union, which holds bargaining rights among all but
office workers of the PTC continued to appeal to the workers to return to their
jobs. The TWU won a collective bargaining election on March 14 by a narrow
margin.

That election was closely contested by the Amalgamated Street Car Workers
(AFL) and the PRT Employees Union. The latter union retained bargaining rights
for the office workers.

Seniority Question

Throughout yesterday James McMenamin, a conductor, who is acting as
spokesman for the committee of workers which engineered the walkout, continued
to insist that the walkout was a result of the strikers' fears over their
seniority rights.

He had previously said that the Negro motormen being placed on the street
cars were claiming seniority from the time they were first employed by PTC as
track repairmen or in other capacities, rather than from the time they were
to be made motormen or conductors.

'No Discrimination'

The upgrading of Negro employes came as a result of a Presidential executive order of June 25, 1941, directing that the Fair Employment Practice Committee recommend to the War Manpower Commission means for full utilization of
all workers, without regard to race, color or creed.

The union contract, recently agreed to by the TWU and at present awaiting certification by the War Labor Board, called for "no discrimination against minorities."

Thus, under the aegis of the WMC, PTC recently began training Negro employees as motormen. Eight had been instructed on trial courses, and on Tuesday, when the walkout began, were to have taken cars on trial runs over the PTC's regular lines.

Philadelphia Inquirer, August 3, 1944.

65. END THIS OUTRAGEOUS STRIKE!

If there must be Federal seizure of Philadelphia's strike-bound transit system to remedy an intolerable situation it is profoundly to be hoped that it comes soon.

Federal action or not, the major imperative is to get the cars, trains and buses running, and keep them running. Philadelphians and the national war effort have suffered enough through this unspeakable PTC walkout. It must be ended.

But Government seizure and operation of the transit system, if such is required, will not solve the deeply disturbing issue from which the disgraceful walkout--clearly a violation of the War Labor Disputes Act--stemmed. Plant seizure in wartime strikes has consistently proved only a stop-gap.

The car and bus operators who stopped work without warning permitted race prejudice to overrule every other consideration, including their duty to the Philadelphia public and to the Nation.

They disregarded completely the fact that, with the aid of Philadelphia war plants and the Philadelphia Navy Yard, the United States is now battling on a global front for the liberty and dignity of individual men and women of every race and color.

In walking out because a few Negroes were upgraded by the PTC in a commendable effort to eliminate racial discrimination the employes disavowed the cause of freedom for which their country, even their own sons and brothers, are fighting.

What did they hope to gain by such a thoroughly unjustifiable act of sabotage on the home front? Rescinding by the PTC of its agreement to remove the color line in the training and advancement of workers? But the agreement to give Negroes fair play, however progressive and praiseworthy, was in compliance with Federal orders. No man or group of men is greater than the Government.

Whatever the opinion of the car workers regarding the War Manpower Commission's ruling and the Fair Employment Practice Committee's directive to the company concerning Negro employees, they had no justification for their shockingly un-American, undemocratic reprisal.

Furthermore, whether or not the WMC order was well timed has no bearing whatever on the issue now. The plain fact is that a group of employees placed their own narrow, selfish, prejudiced demands above the needs of their country and of their fellow men.

With what result? With the result that the output of war goods required for victory over the cut-throat Nazis and Japs was reduced, thousands of persons inconvenienced and Philadelphia business sharply slashed.

With the result, also, that such humanitarian essentials as blood donations to save the lives of our brave service men were cut down because donors could not get to Red Cross stations.

With the result, moreover, that Philadelphia, City of Brotherly Love, has been smeared from one end of the country to the other with the stigma of racial prejudice and lawlessness.

This is not the time to go into complicated dealing with racial and other issues. There will be time later for calm, reasoned consideration of such matters. The first necessity is to get the cars, trains, and buses running.

End this outrageous strike--now!

Philadelphia Inquirer, August 3, 1944.

66. WASTED MANPOWER

The PTC Dilemma

Part II

The provisions of the new contract between the Union and Company are numerous. Among them are the following:

1. A bonus of 5¢ per hour for transportation, shop and maintenance workers.
2. Pension plan.
3. Reduction from 12 hours to 10-1/2 hours in the overall spread on swing runs with payment of half time for swing time in excess of 10-1/2 hours.
4. Upward equalization of rates which will result in raises of from 6 to 21¢ per hour for approximately 2500 hours.
5. Raising lunch allowance to 75¢.
6. Arbitration of disputes.
7. Right to wear the Union button.
8. Union security through maintenance of membership and check off.

Regarding the maintenance of membership clause is on the same principle as industrial insurance. A union member has the assurance that the union will protect him against company injustice, therefore, for the union to give him that protection, they must have some security of membership. If, anyone wants to continue to receive the benefits of insurance, they must keep their payments up. If they do not, they lose their insurance and all its benefits. This same principle applies to maintenance of membership. A member of the union must keep his dues paid up or in trade union language remain in good standing. If a member falls in arrears of a certain number of months (usually three) and does not want to pay up his dues, he is in jeopardy of being dismissed by the company.

Of course, it is an established fact that a Union is no stronger than its membership. I mean, that the more employees belonging to the union, the stronger demands the union can make on the management for the workers.

This is a very important factor. The first step a union must take is to become strong in membership. Prior to any maintenance of membership clause going into effect, there is a fifteen day period known as the escape period. During this period anyone who wishes to withdraw from the union may do so.

It is quite logical to see why the Negro worker at PTC has remained silent on the upgrading issue. The Negro worker realizes that the union is his only salvation, and if there was a lot of "hell-raising for rights" at this particular time, before the contract was signed, it would give ammunition to the Fascists within PTC; and during the Escape Period the A.F. of L. and Company Union stooges would take advantage of the race issue, and encourage the workers to withdraw from the union with the worn line that the TWU-CIO was a n....r loving Union.

Foolish as this may seem, it strikes deep into a strong minority of workers who are being continually antagonized by a combination of the A.F. of L., Company Union stooges, and migrant Southern workers.

Because of this unfortunate situation, the Negro and white press are making a grave mistake. Whether they knock the Union or praise it, the result is the same, the Union is the victim.

Reactionary elements within PTC never rests which is typical of the Fascist gangs. It is true they represent a minority, but so do Rankin and Bilbo. And whose voices are heard more often within the halls of Congress than these two Fascists. This vicious element reads the press with greater interest than the average reader.

Philadelphia Tribune, August 5, 1944.

67. UP TO THE ARMY: END THIS STRIKE!

Continued defiance of the Government and the Army by PTC strikers is an appalling demonstration of lawlessness.

How much longer must Philadelphia and its great war production plants put up with this unspeakable situation? What is the Army going to do about it, and when?

Certainly the PTC employees renewed defiance is not the result of strong-arm methods by Major General Hayes and the men under his command. Their course has been noteworthy for a moderation that approximates extreme caution.

A more positive and prompt effort by the Army toward getting cars and buses moving, with vigorous measures to assure protection, might have been more productive of results.

The same caution extended to other branches of the Government, with Attorney General Francis Biddle ordering an investigation to determine whether the strikers had violated a Federal statue. It seemed plain enough to weary and completely disgusted Philadelphians that the moment the Government took charge the Smith-Connally War Labor Disputes Act went into effect and that thereafter anyone counselling a continuation of the work-stoppage was a law violator and subject to penalties.[128]

A strange anomaly was the request of James H. McMenamin, self-elected chairman of the strikers, for police protection on the ground that he had been threatened by fellow employees.

Having been granted a police guard, did it occur to Mr. McMenamin that there he was, shielded against danger, while on far-distant battlefields American boys were being denied the full help of Philadelphia's great war plants because Mr. McMenamin and his associates were tying up the transit lines upon which war workers depended for transport?

We don't believe he had any such enlightened thought. Yet the truth is that, remote from the blood and the ghastly horror of war, the PTC strikers since early last Tuesday have been double-crossing the millions of GI Joes from Brittany to Guam.

Disregards by the strikers of all appeals to return to work, whether on grounds of patriotism or racial tolerance, is disgraceful.

Their country is at war. Their city is the second greatest war production center in the United States. The company for which they work--when they work-- has been taken over by their Government. The cars and buses which they should be operating are under the supervision of the United States Army. Their refusal to return is, like their attitude toward Negro workers, indefensible.

Getting transit service started in Philadelphia at once is the only issue at this time. Causes of the strike are not the major concern now. There will be time for discussion of the fundamentals, including un-American race prejudice. The immediate imperative is to restore trolley, train and bus service to the outraged people of Philadelphia.

The strikers, as General Hayes has declared, are "apparently more interested in aiding the Axis" than in getting Philadelphia war workers to their jobs. It is a situation that can't be endured.

The War Labor Disputes Act should be enforced at once against conditions in Philadelphia which constitute a betrayal of the Nation and its democratic principles.

How long can the strikers defy their Government and public opinion? It's up to the Army. End this strike!

Philadelphia Inquirer; August 5, 1944.

68. COLLUSION CHARGE SENT TO ROOSEVELT

By Frank Rosen

Local 234 of the Transport Workers Union (CIO), the bargaining agent for Philadelphia Transportation Co. employees, yesterday adopted a resolution to be

sent to President Roosevelt which stated, that "unmistakable surface evidence
points to collusion on the part of important PTC officials in instigating" the
transit strike.

After thanking the President for his "prompt action in ordering the Army
to suppress this conspiracy against the Nation's war effort," the resolution
declared that "we will do everything in our power to make up for the severe
damage to war production and morale resulting from the tragic events of the
past five days."

400 Are Present

Some 400 officers and members of the local, which deplored the strike
from its inception, were present when the resolution was adopted at a special
meeting at the Broadwood Hotel.

Also present was Michael J. Quill, national president of the T.W.U., who
reiterated the nine questions which he outlined publicly here Saturday night
and for which he said "the people of Philadelphia have a right to demand answers from the management" of PTC.

Other Speakers

Other speakers included James J. Fitzsimmon, national vice president of
the union; Douglas MacMahon, national secretary-treasurer; Fred Myers, national vice president of the C.I.O. National Maritime Union, and several T.W.U.
stewards.

At the meeting, Mr. Quill, alluding to the alleged cause of the strike
--the upgrading of eight Negroes to the position of motormen--declared that
"we will fight for the rights and seniority of all workers, whether they be
white or black."

In urging all PTC employees "to go back to work immediately," he said
that "we will clean Fascism out of the transit system in Philadelphia."

Mr. Quill also repeated his charge that Philadelphia police were "useless" during the strike, and that "we have proof" that groups of policemen
and striking employees drank and played cards and took part in crap games
"while this delaying action was going on."

Called Fascist Plot

Mr. McMahon referred to the strike as "a Fascist plot to break up our
union--the U.S. Government knows that the trouble did not start just because
of eight Negroes being upgraded to motormen."

"Every PTC official, he continued, "will have to answer questions before
the Federal Grand Jury," which Attorney General Francis Biddle has instructed
to investigate the strike to determine whether any "criminal conspiracy"
existed.

Philadelphia Inquirer, August 7, 1944.

69. GRAVE STRIKE ISSUES THAT REMAIN

As the PTC strikers go back to work at the firm, if belated, insistence
of the Army, these points merit thoughtful consideration:

Philadelphia has been disgraced before the Nation. All of the transit
employees should unite now in redeeming the city's good name by giving 100
per cent service to the war effort and to the people.

They should hold in abeyance their protests against the upgrading of
Negroes by the PTC.

Meanwhile, the major parties at interest, the Federal Government, the
PTC, the CIO union, the city and the public should make every possible effort,
through calm negotiation and discussion, to settle the racial issue.

But this does not mean that the unspeakable tie-up of Philadelphia's
car and bus lines in the midst of the most terrible war in history can be

lightly dismissed as something past and gone.

On the contrary, Federal, State and local agencies should stop at nothing
to uncover the precise causes of the inexcusable walkout and reveal all of
the persons chiefly responsible for it.

All who had a hand in fomenting it and all of the leaders who defied the
power and authority of the United States Government in wartime should be
penalized to the limit.

In particular the Federal Department of Justice should leave nothing
undone to make the PTC outlaw work-stoppage a stern and unmistakable warning
to every potential wartime striker in the United States.

The Department of Justice was inexplicably tardy in invoking the provisions of the War Labor Disputes Act in this crisis.

The anti-strike law itself has again been shown up as a weak, thoroughly
unreliable protection for the Nation against selfish, lawless groups. But
even the ineffective Smith-Connally measure might have been of some use to the
people of Philadelphia and to the maintenance of war production here if it had
been enforced from the beginning.

In a broader sense the basic issue in the PTC walkout demands earnest and
continuing attempts at solution not only by all Philadelphians but by all
Americans in the North and in the South.

Here was a strike that concerned not rates of pay, not hours of work but
the democratic right of all Americans, whatever their racial origin, to equality
of opportunity.

The contention of the strikers that Negro employees of the PTC should not
be upgraded to car jobs was fundamentally unsound and in conflict with every
American and democratic principle.

But it is the tragic truth that the bigotry and intolerance which came to
poisonous flower in the PTC tie-up have been nurtured by many of our people.

There have been grave faults on both sides of this racial issue but it is
inescapable that since the Civil War far too many Americans have been content
to drift along in the smug hope that the Negro problem would solve itself. It
won't solve itself. It must be solved by all of us, working together.

Into the solution must go better educational methods and facilities, a
clearer understanding, a finer spirit of co-operation, a wider mutual recognition of racial aspirations and, above all, a deeper devotion to America's
democratic ideals.

One national need today towers above all others. It is the prompt, total
winning of the war. But beyond victory we have a racial problem that must be
solved with intelligence, faith and patient perservance.

Philadelphia Inquirer, August 7, 1944.

70.   PHILADELPHIA: POST-WAR PREVIEW

The disgraceful and unpatriotic strike of transit workers in Philadelphia
over the upgrading of eight colored employees is an indication of some of the
serious problems which will confront us in the post-war period.

It shows that the conditioning of the white masses to a bi-racial color-
caste society has gone so far that no sudden change on the part of those in
authority in racial attitudes can be immediately communicated to them.

The decision to upgrade Negro workers in the Philadelphia transit system,
followed a long uphill struggle on the part of the Fair Employment Practices
Committee to overcome the reluctance of the management and the unionized
workers.

The officers of the CIO union, which had become the bargaining agent for
the workers (after an election in which the company union was defeated) favored
the up-grading of the Negro workers, but apparently they had not succeeded
in bringing their members around to the same way of thinking.

On orders from Washington, the Army has taken over and service is normal,
as the military authorities show that they mean business and are not to be
deterred by wildcat strikers.

The outlaw Philadelphia strike poses the question of what will happen
when there is no longer a national emergency, when thousands of factories
close down for lack of war orders, when millions are thereby thrown out of
work, when union officials, therefore, have less power, and when millions
of discharged servicemen join the army of unemployed.

The Army cannot and will not then be called out to operate businesses
whose workers strike because of up-grading of Negroes.

Many of the wartime agencies which have protected Negro labor will be
abolished, and in any event will not dictate to private industry.

These sober considerations should spur us to insistence NOW upon some
post-war plan which will keep down unemployment, increase production and outlaw industrial discrimination because of color.

Neither political party now has such a plan, although both party platforms are filled with platitudes and generalities about the post-war world.

Unless some well-thought-out program is adopted now, before the war comes
to an end, we are destined to have more and bloodier strife over jobs and
upgrading, and efforts to oust Negroes from skilled positions they have
secured as a result of the war effort and the FEPC.

Pittsburgh Courier, August 12, 1944.

71. THE PHILADELPHIA STRIKE

We see two lessons in the Philadelphia transit strike. The first is that
there is no point in wasting time on racial bigots. Neither patriotic appeal
nor polite request by the military could get white Philadelphia transit workers
to call off their ugly stay-out against an FEPC order giving eight Negroes a
chance to work as motormen and busdrivers. The strikers began to go back to
work only after the government showed that it meant business. We approve the
steps the government took, and we hope they will be applied, and more quickly,
the next time there is an outbreak of this kind. The threat to cancel draft
deferments of strikers, to bar them from other work under WMC order, and to
deny them unemployment compensation proved effective. The arrest of four strike
leaders under the Smith-Connally act should prove a deterrent to similar demagogy
in the future. It is time that backward elements in the ranks of labor as
well as capital learned that racial discrimination in employment is contrary to
the public policy and the ideals of this country, and that the government is
prepared to punish those responsible for it.

The second lesson of the Philadelphia strike is that the sooner we take
the FEPC out of the shadowy realm of existence under executive order and give
it full statutory recognition, with power to enforce its decisions, the less
trouble we shall have. The FEPC's present weakness invites disobedience and
stimulates defiance. These Philadelphia transit workers have been working
side by side with Negroes for years; the only difference is that Negroes will
not be given a chance to qualify for some of the better paying jobs. We are
not dealing in Philadelphia, as we might in the South, with ingrown attitudes
and deep-rooted living patterns. We are dealing with the naked, greedy, and
unashamed unwillingness of white workers to give Negro workers a break. That
attitude requires no special understanding; it is racialism in its crassest
form. Congress now has before it the Scantan bill to give the FEPC statutory
authority and powers of enforcement and we hope Negroes and progressives will
press for its enactment now, before the election, when they still have some
bargaining power.

Finally *The Nation* urges Attorney General Biddle and U.S. Attorney Glee-
son in Philadelphia to give the country a thoroughgoing grand jury investigation into all the circumstances of this peculiar strike. We call it peculiar
because a majority of the employees of the Philadelphia Transportation Company
had shown their own opposition to racialism by voting for the Transport Workers
Union, CIO, several months ago in a union election. The TWU had campaigned on
an anti-discrimination platform, in contradistinction to the "independent"
union whose old contract with the company barred Negroes from the better jobs.
The fact that the strike was led by the "independent" union officials and the
readiness of the company's personnel director to give in to the strikers'

anti-Negro demands provide grounds for suspecting that the racial issue was
deliberately exploited to split the workers and hurt the CIO union. This
strike delayed war production and hurt morale, and it disgraced the United
States in the eyes of the world. We want to see it probed to the very bottom
and we want to see those responsible in jail.

The Nation, 159 (August 12, 1944): 172-73.

72. WASTED MANPOWER

It Has Happened Here

Part III

It did happen here. And--up to the time of this writing at least--we have
reason to be thankful for the forms it did not take. There have not been any
wholesale clashes between Negroes and whites.
I walked up Ridge avenue last week and talked to many persons, loitered
near discussion groups and the thought that was utmost in their minds was the
result of the upgrading of eight Negroes to trolley car conductors at 82¢ per
hour. I heard the simple statement iterated and reiterated. (Six thousand
employees strike because they resented the upgrading of eight colored Americans).
In this statement is the link between Philadelphia and Harlem; Philadelphia
and Mobile; Philadelphia and Beaumont. It is not a question in my mind as to
the truth of this statement. What is important is that this statement epito-
mizes what Negroes are feeling not only in Philadelphia, but everywhere throughout the country. It reflects the racial bias of the present PTC disorder.

The Origin of the PTC Strike

In a sense the PTC disorder did not begin on Tuesday August 1. It began
a long time ago when the PTC Company Union was the bargaining agent for the
employees. When last winter the FEPC held hearings on the question of upgrading
Negroes the Company union sat shoulder to shoulder with the employees arguing
against the upgrading of Negroes and also arguing against the constitutionality
of the FEPC. It was then that the seeds of racial hatred were sown. It was in
January that Frank P. Carney, president of the Company Union, refused to accept
the FEPC order. This same Frank P. Carney is one of the ring leaders of the
present strike. In my column for the past two weeks I have mentioned the
position of the TWU-CIO was in ever since the S.L.R.B. election. The company
union with the help of the A.F.L. and both of them being encouraged by the
Company itself has done everything within their power to destroy the CIO. They
never relaxed one moment. Anti-Negro literature was continually being filtered
throughout the Transportation system for weeks prior to the strike.
The stage being set August 1 was the most logical day for the storm to
break loose. The timing of this strike was uncanny and as to its effectiveness, no more need be said.

The Dilemma Facing the Negro

The issue by which the PTC employees are striking is not because of the
upgrading of just eight Negroes; it is the issue as to whether the Negro is
going to achieve his economic rights in industry or not.
If the bell of injustice tolls for these eight Negroes, it tolls for the
entire Negro race. The Negro community in Philadelphia is being torn between
the fight they are asked to wage against strangers for what the white man
tells him is freedom, and concrete discrimination they are asked to endure
from neighbors.
This is not an easy decision for the Negro to make. What has happened in
Mobile, Beaumont, Detroit and now Philadelphia has made it more difficult.
The attitude of the people of the city, the city and state administration,
the army has been distant, neglectful, passive, where they should have been
eager and active in their sympathy and assistance.

Facts That Must Face Reality

1. The PTC Company itself is as much to blame for this strike as the
Fascist elements that engineered it. It was the Company officials of the
PTC that refused to let many drivers take their trolleys out; on the weak
assumption that there may be trouble.
2. The PTC Company has not as yet issued any appeal for the strikers
to return to their jobs.
3. The only solution that the Company offered was the identical one
that the strikers offered, and that was the rescinding of the WMC order in
reference to the upgrading of Negroes.
There is no doubt in my mind that it was the Company's all-out attempt
to break the CIO in Philadelphia for good. The Republican Administration
which is represented on the Board of Directors of PTC and also represents
some of the largest stockholders realizing the growing political strength of
the CIO throughout the community has intentionally been lax in its efforts to
break this disgraceful strike, hoping of course, to discredit the name of the
CIO.

Philadelphia Tribune, August 12, 1944.

73. CIO LEADS FIGHT FOR NEGROES IN TRANSIT

WASHINGTON, Aug. 19--With the destructive race-hate strike broken at the
Philadelphia Transportation Co., seven of the eight Negroes who had been instructed to report for training prior to the strike, this week resumed training
and three of them went out on trial runs, it was reported by the Fair Employment
Practice Committee.
The eighth trainee resigned and the trial runs were made without incident,
the FEPC, which had issued the non-discriminatory order, stated.
As Philadelphia returned to normalcy, it became the tenth American city
to proceed to integrate and upgrade Negroes into the important job brackets of
the transit industry. The employment of Negroes in significant occupations
in the transit industry is by no means new. Since Pearl Harbor, the solution
of this problem has met with some success in several American cities. Today
3,879 Negroes are now operating street cars, buses and other public conveyances
in nine cities.

New York in Lead

New York City leads in the employment of 1,836 Negroes in the operating
job brackets of its transit system, organized by the Transport Workers Union,
CIO. The New York Board of Transportation employs, 1,079 Negro motormen, conductors, bus and streetcar operators. In addition, 702 are employed in other
significant occupations such as clerks, inspectors, station supervisors, train
dispatchers, clerical workers, collecting agents, car and structure maintainers.
The New York Omnibus Corporation employs 20 bus operators and seven
mechanics. The Third Ave. Transit Corporation has on its payroll 14 busmen and
trolley car drivers and the Madison Ave. Coach Corporation employs four Negro
bus drivers and four mechanics.
Detroit is second with the employment of 1,200 Negroes as conductors,
motormen, bus operators and other significant occupations by its Department of
Street Railways. Of this number, 150 are Negro women. San Francisco's Market
St. Railway employs 78 Negro motormen and coach operators and 145 conductors.
Its Municipal Railway system has 10 motormen and 27 conductorettes.
In Chicago 104 Negroes are operating street cars, 30 are driving buses
and 23 are serving as trainmen on its elevated system. Buffalo's International
Railway Co., employs 16 bus and streetcar operators. At Cleveland 319 Negroes
are employed as bus drivers, platform operators and in other significant occupations. Tulsa, Okla., employs 23 bus drivers and Winston-Salem, N.C., employs
40 bus drivers and 25 mechanics and clerical workers. Flushing, Long Island,
employs one Negro bus driver.

CIO News, August 21, 1944.

74. WHERE THE BLAME RESTS

The federal grand jury which investigated the PTC strike and yesterday
indicted 30 employees, made a full report of their findings to the court.
They placed the blame where it belongs--on a rabid, trouble-making minority who manipulated the inexcusable strike and led thousands of their fellow-
workers like sheep, into paralyzing the city's wartime transportation system.
The jury also stipulated that "proper planning beforehand on the part of
the management for such an emergency and quick action by responsible officers
might well have turned the incipient strike into a forceful display of employee
loyalty to their company and to their public duty."
The jury charged that the strike-inciting minority had fed the flame in
the strike in an attempt to prevent upgrading of Negroes to platform jobs for
which they qualified. This was the sole issue, the grand jurors emphasized
and they castigated the strike leaders who defied the constitutional rights
and the inalienable rights of every citizen to "life, liberty and the pursuit
of happiness."
It was the expressed opinion of the jury that the great majority of the
employees were not interested in striking on this basis. The report blamed
the majority of PTC employees for their willingness to follow the rabid minority and the company itself for a "weakness in the PTC management that the
permission to report sick and to be off for the term of illness had become a
much abused term used for any purpose where the employee preferred not to work."
Fear of the term "scab," the grand jury decided had motivated the thousands of striking employees into what the jurors called "a curiously weak
social attitude."
There is no place in this democratic nation for those who would deny any
minority the rights guaranteed by citizenship.
Millions have died in the past four years because of the "master race"
theory. The enemies of this country and of the Allies have used every weapon
they could muster and every sniveling agent they could enlist to spread the
seeds of class and group hatreds.
As the grand jurors emphasized, the scene of the strike was Philadelphia,
"the center of a district of prime importance in the efforts of the nations
allied to conquer those powers (which boast the right to rule and to dominate
the world) and to preserve the rights of man and of nations."

Philadelphia Daily News, October 5, 1944.

75. UNITED STATES OF AMERICA

Executive Office of the President

PRESIDENT'S COMMITTEE ON FAIR EMPLOYMENT PRACTICE

* * * * * *

In the Matter of

PHILADELPHIA RAPID TRANSIT EMPLOYEES UNION

Case No. 55

SUMMARY OF THE EVIDENCE WITH OPINION AND ORDER ON

HEARINGS HELD IN PHILADELPHIA, PENNSYLVANIA, DECEMBER 8, 1943

On November 17, 1943, the Committee, on the basis of an agreed statement
of the facts executed by the Philadelphia Transportation Company, issued its
Proposed Findings of Fact and Directives to said Company and a union of its

employees known as the Philadelphia Rapid Transit Employees Union, were parties
to a collective bargaining contract containing a provision that

> "All existing rules, regulations and customs bearing on the employer-
> employee relationship shall continue in full force and effect until
> changed by agreement between the parties."

The Committee also found that the Company and the Union had interpreted
this provision as prohibiting the employment or promotion of qualified Negroes
in or to all job classifications not presently held by Negro employees of
the Company. The Committee concluded that this contractual provision, when
given the interpretation placed thereon by the parties thereto, violated
Executive Order No. 9346 and it directed the Company to cease and desist from
this discriminatory interpretation, and to consider all applicants for em-
ployment--particularly to position as street car and motor coach operators
and conductors, guards, platform attendants and station cashiers on the
Company's elevated and subway lines--without regard to race, creed, color or
national origin.
Similar findings were made as to the Union and the Committee directed
the Union not to

> "Interpret any section or provision of its contract with the Phila-
> delphia Transportation Company so as to prohibit, limit, or in any
> manner interfere with the employment or upgrading by the Company of
> qualified Negroes in or to"

any job classifications with the Company not presently held by Negroes.

Sufficient factual basis for the Committee's Proposed Findings and
Directives to the Company was contained in the agreed statement executed by
the Company. However, and although representatives of the Committee had held
several conferences with officials of the Union, the Committee was reluctant
to make or to issue final Findings and Directives to the Union before first
giving an opportunity to the Union's membership to consider the question and
to agree as to the relevant facts involved. Accordingly, the Proposed Findings
and Directives to each of the parties provided that the same would become
final on and after November 27, 1943, "unless, prior to that date, either party
shall file with the Chairman at Washington, D.C., a request for a public
hearing."
On November 24, 1943, the Union requested a hearing and by order dated
December 1, 1943, and duly served upon the Union, the Committee directed that
a hearing be held in the City of Philadelphia on December 8, 1943,

> "for the purpose of affording to the respondent Union an opportunity
> to show cause, if any there be, why Executive Order No. 9346 and the
> Directive to said respondent issued pursuant thereto, should not be
> complied with according to its terms."

SUMMARY OF THE EVIDENCE

The "Agreed Statement of Facts" executed by the Company and the Proposed
Findings and Directives issued by the Committee, were introduced in evidence
and are attached hereto. The only testimony presented on behalf of the Union
was a prepared statement read into the record by its Secretary-Treasurer, Mr.
Frank M. Cobourn. This statement, after reciting the issuance of the above
Directive to the Union, asserted the following nine reasons in support of the
Union's opposition to the Directive:

1. The Union does not discriminate against any group.

2. Although the Company is "essential to the war effort," it holds
   no contract with any Government agency, which seems to be necessary
   in order for the Fair Employment Practice Committee to make an order.

3. The Committee and the Company should institute an educational program among the employees first before directing a change in the
   status quo.

4. It is questionable if there is available any idle manpower in the Philadelphia area.

5. Compliance with the Committee's Directives may result in disturbances which will impair the transportation of workers to and from war industries.

6. The service rendered by the Company is adequate.

7. The effect of the Directive is to single out the Company and Union while ignoring other transit systems whose employment practices are no different.

8. Compliance with the Committee's Directive, requiring the Company to reconsider without regard to race or color all applications filed with it by Negroes since June 24, 1941, would disturb seniority and affect the transfer conditions of all employees.

9. The present relationship between the Company and the Union should not be changed without first consulting the Union's 1,000 members in the armed forces.

No factual data or other evidence was presented by the Union in support of any of the above assertions.

After the reading of the Union's statement, the Committee's Chairman informed Mr. Cobourn that his assertion numbered 7 above, "arises from a mis-understanding of the Committee's procedure," and that other cases involving alleged violations of Executive Order No. 9346 by public transportation systems are presently pending before the Committee in the investigatory or negotiation stage. The Chairman stated further that "there was such informal negotiation in this case at one time," and he expressed the view that the Union's "researches" evidently had not been "quite wide enough to find out the places where the Committee has acted."

Regarding the Union's assertion numbered 1 above, Mr. Cobourn admitted on cross-examination that it was the policy of the Union not to permit the Company to replace white employees with Negro employees, nor to replace Negro employees with white employees; that such is the interpretation the Union places upon the "customs" clause in its contract; and that if the Company should employ Negro platform men without first getting the Union's approval, its action would be considered a violation of the contract.

As to the assertion numbered 3 above, the witness stated that education was needed, "for the purpose of breaking down prejudices, if prejudices exist," but that the "Union has not endeavored to carry out any campaign of education on this question." He stated that the matter of employing Negroes as street car and bus operators, etc., had been discussed informally at meetings of the Union Delegates, "but no actual resolution on the floor had been considered." He admitted also that the officers of the Union had been advised of the Committee's proposed action and that the Committee, at their request, had delayed its contemplated action for a period of ten days to allow them "to take the proposition back to the Delegates;" that during this interval of time no meeting of the Delegates had been called or held; and that after the Committee's Proposed Findings and Directives to the Union had been issued, "only these recent communications" were presented to the Delegates. The Delegates then authorized the Executive Board to request a hearing.

Mr. Cobourn was questioned regarding the Union's assertion numbered 4 above and stated: "I haven't heard any representations to the effect that there is available idle manpower in this area." He admitted that his knowledge of the local manpower situation was based on the "several advertisements appearing in the paper, requesting skilled and unskilled labor classifications."

Concerning the disruption of transportation which the Union's assertion numbered 5 above contends "will surely follow any attempt to enforce this Directive at this time, "the Secretary-Treasurer was non-committal," except to observe that "from my observation my contact with the various union members they would not at this time accept such a radical change."

Mr. Cobourn's only explanation of the sixth assertion made in the Union's statement was, that the Company's present advertising for additional employees "might" be due to a desire to have "an extra reservoir there for contingencies." The Union's contention numbered 8 above refers to the Committee's Directive No. 6 to the Company, which requires the Company to,

"Reconsider without regard to race or color all hiring, transferring or upgrading applications filed with the Company by its Negro employees and by Negro applicants since June 24, 1941."

When questioned as to the basis for the Union's statement that this Directive would alter the present procedure by which transfers were made within the Company and would disturb the seniority of present employees, Mr. Cobourn conceded that the "actual wording of the Directive" did not have that effect, but stated that the "implications" to be drawn from the Directive were "that these applications or transfers and hirings were to be considered as being of that date." The Committee's Chairman informed Mr. Cobourn that the date stated in the Directive was intended merely to identify the time from which prior applications to the Company were to be considered, and coincided with the date of the creation of the Committee. The Chairman ruled that the Directive did not, nor was it intended to, affect the seniority of any of the Company's present employees; it "has no relation to any possible seniority of any of the Company's present employees; it "has no relation to any possible seniority rolls of that time."

No further witnesses or evidence was offered by the Union.

* * * * * * * * *

Raleigh Johnson, a witness called by counsel for the Committee, testified that "back as far as 1941" he and other Negro employees of the Company formed a committee and met with the President of the Company and the Chairman of the Company's Committee on Industrial Relations, "to ask that Negroes be employed as bus men, conductors and operators, etc.;" that, at the suggestion of these Company officials, his committee endeavored, without success, to arrange a joint conference on the matter with the Company and the Union; that his committee, eventually did meet with the Union's President, Mr. Frank P. Carney, and one other member of the Union's Executive Board; and that

"Mr. Carney, as we interpreted it, raised the red flag right away. He said he would not consider it; he had not been authorized by the Delegates to consider it, and we got practically nowhere."

Mr. Johnson testified further that, following this conference with the Union's officials, his committee sought the assistance of the National Association for the Advancement of Colored People; and that the Association "got in touch with the Philadelphia Transportation Company also and the PRT Employees Union, but from the information I get, they haven't made much progress."

When questioned by Committee Member Webster whether it was his understanding that the "customs" clause in the Company's contract with the Union, and its reference to past practices, had any relation to races involved, Mr. Johnson stated, "It was never my understanding. We were always led to believe just the opposite." In answer to the question, "Did you know that you and the other Negro members were paying dues into an organization which had written a contract interpreted so as to freeze you in certain positions and prevent you from being employed as a bus driver or street car motorman or conductor in the event the Company desired to so do," the witness replied,

"I did not know that. I thought just the opposite. . . . My interpretation was we knew we would not be able to interrupt the seniority, but I always felt when the time presented itself, we would be able to advance to those positions."

Mr. Roosevelt Neal was called as a witness by counsel for the Committee and testified that he was a Delegate in the Union and was present with Mr. Johnson at the time of the conference with Mr. Carney, the Union's President.

Mr. Neal stated that he recalled the NAACP's letter to the Union requesting
a conference; that the letter was read at the February, 1943, meeting of the
Delegates but no action was taken thereon; that he inquired at the March meeting what answer had been sent and was informed by Mr. Carney that no answer
had been sent. He further testified that at this March meeting a motion was
made and carried "that the letter be ignored;" but "a Delegate got up and
stated, 'Gentlemen, that certainly is an insult to us. If you don't want us
in the Union you shouldn't try to insult us like that;" and that following
this discussion on the floor, the motion was reconsidered and it was voted that
the letter be answered.

No rebuttal testimony was offered by the Union nor did the Union at any
time challenge or object to the above testimony given by witnesses called by
counsel for the Committee.

* * * * * * * * *

The National Association for the Advancement of Colored People filed a
statement at the hearing reviewing its efforts to secure employment by the
Company of Negro platform workers. According to the statement, the Association
wrote the President of the Union on January 18, 1943, requesting "an opportunity
to discuss this matter with you." The Union, by its President, replied on
March 2, 1943, that the Association's communication "was brought before the
Union Delegates and you are hereby advised that the matter of which you write
is not a subject over which the Union has any control. Therefore, no action
was taken." This reply from the Union, according to the statement, was
referred by the Association to the Company and, the statement continues,
"the management stated that the company's contract with the PRT Employees
Union prohibited the extension of Negro employment beyond present customs
'unless the Union should first agree to such extension.'"

A statement urging both the Company and the Union to comply with the
Committee's Directives was filed at the hearing by The Council for Equal Job
Opportunity, an association representing 17 civic, labor, professional, racial
and religious organizations in the City of Philadelphia.

The Catholic Inter-Collegiate Inter-Racial Council of Philadelphia
"comprised of delegates from Catholic High Schools and Colleges and Faculties,"
filed at the hearing a copy of a resolution sent by the Council to the Company,
the Union and to the Mayor of Philadelphia. The resolution urged the Company
and the Union "to reconsider their stand and to follow the example of other
leading cities in the country and open these avenues of employment to qualified
Negro men."

The National Urban League also filed a statement detailing the effect of
public opinion, sympathetic employer cooperation and enlightened Union leadership in securing the employment of Negroes in platform positions with the New
York City, Detroit and Chicago transportation systems.

Finally, there was included in the record of the evidence, a summary
prepared by the Committee's research staff entitled, "Employment of Negroes
in Local Transit Industry." This summary indicated that a total of 2,121
Negroes are employed as motormen, conductors and bus drivers in the cities of
San Francisco, California; Detroit, Michigan; Flushing, Buffalo, and New York
City, New York; Winston-Salem, North Carolina; Cleveland, Ohio; and Tulsa,
Oklahoma.

* * * * * * * * *

O P I N I O N

The Committee has given careful consideration to each of the contentions
asserted by the Union in opposition to the Committee's Directive, and has
reached the conclusion that the Union has shown no cause why Executive Order
No. 9346 and the Committee's Directive to the Union, issued pursuant thereto,
should not be complied with according to their terms.

The Union's first, second and eight contentions are the only ones which
go to the merits of the issue. These will be discussed later.

The remaining contentions of the Union are addressed to a presumed discretion in this Committee to determine whether the President's Order shall or
shall not be obeyed. In advancing such contentions, the Union overlooks the
basic fact that this Committee is charged by the President, as Commander-in-

Chief, with the obligation to "obtain elimination of such discrimination" as
it finds to be violative of the national policy set forth in the Order. In
any case in which the Committee finds discrimination prohibited by the Order,
its obligation to take appropriate steps to eliminate this discrimination is
fixed; and the Committee has no discretion to act or to refrain from acting
according to the wishes of the party or party charged. Moreover, even if the
substantive sufficiency of these contentions be assumed, the Committee is of
the opinion that none of them is supported by any evidence presented at the
hearing and each is refuted by the admissions of the Union's Secretary-Treasurer, or by the several statements presented at the hearing.
     Special mention, however, should be made of the Union's ninth contention,
that its "over 1,000 members" now in the armed forces should be consulted before the Committee requires it to cease its discriminatory practices and
comply with the President's Order. In the opinion of the Committee this contention can only be characterized as a device seemingly conceived by the Union's
Executive Board as a means to forestall compliance. Obviously, however, even
if it were possible to poll the Union's members who are now serving in the
armed forces, their judgment could not be taken to override the President's
Order. The alleviation of the present critical manpower situation, the assurance
of an adequate volume of supplies to our Army and Navy, and the successful
prosecution of the war, cannot be held in abeyance pending the ascertainment
of the racial views of any special group. The Committee will presume that the
members of our armed forces who daily are risking or preparing to risk their
lives in the cause of world democracy, as well as those busily engaged in making America the "Arsenal of Democracy," believe in democracy at home for all
citizens irrespective of race, creed, color or national origin.
     There remains to be considered the three contentions of the Union, the
first, second and eighth, which are addressed to the merits of the issue.
The Union's first contention--that it has not discriminated--must fail because
by the testimony of its own witness it admits that its policy is to exclude
Negroes from jobs held by its white members and to exclude white employees
from jobs held by Negroes. Such a policy constitutes racial discrimination
against both white and colored employees and applicants for employment, and
violates the Executive Order. Admittedly, too, the Union's interpretation of
the "customs" clause in its contract with the Company tends to perpetuate
this discriminatory policy.
     The Union's second contention is regarded by the Committee as a challenge
to its jurisdiction. Executive Order No. 9346, issued by the President on
May 27, 1943, states:
     NOW, THEREFORE, By virtue of the authority vested in me by the Constitu-
     tion and statutes, and as President of the United States and Commander-
     in-Chief of the Army and Navy, I do hereby reaffirm the policy of the
     United States that there shall be no discrimination in the employment
     of any person in war industries or in Government by reason of race, creed,
     color, or national origin, and I do hereby declare that it is the duty of
     all employers, . . . and all labor organizations, in furtherance of this
     policy and of this Order, to eliminate discrimination in regard to hire,
     tenure, terms or conditions of employment, or union membership because
     of race, creed, color, or national origin."
     That Order also created the present Committee and empowered it to "re-
ceive and investigate complaints of discrimination, . . . conduct hearings,
make findings of fact and take appropriate steps to obtain elimination of
such discrimination."
     In the absence of legislative enactments to the contrary, the power of
the President to declare what the public policy of the United States shall be
and how that policy shall be effectuated, cannot be seriously doubted. It
is a power inherent in his position as the Nation's Chief Executive and in war
time it is enhanced by his additional duties as Commander-in-Chief.
     The provisions of the above Order, however, do not "declare" a policy;
they simply "reaffirm" what is and has been our national policy for more than
three-quarters of a century.
     On numerous occasions--especially in recent years--the Congress has
inserted provisions in its legislative enactments forbidding discrimination
based on race, color, or creed. These provisions were designed to give practical effect to the policy of the National Government, implicit in the

Constitution itself, that no citizen should be denied, solely because of his race, creed, or color, that equality of employment opportunity necessary to enable him to work at his highest skill, to earn a livelihood, and to contribute to the defense of his country. This principle, embedded in the framework of our democratic form of government, is not simply a pius platitude to be acknowledged and ignored; it is the cornerstone of our American way of life, amply buttressed by the power of our Government and the moral opinion of all of its citizens.

The President's Order is thus merely declaratory of fundamental Federal policy; and the duties it declares are duties imposed not by the Order itself but by the full force of the national public opinion which it affirms.

Nor can the President's power to create this Committee and charge it with the duty of effectuating this national policy on his behalf, be doubted. The Constitution provides that the President shall "take care that the laws be faithfully executed;" the public policy of the United States is as much a "law" of the United States as any statutory enactment.

The jurisdiction of the Committee in this particular case is likewise clear. The Company has admitted in its "Agreed Statement of the Facts" that it is supplying essential transportation services to the millions of war workers employed in the Philadelphia area; and it concedes that its operations are "within the jurisdiction conferred upon the President's Committee." Moreover, the Union's statement also concedes that the Company's activities are "essential to the war effort." The contention of the Union, however, assumes that the scope of the Committee's powers under Executive Order 9346 is limited to companies holding contracts with Government agencies. This assumption finds no warrant in the Order itself, nor in the purpose stated in the Order. The power of this Committee, according to the Order, extends to all "war industries." There are numerous industries whose successful functioning and the expeditious satisfaction of whose manpower needs directly and intimately affect the successful prosecution of the war, notwithstanding they have no formal contractual arrangements with any Government agency. The Committee has consistently asserted its jurisdiction in such instances with its opinion that its power "to investigate" and to "take appropriate steps to obtain elimination of such discrimination" as violates the Order, extends to all industries classified by the War Manpower Commission as "essential" to the effective prosecution of the war. A fortiori, its power extends to all employees' unions in those industries.

Concerning the Union's eighth contention, the Committee is of the opinion that nothing in its Directive to the Company--to reconsider without regard to race or color all employment and transfer applications filed by Negroes since June 25, 1941--interferes with the seniority or transfer rights of the Company's employees. Accordingly, the Committee approves the ruling made at the hearing by its Chairman on this contention.

* * * * * * * * *

ORDER

By virtue of the authority vested in it by Executive Order No. 9346, the Committee ORDERS:

That the Findings made its Proposed Findings and Directives, attached hereto and heretofore issued to the Philadelphia Transportation Company, and the Philadelphia Rapid Transit Employees Union be, and they are hereby affirmed.

The Committee DIRECTS:

That the Directive attached hereto, and heretofore issued to the Philadelphia Rapid Transit Employees Union on November 17, 1943, be, and the same is, hereby made effective this day.

The Committee further DIRECTS:

That the Philadelphia Transportation Company, as to whom the Directives of this Committee became final on November 27, 1943, comply with the

aforementioned Directives immediately; and that, should the Company's efforts
in this respect meet with any opposition by or on behalf of the Union, or by
or on behalf of any other person, the Company shall report to this Committee
the nature of that opposition together with the names and addresses of the
person or persons responsible' therefore.

BEFORE THE

PRESIDENT'S COMMITTEE ON FAIR EMPLOYMENT PRACTICE

SUMMARY OF THE EVIDENCE, WITH FINDINGS AND DIRECTIVES

in the matter of

PHILADELPHIA TRANSPORTATION COMPANY

and

PHILADELPHIA RAPID TRANSIT EMPLOYEES' UNION

On Friday, November 5, 1943, in the forenoon, the Chairman pursuant to
prior appointment, met at Philadelphia, Pa., with officials of the Philadelphia
Transportation Company and counsel for the Company. As a result of this conference, the Company agreed that the attached "Statement of Facts" embodies a
correct statement of the relevant facts and the position of the Company with
reference to those facts.

In the afternoon of the same day the Chairman met with the President,
Secretary-Treasurer, and counsel for the Philadelphia Rapid Transit Employees'
Union. The above mentioned "Statement of Facts" was discussed with these
officials and their attention likewise was called to the attached "Supplemental
Statement of Facts." The Union's officials and their counsel voiced no disapproval as to the correctness of either the attached "Statement of Facts" or
"Supplemental Statement of Facts." They indicated, however, that they could
not speak for their Union until they had had an opportunity to present the
matter to the Union's delegates. It was agreed that an effort would be made
to convene the Union's delegates for this purpose on or before November 12,
1943.

On the basis of the agreed attached "Statement of Facts" and in the
absence of any objection by the Union to the attached "Supplemental Statement
of Facts," the Committee, by virtue of the authority conferred upon it by
Executive Order 9346 to "make findings of fact and take appropriate steps to
obtain elimination . . . discrimination" does hereby issue to the Company
and to the Union the following proposed findings and directives which shall
become final on November 27, 1943, unless, prior to that date, either the
Company or the Union shall file with the Chairman at Washington, D.C. a request
for a public hearing.

FINDINGS OF FACT

1. The Committee finds the facts as set forth in the attached "Statement of Facts" and "Supplemental Statement of Facts."

2. The Committee finds that the Philadelphia Transportation Company
has refused and still refuses, because of their race or color, to
to employ Negro applicants in, and to upgrade its Negro employees
to positions as street car and motor coach operators and conductors,
motormen, guards, platform attendants, and station cashiers on its
elevated and subway lines; and in or to all job classifications not
presently held by Negro employees of the Company.

3. The Committee finds further that the refusal of the Company to
employ or upgrade Negroes, as set forth in Finding No. 2, above,
violates Executive Order 9346.

4. The Committee finds that the Company and the Philadelphia Rapid
   Transit Employees' Union are parties to a contract which provides,
   in part, "all existing . . . customs bearing on the employer-employee
   relationship shall continue in full force and effect until changed
   by agreement between the parties."

5. The Committee finds that the Company and the Union have interpreted
   the above contractual provision so as to prohibit the employment or
   promotion by the Company of qualified Negroes in or to all job
   classifications not presently held by Negro employees of the Company.

6. The Committee finds further that the above-quoted contractual provision when given the interpretation set forth in Finding No. 4,
   above, constitutes discrimination because of their race or color,
   against Negro employees of the Company and Negro applicants for
   employment with the Company, and violates Executive Order 9346.

DIRECTIVES TO THE COMPANY

Upon the basis of the above findings of fact, the Committee directs that
the Philadelphia Transportation Company, in the interest of the war effort,
shall

1. Cease and desist from all discriminatory practices affecting the
   employment or upgrading of Negroes.

2. Cease and desist from any interpretation of its contract with the
   Philadelphia Rapid Transit Employees' Union which has the effect
   of prohibiting the employment or the upgrading by the Company of
   qualified Negroes to positions as street car and motor coach
   operators and conductors, motormen, guards, platform attendants,
   and station cashiers on the company's elevated and subway lines;
   or to any other job classifications not presently held by Negroes.

3. Give written notice to the Philadelphia Rapid Transit Employees'
   Union, and to all other labor organizations with which the Company
   contracts, that it will comply fully with its obligations under
   Executive Order 9346 and will not discriminate against workers or
   employees, because of race, creed, color, or national origin, in
   recruiting, training, upgrading, or in any other terms or conditions of employment.

4. Issue written notice to all employment agencies whether public or
   private, including the United States Employment Service, and any
   training institution or agency operated by the Company or through
   which the Company recruits or trains workers, that the Company
   will accept workers for any and all job classifications without
   regard to their race, creed, color, or national origin.

5. Issue written instructions to all of its officers, agents, or
   employees having authority to hire or upgrade workers, directing
   them to recruit, hire, train and upgrade workers or employees
   without regard to race, creed, color, or national origin.

6. Issue written instructions to the Personnel Department of the
   Company to:

   (a) Post notices in conspicuous places in the Company's offices,
   stations, garages, shops, and other portions of its premises fre-
   quented by its employees, listing all upgrading opportunities and
   stating that applications will be received from employees, examinations given, and upgrading and training activities carried on,
   without regard to the applicant's race, creed, color, or national
   origin.

   (b) Reconsider without regard to race or color, all hiring,

transfer or upgrading applications filed with the Company by its
Negro employees and by Negro applicants since June 25, 1941.

7. Submit to the Committee's Regional Director at Philadelphia, Pa.,
   a copy of each of the above instructions and notices.

8. Report in writing to the Committee's Regional Director at Philadelphia,
   Pa., within thirty days from the receipt of these directives, the
   steps taken to comply therewith.

9. File with the Committee's Regional Director at Philadelphia, Pa.,
   written monthly reports beginning January 1, 1944, listing the
   color, job classification, and wage rate of each person hired
   during the preceding thirty-day period and the total number of white
   and non-white workers employed in each job category or classification as of the date of the report.

The Company may, at any time after filing the third of such monthly
reports request a relaxation of this directive.

* * * * * * * * *

DIRECTIVE TO THE UNION

1. The Committee directs that the Philadelphia Rapid Transit Employees'
   Union, in the interest of the war effort, shall not interpret any
   section or provision of its contract with the Philadelphia Transportation Company so as to prohibit, limit, or in any manner interfere with, the employment or upgrading by the Company of qualified
   Negroes in or to positions as street car and motor coach operators
   and conductors; motormen, guards, platform attendants, and station
   cashiers on the Company's elevated and subway lines; or in or to any
   job classifications with the Company not presently held by Negroes.

UNITED STATES OF AMERICA

EXECUTIVE OFFICE OF THE PRESIDENT

PRESIDENT'S COMMITTEE ON FAIR EMPLOYMENT PRACTICE

In the Matter of

The Philadelphia Transportation Company

STATEMENT OF FACTS

A. The Company

Philadelphia Transportation Company was formed on January 1, 1940 by
merger of all street railway, bus, trackless trolley and traction companies
theretofore forming part of the leased system of the predecessor operating
company, Philadelphia Rapid Transit Company. The Company is thus the single
owning and operating company of the entire street railway, trackless trolley
and bus system serving Philadelphia with minor extensions into adjacent counties.
This system includes the Market Street Subway-Elevated which the Company
operates under lease from its wholly owned subsidiary. The City-owned Frankford Elevated and Broad Street Subway system and also the Delaware River
Bridge Line high speed line are operated by the Company under leases from the
City and the Delaware River Joint Commission, respectively. Under an agreement with the City made in 1907 and amended in 1939, the City is entitled to
five members on the Company's Board of Directors. The Mayor of the City is
one of these five directors and the City Council elects the remaining four.

Their status on the Board is in all respects the same as that of directors
elected by the Company's stockholders.
      The Company employs approximately 10,900 persons, operates a fleet of
3,264 cars and buses running 325,000 miles daily, and transport daily an average
of 3,300,000 passengers. Many war industries and Government war agencies are
located in Philadelphia and the surrounding area served by the Company. These
industries and agencies employ employees whose only practical means of transportation to and from their places of employment is the system of street,
elevated, and subway lines operated exclusively by the Company. For this
reason the War Manpower Commission has designated the Company "an essential
organization engaged in supplying essential transportation services;" and the
Company is, therefore, within the jurisdiction conferred upon the President's
Committee on Fair Employment Practice by Executive Orders 8802 and 9346.

B. The Complaints

      The Committee has received complaints from several sources alleging that
the Company has refused to upgrade or employ qualified Negroes for operating
(e.g. motor coach operators, street car conductors and motormen, elevated
and subway train operators, guards, starters and platform men) and clerical
positions (e.g. clerks, stenographers, checkers, station cashiers), because
of their race and color. The Committee also has been notified by the United
States Employment Service that the Company has specifically requested that only
white persons be referred to the Company for positions as motormen.

C. The Union

      Most of the employees of the Company are members of the Philadelphia
Rapid Transit Employees' Union, an unaffiliated local employees organization
whose name was taken from the Philadelphia Rapid Transit Company, the corporate
predecessor of the present Company. This Union has been recognized by the
Company as the bargaining agent for all employees and Negroes as well as white
employees are admitted to membership. Eight (8) Negroes are included in the
128 "delegates" who constitute the policy-making body of the Union, and they
represent the white as well as the Negro workers in their shop or "location."
The Executive Committee of the Union is composed of the President, three Vice-
Presidents and the Secretary-Treasurer. The President is the business agent
for the Union.

D. Status of Negro Employees

      Investigation made by the Committee indicates the following facts relative
to the Company's manpower needs and the status of its Negro employees:

      In December, 1942, there were approximately 10,700 employees of the
Company employed in operating its equipment and maintaining its vehicles, tracks
and buildings, and in its offices. About fifteen per cent of the employees
engaged in operating cars and buses had joined the Company since January 1,
1942, and due to the heavy traffic conditions during the summer of 1942, 4,500
employees passed up their usual summer vacations. In recent months the Company
has employed about 220 women as operators of street cars and as starters and
platform attendants on its elevated and subway lines and classes now are being
conducted by the Company for the training of additional women to occupy such
positions.
      The Company now has in its employ 537 Negroes in the following classifi-
cations:

Foreman	10
Welder	45
Paver	1
Grinder	31
Gas Cutter	10
Switch Cleaner	25
Chauffeur	10
Center Setter	2

Trackman	40
Laborer	72
Watchman	4
Rammer	1
Machinist	1
Porter	127
Cement Finisher	1
Material Handler	18
Mat. Handler & Gas Cutter	2
Mat. Handler Tie Mach. Oper.	2
Leaderman	1
Special Work Fitter	1
Punchman & Sawyer	1
Truck Driver & Crane Operator	1
Truck Driver	1
Poleman	10
Crane Operator	2
Sand Dryer Operator	1
Grinder Trackwalker Trackman	20
Trackwalker	14
Grinder Trackwalker Laborer	72
Laborer 1st class	3
Track Leaderman	5
Investigator (Claims Dept.)	1
Conduit Laborer	2
Total	537

Practically all of the foregoing employees who are in a classification other than laborer (or in some cases, other than porter), have been upgraded by the Company. Seven of the foremen and the leadermen have white employees under them. No Negroes ever have been employed as trainmen, busmen, starters, platform attendants, car cleaners or bus cleaners, either by the Company or any of its predecessors. The only Negroes employed as bus cleaners were a few employees by an affiliated company, the interest in which owned by the Company's predecessor and sixteen of them are now porters. Many of the white employees who now hold operating jobs with the Company were upgraded to their jobs from initial employment as bus and car cleaners. Some of the Negro porters have had previous experience as truck drivers and garage workers and several had been employed as railroad brakeman, firemen, or "make-up" men before coming to the Company. The periods of employment of the porters with the Company and its predecessor range up to twenty-three years, with one up to thirty-three years.

E. The Union Contract

The first contract between the Company and the Union was made October 5, 1937 and, except for amendments not material to this case, has remained in effect ever since.

Records of the Committee on Fair Employment Practice, RG 228, Box 343, National Archives.

76. CAROLYN DAVENPORT MOORE (NAACP) TO U.S.
     DEPARTMENT OF JUSTICE, MARCH 10, 1944

Gentlemen:

Enclosed is a photostatic copy of a letter received in our office on January 11, 1944 which is self-explanatory.
The envelope was postmarked from Los Angeles, California, January 7, 1944.

Because of the threats made by officials of the PRT Employees Union, the present bargaining representative of employees of the Philadelphia Transportation Company, we urge that a thorough investigation be made, of officials and PTC Employees who participated in the FEPC Hearing held by the Special Committee Investigating Executive Agencies in Washington on January 11, 1944.

The Congressional Committee is headed by Howard W. Smith of Virginia.

At the Washington hearing, definite threats were made by several PTC employees who testified.

America cannot tolerate this fascist activity and remain a democracy.

Very truly yours,

Carolyn Davenport Moore
Executive Secretary

Los Angeles, California
January 6, 1944

The Nat'l Association for the
Advancement of Colored People

Gentlemen:

Being a father of 2 boys who are now somewhere in the South Pacific and who had hopes of going to work for the P.T.C. as bus drivers, but enlisted in the Navy instead, I was very well pleased to read in todays paper where the P.T.C. Union defied the F.E.P.C. order to hire Negroes.

I sure do think the Negroes of the U.S.A. have a hell of a nerve to try and pull something like this over on the white boys who are doing most of the real fighting in the war.

If you colored people would try as hard to get on the fighting front as you are trying to get the white mens jobs you would be doing some good for yourself. For the past 8 years we have been hearing so much of the great Negro fighters, Joe Louis, Henry Armstrong, Bob Montgomery, Sugar Robinson, Beau Jack, Jackie Wilson, John H. Lewis, Chalky Wright, Jim Bivins, Slugger White, and out here on the West coast we have Turkey Thompson, Willie Joyce, Cecil Hudson, John Thomas, Jack Chase, and several others throughout the country. Out of the whole lot we have Louis, Robinson and Wilson in the Army. And where are they at, over in this country where most of the other Negroes who are in the armed forces are at, safe from gun fire. I was looking at Life Magazine a few months ago and it showed pictures of what a "hard time" Louis, Robinson and Wilson were having in the Army. One picture showed them sitting at a table with a table cloth on it eating with white people, another showed them with their spic and span uniform neatly pressed shaking hands with wounded white soldiers. I noted the look of disgust on two white soldiers to his left. Then it showed the great champion go thru an exhibition bout with another Negro. They should be ashamed of themselves. Why the hell don't a few of these great Negroes fighters get over seas and do some real fighting.[129]

In the last 2 years you colored people are sure showing your true colors, your yellow. What happened out in Detroit last June. There is a city where they put on 1500 Negroes as motormen, conductors, and bus drivers on the D.S.R. and then riots, that is what will happen if the P.T.C. hires Negroes.

Thank God the P.T.C. does not have to depend on the nigger vote, like the politicians are doing in Phila. When you niggers try to force your way into private industry, you are asking for trouble, and you will sure as hell get it.

Hats off to the P.T.C. union, they showed you niggers how the rank and file white people feel toward you.

My sons told me if they should come home and find niggers on the P.T.C. they might mistake them for Japs and shoot them between the eyes.

If I were you niggers, I would be seen and not heard so much. Your
making too much noise lately.

Yours,

John A. Davis

Records of the Committee on Fair Employment Practice, Case 55, RG 228, Box
343, National Archives.

77. RENA CORMAN (PHILADELPHIA) TO FRANKLIN
D. ROOSEVELT, DECEMBER 16, 1943

Dear Mr. Roosevelt:

PM thinks that mail from the people on the FEPC trouble will make it
easier for you to know what action to take at this time.

I am greatly troubled by the attitude of a growing number of people who
refuse to have "industrial democracy" while at the same time our country is
fighting for a theoretical democracy all over the world. Right here in Philadelphia the Phila. Transportation Co.'s fight against hiring Negroes has produced a deplorable situation, and there has been no solution of this problem
yet.

I want you to know that I am in complete agreement with the FEPC policy,
and absolute Negro equality in all fields, for that matter, and am more than
willing to work toward that end. But I don't know what I can do. I talk to
people . . . most of whom just aren't interested, and I am a member of the
NAACP, but that organization seems to be fighting a losing battle against the
lack of interest of the majority and the active Hitlerian work of the powerful
minority.

But you have the power to enforce democratic procedure, haven't you?
Won't you, then, fight for democracy on this count, too? And if there's
anything an ordinary civilian like me can do, I will do it.

Records of the Committee on Fair Employment Practice, Case 55, RG 228, Box
343, National Archives.

THE CIO AND THE BLACK WORKER

78. THE RED CAPS' STRUGGLE FOR A LIVELIHOOD

By Ernest Calloway [130]

Three years have passed since a small group of red caps, station porters
and ushers assembled in Chicago to form the International Brotherhood of Red
Caps. Several months ago, nearly 100 delegates representing 60 local unions
of the Brotherhood met in convention in New York City to review its progress
and to plan the future course of the organization. To meet the growing demand
of an extension of jurisdiction to service employees in allied fields of
passenger transportation, the name of the organization was changed to the
United Transport Service Employees of America.

Today, established firmly upon a community of interests and ideals, the
United Transport Service Employees Union has gone far in uniting Negro, white
and Japanese red caps in its day-to-day struggle for improved working conditions, job security and greater democracy in employer-employee relations.
Today the novelty of a red cap belonging to a union of his own choosing has
worn off, and the union has settled down to the routine tasks of building an
effective economic weapon in behalf of the American red cap. After three
years of struggle, the Union maintains a real practical interest in:

   (a) The security and well-being of the red cap through contractual
relations with the industry and the maintenance of such safety-valves
as adequate social, labor and regulatory legislation in the industry.
   (b) The general public policy of the transportation industry, which,
in the final analysis, has a tremendous effect upon this security and
well-being.
   (c) The development of a well-informed and understanding membership,
able to cope fully with any existing or future problems arising out of
the collective need.

The railroad industry, today, presents itself as a great battleground for
Negro employment opportunities. Present Negro employment figures represent a
drastic and continuous decline in this basic industry. Once the aristocrat
of Negro labor, the railroad worker is being hurriedly shoved out of the
industry by various and sundry forces. Chief among these are: (1) *consolidation and merging of railroads*, (2) *institution of time-saving machinery*, (3)
lack of organization among the bulk of Negro railroad workers, (4) *economic
consequences of racial exclusion as practiced by the dominant standard brotherhoods*.

Not only is this true among Negroes, but many of these factors are responsible for the *general* employment decline in the railroad industry. Of
2,000,000 workers in 1920, less than a million are employed today. The 1930
census figures reveal that approximately 143,000 Negroes were employed. Today
these figures have dropped considerably. Many estimate that they are as low
as 75,000.

As a result, the Negro railroad worker is faced with a double problem;
preserving his job on the one hand, and striving for greater security on the
other. How this problem has been met by the Negro railroad worker is of
tremendous importance. It in part accounts for the general lethargy among the
bulk of these workers. Aside from the heroic and far-sighted struggle of the
sleeping car porters and dining car employees of the American Federation of
Labor, a growing crop of Negro railroad organizations has appeared upon the
scene to add to the confusion and demoralization.

Blinded by the general craft dualism and racial discrimination rampant
throughout the entire railroad labor movement, the general problems have been
shaded from their view. Engaging in the many negative aspects of trade unionism,
they have been hell-bent on building a movement based primarily on extreme self-
protective racial dualism. Impotent in exerting any pressure upon the industry,
they exist more as fraternal orders than trade unions.

The struggle of the red cap for greater security and improved working
standards, to be clearly understood, must be viewed upon this general background and his unusual past relationship to the railroad industry.

Prior to September, 1938, the American red cap had been forced to accept
an inferior employee status compared to that of other workers in the industry.
Disowned as a bonafide employee, the red cap was relegated to a "privileged
trespasser" and "independent concessionnaire" status. Meaning, among other
things, that his sole income depended upon gratuities and tips. Having become
a profitable institution in railway passenger service, he was excluded from all
social and labor legislation designed to improve the living and working
standards of railroad workers.

Under normal conditions, the red cap found it very difficult to maintain
any semblance of the highly publicized "American standard of living." He had
discovered through long experience that tips and gratuities were insufficient
to provide for the needs of a home. He had learned that a family did not live
by the day or week, but by the year. Some days were good; too many days were
bad, and so the real story was told by the yearly average. Because of the fact
that tip income varied sharply each week, a family budget had always been an
unknown quantity with the red cap. These sharp variations in tip income and

its effect upon living standards created the primary impulse for organization, the need for a basic wage to supplement tip income.

Briefly, this was his relationship to the industry when on a cold, bleak day in January, 1938, a group of red caps assembled in Chicago from various sections of the country to give some serious consideration to their problems as workers and citizens. It was at this memorable gathering that the challenging machinery was set into motion which was destined to throw great consternation and additional headaches into the front office of one of America's most streamlined, efficient and powerful trade groups, the Association of American Railroads. It was out of this machinery that the red cap emerged as a consistent and militant trade unionist.

The challenge of the red caps took the immediate and concrete form of a petition to the Interstate Commerce Commission. Citing several Class I railroads, the petition requested the Commission to determine the status of red caps within the meaning of the term "employee" as used in the Railway Labor Act.

The ICC answered this request by ordering all Class I railroads and Class A electric railroads to report on the various duties of red caps employed at their respective stations. Questionnaires were circulated which dealt with the nature of the work, wages received, hours of work, and methods of supervision. The findings of this investigation were reported by the selected examiners to the Commission. Substantiating the charges of the Union, the examiners recommended that the red caps be included within the term "employee" as used in the Railway Labor Act.

On July 14, 1938, attorneys for the United Transport Service Employees Union and the Association of American Railroads gathered in Washington for a public hearing on the whole question before the Commission, the Union in support of the examiners' recommendation and the Association in opposition. Gathering nationwide attention, the case brought representatives from many organizations to appear in behalf of the red caps.

On September 29, 1938, the Interstate Commerce Commission made the following ruling on the case:

IT IS ORDERED, that the work defined as that of an employee or subordinate official in orders of this Commission now in effect be, and it is hereby amended and interpreted so as to include, the work of persons designated by such terms as "red caps," station attendants, station porters, parcel porters, ushers, chief ushers and captains . . . whether such persons received a stated compensation or are entirely dependent upon tips, and bring the persons performing such work within the term "employee" as used in the fifth paragraph . . . of the Railway Labor Act, as amended.

This ruling of the Commission, translated into terms of job protection, meant that the red cap in his new status as an employee had recourse to the provisions of the Railway Labor Act, similar to that of other employees in the industry. Furthermore, it meant that the new organization of red caps had gained a recognized legal status and was ready to take its place as an equal craft or class representative with other labor organizations operating within the railway industry. To do this involved certification from the National Mediation Board as the collective bargaining agency for the red caps employed by the various system and terminal companies. A series of elections among the red cap employees was held for this purpose.

In connection with this, the United Transport Service Employees Union, to date, has invoked the services of the National Mediation Board twenty-one times since the granting of employee status by the Interstate Commerce Commission. These cases and others where the railroads agreed to recognize the Union without the invocation of the Board's services, involved over 2,500 red caps throughout the country, or approximately 65% of the total number of railroad red caps. Of the 2,500 red caps involved, nearly 2,200, or 90%, voted for the United Transport Service Employees Union to represent them. One hundred and sixty three, or 4%, voted for other organizations. Two hundred and one, or 6%, did not vote or their ballots were void.

Following the certification from the National Mediation Board, the Union, to date, has successfully concluded 15 signed agreements, covering nearly 50,000 miles of Class I railroads. These agreements established for the first time, seniority rights, maximum hours of service, equitable distribution of work, and recently, a basic wage. With effective grievance machinery in operation, fifteen railroad companies are covered by contracts with the Union.

HOW RED CAPS VOTED IN THE NATIONAL MEDIATION BOARD'S ELECTIONS

Railroad or Terminal Company	Total No.	No. Voting for UTSEA	Other Organ.	Not Vot.
Chicago, Western Indiana Railroad	59	54	--	5
Cincinnati Union Terminal Co.	95	77	--	18
Delaware and Lackawanna Railroad	32	5	24	3
Missouri Pacific Railroad	29	7	10	12
Indianapolis Terminal Co.	33	20	13	--
Northern Pacific Co.	34	30	--	4
Pennsylvania Railroad	717	564	60	93
New York Central Railroad	651	616	3	32
Cleveland Terminal	66	56	--	10
*Chicago, North Western Railroad	81	81	--	--
Illinois Central	151	104	44	3
Memphis Union Depot Co.	23	22	--	1
Texas and New Orleans Railroad	37	16	--	11
Houston Belt and Terminal Co.	13	12	--	1
Union Pacific Terminal Co. (Seattle)	10	10	--	--
Great Northern Terminal Co. (Seattle)	10	10	--	--
Columbus Union Depot Co.	31	28	2	1
*New York, New Haven & Hartford	80	80	--	--
*Boston and Albany Railroad	26	26	--	--
*Boston and Maine Railroad	27	27	--	--
*Boston Terminal Company	51	51	--	--
Florida East Coast Railroad	58	52	1	5
Penn-Reading Seashore Railroad	23	21	--	2
*Washington Terminal Co.	165	165	--	--
Chicago, Milwaukee & St. Paul Railroad	18	12	6	--
TOTALS	2,543	2,179	163	201

* Companies agreed to recognize Union without invoking the services of
the National Mediation Board.

Without these agreements already signed, and being negotiated, the United
Transport Service Employees Union has jumped its first hurdle in the long-
drawn-out process of building a functioning organization of workers. The full
implications of the Union's victory against the Association of American Railroads before the Interstate Commerce Commission have not yet been recorded.
The far-reaching significance of this struggle can only be revealed by the
passage of time.
     Yet, despite the comparative success of this elementary struggle, a far
greater task lies ahead of the Union in the policing of agreements and the
training of members for effective service and leadership in the organization.
     A comprehensive yet practical knowledge of the industry in which the
red cap works will be a great asset in the handling of these common problems
and the development of an intelligent and well-informed membership. The future
success or failure of the Union depends largely upon the ability of rank and
file members and officers to recognize quickly and understand clearly the
collective problems they face; and above all, to seek their solution on the
basis of this recognition and understanding.

Opportunity, 18 (June, 1940): 174-76.

79.
REDCAPS ACCEPT CIO BID TO AFFILIATE AS NEW INTERNATIONAL

CINCINNATI, O., May 30--Setting its goal for 25,000 members by 1944, the Third Biennial Convention of the United Transport Service Employees of America came to a dramatic close here as the assembled delegates of red caps, dining car employees and train porters voted unanimously to accept the invitation of the CIO to affiliate as an international union.

Realizing its great responsibility to the welfare of its growing membership, the convention adopted plans to institute an insurance department within the organization and a program of liberalization of the Railway Retirement Act which would destroy existing barriers against red caps and station porters relative to their eligibility for full retirement benefits.

President Willard S. Townsend and Secretary-Treasurer John L. Yancey were unanimously re-elected to their respective offices. New vice-presidents elected were John Hoskins of Oakland, California, and J. P. Covington, of Washington, D.C., representing the Dining Car Employees Division. Cleveland, Ohio was selected as the next convention site.

Hit Pegler

The convention went on record condemning the attack of Westbrook Pegler against the Negro press and the trade union movement and voted the institution of a boycott against all Scripps-Howard newspapers and others using Pegler's column. It also called for the passage of stringent federal legislation embodying the principles of the President's Executive Order which created the Fair Employment Practices Committee.

It voted to support the nation's war effort and set as its goal for 1942 the purchase of $250,000 worth of war bonds by the members, and commended the Negro and the liberal press for fair handling of labor news stories.

UTSEA President Willard S. Townsend set the keynote to the mass meeting when he declared that "We of the UTSEA are here to lend every effort towards winning the war. But in this fight, surely one or two things must be sacrificed by those in the control of America. Either they must give up their freedom or they must sacrifice their prejudice, and if they think more of their prejudice than freedom, then surely we will lose our freedom."

CIO News, June 1, 1942.

80.
DETROIT NAACP CALLS ON
NEGROES NOT TO ACT AS
STRIKEBREAKERS FOR FORD

New York--In a long distance telephone call to the national office of the NAACP here April 4, Dr. James J. McClendon, president of the Detroit branch of the association, stated that the youth council and the senior branch had hired a sound truck to urge Negroes in Detroit not to be strikebreakers in the strike at the Ford plant.[131]

The sound truck circulated all through the area adjacent to the Ford plant, Dr. McClendon said, and through the Negro residential and business districts.

"Do not fall for that Homer Martin-AFL stuff," the speakers yelled. They were referring to Martin's proposal, backed by the AFL., that the Ford plant be opened by force, if necessary.

The Ford company, it was reported, is sending letters and telegrams to Negro workers asking them to return to work at once. Ford money arranged a mass meeting of Negroes at which they were told to stay out of the union and stick with the company.

NAACP ASKS FORD STRIKE
ACTION BY DEFENSE BOARD
TO AVERT RACIAL CLASH

New York--Acting on reports from Detroit that an interracial clash might break there after the city election Monday, April 7, the National Association for the Advancement of Colored People on April 4, requested immediate certification of the Ford strike by Secretary of Labor Perkins to the national mediation board.

Walter White, NAACP secretary, wired both Miss Perkins and President Roosevelt urging this step. Fears in Detroit were aroused by the resentment of the striking union against Negro workers who have not joined the walk-out.

Text of the NAACP telegram to President Roosevelt:

"Reports from Detroit state that after city election on Monday, Governor Van Wagoner and others will attempt back to work movement in Ford strike. We are informed by reliable newspaper men and other competent observers that disastrous race riot may take place. Apparently all efforts mediation locally have failed. To avert disastrous riot we are urging Secretary of Labor Perkins to certify immediately to National Mediation Board Ford strike. May we urge you to request such certification by Miss Perkins." [132]

NAACP PROTESTS BIASED
NEWS OF FORD STRIKE

New York--A protest against "news which gives the impression that Negro Ford workers form the majority of non-strikers" was lodged with the Associated Press, the United Press and the International News Service April 4 by the National Association for the Advancement of Colored People.

The NAACP telegram declared this type of news service "is a serious distortion which sharpens feeling against the whole Negro race and may lead to interracial violence."

"The truth is," said the protest wire, "that many Negroes have joined the union and are working shoulder to shoulder with their white fellow workers to win the strike."

The NAACP protest stated that even if the union had a majority of Ford workers signed up out of the 85,000 total, there must be thousands of white workers who have not joined. To feature, in stories and pictures, the Negro non-strikers while saying nothing about the white non-strikers is "unfair news treatment" the NAACP declared.

National Association for the Advancement of Colored People press release, April 5, 1941, Group 2, NAACP Papers, Library of Congress.

81. NAACP PRESS RELEASE, APRIL 9, 1941

Walter White, Secretary of the National Association for the Advancement of Colored People, who has been in Detroit since Monday, made the following statement:

"The Ford strike faces the Negro with the toughest decision he has ever had to make in the matter of jobs and his relations with his fellow workers and employers. Widespread discrimination by some employers, even in national defense industries financed by taxation of Negroes as well as whites, has driven the majority of Negro workers to the ragged edge of existence. Henry Ford has not only hired more Negroes than any other Detroit employer but has given some of them the chance to rise above the menial ranks which contrasts sharply with Knudsen's General Motors.

"The attempt to use Negroes as a club over the heads of those who wish to organize themselves in unions in the Ford plants, however, is a dangerous move in times like these. It may make for increased racial tensions which would hurt the defense program. I regret that a few colored workers, in their desperation for jobs have lent themselves to staying in the River Rouge plant. They are not helping themselves, the cause of the Negro, nor labor relations generally. Especially when every one knows that the Ford company could evacuate the plant in fifteen minutes if it really wanted the thousand or so white and Negro workers out of there. I again plead with the men in the plant

to leave, to remove this source of friction, and to let the issue be peaceably
settled by the vote which has been ordered by the NLRB.

"Gratitude of Negro workers to Henry Ford for jobs which other plants
have denied them is understandable. But I want to remind Negro Ford workers
that they cannot afford to rely on the personal kindness of any individual
when what the worker wants is 'justice.' Death comes eventually to every one
of us. It will some day come to the present heads of the Ford industrial
empire. No Ford employee, colored or white, knows what the future heads of
Ford may do. Honest industrial democracy in the Ford and other industries
of our country offer the only real guaranty of present and future security for
workers.

"The A.F. of L. has played a sorry role in the strike in its futile attempt
to dupe Negro workers who are well aware of the constitutional clauses, ritualistic practices, and other devices by which a number of A.F. of L. unions
maintain "lily white" unions which shut Negroes out of jobs. The UAW-CIO has
conducted itself admirably in trying to remove the color line in this strike.
It needs to do much more to wipe out distrust based on sad experiences of the
past with union labor which Negroes have had and in teaching white labor that
it will never be free as long as black labor can be exploited. If the UAW-CIO
wins the right to represent the Ford workers, as now seem inevitable, it has
a golden opportunity to demonstrate to Negro workers everywhere in the country
that some labor unions are straight on the race question.

"In view of statements made by the UAW-CIO in this particular strike and
in view of the stated policy of the CIO nationally, opposing racial discrimination, I am confident it will take advantage of this opportunity."

Group 2, NAACP Papers, Library of Congress.

82. THE FORD CONTRACT: AN OPPORTUNITY

By Louis Emanuel Martin[133]

*Negro and white workers in the vast Ford plant now have an opportunity,
under the new union contract with the company, to build a model labor community composed of many races, each receiving justice and security.*

A new era for some fourteen thousand Negro workers has begun along the
River Rouge. This vast industrial state of the Ford Motor Company, the largest
industrial unit in the world, which was regarded only a few months ago as the
strongest citadel of the open shop in America, has at last capitulated to the
forces of organized labor. The story of the CIO Automobile Workers Union's
conquest of the Ford empire will rank among the most dramatic in labor history
for years to come.

All of us are aware of the importance this union struggle had for the
Negro workers who are better represented and better integrated in the Ford
Motor Company at River Rouge than in any other large mass production plant.
The employment policies of the company have won the support of Negro public
opinion and Henry Ford has been held as the model industrialist. Skilled as
well as unskilled Negroes found employment in his shops and even the creative
genius of black workers found expression there. The anti-Negro attitude of a
great part of the auto industry made Henry Ford appear by contrast as a heaven-
sent champion of the race and a Christian believer in the brotherhood of man.

When Henry Ford turned his back on unions, many Negro workers felt impelled to follow their kindly master. It was a question of "loyalty" according
to the leaders of the anti-union forces and the time had come to show it. The
thousands of Italians, Poles, hillbillies and immigrants on the other hand,

felt no such impulses and they were deaf to sentimental entreaty.

The majority of white workers saw the tremendous gains the UAW-CIO had
won from every major auto conpany. In General Motors, Chrysler, and others
the Workers had won job security through seniority which removed the constant
threat of arbitrary layoffs. Other auto workers were receiving higher wages
for the same work. There were no inhuman speed-ups. Other workers were free
to vote without fear of spies from a service department that sought to dominate
the political life of the community. The Ford workers wanted to be treated as
free independent human beings who were worthy of their hire.

Negro in Dilemma

The Negro worker no less than the whites, wanted these same things. He
wanted to buy a home and have some assurance that he would be working long
enough to pay for it. He wanted to live without eternal fear. Besides these
things, he also wanted to be loyal to Henry Ford. Seizing upon this dilemma,
both sides pressed for advantage. As the union advanced the tension heightened
and the majority of the black workers found themselves pitted against the vast
army of whites who were signing up with the CIO.

With the sudden advent of the AFL union, the picture broadened and it
was broadcast that Ford looks with favor upon the new organization. The
Negroes who were desperately trying to show their loyalty suddenly shifted
their non-union position and joined up with the AFL. A new bitterness came
into the picture and the CIO redoubled its campaign. The supreme court decision which forced the company to cease its coercion of the workers was hailed
as a CIO victory and the CIO drive got into high gear.

The showdown was not long in coming. CIO workers in the Pressed Steel
Building staged a walkout on the afternoon shift on April 3 and the fight was
on. UAW-CIO officials were themselves surprised by the suddenness of developments. Union men ran from building to building calling the workers out and
before dawn of the next day the UAW officials called the spontaneous walkout
an official strike. Several thousand Negro workers in the foundry stayed at
their posts at the insistence of company agents who promised them full time
and time and a half for overtime. They were told that they should protect
the company against the union vandals.

Threat of Riot

Violence and threats of a race riot alarmed the entire city. The fight
between the union and management had become also a struggle between white
workers and Negro workers who were "standing by." Negro unionists found
themselves at odds with their black fellow workers who were being armed inside the plant to break the picket lines. The stage had been set for a riot
that would have had repercussions all over America. The UAW officials, however, appreciated the impending peril and with admirable foresight they began
immediately a twenty-four-hour campaign among the white workers to prevent a
racial fight. Leaders in the Negro community were asked to appeal to the
Negro workers not to resort to violence and to evacuate the plant.

The wide publicity given this strike only a few weeks ago makes it unnecessary for me to review the details of the strike action or to elaborate
upon the numerous racial incidents which, for all their sensationalism, are
today without significance. Nevertheless, one must pay a tribute to many
intelligent Negro leaders in Detroit who did not hesitate to get in the fray
and restore peace between the workers. The NAACP and the National Negro
Congress were both active and Walter White and John P. Davis flew to the scene
in order to give direction to the efforts of their local branch organizations.

With the ordering of an NLRB election and the settlement of the strike,
the major threats of racial violence abated. Rivalry between the AFL "company
union" and the UAW-CIO sustained the tension but the situation was under control. Walter Hardin, veteran Negro organizer, was placed in charge of the
UAW-CIO organizational activity among Negro workers and, with the aid of an
enlarged staff, he literally argued and debated the opposition into a neutral
corner. It was clear at last that Ford and all of his cohorts were doomed
to defeat.

Negro Among Negotiators

The election passed without incident and the resounding victory of the
UAW-CIO convinced even the most skeptical that organized labor was in the
saddle in the auto industry. Action began immediately upon the heels of this
conviction and negotiations were begun before the NLRB election was even
certified from Washington. A negotiating committee representing the union
went into conference with company officials and a Negro, Shelton Tappes, who
represented some seventeen thousand workers in the foundry, most of whom are
Negroes, sat as a duly credited member of that committee.

No union man dared hope that the company was prepared to do what it immediately set about doing. In the words of Edsel Ford "there must be no
half-way measures" and in such a spirit the UAW-CIO got its first contract in
the auto industry which called for a union shop and a dues checkoff system
collected by the company for the union. Phillip Murray called the contract a
model for the industry and Ford once again had put his competitors in the
doghouse. Ford has given the UAW-CIO new responsibilities and perhaps paved
the way for organizational stability that in the end may pay him dividends.

Briefly, let us look at the contract. In the first place seniority is
established and a Ford worker cannot now be arbitrarily dismissed at the whim
of a straw boss. Craftsmen have plant-wide seniority and unskilled workers
have been given departmental seniority. As one Negro unionist told me, "the
seniority clause alone was worth the fight." It is job security for thousands
of Negro workers who may now plan their own future without fear. It is freedom
from the eternal threats of layoffs for cause or no cause.

The famed Ford service department which rivalled the FBI in the mysterious-
ness of its operations will be eliminated. The Ford worker can now go to the
toilet with a clear conscience and without fear that someone is holding a stop
watch on him. He can now attend any political meeting he chooses and vote for
any party without fear that some spy will report his action. He will no longer
live in constant terror.

Contract Applies to All

According to the contract, "at the beginning of the slack periods, hours
shall be reduced to 32 a week before any worker with seniority is laid off."
Here is further guarantee of a steady job. The contract further declares that
"Wage rates will be brought up to the standard of the highest rates paid in
the several classifications by other automobile conpanies." And believe it or
not, Ford paid less wages in many classifications than other manufacturers.
There are to be no wage reductions in any case.

The clause which is of direct concern to Negro workers, states: "The provisions of this contract shall apply to all employees covered by this agreement,
without discrimination on account of race, color, national origin or creed."

All of the guarantees and safeguards which modern industrial workers have
a human right to demand and expect, have to a large extent, been granted. The
Ford Motor Company still retains the right to hire and that right is affected
only by the stipulation that all employees must join the union within thirty
days. There are many other important aspects of the contract which have not
been discussed. Nevertheless, it is at once apparent that the workers at the
Ford plant, black and white alike, have won security, independence and freedom.

As I write these lines preparations are under way for plant elections in
which Negroes will have the opportunity to shape in a great measure their own
industrial destiny. Within the democratic processes of the union, the Negro
worker can fashion a new place for himself in American labor and develop a new
relationship between the races. White and black workers meet in the union hall
on terms of equality and they will of necessity educate each other. At least,
there is now the opportunity.

Already many Negro workers at River Rouge have shown that they possess
the capacity for leadership which heretofore has been expected only from our
"white collar" class. Shelton Tappes, Veal Clough and a number of other unionists in the plant are now giving leadership to thousands of whites as well as
to members of their own race. The ability to reason out an issue, to state a
problem, to resolve a difference, to express an opinion, all are important
assets in the democratic organization of the union. White workers have shown

the union. White workers have shown a willingness to accept and follow strong
and sure leadership with little regard to color. If the black worker earnestly
seeks to integrate himself into the union life, he has unlimited opportunity.[134]

Must Be Active in Union

No one, however, is deceived. The Negro workers at River Rouge know
that they cannot afford to relax their vigilance and that they must be ever
watchful of their own interests. Here is what they are being told:
"To have your dues checked off each month to qualify as a union member to
hold your job is merely a "half-way" measure. To obtain the fullest benefits
possible under this new regime and to protect your future security, every employee of the Ford Motor Company is invited and urged to take an active part
in the affairs of the union. Attend your departmental meetings. Express your
opinions from the floor. Vote on measures introduced. If you fail to do
this, then you will have no grounds for complaint on measures passed with which
you do not agree."
Indeed, a new day has dawned on the Ford empire. The victory of organized
labor was inevitable from the start. Those who abhorred the union have now
lost their rancor and the cause of the worker has crossed the color line. We
believe in Detroit that the beginnings of a new era in race relations will
be found in the countless union halls of this major industry. White and black
workers are learning fast that they need each other if they are to achieve the
ends for which they were organized.
Within the framework of industrial unionism there is an opportunity for
the kind of democracy that gives status to all regardless of color or national
origin. The Ford plant with its thousands of Negro workers will be something
of a test case for the CIO and the future of our workers in the ranks of
organized labor in America will be determined by the developments at River
Rouge. I believe that there are grounds for optimism and we must now make
certain that our workers take advantage of these new found opportunities. We
cannot afford "to miss the Bus."

The Crisis, 48 (September, 1941): 284-85, 302.

83. NEGROES THANK CIO FOR AID IN DETROIT HOUSING DISPUTE

DETROIT, Mar. 14--Labor's support for Negro families whom the Ku Klux
Klan and other reactionary groups have tried to bar from the Sojourner Truth
federal housing project here, today won all-out praise from Paul Robeson, great
concert singer.
A riot occurred at the project 10 days ago when the Negro families attempted
to move their belongings from their squalid high-rent slum homes into the new
federal development, named in honor of a Civil War Negro woman leader. Police
arrested 109 persons, 107 of them Negroes, but made no apparent effort to stop
the burning of a fiery cross by the Ku Kluxers.
Atty. Gen. Francis Biddle has already ordered a federal grand jury probe
of the affair to determine if a conspiracy exists against the Negroes occupancy of the homes.

Thomas' Comment

Meanwhile, Pres. R. J. Thomas of the CIO United Automobile Workers reiterated his stand in favor of Negro occupancy of the housing project originally planned by the government.
At the same time the union leader asserted that "I believe Ku Klux Klan
and Nazi-minded individuals on the other hand are involved in some of the
opposition to Negro occupancy."
Thomas said he was offering U.S. Atty. J. C. Lehr "eye-witness evidence
of direct invitation to violence by at least one leader of the group that is
opposing Negro occupancy."
Thomas pointed out that "particularly during this war we must have the

cooperation of all races. Neither the Negro nor any other racial strain in
our American life, whether it be Polish, Italian or any other minority, should
be denied the rights of democracy for which our nation's fighting men are now
shedding their blood.
"Any selfish un-American group which attempts to deny such rights must be
held to complete accountability under the law."

Robeson Hails Labor

Robeson, after completing a magnificent song recital under the auspices
of the United Automobile Workers Ford local, discussed the issues involved
before a Sojourner Truth citizen's committee meeting.
"The big thing in this housing dispute," he told a cheering audience, "is
that labor here is firmly on our side."
In a moving, persuasive address, Robeson urged Negro support of the war,
but warned that racial hatred and oppression such as that being stirred up by
the Klan, can only injure national unity and the war effort.

War For Freedom

"This war is for freedom, and particularly for the freedom of the colored
races," he declared, "Don't think that because the Japanese are colored, that
they are leading the fight for freedom.
"A small ruthless minority in Japan persecutes all the rest of the
Japanese and all the other colored races they can reach.
"Don't think that the Japanese propaganda isn't using this Sojourner
Truth issue against the United Nations. That is why it's important to settle
this issue right."

CIO News, March 16, 1942.

84.

FIRST CONVENTION OF THE UNITED STEELWORKERS OF AMERICA, 1942

RESOLUTION No. 5

On Racial Discrimination

WHEREAS, (1) It has always been tne policy and the practice of the CIO
and the SWOC to fight for equal treatment for all workers, regardless of race,
creed or color; and
(2) Inherent in labor's wholehearted support of the Victory Program is its
hatred of doctrines of racial and religious prejudice characteristic of our
Axis enemies; and
(3) Our war effort requires complete unity of all sections of the population regardless of race, creed or color; and
(4) The practices of these industries which discriminate in employment
on the basis of race, creed, or color violate our democratic principles, impede
our program of production for Victory and constitute direct threats to the
success of the national war effort; and
(5) Policies of segregation, Jim Crowism and discrimination in our armed
forces, in housing and in any sphere of our national life undermine our democratic institutions and serve to demoralize and disunite our people; now,
therefore, be it
RESOLVED, (1) That the United Steelworkers of America declares its firm
opposition to any discrimination in industry, in government, and anywhere else
on the basis of race, creed or color; and
(2) That the United Steelworkers of America pledges itself, its members,
and its local organizations to the fight to secure equality of treatment for
all workers, Negro and White, and all races and creeds in industrial employment
and promotion, in vocational training, in union leadership and service in
government and in the armed forces.

This resolution is a substitute submitted by: Local No. 1422, Chicago,
Ill.; Local No. 65, South Chicago, Ill.; Local No. 1743, Buffalo, N.Y.; Local
No. 2600, Bethlehem, Pa.; Local No. 1708, Oakland, Calif.; Local No. 1199,
Buffalo, N.Y.; Local No. 2604, Lackawanna, N.Y.; Local No. 1477, Sharon, Pa.;
Local No. 1193, Farrell, Pa.; Local No. 2523, Sharpsville, Pa.; Local No.
1126, Cleveland, Ohio; Local No. 2590, Bethlehem, Pa.; Local No. 1330, Youngs-
town, Ohio; Local No. 1104, Lorain, Ohio; Local No. 1014, Gary, Ind.; Local No.
1418, Campbell, Ohio; Local No. 1331, Youngstown, Ohio; Local No. 2273, Los
Angeles, Calif.; Local No. 2079.

A motion was made and seconded to adopt the report of the Committee.

Delegate Fountain, Local 1212: I would like to say a few words out of
appreciation. I have listened intently to everything that has gone on here
in this convention. It has made my heart surge to know that the USA-CIO has
gone on record staunchly, pulling no punches, outspokenly against all types
of Hitlerism both at home and abroad.

The delegate from Houston, Texas, this morning hit the keynote. I for
one know that my group must be educated toward unionism. Forthright and outspoken statements are coming from our Resolutions Committee. That in itself
should be the basis or a springboard to launch an educational or a unionization program among my people, particularly in the Southern district.

I know that with the efforts of the CIO that dastardly bill that Mr.
McDonald spoke of, that poll tax will be done away with. That is the thing
that is going to help organize labor.

It is rather ironical. The poll tax law, as you know--at least I hope
you do--was originally intended to keep my people from voting. It so happens
that it was a boomerang; it kept not only Negroes from voting, but the poor
white as well--18,000,000 of my people and almost twice that of poor white
people.

Just as Mr. McDonald said, those who are in the Senate and on the floors
of Congress have perpetuated themselves in office year on top of year--some
of them have been there 50 years--through their political machines, with just
five per cent of representation. Those are the things that helped Huey Long
make a little dictatorship out of Louisiana.

I know I am expressing the sentiments of all Negro delegates here when
I say that the CIO is going to make this work. You know and I know that we
have these laws on the statute books of our Constitution of these United States
of America, but when they were put on they were just put on as a gesture.
They haven't been made to work.

I know from looking into the faces of the delegates here, from the
fellowship that I see throughout the hall and the nods from persons from Coast
to Coast who, when they see you as a delegate--they don't see you as a Negro,
but you are to them, another steel worker--I know, yes, indeed I know, and I
am not ashamed of the fact that there are tears in my eyes right now, because
I feel that way.

After all, every Negro you see represents one out of ten Americans, I
emphasize that fact--Americans--and here in the USA (almost said SWOC), here
in the USA one in every ten. We are Americans; we are not Negroes and we are
not Japanese Americans, and we are not German Americans, nor are we Italian
Americans. We are Americans.

It is along those lines of racial friction that the Axis powers have
been working. Yes, they play up the incidents, the unfortunate incidents
that occur and are blotches to this country, but such things shall not be
said of the USA-CIO. I know.

So, without further say, because I am all choked up, I pledge everything
I have got, everything, to see that unionization and organization among my
people everywhere in these United States is carried out.

The delegates stood and applauded vigorously.

Delegate Burches, Local 1066: I would like to take this occasion to
urge a more practical carrying out of the fine humanitarian principles embodied
in the resolution just presented.

The situation in my Local does not indicate that this is being done at all.
Despite the fact that we have been organized for practically six years and
have been working under a contract for six years, we still have "Jim Crow"
departments--that is departments where no colored people are permitted to work.

Now, this is an indication of laxity on the part of our representatives,

and it should be abolished. I would like at this time to urge all of the
Negro delegates to raise this issue more strongly in their Local Unions, be-
cause as Frederick Douglas, the great leader of the Negro people, has said,
"He who desires freedom must strike the blow for freedom."

Director Bittner: Mr. Chairman and fellow delegates--It will take me
about a minute to explain to you that first the Committee has a report to make
on other phases of this question, such as the Poll Tax and the Civil Liberties,
that will come under resolutions that we have to report to the convention.[135]

In order that every delegate here may understand the substance of the
Committee's report, it is an all-out resolution on legislation against any
kind of discrimination because of race, creed, color, or nationality. That's
what it means; it means that and it is an all-out declaration without any
qualifications whatever. We are all God's human beings, and we should all be
treated as God's human beings.

Delegate Cook, Local 1029: Mr. Chairman and delegates--The resolution
speaks for itself, but I feel that I want to say how much I appreciate the
sentiments embodied in the resolution. So far as racial discrimination is
concerned in my Local, it is scarcely noticed, but in the plant in which I
work there are only nine Negroes, eight of whom are in the Union, five of
whom are holding office. I have been the president since 1937, without any
opposition.

In the Chicago district and throughout some of the Middle Western sections
recently there have been some forms of organization showing up here and yonder
among Negroes. One was the Progressive Negro Steel Workers of America, which
held its meeting last month in Chicago. They said the Steel Workers Committee
had written on paper that there shall be no discrimination against race, creed
or color, and they pointed out all the way back to 1869 at the time of the
Civil War and what happened after that war, and said that it was soon forgotten.
They had high respect for Mr. Murray, but they said that Mr. Murray will not
live always, and we will be hampered with Ku Klux and Black Legions and the
whole CIO will turn against us, as things happened at the time of the Civil
War.

There could not be any finer resolution presented today. There is discrimination against all people, minority groups; and we know that on every
street corner in Chicago, especially in the black belt section, nine Negroes
out of every ten each day are met with some agent of the Axis powers attempting
to destroy the unity which the CIO and the United Steelworkers of America are
now about to create.

We who are in the leadership of our Unions say that they shall not pass.
We are going to work hand in hand with our Union and see to it that the demonstrations of this Union are upheld before the enemies, the reactionary forces
both within and without. We can now return to our people at home and into our
communities, the Negroes and white delegates, and break down the Fifth Column
Nazis who are trying to destroy and weaken our national front, in order to
destroy the morale of the United Nations of the world.

The Japanese are also busy in large cities, not the Japanese themselves,
but they are under cover. You can notice their influence in trying to make
this appear to be a color war. With the agents of Hitler, they are working
within our trade union movement in order to stir up dissension against the
leaders and members of the Union.

This resolution will bury all of that. We, as one of the speakers said
before--and I would like to repeat it to the Negro steel workers of the United
States--we are not going to have any trouble with the members of our Union,
those who are loyal to its constitution and its cause; but we will have trouble
with the forces within our Union who are seeking to destroy this Union by
stirring up hatred among the Negro people.

We ourselves will see to it that all forces of reaction are driven from
the American shores.

The delegates arose and applauded vigorously.

Delegate Tolveroso, Local 1798: I am not questioning the sincerity of
our officers, which I know is sound, especially the sincerity of our great
Chairman, the President of the USA-CIO, Brother Murray. But there is a question
in my mind and in the minds of the delegation from our Local in California,
as to why the Arrangements Committee sent out a notification to all Locals
giving us instructions that white delegates in Cleveland would have arrangements

in different hotels, and the colored delegates would have arrangements made in
other hotels. That is what I would like to ask from the Arrangements Committee,
why they did a thing like that, if we are going to be consistent.
     Chairman Murray: Secretary McDonald can answer the question.
     Secretary McDonald: I think the brother is a bit mistaken. The notice
which accompanied the Call for the convention did not say anything at all about
the colored delegates going to certain hotels, but it just so happens that there
are some colored delegates who want to go to colored hotels. For the information and guidance of those brothers who do want to go to colored hotels, we
put that information in the notice.
     The motion to adopt the Committee's report on Resolution No. 5 was
carried.

Proceedings of the First Constitutional Convention of the United Steelworkers
of America, 1942, Vol. I, pp. 136-39.

85.
CONSTITUTION OF THE UNITED STEELWORKERS OF AMERICA, ADOPTED 1942

ARTICLE I

Name and Affiliation

     This Organization shall be known as the United Steelworkers of America,
hereinafter also referred to as the International Union.
     The International Union shall be affiliated with the Congress of Indus-
trial Organizations.

ARTICLE II

Objects

     First. To unite in this industrial union, regardless of race, creed,
color or nationality, all workers and workmen and working women eligible for
membership, employed in and around iron and steel manufacturing, processing
and fabricating mills and factories in the United States and Canada.
     Second. To establish through collective bargaining adequate wage stand-
ards, shorter hours of work and improvements in the conditions of employment
for the workers in the industry.
     Third. To secure legislation safeguarding the economic security and
social welfare of the workers in the industry, to protect and extend our
democratic institutions and civil rights and liberties and thus to perpetuate
the cherished traditions of our democracy.

ARTICLE III

Eligibility of Members

     All working men and working women, regardless of race, creed, color or
nationality, employed in and around iron and steel manufacturing, processing
and fabricating mills and factories, or in any other place now under the jurisdiction of the International Union, in the United States and Canada or officers,
staff representatives or employees of the International Union or of the Steel
Workers Organizing Committee, are eligible to membership.
     No person having the power, in the management of any mill or factory, to
hire or fire shall be eligible for membership.
     Persons having supervisory power, excluding the right to hire and fire,
shall be eligible to membership subject to the approval of the Local Union
and the International Executive Board.

ARTICLE IV

International Officers, International
Tellers, International Executive
Board and Delegates to the Con-
ventions of the Congress of
Industrial Organizations

Section 1. The International Officers of the International Union shall
be the International President, the International Secretary-Treasurer and two
Assistants to the International President. There shall be one District Director for each District, three International Tellers, and a National Director for
Canada.

Sec. 2. The term of office of the International Officers, International
Executive Board members, International Tellers and Delegates to the Convention
of the Congress of Industrial Organizations shall be two years, except that
the International Officers and Executive Board shall be one year.

Constitution of the United Steelworkers of America, CIO, adopted at Cleveland,
Ohio, May 22, 1942, pp. 3-5

86. CIO's PROGRAM
FOR INTER-RACIAL HARMONY IN ST. LOUIS

*Following is a summary of the program submitted to the late Mayor William
Dee Becker by the St. Louis Industrial Union Council, CIO, to prevent a
repetition of the Detroit tragedy in St. Louis.*

1. Appoint a citizen's committee representative of white and Negro
groups, churches, labor, and industry, to promote racial understanding, and
to study the underlying factors of inter-racial problems.

2. Call upon all citizens to conduct themselves so as to advance national
unity, regardless of race or creed.

3. Call a representative conference of the clergy, labor, and industry,
to promote inter-racial unity for victory in the war, with special attention
to the full use of all manpower for war production.

4. Isolate and suppress any incident that might lead to racial strife by
calling in federal troops to supplant the police in the event of the slightest
incident. Announce a policy that, in the event of a riot, inciters will be
prosecuted for treason.

5. Prevent friction on crowded street cars and buses by equal treatment
of all passengers, and by having persons casting racial slurs for disturbing
the peace.

6. Check the circulation of inflammatory rumors, with the help of the
FBI.

7. Ask President Roosevelt to address the nation over the radio on interracial understanding.

8. Issue a proclamation embodying these actions.

*Mayor A. P. Kaufmann has announced that he will continue the work of the
late Mayor Becker on this program, and will name the committee proposed in
Point 1. Before his untimely death, Mayor Becker had shown a generally favorable
attitude on the whole program. The CIO Council is taking it up further with the
new mayor.*

Flier in possession of the editors.

87. DISCRIMINATION

WHEREAS, 1) The need for war materials is so great and so immediate that the rejection of the services of able men and women by industry because of pre-judice against them for reasons of race, creed, and color is an inexcusable risk to national security, and

2) Prejudice and discrimination in our industrial life, against the Negro particularly, has long been a shameful blot on our national record which becomes less and less tolerable as citizens are called upon to make equal sacrifice in the defense of the country, and

3) The President's Committee of Fair Employment Practice, of which re-presentatives of organized labor are members has already shown in a number of hearings held in various parts of the country that while many corporations working on government war contracts give lip service to the national policy of non-discrimination, in practice they find many subtle ways of evading their obligation to deal fairly and impartially among workers and among seekers for jobs, and

4) The experience of many CIO organizations shows that discrimination for racial reasons, particularly against Negroes, is widespread throughout our war industries, and constitutes a condition which cannot be tolerated indefinitely by a free nation fighting for the rights of plain people everywhere in the world; now, therefore, be it

RESOLVED, 1) That the CIO condemns the practices followed by some employers which prevent the full utilization of our productive man-power in the war effort as a result of the discriminatory exclusion of workers from war production plants by reason of race, creed, or color, and calls upon progressive business management everywhere to direct its attention constructively to this problem, with a view to fostering harmonious relationships among workers of different nationalities, religions, and races within their plants, and the elimination of the discriminatory procedures now as widely practiced by managerial personnel and

2) That the CIO reaffirms its traditional stand against discrimination on grounds against race, creed, or color, in American industry, and urges its affiliates to bend every effort to help in the elimination of prejudices and discriminatory practices in their respective fields.

CIO News, March 30, 1942.

88. NEGRO GROUP TO MEET FDR ON RIGHTS

Washington, July 18--Assurances that a declaration "re-defining the citizenship rights of Negro Americans" will be discussed with President Roose-velt were received by a delegation of Negro union and civic leaders that visited the Justice Department here this week.

The delegation, led by Ewart Guinier, president of the N.Y. District of the CIO State, County and Municipal Workers and Dorothy Funn, of the Teachers Union, of N.Y.C., called at the Department to protest recent Negro lynchings and to point out the dangers to national unity and the war effort that are involved in continued anti-Negro discrimination.

Present Statement

The delegation presented a statement adopted by the Negro Labor Victory Committee in New York, which said in part:

"We call upon our Commander-in-Chief, President Roosevelt, to issue a proclamation re-defining the citizenship rights of Negro Americans; to ask the governors of the 48 states and the mayors of our cities to issue like pro-clamations; and to order all Federal agencies, especially the Department of Justice, to take swift and appropriate action to safeguard the rights of Negro Americans."

CIO News, July 10, 1942.

89.

CIO SEEKS WAR WORK FOR FIRM AS 450 NEGROES FACE JOB LOSS

NEW YORK, July 18--Failure of the Spring Products Manufacturing Co., of Long Island City, to secure war contracts may force the plant to close down, throwing 450 workers, 95 per cent of them Negroes, out of work, unless Government officials heed the protests of CIO and Negro groups.

Local 91 of the CIO United Furniture Workers, which has a contract with the firm, is planning a mass meeting here to arouse interest in the plight of these 450 workers who face the loss of their jobs and $300,000 in annual wages unless War Production Chief Donald M. Nelson acts at once to prevent the sale of the plant at public auction.

Washington Parley

A delegation of CIO union officials, including Morris Muster, international president of the UFW, and a co-chairman of the Negro Labor Victory Committee conferred in Washington with McNutt and other government officials, and also told their story to Senator Robert F. Wagner of New York, who promised to help them.[136]

As explained by members of the delegation, Spring Products, a plant covering more than a city block, manufactured box springs, studio couches, steel beds, inner springs for mattresses and units for upholstered furniture.

A part of the plant had already been converted for the production of war materials. The firm won high praise from the government when it completed a war order for 800,000 bomb springs more than a month ago. It has also turned out thousands of army cots.

For several months, the head of the firm, working closely with officials of the union, has attempted to get war contracts from Washington. He offered to spend $50,000 to complete the conversion of plant machinery for war work, and sent a detailed report to the War Production Board on 16 types of war materials which his plant can turn out. These include ammunition belts, steel helmets, army cots, bunks for ships and other articles needed in the war.

Union Active

A few weeks ago he notified the union that unless he was able to get war contracts, the plant would be forced to close. Horace Small, vice president of the UFW local and a member of the labor-management committee at the plant, called a union meeting, and plans were formulated to conduct a campaign to get war contracts for the plant.

"Loss of these jobs," Small said, "hits Negro workers a body blow, particularly because of prejudice as usual on the part of many employers, makes it difficult for them to get jobs in war industry, despite their skills."

Action in support of the Spring Products workers was taken by the N.Y. CIO Council which sent a request to the War Production Board urging that war contracts be given to the plant.

CIO News, July 10, 1942.

90. UAW-CIO CONVENTION ADOPTS COURIER "DOUBLE V" PROGRAM

By Horace Cayton
(Labor Editor)

CHICAGO, Aug. 13--The United Auto Workers, CIO--the largest body of organized workers in the world--held its seventh annual convention here last week, with approximately 75 Negro delegates among the nearly 1800 in attendance.

Highlighting the convention activities were the resolutions endorsing The Pittsburgh Courier's "Double V" campaign and the strong condemnation of racial discrimination.[137]

The latter resolution, worded in exceptionally strong language, was passed at the insistence of both white and colored rank and file convention delegates. It urged Congress to give FEPC "enforcing powers," asked for a probe of Klan activities, instructed the union to integrate Negro women into industry, sought integration of Negro workers in plants where none are employed, called upon responsible heads in the government to establish mixed regiments in the Army and cited the UAW Constitution which reads in part, "To unite in one organization regardless of race, creed, color, political affiliation on nationality, all employees under the jurisdiction of the International Union."

Issues Draw Fire

This union, which met here last week, is the youngest, largest, roudiest and most democratic union in the country. It came dangerously close to kicking over all traces, as several points came out in direct opposition to the careful plans of the union's administration. Nothing is sacred to those boys in the automobile industry, and the questions of rank and file control time and again upset convention deliberations.

The officers of the union shared to an extent the dissatisfaction of the rank and file delegates as to the equality of sacrificing principle to voluntarily make a pledge of "no strike" for the duration.

They did not want the union to go as far as it did in challenging the A.F. of L. and company unions, who still receive premium pay for overtime and Sunday work. Other issues which the administration lost to the delegates who could not be ruled and in some cases could not even be controlled, were those pertaining to the amount of wage increases for national officers and an increase in dues to build up a post-war fund.

Delegates Fail to Elect Board Members

Negro delegates early in the convention, started working to elect candidates of their own choice in their respective districts.

They also began work towards two major objectives--the election of a Negro board member and the introduction of a resolution on the Negro question "with teeth." The resolution sought to cope with the numerous wildcat strikes in plants upon the introduction of Negroes in the war production program.

Walter Hardin, veteran organizer and chairman of the interracial committee of the International was favored as a strong candidate when the convention opened. He had the personal backing of the international president, R. J. Thomas. Hardin, it was reported, favored the introduction of a constitution change which would make a position for a Negro "board member-at-large." This resolution was reported out of committee and Hardin's chances faded.

Sheffield Beaten in Last-Minute Shift

In a caucus of the Negro delegates called shortly after the convention began, it was agreed to try and elect a Negro from one of the regional offices without attempting to change the constitution.

Oscar Noble of the Pontiac local, young international representative now attached to the Ford plant, was chosen as the delegate to run from his district. With a change in regional lines which affected the Ford plant from which Noble had expected much of his strength, it soon became apparent that he couldn't win.

Most of the delegates then met again, and it was decided that Horace Sheffield should run from the Ford district in spite of a hasty last-minute campaign. Sheffield was defeated for office and no Negro was elected from the convention to the international board.

Strong Resolution Passed by Delegates

Delegates were successful in obtaining a strong resolution on the Negro problem. Seven or eight resolutions were presented to the committee, which voted to present the convention with one which took a "middle-of-the-road" position on the problem of integrating Negroes into the union.

It was here that Sheffield made a stirring speech to the convention,
asking them to take a more forceful stand. Said he:
"In all previous conventions, we have passed these beautiful resolutions
stating we are opposed to discrimination against the Negro race. However, we
have now reached a juncture in American life where Negroes are no longer going
to receive just membership only in a union or in the American way of life.
"We have reached the point where we, too, are human and want a change of
equitable participation in the affairs and economic fruits of American life.
We want full integration into this Union."
Sheffield's speech was wildly applauded. The "middle-of-the-road" resolution was overwhelmingly voted down and referred back to the committee.
The more powerful resolution, referred to above, was then brought in and
immediately adopted.

Pittsburgh Courier, August 15, 1942.

91. MURRAY ORDERS STUDY OF NEGRO JOB EQUALITY

WASHINGTON, Aug. 22--CIO Pres. Philip Murray of the CIO today announced
appointment of a CIO committee to investigate and study the entire problem of
equality of opportunity for Negro workers in American industry.
Named to the committee were James B. Carey, secretary of the CIO; and
Willard S. Townsend, president of the United Transport Service Employees of
America, a CIO affiliate with headquarters in Chicago. Townsend is the first
Negro member of the CIO executive board.
President Murray instructed the committee to report on its investigation
to the next meeting of the CIO's general executive board.
In announcing the survey, Murray reiterated the CIO's affirmative stand
against anti-Negro discrimination as a danger to American democracy, especial-
ly in war time. The CIO head is a member of the Fair Employment Practices
Committee with John Brophy serving as alternate member. This committee has
investigated discrimination against Negroes and other minority groups in a
number of areas throughout the country.

Hit Discrimination

Carey and Townsend, in announcing their survey, charged:
"Discrimination against Negroes and other minority groups has always
been a blight and a paradox in this democracy, the very existence of which is
based on a declaration that 'all men are created free and equal.'
"Since its inception, the CIO has vigourously opposed racial bias and
intolerance. The constitution of the CIO expressly outlaws membership barriers
based on differences of nationality or race. In every national CIO convention,
and in hundreds of regional and local meetings, members of the CIO have indicated their opposition to discrimination.
"The war has taught many Americans a long-needed lesson; that a divided
nation cannot stand up against the Axis, that a solid unity of all the people
is a vital necessity if we are to preserve and amplify our American democracy
against its foes at home and abroad.

Hail Progress

"We are gratified that some progress has been made in recent months toward
bringing about the equality of opportunity which is the goal of labor and
progressive Americans. The Fair Employment Practices Committee has served a
highly useful purpose in putting the spotlight on some of the worst examples
of Hitlerite discrimination and bias in industry, and its work should be supported and strengthened.
"It is the intention of this committee to make a thorough investigation
of race relations among the workers of this country, and of the employment
practices of industry in general. We know that passing resolutions in conventions is not enough.

"We anticipate that the CIO will set an affirmative course of action on the basis of our report to the General Executive Board."

CIO News, August 24, 1942.

92.   CIO TO FIGHT BIAS AGAINST NEGROES: FORMS COMMITTEE

WASHINGTON, Sept. 12--Establishment of a national CIO Committee to Abolish Racial Discrimination was one of the highlights of last week's CIO Executive Board meeting here.   The committee consists of Willard S. Townsend, president of the United Transport Service Employees and James B. Carey, national CIO secretary.

At the same time, the Board adopted a resolution again calling on the government to move strongly against discrimination in war jobs, which is costing the victory effort the services of hundreds of thousands of efficient and patriotic American workers.

Both the resolution and an accompanying report praised the work of the President's Committee on Fair Employment Practices, now part of the War Manpower Commission, and reaffirmed full national CIO cooperation.

Seek Action

They also warned against the possibility that Manpower Commission officials might "be induced to bow to the wishes of big corporative interests, particularly in the Southern states, and throttle the Committee's highly commendable activities," and called on the Commission to give the Committee full aid and scope for its anti-discrimination work.

The report called for legislation to implement the executive order against discrimination and make it permanent, and urged a detailed survey of war plants, community meetings on the problem, and similar steps to abolish jim crow throughout government and industry.

CIO News, September 14, 1942.

93.   NEGROES FAVOR THE CIO

Courier Poll Shows Overwhelming Support for the CIO As Against the AFL

The American Negro, more labor conscious in the last decade than ever before in his history, expressed to The Pittsburgh Courier's Bureau of Public Sentiment this week a preference for the policies of the Congress of Industrial Organization, rather than those of the American Federation of Labor.

In response to the question, "Do you believe the AFL offers more to the American Negro than the CIO?" a completely sampled cross-section of the colored population answered "No" 72.6% of the time; "Yes" 12.5% of the time and a rather large proportion of 14.9% could not make up their minds one way or the other.

"A Raw Deal in Both"

Such answers in the latter classification as: "Don't believe either offers much." "Much room for improvement in both," "The Negro has gotten some raw deals in both," definitely proves that the race is not unaware of the faults in organized labor.

Poll reactions in general, however, gave credit to the attempt made by the CIO in recognizing the industrial worker as a component part of the labor movement.   Resentment is still held by a great majority against the AFL hierarchy and the admitted biased attitude which many in that group possess in regard to the Negro worker and his aspirations for better living conditions.

Randolph Cited

Acts of discrimination as practiced by both organizations were brought
to the front by the alert and sensitive Negro thinkers. The annual "Randolph
humiliation" was a factor strongly involved in anti-AFL sentiment. This yearly
insult to the Pullman porter president hurts that organization's chances for
Negro sympathy, if indeed, say poll followers, they really want it.

On the other hand, the CIO has consistently welcomed the Negro into most
of its locals and one finds him integrated actively into the affairs of that
organization. Appreciation and approval for this trend was expressed more
and more as the poll progressed.

Women Were Different

Other factors favoring the CIO were cited. These included: (a) the admission of the United Transport Workers (Red Caps) into the group and Willard
Townsend's inclusion on the international body; (b) Phil Murray's attempt to
exclude unfair employment practices in industry; (c) recognition of menial
employees as important cogs in the labor movement.

The low percentage of women (53.9%) who approved of the CIO, as compared
with the poll norm, remains unexplained except that the Negro woman has not
entered into the industrial picture in great numbers as yet, at least in those
occupations which are highly organized.

Negroes are labor-conscious. This fact is irrefutable.

Next week's question: DO YOU BELIEVE THE NAVY OFFERS THE AMERICAN NEGRO
GREATER OPPORTUNITY TO SERVE HIS COUNTRY THAN THE ARMY?

Pittsburgh Courier, November 14, 1942.

94. OLD LABOR POLICY IS BLASTED

Murray Demands End of Discrimination as CIO Convention Opens

By Horace R. Cayton[138]

BOSTON, Mass., Nov. 12--A wildly cheering assembly of CIO delegates,
meeting here Monday in the ballroom of the Hotel Statler, heard President
Philip Murray keynote the fifth annual convention by insisting upon labor unity,
which must guarantee the abolition of racial discrimination.

Speaking with studied deliberation, the CIO chief said:

"It is wise to remember that any kind of unity must needs comprehend the
complete abolition of all forms of racial discrimination."

The delegates vigorously applauded Murray's obvious reference to the
practice of some AFL unions, which deny membership to Negroes.

Disclaiming all personal political ambitions, Murray said his prime
interest was in achieving "a real unity, and not a policy of appeasement. The
interests of the CIO and the individual must be protected."

Murray's keynote speech gave added official recognition to the status of
Negroes in his organization. Unlike the 'back-of-the-scene' manipulations
of government, industry and the armed forces, Negroes have had a place in the
policy-making committees.

Willard S. Townsend, a member of the powerful resolution committee, has
been working since the middle of last week, shifting and redrafting resolutions
which have poured in from every national and international CIO union in the
country.

John L. Yancey, secretary and treasurer of the United Transport Service
Employees of America, is doing yeoman work on the convention's constitution
committee.

Other important Negro trade unionists who are here or are expected any
moment are Shelton Tappes of Ford Local No. 600 in Detroit; George Hardin,
chairman of the Interracial Committee of the United Automobile Workers CIO;
Ferdinand Smith, international officer of the National Maritime Union and Boyd
Wilson from steel.

Race Delegates to Represent 250,000

Although there probably won't be over 75 Negro delegates, they will represent approximately 250,000 Negro workers scattered throughout the country in the CIO.

The issues to come up before the convention are of the utmost interest to Negro workers. First, there is the problem of an overall planning and a unified approach to the manpower problem which, incidently, is the heart of the whole war production job. The CIO and its president, Philip Murray, want a voluntary approach to the problem and are against compulsory legislation for the mobilization of men.

Of special interest to the Negro workers is the possibility that the government may "freeze" men to their present jobs, which would be particularly disastrous as it would prevent upgrading of Negroes throughout industry. The opportunity for advancement during the war then would be completely lost and new white workers might even be able to do, in cases of labor shortage, come in over experienced Negroes who were frozen at the unskilled or janitor level.

Another question of great importance to the convention will be the report of the Committee on Racial Discrimination. Although the CIO has been more liberal than the AFL in this respect there are instances where there has been some discrimination and the problem of upgrading has not been met squarely.

Townsend Member of This Committee

Recently, President Murray appointed James B. Carey and Willard S. Townsend as a committee to draw up a program to deal with this problem. An excellent resolution has been prepared and this committee will proceed to work as soon as the convention appropriates the necessary funds for a full time director, and President Murray appoints this individual. In view of the plea for national unity now being voiced on every side, and of the smarting rebuke which the AFL gave to A. Philip Randolph, this resolution will be watched by Negroes throughout the country and will do much to make or break the faith in which Negro workers hold the Congress and its international officers.

There is also the question of John L. Lewis and his miners who will undoubtedly be expelled from the Congress. This relationship between 50-to-75,000 Negro coal miners and the Negro membership of the CIO will undoubtedly follow organizational lines. If Lewis continues his raiding of CIO unions, there will be a civil war in labor, with Negroes lined up on both sides.

No Chance for Labor Double-Cross

Although the opening days of the convention were relatively uneventful, this in all probability, will turn out to be the most important convention of the CIO's history. The role of labor in the national efforts has been under fire from many quarters. The political situation where labor faced the reality of a reactionary congress also gives them much concern. Finally the complete loss of labor's independence by compulsory legislation and the freezing of wages and men in positions may strip union organizations of most of their power.

All these questions affect Negro workers. But Negroes have in addition the problem of racial discrimination and the necessity to push the union towards some sort of action which would be more effective than the important efforts of government to fully integrate black workers into industry.

Pittsburgh Courier, November 14, 1942.

95. CIO CONFAB MAPS ALL-OUT FIGHT ON RACIAL BARRIERS

By Horace R. Cayton

BOSTON, Mass. Nov. 19--"It isn't my object to come to this body this

afternoon and plead for the rights of the Negro," said Willard S. Townsend,
president of the United Transportation Employees of America, before the fifth
annual convention of the Congress of Industrial Organizations in the Statler
Hotel in Boston.

"If you think more of your prejudices," continued Townsend, "than you do
of your freedom, then, by all that is holy, you will lose that freedom."

President Philip Murray of the CIO further said to the 500 delegates:

"The fate of our nation must necessarily comprehend complete abolition
of all forms of racial discrimination."

Keynote Message

These two speeches indicated the tone of the convention which made unprecedented commitments to the Negro and for abolition of racial prejudice in
industry.

Four significant actions of the convention indicated the extent to which
an "all-out" fight against prejudice and bigotry was a central theme of the
convention.

It was unequivocally stated that, on a number of occasions, any labor
unity between the CIO and the AFL would have to have as one of its pre-
requisites abolition of race prejudice in both organizations.

Belated Attack

Murray, the first day of the convention, indicated the convention would
take a stand on this question. It was not, however, until Tuesday, when the
discussions of the non-discrimination resolution was introduced, that the
delegates had a field day on race prejudice.

After the speeches by President Willard Townsend, Ferdinand Smith of the
National Maritime Union, Walter Reuther of the United Automobile Workers,
there could be no question but that the Negro had come into a new day and was
receiving a recognition he had hitherto never obtained even from the Congress.

But later, there was a debate on the Labor Unity Resolution which provided:

"Unity should assume that all forms and practices of racial discrimination
within unions be abolished." At long last, the verbal, and perhaps oratorical,
promise of Philip Murray before the United Auto Workers' convention in Chicago
some months ago, was reduced to writing, in a form which would bind Murray,
the international officers and the executive committee by being unanimously
passed.

Takes Same Stand as Courier

The anti-discrimination clause went further in stating the policy of the
convention than had any previous resolution. Following the precedent set by
the United Auto Workers' convention, the delegates committed themselves to a
similar position for labor as that advocated by The Pittsburgh Courier for
Negroes. The resolution stated in part:

"We of the democracies are fighting Fascism at home and abroad and we
are welding all races, all religions, and all peoples in a united body of
warriors for democracy. Any discriminatory practices within our ranks against
Negroes or other groups directly aids the enemy by creating division, dissension
and confusion."

Following this resolution which held the floor over an hour and a half,
John Yancey, secretary-treasurer of the United Transport Service; Presi-
dent Philip Murray, Van A. Bittner of the United Steel Workers' organization,
Walter Reuther, member of the executive board of the United Automobile Workers;
Ferdinand Smith of the United Maritime Workers and Willard Townsend spoke at
length.

Executive Approval

The appointment of a committee for abolition of racial prejudice in the
CIO and in industry was made some months ago. Members of this committee will
now be able to act as they have the full endorsement and approval of the
executive board.

The board consists of James B. Carey, chairman of the CIO and a liberal
in its ranks; Willard S. Townsend, the militant and fighting president of
UTSEA; Ferdinand Smith, international officer of the NMU which has made such
a splendid record in race relations; Boyd Wilson, special assistant to Murray
in race relations in United Steel, and James Leary, secretary and treasurer
of the Mine, Mill and Smelter Workers.[139]

Negroes shared in an unprecedented fashion in the policy-forming bodies
of the convention. Townsend was a member of the powerful resolutions committee and it can safely be said that the clause on the abolition of racial
discrimination as a prerequisite for labor unity was due almost entirely to
his efforts in the pre-convention discussion of this resolution.

Have Voice

In contrast to government, industry, and the armed forces, it is only in
the ranks of labor that Negroes are finding a method of expressing their wants
and expectations and through this medium it would be possible to influence to
an extent the policies of those sections of the society from which he is
excluded except as puppets to carry out orders. Ferdinand Smith was a member
of the Rules and Order of Business committee, and John Yancy was a member of
the Constitution committee. All these men serve not only the cause of the
Negro but made definite contributions to the respective committees with which
they work.

Fifteen Negroes

There were fifteen Negro delegates among whom were Charles Brown of
Omaha, Nebraska, from the Packing Workers' Industrial Union; Richard Bancroft
of Washington, from the United Federal Workers of America; Rose Burrell of
Baltimore, from the newly formed Domestic Service Workers' Union; Moses Lee
of East St. Louis from the Mine, Mill and Smelter Workers; Leonard Simpson of
New York from the United Sugar Workers, and Noah Walter, New York, of the
Amalgamated Clothing Workers.

A number of visitors were also present, including W. Richard Carter,
member of the international executive board of the Shipbuilders of America;
Boyd L. Wilson, international representative and assistant to Murray in
steel, and Oscar Wilson of the Packing House Workers.

Pittsburgh Courier, November 21, 1942.

96.   PUSH FIGHT ON BIAS---CIO

WASHINGTON, Jan. 9--The Fair Employment Practices Committee of the
federal government must be given additional funds to increase its effectiveness in ending racial discrimination declared this week.

Members of the committee are CIO Secretary James B. Carey, chairman,
President Willard Townsend of the United Transport Service Employees,
secretary; James J. Leary, Mine, Mill and Smelter Workers; Ferdinand Smith,
National Maritime Union, and Boyd L. Wilson, United Steelworkers.

Text of their statement follows:

"The existence of discrimination against Negroes and other minorities
is not only a continuing blot on American democracy, but even more seriously
a drag on the total mobilization of all our people needed to win the war
against Axis slavery.

Every war industry and plant in the country is crying for more manpower,
desperately needed to keep the weapons of war rolling out to the offensive
fighting fronts of our armed forces and our allies.

"Negro Americans are as anxious as any to work for victory, just as they
are fighting for victory in the Army and the Navy. To allow employers or any
other agencies to bar them from jobs as worse than unjust, it is an active
help to Hitler.

Equal Opportunity

"The CIO, in setting up the Committee on Racial Discrimination at its November convention, moved to implement in industry and government the policy it has always held to in its own ranks--of absolute opposition to discrimination in any form, and of complete equality of opportunity for all.

"This policy has been made national in the Executive Order of the President No. 8820 and in setting up of the Fair Employment Practices Committee. The CIO concurs fully in these steps, as it concurs in every move to promise national unity for winning the war.

"At the same time, we must point out that the job of wiping out racial discrimination is far from complete, and at the present rate of progress will scarcely be completed in time to make full answer to the needs of all-out war, or to the needs of a people's peace.

"Too often more lip service is given to the principle of equal opportunity. Too often an employer or a whole industry, ordered to stop discriminating against Negro workers, has evaded the order by offering token employment to a handful in place of opening jobs to all who are qualified. Or again Negro workers are confined to the lowest paid, least skilled or even the menial jobs, regardless of their experience or training.

"Of course there are notable exceptions to these disruptive practices. The exceptions, however, could easily become the rule if the national policy were made completely effective. This cannot be done as long as the Fair Employment Practice Committee lack sufficient funds and sufficient personnel to do the needed job.

FEPC Lacks Funds

"At the present time, the FEPC lacks funds and personnel to do the necessary following up on each of its orders. Trained paid investigators are needed to patrol every section of industry where discrimination is suspected or found. More cooperation from other government agencies responsible for war production is needed.

"The CIO Committee on Racial Discrimination is determined to press for these and all other measures to end this gross injustice and criminal waste of needed manpower. We intend to press for more funds and more authority for the FEPC. We plan to work closely with other government agencies and with employers in the solution of the problem.

"Victory requires the full effort of every person in this country and in the United Nations. Many millions of people among our allies are looking to our country to end inequalities that hold back a speedy United Nations victory."

CIO News, January 11, 1943.

97.   LABOR UNIONIST DISAPPOINTED IN LACK OF INTEREST

By Neil Scott

NEW YORK, Feb. 25--Philip Murray, James Carey and Lin Coe were in town last week to participate in the TWU Madison Square Garden Rally. On Tuesday I succeeded in getting an interview with Mr. Murray, the CIO president, which lasted for the better part of an hour and a half.

I asked Mr. Murray if he thought Negro leaders were giving the labor movement sufficient support.

Mr. Murray replied quite frankly "No." Then I asked why he thought Negro leaders were, as a general rule, so uncooperative. Mr. Murray indicated that he didn't believe the situation could be isolated to any one specific reason but was the accumulated result of numerous and varied attitudes and ideas concerning the trade union movement.

I then questioned if Mr. Murray would be willing to sit in conference

with a representative body of Negro leaders and work out a unified plan for
such common objectives as: destruction of the poll tax laws of the South,
lynchings, and the Dies Committee. Mr. Murray affirmed that he would be glad
to, and had been wanting to do just that for a long time.

Tragic Fact

Now it is a tragic situation which threatens us as a race that our
leaders cannot see the light of hope in organized labor. Even the most illiterate realize that the majority of colored people are unskilled and need
protection from exploitation. Our American heritage has been that of the scab
and forcefully exploited worker. This has been the case largely because
colored men even to this day, have not learned the power of organization.
We have not learned to combine our strength with our friends, regardless
of the color of their skin and fight for a common victory. Every Southern
white man is not a poll taxer and all Northern white men don't feel the same
as Abraham Lincoln. The colored man, north and south, must find his true
friends and then work toward a common goal.

Unionism Has Virtues

Despite many glowing examples to the contrary, unions represent the
medium through which members of the working class, colored and white, can
combine to protect themselves from the brutal lashes of their would be masters.
The manufacturers' association represents a medium through which managements
can operate to keep the working class unorganized and subjected. Manufacturers
have many other mediums--the anti-union press, and radio being the most potent,
while workers only have their unions. "A house divided cannot stand," and it
is equally true that workers divided because of race, creed, skill or color,
will be crushed by any and all who would dominate them.

Stormy Session

James Carey, secretary-treasurer of CIO, said that he was present at a
recent important meeting of colored leaders in Washington during which the
personalities were so hostile that they nearly broke up the assembly. I am
not taking Mr. Carey's statement as the only basis for my belief that even
our Negro leaders cannot get along among themselves. The papers have carried
in detail the difference of opinion between our Northern and our Southern
leaders. Leadership is not an easy capacity to assume. Leadership demands
of those who wear its girdle, correct guidance to a common goal. In the case
of the Negro, we assume that we all have one goal in mind--complete freedom.
Then what do our leaders have to quarrel about? Who is going to be leader of
the movement?   Who should be on the committee to wait on the President or
Mr. McNutt? Or is it, who is to be sergeant-at-arms? Certainly it could not
be for such reasons so petty, for the cause is too great and we've paid so
bitterly for our limited scope.

False Leadership

The fact that we have more than our quota of organizations is one of the
keys to our problem. These organizations are headed by self-styled philosopher
kings who hold their positions by right of "divine authority." These organizations never hold an election of officers and are supported by the wealthy
of the North who own the run-away slave shops of the South. Let us finish
with so many organizations and establish an all-inclusive one. Let that
organization have regularly scheduled elections so that the people might
have their choice for leadership. Colored people could then move under one
leader toward one common goal. Then, for God's sake let this organization
support the union movement!

Pittsburgh Courier, February 27, 1943.

98. NEW HATE STRIKES FLARE UP

DETROIT, March 4 (ANP)--A new wave of protest against working with Negroes was spread by white workers at Packard Motor Car Company during the last two weeks as anti-Negro demonstrationists employed a new technique in "hate strikes" and G. James Fleming, FEPC investigator, pressed for an early hearing in this area.

The new technique calls for short stoppages while Negro workers are booed lustily by whites who ignore the pleas of foremen and union stewards to keep production rolling. All new Negro employees at Packard's are roundly booed as they enter the factory and union stewards report as many as four stoppages have occurred at the plant in a single day because whites protested working with Negroes.

Pittsburgh Courier, March 6, 1943.

99. OSCAR NOBLE TO VICTOR REUTHER (BOTH OF THE[140] UAW WAR POLICY DIVISION), JANUARY 5, 1943

Dear Victor:

Attached is a report that was gathered by the Urban League and our own Research Department covering some 85 plants within this area as to the total number of negro women employed. There is also a confidential report attached. Guard this report as it is not for publication.

These reports along with the report of the Board of Education will give as complete a picture of the available manpower as it is possible to get at this time.

NEGRO WOMEN EMPLOYEES

Ford Rouge	150		12-23-42
Ford Willow Run	7		12-23-42
Packard	6		1-5-43
GMC - Cadillac	none		1-4-43
Chrysler Dodge Main	none		1-4-43
Ford Highland Park	2		12-23-42
Hudson all plants	10	(mostly matrons and government inspectors)	1-4-43
Briggs-Conners	2	(as gov't inspectors)	1-4-43
Chrysler Highland Park	none		1-4-43
GMC-Ternstedt	none		1-4-43
Murray Corp.	250		12-23-42
U.S. Rubber Co.	none		1-4-43
GMC-Detroit Diesel	none		1-4-43
Briggs (Mack and Meldrum)	40	(wives of draftees)	12-23-42
Ex-cell-O Hamilton	15	(matrons and non-productive)	1-4-43
Square D Co.	6		12-23-42
Burroughs	none		1-5-43
N. A. Woodworth	none		1-5-43
Kelsey Hayes Plymouth	18	(expect more soon)	1-4-43
Bendix Corp.	none		1-5-43
Chrysler-DeSoto (Wyoming)	30		1-4-43
Chrysler-DeSoto (War)	none		1-4-43
GMC-Fisher Cen. Engr.	none		1-4-43
Parke Davis	no information		
Holley Carburetor	none		1-5-43
HyGrade Food Prod.	300		1-4-43
Nat'l Auto Fibres	20		12-23-42

NEGRO WOMEN EMPLOYEES (Cont'd.)

Bohn Aluminum	40	12-23-42
Eureka Vacuum	no information	
Essex Wire	none	1-4-43
Farmcrest Bakeries	none	1-4-43

UAW War Policy Division, Walter Reuther Library of Labor and Urban Affairs, Wayne State University.

100. TO ALL
NEGRO FORD WORKERS!
YOUR FUTURE IS WITH THE CIO!!

At the present time the UAW-CIO is conducting a strike against the Ford Motor Company in order to settle discharges, grievances and discriminations. We did not want to strike the Ford Plants. We hoped that our just grievances could be settled around the conference table in a peaceful and democratic manner. The Ford Motor Company evidently does not believe in true collective bargaining that has lawfully been established by the Wagner Act. The company did everything it could to provoke a strike. The discharge of eight (8) committeemen by the company touched off the spark that led to the present strike.

THE FORD MOTOR COMPANY IS UNAMERICAN!

The Ford Motor Company has been found guilty of violating the federal Wagner Act by the Labor Board. The board's position has been upheld by the District Circuit Court and the United States Supreme Court. The Ford Motor Company has been ordered to rehire over a thousand workers with full back pay.

FORD IS NO FRIEND OF THE NEGRO!

The Ford Motor Company has played no favorites in firing Ford workers. Negro Workers as well as white workers have been fired who have dared to improve their status as workers by using their democratic rights of joining a Union.

Today the Ford Motor Company along with the AFL is posing as the champion of the Negro people. The present role that the company is playing is not new to the labor movement. Employers have always tried to divide the workers on racial, religious, nationality and other bases. Today the Ford Motor Company is trying to pit the Negro workers against the white workers in order to attempt to break the strike of the UAW-CIO. The Negro must not allow the company to use them as strikebreakers. They must demonstrate to the world that they recognize the fact that the interests of Negro workers are the same as the interests of white workers. You can strengthen the position of the Ford workers in their struggles by joining with them to bring the present strike at the Ford plant to a successful conclusion. Unity and solidarity of the Negro and white workers will lend to a splendid victory for the Ford workers.

"THE AFL STABS THE NEGRO IN THE BACK !!!"

Our message to you would not be complete unless we said something about the role that the American Federation of Labor (better known as the American Separation of Labor) is playing. The AFL is trying to use the Negro workers in a back to work movement in their futile efforts to break the strike of the Ford workers. These tactics on the part of the AFL are not new, they have performed the same role for the bosses on many occasions in the past.

The record of the AFL does not warrant the support of the Negro people.
The AFL has always followed what is commonly known as a "lily-white" union
policy. Negro workers have been barred from membership in many AFL unions.
This policy of discrimination against the Negro workers by the AFL has led
to serious unemployment problems for the Negro people. The most recent
racial discrimination against the Negro people is found in the Boeing Aircraft
Plant that has a closed shop contract with an AFL Federal Union which bars
Negro workers from employment.

"DO NOT BE MISLED!!"

Do not be fooled or misled by false promises on the part of the Ford
Motor Company or its agents including the agents of the American "Separation"
of Labor. These paid agents of the Ford Motor Company are trying to lay the
burden of the ill treatment of Negro workers on the organized labor movement.
Negro workers have been oppressed and exploited for many years by the bosses.
The CIO is the only labor union that has endeavored to end the persecution
and discrimination of the Negro worker in American Industrial Life. We do
not contend that our union is a cure all for all of the ills of the Negro
people. We do contend, however, that the UAW-CIO is the vehicle through which
the Negro worker can completely emancipate himself.

THE UAW-CIO HAS BENEFITTED THE NEGRO WORKER

In organized shops, the UAW-CIO has given the Negro worker a voice in
settling grievances and other conditions of employment by establishing
grievance machinery which enables the Negro worker to settle his grievances
with the full power and strength of the union. The union has established
"equal pay for equal work" for ALL workers, regardless of race, color, or
creed. The union has established a greater degree of security for Negro
workers through the establishment of seniority rules which govern hiring and
lay-offs. The union has given the Negro worker a higher standard of living
by establishing higher wages and vacations with pay. The UAW-CIO is not content to rest on its laurels. We know that our task will not be completed
until every worker in America can be guaranteed an opportunity of earning a
decent standard of living.

We wish to call upon ALL NEGRO WORKERS to rally behind the Ford workers
in their struggle for industrial DEMOCRACY. UNITED WE STAND--DIVIDED WE FALL!

> Ford Organizing Committee,
> United Automobile Workers of America,
> Affiliated with CIO

THE CIO IS YOUR ORGANIZATION !! "JOIN NOW!!"

Leaflet, April 3, 1941, Nat Ganley Papers, Walter Reuther Library of Labor
and Urban Affairs, Wayne State University.

101. TO ALL NEGRO FORD WORKERS

We of the Detroit Branch of the National Association for the Advancement
of Colored People are impartial towards your view of the Union in the Ford
Strike situation.

Our only purpose in this matter is to avoid race riots and bloodshed.

DO NOT BE USED AS STRIKE BREAKERS

Only those who have official passes should attempt to enter the plant.

Let this Strike be mediated peacefully by the government.

Flier, probably 1943, Nat Ganley Papers, Walter Reuther Library of Labor
and Urban Affairs, Wayne State University.

102.   TO ALL NEGRO FORD WORKERS

The Future of The Negro Worker is With the CIO!

THE NEGRO AND WHITE WORKERS IN THE FORD RIVER
ROUGE PLANT ARE ON STRIKE FOR:

A Seniority System
A General Wage Increase for All Employees
Immediate Reinstatement of All Workers Discharged for Union Activity
Abolition of the Ford Spy System
Recognition of the UAW-CIO as Sole Bargaining Agent
AN END TO THE HELLISH CONDITIONS IN THE FOUNDRY

Equal Benefits for Negro and White UAW-CIO Brothers !!!!!

60,000 Negro Workers ---

--Are Members, Stewards, Chief Stewards, Committeemen, Executive Board
Members and Officers of the UAW-CIO.

Don't Be a Strikebreaker !!!!!

The UAW-CIO is Fighting for Equal Rights for Negro and White Workers
Alike. No Color Prejudices--No Racial Prejudices.

Don't Scab for Ford !!!!!

60,000 of Your Organized Negro Auto Workers Call on You to

JOIN NOW !!!

You Are Invited to Become a Member Today By

LOCAL 600, UAW-CIO--9018 Michigan Avenue
Or at Any Local Union UAW-CIO Office

UNITED AUTOMOBILE WORKERS OF AMERICA, CIO
R. J. Thomas, President
George F. Addes, Secretary-Treasurer
Michael F. Widman, Jr., Director, Ford
Division

CIO IS BEHIND YOU--ONWARD TO VICTORY !

Flier, probably 1943, Nat Ganley Papers, Walter Reuther Library of Labor and
Urban Affairs, Wayne State University.

103.
BOARD MEETING MINUTES INTERNATIONAL EXECUTIVE BOARD
INTERNATIONAL UNION, UNITED AUTOMOBILE, AIRCRAFT
AND AGRICULTURAL IMPLEMENT WORKERS OF AMERICA, CIO,
SEPTEMBER 16, 1941

NEGRO COMMITTEE

President Thomas informed the Board that a committee of Negro workers
desired to appear before the Board to discuss the problem of employing Negro

workers on defense jobs.

Brothers John Conyers, Local Union No. 7; Samuel Fanroy, Local Union No. 7; Horace L. Sheffield, Local Union No. 600; Francis Glenn, Local Union No. 3; J. B. Hill, Local Union No. 490; Otto Johnson, Local Union No. 3; Theon L. Scott, Local Union No. 600; and Dan Carter, Local Union No. 600.

On behalf of the committee, Brother John Conyers asked permission to read the following letter:

Mr. Chairman and Board Members:

We, the committee, composed of Representatives from Dodge Local 3, Chrysler Local 7, Chrysler Local 490 and Ford Local 600 appear before this Board for the purpose of presenting discriminatory conditions as it applies to the Negro section of our International Union.

Our International Constitution and our contracts with these companies clearly states that there shall be no discrimination and promotion shall be based on seniority, also a supplementary agreement enters this picture with the National Defense. Transfers to the Defense Plants should be based on seniority and ability to do the work desired. We have Negroes with both of these requirements who have been constantly denied the right to work in this particular industry.

We have used every avenue of local procedure without any favorable results. It is the consensus of opinion of the Local Officials that this matter cannot be handled adequately by the Local Unions in question, due to many conflicting opinions, recognizing the rights of Negroes, coupled with the hesitation on the part of the Regional Directors to interpret this question in clear language, wholly understandable to the Local Unions. Such has created a situation where outside organization has been sought by the membership in the hope that they will furnish them the leadership, capable of leading them out of this situation.

The committee recognizes this as a union problem and fully believe that the International Executive Board should assume this responsibility, realizing that such has been the position of the Board in a number of other cases involving the welfare of union membership. In each case, the Board acted upon the authority invested in the constitution. While the present controversy may differ in content from previous stands on the part of Board, however, it does involve a question acknowledged by the constitution of our Union.

Therefore, it is only natural that we should come to the highest tribune of our International Union between conventions. With this question, may we further add that the lengthy controversy that has come around this question of defense work as it affects Negro Labor, should carry a public statement from our International Board, fully interpreting the policy of our Union and the position of our leaders on this matter.

Such a statement would serve to reaffirm the membership, together with outside forces that this was a Union problem and would be handled by the Union. It is not our intention here to be looked upon or referred to as a pressure group. Our presence before this International Board is representative of a legitimate grievance and we feel that the International Executive Board is the logical and proper place to bring a grievance, especially when Local Unions are reluctant to act on question of this nature.

Therefore, it is with this thought only, that we seek the audience of the International Executive Board. Having the above mentioned industries, we would appreciate that these workers from industries be heard.

Fraternally,

(Signed)

NAME	PLANT
John Conyers	Local 7
Samuel Fanroy	Local 7
Horace L. Sheffield	Local 500
Francis Glenn	Local 3
J. B. Hill	Local 490

NAME	PLANT
Otto Johnson	Local 3
Theon L. Scott	Local 600
Dan Carter	Local 600

The above mentioned members of the committee each stated their experience in the securing of transfer of Negro workers from non-defense work to defense work. (An itemized list of a number of cases refused non-defense work may be found in the files of the Secretary-Treasurer).

All stressed the fact they desired no special concession, but in the case of where a colored worker has seniority and is able to do a certain job he be given a chance to apply for defense work.

UAW Executive Board Minutes, September 15-23, 1941, pp. 19-21, R. J. Thomas Papers, Walter Reuther Library of Labor and Urban Affairs, Wayne State University.

104.   THE DETROIT RACE RIOT OF 1943

By Earl Brown

On Sunday, June 20, 1943, one of the most serious race riots in American history broke out in the city of Detroit. Before it was brought under control some thirty hours later, twenty-five Negroes and nine white persons were killed and property worth several hundreds of thousands of dollars had been destroyed.

The forces which led to the outbreak in that city exist, to a greater or lesser degree, in most of our cities. Similar outbreaks have occurred elsewhere. A study of the factors leading to the outbreak in Detroit is important because it can show us how to avoid similar outbreaks, not only in Detroit, but in other cities. . . .

My first visit to wartime Detroit occurred in July, 1942. I found that although Detroit is the munitions capital of the United Nations and its war production is essential to victory, there was a disturbing lack of unity of effort. The atmosphere was tense, and the tension was increasing. There were sudden gusts of strikes for unimportant reasons--a strike occurred at the Chrysler Tank Arsenal because the men were not allowed to smoke during work.

But racial feeling was the most alarming of all. Groups of Negro zoot-suiters were brawling with gangs of young white toughs; the determination of Negroes to hold the war jobs they had won was matched by the determination of numerous white groups to oust them. There were many signs of trouble.

Eleven months later, in June, 1943, came the Detroit riot, the most serious racial conflict in this country since the East St. Louis riot in 1917. Said Mayor Jeffries: "I've been conscious of the seriousness of the race problem here for more than a year." "We felt the riot coming," said William E. Dowling, the Prosecuting Attorney of Wayne County. "Race tensions have been growing here for three years."

Here is something of a mystery. If these responsible officials had reason to fear riot, why didn't they take steps to prevent it? Since continuous production of munitions is vital to the prosecution of the war, why didn't the federal government act? In March, 1943, a local newspaperman wrote to Attorney General Biddle about the critical state of affairs in Detroit. Mr. Biddle replied: "Your letter has received careful consideration, although it does not appear that there is sufficient evidence of violation of any federal statute to warrant action by this department at this time." The federal government did not act until nearly midnight on June 21, when President Roosevelt declared a state of emergency and troops began to patrol Detroit--long after the murder, the burning, and the pillage began. . . .

One of the features of Detroit that in many ways sets it off from many other cities is the presence of great numbers of religious and political fanatics. Even before the last war Detroit was known as the city of "jazzed-up religion." Today all shades of opinion are to be found in the city, all races, all creeds, all political attitudes and beliefs. The first figure to attract national attention was Father Charles Coughlin. Railing against Hoover and Wall Street from his radio pulpit, he soon attracted a great following in Detroit and through the Middle West. Next came the Black Legion, an organization of native white Americans and an offshoot of the Ku Klux Klan --with hoods, grips, and passwords. It was organized originally for the purpose of getting and holding jobs for Southern whites, but it quickly developed into an elaborate "hate" organization--its enmity directed against Catholics, Jews, Negroes, and "radicals." After the conviction of the Black Legion leader, Virgil F. Effinger, a former Klansman, for the murder of a Detroit Catholic named Charles Poole, the police had the clues to a long series of unsolved crimes which included several murders, arson, the bombing of Father Coughlin's house and the Workers Book Store as well as the homes of a number of labor organizers. An investigation by a grand jury resulted in the listing of eighty-six persons as members of the Legion. In this list were found names of a member of the state legislature, the manager of the state sales tax, a city treasurer, sheriffs, and other officials.

By the middle 30's Detroit had a representation of every kind of panacea, political nostrum, and agitation. There were the Anglo-Saxon Federation and an anti-Negro organization called the National Workers League. But the most steady, day-in and day-out exhortation came from the sensational preachers. Of these the best known are the Reverend J. Frank Norris and the Reverend Gerald L. K. Smith. Norris was born in Alabama and has held pulpits in a number of Southern towns. He was an energetic politician and brought his brimstone gospel clear to New York City, where he teamed up with the Reverend John Roach Straton and preached in a gospel tent west of Central Park. In 1935 he came to Detroit and took over the Temple Church, commuting to Fort Worth by plane in order to shepherd two flocks.

Gerald Smith has been even more active in politics than Norris. Smith was a minister and had a number of midwestern congregations before he went to Shreveport, Louisiana. He was great for muscular good will; he harangued luncheon clubs; he loved the radio; and then he fell for Huey Long. He fell so hard that he quit pastoring and became one of Huey's lieutenants, only to have his Share-the-Wealth ambitions paralyzed when Huey was killed. There followed a dismal period when the shepherd was busy looking for a flock among the Townsendites and other unhappy souls. Finally he showed up in Detroit as the founder and manipulator of The Committee of One Million, and in Detroit he has stayed ever since. Last year he ran for the Republican senatorial nomination on a "Tires for Everybody" platform and corralled comparatively few votes. But that has neither dampened his restless ambition nor stopped his noise. In April, 1942, he brought out the first issue of a monthly periodical called *The Cross and the Flag*. The magazine announced that its slogan was "Christ First in America" and recounted Smith's fight for justice and his numerous escapes from death by violence. Now he is trying to round up the remnants of the Detroit America First memberships into an American First Party.

These three men--Coughlin, Norris, and Smith--are the best known of the Detroit religious-political demagogues, but there are thousands of others. Some have been in Detroit for years; others came during the recent migrations. It is estimated that there are more than 2,500 Southern-born evangelists of one kind or another in Detroit alone, not counting those in near-by communities. This war has caused an upheaval among the little shouting sects in the South; they have split and split again, and new sects have been formed. When the flow to the war industry towns began, numerous piney-woods and sandy-bottom clerics went along representing the Last Days Church of God, the Church of God (Reformation), all brands of the Assemblies of God, the Firebrands of Jesus, the Pillar of Fire, the Pentecostal Baptists, the Christian Unity Baptists, the Two-Seed-in-Mind Baptists, and various splinters of the Holiness sects. One of the militant sects in Detroit is the American Bible Fellowship headed by a former Methodist preacher who refused to accept the merger of the Northern and Southern Methodist churches. Some of these pulpit-thumpers have gospel tents (complete with oilcloth signs, saxophone, and microphone); some have regular churches; some are radio preachers; the humbler ones have "storefront" churches or work in war plants and preach in their spare time.

There is a connection between the apocalyptic doctrine of these sects
and religious and racial intolerance. The appeal is not only highly emotional
but is grounded on old traditions--which in the South mean White Protestant
Supremacy. A local preacher described it this way: "Their forerunners for
generations preached from the crossroads and schoolhouses that 'Christ came
to His Own and His Own received Him not'--'His Own' being the Jews." On a
Friday night in January, 1943 at Missionary Tabernacle, the Reverend R. H. W.
Lucas said that Jesus had destroyed Jerusalem because it was a Christ-crucify-
ing city. The next Sunday morning it was stated over a national radio hook-up
that the history of the Jews for the last 2,000 years is proof that God punishes
a nation because of its sin. Many of these exhorters are members of the Klan
off-shoot organizations, defiantly "American," suspecting "radicals," and
completely at home with White Supremacy. For more than a decade--and increasingly during the past three years--these rustic preachers have been
spreading their brand of the Word. As feeling in Detroit became more aroused
over the race issue, the effect of this kind of preaching was like pouring
gasoline on a bonfire.

Feelings also have been kept on edge by labor conflicts. Detroit had
never been a union town, but in the bad days of the depression a number of
attempts were made to organize the auto workers. The Communists, through
their Trade Union Unity League, led four little strikes of auto workers in
January and February, 1933. Other groups made several attempts, mostly
futile, to organize the auto industry. These moves excited the alarm of
the local manufacturers, and the Detroit Union League called for strong
measures against labor agitation. Many prominent industrialists were members
of the Union League and its utterances were judged to be the voice of business.[14]

Efforts to organize automobile unions--in the shape of the Associated
Automobile Workers, the Automotive Industrial Workers Association, the Mechanics
Educational Society of America, and others--were increased after the passage
of the National Recovery Act. Gradually, the results began to show. The
early unions were consolidated into the United Automobile Workers (affiliated
with the CIO), and in October, 1936 the Chrysler Corporation recognized the
union. Early in 1937 General Motors also made a contract with the union.

Ford was left as the only big open-shop employer in Detroit. In order
to assure its position with the other firms, the new auto workers' union had
to organize Ford. It hesitated to act, however, not only because of the size
of the job but because of Ford's Negro employees. There were thousands of
Southern whites in the union, and it was too clear what their attitude toward
Ford's Negro workers would be. Further, many of Ford's Negro workers were
anti-union. They were loyal to Ford as the one big industrialist who would
hire Negroes.

When a Negro migrant from the South arrived in Detroit looking for a
Ford job, he generally discovered that it was a good thing to get a letter
from one of the Negro preachers before applying. Many of these pastors
warned the migrants against listening to talk about unions and urged them to
remember at all times that the one powerful friend the Negro had in Detroit
was Henry Ford.

For years Ford had maintained a private police and detective system,
and a part of the system was devoted to the oversight of Negro employees.
What Ford's colored workers did at home and during their hours of recreation
were matters of great interest to these Ford detectives. Organization of
Ford's colored employees by the union meant not only overcoming their devotion to Ford, but also combating the influence of the spy system. Finally,
in 1940, the campaign was undertaken. The CIO sent money and its best
organizers to help in the campaign. The full strength of the UAW was enlisted
in the effort, and the color line was declared to be a thing of the past.

The thing that eventually brought success in this campaign was an un-
expected strike, which was not initiated by the union at all. Once the
strike had developed, it became a question of whether Ford's Negro help at
the River Rouge plant would go out or stay at work and break the strike.
The union decided to make the strike official and redouble its efforts to
win over the Negroes. A group of prominent Negro citizens of Detroit urged
the Ford Negro employees to stand by the union. The result was a tremendous
victory for the union in the ensuing National Labor Relations Board election
and the collapse of the last opposition to the UAW. Today the largest union
local in the world is UAW--CIO, Local 600, the River Rouge Ford plant local.
It has about 90,000 members, of whom 18,000 are Negroes. . . .

It is interesting to note that despite the racial collisions and the
frequent enforcement of Jim Crow practices in Detroit, Negroes have succeeded
in getting some political preferment. There are two Negro assistant prosecuting attorneys, the State Labor Commissioner is a Negro, and one of the State
Senators is a Negro. The Detroit Street Railway Company, which is owned by
the city, employs about a thousand Negroes--both men and women--as motormen,
busdrivers, conductors, and workers of other kinds. With the police it is
another matter, and this has been a burning issue. Out of 3,600 policemen,
only forty are Negroes. In addition, Southern whites have been taken into
the force freely, and they have frequently shown a hostile attitude toward
Negroes.

The local political machine was perfectly willing to cooperate with
Negro gamblers, but they had no interest whatever in the fact that most of
Detroit's Negroes lived in two wretched slum areas. The two principal Negro
districts in Detroit cover about thirty square blocks on the West Side and
a larger district on the East Side called Paradise Valley. This latter name
goes back to First World War days and the wonder of $5 a day. "Goin' to
Paradise" meant going to a job that paid more money than there was in the world.
But the section did not look like Paradise in the beginning and it does not now.
There are few city areas in the United States more jam-packed. Hastings Street,
a dirty thoroughfare lined with dives and gin mills, is filled from dawn to
dark and until the small morning hours with a dense crowd. Here--on the East
Side--live most of Detroit's Negroes. Almost everybody now has plenty of war
wages to pay for lodging, but decent houses simply do not exist. The only
recourse the Negroes have is to cram themselves into the filthy valley tene-
ments. . . .

The war naturally aggravated Detroit's underlying instability. Anti-
Negro sentiment was particularly strong in the Polish districts of Hamtramck,
a suburb. As early as July, 1941, gangs of Polish paper youths provoked a
series of minor riots. An editor of a Polish paper reports that anti-Negro
handbills were distributed on the steps of St. Florian's Church in Hamtramck
during the Sojourner Truth riots.

For many months the Negro press in Detroit and elsewhere busily promoted
a "Double-V" campaign for victory at home as well as abroad. This campaign
was based on the assumption that victory in the war against the fascists
abroad did not mean much if there was Jim Crow at home. Colored soldiers had
told a thousand bitter stories of discrimination and lack of respect for the
uniform. The killings of colored soldiers at Alexandria, Louisiana, and in
other Southern communities were taken to heart. The hopes roused by President
Roosevelt's Executive Order 8802, issued June 25, 1941, forbidding job discrimination in plants with war contracts slowly faded. The Committee on Fair
Employment Practice, set up by the President shortly after the issuance of
the Executive Order, was left to pine away without money or authority and was
finally placed under the War Manpower Commission. If the government would do
nothing, there was nothing left but the union and the determination of the
Negroes themselves. Colored workers who had been promoted to more skilled
jobs were ready to hold on for dear life to their new jobs, and the brimstone
evangelists, viewing with alarm this resolution of the Negroes, whipped up
resentment.

Shortly after the beginning of 1943 a series of anti-Negro strikes broke
out in the plants. Aside from fights between individuals, there was no
violence in the plants, but much bitterness was aroused. The U.S. Bureau of
Labor Statistics lists anti-Negro strikes in the following plants from mid-
March until the end of May: United States Rubber Company; Vickers, Incorporated;
Hudson Motor Car Company; Hudson Naval Arsenal; and the Packard Motor Car
Company. In the Packard strike, which brought the climax, 26,883 men left
work when three Negroes were upgraded. The circumstances of this strike were
so peculiar that union leaders were convinced that it had been engineered by
one of the anti-Negro groups in the city, but nothing was ever proved.

Shortly after the Packard strike Mayor Jeffries called together the
editors of the three local dailies, the *Free Press,* the *News,* and the *Times,*
to take counsel. The conference over, nothing was done. A procession of
Negro leaders and a few prominent white citizens besought the Mayor to take
heed and act before the explosion. The Mayor listened, but appeared to be more
confused after these visits than before. Then everyone relaxed to await the
inevitable. It came on the evening of June 20, 1943.

Belle Isle lies in the Detroit River, connected with the city and Grand
Boulevard by a bridge. There were probably a hundred thousand persons in the
park that hot, humid Sunday, and the greater number seem to have been Negroes.
The atmosphere was anything but peaceful. Tension had increased to the
breaking point. An argument between a Negro and a white man became a fist
fight and the fighting spread.

A hurry call was made for the police, but by the time they arrived the
brawl, involving some two hundred white sailors by this time, was eddying
across the bridge into the riverside park on the mainland near the Naval
Armory. The news that fighting had broken out traveled like the wind. A
young man in a colored night club on Hastings Street is supposed to have
grabbed the microphone about 11:30 and urged the five hundred customers
present to "come on and take care of a bunch of whites who have killed a
colored woman and her baby at Bell Isle Park." The rumor was, of course,
false. It was matched by another story which spread through the white districts,
that Negroes had raped and killed a white woman on the park bridge. By midnight fighting and looting had spread into a dozen different districts and
Paradise Valley was going crazy. By two o'clock that morning a crowd of
Negroes stopped an East Side street car and stoned white factory workers who
were passengers. White men coming from work at the Chevrolet Gear and Axle
plant, three miles away from the center of Paradise Valley, were attacked by
a Negro mob.

Alfred McClung Lee, chairman of the Sociology Department of Wayne University and Norman Humphrey, Assistant Professor of Sociology at the same institution, have pieced together a remarkable time-table of the violence in *Race
Riot,* a report on the riot. Both the authors were present and moved about the
city while the fighting was in progress. Their report shows that:

At four o'clock in the morning (Monday, June 21) there was a meeting in
the office of Police Commissioner Witherspoon to determine action. Mayor
Jeffries, Colonel Krech (the U.S. Army commander of the Detroit area), Captain
Leonard of the Michigan State Police, John Bugas (in charge of the local office
of the F.B.I.), and Sheriff Baird were present. Colonel Krech told the Mayor
that the military police could be on duty in Detroit in forty-nine minutes after
a request from the Mayor had been cleared through the Governor and the proper
U.S. Army officials. Nothing was done about this at the time, and by 6:30 A.M.
Commissioner Witherspoon decided that there was a let-up in "serious rioting."[142]

But there was no let-up. At 8:30 in the morning a Negro delegation asked
the Mayor to send for troops. At nine o'clock Commissioner Witherspoon asked
the Mayor for troops. Mayor Jeffries telephoned to the Governor, who trans-
mitted the request by telephone to the Sixth Service Command Headquarters in
Chicago. By eleven o'clock it was known that troops could not come unless
martial law was declared. Governor Kelly hesitated to do so. By this time
gangs of white hoodlums were roaming the streets burning Negro cars.

The police had already shown themselves to be helpless or negligent. On
the previous night, police had been stationed outside the all-night Roxy movie
theater. A witness reported that a threatening white crowd assembled at the
entrance and every time a Negro came out of the theater the mob went for him.
When the witness asked the police to get Negroes a safe-conduct through the
mob, the officers replied, "See the chief about it!"

At four o'clock on Monday afternoon Major General Aurand arrived from
Chicago. By that time, according to Lee and Humphrey, "the crowds of whites
were increasing in size on Woodward Avenue. Milling packs of human animals
hunted and killed any of the easily visible black prey which chanced into the
territory."

At 6:30 Monday night, just as Mayor Jeffries was going on the air with
a plea for a return to sanity, four white boys, aged 16 to 20, shot down
Moses Kiska, a middle-aged Negro, "because we didn't have anything to do."
Still no troops, and all through the evening, after even the Mayor had admitted
that the city administration and police were unable to deal with the situation,
there went on an endless amount of official confusion until, at last, it was
discovered precisely what had to be done to get federal intervention. Just
before midnight President Roosevelt proclaimed a state of emergency, and by
Tuesday morning 6,000 troops in trucks and jeeps were patrolling the city.
The hold of the city authorities had so completely collapsed that it took the
United States Army to get twenty-nine Negro members of the graduating class
of Northeastern High School away from the closing exercises in safety.

Two days later Governor Kelly decided to ease restrictions a little, and by degrees the city began to breathe again. On Monday, June 28, Commissioner Witherspoon made a report to the City Council justifying his conduct and that of the police. "This was not believed to be the proper time," he said, "to attempt to solve a racial conflict and a basic antagonism which had been growing and festering for years. Such a policy could well have precipitated a race riot at a much earlier date and one of much more serious proportions. The fact remains that this department did not precipitate the riot."

Councilman George Edwards urged that a grand jury be called to investigate fifteen unsolved murders. Both the Council and Police Commissioner rejected the idea.

"Don't get the impression that I'm afraid of a grand jury," Commissioner Witherspoon said, "but it would be an unfair position to put any judge in." In the end the Council smothered any action likely to uncover unpleasant facts, but it did appoint a five-man committee to plan and finance new housing and recreation facilities.

In the succeeding days and weeks there was much dodging of responsibility. The easiest "out" was to blame the Negroes, and this was done. On June 30, Mayor Jeffries said that he was "rapidly losing patience with those Negro leaders who insisted that their people do not and will not trust policemen and the Police Department. After what happened I am certain that some of these leaders are more vocal in their caustic criticism of the Police Department than they are in educating their own people to their responsibilities as citizens."

Shortly after this, Prosecutor Dowling was visited by some members of the Mayor's Interracial Peace Board. Apparently unaware that a reporter was in the room, the Prosecutor not only announced himself as opposed to a grand jury but declared that in his opinion the National Association for the Advancement of Colored People and the *Michigan Chronicle,* the local colored weekly, were responsible for the riot. The report of the Governor's investigating committee, issued August 11, also attempted to whitewash the local authorities. In the official statements about the riot no real effort has been made to deal directly with the more obvious reasons for it.

One of the most extreme proposals for meeting the situation came from Attorney General Biddle--a proposal that has cropped up in other circles. It will be recalled that in the previous March he had written to a Detroit reporter that he, the Attorney General, could see no basis for action by the Department of Justice. But on July 15, he wrote a letter to President Roosevelt in which he suggested "that careful consideration be given to limiting, and in some instances putting an end to Negro migrations into communities which cannot absorb them, either on account of their physical limitations or cultural background. This needs immediate and careful consideration. . . . It would seem pretty clear that no more Negroes should move to Detroit. Yet I know of no controls being considered or exercised. You might wish to have the recommendations of Mr. McNutt as to what could and should be done."

In commenting on this statement, John Chamberlain, economic and political specialist, declared that: "Only a severe case of emotional shell-shock could have pushed Attorney General Biddle into suggesting that Negroes be chained to their places of abode, for all the world as if they were serfs on medieval manors, or slaves on the Roman *latifundia.* In Booker T. Washington's day the Negro might have taken Biddle's suggestion lying down. But no longer. Every Negro leader of any importance stresses the necessity of being polite but firm in insisting on the full protection of the Bill of Rights. This time the Negro is not going to be smacked down without making a fight of it."

Earl Brown, *Why Race Riots: Lessons from Detroit* (New York, 1944), Public Affairs Pamphlet No. 87, pp. 1-3, 6-11, 14-15, 18-24.

105. UAW-CIO PRESS RELEASE, JULY 27, 1943

Statement by R. J. Thomas, president, UAW-CIO

"Prosecutor William E. Dowling's statements are the most serious incit-
ation to race riots we have had since the riots themselves. They contribute
nothing toward solution to Detroit's racial problem. They sound like the
hysterical alibi of a public official who either cannot or will not do his
duty.
     "I have said before that all hoodlums, regardless of color, who were
responsible for the tragic riots should be punished. If Dowling has any
evidence pointing to Negroes as instigators of the riots, I am sure the decent people of the Negro community will join with the non-colored citizens of
Detroit in approving the prosecution.
     "If Dowling believes that the National Association for the Advancement
of Colored People is responsible for the riots, it is his sworn duty to present evidence before a Grand Jury and not to run off at the mouth in public.
I think the NAACP will welcome investigation of all factors in the situation,
including its own role.
     "It is up to Dowling to produce any evidence he may have against the
NAACP, but frankly I am of the opinion that he is attacking that organization
only to cover up his own ineffectiveness or unwillingness to act.
     "The NAACP is an organization of which all Americans, regardless of race
or color, may be proud. It includes among its warm supporters and members
Wendell L. Willkie, Judge Ira W. Jayne, Justice Frank Murphy, General Theodore
Roosevelt, and Herbert H. Lehman.[143]
     "The NAACP is a trouble-making organization in the sense that any organi-
zation that protests against injustice is a trouble-maker, in the sense that
unions are trouble-makers for unfair employers, and in the same sense that
those who believe in liberty are trouble-makers for Hitler.
     "We must have a Grand Jury investigation of the causes and incidents
of the tragic race riots. Thirty-five people cannot be killed in the streets
of an American city without thorough investigation and punishment.
     "It is obvious, however, that Mr. Dowling's office is not the one to
conduct such an investigation. We need a fearless, highly competent attorney
who will not be subject to political or racial pressures of any kind.
     "I suggest that a Grand Jury be constituted and that the American Bar
Association be requested by the City of Detroit to recommend a special prosecutor. He should not come from Detroit. Our choice of such an attorney
will not be a reflection on Detroit but rather an indication to the country
that we are anxious to have an investigation without restriction and without
interference from any individuals or pressure groups."

United Auto Workers of America War Policy Division, Walter Reuther Library
of Labor and Urban Affairs, Wayne State University.

106.   RACE HATRED IS SABOTAGE

     The mob violence and race hatred that have swept like a pestilence
through a number of American cities of late constitute the worst kind of war
sabotage.
     They have halted or diminished war production. They have caused many
deaths and serious injury to hundreds. They have turned Americans to fighting
each other instead of fighting the Axis. They have disrupted national unity.
They have furnished propaganda ammunition to the enemy to divide the United
Nations and to throw scorn on our country.
     Axis agents have unquestionably played a part in provoking this race
hatred and mob violence, which so closely follow the Fascist pattern and so
clearly do Hitler's dirty work.
     The authorities are working to hunt out such agents and their accomplices.
Drastic measures against them are essential for our national security.
     But it is equally important that all Americans should give thought to
the prejudice, discriminations and injustices that provide the powder to which
war saboteurs may set the match.
     Job discriminations, poll tax denials of political rights, unequal com-
munity treatment of racial minorities--these are some of the dark spots in
American life where race hatred is bred.

Organizations like the Ku Klux Klan, as well as direct Axis agents, whip this hatred into dangerous flames. And many Americans unthinkingly contribute to this war sabotage by repeating racial jibes and insults and spreading lying rumors from mouth to mouth.

The sound patriotism of the CIO's position on these questions is amply demonstrated by recent events.

The CIO opposed all forms of discrimination against minorities. It fights to abolish the poll tax and other denials of equal democratic rights.

Its unions organize all workers, regardless of race, creed, color or nationality. They fight for equal treatment and equal job opportunity for all. They carry on educational work against racial prejudice and intolerance. They seek to promote the closest fraternity between all racial and national groups.

This is true Americanism at any time. But it is also a war necessity that such a program should be promoted throughout our national life.

For only so can a recurrence of the recent disasters be prevented.

CIO News, June 28, 1943.

107.
CIO CONDEMNS RACE BIAS, URGES POLITICAL ACTION TO HELP WIN WAR

The last three of eight important resolutions adopted by the CIO Executive Board last week are printed in this week's CIO NEWS. The resolutions, which follow, outline in detail CIO's policy condemning racial discrimination, CIO's recommendation that affiliated unions intensify their legislative work to help win the war, and CIO's proposals for post-war planning, calling for "an income for everyone . . . adequate for health and happiness."

Let Congress Hear from You

WHEREAS, (1) During the past few months events in Congress and out have sharpened the issues before the nation and before the labor movement and have made clear the kind of fight which the CIO faces during the coming months.

Opponents of the Administration in Congress have made clearer than ever the motivation behind their program of sniping and general attack on the Administration's war activities and organized labor.

(2) These forces have opposed effective action to bring about real economic stabilization and to assure full protection against inflation.

They have harried and attacked the price control and rent control policies. They have impeded where possible the institution of grade labeling so necessary to real price control. They have impeded and seek to prevent the adoption of an effective subsidy program so necessary to the complete roll back of prices to the September 15, 1942 level.

They have slashed appropriations of important war agencies carrying on important functions on the home front. Their special targets of attacks have been such agencies as the OWI, the Office of Civilian Defense, the OPA, the National Youth Administration, the National Labor Relations Board, and the United States Employment Service.

They have also, as part of this entire drive enacted vicious anti-labor legislation such as the Smith-Connelly Act, and the emasculating amendment to the National Labor Relations Act.

(3) These are progressive forces in Congress, anxious to furnish their support to President Roosevelt's policies directed against inflation and for economic stabilization as indicated by the coalition of 50 Congressmen, which recently convened a conference of representatives of organized labor, consumer groups, and other interested organizations in Washington in the effort to stem the tide of opposition against the program of our Commander-in-Chief.

NOW, THEREFORE, BE IT RESOLVED:

(1) The CIO must recognize the need of directing its attention to ever more effective action on the legislative front.

Great progress has been made during the past year toward the awakening

of the CIO to the importance of these legislative issues. Legislative committees in local unions throughout the country have begun to function with
great activity because of the growing awareness that labor must act as effectively in the sphere of congressional action as it has heretofore in the sphere
of collective bargaining.

(2) It is extremely important that during the coming recess period of
Congress that the Senators and Congressmen be fully acquainted with the needs
and demands of their constituents and to make sure that on and after their
return to Washington in September Congress will be more attuned to the needs
of the nation.

Toward this end the CIO pledges itself that during this Congressional
recess it will seek to have organized in every community or Congressional
district in which there is CIO membership a conference of representatives of
organized labor, consumer groups, public and civic officials, all other
interested organizations to which the Congressional representatives will be
invited and at which there will be a full discussion and formulation of the
important policies covering our domestic front consistent with the CIO program.

In addition, such conferences should designate special committees to visit
and attend their Congressional representatives for the purpose of obtaining
assurances that their future legislative actions will be in support of this
basic program.

Plan for Peace: Jobs for All

Constructive plans must be made immediately for the months after the war
ends or the nation may suffer economic dislocation even more disastrous than
that of the early 1930's. Preparation for as orderly and speedy transition
to full consumption and employment is nearly as important as victory itself.
Yet Congress has killed the National Resources Planning Board without holding
any committee hearings on its own on post-war problems.

A new agency should immediately be established to plan for peace at home.
War problems cannot be permitted to interfere with the essential minimum of
preparation in defense of the people's welfare in peacetime. The kind of
world we shall have five years from now is being shaped today by inaction as
well as by conscious intent.

A planning body must be given power and responsibility not only to secure
material but, in cooperation with other agencies to draw up concrete detailed
proposals for action.

Otherwise prospects for the post-war period are bleak indeed. Although
the circumstances under which peace will come cannot be foretold exactly,
millions of workers will probably lose their jobs within a few months after
hostilities cease.

Millions of additional men and women will no longer be needed by the
armed forces and will wish to return promptly to civilian life. Although
there will be a large demand for goods, many huge plants will inevitably be
idle for six or nine months as they change over from war production.

The tremendous need for civilian supplies will not in itself guarantee
continued full production and employment. Even more likely than an immediate
depression, is an inflationary boom followed by collapse.

The nation cannot afford to risk such a disastrous outcome of war-time
sacrifices. The danger of economic chaos exists, and therefore must be faced
and averted. Some businessmen and some state and local governments are making
post-war plans on aspects of the problem that are within their own control.
Many governmental and private agencies are studying the question.

Federal Action Needed

But useful as such activities may be, they are far from sufficient for
grappling with a matter of basic importance to the entire nation and affecting
every aspect of its existence. Only the federal government can act for the
nation as a whole and can effectively control economic forces that ignore
state lines.

In rebuilding its economy on a peacetime basis, the nation should seek
not merely avoidance of disaster but the achievement of positive goals which
our productive resources now make possible. These should include:

1. Peacetime jobs as soon as possible for every one, including former
members of the military forces and former war workers.
2. Production of adequate supplies needed here and abroad to maintain
decent levels of living.
3. Improved facilities for education, medical care, recreation, housing,
transportation and so forth.
4. An income for everyone, including the unemployed, adequate for health
and happiness.
5. Full, stable and efficient production and employment, with prevention,
of both inflation and business depressions.
6. Participation by all Americans in political and economic decisions
that affect their welfare.
7. Cooperation with other nations to give all peoples everywhere a
chance to earn a decent living, to enjoy democratic institutions and to live
at peace.

Wipe Out Race Discrimination

The current wave of race riots is seriously endangering the war effort.
The Mobile riot, the Beaumont, Texas, riot, the Detroit riot are but manifestation of an American brand of fascism that is as great a menace as the
Japanese or Nazis. In every instance the riots have followed the familiar
pattern of dissemination of false rumors, the occurrence of a provocative
incident, and the development of mob psychology and hysteria.
The causes of racial tension and conflict arise out of fundamental defects in our democracy. Unless these basic causes are recognized by the entire
nation and effective measures adopted and pursued to eliminate them, racial
conflicts in other crowded industrial areas are inevitable.
Labor must recognize that the forces which foment racial strife are
identical with those that would destroy the organization of the labor movement.
As a means of strengthening democracy and for its very self-preservation,
labor must wage an all-out attack on these disintegrating forces and deal
resolutely with the basic causes in its day-to-day operations.
The absence of conflict in the shops during the recent Detroit riots is a
tribute to CIO leadership in Michigan.
Curative measures are not sufficient. A nationwide program of prevention
is imperative. It must include every segment of our community life.
The CIO through its National Committee to Abolish Racial Discrimination,
working with similar committees set up in our industrial union councils must
make real the basic racial policy of the CIO throughout every community in
which we are organized.

Positive Program

It is incumbent upon the National CIO Executive Board to recommend to the
Federal government that it recognize the conditions that lead to race riots
and take the initiative in formulating a positive program to eliminate these
conditions both in government and outside it. Such a program should include
the following:
1. Development of an overall program for the various Federal agencies to
include full and complete support for the President's Fair Employment Practices
Committee, with White House directives to these agencies for the carrying out
of the program.
2. A national radio broadcast by President Roosevelt on the program,
outlining the situation and the remedies that the Federal government is to
undertake.
BE IT RESOLVED, That the Executive Board of the CIO goes on record again
sharply condemning all evidences of mob hatred and violence against Negro
citizens and people of other minorities, wherever they occur or under whatever
circumstances.
We petition President Roosevelt to order the Department of Justice and
other appropriate agencies to make the fullest investigation of the origin and
perpetrators of these outrages, with special attention to the presence and
activity of Axis agents among them, to punish those guilty with the utmost
severity, and to proceed immediately against such individuals as Gerald E.
Smith of Detroit and the Ku Klux Klan who have notoriously been fomenting the

very mob hatred and violence against Negro citizens and people of other
minorities.

We express our solidarity again with our Negro fellow citizens and fellow
workers, and renew our fight against discrimination and persecution of any of
our people as a necessary part of our common fight against the enemies of our
country and of the United Nations.

CIO News, July 19, 1943.

108. CITIZEN CIO

By Willard Townsend

*The distinguished president of the United Transport Service Employees of
America describes the efforts of the Congress of Industrial Organizations in
combating racial prejudice and discrimination in labor movement and the war
effort.*

One of the bright spots, in an otherwise dark picture of race riots,
lynching, job discrimination, and the brutal treatment of the Negro in the
armed services, is the aggressive fight being waged by the Congress of Industrial Organization along the racial front. Today the CIO has two new powerful
weapons in its battle against discrimination--the Committee to Abolish Discrimination, formed to eliminate racial discrimination within its own ranks;
and the National CIO War Relief Committee, set up to administer the collection
of war relief funds from organized labor.

The CIO War Relief Committee, in existence two years before the Anti-Discrimination Committee, collected more than $17,000,000 last year for relief
to the United Nations. But vastly more important is the fact that half of
this enormous fund goes to local community agencies in 400 cities throughout
the United States. And now that the organized labor movement has entered
the fund-raising field, CIO can bring its powerful forces of five million mem-
bers--500,000 of them Negroes--to the fight against racial discrimination in
the new field of social agencies.

This development should be acutely the concern of Negroes. For the CIO
holds that since there was no color line in the shops and factories when
Negroes and whites alike pledged "one hour's pay a month" to raise war relief
funds, there certainly should be no discrimination in the administering of the
funds directed to local community agencies.

How does the CIO implement its declared policy of "no-discrimination"
among the social agencies with whom it deals, and those who are beneficiaries
of organized labor's contributions?

Listen to Monroe Sweetland, national director of the CIO War Relief Committee. "From its inception," he declared, in a speech before the Secretaries
of the YMCAs boldly scoring race separatism, "the CIO broke with much of American labor's tradition and has tackled this horny problem--of race discrimination
--and segregation--where it hurts--at the job level. By bold insistence on a
pan-racial membership and employment policy, CIO defied the whole tradition of
segregation and 'keeping the Negro in his place' by affirming that the place of
the Negro worker is alongside the white worker--and with no 'but' clause to
provide regional or individual escape."

Anti-Negro elements have taken advantage of this policy, he said, "We have
lost important labor board elections to other labor groups because the voting
workers were whites whose prejudices were aroused. We have had internal revolts among white workers against the first Negroes who went to work. But by
educating and fighting on this basic issue there are today literally hundreds
of thousands of Negro families whose wage-earners work at union scales in
American industry.

"If a new organization on the American scene like the CIO," he challenged,
"without friends or security, can accomplish this much in seven years, why
can't the powerful YMCA do as much in its field?

"The YMCA can do much, not through a segregated, Jim-Crow set-up, but by
leading the community in pulling our various racial and national strains
together."

He asked: "Are we right in our estimate that generally the YMCA followed
community prejudice and custom, instead of leading away from them?

"Isn't this the year to abolish Jim-Crow restaurants and dormitories in
your institution everywhere?"

Policy Produces Results

Such a policy has produced tangible results. By the end of 1943, three
thousand CIO representatives—Negro and white—will be serving on the directing boards of social agencies and relief organizations. The catalogue of
agencies includes everyone from Boy Scouts of America to YMCA, to visiting
nurses. These CIO people are attending luncheon meetings, round table discussions, talking with men and women who have been consistently guilty of
Negro discrimination.

The full weight of the CIO's progressive policies is felt at these meetings. Thus, these labor representatives—Negro and white—allow no Jim Crow-
bookkeeping or racial differentials by social agencies when relief money is to
be spent. They insist—with the organized power of the CIO backing them—
that Negro social agencies receive adequate appropriation and that other
social agencies give increased services to Negro recipients. They are keenly
aware of the need.

These activities extend to war agencies. Last year CIO members gave
$4,000,000 to USO. It was the largest single contribution on that organiza-
tion's books, and with the money went labor's pledge, "Our funds shall not
support any kind of minority discrimination." Men in uniform—white and
Negro—listen to juke boxes, dance, read magazines, every night at labor's
first USO canteen, built and operated by CIO and AFL in Philadelphia. White
and Negro girls act as hostesses. For before construction started on the
canteen, labor reminded USO officials that there could be no segregation or
exclusion of Negroes in any labor canteen.

This development is not localized. In Detroit members of the Women's
Auxiliary—again Negro and white—of the United Automobile Workers CIO are
serving doughnuts and coffee at the "John R" USO center for Negroes; enter-
taining some fifty thousand servicemen who have visited the club during the
last six months.

Supplied Musical Instruments

Sweet music in CIO's ears is the topnotch bugle and drum corps of the
514th Negro regiment at Fort Meade, Md. At the request of the men stationed
there CIO furnished 27 bugles, three big drums for the corps—a number of the
men in this outfit were former members of the big "name" bands. Colonel Krokus
at Fort Meade wrote to the CIO War Relief Committee, "I know of no other medium,"
he said, "by which the morale of our men could have been brought to its present
high level. The new bugle and drum corps in a short time should rank with some
of the best in the country."

CIO goes in for interior decoration at Army posts, too, where this will
help the morale of the troops. At most camps the Army sets aside recreation
rooms but makes no provision for furnishing them. At least half of the money
the CIO spends on Army interior decorating goes to Negro camps, because at
many posts Army indifference and Jim-Crow communities leave the Negro soldier
with no place to spend his leisure time.

CIO did its first interior decoration job at Camp Butner in North Carolina,
where Negro soldiers are stationed. Before being refurnished, Monroe Sweetland,
National Director of CIO's War Relief Committee, visited in one of the recreation rooms there. He found cobwebs along the walls, a rusty potbellied
stove, a large and shabby newspaper rack, with only two newspapers. He went
shopping with some five hundred dollars, and he bought davenports, easy chairs,
material for drapes, card tables, reading tables, radio, phonographs, two
pianos, band instruments and subscribed to a number of newspapers.

War relief funds of CIO people also aid the colored peoples abroad. There
are 10 million Negro French subjects today sharing in the Free French relief

funds to which CIO contributes. There are 6,500,000 Negro Frenchmen in
French Equatorial Africa, the most vital strategic area on the African continent. Added to them are 4,000,000 natives and refugees in Syria and Lebanon,
on Tahiti and New Hebrides in the Pacific and Martinique at the foot of the
United States.

They receive food, clothing and medical supplies to help them continue
their fight for freedom. The world knows the courage of the natives of French
Equatorial Africa under M. Felix Ehoue, its black governor-general and of the
courage of the Sengalese troops who fought for the old France and now under
the banner of the Free French movement.

The CIO War Relief Committee's Servicemen's Manual, an item that acquaints
the soldier with his civilian rights, which has been distributed to more than
a hundred thousand servicemen, speaks plainly on the race question. The 34-
page booklet tells the man in uniform about his special civil and military
rights and what his status is when he returns to civilian life after the war.
The section entitled "United We Stand; Divided We Fall," is an eloquent plea
for racial equality and somewhat in line with the NAACP's request to the War Department that literature should be prepared for the servicemen about the race
problem.

Straight Thinking Needed

"Straight thinking is the duty of every citizen on the problems of
religious and racial prejudices"--runs a typical section. "The Nazi game is
to stir every racial and religious prejudice to try to divide the American
people. CIO men are doing much in the services and with the public to demonstrate by work and example the unity of all Americans against the Axis . . .
Hundreds of thousands of CIO members are among American minority racial and
religious groups. If you happen to be among them, you know your CIO is always
ready to go to bat to protect you against discrimination on the job or wherever
you may be."

While the National CIO War Relief Committee recognizes the rights of
white and Negro servicemen in the Army and Navy, CIO fights for racial democracy in the local unions and factories. That fight starts on the production
line.

CIO has adopted an aggressive "no discrimination" job policy to prove to
thousands of new workers that the democratic processes at work in the labor
movement make no distinctions because of race, religion, color or nationality.
The union knows that if it fails to utilize the skills and strength of every
American workman, it prolongs a bloody and destructive war. This line of
thinking was expressed at the November 1942 convention, when the CIO established its Committee to Abolish Racial Discrimination. Sincere, hard-fighting,
the Committee is tackling a rough job with vigor and courage. By demanding
full utilization of manpower in all industries, it has broken down racial
barriers that were a half century in the making.

The National Executive Director of the Committee is a Negro, George Weaver,
an officer of the United Transport Service Employees of America. He presents
CIO's position on racial discrimination to the press, to government and
industry, as well as among the rank-and-file of CIO people. He takes a stern
hand when international unions find it necessary to discipline union locals
and members who rebel when Negroes are given their full upgrading and seniority
rights. He insists that CIO locals take the lead in securing equal rights on
the job for Negro members.

Regional, state and local councils in CIO as well as local unions have
set up committees on fair employment practices and race relations. A further
safeguard against racial discrimination is the election of Negroes to serve
as stewards, shop committeemen, and as members of bargaining committees, labor-
management and grievance committees.

However, CIO's Committee To Abolish Racial Discrimination is opposed to
any form of departmental segregation because it "continues misunderstanding
and lack of sympathy between the two races."

George Weaver warns that management often attempts to use the Negro as a
pawn in management-labor controversies. Sometimes the Negroes become a football
in local union politics. "In most of the cases that the CIO Committee to
Abolish Racial Discrimination has investigated, we have found one of the above
factors present, in some instances both," he reports.

Meeting the Problem

Weaver has revealed the manner in which this problem has been met. At
the Timken Roller Plant in Canton, Ohio, for instance, twenty-seven Negroes
were suddenly upgraded by management without warning or system. The foremen
and shop stewards were not consulted, and the department picked for this
experiment was relatively new. The white workers, most of whom had been recently imported from the South, all had less than two years' union experience.
"The results were a foregone conclusion," Weaver relates in an article
in the Michigan CIO News. "A checkback on the labor-management relations record indicated that their labor policies were bad and they had fought the union
bitterly, step by step. The obvious conclusion was that management hoped to
create an additional problem with the racial issue."
The union, in this case the United Steelworkers, insisted that Negro entitled to promotion remain in the upgraded positions. The company, realizing
that it could not embarrass the union by these tactics, receded and demoted
the Negroes.
This act by the management brought a second walkout, this time on the
part of the Negroes. But the union and the Government settled the question by
insisting that those entitled to the upgraded positions retain their promotions.
The union has carried its fight against racial discrimination into the
Government. It is represented on FEPC by John Brophy, CIO's Director of
Industrial Councils.
CIO is doing vigorous work in teaching its own members that whites and
Negroes can work together harmoniously--and is proving it by day-to-day developments. During the Detroit riots, for instance, there was no trouble in any
of the shops where white men and Negroes worked on the assembly line. Nor
did fighting flare up in the neighborhoods where both races live peaceably
together on the same city block. Rioting broke out in the segregated neighbor-
hoods--the so-called "white spots" and the "black pockets." CIO took a lead
in exposing the causes of the riots and in calling for immediate action to
remedy those causes and to avoid future outbreaks.
This is the trend in the progressive wing of the organized labor movement
today. The Negro is not without white allies in his struggle for equality.

The Crisis, 50 (October, 1943): 299-300, 312.

109.   THE CIO AND THE NEGRO AMERICAN

By Monroe Sweetland

New jobs and classifications have been opened to thousands of Negroes
in war industries. These workers have found improved working standards and
security through their industrial unions.

To the American Negro the coming of the CIO has been the most important
historical experience in 75 years of struggle for a chance to live and achieve.
This is true also for millions of white industrial workers, but it is true in
double measure to the forgotten black workers of American industry.
Nearly all Negroes are workers in industry or agriculture. On the farm
there is still nothing approaching security for farmers, either black or
white. But in industry Negro workers were at a special disadvantage under the
old regime--they had neither jobs nor security. CIO, with its insistence on
equality, has meant that Negro membership in organized labor is today six
times what it was six years ago. With this has come opportunity for promotion,
seniority protection, recognition of ability, and increased and stable income.
Thousands of new jobs and classifications, heretofore for whites only, have
been opened to Negroes and other minority races.
There is a long, long row to be hoed before Negroes have anything like
equal opportunity, but the row is being hoed. No longer do you have to set
stakes to measure the progress. Support from Government, the press, and large

sections of white public opinion has been won by Negroes in the last 5 years.
Much of this support has grown out of the rejection by CIO of the self-defeat-
ing anti-Negro policies of the old regimes in American labor.

Until the coming of the industrial unions of CIO the comparative standards
of American Negro life had been only slightly ameliorated. In a number of
fields occasional Negro celebrities won recognition--all too often for themselves and all too seldom for the race. Occasionally a concession was wrenched
from the indifferent or hostile white majority, but by and large the gains
made in one salient would be cancelled off by set-backs elsewhere. A base for
future progress was laid in the improvements in Negro education, but the number
of college graduates among the porters, waiters and Red Caps of American railways bear testimony to the narrowness of opportunity. None of the palliatives
offered by the well-intentioned-acquaintance, good-will, proximity, or educa-
tion--provide any solution in themselves so long as the poison of economic
inequality is present. Democratic understanding grows out of job equality,
and is not a condition precedent to it.

Only with the coming of industrial organization in steel automobiles,
stockyards, packinghouse and other mass production industries where Negroes
are largely employed, did the clouds begin to lift for the scapegoat of American industry. The old, indisputable truism that the Negro was the "last to be
hired and the first to be fired" began to lose its validity. Today the Negro
worker finds tens of thousands of jobs open to him which heretofore were closed.
Even the labor shortages of the war boom would not have opened factory gates
for him had he not had the protection of the pan-racial policy of CIO. This
policy, together with the union grievance committee and seniority rating, make
many exceptions to the old truism.

The self-conscious period, when the Negro members were strange and new in
the CIO unions, is passing. The leaders of the CIO knew from the beginning
that their policy was to organize every worker, black or white, and that
effective industrial unionism was color-blind. But this theory did not take
effect gracefully, noiselessly and automatically. At the outset many unions
placed one Negro on the executive committee--usually as vice-president--with
a flourish of patronizing sponsorship. This period is passing rapidly, and
in the older locals we now find Negroes elected or defeated for union office
on the basis of their ability to do the job. A few Negroes have now been
elected to responsible offices in international CIO unions by preponderately
white membership. They also serve as shop stewards, and are on hundreds of
important grievance and negotiating committees.

There are many ragged edges on the race front in CIO. A smooth pattern
was not guaranteed by the national policy of equality. White men and women in
CIO ranks do not abandon automatically a life-time accumulation of prejudice
when they sign a CIO membership card; neither do all Negroes discard automatically all Uncle Tom-ishness in the presence of their white brothers and
sisters. For the most part the rank-and-file has accepted and supported the
policy of job equality.

Social idealism was not the overwhelming factor in bringing about CIO's
policy. It was the practical necessity of organizing all the workers into
one big union. The growing political power of Negroes in the Northern and
border states also assisted the development, although that power in turn is
reaching new pinnacles as part of the general labor movement.

It is no political accident that the first Negro member of the Michigan
Legislature is a member of the United Automobile Workers, elected largely by
labor votes, or that the first Negro member of the New York City Council is
elected on the American Labor Party ticket, or that the fight against the poll
tax, against the Red Cross blood-segregation policy, for decent Negro housing
and for abolishing Southern wage differentials has been led by CIO.

CIO has paid a price for its policy. More than one Labor Board election
has been forfeited to the AFL or to company unions because CIO locals stood
by their guns on the score of race equality. Only recently CIO's convictions
were tested in a bitter New Jersey aircraft election, where victory was of
great importance to CIO's aircraft drive nationally. Some compromise or
hedging on race policy was warranted here, the argument went, to insure other
open-shop citadels which would fall thereafter. But CIO stood its ground and
was defeated by a company union which waved the bloody shirt of white supremacy
during the campaign. In Detroit, Columbus, Indianapolis and other cities
the powerful automobile workers have been confronted with organized resistance

to their policy of equality. In some plants strikes occurred against giving
seniority to Negro workers, or against the first Negroes placed in skilled
jobs. But in every case R. J. Thomas, Walter Reuther, and the other leaders
of UAW-CIO have carried out the CIO policy by persuasion or by heavyhanded
discipline. R. J. Thomas, president of UAW, has risked the wrath of the un-
enlightened thousands of transplanted Southerners in his union by his firmness
in enforcing the union policy, and in pressing an educational program which
will make it understood by the shocked and bewildered Southerners.

But still CIO wins some two-thirds of its NLRB elections, and the battle
for pan-racial industrial unionism is being won. The AFL, under the impact
of CIO competition, has also relaxed its discriminatory policies. Some of
its affiliated international unions have large Negro membership, but the
powerful Machinists and most of the railroad affiliates still discriminate by
policy and practice.

The full effect of CIO's pioneering upon the life and character of America's Negroes will not be apparent for a generation. Already it has changed
the way of life of the million-and-half Negroes in CIO families, and for un-
counted millions of white Americans who see things differently because of their
experience in CIO.

CIO's policy has given the Negro a stake in American democracy he never
had before. The war may be won by that sound and courageous action. Every
Negro family which has won a degree of security and status in industry, which
has enough income to give its children a chance, and which shares in community
life, is an anchor of loyalty in a Negro population which has been rocked by
Axis propaganda. CIO's policy has already shown the Axis that Negro and white
America can live and work together in peace. CIO's policy has eased the tense
labor supply problem, which could never have been surmounted under the old
system of "whites only." In short, a substantial percentage of America's
Negroes now have something to fight for. It is very largely this hope for
the future which gives our polyglot nation the degree of unity we have achieved
in the midst of war. Only a beginning has been made. But in that beginning
hope is replacing fear--faith in the future replacing distrust--as the dominant
undertones in American Negro life.

Opportunity, 20 (October, 1942): 292,294.

110. CIO FIGHTS DRIVE AGAINST NEGRO WAR WORKERS

WASHINGTON, Mar. 4--A double-barreled polltaxer attack on the Fair Employment Practices Committee, which fights anti-Negro and other minority discrimination, shaped up in Congress this week, with an affiliate of the AFL playing
the shameful role of stooge.

In the Senate, the polltaxers, led by Sen. Russell (D., Ga.) are openly
seeking FEPC's abolition, through the familiar trick of cutting off its funds.
The pretense is that all FDR-established agencies must be subject to Congress
review after 12 months of operation; the real intention, as Russell admitted,
is to get FEPC.

The second barrel is being shot off in the House, where the Smith (polltaxer, Va.) smear committee is holding what it likes to call hearings on
whether or not the FEPC is "exceeding its authority" as a U.S. war agency.

With the exception of one member, Rep. John Delaney (D., N.Y.), the whole
committee is sure that the FEPC is committing a serious offense by trying to
get Negro war workers into war jobs where they are needed to keep up war output. 144

Also being smeared by the Smith gang is the War Shipping Administration,
which is "guilty" of assigning Negro seamen to ships carrying war cargoes.
And the sorry stooge that give them a dash of union color is the AFL's Sea-
farer's International Union, hollow relic of the old, corrupt and very dead
Intl. Seamen's Union that was sent to the junkpile by CIO's Natl. Maritime
Union some years ago.

The SIU, which has about 5,000 members on the east coast compared to the
NMU's 85,000, believes in anti-Negro segregation, admits it, and is proud of it.

John Hawks, one of its officials, said this during Smith committee testimony.

What's more, the SIU takes the amazing position that the FEPC and the War Shipping Administration are violating the President's order against discrimination by shipping Negro seamen together with white seamen, since this promotes "racial friction." The FEPC and the WSA, therefore, ought to be abolished, and besides, their officials are all a bunch of "fellow travelers."

Sharply contrasted with this is the NMU-CIO policy of an absolute ban on discrimination in the union and its record of Negro and white seamen working and risking their lives together with a total absence of friction.

This is what Frederick N. Myers, NMU vice-president, had to say this week in his testimony before the Smith committee, after he had pointed out that more than 8,000 of NMU's 85,000 are Negroes:

"Not one NMU ship has been delayed or missed a convoy because of a shortage of manpower. Our vessels have been fully manned with skilled and experienced seamen . . . We have been able to do all this by strict adherence to a policy of no-discrimination and by giving full opportunity to all seamen to make their contribution to the war effort, regardless of race, creed or color.

"The war has now reached the stage where a showdown is in the offing. The coming land invasion of Europe will call for a more extensive application of this policy than ever before. In such a perspective, there is no room for segregation or discrimination."

The lynch spirit being whipped up against Negro war workers isn't confined to the polltaxers in Congress alone. This week, the South Carolina state legislature passed a resolution praising the segregation policy and threatening to kick the "damned Northern agitators" out.

This resolution, written in the true Hitler style of race baiting, was loudly applauded by Sen. Smith (polltaxer, S.C.) on the Senate floor and was widely distributed to the daily newspapers by the Associated Press.

This is a campaign year, and every year polltaxers have tried to use race hatred to defeat the New Deal. This time there's also a war on, a war that Hitler tries to win by promoting race hatred in America and in all his enemies.

CIO News, March 6, 1944.

111.
SECOND CONVENTION OF THE UNITED STEELWORKERS OF AMERICA, 1944

Negro Steel Workers

During the war the number of Negro members of the USA-CIO has doubled. In 1940 there were approximately 35,000 Negro members of the union. Approximately 20,000 were members of local unions in steel producing mills and 15,000 were members in fabricating and processing plants. At the end of 1943 the Negro membership of the union had increased to 70,000 members. Roughly, half are in steel-producing mills and the other half in the fabricating and processing plants.

Since the inception of the union the employment of Negro workers in the steel and allied industries has steadily increased and their position inside the plants has been constantly improving. The war has increased the opportunities of Negro workers for greater employment and improved jobs in the steel and allied industries.

The policy of the USA-CIO from the outset has been to advance the interest of all of its members, regardless of race, color, creed or nationality. In a comprehensive study of ORGANIZED LABOR AND THE NEGRO, by Dr. Herbert R. Northrup, it was found that "the CIO and its constituent unions have sedulously adhered to (their) non-discrimination policy in organizing Negroes . . . (and) the national officers of the CIO unions have, by and large, a consistent record of practicing what they preach in regard to the treatment of Negroes."

In improving the position of Negro workers, the union's work and record have been outstanding. Following the 1942 convention, Boyd L. Wilson, international representative, was assigned to look into, survey, and assist in the solution of any problems which arise in connection with Negro members and potential members. Not only has the union improved the economic position of all of its members, but it has also afforded greater opportunities to the Negro workers in the steel and allied industries.

Throughout the duration of the war the union will continue to afford the full protection of collective bargaining to all of its members, white and Negro alike.

In the post-war period the union will likewise pursue its untiring efforts to extend the full protection of collective bargaining to all workers in the steel and allied metal industries. Seniority provisions of the union's collective bargaining contracts will be strictly adhered to without discrimination because of race, color, creed or nationality.

Resolution No. 9

Negro Steelworkers

WHEREAS, (1) It is a cardinal principle of our Union that all steel workers, regardless of race, creed, or color, shall be admitted into membership and receive equal treatment;

(2) We have not rested upon pious hopes or expressions but have effectively improved the economic conditions of the Negro steel workers and afforded the full protection of our Union to collective bargaining contracts to all of our members, white and Negro alike;

(3) Today more than ever as a demonstration of the full meaning of American democracy as against the practices of the Nazi regime, we must make certain that every vestige of Negro or other discrimination be eliminated from our national life; now, therefore, be it

RESOLVED, (1) Each member and officer of our Union must recognize his solemn obligation to prevent and eliminate the exercise of any discrimination within our organization, by any employer, by the government or elsewhere. We must persist with untiring efforts to protect all our members against any form of discrimination, because of race, creed, or color;

(2) This convention desires to express its vigorous condemnation of the specific acts of brutal treatment and vicious discrimination that have occurred or is being practiced against the Negroes in our armed forces and call upon responsible Army and Navy officials to forthwith eliminate this evil.

Substitute for resolutions submitted by Local Unions 65, 1011, 1299, 1330.

Committee Secretary Millard moved the adoption of the resolution. The motion was seconded.

Delegate J. R. Moore, Local Union 1331, Youngstown, Ohio: I rise to support this resolution. No doubt many of you in this hall remember many, many years ago when you white brothers caused strikes that the colored brothers were used as human guinea pigs and to break strikes caused by white brothers.

I am here to say that that era is passed. For years colored brothers were used to break strikes and for a time it seemed like that would be his only destination. But, thank God, things have changed. There was a time, as undoubtedly you all know, when many labor unions were getting organized he was looking for something he would be able to find and in looking he didn't find anything that was quite suitable to give him the situation that he was looking for. Then there appeared on the scene the Congress of Industrial Organizations and he thought for a time that this was not his salvation. But, looking forward and looking ahead and reading its constitution and the constitution of the International Union, he found that truly in trade unions, and especially in the United Steelworkers of America, this was, his salvation.

He immediately began to take steps to come into this great Union, and when he came in he found the doors open wide, he found that he was to take a part, not as a back-seat driver, but that he was to attain all the advantages he was ever able to attain, if he was able to do the job and do it in the right way. And to that end he came in and took his rightful place and in the United Steelworkers of America he found consolation and peace that heretofore had never been known to him. And in that peace he found that all he had to do was to qualify, and in his qualifications he gained the seat of high rank.

We wish to thank the International Union and the United Steelworkers of America for this great opportunity, for this privilege. We wish to thank them who have taken the stand on the armed forces which, no doubt, not one

of you in this hall have not read about and how Negro people in the armed
forces are being treated. That is what I like about the United Steelworkers
of America. When they believe in doing a job they do a big job. They will
bring satisfaction to every human being on the face of the earth. To them
and to our boys in the armed forces when the time-will come when they return
home again, we know that the United Steelworkers of America will keep that
light burning, not only burning, but it will be brighter, that they will
find the peace they are longing for and the comfort that they all need when
they return home.

Delegate Marsden, Local Union 2457: Mr. Chairman and the delegation, we
in America are just one great big American family, 130,000,000 strong, representing one of the greatest commonwealths on the face of the earth. We
realize that if we keep our shoulders to the wheel and the workers agree with
one another, there is no Axis power on the face of the earth that can defeat us.

I realize it is necessary to have the cooperation of the two races in this
country, and the only way to do that is for each and every one of us to be
fair to one another.

I thank God for the existence of the CIO. I thank God that it came into
the South to organize the workers in the South, because all of us have benefitted, white and Negro.

With the coming of the CIO into the state of Texas I was one of the first
Negroes in that state to get behind this movement. I said on this floor two
years ago that I hoped the time would come when the entire South would be
organized. I am happy to say that since that time we have made wonderful
progress in our District. The job is not done, but we are well on the way.
I am thankful for the effort that the CIO has put forward to eliminate discrimination in the plants throughout the country and in the armed forces.
This is going to be necessary in our war effort. It is going to be necessary
that all manner of discrimination be eliminated, because it is so vitally
important to the thing that we are trying to do.

I am glad to speak in behalf of the resolution, and I thank you.

Delegate Sallie, Local Union 1557: Unless this resolution is carried
back home, not by word and not by deed, but physically, it is not going to be
worth the paper it is written on.

There has been a seniority clause in our contract since the inception,
back in 1937, but that seniority section was an empty clause so far as the
Negro worker was concerned. He would move so far, then stop. Other workers
would come in and detour around him. In the last two years it has been possible, through the process of education in the various groups, to bring about
a reality as far as seniority was concerned. But then what happened? Whenever a Negro was placed on a job, especially when it upgraded him, the other
boys decided they wanted to go out on strike. What for? To stop a fellow
member from progressing.

I can speak from experience on this particular angle because it happened
to me. So you see the job is up to the membership of the Union itself to
solve this problem.

In the course of two years we had eighteen cases that went into the fourth
step dealing with seniority, and each one of those cases was turned back--"no
ability"--in spite of the fact that some of the men had as much as twenty-
five years, had worked at the job effectively seventeen or eighteen years,
but yet "no ability," and the cases were turned down. Within the last year
we have been able to advance exactly one man to the top in a particular department.

We had a stoppage a few months ago dealing with the very same problem,
but now there has been set up a promotional sequence and the boys are beginning
to move. But they can't move if the rest of the boys decide they are not going
to by shutting the plant down. So if we are going to stick together we will
have to do it that way or else hang separately when this thing is over.

Delegate Branzovich, Local Union 2726: I was going to talk on the same
line as the brother who just spoke. Now I will have to change my little talk.
What I want to bring out is that some of our labor leaders, for some reason
or other, hesitate to put into effect a clause of no discrimination because of
race, creed or color. They use little, petty arguments that they may cause corruption within a Union. I don't think so, because a number of times things
like that have come up in our Local, and if the white brothers get behind the
colored brothers I don't think there will be any corruption.

As the colored speaker just pointed out on that, what really is lacking
is a real understanding of the problems of the colored people. We are taking
an interest in it, because in my opinion I don't think the white brothers
wholeheartedly want to discriminate against the Negroes of our Locals, any more
than you or I or anyone else. Under our own constitution they have the same
right we have, because they are American citizens.

I firmly believe, as the last speaker pointed out, that if everyone of us
will get behind it, not in lip service but in reality, it is possible that
with the poll tax bill coming up and with the possibility that Negroes will
be permitted to vote and express their opinions, in the future we can have a
greater Union, with more representation by the colored people. I think if we
all get behind it we can have a successful organization.

Delegate Owen, Local Union 1044: Mr. Chairman and delegates, I am happy
to be within your midst. Some of the things I had in mind to say have been
covered by other delegates, but there is one particular point I would like to
bring out, and before I get to that I want to say something else. I have been
in the labor movement for over twenty-seven years. Our wonderful President
was my President years ago in the coal fields of Pennsylvania, District 5. I
was on the picket line when John _____ and Fanny Sellins were shot down in
Brackenridge. I have followed the labor movement from there to the steel mills.[145]

In 1917, at the Allegheny-Ludlum Steel Company in Brackenridge there were
only two colored persons working at that time, and when that strike was called,
as the brother mentioned a few minutes ago, you know and I know that the
industry went throughout the length and breadth of this country and brought
Negroes here in order that they defeat the progress of organized labor. Some
of you called them scabs, etc., at that time, but they were not union men, they
had no other chance to advance, and they took the jobs for the betterment of
their own conditions at that time because they were not welcome in the ranks
of organized labor.

We are happy that organized labor has awakened to the fact that no substantial progress can be made unless all of us pull together, not from the
standpoint of lip service, but from our hearts.

You delegates must have some influence, you must have a certain measure
of intelligence, otherwise you would not have been elected over and above the
rest of the membership of your Local Unions. We can resolve and whereas from
now until doomsday. I am heartily in cooperation with this resolution and I
intend to vote for its adoption, but here is what you delegates can do: You
can go back home, as I have heard said so often here, and roll up your sleeves.
Within this great organization we have locals where a Negro as a skilled man
cannot get a job. That is true of the puddlers in the wrought iron industry.
I have been a puddler now for twenty-two years at the Penn Iron and Steel in
the Allegheny Valley. Ninety per cent of the puddlers are colored men. In
our mill any white puddler from any other mill can come there and get a job.
We are carrying out absolutely the no-discrimination propaganda that has been
put out by our organization, but there isn't another puddling mill in the whole
United States that a Negro puddler can go in as a brother of the organization
and ask for a job and get it. Why? When the committee went down and asked
for a job for a man the superintendent would tell us that the men wouldn't
work with a colored man. All right, we went out in the mill and asked the
committee and they told us that the company wouldn't hire us. We all belonged
to the same Union. That is only one mill, and all except one belongs to this
organization, and we can't get a job. If we want to break down discrimination
we should clean it up in our own homes before we send our resolutions and
whereases to the Congress of the United States. If we do that we will not have
one group looking down on us, we will have a united front and we can carry
out what we are asking them to do and we will be recognized.

I have boys in the Army and I know about the discrimination. The 15th
day of June one boy will be in four years, and I know all about the discrimination and I don't agree with it. I am happy to see this sentiment here,
and I am praying to God that when this war is over and my boys come back, or
if they are lying under the clods in some foreign country, I want the boys
that come back to be in a position where they won't say that it was like 1918,
when we went out and fought for democracy and came back and found it a mockery.
I want it to be the United Nations with the Four Freedoms that Roosevelt has
declared for to be spread throughout the length and breadth of this and every
other country, so that we can work hand in hand, because some day we must meet
on the other side, and we might as well get together here. I thank you.

President Murray: I might remind the delegation that we are running against time, of course. This convention has got to conclude its sessions tomorrow at noon, and I am merely passing that reminder on for whatever it may be worth to you, because you will have to have your tickets and your bags ready for tomorrow noon.

Delegate McCloskey, Local Union 1193: I have come up here to talk on the colored members, and I mean our new members that are coming in here during the war. I mean the colored women. Down in our plant they are using colored women to take the place of the men. They expect those colored women to do the same work as a man, driving them like they did down in the South. There was a war on that to do away with slavery, but you are bringing it right back into the North. We have been fighting to do away with that, too.

Under your contract you have a provision for a probation period of three months. They can start these women out to work, work them eight or nine days and use them to put the fear of hell in their hearts of the other women that are working there, use them to fire these other women.

We have a grievance up now that has been in the fourth step, and I am going to ask Brother Murray to see that that is carried through with the Farrell Steel Plant.

Another thing we had in our last election of Local officers. I didn't go out there to use politics on it. We got out and talked to the boys. We have in our plant officers of all nationalities. We have one man here today, delegated here by his Local Union, a colored man, a Vice President, and he is doing a fine job. He has been organizing these people, not only organizing them as a Union, but by way of political action also.

I think our Local can go on record, even before political action was started down in our end of Pennsylvania, as bringing out people who never registered before. These colored people got out and worked, and we know how they have been using these colored people for years back, your corporations bringing them up from the South and using them to vote for one purpose.

I promised President Murray I would be brief, but I am going to ask him to go along and see see that these grievances are carried along, where these two colored women have been fired in our steel plant. We feel that is discrimination not only against the colored people but the white people as well.

Delegate Merriweather, District 4, Local Union 2603, Buffalo: I would like to speak in favor of this resolution. I am very much in favor of this resolution, but the thing that aroused me to speak is the way resolutions are handled after being acted upon and passed.

I realize we have various committees throughout our organization which are functioning in certain capacities, but they can do nothing without the support of the rank and file. I hope that this resolution is passed. But, I say this, in the event that you do not mean to put the resolution in action, then I would ask you to vote against it. Of course again there is the question in my mind whether you actually mean to put this resolution in action or not, and if you do not mean to put this resolution in action, then I will ask you to vote against the resolution because the common class of people or the working class, or particularly the Negro are no longer satisfied with just merely resolutions. We realize that the resolution is a step forward for breaking the bars before the Negro people, but we do not hope to realize the delegation taking this step if that step is to remain for the next Constitutional Convention.

So, delegates, we call upon you to vote in favor of this resolution, but if you do not mean to put the resolution in action, then we will ask you to vote against it and thereby you will avoid all acts of hypocrisy.

The question was called for.

President Murray: I merely wanted to make a few observations about the resolution in order that our delegates may have an appreciation of what the organization is doing to eliminate all forms of discrimination. The CIO movement and the United Steelworkers of America have done more in the past seven years to eliminate the causes of discrimination in American industry than any other group in the United States of America.

Our Constitution, the Constitution of this organization, provides that there shall be no discrimination against anyone regardless of creed, color or nationality. That is basic. That is fundamental. That is essential, and no individual affiliated with our Union is entitled under our Constitution to retain his membership in the organization if he practices discrimination.

Who is it in the United States of America, outside of the CIO movement and
the United Steelworkers of America, the past six or seven years in the steel
industry, that has fought harder for the economic emancipation of all groups
employed in industry than has the CIO and this Union? Who is it that is constantly to the forefront in the newsprints of the nation advocating the
elimination of all forms of discrimination, racial or otherwise? It is the
CIO, and of course organizations like the United Steelworkers of America.
Who is it that has assumed the leadership in the United States for the elimination of the poll tax and inequities in the Southern States of the United
States? It has been your Union. It has been the CIO. Who has been organizing the South for the economic and political emancipation of the workers
down there, both white and black? It has been the CIO. Who has stood four-
square against intolerance in any form in the United States of America? It
has been the CIO; it has been the United Steelworkers of America and other
affiliated organizations attached to the parent body.

I don't think that I need make any extended speech here about these
services your organization, the United Steelworkers of America, has rendered
the workers employed in this great industry, particularly the colored groups.

We have incorporated in almost every collective bargaining contract
negotiated between employers and this Union provisions to protect the rights
of colored workers against discrimination. We have created grievance committees to see to it that those rights are fully guaranteed. The position of
your International Union has been one of insisting constantly upon the rights
of colored workers being protected whilst on their jobs under collective
bargaining contracts. The only hope that I know of that colored workers have
anywhere in the United States of America is in affiliation with some CIO
organization. Their eventual emancipation, lies in their willingness to
affiliate with the CIO labor organization. We practice what we preach. We
preach the elimination of all forms of discrimination and we practice that
one thing. We do it in the shops. We do it in the factories. We do it where-
ever the CIO movement is.

I know that the colored workers all over this country have a deep seated
affection for this CIO movement. Just as the colored brother from the Allegheny Valley said a few minutes ago, a colored man whom I have known for over
twenty-five years, a former coal miner, he knows what discrimination means.
He knows that up until a few years ago a colored worker employed in heavy
industry in the United States of America outside of coal mining could not
hope to affiliate himself with a labor union. But the CIO was created and
it embraced all groups, regardless of creed, color or nationality. It says,
"Come on. We're all the same. We've all got the same aspirations." We are
against discrimination. We mean it. We are going to practice it. I think
that is understood. It requires no extended argument to prove the position
of either this Union or the CIO.

The day that this organization of ours loses interest in protecting the
colored worker or any other group, that day this organization will start
to decay. It will begin to go down. It must constantly and militantly fight
all forms of persecution and discrimination. That is your job. That is my
job. That is the job of the CIO. That is the job of the United Steelworkers
of America. Now remember that.

We are not merely passing a resolution here and going back home to forget
all about it. We have not been doing that. It is the job of our grievance
committees in our Local Unions and our District Directors to make this provision in our Constitution and in our collective bargaining contracts workable,
to apply it diligently, equitably, to all groups, regardless of creed, color
and nationality. That is your business. That is my business. That is my job
and that is your job.

The colored worker, like all other workers, is entitled to the fullest
measure of protection that this organization can give him. Well, I shan't go
any further with this thing, because I imagine we could talk for days about
it, a lot of matters could be brought to the attention of the convention concerning discrimination.

The question of discrimination against the colored men in the United States
Army is brought out in the resolution, but it is equally true and has been
proven that active members of our Union, CIO Unions, who have either enlisted
in the Army or have been inducted into the armed services, whether they were
black or white, have been discriminated against, and I know it. I have brought
those matters to the attention of the authorities in the city of Washington
repeatedly.

There are many instances of actual, forthright acts of discrimination that have been practiced against men simply because they were members of the CIO Union. There are men in this hall who perhaps a week from now may be in the United States Army, not black men but white men who have gone before draft boards in the state of Ohio, and who have been told by officials of city draft boards in this state that because they were officials of CIO organizations here in this state they were going to see to it that when they got into the Army, this question of advocating the upbuilding of trade unions was going to be driven out of them. We have had cases brought to our attention affecting representatives of this Union who were actually enlisting in the Army only a few months ago and who were told in the offices to which they reported for enlistment, "Well, we're glad you came, and when we get you in here we're going to see to it that you are not going to be a union man when you get back home." So these discriminations are not confined merely to the colored people. No. I have hundreds of letters from colored people and white people over in my office in the city of Washington, members of CIO Unions who have reported to me these acts of discrimination against them because of their affiliation with a CIO Union, and don't forget we can't make these problems of discrimination merely Negro problems. The Negro, to me, is a creature of God just the same as a white man. As an American citizen he is entitled to equality of treatment. I believe deep down in my own heart and soul that the problem of discrimination, particularly racial discrimination, leads to religious and other kinds of hatred. You can't tolerate racial discrimination, because if you do so, unquestionably you will have to meet the problem of other kinds of discrimination. So this organization, being a democratic institution, dedicates itself to the furtherance of these democratic principles to which we will adhere, and it must of necessity, see to it insofar as we are able, all forms of discrimination, racial or otherwise, should be eliminated from our life. That is our goal. That is our objective. That is why we organize. We don't organize to create prejudice and hatreds amongst groups. We bring people together to have people work together and be happy working together. If I thought this Union that I preside over, the Steelworkers' Union, is going to practice racial discrimination or religious discrimination or any other form of discrimination, if I thought that this Union was going to do that I would say to you, "Boys, give this job to some other man. I don't want you. I don't want you." That's how I feel about it and I know that you feel like I do.

Discrimination is ungodly; discrimination breeds distrust, it breeds hate, it breeds prejudice, it creates disunity. Discrimination has broken up families—yes, it has broken up homes. Discrimination has wrecked lives. Discrimination has perpetrated many injustices upon the human race, not only in the United States but all over the world.

It is important, therefore, that this Union of yours and mine should constantly dedicate itself to the provisions of this one task, to the elimination of all forms of discrimination. That is your job and that is my job.

Now I will put the motion, with your permission.

The motion to adopt the resolution as submitted by the committee was carried by unanimous vote.

Resolution No. 10

Discrimination

WHEREAS, (1) Discrimination against any individual or groups of people because of race, religion, or country of origin is an evil characteristic of our Fascist enemies. We of the Democracies are fighting Fascism at home and abroad by welding all races, all religions, and all peoples into a united body of workers for Democracy;

(2) Any discriminatory practices within our own ranks against any group directly aids the enemy by creating division, dissension and confusion. Such discrimination practiced in employment policies hampers production by depriving the nation of the use of available skills and manpower.

(3) We have already seen in this country in Los Angeles, Beaumont, Texas; Detroit and elsewhere the results of the effort of the fifth column in the United States as represented by Gerald L. K. Smith and the Ku Klux Klan who are doing the work of our Axis enemies to foment riots and insurrection, to stir up Anti-Semitism, thereby creating division and disruption to weaken our war effort, now therefore, be it

RESOLVED, (1) This convention reiterates its firm opposition to any
form of racial or religious discrimination and renews its pledge to carry on
the fight for protection, in law and in fact, of the rights of any racial and
religious or minority group, to participate fully in our social and political
life.
(2) This convention commends the work of the Fair Employment Practices
Committee established by President Roosevelt under Executive Order, to eliminate practices of discrimination in industry, urges such committee to carry
forward vigorously to effectuate this vital policy and urges Congress to enact
appropriate legislation to place the committee and its work on a permanent
basis with effective enforcement authority.
(3) This convention calls upon President Roosevelt and the Department
of Justice to take immediate steps to prosecute those individuals and groups
within the nation, such as Gerald L. K. Smith, the Ku Klux Klan, and the
seditionists, which deliberately seek to foment civil strife and discord by
setting one race against another, whipping up hatred against minority groups
and encourage discrimination. Any vestige of Nazism which rears its ugly head
tc our glorious Democracy must be immediately and decisively eliminated.
(4) This convention rededicates itself to continue with determination
its efforts to eliminate completely the economic factors which are the fundamental causes of discrimination in its most vicious form.
Substitute for resolutions submitted by local unions 65, 1014, 1066, 1104,
1330, 2860, 3126.
Committee Secretary Millard moved the adoption of the resolution.
The motion was seconded.
Delegate Trallo, Local Union 2715: Mr. Chairman and fellow delegates:
I was not going to speak on this subject because I thought the matter could
best be handled by one of the colored delegates speaking for themselves, but
something has occurred in our own delegation that I think should be brought
to the attention of this convention. Personally, I think it is a serious problem, not only because it involves discrimination against one of the colored
race, but because it involves discrimination against the rest of the delegation.
Upon arriving in this city Sunday evening, we of Local Union 2715, had in
our delegation a colored man. We made reservation at a hotel, and after the
hotel found out we had a colored man in our delegation, we were refused admittance to the hotel. You can well imagine the feeling of the rest of the
delegation, after traveling all day long, arriving in Cleveland tired, dirty,
wanted to wash up and rest a bit. We arrived in the city at 8:20. Finally,
after a lot of bickering--incidentally we found other quarters for our delegates
--we finally got our rooms at about ten-thirty or quarter to eleven.
You can well imagine that this delegation is pretty sore. I wonder what
Abraham Lincoln would think. I wonder, if Abraham Lincoln was here today and
he could see the discrimination that is practiced against the colored people--
well, I would hate to think what he would say. If he knew what was going on
today he would turn over in his grave.
Do you think that President Roosevelt and Prime Minister Churchill, when
we said that we should have the Four Freedoms, and especially freedom from
want and freedom from fear, were excluding the Negro race? No, they meant
all races.[146]
Therefore, gentlemen, I am not going to take up much of your time, but
I would like to impress upon you that in our resolution it says in part that
it renews its pledge to carry on the fight for protection, in law and in fact,
of the rights of any racial and religious or minority group, to participate
fully in our social and political life.
A motion to close debate was adopted.
The motion to adopt the resolution was carried by unanimous vote.

Proceedings of the Second Constitutional Convention of the United Steelworkers
of America, 1944, Vol. I, pp. 43-44, 188-96.

112.   CIO SPURS NEGROES IN WINSTON-SALEM

Revolutionizes Politics and Labor in
North Carolina Tobacco Metropolis

By Rev. Marshall Shepard

It is not safe to speak against the CIO anywhere among the Negro workers of Winston-Salem, N.C., the largest tobacco manufacturing city in America. Of the 12,000 employees of the R. G. Reynolds tobacco factory, about 9,000 are Negroes and over 6,000 are CIO members with a passion.

Negroes Go CIO

At the first few meetings in October, 1941, to organize the tobacco workers of the Reynolds plant, there were only a half-dozen persons in attendance, but by the spring of '43, the meetings increased to six to seven thousand. When the election was ordered by the U.S. Labor Relations Board, June, '43, seven thousand Negro workers were holding membership cards in the R. G. Reynolds Employees' association, but when the election figures were tabulated, the Reynolds Employees' association polled only 3,175 votes, while 6,833 had voted for CIO. The officials of the association denounced the workers for what they termed a "double cross."

CIO Denounced as Race Agitator

Jasper Redd, president of the R. G. Reynolds Employees' association said in an interview that the CIO was menace to interracial goodwil. It had taught Negroes to disrespect white leaders and had brought about ill feeling between the masses of Negro workers and their own business and professional leaders. Mr. Redd was bitter in his denunciation of the Negro pastors, many of whom he charged were bribed by CIO.

According to Mr. Redd

There were two ministers, Rev. A. H. McDaniel, pastor of the Union Bethel Baptist church and Rev. S. G. Thomas, pastor of the Congregational church, who refused to support the CIO and were almost forced to leave their pulpits. Rev. Thomas was taken back into his church only after he publicly recanted. Rev. Thomas has ceased all anti-CIO activities. Mr. Redd said that in his own church and Sunday school, the people avoid him.
Dr. A. H. Ray, a prominent physician of the Twin city was dropped from his position as company physician for the Safe Bus company, an all-Negro concern, after CIO protested his anti-union activities.

Negroes Registering to Vote

Heretofore, the number of registered Negro voters in Winston-Salem were only a few hundred. The CIO and NAACP put on a drive for increased Negro registrants. Speakers were sent to churches and fraternal meetings to urge the people to register. It is estimated that CIO alone registered over 2,000 of its members and the total registration of Negroes will perhaps reach 5,000 in Winston-Salem. Many of the registrars at some of the polling places it is charged were officials of the Reynolds Tobacco company, and they resorted to many and devious methods to slow up Negro registration.

Negroes Register Democratic

The CIO claimed their members were registering Democratic because they intend to support President Roosevelt for a fourth term. Also they said to vote Republican in North Carolina was a waste of time. All candidates for public office have been sent questionnaires seeking their views on labor and race issues.
I accepted an invitation to attend a weekly meeting of the shop stewards

of the CIO union. There were about 500 in attendance. They met at 7:30
promptly. The meetings are held in a Holiness church. It seems that the
Holiness pastors, many of whom work in the factory side by side with other
workers are close to the working masses and are not easily influenced by
pressure from the owners.

The meetings were opened by a 15-minute devotional service led by ministers, four of them elected chaplains of the local.

Workers Instructed

Then the workers are carried through a quiz program on a well-thought out
plan of workers' education. The enthusiasm with which this program was received and the intelligent grasp of labor problems that these people were
getting was indeed thrilling to one who had once been appalled by the lack of
all these things among the Negro workers.

As I moved among these workers, white and black, and talked to many of
them in all walks of life, I was conscious of a growing solidarity and intelligent mass action that will mean the dawn of a New Day in the South. One
cannot visit Winston-Salem and mingle with the thousands of workers without
sensing a revolution in thought and action. If there is a "New" Negro, he
is to be found in the ranks of the labor movement.[147]

Pittsburgh Courier, June 3, 1944.

113. PITFALLS THAT BESET NEGRO TRADE-UNIONISTS

By George L. P. Weaver

The Congress of Industrial Organizations, like other forward-looking
groups, began to demand the full utilization of all available manpower as soon
as the defense program got under way in 1939 and 1940. That demand, backed
up by unremitting efforts, has broken down many barriers that have been a
half-century in the making. A great number of industrial plants now hire
Negroes that had never hired them before. Similarly, Negro workers are joining unions in greater numbers than ever before. But even with this decided
progress, the job that must be done has just begun.

One direct result of this new union membership of Negroes is an increase
of problems that grow out of our varied racial community practices. Another
result is the emergence of a new Negro trade-union official, particularly in
the CIO. These officials are operating on all levels of authority with a
growing number of Negro local presidents, local grievance committeemen, and
members of other key local committees. In the larger Internationals we tend
to have an ever increasing number of Negro International Representatives. And
this thread of progress leads up to the highest councils of the CIO, where
there are now two Negro members serving on the CIO Executive Board. The first
to be placed was Willard S. Townsend, President of the United Transport Service
Employees, who blazed the trail for other Negroes to follow. The second was
Ferdinand Smith, Secretary of the National Maritime Union, who was selected
by his union at the 1943 CIO Convention.

No Special Group Problems

Willard Townsend's service on the CIO Board has been marked by his interest
in all trade-union problems, instead of problems that can be considered as
solely "Negro problems." In this Mr. Townsend offers the key that all Negro
trade-unionists must use in order to advance their racial as well as their
general interests in the labor movement. All of us need to realize that so-
called racial problems are in reality only part of a worker's problem. The
Negro neither wants nor needs special attention--he is looking to his trade-
union for equal opportunity and the right of an American worker to advance up
the ladder in whatever industry he may be employed. One of the most dangerous

pitfalls that Negroes in the labor movement can fall into is that of allowing
themselves to be maneuvered into a position of demanding special racial rights
and consideration. In far too many instances, Negroes have fallen into this
very pitfall.
     The National CIO Committee to Abolish Racial Discrimination has received
complaints from Negro workers, Mexican workers, Jewish workers, Japanese-Americans, and the largest minority of all--women workers. Investigation discloses
that each one of these groups thinks its problem the most important of them all.
Our Committee's approach to all minority problems follows the theory that are
all *workers'* problems--part and parcel of the same fabric. As long as one of
these vexing racial or cultural problems remains unsolved, the rights and privileges of all other workers are threatened.

Dangerous Trends

     If we Negro trade-unionists allow ourselves to become engrossed in the
Negro's problem to the exclusion of the others, we run the risk of creating
a dangerous racism, an evil that no one has ever been able to control and
direct constructively. There are dangerous trends leading in this direction.
The March on Washington Movement is the most outstanding manifestation of
this "black chauvinism." And this writer has been puzzled and alarmed at the
attitude of many local Negro trade-union officials. Too frequently ordinary
trade-union grievances are blown up into charges of discrimination. Every
local problem involving a Negro is laid on the doorstep of discrimination,
regardless of the attitudes and principles of the white officer or brother
union member involved. Such an approach robs the complainant of the necessary
objectivity that he must possess to be a useful trade-union official in his
local. A Negro elected to a post in a local union is expected to function
as an officer for all the members, not for a Negro minority--or even majority.
Then, too, by placing primary emphasis on the whole trade-union point of view,
Negroes are much more apt to win the support of white members who recognize
the trade-union approach, but who might become opponents if the issue were
presented as a race issue.
     The recent convention of the United Auto Workers, held in Buffalo,
furnishes an example of this kind of danger. That union's race relations'
record is second to the record of no other American union. Its convention was
thrown into an uproar by a minority report on an amendment to the constitution
which would create a Minorities Department in the International, headed by a
Negro who would also have a seat on the Executive Board.
     Thoughtful observers must agree with the position of R. J. Thomas, UAW
President, who firmly opposed this proposal. If Negro workers are entitled
by race alone to a special place on a union Executive Board, that same argument could be used to justify segregation on a streetcar, in a hotel, and in a
restaurant. To carry this principle to its logical conclusion would mean in-
suring places on the Board for women, Poles, Jews and Catholics, since there is
a sizable representation of each group in the UAW. Many union officials would
be strongly tempted, if this proposal were adopted, to pass on to the Negro
Board member problems that should be solved by the whole Board.
     A number of Negroes took this position at the UAW convention because they
recognized the inherent dangers contained in the proposal. Oddly enough, they
were castigated as anti-Negro and reactionary. Horace Sheffield, a Negro International Representative, was bitterly condemned and several Negro delegates
have stated to this writer that "they are out to get him." Paul P. Shearer,
labor editor for the *Ohio State News,* and an officer in Local 927, UAW, Columbus,
Ohio, lumped together all opponents of the plan as members of anti-Negro factions and reactionaries. His list included Victor and Walter Reuther. When
Shearer had pointed out to him the dangers and inconsistencies of this line of
reasoning, he agreed and unconsciously explained the predicament that many Negro
trade-unionists are in. They ride into office on the race issue in locals with
large Negro memberships, and their thinking and approach to most trade-union
questions constantly starts off from the point of "how do they affect Negroes?"
     Negroes are also pushed along toward their pitfall by certain kinds of
white support. For example, at the recent National CIO Convention in Philadelphia, Abram Flaxner, President of State, County and Municipal Workers, in
speaking on the anti-discrimination resolution, said, in part, that he felt it

would be in the interest of the CIO to elect a colored Board member to the
International Executive Board--not from any one organization, but as representing all of the organizations on that Board. When the Flaxer proposal is
examined, it seems patronizing, to say the least. Why should a Negro be
elected to the Board, floating around without any anchor when all other members
of the Board represent their International Unions? If the Board lacks Negro
membership, there is nothing to stop Brother Flaxer's organization, or any
other organization from electing a Negro to represent it.

Separation Creates Ignorance and Suspicion

To think clearly on this question, we must keep firmly before us our
long-time objectives. If we are working towards the goal of complete economic
equality and are using the trade-union structure toward that end, it seems a
tragic paradox to consider any kind of proposal that dignifies separation. It
may be held axiomatic that anything which separates people into sharply dis-
tinguishable groups--whether it be a racial difference, a difference of religious groups, or a class distinction--will produce between the groups thus
separated: first, ignorance of one another; then, suspicion growing out of
that ignorance; then, misunderstanding growing out of that ignorance and suspicion, and finally conflict. A safe general approach for Negro trade-
unionists is one that considers questions affecting the black worker's welfare
from the standpoint of sound trade-unionsm, rather than the much narrower one
of race. Time will prove the wisdom of this view. What harms the Negro harms
all workers. What harms workers in general also harms the Negro. Trade-union
leadership has come to recognize today--certainly in the CIO--that if the
rights of Negro workers are not made secure exploitative management will not
long hesitate before pushing white workers down to the Negro's level. Just as
white workers through their leaders have rapidly come around to this point of
view, so Negro workers and members of their race who aspire to leadership in
the trade-union movement must accept their responsibility for protecting the
interests of organized labor itself.

Opportunity, 22 (Winter, 1944): 12-13.

114. NEGROES RATE CIO FAIRER, POLL SHOWS

A round table discussion on "Which Union Is Fairer to the Negro: AFL or
CIO?" is featured in the June issue of Negro Digest. CIO Pres. Philip Murray,
Willard S. Townsend, pres., Transport Service Employees and Ferdinand Smith,
sec., Natl. Martime Union, present the CIO's case.
The AFL position is given by Pres. William Green and Dr. D. G. Garland,
Negro organizer in the South.
"In all the history of the American labor movement," states Pres. Murray,
"no union can match the sterling record of the CIO in battling racial dis-
crimination."
Contrasting the CIO and the AFL policy on race discrimination, Murray
asserts that unlike the AFL, not a single CIO union bars Negroes from membership, or sanctions Jim Crow locals, but on the other hand, Negro trade union
leaders hold high office in most CIO unions.
"The enemies of the Negro are the enemies of the CIO," he declares.
Mr. Townsend explains that Negroes do not expect or want special treatment in the labor movement, but only their democratic rights, and this is what
they get in the CIO, which offers them "an equal opportunity to assume their
responsibilities and obligations as organized working men and women."
A poll taken by Negro Digest of a cross-section of the Negro population
shows that most Negroes favor the CIO over the AFL: Here are the figures:

	AFL	CIO	Unde- cided
North..........	14%	79%	7%
West..........	11%	82%	7%
South..........	19%	67%	14%

CIO News, June 11, 1945.

PART IV

THE AMERICAN FEDERATION OF LABOR
AND THE BLACK WORKER, 1936-1945

Part IV

THE AMERICAN FEDERATION OF LABOR AND THE
BLACK WORKER, 1936-1945

By incessant appeals and expensive litigation, blacks fought racial
discrimination in the AFL unions during World War II. The AFL representative
of the FEPC regularly opposed any action against unions which practiced discrimination. When the Smith Committee, headed by Howard Smith, the segregationist, antilabor congressman from Virginia, held hearings to discredit the
FEPC, leaders of key AFL unions readily appeared as witnesses to complain
against the government agency forcing unions to practice racial equality.

The railroad brotherhoods, the Building and Metal Trades Councils, and
the International Brotherhood of Boilermakers were among the worst of the
unions for practicing racial discrimination, although they were not alone. In
1942, it was reported that nineteen international unions, ten of which were
affiliated with the AFL, practiced racial discrimination against black workers.
Even when unions pledged nondiscrimination in their charters, they often employed subtle means, such as the initiation oath, to exclude Negroes. Representative of the attitude in many of the trade unions was that of William
Hutcheson of the carpenters' union, who retorted to charges of racial bias:
"In our union we don't care whether your're an Irishman, a Jew, or a Nigger."

Meanwhile, at AFL conventions during the war years, A. Philip Randolph
and Milton P. Webster of the Brotherhood of Sleeping Car Porters, continued
their efforts to end racial discrimination in the federation. At nearly every
convention the "Randolph resolution" called for the AFL to establish an in-
vestigative committee to inquire into charges that affiliates employed such
practices, but for the most part the delegates refused to comply. When
Randolph and Webster introduced their resolution again at the 1941 convention,
a heated debate developed. Randolph listed case after case in which AFL
unions discriminated against black workers, but the response was that the convention could not intrude upon the rights of autonomous unions.

At the 1942 convention, Randolph again presented a detailed summary of
the facts on discrimination, but once again he failed to get action. The 1943
convention was again the scene of a heated debate on the Negro labor issue.
As at previous conventions, Randolph attacked the AFL's lack of action, and
condemned auxiliary unions as the equivalents of "colonies." The union leaders
responded by denouncing Randolph for being a "professional Negro" and "trouble-
maker" at a time when unity in the ranks of labor was essential for a victory
over fascism. William Green, president of the AFL, brought the debate to a
close with a gesture to Randolph. He conceded that problems existed, but
lectured Randolph that change could not come without much time and education.
The same outcome followed a repeat performance of the Randolph-AFL debate at
the 1944 convention, with Green again counseling black workers that they would
have to wait and practice "good judgement" during the interim.

By the end of World War II, not much had changed for blacks in AFL
unions. As sociologist Gunnar Myrdal put it: "The fact that the American
Federation of Labor as such is officially against racial discrimination does
not mean much. The Federation has never done anything to check racial discrimination exercised by its member organizations."[148]

THE AFL AND RACIAL DISCRIMINATION

1. OLD GUARD VS. A. F. OF L.

By Lester Granger

On the surface, so far as Negro workers are concerned, the American Federation of Labor's convention at Atlantic City was "just another of those affairs." It is true that the stage was set for dramatic fireworks, with the San Francisco convention of 1934 as a background. Delegate A. Philip Randolph, president of the Brotherhood of Sleeping Car Porters and fiery leader of Negro workers, had demanded at that convention an end of evasive resolution-passing by the A. F. of L. on the question of racial discrimination in unions. He submitted a resolution which if adopted would have given unions the choice of dropping their barriers against Negroes or loss of their charters.

The resolutions committee of that convention, as was expected, reported non-concurrence, but when the eloquent Randolph took the floor in defense of his motion the response of delegates to his address was so enthusiastic that there seemed real danger of a defeat for the hitherto impregnable political machine of the old guard. A compromise, hurriedly adopted, appointed a committee to study the issue of racial discrimination and report its findings to the 1935 convention.

The Committee on Problems of Negro Labor met in Washington last July and called witnesses to present definite testimony. The National Urban League was represented at that hearing, as well as the N.A.A.C.P., the Joint Committee on National Recovery, and similar organizations, backing up the labor leaders who exposed subtle and flagrant Jim Crow tactics by local and international unions.

The findings of the committee were turned over to the Executive Council of the A. F. of L., which promptly buried them. No mention was made of the issue in the council's annual report to the convention, and the committee's report was referred to the tender care of George L. Harrison of the Brotherhood of Railway and Steamship Clerks, an international whose constitution specifically bars Negroes from membership. Randolph's efforts to get action from the floor of the convention were smothered with the usual parliamentary technicalities and the bland statement that "the Federation must not violate the autonomy of internationals with respect to their memberships." This attitude from a group of officers who had just been defeated in their attempts to expel communists from unions affiliated with the A. F. of L.!

Thus described, the convention seemed truly "just another of those affairs." But this bare report does not tell the real story. For instance, there is the fact that the Committee on Problems of Negro Labor, headed by John Brophy of the United Mine Workers, made an honest and courageous report to the Executive Council--much to that diplomatic body's dismay. The report verified the justice of Negroes' protests and recommended adoption of the Randolph resolution in substance.

Finally on September 15, 1935, another resolution which Randolph immediately submitted tied up business in the council and the resolutions committee for half a day, while their members debated on ways and means to bury this unwelcome ghost of a dusky Banquo. In the old days both report and resolution would have been brought out on the floor to be crushed speedily under the convention machine. This year, however, the old guard knew perfectly well that there were a hundred delegates at the convention who were waiting for a chance to support any resolution that would give a finishing blow to Jim Crow in organized labor. The politicians simply couldn't take the chance of bitter conflict and possible defeat on this issue, leading the way to further and more fatal defeats on other convention issues. [149]

Several lessons to Negro workers, developed at the San Francisco convention, were brought out even more sharply at Atlantic City. First, that it is more and more inaccurate to speak of "A. F. of L. attitude" as if it were fixed or unanimous. Within the Federation, on the Negro issue as on other matters, there is a constant conflict between progressive and reactionary forces, with the progressives steadily growing in strength. Negroes who blindly condemn "the A. F. of L." as being a Jim Crow body seriously embarrass their own champions within the ranks of organized labor. Intelligent and helpful criticism will distinguish between friends and foes and support the former.

Second, labor leaders are perfectly correct when they say that the problem of Negro workers will be solved eventually, not at the A. F. of L. conventions but within the internationals and locals. Though the Federation can and should set the pace toward labor democracy, the goal will not be reached without patient educational work in the ranks of organized labor. That work has been begun in the rank-and-file movement, so-called, in union locals, but it must be supported by active efforts on the part of Negroes themselves. The lobby conducted at Atlantic City by the Urban League disclosed many officers of internationals who were perfectly ready to vote for the Randolph resolution, but who were frank in stating that its results would be disappointing without thorough follow-up work in the internationals and locals.

Finally, Atlantic City showed again the need for a louder and better organized Negro voice within the Federation, on the floor of its conventions, taking part in its committee meetings. Six or eight colored delegates were in evidence this year, including A. Philip Randolph and Milton L. Webster of the Sleeping Car Porters. Every Federal local with at least a majority of colored workers should strain its resources to send a delegate to the convention. Merely the presence of Negroes, sprinkled throughout the meeting, is bound to influence the convention vote on issues affecting interests of Negroes.[150]

On the Negro question, on the issue of industrial unionism, as on that of a Labor Party, the Atlantic City Convention resolved itself into a struggle between an entrenched Old Guard of politicians and a newly-arising progressive faction. The Old Guard stands for conservatism, protection of fat jobs, extirpation of every tendency that seems militant--and therefore threatening to the Old Guard. And yet, the welfare of labor today demands more militancy, more radical departure from old ways than ever before. The Old Guard therefore is opposed to the A. F. of L.--the real Federation. It should not be difficult for Negroes to decide on which side they will line up.

Race, 1 (Winter, 1935-1936): 46-47.

2.   ORGANIZED LABOR'S DIVIDED FRONT

By Charles H. Wesley

Organized labor in the United States has presented a divided front throughout the period of its history. Class, race, craft and organizational lines have been barriers against union. None has been more important in influence than that of race. In the midst of the economic expansion and the centralization of industry which followed the Civil War, voices in the wilderness of our economic divisions have been urgently demanding that labor should close ranks and present a united front. . . .

The Knights of Labor, organized in 1869, held its first national convention in 1876. The resolutions which were adopted by this and subsequent conventions and the practices which were urged upon the local unions led to the admission of large numbers of Negroes into the organization. The decline of the Knights of Labor was paralleled by the rise of the American Federation of Labor which was formed in 1884. In its early years the Federation refused to admit to its membership associations which raised the color bar in their membership. When the international Association of Machinists applied for admission with the word "white" in its constitution, this was refused until the word was removed. The Federation declared that there were to be no differences of creed, color or sex.

Separate Charters for Negroes

From 1897 to the present time the conventions of the Federation have affirmed their welcome to all labor "without regard to creed, color, sex, race or nationality." The Convention of 1897 met the issue squarely when it declared that no affiliated union had the right to bar Negroes from its membership. In 1902 the convention passed a provision for the issuance of separate charters to unions composed entirely of Negro workers. This action was representative of a shift in policy. Fences were to be erected between the two races. Rapidly the policy degenerated into one in which the Federation declared that it would not force its declarations "upon individual or affiliated unions without their consent."

This policy has been followed consistently by the American Federation of Labor from 1916 to the present time. Resolutions were passed declaring that there is no distinction of race in labor's ranks and that Negroes ought to be brought into labor organizations. In 1917, it was decided that a Negro organizer would be employed by the Federation. It was stated later that funds did not permit the employment of such an official. For one reason or another, convention after convention led by reactionary leadership evaded the racial issues which were brought before the meetings. This result was repeated at the convention of 1920, 1921, 1924 and 1925.

The situation created by these repeated rebuffs led to action by Negroes themselves. Resolutions and the expression of intentions alone were not strong enough to hold the leadership of Negro labor. In 1925, the American Negro Labor Congress meeting in Chicago declared that "the failure of the American Federation of Labor officialdom, under pressure of race prejudice benefitting only the capitalists of the North and South, to stamp out race hatred in the unions, to organize Negro workers, and to build a solid front of the workers of both races against American capitalism, is a crime against the whole working class."

Porters' Brotherhood

Almost in response to this declaration, the announcement was made in June, 1925, of the organization of the Brotherhood of Sleeping Car Porters. Under the leadership of A. Philip Randolph, then editor of *The Messenger*, Ashley L. Totten, and M. P. Webster, following the failure of a wage conference between the Pullman Company and the porters in accordance with a Plan for Employee Representation, the decision was reached to launch an independent Negro labor organization. The Pullman Company declined to recognize the Brotherhood. In spite of this opposition and with the small funds contributed by the porters, the Brotherhood undertook a fight which culminated in partial recognition under the Railroad Labor Act of 1934. In the following year, the American Federation of Labor, convinced by this evidence of strength on the part of a Negro union, granted the Brotherhood an international charter. This gave an impetus to the organization of the porters. In August, 1937, an agreement was signed with the Pullman Company which granted wage increases totaling a million and a quarter dollars to some 8,000 Pullman porters. This is regarded as one of the important milestones in the march of Negro labor towards an improvement in its economic status, although there are those who deny that this result is a victory. This Negro labor experiment shows the strength of a racial organization when it is used to break down opposition within the ranks of labor and at the same time to seek affiliation with white labor upon a basis of an independence which demands self-respect.[151]

A slightly different result was reached by another organization of Negro workers. The Brotherhood of Dining Car Employees, established in 1919, has had to wage a similar fight for recognition. The Pullman porters, as employees of a single management, could become unified in purpose and objective. Each of the railroads operates its own dining cars and has full jurisdiction over them. During the war when the roads were under the control of the Railroad Administration, a 240-hour-month was agreed upon through the leadership of Rienzi B. Lemus. This agreement, together with overtime pay provisions and increases in pay, were preserved by contracts between the Brotherhood of Dining Car Employees and the large eastern railroads. The National Brotherhood of Dining Car Employees, a smaller and less significant

organization, confined its activities chiefly to the railroads which operated
west of Chicago. The Brotherhood of Dining Car Employees, and the western
organization, as well, were largely superseded by the action of the Hotel and
Restaurant Employees' International Alliance, an affiliate of the American
Federation of Labor, in sponsoring an organization known as "The Dining Car
Employees Union." The contracts formerly negotiated by the independent
Brotherhood have been maintained through this union, although at the present
writing some railroads are threatening reductions in pay. However, the
divisions along racial lines have continued and the Negroes remain in a "Jim-
crow" organization under the dominance of a white international.[152]

Significant Fight

The fight which has been pressed from the vantage ground of Negro independent labor organization upon American Trade-Unionism is one of great
significance to Negro labor.
With relief figures mounting for Negroes as contrasted with whites, with
the level of wages rising in several occupations in spite of the depression,
and the adoption of minimum wage standards, evidences of discrimination become
more apparent. Discrimination against Negroes in employment is being courageously met in several cities. Jobs which were formerly filled by Negroes are
now being taken by whites who would not have them before but they readily
accept them because of the wages, and the employers seem eager to hire them.
In order to combat this rising tide of job losses, movements have arisen, such
as those sponsored by The New Negro Alliance of Washington, which has recently
won its Supreme Court case against the Sanitary Grocery Company and the Harlem
Job Committee and the Coordinating Committee for Employment of New York City.
The National Negro Congress has made the cause of labor one of its major
topics of discussion. Labor councils have been organized and labor representatives have worked among Negroes. The results are far from satisfactory.
Such efforts treat the symptoms and often neglect the malignant disease of
disunion.

Exclusion Widely Practised

Negro workers today continue to meet exclusion and discrimination from
the unions. Twenty-one large unions discriminate against Negroes by clauses
in their constitutions or rituals. One of the railroad brotherhoods also
excludes Mexicans and American Indians. Other important organizations which
are affiliated with the American Federation of Labor exclude Orientals.
Limitations by the use of the word "white" as a qualification for memberships
are found in the regulations governing the Brotherhood of Railway and Steamship
Clerks, Freight Handlers, Express and Station Employees, Order of Sleeping Car
Conductors, Grand International Brotherhood of Locomotive Engineers, Brotherhood of Dining Car Conductors, Air Line Pilots' Association, and many other
unions. Other unions bar Negroes from representation in conventions, in
executive bodies of unions and from office holding. On the contrary, there are
unions which specifically legislate against discrimination. The Lather's
International Union, Wood, Wire and Metal states that "no one shall be discriminated against for race or color." The Cigar Makers' International states
that "all persons engaged in the cigar industry regardless of color or
nationality shall be eligible for membership." There are unions which specify
that Negroes shall be organized in separate locals. Among these there is the
Sheet Metal Workers' International Association. This organization provides
that Negro sheet metal workers shall be organized into separate locals with the
consent of "the white local of the locality" or in "auxiliary locals," if the
consent of the white local is not obtained. It is further provided that Negro
locals should be under the jurisdiction of the white locals. Still other
unions provide apprenticeship provisions which are so operated that they
exclude Negroes from both the industry and the union.
Various subtle methods well known to students of race in the United States
are practised in order to accomplish the exclusion of Negroes from membership
in trade unions. Negroes are frequently denied jobs in the building trades
because they do not have local union cards. When they apply to the unions they
are denied cards or they are told that they must have jobs first before cards

can be issued to them. There are employers who want to give Negro labor,
unorganized as it is, an opportunity for jobs, but they are held up by powerful unions which refuse to work on the same jobs with non-union workers. They
exclude Negroes from their unions and then refuse to work with them because
they are non-union men. Negro labor finds itself between these two fires, and
the employer is finally compelled to yield to the organization which strikes
and pickets the non-union job.

There are also those who claim that Negroes are not good "union" material,
that they will not strike, or the contrary that they are strike-breakers and
"scabs," that whites will not work with Negroes and that if Negroes organize
they prefer to be by themselves. However, all of these assertions have been
disproved by the recent activities of the United Mine Workers of America, the
International Longshoreman's Association, the International Ladies Garment
Workers Union and scores of labor organizations in strikes, lockouts and labor
demonstrations throughout the country.

The C.I.O.

Widespread trade unionism, Labor's Non-Partisan League, the American
Labor Party, and the encouragement given to organized labor by the Wagner
Labor Relations Act, the National Labor Relations Board, and the discussion on
the Wages and Hours Bill seem to be introducing a new period in labor history.
The Committee for Industrial Organization in its development of a new unionism
among American workers has announced and consistently adhered to a program of
non-discrimination in admission to its membership. This position was presented
in a letter to the N.A.A.C.P. during the negotiations in December, 1937,
between the American Federation of Labor and the Committee for Industrial
Organization. This is an advance from the position of non-intervention which
is practised by the American Federation of Labor. If the competition between
the A. F. of L. and the C. I. O. continues, it is conceivable that the Negro
may gain in economic organization similarly as he has gained by the division
between the political parties in reference to his party alignment. The C. I. O.
has not yet undertaken to break down the lines which make it an impossibility
for Negroes to move into the better types of employment, nor has it begun to
discourage separate organizations of Negro workers and to insist upon the
complete solidarity of labor. The Southern Tenant Farmers' Union with headquarters in Memphis, Tennessee, has led the way since 1934 in the organization
of white and black workers which has demonstrated in Tennessee, Alabama,
Mississippi, Arkansas and other southern states that labor can have a solid
front and that it can destroy the color line. In other places Communist
organizers have decreed the abolition of color and racial barriers among
workers and their appeals are being heard by Negro workers.

Should Close Ranks

After three score and ten years of the divided front, through which only
partial victories have been gained, white labor and black labor should now
present a united front in a Second Emancipation to include all ranks of those
who labor. The laboring classes in the United States cannot attain their
objectives without the Negro workers. The opposition of white workers to black
workers should be challenged in their interest as well as in the interest of
the black workers. Ambitious politicians and unwise labor leaders have misled
the labor movement by encouraging racial barriers. With the Negroes forming
about one-seventh of the American labor force, and about 30 per cent of the
total working population in the South, it is unthinkable that labor can go
forward with this weighty mass tugging at its feet. Laborers of all colors
should join hands and go forward towards better living conditions together.
The Negro is ready to cooperate although he distrusts the white union member.
In turn, the white union member is of the opinion that if Negroes are admitted
to their unions, this would be a social recognition, as well as an economic
one. Thus by the decadent shibboleth of white superiority, labor's ranks are
divided.

Here then are vital questions which face Organized Labor today. Can a
divided labor front based upon race win its way in a Democracy? Does
Organized Labor propose to advance the cause of white labor and to neglect and

retard the cause of black labor and expect to be secure in its own gains? Will Organized Labor permit a united front without regard to race to be advocated and practised only by ultra-left wing organizations? Will Organized Labor fold its arms in satisfaction and join the Fascist ideology and practise which searches for a scapegoat among the racial minorities in American life? Answers to these questions will determine whether Organized Labor in its struggle with a self-seeking capitalism will unite race and class in a permanent economic advance or will limp along with its divided front of temporary and fluctuating divisional gains and losses.

The Crisis, 45 (July, 1938): 223-26.

3. NEGRO MEMBERS DRIVE IS PAINTERS COUNCIL PLAN

Weinstock, Certain of Election as District's
Secretary, Announces Program of Special
Activity in Harlem

A new deal for Negro building trades workers became a distinct possibility yesterday when Louis Weinstock, leader of progressives in District Council 9 of the Brotherhood of Painters, running for secretary-treasurer, announced his platform.

The platform, which has the almost unanimous approval of the 10,000 organized painters affiliated with the council, provides as one of its eleven points.

"A special organizational drive in Harlem to organize the Negro painters without discrimination and to unionize the jobs."

Part of Drive

Weinstock, a member of Local 848, estimates 1,500 Negro house-painters in Manhattan, Bronx and Staten Island. He explained that the plan to pay special attention to Harlem is part of a drive which is to be instituted for the organization of all of the 20,000 unorganized painters in New York.

"There are now a scant dozen Negro members in the local unions affiliated with District Council 9," Weinstock said. "It is not surprising to anyone who knows Negro workers that they have displayed devotion to the organization.

"Whatever the causes have been for the apathy of the union's officials toward organizing the Negro painters, the membership will no longer tolerate it. They realize that the large group of Negro painters have always been used to hammer down standards. Such a situation could never have existed if some effort had been made to enroll them," Weinstock said.

"It is not enough merely to accept the applications of those few Negro painters. From now on we're going out to get Negro members and that means not merely the privilege of paying dues and attending meetings, but the willing and eager extension of the hand of brotherhood."

The election will be held February 29. It was ordered as a result of the resignation of Philip Zausner, former secretary-treasurer of the District Council, following an investigation which substantiated the charges that Zausner and business agents of locals under his control had been fraudulently elected in June 1935.

Local 905 of the painters' union, affiliated with District Council 9, has sent Joseph Lenoff as a delegate to the National Negro Congress which is being held over the weekend in Chicago.

Enthusiastic ovations greeted Weinstock when he appeared on Friday night before three local unions for the official opening of his campaign.

Unanimous endorsement of his candidacy by Local 905, with headquarters at 870 Freeman Street, Bronx, was the result of his first appearance of the evening.

Certain of Election

Although he asked no vote of endorsement at any of the three local
meetings in which he appeared, the overwhelming enthusiasm of his audiences
indicated how completely certain is his election to office on Feb. 29.
"There is only one guarantee that our union is really entering a new
era, a period of democratic reconstruction and unified effort to compel the
bosses to live up to their agreements," Weinstock said. "That guarantee is
the unflagging vigilance of every painter in District Council 9."
Weinstock emphasized that his election is not to be regarded as a victory
for an individual or a group of individuals but for a program which has long
been the dream of the vast majority of the membership.

Daily Worker, February 17, 1936.

4. STRIKE MEDIATOR WILL ARRIVE HERE

Work At Smithfield Court Is
Practically At Standstill

Contractors in charge of construction of the $2,500,000 Negro model
housing project at Smithfield Court today awaited arrival of a Federal con-
ciliator from Washington to settle the six-day-old strike of 150 workers on
the project.
Work is practically at a standstill. A small number of plumbers are
carrying on despite inclement weather.
A hundred common laborers went on strike Friday, demanding an increase in
wages from 30 to 40 cents an hour. Fifty semi-skilled laborers quit work in
sympathy with the others.
Representatives of Algernon Blair, Montgomery contractor in charge of
construction of the superstructures for the project, said the Public Works
Administration, which is furnishing funds for the work, has set wage scales
and that they are abiding by these regulations.
The strike was called by G. A. Harris, president of the Birmingham local
of the International Hod Carriers Building and Common Laborers' Union of
America.

Birmingham Post, January 20, 1937.

5. PICKET LINE PROTESTS USE OF WHITE WORKERS
IN COLORED NEIGHBORHOOD

*Black Skilled Workers in St. Louis Building $55,000
Theater to Prove They Are Qualified--Urban
League Active.*

ST. LOUIS, Aug. 26--(ANP)--As Negro skilled workers continued construction
of a $55,000 theatre to prove themselves worthy of admission into the Building
Trades Council of the American Federation of Labor, members of the workers'
council, an organization of Negro laborers, this week are picketing a construction job employing whites. Both building projects are in colored neighborhoods.
The pickets, carrying signs stating, 'Job Unfair to Negro Labor,' are
stationed at a corner where stores are being erected. The construction firm
is under contract to hire members of A. F. of L. unions.
The workers' council is affiliated with the St. Louis Urban league, which
is fighting to get recognition of Negroes in the building trades council for
something other than common labor. Both the all-Negro construction job and the
picketing are being done because of this fight.
John J. Church, white, secretary of the Building Trades Council, denied

Negro skilled workmen are barred from membership, stating, "If skilled Negro
workmen come up to the standards set by the union examining boards, they will
be admitted to membership. It's true there are no Negro members of the
skilled workmen's unions, but that's not our fault. Several have applied for
membership, but failed to pass the examination."

But according to John T. Clark, Urban League secretary, "The Building
Trades unions are hostile, evasive and unfair in their attitude towards Negroes
joining them. Our criticism is not against the American Federation of Labor,
which permits Negroes to join their building unions in other cities, but
against the Building Trades council here."[153]

He declared skilled workers have obtained transfer cards in other cities
but the local council refused to honor them. Three of the bricklayers on the
theatre job hold transfer cards the white unionists here have refused to
recognize.

Pittsburgh Courier, August 28, 1937.

6. WHITES STRIKE OVER HIRING OF RACE EMPLOYES

MEMPHIS, Tenn., Aug. 26--(ANP)--Because Negroes were employed in the same
department in which they work, 15 white employees of the rug department of
McCallum and Robinson, Inc., walked out of the plant Wednesday on strike.

After the strikers called at the office of Lev Loring, president of the
Memphis Trades and Labor council, Loring said, "I'm going to do whatever I can
to help them. They don't have a complaint about wages. They said they
received from 20 to 22 cents an hour. The complaint is they are afraid they
will be replaced by Negroes who are already being brought into the division."

W. W. Robinson, president of the company, said his white workers should
have no fear of losing their jobs to colored inasmuch as a number of Negroes
work in the same department with some having been there for over 10 years.

Pittsburgh Courier, August 28, 1937.

7. EDITORIAL OF THE MONTH:
Labor Points the Way

Labor . . . is leading the way to accord between blacks and whites. Signs
of the new understanding are everywhere. A few weeks ago the hotel and
restaurant workers, assembled in San Francisco for their international meeting,
decided unanimously to leave the hotel which had been chosen for their headquarters when it sought to discriminate against their Negro delegates. The
American Federation of Labor, at its meeting in Tampa, followed its own, not
Florida's standards, in the treatment of Negroes in attendance.

In other relations progress is slower. The Democratic party in national
convention in Houston, Texas, put Negroes behind a screen. The Republican
party meeting in Kansas did not share the headquarters of their states. Even
Christianity for which brotherhood is a cornerstone has bowed the knee to Baal.
The young people's international group, headed by Dr. Daniel A. Polling, found
its religious convictions unequal to meeting young people of color on an
equality when its annual gathering was held in a border state.

In the light of these failures of accord within groups who are associated
together in a limited way, labor's acting all for one and one for all in the
one most important matter of making a living is Gargantuan, overwhelming,
incontrovertible evidence of lessening friction between the races. Granted
that some unions and some union men still live in the past, the rapid increase
of those that incorporate the Negro into unionism whole-heartedly is the real
weather vane of what is happening.

Nothing short of this depression which upturned established custom could have hastened the entry of Negroes into labor and into industry. They used to get a chance to work as strike breakers. But there could be only a limited amount of that sort of employment and it was short lived. Today, in a greater variety of crafts and in larger volume than ever before the Negro's right to a job is conceded.

Some see race progress in what Negroes do only in politics. A minister appointed to Liberia, or an official elected for them is noteworthy. But measured by consequences, both immediate and far-reaching, Negroes answering the roll call when some factory resumes production, is the more important.

At the same time that Negroes find this new tendency heartening, labor unions are getting the thrill of doing that which is in keeping with conscience. Less black-balling of the Negro is a duty owed to the race. Instead a sober consideration of what will give labor its rightful share of its production.

This more thoughtful action is bound to continue. It is in keeping with the eternal verities. It will pay! Men of sense all know that Negroes must share work if they are to carry responsibilities. Whites are beginning to see how they sacrifice themselves whenever prejudice supersedes sense.

The "race question" bids fair to fade out of American life in this century. "Cotton Ed" Smith of South Carolina and his ilk may drag the Negro into politics just as Tillman used to do to divert attention from the really important public questions, but as fast as whites tolerate the Negro in labor, they will refuse to ban him in politics.[154]

The Crisis, 45 (October, 1938): 331.

8. NEGRO DOCKERS STRIKE IN GEORGIA FOR PAY INCREASE

SAVANNAH, Ga., Oct. 13 (UP)--Negro longshoremen went on strike here again today several hours after they returned to work under a 48-hour truce pending conferences with deep-water shippers on a new union contract.

Officials of the International Longshoremen's Association here refused to comment on the new walkout, but it was understood it was called because one shipper continued to work non-union stevedores.

V. E. Townsend, southern representative for the union, was enroute to Savannah from Charleston, S.C.

The strike did not affect coastwise shipping. Members of the union are demanding 50 cents hourly wages be increased to 75 cents, and greater sub-division of hatch crews.

The original strike became effective Saturday.

Daily Worker, October 14, 1938.

9. LONGSHOREMEN IN NEW ORLEANS;
The Fight Against "Nigger Ships"

By Robert C. Francis

New Orleans is a quaint old city, noted for many things, chief among which is the river-front and the disturbances which have occurred there particularly since 1919. It may be well to recall, at this time, that the entire labor movement in this city is backward as compared with that of northern industrial centers. There is a greater union mortality rate, especially among Negro organizations than one encounters elsewhere. The story of unionism on the river-front, in which the black worker has played a significant role, is indeed replete with examples resulting from a state of development not far removed from the embryo.

A number of phenomena have united to make the plight of the black long-shoreman precarious. The great amount of unemployment in recent years in New Orleans has decreased the Negroes' opportunity to hold a job because, as elsewhere in the South, many of those jobs that only the colored man handled have been taken by the whites and in larger numbers they have looked for work on the river-front. Along with unemployment, politics has taken an increas-ingly important part in curtailing the range of Negro longshoremen, and this has only been offset by gains they have made by acting as strikebreakers. In a number of places it is believed that a few years ago Negroes lost out on certain docks and were replaced by white men as a means of obtaining votes for those in control of the state administration. Those persons who have learned from experience feel that the Negroes who picketed during the 1935 strike did so through ignorance, for they believe that after the settlement is made, white longshoremen will get the work.

The International Longshoremen's Association, (I.L.A.) a strong organiza-tion, and one of the American Federation of Labor Unions which has no color bar, has been trying to effect a contract with the New Orleans Steamship Association for a number of years. Of course, in the southern seaports, the I.L.A. generally maintains separate colored and white locals. In New Orleans, a rather unique situation prevailed, i.e., the Negro organization was affiliated with the I.L.A. and known as Local 231. The white union was recognized by the national body through the black one. In New Orleans, both unions continued to exist between 1919 and 1923, although no contract had been signed. The agreement of the first named year, however, called for 60 cents per hour, while 80 cents was paid during the four-year period because of a scarcity of men. In 1923, the unions demanded a contract calling for 80 cents per hour, and at the same time, they asked the inclusion of the screwmen over which issue a controversy arose.

The function of the screwmen, before the introduction of the compressor, had been to tighten the loosely packed bales of cotton in the hold of the ship by means of a screw-press made for the purpose. Shortly before the World War, the compression of cotton in the gins relegated the task to the past, but for a time, as is usual in such cases, the screwmen held on. The strike of 1923, which ended in the defeat of the unions, was occasioned by their effort to negate the result of increased mechanization by attempting to have the occupa-tion of the screwmen remain unmolested.

This, the operators refused to do. The two organizations proceeded to take a strike vote, which resulted in the Negroes deciding to work by a majority of 440 to 160, while the white longshoremen, 500 strong, went on record as unanimously in favor of a walkout. Hearing of the outcome of the vote, the white president led his entire organization to the Negro Hall, and at a joint meeting, overruled those who wanted to work. Many of the colored longshoremen who had voted against the strike, reported for work the following morning, but were unable to find employment because the foremen, all of whom were white, were on strike.

The strike is, of course, the strongest weapon of organized labor and yet it is costly to all concerned. In 1923, the colored longshoremen sustained a loss from which they have never recovered. At that time, they owned the premises known as the Longshoremen's Hall, so in order to protect the property, twenty-five of the unionists, who were not in favor of the strike, obtained a Federal Injunction prohibiting those members who had struck from disposing of the property; moreover, the injunction stated that the Negro was not a scab, because his organization had voted almost by a plurality, to work; consequently, in so doing, he was only carrying out this mandate. This group, which is known as the Longshoremen's Realty Organization, is still the owner of the Hall, but the split of 1923 has kept the majority of those working from using the building.

Just about the time the Steamship Association was beginning to wonder about a way out, one A. E. Harris, of New Orleans, approached the employers and told them that he would handle the work for them. Harris had worked on the river-front in his earlier years, and knew the game. He rounded up a gang of men, none of whom had ever worked as longshoremen. The operators were dubious but desperate, so they agreed to his proposition. Harris's men, all-around good hands, soon became familiar with the work; in fact, most of the members of Local 231 soon joined the new men. As a result after a few weeks, the strike was given up,--a complete failure.

A noteworthy gain was made insofar as individual workers were concerned, because previous to 1923, there had been no Negroes acting as foremen nor any in positions of responsibility. The close of the strike found 14 black men running gangs; at the present time, there are about 8 or 10. The decrease in the number may be accounted for in one way only--the men who have lost out were not capable of holding down the jobs. After the strike, Negroes were to be found driving winches, operating derricks, working as overside men, etc. At that time, there were about 27000 regular longshoremen--only 125 of whom were white. Between 1923 and 1927, longshoremen worked independently as employees of the Steamship Association. During the interval, Harris was given the task of supervising the hiring of all men. A badge system was adopted and only men possessing credentials given by the representative of the Steamship Association were permitted to work.

In addition to a great increase in the black personnel on the river-front, another distinct gain was made in the spread of the Negro over the whole field. Prior to 1923, there had existed what was known as "Nigger ships"--that is, all of those ships which came to port with cargo that was difficult to handle or obnoxious to the senses. White longshoremen would not handle these boats, but left that for the black man to do, while the former took all of the easier work. Boats loaded with creosote timber, iron ore, cement, sugar, cottonseed oil cake, and the like, were some of these ships. During the strike, the Negro proved himself to the extent that the employers became convinced that he could do the work faster, more efficiently, and seemed to withstand the heat of the summer better than the white man, who also, in contrast to the attitude of the black, would not do all types of work. Steamship owners did not continue to hire the Negro because of any love for the colored man, but for the simple reason that it was to their economic advantage.

In 1927, a series of events transpired;--events that were destined to keep the longshoremen in a state of upheaval that has had as a result the present trouble. That was the year in which Francis Williams ran for Mayor of New Orleans against Walmsley. An article was printed stating that the New Orleans Steamship Assn. had Africanized the water-front through A. E. Harris;--further that "N-----s were riding to work in automobiles while whites were starving." Williams stressed these facts throughout his campaign, thus making the whole issue a political one. About the same time the remnants of the white organization, many of the former members of which had gone into other occupations, elected a person known as Terrence Darcy to the presidency. Their new president immediately attempted to make inroads upon the gains the Negroes had achieved.

In the meantime, under the leadership of Mose Johnson, who was president of the organization from 1925 to 1927, Local 231 was reinstated in the I.L.A. by paying up all of the past obligations. Johnson proved to be honest, and in his fourteen months in office the treasury accumulated $14,000. In 1927, when trouble was brewing, Johnson advised the men to have nothing to do with any dispute, but to continue working as usual. At that time, there were about 700 members in good standing in Local 231. The reason for the comparatively small number was because the initiation fee required for entrance into the organization was $66.00. (In contrast to this, the white longshoremen paid $1.00 to join their union). The high fee kept those who did not work rather steadily out of Local 231. Some of those Negroes who were outside of the Local gave Darcy a fertile field in which to work. And this he was quick to grasp.

Darcy organized what was known as the "Get-Together Club," included in whose roster was a Negro named Sylvester Pete, a man who has played an important role in the affairs of the longshoremen. Each Sunday afternoon, members of the club, numbering about 2500, composed of colored longshoremen, roustabouts and others, hoping to get jobs, met at the white longshoremen's hall. A plan was outlined by Darcy, calling for a strike and the assumption of the work handled by 231, by members of the "Get-Together Club." Local 231 refused to take the members of the club into its fold as had the white union. Darcy, however, influenced Joseph Ryan, the President of the I.L.A. to force Local 231 to take the entire "Get-Together" membership into its ranks at $1.35 per man. Late in 1927, when this occurred, there was only enough work for the regular men in the local. The Sunday after the induction of the clubmen into the union, the former, following Darcy's orders, voted to strike, while at the same time, white unionists decided to work. A very pretty trick designed to make it appear to the operators that Local 231 had caused the trouble, and to give the white union an opportunity once again, to control labor conditions along the water-front. But the New Orleans Steamship Association failed to see eye to eye with Darcy, so the white union failed in their plan to take over all of the work.

Johnson and Darcy, as presidents of their respective unions, were summoned to appear before the Mayor that he might ascertain whose was the responsibility for the calling of the strike. Johnson rightly claimed that the Negro longshoremen were not striking, but that the "Get-Together Club" was;--on the other hand, Darcy was able to show, in his union's minutes, that its members had voted to work. The outcome of the whole fiasco was that Darcy succeeded in having Johnnson impeached. In the interim, between the deposition of Johnson and the installation of a man under Darcy's control, old members of Local 231 approached Harris and asked him if they could work, to which he, as representative of the Steamship Association, replied that they "and any bona-fide white longshoreman" could work.

Spencer, the new President of Local 231, immediately attempted to carry out Darcy's policy. His first act was to bring charges of insubordination against the old members of the local, some of whom were fined as high as $24.00. All of the men who were in this category, left the organization and worked as independents, the majority of them remained in the employ of the United States Shipping Board until it went out of business. The strike of 1927, succeeded in accomplishing nothing but the complete disruption of Local 231.

Things remained in this condition until 1931, when, because of the withdrawal of Shipping Board work, Negroes decided to work for 65 cents per hour. Darcy refused to agree to the terms, but demanded 80 cents per hour. Instead of responding, however, black longshoremen notified their superintendents that they would work. The strike of 1931, like the previous ones, was lost and the Negroes became more firmly entrenched.

Darcy then attempted another method; one in which politics was to play a significant role. He caused Spencer to have those remaining in Local 231 to adopt a resolution reading to the effect that no one but a certified registered voter could do work on the water-front. The fact that the individuals in the organization would do such a thing is commentary enough on their caliber. To date, less than 1,000 Negroes have qualified to vote in New Orleans. At that time, the number was less, and it is safe to say, not a dozen of them were working on the river-front. Darcy had tried, without success, to get Local 231 to do this before and had been told that he had "a lot of nerve coming into a Negro organization and into a Negro Hall with such a proposition."

The proposition, stating in part, that only certified registered voters should be employed in "loading and unloading on publicly-owned and operated trucks, freight cars, ships, vessels, or similar vehicles within the territorial limits of the city," was made an ordinance by the City Fathers. There was widespread and bitter protest. Negro longshoremen marched to the City Hall in a body, and they were joined in their protest by other Negroes representing all walks of life. The outcome was the changing of the original ordinance to require that a person must have a two year old poll tax certificate in order to be employed, as above mentioned. This would have made no difference, because Negroes, knowing they could not qualify to vote, did not bother to pay the poll tax. At the City Hall, Darcy made a public speech concerning the adoption by the New Orleans Steamship Association of a system where everyone employed regularly at every line had to wear a badge and be photographed as a means of identification, with the end in view to keep their regular men on the job. He held up a badge and a photograph and lamented such a disgraceful thing as a white man not being able to work on the river-front unless the N-gg-r A. E. Harris said he could do so.

Of all the attempts to get the Negro off of the water-front, this was the most flagrant. The effort to politicalize longshore work in New Orleans, was not a success because the important business concerns of the city prohibited the enforcement of the ordinance. It is necessary to use the wharves and thoroughfares in getting to and from the docks; moreover, most of the drivers of trucks and teams are Negroes, so 68 different injunctions were taken out against the City Ordinance by "big business."

Local 231 had made a pretence of keeping up its obligations with the I.L.A., but after 1931, it became defunct. Thus, what was once a progressive Negro Union, passed into oblivion.

In 1933, under the labor clause of the National Recovery Act, the longshoremen again came together for union action in two separate groups known as
the Independent Colored Longshoremen's and Independent White Longshoremen's
Associations. The men in both organizations were old-time longshoremen, the
present colored officers are former officers of Local 231 and would still be
connected with it, had they been permitted to conduct their own business and
not been subjected to outside interference. After the organizations had
signed contracts at 75 cents per hour with the Steamship Association, President
Ryan influenced them to consider re-affiliation with the I.L.A., which
question, after due deliberation, the unions decided affirmatively. The Negro
organization paid $300, the entire sum needed for reinstatement, while the
white union paid $25, the balance of which was to be sent to I.L.A. national
headquarters upon receipt of the charter. In the meantime, Darcy and his
henchmen intercepted the granting of the charters to the two newly formed
groups. Ryan rescinded his action on the grounds that he was unaware of a
point brought to his attention subsequently, i.e., that the Independents were
company unions and as such, could not be taken into an A. F. of L. Federation.
The money was not returned to the outcasts and although entered in the 1934
directory of locals of the I.L.A., they have never actually functioned as such.
    The strike which began on October 1, 1935, was called by the few remaining
adherents of the I.L.A. led by the same Darcy, for the purpose of destroying
the Independent unions. The walkout had been planned for earlier in the year,
but was postponed until October, when I.L.A. officials decided their only hope
lay in making trouble. At the outset it was apparent that of the 2700 Negro
and 400 white longshoremen regularly employed, comparatively few blacks would
stop work. The first morning a number of whites failed to appear along with 2
or 3 per cent of the colored workers, but there was a surplus of new men on
hand, looking for jobs, and this has been true every day since October 1st. To
date, in the neighborhood of 300 vessels have sailed on schedule—which proves
decisively that the strike in the Gulf Ports, which had its inception in New
Orleans and has retarded work elsewhere, has done nothing to slacken it there,
—on the contrary, business for the port as a whole, has been greater for the
past two months than in any like period during the past four years.
    The men meet at a central point, (foot of Canal Street) before six A.M.
There they are hired by the respective foremen and since the strike began, they
have been transported to their respective jobs in trucks and tugs under police
protection. For a few weeks they were returned to the hiring place in the
evening, but the attacking of workers by the strikers, on their way home,
caused the employers to send the men to the vicinity of their homes in police
protected trucks.
    Motivated by the outbreak of violence, which the police thought might
develop into something serious, the Steamship Association put into effect an
injunction which was granted in 1927. Its effect was instantaneous,—aside
from quieting the strikers, it compelled the leaders to spend their time in
seeking to have the order of the Federal District Court reconsidered under the
Norris-LaGuardia Act. Despite the anti-injunction law, the employers' weapon
remained in effect, while what Professor Commons states in his recent book,
"Institutional Economics" is a truism, namely: "If the courts would observe
them, anti-injunction laws would keep the courts out of politics and place
labor associations somewhat on an equality before the law with employers'
associations," Professor Commons was considering the organized labor movement
in its entirety, and not the problem of Negro labor in the South.[155]
    The I.L.A. would have lost out completely in New Orleans weeks ago had it
not been for the boycott which was carried on in other ports against the
handling of cargo loaded by independent labor. As it is, the one thing that
kept it from utter rout, was the appointment of a Mediation Board by the
Secretary of Labor. It appears now that the organization will hold what it had
before the strike, while the only possibility of its making a gain is this: The
Board may succeed in effecting a compromise measure, in which case the
Independent unions may again take up the banner of the I.L.A. A compromise,
however, is never satisfactory and in that event, trouble may be expected in
the near future. This has already been presaged by a recent petition filed in
the Federal Court by the Negro and White Independent Longshoremen Associations
for an injunction to restrain members of the I.L.A. from interfering with
workers on the docks. In fine, the two non-I.L.A. unions are attempting to

prepare against expected difficulties, for knowing the method of the International Longshoremen's Association, they expect it to try again.

It is a pathetic situation that has existed in New Orleans, for most of
the physical fighting was done by Negro strikers and Negro strikebreakers.
This is brought more forcibly to mind, when we realize, as shown above, that
every move on the part of the New Orleans representatives of the I.L.A. has
indicated their desire to drive the black man from the water-front. There is
no complaint against the I.L.A. as an organization, for theoretically it does
not discriminate against the Negro. But the machinations of the representatives in New Orleans have made the colored longshoreman wary. The requests of
the strikes, for an increase in the hourly wage from 75 cents to 85 cents
straight time and for an improvement in working conditions, were felt to be
quite sane and much needed by those who did not strike, but they did not want
to see the crystallization of the main part of the plan--the ascendency of the
International Longshoremen's Association to absolute control of the labor
market on the New Orleans water-front.

This type of guerilla warfare does not do the black or white laborer any
good, but until the white laborer learns that his interest is identical with
that of the Negro working man, we must seize every opportunity for momentary
gain. In New Orleans, for the present at least, it is best for the Negro to
be independent of the I.L.A.

It is well to remember that the South is still the South--and its
prejudices are deeply rooted,--particularly where, in his efforts to gain a
livelihood, the black man competes directly with the white laborer. In view
of this, the Negro worker has to grasp every opportunity to make a living.
Necessity has forced the black longshoremen to view affiliation with the I.L.A.
from one aspect alone: Will they gain more by going into the organization or
by remaining without? Unfortunately, the colored man is not a part of the
Labor Movement in the South, and is only tolerated as a means of avoiding
competition. He will never be a part of such a movement until a change of
heart occurs on the part of the poor whites--if this is possible.

Opportunity, 14 (March, 1936): 82-85, 93.

10. JOHN FITZPATRICK TO WARREN N. CLARK AND
SHAILER MATHEWS, CHICAGO CHURCH FEDERATION, MAY 26, 1937[156]

Gentlemen:

We received your letter of May 21st, requesting information in reference
to the attitude of labor unions towards Negro workers and in answer to your
first question, "Are Negroes admitted to any or all unions in Chicago? will
say:

The answer is that this matter is determined by employers. If employers
employ Negroes, we strive to bring these Negroes into our unions, if for no
other reason, than out of necessity to maintain our hour and wage standards.

In reply to your second question, "Are there special units for Negro
members?" we would say that fundamentally, the labor movement is opposed to
special privileges under any and all circumstances. Where white men and
Negroes are employed in the same employment, they are accepted into the union
on an equal footing, but if only Negroes are employed, they can secure a
charter just the same as if the group were all white. In other words, there
would be nothing in the charter to indicate that it was issued to Negroes or
white men.

In reply to your third question, "Are there restrictions as to where they
may work, if Negroes? the answer is yes and no. The unions do not inject any
restrictions, but the employers do. Employers can and do restrict their
employees to all Negroes or all whites. We have no say in such cases. We just
proceed to organize the workers, regardless of creed, color or nationality.

In reply to your fourth question, "Are there wage differentials of any
sort?" The labor movement declares for equal pay for equal work, whether

performed by men or women employees. Employers, on a basis of 99 out of every 100, try to punish the Negro because of his color. Organized labor is the only institution that stands for equality for the Negro as far as his economic interests are concerned.

I hope I have given understandable answers to your questions. If I have failed to make myself clear, point out such instances and I will be glad to try again.

I may add that in each recurring convention of the American Federation of Labor for the past forty or more years, some resolution or some declaration has emanated therefrom, urging organization of Negro workers as the only means of preventing exploitation of the Negro by employers and the only means of safeguarding the standards of life and labor secured by white workers.

The Negro worker is more "prone" to "Jim Crow" himself than to be "Jim Crowed" by white workers. The Negro worker attempts to secure special consideration because of his color and in order to prevent the Negro from "Jim Crowing" himself, we accept him on an equal footing with white workers.

As workers, our problems are exactly the same. We have a common cause and as some one said, "A house divided will surely fall," and we do not propose to let our house fall because of such division.

Out of 106 National and International unions affiliated with the American Federation of Labor, I know of only two organizations whose constitutions declare "This is an organization composed of white men," and these organizations have been urged to change this language. We are in hopes that they will soon see the wisdom of making this change.

If the foregoing statements call for further clarification, please let me know and I will be glad to go into further detail.

Yours very truly,

President
CHICAGO FEDERATION OF LABOR.

John Fitzpatrick Papers, Chicago Historical Society.

11.   WARREN N. CLARK AND SHAILER MATHEWS TO THE
CHICAGO FEDERATION OF LABOR (JOHN FITZPATRICK), MAY 21, 1937

Gentlemen:

A recent joint meeting of the Commission on the Church and Industry, and the Commission of Interracial Relations of the Chicago Church Federation heard a presentation of the difficulties encountered by Negroes in securing employment, especially in skilled trades.

In the discussion following the presentation the Commission felt the need of factual data to guide appropriate action. It was therefore ordered that your organization be addressed with a request for a statement of its policies regarding Negro labor. Are Negroes admitted to any or all unions in Chicago? Are there special units for Negro members? Are there restrictions as to where they may work, if members? Are there wage differentials of any sort?

The commissions would greatly appreciate your statement in order that they might have a clear picture of the Negro's problem as regards organized labor.

Very respectfully,

Chairman, Commission of Church and Industry

Chairman, Commission on Interracial
Relations

John Fitzpatrick Papers, Chicago Historical Society.

12.   PACKERS JOIN AUTO HANDS IN SIT-DOWN STRIKE

By Russ J. Cowans

DETROIT--Chief battleground of the sit-down strikers, Detroit last week
saw workers in many other fields adopt this latest form of labor protest which
has practically riddled the automobile industry.

Most outstanding was the strike at the Newton Packing Company, under
A. F. of L. auspices, in which more than fifty colored butchers, sausage
makers, cutters and slaughterers joined.

Efforts of Sheriff Thomas Wilcox to serve an arrest order on the group
met a setback when Circuit Court Judge Allen Campbell on Monday announced that
he would withhold decision on a petition for permission to deputize 600 men for
the task.

Shortly before, Judge Campbell granted the Chrysler Corporation an injunction restraining strikers from occupying the Chrysler plant after Wednesday.

Many of the 3,000 colored employees of the firm were among the group
ordered to evacuate. Other thousands are helping to retain possession of the
Dodge, Plymouth, DeSoto and Hudson plants.

The ranks of some 10,000 colored automobile workers are seriously divided
over the question of affiliating with the United Automobile Workers, division
of John L. Lewis's Committee for Industrial Organization.

While many thousands readily fell into line, other thousands remained
definitely aloof, while many are in a quandary as to the best policy.

John King, Dodge employee, who sought to leave the plant last week, was
severely beaten by strike guards who have been thrown around the plant to
frustrate any attempt on the part of workers to abandon the sit-down campaign.

Pay Held Up

Approximately thirty colored workers stormed the Chrysler plant, Saturday
morning, in an effort to get their pay from the paymaster. They had to club
their way through the strong guard stationed at the gate, but were unable to
get their pay as the paymaster told them the records were in the office held by
the strikers.

Although no sit-down strikes have been pulled in any of the restaurants
and beer gardens in the colored districts, plans are already afoot for the
unionization of the waiters and waitresses.

Frank Loftis, official organizer for the waiters' and waitresses' union,
an affiliate of the A. F. of L., has been working in this direction.

Edwards on Committee

Marshall Edwards, 29, was chairman of the strike committee and a member of
the negotiating committee which was in conference with officials of the Michigan
Malleable Iron Foundry before the settlement of the strike there, last week.

The workers in the automobile plants are asking a minimum wage of 75 cents
an hour for men and 65 cents an hour for women. They are also demanding that
the United Automobile Workers be recognized the sole bargaining agency for the
employees.

Baltimore Afro-American, July 20, 1937.

13.- PACKING CO. EMPLOYEES DISARMED:
HAULED TO JAIL

DETROIT.--Filing out of the Newton Packing Company, 5075 Fourteenth Street,
when 400 policemen and deputy sheriffs, armed with tear gas, dislodged the 82
sit-downers, including 20 women, were 8 colored employees of the company.

Along with the other strikers, these eight were taken to the county jail,

where they were held until a preliminary hearing before Judge Allen Campbell
of the circuit court, who suspended sentence on the men upon their plea of
guilty to a charge of contempt of court.

Judge Campbell last week issued an injunction ordering the strikers from
the plant, but they refused to obey.

As the officers broke into the plant, 100 of them lined up outside
prepared to fire tear gas. A search of the first floor of the office building
revealed only one man, guarding a door leading to a large yard between the
office building and refrigerator plant.

Had Improvised Weapons

The sit-downers, including the eight colored workers, were standing in
the yard, armed with clubs, milk bottles, red-hot meat hooks, small cleavers
and large ones that needed two hands to swing them. Some of them had short
lengths of pipe.

A fire was burning in the yard, in which the hooks had been heated.

The officers ordered the strikers to line up against the wall. Those
with the hooks refused to move. When the police approached they shouted, We
are American citizens. You can't touch us."

The officers rushed the strikers, dislodging them from the large drums,
and lined them up with their companions, their weapons abandoned.

The doors and windows had been barricaded with boxes and other obstruc-
tions. Officers found mattresses on desk tops on the second floor. Also laid
on the floor were rugs and canvas bags, used for pillows.

Strikers Fare Well

Ben Downey, 24, of 973 East Warren Avenue, said he had fared well during
the twenty-four days the sit-downers had occupied the plant. Officers said
they had discovered a large ham boiling in a pot over one of the fires.

In the meantime, those colored workers in the Chrysler, Dodge and Hudson
plants, are preparing for a raid on the part of the police, sometime this week.
The Chrysler officials have secured an injunction order for the eviction of
the workers from the eight plants now being held. . . .

A sit-down strike at Frank and Seder Department Store was averted when
police dislodged the sit-downers less than an hour after an organizer had
blown his whistle in the store to announce a strike.

It would have involved several porters and maids employed at the store.

Baltimore Afro-American, March 27, 1937.

14. JIM CROWISM IN A. F. OF L. SCORED AT HARLEM RALLY

By Cyril Briggs[157]

Support for the work of organizing Negro workers into the American labor
movement on a basis of full equality and for the fight to break down the
jim-crow barriers that still exist in some of the A. F. of L. unions was
pledged by prominent trade union leaders of New York, and by Norman Thomas,
Socialist leader, at the dedication of the new Harlem Labor Center, at 312 West
125th Street, on Sunday afternoon.

The dedication ceremony, held in the beautifully-equipped center, was
attended by 500 workers, most of them Negroes, with Jacob Mirsky, president of
Bricklayers Union, Local 37, presiding.

The meeting was opened by Noah O. A. Walters, secretary of the Socialist-
led Negro Labor Committee who, before introducing Mirsky, gave a brief outline
of the organization of the committee six months ago, its work in combatting
discrimination in the labor movement, and its achievement in creating a center
"for the use of all trade unionists, Negro and white, in the community."

Mirsky Sounds Keynote

Mirsky sounded the keynote of the meeting with a call for "unity of black and white workers for betterment of economic as well as of social conditions."

The meeting gave a tremendous ovation to Norman Thomas, Socialist leader, and vigorously applauded when the chairman praised the Socialist Call, spokesman of the newly constituted City Central Committee, which is leading the fight in the Socialist Party against the Old Guard.

Thomas praised the work of the Negro Labor Committee, and declared that there is no chance, whatever, that this country will escape fascism unless the unity of Negro and white workers is forged. The beating of three labor organizers in Tampa, which resulted in the death of Joseph Shoemaker, Socialist leader, is an example of what the workers of the United States will have to face, unless colored and white workers are organized in the labor movement without discrimination, he said.

Urges A.F.L. Boycott of Tampa

He urged that all A. F. of L. workers exert pressure on the A. F. of L. Executive Committee to force a change in its plans to hold the next A. F. of L. convention in Tampa.

Fascist Italy's robber war on Ethiopia was vigorously assailed by Luigi Antonini, First Vice-President of the International Ladies Garment Workers Union, who was one of the delegates from this country to the recent World Congress of Italians abroad, demonstrated last Saturday night against the fascist meeting in Madison Square Garden, at which Mayor La Guardia and several New York State judges spoke.

The meeting heard a message read from William Green, president of the A. F. of L., in which the A. F. of L. head declared that "Negro workers were turning to the A. F. of L. with increasing conviction," and "were becoming more responsible trade unionists," but was silent on the burning issue of continued discrimination in many of the A. F. of L. unions, and the responsibility of the top leadership by the progressive and the rank and file movement in the A. F. of L.

Crosswaith Speaks

Frank Crosswaith, chairman of the Negro Labor Committee and an organizer of the I. L. G. W. U., expressed appreciation to the numerous unions and individuals that were supporting the work of the Committee. Scoring the continued hostility to Negro labor of the reactionaries in the A. F. of L., Crosswaith declared that the working class "cannot win power by remaining divided on a basis of race or craft."

Other speakers, all of whom pledged support to the fight to root out prejudice and discrimination from the labor movement included Thomas J. Curtis, a former vice-president of the A. F. of L., Thomas Young, Negro vice-president of Building Service Workers Union, Local 32B; Sascha Zimmerman, Business Manager of Local 22, I. L. G. W. U., Murray Baron, Business Manager of the Suitcase, Bag and Portfolio Workers Union.[158]

Telegrams of greetings to the meeting were received from Leo Krzycki, chairman of the National Executive Committee of the Socialist Party; Clarence Senior, National Secretary of the Socialist Party; Jack Altman, temporary chairman of the newly constituted City Central Committee of the New York Socialist Party and Morris Feinstone, secretary of the United Hebrew Trades.[159]

Daily Worker, December 17, 1935.

15.   RESULT OF GREEN PROBE IS AWAITED

ST. LOUIS, Sept. 16--(By ANP)--A special probe of protests by Negro organizations that members of the race skilled in building trades are being discriminated against by A. F. of L. unions of skilled mechanics is being conducted under orders of William Green, national president.

Investigating the charges is Al Towers, white, organizer for the International Moulders' Union, at Erie, Pa. For over a month Towers has been conferring with officials of the Building Trades Council, and with representatives of Negro groups. Other meetings are planned for the near future, after which Towers will submit a report to Green.

The president acted after receiving protests from locals of the Brotherhood of Sleeping Car Porters, Dining Car Employees' Union and other A. F. of L. affiliates which have colored members here. They pointed out that for years skilled Negro workers have been trying without success to gain admission to the Building Trades Council here, although the council has taken in Negro hod-carriers and laborers.

Just what official standing the conferences will have is doubtful. Towers explained that international unions affiliated with the A. F. of L. are autonomous and each has the right to determine its own standards of eligibility, so that apparently all that can result is a "recommendation" as to policy in St. Louis. The unions in the Building Trades Council admit skilled Negro workers in some cities, but in others do not.

Pittsburgh Courier, September 18, 1937.

16. LILY WHITE UNIONS STEAL NEGRO JOBS

The people who preach about labor unity to Negroes will find the reason for much of the skepticism with which they are greeted if they will consider the situation in Tampa, Fla. In that city the Tampa Shipbuilding and Engineering Corporation employed about 1,200 men, of whom about 600 were Negroes. When the corporation secured a government contract for building ships, two A. F. of L. unions secured a closed shop agreement and promptly booted the Negroes out of about 500 of their 600 jobs. Of the 118 colored men now on the job, 116 are doing menial and unskilled work. One Negro hoisting engineer with 20 years of experience is picking up paper in the yard because the union, which has taken his dues, refuses to certify him for anything except picking paper. Scores of other Negroes are paid up union members, but cannot get work.

Now, the employer has had many years of experience with Negroes and wants to employ them. But the union says he cannot. Here is a case where a demonstration of a little labor unity on the part of whites would help erase some of the justifiable reluctance of the Negro to join wholeheartedly in the labor movement.

The Crisis, 46 (September, 1939): 273.

17. THE A. F. OF L. SLAMS THE DOOR AGAIN

There can be little surprise over failure of the annual convention of the American Federation of Labor which met in Seattle in October to take any action against the flagrant racial discrimination of its member unions. The A. F. of L. has been ducking and dodging on racial discrimination these many decades.

A. Philip Randolph, scholarly president of the A. F. of L. Brotherhood of Sleeping Car Porters, made a masterly plea for his "brothers" in the federation to strike a blow for tolerance *in America* at the same time they were yelling for an all-out smash against Hitler's intolerance abroad. He cited chapter, verse, and line of discriminations by unions against Negro workers, especially in the national defense program. But the brothers turned a deaf ear.

Not only were they deaf, but they were insulting. William L. Hutchinson, president of the carpenters' union (which has been a leader in jim crowing

Negroes in national defense work) told Randolph to mind his own business and
is reported to have added: "In our union we don't care whether you're an
Irishman, a Jew, or a nigger."
        Which, of course, is not true.
        Latest and most sinister aspect of the whole picture of the A. F. of L.
and the Negro is the so-called "stabilization" agreement entered into between
Sidney Hillman of OPM and the A. F. of L. building trades unions whereby the
latter are given a virtual monopoly of defense building construction. This
means, in effect, that the government has handed a monopoly to unions whose
policies, with but few exceptions, exclude Negro workers from full-fledged
membership.
        Labor today is more on the defensive than it has been in the last decade.
A dozen anti-labor bills are in the Congress. There is great and heavily-
financed activity by manufacturers and trade institutes and associations to
curb labor under the pretense of building national unity. Already organized
labor is calling upon Negro voters to mobilize and help defeat "the bosses."
        Well, what is the Negro offered? To date he has been not only offered,
but given, a kick in the pants, and no playful one at that. The other week in
Chicago one Harry O'Reilly, regional director of the A. F. of L., offered the
Negro his opinion that the race is "an evil" in the labor movement.
        The important section of organized labor represented by the A. F. of L.
has spoken plainly to us. We can look for no help there. While we must
continue to fight for our rights in the A. F. of L., we can do better than mark
time by working with the C.I.O., which has accorded our workers much better
treatment. In this new wing of organized labor we may be able to go forward as
we should: within the ranks of the labor movement. It would be the greatest
tragedy for all concerned if the millions of normally gainfully employed Negroes
in America were driven to explore what alliances they could make *outside* the
labor movement.

The Crisis, 48 (November, 1941): 343.

18.   FINAL FORUM GATHERING CONDUCTED

Walter White Raps American Labor Federation for
Refusal to Recognize Colored Persons

RACIAL DIFFICULTIES ATTRIBUTED TO SETUP

National Association Secretary Cites Menial
Position of Race in Address at Central High School

        Refusal of the American Federation of Labor to recognize the colored people
of America in industry was cited as one of the chief reasons for difficulty in
racial relations by Walter White, secretary of the National Association for the
Advancement of Colored People, in the final lecture of the Civic Educational
Forum last night in Binghamton Central High School.
        Speaking under the auspices of the Binghamton Inter-racial Commission and
the Civic Educational Forum committee, Mr. White said that the drawing of the
color line by the A. F. of L. and the subsequent wholesale lack of employment
for colored people is one of the biggest barriers in the path of better racial
relations.
        "In the recent depression," he pointed out, "the Negroes were forced out of
even the positions which have always been occupied by colored people, such as
bootblacking, porter work and other menial tasks.
        He called attention to the fact that there is not a single Negro employe
in many of the major industries of the country and said that the people of
America must begin to realize that qualified Negro workers must be recognized
in industry if we are going to solve the racial problem.
        "Lines of demarkation in the skin and color problem are of little
importance in the light of the major problems which face the entire nation,
white and colored.

"If the present spirit of bigotry and intolerance which exists today in the South is allowed to continue we will find that infamous Ku Klux Klan back at work. Denial of justice and opportunities to the Negroes will only complicate the situation by increased crime and the country will eventually pay the bill."

The speaker saw a glimmer of hope in the fact that the collapse of the cotton market in the South has brought the poorer classes together in poverty and is creating a better understanding between some white people and Negroes.

"Negroes are always permitted to pay taxes but are discriminated against in the spending of the revenue obtained through these taxes," he said.

He explained that amounts of the appropriations for education in the South are very unevenly distributed, favoring the white children.

Mr. White urged taking of Negroes into industry in order to improve their economic condition and give them a fair opportunity away from partiality and bigotry.

Birmingham Sun, March 12, 1937.

19. NEGROES MAP NATIONAL CAMPAIGN TO BREAK
COLOR BAR IN R.R. UNIONS

At a meeting of representative trade unionists and other Negro leaders held at the Harlem Y.M.C.A. last Sunday plans were made for a nationwide attack on discrimination against Negro railroad workers in the matter of jobs on railroads and membership in railroad unions. Immediate action on a national scale was declared necessary if the Negro is to hold his own in employment in the railroad industry.

The plans made at the meeting include: (1) Conference with leaders of railroad unions to urge a change of policy towards Negroes; (2) Court action to compel federal labor boards to act in the matter; (3) Injunctions to prohibit unions which bar Negroes from having the benefit of the protection of federal legislation; (4) A nationwide campaign for legislation to protect Negro railroad workers.

Local actions around specific problems faced by Negro railroad workers are also planned. James E. Baker Jr., chairman of the Greater New York Federation of the National Negro Congress has already begun to rally other groups to the defense of Negro railroad workers of New York City. Other localities have begun to plan similar action.

The meeting was held in response to a letter sent out to national leaders by John P. Davis, secretary of the National Negro Congress and James W. Ford. Representatives of Negro Railroad groups were present at the meeting and other national leaders sent messages pledging cooperation. These latter included George Brown of New York City and Layton Weston of St. Louis, Missouri, representing Locals 370 and 354 respectively of the Dining Car Employes Union; T. Arnold Hill of the National Urban League; A. Philip Randolph of the Brotherhood of Sleeping Car Porters and Roy Wilkins, editor of the Crisis magazine.

Barred From Jobs

Pointing to the use of membership color bars as effective devices for keeping Negroes from jobs in the industry, speakers at the meeting pointed out that recent federal legislation governing labor relations on railroads made it imperative that speedy action be taken against the color bars if the Negro worker is to keep his hold on jobs in the industry.

Typical working agreements between railroads and unions were discussed. Many of them were found to provide for no further employment of Negroes and for the gradual elimination of those already employed. "If these working agreements continue to be made and remain in force," declared John P. Davis, "it will be a matter of but a few years before practically no jobs exist for Negroes in the railroad industry. Already as a result of these contracts the number of Negroes employed in the industry has seriously declined, leaving thousands of Negro workers and their families unemployed."

These working agreements, it was pointed out, are enforced in the courts and are aided by federal legislative acts, although they are against public policy and serve to deny to Negro workers their constitutional rights.

Particularly vicious in their terms are clauses in the constitution of the Brotherhood of Railway Carmen, it was indicated. In this union, Negroes are forced into separate locals where they pay dues but where they have no right to elect Negroes to represent them.

Daily Worker, March 12, 1937.

20.   NEGRO LEADERS ASK END OF RAIL UNION DISCRIMINATION

Railway Employes Department Convention Is Sent Appeal Asking Clauses Against Negroes Be Eliminated From Constitution

Eight prominent Negro leaders of unions and organizations yesterday addressed a letter to the National Convention of the Railway Employes Department of the American Federation of Labor now in session at Hotel Morrison, Chicago, appealing that action be taken to eliminate from constitutions of affiliated unions clauses discriminating against Negroes.

The letter mentioned nine unions in the railroad field which have such discriminatory clauses or practice devices which have the same effect.

The Letter

The letter follows:

"Your Convention is meeting at a grave moment in our country that calls for the unity of all forces of labor to protect and defend all the workers' interests and rights.

"We, the undersigned, representatives of the Negro people and of Negro labor, wish to call your attention to the special injustices that face Negro workers in the railroad industry. These injustices are the following: (a) the barring of Negroes from employment in the industry and an alarming tendency to eliminate them completely; (b) the lack of seniority protection and promotion rights for them where they are employed; (c) the failure to admit them at all or to full membership in unions of the railroad industry, with consequent failure to extend union protection to their wages, working conditions, etc.

"Several of the organizations affiliated to the Railway Employees Department of the A. F. of L. have clauses in their Constitutions specifically barring Negroes from becoming members, while others use various discriminatory devices to the same effect. Among these unions are the Brotherhood of Railway Clerks, the Brotherhood of Maintenance of Way Employees, the Brotherhood of Railway Carmen, the Switchmen's Union of North America, the Order of Sleeping Car Conductors, the Order of Railway Telegraphers, the International Brotherhood of Electrical Workers, the International Brotherhood of Blacksmiths, and the Sheet Metal Workers International Association.

Ask Practice Condemned

"We wish to protest to you that these discriminatory practices against Negro workers violate the collective bargaining provisions of the Railway Labor Act and the Wagner Labor Relations Act, and thereby also the rights of Negroes as guaranteed by the Constitution of the United States. They are also against all principles of democracy upon which our country is based.

"Moreover, such discriminatory practices are injurious to white labor as well as to Negro workers on the railroads. The employers have resisted, over a long period of years, the efforts of Negro workers to break down Jim-Crow practices against them in the unions and in the industry. But Negro workers have become trade union conscious and are now a big factor in all struggles of labor, both trade union and political. They are supporting organized labor

wholeheartedly wherever bars are dropped from against them in the unions.   The
railroad labor organizations cannot afford to reject such powerful, potential
support.

"We request your convention to condemn these discriminatory practices
against Negro railroad workers and to call upon your affiliated organizations
to eliminate their Constitutional clauses or other practices that bar Negroes
outright from union membership and limit them in such membership, and that your
convention take the necessary steps to see to it that the question of the
rights of Negro workers on the railroads is placed before forthcoming conventions of your affiliated unions.

"Fraternally yours,

"John P. Davis, Secretary, National
Negro Congress of Washington, D.C.
"Roy Wilkins, Assistant Secretary,
National Association for the Advancement
of Colored Peoples.
"George E. Brown, Regional Director,
Dining Car Employees Union, A. F. of L.
Local No. 370.
"Ashley L. Totten, Int'l Secretary-
Treasurer, Brotherhood of Sleeping Car
Porters.
"Manning Johnson, Business Agent,
Cafeteria Employees Union, Local 302.
"William Gaulden, State, County &
Municipal Workers of America, C.I.O.
"Bill Russell, Painters District Council
9, Delegate.
"A. C. Powell, Jr., Pastor, Abbysinian
Baptist Church."

Daily Worker, April 8, 1938.

21. FIGHT ON DISCRIMINATION SHIFTS TO
A. F. OF L. UNION

Brooklyn Committee Seeking Jobs for Negroes Told
Stores Have 'Closed Shop' with A. F. of L., But
Union Says Books Closed

After fourteen weeks of run around the Citizens Civic Affairs Committee
was still making attempts to break through the anti-Negro policy of Dilbert
Bros., Inc., operators of 45 food stores in Brooklyn, Queens and Long Island.

The committee, which represents a number of civic, labor, church and
fraternal organizations interested in promoting equal job opportunities for
Negro people, has been picketing the company's stores. Signs carried point
out that the company hasn't a single Negro among all its employees and refuses
to hire any, although certain of its stores depend mainly upon Negro trade.

After several vain attempts for a conference with company officials, the
Citizens Committee was finally told that "Negroes would be hired if business
requires them." At the same time the committee was referred to Local 1204 of
the International Retail Clerks Protective Association of the A. F. of L., with
whom the company claimed it has a "closed shop" contract. This was in May.

Union Books "Closed"

Since then, the committee has made efforts to break through an equally
air-tight discrimination wall of Grocery Clerks Local 1204 of the A. F. of L.,
which operates under the guise of a "closed shop" contract.

Frank Elia, business manager of Local 1204, told the committee's representatives that the "closed shop" contract forces the company to employ only union people, but the union's books are "closed" to new members.

Mr. Elia did, however, hasten to assure the Citizens Committee that his union does not discriminate against Negroes and offered to unionize any Negro clerks under a "sub charter," in a separate local that would be "autonomous" and "you could run it yourself." The dues would of course go into Local 1204 and the International's treasury, it was explained. This offer of a jim crow local was declined by the committee.

Inquiries among workers of the Dilbert chain gave some details on how Local 1204 obtains its "closed shop" agreements. As the United Retail Employes of the CIO made rapid headway organizing stores in New York, Dilbert Bros. was one of the firms that sought protection from the Retail Clerks Protective Association of the A. F. of L. A conference between company and union officials struck a bargain whereby every worker is to be forced to join 1204, dues to be checked off by the company.

Seldom are any meeting or election held in the local. The agreements are first entered into with employers, then the union officials get acquainted with the members they are to take in.

Daily Worker, July 28, 1938.

22. BROTHERHOOD WINS OVER HALF MILLION DOLLAR INCREASE FOR PULLMAN PORTERS

In the Pullman Building in Chicago, Illinois, Friday, April 18th, a revised Agreement for Pullman Porters, Maids, Attendants and Bus Boys was negotiated and signed by Champ Carry, Executive Vice-President for the Pullman Company, and A. Philip Randolph, International President, for the Brotherhood . . . .

After long and hard debates day in and day out, definite progress was reflected in the settlement upon rule after rule, including monetary compensation as well as the clarification and refinement of working rules, observed the International President of the Brotherhood at the International Headquarters in New York City. Rules were secured increasing the in-charge porter's rate of pay from $13.50 a month to $20.25, which is a 50 per cent boost. Attendants confined to kitchen work also received a differential of $20.25, which represents a differential of this amount above what they formerly received. Whereas before, attendants only received the established monthly rate of pay for work when confined in the kitchen. Porters assigned to training student porters and private car porters will also receive the in-charge differential of $20.25 per month. Attendants confined to kitchen work will receive an increase of $20.25 per month.

The basic work month remains the same, but the elapsed time prior to compensation of punitive time at time and one-half was reduced from 20 hours to 10 hours. This change represents a considerable increase in income to the porter, especially those engaged in troop movements. Attendants deadheading, who formerly received the standard car work rate, under the revision of the contract will receive the established attendants' rate of pay, which is higher. . . .

According to the representatives of the Brotherhood and Mr. Randolph, one of the most important features of the revision of the contract is that it was consummated through direct negotiations between the Management and the Pullman Company, which showed a splendid spirit of cooperation, and the Brotherhood, without the intervention of the National Mediation Board. . . .

The Brotherhood insists upon this arrangement so that the Organization's hands will not be tied in the event that a wage movement is begun among railroad workers for pay increases. Under the present arrangement, if a wage movement should begin in the railway industry in the next six months or year, the Brotherhood can move in to secure these wage increases for the Pullman Porters, Maids, Attendants, and Bus Boys upon 30 days' notice, without difficulty, concluded the porters' leader.

Members of the Agreement Committee that negotiated the contract for the
Brotherhood were the International President; First International Vice-
President, M. P. Webster; Second International Vice-President, Bennie Smith of
Detroit; Third International Vice-President, E. J. Bradley of St. Louis; Fourth
International Vice-President, C. L. Dellums of California; T. T. Patterson,
Claims Adjustor for the Eastern Zone of the Brotherhood, and Vice-President of
the New York Division; and Ashley L. Totten, International Secretary-Treasurer.
The Negotiating Committee for the Pullman Company were represented by the
Executive Vice-President, Champ Carry; George Kelley, Vice-President Public
Relations; B. H. Bowman, Assistant to the Executive Vice-President, and H. R.
Larry, Director, Industrial Relations.[160]

The Black Worker, April, 1941.

23. AFL IGNORES RANDOLPH

Union Votes Down Proposal For Group To Fight Jim-Crow

TORONTO, Oct. 22--Despite the annual eloquent and dramatic plea of A.
Philip Randolph, president of the Brotherhood of Sleeping Car Porters, the
62nd convention of the American Federation of Labor, meeting here for its
annual session made no definite attempt to solve the far-reaching discriminatory
practices against Negroes which exist within the organization.

Randolph Assails A. F. of L. Leaders

For 20 minutes the delegates last week heard A. Philip Randolph assail AFL
leaders for "dodging" a proposal that the group create a committee to fight jim
crow.
Randolph said:
"We have heard many grand and splendid speeches at this convention, and if
a man from Mars had come here he would have thought most of the speechmakers
believed in democracy. When he learned that many of the same men denied
Negroes the right to join their unions he would reach the conclusion that these
speeches are baloney!"
In one minute, Randolph was voted down as his proposal was rejected. The
only dissenting vote came from Milton J. Webster, his co-delegate from the
Porters' union.

Tobin Blasts Randolph

Daniel Tobin, head of the Teamsters' union, let loose a blast against
Randolph the next day in answer to his speech when he accused the race delegate's speech of "helping to light the torch of dissension and destruction
among a large section of the population."[161]
Tobin also condemned Randolph's plea for immediate independence for India,
wherein the Sleeping Car Porters' president had said:
"It is proper, fitting and timely that the American Federation of Labor,
which has been under attack from open shop, anti-labor, big business interests
and some labor-baiting government officials, should raise its voice in behalf
of the freedom and independence of India and its downtrodden, over-taxed, debt-
ridden, half-starved peasant masses.
When Randolph attempted to gain the floor to answer Tobin, he was ignored
by AFL President William Green, who is now starting his 19th year as head of the
Federation.

Webster Asks Support For FEPC

Milton Webster, first International vice-president of the Sleeping Car
Brotherhood, and a member of the President's Committee on Fair Employment
Practice, asked the convention's support in calling for a restoration of the
FEPC to its original status of independence and responsibility to the President.

He indicated that the committee was handicapped by lack of funds and a small staff with which to police the Executive Order 8802.

As Randolph was swept under in the protest of unfair treatment of Negroes in AFL unions, he listed four types of bias within the AFL, including 15 unions which have "color clauses" barring Negroes, many others which have unwritten understandings to keep Negroes out, internationals which have no written clauses but permit locals to do as they like, and unions which create "undemocratic auxiliaries" or jim-crow units for Negro members.

"Wait For Educational Processes"--AFL

The official answer to Randolph was embodied in the AFL Resolutions committee report, which said:

"We are doubtful whether any other method than the educational one can make the progress which is necessary, for experience has been that where compulsory methods are applied, prejudices are increased instead of diminished."

Pittsburgh Courier, October 24, 1942.

24. AFL UNION HEAD FAVORS CONDUCTORS

WASHINGTON, Dec. 31--Replying to a letter from President J. G. Bigelow, of Local 689, Amalgamated Association of Street, Electric Railway and Motor Coach Employees of America, AFL, in which he said he was confronted with the race problem in his division and requested information regarding colored men in other divisions of the association, W. D. Mahon, international president of the union, made emphatic his position in the matter.[162]

Mr. Mahon urged Local 689, which has a contract with the Capital Transit Company of this city, "take into consideration the fact that we are now engaged in a war in which the colored man is called upon to do the same line of duty that the white man is called upon to do."

Emphasizes Non-Discrimination

Mr. Mahon further said:

"Our organization is a part of the American Federation of Labor whose policy is not to discriminate against a fellow worker on account of creed, color, or nationality--that's the policy of this organization that you must always keep in mind when dealing with this matter.

"I know of no complaints in our organization anywhere over this matter. There was some little complaint in San Francisco some time ago, but that has disappeared and there is nothing of it at the present. In many places, colored men are employed in this line of transportation and in many of our organizations there have been colored men holding memberships for years."

Finds Races Equally Efficient

Mr. Mahon, answering Mr. Bigelow's request concerning the Negro's accident record, declared that, as far as he could ascertain, there is no difference in the accident record of white and colored operators.

The President's Committee on Fair Employment Practices was officially notified Tuesday, Dec. 22, that the Capital Transit Company, which has been declared a war industry, will abide by the directions issued to it to bring the employment policy of the bus and trolley system into line with Executive Order 8802. This order forbids discrimination against war workers because of their race, color, creed or national origin.

Pittsburgh Courier, January 21, 1943.

25. "WE MUST USE ALL LABOR," AFL TOLD

ATLANTA, Ga., Jan. 28--Director Wendell Lund of the Labor Division of the
War Production Board pictured in glowing terms to the South here last week its
great industrial importance in the present war crisis and emphasized that, in
1943, it would be necessary to double the production of the previous year.

According to Rob F. Hall, who covered the American Federation of Labor's
Southern War Labor Conference here, Mr. Lund is calling the attention of 11
Southern states to their new responsibilities.

Must Use All Available Labor

"If we are to achieve these goals, we must expand our labor force. Five
to six million war workers--women, older workers, handicapped workers, Negroes
--loyal Americans of every race, creed, color and national origin--must be
added to our present labor force. To win the war this must be done and I know
you will do it."

Mr. Lund said there are labor shortages and that these bottlenecks in
production must be eliminated by two methods: (1) integrating more available
manpower and (2) by working longer hours without basically changing the
conventional forty-hour week.

Nation Aware Of "Bottlenecks"

"The nation knows where labor stands on work stoppages and that labor will
not tolerate them in the critical year," Mr. Lund asserted and he received loud
applause from the more than 5,000 delegates when he concluded by saying:

"Nor can there be any toleration of those who would exploit the 'no-strike'
pledge of labor while the common enemy stands at our door."

Pittsburgh Courier, January 30, 1943.

26. PROTEST AGAINST AFL JIM CROW LOCAL NO. 92

By Herman Hill
(Courier Coast Correspondent)

LOS ANGELES, Calif., Mar. 4--Several hundred Negro workmen affiliated with
the American Federation of Labor Boilermakers' "Auxiliary," who are employed in
the California Ship and Consolidated shipyards and the Western Pipe and Steel
Company at the Los Angeles harbor, united in protest last week against the
"taxation without representation" policy of the union. Colored members, it is
alleged, are herded into the jim crow Local 92, but pay the same dues and
receive less insurance benefits, little or no protection, and are, in most
cases, the last persons to be upgraded.

For some time the present strife has been brewing and finally burst into
the public eye last week, when the employees in question enlisted the aid of
civic organizations and the press. Previous protests to union heads here have
resulted in nothing but promises and buckpassing to the main headquarters in
Kansas City. The AFL has a closed shop agreement with the plants in question.
Protest wires have since been dispatched to the Committee on Fair Employment
Practices headquarters in Washington, D.C.

Other Jim Crow Locals

The AFL has already set up such auxiliaries in Portland, Ore., at the
Kaiser Shipyards and at other coastal points.

Filipinos and other nationalities are permitted to join the regular union
body at the three plants. It is further claimed that there is no racial
exclusion clause in the union constitution or by-laws, but, rather, the jim crow

rules have been self-willed by the various locals. Pointing out that such
un-American tactics are injurious to the all-out war efforts, the protestants
are demanding complete integration.

One Such Local Clicking

The signal success of the all-Negro Boilermakers' Local 26 in Oakland,
which boasts of more than $20,000 and a membership of more than 500 workers,
has been suggested by some as a solution to the problems of the Southern
California group. Although labeled as a jim crow local by certain factions,
the Oakland Bay Region local was born of a desperation of a pioneering few who
felt the Negro should be given a share of skilled and semi-skilled jobs in
defense yards and plants in the locale. Battling tooth and nail for a foothold,
the Northerners have won the respect of both management and labor alike. They
have affected many reforms, such as insurance rate adjustments and wages and
hours. Its housing committee, working in conjunction with Federal and city
housing authorities, is making a determined effort to solve the Bay Area's
desperate housing situation. A short while ago, Local 26 purchased its present
location. When officials of the local visited Los Angeles last month, a hue
and cry went up that they were planning to "move in" here. This accusation
was firmly denied later.

Torn between the schools of thought, the Los Angeles auxiliaries are
exploring all angles and are deliberately and carefully plotting their futures.

Pittsburgh Courier, March 6, 1943.

27. GREEN ASKS PLAN TO END AFL BIAS

WASHINGTON, D.C. (ANP)--The National Urban League was asked by President
William Green, of the American Federation of Labor, to submit to him immediately
its idea of the type of machinery which should be established within the AFL
designed ultimately to secure full recognition of, and status for, the Negro
worker as an integral part of the labor movement.

Green promised to lay the proposal before the mid-winter meeting of the
Federation's executive council, which was scheduled to convene in Miami on
Monday, and to give it his support.

Says Conference Was Significant

- This comes probably as the outstanding development growing out of the hour
and a half long conference which executives of eight branches of the league and
officials of the national office held here on Wednesday with Green. At the
conclusion of the meeting separate statements were made by the labor leader and
by Lester B. Granger, executive secretary of the league.

"I attach deep significance to this conference," Green declared. "I am of
the opinion it will serve to promote co-operation between the Urban League and
the AFL. Such co-operation will be in the interest of both Negro workers and
the membership of the AFL."

Pittsburgh Courier, January 22, 1944.

28. NLRB EXAMINER CRACKS DOWN ON AFL JIM CROW

WASHINGTON, Feb. 27.--In a precedent-setting move, a National Labor
Relations Board trial examiner yesterday threatened to cancel the collective
bargaining rights of an AFL local unless it immediately abolished a jim crow
local for Negroes.

The ultimatum, directed to the AFL Tobacco Workers International Local
219 at Richmond, Va., is the first of its kind issued by the NLRB. Heretofore,
all such cases have been handled by the President's Fair Employment Practices
Committee (FEPC). The examiner's findings may have sweeping repercussions in
the South where AFL unions frequently maintain segregated locals.

Establishment of the Jimcrow local at Larus & Bros., Inc., Richmond, runs
counter to the President's executive order banning discrimination, contravenes
NLRB regulations by denying Negro workers adequate representation, and violates
American constitutional policy the examiner, Frank Bloom, held.

The case came before the NLRB through the petition of the CIO Food &
Tobacco Workers which asked the board to rescind AFL certification at Larus
Bros. and to schedule a new election there.

Separate Local

The AFL had won a collective bargaining election at the plant March 14,
1944, defeating the CIO union 315 to 179. Two days after the election, George
Benjamin, an international vice-president of the AFL union, himself a Negro,
met with Negro workers and advised them to apply for a charter for a separate
local. This was later established as Local 219-B.

Hearings held by Bloom revealed that management, which signed a contract
with Local 219, did not consider itself bound contractually to the Jimcrow
unit, which was not a party to the agreement.

Daily Worker, February 28, 1945.

29. LARUS CASE SPOTLIGHTS AFL'S POLICY ON NEGROES

The AFL's practice of Jim Crowing its Negro members into class B locals
where they are deprived of their full union rights, is under attack in a case
brought before the Natl. Labor Relations Board by the CIO Food, Tobacco,
Agricultural & Allied Workers. Hearings on the charges started this week in
Washington.

The case involves the formation of an AFL union of a separate local for
Negro workers at the Larus & Brother tobacco plant in Richmond, Va. After
preliminary hearings on the case last February, NLRB Trail Examiner Frank
Bloom, recommended that certification of the AFL local be withdrawn unless the
union notified the Negro workers that they were eligible for membership in the
white local and cancelled the Negro local's charter.

The story of unionization at the Larus tobacco plant dates back to 1937
when, at the request of the AFL, the NLRB held an election based on two units--
white and Negro. The AFL won bargaining rights for the white workers, and the
Negroes voted for the CIO.

In March, 1944, a new election covering the entire plant was held at the
request of the AFL. The AFL local won and was certified by the NLRB as the
union for both Negro and white workers. Instead of including the Negroes in
the regular local, the AFL set up a separate B local for the Negroes with its
own officers and committees, which was not mentioned in the union contract.

The issue presented in the case is considered of great importance for the
labor movement. A resolution supporting the FTA's fight was passed at the
April 12 meeting of the Natl. CIO Executive Board. The NLRB's action in the
case, the resolution stated, "will represent a vital test of the Wagner Act at
a time when this country is engaged in a bitter struggle for democracy and
against racial discrimination."

FTA Pres. Donald Henderson declared that "the fundamental principle of
democracy in the trade unions is involved in the Larus case. The CIO firmly
believes that you cannot exclude any group of workers from the benefits of
collective bargaining without jeopardizing the rights of all workers."

CIO News, June 25, 1945.

30. THE AFL CONVENTION

A. Philip Randolph touched off the fireworks at the recent convention in New Orleans in driving home his proposal to eliminate the Jim Crow "auxiliary" unions of the AFL.

Randolph specifically accused the Boilermakers, the Machinists, and the Electrical Workers unions of resorting to auxiliaries in order to deny Negroes the right to vote in conventions, to take part in negotiating contracts, or to assist in the management of the unions.

"It is," Randolph said, "trade union imperialism, a form of dual membership in the AFL, under which first class membership is given to white workers and second class membership to Negroes.

"The reason we have these auxiliaries is because certain powerful unions want them," he continued. "There's no use letting the Boilermakers, the Machinists, and the Electrical Workers get away with it. These unions should either toe the line or get out of the AFL."

These statements caused the astute AFL conventioneers to gasp. Brother Randolph was not behaving like a "brother." The impact of the speech is revealed by the reaction coming from those whom he accused.

Said Brother Charles J. MacGowan, president of the Boilermakers, he had never heard "a more offensive address in all his years at AFL conventions." He termed Randolph's statements "arrogant and insolent," then added, "From some of his utterances, I wonder if he's in the right organization."[163]

It is just possible that Brother MacGowan, without intending to do so, has raised a highly legitimate question. Considering the meager gains offered to Negroes affiliated with the AFL, we cannot help wondering if Brother Randolph and his 1,000,000 Negro co-unionists are "in the right organization."

Truly, Randolph made a strong appeal, but did it in any way soften up the attitudes of the reactionaries who control the policy of the AFL? We think not, if the statement made by the president of the Tennessee Federation of Labor can be taken as a sample of opinions. In commenting on Randolph's speech he said, "I object to the Pullman car porters telling us who to take in."

The principle of democracy is not even considered, but the question is whether Negroes shall tell the unions of the AFL whom they shall accept. Apparently many representative AFL leaders feel that Negroes should "know their place" and sit quietly in the back seats while their betters make momentous decisions.

The convention did not pass Randolph's resolution "abolishing the auxiliaries." Are the 1,000,000 loyal Negro members paying dues and supporting the wrong organization? We wonder.

Chicago Defender, January 6, 1945.

SELECTED AFL CONVENTION RESOLUTIONS ON BLACK LABOR

31. 1936 CONVENTION

Negro Labor Organizer

Resolution No. 80--By Delegate A. Philip Randolph, Brotherhood of Sleeping Car Porters.

WHEREAS, Aroused and victimized by the depression sentiment for trade union organization among negro workers throughout the country is stronger than it has ever been before; and

WHEREAS, the heroic fight of black workers in the ranks of trade unionists,

such as the needle trades workers, miners, longshoremen, teamsters, motion
picture operators, musicians and building trades workers, etcetera, has
demonstrated that negro toilers will and can battle for union conditions
against the employers, and no more desire to be strike breakers than the white
workers; and

WHEREAS, There is no negro organizer now under the direct supervision of
the American Federation of Labor, and since previous conventions have only
given perfunctory approval of resolutions calling for an appointment of negro
labor organizers, but have actually never done anything about it; therefore
be it

RESOLVED, That the fifty-sixth annual convention of the American Federation of Labor, assembled in Tampa, Florida, go on record as authorizing
President William Green to appoint one or more paid negro general organizers
so that they may help promote, in cooperation with the national, international
and federal unions, a program of organization and education among the black and
white workers of America.

Your committee recommends that the resolution be referred to the Executive
Council.

The report of the committee was unanimously adopted:

The Scottsboro Boys

Resolution No. 84--By Delegate A. Philip Randolph, Brotherhood of Sleeping
Car Porters.

WHEREAS, The Scottsboro boys have become a symbol of American persecution
and torture of the American Negro, since these nine boys have been sentenced
to die in the electric chair, despite overwhelming evidence to establish their
innocence of the crime of which they have been accused, and have languished in
prison for more than five years, with a recent tragic and unhappy attack upon
one of the boys by a guard; and

WHEREAS, Every respectable national Negro organization, religious, civic,
economic, political and social service, have endorsed the fight for the release
of these boys, and a National Committee, headed by Rev. Allan Knight Chalmers,
Pastor of the Broadway Tabernacle of New York City and Colonel William J.
Schiefflin, treasurer, with a large number of outstanding citizens, have
examined the evidence in the case and are convinced of their innocence; and

WHEREAS, The continued imprisonment of the boys and their death would
tend to injure the cause of working class solidarity between the black and
white workers, and since a large section of white workers in Alabama desire the
boys' release, and since the case of the boys will come up for trial in the
courts some time in January; therefore be it

RESOLVED, That the Fifty-sixth Annual Convention of the A. F. of L.,
assembled, in Tampa, Florida, go on record as condemning the cruel persecution
of these boys, and call for their unconditional freedom.

In lieu of the resolution your committee finds that despite the action
taken by the Alabama Courts in these cases, that the Supreme Court of the
United States has, on two occasions, reversed the procedure and the law as
applied to them, an action clearly indicating that the nation's highest judicial
tribunal was active and definite in protecting the constitutional safeguards of
every citizen, regardless of color or of membership in a minority group.

As a result of the United States Supreme Court's decision, these cases are
to be brought to trial again in the Courts of Alabama.

In view of this impending trial your committee is of the opinion that this
convention should not inject itself upon a due process of the law, unless it
becomes evident that the defendant's legal and constitutional rights are being
invaded.

A motion was made and seconded to adopt the report of the committee.

Delegate Randolph, Sleeping Car Porters: Mr. Chairman and delegates of
the convention, I do not think that the reasons assigned by the Resolutions
Committee for its refusal to affirmatively concur in the resolution are
sufficient. As a matter of fact, there are cases that have come before the
convention before that were similar to the Scottsboro case and they were before
the courts, and yet resolutions favoring those cases have been concurred in--
for instance, the case of Tom Mooney.

Moreover, the convention has not followed that policy in relation to measures pending before the courts of law. Take for instance the Wagner Labor Disputes Bill, and the Railway Retirement Act. If we follow the policy of not taking any action upon a case until that case has had final action in the court, the implication of that position is that we will not do anything about the matter until the individual is convicted. That certainly does not seem to be a sound policy for the American Federation of Labor.

On the matter of the due process of law aspect of the resolution, that especially is inadequate in relation to the Negro in the South. All of us know that the Negro in the south has no rights in the courts of law. As a matter of fact, the Negro is convicted upon his color when he appears in court. The Negro has no right to secure proper representation by way of counsel.

This case of the Scottsboro boys is a case of mob rule, of lynch terror. There are some outstanding facts in connection with it. For instance, when the case was being tried there in the court they had a condition which was calculated to create an emotional outburst against the boys. The attorneys against the boys appealed to the basest passions of the jury. They attempted to inflame and stir up the people against them. Threats were made against the boys. As a matter of fact, it was a shot gun, lynch law atmosphere in the court. The Judge himself virtually slobbered vengeance against the boys, and they had absolutely no proper and fair consideration in the court. There was a bloody shirt spirit against them.

This is one outstanding reason why this convention should take some action on this case. Second, one of the girls who it is alleged the boys had attacked testified to the innocence of the boys, and yet there was no disposition to seriously consider that testimony by the court.

Third, the United States Supreme Court has reversed the opinion of the lower courts and remanded the case back to them, but that certainly is not going to have any great effect upon the courts of Alabama in relation to this case. Nothing but mobilized public opinion can save the boys.

We find, for instance, another important aspect of the case, and that is the torture and the terrorizing of these boys in prison. They have been tormented in a barbarous and inhuman way by the guards. In one instance one of the boys had part of his face shot off by one of the guards. This is a case of terrorism against the helpless and defenseless boys, and therefore, it seems to me that this convention, composed of working men who themselves have been victims of persecution, should take an affirmative position on the resolution.

In connection with this case we have a national committee composed of prominent citizens throughout the country seeking to bring about the liberation of the boys. The head of the committee is Rev. Allan Knight Chalmers, pastor of the Broadway Tabernacle Church of New York. There is also Colonel Schiefflin, who is Treasurer of that committee. Colonel Schiefflin is the Chairman of the Citizens Committee of New York and head of one of the largest drug companies in New York.

Now, my friends, in view of the fact that practically every outstanding Negro organization has endorsed the plea of these boys, knowing that they have no right before the Alabama court, it seems to me this convention ought to take some action in their behalf. This case involves the whole question of liberty and democracy, not only for the Negroes but also for the White workers.

This terrorism and the attitude of hostility against the boys is transferred to practically every institution in this section. For instance, since myself and my colleague, Brother Webster, have been here in Tampa, Florida, when we went to the Floridan Hotel to register one of their uniformed representatives stepped up and said, "Now we will conduct you to the place where you register." In other words, they did not want us to ride up on the elevator. We did not give them any attention. We stepped on the elevator and rode up. But there is this studied and deliberate attempt at discrimination, insult and humiliation which is characterized in the persecution of the Scottsboro boys.

I hope this convention will vote down the report of the Resolutions Committee. I don't cast any reflection upon the spirit of the committee. I think the report of the committee does not reflect the logical analysis which we ought to expect from the able leadership of that committee. It seems to me that the report is skimpy and nondescript and fragmentary. It does not meet the issue. I don't know why we should be afraid to face this thing here because we are in the south. I hope the convention will see the great importance of this case and take the proper action. If these boys cannot plead with the American Federation

of Labor for help, where will they go? There are high forces in the south
opposed to the liberation of the Scottsboro boys, the best people, the
capitalist people. Let us give the workers of Alabama some encouragement in
fighting for these boys.

You know what the attitude generally is when there is any question raised
with respect to lynch laws. Whenever that matter is raised on the floor of the
Senate, somebody steps forward and raises the doctrine of state's rights and in
the name of the liberal traditions.

The best capitalist people, as a matter of fact, do not participate in
lynchings, they do not soil their hands in the blood of the black victims,
they do not listen to the screams at the burning of the negro. They stand in
churches and they listen to the preacher say "Blessed are the poor in spirit
for they shall see God." They make their contributions to foreign missions
and such as that. No, they don't soil their hands in the blood of the black
victims, but they soil their souls, and I hope the American Federation of Labor
will not soil its soul by pandering to the sentiment of the lynch spirit of
the south, in not taking an affirmative position upon this resolution.

Delegate Watkins, Fire Fighters' International Association: Mr. Chairman,
I regret very much that it becomes my duty to speak on a subject so foreign to
what should be considered in this convention, but before I go into that matter
I desire to state that I am speaking as a delegate to this convention and not
as a representative of my international union. It is my privilege to concur
in the report of this committee. I want to congratulate the committee on its
decision. I think it has acted wisely in non-concurring in the resolution.

I regret that this resolution should have been brought here by someone
who does not recognize the right of democracy. The Alabama State Federation of
Labor has held conventions annually for the past five years in which this case
has been under trial and in course of disposition by the court, and in not one
instance has the Alabama State Federation of Labor seen fit to intervene in
behalf of the Scottsboro boys. There has not been a resolution before that
convention. Neither has there been a resolution sent from that State Federation
to the American Federation of Labor. I believe that the Alabama State
Federation of Labor is capable and has sufficient courage to protect the rights
of any citizen of Alabama, and I believe, as they believe, that if an injustice
is being done in this case they would have appealed to this body for some
support.

Mind you, my friends, in the last two conventions of the Alabama State
Federation of Labor at least one-fourth of the delegates have been negro
delegates, and they, too, have not up to this time made any mention of the fact
that there has been an injustice done to these Scottsboro boys. I believe they
have sufficient courage and sufficient intellect to appeal their case to the
American Federation of Labor if the colored delegates in the state of Alabama
to the Alabama Federation convention had felt there was an injustice being done.

Not a single one of this group of boys is a member of the American Federation of Labor. It is a matter entirely without the jurisdiction of the American
Federation of Labor until such time as the courts of Alabama have tried these
men and found them guilty or not guilty, and if the American Federation of Labor
feels that an injustice has been done.

It has been mentioned here by the previous speaker that a negro has no
right of representation in the courts of Alabama. I deny that fact, I deny that
emphatically. It is not a fact and it is made, not in the interests of justice
to this or any other case, but to prejudice the minds of this convention against
the courts of Alabama. These negro boys had their representatives. The
American Defense League of New York sent Count Von Lubowitz down there and spent
much time and money in this case in an attempt to give these boys justice, when,
as a matter of fact, in my opinion, they did not want justice, neither do they
want these cases disposed of. They want to exploit the negro of the entire
country.

I have in my mind a general subscription being taken up all over the United
States for the defense of these negro boys, and that is true as far west as
California, and you heard the man say it had been done in New York. So why is
all this? They have had their counsel. I make the claim to this convention
that the continuous interference with state's rights of Alabama is not doing
the Scottsboro boys any good, and it will in the end do them an injustice. I feel
that this convention, in the name of democracy, in the name of the courts of

Alabama, in the name of justice, should concur in the report of the committee.

Secretary Frey: Mr. Chairman, the committee had referred to it a resolution.   After examining the whereases and the resolves, the committee was of the opinion that approval was impossible.   But the committee was unwilling to bring in a report of non-concurrence because then the action of the committee would have been misunderstood and would have been misinterpreted. Now the action of the committee was to bring in a report in lieu of the resolution which would make it clear that this convention intended that if there is any evidence at the next trial of these Scottsboro boys, or any action by the authorities which indicated an invasion of the rights as American citizens, then we would interfere.   But the committee called attention to the fact that the case now is about to proceed under orderly forms, that the Supreme Court of the United States on two occasions, because of questions raised, had referred the case back to the Alabama courts.

The committee, in defending this report, had no intention of examining the record or of making reference to some of the unfortunate instances which are happening.   Certainly we intend to make no reference to what preceded the shooting of one of the Scottsboro boys, because he is still on trial for his life.   Let me call your attention for a moment to what this resolution asks us to do, and what it says.   First of all it tells us that every respectable national negro organization and others have approved of the purpose of this resolution.   No evidence has been submitted to your committee that such is the case.   Then another whereas says that the continued imprisonment of these boys and their death would do what?   Injure the cause of working class solidarity between the black and white workers.

Your committee was unable to see anything in connection with the case, anything in connection with the alleged injustice and the miscarriage of justice which in any way had any bearing upon the relationship between white and colored workers, and particularly in our trade union movement.

Then what does the resolve ask this convention to do, in view of the fact that this case is about to go on trial in the duly constituted courts of Alabama?   It asks us to prejudge what that court will do and to declare now and here in convention that we, having no confidence in this court, intend to determine what the result must be.   I want to read the language to you.   I am sorry that it is necessary for your committee to go into the body of this resolution, so unfortunately and ineptly drawn, if I understand the purpose of those who introduced it.   Listen to this language:

"That the fifty-sixth annual convention of the American Federation of Labor, assembled in Tampa, Florida, go on record as condemning the cruel persecution of these boys, and calling for their unconditional freedom."

This convention is to prejudge what the court is to do itself and take action before the court again has heard this case, and as an American Federation of Labor, commit us to the proposition that we now, before that trial, demand their unconditional freedom.

It seemed to your committee that the American Federation of Labor, never put itself in such a position before, should not now attempt to set aside due process of law and substitute the opinion of this convention.   And so your committee presented a report to you which we think adequately safeguards the rights of these Scottsboro boys.   It puts itself on record as supporting the action of the United States Supreme Court in referring the case back twice to the Alabama courts, and then it concludes with the statement that if anything in that trial should indicate that these boys have been denied every right of citizenship, we will then again voice our opinion.

So I hope that the committee's report will be heartily supported.

The report of the committee was adopted.

At 12:30 p.m. the convention adjourned at 2:30 o'clock p.m. of the same day.

Proceedings of the 56th annual convention of the American Federation of Labor, 1936, pp. 234-36, 631-35, 657-64.

32.   1938 CONVENTION

Report of Committee on Organization

President Green: The Chair now recognizes the Chairman of the
Committee on Organization, Vice President Duffy.[164]
Vice President Duffy requested Secretary Ozanic to come to the platform.
President Green: When we adjourned yesterday afternoon we had under
consideration Resolution No. 9, introduced by Delegates A. Philip Randolph and
M. P. Webster, Brotherhood of Sleeping Car Porters.
Vice President Duffy: When we adjourned last night the committee had
submitted its report on Resolution No. 9. At that time Delegate Randolph was
on the floor, and President Green asked him if he would mind holding over
until morning, which he agreed to do. The question is now before you.
Resolution No. 9 and the report of the committee are as follows:

Protesting Constitutional Provisions of Trade
Unions Barring Negro Membership

Resolution No. 9--By Delegates A. Philip Randolph, M. P. Webster,
Brotherhood of Sleeping Car Porters.
WHEREAS, The color bar and various subtle forms of race discrimination,
some open and others disguised, operate to curtail the right of Negro workers
to various jobs, without regard to skill, training and experience; and
WHEREAS, Race discrimination by trade unions tends to divide the workers
upon a basis of race and color, thereby playing into the hands of the employer
who fundamentally cares no more for a white worker than he does for a black
worker; and
WHEREAS, Whenever a trade union excludes a worker merely because of race
or color, such exclusion weakens the entire labor movement, and lessens its
power to fight for decent wage rates, humane hours of work and improved
working conditions that will assure living standards commensurate with health,
comfort and decency; therefore be it
RESOLVED, That this 58th Annual Convention, assembled in Houston, Texas,
go on record calling upon all national and international unions and departments
to eliminate the color bar and all forms of discrimination which serve to
exclude workers from membership on account of race or color; and, be it further
RESOLVED, That the President and Executive Council of the American
Federation of Labor call upon the conventions of national and international
unions whose constitutions have color clauses and that practice discrimination
against Negro workers, to create a committee to report on the question of the
color bar and various forms of race discrimination to their next convention,
for discussion and abolition.
Your committee concurs in the intent of this resolution and recommends
it to the Executive Council in the spirit in which it is submitted.

President Green: The Chair recognizes Delegate Randolph, who will speak
upon the resolution and upon the committee's report.
Delegate Randolph, Sleeping Car Porters: Mr. Chairman and delegates to
this convention--I rise to support the report of the committee and to add a
few remarks. The members of the committee discussed this question to some
extent. There were no dissenting voices, although there was some expression of
apprehension with respect to the question of autonomy of national and
international unions. However, I explained to the committee that I thought
the convention could at least call upon the national and international unions
to eliminate the color bar and provide some basis for discussion of this
question by this convention, and so the committee concurred in the resolution.
Now the American Federation of Labor itself has frequently taken a
position on this question of negro workers. Whenever the colored workers have
been excluded from national and international unions, Federal charters have
been issued and these negro workers brought into the American Federation of
Labor. Of course Federal charters are not always effective agencies in
organizing the workers, especially if the locals are small, because of the lack
of financial resources. Nevertheless, it must be stated that the Federation

as such has always taken a position in favor of organizing the negro workers.
There are about twenty national and international unions that exclude
negro workers by the color bar and various other forms of discrimination.
There are many international unions that take in negro workers. There is
Vice-President Joe Ryan's organization, the International Longshoremen's
Association. There are several international negro vice-presidents of that
organization. There is the Hod Carriers and Building Laborers' organization.
They have had a negro international vice-president for some time. The
International Hotel and Restaurant Employees have recently seated and elected
a negro international vice-president. The Musicians' Union has thousands of
negro workers in its ranks.[165]

But as I have before indicated, there are twenty or more unions that do
not permit negro workers to join at all, and it is an outstanding disgrace to
the trade union movement. There is no doubt about this matter.

There is no international president who would himself attempt to justify
the exclusion of a worker merely upon the basis of race or color. I have had
some of the international presidents tell me that they are in favor of negro
workers joining their union, but that their southern constituency was opposed
to it, that the southern members would not stand for it. And so this
resolution is calculated to help educate the workers in the South to realize
that they have everything in common with their black brothers and nothing in
opposition.

As a matter of fact, the black men and the white men of the South are
both in proverty. We are being exploited and oppressed and outraged by the
employers, and they have everything to gain through power that can emanate
from organization. Therefore, the black brothers and white brothers of the
South should not fight each other. Their salvation lies in helping each other,
and that is the purpose and intent of this resolution.

I think this resolution is a distinct improvement upon the handling of
this question by previous conventions, and it is calculated to have a wholesome
and educational effect upon the negro people of the country.

May I say that President Green has always responded to the call of the
Brotherhood of Sleeping Car Porters. The Brotherhood of Sleeping Car Porters,
its officials and members have a deep affection and high esteem for President
Green. Even before we had Federal charters he came to the rescue of the
organization in giving co-operation.

And so the Brotherhood of Sleeping Car Porters takes the position that in
order to help bring the negro workers into the American Federation of Labor,
some bona fide attempt must be made by the American Federation of Labor itself
to get negro workers in. That is why I hope this convention will adopt this
resolution, because it certainly will work for the betterment and the advancement of the relations between the negro and white workers throughout the nation.

President Green: The Chair recognizes Delegate Davis, of the Teachers'
Union.

Delegate Davis, American Federation of Teachers:

Mr. President, on behalf of the organized teachers of America, I rise to
support the motion by Brother Randolph. If there is any one principle that the
American Federation of Labor has always stood for, it has been the principle of
equality and brotherhood and against prejudice in any of its forms. One of the
greatest obstacles to the solution of exploitation is class prejudice and race
prejudice.

Another great principle which the American Federation of Labor has stood
for has been opposition to Fascism. I have just returned from Europe, where I
have seen the Fascist countries in action, and one of the basic principles of
Fascism is racial prejudice. I saw it in action in Germany, where they shaved
the heads of the Jews, where they put them in concentration camps, where they
smashed the labor unions.

Prejudice is one of the basic factors in the Fascist system which the
American Federation of Labor has frequently gone on record against. Now we
cannot speak against prejudice in Fascist countries while we retain in our own
country prejudice in any international union of workers. Therefore, it is
essential that while we stand absolutely opposed to dictatorship and Fascism
abroad, we should also stand absolutely opposed to any form of prejudice within
our own ranks.

One of the methods of demonstrating to the world that we are genuinely
opposed to every Fascist method is to pass the resolution proposed by Brother
Randolph. I could have wished that we might have adopted this resolution from
the floor of the convention, but it seems to me it is a great step forward.
We can pass this on to the Executive Council for them to take constructive
steps in really building brotherhood and fraternity in fact in every union
affiliated with the American Federation of Labor, as we always do in theory.
I therefore hope this resolution will receive the support of every delegate.

The motion to adopt the committee's report was carried by unanimous
vote. . . .

Protesting Discriminations Against Negroes

Resolution No. 5—By Delegates A. Philip Randolph, M. P. Webster,
Brotherhood of Sleeping Car Porters.

WHEREAS, The Negro people are the victims of varied forms of discrimination which result in limiting their right in the purchase and use of property;
and

WHEREAS, Race discrimination serves to deny their right to certain types
of employment, thereby creating the unfair and unAmerican practice known as
"white man's jobs," regardless of merit and ability, which makes for the
economic impoverishment of the Negro people; and

WHEREAS, Hotels, restaurants and theatres, colleges and universities,
hospitals and recreational facilities, together with railway carriers and
other means of transportation and places of general public convenience,
licensed by city, state or federal agencies, refuse the Negro people accommodation on account of race or color, or humiliate and exploit and rob them by
segregation or jim-crow practices that are extremely despicable and offensive
to Negroes of a similar plane of culture and education of the white people that
have access to such conveniences; and

WHEREAS, The denial of these elemental and necessary privileges of
accommodation to the Negro people, involves their basic civil rights,
guaranteed by the federal constitution; and

WHEREAS, Negro blood, brain and brawn have helped to make these United
States of America what they are today; and yet the Negro people are disfranchised by various unconstitutional devices, and held in peonage; therefore,
be it

RESOLVED, That this 58th Annual Convention of the American Federation of
Labor, assembled in Houston, Texas, go on record for the abolition of all
forms of discrimination on account of race or color, and call upon the
Executive Council, State and City bodies, as well as federal locals, national
and international unions and the various departments, to express their definite
moral opposition to this sinister and destructive practice of race discrimination, and to support the fight for legislation which purports to secure for the
Negro people their civil and political rights.

The resolution relates to discrimination against negroes, but the
principle involved applies with equal force to all other groups against whom a
passive or active form of discrimination exists in our country. Such discrimination exists in our country. Such discrimination is to be regretted.

Involved in these discriminations are questions of individuals and group
preferences and the social intercourse between individuals. It is not for your
committee to discuss the origin of these discriminations, but rather to face
the practical fact that they do exist, but that most fortunately they tend to
modify themselves.

Your committee is of the opinion that there are elements in the field of
racial discrimination which cannot be adjusted by law, but must find their
solution in the intelligent thought of those who recognize that the solution of
some human problems depend primarily upon time and experience rather than upon
legislative enactments.

The position of the American Federation of Labor upon the question of
racial discrimination, and specifically discrimination against negroes, has been
definite from the time we were organized as a federation in 1881.

In 1932 there was an exhaustive report presented to the convention on
this subject, the report containing a review of the action taken by preceding

conventions of the American Federation of Labor on the subject. The 1920
convention of the American Federation of Labor declared that

> "The American Federation of Labor has never countenanced
> the drawing of a color line of discrimination against individuals
> because of race, creed, or color. It recognizes that human
> freedom is a gift from the Creator to all mankind, and is not
> to be denied to any because of social position, or the limitation
> of caste or class, and that any cause which depends for its
> success on the denial of this fundamental principle of liberty
> cannot stand."

Your committee recommends that this declaration of the 1920 convention be
reaffirmed in lieu of Resolution No. 5.

Delegate Randolph, Sleeping Car Porters: Mr. Chairman and delegates of
the convention--The report of the committee is rather involved and somewhat
indefinite. The committee sets forth the position that you cannot legislate
race prejudice out of existence or abolish discrimination against the Negro
people by law, or something to that effect. However, the resolution calls
for legislation that will prevent the Negro people the right of access to
public conveyances, public utilities, places that the public use from time to
time, for instance, the hotels, the restaurants, the various surface cars, the
trains and all of the various agencies that the public generally use.
The committee does not seem to realize that, as a matter of fact, civil
rights laws have been enacted in a number of states of this country. You have
a civil rights law in New York and in the recent constitutional convention a
definite provision was made that no discrimination shall be made against a
group of people on account of race or color. That is in the new constitution
of the State of New York. And you have civil rights laws in Pennsylvania; you
have them in Ohio and in a number of other states. Why cannot the American
Federation of Labor convention go on record in favor of the enactment of laws
against all forms of discrimination against people on account of race and
color? Why should Negro people any more than any other sort of people be
denied access to any public agency? Why should Negro people be denied these
rights in Texas or any other Southern state? Why should they be denied access
to the hotels in Texas? They are citizens, they have fought in every war from
the time of the War of the Revolution for the establishment of the United
States of America and the independence of this country. Why, then, if people
can be used in wars to defend the nation they should not enjoy all the various
civilizing agencies of the nation just like any other people?
Now, the delegates of the Brotherhood of Sleep Car Porters call upon this
committee to endorse the resolution that there be no discrimination of any kind
because of race and color. When Brother Webster, my colleague, and myself came
here and went to the Rice Hotel in order to get our badges and to deposit our
credentials, some people said, "Why, Negroes don't go in the front entrance of
the Rice Hotel." Think of it! American citizens not allowed to go in the
public entrance of a hotel! It is ridiculous, it is preposterous! As a matter
of fact, it stands as a point of division of the American labor movement, and
the American labor movement will not develop solidarity until it puts its foot
down squarely on this question and not pussyfoot about it. Brother Webster and
I went into the Rice Hotel and asked the colored man in front, "Where do the
delegates go?" The colored man looked scared, he wouldn't say a word.
We walked by him and went into the hotel. Then I went to the information
desk and asked the man there, "Where is Mr. Morrison's office, the Secretary-
Treasurer of the American Federation of Labor?" And the white man at the desk
was scared, too, and he began fumbling with paper and pencil and said something
about asking the management where Mr. Morrison's office was. Everybody knew
where it was. Here was a negro, a delegate to the American Federation of Labor,
and they did not want to permit him to have the rights of other delegates
because of the question of color. [166]
Now, my friends, the South has taken this position. We know something
about the historic background of this question. The South has taken this
position for economic reasons. As a matter of fact, demagogic congressmen and
Southern senators rise in Congress and defend this discrimination against people
because of race and color. Cotton Ed Smith of North Carolina, Senator George

of Georgia, and various other Southern senators and congressmen come out and
tell the people that we must oppose the Negro people. Now they are not workers.
They don't work for a living, but the common white workers in the South where
they come from are considered poor white trash. They are looked down upon,
they are spat upon, as a matter of fact, the common white longshoremen and the
common white teamsters of the South have no more in common with Cotton Ed Smith
than they have with Hitler in Germany, and if it is right for you to put your
foot down against the discrimination against Jews in Germany by Hitler, it is
right to put your foot down against this discrimination of the Negro people of
the country. [167]

This is an important question; it is labor's question and, as a matter of
fact, you cannot legislate virtue into the people and vices out of the people,
but who has ever taken the position that he does not have power to bring about
corrections of evil? You are making a great demand for the amendment of the
National Labor Relations Act. If it is necessary, my friends, to use legislation in order to protect one group, it is important to use legislation in
order to protect other groups. I don't know whether workers in the Rice Hotel
are organized or not, but I want to say to the International Hotel Workers
Union that if the workers in the Rice Hotel are organized, you ought to talk to
them and say something to them, say that no union workers should lend themselves
to discrimination against other workers because of race or color, and that was
practiced by the workers in the Rice Hotel.

There are 15,000,000 Negroes in America. There are more Negroes in
America than there are people in Canada, there are more Negroes in America than
there are people in Czechoslovakia, and you cannot ignore 15,000,000 of any
race.

I know the American Federation of Labor is not responsible for this
condition of race prejudice. I know that the American Federation of Labor is
not responsible for discrimination and things of that sort. President Roosevelt has appointed a Commission to investigate conditions in the South, maintaining that the South is the Nation's No. 1 problem. Is there any reason why
you would not have an economic burden on a section where you have economic
duplications? Certainly not, and the Brotherhood of Sleeping Car Porters,
realizing the importance of this question, realizing that the American
Federation of Labor has always opposed discrimination, asks for the adoption
of this resolution. It is certainly not the intention of the delegates to
charge the American Federation of Labor with responsibility for this
condition, but we are calling upon the American Federation of Labor to use its
moral power to break down this condition, and there is no better place to begin
than right here in this convention.

A few days ago we had Congressman Thomas from Houston, Texas, on this
platform. In a part of his speech he told stories about the Negroes, holding
up the Negroes as a joke before the nation. We resent any kind of jokes being
told that hold the Negro people up as objects of fun and ridicule, and we want
to tell the people of Houston, the delegates, and everybody now that we don't
like it. And so, we presented this resolution, not only for the benefit of the
Negro people, but for the benefit of the poor white people of the South. Poor
white women wear gunny sacks for dresses and poor colored women wear gunny sacks
for dresses; poor white children go barefoot and poor colored children go
barefoot. And so you have demagogs in politics playing upon the passions of
the people to keep them divided in order that they won't unite and fight for
better conditions. [168]

And so in raising this question to abolish discrimination, it is in the
interests of greater solidarity, it is for the purpose of making a stronger
labor movement in the nation. You can't do it by putting your foot down on one
worker, because he happens to be black or white. Booker T. Washington once
said that one of the reasons for the backwardness of the South is that you don't
keep a man down in the ditch unless you stay down in the ditch with him, and
that has been the very situation and the result of the practice of this
discrimination against the negro people of this country.

And so I know that the members of the Resolutions Committee themselves are
certainly opposed to discrimination and things of that sort, but the report of
the committee is involved, circumlocutory and rather indefinite, and I should
like to have the committee come out very frankly, very candidly and very
unequivocally and say that they are opposed to all forms of discrimination

against the negro peoples and that they are in favor of the enactment of civil legislation to protect the interests of American citizens who are born here.

I was born in America. My people were born in Florida. My forebears go back as far as any man's forebears who sits in this convention, and the Negro people have a right to be here. They are not here on sufferance.

And so the delegates of the Sleeping Car Porters have presented this matter to this convention because the conscience of the American people will realize ultimately that in order that there may be peace, harmony, prosperity, and plenty and real brotherhood of man, no man because of color shall be down and another man up because of a different color.

I thank you.

Delegate Frey, Secretary of the Committee: Mr. Chairman and delegates-- Mr. Chairman, the delegate has not attacked the committee's report, but he has left the inference that the committee in its report endeavored to avoid the issue. We are dealing with a reality. We are endeavoring to lay down principles broad enough and definite enough to cover the entire subject contained in the resolves of the resolution.

Your committee, however, noted that the delegates who introduced the resolutions sought to avoid making their own resolution all-inclusive. The third whereas reads--and here the delegates introducing the resolution enumerated the specific places where they wanted discrimination removed and abolished--"hotels, restaurants, theatres, colleges and universities, hospitals and recreational facilities, together with railway carriers and other means of transportation and places of general public convenience, licensed by city, state or Federal agencies."

Now those who understand the unfortunate and difficult problem which the delegate has just discussed so eloquently recognize the fact that one very definite form of discrimination was omitted from their resolution, and that is the segregation of whites and the negroes by some of the largest Protestant denominations in the South.

I have never yet in these conventions heard any representative of the Negro race raise a question for the convention to pass upon because the Methodist Church South and the Baptist Church South have churches and pastors and congregations for whites and they have a similar condition for the negroes. I don't hear the negroes raising any question about religious discrimination in the South.

I think it is unfortunate that the inference is left from the remarks just made that this American Federation of Labor tries to evade, through a committee's report, what the issue is. The delegate knows what is is. It has been growing in this country from the time his remote ancestors came over here.

So far as negro churches and negro pastors in the Methodist, Baptist and some other Protestant denominations are concerned, the delegate recognizes that that cannot be changed by law. Now, in fairness to the committee, I wish the delegate would withdraw that statement that the committee used circumlocutory language for the purpose of evading an issue. We have not. Instead of that we have brought in a recommendation in lieu of the resolution which is as strong, as detailed and as definite a pronouncement upon racial discrimination as has ever been adopted by any convention of any organization in the United States.

For the information of the delegates may I reread the latter portion of the report:

"The American Federation of Labor has never countenanced the drawing of a color line of discrimination against individuals because of race, creed or color. It recognizes that human freedom is a gift from the creator to all mankind, and is not to be denied to any because of social position, or the limitation of caste or class, and that any cause which depends for its success on the denial of this fundamental principle of liberty cannot stand."

Delegate Randolph, Sleeping Car Porters: May I say I think I have made it definitely clear that the American Federation of Labor was not responsible for this condition and that the American Federation of Labor has in convention after convention taken positions against discrimination against the negro people. But I have reference to that part of the report dealing with the futility of the law in trying to correct some of these conditions.

I said that the part of the report was involved, and it is involved.
Delegate Frey and Delegate Woll know that. It is not definite, it is not
clear. As a matter of fact, they know that the law has been employed for the
protection of the civil rights of negro people in other states, and all we are
asking for is that that position be taken here.

Now, so far as the separation of negroes and white people in the Protestant
churches in the South is concerned, for the delegates of the Brotherhood of
Sleeping Car Porters we are opposed to that. We are opposed to any kind of
separation. We are opposed to any kind of segregation because we know it is
unsound, and we know that it plays into the hands of the ruling class, it plays
into the hands of employers--and it is not our fault that you have a negro
Methodist Church and a negro Baptist church. They were here and they are being
carried on because of certain conditions, but as far as we are concerned we are
opposed to any kind of segregation, and I want that to be clear.

Now there is no question with respect to the attitude of the American
Federation of Labor and their spirit on the matter of negro people, but I am
talking about this particular aspect of this report--and Brother Frey knows
that the report is indefinite--in speaking about the futility and impossibility
of a law to make certain corrections of social evils.

As a matter of fact, why seek any kind of law? We are not able to abolish
crime, for that matter, but does that mean that we do not adopt laws against
crime? Certainly not.

Consequently, the Sleeping Car Porters call upon the convention to take a
position for the adoption of legislation that will make for the elimination of
all forms of discrimination.

Delegate Frey: I would like to ask the delegate a question.
President Green: Delegate Randolph, will you please answer?
Delegate Randolph: I will.
Delegate Frey: Is it the opinion of the delegate that state or federal
legislation would abolish the present segregation of certain denominations in
the South?
Delegate Randolph: I am not certain to what effect any legislation would
have on the question of religious relations. That is highly a speculative
question, and I think Brother Frey knows that neither he nor I can answer that
question.
Delegate Frey: One more question. That being so, the committee would like
to know whether the delegate will recommend to this convention that it seek
legislation to abolish that division between colored and white in these
Protestant denominations.
Delegate Randolph: Yes, I would be in favor of seeking legislation that
will make for the elimination of any form of segregation or separation of the
races. Now that is all-inclusive.
The report of the committee was adopted.

Ethiopia

Resolution No. 6--By Delegates A. Philip Randolph, M. P. Webster,
Brotherhood of Sleeping Car Porters.
WHEREAS, Ethiopia, one of the most ancient kingdoms of Christiandom, has
been cruelly betrayed and "sold down the river" by her alleged allies, and,
especially, England, with a smirk and genteel hypocrisy, resulting in the
murderous usurpation of the sovereignty of a free and peace-loving people by the
barbarous legions under the pompous dictator, Mussolini of Fascist Italy, in
contravention of the Kellogg-Briand Pact, the various declarations of the
League of Nations, the Good Neighbor policy of President Roosevelt's Administration and all principles of international law; therefore, be it[169]
RESOLVED, That the 58th Annual Convention of the American Federation of
Labor, assembled in Houston, Texas, go on record as condemning the ruthless
policy of aggression by Fascist Italy against an orderly nation, expelling and
exiling its great Ruler, Hailie Salassie, the Lion of Judah, the heir of King
Solomon, and demand the restoration of Ethiopia to the people of Ethiopia, and
urge the United States, the League of Nations and civilized society never to
recognize the Italian conquest of Ethiopia.[170]

Your committee recommends reaffirmation of the action of the Denver
Convention, 1937, on this subject.
A motion was made and seconded to adopt the report of the committee.

Delegate Randolph, Sleeping Car Porters: Mr. Chairman, I just want to
make a few remarks on this matter because we have talked a whole lot about
peace in this convention. Only a few days ago the world was disturbed about
the question of Czechoslovakia. People were all aroused over the possibility
of Hitler going into the Sudeten territory and taking it away from the
Czechoslovakian people. Now, then, the question was raised that people have
the right of self-determination. Of course they have, but this question of
self-determination has not just risen. It arose when Mussolini, with his
Fascist legions, rode into Ethiopia and murdered the people there and destroyed
their sovereignty. As a matter of fact, England is unquestionably the most
hypocritical, the most deceptive, the most unreliable government in the world
so far as keeping its word is concerned, an international pact--and I make a
distinction between the British people and the British government--but it is a
matter of record that England sold the people of Ethiopia down the river.
There is no question about that, and the corpse of Ethiopia must be placed
upon the doorstep of No. 10 Downing Street, in co-operation with France.
And so after Ethiopia was raided, after the sovereignty of that great
people was destroyed, then they took over Austria, and from there the Fascist
legions went on into Spain. Then you have had Japan taking territory from
China. In other words, this whole question of the self-determination of
smaller nationalities has been practically disregarded.
But we did not give any thought to the question of Ethiopia. We did not
care very much about Ethiopia, because they were not white people.
And so I want to raise this matter to the delegates here, that the
question of democracy, the question of the principle of self-determination of
smaller nationalities, must be applied to peoples without regard to race, creed
or color. Unless that is done, then what will happen to Ethiopia today will
happen to Austria tomorrow, and from Austria to some place else.
And so the delegates raised the question in this convention some time ago,
but not very much notice was taken of it. We called for the boycott of Italian
goods, just as you are boycotting the goods of Germany, because of the action
against the Jews. But we could not get the convention to go on record in
favor of boycotting Italian goods. Now we see what the result is, and who
knows where it will lead to? Austria is destroyed, Czechoslovakia is destroyed,
and perhaps it may result in another world war.
The motion to adopt the committee's report was carried.

Protesting Displacement of Colored
Railroad Maids

Resolution No. 11--By Delegates A. Philip Randolph, M. P. Webster,
Brotherhood of Sleeping Car Porters.
WHEREAS, Colored Maids have been taken off the Union Pacific trains and
are gradually being taken off all of the railroads, and are being replaced by
white Stewardess Nurses in utter disregard of their seniority, some of the
Colored Maids having put 25 and 30 years in the service, and
WHEREAS, The Colored Maids performed practically all of the duties now
being performed by the white Stewardess Nurses, besides giving the additional
service of manicure and hairdressing; and therefore, be it
RESOLVED, That the 58th Annual Convention of the American Federation of
Labor, assembled in Houston, Texas, condemn this violation of the principle of
Seniority for which the trade union movement has fought so long and hard, by the
Union Pacific Railroad and other railway systems, as unfair to a group of maids,
regardless of color or race, who have given the best of their life to a railroad
company, only to be thrown upon the scrap heap, into the discard in order to
experiment with some fad of service, while these maids walk the streets, with
no prospect of ever getting employment again, and yet deprived of the old age
service pension benefit; and be it further
RESOLVED, That the delegates of the Brotherhood of Sleeping Car Porters do
not make this protest against the Stewardess Nurses being placed on the trains

because they are white, but because their being placed there has broken down a
well established trade union principle of Seniority. The Brotherhood delegates
would protest against Negro Stewardess Nurses displacing colored or white maids
who have given satisfactory service for a quarter of a century or more, and may
we add that these maids were union maids of the Brotherhood and affiliated with
the American Federation of Labor; and, be it further
    RESOLVED, That President Green be authorized by the convention to address
a letter of protest to the President of the Union Pacific Railroad and other
railway systems, against this outrageous abuse of the Seniority rule which
organized labor so dearly prizes, the abrogation of which has resulted in the
elimination of the Colored Maids and the substitution of white Stewardess
Nurses.

    Secretary Frey: So that the committee's report may not be misunderstood,
it may be well to read a part of the resolution, beginning with the first
"Whereas":
    "Whereas, Colored maids have been taken off the Union Pacific trains and
are gradually being taken off all of the railroads, and are being replaced by
white stewardess nurses in utter disregard of their seniority, some of the
colored maids having put 25 and 30 years in the service; and
    "Whereas, The colored maids performed practically all of the duties now
being performed by the white stewardess nurses, besides giving the additional
service of manicure and hairdressing; therefore, be it
    "Resolved, That the Fifty-eighth Annual Convention of the American
Federation of Labor, assembled in Houston, Texas, condemn this violation of
the principle of seniority for which the trade union movement has fought so
long and hard, by the Union Pacific Railroad and other railway systems, as
unfair to a group of maids, regardless of color or race, who have given the
best of their lives to a railroad company, only to be thrown upon the scrap
heap, into the discard."
    So much of the resolution gives the delegates the import of the resolution.
    This resolution calls for jurisdiction over employes based on color and
race. The basic policy of the American Federation of Labor, from the beginning,
has been that there should be no discrimination because of race, color, or
religion. The adoption of this resolution would be to declare that one
occupation should be given exclusively to Americans who are members of one race.
Such action would be definitely establishing racial distinction. For this
reason your committee recommends non-concurrence in the resolution.

    Delegate Randolph, Sleeping Car Porters: The committee evidently misread
the resolution. Now the resolution said definitely that the Sleeping Car
Porters would be opposed to displacing black stewardess nurses on a basis of
color, that we were not taking the position in this case with regard to race,
but clearly from the point of view of the seniority rule. Now, read the
resolution in full, and you will see that very definite statements were made to
the effect that the Brotherhood of Sleeping Car Porters would be opposed to
displacing any group of workers on a basis of race alone. But this is a question
of seniority. The colored maids have been on these trains for 25 or 30 years.
They just incidentally are colored, that's all, and the only way to describe
them was to say that they were colored. But so far as the race question is
concerned, that is not involved at all. I think the Resolutions Committee
evidently misread this thing. They did not read the entire resolution because
the thing is very explicit, very clear, very definite, and there is no element
there with respect to race, calling for any action in the interest of those
maids because they are colored, but because of the fact that they have
seniority rule, seniority rights, and that those seniority rights have been
ignored.
    Let Brother Frey read the resolution in its entirety to the delegates in
this convention, so that they will understand that the delegates of the
Brotherhood of Sleeping Car Porters are not trying to raise any race question
here in favor of the colored maids. We used the word "colored" merely to
describe the maids, that is all. But the principle of seniority rights is the
only principle involved, and the Resolutions Committee certainly know that.

    Secretary Frey: The delegates have copies of the first day's proceedings
and they can all read the resolution. It is true that a part of the resolution

is based upon seniority rights. It is equally true that under these seniority
rights white maids could not go to work on these trains where the management
desired to employ them. White maids never would be able to be employed on
these trains if the resolution as a whole were adopted and the railway companies
would be guided thereby. You don't have to read the entire resolution to find
out what the purpose is. If the delegates will read the resolution they will
find that in a very able way the question of seniority is used to cover the
question of establishing employment by the one race in one occupation, and that
is why the committee recommends nonconcurrence in the resolution.

Let us read the first "Whereas" once more:

"Whereas, Colored maids have been taken off the Union Pacific trains and
are gradually being taken off of the railroads, and are being replaced by white
stewardess nurses in utter disregard of their seniority, some of the colored
maids having put 25 and 30 years of service" . . . the substance of all that
follows is in that first "Whereas." The delegates can read that. They have the
proceedings in their hands.

Bringing in a question of seniority is done to mislead the purpose of the
first "Whereas," and it is astounding to your committee, and it must be
surprising to the delegates after the years during which we have heard the
eloquent delegate discuss discrimination, that he should subscribe to a
resolution which would establish discrimination against whites and prevent
their employment so that the negro race would have the exclusive right to work
in a certain occupation.

Delegate Davis, American Federation of Teachers: I rise to support the
contention of Brother Randolph. If the delegates will read the resolution as a
whole, they will find that the delegates of the Brotherhood of Sleeping Car
Porters do not protest against the stewardess nurses being placed on the trains
because they are white, but their being placed there has broken down a well-
established trade union principle of seniority. The Brotherhood delegates would
protest against negro nurses displacing white maids who have given satsifactory
service for a quarter of a century or more, and may we add that those maids were
union maids, and affiliated with the American Federation of Labor.

Now I think it is the clear sense of this resolution that the Brotherhood
of Sleeping Car Porters have no objection to the railroad employing white maids
if they wish, but solely because they are employing white maids to displace
negro maids who have had 25 years of service. Therefore, it seems to me in
fairness to Brother Randolph we should concur in the resolution, which merely
asks authorization for President Green to protest the seniority rule to the
President of the Union Pacific Railroad.

Delegate Webster, Sleeping Car Porters: Mr. Chairman and delegates to the
convention--The Brotherhood of Sleeping Car Porters and its delegates wish to
clarify the situation which has been stated to you here by Delegate Frey,
raising the issue that it was the intention of the delegates of the Brotherhood
of Sleeping Car Porters to cover up an effort on their part to bring about the
employment of colored maids specifically and exclusive of all other nationalities
in connection with this resolution.

It has been the purpose and the principle of this organization to approach
these problems from their economic point of view, rather than from their labor
point of view, and in our negotiations of our agreement under which these maids
and porters work the most controversial point wherein we had a threatened strike
was over the question of insisting upon one other nationality which was hired to
work in these capacities being included in this contract.

It might be interesting for the delegates here to know that the white
barbers employed by the Pullman Company and operating on the various trains
throughout the nation have made application and have been accepted in the
Brotherhood of Sleeping Car Porters. There is absolutely no desire on the part
of this organization to dictate what race, nationality or color of employees
should be hired by these particular corporations. The idea was that these maids
that had been working on these cars 25 or 30 years had established certain
seniority rights and that they had been very definitely relieved of that job by
the introduction of this other service.

We believe that those maids who have served the public long and well, who
are good union maids and members of this American Federation of Labor should
not just be eliminated by the stroke of a pen, and we brought this resolution to

this convention in the hope that we might be able to get some co-operation in trying to emphasize upon the Union Pacific Railroad and other railroads that some consideration should be given to these maids by virtue of the long years of faithful service they have rendered to the railroad industry.

There was no intention on our part at all, and we submit that we are not inconsistent with our general policy of promulgating that workers should be considered, not with reference to their race or nationality, but with reference to their position on the job. We hope the delegates will understand our position in that matter. We happen to have in our organization not only negroes, we have Chinese, Filipinos, and as I stated a moment ago, fifteen or twenty white barbers operating on the Pullman cars throughout the nation have made application and have been accepted as members of our organization.

Secretary Frey: Mr. Chairman, in view of the explanation which has just been made by the introducers of the resolution, and the very definite commitments just voiced, the Chairman and the Secretary of the Committee, if it is agreeable to the other members of the committee, will move that the entire subject matter be referred to the Executive Council.

Vice President Woll, Chairman of the Committee: I second the motion.

President Green: You have heard the motion offered, that in view of the explanations regarding the true intent and meaning of this resolution, it be referred to the Executive Council for action.

The motion to refer the subject matter to the Executive Council was carried.

President Green: Let the Chair make this statement, that so far as the American Federation of Labor is concerned, we will do everything that lies within our power to preserve the seniority rights of workers regardless of color or creed. That is a very fundamental principle, and particularly on the railroads. I understand it perfectly well, and I can assure you that this resolution, referred to the Executive Council, will be taken up, and in the light of the interpretation placed upon it we shall be glad to co-operate with the Brotherhood of Sleeping Car Porters in protecting the seniority rights of their members.

Scottsboro Boys

Resolution No. 7—By Delegates A. Philip Randolph, M. P. Webster, Brotherhood of Sleeping Car Porters.

WHEREAS, Court trials and investigations have demonstrated that the nine (9) Scottsboro Boys were the victims of an infamous frame-up, having been tortured almost a decade in jail; and

WHEREAS, Rescued from Alabama judicial and mob terror by the United States Supreme Court, at different strategic times, the stricken conscience of Alabama, under the pressure of an aroused public opinion, was forced to set free four (4) of the Scottsboro Boys charged with the very same crime the five (5) boys are charged with that are still held in prison awaiting their doom; and

WHEREAS, It is clear and obvious to friend and foe of the boys that it was fair and just to give four of the Scottsboro Boys their freedom, when the State of Alabama contended that the nine (9) boys were guilty of the same crime, then it is just and fair to release from the Alabama prison dungeons the remaining five boys, some of whom have suffered from the brutal assaults of prejudiced prison guards; therefore, be it

RESOLVED, That the 58th Annual Convention of the American Federation of Labor, assembled in Houston, Texas, call upon the state of Alabama, in the name of justice and humanity and fair-play, to let the other five Scottsboro Boys go, and cleanse the hands of Alabama from the blood of the innocent Scottsboro Boys.

Your committee recommends concurrence with the resolution.

The report of the committee was adopted.

Protesting Discrimination Against Negroes in
Primary Elections in Southern States

Resolution No. 8--By Delegates A. Philip Randolph, M. P. Webster,
Brotherhood of Sleeping Car Porters.

WHEREAS, Lily White Primaries in Southern states are unconstitutional
since, by denying Negro citizens the right to vote, they are a violation of the
14th Amendment to the Federal Constitution; and [171]

WHEREAS, Lily White Primaries elect representatives to city, state and
federal offices that make laws and hand down decisions that affect all of the
people of these Southern states, and yet Negro citizens, a part of the population, are not permitted to vote in these primaries, whose results are
equivalent to election, merely because of race or color, which is a flagrant
form of taxation without representation, which was the cornerstone of the
American revolution which resulted in the independence of the thirteen colonies
from the tyranny of King George of Great Britain; therefore, be it

RESOLVED, That the 58th Annual Convention of the American Federation of
Labor, assembled in Houston, Texas go on record as condemning the Lily White
Primaries as un-American, unjust and unfair, and against the principle of trade
union organization as represented by the American Federation of Labor, since
Lily White Primaries divide the workers upon a basis of race and color, and
call upon the Southern states to rid themselves of the stigma and disgrace of
the Lily White Primaries, and permit all citizens to vote in all primaries
regardless of race or color.

Inasmuch as the American Federation of Labor from the beginning has worked
to secure legislation which would give to all wage earners full use of the
franchise, your committee recommends that this resolution be referred to the
Executive Council so that careful consideration may be given to such measures
as may be proposed from time to time.

A motion was made and seconded to adopt the report of the committee.

Delegate Randolph, Sleeping Car Porters: Mr. Chairman and delegates, I
don't arise to oppose the report of the committee, but just to make a few
observations on the resolution. The question of democracy has been discussed
in this convention rather extensively, and as I see it, the cornerstone of
democracy is the right of free speech, the right to express one's voice in the
affairs of state. Now you have here in the South ten or twelve millions of
negroes. They pay taxes. They are workers, but they are denied the right to
vote. And why? Because of the operation of what is known as white primaries.
You talk about the totalitarian state of Germany, the totalitarian state of
Italy, but you have a totalitarian state right here in Texas. You have a
totalitarian state in all of the Southern states where you have the one single
political organization. When you nominate a man in the white primaries that
is equivalent to his election.

In other words, the negro people, citizens of the nation--think of it!--
have not the right to express their voice with respect to the election of a
sheriff, with respect to the election of a mayor, with respect to the election
of a congressman in any of the southern states. The other day you had
Governor Leche, who made a very splendid talk here and called himself a liberal,
and yet no word was said about the right of the negro people to vote. Think of
it! Twelve million or more people absolutely denied the right to express their
voice in any form of government in the South.

Now that is a condition that must be changed, and the only way in which it
can be changed is through the abolition of white primaries. You have negroes
here. They pay taxes on property, and even if they do not pay taxes on property
they are workers and they have just as much right to express their voice with
respect to the election of officers, also to be elected as officers as any one
else in this country.

And so, my friends, this question is fundamental to the power of the labor
movement in the South. You have a strong longshoremen's union right here in
Houston, but one-half of the longshoremen are not allowed to vote because they
are colored. I heard one representative get up here and say that they have
what is known as a Legislative Committee for the State of Texas. What is the
use in having a Legislative Committee if they are going to deny one-half of the
workers the right to support the policies of a Legislative Committee?

And so the negro people are demanding the right to vote because they are citizens of this nation. For instance, a Japanese who is born in America can vote anywhere in this country. A Chinese who is born in America can vote anywhere in this country. I do not object to that, absolutely not. Any one from any foreign nation in the world may come here and be naturalized and vote for any official in any state in the South, but a negro who is a citizen of this country, who has fought and bled to defend it, who has made his contribution to this nation, is denied the right of free speech.

That is a serious question, my friends. I submit that that is one of the most important questions before the South today. I hope the Southern delegates will have the courage to meet that question and go back in their central labor bodies, in their state federations, in their local bodies and fight for the abolition of white primaries.

What is a totalitarian state? It simply means the depositing of power in one political agency. That is all a totalitarian state means, and it means the depositing of power in one particular group, whether it be racial or what not, and that is a condition that you have in the southern states.

So, this question of the right of the negro to vote is one of the most important questions before the American people. President Roosevelt has recently expressed himself against the poll tax. You have poll taxes that prevent both black and white workers from voting, but specifically black workers. I know black workers who pay their poll taxes and are yet denied the right to vote. As a matter of fact, in certain places if they even present themselves to vote, they are brutalized. How can the negro people get better streets, better schools, longer school terms, how can they improve their social conditions unless they possess political power?

That is the purpose and intent of this resolution. As aforesaid, I am not opposing the report of the committee, but I want the delegates here to know the basis of this resolution and what it means not only to the negro people, but to the poor white people of the South.

The report of the committee was adopted. . . .

Protesting Discrimination Against Workers on Account of Race, Color or Creed

Resolution No. 25--By Delegates Edward Flore, Robert B. Hesketh, Chris Lane, Nat Messing, Emanuel Koveleski, Louis Koenig, Helen Caren, Hotel and Restaurant Employees' International Alliance and Bartenders' International League of America.

WHEREAS, In the face of increasing threats of reaction and fascism, the policy of disunity caused by discrimination on account of race, color, creed or political affiliation weakens the forces of labor and labor's bargaining power; and

WHEREAS, Such discrimination in hotels, parks, playgrounds, restaurants, public places and the like as practiced against persons on account of race, color or creed, throughout the United States, is in violation of the principle and spirit of the Thirteenth, Fourteenth and Fifteenth Amendments to the United States Constitution and the Civil Rights Laws of most States, and does not make for unity; and

WHEREAS, Such discrimination is an un-American practice, that in a large measure is carried out by workers against other workers, workers as agents of employers, workers who may be members of the Hotel and Restaurant Employees' International Alliance and Bartenders' International League of America, playing into the hands of reaction; and

WHEREAS, On page three of the International Constitution in the first paragraph of the Preamble it is pointed out: "Recognizing the fact that organizing is necessary for the amelioration and final emancipation of labor, therefore, we have organized the 'Hotel and Restaurant Employees' International Alliance and Bartenders' International League of America'," a principle which can't be carried out without unity of all workers regardless of race, color, creed or political affiliation, as bulwark against the open-shoppers, reaction and the enemies of all labor; therefore, be it

RESOLVED, That the Twenty-ninth Biennial Convention of the Hotel and Restaurant Employees' International Alliance and Bartenders' International

League of America go on record for the enforcement of the Thirteenth, Fourteenth and Fifteenth Amendments to the United States Constitution and the Civil Rights Laws of the State; and, be it further

RESOLVED, That this convention go on record condemning the practice of discrimination against persons on account of race, creed or color in hotels, parks, playgrounds, restaurants, and public places; and, be it further

RESOLVED, That this International Union immediately set up machinery to educate the members of our International Union against such practice; and, be it further

RESOLVED, That this convention go on record condemning any member of the International Union guilty of being a party to discrimination, either as direct agent, or witness, in behalf of employers and owners who do so discriminate--in violation of the Thirteenth, Fourteenth and Fifteenth Amendments to the United States Constitution and Civil Rights Laws of the States--against persons and workers on account of race, color, or creed, and that any one found guilty will be subject to fine by the International Union and publicized in the International magazine; and, be it further

RESOLVED, That copies of this resolution be sent for adoption to the American Federation of Labor Convention and the Committee for Industrial Organization and released to the Nation's press and published in the International magazine.

Your committee finds that this resolution is an instruction to the officers of the Hotel and Restaurant Employes International Alliance and Bartenders' International League of America, given to them by their last convention, to forward copies of the resolution to the American Federation of Labor Convention and the Committee for Industrial Organization.

Inasmuch as the resolution is instructions to the officers of the above named organization, your committee believes that no action is required by this convention on this resolution and so recommends.

The report of the committee was unanimously adopted.

Proceedings of the 58th Annual Convention of the American Federation of Labor, 1938, pp. 300-01, 352-62, 396-97.

33. 1941 CONVENTION

Trade Union Committee to Abolish Discriminations on Account of
Race, Color, Religion or National Origin

Resolution No. 18--By Delegates A. Philip Randolph, Milton P. Webster, Brotherhood of Sleeping Car Porters.

WHEREAS, Discriminations on account of race, color, religion or national origin is undemocratic, un-American and opposed to sound and progressive trade union principles, and

WHEREAS, Discriminations because of race, color, religion or national origin are practiced by certain trade unions, constitutional provision, ritualistic practice and other devious and subtle methods, which divide the workers, thereby playing into the hands of anti-union employers, while seriously limiting employment opportunities to those victims of discriminations, and weakens the American Federation of Labor and the entire labor movement, and

WHEREAS, These discriminations result very largely from ignorance, false and demagogic propaganda and illusions about race, color, religion and national origin; therefore, be it

RESOLVED, That the American Federation of Labor in its 61st Convention in Seattle, Washington, assembled, go on record for the establishment of a trade union committee on discriminations based upon race, color, religion or national origin, composed of seven (7) members of trade unions affiliated with the A. F. of L., appointed by the President of the A. F. of L. in consultation with the Executive Council, for the purpose of hearing and investigating cases of discriminations concerning membership in unions or employment opportunities due to race, color, religion or national origin, report findings of hearings and investigations, together with recommendations to the President and the Convention

of the A. F. of L. for decision and action, and that the expenses of the above
mentioned committee entailed in the conducting of said hearings and investigations concerning discriminations because of race, color, religion or national
origin, be paid by the Secretary-Treasurer by order of the President; and be
it further

RESOLVED, That a campaign of education in the form of lectures, leaflets,
forums, study classes, seminars under the direction of the Trade Union
Committee on Discriminations in cooperation with the President of the A. F. of
L. in the interest of and to the end of abolishing discriminations resulting
from race, color, religion or national origin be carried on.

This resolution in purpose and in substance is similar to Resolution No.
17 introduced in the New Orleans convention of the American Federation of
Labor, 1940, by the same delegation. Your committee recommends that this
convention reaffirm the action taken on Resolution No. 17 last year.

Secretary Frey moved the adoption of the committee's report.
The motion was seconded.

Delegate Randolph, Brotherhood of Sleeping Car Porters: Mr. Chairman and
delegates of the convention: It was the hope of our delegates of the Brotherhood of Sleeping Car Porters that the Resolutions Committee this year would
have seen the advisability of concurring in the resolution for the establishment of a committee to study discriminations practiced against workers on
account of race, color, religion or national origin. Recent experiences in the
labor movement it seems to me, ought to have dictated and encouraged the
Resolutions Committee to have changed its policy.

Last summer during the election of the Ford workers, President Green wired
me while I was in Jacksonville, Florida, to come to Detroit for the purpose of
working with the Ford men in the interest of the American Federation of Labor.
That is to say, the American Federation of Labor wanted to win the election.
I was unable to go there, I didn't get the telegram in time, but even if I had
it is doubtful that my presence in Detroit would have been very effective in
winning support for the American Federation of Labor when the Federation admits
that it cannot do anything to remove discriminations practiced by some of its
Internationals.

Now here we are in the midst of a great program of national defense, and
the Government calls upon all able-bodied workers to respond in the interest of
production, believing that the issue of this war rests upon production. But we
find numerous cases of discriminations against Negro workers, depriving the
Government of the use of the skill of these workers, which results in the
retardation of the defense program.

I want to cite a few of these cases, because the recitation will prove the
advisability of establishing a committee to hear and study discriminations in
the labor movement.

Negro painters in Omaha cannot get into the Painters' organization, nor
can they secure a charter.

Plasterers and cement finishers in Kansas City, Missouri, cannot get into
the organization nor can they get a charter.

The A. F. of L. unions in the shipbuilding yards in New Orleans refuse
membership to Negro workers, although the company has expressed a willingness
to employ them.

Recently, Metal Trades Department unions have secured at some yards,
through training formula, a monopoly of trainees who will be up-graded in these
yards.

Stabilization pacts between O.P.M. and certain of the building trades have
resulted in disqualifying qualified colored artisans from defense employment,
and thereby retarding defense efforts.

In St. Louis Negro artisans cannot get work but white workers come from
outside of St. Louis and are put to work.

At Columbus, Georgia, in April, 1941, a business agent of Local No. 15 of
the Bricklayers Union, by the name of Willett, refused to certify two Negro
bricklayers by the names of G. J. Marks and Robert Whitted, members of Local
No. 1, of Alabama, who had been sent to Columbus in response to a request from
R. J. Gray, international secretary, in Washington, D.C. Secretary Gray had
informed the Birmingham local that several hundred masons were needed urgently
in Columbus, Ga. When Marks and Whitted arrived, under instructions from
George N. Scott, business agent of local No. 1, Willett is said to have told

them, "We didn't send for any Niggers, and I am not going to work any on this
job." Despite their credentials, they were unable to secure work there.
They moved northward into Alabama at Gadsden, where they ran into the same
situation. But white workers with transfer cards, find no difficulty in
securing employment. [172]

(2) At Ft. Leonard Wood in Missouri, five Negro painters, namely M. C.
Howard, James Simms, W. M. Fowler, Ollie Granberry, and W. F. McCrary, applied
for work on April 7, 1941. They were interviewed by Dwight Rench, business
agent of Painters Local No. 1265 at Devil's Elbow, Missouri. Rench is quoted
in an affidavit as having said: "I will not issue permits to colored painters
to work on this job. I will issue permits to whites only. I think where white
men can be found to do this work, they should have it. This is the way I feel
about this matter. You may take any steps about it that you want to."

(3) In the spring of 1941, Negro members of local No. 804 of the Cement
Finishers Union at Beaumont, Tex., attempted to secure employment on two
defense projects in Orange, Texas, namely, the navy yard, and the housing
project. According to H. W. Pierce, secretary-treasurer of the local, they
were refused because of their race. The men made application also through the
Plasterers' Local No. 200 with the same result. Secretary Pierce's statement
says "Our local No. 804 has white members and also colored members; some of
the whites have been employed, but not one Negro has been. Mr. Fields of the
housing project said that he did not plan on using any colored skilled labor
at all."

(4) The A. F. of L. Painters Union in Kansas City, Mo., was reported on
March 8, 1941, by 70 Negro organizations operating there as a Negro defense
committee, as following a policy of excluding Negro applicants from membership
by giving only two out of thirty a passing grade in an examination. Seven
members are required to establish a separate local. Thirty of the fifty-five
Negro painters who sought enlistment in the union had had experience of from
three to twenty years in the trade.

The most conspicuous and consistent denial of employment for Negroes which
can be attributed almost directly to union influence is found at the Boeing
Aircraft Corporation in Seattle, Washington. From the very beginning of the
national defense program, the Boeing company has given as its excuse for not
employing Negroes the fact that it has a contract with the Aeronautical
Mechanics Union, Local 751, International Association of Machinists, A. F. of
L., and that the union accepts white members only. Paul Frederickson,
personnel manager, has written a letter to the N.A.A.C.P. branch in Seattle,
Washington, stating that his company has an agreement with the Machinists
union obligating it to employ only union members. Several of the large
aircraft corporations holding national defense contracts have changed their
policy, and are now employing Negroes, but not Boeing.

(5) In Portland, Oregon, local 72 of the Boilermakers union is said to be
blocking the employment of Negro workers by four local companies, namely, the
Oregon Shipbuilding Corporation, the Williamette Iron and Steel Company,
Commercial Iron Works, and the Albina Machinist Works. These companies are
said to have expressed their willingness to employ Negro labor, but because of
their contract with the union are prevented from doing so. The union is
reported to have refused to relent in its policy of barring Negro members, and
to have written a letter stating "The available supply of Negro labor in this
area can be absorbed as janitors."

Another notorious case involving the boilermakers and machinist unions is
one at Tampa, Fla., at the Tampa Shipbuilding Corporation. This case has a
long history, and has been brought to the attention of President William Green
in the greatest detail. Briefly, it arose in 1939, when after a successful
strike for recognition, the Tampa Shipbuilding Corporation signed a union
contract. Prior to this time, approximately 600 Negroes had been employed in
the yard in various skilled and unskilled capacities. After the contract was
secured, the Negro workers were excluded altogether from the union, or were
sidetracked in a separate Negro local, and eventually frozen out of work. Those
who were kept at work were given the most menial of unskilled labor, and one
instance has been cited of a Negro hoisting engineer being assigned to the job
of picking up paper in the yard. The A. F. of L. is supposed to have made an
exhaustive investigation of this case, but its report did nothing to relieve
the plight of the 600 Negro shipyard workers who had supported the strike for
union recognition only to be frozen out of their jobs after the battle was won.

Latest information on the Tampa situation is contained in a letter to the N.A.A.C.P. dated July 18, 1941, which declares:

May I say in connection with the Tampa situation I took this matter up with Mr. John P. Frey, President of the Metal Trades Department, and Mr. Frey took the position the unions were not responsible for the plight of the Negro workers in relation to the Tampa Shipbuilding Corporation. He assigned as the cause for the condition the general social condition of the city of Tampa, indicating Tampa was under the influence and control of the Ku Klux Klan. Now, upon analysis, Mr. Frey's argument is unsound. Why? Because the Ku Klux Klan, we admit, is in control of Tampa. Incidentally, it is also in control of the Central Labor Union of the A. F. of L. in Tampa. Now, the Negro workers, 600 Negro workers were in the shipbuilding yards before the unions had negotiated a closed shop contract with the shipbuilding company. At the same time the Ku Klux Klan was in control of Tampa when these 600 Negroes were in the shipbuilding yards. Now, if the Ku Klux Klan is responsible for elimination of the Negroes from the shipbuilding yards why is it they were not eliminated before the closed shop contract was negotiated with the shipbuilding company? So the position that has been taken by Mr. Frey in this matter is entirely undefensible and as a matter of fact it will not bear examination.

Now, we know that the Ku Klux Klan burned crosses before the homes of Negro boilermakers in Tampa, and they sent letters with cross bones and skulls to Negro workers in the Tampa yards, but that did not intimidate the Negro workers. They even held a parade in St. Petersburg, the Ku Klux Klan did, to intimidate the Negro workers, and the Negro workers tore the hoods from the faces of the Ku Klux Klan. As a matter of fact, the Negro workers don't give a damn about the Ku Klux Klan. What they want is the opportunity to work, and they will cross the line of any Ku Klux Klan for the possibility of getting a job. And so, my friends, the disposition assigned to the Ku Klux Klan as the cause for the condition of the Negro workers, which is fundamentally assignable to the Metal Trades Department that controls practically most of the shipbuilding yards, is entirely one which will not pass muster, and I think that Mr. John P. Frey is obligated to make a statement to the public, to the American people, on this question of the exclusion of Negro workers from various of these shipbuilding yards. The people want to know why this is done. The union is being charged with keeping Negroes out of jobs, and the unions that are chargeable we think certainly have a moral obligation to make some public statement on this question.

Now, no doubt we all know that Mr. Frey has a fine spirit and believes in sound trade union principles, but when it comes to the application of these principles with relation to the Negro they do not always seem to hold up.

A committee of six called on Mr. Howell, President of the Tampa Shipbuilding Company. He told them he had received the President's order, that he was willing to hire Negro labor, but that his yard was under a closed shop contract. He said he had turned the order over to the Boilermakers and advised that it be seen. So this a.m. I went with them to see Mr. Hatfield, manager of Local 433, Boilermakers. We told him our mission. He said that we should know that no one could join their union unless he was employed at his trade at the time he made application. I asked him if he knew that the order said it was the duty of labor organizations to see that all citizens participated fully, etc., but nevertheless, he said there was no chances for us. He said there was no aid or advice that he could give us.

Now of course that is mere evasion. In other words, the leader of the union tells the committee of Negroes that no Negro can join the Boilermakers Union unless he is employed at the trade, and when the Negro worker goes to the employer the employer tells him, "You cannot get a job unless you are a member of the union." In other words, he cannot get a job unless he has a union card and he cannot get a union card unless he has a job. Of course that is a runaround that beats anything that Hitler can devise for an oppressed or a minority group.

At Milan, Tenn., there is a vast ordinance plant now under construction by the Ferguson-Oman Company. The contractors have repeatedly expressed willingness to employ skilled Negro workers and have used them in all instances where these colored artisans could secure union clearance. In the area from which labor has been and is being recruited for this project, there are several all-Negro locals of the International Brotherhood of Carpenters and Joiners of America. These Negro craftsmen pay their dues to the International and have

been employed successfully on United States Housing Authority-aided housing
projects, and (prior to the stabilization pact) on the construction of Fort
Forrest in the Tennessee area. Skilled Negro carpenters have been denied work
on the Wolfe Creek Ordnance Plant at Milan, Tennessee, however, because the
all-white Carpenters' Local, No. 259, of Jackson, Tennessee, which has jurisdiction over this project, has steadfastly refused to grant clearance to any
Negro worker. George M. Johnson, Business Agent of this white local, told
R. F. Jones, Business Agent of the Negro local, No. 1986 in Memphis, that "I
don't care what cards you hold; I don't recognize no Negro as a union man."
Mr. Johnson has refused to alter his position even at the insistence of
government representatives.

Now, brothers and sisters, these are actual instances, bona fide and
authentic instances of discriminations practiced by various local unions of
International Unions.

Now some of the local unions of the International Brotherhood of Carpenters
and Joiners accept Negroes. For instance, in New Orleans you have a Negro
local of the Carpenters' organization which is able to get work and is doing
splendidly. In New Orleans the Negro bricklayers dominate the bricklaying
trade. Therefore, you have instances where the locals of the International
Unions do accept Negroes and Negroes get jobs, and instances where those
locals discriminate against them.

Now it seems to me that the International Unions ought to do something
about this. We have the Machinists organization, with the able presidency of
Brother Harvey Brown. Now the Machinists organization is definitely keeping
Negroes out of the Boeing Plant. Brother Brown has an obligation to make a
statement to America on this matter. Here we are in the period of defense.
We are fighting to break down totalitarian forces throughout the world. We
know that production is necessary. Every hand available ought to be used, and
yet we have the Machinists telling the worker because he is a black man he is
not going to be permitted to work. This is certainly against sound trade
union practices, and it seems to me that Brother Brown, President of the
International Machinists Union, owes it to the people of America and to his own
organization and to the American Federation of Labor to make a statement on
this question.

The same thing ought to be done by other organizations, and if the
Machinists Union is going to persistently defy the President's executive order,
then the American Federation of Labor ought to put the Machinists Union out.
We ought to have some way of washing the hands of the American Federation of
Labor of the stigma of discrimination. We know that the American Federation
of Labor as such does not discriminate against Negroes, but there are numberless
unions affiliated with the American Federation of Labor that discriminate
against them, and the people cannot differentiate between the American Federation of Labor and the unions affiliated with it that discriminate against Negro
workers.

Consequently the International Carpenters' organization, with its fine and
splendid president, Brother Hutcheson, should make some statement on this
question and the locals of his organization ought to know what position he is
going to take when they are disregarding the President's Executive Order in not
permitting Negroes to work.

So, my friends, we call upon the convention to enact and adopt this resolution, setting up a committee for the purpose of studying this question. That
is all it is for, to study the question of discrimination among Negroes and hold
hearings that labor itself will begin to set its house in order.

And of course the Resolutions Committee, in its characteristic manner of
holding to its customary path, just summarily says: "We re-affirm the position
taken by past conventions." Now, have we come to the point where it is
impossible for us to make any progress on this question, and whenever the issue
is raised we are simply going to re-affirm the old attitude of do-nothing that
has been taken in the past? If that is done, surely we are planting here the
seeds of Fascism, of Nazism and of Communism.

And so, my friends, we have raised this question with a view to having you
give some thought to it. You ought to vote down the report of the Resolutions
Committee. The Resolutions Committee has given no careful consideration to this
matter. They have simply brought the matter in and summarily dismissed it.
Now the delegates have got to take a position on it sooner or later and you
ought to put your house in order and not have the government do it, not have it

done by legislation.

There are almost twenty millions of Negroes in America and they are not going to continue to be discriminated against by anybody denying them the right to work. I don't believe that the American people will sustain the position of the Resolutions Committee in utterly and flagrantly throwing this whole matter aside. I believe that the American people's heart is sound on the question of democracy. They believe in the right of the people, the Negro people as well as other people, to work and to live and to enjoy the benefits of democracy.

Negroes are not begging you for anything. We are calling upon you for these things as a basis of right. We have earned the right to call for liberty and equality of consideration on matters of work and other issues affecting the citizens of this country. Negroes have helped to make this nation. Negroes, with their blood and tears have defended this nation, and I don't believe that any labor organization is strong enough, I don't believe you have the power to defy public opinion on a sound, moral issue. You may have more power than I think you have, but I believe that public opinion is going to take some position on the question, and I don't think you are going to be able to withstand it merely because you may have negotiated some stabilization pacts.

I am not opposed to the closed shop in principle if it includes Negro workers, all workers without regard to race or color. But now if we are going to exclude some and take others, you know that is not sound Americanism.

Negroes are not the only people in America who are the victims of persecution and discrimination. There is a rising wave of anti-Semitism in America. The Jews are the victims of this wave of persecution. There is also a wave of anti-Catholicism in America. You remember when Alfred Smith ran for President of these United States, and a wave of hysterical bigotry and intolerance swept the country. Five Southern States went against the Democratic party for the first time in history. Why? Because they hated the Catholics. In the Midwest and the deep South the flames of bigotry rose high. They said that if Alfred Smith was elected President the Pope would sit in the White House.[173]

And so, my friends, there grew up in America what is known as a Know Nothing Party, designed for one thing—the destruction of the Catholic Church. And so the Negroes, the Jews and the Catholics are the victims of this discrimination, and these forms of discrimination constitute the foundation of Fascism. If we want to save the nation from what overtook Germany and other nations of Europe, like Italy and Japan, we must set our foot down upon any form of religious intolerance, any form of racial intolerance, and accept the worker, accept the American citizen whether he is Catholic or Jew, whether he be black or white, whether he be Protestant or what not. This is the only type of democracy that is worth living for.

And so, my friends, you ought to reject the report of the Resolutions Committee and have something done about this question of setting up a committee for the purpose of studying discrimination in order that the American Federation of Labor may make some solid and genuine and progressive progress on this matter. Thank you.

Delegate Lindelof, Painters: Mr. Chairman and delegates, the inference that has been made by Delegate Randolph that certain organizations are discriminating against the Negro workers is a serious accusation. Among the organizations which he claims is discriminating against his race is the Brotherhood of Painters and Decorators of America. I take the floor here because I want to deny that the Brotherhood of Painters are discriminating against the Negro race.

Delegate Randolph, in talking to you, did not state some other facts which he is in possession of. He did not tell you that the Brotherhood of Painters have sixteen Negro local unions chartered under the International organization. He did not tell you that we have several hundred Negro painters affiliated with white locals scattered throughout the entire country, even in the Northwest territory here. He did not tell you that recently at our convention in Columbus, Ohio, we had four Negro delegates, enjoying the same privileges as any white delegate present in that convention. He did not tell you that in New York City for the past year and a half we have been trying to organize the Negro painters in Manhattan. They were willing to be organized, they were willing to accept a charter from the International Union, with the stipulation that they would be in no way responsible or affiliated with Painters District Council No.

9 in the City of New York, in that they wanted to run their local union
independent of any interference either from District Council No. 9 or the
International Union itself.

Delegate Randolph did not tell you that as far back as 1914, I, as
Secretary-Treasurer of District Council No. 14 in Chicago, organized the Negro
painters in that city into a local union, No. 1332, a local which is still in
existence in the City of Chicago and is one of the outstanding Negro local
unions. He did not tell you that I, as Vice-President of the Southern District
some years ago assisted the Negroes in organizing in the South.

The only thing he told you was that the International Brotherhood of
Painters and Decorators were discriminating against the Negro. During the past
two years I have had numerous communications from President Green on this
question. As recently as a month ago I have had numerous communications from
the Labor Department and communications from Negro associations in St. Louis,
in Kansas City and in New York City. The three localities that have been
mostly affected are Kansas City, Omaha, Nebraska, and St. Louis, Missouri.

I want to be frank with you and say I would like to institute a Negro
charter in Kansas City, as well as in Omaha, Nebraska, and I have explained
in my communications to President Green, to the Labor Department, and to the
various organizations of Negro orders the reason why the charter has not been
issued in those cities. I don't see why I should have to repeat those statements time and time again when everyone knows the reasons why.

The laws of our International organization prevent us from putting in a
local union of white workers in the city, let alone a local union of Negro
workers. The law provides that the International Union cannot issue a charter
in any location where a local union is already established, unless we have the
consent of that local union. It so happens that in Kansas City, Omaha and in
one or two other places we have not been able to receive the consent of the
local unions in those cities, and that is the reason why charters have not been
issued.

During the past month two new charters have been issued in the South, one
in Missouri and one in Alabama. I don't want to bother the delegates with the
troubles between our International Union and the Negro situation. We are for
the organizing of all workers, regardless of race, color or creed, but we have
certain laws that we must observe, and as long as those laws are on the statute
books of our International Union I, as President of the International organization, will abide by those laws, I will comply with those laws until such time
as they are changed by the proper authority, which is the membership of our
International organization.

I thank you.

Delegate Frey, Secretary of the Committee: Mr. Chairman, the address that
we have just listened to from the delegate has disturbed me more than any
statements in connection with the racial problem in this country which have ever
been made in a convention of the American Federation of Labor. It is evident
that the delegate came here with one specific object in mind, and that was to
present an indictment, and that considerable research work has been done, and
now we have the indictment as a part of our record. It would not be surprising
if that indictment, standing by itself, would find its way in pamphlet form,
distributed in those sections of the country where the most prejudice prevails,
and there be used to make our task of organizing the colored worker infinitely
greater than it has been.

The delegate, who was quite personal in his references, has an advantage
over every other delegate who is present. He is the only one who has had the
full advantages of an education in Harvard University. He studied logic, he
studied philosophy, he studied ethics, he studied the humanities and human
nature as well, and I again express regret that a trade union delegate should
rise and present the type of indictment which this highly cultured individual
presented this morning. If this indictment is spread in pamphlet form, if it
is reproduced so that members of his own race may read it, I doubt very much
whether it will be accompanied by the statement that President Lidelof made a
moment ago and the statement which I desire to make.

If there is any institution in these United States to whom the colored race
owes more than to any other, it is this American Federation of Labor. The
delegate's organization could have not come into existence, in all likelihood,
had it not been for the assistance given to the Railway Porters by organizers

of the American Federation of Labor, by the officers and committees of Central
Labor Councils and State Federations of Labor and by International Presidents.
And yet, instead of hearing one word of appreciation for what the American
Federation of Labor and its constituent unions have done, instead of one word
of appreciation that from the beginning we have endeavored to break down
racial prejudice and help the Negro to organize, all we listen to is an
indictment.

And let us look some facts in the face, because possibly what we may say
now may accompany the indictment if it is published. The delegate's organization is composed exclusively of members of the colored race, and no white
individual is permitted to become a member. So we have a gentleman rising here
and accusing us of willful, deliberate race prejudice when the great organization he heads will not permit a white person to become a member.

Now this is all unfortunate. It is greatly to be regretted. The delegate
knows that in some of the specific references in his wholly unjustified
indictment, that when he was enjoying the advantages of a university education,
delegates who are seated in this hall today were organizing Negroes in the
Deep South, and I am one of them, for I organized Negro molders in the city of
Chattanooga, Tennessee, 41 years ago. That is why I regret the method by which
this highly intelligent and highly cultured delegate has chosen to bring this
question into this convention. I think sometimes that those who injure their
own people the most are those in a position of leadership who permit a biased
attitude to influence them when they come into a convention, whether of the
American Federation of Labor or of any other organization.

The record of the American Federation of Labor is not perfect. It is a
human institution, but the records of the American Federation of Labor from the
beginning indicate that this Federation has continually endeavored to wipe out
those dividing lines of race and color, and that so far as the colored workers
are concerned they are members in very large numbers of the American Federation
of Labor Unions, and their membership in those unions is due to the attitude of
the white officers and the white members of those unions. We get no credit for
that. We are not to receive a single statement of appreciation for all that we
have done. Instead, the more we do the more unjustified the criticisms are,
the more unjustified the indictment when this question of racial prejudice is
discussed in this convention.

Racial prejudice was developed in these United States long before the
American Federation of Labor came into existence. The American Federation of
Labor cannot change men's minds and men's attitudes in every portion of the
country. What we can do is to carry on a continual campaign of education among
ourselves and among those who are not organized. No one knows better than the
delegate that the type of a statement which he made this morning, instead of its
making it easier for us to organize the Negro, makes it infinitely more difficult. It almost seems as though he was deliberately endeavoring to inject a
statement into this convention which would make our task of organizing the Negro
workers ten thousand times more difficult than it has been in the past.

I intend to say nothing relative to the personal references. My record is
pretty clear so far as the Negro worker is concerned. It began 41 years ago and
it is just as consistent now as it was then.

The record of many International Unions is identically the same. We are
opposed to racial prejudices. This Federation has consistently endeavored to
break them down wherever we encounter them.

But I do want to submit for your earnest consideration that those on whom
the responsibility falls of bringing about this education should not be
unnecessarily handicapped by the type of statement we have just listened to from
the delegate.

The inference is that your Committee on Resolutions is uninterested in the
question, that all it had in mind was finding the most convenient way to dispose
of the question and of leaving our good friend in a position where he could say,
well, again the Committee on Resolutions was unfair. The Committee on
Resolutions gave this question the same long, serious consideration it has given
to such questions every year. The committee's action on the matter finally was
unanimous, and the committee's purpose was not to handicap the delegate or to
handicap his race, but to prevent the flaming up of racial prejudices in every
community at the present time.

Supposing we hold public hearings in Seattle for the purpose of diminishing
racial prejudices that may exist. We hold public meetings and we listen to the

same type of indictment. We hear the question presented as it was this morning.
Would that tend to assist International Officers in preparing their members'
minds more readily to break down these prejudices? For myself I had this in
mind as a member of the committee that we do not want the American Federation
of Labor to take any action which would afford a sounding board for the public
inflaming of racial prejudices. We have done something without all of this in
the past. Thousands and thousands and thousands of colored workers are
organized in their unions all over the country--more today, thank heaven, than
ever before, and we want to see that continue. We believe it is essential to
the preservation of our own race to see that it continues, and it was with all
these things in our minds that your committee recommended as it did.

In closing I want to call the attention of the delegates to the fact that
there is racial distinction in the field of religious organizations. I am
familiar with the South. I spent many, many years there as an organizer and
otherwise, and I know that in some of the denominations the whites go to their
church and the colored go to their church buildings of the same denomination.
They get along as Christians should. In fact, the colored members prefer to
have the privilege of employing and of discharging their own pastors.

The point I want to make is this: What would be the result in the field
of religion if you began to hold public meetings in the South, so that a story
could be told of the racial prejudices which exist in some of the great Christian
organizations of this country? For these reasons I sincerely hope that the
report of the committee will be adopted, with the understanding that instead of
its being directed against organizing the members of the colored race, the
committee had only one purpose in mind--the purpose every delegate here has in
mind, which was to do everything which lay within our power to be helpful to
the members of the colored race and to break down racial prejudices which
handicap them.

Delegate Webster, Sleeping Car Porters: Mr. President and delegates of
the convention, I rise to answer in some respects the statements made by the
Secretary of the Committee, Brother Frey, in reference to the remarks of the
delegate from the Sleeping Car Porters' organization. In the first place I
would like to correct the statement that he made here with reference to
President Randolph having spent so many years at Harvard University. I have
known Brother Randolph all his life and I never did know him at the time he
attended Harvard University. That statement is incorrect.

Second, I would like to correct some misinformation that has been given
by the delegate in reference to the Brotherhood of Sleeping Car Porters barring
everybody from its membership except Negroes. It so happens that the constitution of the Brotherhood of Sleeping Car Porters does not bar anybody of any
race, creed, or nationality who works in the particular craft over which we have
jurisdiction, and in our organization at the present time, while it is true the
large majority of its members are Negroes, we have Filipinos, we have Mexicans,
who are considered white in this country, we have a large number of Mexicans in
the City of San Antonio who are full-fledged dues-paying members of the
Brotherhood of Sleeping Car Porters. We have Chinese, and, perhaps much to
your surprise, we have two white men who are members of this Brotherhood of
Sleeping Car Porters. Evidently the delegate is not so familiar with the
movement of this Brotherhood of Sleeping Car Porters.

Then, too, I want to call the attention of the delegates to the fact that
this resolution does not call for this committee to hold any public hearings.
The purpose of this resolution was to try to do something definite and concrete
within the confines of the American Federation of Labor itself. It calls for
a committee to be appointed by the President of the American Federation of Labor
to work within the American Federation of Labor, in collaboration with the
Executive Council.

It is our opinion, based upon the results that have been obtained in other
International labor unions of this American Federation of Labor, that something
can be worked out, but nothing can be worked out if we continue to shove this
question aside convention after convention.

At the San Francisco convention, which no doubt was the first convention
where this question of race discrimination had an airing, a committee was
appointed by the President of this Federation of Labor to investigate the
question of discrimination against Negroes within the American Federation of
Labor. It made its report, a very splendid report to the Atlantic City

convention, and since that time nothing has been done. All that this resolution asks for is that a committee such as the one that was appointed as a result of the action of the San Francisco convention be made a permanent committee, not to hold public hearings, not to spread propaganda throughout the country relative to this situation, but to try to sit down around the table with the white members of organized labor in this Federation to work out some common-sense solution of this problem, which unfortunately is denying to many loyal Negro citizens of this country the right to work.

Fellow delegates, that is all that the resolution asks for, and we urgently ask that you vote down the report of the committee and sustain the resolution.

Delegate Turco, News Boys: Mr. Chairman, the reason I am interested in the question before the house is because 28 years ago the same question came up and I happened to be in New Orleans, and the only time the white worker was interested in the Negro was when the boss was using the Negroes to take their jobs. The only time we favor them, the only time we do anything for them is when we need their support.

Back in the last World War, in Seattle the Negro got some of the jobs which came along, and he applied for membership in the union, in place of going to the employer for a job first. First they came to the Labor Assembly to find out if they could join the union, and they were denied their rights.

You people talk about the Communists and the C.I.O.--you give them all the chance in the world to organize these men when they deny them the right to a union of their own.

Brother Frey and Brother Woll of the Resolution Committee--that is the history of the Federation, they are trying to smother things out the best they know how for their own individual gain. They might think I am silly to say these things, but I have been following the Federation.

I am not a young man in the Federation, I have been carrying a card for 41 years myself. I came from the Miners, the same organization that President Green came from, and I tell you right now the greatest salvation of the Miners' Union was when they took everybody in. That made their organization and that will make all your organizations.

But when you deny the right to the Negro because he cannot help it any more than the white man can help it--he was born without his consent and so were you--you are not treating him fairly.

Now, Mr. Chairman, if the colored boy went to college that is no crime. I am only sorry I never had the opportunity. If he can state his case as ably as he has done this morning, I wish I could, and I will ask this convention to do something for them, not only for the Negroes, but for the Filipinos and the rest of them. I tell you right now, you are leaving the door open to them to go to a dual organization. The biggest argument John Lewis and his gang used to organize the Negro was to go in and start discontent among the American Federation of Labor, because the high officials discriminate and they cannot see any further than their own noses. John Lewis used that very, very effectively with all his organizers all over the country, and we are now in a position in this convention to try to clear that situation.

International officers can deny that they discriminate against the Negroes, they can't do this and they can't do that. Mr. Chairman, if the International Union has no power to issue a charter in Omaha or St. Louis or any other city, then let the Federation issue a Federal charter and take in those boys who are willing to be organized.

I know one time in Louisiana a white man went up there to organize at the time of the Harriman strike. Maybe Mr. Frey recalls the Harriman strike in 1911. When some of the Negro workers said they wanted to be organized, they did not want to scab, they were denied the right to organize because they were Negroes, and the Harriman strike was lost from the standpoint of unionism.

So I only hope you give them some consideration. I hope this convention will deny concurrence in the report of the committee, and that President Green will appoint a committee to go over the situation and give the Negroes and the rest of the people who are not white a fair chance. I would rather have the friendship of some of these fellows who are black in their face and white in their hearts than I would to have the friendship of some of those who are white in the face and dark in their hearts.

Vice President Woll, Chairman of the Committee: I fear that the
convention is entirely misled as to the direct issue involved in the resolution,
by statements that have been made upon it.
The Committee on Resolutions certainly is not in favor of discrimination
of race or color on the part of the wage earners. To the contrary, it is
keenly alert and anxious that our affiliated trade unions remove whatever
degree of discrimination may exist and wherever it exists. We believe that
nearly all of our national and international unions have amended their constitutions to avoid discrimination against workers either on the race or color
basis. I don't think that is the question at issue.
The resolution asks that a committee of seven men be appointed, a committee
that shall be permanent in character, that shall hear every grievance of a
racial or religious discrimination. The committee shall proceed to that
particular locality to make its investigation, have an open hearing, make its
findings to the Executive Council and in turn to the convention for action.
The introducer of the resolution has made clear what he proposes to do by
that action, and that is that national and international unions that may not
comply with the wishes or instructions of that committee might have their
charters removed. Thus it is clearly evident that the resolution is designed
to infringe upon the jurisdictional rights of our various national and international unions in the matter of discrimination of race, color or creed.
Your committee is not prepared to recommend such a procedure to this convention, because if the American Federation of Labor could intrude itself upon
the autonomous rights of national and international unions in that regard, it
may equally well intrude itself upon the jurisdictional and autonomous rights
of national and international unions in other regards. That is why the
committee is not in sympathy with the appointment of a permanent committee and
for the purposes indicated and made clear by the delegate having introduced his
resolution.
Now, what does the committee say? It asks that this convention reaffirm
its declaration of a year ago and of previous years. And what is that declaration. I just want to read that to you. This is the committee's report on a
similar resolution a year ago:
"This resolution calls for the creation of an intra-racial
committee appointed by the American Federation of Labor, which
would investigate instances of racial discrimination. The
American Federation of Labor, in past conventions, has definitely
declared its opposition to racial or religious discrimination
within the trade-union movement or within the nation. In lieu
of the resolutions your committee recommends that affiliated
national and international unions be requested to give the most
sincere consideration to policies which will assist to eliminate
any tendency to discriminate against workmen because of race,
color, or creed."
What more can we do as a Federation than that, even though we may have a
multitude of investigations and reports, unless we proceed to follow that up
further with what the introducer has indicated and have the convention then to
assume power to discipline national or international unions who may not have
followed the recommendations contained in such an investigation?
Therefore, the issue clearly is one of how far this convention will want
to intrude itself upon the rights of autonomous National and International
Unions, and it is not a question of the degree of interest we shall display in
removing discrimination, racial, religious or otherwise on this very deep and
fundamental issue insofar as the Federation is concerned. It is not a question,
as I have indicated, of race, creed or color, because on that subject we are all
united and the record and findings of the American Federation of Labor are clear
along that line.

President Green: I wish to preserve the good name and standing of the
American Federation of Labor if I can and to present its real attitude to the
public and to public opinion. For that reason I am going to beg your indulgence
for just a moment while I endeavor to restate, if I may, the position of the
American Federation of Labor towards the subject that has been discussed so
enthusiastically here this morning.
First of all, I declare without equivocation that the American Federation
of Labor has placed itself on record as opposed to discrimination against any

person because of race, creed, color or nationality. And when that declaration was made a convention of the American Federation of Labor supplemented that declaration by instructing the President of the American Federation of Labor and the Executive Council that where any National or International Union affiliated with the American Federation of Labor discriminated against Negro workers who desired to become organized and to become a part of the American Federation of Labor, that the American Federation of Labor itself organize those Negro workers into a union directly chartered by the Federation. Is that discrimination? That is the position of the American Federation of Labor, and that position is being confused here this morning because of criticism directed against some National and International Unions. But the line ought to be clearly drawn between the official attitude of the American Federation of Labor itself and the action of some International or National Unions. It is unfair to place the American Federation of Labor before the public as opposed to the organization of Negro workers into the American Federation of Labor. That hurts me very much, when an attempt is made to place the American Federation of labor in that position. It is not correct. The record shows that the American Federation of Labor itself has declared and restated over and over again its determination to organize Negroes or other workers, regardless of nationality, into unions directly chartered by the American Federation of Labor. Proceeding in accordance with that declaration, we have organized thousands of Negro workers into unions directly chartered by the American Federation of Labor, and if I find any officer in a federal union discriminating against Negro workers who desire to become members of a Federal Labor Union, as long as I am President of the American Federation of Labor I will remove him.

In order that I might bring this point home to you clearly, may I tell you about some of our experiences during the past year? We attempted to organize the employees of the Ford Motor Company into a federal labor union to be directly chartered by the American Federation of Labor. A large number of the employees of the Ford Motor Company turned their faces towards the American Federation of Labor. More than 25,000 of them voted to become a part of the American Federation of Labor. And in accordance with our policy of no race discrimination we appealed to the Negro workers of the Ford Motor Company to become a part of the American Federation of Labor and to belong to a federal union, on the same basis as every other person employed in the Ford Motor Company plant. Our organizers carried on a vigorous campaign, we presented the issues, we sent Negro organizers employed by the American Federation of Labor there to engage in organizing these workers into the American Federation of Labor. Unfortunately the race issue was raised in that instance, and the American Federation of Labor was falsely accused of being against the Negro worker, and yet we were appealing to them to come into this federal labor union without discrimination.

Paul Robeson, that great Negro artist and singer, was called in, and he denounced the American Federation of Labor and appealed to the Negro worker to stand against us, the parent body. They were not being asked to join the National Union, they were being asked to join a federal labor union chartered by the American Federation of Labor. The leader of the organization called the Organization for the Advancement of Colored People, I think, the representatives of the Urban League, practically every organization made up of colored workers had their representatives there in opposition to the American Federation of Labor. Complaint has been made against unions, national unions chartered by the American Federation of Labor. They were not there, the ones that were complained against; they were not trying to organize Ford workers. It was the parent body, the American Federation of Labor, begging, pleading, entreating these workers to come with us and occupy their place in the house of labor.

I tried to appeal to President Randolph to come and tell the story, and I tried to reach him by telephone and telegram for days, and I could not. I know that unfortunately it was because he was unavoidably delayed, he was occupied and could not come, because I believe he is devoted to the American Federation of Labor that if he could have come he would have been there to have offset or tried to offset at least these accusations made against the American Federation of Labor.

I ask you fellow delegates if it is the policy of the American Federation of Labor, finally settled, to organize these Negro workers into federal labor unions, are we then to be opposed when we attempt to organize them on the ground that we practice race prejudice and race discrimination?

That was unfortunate, but it seemed to me I should tell you this story now because it is a true one. I was tremendously disappointed when we were forced to meet that issue. As you know, thousands of Ford workers are Negro workers, and they ought to be in the American Federation of Labor, they ought to be a part of the great American Union, the American Federation of Labor, but the leaders of these organizations opposed us vigorously, their speakers assailed us, they charged us with being guilty of practicing race discrimination and of developing racial prejudice. Now, that could not be true in that instance because it was the parent body bringing them into a Union, begging them to come in.

My good friend here this morning indicts us because they won't take them in, and here is an instance where we are begging them to come in. In accordance with the traditional policy of the American Federation of Labor there is no man in America that has a greater, a deeper interest in the welfare of the Negro people, and it has ever been my purpose to shape the policy and destiny of this great movement so that it would stand in support of all classes of working people regardless of race, creed, color or occupation. I have endeavored to have this American Federation of Labor stand four square in its determination to accept Negroes into membership in all organizations affiliated with the American Federation of Labor when they desire to belong to us, and in pursuit of that policy I attempted to organize these workers into a federal labor union in accordance with the traditional policy of the American Federation of Labor.

I am blaming nobody for the results, but I wanted to state to you these facts.

We have, I think, succeeded in breaking down prejudice. We must deal of course with this question as a realistic one, we must face the facts, and we cannot force men, but we can appeal and we can educate and ultimately we can overcome. I think we have made great progress because most of our national unions accept Negroes into membership; the Ladies' Garment Workers, the Hod Carriers, Building and Common Laborers, the Actors and Artistes, and Musicians take them in and we hope ultimately if there is any barrier anywhere that it will be broken down. But surely when we are all trying and earnestly trying to break down the barriers, we ought to receive the support of those who believe with us.

This question has been with us since long before the Civil War. They had the Methodist Church, North and South, for I think 60 or more years after the Civil War, and religion was divided because of the race question. It was indefensible and wrong, but it was the Church, religion itself, that preached the brotherhood of man, divided until they had the Methodist Church, North and South. It takes time to break it down; it is being broken down and will be broken down, and this race discrimination and prejudice will be broken down by those who are earnestly seeking to break down race prejudice and race discrimination in the United States of America.

Now, I want to place the American Federation of Labor right. I want the public to know where we stand. The American Federation of Labor does not discriminate against Negro workers. It accepts them into unions directly chartered by the American Federation of Labor whenever they are willing to come, and we are spending the money paid in by national unions into the treasury of the American Federation of Labor in trying to organize Negro workers into federal labor unions directly chartered by the American Federation of Labor. If we are doing that, are we failing? There is where we stand; there is where we will stand; those are our virtues, and we seek to exploit them so that the people of America may know where we stand in our effort to organize Negro workers.

Vice-President Hutcheson, Carpenters: Mr. Chairman, I have been one who has always had a sympathetic consideration for the Negro worker. Past records will show that. I am somewhat surprised, however, at the remarks of Delegate Randolph this morning. It would seem that one with his ability should have looked into the situation farther than he apparently did, considering his remarks. If he, as a delegate here from the Pullman Porters, is taking the responsibility of representing all the Negro workers in the country, then he should familiarize himself with the conditions of the Negroes in some of the organizations that accept them into membership. If he would take the trouble to investigate, he would find the Brotherhood of Carpenters has many locals of

Negroes in its organization. He would also find in many of our white locals
we have Negroes as members along with the white men of our organization. He
would find we have locals scattered all over the United States, even in the
city of New York. He would find, if he would take the trouble to look it up,
in the city of Savannah we have one local of Negroes of 690 members as against
a white local with 970 members. He would also find, if he took the trouble to
investigate further, there are more Negroes carrying cards in the city of
Savannah than there are white men. He would also find that under the recent
Government housing project in the city of Savannah 430 Negro Carpenters worked
on that project along with white Carpenters.

Now then, if in his desire to bring about a condition that would help the
Negroes of this country as a whole, he would have done more toward that end if
he had told some of the good things that some of the organizations have been
doing for the Negroes and not merely criticize and tell the things that did not
sound so well, at least to the public. I would advise Delegate Randolph to not
oppose the adoption of the committee's report, but to see that it is adopted,
because by that procedure and by the procedure in the future of telling some of
the good things done for the Negro race rather than all the things that could
be complained of, he would do much more good for his race.

If the situation were reversed and a resolution was introduced to this
convention to try to direct the internationals as to what their membership
could consist of, what does he or any other delegate think the internationals
would say to this convention? As far as our organization is concerned, we
would tell you to go plumb to and stay there, if you chose.

The qualification for membership in our organization is if they can qualify
and are an American citizen they can become a member of the Brotherhood,
regardless of race, color or creed. Whether an Irishman, Swede, Negro or Jew
does not make any difference to us, as long as you are a qualified Carpenter.
That is the policy of the Brotherhood, and has been for years, and we have had
Negro members who have held membership in our organization for over a third of
a century and who have participated in our conventions, and perhaps will again
in time if they see fit to send them. I cannot see why any delegate here should
oppose the report of the committee.

Vice-President Bates, Bricklayers International Union: During the course
of the remarks of Delegate Randolph, he made the charge that two Negro Bricklayers were denied employment at Columbus, Georgia. I think an investigation
of this charge would show that Delegate Randolph was making a charge that was
unjustified and unwarranted under the circumstances. It is well known to
Delegate Randolph and the delegates to this convention that the organization
that I represent, the Bricklayers, Masons and Plasterers International Union of
America have many exclusive Negro charters in different sections of this
country. We have mixed unions, and we take into our organization all who are
qualified mechanically, regardless of race, creed or color. Any statements
made to the contrary by Delegate Randolph are not warranted and borne out by
the facts.

Delegate John E. Rooney, Plasterers: I might add to the statements that
have already been made by the Bricklayers that as far as the Plasterers and
Cement Finishers International Union is concerned that we have many Negro
members in our organization. Brother Randolph did state this morning there was
one city, and I believe that is the only city he mentioned, Kansas City,
Missouri, and that matter was taken up with me last week, and I intend to have
that remedied as soon as possible. Other than that, we have Negro members,
thousands of them, in our organization. Not only do they belong to the
organization but they also hold office in many of the unions; and I might add,
too, at our last convention, just adjourned, we had several colored delegates
at that convention, and we do not discriminate against the colored race.

Delegate Randolph, Pullman Porters: Brother Chairman, I rise to state that
I am able to sustain every charge I have made on this floor, and that I don't
retract a single one I have made.

I don't need Delegate Hutcheson to tell me what to do about this resolution.
I am perfectly able and prepared to take a position on this question according
to my own judgment, and I don't care anything about the opinion of Brother

Hutcheson so far as advising me what I shall do in regard to this resolution.
I want to say this to Brother Green, a herring has been drawn across this
issue. No statement was made here to the effect that the American Federation
of Labor, as such, discriminates against Negroes. Now, everybody knows that.
Why is there a disposition to prostitute and distort this question? There is
a desire to evade the issue, and therefore a tendency to draw a red herring
across the issue.

President Green: Brother Randolph, just a moment. I said you know at the
Ford Plant we were charged, the American Federation of Labor, with discriminating
against Negro workers.

Delegate Randolph: But I had nothing to do with that, Brother Green.

President Green: Is that right?

Delegate Randolph: Well, I don't know about -- yes, that is right.

President Green: You know, yes.

Delegate Randolph: I had nothing to do with that. Those were Negro
organizations. They stated that discrimination exists in the American Federation of Labor. They stated there were organizations affiliated with the
American Federation of Labor that denied Negroes membership. Now, that is true.
That does not mean, however, that the American Federation of Labor itself
discriminates against Negroes. But I stated here that it is difficult for the
public to differentiate between the American Federation of Labor discriminating
against Negroes. Now, that is a simple matter of fact, Brother Green. You know
that is true. It is hard for the public to differentiate between the two
positions. Now, that is what I pointed out here in my discussion. But it is
also important to observe that the purpose of this resolution is to get the
American Federation of Labor to provide some machinery for the study and
investigation of discriminations in order that the facts revealed may serve as
a basis for the formulation of policies to the end of trying to remedy the
condition. Now, that is the sole purpose of the resolution.
Brother Woll raises the question that the intention is to infringe upon the
jurisdiction of national and international unions. This is a pure appeal to the
prejudice of the national and international unions in this convention. That is
all it is, a pure appeal to the prejudice of International Unions. The assumption is now if the purpose of this resolution is to infringe upon the jurisdiction of national and international unions. "You national and international
unions had better vote against it." Now, that is the inference.
And so with the question, too, that was presented about the Church having
been divided into the North and South. Well, we all know that. That is old
history. But as a matter of fact, the American Federation of Labor should point
the way for the churches in this country on the question of the races, because
this involves a question of life, the right to work.
And so, Brother President, the Brotherhood of Sleeping Car Porters takes
this position definitely in favor of the fact that the American Federation of
Labor itself does not discriminate against Negroes, you accept Negroes in the
federal unions, but I want to make this remark, Brother Green, too, and you know
this to be the truth, that in a large convention you permitted the Brotherhood
of Railway Clerks to take over the freight handlers that were federal unions and
wiped out these federal unions, and these freight handlers now are in Jim Crow
auxiliary unions, and they don't have the right to vote, they don't have a voice
in the determination of the policy of that international union. Now, that is a
fact. How are we going to beat that down?
To that extent the American Federation of Labor has not kept faith with the
Negro workers because the American Federation of Labor took the position that
"If a national union will not accept you, we will give you a federal charter."
But here they have taken away the federal charter from the freight handlers, and
gave them over to an international that had . . .

President Green: (Interposing) Brother Randolph, I want that stated clearly.
I must interrupt you. First of all, that organization would not accept Negroes
into membership.

Delegate Randolph: Exactly.

President Green: Pursuant to the policy of the American Federation of Labor we took them in, organized them into Federal Labor Unions, but freight handlers come under the jurisdiction of the Brotherhood of Railway Clerks. Finally, after some years of experimenting along that line, the Brotherhood of Railway Clerks amended their constitution so as to provide for the creation of auxiliary locals, and then they were turned over to the Brotherhood of Railway Clerks, but there is a vast difference between the statement you made regarding their rights in the Brotherhood of Railway Clerks and what President Harrison states is their right, and we have to keep the faith in that respect.

Delegate Randolph: Brother Green, I wanted to have this clear and that is, yes, they are in an auxiliary local to the Brotherhood of Railway Clerks, but they don't have the right to vote, they don't have a voice in the conventions of that organization. Now that is a question of fact. And so in that respect it is the position of our delegates that the federal charter should be returned to the Negro workers if they are not permitted to join a national or international union.

Delegate Marshall, Hod Carriers: Mr. Chairman, I desire to draw to the attention of the delegates to this convention that the International Union of Hod Carriers and Laborers, have organized over 70,000 colored workers within the United States. In the Southern states of this country we have advanced and increased their wage scales. They were working prior to our organizing them for 12 or 15 cents an hour. Today they are receiving from 60 to 70 cents per hour. We have a colored brother who is a member of the Executive Board of our International Union, and at our recent convention we had over 250 colored delegates sitting in that convention with voice and vote.

Now what I want to know is what has Randolph ever done for the laborers of the South who work on building and construction work, that is, the colored laborers? He was never interested in them. The only thing he is interested in is coming to this convention year after year and criticizing the activities of the international unions and the American Federation of Labor.

President Green: The question now recurs upon the motion to adopt the committee's report. All those who favor the adoption of the committee's report please say "aye"; those opposed say "no."

The motion seems to be carried. The Chair declares the motion carried, and it is so ordered.

Report of Committee on Resolutions

Vice-President Frey, Secretary of the Committee, reported as follows:

Auxiliary Locals

Resolution No. 19--By Delegates A. Philip Randolph, Milton P. Webster, Brotherhood of Sleeping Car Porters.

WHEREAS, Auxiliary locals organized by some international unions, affiliated with the A. F. of L. is a grave violation and nullification of American democracy and sound trade union principles, since they are a notorious specie of taxation without representation and creates a separation and division of the workers which makes for weakness; therefore, be it

RESOLVED, That the 61st Convention of the A. F. of L. at Seattle, Washington, go on record as condemning the auxiliary form of organization, since it denies workers, because of race, color, religion or national origin, the privileges of full fledged membership, in the national or international union, enjoyed by the other workers, and that this Convention, in harmony with sound trade union principles, calls upon the national and international unions that have auxiliary local unions to disestablish said auxiliary local unions.

Your committee is aware that many International Unions, for most advisable reasons, have established auxiliary local unions, and that the membership of these auxiliary locals is not based upon any distinction or discrimination of race, color or creed, but are intended solely to increase the field of organization.

Attention must be called to the valuable support given to many International Unions through the organization of Ladies Auxiliaries.

Your committee would further call attention to the fact that several organizations against whom there have been charges of discrimination because of color, have established auxiliaries for the purpose of bringing colored workers into the trade union movement.

As this resolution, if adopted, would condemn all such auxiliaries, your committee recommends non-concurrence.

Secretary Frey, moved the adoption of the committee's report.

The motion was seconded.

Delegate Randolph, Brotherhood of Sleeping Car Porters: Mr. Chairman, I want to make a few brief remarks on this resolution. The auxiliary form of organization does not provide for the members of the auxiliary unions the status of full-fledged membership. In other words, members of auxiliary unions do not possess the right to vote on policies affecting the national organization or the auxiliary unions. For instance, no member of an auxiliary union can attend a national convention of a national organization. He has not the right to vote for a delegate to the national organization nor has he the privilege of being voted for as a delegate to that convention. It seems to me that if there is no objection on the part of certain national or international organizations to take in workers without regard to color, race, religion or national origin, there would be no auxiliary union, because the primary purpose of the auxiliary unions is to give the impression that these national unions are taking Negro workers in when they are actually keeping them out.

These are the grounds of the objection of the Sleeping Car Porters to the auxiliary locals. You will notice in this convention there are only two colored delegates. In the last convention there were about 15 or 20. These delegates who lost out came from various federal locals, but the charters of these federal locals have been taken up on the grounds that the national organizations had jurisdiction over these workers and that they were going to grant them auxiliary charters. That has been done, and as a consequence the voice of the federal local is no longer heard in this convention. It is a strange interpretation that is being given to the auxiliary local when it is contended that they do not represent any form of discrimination. Why have them at all?

And so, fellow delegates, it is the hope that ultimately by a process of education that various National and International Unions will recognize the validity of accepting workers as members into their national organizations as such and not establish these Jim Crow auxiliary forms of organization.

Secretary Frey: Mr. Chairman, this convention should be under no misunderstanding as to the resolution which the committee recommends non-concurrence with. The resolution is directed against all auxiliary unions. It is very definite on that point. And a number of the International Unions seated here have had auxiliary unions which have had nothing at all to do with any kind of race, color or creed. These auxiliary unions have been of great advantage not only to their members but to their Internationals and to the trade union movement in general.

There was one hopeful word in the statement that has just been made, and that was that education would be helpful in working out the problem. That has been the position of the American Federation of Labor from the beginning. We must take men and women and communities as we find them, and we must educate them to a point of view or else drive them unwillingly into some form of organization they know little about or care less.

It was not so many years ago we listened to the complaint, and a justifiable one, that the Negro worker was unorganized and could not elevate his social and industrial position except through trade union organization. This American Federation of Labor undertook a campaign of education, and as a result hundreds of thousands of Negroes are now not only organized but they are within the fold of the American Federation of Labor. If in some communities, because of

conditions which the American Federation of Labor had nothing whatsoever to do
in creating, it has been found difficult to organize the Negro and bring him
into the white local unions as a member, then certainly it is a long step in
advance from conditions as they were when we bring him into the fold of trade
union organizations. I am thankful that the note of criticism, bitter, biting,
unjustified criticism which we listened to yesterday was not in the address of
the delegate made a few moments ago.

Now, this convention will not place itself on record, in the committee's
opinion, as opposed to auxiliary unions which we have organized, the auxiliary
unions, created from the wives and the daughters and the sisters of trade
unionists, or from the other auxiliaries that we have, like the Apprentice Boys
Auxiliary Unions to our International Unions, which are the means by which we
help to educate the apprentice to understand what the trade union movement
really means to him the moment he becomes a journeyman, and so your committee,
because of the wholesale condemnation of the policy of organizing auxiliaries
embodied in the resolution, made its recommendation on non-concurrence.

The motion to adopt the report of the committee, non-concurring with
Resolution No. 19, was carried.

Lend-Lease Aid to Ethiopia

Resolution No. 20--By Delegates A. Philip Randolph, Milton P. Webster,
Brotherhood of Sleeping Car Porters.

WHEREAS, Ethiopia has played and is now playing an heroic role in the
struggle against the Axis powers, having been the battleground of some of the
fiercest and bloodiest encounters of the democratic forces against sinister
totalitarian states; therefore be it

RESOLVED, That the A. F. of L. in its 61st Convention assembled in Seattle,
Washington, endorse and support lend-lease aid by the United States to Ethiopia,
since lend-lease aid is intended for all countries allied with the democratic
nations in the fight against Nazism and that a military and scientific and
economic commission be sent to Ethiopia to help in her defensive and offensive
struggles.

Your committee recommends concurrence with this resolution.
The recommendation of the committee was unanimously adopted.

Poll Tax

Resolution No. 21--By Delegates A. Philip Randolph, Milton P. Webster,
Brotherhood of Sleeping Car Porters.

WHEREAS, The Poll Tax is a pernicious device of a small oligarchy to disfranchise the great mass of black and white workers in eight states of the
South; therefore, be it

RESOLVED, That the 61st Convention of the A. F. of L. in Seattle,
Washington, go on record as endorsing and supporting the anti-Poll Tax legislation and court action.

Your committee endorsed a similar proposal, submitted by the same delegation, a year ago, and recommends that the former action of the convention be
reaffirmed.

The recommendation of the committee was unanimously adopted.

Fair Employment Practice Committee

Resolution No. 22--By Delegates A. Philip Randolph, Milton P. Webster,
Brotherhood of Sleeping Car Porters.

WHEREAS, A Fair Employment Practice Committee has been set up by President
Roosevelt under an Executive Order to abolish discriminations in national defense
on account of race, creed, color, religion or national origin, for the purpose
of utilizing the skill and labor of every available worker and to practice the
principles of democracy we preach that coincides with the repeated declarations

of the American Federation of Labor; therefore, be it
    RESOLVED, That the 61st Convention of the A. F. of L. assembled in Seattle,
Washington, go on record as endorsing the Fair Employment Practice Committee.
    Your committee recommends approval of this resolution.
    Secretary Frey moved the adoption of the committee's report.
    The motion was seconded.

    Delegate Milton P. Webster, Sleeping Car Porters: Mr. President and
delegates to the 61st Annual Convention of the American Federation of Labor, I
arise as a representative of the Sleeping Car delegation that introduced this
resolution to offer commendation to the Resolutions Committee for its approval
of this resolution endorsing the Fair Employment Practice Committee. I wish
also to take this opportunity to extend our thanks and appreciation to President William Green for complying with our request in inviting Mark Etheridge,
the Chairman of the Committee on Fair Employment Practice, to address this
convention. Mr. Etheridge delivered quite a scholarly and informative address
on the functions of this particular committee.
    I wish to take this opportunity to acquaint the delegates of this conven-
tion with some of the background that has been responsible for prompting the
President of the United States to appoint this Committee on Fair Employment
Practice.
    Almost immediately at the institution of the widespread defense program
the Negro workers of the nation found themselves in an almost unprecedented
position of not being allowed to work in many of the defense industries. The
agitation among the Negro workers of the nation became so great that some of
the Negro leaders in the trade union movement, particularly the American
Federation of Labor, stepped into the situation and organized the widespread
protests that were being made throughout the nation by Negro workers and
other representatives of Negro organizations against this practice of not
allowing the Negro workers to be integrated into the national defense program.
As the result of the organization a committee was organized and prevailed upon
various officials of the Government to take some action in reference to this
particular situation. After a large number of conferences with many of the
officials of the United States Government, the Committee finally got a
conference with our great president, President Roosevelt, and after going into
an exhaustive investigation of this particular situation, the President agreed
with the committee that this was an unusual situation which called for some
unusual action, and at the request of this committee the President issued an
executive order in connection with the question of discrimination against Negro
workers in the defense industries.
    The Negro representatives of the American Federation of Labor played quite
an important part in the conferences with the officials of the United States
Government and the President of the United States, which was responsible for the
issuance of this Executive Order and the appointment of a Committee on Fair
Employment Practice. We had as members of this committee representative Negro
trade unionists from the International Ladies' Garment Workers, from the
International Hotel Workers' Alliance and Bartenders' League, from the National
Teachers' Federation, and from the Brotherhood of Sleeping Car Porters.
    The committee has been appointed, and there is a good representation of
trades unionists on the committee, including President William Green, President
Philip Murray of the C.I.O., and myself from the Brotherhood of Sleeping Car
Porters. The committee has had a number of meetings and there have been a
large number of complaints forwarded to the committee affecting all forms of
discrimination against Negroes, preventing them from being integrated into the
defense industries, and unfortunately many of them have been directed towards
some of our trade unions; and so this committee is starting out on this program
with the purpose of trying to solve some of these problems.
    We very greatly appreciate the action of the committee in recommending
approval of the Committee on Fair Employment Practice, and we feel this
recommendation coming from this convention will be able to influence many of
the national and international unions against which these complaints are made,
to cooperate with us to the utmost extent, to the end that a large number of
workers in this country who have heretofore been prevented from being integrated
into the defense industries because of the unfortunate discriminatory practices
that have prevailed in America, may so be employed. We wish to express our
thanks and appreciation, and I am sure the committee is willing to cooperate

with the national and international unions. We certainly hope we get the
cooperation from the national and international unions to the end that this
problem, insofar as the defense industries are concerned may be settled in
some degree of equity with the least disturbance in connection with the
carrying out the program and practices of the Committee on Fair Employment
Practice.
   The motion to adopt the committee's report, concurring in Resolution No.
22, was carried unanimously.

   Secretary Frey: Mr. Chairman, the committee was proceeding with the
resolutions in their numerical order, but believes it advisable to bring in
some of its report on the Executive Council's report. We would like to submit
two portions of the Executive Council's report at this time.

Proceedings of the 60th annual convention of the American Federation of Labor,
1940, pp. 475-92, 536-37, 538-39.

34. 1942 CONVENTION

Race Discrimination

   Resolution No. 10—By Delegates A. Philip Randolph, Milton P. Webster,
Brotherhood of Sleeping Car Porters.
   WHEREAS, The victory of the United Nations in this global war against the
Axis Powers depends upon national unity and since national unity cannot exist
if there is discrimination against persons on account of race, color, religion
or national origin, and because this war has its roots in a mythical racial
superiority advocated in "Mein Kampf" to Adolph Hitler, therefore, be it[174]
   RESOLVED, That the sixty-second convention of the A. F. of L. go on record
as condemning all the forms of discrimination on account of race, color,
religion or national origin as being inconsistent with the fight of the United
Nations for a free world and also constituting the basis of a Fascism which is
the mortal enemy of a free trade union movement and of the democratic way of
life.

Trade Union Committee to Abolish Discrimination on
Account of Race, Color, Religion or National Origin

   Resolution No. 12—By Delegates A. Philip Randolph, Milton P. Webster,
Brotherhood of Sleeping Car Porters.
   WHEREAS, It is necessary that the complete manpower of the nation be
mobilized for use in the armed forces and defense industries for the victory of
the United Nations and since discrimination on account of race, color, religion,
or national origin is a bar to this effort; therefore, be it
   RESOLVED, That the sixty-second convention of the A. F. of L. set up a
minorities committee composed of representatives of the various minority groups
in the A. F. of L. such as Negroes, Jews, Catholics and others for the purpose
of thoroughly exploring the question of discrimination practiced against
minority groups by unions affiliated with the A. F. of L. and various industries
with a view to mapping out plans and making recommendations to the Executive
Council and subsequent conventions, to abolish these forms of discrimination as
being against sound trade union principles and giving aid and comfort to Fascism
in America, and be it further
   RESOLVED, That the President of the A. F. of L. be authorized, in cooperation with the Executive Council, to set up a minorities committee on discrimination on account of race, color, religion or national origin, to investigate
various forms and cases of discrimination that may be presented to it, or that
may come to its attention in any way, and that funds be provided for transportation and stenographic services and other incidental expenses to the carrying out
of the purposes of this resolution of the complete abolition of discrimination
in unions affiliated with the A. F. of L., and be it further

RESOLVED, That this committee plan a systematic educational program among the members and officials of the A. F. of L. for the enlightenment of the workers on the necessity and value of unity in the labor movement without regard to race, color, religion or national origin.

Racial Equality

Resolution No. 13--By Delegates A. Philip Randolph, Milton P. Webster, Brotherhood of Sleeping Car Porters.

WHEREAS, The present world war is largely due to vicious and fallacious concepts of racial superiority and since there can be no peace in the world so long as one billion and seven-hundred millions of peoples of color throughout the world are looked upon as inferior and treated as vassals and slaves such as obtains in Africa, India, China and the isles of the sea; therefore, be it

RESOLVED, That this sixty-second convention of the A. F. of L. go on record as supporting the principles of racial equality as essential to national unity and the unity of the darker peoples back of the fight of the United Nations to put an end toward aggression and that this principle of racial equality be duly recognized and accepted as a basic factor in the reorganization of the world at the peace table when the war ends.

In connection with the subject of race discrimination your committee has considered Resolutions Nos. 10, 12, and 13, all of which deal with one or more phases of race discrimination.

The American Federation of Labor, at every convention where the subject has been introduced, has vigorously and unequivocally, declared against race discrimination--any discrimination because of race, color, religion or national origin. The American Federation of Labor has been the outstanding organization in the United States and Canada to make such declaration, and to further the interests of the colored race.

It is unfortunately true that because of geographical situation and other reasons, there still remains a degree of discrimination, not only against the colored race, but against other groups, because of their racial origin; but we have no hesitancy in comparing the record of the American Federation of Labor on the question of race discrimination with the activities of any other organization in the United States and Canada.

It was the American Federation of Labor which pioneered the organization of the colored people. Experience has led us to believe that the most effective way of eliminating race discrimination is the education of the trade union movement and of the public. Without this education the progress which has been made in organizing America would not have made the progress which it has. We are doubtful whether any other method than the educational one can make the progress which is necessary, for experience has been that where compulsory methods are applied, prejudices are increased instead of diminished.

Your committee voices its approval of the recent Executive Order of the President intended to accomplish the praiseworthy elimination of racial distinction between the wage earners and the citizens of the United States.

Your committee therefore recommends the adoption of this statement in lieu of separate action on the resolutions presented.

Committee Secretary Frey moved the adoption of the committee's report. The motion was seconded.

Delegate Randolph, Sleeping Car Porters: Mr. Chairman and delegates to the convention, I want particularly to discuss the resolution suggesting the creating of a committee, a Minorities Committee, for the purpose of exploring the question of race discrimination in order that we may ascertain the extent of racial discrimination, the forms and manifestations of racial discrimination and their general influences and effects. This resolution calls for the systematic conducting of a campaign of education through this machinery of a Minorities Committee. The suggestion of a campaign of education is based upon the theory that racial discrimination arises out of ignorance and fear. Were it possible for the workers and also their leaders to know something about the origin and basis of race discrimination they would not so readily lend themselves to it.

For instance, in the South, the South is the No. 1 economic problem of America. The South is culturally and educationally and politically the most backward section of America. Why is this? The reason for this is that one-third of the population of the South, the Negro workers, are exploited and oppressed, not only by the monopolistic capitalist interests, but by an alliance of misinformed and ignorant workers, who with the employers, have made a virtue and a career of being white. The ordinary poverty stricken, uninformed workers has been made to believe that there is some special virtue in being white. As a result of the conflict between the black and white workers over this imaginary question of superiority of race, they are unable to get together and form powerful trade unions. Because of the division on race the workers' movements of the South are weakened, and since they are weakened the employers are able to oppress and repress them, thereby paying them low wages and providing them worse working conditions and longer hours of work than exists in any other section of the country. In other words, the white workers of the South are down economically and organizationally because they are trying to keep the black workers down. They can't get up because they won't permit the black workers to get up.

This is the result and the consequence of ignorance and fear. The workers have had the idea that if they extend democratic rights, equality of opportunity to the black workers they will, ipso facto, reduce and minimize their opportunities in the general southern community. We all know that is wrong, unsound, fallacious, but until this information becomes a part of the thinking of the workers they still will act upon that idea.

Now discrimination against the Negro workers in the Unions affiliated with the American Federation of Labor falls into four categories. One is that you have a number of Unions, about fifteen or twenty, affiliated with the American Federation of Labor that have color clauses in their constitution, or ritualistic provisions against the membership of Negro workers. For instance, the Boiler Makers' Union, the International Machinists' Association, and practically every Union which is a part of the Department of Railway Employees of the American Federation of Labor has a color clause or ritualistic provision against the membership of Negro workers. Then in addition to that you have Unions that do not have color provisions in the constitution, but by practice and custom, do not permit Negro workers to join. These unions are, for instance, the Electrical Workers, the Plumbers, the Pipe Fitters. When workers go to those Unions for membership, when Negro workers go to them to join there is nothing in the Constitution that says no, you can't join, but they have a policy of not permitting Negro workers to join. They have some provisions that some of the members must suggest or recommend members for membership, and of course the Negro worker is never recommended.

Then we have Unions connected with the American Federation of Labor that permit Negro workers to join, but some of their Locals deny Negro workers the right of membership and also use their power to prevent these Negro workers from securing employment. For instance, the Carpenters' Union accepts Negro workers as members, but the Carpenters' Local in San Antonio, Texas, not only refuses Negroes the right to become members, but threatened to strike on the housing project which was in the interests of Negro tenants if there was any effort to compel them to accept Negro workers or to put Negro workers on the job.

In St. Louis there were International Unions that had Locals and some of these International Unions accept Negro workers as members, but their Locals in St. Louis will not accept Negro workers and also negotiate closed shop contracts that prevent Negro workers from even securing employment.

Then you have another category of discrimination. We have unions that have color clauses in their constitution but they organize what are known as auxiliaries, which Negroes are permitted to join. The auxiliary form of organization is undemocratic and serves to disfranchise the worker. For instance, the Brotherhood of Railway Clerks has a clause in its constitution denying Negroes the right to join, but it creates auxiliary Locals. In these auxiliary unions the Negro workers pay a certain per capita tax, along with the white workers, but they have no right to send a representative or a delegate to the International Convention of the Brotherhood of Railway Clerks. They have no voice or vote in the formulation of policies and the determination of the general machinery of the organization. In other words, it is a form of taxation without representation.

Now, the question may be raised as to the necessity of this committee. If there is no necessity for this committee then it ought not to be created. If there is necessity for this committee then it ought to be created. How can we find out whether there is necessity? You can only determine that by searching

for conditions that this resolution is designed to remove. These conditions
are discriminatory practices. Now, for instance, only recently in Portland,
Oregon, 30 Negro workers were imported from New York to Portland to work.
Nineteen of these workers were skilled men. They had experience as welders
and as all different sorts of mechanics. When those workers arrived in
Portland one of the union representatives boarded the train and reclassified
those Negro workers, and put them all in the category of laborers. Now, the
laborers in the Henry J. Kaiser Shipbuilding Yards received 95 cents an hour,
but the welders and other mechanics received a higher rate. The Secretary of
Local 72 of the Boiler Makers, Shipbuilders, Iron Workers and Helpers Organization read the riot Act to the Negro workers who had come all the way from
New York to Portland for jobs, for jobs that had a higher differential in pay
than the laborers because of skill.

Now, we listened here yesterday and today to many grand and splendid
speeches about democracy. As a matter of fact, if a man from Mars had dropped
in on this convention and listened to the oratory about democracy he would have
come to the conclusion that most of the people who are making these speeches
really believe in democracy; but if he had examined the situation closer and
found out that some of the men that were making those speeches were members and
representatives of organizations that deny workers membership in those
organizations, not because of lack of competency, not because of lack of skill,
but merely because they were black, certainly he would come to the conclusion
that these speeches all about democracy were pure baloney. We had, for instance,
a statement made here by Brother MacGowan yesterday to the effect that if there
was anything in the shipping yard that tended to increase the number of days
necessary for putting out a ship that that borders on sabotage or treason. I
agree with him, but I want to ask how he classifies race prejudice? How does he
classify racial discrimination which definitely limits the manpower available
for use in the shipping yards? Certainly any institution, any agency, whose
practices and policies and customs now limit the manpower that may be available
for production of ships, of munitions of any kind, certainly that borders upon
treason and it represents sabotage of the war effort and of the victory of the
United Nations.

Now, my friends, certainly no one can contend that any union that denies a
worker membership in it merely because of race is not sabotaging the war, is
not sabotaging the program of the United Nations; but yet you have unions
connected with the Federation that openly say that you can't become a member of
the organization. Now, we men get up and talk about democracy and about the
democratic processes, as was done by the representatives of the Machinists and
the Boiler Makers and other groups, and then the Negro workers come to them for
membership in their union and they say, "You can't become a member until you get
a job." And when the Negro goes to the employer and asks for a job the employer
says, "No, you cannot get a job unless you get a union card." There this Negro
worker is between two forces, both of which are against him. He can't get work
unless he has a union card and he can't get a union card unless he has work.
This is the condition in which the Negro worker finds himself.

Now, the American Federation of Labor takes the position that this is a
federated body; the International Unions are autonomous. We have no power to
compel the International Unions to admit anyone as a member in them. Well, now,
you cannot expect a Negro worker to understand that. You can't expect even the
public to see that point. As a matter of fact, it is recognized as a dodge. It
is recognized as a refuge in a smoke screen where we don't have the moral courage
to face the issue. I am definitely able here to state that the American Federation of Labor has never faced this question on racial discrimination with any
measure of moral courage. We have adopted resolutions and find proclamations
have been made, splendid declarations have been issued, but they have amounted
to nothing. They have been mere lip service on the question of discrimination
in this great organization. Therefore, the American Federation of Labor faces
a moral challenge.

Something should be done about this thing now. We have suggested a concrete,
tangible and practical method, and that is this committee that we wanted to have
created in order that it might explore this question and then set up adequate
machinery to carry on a program of education. That has been rejected by the
Resolutions Committee. Of course, I was not really surprised, because
unfortunately it seems that our Resolutions Committee never learns anything about
the question of race and never forgets anything about it. As a matter of fact,

at this time in our world history when race plays so great a part in the
determination of international affairs, it is unfortunate, it is pitiful,
that a committee which really sets down the policy of this Federation does not
have the broadness of vision to see that unless this question is fundamentally
met, realistically dealt with some degree of courage, there never will be any
peace in the world, there never will be any peace in the labor movement of
America.

Now, the Brotherhood of Sleeping Car Porters has organized a powerful
International Union which demonstrates the adaptability and the capability of
Negroes for organized labor action. You have hundreds of thousands of Negroes
in the American Federation of Labor now. I would estimate that there are from
250,000 to 300,000 Negroes in the American Federation of Labor, but you have
only two delegates here at this convention. They are from the Sleeping Car
Porters' Union. Why? There are thousands of Negro workers in the other
International Unions but these unions never send a delegate to this convention.
My friends, it is based upon the fallacy, it is based upon the false position,
it is based upon the lack of information as to the relationship between peoples
different in color.

Today we are facing a situation when the world itself is in flames, largely
because of this doctrine of racial supremacy of the white race and of the
inferiority of the peoples of color. All of the struggles in the past, international struggles, have been around an attempt on the part of Europeans and
white-power nations to grab the land and natural resources of the peoples of
Africa, India, and China, and the isles of the sea. We all know that Hitler
himself built up Fascism around the persecution of the Jews, and the same thing
can happen here in America. So long as any form of discrimination exists,
whether it be racial, religious or national, it constitutes the grounds in which
the seeds of Fascism may be sown, and just as the Nazi party broke down the
social democracy in Germany, overthrew the republic as the result of the
accumulative power built up by the leader of the Nazi party, Hitler, the same
thing may happen here in America, because you have the fertile ground for sowing
the seed of Fascism.

We have, for instance, the Ku-Klux-Klan. We have a number of organizations
that definitely and openly state their opposition and condemnations of the Jews.
We have organizations that condemn the Catholics. You very well remember when
Al Smith ran for President. Al Smith was one of the most democratic men in
America. He was loved by everybody, but Al Smith met the most bitter persecution, opposition and propaganda that any man has ever met who ran for public life
in this country. They stated that, "If Al Smith wins the Pope will move to
Washington and go into the White House." That was the kind of propaganda that
was carried on against him, because he was a Catholic.

You who have read anything about American history know about the Know-
Nothing Party, a political organization committed to the program of persecution
of the Catholics. [175]

Now, we have that situation here with respect to the Negroes. The Negroes
are the victims of a persecution, but they will transfer this persecution from
the Negroes to the Jews to the Catholics and to the workers. Recently in
Congress the reactionary Senators and Congressmen introduced 50 bills for the
purpose of stripping labor of its rights, emasculating the principle of
collective bargaining, and throwing back labor from its present position and
destroying our labor and social gains.

My friends, when this war is over you are going to meet a situation far
different from that ever witnessed in this country, whether the Axis powers or
the United Nations win. You are going to have a trend toward conservative
policies in the nation, and the only hope of the workers, the only hope of even
the American Federation of Labor is that it adopt a policy embracing all of the
workers, regardless of race, creed, or color.

You know that the German trade movement was the most powerful movement in
the world, absolutely more extensive and with the basic philosophy and understanding of the practices and policies and programs of the organized workers.
You know that, and consequently these agencies will use any point, they will use
any particular situation in order to work up sentiment, in order to work up
hysteria that may break the morale of the workers of America and set them back
a hundred years.

And so, my friends, the Brotherhood of Sleeping Car Porters raises the
question before you not alone for the benefit of the Negro workers, but for the

benefit of organized labor, for the safety and salvation of the workers, and
for the preservation of our democratic processes. It is not enough for you to
get up on this floor and say, "We stand for Democracy and freedom; we stand for
the brotherhood of man; we stand for the spirit of tolerance, and we want to
see that the principle of free speech, freedom of the press, freedom of assembly, the right to petition, of trial by jury, freedom of worship--we want to
see those freedoms preserved."

It is all right, my friends, to get up on the floor and make those
splendid statements, but they don't mean anything unless you practice them.
That is the position of the Negro workers today. The Negro workers may be the
means of saving America from the flames of Fascism, because the Negro people
are dedicated and consecrated to the cause of democracy. We know that no men
of authority in the world, regardless of color, can ever expect to make progress,
can ever expect to take their places among the peoples of advancement and
enlightenment, except under the democratic system.

Therefore, the Negroes know already the meaning of Fascism; the Negroes
know already the force of a national race prejudice. The Negro knows already
something about the victimization of a people, because of the fallacy hailed by
others who are committed to the ideals of a heterogeneous democratic system.

And so, we stand upon the principle that the American Federation of Labor
will never be able really to take the position that it is thoroughly democratic
until there is not a single organization affiliated with it that bars a worker
because of race, color, nationality, or religion.

The hope of the American Federation of Labor in serving as the creative
and constructive agency of a democratic economy, is that it will clean its
skirts, clean its hands and come into court and say, regardless of color,
religion, nationality, creed, or sex of the workers, eligible for membership
in any Union which is a part of this Federation, and that any International
Union that hasn't the spirit of democracy, that does not show that it is
committed to the ideals of a brotherhood of man, will be expelled from this
Federation if it refuses to accept the worker merely because of the fact that
that worker's pigmentation is more heightened than the pigmentation of another
worker.

And that is the only difference between the peoples of the world. The
peoples of India and Africa and China are dark merely because of the geographical condition. Skill, genius, and color are not the monopoly of any race in the
world. It is the common property of mankind. I can point out to you some of
the greatest scientists of America who are black, some of the greatest
philosophers of the world who are black. Pushkin, the Russian poet, was black;
and the Dumas, some of the greatest writers of literature of France, were
Negroes. 176

So, my friends, this question of racial discrimination strikes at the heart
of the workers, at the heart of democracy, and there will be no freedom in this
world so long as one group of men say, "I am white, you are black, and
consequently because you are black and you are not entitled to the privileges
and opportunities that I enjoy."

As long as that spirit persists there will be no peace, there will be no
brotherhood of man, but we will be facing a conflagration even more catastrophic,
even more disastrous, even more destructive than the world war in which we are
now engaged.

And so, my fellow delegates, I appeal to you that you adopt some machinery
to deal with this question. President Green, Brother Woll, and Brother Frey
know very well that these declarations do not mean a thing so far as actually
getting discrimination eliminated is concerned. Right here in Tampa, Florida
Negroes cannot work as boilermakers, but they are boilermakers.

So, my friends, we want you to do something that is positive, something
that is practical by way of setting up some machinery. Of course, I hoped that
the convention would take some definite position on it and not leave it to the
Executive Council. We can't say that all members of the Executive Council are
our pals, and we know that sometimes popular issues find a graveyard in the
Executive Council. But we know that President Green has some definite convictions on this matter. We know also that the International Unions have power
and that he cannot do everything he wants to do.

I remember this morning or yesterday Brother Harvey Brown said it was a
bad thing that in an organization you may have a monopoly of power in the hands
of one or two organizations, and that principles may not be given their adequate

expression and application. Well, my dear friends, that same thing may be said with respect to racial discrimination in the American Federation of Labor, and the position the Executive Council takes upon these matters.

You have sitting on the Executive Council men who represent organizations that have color clauses in their constitution. And so when you call for democracy in one respect, we ought to be willing to extend it to the other respect. But that has not been the case, and we ought to be honest with ourselves, we ought to be fair with ourselves, and fair with the public. We haven't met this question of race discrimination with courage, with spirit, and with determination to eliminate it. Until we do it we are going to have trouble in this country, because the Negro people are not going to continue to take it. They are determined to fight for their rights, regardless of what happens.

Upwards of twenty millions of people cannot be kept down. It doesn't make any difference, my friends, what they eat or what the attitude of the people that are trying to keep them down is, 20,000,000 people cannot be kept down.

And so the Negro people come to you because you are a body of workers, you are victimized, you are exploited. They said the National Labor Relations Board was not doing the right thing, and yet these Unions that say the National Labor Relations Board is not doing the right thing, these very same Unions are violating the principles of the National Labor Relations Act, because the basic principle of that Act is that every worker shall have the right to choose and select his bargaining agent. But the Negro workers can't do that. And so, my friends, the position taken by these powerful organizations with respect to democracy really means democracy for themselves and nobody else. But the time must come, and it must come soon, when the American Federation of Labor will take the position that they will not tolerate the position of any Union in it that says you cannot become a member merely because you are black.

President Green: Are there any further remarks?

The question recurs on the motion to adopt the committee's report. All in favor will please say "aye." Those opposed will say "no."

The motion is carried and it is so ordered.

Race Discrimination in Trade Unions

Resolution No. 14--By Delegates A. Philip Randolph, Milton P. Webster, Brotherhood of Sleeping Car Porters.

WHEREAS, Millions of American workers will fight on all fronts throughout the world to put down the evil of totalitarian slavery that democracy and freedom may live in the world and trade union movements be preserved; therefore, be it

RESOLVED, That workers who are now in Uncle Sam's uniform to fight for the freedoms and the Atlantic Charter be given the freedom and eligibility to join any union affiliated with the A. F. of L. at the end of the war without regard to race, color, religion or national origin for one-half the regular joining fee and that any international union refusing said workers membership now in Uncle Sam's uniform on account of race, color, religion or national origin be expelled from the A. F. of L. until said worker is permitted to join, as a gesture for strengthening the cause of national unity now.

Resolution No. 14 cover two subjects, one race discrimination, and secondly, a reduced initiation fee of those who have had a period of military service.

Your committee has already dealt with the subject of race discrimination, and has also presented its report on the question of reduction of initiation fees. It therefore feels no further action is required on this resolution.

Committee Secretary Frey moved the adoption of the committee's report.

The motion was seconded and carried.

At 5:45 o'clock, p.m. Delegate Bugniazet, Electrical Workers, moved that the rules be suspended and the convention remain in session until the report of the Committee on Resolutions was completed, which he said he understood would take about 45 minutes.

The motion was seconded but was lost on being put to vote.

Proceedings of the 62nd Annual Convention of the American Federation of Labor, 1942, pp. 573-80.

35. 1943 CONVENTION

Racial Discrimination

Resolution No. 111--By Delegates W. G. Desepte, C. C. Coulter, G. A. Sackett, Retail Clerks International Protective Association.

WHEREAS, Our Nation is engaged in a war for the preservation of democracy and the defeat of Nazism and its medieval theory of race superiority, and

WHEREAS, We cannot conduct a democratic war abroad without practicing complete democracy at home, and it has always been the commendable position of the American Federation of Labor that the right to work or admittance into Union membership should not be based on race, creed, color, or national origin, and

WHEREAS, President Roosevelt has deemed it necessary to issue Executive Order No. 8802, as well as to set into motion a governmental body known as the "Fair Employment Practices Committee" to assure that there will be no discrimination in industry on the grounds of race, creed, color, or national origin, and

WHEREAS, In spite of this clear policy in the interests of justice and national unity in war, some few locals in the American Federation of Labor are following contrary policies of either not accepting minorities into their Unions or putting them into auxiliaries aiding the Fascists who claim this country is not truly democratic and defaming the name of the American Federation of Labor, therefore be it

RESOLVED, That this convention of the American Federation of Labor go on record as:

1. Opposing all discrimination based upon race, color, creed, or national origin;
2. Calling upon all the Internationals and their affiliated unions to accept all workers into membership without discrimination or segregation, and
3. Calling for complete support and cooperation of all unions with the Fair Employment Practices Committee.

Your committee has given lengthy and most sincere consideration to Resolutions Nos. 24, 28, 29 and 32 introduced by the delegates of the Brotherhood of Sleeping Car Porters; and Resolution No. 79 introduced by the delegate of the Minnesota State Federation of Labor; and Resolution No. 111 introduced by the delegates of the Retail Clerks International Protective Association, all of which deal with some phase of discrimination because of race, color, religion or national origin. Instead of reporting upon each resolution separately, your committee believed it advisable to present a substitute for all of them as follows:

The founders of the American Federation of Labor since their inception, were opposed to any prejudices, traditions, social or religious demarcations which could be applied to interfere with, or prevent thorough-going organization of all wage earners. They made one of the corner-stones of the great trade union structure they were determined to erect--the principle that the right to work, or membership in a trade union should not be limited, or restricted in any manner, because of creed, color or race.

The American Federation of Labor at that time, and ever since, has been the principal constructive and influential force in our country in giving practical application to that basic principle. We can examine the record of progress made in eliminating prejudices against so-called minority groups, with gratification and sincere pride.

The principle announced over sixty years ago has been given increasing practical application. Distinctions, because of national origin within our trade union movement, have been very largely eliminated. The color bar has been removed to such an extent that labor representatives of our colored members inform us that over half a million of their race are now dues paying members of the American Federation of Labor. This is the largest organization of colored workers in the world.

It is evident, however, that in some portions of our country there still remain among workers lingering suspicions, prejudices and traditions fostered by conditions long since passed, but which still operate to prevent the complete application of that great principle upon which our trade union structure has been erected.

The world war in which our country is now engaged, which involves safe-guarding the vital principle of free institutions under government by law, enacted by the peoples' representatives for the people, demands that national unity must be had and that all prejudices which interfere with this unity must be eliminated.

Those in our armed forces are risking their lives in our country's defense, without thought of national origin or the color which nature has given them. All of them are the nation's defenders. When the war ends those who are wage earners must be free to return to peaceful occupations as equals in the enjoyment of all the rights and opportunities enjoyed by others in our trade union movement.

National origin, race or color must in no manner or form restrict any American from a free opportunity to prepare himself to become a skilled mechanic, a craftsman, and take his place as such in any employment requiring the skill which he has acquired. The doors of our trade union movement must be open. This country must not maintain an industrial standard which discriminates against a wage earner because of his color.

Substantial progress has been made in eliminating prejudices, but there still remains an obligation upon the American Federation of Labor to carry on and expand the good work it has already done, so that the principle of industrial equality of all men will be established beyond question in every section of our country.

It is obvious that the goal we aim for, the best interests of the American people as a whole, and our democratic way of life, cannot be secured by one stroke or through the method of decrees, mechanical orders or threats handed down from on high. What is required is the intelligent, systematic, educational efforts to speed the day when there will no longer exist in the industrial field any prejudices or handicaps because of racial origin or color.

So that vitality and action can be given to this declaration of principle and of policy, your committee recommends that these declarations be given the widest possible publicity, and that all of the educational facilities of our trade union movement be used in furthering the objectives which have been herein set forth.

Your committee recommends reaffirmation of the action taken by the last convention endorsing the President's Committee on Fair Employment Practice.

The Post War Problems Committee of the A. F. of L. has appointed a sub-committee to deal with this and other minority questions. On this subcommittee the minority groups, including the colored race, are represented. Your committee is confident that as a result of this committee's work definite progress will be made.

President Green: You have heard the reading of the report of the committee; the motion is to adopt. Are there any remarks? Delegate Randolph.

Delegate Randolph, Brotherhood of Sleeping Car Porters: President Green and fellow delegates to the Sixty-third Convention of the American Federation of Labor: I want, on behalf of the Sleeping Car Porters' delegates, to express our appreciation for the sincere and serious efforts made by Chairman Woll and Secretary Frey of the Resolutions Committee to arrive at some formula for dealing with the problem of discrimination in the trade unions here at this convention. We, however, are in disagreement from the viewpoint of the scope of the report. The purpose of the report, the aim and objective of the report are all commendable, but we feel morally bound to discuss a very important phase of the trade union movement, at this time in connection with Negro workers, and I may say that we talked with Secretary Frey about this question at length and we certainly were impressed with his sincerity and concern with his interest in attempting to deal with this question. The same may be said with respect to Chairman Woll. But the matter of the material that should be included in the report was one upon which we could not agree. Thus, I want to present objection at this time.

The race problem is the number one problem of America today. It is the number one problem of American labor. It is the number one problem of the American Federation of Labor.

The fact that the U.S.A. organized labor, or the A. F. of L. may not be conscious of it, does not alter the fact that it is so.

It is for this reason, Mr. President, and delegates, that the conventions of the American Federation of Labor will always hear the voice of Negroes crying out against the color bar and discrimination in the constitutions, rituals, and policies of certain trade unions. When the Negro delegates that are now here are gone, others will come out and take their places and continue to cry out against membership exclusion policies by unions on account of race, color, religion, or national origin until it is wiped out. And we Negro delegates now amongst you are confident that day will eventually come. For the American Federation of Labor cannot continue to exist with a part of its members who are white as first-class union men and another part who are colored as second-class union men. This division of the house of labor is vital to its existence and future.

Influence of Southern Membership: But when you raise the question of the right of Negro workers to join certain trade unions, the leaders of these unions present the alibi of antagonism and opposition from their southern members. These officials privately proclaim their liberal attitude upon Negro workers joining their unions but express fear of sticking their necks out by championing the Negro workers' cause. This raises a moral and educational problem. The moral problem is: Can a true leader of labor shirk the responsibility to challenge and condemn the policy of his union's violation of the most fundamental tenets of trade unionism; namely, the right of a worker to join the organization of his choice of his craft or class or industry, without regard to race, color, religion, or national origin?

When a labor leader refuses either from fear or prejudice to fulfill this mission, is he not the foe rather than the friend of his own union? Moreover, each member of a union has a responsibility, second only to that of the leader, to see to it that his union does not violate the moral right of a worker to join the organization of his choice, to protect his economic interests and rights. It is enlightened self-interest for every union worker to fight for the right of every other worker to join the union of his choice, for the rights of no white union worker are secure as long as the rights of a black worker are insecure.

The denial to a worker union membership on account of race, color, religion, or national origin under a system of government support of union rights and interests is tantamount to denying the worker the right to work and to deny a worker the right to work is just like pointing a gun at the worker's head and telling him he shall not eat. That this is morally wrong and indefensible, not even a Robin Hood could gainsay.

Now, an A. F. of L. labor leader would consider it criminal for a man to take bread out of the mouth of another man solely because he had the power to do so. But certain A. F. of L. officials like Tom Ray, little Tin Horn Hitler, not only condone this very act by their own union, but are a party to it. Certainly this is an anti-social and anti-labor position. Let us remember that an individual's moral responsibilities don't end at the threshold of an organization. This is true of a member or leader of a union. A union may be criminal and immoral just as an individual, and its conduct may justify the moral condemnation of the community. If this were not true, then it would be improper and unjust to impose any penalties upon the German, Japanese, or Italian nations after Hitler, Hirohito, and Mussolini pass out. A nation is morally responsible for the conduct of its people, and the people are morally responsible for the conduct of their nation. This logic holds true with an individual union or international. It also holds true with the American Federation of Labor.[177]

The A. F. of L. cannot expect the public to give it moral immunity from condemnation for racial discriminations by its international unions on the grounds that it is a federated body. If the A. F. of L. claims that it is the house of labor, then it cannot escape criticism for the wrongs committed in that house. If the A. F. of L. is justified in claiming credit for the numerical increase of general union membership, it must bear the guilt for the lack of increase of Negro union membership because of a narrow racial policy. Can the United States of America justifiably take refuge in the thread-bare doctrine of states' rights when it is condemned because of the Poll Tax disgrace? Hardly!

Now, the educational problem consists in exploding the myth of racism and its danger to the working class solidarity, the salvation of labor.

How Does Racial Discrimination Function in Unions? Let us take the case

In very truth, the question of race and color is the central, historical, social issue of these times. There are several reasons for this. One is the fact that two-thirds of the population of the world are colored. Second, the peoples of color have reached a higher level of moral, spiritual, and intellectual maturity, and have thus raised the question of world political issue.

In the U.S.A., the question of freedom, equality, and justice to the Negro people has assumed the status of a major, national, political issue. This problem must be met. It cannot be continuously evaded. Its solution does not involve, will not involve, Negroes alone. It involves all of America. Until this problem is frankly and courageously met and solved, the major problems of America and world democracy will continue to baffle the American people and world governments. Until the A. F. of L. realistically attacks this question of racial discrimination it cannot mobilize the complete strength of American labor or develop a healthy and sound and progressive existence.

Thus, racial discrimination should be abolished by every union affiliated with the A. F. of L. not only for the benefit of the Negro and other minorities, but for the sake of the A. F. of L. itself—to square its practices with its professions. This Federation is challenged in this hour of national and world crisis to make up its mind as to whether it shall shape and measure the soundness, value, and worthwhileness of its policies and programs upon solid and universal moral laws and principles, that the civilized world accepts and supports, or whether it will ignore, disregard, and flout these laws and principles, and formulate tactics and methods that give it the power to override opposition and squelch valid criticism. If it recognizes and accepts the tenets and standards of the christian and democratic moral order, it will wipe out all distinctions between workers based upon race, color, religion, or national origin, and justify its existence as a symbol and expression of the age-old struggles of the working people in particular and mankind in general to achieve justice, freedom and equality. If this federation refuses to cleanse its house of labor of the poisons of discrimination on account of race, color, religion, or national origin, it will, despite its material and economic power, forfeit and lose the confidence and faith of the enlightened and liberal people of America and the world. The leaders of the A. F. of L. must realize and understand that material strength and economic power that have no moral sanction and spiritual or social justification, are hollow, superficial, and impermanent. And the unions affiliated with the A. F. of L. must eliminate the color bar because of common horse sense, self interest to save its own hide.

We are witnessing now in Nazi Germany an arrogant, irresponsible, and reckless use of power—military power—spreading battle and blood, death and destruction, terrorism and tyranny, over the face of the globe.

Why is this? The answer is that Hitler, Mussolini, and Hirohito possess no code or concept of moral righteousness; no answer to the questions: What is wrong or right except material and military power? Their philosophy is that the structure of relationships of society will always and inevitably be the dominator and dominated, master and slave, oppressor and oppressed, top dog and bottom dog. This is a dog eat dog, tooth and claw, beak and fang doctrine. It is the doctrine of destruction. It is the doctrine of destruction even for the oppressor, the top dog. In the language of the discriminating unions, it is "A" or first class membership and "B" or secondary membership. The right to rule is not based upon blood and sword, gun and force and color or race. Under this creed, the bottom dog will always remain the bottom dog unless he can mobilize more and greater brute-force than the top dog. The unavoidable implication of this philosophy is eternal war, conflict, chaos, and confusion. Why? Because the oppressed, the bottom dog, will not calmly remain the bottom dog without a struggle to the death for freedom, justice and equality.

In the nature of things, no human being will forever accept the status of a slave and acknowledge another man as his master. By the same token, no people will be content to exist as second-class citizens or second-class union men.

Men, regardless of race, color, religion, or national origin, will ever protest and fight against this condition. It is this ceaseless struggle of the oppressed for justice, freedom, and equality which is the great insurance of the preservation of the democratic, liberal tradition. Without this agitation of the forgotten man, the conscience of the tyrants will be undisturbed, their ruthless rule unquestioned, and the creative and liberal spirit would die.

involving the controversy over the representation of employees in a shipyard
when the National Labor Relations Board is called upon to determine what effect
it shall give to racial discrimination by a labor union when, on the one hand,
that union seeks to represent a unit composed in part of workers which it
excludes from membership rights because of their race.

More specifically, the Bay Cities Metal Trades Council of the A. F. of L.
sought to define the appropriate unit for collective bargaining on a plant-wide
basis and to have an election ordered solely within that unit. The records
show that substantial numbers of Negroes and other non-white employees are
working within the plant and within the smaller functional areas whose demar-
cation as appropriate units was in issue.

The record also shows the extent of the practice of racial discrimination
by the constitution and by-laws of the Bay Cities Metal Trades Council and the
International Brotherhood of Boilermakers, Iron Shipbuilders and Helpers,
principal constituent member of the Trades Council involved in the case.

Now, representation by the Trades Council would be representation by an
affiliated group of unions among which the Boilermakers claim and exercise
exclusive jurisdiction over a large part of the work and the great majority of
the employees required for shipbuilding. The record and the basic law of the
Boilermakers show that Negroes under jurisdiction of that union must be
organized into so-called "auxiliary lodges" of which there are two in the
plants where the controversy in question arose; namely, the Bethlehem Almeda
Shipyard, Inc., on the Pacific Coast. But the record further shows that the
so-called "auxiliary lodges" are excluded from membership in the aforementioned
Trades Council. Thus, the Trades Council, through the neat but questionable
device of forcing Negro workmen into "auxiliary lodges" and excluding these
auxiliaries from the Council, effectively denied Negro workmen a measure of
participation in or control over the conduct of the proposed bargaining agency
set up under the laws of the Federal Government.

If a labor organization which in substance excludes Negroes from membership,
as do the Trades Council here and the Boilermakers, should be accorded exclusive
rights or representation for a group including Negro workmen, those Negroes,
because of their race, would arbitrarily be denied that measure of participation
in and control over their "representatives" which is enjoyed by white union
members and inheres in the very concept of collective bargaining. The processes
of the National Labor Relations Board designed to insure workers substantative
benefits of collective bargaining would in such case, or in case of any similar
denial or exclusion predicated on sex, creed or national origin, be employed
to exclude the injured group altogether from any real participation in collective
bargaining. Such misuse and perversion of its processes should not be tolerated
by the National Labor Relations Board.

In this connection, it is believed that the National Labor Relations Board
may and should properly be influenced by the fact that throughout the history
of American organized labor the exclusion of Negroes from labor unions and the
resultant promotion of strife between white and Negro workmen have been disturbing factors of major importance in industry and commerce. Thus, to the
extent that the Board, in its adjudication of particular cases, can achieve
participation of workmen in the processes of collective bargaining without
discrimination as to race, sex, religion, or national origin by so much will
the Board promote order and harmony in commerce and industry and thus advance
the purposes of the National Labor Relations Act.

Not only are the special purposes of the National Labor Relations Act
defeated by the discriminatory practices herewith considered, but the national
policies of the United States in furtherance of war production as well.

The National Labor Relations Board should also consider that the Negro
worker, no less than any other, has viewed the National Labor Relations Act as a
charter for orderly and just processes in labor relations. Such confidence is
essential to the successful administration of the law. It would be catastrophic
for Negro workers to find that the Labor Relations Act could be used to force
them to accept as a bargaining agent, a union from which they are excluded
bluntly or by sophistical devices. The progress which Negroes are making toward
equality of status in organized labor would be arrested by the very legislation
to which all labor looks for a new measure of justice and security. The Negro
as a substantial minority group, outraged and disllusioned, would become a source
of continuing discord and strife, and would serve dissident employers as a ready
tool for exploitation of black and white workers alike.

One of the consequences most likely to result from exclusive representation under sanction of the National Labor Relations Act is the negotiation of a closed shop contract between the employer and the exclusive bargaining representative. The union seeking a still stronger position, and the employer seeking stability in labor relations are both impelled toward such a contract. But to the worker of a minority group who is arbitraily denied status in the union, such a closed shop contract becomes the means of his total exclusion from employment. Thus, to the Negro worker, the greater calamity of total denial of employment is the probable consequence of granting exclusive bargaining rights to a discriminatory union.

The injustice of enforced representation by a union which excludes from membership a group of Negroes whom it claims to represent has most recently been recognized by the Court of Appeals of the District of Columbia in a case arising under the Railway Labor Act, but enunciating a principle entirely applicable to the present case:

> "It will be observed that Congress granted employees certain positive rights, both affirmative and negative in character. They have the right to organize and bargain collectively through represenatives of their own choosing which carries the corollary right to bargain collectively. And yet the employees in the case at bar are ineligible to organize with the only labor union that their employer will recognize as their bargaining agent."

The Appropriate Record: The National Labor Relations Board enjoys wide discretion to determine on the facts of each case whether a proposed unit is appropriate for collective bargaining. For the reasons above stated, the Board should not recognize or certify a unit as appropriate if the effect of exclusive representation by the only petitioner who proposes that unit and seeks exclusive bargaining rights therein would be to deny to persons of any race, sex, creed, or origin the real participation in the collective bargaining process enjoyed by other employees within the unit. On the other hand, if such full participation of all workmen in the collective bargaining process would be promoted by setting up a proposed bargaining unit, this fact should be one of the controlling considerations in favor of the determination that such a unit is the appropriate one under the circumstances of the case.

Consistency of the Proposed Rule with Prior Adjudications of the Rule: This National Labor Relations Board has consistently held that a unit is not appropriate for collective bargaining if it is differentiated and established on the basis of the race and the employers who would constitute the unit. A "white" unit or a "Negro" unit is not appropriate. But if a white unit or Negro unit is not appropriate, a white union is not appropriate.

The soundness of this doctrine seems clear. The Utah Copper case shows that the exclusion of Negroes from a proposed unit may properly be a controlling factor in the Board's refusal to order an election therein. As a corollary, it seems proper that, since both colored and white employees whose functions are not differentiated must be included within a single bargaining unit, the Board should find the proposed unit appropriate, and certify a representative only if real representation and bargaining rights would be afforded to both white and Negro workmen by the union, or by one or more of the unions, seeking status within that unit.

The National Labor Relations Board has not heretofore found it necessary to decide the issue now before it, although within the month, the issue has been noted and expressly reserved for future decision. But its recurrence in future cases can reasonably be anticipated.

Only a minority of unions practice the discrimination herein complained of. Yet the minority is great enough to affect a large area of industry and commerce. The most recently published survey of the extent of such discrimination and exclusion is the study by Herbert R. Northrup, Organized Labor and Negro Workers, 51 *Journal of Political Economy,* 206 (June, 1943). Northrup lists the major unions which exclude Negroes or discriminate against them as follows:

   I. Union which excludes Negroes by provision in ritual: Machinists, International Association of (A. F. of L.).

  II. Unions which exclude Negroes by provision in constitution:

A. F. of L. affiliates:

Airline Pilots Association
Commercial Telegraphers Union
Masters, Mates and Pilots, National Organization
Railroad Telegraphers, Order of
Railway Mail Association
Switchmen's Union of North America
Wire Weavers' Protective Association, American

Unaffiliated organizations:

Locomotive Engineers, Brotherhood of
Locomotive Firemen and Enginemen, Brotherhood of
Railroad Trainmen, Brotherhood of
Railroad Yardmasters of America
Railroad Yardmasters of North America
Railroad Conductors, Order of
Train Dispatchers' Association, American

III. Unions which habitually exclude Negroes by tacit consent:

All A. F. of L. affiliates:

Asbestos Workers, Heat and Frost Insulators
Electrical Workers, International Brotherhood of
Flint Glass Workers' Union, American
Granite Cutters, International Association of
Plumbers and Steamfitters, United Association of Journeymen

IV. Unions which afford Negroes only segregated auxiliary status:

A. F. of L. affiliates:

Blacksmiths, Drop Forgers and Helpers, Brotherhood of
Boilermakers, Iron Shipbuilders, Welders and Helpers,
    Brotherhood of
Maintenance of Way Employees, Brotherhood of
Railway Carmen of America, Brotherhood
Railway and Steamship Clerks, Freight Handlers, Express
    and Station Employes, Brotherhood of
Rural Letter Carriers, Federation of
Sheet Metal Workers' International Association

Unaffiliated organizations:

Rural Letter Carriers' Association
Railroad Workers, American Federation of

It is to be noted that this list includes unions, among them the boiler-makers, which have their historic roots in the highly restrictive organization of precisely defined crafts but currently are in process of rapid transformation into vast industrial unions. Thus, racial, religious and sex discriminations stand as irrational surviving impediments to the present course of union development in an area which widens as the discriminatory unions become increasingly industrial in character.

The question of Local Auxiliary Unions is of paramount and far-reaching importance, if the American Federation of Labor seeks to chart a new path of democracy for the workers. An examination of the nature and function of the Auxiliary Union reveals that its relationship to the International Union is quite similar to the relationship of colonies of colored people to the empire systems, particularly the British Empire. Colonial natives are economic, political, and social serfs, since they possess none of the rights that the white population in the mother country enjoy, except the right to be taxed. They can't vote; they can't hold offices, except of a perfunctory nature; and they can't participate in any of the policy-making bodies. They, however, have the right to be used as cannon fodder in defense of their oppressors when wars break out.

Now, the members of the Auxiliary Unions do not have any voice or vote in the selection or election of representatives that make and maintain agreements,

adjust grievances and claims, and execute and administer the affairs of the
International Union. They can't attend national conventions, and they play no
part in the management of the movement. They are, of course, permitted to pay
dues and assessments. This is a taxation without representation--the cause of
the rebellion of the thirteen colonies against British rule. Thus, Negro
workers cannot be condemned for seeking to abolish this species of trade union
misrule and imperialism.

I want to give this convention the testimony of the constitution and
by-laws of an International Union which maintains auxiliary locals so that it
may be clear that all I am doing here is making an objective analysis of
Auxiliary Locals without prejudice, but only with a desire to have the delegates
and officers of these international organizations see and understand that the
Auxiliary Local reflects a system which is ancient, feudalistic, and tyrannical
and is inconsistent with the avowed purposes of the American Federation of
Labor, that seeks to preserve the principle of free and equal workers.

This system of Auxiliary Unions is undemocratic, unAmerican, and violative
of the fundamental principles of trade unionism that insure the right of all
workers regardless of race, color, religion, or national origin, to associate
as equals in a common movement to resist exploitation and oppression. The
separation of the workers that Auxiliary Unions make necessary, creates
suspicions and prejudices that grow out of the idea that this separation is
based upon some fundamental difference among the workers, and thereby fosters,
ingenders, and inculcates hatreds, rancor, ill-feeling, and antagonisms that
render working-class solidarity impossible.

I shall read from the constitution and by-laws of the International
Brotherhood of Boilermakers, Iron Shipbuilders, and Helpers of America as
adopted January 1, 1938, and amended July 15, 1942.

Article VII of the Auxiliary By-Laws provides that auxiliary lodges shall
be composed of "colored male" persons. The regular local lodges are protected
against the admission of Negroes by racial restrictions embodied in their
ritual. With the segregation of colored and white workmen thus accomplished,
various provisions in the International Constitution and the Auxiliary By-Laws
restrict the Negro "members" and their auxiliary lodges to merely nominal
status. The following requirements are specially noteworthy:

1. Article II, Section 14 of the Auxiliary By-Laws provides that the
business agent appointed by and acting for the local white lodge "supervising"
the colored auxiliary "shall perform the same duties for the auxiliary lodge as
are performed for the supervising lodges, including the dispatching and assigning of members to jobs." Thus, Negro members of auxiliary lodges have no voice
or vote in the selection or control or dismissal of the man who is arbitrarily
set up as their representative in the most important and fundamental contacts
with the employer.

2. The Shop Committee of the "supervising" white lodge established under
Article XIV of the Subordinate Lodge Constitution to handle shop disputes and
grievances is designated in Article XIII of the Auxiliary By-Laws to exercise
the same functions for the auxiliary lodge. The members of the auxiliary
lodge have no voice or vote in selecting or controlling such shop committees.

3. Article II, Section 13 of the Auxiliary By-Laws provides that the
Grievance Committee of the "supervising" lodge shall act for the auxiliary
lodge as well, yet limits the auxiliary lodge to one member who may function
with the committee regardless of the relative size and membership of the
auxiliary and "supervising" lodges.

5, An auxiliary lodge has no voice or vote in the Quadrennial Convention
which is the ultimate legislative authority of the International Brotherhood of
Boilermakers, Iron Shipbuilders and Helpers of America. In contrast, at each
such convention, each white local lodge is entitled to voting representation
proportional to the number of its members. See Article II, Section 2,
International Constitution.

Moreover, Negro workmen and their auxiliary lodges have no security even
in their nominal status. Article I, Section 4 of the Auxiliary By-Laws
authorizes the International President within his uncontrolled discretion to
suspend any auxiliary lodge or any officer or member of an auxiliary lodge,
thus arbitrarily depriving the Negro even of limited status within the union.

In contrast, the International Constitution contains no provision for the suspension of a white local lodge, but provides for revocation of the charter of a subordinate lodge only by the International President, in conjunction with the Executive Council and only after such lodge shall have been proven guilty of violation of the said Constitution. See Article IV, Section 2. Members of white local lodges can be suspended or otherwise disciplined only after formal trial following the procedure prescribed in detail in Article XIV of said International Constitution.

The net effect of this scheme is to make it lawful for a white local lodge and its business and other bargaining agents at their whim and caprice to permit Negroes to work on union jobs, reserving arbitrary control over their status, upgrading, and even their continuation in nominal good standing. All significant rights of union membership, including all participation in collective bargaining are denied to the Negro. In substance, he pays his dues and gets in return only a work permit revocable at will. This travesty designed to sanction the inevitable temporary utilization of Negro workmen in these times without conferring any significant status upon them, does not merit characterization as union membership.

In the New Orleans Convention of 1941 there were 25 or 30 Federal Locals of Negroes composed of Freight Handlers and Red Caps who were given federal charters by the A. F. of L. because the International Union which controls the jurisdiction over the work, had color clauses in their constitutions and therefore excluded Negro workers. These Federal Unions were ordered by President Green and the Executive Council to go into the local auxiliary unions of the Brotherhood of Railway Clerks, and their charters were lifted. President Green told Brother Webster and myself that he understood that the Negro workers in the auxiliary unions could attend the National Convention of the Brotherhood of Railway Clerks, but of course, this is not the case. The Negro freight handlers and red caps were so incensed and disgusted with this policy that most of them refused to go into the Railway Clerks and established an independent Freight Handlers Union and some of the Red Caps went into the C.I.O.

Thus auxiliary locals of International Unions that have racial bars have taken the place of Federal Locals. The Federal Locals directly chartered by the A. F. of L. provided the one agency which Negro workers could join when refused membership by an International Union. Now this hope is gone. I consider this a step backward.

If these Negro Freight Handlers and Red Caps representing some 25,000 or 30,000 workers had been permitted to retain their federal charters, they would be in the fold of the A. F. of L. now.

And even though some of the delegates may have arrived at certain deductions and conclusions, the fact remains that until the International Unions abolish discrimination there can be no pretense of democracy in the labor movement. And, my friends, this is not said in the interest of Negroes alone but in the interests of the American Federation of Labor itself.

Now it was stated from this platform that the American Federation of Labor is concerned about a representative at the peace table. In other words, organized labor wants to be heard at the peace table. Organized labor wants a voice in the determination of world policies. Well, what about the Negro? Don't you think the Negroes are concerned about democracy, too? As a matter of fact, it seems to me that men are naive who will get up on the floor merely because that delegate is calling for freedom for Negro workers and is pointing out that all discriminations on account of race are un-American, un-democratic and absolutely unethical. Now if any delegate believes that by getting up and de- nouncing a Negro delegate here because he fights and condemns discrimination that that Negro delegate is going to abandon that fight, he certainly is absurd and preposterous, because so far as Negro delegates are concerned they are going to fight and condemn and oppose racial discriminations, regardless of what happens, because we believe in doing that we are serving the cause of democracy, not only for the American Federation of Labor but for the American people.

Do you not know that the agents of Japan, that Goebbels of Germany and that the propaganda organization of Italy, Fascist Italy, have used the various incidents of discrimination against Negroes in spreading propaganda among the colored peoples of the world, to the end that they contend, how can you have any faith in the democracy that is pretended to exist in America when they will not give democracy and justice and equality to their own Negro citizens.

My friends, this convention is meeting in a city which is historic. Go
to Boston Common, where President Green will speak, and there you will see a
monument of Crispus Attucks, a black man who was the first to give his blood
and life for the cause of his country. Right here in Boston, in Faneuil Hall,
a Negro slave woman got up when the great agitation against slavery was going
on and served as the inspiration for Wendell Phillips and Sumner. In other
words, the Negroes have played their role for the advancement of Democracy in
America. [178]

Right here you have talked about the fight now being made against labor,
the anti-labor legislation in various states, and Judge Padway has indicated
that cases were going to be brought up under the Fourteenth Amendment. Do you
know why you have a fourteenth Amendment? The Fourteenth Amendment was
adopted primarily to have human rights, primarily to protect the rights of
Negroes in this country, but the Fourteenth Amendment is now being resorted to
by various other agencies for their own protection. You ought to be aware of
this; you ought to realize this also, that the same enemies that are turning
their guns of reaction against Negroes are turning their guns of reaction
against others. And, brothers, let me warn you that unless a sound, unequivocal
and definite position is taken on the question of democracy for Negroes in the
American Federation of Labor and other agencies, the tides of Fascism are going
to rise in this country and wipe out not only the Negroes but organized labor
as well. Fascism came to Germany, and the most powerful trade union in the
world was squelched and destroyed. The same thing happened in Italy. Fascism
will use the Negro as the scapegoat, but while they are attacking the Negroes
today they will attack the Jews tomorrow and they will attack the Catholics the
next day.

You remember when Al Smith ran for President. All throughout the South
propaganda raged against Catholics. Five southern States seceded, and why?
Because they spread the propaganda that if you elect Alfred Smith President of
the United States, the Pope would sit in the White House.

And so, my friends, I tell you it is to the interests of workers regardless
of race, creed or color to fight for the abolition of prejudice and discrimination against any particular group within our Commonwealth.

I thank you.

President Green: The hour of adjournment has arrived because we must
vacate the hall a little earlier tonight in order that the hotel management may
prepare for the banquet. They requested that we be out of the hall by five
o'clock. It is now just a few minutes after five.

We will take up further discussion of this subject promptly tomorrow
morning.

At five o'clock P.M., under suspension of rules, the convention was
adjourned to 9:30 o'clock Tuesday morning, October 12th.

President Green: We will now proceed with the regular order of business.
The discussion will take place upon the report of Committee on Resolutions
which was before us last evening, and the Chair now recognizes Delegate
MacGowan, of the Boilermakers and Shipbuilders' organization.

Delegate MacGowan: Mr. Chairman, and delegates--I want to present for the
record certain factual information which was made necessary by certain allegations made on the floor of this convention yesterday afternoon.

I think it unnecessary to assure the delegates that what I have to say may
not be in polished Harvard accents, nor in the refined cultural language of
Washington drawing rooms. The language that I have learned to speak as a trade
unionist is the rather picturesque and sometimes lurid language of the boiler
shop, and about the only connection I ever had with a drawing room for many
years was those which had side door entrances and were labeled 60,000 pounds
capacity. But in that status, like a lot more men seated in this hall, I
learned many things about the underprivileged and the unfortunate and the lowly
among mankind.

Yesterday afternoon we listened with rapt attention to the speech of
Delegate Webster and to about half of the speech of Delegate Randolph. Those
portions, or that portion of Delegate Randolph's speech which followed the
pattern of Delegate Webster, no man can find fault with. It was the outcry of

an oppressed and underprivileged people, appealing to the fairness and decency of others for proper treatment and proper consideration, and had Delegate Randolph stopped at that point I would not now be consuming the time of this convention. But he elected to fish in troubled waters and he elected to make allegations and interpretations of our law--and I use the word "interpretation" most charitably. So it therefore becomes necessary, in the language of a famous statesman of this generation, to take a look at the record and let us see what the record discloses.

In the first place, in case Delegate Randolph may have overlooked it, Section 2 of Article II of the Constitution of the American Federation of Labor provides for the establishment of national and international unions based on each trade. This institution is, as its name implies, a federation of autonomy and independent and self-governing international unions. It is, as its founders have often declared--and with which I am in full accord--a purely voluntary organization, and as long as it remains voluntary and concedes to each International Union the right to manage its own affairs it will remain the guiding star of the American labor movement.

There have been some noticeable trends in recent years to exchange the voluntary principle for one of compulsion, and in my humble judgment, unless that trend is checked we have compounded our own destruction.

The argument advanced by Delegate Randolph, based upon Resolution 28, contemplates compulsion--compelling International Unions to do thus and so, and I respectfully submit that when we reach the point of declaring "Thou shalt not," we have reached the point of disintegration in the American Federation of Labor.

Our International Union for many years gave extensive consideration to the Negro problem in its several conventions, and the speaker now addressing you has a long record in our convention of advocating the organizing and the protection of the colored workers. As in every convention of trade unionists, none of us always have our way. Compromises are arrived at. It is by compromise that we make progress, and when our International convention speaks on the issue, their decision must needs be my decision. There were conflicting schools of thought, as many other organizations here have experienced. Finally in 1937 at our last convention, the International Executive Council recommended a system providing for the organization of the colored men of our trade. The convention did not see fit to accept in toto the recommendation of the Executive Council. Another compromise was arrived at and finally the Auxiliary system was established. We meet on January 31st of next year in regular convention and the progress made and the difficulties encountered in the experiment of the last five years will be studied and upon that record will depend our future policy.

No act of this convention can compel our convention to do other than that which it elects to do of its own free will, and I say in all earnestness to Delegate Randolph and those of you who think as he does that the allegations made here yesterday are not helping the cause of the Negro in our International Union or in others. The statements made by him constitute one of the greatest disservices that he has ever rendered his people.

For the information of the delegates, let me submit a bit of our experience. We had our numerous Auxiliary locals operating without difficulty. They were operating in fine shape until the shipbuilding boom hit the Pacific coast. We installed an auxiliary Local Union in the city of Oakland, California, and after a few months we began hearing strange stories. We finally instituted an investigation, and later the officers of that Auxiliary were brought in before our International Executive Council for further investigation.

And, behold, what did we find? That a group of people claiming to be Negro leaders had organized what was known as the Miscellaneous Workers Incorporated. They had opened an office adjoining our Auxiliary office, and every Negro that was brought into Oakland for referral to the shipyards of that area was not only required first to become a member of the Miscellaneous Workers' Incorporated, but he was required to sign an authorization delegating to that body all bargaining rights. The result was that we had an Auxiliary Local Union of several thousand members but we had no bargaining rights. The bargaining rights were vested in this strange institution which was collecting monthly dues from the membership of our Auxiliary Local. We ordered the discontinuance of that practice and from that day until this, the Boilermakers International Union has been Peck's bad boy. We broke up somebody's playhouse, and that may be the

answer why Delegate Randolph took such an extended amount of time to point out
the sins and vices of our International Union.

I could go on at length discussing other developments in this situation,
where our Auxiliary headquarters was picketed in the city of Los Angeles, where
so-called Negro leaders went out among the shipyard workers in Portland,
Oregon, and told them not to pay dues; they said, "we are going to challenge
this thing." Then they went to the President's Committee on Fair Employment
Practices and filed a bill of particulars consisting of ten legal pages, which
I have before me , and they called upon the President's Committee on Fair
Employment Practices to instruct us to disestablish our Auxiliaries and to
admit the Negro to full membership in other Locals.

Now I respectfully submit that the Committee on Fair Employment Practices
is charged with certain duties--the duties contained and spelled out for them
in the President's Executive Order, and I make the statement here and now
without fear of contradiction, that our International Union, none of its
officers or representatives have discriminated in the hire, tenure, wages, or
working conditions of any person, regardless of race, color, creed or national
origin. The proof of that lies in the fact that today there are over 15,000
members in our Auxiliary Local Unions.

In the city of Portland where this charge which I refer to--the ten-page
allegation--was filed, the names of two men were submitted and the general
blanket indictment made was that there were 300 men removed from that employment. As a matter of fact of the two men whose names were used, one was a
sheet metal worker and the other was a draftsman, and the names of the 300
alleged victims have never yet been submitted to us.

Let me look at the record again. In the Portland area, as of September
11th, there was a total of 1592 Negro persons employed in the shipyards in that
area. Of that number 664 were receiving the mechanic's rate of pay, or 42% of
the total employed, and practically none of those men, or women either, had
ever seen a shipyard, much less work one 12 months ago. And yet under our
trainee program and our upgrading, here we find 42% of the 1600 that are
employed being upgraded to mechanic's rates of pay in a year's time. Does that
spell discrimination? And of the 300 men that have been alleged to have been
removed, our check of the record shows that there were 20, and those 20 were
removed with hundreds of white workers for the simple reason that they refused
to pay dues and keep in good standing, and for that reason only.

I repeat again, our Auxiliary Local Unions in nowise interfere with the
hire, tenure, wages or conditions of employment.

The Auxiliary charter which Delegate Randolph referred to yesterday contains in substance about 85% of our international law. He likewise referred to
the fact, and tried to leave the impression, that these Auxiliary Locals were
conquered provinces, where some importing Quisling was dominating the affairs
of the Auxiliary. He failed to read the most important section of all:

"The officers of each Auxiliary Lodge shall consist of a president, vice
president, treasurer, inspector, inside guard, outside guard, recording
secretary, financial secretary, corresponding secretary, and three trustees."

He complained about the fact that the Auxiliaries were only entitled to
minority representation on the collective bargaining committee. Would he have
us turn majority control over to their Auxiliary in a shipyard where there are
20,000 white employees and 500 or 600 colored? Is that what he is asking?

Mr. Chairman and delegates, no man has more sympathy and more understanding
of an oppressed peoples' problems than I think I have. All my life I have been
a champion of the underprivileged, and I say with the utmost kindness of
Delegate Randolph, this Auxiliary proposition may not be the entire answer, but
you have got to meet conditions as you find them, not as you would wish them to
be.

There may come a time when the entire organization has reached that point
in its thinking, to admit all people on a basis of equality to membership, but
until our convention speaks--as an officer of that organization--I am duty
bound to carry out its mandates and I am duty bound to object to interference
in our autonomous affairs on the part of the American Federation of Labor. But
I say to you most sincerely, accusations such as were hurled at us yesterday do
not promote the cause for which Delegate Randolph undertakes to speak.

Let me read from the record what he said: "This system of Auxiliary Unions
is undemocratic, un-American and violative of the fundamental principles of
trade unionism." Delegate Randolph has the right to disagree with me, with our

organization and its policies, but in the middle of a great all-out war, when
the fate of civilization hangs in the balance, it comes with poor grace for
Delegate Randolph to condemn us for being un-American.
   I shall not attempt to exalt the International Union that I speak for or
the contribution that it has made in time and money and effort and the 50,000
members in the uniform of the nation. That record speaks for itself. But
there sits on the floor of this convention a man who thirty-five years ago
laid aside his tools and overalls and came out to take a struggling, weak
child in the form of our International organization. He struggled with it,
he fought for it and he fought with it. He fought the discordant elements
within it and the enemies from without, and now, in the closing days of his
life, to find him standing accused on the floor of the American Federation of
Labor as sponsoring an organization that is undemocratic and un-American and
as sponsoring an Auxiliary system that is a cheat and a fraud, is just too
much to take. It is not a pleasant tribute to hand to Joe Franklin, after the
thirty-five years of effort that he has put into the trade union movement
without a whisper against his character and his integrity.
   Mr. Chairman, as a final thought, I once heard Samuel Gompers in the
convention of the American Federation of Labor in the city of St. Paul--in a
perennial discussion of Irish freedom, make this statement, and many of you
that are here today heard it. He said, "One of the greatest obstacles confronting the cause of Irish freedom is the professional Irish." One of the
greatest causes contributing to the failure of the Negro to advance further is
the professional Negro. We have no difficulty with the workers in the shipyards
and plants and railroad shops. We meet with them, we confer with them and
sympathetic understanding prevails, but when those people come around who seek
other things than the pure and simple advancement of the economic welfare of
all people--regardless of color--then trouble begins. This is an economic
question--the well-being of the Negro is my interest as much as it is the white.
The unorganized and underpaid Negro is a menace to the men of my trade, the
same as the white, and I have battled and will continue to battle for the advancement of all men that work at our trade. We have Filipinos, we have
Chinese, we have Latin Americans of all grades. The Negro question is safe in
our hands. It will be handled wisely without the interference of those who
would indict us at this time.
   Mr. Chairman, I am heartily in favor of the report of the Committee on
Resolutions. It is a masterful approach to the question. It is statesmanlike.
It is an appeal to the hearts and the minds and the consciences of the delegates
to this convention. It is sound doctrine and I hope it will be adopted.
   Thank you.

   President Green: The Chair recognizes Delegate Bugniazet.

   Delegate Bugniazet, Electrical Workers: Mr. Chairman and delegates, I had
no intention of burdening you with any statement on this question, because in
my humble opinion I believe the attacks made on the organizations of this
Federation by Delegate Randolph are only made here as a sounding board for his
work on the outside. [179]
   He used to charge our organization with discriminating against the Negro,
with refusing to organize them. I have discussed that at meetings with him
before the Executive Council and elsewhere, and now he has changed his attack
and uses it in this language. And he has got us in the group that habitually
excludes Negroes by "tacit consent." He can't go further, because he has seen
our laws, and if either he or any other person can find or interpret anything
in there that discrimination against either race, creed or color, or other
things, why he is going to show me something that I have never seen, and I
think I ought to know as much about our organization as he does--maybe a little
bit more. Our organization has never excluded Negroes or any race, or any
color, and we don't take men or women into our organization just because they
want to join it and exploit it. They have got to be competent to join our
organization, and I could say many things here that might hurt the Negro and
let him know why he hasn't progressed in our line of industry, but I don't
intend to injure his cause. I just want to make the record straight.
   Long before Randolph thought of coming to A. F. of L. conventions or to
champion the cause of Negro workers, when we had a vacancy in one of our International Vice Presidencies in the early 1900's--and I think that is a little

before his time--our President appointed a full blooded Negro as the International Vice President for a whole District and he didn't have many Negroes under him, and Randolph can't say we did that to play to the gallery, because in the early 1900's you didn't hear anything about Negroes being kept out of organizations.

For his information, in the historic city of Boston one of our largest Local Unions has sent Negroes to our International Conventions, I believe about three in number, and that same Negro until his death three or four years ago had been for fifteen consecutive years the treasurer of that Local Union, elected by white men. And they weren't playing to the gallery because there weren't any Negroes to organize. We have many Negroes and we have the problem that everybody has in the South. You can't mix oil with water, even if you want to.

Some people in the South are still fighting the Civil War. The government has not cured that, and agitation such as Delegate Randolph is indulging in is not going to improve that. That only delays it. We have a Chinese secretary of one of our Local Unions. We, at least, could have let him remain a member and not put him in office.

Now I wonder, is Delegate Randolph consistent? I say he is not, and I have the right to my opinion, as he has to his. I will give him my reasons so that he cannot say I was trying to pull some parliamentary trick by making a statement and not supporting it.

He came before the Executive Council several years ago on a complaint of the Pullman conductors, claiming transgression of jurisdiction and undercutting the conditions. I am not going to discuss that case, only just enough to recall his mind to the incident. There was quite some discussion in the Council room while he was present and he was asked this question: If the Pullman Company employed some white men as Pullman porters would you admit them to your organization? He said, "No, that is a colored man's job." He claimed that the whites should organize the colored, but he has a monopoly in the Pullman porters for colored people, and the white people have no right there. Consistency, thou are a jewel, even with an education.

I want to say now, definitely, for our International Union that the only bar to entry is competency. Our Locals have complete autonomy in the matter of admitting members, they have the right to examine them and they are put up for a vote. Some large Locals refer it to the Executive Boards of these Local Unions.

We have no Auxiliaries. We issue only one charter for one class of workmen in a locality. We have several charters but they have different jurisdiction. We do not issue Jim Crow charters, although we have had requests to do so. Where they are organized, they go into the Local Union with the white men and if there is a Negro majority there, they will go into that Local and they will not get a separate charter.

The biggest fault we have found is the employer. He is choosey on who he wants and I have told our organization convention, and the records will show it, away back about 1917, that we cannot let any feeling influence us in the matter of those we take in, except in the matter of competency, and there is going to be discrimination, let the employer be guilty of it, and let us get the conditions for all those who are doing the same class of work, be they women, black, white or any other color.

It is getting tiresome in convention after convention to hear someone who is out shouting from the housetops. Maybe he thinks he is doing a good job for the people he is representing, but I share the views of others that he is doing them a great disservice. He is agitating and not doing anything concrete. All he is doing is attacking, charging.

I feel the committee brought in a magnificent report. I think they went as far as they could in language, and I, for one, am wholeheartedly behind it and in full accord with their report.

I thank you.

President Green: The Chair now recognizes Delegate Horn of the Blacksmiths, Drop Forgers and Helpers.

Delegate Horn, Blacksmiths, Drop Forgers and Helpers: Mr. Chairman and brother delegates: I will tell you the truth about the International Brotherhood of Blacksmiths, Drop Forgers and Helpers and its colored members. For

quite a number of conventions in the past years, I have sat quietly by and
listened to allegations made against the organization of which I happen to
have the honor of being its chief executive, allegations which were not true,
and I thought the best thing to do was to laugh it off. But there are times
in the lives of men when patience ceases to be a virtue and I have reached
that time.

I will go back thirty years during the period that I was vice-president of
our organization. I represented our organization in every one of the States
of the United States and throughout the Dominion of Canada. I organized white,
black and yellow men for all the organizations as well as my own.

In the city of New Orleans thirty years ago I held up a conference for
ten days until we got the same rate of pay for colored blacksmiths' helpers
that we got for white blacksmiths' helpers. I even became persona non grata
with my colleagues in other organizations, who told me they were disgusted.
The employer asked me this question: "Mr. Horn, were you ever in the
South before?" And I answered, "Many times, I have been all over the country."
Then he said, "Well, we thought probably you hadn't. The large majority of
these blacksmiths' helpers are colored men." I said, "They were colored when
I came down here I didn't have anything to do with that, but I am here
representing the Blacksmiths, Drop Forgers and Helpers, regardless of color."
I left that conference with the same rate of pay for colored helpers as I got
for the white helpers, although at that time our organization did not take
colored men in.

Twenty-four and a half years ago, in the city of Indianapolis, Indiana,
our organization passed the necessary legislation to organize the colored
blacksmiths' helpers of our trade. We have been doing it ever since, wherever
we could get them to join the organization. We find many of them today who
can think of just as many excuses why they should not pay dues into a labor
organization as any white man that ever made an excuse, and you gentlemen know
the white men know most of the alibis.

Our blacksmiths' colored helpers have been mentioned. Those members have
the same standing in the International Brotherhood of Blacksmiths, Drop Forgers
and Helpers as the chief executive of that organization. They vote on all
questions; they vote on who their International officers shall be; they vote on
who their delegates to the American Federation of Labor shall be. They receive
the same consideration with regard to our funeral funds as any other member.

I have visited many of these colored Auxiliary Locals and I am proud of
them as members and as citizens. Some of the finest letters of comment we
receive from our Local Unions come from colored Local Unions. There is no
dissatisfaction among them, they haven't had a complaint.

Now what happened? Mark Twain said there were three kinds of rogues--
plain rogues, damned rogues, and pothouse politicians. Only recently pothouse
politicians went up and down a certain railroad and persuaded the colored
helpers on that road not to vote for our organization, even though we, in
conjunction with fourteen other organizations, had just secured an increase in
pay of eight cents an hour for them, which is now being held up by that great
dictator down in Washington, Mr. Vinson, and his decision has not yet been
overruled. But we did our part and we did it well.[180]

I received letters from down there which were not composed by the colored
helpers of these shops, wanting to know how many colored delegates they would
have in the American Federation of Labor if they voted for our organization.
I wrote them a letter and sent them a copy of our Constitution, explaining that
the delegates to the American Federation of Labor were elected by referendum
vote of the rank and file of our Brotherhood at the same time they elected
General Officers. I asked them to communicate with those well satisfied
Auxiliary Locals that we had and find out what those members thought of our
organization. And in the face of all that they went up and down that railroad
and inveigled enough of those men to vote against it, so that they are still
under the domination of a company union, although our organization, working in
conjunction with the other organizations, secured for them everything they have
in wages and in working conditions.

We make no discriminations. If those who are representing the colored race
in this convention want to do something really helpful for themselves as well
as the labor movement in general, they will say to the colored men, especially
in the blacksmith shops and the forge shops of this country, go in and join the
organization that is your friend and benefactor, the organization that has done

for you what you are unable to do for yourselves. Don't wait around on the
outside for something that somebody else thinks is perfect.

I don't think it is necessary for me to dwell on that. We have heard
enough in this convention about imperfect people.

I have no apology whatever to make for the manner in which our International Brotherhood is conducted. We have been honorable and fair at all times
and it will be conducted in the same manner in the future as it has been in
the past.

I thank you.

President Green: The Chair recognizes Delegate Frey, Secretary of the
Committee.

Secretary Frey: Mr. Chairman, I rise with a heavy heart, because something was done yesterday afternoon which I feel is the greatest injury done the
Negro race since the question has come into these conventions.

The committee, in its report, endeavored to do what the English language
was capable of in laying down a basic principle and in stating the policy that
should be applied to that principle, so that racial prejudice would be entirely
removed from our trade union movement. There was deliberately put into
yesterday's record a statement calculated to place the American Federation of
Labor in a false position as to its basic policy, a statement deliberately
prepared, which contains much more misstatement of fact than of truth. That
statement may have been prepared for the delegates. I do not want to believe
that there was any other motive, but I fear that the statement will be printed
in pamphlet form, and sent throughout our country for the purpose of prejudicing
Negroes against the American Federation of Labor. To me, that is little short
of a moral crime. I feel very deeply about this question. I have a right to
speak upon it. Forty-two years ago in the city of Chattanooga, Tennessee, I
organized a union of colored molders, a union of craftsmen and white people in
Chattanooga and some of the members of our union seemingly considered the
question of lynching me. I took my position because I believed it was sound;
I believed that the Negro worker was entitled to the same opportunity as any
other worker in our country, and that he must receive the same remuneration
when he performed work as was given to white men. I have never deviated from
that position since then. I have done what I could, through the written word
and the spoken word, to remove prejudices which I thought were harmful to our
movement and harmful to the colored race.

And now we have this statement, the accusations, the specified charges,
a part of the record of this convention which, without doubt, will be given
much more publicity, and what we may say in response will receive no publicity
at all except as our members read the proceedings of this convention.

I said I have a heavy heart. It is difficult for me to understand how a
representative of a race that has been helped more in this convention by the
American Federation of Labor than any other organization would stand up in our
convention and deliberately misstate the facts for the purpose of arousing a
feeling against us on the part of the Negroes we are trying to help by bringing
them into our trade union movement. I could not remain silent when charges
were made against some of the splendid Metal Trades Councils which we have.

The delegates spent some time making charges against the Bay Cities Metal
Trades Council, an organization that came into existence before the Metal
Trades Department was born. Every delegate here has heard about that Council,
about its even balance between all affiliated unions. The Metal Trades Council,
or the Bay Cities Metal Trades Council, as it is known, has never shown any
racial prejudice on the part of its delegates or in its official actions.

As a matter of fact, eighteen months ago no Negroes were employed in the
shipyards in the San Francisco Bay. At the present time over 8,000 are there
employed and they are loyal members. I have talked with them. I know what is
on the minds of those that I discussed this very problem with, and they tell me
it is not the International Unions or their representatives that constitute
their problem. Their problem arises because of the continual activity among
them of men on the outside, men of their own race, who endeavor to stir up all
the trouble possible.

Yes, trade unionists, representatives of the Negro race in San Francisco,
in Los Angeles, in Portland, Oregon, in Seattle, Washington, for months have
spent their time setting up a separate organization and advising Negroes to

cease paying dues into the Union where they now have the benefits of membership.

Yes, there are prejudices and they are not confined to any one group, and the men of the colored race who spend their time trying to stir up prejudice against us, among the members of their race, are rendering the greatest disservice the Negro in this country has ever suffered from.

These are things that we have to keep in mind. I may not be entirely free from prejudices because I am a human being. I do understand, however, the prejudices in some of our shipyard centers on the Pacific Coast. One city, and it seems to be the one that disturbed the delegate more than any other on the Pacific Coast, Portland, Oregon, still has a prejudice against the Negro. It is an understandable one. After the first World War the largest shipyard in that port believed that it could force a reduction of wages. It did. Our members struck. They remained on strike for months. The strike was broken through the importation of Negro strike breakers, and I find it difficult, in talking with some of the old timers, to remove the prejudice against the Negro workers which I believe must be removed.

I feel that there was as great a lack of statesmanship in the statement made by the delegate yesterday afternoon as I have ever listened to, and this morning we find that others feel the same way.

Perhaps the individual most prominent in our country for some time whose voice has been raised in defense of the Negro, insisting upon his receiving equality of treatment, is the first lady of the land--Mrs. Eleanor Roosevelt. This morning's paper carries a United Press dispatch. I want to read it so that this also will be in the record, along with the statements made by the delegate yesterday afternoon. It is dated October 11th, which was yesterday, from Chicago, and it reads:

"Mrs. Franklin D. Roosevelt in an article entitled 'If I Were A Negro,' appearing in the October issue of the *Negro Digest* published here, counsels that representatives of that race should not do too much demanding. Mrs. Roosevelt wrote 'If I Were A Negro, I would take every chance that came my way to improve my quality and my ability and, if recognition was slow, I would continue to prove myself, knowing that in the end a good performance would be acknowledged.'"

If she were a Negro, Mrs. Roosevelt wrote, she would have moments of great bitterness and would find it hard to sustain her faith in democracy and men of other races. She emphasized, however, that she would participate to the full in this war. She would accept every chance that was made in the Army and the Navy although "I would not try to bring about these advances any more quickly than they were offered."

If the delegate measured up to the viewpoint declared by Mrs. Roosevelt yesterday there would be no such record as appears in yesterday's proceedings --the most unfortunate, the most dangerous statement which has ever been made in connection with the efforts of the American Federation of Labor to wipe out racial national prejudice so that every wage earner would be looked upon as an equal.

Delegate Randolph may not realize it, but I want to repeat it is my conviction that he rendered the greatest disservice to the colored race that has ever been rendered at any time since the Negro became a free man.

President Green: The Chair recognizes Delegate Allen.

Delegate Allen, Commercial Telegraphers Union: In his address yesterday, Delegate Randolph included the Commercial Telegraphers Union among those organizations which exclude Negroes from membership.

That is not so, Mr. President, in the case of our organization, and I would like to have the record corrected accordingly. At our convention eight years ago, in 1935, our Constitution was amended and the bar to membership of Negroes in our organization was removed. It is true that all of our subordinate unions enjoy full Constitutional autonomy in the admission of applicants to membership. So far as I know, since that time, no Negro applicant for membership has been denied membership in any of our subordinate unions.

Thank you.

President Green: Has everyone spoken who wishes to speak on this question?

Delegate Randolph, Sleeping Car Porters: Mr. President.

President Green: Delegate Randolph has already spoken on the question and in accordance with parliamentary procedure, he could not be recognized if other delegates wished to speak. If there are no others the Chair will recognize Delegate Randolph, but please, please avoid this awful controversy.

Delegate Randolph, Sleeping Car Porters: Mr. Chairman and delegates of the Convention--I want to make a few remarks on the statements made by the various delegates concerning racial discrimination in the trade unions that I discussed yesterday.

In the first place, Delegate MacGowan referred to the Constitution of the American Federation of Labor, which emphasizes the autonomy of International Union. Well, that seems to me simply a statement of justification of the policy of discrimination on the part of International Unions that do discriminate against Negroes. The question of autonomy and the question of racial discrimination are questions at issue here. If under the smokescreen of autonomy, International Unions are going to continue to discriminate against Negroes and assume that the mere fact of autonomy gives them the right to carry on this discrimination, why then there is little hope in introducing any real and genuine democracy in International Unions that discriminate against Negroes.

On matters relating to jurisdiction, this American Federation of Labor has taken positive action, and International Unions that have invaded the field of jurisdiction of other unions have been curbed--they have been curbed by expulsion. If the American Federation of Labor would use one-tenth of its energy and concern in the interest of eliminating discrimination as it does in attempting to protect the jurisdiction of International Unions, we would not have a whole lot of trouble about the question of Negroes being admitted into the various unions. Although the American Federation of Labor may not attempt to use compulsion, if it will simply use consistent and systematic education, it is possible to abolish discrimination in the various unions. But the American Federation of Labor has not used consistent and systematic educational methods. The resolution that was introduced by the Sleeping Car Porter delegates called for the establishment of a committee merely for the purpose of exploring the question of discrimination, with a view of adopting some policies of education that would bring these various unions around to the recognition of the fact that racial discrimination prevents working class solidarity and is, therefore, a fool and an enemy of the worker and the Union.

Now, Delegate MacGowan talked about Auxiliary Unions, but did not deny that they exist. All I claimed in my statement yesterday was that racial Auxiliary Unions are undemocratic; that they violate the principles of trade unionism and that they are un-American. Now, is there anybody in this convention who is going to take the position that the organization of racial unions can be justified? Is anybody in this convention going to take the position that a worker must be deprived of certain privileges merely because of the accident of race? No one here will contend that Jewish unions ought to be organized, or Catholic unions ought to be organized. No one will contend that particular unions that have any special identity ought to be set aside especially when they interfere with the rights of the workers.

Delegate MacGowan has not shown that the Auxiliary Unions have absolutely no voice in the determination of the policy of the International Union, the International Union that controls the Agreement Committee, the Agreement Committee that regulates and shapes the wage standards and the working rules. Now if a worker is a part of a system in which he has no voice, no rights, to exercise an influence on the policies that affect his wages, certainly no one can contend that that worker is being benefited. Now an Auxiliary Union is either democratic or un-democratic. If it is right it ought to be justified and defended. If it is wrong, it should be condemned and exterminated.

The delegates of the Sleeping Car Porters contend that the racial Auxiliary Unions are comparable to the colonists of the various empires of the world because the colonists are serfs--they have no rights that other

citizens enjoy. The same thing is true of members of Auxiliary Unions. They
have absolutely no right to exercise their voice in the policies of the International Union.

There seems to be some spirit in the convention on the part of delegates
that criticism of policies that are obviously unsound is unjustified. Now
whenever an organization that proposes to be democratic takes the position
that criticism of policies that are obviously unsound is unjustified, then
that organization is moving backward and not forward. Certainly it is
recognized that in the arena of criticism sound policies, truth and programs
are developed. When policies are permitted to remain in secrecy, nobody can
tell just what the effect of those policies will be upon the ultimate future
of the workers of the organization.

Now it is said here that there is an organization known as Miscellaneous
Workers' Incorporated, that Negroes are in that organization and that organization is telling Negroes not to join the Auxiliary Unions. Well, I don't
know anything about Miscellaneous Organizations, but I take it that it is a
company union. The company perhaps organized a miscellaneous organization of
Negroes. That is no reflection upon the Negroes. There are company unions
of white men that are used to oppose the organization of other white men and
therefore, Negroes ought not to be condemned because they are in a company
union.

Moreover, perhaps some of them would rather be unorganized at all than
to be in a Jim Crow union, such as those organizations are. I can understand
why some unions are picketed by Negroes because they recognize that the
Auxiliary Union is a step backward and they want to express their opposition
to it and therefore they use the method of picketing. That is taxation
without representation. Can anyone in this convention get up on the floor and
justify taxation without representation? Well, that is what the Auxiliary
Union is.

Now the contention is made here that because there are 15,000 Negroes in
the Auxiliary Unions that makes the Auxiliary Union Kosher. Well, Negroes
are compelled to buy tickets in a Jim Crow car, but does that imply they want
to be in a Jim Crow car? By no means. And it is also said that Negro
agitation, or Negro so-called professional men are doing the Negro an injury.
Negroes who point out injustices that are practiced upon Negroes are not doing
the Negroes or anybody else harm, but are doing them a great benefit. As a
matter of fact, the claim that by pointing out injustices to the public is
creating agitation and creating conditions is like contending that a meteorologist that points out a storm is coming creates the storm. Negroes who indicate
that unfair conditions to Negroes exist are merely playing the role of the
meteorologist who indicates that a storm is coming and that you ought to
prepare for that storm. No one denies that discrimination exists in these
unions. Then why attempt to hide it? And why attempt to condemn people who
point it out? We are not doing any disservice to the American Federation of
Labor. We are helping the American Federation of Labor by bringing the issue
out into the open, and I want to say that I think some progress is made after
all, in that at least there is some disposition to give this question some
serious consideration.

Now it was said by one of the delegates in the Executive Council meeting
of the American Federation of Labor that I said that the Brotherhood of
Sleeping Car Porters would not accept white men if they worked as Pullman
porters. That is not true. I never made that statement. As a matter of
fact, in our organization now there are white barbers on the Pullman cars that
are members of the organization, and there are white Pullman car cleaners in
the organization. We have Filipinos and Chinese and Mexicans along with
Negroes in the Brotherhood of Sleeping Car Porters. I don't understand how
he got that idea in his head. As a matter of fact, our Constitution provides
that there shall be no discrimination against a working man becoming a member
of the organization on account of race, creed, color or national origin.
Certainly we would be the last organization in America to raise any bar
against anybody, in view of the fact that we Negroes are members of a group
that are victimized as a result of these discriminations.

Now it is said that in the Portland shipyards these discriminations among
the Negroes have not militated against upgrading Negroes. Well, the records
do not bear out that statement. As a matter of fact, already plans are being

made to make an investigation of the Portland shipyard with respect to its
policies of discrimination by Tom Ray, the Little Tin Horn Hitler, out there.
As a matter of fact, Negroes are now revolting against the fact that they are
not given upgrading in accordance with their skill and qualifications. Therefore that statement is not borne out by the record.

It is also pointed out that Negroes were strike breakers in some strikes
in Portland, and that was responsible for the prejudice against Negroes. What
about white men who are strike breakers? Is there anyone here who contends
that Negroes are the only strike breakers in America? The great labor strike
breakers in America are white men. Therefore, the contention that the
prejudice is justified against Negroes on the grounds that they are strike
breakers is naive and credulous, and anyone who believes in such a thing as
that is incredulous.

On the matter of the Auxiliary Locals having a roster of officers, well,
what about it, what does that mean? Some one mentioned the fact that
Auxiliary Unions have a roster of officers. They have no power, they don't
mean anything, they can't do anything, they can't shape any policy of an
International Union, so that they are mere window dressings and those things
are simply raised here for the purpose of making it appear that the condition
is not as bad as it is.

So far as the matter of the Brotherhood of Sleeping Car Porters or the
delegates in this convention following the advice of Mrs. Roosevelt, may I
say that we have the highest regard for Mrs. Roosevelt and her opinions. She
has been a great benefactor, not only to the Negro people but to the oppressed
peoples of America and the world, and certainly we have absolutely no criticism
of the attitude and the history in her conduct with respect to the Negro
people or anybody else. But of course we have a right to our own opinions;
we believe that Negroes have a right to make demands. Everybody may not agree
with our demands, but certainly we have a right to make them. If you were in
the Negro's place and you were put into an Auxiliary Union and had no rights
except to pay dues, what would you do? If you were in the Negro's place and
you want to show your patriotism in order to give your blood and life for this
nation, and yet you were not permitted to exercise your skill and ability and
knowledge in rising and being promoted, what would you do? Negroes have all
of the eagerness and all of the ambition that other people enjoy and have, and,
as a matter of fact, merely by disputing the policy of Negroes to fight for
their rights is not going to change that policy.

On the matter of the Commercial Telegraphers, although it may be that the
International Union has eliminated the color clause, we are in possession of
facts that there are certain Local Unions that do bar Negroes. We do not want
to enter into any controversy with the Commercial Telegraphers Union, because
we appreciate the spirit that has been manifested here in indicating that it
is opposed to the color clause in the International Constitution.

On the matter of the question of the Negro people not making progress
because of some unfair criticism that may be made by the Negroes that are
concerned about changing the situation, you have as a matter of history
progress being made only upon a basis of exposing conditions that are evil
and that are retrogressive and backward, conditions that are inimical to the
interests of any particular group. We contend that the white workers here are
not safe until every Negro is protected. We contend that the American
Federation of Labor itself is not secure so long as Negroes are not given the
same rights that other workers in the Federation enjoy.

We know that Negroes and white workers can be organized together and they
are being organized together. Therefore, we are trying to point out to the
Federation that it must have the courage to take the position that even though
these International Unions are autonomous, it ought to have the courage to
say to them, "Your policy is wrong and it is up to you to bring your policy
in harmony and in conformity with the basic principle of the American Federation of Labor as expressed in the Constitution."

Nothing has been said on this floor which causes me to alter one word
that I have said. Nothing has been said on this floor that causes me to
retreat from the position I have taken.

With respect to the Electrical Workers, it is good to hear that so many
Negroes are being organized into the Electrical Workers Union. But where are
they? I go all around this country, and I would like to see some of them.

Negroes are coming to me who are licensed electricians and who cannot get into the Union, so that those statements about what is being done in the interests of breaking down bars and the escapements may sound all right, but let's see some action.

That is all the Sleeping Car Porters' delegates are calling for. And so, my friends, we want to reiterate our position here; that nothing has been said here to show that Auxiliary Locals do not exist. Nothing has been said to show that Auxiliary Unions based upon race are not necessary, they are undemocratic and un-American, and upon that we rest our case.

Committee Chairman Woll: May I say just a word? I merely wish to say to the convention that there has not been a single word uttered against the committee's report. Hence, it is not necessary to speak further in behalf of the report, but only necessary for the convention to act upon it.

President Green: May I impose upon your patience for a moment while I indulge in the presentation of some facts and express, if I may, my official and personal point of view toward the subject that has been so sincerely and earnestly discussed on the floor of this convention since yesterday afternoon. You yourselves in this convention, in this open forum of debate have demonstrated your interest in the subject, because you have been tolerant, you have been patient, you have exercised good judgment in that you have sat quietly by and have listened with rapt attention to the discussion which has taken place. I ask that you accept that as evidence of the desire of the American Federation of Labor to understand this question and to find a correct solution for it.

I am conscious of the fact that it is a live question, one that is attracting the attention of people everywhere. It is like a mounting current running through our economic, our social and our national life. I think we ought to manifest a sense of understanding toward Delegate Randolph, because I can understand how he is moved by a deep sense of injustice, speaking as he does for a race that has suffered much and that is seeking to lift its economic and racial standards to a higher and still higher level. I know that all of you possess such an understanding of the attitude of Delegate Randolph and his associates.

But this is a question that runs deep, I repeat, through our social, ecnomic and industrial life. It is not a problem that is grappled with solely by the American Federation of Labor. We see evidence of the tensity of the problem here and there and everywhere because of the developments that take place.

Now surely those of us who are sympathetic toward the aims and purposes of the Negro race to lift their standard of life and living to higher levels and promote economic equality at least realize that it is a question that will only be solved through understanding and education. There must be a convincing appeal made to the hearts and the minds and the consciences of all classes of people. It will never be solved through the application of forced methods or through the presentation of demands that groups here, there and everywhere comply with said demands. We learn much in the broad field of experience, and I think we have learned much in dealing with this question as a result of experience. Experience shows that progress has been made and is being made, and if we pursue a wise policy, a policy which provides for education, a presentation of the facts, an appeal, not a demand, an appeal to the hearts and the conscience and the judgment and the tolerance of the people of this country will bring about a solution of the question.

So far as I am concerned, representing the American Federation of Labor, I have always taken a most advanced and progressive position upon this subject. If I had my way every organization affiliated with the American Federation of Labor would admit Negroes to membership on the same basis of equality as other workers. In our conventions I have tried to influence the committee, the Executive Council and the Convention itself in the adoption of policies and declarations placing our great parent organization upon a basis which ought to command and secure the support of the Negroes of the country.

As Chairman Woll has said, nobody has found fault with the report of the committee, not even Delegate Randolph, and Delegate Webster, who is serving as a member of our Post-War Committee, made a fine statement yesterday when the report of the committee was presented upon the Fair Employment Practice

Committee's work. These official declarations adopted by the convention
represent the real attitude of the American Federation of Labor toward the
subject.

Now I want to make a report to you upon some of our experiences where we
have endeavored to carry out these declarations.

They speak for themselves, they have been repeated over and over again--
these declarations of the American Federation of Labor, the parent body, the
instrumentality through which the representatives of organized labor express
the opinion of the workers, are on record, they are printed, published and
distributed for educational purposes, but notwithstanding that fact, for some
reason or other--I know not why--we find that in our efforts to organize the
Negro workers of the country we are boycotted by the representatives of the
prominent Negro organizations of America. No one can successfully say that
our American Federation of Labor discriminates against Negroes who are
employed in manufacturing or industrial plants, when we seek to establish
Federal Labor Unions--and we have organized hundreds of thousands of workers
in Federal Labor Unions. I think the report of the Secretary shows that we
have over 300,000 members in these Federal Labor Unions. That is the policy
of the American Federation of Labor--no discrimination.

We go into an industrial plant; we appeal to all working in that plant to
come with us. There is no discrimination against any man because of race,
creed, color or nationality, because I take the position that if any representative of the American Federation of Labor attempts to discriminate against the
workers because of race, creed or color when we seek to organize them into
Federal Labor Unions, he can no longer represent the American Federation of
Labor.

We have employed a number of Negro organizers to carry on work among
those Negroes whom we seek to organize. Does that mean anything? Does that
act in itself mean that the American Federation of Labor is trying to live up
to its declarations? My experience has shown that during the last few years,
under the impetus of the war effort, large number of Negroes have been employed
in war material production plants. Many of the employees of these plants do
not come under the jurisdiction of a national union chartered by the American
Federation of Labor. So the American Federation of Labor goes there, it seeks
to organize them into Federal Labor Unions directly chartered by the American
Federation of Labor. We assign Negro organizers to carry on organizing work,
and together with our other organizers they cooperate in a fine, wonderful way.

But in every instance where we seek to carry on this organizing work
Negro representatives of prominent colored organizations in the United States
appear on the scene and appeal to the Negro workers to boycott the American
Federation of Labor and to unite with the dual, rival organizations.

At the International Harvester Company in Chicago we sought to organize
those employees into the American Federation of Labor, we found that the
representatives of the Urban League, the representatives of the organization
called the National Association for the Advancement of Colored People and
other representatives of Negro organizations in America appeared at Chicago
and opposed the American Federation of Labor representatives in their efforts
to organize the Negroes into the A. F. of L. As a result of it what happened?
All these Negroes voted to stay out of the American Federation of Labor. Now
it seems contradictory, when complaint is made that we won't organize them,
and yet when we attempt to organize them prominent representatives of colored
organizations appear in opposition to our efforts to organize them.

When the campaign was launched at the Ford Motor Company in Detroit we
carried on our campaign there. We appealed to the Negro workers employed by
the Ford Company to come with us, and in the campaign that was carried on
many of the artists, outstanding artists like Mr. Robeson, who entertains
audiences on the stage throughout the country, the representatives of the
organization known as the National Association for the Advancement of Colored
People, colored preachers representing the colored churches of the country all
united and every one of them were against the American Federation of Labor.
The result was that those Negroes were influenced to vote against us.

That is going on in many sections of the country. If they want us to
organize the Negro workers and we spend your money in an effort to do that,
and we assign our people to the work, why don't they line up with us and help
us to organize these Negro workers? It seems very contradictory to rise and
challenge and charge and complain that we are discriminating against Negro

workers, and then when we try to organize them oppose us in our efforts to organize them.

Our organizers in the field report to me that this is repeated over and over again. Men, listen! I cannot prevail upon the outstanding representatives of any Negro organization in America to join with our representatives in appealing to Negro workers to join the American Federation of Labor Unions. These are facts and they are given to you so that our representatives here, the Negro representatives, might try to help us to overcome this prejudice against the American Federation of Labor. We talk about racial prejudice, racial boycotting, putting organizations in the doghouse and telling them to remain there. We complain against that. But what about putting the American Federation of Labor there? We find prejudice against us, opposition to us, opposition of the worst kind when we seek to organize these Negro workers into the American Federation of Labor.

There is only one other point and that is this. There are 107 National and International Unions affiliated with the American Federation of Labor and hundreds and hundreds and hundreds of federal labor unions. Out of these 107 unions Delegate Randolph classifies seven, according to the report of Herbert R. Northrup, which exclude Negroes by provision in the Constitution. The representative of the Commercial Telegraphers Union arose this morning and said that was not true, so that ought to eliminate that one. Other organizations here have declared that that statement is not in accordance with the facts. Then he has classified unions which habitually exclude Negroes by "tacit consent". That is susceptible of various interpretations. In that group there are five.

In another group are listed unions which afforded Negroes only a segregated auxiliary status, and in that classification he has six, but these unions accept Negroes into membership, but on an auxiliary basis.

Now of course the objection is to the organization of them on that basis. If I had my way I would have it the other way, but I have found in life's experience that I don't have my way in a good many things, and many times I have to wait a good while before I can have my way, and sometimes I never get it.

But that is a small percentage of our unions out of the 107 National and International Unions affiliated. I am not defending this action on our part, but simply referring to it to point out that this certainly represents progress. I hope that eventually we will break down the barriers of prejudice that have been raised by these unions until you will not be able to submit even a list of that kind. Education will do the job. Appeal to the heart and the conscience and the judgment of the people of our country, I repeat, will do the job.

I wanted to make these remarks, not in a critical way but for the purpose of presenting the facts to you. I have dealt only with facts and I have tried to approach a brief consideration of the subject in a realistic way.

Delegate Webster, Pullman Car Porters: I just want to make a few remarks on the subject in behalf of the Brotherhood of Sleeping Car Porters. We have been in the American Federation of Labor since 1929. Of course when we first came in we had problems of our own that affected the Sleeping Car Porters, but our organization has been fairly successful in organizing that group of workers in the nation into an international organization which we are proud of, in the American Federation of Labor.

After having accomplished our own purposes to a large extent we have rendered the best possible service we could render in an effort to prevail upon the Negro workers of the nation to realize that the American Federation of Labor was the labor institution in which Negroes should be organized. We have participated and cooperated with many of the international organizations, even some of those who have color clauses in their Constitutions, to organize the Negroes into the American Federation of Labor.

We had a good deal to do with the rapid organization of the dining car waiters into the Hotel and Restaurant Employees' International Union. We did a good job in attempting to organize the Red Caps into an A. F. of L. Union, and as we go about the country looking after our own business we never fail to analyze the problems that Negroes are confronted with, often agitated to a large extent by the so-called rival organizations. Even in very recent months, where there have been contests between the American Federation of Labor unions and the unions of the rival organizations, we have not only given them our moral support but we have helped finance campaigns to carry on an educational program, to the end that the Negro workers might come into the American Federation of Labor.

It has only been very recently that in the city of Chicago we had four or five contests between an A. F. of L. organization and an organization of the rival group, and due almost entirely to the activities of the Brotherhood of Sleeping Car Porters, when the votes were counted the votes were in favor of the American Federation of Labor. It is true that we are not satisfied with everything that goes on in the American Federation of Labor and we don't expect anybody to pull any rabbits out of their hats in an effort to try to wave a wand and solve these problems over night. But we are conscious of the fact, as an International Union affiliated with the American Federation of Labor, that we are attempting to prevail upon those who are part of the American Federation of Labor to make the job we are trying to do in building up and organizing Negro workers into the American Federation of Labor a little easier than it is, with many of these handicaps of racial discriminations and practices provided for in the constitutions of some of our International organizations.

President Green: Are there further remarks? If not, the question presented is, shall the report of the committee be adopted. Those in favor will say, "aye", those opposed will say; "no". The motion is carried and is so ordered.

The Secretary of the Committee points out that the vote on the committee's report was unanimously adopted, and the Chair so decides.

Proceedings of the 63rd Annual Convention of the American Federation of Labor, 1943, pp. 421-45.

PART V

THE POST-WAR DECADE, 1945-1955

Part V

THE POST-WAR DECADE, 1945-1955

On September 2, 1945, World War II came to an end, but the dream that
the war would bring a permanent improvement in the economic status of the
black workers had ended even before that. As victory approached, war industries began cutbacks in production, and Afro-Americans, being the most
recent newcomers to many industries, were the first to lose their jobs. When
the FEPC ended in 1946, the employment of black workers on equal terms with
whites ceased to receive even "lip service" from the federal government.
What gains had been made occurred during the war, and when the guns were
silenced retrogression had already begun.

Nor did job opportunities for blacks develop either in number or in
status in war production after armed forces were sent to
Korea in 1950. Many blacks who had worked in defense plants during World War
II were bypassed in favor of new white recruits. The plight of black workers
was exacerbated by a technological revolution which was eliminating menial
and unskilled jobs in industry at the very time that mechanization in southern
agriculture was driving blacks off the land and into the cities. Thus, as the
demand of basic industries for unskilled labor was declining, the influx of
rural blacks into the industrial centers was increasing.

It came as no surprise to black workers and community leaders alike
that the AFL's racist posture persisted after World War II. But they were
seriously disappointed that the CIO seemed to lose interest in the plight
of black workers during the postwar period. By 1950, there was no organization concerned specifically with the rights of black workers. To fill this
void 900 delegates met in Chicago in June, 1950, at the National Labor Conference for Negro Rights. The conference formed a committee which would lay
the groundwork for establishing a permanent organization. On October 27,
1951, a convention was held in Cincinnati, Ohio, to found the National Negro
Labor Council. The convention adopted a Statement of Principles and a Program
of Action, based on the premise that blacks could attain first-class citizenship only if black workers organized to fight for full economic opportunity.
The NNLC set two basic tasks for itself: to break the pattern of job discrimination against blacks in industry, and to eliminate racism in the unions.
However, 1951 was the height of the anti-Communist hysteria, and the NNLC
was branded subversive by the House Un-American Activities Committee. NNLC
leaders were hounded by the Committee, and by the Subversive Activities
Control Board. Confronted with defense costs of $100,000, the NNLC's leaders
voted to dissolve the organization.

One of the staunchest supporters of the NNLC, and unionism among blacks
generally, was Paul Robeson (1898-1976). The son of a former slave, Robeson
graduated from Rutgers University with Phi Beta Kappa honors, and received a
law degree from Columbia, before distinguishing himself internationally as an
actor and baritone. A trip to the Soviet Union early in his career was the
beginning of a life-long attachment to the USSR, which awarded him the Stalin
Peace Prize in 1952. After World War II, Robeson took a firm and vocal stand
against oppression throughout the world, particularly against European
colonization in Africa, and segregation in the United States. As editor of
Freedom, a black monthly published in Harlem, Robeson attacked the anti-
Communist witchhunting of the post-war era, and called for a return of peaceful relations with the socialist nations of the world. Because of this
position, Robeson was harassed by the U.S. government, which also lifted his
passport, and thereafter was deprived of earning a living as an artist. The
last years of his life were spent in self-imposed seclusion.

Robeson was an articulate spokesman for the view that workers themselves must save the labor movement. By 1954-1955, Robeson could point to
the movement to merge the AFL and the CIO into one organization as evidence
that the CIO had become as conservative as the AFL.

THE POST-WAR DECADE

1. EMPLOYMENT AND INCOME OF NEGRO WORKERS: 1940-52

By Mary S. Bedell

Negro workers, in terms of employment and income, were less well off than
white workers in 1952, although the comparison was more favorable than in 1940.
The improvement was due almost entirely to the fact that Negroes, in shifting
to nonagricultural industries, were able to get better jobs and were, therefore, less heavily concentrated in the traditionally unskilled and low-wage
occupations. The relatively greater gains of Negroes during this period of
unprecedented levels of economic activity suggest their particular sensitivity
to economic developments.

Factors in the Changing Employment Picture

The narrowing of the differentials in the employment status of Negro and
white workers reflects the combined effect of broad economic and social forces.
Many authorities have expressed the view that the high level of economic activity prevalent during virtually all years from 1940 to 1952 was the more directly responsible for the recorded improvements in the Negro's employment
position. Support for this position is found in the fact that employment
rates increased twice as much for Negroes as for whites from 1950 to 1951,
when total employment expanded by about 1 million. Conversely, there is some
evidence that reconversion affected Negroes more severely than white workers;
from July 1945 to April 1946, for example, unemployment rates among nonwhites
increased more than twice as much as among whites. And when the unemployment
rate reached a postwar peak early in 1950, the proportion of Negroes employed
in nonagricultural industries, particularly in manufacturing, decreased
markedly.
   However, changes in the employment status of Negroes have been attributed
partly, by some observers, to the effects of such other forces as growing
governmental concern with the question of racial and group discrimination.
The Federal Government, early during the World War II period, initiated executive action to promote fair employment practices; the Committee on Fair
Employment Practice continued in operation until July 1945, when the Congress
discontinued its appropriation. Subsequent Executive Orders prohibited discrimination in the Federal Civil Service and the Armed Services. Since 1943,
Federal contracts and subcontracts have contained fair employment clauses;
and in 1951, President Truman established a Committee on Government Contract
Compliance to find ways of strengthening compliance with those provisions.
All of these measures have diminished discrimination in Federal employment
(both direct and indirect). [181]
   In addition, 11 States and 25 municipalities had adopted some form of
fair employment practice legislation between 1945 and mid-1952. On the latter
date, it was estimated that "enforceable FEP laws [were] in operation in areas
that include about a third of the Nation's total population . . . and about an
eighth of the nonwhites." Administrators of these laws have reported the
opening of many job opportunities to workers formerly barred by reason of their
race, color, religion, or national origin. Some have expressed concern, however, that the fairly small number of complaints alleging discrimination does
not fully measure the extent of noncompliance, although their experience has
been that the mere existence of enforcement powers is a potent factor in promoting merit employment. In fact, no comprehensive measure of the effect of
such legislation is available, and some interpretations of existing data recognize that favorable economic conditions may have influenced the operation
of these laws. One reporter commented: "That these laws appear to have worked
satisfactorily under existing conditions does not give assurance that they would
continue to do so in a period of widespread unemployment . . . [for] the

tendency to discriminate on the basis of race, color, or religion is obviously rather slight [in a tight labor market] as compared with the temptation to do so under adverse economic conditions."

Quite apart from legal sanctions, the administrators of fair employment laws have relied heavily upon educational efforts to build up public sentiment, and particularly to influence the attitudes of both employers and workers. A recent report indicated that "Many [employers] have . . . expressed their belief that such legislation has not prevented them from hiring the most competent employees available and has had positive beneficial effect." Some evidence of workers' attitudes on this subject was revealed in a survey conducted by Factory magazine in 1949 to find out, among other things, how factory workers felt about Federal fair employment legislation then pending in Congress. About two-thirds of the workers favored the legislation: the percent of those who approved ranged from 48 in the South to 85 in New England. Slightly more than a fourth disapproved, and the remainder expressed no opinion.

Paralleling governmental action, many private groups, both national and local, have become increasingly interested in ameliorating or checking discrimination. Some leaders of organized labor, particularly in recent years, have been outstanding in such activities; both the American Federation of Labor and the Congress of Industrial Organizations, are active proponents of Federal fair employment practices legislation, and several national and international unions have special programs designed to eliminate discrimination in employment. Recognizing this, the President's Committee on Government Contract Compliance commented, however, that "At local levels, union discrimination against Negroes and other minorities persists. The Committee has witnessed examples of union discrimination which have hindered employers from complying with the nondiscrimination clause in their Government contracts."

Employment and Unemployment

Relatively fewer Negroes than whites who wanted to work could find jobs in 1952, although, percentagewise, more Negroes were actually in the labor force. This was also true in 1940. During this 12-year period, of course, total employment and the size of the labor force expanded sharply for both groups, with marked declines in unemployment rates.

To get an overall perspective of the separate figures, it is useful to note that in 1950 about 16 million Negroes represented 10.5 per cent of the total population. Birth rates have been consistently higher for Negroes than for whites, but so have mortality rates, and the age structures of the two populations are quite different. In consequence, Negroes 14 years old and over comprised only 9.8 per cent of the population of working age.

The civilian labor force in 1952 totaled nearly 63 million and included 56.9 per cent of the white and 62.2 per cent of the Negro population of working age. Virtually all of the difference was due to the fact that 44.2 per cent of the Negro women, compared to 32.7 per cent of the white women, were working or seeking work. In 1951, only in the age group from 18 to 24 years was the proportion of Negro women in the labor force below that for whites. The rates for men were practically identical, although in 1951 a significantly higher proportion of Negro men under age 20 and over age 65 were in the labor force. In 1940, the civilian labor force was 55.6 million; no participation rates comparable with those for 1952 are available. There is, however, evidence that the differential between Negro and white rates narrowed over this 12-year period, due almost entirely to a relatively greater increase in the proportion of white than of Negro women in the labor force.

About 1 in 4 white women was in the labor force in 1940; the ratio was approximately 1 in 3 in 1952. Married women were responsible for most of this increase, the proportion of white married couples with the wife in the labor force having grown from about 11 per cent in 1940 to more than 22 per cent in 1950. Among Negro couples, the comparable figures were 24 and 37 per cent--considerably above those for white couples on both dates, although the relative difference was less at the end of the 10-year period.

Unemployment rates also are consistently higher for Negroes than for whites. From 1940 to 1952, unemployment decreased from 8.1 million to 1.7 million--from about 14.5 per cent to 2.7 per cent of the Negroes and 2.4 per cent of the whites in the labor force were unemployed--the lowest rates for both groups recorded in any year since the end of the war. Further, a comparison of 1950 unemployment rates for Negro and white men in different age groups reveals that the most significant difference is within the age group 25 to 34--the workers most sought by employers. The overall unemployment rate was then 5 per cent; among men in this age group, the rates were 10.5 per cent for Negroes and 3.8 per cent for whites.

Total employment rose from 47.5 million in 1940 to 61.3 million in 1952. In April of the latter year, 9.6 per cent of all persons with jobs were Negroes. This was slightly less than the 1940 ratio because, as relatively more white women entered the labor force, the proportion of employed women who were Negroes decreased. The proportion of Negroes in the number of employed men was practically unchanged.

Industrial and Occupational Distribution

In terms of the types of employers for whom they worked and the kinds of jobs they had, the differences between Negroes and whites narrowed somewhat more between 1940 and 1952 than did differences in the overall employment ratios. The most striking change in both the industrial and occupational composition of employment was a much more pronounced shift away from agriculture for Negroes than for whites. The geographical distribution of Negro employment also changed, because 90 per cent of all Negro agricultural workers in 1940 were in the South. Many of them moved to urban areas--in the North and West, as well as in the South. As a result, during the 1940's the proportion of all employed Negroes working in the South fell from three-fourths to two-thirds and the Negro population became predominantly urban, for the first time.

Agriculture, in 1950, still represented about a fifth of all Negro workers, and the service industries continued to provide jobs for about a third. While these two industry groups remained the largest sources of Negro employment, they were considerably less important in the total than in 1940, when more than two-thirds of all employed Negroes worked in one or the other. In contrast, less than a third of all white workers were so employed in 1950, as shown in table 1.

Negroes made many gains in nonagricultural employment during World War II, when new opportunities for industrial employment were opened to them. In general, their wartime position has been retained in the postwar years, and, in fact, even larger proportions of employed Negroes were working in nonagricultural industries in 1952 than in 1950. These recent increases more than offset the interruption of the trend away from agriculture which occurred in 1949 and 1950 when unemployment rates reached postwar peaks.

Negroes made notable employment gains in manufacturing, construction, and trade from 1940 to 1952, and the proportion employed in the domestic and personal services segment of the service industries declined in spite of a slight postwar upswing which culminated in 1950. An even larger proportion of Negro men worked in the first two industries in 1952 than in 1950; the proportion of Negro women in manufacturing, on the other hand, had declined slightly, but this decrease was more than offset by a somewhat higher proportion employed in trade. The percentage of Negro women working in professional services increased sharply after 1950, accentuating a steady growth since 1940. By 1952, this industry group accounted for nearly 14 per cent of all employed Negro women; work in domestic and personal services, however, still comprised more than half the total.

With the shifts in the industrial distribution of Negro employment came changes in their occupational patterns, particularly in farm and manufacturing jobs. The proportion of Negroes working in all nonagricultural occupations except domestic service increased, with a marked rise in the semi-skilled "operatives" classification. In spite of substantial reductions in the percentage of Negro workers who were either laborers or service workers, in 1950 these occupations were still the most important for Negro men and women, respectively. They accounted for more than half of all employed Negro workers; in contrast, less than one-fifth of white workers were so employed. . . .

Negro men, by 1952, had made additional gains as operatives, and in April of that year accounted for nearly 10 per cent of all men employed as operatives, although fewer than 9 per cent of all employed men were Negroes. They continued to hold about the same small share of professional, clerical and craftsman jobs as in 1950. In these three occupational groups, the proportion of Negroes in

total employment increased relatively more between 1940 and 1952 for women
than for men. However, in the latter year, the proportion of women employed
in such jobs who were Negroes was very small in comparison with the 11.4 per
cent of all women workers who were Negroes. In even more striking contrast
with this overall ratio, more than half of all women employed in private house-
holds were Negroes.

Another important aspect of the Negro's employment pattern was the heavy
concentration in occupations characterized by lower job stability and by casual
and part-time work which interrupts job tenure. A Census survey in early 1951
showed that whites had consistently longer tenure on their current jobs than
did Negroes--the median number of years being 3.5 compared to 2.4. The difference was least for nonfarm workers--about 8 months for men and 7 months for
women--but it prevailed for both men and women and for farm and non-farm residents. Significantly, the percentage of white workers who had started on
their jobs before 1940 was 18.3; for Negro workers, it was only 10.7

Lower levels of education and vocational training of Negroes in comparison with whites have been cited frequently as an important underlying factor
for their occupational employment pattern. In 1950, Negroes aged 25 and over
(comprising about four-fifths of the Negro labor force) had completed only 7
years of school, almost 3 years less than the average for white persons. Although the educational differences narrowed between 1940 and 1950, the 9 per
cent of Negroes of high school and college age who were in school was still
below the comparable figure of 14 per cent for white young people. In addition, recommendations of the President's Committee on Government Contract
Compliance pointed up the existence of discrimination against minority groups
in some vocational apprenticeship, and on-the-job training programs. Furthermore, recent court decisions held that the facilities provided for Negro
students were inferior in the southern localities involved in the test cases.
Throughout the South, the public schools are segregated on the basis of race,
under the prevailing "separate but equal" doctrine.

Income

The cumulative effect of all these differences in the number and type
of job opportunities for Negro and white workers was evidenced by the particularly sharp contrast in their average income. In 1950, Negroes' income
averaged but little more than half that of whites, although their position
was relatively better than prewar. Not only did the Negro have less purchasing
power than the average white worker, but he faced a less secure old age and
his dependents were not so well provided for in the event of his death.

The median income of Negro wage earners and salaried workers was $1,295
in 1950--48 per cent less than for comparable white workers. (The overall
ratio showed the combined effect of a much less favorable comparison for
women than for men and the considerably larger proportion of Negro than of
white earners who were women). The difference was smaller than in 1939,
largely because of a greater relative increase in the earnings of Negro men.
Family income told about the same story, although a substantially higher proportion of Negro families had more than one earner. In 1950, the median annual
income of Negro families was $1,869--54 per cent of the $3,445 average for
white families and more than 80 per cent of the Negro families had smaller incomes than the median for white families. Concealed within these figures is
a major incentive for Negroes to shift to nonagricultural employment during
the 1940's; the Negro who left the farm in 1950 could improve his money income relatively more than could the white farm worker. Average family income
derived chiefly from farm wages was 37.7 per cent of that from nonfarm wages
or salaries for Negroes, compared with 47.5 per cent for whites.

Lower income also will affect the amount of benefits for which a worker
is eligible under the Old Age and Survivors Insurance program. For the great
bulk of Negroes working in agriculture and domestic service, the benefits they
can look forward to are also seriously affected by the recentness of their
coverage under the OASI program (although all eligible workers are guaranteed
minimum retirement benefits of $25 a month). Such workers have been able to
accumulate OASI credits only since 1950, and then only if they met the minimum
tests of earnings and days worked. These standards are particularly important
for Negroes in view of the casual and part-time nature of much of their employment. . . .

TABLE 1.--*Per cent distribution of employment among major industry groups by color and by sex, April 1950 and March 1940*

Industry group	1940						1950					
	White			Nonwhite			White			Nonwhite		
	Total	Male	Female	Total	Male	Female	Total	Male	Female	Total	Male	Female
Agriculture........................	17.0	21.5	2.4	33.1	41.7	16.1	12.0	15.3	3.1	20.1	25.2	10.7
Mining.............................	2.1	2.8	.1	1.2	1.7	*	1.8	2.5	.2	.7	1.1	*
Construction.......................	4.7	6.1	.3	3.1	4.7	.1	6.3	8.4	.7	5.3	8.0	.3
Manufacturing......................	25.0	25.4	23.7	11.4	15.4	3.5	26.0	26.6	24.6	17.9	22.3	9.6
Transportation, communication, and other public utilities.........	7.2	8.3	3.5	4.4	6.5	.2	7.8	8.8	4.9	6.0	8.5	1.3
Wholesale and retail trade.........	17.8	16.9	20.5	8.3	10.4	4.2	19.2	17.5	23.9	12.7	14.0	10.3
Service industries.................	21.0	13.9	43.8	35.6	15.9	74.3	20.4	14.7	35.9	32.4	15.1	64.8
All other industries...............	3.6	3.8	3.2	1.7	2.2	.6	4.8	5.0	4.2	3.6	4.6	1.8
Industry not reported..............	1.6	1.3	2.3	1.3	1.5	.9	1.6	1.2	2.5	1.2	1.3	1.1
Total †	100.0	100.0	100.0	100.0	100.0	100.0	100.0	100.0	100.0	100.0	100.0	100.0

* Less than 0.1 per cent.
† Figures do not necessarily add to totals because of rounding.

Source: U.S. Bureau of the Census

It should be pointed out that white workers with low incomes are also insecure, and of course their number is much larger, although smaller in proportion to total white employment; however, many Negroes face a less secure old age than do white workers in the same income classes. Both groups find it difficult to finance private insurance, but only 7 States prohibit discrimination on grounds of color in life insurance premium rates and benefits; higher premiums for Negroes than for whites are common. In the South, however, Negro insurance companies service Negro clients on a nondiscriminatory basis.

In addition, the shorter length of a Negro man's working life has significant effects upon the security of his dependents. In 1940, the median age of separation from the labor force was 57.7 years for Negro and 63.6 years for white men, principally as a result of higher death rates for Negroes at all working ages. Particularly significant for urban workers were the higher incidence of disability and a much greater concentration of Negroes in jobs in which age and physical disability were likely to be greater handicaps to continued employment. Negro men working on farms retired later in life than white farm workers, with the result that the average retirement age for all Negro men was about 8 months above that for white men.

Monthly Labor Review, 76 (June, 1953):   596-601.

2.   POSTWAR JOB RIGHTS OF NEGRO WORKERS

Negro workers who have contributed mightily to the cause of victory for the United Nations want to be assured that the jobs they filled during the war will not be ruthlessly snatched away from them with peace. At the CIO Political Action Conference, the issue was discussed by Sidney Hillman, chairman of the Political Action Committee and president of the Amalgamated Clothing Workers, and by Pres. Willard Townsend of the CIO Transport Service Workers, and Ferdinand C. Smith, secretary of the NMU.

By Willard Townsend

"Basically, the racial problem is a worker's problem. For as long as the Negro workers' rights are insecure, all workers' rights are in jeopardy.

This summer more than a million Negroes were in war plants. The vast majority entered war work during the latter half of 1942, and the first quarter of 1943. Unemployment among Negroes has reached a new low, and occupational progress has moved steadily forward.

Full employment for the Negro in war time, in certain selected war industries, means that the total number employed is 5% for Agricultural Machinery; 5% in Aircraft; 12% in Steel; 25% in Iron and Steel Foundries; 4% in Communications; 2% in Electrical equipment; 10% in Smelting and Refining of Nonferrous metals; 10% in shipbuilding.

The Negro worker is definitely worried. He is worried about today, he is worried about tomorrow. He is restless. He remembers only too well the broken promises.

The big question--what of the Negro worker after the war--is causing as much concern among Negro workers as any other segment of our population. Will peace destroy the gains toward full employment for the Negro? What will be his status at the end of hostilities? A depressed economy has always meant but one thing for the Negro worker--widespread unemployment.

If we have an economy of full employment, it will establish a framework favorable to the continuing occupational advancement of the black worker; and to the removal of the white worker's fear of him as an economic rival.

By Ferdinand C. Smith

The CIO has proved itself the leading force in America that stands four-square behind the just aspirations of the Negro people and actively implements its no-discrimination policy on a national scale.

It must continue that leadership on the vital economic front. Even in
wartime, despite the manpower shortage, we know that jobs have not been made
fully available to Negro workers. The prospect, therefore, of full employment
for Negroes in the post-war period becomes a serious problem which must be
considered in the planning stage.

What the Negro people want is what every decent American wants--full
citizenship in a democracy.

If every trade union opened its doors to Negroes and removed the stigma
of second class membership and its attendant inequalities, you can be sure the
time would not be far off when the second class citizenship of Negroes in our
democracy would be wiped out, the polltax Congressmen notwithstanding.

We in the National Maritime Union have deep pride in the knowledge that
full and equal opportunities of employment are offered to our Negro brothers
through our rotary hiring halls in every section of the country. The men who
Keep 'Em Sailing and Deliver the Goods know that torpedoes and bombs don't
discriminate.

They know that the color of a man's skin doesn't affect his ability to
fight fascism nor make him a less patriotic American. That's a Hitler concept
which has no place in American democracy.

This policy of equality on the job which the members of my union have
upheld since its inception has been a vital factor in the effective manning
of the bridge of ships to every battlefront. You can picture for yourself the
tragic situation the nation and its Allies would be facing if the delivery of
war supplies were held up because of race conflicts aboard our ships.

By Sidney Hillman

The CIO Political Action Committee has as a primary objective the organizing of labor's vote. The Negro working man and woman are important and
necessary parts of this group. No drive of this nature, therefore, could be
undertaken without an awareness of this fact and a determination to make it
count.

If re-emphasis be necessary, we state now that a genuine effort will be
made to win the support of the Negro trade unionist and the trade unionists
of all minority groups, for it is with labor that minorities have their biggest
stake. To this end we shall place our arguments with the Negro people in the
South as well as in the North, and with equal vigor.

The Committee knows that in readily identifiable sections of our country,
unfortunately, there are still certain hazards and obstacles between the desire to vote and the ability to vote. We know, for example, that the polltax
prevents 10 million Negroes and whites from voting. We know that registration
is not always freely permitted to many of those who pay their tax.

Today we are engaged in a total war. Nothing less than total organization for victory can secure us of a successful conclusion. Labor sees its
task and intends to meet it. Negro people are sharing the burden and must
share the victory. To this the CIO Political Action Committee is squarely
committed.

CIO News, January 24, 1944.

3. POSTWAR JOBS FOR NEGRO WORKERS

By William Green, President, AFL

As the battles on the German front and the fighting in the Pacific area
are reaching the height of intensity, so the full force of the purpose behind
every attack and every landing is reaching deeper in the hearts of all Americans. The American soldiers at the fronts did not retreat before the massed
attack of the mechanized Nazi divisions. Americans everywhere will not retreat from their objective of liberation of those oppressed and enslaved by
the dictates of the fascist terror. This goal of freedom which is the foremost issue in mankind's most decisive struggle of modern times cannot be set

apart from our own major peacetime goal--freedom of opportunity for everyone
willing and able to work here at home.

Freedom of opportunity in employment without discrimination because of
color, race or creed is a goal which cannot be reached by any one magic formula.
There is much work to be done by all of us, including labor, management and
the government, to speed its attainment. In this task, demobilization when the
war ends is bound to raise many challenging problems. This is especially true
in the fulfillment of the objective of assuring full employment opportunities
to Negro workers. In many sections of our community prejudice, intolerance
and outright discrimination still prevail. The coming new shifts of employment
are bound to result in new strains and stresses of large-scale readjustment.

Positive measures must be taken without delay to relieve these inevitable
strains. First comes the educational work that must be done. It is the most
important because education strikes at the roots of prejudice. Every American
should know the facts, the dramatic and unassailable facts, of the Negro's
contribution to the winning of this war--in the battle and here at home. How
many know that Negroes, who comprise 9.8 per cent of our population, have given
the nation over 16 per cent of Army volunteers in the very first two years of
defense mobilization? How widely known are the factual reports of valor and
heroism beyond the call of duty shown by Negro servicemen in all branches of
the service? How much has been told of the Negro workers' record in war jobs
in exacting and highly skilled tasks in which their performance is to further
the war effort has been a match for anyone? These facts now buried and obscure should be widely disseminated--not as unique exceptions which they are
not, but as a record of natural, matter-of-course accomplishment which they
are.

Second, we should provide the widest opportunity for vocational training
to equip the demobilized Negro soldiers and war workers for remunerative employment. To be most effective such training must be given on real jobs. The
motivating power to accomplish this objective, to make work training acces-
sible to the Negro, must therefore come from both management and labor in the
various industries and in all communities.

Third, we must assure the Negro access to the job. Non-discrimination in
hiring and in job tenure is the final test of equality of employment opportunity for the Negro worker and veteran. In the past, the largest single
source of pressure behind discrimination has been the disparity in the standards of wages paid Negro workers. In many sections of the country, wage
differentials have been racial differentials. A firm policy designed to eliminate such wage differentials will do much to stamp out job discrimination.

No less important is the need for affirmative action on the part of labor,
management and the government to safeguard the Negro worker's rightful claim
to equality in hire and job tenure. The doors to union membership for mutual
aid and protection to them and to all workers must be opened to all qualified
Negro wage earners willing and able to work. A corresponding responsibility
rests upon management not to discriminate in the recruitment of workers or in
the maintenance of the standards of wages and employment conditions. Employers
must not yield to the temptation, which in the past competition has made strong,
to use the Negro worker as a tool for lowering wages and work standards of all
workers. In the end such policies would spell disaster, not only to Negro
labor, but all labor and to our entire economy.

Finally, there is the responsibility of the government to help effectuate
a non-discrimination policy. The employment services of the government should
adhere to this policy in all procedures of referral and placement. Where discrimination does occur, a permanent Fair Employment Practice Commission should
provide the means for hearing and adjustment of all complaints.

Only through such a three-sided but unified effort, with complete teamwork on the part of labor, management and the government and with the full
backing of the entire community, can we meet the challenge of orderly readjustment from war to peace without disruption to our economy and to the national
unity. Only through such a forward looking program, in which there is widest
participation of representative citizens in every community, can we achieve
full freedom of equal opportunity in the future peacetime years.

Opportunity, 23 (April-June, 1945): 80-81.

4. POSTWAR JOBS FOR NEGRO WORKERS

By Philip Murray, President, CIO

We have *all* been working to produce weapons to win the war. With the
winning of the war our task is to have *all* working to produce the products of
peace.

An army of people *not* working and without income, plus a working force
with greatly reduced income, means depression. When the working people do not
have wages to spend, there is tremendous loss to the butcher, the baker, the
landlord and the farmer, who consequently have their purchasing power reduced.

Competition for jobs which are scarce brings new tensions. Race riots
would follow; worker will be competing against worker for jobs; groups competing against groups; veteran competing against civilian; black worker competing
against white worker, in order to earn the wherewithal to live.

The CIO is deeply interested in the security and prosperity of every section of the nation. We want real prosperity for the farmers. We are concerned
with the problems of independent businessmen and professional people. We are
vitally interested in the welfare of returning veterans. We champion the cause
of all racial and national minorities.

Every veteran of both this and the earlier war must have his job opportunity
in a national program of full production and full employment. The same is true
of the large group of women who through necessity or choice will be in the labor
market when the war is over. Women must not only have democratic employment
opportunities; they must receive equal pay for equal work.

The Negro worker has given his efforts to production for Victory; he must
be given the opportunity to produce for peace. His employment opportunities
must not be tampered with because of his color. An economy to which all can
contribute their best efforts and from which all can obtain an adequate living,
must be the goal towards which we must strive.

We believe the following eight-point program is absolutely necessary to
insure a high volume of purchasing power to maintain full employment:

1. Strong unions and high wages.
2. Teamwork for full production and full employment.
    a. A National Production Council should be set up, linked with the
        War Production Board and other war agencies, which will be re-
        sponsible for taking the country through reconversion and keep-
        ing it prosperous. It should be composed of representatives
        of labor, industry, agriculture and government.
    b. Industry Councils should be established in the great basic and
        mass production industries, composed of representatives of labor,
        management and government.
    c. The National Council and the Industry Councils should work out
        an over-all national program and component industry programs
        for changing over to peacetime production and operating at
        capacity thereafter.
3. Construction of a modern transportation system which should include
    a highly developed airway system, railway and highway.
4. Housing and city reconstruction.
5. An expanded program of regional developments.
6. Increased foreign trade.
7. An expanded health and education program.
8. An expanded adequate social security program.

It is only by achieving full employment that we can hope to establish the
climate that will enable us to continue to improve the economic, social and
political status of the Negro. To this end, the CIO Committee to Abolish
Racial Discrimination was created, with James B. Carey, Chairman, Willard S.
Townsend, Secretary, and George L-P Weaver, Director. This committee has
greatly strengthened our efforts to achieve human dignity and freedom.

The CIO believes that by advocating and working toward the attainment of
these objecttives, it is working towards a better America, towards a better
world.

Opportunity, (April-June, 1945): 81.

5. THE GOVERNMENT'S ROLE IN JOBS FOR NEGRO WORKERS

By Major General Philip B. Fleming

In this war, as during the first World War, the Negro has made large economic gains. Traditionally an agricultural laborer or domestic servant, total war has made it possible for him to acquire and utilize higher skills both for the welfare of his country and for the enhancement of his own position.

Even in Government service doors are opening to the Negro that formerly were closed to him. For example, a recent tabulation showed 8,602 Negroes on the payroll of the Federal Works Agency, or 43 per cent of total employment. While a majority of these workers scrub floors of the Government's buildings, wash the windows, operate the elevators, run errands as messengers and fire the boilers, the amount of upgrading brought about by the war is significant. Of some 2,700 guards protecting Government buildings, 900 are Negroes. Five guard sergeants are supervising both white and colored men. Two hundred Negro girls are working in FWA clerical and stenographic positions and twenty Negro men and women are in administrative or professional positions as engineers, supervisors, and technicians.

I have promulgated regulations prohibiting discrimination in employment on racial or religious grounds on all construction carried out by the Federal Works Agency under the community facilities provisions of the Lanham Act. Contractors are required to employ skilled Negro labor in the proportion that the number of available skilled craftsmen of that race bears to the total number of skilled building workers in the community in which each project is built. A recent check showed that of a total wage bill of $40,993,806 on Lanham Act construction projects, more than 20 per cent had been paid to Negro workers and $1,210,417, or 4.7 per cent, to skilled Negro craftsmen.

Data for other agencies, as reported recently by the Fair Employment Practice Committee, are comparable. For example, of 37,012 civilian employees of the War Department, 8,179 were Negroes; of 4,698 employed by the Office of Price Administration, 345 were Negroes; of 1,788 at the War Manpower Commission, 231 were Negroes. These are "departmental" positions as distinguished from the field service. An analysis of the employment records of the war agencies showed that 12,849 positions were held by Negroes, or 17.9 per cent of all positions. Forty-five of these positions held by Negroes were classified as professional, 31 as sub-professional, and 2,987 as "clerical, administrative or fiscal."

These figures furnish some clue to the wartime advances made by Negroes throughout the whole economy.

The Negro's hold upon the economic gains of 1917-18 became increasingly tenuous during the 1920's and was almost completely snapped in the depression of the '30's. The status of the Negro in the next postwar period also will depend upon what happens to American economy as a whole.

If the war is to be followed by another depression, the old rule that the Negro is last hired and first fired will again come into operation. His social stature, as well as his economic gains, will be in jeopardy if there are not enough jobs to go around. It is characteristic of any people in times of economic stress to nominate scapegoats, and thus race is aligned against race, creed against creed, and color against color. Periods of severe business depression sow seeds of fascism as well as hunger.

It must be the policy of Government hereafter to see that every man able and willing to work shall have employment at the highest level of his talent and ability. I believe that policy can be expressed, in part, through a program for the construction of needed public works, made ready and held in reserve for use at the first warning of contraction of business and employment.

White and black, Jew and Gentile, Catholic and Protestant, native sons and foreign born--we are all in the same economic boat. What injures any one of us will, in the long run, injure all of us; whatever improves the status of one helps in some degree to improve the status of all.

Opportunity, 23 (April, June, 1945): 82.

6. LABOR AND FAIR EMPLOYMENT

By Jacob S. Potofsky[182]

Excerpts from a speech delivered before the New York Chapter of the
Southern Conference for Human Welfare on September 23.

With pardonable pride I refer first to the Amalgamated Clothing Workers
of America and how we have met the problem of minorities. I think then certain object lessons can be drawn that may have direct application to other
unions, nonunion workers and the question of federal legislation to prevent
discrimination in industry.

The Amalgamated, by itself, is a sort of League of Nations. Our 325,000
members, living and working in 32 states of the Union and three Canadian provinces, are made up of minorities. There is no racial or national lineage
which dominates or can dominate this union, nor discriminate against any other
group. This holds true as to the right to a job, skilled opportunities, a
voice in union affairs, running for and holding office.

The members of the Amalgamated are Americans all--of Italian, Jewish,
Negro, Polish, Bohemian, Czech, Russian, French, Anglo-Saxon and every other
conceivable extraction. We have Chinese members in our union.

The disabled pharmacist's mate, Edward Bykowski, an American of Polish
extraction, who picketed Senator Bilbo's office and home in Washington for
sixteen days at his own expense in protest against Bilbo's vile assaults upon
Americans of minority stock, is a member of the Amalgamated Clothing Workers
of America. We are proud of Ed Bykowski.

The Amalgamated Clothing Workers of America operates in the North, South,
East and West. We have thousands of Negro members in New York; we have Negro
members in Southern cities. Wherever Negroes are employed in industries in
which we have jurisdiction, they are admitted on the same basis as everyone
else.

It would be offensive to the spirit of our great membership to discriminate
against any single member of our union because of race, color, creed or sex.
Our members receive the same pay for the same type of operations, regardless
of the color of their skin or where they are born or where their parents were
born. They are protected in their jobs by our union constitution, our by-laws,
our conventions and our contractual agreements with our employers.

We operate in 32 States of the Union and not in 48. But we have laid
down a pattern for other enlightened unions to follow, whether they are large
or small, whether they operate in all 48 states or not, whether they are in
interstate commerce or not.

Undoubtedly, there is the greatest moral and economic obligation upon
labor unions not to discriminate against any worker . . . if he wishes to
share the obligations, as well as the benefits, of membership in the union.

But, because there are large sections of American labor still unorganized,
because they have no enlightened unions to speak for them and to protect their
economic interests, federal legislation against discrimination is an elementary
must proposition.

Obviously, the Federal government must protect those who have no protection through their unions. This involves not only the right to work, but the
right, also, to work at decent standards, comparable with the best that have
been obtained through our years of struggle up from economic, and, in the case
of the Negro, from chattel slavery as well. The right to work is meaningless
if it means only at inferior and menial tasks, inadequately paid, with little
or no hope of promotion to higher skills with commensurate improvements in
economic standards.

Those who urge 48 different Fair Employment Practice statutes, instead of
federal legislation, are asking for a hollow sham. They know it won't work.
It will pit state against state. There will be large migrations of Negro and
other minority groups from state to state in an effort to beat discrimination,
only to find that the jobs are not there.

Whether it has been the question of a minimum wage, or recognition of the
principle of collective bargaining or any other matter vital to American labor,
we have argued that only federal statute, rather than state legislation, must
be the controlling factor. Otherwise, you get cutthroat competition with state

pitted against state, worker against worker. You get migration of plants to
so-called cheap labor centers and you encourage a spiral downward which results in the debasement of labor and living standards.

Full employment means work for all Americans--union workers, as well as
non-union workers, displaced war workers, returning veterans, black and white
--all able and willing to work. It means work without discrimination.

We support fully the proposal for a permanent federal Fair Employment
Practice Commission.

Opportunity, 23 (October-December, 1945): 209.

7.   AFL CONVENTION, 1946

Sleeping Car Porters

Resolution No. 158--By Delegate F. N. Aten, Railway Employees' Department.

WHEREAS, All organizations affiliated with the American Federation of
Labor are required to respect the jurisdictional rights of other affiliates,
but the Sleeping Car Porters are, notwithstanding the regulations, raiding
the jurisdiction of the shop craft organizations, composing the Railway
Employees' Department, therefore, be it
RESOLVED, That as all efforts to adjust this dispute by President Green,
meeting with President Randolph, President Knight of the Railway Carmen representing the shop craft organizations meeting with President Randolph and
the Sleeping Car Porters being summoned to appear before the Executive Council
of the American Federation of Labor, August, 1945, and they did appear but
nothing was accomplished in any of these efforts, the Pullman porters stating
their position quite clearly that they intended to go through with efforts to
organize mechanics, helpers, apprentices, coach cleaners, and laborers of the
shop craft organizations, and be it further
RESOLVED, That the Sleeping Car Porters be suspended unless they immediately cease and desist from their raiding of the jurisdiction of the shop
craft organizations and notify the Pullman Yard and Terminal employees of
their withdrawal from the Pullman campaign.

Your committee deplores the fact that the Sleeping Car Porters are going
far beyond their charter rights which are as follows: "Porters, attendants,
maids and bus boys" in their attempt to organize mechanics, helpers, apprentices, coach cleaners, laborers and storeroom employees, all of whom have for
years been recognized as coming within the jurisdiction of the shop crafts
organizations composing the Railway Employees' Department, A.F. of L., and
the Brotherhood of Railway Clerks, and condemns the Sleeping Car Porters for
their failure or refusal to heed President Green's request as contained in
his letter to President Randolph under date of July 13, 1945, reading as
follows: "Certainly the Brotherhood of Sleeping Porters' organization, of
which you are president, cannot claim jurisdiction over boilermakers, blacksmiths, carmen, machinists or any other mechanics employed by the Pullman
Company. For this reason, I must, in a most friendly but emphatic way, call
upon you to immediately cease and desist from attempting to organize workers
such as are referred to in this correspondence or other employees of the
Pullman Company who do not come under the jurisdiction of your Sleeping Car
Porters organization."
Therefore, the committee recommends that Resolution 158 be referred to
the Executive Council of the American Federation of Labor, with authority to
suspend the Sleeping Car Porters at the January, 1947, Council meeting unless
the Sleeping Car Porters notify the Council before that meeting that they (the
Sleeping Car Porters) have discontinued their efforts to organize Pullman
employees coming under the jurisdiction of other A.F. of L. affiliates and
will hereafter confine their efforts to the organizing and servicing of porters, attendants, maids and bus boys.

Committee Secretary McCurdy moved the adoption of the committee's report. The motion was seconded.

DELEGATE RANDOLPH, Brotherhood of Sleeping Car Porters: Mr. Chairman and fellow delegates of the convention: I want to give you a little background of this controversy. The Brotherhood of Sleeping Car Porters is organizing the car cleaners, the non-clerical storeroom workers, the upholsterers' apprentices and helpers, the painters' apprentices and helpers, the mechanics' apprentices and helpers in the Pullman yards. We have never been concerned about the organization of mechanics or any group of workers in the shops.

Now, the car cleaners, the non-clerical storeroom workers, the mechanics' helpers and apprentices, painters' helpers and apprentices, upholsterers' helpers and apprentices have constituted one bargaining unit in the Pullman yards. The existing agreement between the Pullman Company and the Independent Federation of Pullman Workers covers the classes of employees I have afore-mentioned.

Now, the Brotherhood of Sleeping Car Porters is concerned about the organization of the car cleaners because they are close to our group of workers. They are related to the porters. In other words, sometimes porters are transferred to the yards to serve as car cleaners. Then car cleaners are transferred to the cars to serve as porters. This fact is recognized in the agreement between the Pullman Company and the Independent Federation of Pullman Workers.

Now, the Independent Federation of Pullman Workers is a company union. Not until the Brotherhood of Sleeping Car Porters started into organizing this group of workers did the Brotherhood of Railway Carmen show up on the scene. As a matter of fact, the car cleaners sought the Brotherhood of Railway Carmen some 20 years or more ago, calling upon them to organize them, to permit them to come into the union. Officials of the Brotherhood of Sleeping Car Porters requested the Brotherhood of Railway Carmen officials to do something about the organization of this group of workers. Nothing was done. We recognized that were the porters to be involved in a crisis and the car cleaners were under the control of a different organization we would have great difficulty in maintaining our position because of the close relationship of these two groups of workers.

Now, the Brotherhood of Railway Carmen came in after we had started the campaign and claimed that we were raiding their jurisdiction. We are not raiding their jurisdiction. They don't have any car cleaners--not in the yards. Nobody has the car cleaners except the company union. The various organizations are trying to get hold of the car cleaners.

At this very moment there is a mediator in Chicago sent here by the National Mediation Board for the purpose of planning an election to determine the bargaining agent of these groups of workers. We are perfectly willing to abide by the results of the election, but we don't think it is fair for the Brotherhood of Railway Carmen to come into the American Federation of Labor and into the convention and seek to get the support and cooperation of the convention in winning the election.

Now, if the convention goes on record for suspending the Brotherhood of Sleeping Car Porters, it is *ipso facto* helping the Brotherhood of Railway Carmen to win the election, because the Brotherhood of Railway Carmen will go out and tell the car cleaners and other workers, "See, they were kicked out and they were kicked out because the convention recognized that they had no right to organize the car cleaners and related workers."

We consider this a rather low form of trade union organization morality. We think it is unethical, definitely unfair. Now, if the Brotherhood of Railway Carmen think that they can get the car cleaners to come along with them, go out and get them. You are perfectly welcome to them if you can organize them, but they didn't do anything about organizing them for over 25 years, or some 20 years ago. Now, they want to come along, want to get the benefit of the educational program the Brotherhood of Sleeping Car Porters has conducted among these workers. We have about made these workers trade union conscious now. They are ready to give a bona fide trade union organization serious consideration. I am not saying that we will win the election. I don't know whether we will or not, but we are perfectly willing to abide by the results and we are willing to wage the campaign on our own merits, and we are not seeking the cooperation of the convention to discredit the Brotherhood of Railway Carmen and the work of President Knight, not at all. We want this matter to rest on its own merits.[183]

It was my understanding or feeling in the last meeting of the Executive
Council that we were going to leave the thing to the determination of an
election and may the best man win. I didn't know that they were going to
write a resolution of this sort and bring it to this convention. I had the
idea that all of us were going into this election and carry on and wage a
campaign upon sound ethical standards and abide by the decisions of the collective will and feeling of the workers in the Pullman car yards. That is
our position.

The Brotherhood of Railway Carmen, moreover, only recently, so I have been
told, took the color clause out of their constitution. For some years the car
cleaners and others in the Pullman yards were excluded from full-fledged
membership in the Brotherhood of Railway Carmen. Now, one would believe or
have the feeling that workers could make some sudden and miraculous change in
judgment to turn around and place their confidence in an organization which
is just now taking the color clause out of the constitution in order to win
the election, perhaps.

The Brotherhood of Sleeping Car Porters is glad that the Brotherhood of
Railway Carmen have taken the color clause out of their constitution. We bid
them forward. We congratulate them on that fact. Nevertheless, I have not
heard that the Jim Crow locals have been abolished, and as long as there are
Jim Crow auxiliary locals the workers in those locals do not have full-fledged
economic citizenship. They don't have the right of voice and vote in determination of the policies that govern the union. They don't have voice and
vote in the election of the representatives that negotiate agreements concerning rules and regulations governing working conditions.

Therefore, in addition to abolishing the color clause in the constitution,
I want to hear President Knight say that he also has abolished the auxiliary
Jim Crow unions. So, Mr. Chairman and fellow delegates, we consider that the
resolution is decidedly unfair, out of order, and, as a matter of fact, ought
to be rejected by the convention. We believe that if you are going to refer
this resolution to the Executive Council, the Executive Council should not be
bound by the mandate to suspend the Brotherhood of Sleeping Car Porters under
any conditions.

In the Executive Council's report this morning the statement was made that
the International Machinists' Union should be called upon to come back into the
organization, the American Federation of Labor, and here plead their cause
within the framework of this great institution and not remain on the outside
of the American Federation of Labor. Why not apply that same policy in the
Brotherhood of Sleeping Car Porters? Let us plead our cause here within the
framework of the American Federation of Labor. If the cause of the Brotherhood of Railway Carmen is sound, it will bear examination. If it isn't sound,
it won't bear examination and the Brotherhood of Railway Carmen should not be
afraid for the Brotherhood of Sleeping Car Porters to remain in the American
Federation of Labor to fight this issue out on its merits. Why attempt to
take advantage of one group by putting them out where they will then be denied
the privilege of challenging the decisions of this Federation to establish
the validity of their position, whereas the other group is here and is able to
take advantage of their various designs to make their cause secure?

So, Brother President and fellow delegates, the Brotherhood of Sleeping
Car Porters maintains that it is not raiding the membership of the Brotherhood
of Railway Carmen, because they haven't got these workers. They never attempted
to get them for years, and second, we hold that these workers are related to
the porters, they are closer to the porters, and consequently upon those
grounds we believe that our position is sound and that the resolution should
be turned down.

Thank you.

DELEGATE ATEN, Railroad Employees' Department: Mr. Chairman, Brother
Randolph made a very interesting speech, but he evaded the vital issues in
this question. The Pullman porters have been getting jurisdiction over a
certain class of workers. It was made very plain in the reading of the report
of the committee that no one was ever extended that jurisdiction because of
any class of workers beyond those named in the charters of that organization.

Now, I want to get a few facts before the convention, and I want you to
bear with me just a little bit. I will have to go into three or four details

of history. One is the Pullman Company, that is, the operating company that
operates the sleeping cars, is a common carrier in the same meaning that any
railroad is a common carrier. It is subject to the Interstate Commerce Act
and subject to the Railway Labor Act. This company is regulated by the regulations of the Interstate Commerce Commission and is regulated as to labor
matters by the provisions of the Railway Labor Act.

Mr. Randolph made a statement that we have made no attempt to organize
the Pullman employees for a long period of years. Well, it just happens that
I was chairman of a committee that negotiated the first agreement that shop
men ever had with the Pullman Company in 1921. That agreement remained in
effect until the 1922 strike of the shop men, and we lost that agreement. We
not only lost the Pullman agreement because the company refused to settle with
the men on strike, but we lost the majority of our agreements covering shop
men on the other common carriers, the railroads of this country. It was a
long road back. Since that time we have recovered the right to represent the
shop craft employees on the more than 100 railroads that we lost in the 1922
strike, and the Pullman Company and the Pennsylvania Railroad are the only
two large car carriers today on which we do not represent the shop men.

There is one other thing that should be cleared up. That is the Brotherhood of Railroad Carmen of America is not the only organization involved in
this matter. The Railway Employees' Department performs certain services and
represents in various ways all of the shop craft organizations in dealing with
management, negotiating agreements, representation before the National Mediation Board and in various other ways. These organizations are the International Brotherhood of Blacksmiths, International Brotherhood of Boilermakers, the
Brotherhood of Railway Carmen, International Brotherhood of Electrical Workers,
Sheet Metal Workers' International Association and the Firemen and Oilers, at
present affiliated with the Railway Employees' Department.

So, all these organizations, with the exception of the Boilermakers, are
interested in this campaign on the Pullman Company. We have had a crew of
organizers on that road for over a year. I don't know when Brother Randolph
started his campaign, but it doesn't seem to matter to me if we, the Railway
Employees' Department organization, undertook to represent employees of any
class covered by his charter I am sure that he would say we were trying to
invade his jurisdiction, whether the people we were after are present members
of his organization or not.

Now, as I said, it has been a long way back since the 1922 strike. We
have done this work of recovering our representation and our agreements on
these roads as rapidly as conditions would permit. With such an enormous job
to do it was, of course, obvious that we would first tackle those roads that
seemed easy to get, and that is just what we have done. The Pullman Company
has been canvassed several times in this period of years, and not until within
the last two years has there appeared any likelihood that the employers would
respond to an organizing campaign put on by the organization operating through
the Railway Employees' Department. When that time appeared we put a crew on
the system because it is not just like a railroad. It is a nationwide system.
There are 200 points, 200 towns and communities where Pullman employees are
employed in the yards and towns. There are six heavy repair shops of the
Pullman system that do the overhauling for the Pullman cars. The Pullman
porters' organization is not trying to represent or not seeking to represent
the employees in the six repair shops where about 40 per cent of the total
number of employees are employed. They are seeking to represent all the
employees in the yards where 60 per cent of the employees ordinarily represented by these shop craft organizations are employed.

This present representation election now coming on is brought on because
of the fact that the Railway Employees' Department invoked the services of the
National Mediation Board to determine who shall represent these crafts employed
in the Pullman Company. You men in the American Federation of Labor know what
a craft is. I don't need to give you any definition of that, but that word as
applied in the railway industry and the Pullman Company, to all intents and
purposes, is a part of the railway industry because it is a common carrier
under all the acts of that regulation and has been treated as such all through
the history of the organization, and these crafts on railroads are not the
boilermakers and helpers' apprentices, for example, employed in one shop, like
the Topeka shop on the Santa Fe Railroad. They are the boilermakers employed
on the Santa Fe Railroad from Chicago to San Francisco, the Gulf Coast lines
and the coast lines from the western region. In other words, the entire oper-

ating carrier under the Railway Labor Act is the unit on which a craft vote
is taken. Even the employees in marine shops on the coast are voting along
with the mechanics' helpers and apprentices in the actual railroad shops
where cars and locomotives are repaired, so a craft on a railroad means the
employees such as electrical workers, their helpers and apprentices, employed
in the six heavy repair shops and in the 200 yards and termination points on
the Pullman system.

Now, there are two company unions representing employees in the Pullman
Company at the present time. One is an organization representing those in
the six heavy repair shops only. The other is another company union representing employees in the yards and termination--these 200 points outside
the shops. There is a CIO organization undertaking to represent the employees
in the six heavy repair shops. There are the Pullman porters undertaking to
represent the employees in the 200 yards and terminal points. That makes
four different organizations against us in this campaign. The Pullman porters'
president says, "Let the best man win," with the full knowledge, without a
doubt, that if he has any conception of what the Pullman system means as to a
mechanics' helper and apprentices nobody will win this election if they continue in the election. It means there is a vote for five different organizations which will have to be placed on the ballot. We would expect such an
experience from a CIO outfit that is trying to organize and represent the men
in the repair shops, but we certainly have a right to expect cooperation instead of interference from an American Federation of Labor organization.

Then, suppose that no organization receives a majority of all the votes
in any one craft. That simply means that under the procedure of the Railway
Labor Act, if a representation election is held and no organization receives
a majority of all the votes cast in a craft over the entire system, mind you,
shops and outside points, no organization receives a majority of that craft
vote, there is no change in representation. In other words, it means a cinch
for the company union if no one of the three contesting organizations, the
CIO, the Pullman porters, or the Railway Department organization, wins a
majority of any one of these crafts. They will still be represented by the
company union because there has been no vote for a change in representation.

Now, under the procedure of the Railway Labor Act, as I stated, the
Electrical Workers, for example, their helpers and apprentices on the entire
operating system, which is the entire Pullman Company, six repair shops,
200 outside plants, are one unit. There was a hearing in Washington before
the National Mediation Board some time in July and at that hearing the Pullman
porters were represented by a very competent attorney and certain other of
their representatives. They contended that they wanted the National Mediation
Board to recognize as the bargaining unit only the employees in the yards and
termination points and not include those in the six repair shops. They want
them not only to recognize that as the bargaining unit, but they want the
National Mediation Board to order an election of everybody as one voting unit,
with those distinctions as to crafts.

Well, after that hearing the attorneys for the several contesting parties
exchanged briefs, filed answers and a decision of the National Mediation Board
was made a couple of weeks ago. That decision was that the vote would be taken
by crafts on the entire system, including the six heavy repair shops and the
200 yards and terminals, so the carmen have got to win a majority of the votes
in the six repair shops and in the yards. The electricians have to do the
same--the blacksmiths have to do the same if they are going to win this vote.

Now, I don't know that I can add much more to that, I just wanted to get
these facts before you. There is a considerable difference in the way representation elections are handled under the Railway Labor Act and the way they
are handled under the National Labor Relations Act. The National Labor Relations Board can say what will constitute a voting unit. They might vote the
employees of the General Motors Company in Buffalo and one in San Francisco as
separate, but the National Mediation Board under the Railway Labor Act and the
procedures established thereunder cannot split up any common carrier for
voting purposes, and they have made numerous decisions sustaining that procedure.

So, I just wanted you to have these facts, and I am sure that President
Knight of the carmen has certain documentary evidence that he may want to give
to the convention.

DELEGATE WEBSTER, Brotherhood of Sleeping Car Porters: We judge, from the remarks just made by the last speaker, that all we had to do was to get out of this election and it would be a cinch for the American Federation of Labor. Now, the question of the arrangement or the voting for these crafts was an action on the part of the National Mediation Board. When we went into this situation some four or five years ago these people in the yards were orphans. The Carmen's Union or the shop craft employees--the shop crafts' organizations were not giving any attention to these people. Naturally, having an organization of Pullman porters and having the same field to cover, we came in close contact with these people. Many of these people who had been porters were not working in the yards. Many of the men who work in the yards have come on the road as porters. In fact, in the company union agreement specific arrangement is made for the so-called upgrading of people working in the yards to porters operating on the roads.

Then, incidentally, a large percentage of these workers are Negroes, and at the time we started this campaign these Negroes could not come into the Carmen's Union or any of the shop craft unions that we know of, unless it was the Electrical Workers' Union. Nothing had been done. As a matter of fact, as an organization we have attempted to operate with the Carmen's Union to try to get these people organized. I have spoken at meetings held by the officers of the Carmen's Union 15 or 18 years ago, but all of those efforts were out.

All these people were struggling along under the yoke of a company union. Originally they operated under what was called the plant employee representation. Then after the Railway Act was amended and these interested organizations were inaugurated they started to operate under the auspices of these independent organizations, which was a glorified company union.

Now, what was our position? We represent a large substantial group of people employed by the Pullman Company, and who have we got surrounding us? We have three company unions. There are three company unions--not two. One in the shops, one in the yards and the clerks, all operating under the jurisdiction of company unions. Then along comes the CIO group and, of course, we didn't have jurisdiction over the laundry workers. We didn't take any part in the campaign, even though the laundry workers solicited our help. Who do we find represent the laundry workers? The CIO. We have a laundry workers' organization there, too, but the CIO moved in and they now represent the laundry workers and are moving in to represent these other groups, and until we started in this program not one thing was done by the Carmen's Union or any of the other organizations to get these people into an organization.

Now, as a matter of fact, it is a question of self protection. If the CIO did encroach and get the laundry workers and then we stood idly by and the others encroach and get those people who are close to us, it is only going to be a short space of time before they make trouble for us. It is amusing as we read this resolution to hear these people talk about raiding their jurisdiction. They have admitted that they have done nothing to organize these people for many years. Before the Committee on Adjustment the speaker who preceded me pointed out that they did have a contract in 1921 and '22. Now, that is 24 years ago. Twenty-four years is a long time. Yet they have allowed these people to come under the yoke of this company union, and the company union at the present time has a contract covering the wages and working conditions of this particular group of people.

Now, this isn't a jurisdictional dispute, as we see it, as many jurisdictional disputes we have heard argued in these conventions from time to time, but here are a group of workers that they did not attempt to organize until we got into the picture a little over three years ago. Now, should we stand by and wait until they get ready, wait until they take the color clause out of the constitution and let our own interests be jeopardized? We have no special desire to usurp anybody's jurisdiction, but we are confronted with a practical, everyday problem. A large number of these people in these yards are Negroes and they were being exploited. They don't exercise their rights, their seniority rights under this setup. They were being pushed out of jobs without having access to go to the National Railway Adjustment Board, and all of these complaints were brought to us from time to time, so we as an organization are interested primarily in the organization of the Negro workers and we are trying to bring these people under our wing in an effort to bring to them some sort of organization.

There is no certainty of who is going to win the election. There is no certainty that the Carmen are going to win their share of it and there is no certainty that the company unions are going to win their share of it. As a matter of fact, had we known that there was any qualified representative on the part of the Carmen's Union or any of the groups in the shop yards to go out and organize these people we would have been glad to help them rather than to take on this responsibility. But we know the conditions of these people. Negroes are being driven off of the railroads because organized white organizations are bringing pressure on the railroads to drive these Negroes off. Can we stand by and wait until the Carmen get ready to organize these people to try to put forth some effort to put these people back into an organization?

Now, we are thoroughly convinced that our position is sound. We ran into this thing with our eyes open. We have tried to bring these people into the American Federation of Labor. We believe that we have as much chance, and maybe a little more, to bring these people into the American Federation of Labor than anybody else on the ballot. We do feel that an injustice is being perpetrated upon us by this organization which admits they shamefully neglected these people, coming in here at this late date and who are trying to throw the Brotherhood of Sleeping Car Porters out because they dared to sympathize with a number of their brothers who have long been exploited not only in the railroad industry but in America as a whole.

We plead with you delegates to this convention to turn the report of the committee down.

DELEGATE BURKE, Pulp, Sulphite and Paper Mill Workers: Mr. Chairman, I request that the Secretary of the Committee read in that portion of the committee's report referring to the suspension of the Brotherhood of Porters. Read that portion of the report again.

PRESIDENT GREEN: We will accommodate you. The Secretary will please read that section of the report.

COMMITTEE SECRETARY McCURDY read the following portion of the committee's report:

"Therefore, the committee recommends that Resolution 158 be referred to the Executive Council of the American Federation of Labor with authority to suspend the Sleeping Car Porters at the January, 1947, Council meeting unless the Sleeping Car Porters notify the Council before that meeting that they, the Sleeping Car Porters, have discontinued their efforts to organize Pullman employees coming under the jurisdiction of other A.F. of L. affiliates and will hereafter confine their efforts to the organizing and servicing of porters, attendants, maids and bus boys."

DELEGATE BURKE: Now, Mr. Chairman, I move that the report of the committee be amended by striking out that part referring to the suspension of the Brotherhood of Sleeping Car Porters.

DELEGATE LYNCH, Pattern Makers: As President of the Pattern Makers' League of North America, I wish to second that motion.

PRESIDENT GREEN: You have heard the motion to amend the committee's report. The Chair recognizes Chairman Knight of the committee.

COMMITTEE CHAIRMAN KNIGHT: You would think from the discussion that the Brotherhood of Railway Carmen was the only organization involved here. Here is the original resolution that was submitted to the A.F. of L., and it is signed by Fred N. Aten, President of the Railway Employees Department, myself as President of the Railway Carmen, G. M. Bugniazet, of the Electrical Workers; George M. Harrison, Brotherhood of Railway Clerks; Charles MacGowan, of the Boiler Makers.[184]

Now, he says no Boiler Makers are involved. They have six rebuilding shops and they have a repair plant at every one of those places with boilers in all of them.

It was also signed by Robert Byron of the Sheet Metal Workers, John Pelkofa of the Blacksmiths and President McNamara of the Firemen and Oilers.[185]

It is difficult for me to touch on these various subjects because they are so far from the facts. As I recall, President Randolph said we hadn't

done anything for 25 years. There is an agreement in evidence that we had
with the Pullman Company that covered white, black, red and yellow employees
of that company in the shops and yards that we lost in the shop strike in
1922.

It has been said that coach cleaners and Pullman porters are interchang-
able. Well, that was in existence many, many years ago, even before these
shop organizations had a signed agreement with the Pullman Company for
all of the employees involved in this representation campaign.

We lost that agreement in 1922 in the strike. It has been said here that
we haven't attempted to do anything with these Pullman employees for 25 years.
Well, these shop craft organizations have learned from long experience, experience going far beyond the time that the Pullman porters were organized,
that when a limb shakes, the tree is not full of squirrels, and when some
Pullman employee becomes dissatisfied and goes out and looks for the organization that that doesn't mean there is any great dissatisfaction among those
employees.

We have organized lodges of Pullman employees in the last seven years,
notwithstanding the statements to the contrary. We could have organized more
of them. We don't want their money until such time as we are authorized by
the National Mediation Board and are given that authority under a Federal law.
When they say that we are the bargaining agency then we will organize them and
accept their money, and not until then.

Now, the hazard that the Pullman porters might experience with the coach
cleaners that they talk about mostly--what did the shop men experience in the
1922 strike when these same mechanics, helpers and apprentices, coach cleaners,
laborers and storehouse employees went on strike? I do not think if the coach
cleaners and others that were not organized could do the porters any more
damage if the porters went on strike than they did to the shop craft organizations in our 1922 strike. However, the Pullman porters were not organized then
on the Pullmans. They haven't anything to do with what did that. Who is
closer to the employees in the shop--these mechanics' helpers and apprentices,
coach cleaners and laborers working on the same car, in the yard or in the
terminal that the Pullman employee works on, sometimes working side by side on
the same car. There was no group that had more to do with the organizing of
the Pullman employees than these shop men working in the terminals and yards,
because every Pullman employee that is operating the Pullman car rides that
car into the yards where these shop men are working and they are in contact
with them every day. They all know one another, and there was a great influence exerted upon the Pullman employees by these shop men, coach cleaners
and laborers in the organizing of President's Randolph's organization.

It has been said here that if the Pullman porters had known that these
shop craft organizations or the clerks were interested they wouldn't have got
in the campaign. It would not have been much trouble for them to ascertain
if that was a fact. However, they did not go to that trouble. The first
time the activities of the Pullman porters came to me was through the Vice
President of the Electrical Workers, and I wrote President Randolph on March
24, 1944. I was asked by these shop men to handle it for them, and I did.
Perhaps that is the reason that the Carmen are the greatest culprits in this.

The last paragraph of President Randolph's reply of April 14 reads:

"Of course, the Brotherhood of Sleeping Car Porters is not organizing
the Pullman car cleaners. I hope this explanation will be satisfactory, but
be assured that it is not my desire to have any conflict of interests with
yours or any other organization which I may have anything to do with.

                              "A. PHILIP RANDOLPH."

Now, I accepted that as the whole clause, but just before the A.F. of L.
Convention in New Orleans in November of 1944 other rumors came to me, and I
went over to President Randolph's table and sat down and talked to him about
it. He told me substantially the same thing there, but when the sentiment
among the Pullman employees indicated that there was a possibility of these
shop craft organizations taking over we started a campaign and then we found
out what the Brotherhood of Sleeping Car Porters had done and was doing--they
organized numerous locals throughout the country. They called a meeting here
in Chicago. I think it was on May 4 and 5, 1944--or somewhere back there and
they brought these people in here and adopted resolutions and all of those things.

They talk about ethics and so on. I could read those resolutions to them.
If there is any ethics in those resolutions and fair dealings with these employees that are being exploited, as has been said here, I don't know anything about that language.

After learning just what the Pullman Car Porters were doing I wrote
President Green. He wrote President Randolph several letters. He had a conference with President Randolph and some of his associates in President Green's
office in which President Green tried to get him to discontinue his tactics.
He failed, and then he requested President Randolph to confer with me, and
President Randolph and Vice President Webster came into my office in Kansas City
on June 15 last. We talked the situation over at great length, but they were
very adamant in their position that they were going ahead. I asked President
Randolph if he knew what the ultimate outcome of that might be. "Well," he
said, "I don't know. It might mean that we would be kicked out of the A.F.
of L." Now, he fully realized what he and his associates were doing and what
the possibility might be in their doing that.

Here is a letter from President Green to me, dated June 21, 1945. I will
not read all of it, but the last paragraph on the first page will be interesting.

"I submit the following quotation from a letter I received from President
Randolph acknowledging receipt of my communication and advising me that he was
planning to meet with you. The quotation is as follows:

" 'May I say, however, that I cannot agree to discontinue the work of
organizing the Pullman car cleaners and yard forces, who have been without
organization for 50 years or more, except that they had a company union since
1920. Moreover, some of the car cleaners are colored, and as I understand it
are not eligible for membership in the Brotherhood of Railway Carmen because
of a color clause in their constitution.' "

The statement that they hadn't any organization for more than 50 years
is disproved by the fact that we had an agreement to strike in 1922, and the
statement that they have had a company union since 1922 likewise is not a
fact, because we had the agreement and we lost it in 1921.

During the strike of July 1, 1921, the National Railroad Labor Board,
meeting here in Chicago on July 3, 1921, adopted a resolution calling upon the
management of the railroads, every railroad in the United States, because
there was in excess of 500,000 shop men out on strike because that board had
abrogated their agreement on every railroad in the United States, and imposed
upon them two reductions in pay.

That resolution of July 3 called upon the management to form an organization to deal for the employees that remained in the service and those that
might come in during the strike. That was the starting of so-called company
unions. The management of the railroads wrote those agreements. They appointed the officers of that company union and there are two of them still in
existence. That is the Pullman Company and the Pennsylvania Railroad, and we
now have a campaign on the Pennsylvania that we expect to take over in a short
while.

Here is a letter that President Green wrote to President Randolph on July
13, 1945. It reads in part as follows:

"The complaints which reach me alleging that you are transgressing upon
the jurisdiction of metal trades organizations affiliated with the American
Federation of Labor in the campaign which you have launched to organize certain employees of the Pullman Company have increased. As evidence of this
fact I enclose a copy of the letter I received from President MacGowan of the
International Brotherhood of Boilermakers, Iron Shipbuilders and Helpers, a
copy of a letter I received from President Brown of the International Association of Machinists, and a copy of a letter I received from President Horn
of the International Brotherhood of Blacksmiths, Drop Forgers and Helpers.

"I cannot help but believe that after you have read these copies of letters
I am enclosing you will agree with me that the situation dealt with in the
correspondence has become quite serious. Certainly the Brotherhood of Sleeping
Car Porters' organization, of which you are president, cannot claim jurisdiction over boilermakers, machinists, blacksmiths and drop forgers, or any
mechanics employed by the Pullman Company. For this reason I must, in a most
friendly but emphatic way, call upon you to immediately cease and desist from
attempting to organize workers such as are referred to in this correspondence,
or other employees of the Pullman Company who do not come under the jurisdiction
of your Sleeping Car Porters' organization."

Here is a letter that I prepared and which went out over the signature
of the shop craft organizations--seven of them--including the officers of the
Railway Employees' Department, under date of September 4. It is addressed
to the Pullman Yard Employees:

"No doubt your attention has recently been called to a four-page handbill
or circular, the first page of which is headed 'Attention Pullman Yard Forces'
over the signature of President A. Philip Randolph of the Sleeping Car Porters.
The second and third page are entitled 'An Open Letter to All Members of the
Pullman Yard Forces,' three columns over the signature of International Sec-
retary Ashley L. Totten.
   "The first paragraph of the open letter reads as follows:
   " 'The writer believes in striking the iron while it is hot. The best
time to kill a snake is when it shows its head.'
   "We agree with the contents of the above quotation and believe that the
Sleeping Car Porters can be likened to the snake in that case, because they
have raised their head in violation of their charter rights with the A.F. of
L. and are encroaching upon the charter rights and raiding the jurisdiction
of the organizations signatory to this circular."

Here is a letter from President Green to President Randolph of August 15:
   "Following the conclusion of the hearing which was held by the Executive
Council, in which you participated, of the complaint filed by President Knight
of the Brotherhood of Railway Carmen and a number of representatives of other
railway shop craft organizations against the Brotherhood of Sleeping Car
Porters, the Executive Council directed me to communicate with you requesting
that you discontinue organizing employees of the Pullman Company and railroad
companies who, it was pointed out at the hearing, come under the jurisdiction
of the Brotherhood of Railway Carmen and other shop craft organizations. The
Executive Council requests that you discontinue the efforts you are putting
forth to organize these workers into the Brotherhood of Sleeping Car Porters,
otherwise the Council will be compelled to take further action."
   Here is a circular put out over the signature of President Randolph:
   "Dear Brothers and Sisters:
   "Little David slew Goliath and the Brotherhood of Sleeping Car Porters
can lick the Carmen's Union and its allies."
   Well, now, it seems to me that that is a pretty big undertaking. If I
understand the American Federation of Labor, the Brotherhood of Railway Carmen
as an affiliate of the American Federation of Labor, is an ally to all other
affiliates of the American Federation of Labor. Or turn it around the other
way--all affiliates to the American Federation of Labor are allies of the
Brotherhood of Railway Carmen, so they are saying here that they can whip the
carmen and their allies.
   Then the next paragraph reads:
   "The Brotherhood of Sleeping Car Porters is out to represent all of the
yard and shop forces--all of the yard and shop forces, including mechanics,
helpers and apprentices; painters, helpers and apprentices; upholsterers,
helpers and apprentices; electrical repairmen, helpers and apprentices, and
car cleaners."
   There is a lot more here, but it is getting late, so I will just take up
this and it will be the last.
   This representation vote that is going to be taken in a few days among
the shop craft employees and the yard and terminal employees of the Pullman,
the same as if they were all working under one roof--by the National Mediation
Board, Case No. R-1625--Washington, involving machinists, their helpers and
apprentices; blacksmiths, their helpers and apprentices; sheet metal workers,
their helpers and apprentices; electrical workers, their helpers and apprentices; carmen, their helpers and apprentices; powerhouse and shop laborers;
storeroom, non-clerical--now, can you conceive of the Pullman porters having
a place on the ballot when that is the vote that is going to be taken? Of
course, I may not have a college education and I might not be competent to
realize just what that means, but I do know what it means at a 147 properties
where these shop craft organizations have taken the representation vote since
the amending of the Railway Labor Act in 1934, and they have voted in that way
in each and every instance, and we have been certified to as the bargaining
agent and we expect to be certified to on the Pennsylvania when the vote is
taken shortly. But under the present conditions I doubt if any crafts or any

class will get a majority of the eligible votes in the 200 railway terminal
yards and six rebuilding plants, and if they don't the company unions will be
certified as the bargaining agent sometime later.

Now, then, I do not think that an amend to the committee's report, with
these facts before us, is a proper motion, and I, therefore, trust that you
will vote it down and approve the committee's report. That leaves it in the
hands of the Executive Council of the American Federation of Labor.

DELEGATE LYNCH, Pattern Workers: Delegate Lynch, in parliamentary fashion, applies himself to the question before the house, which is the matter of
amending the committee's report. First, let me say that I listened attentively
to Brother Knight. It is not my intention here or now to enter into the merits
of a jurisdictional dispute. I heard some reference to some language that was
reminiscent about taking apart all of these railway organizations, but that
is not strange language in this convention. If my memory serves me right I
think I heard that same language employed in 1935 by no less eminent a man
than John L. Lewis himself. I think I have heard that same language come
from other representatives of the so-called craft unions in this convention.

But I want to make one thing clear, President Green, that in all of these
matters that come in the nature of jurisdictional disputes which are never
solved, they usually come before this convention with a recommendation to refer
it to the President of the American Federation of Labor or to the Council without a dire threat in the first instance. You have had jurisdictional disputes
on this floor this afternoon and they were referred, not once, as I understood
President Stevenson, but twice, and for three or four years, and so I want to
make clear that I am not entering into this jurisdictional dispute, despite
the fact that President Knight has some pattern makers which he is welcome to.
I don't want them.

But I say this, that when you come before this convention with a threat
to George Lynch or Philip Randolph or anyone else in the first instance, you
will behave worse than the National Labor Relations Board, which you criticized on this convention floor.

I have no objections to referring it to the Council. We might have to
refer District 50, and are we going to throw out the Mine Workers if the Paper
Makers or Pulp and Sulphite Workers ask for their jurisdiction there? I guess
not. The Miners have 500,000 votes. That is a couple of more than Philip
Randolph or George Lynch.

What I am objecting to, Mr. President, is the threat. I don't like it.
Perhaps that is because I am Irish, and the Irish don't take anything, even
from the King.

DELEGATE BURKE, Pulp and Sulphite Workers: I made the amendment. As a
delegate to this convention I feel a keen sense of responsibility in casting
my vote upon this question. In deciding a jurisdictional question of this
kind the delegates are placed in the position of a jury, the delegates have
to make the decision. I think every delegate should feel as I do, that it is
a very grave responsibility that is put upon us in voting upon a question of
this kind.

I have listened to the arguments from both sides. After listening to the
arguments it seems to me that this is one of those borderline cases where
something can be said on both sides. Now it would seem to me that, instead
of talking at this time about suspending the Brotherhood of Sleeping Car
Porters, the proper procedure would be to refer it back to the Executive
Council for further conferences and further efforts to settle this dispute.

As we look back a few years and look at the records of the American
Federation of Labor, I find a great many unions have been suspended or expelled.
I remember that the United Mine Workers were suspended or expelled--I have
forgotten which. I voted against the suspension or expulsion of the United
Mine Workers. The record of the American Federation of Labor convention will
show that the delegates from the Pulp, Sulphite and Paper Workers' Union voted
against the suspension of the United Mine Workers. After the Mine Workers
were out for a number of years we voted three years ago at the Boston convention to give the Executive Council power to enter into negotiations with the
Mine Workers to try to bring them back into the A.F. of L., and after three
years of negotiations we are happy to have delegates of the United Mine
Workers of America sitting at this convention.

But how was that brought about? I suppose that negotiation after negotiation was held between the leaders of the United Mine Workers of America and
the Executive Council of the American Federation of Labor. This is what usually
happens after we suspend an international union. That union either comes back
or somebody from the Executive Council or someone else goes to that union and
tries to get it back. Then conferences are held--conferences and conferences,
until finally, as in the case of the United Mine Workers, the union comes back.

Why not have these conferences and discussions and efforts before we
suspend the union? Does that make sense?

Then we suspended the Brewery Workers' Union. I voted against it. Where
are the Brewery Workers today? In the CIO--is that right? Yes, they are in
the CIO, affiliated with the CIO.

We suspended the Lithographers. Where are they? In the CIO. Let's not
forget, brother delegates, that when we suspend an organization from the
American Federation of Labor today there is another powerful organization of
labor with its arms wide open to receive that suspended organization.

Suppose we suspend or talk about suspending this organization composed of
colored workers. Just imagine what a nice morsel that would be for the Communist press of this country! Can you picture the headline in the "Daily
Worker?" You delegates to this convention must know the damnable propaganda
that is being circulated among the colored workers in this country by the
Communistic elements in the CIO. We have Labor Board elections in the South
where the colored workers have voted solidly against our organization, because
they have been fed on this damnable propaganda that the American Federation of
Labor is discriminating against the colored workers, and they are making the
colored workers believe it.

I am warning the delegates to this convention to be careful in voting on
this proposition. I urge the delegates to vote for my amendment. I urge you
to think carefully before you vote. You are the jury. If you want to do the
American Federation of Labor a service, vote for my amendment and let the
Executive Council make another effort to settle this jurisdictional dispute
before we talk about suspending the Brotherhood of Sleeping Car Porters.

DELEGATE CLARK, Typographical Union: I have listened very carefully to
all of this testimony from both sides on this question, and as one delegate I
feel I cannot be free to vote any other than to support the amendment that
has been made here, for this reason, that I believe that every delegate in this
hall believes in ironing out our differences by conciliation and collective
bargaining, and certainly when we hold a club over one organization's head,
such as a definite threat to suspend them if they don't accede, that is not
collective bargaining. It is holding a pistol at their head.

I don't want to take any part or be any judge in a jurisdictional matter,
for this reason. First, I have listened to these arguments, I have found
conflicting statements, and even the labor paper that was laid upon our desks
carries a picture of President Knight, and under the picture it says:

"President Felix Knight, of the Brotherhood of Railway Carmen, A.F. of L.,
presided over the Union's recent convention in Chicago. Knight supported a
proposal to eliminate the color bar from the union's constitution, but the
delegates voted it down."

I have heard here in the discussion that the color bar was removed from
the constitution. This paper is dated October 10, the *Colorado Labor Advocate*.
It is all the more confusing, and I do believe that the only wise course, the
only sane course we can take is to support the amendment and not place a
definite threat over the Brotherhood of Sleeping Car Porters.

PRESIDENT GREEN: Are there any further remarks?

DELEGATE RANDOLPH, Brotherhood of Sleeping Car Porters---

PRESIDENT GREEN: Delegate Randolph, the Chair can only recognize you if
there are no others who wish to speak who have not yet spoken. Are there others
who wish to speak who have not spoken? It seems not, and the Chair will recognize you.

DELEGATE RANDOLPH, Brotherhood of Sleeping Car Porters: I simply want to
say that the delegates of the Brotherhood of Sleeping Car Porters are in agreement with the amendment proposed by Delegate Burke. We feel that this question

is too complex, it is too far-reaching to be disposed of summarily and hastily, as it is being disposed of, according to the report of the Adjustment Committee.

It was a rather strange procedure, anyway, that in the Adjustment Committee President Knight served as the chairman, the prosecutor and the jury. He produced all of the documents and presented documents to support his argument against the Brotherhood of Sleeping Car Porters. That does not smack of the democracy we have been talking about here.

I do not think we have ever had in the history of this organization a case comparable to this. Here you are calling upon a convention, where a question is raised before it for the first time, to take drastic action in suspending an organization which is charged with trespassing upon the jurisdictional rights of another organization. I never heard of that before.

Why do you have this desperation on the part of the Brotherhood of Railway Carmen and the other organizations? The reason is simple, it is plain. The Brotherhood of Railway Carmen and other organizations are in desperation because they think they are going to lose the election which is going to be staged in the next few weeks, and they want to use this convention as a public forum to propagandize the workers in the Pullman yards and get them to vote for them. That is the reason for this desperation.

There is no precedent for this action. It is extraordinary for an organization which is brought upon the charge of trespassing the jurisdiction of another organization to be suspended by the convention in which that question is first raised.

We are perfectly willing for this matter to be referred to the Executive Council and Brother William Green, without that threat of suspension which is a part of that resolution.

The question was called for.

PRESIDENT GREEN: The question now recurs upon the amendment to the committee's report. I presume that every delegate here understands the report quite well and the amendment to the report now pending for decision. The question will recur upon the amendment.

All in favor of the adoption of the amendment to the committee's report will please say aye. Those opposed will say no. The ayes seem to have it, the ayes have it, and it is so ordered.

The question now recurs upon the adoption of the report as amended. All in favor of that motion please say aye. Those opposed will say no.

The ayes have it, the motion is carried, and it is so ordered.

The convention will stand adjourned until tomorrow morning.

At 6:20 o'clock p.m., the convention was adjourned to 9:30 o'clock, Tuesday morning. October 15.

Proceedings of the 66th annual convention of the American Federation of Labor, 1946, pp. 452-62.

8.   OUR STAKE IN THE LABOR FIGHT

By Clarence Mitchell[186]

A raw January wind was threatening to tear away the handful of circulars she carried explaining the issues of the strike. Except for the hostile light in the doorway of the building, which housed a cafeteria, the street was dark. A few drops of water made me know that a cold rain was coming up in a matter of minutes. A uniformed guard was standing a few feet away, but he was there at the request of the employer. She had no assurance that he would give adequate protection against strike-breakers--one of whom had threatened some of the pickets with a knife earlier in the day.

This woman, trudging up and down in a lonely picket line, was one of 2,000 other Government Services, Inc., employees. Their employer operates most of the government cafeterias in Washington. They were on strike for better

wages, time off when sick, and a few other elementary forms of protection
that many industrial workers and almost all government employees take for
granted.

With Thomas Richardson, international vice-president of her union, I had
been trying to enlist support of persons who used the cafeteria she was picketing. For some reason, the employer in this case had seen fit to keep the place
running as though there had been no strike. Most of the customers were government girls who lived in near-by dormitories. As the union official put it,
"Many of the cafeteria workers didn't earn as much as the government girls
paid for rent." This situation and the need for public support of workers may
be duplicated many times about the country.

We Negroes have a definite stake in such struggles for there are approximately a million-and-a-half colored persons in the AFL and CIO unions, and
their economic well-being depends on the success of the great trade union
movements of the country.

AFL employees of a chemical company in Alabama in April threatened a
strike when management attempted to include a five cent wage differential between the races in a new contract. Insisting that colored and white workers
did not want to be divided, the union members forced the company to give all
workers a twenty-five cent increase retroactive to six months. In Atlanta,
the AFL Bridge and Structural Iron Workers fought for and won a clause in their
contract which provides that there shall be no discrimination in hiring, firing,
or promotion because of color.

In Baltimore, colored members of the Wholesale, Retail and Department
Store Employees began picketing for a living wage just before Christmas. It
probably cost the employers money to have no customers during the Christmas
rush, but it required real courage upon the part of the employees to go on
strike. Many of them have children and Christmas without a pay check is dull
indeed.

Living Cost Responsible

The increased cost of living is the major factor responsible for the recent larger work stoppages. The *Monthly Labor Review* for December, 1946, reports that over seventy-seven percent of all workers involved and about eighty-
six percent of the man-days lost in strikes of 1,000 or more workers centered
around wage issues. This was for the period from VJ-Day to June 30, 1946.

These disputes--the fight of the mine workers for wage increases, the
struggles of the auto workers, and the needs of men in steel--are what well-
fed Congressmen and some smooth talking executives refer to as the "labor
problems." These gentlemen and a lot of other Americans who are taken in by
their propaganda have decided that now is the time to give labor the works.
"This time," they say, "we shall amend the Wagner Act, cut out the closed shop,
and give the employer the same rights of free speech as the employee."

It is interesting to note in passing that when those who control the sale
of meat throttled the country by snatching bacon from the breakast tables in
order to get a higher profit, their use of "educational" devices forced the
president of the United States to eat crow and abolish controls. Furthermore,
most of the screaming headlines blamed OPA for the shortage of meat instead of
the real culprits. On the other hand, when unions work for pay raises, these
same devices are used to lambast them for being too arrogant.

Since three-fourths of the gainfully employed people in this country are
wage and salary earners, it is not possible to pass repressive labor legislation without first dividing the workers into "warring camps." As Walter
Reuther said at the National CIO Convention, "They slip it to you while you are
off guard." Between the "Afternoon of a Faun" and the "Moonlight Sonata," a
silky voice on the radio identifies your interest with those of the big companies by telling you how hard they are working to get that new car for you,
to make your home a palace of comfort, and to provide jobs for veterans.

Your Aunt Minnie

A sign in a gift-wrapping department tells you that a present for Aunt
Minnie can't be wrapped the way you want it because there are strikes in the
paper mills; and, of course, when faced with the unpleasant prospect of freezing because your coal bin is empty, you are likely to be proded into taking a
short cut to the nearest person who says he can do something about it.

And in the 80th Congress, there are dozens of experts who say they can do something about it. Yet many of these same men scuttled price control in the last Congress. They are also the ones who let the FEPC bill die a quiet death. Now they propose to make it almost impossible for working people, through collective bargaining, to earn sufficient wages to meet the higher cost of living. They want to break up industry-wide bargaining. They want to have you believe that once unions have "been cut down to size," the nation's economy will be in perfect working order.

One particularly iniquitous argument offered to colored people is that you must be against the closed shop if you advocate FEPC legislation. Some editorial writers have already swallowed this bait, and far too many believe it. These people haven't bothered to read the "fine print" which shows that this same legislation would also strike at union shops, maintenance of membership, and a lot of other things which have been won through the years. Section two of Senate Bill 105 provides that: "No employee and no individual seeking employment in an industry affecting commerce shall be required as a condition of obtaining or retaining employment to join or remain a member of or to support, or to refrain from joining or remaining a member of or supporting any labor organization."

Such a law would be a blow to the 95,000 colored members of the Steel Workers, the 50,000 members of the United Mine Workers, and the 30,000 members of the Packing House Workers. It would cripple the thousands of hotel and restaurant workers who, for the first time, have gotten a toe-hold on security through the use of some of these very contractual provisions.

Union Agreements

The Bureau of Labor Statistics reports that of the 12 million eligible workers in manufacturing in 1945 about sixty-seven per cent or eight million were covered by some kind of union agreement. However, less than twenty per cent of the workers in manufacturing were covered by closed-shop agreements under which the employer hires new workers through the union. About ten per cent were covered by union-shop agreements under which the employer does not hire through the union though new workers must join after a certain period. In non-manufacturing employment, where seventeen million workers were eligible, considerably less than a fifth are covered by closed-shop agreements. Since the closed shop only requires that persons be union members at the time they are hired, no reasonable person can say that employment discrimination will end if we get rid of the closed shop. Some of the industries in which there is the worse discrimination are those which have no closed shop. A good illustration is the railroad industry. It has been the closed mind rather than the closed shop which has kept colored men from being engineers, conductors, and from being many other types of skilled work.

Of course, if the "friends of the colored people" really want to crack discrimination in employment, they will pass an FEPC law with teeth in it. These "pals," however, are just as much against an FEPC as they are in favor of anti-labor legislation. One of them is Senator Clyde Hoey of North Carolina. Speaking at the Waldorf Astoria in New York on December 13 the senator expressed his profound knowledge of the Negro and his problems with this observation: "I read Hambone in the papers. You know Hambone is a character who represents the Negro race." He then explained to the gathering, which happened to be the Fortieth Annual Meeting of Life Insurance Association of America, that the first "long speech" he made in Congress was against the FEPC. A few seconds later he was saying, "I think we have some very unwise and very unfair labor laws now in force. I have been in favor of modifying the Wagner Act. I think it ought to be."

When Senator Hoey referred to his long speech, he meant filibuster. When he said modifying the Wagner Act, he meant destroying it.

The present anti-labor legislation before Congress must be fought by all persons who believe in civil liberty and justice. These attacks on labor can only lead to industrial strife and the destruction of job security. They also result in assaults upon social legislation in general. We must let Congress know, by wire, telephone, and letter, that the people have not given a mandate to Congress to return us to industrial chaos and wage slavery.

The Crisis, 54 (April, 1947): 106-107.

9.   WORLD TRADE UNION PARLEY AND NEGRO LABOR

By James W. Ford

One of the most promising signs of the times is the editorial comment of
the London Times of Feb. 19 on the World Trade Union Conference. The Times
says the World Trade Union Conference "has ended with a notable success," and
adds that "the chance of uniting 'the trade union bodies of freedom-loving
nations irrespective of racial, creed, political, religious or philosophical
differences' has never before been greater.'

This announcement by Britain's most powerful newspaper which exerts wide
influence on British policy throughout the Empire holds special significance
in regard to the establishment of democratic and unmolested trade unions in
colonial countries and particularly in the British colonies of Africa and the
West Indies. It is indeed a hopeful sign when the London Times favors a world
trade union movement based upon freedom-loving peoples irrespective of race or
creed.

On July 1, 1931, the International Conference of Negro Workers was scheduled to be held in London. The British government prohibited the holding of
the conference in London, and leading English dailies fully supported the
policy of the government. The conference was subsequently held at Hamburg,
Germany. In attendance were delegates of trades organizations of labor from
South Africa, from Accra, Gambia, Nigeria and Sierra Leone in West Africa;
from Jamaica and Haiti in the West Indies, as well as representatives of
Negro labor from the United States.

What the British government and the English press seemed to fear at that
time was the perspective of the organization of free trade unions of Negro
laborers. This policy was however, only the policy and attitude of the International Federation of Trade Unions (Amsterdam) towards colored and colonial
labor. The IFTU was essentially a European and American labor organization.
For the leaders of Amsterdam the world did not include colored and colonial
labor in the brotherhood of labor. At times it made pretenses of friendship
for colonial labor by having government-dominated representatives from certain
colonial areas. The record shows that on numerous occasions many of these
fraternal delegates, finding out the true character of the IFTU, protested and
left these international gatherings in disgust. So far as Negro labor was
concerned the IFTU was completely degenerate. The apathy growing out of this
attitude led to the calling of the First International Trade Union Conference
of Negro Workers in 1931.

Present at the conference were regularly elected delegates from the Gold
Coast Carpenters Association and the Gold Coast Drivers Association of Accra;
the Colored Labor's Organization of South Africa; the Gambia Labor Union; the
Nigerian Democratic Workers' Association; the Railroad Workers' Union of Sierra
Leone, and the Railway Workers' Union of Jamaica, West Indies. The conference,
after listening to the reports from the various countries, adopted a program of
simple trade union organization, including the right to organize, shorter hours,
a living wage, social benefits, against forced labor and repressions and a
petition for democratic rights in general in their respective countries. "We
are here for no political controversies," declared the basic report of the
conference. The years following proved particularly fruitful in the stimula-
tion of trade unionism among Negro workers.

The war against fascism has also resulted in the liberalization of trade
union policy towards many Negro colonies. In the British colony of Jamaica,
a strong labor movement has grown up. Concessions have been won from the
British government for a legislative council and in recent elections the Jamaica
Labor Party came out with more than two-thirds majority in the House.

Today we see a new world body of labor formed which does not despise
colored and colonial labor peoples; but which on the contrary, encompasses
delegates from Nigeria, Jamaica, India, China and Latin America as equal
brothers of the world labor movement. Obviously this is a firm democratic
foundation. It is in line with the policies laid down at Teheran, Cairo and
Crimea.

Daily Worker, February 22, 1948.

10. WARN NEGROES OF MATT SMITH

PITTSBURGH, March 7.--Matt Smith has gotten a sharp rebuff from the
Pittsburgh Courier, Negro weekly. The Courier advises workers to join the
CIO and AFL and steer clear of the Confederated Unions of America. This latter
group is the catch-all of company and "independent" unions, which its president Smith, notorious for his strikes and his opposition to the war, is trying
to build up in the East. Affiliates are now confined mostly to Ohio and
Michigan.
     A correspondent for the Courier, Nat Middleton, attended a CUA meeting
in Philadelphia last Sunday, and interviewed the only Negro present, C. E.
Hendricks. He is president of the so-called "Pullman Porters Independent Union of New York City," which claims a national membership of 800. "He admitted," Middleton writes, "that the Confederate Unions of America was not as
liberal on the race question as he had hoped."
     "Mr. Kendricks is attempting to attract other Negroes to this organiza-
tion. . . . I can see no reason why Negro workers should pay the slightest
attention. . . . The wiser course seems to be to join the CIO and AFL in
greater numbers and become a factor in these old-established labor organizations."

Daily Worker, March 8, 1948.

11. FOUL EMPLOYMENT PRACTICE ON THE RAILS

By Charles H. Houston[187]

     This is the story of the fight for economic survival by two groups of
Negro workers on American railroads. I am not talking about the shop craft
men who help keep the rolling stock in repair and running condition. I am not
talking about the maintenance of way men who look after the tracks and the
roadbed. I am not talking about the cooks and waiters, the Red Caps, or the
Pullman Porters. I am talking about the men out on the mainline who help
speed the traffic from terminal to terminal, and the men in the yards who
switch the engines and cars about and make up the trains to go on the road. I
am talking about the Negro firemen and brakemen and switchmen who used to be
all over the South and Southwest forty years ago, but who are vanishing now thru
the organized prejudice and discriminations imposed on them by the national
white operating railroad unions.
     The Bureau of the Census did not make a separate breakdown on Negro and
white firemen, brakemen and switchmen until 1920. The 14th Census in 1920
showed 6,505 Negro firemen in that year. By the 1940 Census the Negro firemen had dwindled to 2,263. The 1920 Census showed a total of 8,275 Negro
brakemen, switchmen, flagmen and yardmen. The 1940 Census gave the total of
Negro brakemen, switchmen, flagmen and yardmen as 2,739.
     Figures are not available showing the number of Negro firemen, brakemen,
switchmen, flagmen and yardmen as of 1949; but if we had them they would show
figures much lower than those for 1940 due to deaths, retirement, discharge
and other reasons. There were no Negro replacements by way of new hiring.
The big-four operating brotherhoods (Brotherhood of Locomotive Engineers,
Brotherhood of Locomotive Firemen & Enginemen, Brotherhood of Railroad Trainmen and Order of Railway Conductors) presented a solid front against the hiring
of Negroes even during the manpower emergency shortage in World War II.
     It is reasonably safe to say that practically no Negro firemen, brakemen,
switchmen, flagmen or yardmen have been hired on Class I American railroads
since 1928.
     On many railroads hiring of Negroes in train and engine service stopped
before that. On the Norfolk & Western Railroad, as the result of a secret
agreement between the railroad and the Brotherhood of Locomotive Firemen and
Enginemen and the Brotherhood of Railroad Trainmen 1909, not a single Negro
fireman or brakeman has been hired in the last forty years, and the last Negro

fireman on the Norfolk & Western has now retired. There are a few Negro
brakemen still left, but they too will soon be gone. For the past fifty years
the Big-four Brotherhoods have been using every means in their power to drive
the Negro train and engine service worker out of employment and create a
"racially closed shop" among the firemen, brakemen, switchmen, flagmen, and
yardmen. They have just about succeeded on the Norfolk & Western and will soon
succeed on all the other railroads in the South and Southwest unless they are
checked by judicial decision and the force of public opinion.

Key Workers

White collar or professional workers often look down on the Negro firemen and brakemen without realizing the strategic role they play in the struggle to democratize the industrial structure of the United States. Transportation workers are always key workers in the industrial structure. A major
transportation strike can paralyze the country; and the Government always
steps in and seizes the railroad on which such a strike is threatened in order
to avoid this economic paralysis.

The transportation workers are usually the most favored industrial workers so far as rates of pay and working conditions are concerned. Hour for
hour of service the firemen and brakemen make more money than most white collar and professional workers. The average brakeman earns from $350.00 to
$400.00 a month; the average fireman from $400.00 to $500.00--with vacation
with pay, and liberal compensation laws. On a fast passenger or fast freight
the fireman or brakeman makes his run in from 90 minutes to three hours and is
then thru for the day. He works on an average of from 20 to 25 days a month.
Unless something goes wrong, a fireman or brakeman does less than thirty
minutes physical work on a road trip; the rest of the time he is sitting still
watching the road and his train. The next time you go to a station or pass by
a railroad switching yard, or ride a fast streamliner, watch and see just how
much physical work the fireman or brakeman is actually doing.

That is part of the secret; the jobs are too soft and the pay too good
for these Big-four Brotherhoods to permit these jobs to be held by Negroes.

Negroes are not the only minority that these Big-four Brotherhoods fight.
Get railroad conscious and ask yourselves how many Latin-American firemen or
brakemen have you seen; how many Japanese-American, or Jewish or Italian?
These Big-four Brotherhoods have the railroad train and engine service tied up
tight for a white monopoly, for a "Nordic closed shop." Every race, color,
and creed has to use the railroads. Every race, color, and creed has to pay
taxes to help support the railroads; but the Big-four Brotherhoods have the
train and engine service reserved for 100 per cent pure Gentile firemen and
brakemen. The census figures for 1940 show the whites have 99.9 per cent of
the railroad conductors, 99.4 per cent of the locomotive engineers, 94.8 per
cent of the locomotive firemen, and 97.4 per cent of the brakemen, switchmen,
flagmen and yardmen. This sounds like an advertisement for "Ivory Soap--99.44
per cent pure."

The Big-four Brotherhoods are rich and powerful. President Whitney of
the Brotherhood of Railroad Trainmen threatened to spend one million dollars
in 1948 to defeat President Truman. He could afford to do this. The Brotherhood of Railroad Trainmen has over 200,000 members. The Brotherhood of Locomotive Firemen & Enginemen has over 100,000 members; the Brotherhood of Locomotive Engineers about 80,000 members and the Order of Railway Conductors some
60,000 members. The four brotherhoods maintain an independent legislative
lobby in Washington. In fact theirs is the oldest labor lobby in Washington.
They helped write the 1934 Railway Labor Act, and each one of the four brotherhoods has its representative sitting on the First Division of the National
Railroad Adjustment Board which has jurisdiction over all grievances affecting
train and engine service employees, including firemen, brakemen, switchmen,
flagmen and yardmen.

Shocking Testimony

During World War II the President's Committee on Fair Employment Practice
was able to integrate minority workers in many industries, but it was not able
to budge the Big-four Brotherhoods one inch. The FEPC in 1943 cited the four
brotherhoods because all of them have clauses in their constitution excluding

Negroes from membership and because of their hostile and discriminatory acts
against Negro train and engine service workers. The Big-four Brotherhoods
ignored the charges. The FEPC held a four-day hearing in Washington in September, 1943, on discriminations against minority railroad workers as impeding
the war effort. The Big-four Brotherhoods refused to attend the hearings,
send representatives, or to submit any evidence. The FEPC issued its directives against the carriers and the railroad unions. Neither obeyed the directives, but instead both the carriers and the unions preferred charges
against the FEPC before the Smith Committee of the House of Representatives.
The lawyer for the Railway Labor Executives Association stated to the Smith
Committee that if the directives of the FEPC ordering elimination of the color
bar in the brotherhood constitutions and of the discriminatory working conditions were carried out the organizations would not be responsible for what
their membership might do.

The Big-four Brotherhoods never felt the necessity of defending their acts
of discrimination, any place, except in court, until this spring. Then they
were called before a sub-committee of the House Committee on Education and
Labor presided over by Congressman Adam C. Powell of New York, who was holding
hearings on his FEPC Bill H.R. 4453.

Congressman Powell was so shocked by the testimony of discrimination put
in the record against the Big-four Brotherhoods that he issued telegrams to the
heads of the four organizations requesting them to appear. He dropped a hint
that if they did not appear he was going to issue subpoenas, that he wanted
them to know they were dealing with a committee of the Congress and not with
a war-time FEPC. The four brotherhoods appeared on schedule. The presidents
did not come. Even when they were licked they wanted to make a last show of
defiance. But the vice-presidents came, and if you ever read their testimony
before the Powell committee you will see how the most powerful can squirm when
they are finally exposed in the floodlight of public opinion.

This article might sound anti-labor or anti-union; but basically we are
not fighting the brotherhoods as such. What we are fighting is discrimination
and jim-crow in the brotherhoods. Nobody recognizes more than the Negro firemen and brakemen how much the Big-four Brotherhoods have done generally to raise
wages and improve working conditions on the railroads. What the Negro firemen
and brakemen complain about is that the Big-four Brotherhoods raise wages and
improve working conditions, then just as soon as the wages are raised and
working conditions improved, they set about to limit or to completely eliminate
the Negro from the road.

Origin of Brotherhood

The history of aggression of the Big-four Brotherhoods against the Negro
firemen and brakemen goes way back. In every major war the United States has
fought since railroading began the unions have put their prejudices over and
above the national safety. The Brotherhood of Locomotive Engineers is the
oldest of the big-four. It started under the name of the Brotherhood of the
Footboard on the Michigan Central in 1863. Part of the reason was resentment
against the Michigan Central's proposing to hire some Negro firemen during the
manpower shortage caused by the Civil War.

In World War I the Baltimore & Ohio and the New York, New Haven & Hartford,
which up to that time had hired only white firemen, proposed to hire some Negro
firemen to tide them over the war emergency. Both the Grand Chief Engineer
of the Brotherhood of Locomotive Engineers and the President of the Brotherhood
of Locomotive Firemen & Enginemen instructed their members to refuse to work
with Negro firemen on any railroad which up to the War had had a pure white
hiring force. The Brotherhood of Railroad Trainmen in its official journal in
October, 1917, announced that its organization was in full accord with the
Engineers and Firemen, and advised its membership to notify the President of the
Brotherhood of Railroad Trainmen as soon as they received an intimation that
any railroad was contemplating hiring Negroes for freight, yard or passenger
service on jobs theretofore held by white men.

In World War II the Brotherhood of Locomotive Firemen & Enginemen put out
a strike ballot to prevent the hiring of additional Negro firemen on the
Atlantic Coast Line where Negroes had been working as firemen ever since there
had been an Atlantic Coast Line. Hundreds of white firemen had been hired by
the Coast Line during World War II. But not a single Negro fireman had been

hired by the Coast Line since 1929. Yet the Firemen's Brotherhood was willing
to strike, without regard to its effect on the war effort, rather than let a
single new Negro fireman be hired.

On the St. Louis-San Francisco Railroad not a Negro fireman or brakeman had
been hired since 1928 due to a blanket agreement the four brotherhoods had
forced the Frisco to sign under strike threat not to hire any more Negro firemen or brakemen. In 1944 after the Battle of the Bulge, when the United States
was straining every nerve and sinew against Germany and Japan, the Frisco
management approached the four Brotherhoods to get their consent to hiring
some Negro firemen and brakemen during the war emergency on the Southern Division from Memphis to Birmingham, where Negro firemen and brakemen had been
working since 1894. All four brotherhoods replied that they were unalterably
opposed to the hiring of a single Negro fireman or brakeman.

Negroes Not Wanted

Inch by inch, and yard by yard, down thru the years, the brotherhoods
have been choking off the employment rights of Negro train and engine service
employees. In 1890 the Trainmen, Conductors, Firemen and Switchmen's Mutual
Aid Association demanded that all Negroes in the train, yard, and locomotive
service of the Houston & Texas Central Railway System be removed and white men
employed in their places. In 1898 the Trainmen tried to get all the Negro
brakemen removed from the Missouri Pacific System. In 1899 the four brotherhoods had all the colored porters on the Gulf, Colorado and Santa Fe Railway
passenger trains removed and replaced by white brakemen.

In 1908 the Brotherhood of Locomotive Engineers voted to organize the
railway engineers in South America and sent a vice-president down for that
purpose. In 1910 that officer reported back to the Engineers' convention that
the reason he did not attempt to organize the railway engineers in Cuba was
because there was no way of telling the "nigger" from the white man.

In 1909 the Firemen's Brotherhood staged a bitter and violent strike
against Negro firemen on the Georgia Railroad, demanding white supremacy and
the replacement of Negro firemen by whites. In 1910 the Trainmen and the
Conductors negotiated what is called the Washington Agreement with most of the
Southeast railroads providing that no more Negroes were to be employed as bag-
gageman, flagman, or yard foreman; they followed up in 1911 by negotiating a
similar agreement with some of the railroads in the Mississippi Valley.

In 1914 the four brotherhoods joined in a letter to Colonel Goethals of
the Panama Canal demanding the removal of Negro engineers, firemen, conductors
and brakemen from the railroads at the Panama Canal, stating that it was the
policy of the four brotherhoods in the United States to oppose the use of
Negroes as engineers, firemen, conductors, or brakemen on the railroads in the
United States.

In 1919 while the railroads were under Federal Control in World War I the
Brotherhood of Railroad Trainmen demanded of the United States Director General
of Railroads that he guarantee the brotherhood a majority of men employed, so
that contracts made by the brotherhood could be protected by the brotherhood.
The Trainmen further notified the United States Southern Regional Director, Mr.
Winchell, that it desired to negotiate an agreement which would thereafter prevent the employment of Negroes in train and yard service.

The list is too long for all the acts of aggression to be pointed out.
We have already pointed out the attitudes of the brotherhoods in putting their
prejudices above the national safety in World Wars I and II. We close this
part of our survey by noting that in 1940 the Firemen's Brotherhood served a
notice on the Southeastern carriers which if adopted would have driven every
Negro fireman out of service within a year. Also in the 1940's the Brotherhood
of Railroad Trainmen, facing losses of jobs for their members because of streamlined trains, diesel engines, and competition of bus and air lines, began raiding
or trying to drive off all the Negro train porters, who are really passenger
brakemen on the head-end of the passenger trains, and have them replaced by
white brotherhood members. They have tried this on the Santa Fe, the M.K.T,
the Frisco, the Missouri Pacific and other roads.

Negro Trainporter (Brakeman)

The story of the Negro train porter is a story in itself and illustrates

how the Negro has been exploited by railroad management as well as persecuted
by white railroad labor which has refused to recognize the essential economic
unity of interest between white and black workers in the same craft.

The Negro trainporter on the head end of the passenger trains does all
the braking work, and in addition handles mail, baggage, takes care of the
passengers and sweeps out the coaches enroute; but because he is black, the
railroads classify him as a "porter" and refuse to pay him even a brakeman's
pay. During World War I while the railroads were under federal control the
Negro trainporter was actually classed as a passenger brakeman and paid standard brakeman's pay. But when the railroads were turned back to private ownership, the private management reclassified the Negro as a trainporter and cut
his pay in half. The Negro is the only American railroad worker who the more
he does the less he is paid.

Most people are familiar with the subterfuge the Pullman Company used to
employ of sending a Pullman car out in charge of a Pullman porter, calling him
"Porter-in-charge" in order to keep from recognizing him as a Pullman conductor and paying him a conductor's pay altho he did everything a Pullman conductor iid.

Equally familiar is the subterfuge of the railroad companies in sending
out dining cars in charge of waiters who do everything a steward does, but to
keep from recognizing the waiter-in-charge as a steward and paying him steward's pay, the railroads call him "waiter-in-charge" and give him a pat on the
head and a few pence in his palm. During the War the FEPC tried to find out
the difference between a steward and a waiter-in-charge, and finally came to
the conclusion that outside of recognition and pay the only difference was that
the steward had a white face and black coat, while the waiter-in-charge had a
black face and a white coat.

Hat in Hand

For a long time the Negro railway worker did not know their rights, did
not know how to fight. They depended on making friends and being humble to
management, as in the pitiful tragic letter of April 7, 1928, which the Negro
brakeman wrote to the president and vice-president of the Frisco lines in
1928 when the four brotherhoods clubbed the Frisco into agreeing never to hire
any more Negro firemen or brakemen:

Dear Sir:
We the undersigned colored (freight) brakemen of the Tupelo and Birmingham Sub. Div. wish to petition your sovereignty by asking you farther privilege
to meet you in a personal conference which is of a very serious nature and
vital interest to us. Dear Mr. Kurn, we feel with all due respect to our
superior officials that you are our only refuge in this most (terrible) calamity that has happened in the history of this your magnificent railroad.
Hoping you will give this your earliest attention, Yours truly,

Limit Brown, Gen. Chr (man) 17 yrs. service
Jim Judge, Local   "   13 yrs. service
Abe Smith, Local   "   14 yrs. service

or in this follow-up letter of April, 1928:

Mr. J. E. Hutchinson, Vice President of St. L. and S.F. RR
Dear Sir:
We the undersigned Colored freight brakemen are the humble and submissive
voices of the colored brakemen of the Tupelo and Birmingham Sub. Div. wish to
petition your *majesty* to meet you in a conference to ascertain why and what
accusations you have against us and our posterity to cast us off in old age
after serving you most faithfully for over a decade and almost half our lives.
Dear Mr. Hutchinson. If it be possible for us to remedy such an accusation we are more than willing to do all there is in our power to remove the
obstacles which hinder the free and embarrassed actions of those about us,
thanking you in advance for any consideration you may give us, we beg to remain your servants for ever.
Limit Brown, Chr., 17 yrs. service
Abe Smith

Of course Mr. Kurn and Mr. Hutchinson did absolutely nothing.

To bring the story to a close, about ten years ago two small Negro organizations of firemen and brakemen started to fight. It probably sounds like David and Goliath when one realizes that the Trainmen alone had 200,000 members while there were just 2,739 Negro brakemen, switchmen, and yardmen both in and out the two Negro organizations; 100,000 members in the Brotherhood of Locomotive Firemen & Enginemen while there were only 2,263 Negro firemen in the entire railroad industry; most of them unorganized.

There was no use in the Negro workers going to Congress and asking for remedial legislation. Congress, unfortunately, on most occasions shows itself more concerned with votes than principle. In addition the Negro firemen and brakemen were all in Southern states, and *Smith v. Allwright* had not been handed down ten years ago to crack the white primary. The only place the organization could wage their fight was in the courts.

So the Association of Colored Railway Trainmen & Locomotive Firemen with headquarters in Roanoke, Virginia, and the International Association of Railway Employees with headquarters in Memphis started out. They have been joined by the Colored Trainmen of America from Kingsville, Texas. And recently five Negro railway labor unions: the Association of Colored Railway Employees, the Colored Trainmen of America, the Southern Association of Colored Railway Trainmen and Firemen from North Carolina, and the Dining Car and Railroad Food Workers Union of New York have joined hands and formed the Negro Railway Labor Executives Committee, which issues its own bi-monthly bulletin to educate the Negro railroad workers as to their rights and to keep them advised of the cases which are being carried thru the courts.

In their first bulletin issued June, 1948 they stated:

We Negro workers are no strangers, no newcomers to the industry. We were at work, firing and laying tracks when railroading was still in its infancy. . . . the first steam locomotive to run on U.S. tracks . . . was called the "Best Friend of Charleston" and in December 1830 first ran the six-mile stretch of the Charleston & Hamburg RR. *The firemen on that first engine was a Negro fireman. . . .*

Our fathers and grandfathers pioneered the industry. We will not be driven out more than 100 years later.

The Association of Colored Railway Trainmen & Locomotive Firemen and the International Association of Railway Employees carried the Steele and Tunstall cases to the Supreme Court of the United States, which established the basic principle that a majority union under the Railway Labor Act cannot make contracts which discriminate against the non-member minority workers (323 U.S. 192,210). They are now working on cases in the United States District Courts in the District of Columbia, Louisville, Kentucky, and St. Louis, Missouri, which, if won, will establish the principle that a railroad union has no right to represent a non-member minority worker unless it gives him the chance to elect the officials who conduct the collective bargaining process, to censure and remove them, as possessed by the union members. If these cases are won the jim-crow union membership will be nothing but an empty shell.[188]

In the federal courts in the District of Columbia and Louisville, Kentucky, the International Association of Railway Employees has obtained injunctions against the Firemen's Brotherhood putting forth proposals affecting Negro firemen's working conditions without first calling in the Negro firemen and giving them an opportunity to be heard and to vote on the propositions. Then, even if outvoted, we can still fall back on the Steele and Tunstall cases which establish the principle that the majority union cannot make a contract which unfairly discriminates against the non-member minority workers.

In the federal court in St. Louis the Association of Colored Railway Trainmen & Locomotive Firemen is conducting the Tillman case against the four brotherhoods and the Frisco in one lump trying to obtain a ruling that it violates the Railway Labor Act, the Federal Civil Rights Act and the Constitution of the United States for a railroad and a union to make a contract not to hire any qualified worker on the irrelevant and invidious distinctions of race, color, creed or national origin. That case is not over, but we are happy to report that on April 25, 1949, the Association forced the four brotherhoods to come into court and cancel the iniquitous contract of March 14, 1928, wherein they had forced the Frisco to agree never to hire any more Negro firemen or brakemen.[189]

In Chicago the International is striking at the packed National Railroad
Adjustment Board which has its First Division packed with representatives from
the four big brotherhoods, all of which exclude Negroes from membership. And
credit is due to Richard R. Westbrooks of Chicago, representing the trainporters
on the Santa Fe, who saved their jobs by an injunction against the Santa Fe and
the Brotherhood of Railroad Trainmen against a decision of the packed First
Division of the Adjustment Board giving the Santa Fe trainporters' jobs away to
the white brotherhood brakemen.

The Negro railway labor organizations have now been battling ten years.
They are prepared to battle ten or twenty years more, because what they are
doing is basic to the whole concept of economic democracy. Every principle
which they establish for railroads can be applied to every other public utility:
gas, electricity, telephone and telegraph, bus lines and air lines, every
industry affected with a public interest. As the Negro Railway Labor Executives Association announced: "Other fathers and grandfathers pioneered the
railway industry, and we intend to hold this employment and broaden its base
until every vestige of segregation and discrimination, and every limitation on
a man's right to hold a job on the railroad based on race, creed, color or
national origin, is wiped out. When we do this we shall have gained a victory
not only for ourselves but we shall have gained a victory for the white railroad workers by freeing them from their prejudice and their fears; because
they are imprisoned just as much as we are."

The Crisis, 56 (October, 1949): 269-71, 284-85.

12. AFL CONVENTION, 1949

PRESENTATION OF PLAQUE TO PRESIDENT GREEN BY THE
BROTHERHOOD OF SLEEPING CAR PORTERS

DELEGATE RANDOLPH: President Green, officers, members and delegates to
the Sixty-Eighth Annual Convention of the American Federation of Labor:

On behalf of the officers and members of the Brotherhood of Sleeping Car
Porters and the delegates to this convention, Milton P. Webster, First International Vice-President, and Frank Boyd, Secretary-Treasurer of the Twin
Cities Division, we take the highest pleasure and privilege and honor in presenting to you, President Green, a symbol of the esteem, affection and love of
the officers and members of the Brotherhood of Sleeping Car Porters entertain
and hold for you. We hold you in high esteem because of your support and
cooperation with our organization in the days of its darkest struggles, and
also because of your fight for the elimination of discrimination because of
race, color, religion, national origin or ancestry.

Division in the ranks of labor because of race, color, religion, national
origin or ancestry weakens the labor movement and disarms it in its fight to
achieve higher wage rates, improved working conditions, shorter hours of work,
democracy and peace. You, Brother William Green, President of the American
Federation of Labor, have given of your talents and ability and the prestige
and power of your office, as the head of the great American Federation of
Labor to help eliminate all forms of discrimination and segregation from the
labor movement. The Brotherhood of Sleeping Car Porters, which is committed
to protect and safeguard the rights and advance the cause of its members, and
also dedicated to fight to abolish racial and religious discrimination, takes
great joy in presenting to you this plaque as a token of appreciation of the
important, far-reaching, constructive and uncompromising role you have played
and are playing to fulfill the historic mission of the trade union movement in
seeking to achieve the well-being of all wage earners regardless of race, creed,
color, national origin or ancestry.

In the early days of the struggle of the Brotherhood of Sleeping Car Porters, you, whenever called upon for support and cooperation, never failed to
respond.

A cursory examination of the problems of minorities and labor will reveal
that the struggle to exterminate racial and religious discrimination cannot be

separated from the fight against inequality and insecurity, as well as the
social and psychological uncertainties and frustrations that arise therefrom.

We of the Brotherhood of Sleeping Car Porters are happy to take this
occasion to express our thanks for the fact that you, along with other officers
of the AFL, have invariably and consistently made it known that the AFL regards
racial and religious intolerance, bigotry and discrimination as a grave menace
to the trade union movement.

In your speeches to the annual conventions of the AfL, and at conventions
of the Brocherhood of Sleeping Car Porters, you have pointed out in unmistakable
terms, that the practice of playing upon prejudices, racial, religious and
national, is followed by brutal attacks upon the labor movement itself.

The Brotherhood of Sleeping Car Porters congratulates you and the AFL on
the fight you are making for the enactment of federal legislation for a Fair
Employment Practice Committee.

We honor you because you have fought and still fight to abolish the Poll
Tax that all men may vote.

We honor you because you have fought and still fight to eradicate the
disgrace of lynch-law from our land.

We honor you because you stand against jim-crow and discrimination in our
armed forces, believing that every boy who gives his life for our country
should have the right to die as a free man.

We honor you because of your support of federal aid to education, without
discrimination.

We honor you because of your uncompromising opposition to Communism and
Fascism that are bent upon the destruction of free trade unionism everywhere.

Our Brotherhood realizes that the fight against racial discrimination and
segregation cannot be separated from the fight against discrimination and hatred
against all groups, Jews, Catholics, Orientals, Mexicans, foreign born and
labor.

Anthropological and psychological studies of prejudice unequivocally
establish that in the main, people who are prejudiced against one minority
group, are hostile to other minority groups. Thus, an attempt to fight discrimination on account of race, while disregarding movements of anti-Semitism,
anti-Catholicism, anti-foreignism and anti-liberalism, would be ineffective,
futile and naive. So long as a Jew in Poland, or a Catholic in Czechoslovakia,
or a Japanese in California, or a Hindu in Vancouver, Canada, or a Mexican in
Texas is denied fundamental human and civil rights, the security of the Negro,
or for that matter, a white-Protestant in the labor movement or anywhere,
cannot be assured.

Verily, the fight for justice and freedom for minorities and labor is
indivisible, because freedom and justice are indivisible.

Because of the aforementioned reasons and facts, the Brotherhood of Sleeping Car Porters, seeing that the powerful and menacing forces of Communism in
the United States, Europe, Asia and Africa are seeking to split or control the
labor movement and minorities, white and colored, takes this occasion of viewing
this presentation of this plaque to you, President Green, as a challenge and
refutation to the vicious misrepresentations and violent psychological warfare
being waged by totalitarian Communist Russia and her satellites against a free
trade union movement, the Negro liberation movement, and the cause of the
Western democracies in general and the democracy of the United States of America
in particular.

We believe that labor's and democracy's best answer to Communism is to be
true to itself, true to its traditions and struggles, its hopes and faiths.
Democracy can only answer Communism with a frank and honest recognition of the
essential worth, value and equality of every human personality, without regard
to race, color, religion, national origin or ancestry. Any equivocation of this
principle of equality will be fatal to the cause of democracy.

Neither armies nor atomic bombs are as potent in the protection of democracy and our judeo-Christian heritage as the high moral principle of the
Brotherhood of Man and the decent and honest respect for every human being,
whether he be Catholic or Jew, native or foreign, white or black, brown or
yellow, man or woman, rich or poor.

The grave question before the workers today is which ideology, democracy
or Communism, will win the minds, wills, hearts, allegiances and souls of the
millions of workers in America and Europe; which ideology will capture the

imagination and minds of the teeming missions of the peoples of color in the
United States, the West Indies, Africa, Asia and the Isles of the Sea.

Let us be warned that this is the issue and we don't have long to decide.
The sands are running out and if we fail to build a bastion of freedom among the
peoples of color of the Americas and the world and the workers everywhere outside the Soviet orbit, we may not be able to withstand the rising tides of red
tyranny.

Mighty militant ideas are on the march across the world. This is an
ideological age. We are in the midst of an ideological war. A program of
mere anti-Communism is not enough. We need a dynamic program of pro-democracy;
yes, Christian democracy not only political but industrial, economic and ethnic.

Verily, labor still has some way to go to remove all barriers of race or
color, but thank God, we are on our way.

Let us weld our diversities into a creative unity for the victory of the
principles of a free trade union movement and the dignity of the human spirit
over the deadening forces of materialism, hate and war.

It is possible that this occasion of expression of the simple and common
principles, ideals and values of love, respect, cooperation and unity, with
high moral purposes between representatives of two great racial groups, may at
this time of great world tension, serve as one of the decisive factors in
directing the destiny of peoples of color and labor along the path of democracy
and human rights.

Men of all races, colors, religions and climes are hungry for peace. They
are hungry for love. They are hungry for a living faith in themselves and their
fellow men. Yes, millions, too, hunger for bread. They stretch out their arms
to our great country, and they look to the mighty millions of men of labor in
our land for hope and help.

But, we cannot give them peace. We cannot give them faith. We cannot
give democracy. We cannot give them leadership and love until we create and
nourish and practice them here, ourselves; practice them with each other.

Yes, we are rich in land and machines. We have powerful unions in members
and money. We excel in material resources. But, this is not sufficient. We
need riches of the spirit. We need new and vital, dynamic resources of the
soul. Yes, we must develop a moral rearmament which can and will conquer the
arrogant, ideological minions of Stalinist Russia and give man the fresh,
living waters of peace and good will toward all mankind.

Humble porters, and their officials, on the trains that cover the nation,
giving of themselves for service, salute you, President Green. Forward with
the torch of human dignity and liberty under the banner of the American Federation of Labor and the free trade union movement of the world.

At the conclusion of his remarks Delegate Randolph presented to President
Green a plaque with a copper engraving mounted on mahogany and bearing the
following inscription:

*For Distinguished Service in the Fight for the Abolition of Racial Dis-
crimination in the Labor Movement, Presented to William Green, President of
the American Federation of Labor, Sixty-Eighth Annual Convention, October 3,
1949, Saint Paul, Minnesota, by the Brotherhood of Sleeping Car Porters International Union, Affiliate, A.F. of L.*

In the center of the plaque was a replica of a sleeping car porter in
uniform.

PRESIDENT GREEN:

President Randolph, Mr. Webster, and associates: I am deeply touched by
the eloquent statement you made and by your presentation to me of this beautiful
plaque. I cannot find words or language at the moment that will adequately
express my thanks, gratitude and appreciation for this plaque which you have
presented me on this occasion.

But aside from that, I am sure that every delegate in attendance at this
convention was tremendously impressed by the impressive and eloquent address
which you delivered. Coming as it does from you, the President of the Brotherhood of Sleeping Car Porters' organization, and those you represent, it must
be regarded as most significant and wonderful. I ask you, fellow delegates,
isn't it wonderful?

Here is a splendid organization made up of colored workers organized in
the American Federation of Labor some few years ago, that has grown and expanded and developed until it is now a very vital and effective force in
collective bargaining, and in our great organized labor movement. Surely we
must interpret this impressive address as meaning that as a result of af-
filation with our great movement there has developed among these colored
workers who make up this splendid organization, a new, a keener, and more comprehensive sense and understanding of the economic, social, and industrial
philosophy of the American Federation of Labor.

Along with my colleagues connected with the Federation of Labor we have
learned and understood early in life that it was impossible to establish the
brotherhood of man--and our organization is based upon that principle--until
we first recognize that every man of character and standing, regardless of
creed, color, or nationality, must be permitted to join and work with all
other workers in the nation. I cannot conceive of the establishment of that
principle and that organization anywhere or anyplace until those who advocate
brotherhood practice brotherhood and express themselves repeatedly over and over
again as opposed to discrimination because of creed, color, or nationality
anywhere, anyplace in the United States of America.

We have grown and developed and expanded, serving in that capacity and
preaching that unchallenged doctrine. We are advocating that unchallenged
doctrine. We are advocating it. We stand for it. We are united. We are
going to make it more effective in the future than we have in the past.

I want these brothers to carry that message back, tell them that they
can rely upon this brotherhood, the American Federation of Labor, to practice
and preach brotherhood everywhere, every place, and to fight against discrimination because of race, creed, color, or nationality anywhere or any
place.

I want to thank you from the bottom of my heart for this beautiful plaque
you presented me this morning, and I want to assure you that I shall always
retain it among my priceless possessions, placing emphasis upon its intrinsic
value and still more, upon the sentiments which I know it expresses.

Proceedings of the 69th annual convention of the American Federation of Labor,
1949, pp. 328-31.

13. BLACKS IN THE LABOR UNIONS: NEW ORLEANS, 1950

New Orleans does not have a large number of major industrial plants.
There are only five industries which may be considered in the category of
large industries. These are:
    Todd Johnson Shipbuilders and Dry Dock--now engaged primarily in ship
repairs.
    Higgins Shipbuilding Company--since the war, engaged mostly in the build-
ing of pleasure crafts.
    Celotex
    Penick-Ford--engaged in molasses manufacturing
    Lane Cotton Mills

All of these plants employ Negroes, but mostly as unskilled workers.
Negroes are members of labor unions in the above industries. Lane Cotton Mills
has the largest number of Negroes of any single employer, using approximately
300 in a total force of 1,600.
    According to officials in both the AF of L and CIO unions, there are
approximately 30,000 Negroes in labor unions in New Orleans, many of which
(unions) are interracial.
    The General Longshore Workers Union, Local #1419, with a membership of
approximately 3,200 Negroes, is perhaps the largest Negro union in the nation.
Negro and white longshoremen are members of separate unions but work on the
same job and sign the same contracts. The union has five representatives in
the Central Trades Labor Council and is entitled to twelve delegates to the

State Federation of Labor. Members of both Negro and white longshoremen's unions are members of the same Council. One Meeting is held each quarter among the total Negro and white membership. At one meeting the Negro president presides and the white president serves as secretary. In the following meeting the order is reversed. Local #1419 has been one of the politically active groups in the city. Recently a person was employed by the union on a full-time basis to teach union and non-union residents how to qualify to vote and how to use voting machinery. . . .

Both Negro and white union officials expressed the opinion that, on the whole, labor relations between Negroes and whites in New Orleans are exceptionally good. They agreed, however, that there have been evidences of discrimination toward Negroes which have impeded the building of a strong united front in labor.

The National Union of Marine Cooks and Stewards has done more to protect the interests of its Negro membership than any of the other local unions. . . .

In the International Brotherhood of Teamsters, Local #965, which is a mixed AFL local, Negroes hold positions of president, vice-president, secretary-treasurer, and trustees.

Louis Stark, manager of the Laundry Workers of America, stated that the relationship between Negroes and whites in his local is good. The president of the union is colored. Negroes are also stewards and committeemen.

The president and general manager of the General Truck Drivers and Chauffeurs Union stated that there may be internal feelings between Negroes and whites toward each other, but these are not allowed to affect affairs in the union. The Negro elected officers, he stated, were chosen with good white support. The assistant business manager and organizer of the union are Negroes.

There are six Negro members in Local #2369 of the United Steel Workers of America, CIO, and all of these are good members according to Ralph J. Levison, president. . . .

Negro plumbers are consistently denied membership in the local plumbers union. The local policy of the union states that a prospective member must have his application vouched for by a member of the organization. This rule is a disadvantage for Negroes because no white member has ever vouched for a Negro. Negroes in New Orleans who engage in plumbing work are under the supervision of white licensed plumbers. There are two certified Negro plumbers in the city; both are certified by the union and the city. Because of the union policy they have not been elected into membership in the union.

There is an almost unanimous acceptance in all AFL and CIO unions of equal pay for equal work among Negro and white union members. The major problem among Negro union members is in the shipbuilding industry where they have difficulty in getting upgraded. . . .

It was the opinion of observers. . . that there are employers who refuse to employ Negro union workers if their wages are to be the same as white workers. Several Negro craftsmen advised the writer that some contractors still just refuse to employ Negro union members. In the construction of the Le Garde Hospital in 1941, it is claimed that the white union painters refused to work on the job with Negro painters who were also union men in another local. The engineer in charge of the job designated a number of the buildings for Negroes to work on in order to provide them with employment. It should be pointed out that this type of discrimination no longer exists among white union painters.

Little is done in an organized way to foster workers' education by the AFL or CIO.

The AFL recently sponsored two workers' education meetings for business agents of their unions. These meetings, held at Dillard University, were attended by approximately 80 per cent of the business agents of all AFL locals.

George Snowden is the leading Negro spokesman and a person of special influence in the AFL union. He is a member of the Central Trades Council and head of the workers' education program which he initiated and had adopted by the Council. In 1948 he became a vice-president of the State Federation of Labor, the first Negro to be elected to that position in Louisiana.

PARTIAL LIST OF AF OF L AND CIO UNION MEMBERS
New Orleans, Louisiana: 1950

Union	Total Member-ship	White	Negro
International Union of United Brewery Workers and Beer	141	141	0
International Brotherhood of Teamsters Local #965, AFL	500	100	400
United Steel Workers of America Local #2369, CIO	280	274	6
Ship Carpenters, Caulkers and Joiners of America, #584, AFL	325	300	25
Laundry Workers Join Board Amalgamated International Workers of America	900	300	600
General Truck Drivers, Chauffeurs and Helpers, Local #270, AFL	1,430	770	630
Distillery Workers, Local 168, CIO	120	80	40
United Steel Workers of America Local #2179, CIO	103	103	0
United Wholesale, Warehouse Workers, CIO	200	–	200
Textile Workers of America	2,500	1,997	503
Amalgamated Lithographers, Local #53	75	75	–
National Union of Marine Cooks and Stewards, CIO	6,000	3,500	2,500
Building and Common Laborers, AFL	2,000	160	1,840
Longshoremen's Locals, #1418, # 1419 AFL	3,500	300	3,200
Transport Workers, Local #206, CIO	500	48	452

"A Review of the Economic Problems of New Orleans, La., February – March, 1950," Department of Research and Community Projects, National Urban League report, pp. 44-58.

14. CIO SEEKS END OF SEGREGATION IN OKLAHOMA UNIVERSITY

The CIO last week hopped into the middle of a major legal fight against state-enforced segregation of Negroes.

In the U.S. Supreme Court the CIO filed a "friend of the court" brief backing up G. W. McLaurin in his fight to put an end to segregation practices at the Univ. of Oklahoma Law School.

The university, having lost a fight to bar Negroes from the school, instituted a strict segregation set-up. McLaurin was forced to sit in a special section of the classroom, eat in a corner of the cafeteria, use a special desk at the law school library.

McLaurin protested in the courts that this scheme was in violation of the Fourteenth Amendment to the Constitution. The CIO brief was filed in support of his case, which comes up before the nation's highest court this week.

Two other important discrimination cases are due to come up at the same time. One of the cases is Henderson vs. U.S., which challenges the right of Southern railroads to set up segregated dining car services for Negroes.

The Interstate Commerce Commission had approved the railroad's policy, but U.S. Solicitor General Philip Perlman, who represents Uncle Sam in arguments before the Supreme Court--has agreed with Henderson and opposed the ICC position.

The other case is Sweatt vs. Painter which involves the refusal of the Univ. of Texas Law School to admit a qualified Negro as a student. The CIO was barred from filing a friend-of-the-court brief in that state by the objections of the Texas attorney general.

The CIO brief in the McLaurin case was filed by General Counsel Arthur J. Goldberg.

"The question is only whether a state may require segregation for the sake of segregation, nothing more," Goldberg said in his McLaurin argument.

The Oklahoma Univ. rule, he charged, "is not to permit them (the students) to practice segregation but to require them to do so."

Objective of this type of regulation, the CIO added, is not to preserve public order--since there had been no evidence of disturbances or threats. "The purpose and intent . . . whatever may be the justification offered, is to stamp the Negro as inferior and to require, in the field of higher education, the preservation and maintenance of the policy of 'white supremacy.' "

"The issue which the Court must decide is whether such regulations meet the requirements of the Fourteenth Amendment that no state shall deny to its citizens 'the equal protection of the laws.' Once the issue is clearly seen, we submit that only a negative answer is possible."

The issue in the case, Goldberg's statement added, can be confused only by use of the "false assumption" of Negro inferiority and of the belief that no white persons ever want to associate with Negroes.

"The assumption is false," the CIO brief said. "The CIO is living proof that it is false. And, apart from matters of proof, certainly such an assumption . . . has no place in our constitutional doctrine.

"The Court should hold that such compulsory segregation is, per se, unconstitutional because it deprives both whites and Negroes of freedom of choice because of color, and nothing else."

CIO News, April 3, 1950.

15.

NEGRO WOMEN WORKERS: UNION LEADER CHALLENGES PROGRESSIVE AMERICA

By Vicki Garvin
(Vice President, Distributive, Processing and Office Workers)

If it is true, as has often been stated, that a people can rise no higher than its women, then Negro people have a long way to go before reaching the ultimate goal of complete freedom and equality in the United States.

Latest figures on the job status of Negro women dramatically point up the inescapable fact that they are at the very bottom of the nation's economic ladder. A glance at the record shows that the average Negro woman in the U.S.:

Earns only $13 per week.
Is forced into the dirtiest, least desirable jobs.
Puts in abnormally long hours.

By and large, Negro women today are living and working under conditions reminiscent of the plantation era, even though slavery was ostensibly abolished by constitutional amendment some 85 years ago. When it's considered that seven out of every 10 Negro women workers are chained to menial service jobs as farm hands, domestics, etc., where in addition to low pay and deplorable working conditions, human dignity is least respected, it can readily be seen that raising the level of women generally and Negro women in particular is an acid test for democracy at this crucial point in history.

Low Pay in Boom

Even during the peak period of World War II when pay envelopes were considered to be fatter than ever before, domestic workers, both Negro and white, averaged a take-home pay of only $339 per year.

In New York City, where one-half of all Negro women at work are domestics, labor officials admit that the present average work day is 13 and 14 hours long.

In the South, the situation is complicated by the fact that while only
50 per cent of white women workers have found employment as clerks, saleswomen
and factory workers, Negro women for all practical purposes are barred from
these "white collar" and semi-skilled jobs. In fact, the income of the average
Negro family in southern rural areas is a substandard $942 yearly.

The Negro woman worker, whether married or single, faces the additional
burden of feeding one or more dependents besides herself. As a member of a
family whose average income in urban centers is but $42 a week, Negro women
have no choice but to find employment to help meet basic food, clothing and
shelter needs.

In the case of white families, where the average income is $75 weekly,
the pressure upon children to leave school and seek work is not nearly so
severe as it is among Negroes. Yet, significantly, more than half of all
Negro college students are women. The reverse is true of white students.

Getting a husband is not the answer for the Negro woman's search for
security and release from back breaking toil, for the proportion of Negro
women who enter the labor force after marriage is much higher than the one
out of five rate for white women. When most Negro women think about marriage
and children, it is almost a foregone conclusion that she will become a co-
breadwinner.

Freedom, November 1950.

16. COURT OUTLAWS RAILROAD-UNION JIM CROW DEAL

Charlotte, N.C.--". . . *No railroad in the United States has ever employed
a Negro as engineer. . . . Because railroads do not permit Negroes to hold
engineer's posts is no reason that the bargaining agent representing them
should use bargaining power to deprive them of desirable positions as firemen,
which railroads permit them to hold."*

This was the gist of an opinion handed down by the U.S. Fourth Circuit
Court of Appeals January 3. The court reversed a lower court decision which
permitted railroads to restrict hiring of Negroes as firemen. Senior Judge
John J. Parker delivered the opinion which voided an agreement by railroads
and railroad brotherhoods to restrict the hiring of Negroes to no more than
50 per cent of those employed as firemen.

The original suit was filed in the U.S. District Court of Virginia by
William J. Relax and others against the jim crow Atlantic Coast Line Railroad
and various railroad unions.

Judge Parker's decision noted that the Brotherhood of Locomotive Firemen
had urged that Negroes be excluded from employment as firemen because they
were non-promotable to engineers. A spokesman for the Brotherhood contacted
in Cleveland, said the union had no comment right now.

Freedom, January 1951.

17. NEGRO WORKERS GAIN NEW JOBS WHEN UNION FIGHTS JIM CROW

By Ernest Thompson

United actions of Negro and white workers in a union is the most effective
way of wiping out Jim Crow. Here's how it was proved in a number of instances.

CLEVELAND, Ohio--Between 30 and 50 Negro workers, largely women, have
been hired at the General Electric plant following insistence of UE that terms
of a national agreement against discrimination be put into operation. This
plant has been traditionally lily-white.

CHICAGO, Ill.--After demands by UE, the management of the Harvester Tractor Works reached an agreement with the union on no discrimination in upgrading and bidding for open jobs. As a result of a job-posting plan, the union has obtained jobs for a number of Negro workers at various skills such as precision grinding, mill wrights and others.

SOUTH BEND, Ind.--Here UE is engaged in one of its most significant fights against discrimination. The large and important Local 112 was facing dangerous inner disunity.

The reason: some 800 of the local's 2,000 members are Negro. Justifiable grievances of these workers included failure of the local union leadership to understand and act on such issues as discrimination in hiring against Negro women by the Oliver Plough Co. and rampant Jim Crow policies in restaurants and taverns in the area of the local union office--including the very building where the office is located.

When the UE National Fair Practices committee entered this situation, we had these grievances brought forth clearly and with their full importance.

The result: management has been approached on its hiring practices and, to date, has for the first time at least made promises. The locally organized UE Fair Practices committee is pushing for action as well as promises.

Furthermore, a boycott against the tavern using Jim Crow practices has been instituted and the local union has joined a lawsuit already filed against the restaurant owner for discriminatory practices.

These acts--with indications of more to come--built unity in Local 112. And unity around UE's progressive policies came just in time to turn back a raid launched on the shop by UAW misleaders who use any disunity that may exist to further their raiding schemes.

This case illustrates UE's disunity in action.

The program for Negro and minority rights, adopted at our convention last September, was itself a landmark of progress in the American labor movement. Our efforts to put it into effect have clashed head-on with the intensified drive of white supremacists. This drive, contrary to what many people think, is intensifying itself day by day and threatens to wipe out those gains that have been made in the fight for Negro rights.

In spite of the forces of reaction, we have made considerable progress in carrying out the convention decisions and the program of the great Chicago Conference for Negro Rights held a year ago June.

The key planks in the Chicago program, in my opinion, were:
The model contract clause.
An all-out fight for the hiring of Negro workers in lily-white shops.
Apprenticeship and job training opportunities in all trades.
An intensified campaign for upgrading.
A consistent day-by-day fight for the civil rights of the Negro people.
We have conducted campaigns on every one of these planks which have had a significant effect on all our members.

For the Negro worker it has meant a new opportunity to fight for economic equality with effective machinery backed up by the whole union. This has brought forward many new Negro leaders on the General Executive Board, on district and local levels.

To the white worker, the program has brought a greater realization of the devastating effect of Jim Crow and division on all workers.

UE's participation in the cases of Lt. Gilbert, the Martinsville 7, Willie McGee and the Trenton 6 has further cemented the unity of our Negro and white members in the union's fight against discrimination.

Freedom, April 1951.

18. UNITY FORGED IN LOCAL 600; NOW IT LEADS AUTO INDUSTRY

DEARBORN, Mich.--Two giants face each other across the railroad tracks of this Detroit suburb--Ford's River Rouge plant, the biggest self-contained auto factory in the world, and the world's largest union local, Local 600, UAW-CIO. Forged from the blood and sweat of thousands of Negro and white workers, Local 600 has survived 10 years of attacks from the company and internal splits.

Today, it stands out as a more militant and more consistent fighter for workers' rights than its parent body, the International Auto Workers.

Key to its unquestioned position as leader among workers in the auto industry is the unity among its vast Negro membership and an increasing awareness among white members that their problems will never be solved until the Negro is granted full economic, social and political freedom.

Backed by some 60,000 members, President Carl Stellato and other Local 600 officers have in recent weeks:

Supported Sen. Johnson's peace resolution.

Tossed a bombshell into the nation's labor scene by inviting John L. Lewis to 600's 10th anniversary.

Issued a call for a conference of UAW leaders to stem the rising tide of layoffs and speedups.

Backed the petition drive for an FEPC in Detroit.

Action on these issues alone is enough to make Local 600 noteworthy, but it is in integration of Negro workers that the Ford local surpasses the International UAW and points the way to increasing participation of Negroes in the top echelons of labor.

From the days of the bloody battles with company goons, Negroes have been active in Local 600. Many of them who helped break the resistance of Ford's, last auto company to be organized, are still around, some still holding positions in the local. Others, however, were too militant for both the company and their union, and have been ousted one way or another.

Top-ranking Negro officer in Local 600 is William P. Hood, recording secretary, now serving his fourth term. Other elected officials are Bill Shuford, guide, Clarence Saunders and George La Marque, trustees. Administrative assistant to President Stellato is young Bill Johnson, former Production Foundry Unit Chairman.

Seven of the 35 women on the office staff are Negro women, all of whom have been with Local 600 for at least five years, some as long as 10. Among them are Thelma Rowman, who handled workmen's compensation for 7 years, and Roxie Simpson, who handles grievance procedure.

The local is set up on a unit basis, one for each of the 17 different departments at the Ford plant; Gear and Axle, Iron Foundry, Pressed Steel, 'B' Building, etc. Every unit elects nine officers, and two of them have Negro presidents, Joe Morgan, chairman of the Frame and Cold Heading Unit, and M. Johnson who heads the Foundry Unit. Morgan was elected last April on a broad progressive program of peace, jobs, and unity, the first time a Negro has headed the unit.

Three units have Negro vice-presidents, among them Dave Moore, a veteran 17-year-man at the Rouge, who was elected to the Gear and Axle Unit, and Nelson Davis, chairman of the Foundry's mammoth picnic. In all but two units, Negroes hold important positions as officers or committeemen.

Director of Local 600's active FEPC department is James Watts, appointed to the staff recently. An administration assistant to UAW chief Walter Reuther for two years, Watts broke with Reuther at the last convention over the question of Negro representation on the International UAW board to date. To date there are no Negroes in this top policy-making body in the union. Joe Crenshaw is the director of the education department.[190]

Officers and members all agree that Local 600 is in better position today than ever before to tackle problems confronting auto workers, and all agree that it is the result of hammering out unity among various factions within the organization. Alert now to the growing demands of its Negro membership, 16,000 to 20,000 strong; for "deeds, not words" the local has found that adhering strictly to real trade union principles can produce results.

The world's biggest union local stands as monument to what men united in common cause can accomplish and is a challenge to what they can accomplish in the future.

Freedom, August 1951.

19. U.S. IS THE BIGGEST JIM CROW BOSS

By Ewart Guinier
Secretary-Treasurer, United Public Workers of America

The U.S. Government is the nation's biggest Jim Crow employer. Segregation and discrimination still make a mockery of the President's tongue-in-
cheek fair employment practices order. Negroes on the federal payroll generally perform the most menial, low-paid work there is--and the big stick of the
loyalty order is poised like the plantation owner's whip to make sure that
nobody gets out of line.

People are getting out of line, though. They are standing up together and
demanding equal rights. And wherever the struggle is made, there are the gains
to show that organized action is stronger than the whip.

How many Negroes are employed by the U.S.? During the last war the figure
rose to something like 16 per cent. Today I would say that it is 10 per cent,
or less. Gains made during the New Deal are being taken away and the door
closed to further gains except when the most intense campaign is made.

The union decided to tackle one of the sorest spots in this sorry situa-
tion--the Bureau of Engraving. These were the conditions: over half of the
6,000 workers were Negroes, but they received only about a quarter of the payroll. Less than half of one per cent held any but menial, unskilled jobs.
And by way of salt in the wounds, there were separate toilet facilities and
segregated work areas for people doing the same jobs.

For several years we waged a fight against discrimination in this bureau. We
had the cooperation of most Negro organizations and many unions, and we startled the whole town with our mass picket lines at the Bureau of Engraving and
at the White House. We made it clear that the President has the authority to
enforce fair employment practices in the federal government.

In January of this year we won a significant and historic victory. For
the first time since the Bureau was established in Civil War days, the barriers
went down and 17 Negroes were hired to work as apprentice plate printers.

Though Jim Crow rides high in Washington, the most flagrant discrimina-
tion is practiced officially by the U.S. Government in the Panama Canal Zone.
The double standard set up there for colored and white workers condemns
Negroes to degrading conditions.

When the canal was being built, the pattern of discrimination was set
with white workers paid in gold and Negro workers in silver. In 1946, when
the United Public Workers waged a fight against this arrogant, bloated Jim
Crow, wages for "silver" workers were running four and five times lower than
those paid "gold" workers on identical jobs.

The same sharp contrast exists in housing, schooling and general living
conditions. Recreational facilities are strictly lily-white, and signs at
clubhouses, movies, bowling alleys and athletic fields warned "silver" workers
to keep out.

The union was able to get the humiliating "gold" and "silver" signs removed and got the minimum wage raised from 12 to 26 cents an hour; a 40-hour
week (it was 48 to 54 before); time and a half for overtime; double time for
ten paid holidays; wage increases for many "silver" workers, and other improvements.

Wherever the union tried to improve conditions for government workers, we
had to tackle the barrier of discrimination first. And just because of this
ancient device for exploiting all workers--Jim Crow--the Negro workers were
hit most viciously by the loyalty order.

This is particularly true in the Post Office Department, where tens of
thousands of Negro workers are employed. Negro postal workers were fired
because they belonged to the NAACP or participated in NAACP activities. Any
activity aimed at Jim Crow made a person "disloyal."

White workers, too, got caught in the "loyalty" net when they joined
Negroes in the common aim of winning better working conditions. Some of the
questions that determined a person's "loyalty" went like this:

"Have you had any conversations that would lead you to believe (the accused) is rather advanced in his thinking on racial matters?"

"Have any of your neighbors made complaints about having Negroes in your
home?"

The United Public Workers has shown the way to break through this pattern. The struggle must be intensified because the repression is getting worse all the time. FREEDOM must begin at home, and the best place to start is in government employment.

Freedom, August 1951.

20. ALL-WHITE AUTO UNION JURY OUSTS 13 DETROIT LEADERS

The Negro membership of the United Auto Workers is fighting mad over the outrageous action of the lily-white international executive board against militant Leland Unit of Local 205 in Detroit. Thirteen plant leaders—12 of them Negro—are expelled while a white administratorship, which candidly calls itself a dictatorship, still sits on the 90 per cent Negro plant.

It was when the bosses announced they were "tired of having Negroes running their plant" that the Reuther people began to cuddle up to this Dixiecrat management of the Allen Industries' Leland plant.

For ten years since the plant was organized the management had been forced to hand out raises and improve conditions. So they decided (they admitted) to get rid of James Walker, chairman of the plant committee, and his two fellow committeemen. They decided the easiest way to accomplish this was through the notoriously white-supremacist leadership of the international union.

That is just what happened. The company refused to discuss grievances, and the workers called a 45-minute work stoppage in January 1950. All three members of the shop committee were fired and the rest of the workers sent home. They refused to return to work without their committeemen. Three other Allen Industry shops went out in sympathy.

At this point, the president of Allen Industries said later, the three committeemen would have been reinstated if the international had requested it. Instead, the Reuther men joined the company in telegrams instructing the workers to return or lose their jobs. White UAW members paraded with the police before the plant to intimidate the strikers. They finally returned to work.

Later, two of the committeemen were reinstated—but Brother Walker stayed fired and many more were fired for their union activities.

Under the white dictatorship imposed on the plant by the international, no election of officers was allowed; the union contract expired in June, 1950 and the plant has been working without a contract since then. No grievances were processed, workers were speeded up by slap-happy foremen and the firings went on.

With no other way to make their union function for them instead of for the boss, the workers petitioned for a decertification election. It was held in June 1950 and the vote was 279 to 194 for the UAW. It was for this that charges were filed against 19 plant leaders, all Negro but one. Six of the 19 defendants were fired by the company.

The dictatorship has been in force for over a year now, though the UAW constitution provides for only 60 days. The trial was held July 17, with an all-white jury. Seven were expelled from the UAW for life; six were suspended for five years and fined $100 each. And now the international figures it's in control enough to risk an election in the plant.

Those who have lost their jobs in the industry have long records of activity in the union. Three were members of the executive board of Local 205. Three were women.

The case of the Leland workers will be taken to the next convention of the UAW, in 1952. Meanwhile, Negro members throughout the industry and their white allies are determined to change the brazenly anti-Negro policies of the Reuther administration.

Freedom, September 1951.

21.   FERDINAND SMITH LEAVES: "REACTION WILL PASS,"
SAYS LABOR LEADER ON DEPARTURE

"I helped to build a union which enabled sailors to marry and have children and a home just like other workers, instead of being kicked around like
bums. For this I earned the enmity of the shipowners and their agents, in and
out of the government."

The mellow, steady voice came from a man who had reached the top position
achieved by any Negro in the modern American labor movement and who was now
giving his last interview to the American press. Ferdinand Smith was surrounded
by a hundred-odd close friends and wellwishers as he waited in New York's International Airport for the plane that would take him to London. Victim of the
current deportation hysteria under which the administration had branded him an
"undesirable alien" he had elected to leave the country which had been the
scene of his tremendous contributions to the struggle for Negro rights, workers'
unity and peace.

The AP reporter kept prodding. He wanted to know what Smith would do next,
how he was going to live. "Ferd" quickly answered that seamen know their way
around in the world and that he wasn't worried about finding a job, and then
he went on to say what was in his heart.

"I have no bitterness in leaving," the Jamaica-born labor leader said,
"I have worked and lived among the American people for 33 years in the United
States and before that for five years in the Canal Zone. They are as fine as
any people in the world, but now they are passing through a stormy night of
reaction. This will pass away and I am confident the American people will return their government to the hands of the masses to whom it belongs."

Paul Robeson and William L. Patterson were among those who shook hands
with "Ferd" as he left. There were many of his old buddies from NMU, but not
president Joe Curran, who has sanctioned the Coast Guard "loyalty" screening
program which has yanked off the ships hundreds of progressive sailors, the
majority of them Negro and Puerto Rican.

Among the crowd was a quiet, dignified man, master mariner for 30 years,
who was not permitted to sail an American ship until Ferdinand Smith and the
NMU led the fight which placed him at the helm of the Booker T. Washington
during the anti-fascist war. Recently Capt. Hugh Mulzac had received a notice
that he had been "screened" out of the merchant marine.

One of the last things Ferdinand Smith, ex-secretary of the NMU and former member of the executive committee of the CIO, said as he waved goodbye was
that he hoped American progressives and trade unionists would wage a real
struggle to place Captain Mulzac back on the Booker T. You just knew, as the
plane took off, that wherever "Ferd" is there'll be a struggle for Negro
rights.

Freedom, September 1951.

22.   THE NEGRO LABOR COMMITTEE

By Frank R. Crosswaith

In 1935, at a delegated conference similar to this, the Negro Labor Committee was born. At that time the organized labor movement of the United
States faced one of the most disturbing problems of its life. Our country was
then in the midst of that never-to-be-forgotten unemployment period with millions
of workers moving through the streets of their cities poorly clad and poorly
shod, while garment workers and shoemakers were looking for work; millions of
workers were sleeping along roadways and on river banks, while millions of
carpenters, bricklayers, steelworkers and other construction workers were unable to find employment. Hunger, poverty, want and misery were the daily diet
of the average worker. I repeat, this was a most disturbing condition facing
the working class and our democratic form of government.

It was then that three things of historic importance occurred. The first
was the passage of the immortal Wagner-LaGuardia labor law which gave to labor
the right to organize--a right which the Manufacturers' Association and the
Chamber of Commerce had always enjoyed. The second occurrence of historic
importance was the organization of the unemployed, which compelled both
federal and local governments to become a little more socially enlightened
and thus make relief provisions for the unemployed millions of the nation.
The third event to occur at that time was the birth of the Negro Labor Committee. Of the three events thus listed, I consider the birth of the Negro
Labor Committee to be most significant and fundamental--as its history, when
it is written some day by some unbiased historian, will prove.

With labor now enjoying the right to organize, a campaign was started to
organize workers, reduce the work day and thus open the door of employment to
the unemployed. As this campaign got under way, the responsible leaders of
labor soon discovered that in addition to facing the natural hostility of
employers they also had to face the antagonism of the millions of Negro workers.
This antagonism was the product of experience. Negroes in the world of toil
always had to face ignorance, prejudice and discrimination. The Negro was
always the last to be hired and the first to be fired. A large number of
labor organizations had early established in their constitutions and bylaws
provisions which relegated the Negro to the status of an auxiliary worker or
denied him membership in their union. This experience drove the masses of
Negro workers into the oasis of domestic service and agricultural labor; it
made the average Negro workers unsympathetic to the claims and appeals of
organized labor, and friendly to the employer's interests, for it was the
employer--in his efforts to meet and overcome the increasingly loud demands of
labor for "more pay and less work"--it was the employer who became the friend
of the Negro by giving him a job outside a kitchen, a dining room, or operating an elevator. It was the employer who gave him a chance to move out upon
the broad industrial plains of the nation and away from those low menial confines of service which the Negro inherited from 245 years of chattel slavery.
In addition to the apathy of the Negro worker, we had to face two other
obstacles. One was the opposition of the extreme leftists, whose main objective, as we all know, is to use the Negro to advance the ungodly, unmoral
and barbaric objectives of Communism.

This then, in brief, was the world in which the Negro Labor Committee
was born in 1935. Fortunately for the Negro and fortunately for labor,
those of us who were privileged to shape and direct the course of the Committee understood and appreciated our responsibility, thus enabling the Committee to render the Negro and labor a service the value of which only a united
and economically emancipated working class can adequately appraise. This duty
we modestly place in the lap of the working class of the future.

For the present it is sufficient to state, that as a result of the work
and influence of the Negro Labor Committee millions of Negro workers are today
an integral part of the organized labor movement of the United States and the
world. In many instances, many Negroes today occupy important and responsible
posts in their unions, having been chosen for such posts not because of their
color, but rather because of their demonstrated ability and devotion to the
lofty ideals of labor and labor's inseparable destiny with the fate of democracy, freedom and justice.

Today, we face a problem equal in importance to those faced by organized
labor in 1935, when the Negro Labor Committee was born. The Negro is now a
part of the organized labor movement, but many of the problems which have
haunted him down through the ages, during and after chattel slavery are still
to be met and solved. He can only meet and solve such problems as lynching,
segregation, race prejudice, inadequate educational facilities and opportunities,
et cetera, if and when organized labor recognizes its common interest with
the Negro and through education and organization joins with him to meet and
solve them.

Out of this conference can come the machinery and the movement that spell
victory for all of us as workers in our desire to justify our birth, justify
our common divine origin and common destiny.

Speech presented before the Committee, March 6, 1952. Text furnished by the
Negro Labor Committee and published with the Committee's permission.

23. SPEECH OF FRANK R. CROSSWAITH
MADE AT
NEGRO LABOR COMMITTEE CONFERENCE, FREEDOM HOUSE, JUNE 28, 1952

Fellow trade-unionists and fellow Americans! First of all permit me to
express in behalf of Brother Iushewitz and myself, our sincere and profound
thanks, and appreciation to you, for having chosen us here this morning to do
the task of co-chairmaning the work of the Negro Labor Committee to be known
as Branch #1 affiliated with the Negro Labor Committee, USA.

I am sure, I also speak for Brother Iushewitz, when I say, that whatever
it is humanly possible for us to do, to advance the ideas and deals expressed
in your action here today we will do it to the best of our ability. Having
said that, permit me first to assure you that I am not going to burden you with
a prolonged speech. I want to just briefly, express a thought or two to you,
so that during the days and months and years ahead, as you return to your
separate trade unions or meet with us in the Assembly some of these thoughts I
throw out to you today, may be of some value to you. First of all let me assure you, that I have no personal ambition in this matter, none whatsoever.

Over a quarter of a century ago when I shed the uniform of an American
sailor and came to live in the City of New York, I saw some things that made a
deep imprint upon my mind, and which more than any others have steered the
course of my life. One of the things I saw was that the Negro race, the race
to which I accidentally belong, was utterly unaware of the economic nature of
its problems. In those days, the average Negro felt, that if ever he was to
win his rightful place in the United States, the only way open to him to win
that place was to be a beggar. Although the son of a painter and the son of
a cook, I rejected that idea, because I had long been convinced even as a boy
in the Virgin Islands of the United States where I was born, that no group
could ever win its rights anywhere in the world, by merely begging for these
rights. (Applause)

To get what you deserve you must fight for them, and in fighting for
these rights, sacrifices will have to be made; sometimes by individuals and
sometimes by large numbers; but in a fight you must make sacrifices. One of
the first things I did, in New York City, was to become affiliated with a
Union before I even got a job. I later went to school at nights, and among
the things I tried to learn was the ability to express myself upon a platform.
I don't know how successful I have been in that respect, I leave the answer
to you, (LAUGHTER). But in the course of the years that followed immediately
after, I was found speaking on the street corners of New York almost every
night, after working all day for $8.00 a week.

Instead of being home with my wife and my children, I was speaking on the
street corners; and one of the thoughts I threw out there, on many of those
nights--together with A. Philip Randolph and others--were intended to strengthen
the economic life-line of the New Negro. Do you remember that term my friends?
THE NEW NEGRO! Until that expression was coined by us, America was thinking
of the Negro in the terms of yesteryears; thinking of the old-time darky who
wanted to beg his way to the top, who wanted to sing a song in order to avoid
being lynched or being discriminated against. We coined the expression, the
New Negro, and it wasn't very long before that expression and the thoughts it
involved, became the rallying cry of my race throughout the United States.
Everyone began talking about the NEW NEGRO. THE NEW NEGRO who recognized that
if he is to successfully fight for his rights, his place must be alongside his
brother who's skin may be white who's economic needs are exactly those of
the Negro. And so we attempted to bring the Negro within the trade-union movement. How successful we have been the unbiased history of America and the
history of the world will tell that story, for more eloquently than Frank R.
Crosswaith can tell it to here this afternoon. But that we have succeeded,
there is no doubt about it.

Today, you have Negroes practically in every union, in every industry in
the nation; many of them are occupying important posts in their union, they
were chosen for their posts not because of the color of their skins primarily--
I hope, but chosen because of their demonstrated devotion and loyalty to the
ideals and principles of the organized labor movement of the United States.
We have made definite progress. We could have made much more that we did, but

unfortunately we didn't. Upon some other more appropriate occasion I'll tell
you why.
     I hope however, that as a result of your action here this afternoon we
will learn another lesson; namely, the importance of cooperation. Cooperative
thinking and cooperative acting, represent the most dynamic force in human
progress. When people can appreciate and understand their common interest the
speed of progress is hastened. Do you understand? I hope you do! (Applause)
     Early in life, I also learnt another lesson. Let me throw that out to you
too. You know life is a rather interesting thing. And when I say life, I am
thinking not only of human life, I am thinking of anything, any object that
lives. In order for life to progress there must be changes; please don't forget that. When life--whether it be human or otherwise,--when life can no
longer affect changes it dies. Watch a human being, as he leaves his little
cradle and he can run and jump and carry on, and climb fences; watch him changing upward through the years; and then he reaches a certain height. Even
though he has reached that height and he can go no higher, in order for him not
to die he must still affect change. He begins to bend, his hair turns gray,
his head is bowed and his back is bent; but he keeps on changing downward until he reaches that point where he can no longer affect change; then he passes
out of the picture. This thought that I have just thrown out to you applies to
the Negro. That original New Negro that I spoke of earlier has passed away;
in his place today stands a NEWER NEGRO. A Negro with the knowledge for instance, that one billion, two hundred million of the world's population are
non-white--may I repeat those figures for you--one billion, two hundred million
non-white people in the world as against five hundred million whites. What a
difference! But you will note, that the lands and the labor of this one billion, two hundred million have been controlled by a relatively small segment
of this five hundred million. THE NEW NEGRO understands that! And he knows,
that if he is to correct this age-long injustice to the non-white peoples of
the world, he has got to close ranks with the working class of the world and
together correct this injustice. To do that, he must plant his feet solidly
in the soil of democracy. Because since democracy is regulated by a majority,
we can never lose, for we are the majority.
     So this NEWER NEGRO which by your conduct here today, you have given some
encouragement to,--I hope, he will be able to meet every obstacle in his
pathway. I hope we will be able to become so thoroughly and effectively
united that neither the Communists nor any other reactionary group, whether
of the right or of the left,--will be able to move us from our common objective; and that common objective is, equality for every member of the human
race, and justice for the working class of the world. (PROLONGED APPLAUSE)

Copy in possession of the editors.

                    24. COLORED UNION WINS COSTLY SUIT

               Action Instituted By Headquarters In Roanoke, Va.

     WASHINGTON, D.C. (NNPA)--The United States Supreme Court, in a 6 to 3
decision, ruled last Monday that the courts have power to protect colored
railroad workers from loss of their jobs under compulsion of a bargaining
agreement, which, to avoid a strike, the railroad made with an exclusively
white man's union.
     The ruling, which has the effect of preserving for Negroes the jobs they
have held for many years as train porters, came as the result of a suit filed
in 1951 at the instance of the Association of Colored Railway Trainmen and
Locomotive Firemen of which S. H. Clarke, Roanoke, Va., a brakeman for the
Norfolk & Western is president.
     Justice Hugo L. Black delivered the opinion in the case of Simon L.
Howard, Sr., an employee of the St. Louis, San Francisco Railway Company for
nearly 40 years, who brought a class suit on behalf of himself and other
train porters of that railroad.

The justices who voted to uphold the decision of the United States Court
of Appeals at St. Louis were, in addition to Justice Black, Felix Frankfurter,
William O. Douglas, Robert H. Jackson, Harold H. Burton and Tom C. Clark.[191]
Dissenting were Chief Justice Fred M. Vinson, Stanley F. Reed and Sherman
Minton. Justice Minton delivered the dissenting opinion.[192]
Bargaining agents who enjoy the advantages of the Railway Labor Act's
provisions must execute their trust without lawless invasions of the right of
other workers. Justice Black declared, adding:
"We agree with the Court of Appeals that the District Court had juris-
diction to protect these workers from the racial discrimination practiced
against them."

Norfolk Journal and Guide, June 21, 1952.

25. SUPREME COURT DECISIONS PROTECT NEGRO RAILROAD WORKERS

By Louis Lautier

The class suit, originally brought by Simon L. Howard, Sr., a "train
porter" on the St. Louis-San Francisco Railway for nearly forty years and decided favorably to train porters of the Frisco and its subsidiary, the St.
Louis-San Francisco & Texas Railway Company, is a part of the continuing fight
waged by several colored railway organizations to eliminate racial discrimination in employment in the railway industry.
These organizations are the International Association of Railway Employees and the Association of Colored Railway Trainmen and Locomotive Firemen.
The decision of the United States Supreme Court in the Howard case represents an extension of the doctrine laid down in the cases of Bester
Williams, a fireman on the Louisville & Nashville Railroad, and Tom Tunstall,
a fireman on the Norfolk Southern Railway.
In these later cases the Supreme Court ruled that the collective bargaining representative under the Railway Labor Act must represent all members of
the craft or class without discrimination and cannot use its statutory position to make unlawful discriminations within the craft.
The court in the Howard case extended that doctrine by holding that "The
Federal Act thus prohibits bargaining agents it authorizes from using their
position and power to destroy colored workers' jobs in order to bestow them
on white workers. And courts can protect those threatened by such an unlawful
use of power granted by a federal act."
The immediate effect of the decision is to save the jobs of some 125 or
more train porters employed on the Frisco railroad. The ultimate effect will
be the establishments of a broad principle for the use and protection of
colored workers against discriminatory practices of lily-white railroad unions.
The fight for protection of colored railroad workers, by the use of legal
action, began in 1939 when the Association of Colored Railway Trainmen and
Locomotive Firemen and the International Association of Colored Employees
commissioned the late Charles H. Houston and Joseph C. Waddy to study the
problem in its legal aspects and prosecute suits against the unions and railroad companies for discrimination against colored workers.[193]
The first case filed, jointly sponsored by the two organizations, was
known as Ed. Teague against the Gulf, Mobile and Ohio Railroad. This case
was lost in the United States Circuit Court of Appeals.
In 1941 the Steele and Tunstall cases were brought, the Steele case being
filed in the state courts of Alabama and the Tunstall case in the Federal
District Court for the Eastern District of Virginia. The Steele case was
sponsored by the International Association of Railway Employees, and the
Tunstall case by the Association of Colored Railway Trainmen.
After these cases were won, the International filed seven suits against
southeastern railroads and the Brotherhood of Locomotive Firemen and Enginemen.
These cases were all settled within the last few months by injunctions against

the Brotherhood and the railroads, restraining them from enforcing an agreement limiting the number of colored firemen to a certain percentage of the
total and prohibiting them from barring colored firemen from jobs as helpers
on Diesel engines.

In the settlement the brotherhood also agreed that it would voluntarily
end percentage agreements and restrictive Diesel engine agreements on railroads in the Southeast where suits had been filed. The Brotherhood also
agreed that it would not interfere with the employment of colored firemen by
seeking agreements with railroads opposing such employment or by striking or
threatening to strike against the carriers.

The Howard case represents a portion of the activities of the Association
of Colored Railway Trainmen against the Brotherhood of Railroad Trainmen in an
effort to compel the BRT to cease its discriminatory practices.

Among the cases sponsored by the Association for this purpose was the one
brought by James Tillman, a train porter on the Frisco, which resulted in the
breaking of an agreement, made in 1928 by the BRT and the Frisco. This agreement provided that no colored person would be hired in train, engine and yard
service on the Frisco.

The architect of the entire plan to wipe out racial discrimination in
employment on the railroads, through court action, was the late Dr. Houston,
who, with Mr. Waddy, his law partner, handled all of the precedent-making
cases, and since his death the work has been carried on by Mr. Waddy, who
argued the Howard case in the Supreme Court.

Norfolk Journal and Guide, June 21, 1952.

26. N.C. FURNITURE WORKERS BLAZE UNION TRAIL

By George Johnson

THOMASVILLE, N.C.--When I started at the Thomasville Chair company twenty
years ago, I worked ten hours a day for 20 cents an hour. It was a long time
before the union came, but when it did everybody in Thomasville knew it. For
17 long weeks in 1946 Negro and white workers in this Jim Crow town walked
the picket lines together, ate out of the same soup kitchens and won a strike
which established Local 286, United Furniture Workers of America, CIO, as our
bargaining agent.

Today we're out on strike again. This time we're fighting to keep our
union which has won more benefits for the workers at Thomasville Chair in the
past six years than the company had granted in all its past history.

For six months we negotiated for a measly five cent wage increase and for
six months the company refused to budge. It offered--nothing! Now we've been
out for 12 weeks and Thomasville Chair has already lost more than the wage
increase would have cost them for a year. It seems the company has one aim:
to smash our union.

Union Brought Dignity

When the union came in 1946 the average worker at the plant was making
about 40 cents an hour. The union has won a wage increase every year except
1951, so that the average wage is now around 90 cents. We now get insurance,
sick benefits and paid vacations.

But mostly, the union has won dignity. There was a time when if a foreman
didn't think you were working hard enough and fast enough, he would just walk
over and kick you good. If you complained, you lost your job. It was usually
the Negro workers who got most of that, but they used to kick the white workers
too.

Negro workers in the plant average between 85 and 90 cents an hour tops
and as usual do the dirtiest work--in the lumber yard, the filler room and the
glue room. My own hands are stained white from having to clean them with
strong solutions to get the varnish off. For this, I draw 99 cents an hour.

Jim Crow Wages

The big job is to get the white workers at the plant to understand how white supremacy hurts them. For instance, only whites are hired in the higher skilled jobs in the cabinet, machine and upholstery departments. They average around $1.10 an hour. Now this is a little more than the Negro workers get, but it is a lot less than all workers, Negro and white, could get if the discriminatory hiring policy were wiped out and the union's bargaining strength increased. Compared with a New York upholsterer who makes an average of $2.50 an hour, the Thomasville upholsterer, in his "white-only" job, loses about $1.35 an hour to the bosses pocket and to Jim Crow.

Thomasville Chair works about 1500 men and women; between five and six hundred of them are Negroes. At present the company is trying to keep the plant going with about 350 scabs, and among these you will only find four or five Negroes. In fact, most of the white workers on the picket lines will tell us that if the white workers would stick together like the Negroes are doing, we could make a whole lot of trade union progress in this town.

It wasn't easy to build a union in a company town like Thomasville, especially a union with Negro and white workers together. The Finch family which owns the plant also owns the bank, most of the land, controls the newspaper and owns most of the houses the workers live in. But the coming of the union changed a lot of things. Even those who aren't in industry don't bow and scrape to the Finches as they used to.

That's why they want to get rid of the union so bad. The company offers the workers a little more money and better jobs if they quit the union. Sometimes the union signs up 150 workers in a month, and the next month maybe 100 of them have been fired. The bosses tell the white workers: "Are you going to join that Negro union? They know, of course, that most of our members and officers are white, but they try to stir up the worst prejudices, to keep the workers divided and the union weak. But still in spite of these things, the union has stuck.

Worked Night and Day

That's why our strike is so important. It will affect the trade union struggles of 50,000 furniture workers in North Carolina and Virginia. It is a trail blazer in unity of Negro and white workers in Southern unions.

The company has no use for those of us who have fought for decent living wages, and they have tried to intimidate me in every way they know how.

I am just a plain working man who has worked day and night for many years to educate my seven children. Two of my daughters are nurses, my son is a vet and goes to A & T College in Greensboro, and I have another daughter who went to Johnson C. Smith College in Charlotte. I haven't had much education myself and there must be many things I don't know, but I figure like this: there is one thing a man has got to have and that is the guts to stand up and fight for himself and his people.

One thing is sure. When this strike is over, the workers are going to be a lot more interested in political issues. They have seen how the elected officials treat their strike. I was one of the men who handed out leaflets asking Negroes to register to vote.

I believe that if we can keep our union strong and build up the voting power of the workers and the Negro people, we can make Thomasville a happy place to live in--a place where folks won't have to worry about being hungry and living in shacks and not having enough to send their children to school.

That's the kind of country our union stands for and I hope all the people who read this article will do all they can to help us win it.

Freedom, June 1952.

27.
BRUTAL CAPTAINS, FEDERAL SCREENING TAKE NEGROES' LIVES AND JOBS AT SEA

About a year and a half ago, the National Maritime Union attempted to have one Franklin B. Weaver, the Chief Mate aboard the Isbrandtsen ship Flying Trader, removed as "trigger happy". Weaver instead was made captain of the freighter.

On October 25 of last year, the Alabama-born Captain pumped three bullets
into the body of a young Negro seaman. Before he went to his room to get the
revolver, Weaver admittedly beat 24-year-old Harvey, with a blackjack and hand-
cuffed him.

The entire unlicensed crew of the Flying Trader walked off the ship following the killing and refused to return with Weaver in command. Although the
Captain threatened them and finally logged them as deserters, the men would not
budge, and returned to press charges of murder against Weaver.

These charges were later reduced by a grand jury to voluntary manslaughter
"in the heat of passion."

Two lily-white Federal Court juries heard the charges against the burly,
six foot, 200 pound Weaver. Both failed to find the Captain guilty. Weaver
had pleaded "self-defense" in the shooting of Harvey who weighed 125 pounds
and was about five feet six inches tall and handcuffed at the time he was shot.

On June 19, a jury which included a bank vice president and a real estate
broker split 8-4 in favor of convicting the captain after 11 hours of deliberation. Weaver was set free for the second and perhaps the last time.

The Isbrandtsen Co. has an especially bad reputation among seamen. Known
among seamen as the "Hungry Goose Line" because they are constantly being
forced to sue for wages withheld for "disciplinary" reasons, the company has
gone openly to war with the union on the Weaver issue.

Throughout the trial defense attorney Mahlon Dickerson tried to show a
"conspiracy" of the union against Weaver, and that mutiny was imminent on the
part of the union members. Capt. Clayton McLaughlin, operating manager for
Isbrandtsen, told reporters that the union would "be the death of the U.S.
Merchant Marine" as soon as the Korean War ended.

Constantly, during the last 10-day trial it was repeated by the defense
that the captain is absolute master of the ship, and that no land-locked bunch
of jurors had the right to judge the actions of a "master" while at sea.

Coast Guard hearings on the possible revocation of Weaver's license have
been suspended pending the outcome of the criminal prosecution. It is doubtful
however, if the Coast Guard, busy "screening" militant Negro seamen, will act,
should the government declare it will not prosecute.

It is to be noted that Joe Curran of the NMU and the NAACP lashed out at
those who would free the Alabama-born killer, Weaver. Walter White said that
his organization would press to see justice done, "no matter how many trials
it takes," and Curran stated that "it is highly improbable that an NMU crew
can be found that will ship with Capt. Weaver." Curran also said he would
press the Coast Guard to declare Weaver unfit to carry a master's license,
and has asked union members to write to "everyone from Truman on down" to get
justice in this case.

The NMU leader has not come out against screening, however, which under its
phoney "war emergency" front, threatens to break the entire trade union movement
on the sea. and to drive Negro workers off the ships and the waterfront.

Freedom, July 1952.

28. A LEADER OF THE FURRIERS UNION

By Kathryn Cooper

New York--As a child in Edgefield, South Carolina, and later as a young
woman in Augusta, Georgia, Fannie Washington wrote plays for her school classes
and acted in them. She took part in church programs.

Those were the happy memories she recalls. She also remembers vividly
the $3.00-a-week domestic workers in the South in the 1920's, the working con-
ditions of the tenant farmers. "Wherever I was," she said, "I always wondered
why some people had so much and some had so little."

"My father died when I was very young. I don't remember my mother. He was
a very religious man, but what I remember most about him was that he was always
trying to help other people. After his death an uncle in Augusta, Georgia,
reared my sister and me."

$18 a Week

In 1940 Mrs. Washington came to New York to be with her "side-kick," her older sister, and now instead of just wondering about the great differences in the way people lived, she asked questions and searched for answers.

It wasn't easy working in the fur industry when she started. Her first job as an operator trimming the inside of fur coats only paid $18.00 a week.

She joined the International Union of Fur and Leather Workers as a rank and a filer. At one of the meetings during elections she was nominated to the Executive Board, and she was elected. There too, she was always asking questions , always wanting to know why. At that time she was the only Negro woman on the Executive Board--and was a member for about 8 years.

In 1948 the secretary-treasurer of Local 64 left the industry and she was appointed to fill out his term.

Learned from Mistakes

"One afternoon," she said, "one of the officers of the local came into my office and told me that he had suggested my name as financial secretary of Local 64. Not knowing anything about the work, I was a little taken aback."

He gave her a sketchy outline of her duties and told her that people would help her. "I found out though, that it wasn't as easy as that. I made mistakes and no one on the committee bothered to help me. It seemed to be their thinking that if you made a mistake--well, you made a mistake. I became involved in the work and made lots of mistakes, but learned from them."

The former secretary-treasurer of Local 64 did not return and Mrs. Washington was nominated to fill the job--no one ran against her.

Aside from being secretary of the Joint Board of the Fur Workers Union, chairman of the Credit Committee, member of the Board of Directors and trustee of the Pension Fund, Mrs. Washington "in her spare time" is taking a dressmaking course at the Needle Trades High School twice a week.

Supports Menhaden Fishermen

She has been involved in many struggles in her union since 1940 and things have changed for the better for the workers since then. They now have an insurance plan, a pension fund, and better wages. She has been involved in the struggle to upgrade women workers. Today she is working as a finisher in the cleaning section.

"Organized labor is about the best way for any minority group to solve their problems," she continued. "The unity of workers, Negro and white, is the key to better working conditions."

Thinking back over her early days in the South, Mrs. Washington is thrilled by the fight being waged by her international union to organize the Menhaden fishermen along the Southern coasts.

"The courageous struggle of these fishermen and their wives for better working conditions is something I'll long remember--how these women stand with their husbands because they know it means books for their children, better food, improvements in their living conditions. They won't take 'No' for an answer but fight for what is rightfully theirs. All labor should take a lesson from them."

Mrs. Washington is the mother of a 27-year-old son, who is also employed in the fur industry. She is an active member of Emanuel AME Zion Church in Harlem.

Freedom, May 1953.

29. INT'L. HARVESTER STRIKERS FIGHT WAGE CUT

CHICAGO--Prices up--wages down! This seems to be the slogan of the International Harvester Company which has set off a strike of some 12,000 farm equipment workers in three Chicago plants. These workers, part of 22,000 members of the Farm Equipment-United Electrical Workers Union which has walked

out of International Harvester shops in Illinois, Indiana and Kentucky, are
fighting against proposed down-scaling of pay rates which would slice $26
million out of their pay envelopes in the next three years.

Efforts of the company to break the strike by herding scabs on the Southside and in other areas have been to no avail. The Negro people of Chicago
are well acquainted with the record of the FE-UE locals in improving the living
standards of its members, many of whom are Negroes who are fighting for un-
segregated housing in the face of the attacks of organized vandals. Among the
union leaders rallying the membership and the people of the Southside in support of the strikers' reasonable demands is Frank Mingo, vice president of
FE-UE Local 101.

Freedom, October 1952.

30. LABOR DEFENDS LIFE OF NEGRO UNIONIST IN HARVESTER STRIKE

On October 5, by order of Illinois State's Attorney John Boyle, Chicago
police arrested trade union leader Harold Ward and held him for grand jury
investigation on suspicion of murder.

The arrest was immediately declared a frameup by trade union leaders who
saw Ward's arrest as another desperate attempt to break the then six weeks-old
solid strike of 30,000 United Farm Equipment and Metal Workers of America
against Chicago's notorious anti-union corporation, the giant International
Harvester Company.

William Foster, the murdered man, was a strikebreaker. Early on October
3 he was found in front of his Southside home, brutally beaten to death. For
the first time in the memory of Chicagoans the police became interested in
bringing to justice the murderers of a Negro. The president of the company
where Foster had been crossing picket lines and scabbing against Negro and
white workers, offered a $10,000 reward for Foster's killer.

Jack Burch, Vice-President of FE-UE's District 11, called the arrest of
Ward in connection with the Foster slaying "a rotten frameup engineered by
Harvester bosses who know as well as we do that neither Ward nor any member of
our Union had anything to do with Foster's tragic death."

Ward was born in Tennessee and worked at Harvester since 1944. He is
the financial secretary for Local 108, FE-UE. He had been active in the
heroic struggle of the Harvester workers to hold solid their strike against
the wage-cutting, union-busting activities of International Harvester. The
30-year-old father of two small sons has gained a reputation among his fellow
workers as a militant and courageous trade unionist who was never afraid to
speak out and act in defense of his Union or his people.

The Ward case is seen as an attempt to revive the most infamous of anti-
labor traditions in American history. In May, 1886, Chicago police fired on
and murdered six workers at the International Harvester Company who were engaged in a strike to win the eight-hour day.

When thousands of AFL workers massed in Haymarket Square to protest the
cold-blooded police murder and to further the fight for shorter working hours,
eight of their leaders were framed, railroaded through a trial that was a
mockery of justice, and eventually four of them were executed by the State of
Illinois.

Today International Harvester is one of six giant corporations which
dominate the economic life of Chicago. The others are Montgomery Ward, the
Armour and Wilson meatpacking companies, U.S. Gypsum Co., and Marshall Field
& Co. Together these six industries command assets of $2.1 billion. The
Harvester Company itself, is the nation's leading producer of farm equipment
and owns 45% of the industry's assets. The McCormick family of International
Harvester includes Col. Robert McCormick, owner of reactionary Chicago and
Washington newspapers and backer of such fascist causes and organizations as
American Action and the Crusaders.

Chicago workers see in the fight to free Ward a battle against the return
of the anti-labor violence, legal-lynch tactics, and frame-up practices which

International Harvester has helped to make infamous in U.S. labor history.

The alliance of the police with company strike breaking was attacked by union officials who declared: "To assist in its dirty work, they (Harvester) have enlisted the aid of State's Attorney Boyle. It is significant that the State's Attorney who is so zealously seeking the prosecution of Ward, a Negro militant, is exactly the authority who tried to indict the Negro victims in the Cicero riots of last year."

In mobilizing its full strength to fight the case the FE-UE leadership called for the support of the entire Negro community of Chicago, and stated: "Harold Ward is innocent of the charges brought against him and a fair trial will result in his acquittal and quick return to stand again with us in demanding decent wages and working conditions for our members."

Negro communities all over the nation will watch the program of the Ward case and will join in the demand for a fair trial in order to guarantee that the hysteria of 1886 which sent four innocent men to their death will never return.

Freedom, November 1952.

31. HARVESTER STRIKERS BATTLE COMPANY ATTACK;
BEAT COMPANY PLAN TO HERD SCABS ON SOUTHSIDE

CHICAGO--This is a story of 30,000 hard-working men and women--and their families. It is the story of 10 weeks without a pay check--10 weeks with no money coming in for food and rent and doctor bills, for shoes, rubber boots, or clothing for the kids going back to school.

It could be your story, if you work for a living. And, whatever you do to make ends meet, it concerns you.

Ten weeks ago, 30,000 workers in the mid-West empire of the International Harvester Company went on strike. They are members of the Farm Equipment Workers Union-UE and turn out farm implements and machines in plants at Chicago, Rock Falls, and Rock Island, Ill.; Richmond, Ind., and Louisville, Ky.

5,000 Negro Workers

Of the 17,000 strikers who live in the Chicago area, 5,000 are Negroes. And therein lies a special feature of this bitterly contested labor struggle.

International Harvester has used every trick in the book to break the united stand of Negro and white workers. It has sent its goons and other questionable characters into the populous and poor Southside trying to herd scabs to break the strike. It has harassed the wives of strikers with telephone calls, trying to influence them to urge their husbands back to work. It has enlisted the police in violent attacks against the workers, with special attention to Negroes. It has framed a militant strike leader, Harold Ward, on a transparently phony murder charge and is trying to send him to the electric chair.

But still the strikers hold. In the past ten weeks little or nothing has been manufactured in the struck plants. Why? Why do workers, family breadwinners, face the attacks of hostile police and company hired goons--and remain solid for two-and-a-half months?

When the contract with Harvester came up for renewal in May, FE-UE presented a list of demands as a basis for negotiation. The union wanted a 15¢ general wage increase to keep up with the mounting cost of living. It called for an end to speed-up which was wrecking the health and endangering the lives of its members. Other demands included a company-financed health and welfare plan to be administered by the union, special wage increases for skilled workers, improved vacation and holiday provisions, and a guaranteed annual wage.

Could Harvester meet these demands? All signs point to the answer--yes. Last year the company NETTED a profit of $86 million, or three-and-a-half times the $24-1/2 million it coined in 1945, the last year of the war. HI's president McCaffrey had boosted his own salary at the rate of $7.40 an hour to give himself an annual wage of $196,000.

Yes, Harvester could meet the demands, and the workers deserved the
raises. By 1952 they were taking home less real pay than in 1950. High prices
and higher taxes accounted for this. And each worker was turning out much more
for the company than two years ago. Backbreaking speedup accounted for that,
and the record-making profits of the huge corporation added up to more than
$2,500 on every worker.

Harvester could actually have raised wages 60¢ an hour last year, paid
all taxes, and wound up with double the healthy profits of pre-war years.

But the largest stockholders in Harvester are the McCormicks, notorious
for their record of crushing the workers and trying to break their unions.

Downgrade Work

The management answered the workers' demands, not with counter-proposals
for smaller increases, but with proposals for wage cuts. The company suggested and began to institute a plan for downgrading day work and retiming
piece work which amounted to wage cuts of 30¢ to $1.00 an hour.

And that was when, and why, the Harvester workers struck.

Will they hold out with their demands? Everyone who knows the fighting
history of the FE-UE union and the militant spirit of its Negro and white
members believes that they will.

They will hold out if other unions and organizations in the communities
where these workers live realize their stake in the Harvester strike and lend
a helping hand.

Community Support

Recently a man walked into the Southside strike headquarters of the union
at 123 East 39th Street and placed $2.00 on the table. He had walked ten blocks
from the Ida B. Wells housing project which had been covered that morning with
a newspaper telling about the strike and asking for help. He said, "I don't
work at Harvester--I'm a hotel worker. But I know what you men and women are
up against, so I want to do my part. If all workers would pitch in with a
dollar or two to help you win, it will make it easier for us the next time
contract time rolls around in our industries."[194]

There are always people coming and going at this busy strike headquarters
--four to five hundred a day. The wives of the strikers have organized to put
on a children's Halloween party, solicit food and get the help of their ministers.

Leaders of the union have spoken to the congregations of 15 of the largest
Southside churches and to 300 Baptist ministers in conference. They are asking
for letters condemning the company's scab-herding program which is concentrated
in the Southside community and aims at breaking the bond of unity between white
and Negro workers which has been built up during many years of intense labor
struggles. They are asking for sermons on the strike and contributions through
special collections and petitions.

Chicago has long been a major center of organized labor strength for tens
of thousands of Negro working men and women who came to this city seeking an
equal chance to educate their children and live in security and dignity. No
single institution has made a greater contribution to the pursuit of that goal
than the trade union movement. Much that has been won in recent years is at
stake in the International Harvester strike. The 30,000 hard working men and
women of FE-UE--and their families--deserve all aid that can be sent to them
through their strike headquarters at 123 East 39th Street, Chicago, Ill.

Freedom, November 1952.

32. RACIAL DISPUTE IRKS REUTHER

CHICAGO, May 1--Walter P. Reuther, president of the United Auto Workers,
CIO, said today that an employer might discipline any member of the union who
tried to interfere with promotions because of racial discrimination. He made
the statement in a telegram to John L. McCaffrey, president of the International

Harvester Company, who had informed Mr. Reuther that a "wildcat" strike had
occurred in the company's Memphis, Tenn., plant over the promotion of a Negro
to welder on the basis of seniority.

New York Times, May 2, 1953.

33.   UNION GOAL: END JIM CROW!

When a major trade union sets a target date for ridding its industry of
discriminatory practices against Negro workers, that's big news for the labor
movement and for all Negro Americans.

And, even though little attention has been given to the event in the commercial press, this is exactly what the United Packinghouse Workers, CIO did
at its First Annual Anti-Discrimination conference in Chicago, October 30,
November 1-2.

Almost 400 union workers from shops in all parts of the country enthusiastically supported a resolution which declared: "That the UPWA set as a major
goal the complete breaking down by 1954 of all lily-white situations so that
every UPWA plant employes minority group members without discrimination."

The delegates heard reports of victories already won in the union's
battle against Jim Crow. One of the most exciting stories was that of Local
54, District 8, in Fort Worth, Texas, in which the leadership beat back an
attempt of a "white-supremacy" rump caucus to prevent removal of a partition
in the dining room and of "white" and "Negro" signs on other facilities.

Freedom, October 1953.

34.   CIO BAN ON SEGREGATION IS REAFFIRMED

The long-standing policy of segregated facilities in all CIO offices, union
halls, etc., was restated last week by Pres. Walter P. Reuther.

In a letter to all CIO regional directors and industrial union councils,
he recalled correspondence sent them in April 1950 by CIO General Council
Arthur J. Goldberg with the expressed approval of the late CIO pres. Philip
Murray.[195]

Goldberg's letter stated the CIO position that any statute, ordinance
or lease "which requires CIO organizations or bodies to practice segregation
in any form" is unenforceable.

Reuther wrote that the original statement "represents the continuing
policy of the CIO and is as applicable today as it was at the time of its
issuance."

"It continues to have the full support of all CIO officers," he said.

"Furthermore, this CIO position and policy against segregated facilities
in CIO offices and halls applies with equal force and effect to all functions
held under the auspices of CIO organizations or bodies.

"I am confident that I can depend upon all CIO regional directors and
the officers of all CIO industrial union councils and committees to see to it
that the CIO policy against segregation in CIO offices, halls and functions
is enforced."

CIO News, March 1, 1954.

35. NEGRO GAIN SHOWN IN SOUTH'S PLANTS

Research Study of 5 Concerns Cites Equal Pay Rates
and Lack of Friction

WASHINGTON, May 23 (UP)--A private nonprofit, nonpolitical research
organization today disclosed new cracks in the wall of Negro segregation in
Southern industries.
The group reported that Negro workers had seized their new opportunities
and performed their better jobs "satisfactorily."
The research organization, the National Planning Association, noted that
Southern employers had made "significant departures from traditional bi-racial
employment practices."
The association's Special Committee of the South based its findings on a
study of five Southern companies--three in New Orleans and two in Little Rock,
Ark. The group cautioned that its findings "of necessity" were "very limited"
and did not necessarily reflect over-all labor conditions in the South.
But the committee, composed of eighty-one leaders in the South's agriculture, business, industry, labor, press and government, said its report
indicated "what is possible in the way of bi-racial employment patterns and
relations" in the South.
It emphasized that in none of the five companies had any of the increased
opportunities for Negroes caused "friction" with white workers.

Rates of Pay Equal

It also said most of the opportunities for Negroes to get better jobs
resulted from the severe labor shortages caused by World War II.
The Negro workers in the five companies received "identical" or equal
rates of pay with the white workers in the plants, the committee said.
The group's aim is to help develop the "great reservoir of undeveloped
resources" in the South, its "untapped markets and manpower available for jobs
in new industries and business."
In Little Rock, the two companies studied manufacture low-cost women's
clothing and are owned by the same family. One is the Ottenheimer Brothers
Company and the other the Rocket Manufacturing Company.
The committee found that through "careful planning" the employer had
been able to hire "a carefully selected group of Negro women" for the skilled
jobs in the plants. None of the Negroes received supervisory or clerical
work and none worked "side by side" at the same jobs with whites. But "the
two races intermingle constantly in the course of their work" and intermingle
without "unpleasant incidents," it said.
The report noted that the few attempts the companies had made to promote
Negroes to supervisory posts failed "apparently because the workers did not
like to work under the supervision of members of their own race."

Incentive System Lifts Pay

It quoted the manager of one of the plants as saying the Negro and white
women were about equally capable of handling the same work if it was the same
task "for a long period." He said, however, that the Negro women showed "less
speed" in adapting themselves to new routines.
The three New Orleans companies were not named in the report. One manufactures roofing and siding materials, one clothing and the third processes
food.
The committee said one company had an "incentive system" and as a result
some Negroes earned more than whites doing the same work. Negroes generally,
however, earned less because the higher paying jobs were given "predominantly"
to whites.
In another, unionization has had "far-reaching effects" in modifying pre-
war promotion and lay-off policies, in raising Negroes' eligibility for better
jobs and in "altering the status of Negroes as employees," the report said.
The union "buttressed" these changes with a "no discrimination" clause in the
company contract, it said.

But in no cases, the report said, have Negroes supervised white workers. "Where whites and Negroes worked in the same groups," it said, "Negroes were automatically barred from any jobs that entailed even the smallest degree of delegated authority or direction."

New York Times, May 24, 1954.

36. NEGRO EMPLOYMENT IN THE BIRMINGHAM AREA (1955)

By Langston T. Hawley

The smallest proportion of Negro employment found is [in] the apparel industry where only 10 Negroes were employed out of over 400 workers in two apparel manufacturing firms. In sharp contrast, Negro workers make up 40 per cent of the work force in the basic iron and steel industry and 50 per cent in transportation equipment manufacture. [The] table [page 310] presents a summary of the percentage of Negro workers to total employment in the various industries represented by the firms included in the survey.

The figures upon which these percentages are calculated are in some cases the employer's best estimate and do not represent an actual payroll count. This is particularly true of the figures for 1939. For this reason, a change from 1939 to 1951 of only a few per cent is probably not significant. It should also be pointed out that the nature of the building construction business makes it difficult to give a precise proportion of Negro employment, which will vary considerably according to the character of the particular construction job. The estimate shown here was concurred in by officials of all

Percentage of Negro Employment to Total
Employment in 43 Firms, By Industry Group
1939 and 1951

INDUSTRY GROUP	1951	1939
Manufacturing:		
Food	37	26
Textiles	11	9
Apparel	2	3
Lumber and wood products	34	**
Paper and allied products	18	30
Furniture and fixtures	60	60
Stone, clay, and glass	48	45
Primary metals*	40	46
Fabricated metals	22	25
Machinery (except electrical)	19	20
Transportation equipment	50	50
Bituminous coal mining (commercial)	29	31
Building construction	40	40
Transportation	19	19
Public utilities:gas electric and water	16	18

* Includes captive iron and coal mines
** Data not available

construction companies interviewed.

Since the figures presented in [this] table are averages, they tend to obscure important variations in the percentage of Negroes employed by the specific firms within the several industry groups. In the food industry, for example, the proportion of Negroes employed varies from 11 per cent in a coffee

plant to 63 per cent in a grain and flour mill. Officials of these firms
state there is nothing unusual about their proportions of Negro employment to
total employment for their specific kinds of business in the Birmingham Area.
In the case of two meat packing concerns, one has 20 per cent Negro employment
while the other has 40 per cent. This came about during the war when the latter concern increased the employment of Negroes to alleviate a labor shortage
and kept all of them on after the war in view of their satisfactory service. The
firm with only 20 per cent hired a somewhat larger percentage of white women
during the war when pinched for labor.

Again, in the case of firms in the primary metals group there is wide
variation. A small jobbing foundry has 90 per cent Negroes comprising its
work force, and the president of this company states that this is not at all un-
common for firms of his size (65 employees) in the foundry business in the
Birmingham Area. Those firms in the primary metals group operating blast
furnaces, rolling mills, and iron ore and coal mines have from one-third to
one-half of their work forces made up of Negroes. Other firms making up an
important part of the primary metals group manufacture cast-iron pipe, fittings,
and industrial valves. These firms have from one-half to two-thirds of their
total employment made up of Negro workers. The higher proportion of Negroes in
this branch of the primary metals industry is due largely to the importance of
foundry work in the manufacturing process.

In the fabricated metals group the proportion of Negro employment to total
employment ranges from 6 per cent to 31 per cent for the individual firms surveyed. The firm having only 6 per cent Negroes is a small (150 employees)
manufacturer of metal lawn furniture, fire escapes, and stairways. Its work
involves a fairly high degree of skill and it has relatively few common labor
jobs; also, it has a long tradition of employing only white craftsmen and
helpers. In general, each of the firms engaged in manufacturing light, structural steel shapes employs a smaller proportion of Negroes than is the case in
the firms of the primary metal group.

As would be expected, wide variations in the number of Negroes employed
relative to whites were observed in the transportation and public utility firms
in the area. The proportion of Negro employees ranges from 7 per cent in an
electric utility company to 44 per cent in the maintenance shop of a common
carrier bus company. One of the two major railroads included in the study has
20 per cent Negro employment, and the other 14 per cent. About one-third of
the employees of the City of Birmingham's Water Works Board are Negro, while
only 23 per cent are employed in a large gas company where the work of the
Negro--the installation and repair of pipe line systems--is very similar. The
large proportion of Negroes in the maintenance shop of the bus company is due
largely to the heavy use of Negro women in cleaning the interiors of the
buses. . . .

The higher proportion of Negroes employed in the food industry is accounted for largely by a meat packing firm of 250 employees which turned to
Negroes during the war as a result of a tight labor market and retained the
Negroes after the war's end. In 1939, this firm had 20 per cent Negroes in its
work force. It is a unionized plant, paying the same wage rates to Negroes
and whites for the same work classifications. No other significant change in
the use of Negro workers was found among the firms representing the food industry.

Two companies in the basic iron and steel industry reduced their proportions of Negro employment to total employment during the period 1939 to 1951.
In the larger of these firms, the reduction was from 43 per cent to 36 per cent,
while the smaller firm's proportion of Negro employment fell from 54 to 50
per cent. A management official of one of these firms explained the decline
in his company on the ground that improved technology, particularly in materials
handling equipment, had displaced some Negro workers. No explanation was
given by the other firm.

The slightly decreased proportion (from 25 per cent in 1939 to 22 per
cent in 1951) of Negro employment in the fabricated metals industry is trace-
able to three fabricators of structural steel products. These three firms
experienced considerable expansion in their total employment from 1939 to 1951.
The character of their operations led to a larger expansion of relatively
skilled jobs than of unskilled and semiskilled jobs. Since skilled jobs are
traditionally filled by white workers, the employment expansion led to a
relative decline in their use of Negro workers. This process of expansion

was accompanied to some extent by the adoption of mechanical materials handling equipment which tended to hold down an increase in the employment of
Negroes that probably would have occurred had such equipment not been available. The proportion of Negroes employed by fabricators of heavier iron and
steel products--such as cast-iron pipe--which involve extensive foundry operations, remained remarkably stable during the period.

One large manufacturer of paper products (writing tablets, paper boxes,
etc.) employed 30 per cent Negroes in 1939 but only 19 per cent in 1951. This
decline in the proportion of Negroes occurred during a period when the company's total employment expanded 93 per cent. The management of this company
offered two principal reasons for this relative decline in the use of Negro
workers: 1) the company shifted from hand trucking on its loading dock to
gasoline and electric lift trucks, and 2) since the Fair Labor Standards Act
requires the company to pay a minimum wage of 75 cents an hour, and there is
an adequate supply of white labor willing to work for this rate, the company
prefers white workers. The management official interviewed stated that this
preference is based on the company's experience that white workers are better
educated, understand instructions more readily, are more reliable, and, in
general, are more productive than Negro workers.

Two cases of what may be termed "mass substitution" of white for Negro
workers deserve special mention.

In one case a lumber manufacturer employing 235 people in 1951 was found
to have had approximately three-quarters of his total employment comprised of
Negroes in 1939 but none in 1951. This replacement of Negroes with all white
workers was apparently the outgrowth of a labor dispute. An attempt was made
to organize the company's workers, and a strike for recognition ensued. The
company refused to recognize the union as bargaining agent and replaced the
strikers with other workers. In the course of this replacement none of the
Negro workers were taken back and an all-white work force resulted. The
management official interviewed in this firm indicated that the reason Negroes
were no longer employed is that they are "too susceptible to union organization."

The other case involved a coal mining company that employed 300 workers
in 1951, about 4 per cent of whom were Negroes. In 1939 this firm employed
approximately 600 people of whom about 22 per cent were Negroes. The company
operates two mines in the Birmingham Area. The company president attributed
the relative decrease in the use of Negro workers to what he believed to be
a policy of the union (United Mine Workers of America) on upgrading. This
policy as applied to Negroes would broaden the base of Negro job opportunities
in and around the mines, and would require upgrading of the Negro to the more
skilled jobs traditionally held by white workers.

The result of this union policy, stated the employer, is to create friction between white and Negro workers. He related that in one of the company's
mines, as a direct result of the union policy, the white workers forced segregation upon the company. This segregation took various forms, both within and
without the working environment. On one occasion, a deputation of white miners
who were members of the local union told the company "point blank" that the
whites would no longer work with Negroes. After this experience the company
stopped hiring Negroes entirely at one mine, and apparently greatly reduced
such hirings at the other mine. At present, the company's policy is not to
hire Negroes in any circumstance which might lead to friction. . . .

On the whole, ignoring relatively minor changes in the proportion of
Negroes employed between 1939 and 1951, only three cases were found among the
43 companies surveyed where there was a significant increase in the relative
importance of Negro workers in the total work force. On the other hand, eight
firms (including the two cases of mass substitution) reported that they were
using Negroes in significantly smaller proportions in 1951 than they had in
1939. From the standpoint of the absolute numbers of Negro workers involved,
the decreases substantially overshadowed the increases.

In the firms surveyed, the overwhelming proportion of Negro workers was
found among the unskilled and semiskilled occupations. With few exceptions
these occupations break down into certain basic types of work: common, manual
labor jobs, requiring only a few days training time and very little education;
journeyman or craft-helper jobs, requiring very little skill and often calling
for considerable physical exertion; and machine operations, both heavy and
light, requiring at most a few weeks learning time and typically repetitive in
nature. With respect to the unskilled jobs, it was found that while they are
performed by both white and Negro workers, the latter do the dominant portion

of this type of work. In the building construction industry, for example, it
was estimated by the management officials interviewed that from 90 to 95 per
cent of all common labor is performed by Negroes. Much this same situation
exists in the heavy industries which were investigated particularly in the
basic steel industry.

Howerver, in the case of semiskilled jobs, such as machine operators, it
was found that in most cases both white and Negro workers fill such jobs, and
there was no discernible predominance of Negroes in them. This was not true,
however, of the semiskilled jobs of packer, mortar mixer, chipper and grinder,
garage helper and chauffeur, mule driver, air hammer operator, and tire
changer. The Negro was definitely found to be predominant in these occupations.

Relatively few Negroes were found in the skilled and clerical occupations
of the companies studied. Less than half--44 per cent--of the companies interviewed had any Negro workers in skilled jobs, and only 9 of the 43 firms indicated that they had Negroes doing some degree of clerical work. No Negro
workers were found in skilled occupations in the participating firms in the
following industries: textiles, apparel; lumber; transportation equipment
manufacture; gas, electric, and water utilities; paper and paper products;
cement; and bed springs and mattress manufacture. Only one skilled Negro
worker--an oven operator in a bread bakery--was found in the six firms interviewed in the food industry.

Negroes in skilled occupations were found most frequently in coal mining,
train and engine service of railroads, foundries, and building construction.
A special word of comment is in order about skilled Negro workmen in railroads
and building construction. In both of the major railroads included in the
study, all of the skilled Negroes found were in train and engine service--that
is, were firemen, brakemen or switchmen. These Negroes were all long-service
employees, and the officials contacted in both railroads stated that they had
not hired Negroes in train and engine service for over twenty years. Thus,
skilled Negroes on the railroads are apparently being gradually replaced with
whites through the attrition of turnover, principally by retirement.

Officials of the three building construction firms interviewed stated that
they rarely employed Negro bricklayers or carpenters. It was their opinion
that in the Birmingham Area, Negroes are employed in insignificant numbers--
both absolutely and relatively--in these trades. . . .

Langston T. Hawley, "Negro Employment in the Birmingham Area," Case Study
No. 3 *Selected Studies of Negro Employment in the South* (Washington, D.C.:
National Planning Association, 1955), pp. 232-43.

THE NATIONAL NEGRO LABOR COUNCIL

37.   FOR THESE THINGS WE FIGHT!

William R. Hood

Keynote Address at the Founding Convention of the National Negro Labor
Council, October 27, 1951, Cincinnati, Ohio.

Brothers and Sisters: This is a historic day. On this day, we the
delegated representatives of thousands of workers, black and white, dedicate

ourselves to the search for a new North Star, the same star that Sojourner
Truth, Nat Turner and John Brown saw rise over the city of Cincinnati over a
century ago.

We come conscious of the new stage in the Negro people's surge toward
freedom. We come to announce to all America and to the world, that Uncle Tom
is dead. "Old Massa" lies in the cold, cold grave. Something new is cooking
on the Freedom Train.

We come here today because we are conscious at this hour of a confronting
world crisis. We are here because many of our liberties are disappearing in
the face of a powerful war economy and grave economic problems face working
men and women everywhere. No meeting held anywhere in America at this mid-
century point in world history can be more important nor hold more promise for
the bright future toward which humanity strives than this convention of our
National Negro Labor Council. For here we have gathered the basic forces of
human progress; the proud black sons and daughters of labor and our democratic
white brothers and sisters whose increasing concern for democracy, equality
and peace is America's bright hope for tomorrow.

We, the Negro working sons and daughters, have come here to Cincinnati to
keep faith with our forefathers and mothers who landed right here from the banks
of the Ohio River in their dash for freedom from chattel slavery through the
Underground Railroad. We come here to pledge ourselves that the fight for economic political and social freedom which they began shall not have been in vain.

Yes, we are here as proud black American working men and women; proud of
the right to live, not humiliated any. We are proud, too, because of our
democratic white brothers and sisters who have come here; proud because these
stanch allies are not afraid to stand shoulder to shoulder with us to fight for
that which is right.

The Negro Labor Council is our symbol, the medium of expression of our
aims and aspirations. It is the expression of our desire and determination to
bring to bear our full weight to help win first-class citizenship for every black
man, woman and child in America. We say that these are legitimate aims. We
say that these aspirations burn fiercely in the breast of every Negro in America.
And we further say that millions of white workers echo our demands for freedom.
These white workers recognize in their struggle for Negro rights the prerequi-
sites of their own aspirations for a full life and a guarantee that the rising
tide of fascism will not engulf America.

And we say that those whites who call the National Negro Labor Council
"subversive" have an ulterior motive. We know them for what they are--the
common oppressors of both people, Negro and white. We charge that their false
cry of "subversive" is calculated to maintain and extend that condition of
common oppression. We say to those whites: "You have never seen your mothers,
sisters and daughters turned away from thousands of factory gates, from the air
lines, the offices, stores and other places of desirable employment, insulted
and driven into the streets many times when they tried to eat in public places--
simply because of their color. You have never been terrorized by the mob, shot
in cold blood by the police; you have never had your home burned when you moved
out of the ghetto into another neighborhood--simply because you were black. You
are not denied the franchise; you are not denied credit in banks, denied insurance, jobs and upgrading--because of the pigmentation of your skin. You are
not denied union membership and representation; you do not die ten years before
most of the people because of these many denials of basic rights.

"Therefore, you who call this National Negro Labor Council 'subversive'
cannot understand the burning anger of the Negro people, our desire to share
the good things our labor has produced for America. You do not understand this.
So you sit like Walter Winchell, one of our attackers, in the Stork Club in
New York and see that great Negro woman artist, Josephine Baker, humiliated and
not raise a finger.

"The Negro Labor Council is dedicated to the proposition that these evils
shall end and end soon. The world must understand that we intend to build a
stronger bond of unity between black and white workers everywhere to strengthen
American democracy for all. If this be subversion--make the most of it!"

A most significant event took place in Chicago in June of 1950. Over nine
hundred delegates, Negro and white, gathered there to chart a course in the
fight for Negro rights. They came from the mines, mills, farms and factories
of America. Many of them were leaders in the organized-labor movement: seasoned
militant fighters. They voiced the complaints of Negro America.

The delegates were told that as you looked throughout the land you could see Negro men and women standing in long lines before the gates of the industrial plants for jobs, only to be told that no help was wanted—while at the same time white workers were hired. Negro women are denied the right to work in the basic sections of American industry, on the airlines, in the stores and other places. Those who were hired into industry during World War II have for the most part been systematically driven out—often in violation of union contracts. Vast unemployment since the war has struck the Negro community a severe blow.

In thousands of factories throughout the land Negroes were denied upgrading and better job opportunities. Too often the unions did not defend or fight for the right of the Negro workers to be upgraded.

We heard there in Chicago that Negro workers were denied any opportunity to participate in the great number of apprenticeship-training programs either in industry or in government, in such fields as the building trades, machine tools, printing and engraving, and other skilled fields.

We found out there that thousands of lily-white shops exist throughout the land, where no Negro has ever worked.

We discovered that federal, state and city governments maintain a severe policy of Jim Crow discrimination, beginning with the White House and moving on down to the lowest level of municipal government.

Our black brothers and sisters from the South told of unemployment, low wages, wage differentials, Jim Crow unions, peonage, sharecrop robbery and miserable destitution. They described the perpetuation of conditions in twentieth-century America that are cruelly reminiscent of slavery.

Black firemen and brakemen came to tell of the collusive agreements between railroads and the railroad brotherhoods to throw Negroes out of the railroad industry after a hundred years or more, and of the denial of union membership in these unions and no representation. A number of AFL unions were singled out for their policy of exclusion and job "monkey business" as regards black workers. We also learned that the CIO had joined the war crowd of colonial oppression and exploitation and was running fast from its early position of the thirties, when with John L. Lewis at its head it really fought for Negro rights.

Many of the delegates were stunned to hear of the thousands of denials of civil rights in public places in every state in the union. We were saddened and angered when we heard about the frameups of the Martinsville Seven, Willie McGhee, the Trenton Six, and countless other Negroes because they were black and for no other reason. We were horrified to hear of the many police killings of Negroes from New York City to Birmingham, Alabama.

Negro families were still hemmed into the ghettos, charged higher rents, chained by restrictive covenants, mob terror and finally even bombed if they were not lucky or able to move out in time. The rats are given ample opportunity to wreak their damage upon human beings, their destruction through disease and death.

Our delegates made it clear in that 1950 convention that inferior Jim Crow schools are still the policy in the South and Jim Crow quotas in the colleges of the North. The desire of black children for education and a full, useful life is yet a dream unrealized.

Is there any wonder then that this great gathering of the black working sons and daughters of our land said that this oppression can no longer exist in our America? Or is it any wonder that we received the full support of these stalwart democratic white workers present there who truly love democracy and recognize our common, basic unity of interests? So it was that they, in all righteous indignation, gave unto us, the continuators' organization, a mandate. They said to us: "Go out and build strong the Negro Labor Councils throughout the land. Build them into instruments of democracy, equality and unity."

They gave unto us the main task of fighting on that front which we knew best—the economic front for jobs, upgrading, for an end to the lily-white shops, for apprenticeship training, government jobs, local and state fair-employment-practices legislation, the nondiscrimination clause in union contracts and finally, with emphasis, the right of Negro women to work anywhere and everywhere.

They gave unto us the mandate to build an organization composed in the main of Negro workers, united and determined to wage an uncompromising struggle against Jim Crow—to build an organization which can unite with white workers who are willing to accept and support our program—to exclude no freedom fighter!

That mandate commissioned us to cooperate with those existing organizations, community and trade-union, which have undertaken genuine campaigns for
the full citizenship of the Negro people.

We were directed to build a new type of organization--not an organization
to compete with those organizations of the Negro people already at work on many
civil rights struggles. The delegates who met at Chicago demanded an organization of Negro workers from a wide variety of industries, organized and unorganized, from the great industrial centers of the North, the urban communities
of the South and the farm workers from the great rural areas. Such an organization will encourage Negroes to join unions and urge to organize Negroes.
It will call upon the entire Negro people to support labor's fight. . . .

During the course of our Council building there has been opposition from
some of the trade-union leaders, particularly to this convention. They have
accused us of attempting dual unionism, and some of them have gone so far as
to advise Negro workers not to participate in this convention. To them we
say: "Look at the Bill of Particulars, then tell us if it is not true that we
are second-class citizens in this land. Negro are still barred from many
trade-unions in this country, denied apprenticeship training, upgrading, and
refused jobs in many, many places."

We are not represented in the policy-making bodies of most international
unions. We say when the mobs came to Emerald Street in Chicago and to Cicero,
Illinois, we did not see the great trade-unions move. Yet, the basic right to
live in Cicero was denied, not only to the family of Harvey Clark, but to the
Negro people as a whole. We say that we will no longer permit the denial of
these basic rights in our country, and are pooling our strength for that purpose. We intend to do it on the basis of cooperation and unity, wherever
possible, with the organized labor movement.

We wish to say further that the day has ended when white trade-union
leaders or white leaders in any organization may presume to tell Negroes on what
basis they shall come together to fight for their rights. Three hundred years
has been enough of that. We ask for your cooperation--but we do not ask your
permission!

We believe it to be the solemn duty of trade-unions everywhere, as a matter
of vital self-interest, to support the Negro workers in their efforts to unite
and to play a more powerful role in the fight of the Negro people for first-class
citizenship based upon economic, political and social equality. We believe,
further, that it is the trade-unions' duty and right to encourage the white
workers to join with and support their Negro brothers and sisters in the achievement of these objectives. . . .

Brothers and sisters! Eloquence is a mighty weapon in the struggle for
our just demands. But what is more eloquent than the struggle itself? The big
white bosses, the men in Washington, will move far more rapidly when they see
millions of us in struggle than when they hear speeches alone.

The Negro Labor Councils are, above all, organizations of struggle. We
stand for the unity of all Negro workers, irrespective of union affiliation,
organized and unorganized; for the unity of Negro and white workers together;
for the unity of Negro workers with the whole Negro people in the common fight
for Negro liberation; and for the alliance of the whole Negro people with the
organized labor movement--the keystone combination for any kind of democratic
progress in our country. . . .

We face a number of grave tasks. We are called upon to chart a course that
will win thousands of new job opportunities for Negro men and women, that will
convince the organized-labor movement to complete the organization of the South
on the basis of equality and nonsegregation, that will help bring the franchise
to all the peoples in the South.

We are on the high road to a more democratic America. We are on the way
toward breaking the grip of the Dixiecrats and the Northern reactionaries on our
national life. I know that as you hammer out a program in these two days you
will speed up the Freedom Train; you will give greater spirit and meaning to the
Negro labor Councils; you will adopt the battle cry of the great Frederick
Douglass--"Without struggle there is no progress."

We move on, united--and neither man nor beast will turn us back. We will
achieve, in our time, for ourselves and for our children, a world of no Jim
Crow, of no more "white men's jobs" and "colored only" schools, a world of
freedom, full equality, security and peace. Our task is clearly set forth.

Brother and sisters, we move on to struggle and to victory!

Excerpted from the pamphlet, *For These Things We Fight* (Detroit, 1951).

36. NEW COUNCIL MAPS NEGRO JOB BATTLE

Labor Group Votes '52 March
on Washington to Demand
National F.E.P.C. Order

CINCINNATI, Oct. 28--The National Negro Labor Council formed a permanent organization here this afternoon and voted to lead "a national march on Washington around May 1, 1952."

The 1,052 delegates in a two-day session in the former headquarters of the Hamilton County Communist party, decided to deliver in the Capital a million signatures demanding an equal job opportunity for Negroes equal to that of all other Americans.

The plan for the march was part of a resolution calling upon President Truman to issue a Fair Employment Practice Committee order similar to that issued by President Roosevelt, and for establishment by Congress of a Federal Fair Practices Committee to enforce the order.

The resolution asserted that more than 15,000,000 Negro Americans did not have job opportunities equal to whites, and that the average Negro family's average annual income was 55 per cent below the general average and was only 40 per cent of the income estimated as necessary for minimum health and decency.

Job Struggle Called Basic

The resolution said:

"While big business and its stooges in Government on one hand proclaim to all the world that it stands for freedom and democracy, on the other hand a new tide of attacks is launched against Negroes.

"The struggle on economic issues and for a job is basic to the struggle for Negro rights. It is this struggle that is the weakest in the fight for Negro liberation.

The other principal resolution called for "a nation-wide fight for a minimum of 100,000 new jobs in the industries, shops, departments, office, crafts, skilled trades and Government employment which now deny equal job opportunities for Negro workers."

"This campaign," the resolution said, "must center around three main objectives--jobs for Negro women: cracking lily-white shops; and a general fight for upgrading throughout industry.

Asks Backing for Drive

"We call upon our affiliated councils, white allies, trade unions and all fighters for freedom to support this campaign for 100,000 new jobs and guarantee its successful conclusion by May 15, 1952," the resolution added.

A third urged special attention to jobs in industry for Negro women.

Of the 1,052 delegates, a convention spokesman estimated that 20 per cent were white.

The delegates elected as president William R. Hood of Detroit, secretary of Ford Local 600 of the United Auto Workers, CIO, Coleman Young, former director of organization for the Wayne County (Detroit) CIO Council, was chosen executive secretary. Miss Octavia Hawkins of Chicago was elected treasurer.

Ernest Thompson of Jersey City was chairman of the resolutions committee and was elected director of organization. He is Fair Employment Practices director of the United Electrical Workers, unaffiliated.

M. E. Travis of Denver, secretary-treasurer of the International Union of Mine, Mill and Smelter Workers, was elected a vice-president.[196]

New York Times, October 29, 1951.

39.   LABOR WILL LEAD OUR PEOPLE TO FIRST CLASS CITIZENSHIP

By William R. Hood

The immediate consideration in the experiences of the black people of
America, it seems to me, is that they come head-on daily with the following
things: They see the rebirth of the KKK, not only in the South but in the
North as well. They see seven Negroes judicially murdered in Richmond, Va., by
the state. They see Willie McGee murdered in the same manner. They see trigger-
happy policemen shooting down Negroes in cold blood in cities throughout the
nation. They see the First Amendment of the Constitution being destroyed.
     They see men like Ferdinand Smith, William L. Patterson, Dr. W. E. B.
DuBois and other Negro fighters for complete liberation of the Negro people,
becoming victims of a hysteria conceived in Wall Street and carried out in
Washington.
     They see an unimpeachable fighter for complete liberation of black people
of America and colonial people of the world like Paul Robeson, being put under
virtual house arrest, denied a passport to travel abroad and give to the people
of the world of his talent.
     They see the despicable and unforgiveable Cicero, Ill. incident. They see
the authorities there indict the legal counsel for the Clarke as well as others
who felt that all people should have the right to the pursuit of happiness. All
this they see happening in this America. Therefore it becomes imperative that
Negro men and women meet together and devise ways and means of putting a stop
to these outrages in order that they can help themselves as well as America.
     The convention of the Negro Labor Councils will be unique because its
purpose will be primarily to nail down in no uncertain terms a blueprint for
the complete liberation of the black people of America; having a clear understanding of the need for a complete break with the old methods and gradualist
theory of the past.
     We will consciously call upon organized labor, labor unorganized, share-
croppers, professionals, small businessmen, the churches, and all people and
organizations of good will to come together to take their position unequivocally on the question of right against wrong.
     This convention will be under the leadership of Negro working men and
women. It will take into consideration the part that must be played by the
Negro masses in the South. It will strike a new note for complete freedom of
the Negro people and call for rededication to an all-out struggle to attain
that freedom.
     The interests of Negro and white workers in America are basically the same.
They must work to live. They must struggle against the same common enemies--
the bosses of industry and of farms and plantations. We will make clear to our
white brothers and sisters that it is in the complete freedom of black America
if they are to be free themselves. We are certain that starting on this premise,
the unity of Negro and white workers will be straightened.
     While we shall fight for Negro and white unity in America, we are conscious
of our international responsibility. The great struggle for Negro liberation
is also tied with the struggles of the colonial peoples of the world in their
effort to throw off the shackles of foreign domination. We will come to Cincinnati conscious of the fact that the rulers of our country are at this point
the leaders of world reaction and the drift toward war and fascism. We will
understand that these leaders are the main oppressors of the darker people of
the world. And we will understand that it is impossible to carry on a war of
oppression and subjugation and at the same time have freedom for the darker
people of America and independence for the darker people of the world.
     I want to call upon, first the Negro people to come to Cincinnati with a
new song in their hearts, with an unshakable determination to see and get
freedom, not in the far distant future, but soon. I call upon them to come
with the approach that no matter what the cost, we will have freedom--and
freedom NOW. I call upon white people of good-will to come with the spirit of
joining this over-all struggle.

Freedom, October 1951.

40. LABOR COUNCIL MEETS, CHARTS FIGHTING PATH

By Viola Harrison

The Freedom Train, jam-packed with fifteen hundred fighters, rolled out of Cincinnati Sunday, Oct. 28, with the National Negro Labor Council well launched and put into working shape. The singing, cheering, determined delegates and observers--spent with their tireless efforts, resteamed the old train's engine and opened up the throttle to push on up the Freedom Road hewed out by their forefathers.

From the mines, from the mills, from the shops, from offices and schoolrooms, Negro working-class leaders and rank and file workers, organized and unorganized, took their battle posts and girded for action in a nationwide fight not only to attain economic, political and social status equal to white people, but to make America a better place for all people.

This historic two-day conference, the first of its kind, took appropriate notice of the background of its convention city, the most important gateway to freedom on the Underground Railroad of antebellum days. The spirits of Sojourner Truth, Denmark Vesey, Harriet Tubman, Frederick Douglass and John Brown rose again as the hall rang out with robust ayes and nays.

The theme running through the convention, in the words of its chairman, William R. Hood of Detroit, secretary-treasurer of UAW 600, largest single local in the world, was "to build a stronger unity between black and white workers everywhere to strengthen democracy for all." He reflected the attitude of all present when he defied those who labeled the conference "subversive" before the ink was dry on the sheets of the convention call by crying out, "If this be subversion--make the most of it."

Freedom, November 1951.

41. THESE WERE THE PEOPLE ON THE FREEDOM TRAIN

In order to find out what kind of people made the Freedom Train run at the NNLC convention, FREEDOM talked with the delegates. Here are some of the interviews.

"It's the lack of power, and not just the color of our skin that is the basic problem. The reason I'm sold on the NNLC is that it represents power."

The man talking in a quiet, husky voice was Asbury Howard, regional director of the Mine, Mill & Smelter Workers Union for Alabama and Mississippi. And all the experiences of Brother Howard's life have taught him the meaning of power.[197]

In 1933 he joined the union at the big Muscootia ore mine of the TCI in Bessemer, Ala., and he saw the power of the union transform the mines in that region from hell holes and death pits to places where the worker had a fighting chance to stay alive and eke out a living. Thirteen thousand out of Bessemer's 22,000 population are Negroes and Brother Howard knows that the reason the steel and ore center is Klan-dominated is fear of the power of the Negro majority. And he knows that the only thing that will stop the Klan is more power, not less.

He is clerk of the Starlight Baptist Church and superintendent of the Sunday school. He is active in the local Masons and V.P. of the Bessemer branch of the NAACP. As president of the Bessemer Voters League he has sparked a major registration drive to increase the number of Negro voters. During the drive every Negro teacher except two have registered, many of them paying $36 in back poll taxes.

"I'm fighting for my freedom. We've been slaves or half-slaves all our lives. It's like living in a dark place where you never see the light. But in the leadership of our own Paul Robeson the sun is beginning to shine. I know now that we're going to reach the top and have freedom and peace and no discrimination."

An expression of serene confidence in the face of Mrs. Estelle Holloway as she talked about conditions in the Eastern North Carolina tobacco country--the section where Paul Robeson's father was born a slave.

"Before the union came," Mrs. Holloway said, "the bosses were cruel. They're still cruel, but they can't tell us, 'Go home and stay so many days till I call for you!' like they used to. And even though the women workers make only 78¢ an hour, that's twice as much as we used to make before we had a union.

"Our big problem now is to win some kind of year-round security. The season in the leaf houses only lasts from August through the middle of November. Then the workers have to look for jobs as domestics at $10 or $15 a week. And if we don't accept any old kind of cheap job offered at the agency, we're cut off the unemployment compensation."

Mrs. Holloway is an active member of the St. James Baptist church, a member of the NAACP and a charter member of the Tri-State Negro Labor Council.

Workers were getting 40¢ an hour in the leather factory where Joseph Oliver works when the Int. Fur & Leather Workers Union stepped in in 1941. Now their contract calls for a $1.09 minimum and scores of abuses have been eliminated.

These improvements are largely due to Brother Oliver, who is not only president of the local, but a leading community figure as well. He is a member of the senior choir of the Watchco Methodist Church, chairman of the Sunday school and president of the Methodist Men of the Church. He also finds time to serve as Worshipful Master of his Masonic lodge.

Freedom, November 1951.

42. "BIG TRAIN" SPEAKS OF THE "NEW NEGRO"

By Yvonne Gregory

"Hey daddio! I see you here, man I see you with it."

"You listen when I tell you, man. Simple is solid here to speak his natural mind."

Time: Oct. 27, 1951.

Place: Lobby of the Hotel Manse, 1004 Chapel Street, Cincinnati, Ohio.

Persons: Leaders of the founding convention of the National Negro Labor Council.

They came from Cleveland, Birmingham, San Francisco, Chicago, Houston, New York, Detroit, Denver, Louisville, Winston-Salem, Pittsburgh, New Orleans, Seattle, Minneapolis, Buffalo, Jacksonville, St. Louis, Philadelphia and Newark.

One of them was Ernest Thompson, national secretary of the Fair Practices Committee of the United Electrical Workers. The others referred to him warmly and humorously as "Big Train."

It is always hard to tell how nicknames arise. But it would be a fair guess to assume that Ernest Thompson's nickname had grown out of the fact that his eyes glowed and his voice deepened when he talked on his favorite theme . . . "the Freedom Train." Thompson sees the National Negro Labor Council as one of the main pieces of machinery that will get the Freedom Train for the Negro people headed straight down the rails in the complete and final end of Jim Crow.

"Big Train" introduced the keynote speaker, William R. Hood, recording secretary of Ford Local 600, United Automobile Workers, CIO, who came out of the founding convention as first president of the Labor Council. He said:

"The new wind of freedom is blowing from the seven seas . . . it has brought upon the American scene a new Negro, sons and daughters of Labor. This new Negro comes with the song of freedom on his lips, and believe me when I tell you, that Negro is here today with some tried and true allies. And that new Negro just isn't fooling about where he means to go from here."

The 1,200 new Negro sons and daughters of Labor leaned forward in pride and wonder as they shared the rare experience of listening to an American trade union leader using the poetry of his people to illustrate and strengthen his message. "Big Train" quoted Paul Lawrence Dunbar's poem "Frederick Douglass" in full; referred to Dr. W. E. B. DuBois; quoted parts of Sterling Brown's "Strong Men" and wound up with a reference to Langston Hughes' "Simple Speaks His Mind."[198]

The reading of the Dunbar poem was particularly eloquent. He recited it
as though he had been remembering it all his life; waiting for the chance to
stand on a platform in Cincinnati, O., as the representative of a new Negro
organization dedicated to the fight for full freedom and say the poem which
included these words about Frederick Douglass:

> "We weep for him, but we have touched his hand,
> And felt the magic of his presence nigh,
> The current that he sent throught the land,
> The kindling spirit of his battle cry.
> O'er all that holds us we shall triumph yet,
> And place our banner where his hopes were set!

Freedom, November 1951.

43. SOUTHERN WORKER CALLS FOR LABOR COUNCIL DRIVE

By Joseph Reynolds

MEMPHIS, TENN.--I was unable to attend the Negro Labor Council convention
in Cincinnati due to my physical condition, but I have read the keynote speeches
of Brother Bill Hood, Sister Pearl Laws, Paul Robeson and others and I think
they express the real down-to-earth feeling of the Negro masses, especially
here in the South.
It is my firm conviction that this conference and its leaders have a job
to do in the South now. That is the job which hasn't been done by these labor
leaders who have betrayed and deserted the Negro people's struggle for freedom
in the South, such as the Murrays, the Reuthers, the Bill Greens--and we can by
no means overlook the deeds of John L. Lewis, how he has also played his part
in deserting the Negro coal miners in the South, who were the first to bleed
and die in the mountains of the South to build the union in these mines.
The job that must be done is the job of organizing the unorganized. By
this I mean to a great degree the Negro masses. In my opinion the job of
building the Negro Labor Councils in the South is more vital today to the whole
nation than the birth of the CIO was in 1935-38. I am not attempting to overlook the gains that we made here in that period; but in those days we had to
face only the company dicks, city and county officials. Fighting for our rights
today, it is the city, county, state and the federal government's FBI Hitler-
like police that we have to face in the South.

FBI Snoopers

These Truman police can't find the lynchers of the Negro people. They
don't dare to trail the KKK leaders but on the contrary, spend 24 hours a day
looking and snooping behind rank-and-file Negroes--and also the whites who dare
to speak up for the rights of the Negro people. So this is why organizing the
unorganized Negro masses is vital today to the whole nation.
The program calls for hundreds of thousands of jobs in lily-white industries.
That's fine. But let me also state that there in the South Negroes are being
kicked out of jobs right and left, and many of them are members of some of these
big labor unions, and these big labor leaders and their local lieutenants are
doing nothing about it.
Among the millions of Negroes here in the South there are unorganized
lumber workers, sharecroppers, tenants and small farmers who need an organization of some kind for their security, and they are looking and hoping for a
chance to free themselves.
I would say there are at least a million or more domestic workers in the
South, and I dare say two-thirds of the workers are Negro women. Among these
women are wives, daughters and sisters of steel, coal, railroad and all kinds
of Negro workers. Many of these women are members of sharecropper, tenant and
small farmer Negro families.

Action Counts

We in the South have been in these founding conventions before. We have
heard many big-sounding words from various speakers. But action is what's
going to count today. Action is what is going to win over these would-be slave-
holders of the Negro people of the South and the working masses of this country.

What is to be done from this founding Negro Labor Council that has closed
its sessions in Cincinnati, Ohio?

There must be an organizing drive in the South, to do this job of organizing these millions of unorganized Negro people, a drive like that put on in
the early days of the CIO in the South.

There should be a Southern organizational director, with finances and
manpower known as the organizing committee (a) to build Negro Labor Councils on
a city and state basis among existing Negro trade unionists and their white
allies, and (b) to organize the unorganized domestic workers, farm labor, sharecroppers, tenants and small farmers.

These so-called left labor leaders who head these so-called left unions
should be called upon by the national leaders and members of this Council to
get off the fence and show what side they are on in this fight for Negro rights
in their unions and in the South.

They should come together and pool their financial resources behind this
Council's drive to organize the unorganized of the South.

Plans should be made to organize a series of affairs, of Robeson concerts
with talent from the South such as speakers, singing groups and soloists taking
an active part. Those who say they are interested in helping the cause of freedom of the Negro people should be called on, to give them a chance to put words
of sympathy into deeds.

There are many Negro veterans of struggle who are waiting for a chance to
come forward and again show their ability in the struggle for freedom, who have
been made victims here in the South by the white supremacists in the labor unions.

Freedom, December 1951.

44.
HEARINGS
BEFORE THE

COMMITTEE ON UN-AMERICAN ACTIVITIES[199]
HOUSE OF REPRESENTATIVES

Testimony of Coleman A. Young, Accompanied by His
Counsel, George W. Crockett, Jr.

Mr. Wood. Are you represented by counsel, Mr. Young?

Mr. Young. May I get my brief case?

Mr. Wood. Are you represented by counsel?

Mr. Young. I am.

Mr. Crockett. I represent Mr. Young. My name is George W. Crockett, Jr.
I am a member of the bar of Michigan and the United States Supreme Court. My
office is located in the Cadillac Tower in the city of Detroit. I am appearing
as counsel for the witness, Mr. Coleman Young.

Mr. Tavenner. Will you state your full name, please, Mr. Young?

Mr. Young. Coleman A. Young.

Mr. Tavenner. When and where were you born?

Mr. Young. May 24, 1918, Tuscaloosa, Ala.

Mr. Tavenner. Will you tell the committee, please, briefly, what your
education training has been?

Mr. Young. I am a high school graduate.

Mr. Tavenner. Do you now reside in Detroit?

Mr. Young. I do.

Mr. Tavenner. How long have you lived in Detroit?

Mr. Young. Approximately 30 years.

Mr. Tavenner. Will you give the committee, please, a general background
of your employment record, say, over the past 10 years?

Mr. Young. Well, I came out of high school and I went to work at Ford
Motor Co.--that was in 1937--for about a year and a half. I subsequently
worked in a dry-cleaning plant; I worked for the United States Veterans' Administration, at the hospital here; I worked for the post office before I went
into the Army. I was discharged from the post office for attempting to organize
a union. I went into the Army about a month later. After coming out, I worked
for the post office about 2 months. I quit the post office because they refused to give me a leave of absence so that I might work for the union organization, the International Union of United Public Workers; director of program for
the Wayne County CIO; State director for the Progressive Party of Michigan;
presently, national executive secretary of the National Negro Labor Council.
    Mr. Tavenner. What was the last of the employment you had:
    Mr. Young. I am national executive secretary of the National Negro Labor
Council.
    Mr. Young. It is.
    Mr. Tavenner. What was the position you mentioned you had with the organi-
zation of the CIO?
    Mr. Young. Director of organization for the Wayne County CIO Council.
    Mr. Tavenner. Over what period of time?
    Mr. Young. During the period of 1947 and 1948.
    Mr. Tavenner. Mr. Young, I want to state to you in advance of questioning
you, that the investigators of the committee have not produced or presented any
evidence of Communist Party membership on your part. The purpose in asking you
to come here is to inquire into some of the--into the activities of some of the
organizations with which you have been connected, to see to what extent, if any,
the committee should be interested in them from the standpoint of those manifesting communism. Now, you mentioned--
    Mr. Young. Mr. Tavenner, I would like to say this: First of all, I have
understood, from official pronouncements of this committee, and yourself, that
this is a forum; you call it the highest forum in the country, being that of the
Congress of the United States. I have been subpoenaed here. I did not come by my
own prerogative.
    Mr. Tavenner. I understand.
    Mr. Young. I can only state that in being interviewed and being asked
questions, that I hope that I will be allowed to react fully to those questions,
and not be expected to react only in such a manner that this committee may desire me. In other words, I might have answers you might not like. You called
me here to testify; I am prepared to testify, but, I would like to know from you
if I shall be allowed to respond to your questions fully and in my own way.
    Mr. Tavenner. I have no objection to your answers, if they are responsive
to the questions.
    Mr. Young. I will respond.
    Mr. Tavenner. But I desire to ask you the question which I have asked
other witnesses: Are you now a member of the Communist Party?
    Mr. Young. I refuse to answer that question, relying upon my rights under
the fifth amendment, and, in light of the fact that an answer to such a question,
before such a committee, would be, in my opinion, a violation of my rights and
privacy of political beliefs and associates, and, further, since I have no purpose of being here as a stool pigeon, I am not prepared to give any information
on any of my associates or political thoughts.
    Mr. Tavenner. Have you been a member of the Communist Party?
    Mr. Young. For the same reason, I refuse to answer that question.
    Mr. Tavenner. You told us you were the executive secretary of the National
Negro Congress--
    Mr. Young. That word is "Negro," not "Niggra."
    Mr. Tavenner. I said, "Negro." I think you are mistaken.
    Mr. Young. I hope I am. Speak more clearly.
    Mr. Wood. I will appreciate it if you will not argue with counsel.
    Mr. Young. It isn't my purpose to argue. As a Negro, I resent the slur-
ring of the name of my race.
    Mr. Wood. You are here for the purpose of answering questions.
    Mr. Young. In some sections of the country they slur--
    Mr. Tavenner. I am sorry. I did not mean to slur it. I was mistaken in
referring to your having said you were the executive secretary of the National
Negro Congress; but, I will ask you a question, if you were, at any time in the
past, executive secretary of the National Negro Congress?

Mr. Young. I refuse to answer that question under the fifth amendment.

Mr. Tavenner. Your position is that to answer any question with relation to your connection with the National Negro Congress might tend to incriminate you, is that your position?

Mr. Young. The National Negro Congress, as I understand it, has been labeled by not only the Justice Department, but by this committee, which also labeled the National Association for the Advancement of Colored People as subversive, and I don't intend to discuss any organization that, properly or improperly, has been designated by you or any other committee as subversive.

Mr. Tavenner. Were you, at any time, a field organizer for the National Negro Congress?

Mr. Young. The same answer will apply in regard to the National Negro Congress.

Mr. Tavenner. I understood you to state--you answered a moment ago that this committee had labeled the NAACP as subversive.

Mr. Young. That is correct.

Mr. Tavenner. When was such action taken?

Mr. Young. I refer you to the Negro Yearbook of 1949.

Mr. Tavenner. Can you refer to any record of the committee which has so designated the NAACP?

Mr. Young. I am sure this committee is in possession of its own records. I would suggest a search of those records.

Mr. Tavenner. It is on record? You are sure I have evidence of such designation with regard to the NAACP, a national organization?

Mr. Young. I refer you to--

Mr. Tavenner. There was a local in Hawaii which had some special problem, but, as far as the national organization is concerned, this committee has not so cited it, nor has the Attorney General's office, in my opinion.

Mr. Young. Was Mr. Rankin ever a member of this committee, Congressman Rankin; I refer to Congressman Rankin. He is the person who designated the NAACP, the National Association for the Advancement of Colored People, as being a subversive organization, and thus preventing them from any early considerations in projects for Negro rights.

Mr. Potter. Mr. Young, Congressman Rankin is not a member of this committee.

Mr. Young. Mr. Potter, Congressman Rankin was one of the foremost members of this committee, following the same purpose.

Mr. Potter. We are not here to discuss Congressman Rankin. We are here to find out the extent of the Communist activities in this area. You are in a position to help and aid, if you will, but the attitude you are taking is uncooperative to such an investigation.

Mr. Young. I am not here to fight in any un-American activities, because I consider the denial of the right to vote to large numbers of people all over the South un-American, and I consider--

Mr. Potter. I will join you in the same thing, but, at the same time, a member of the Communist Party is a person who carries on un-American activities.

Mr. Tavenner. Do you consider the activities of the Communist Part un-American?

Mr. Young. I consider the activities of this committee, as it cites people for allegedly being a Communist, as un-American activities.

Mr. Wood. Just a moment. Your answer is not responsive to the question. He asked if you regarded the activities of the Communist Party as un-American?

Mr. Young. I am not in a position to answer that question.

Mr. Tavenner. Are you acquainted with any of the activities of the Communist Party in the city of Detroit?

Mr. Young. I have made it clear, or sought to make it clear--

Mr. Tavenner. That you might aid the committee, as you suggested awhile ago you would like to do.

Mr. Young. I sought to make it clear that I consider any questions that deal with my political beliefs, or with the beliefs of people I may or may not have been associated with, a violation of my rights under the fifth amendment, and an invasion of my privacy guaranteed me under the first amendment.

Mr. Tavenner. I asked you no question regarding your individual views. I asked if you knew of any activities of the Communist Party in this community, which might be of some assistance to this committee in its investigation of un-American activities. I understood from your statement you would like to help us.

Mr. Young. You have me mixed up with a stool pigeon.

Mr. Potter. I have never heard of anybody stooling in the Boy Scouts.

Mr. Young. I was a member of the organization.

Mr. Potter. I don't think they are proud of it today.

Mr. Young. I will let the Scouts decide that.

Mr. Potter. I think they would.

Mr. Tavenner. I would like to take you at your word, that you would like to help this committee in its investigation of anything that may be of an un-American character, and one of the things the committee, as I mentioned to you a moment ago, desire you to do is to relate some of the activities of the persons of some organizations with which you have been connected. You are certainly in a position to give that information if you were actually a member of the organization. Now, we are anxious to know about the origin of the organization, of which you are now, I believe, the executive secretary, the National Negro Labor Council.

Mr. Young. I will tell you about my organization.

Mr. Tavenner. I want you to try to go back to the beginning. I have asked you about the National Negro Congress, which you have declined to advise us about, and, I want to ask you, further, whether or not you and a group of others were active in the organization of a city-wide veteran council in January 1946, and if there was any connection of any character between it and the National Negro Congress?

Mr. Young. I refuse to answer that question, taking advantage of the privilege granted me under the fifth amendment. However, if you want to know about the National Negro Labor Council, I will tell you about it.

Mr. Tavenner. We will come to that.

Mr. Young. You are going to tell me about it, is that it?

Mr. Tavenner. No, no, no. Would it not be correct to say that the Veteran's Council, which was organized in January 1946, was converted into and became the Detroit chapter of the National Negro Congress?

Mr. Young. I have already indicated to you that I have no information for this committee concerning the National Negro Congress. I am willing to discuss my organization, the National Negro Labor Council.

Mr. Wood. Just answer the questions that are asked. Let's get along with the hearing. He is asking you if it is correct--

Mr. Young. Congressman, you invited me here to testify, and, I intend to testify.

Mr. Wood. I want you to answer the questions as they are asked.

Mr. Young. I will answer them in my own way.

Mr. Wood. There isn't but one way to answer them, and that's the right way.

Mr. Young. And, that's the way you want me to answer it.

Mr. Wood. That is the only truthful way to answer it.

Mr. Young. I am not allowing the committee to put words in my mouth.

Mr. Jackson. The committee might put some words in your mouth that are a great deal better than the ones you are uttering.

Mr. Young. Sir, you have been making lectures for a long time--

Mr. Wood. I am not going to allow you to argue. If you want to answer the question, answer; if you don't want to answer it, decline. This is not a vaudeville here; this is serious business.

Mr. Young. I regret not being given the opportunity to answer. You said this was going to be a forum. When the Congressman addresses me, I will expect the courtesy to answer the Congressman.

Mr. Jackson. As far as I am concerned, you will have opportunity to answer me at any time I say anything to you.

Mr. Young. You just got through addressing me.

Mr. Jackson. You will have the opportunity to answer any questions I ask.

Mr. Young. Do you have anything to say to me?

Mr. Jackson. I will have something to say to you in due course.

Mr. Young. I will have something to say to you, too.

Mr. Jackson. That is your privilege.

Mr. Tavenner. Were you affiliated, at any time, with an organization known as the United Negro and Allied Veterans of America?

Mr. Young. I refuse to answer that question, taking advantage of the fifth amendment, Mr. Tavenner. You told us, in giving us the background of your record of employment, that you are now the executive secretary of the National Negro Labor Council?

Mr. Young. That is correct.

Mr. Tavenner. When was it formed?

Mr. Young. It was formed in Cincinnati, Ohio, formally organized on October 27 and 28 of the past year. That would be 1951.

Mr. Tavenner. Nineteen fifty-one?

Mr. Young. That is right.

Mr. Tavenner. Who is its president?

Mr. Young. President William R. Hood, whom you have also subpenaed.

Mr. Tavenner. Is there any difference in the objectives of the National Negro Labor Council and the National Negro Congress?

Mr. Young. I am prepared to discuss the objectives and the program of the National Negro Labor Council. I am not prepared to discuss the objectives of the National Negro Congress. If you will separate the question, I will answer.

Mr. Tavenner. Why aren't you prepared? Is it you are not familiar with the objectives of the National Negro Congress? What do you mean, by saying you are not prepared?

Mr. Young. As far as the National Negro Congress is concerned, I have stated my objection under the fifth amendment, as well as the first amendment. I have also indicated to you it isn't my intention to discuss here any organization labeled by your committee or any other committee as subversive. I have here a copy of the preamble of the National Negro Labor Council, which will explain its objectives, if you want to hear it.

Mr. Tavenner. I would like to have it filed.

Mr. Young. You don't want to hear it, you want to file it.

Mr. Tavenner. I would like for you to tell me wherein it differs from the National Negro Congress.

Mr. Young. Are you a congressman?

Mr. Tavenner. No, I am not. I had in mind, from the investigation we made, you would know something about the National Negro Congress; in fact, our information has been that you were the field organizer of it, and, if you were, you would be bound to have some knowledge of its objectives, if you worked as an organizer for it.

Mr. Young. If your information comes from stoolpigeons and paid informers, you might have any kind of information.

Mr. Wood. Well, let's get the information from you. Were you or were you not an organizer for it?

Mr. Young. I have stated, and I restate, I refuse to answer any questions concerning the National Negro Congress, relying upon my rights under fifth amendment.

Mr. Tavenner. Wherein does the objectives, purposes of your organization, which you are now executive secretary differ from that organization?

Mr. Young. The purposes of the organization which I am now connected with, and that is the National Negro Labor Council, are as follows:

We, the members of the Negro Labor Council, believe that the struggle of the Negro people for first-class citizenship based on economic, political, and social equality is in vain unless we as Negro workers, along with our white allies, are united to protect our people (Negro) against those forces who continue to deny us full citizenship.

Realizing that the old forms of organizations which were dedicated to the fight for first-class citizenship for Negro people have been unable to bring full economic opportunity for the Negro worker in the factory, the mine, the mill, the office, in government; to stop wanton police killings of Negros throughout the land; to stop mob violence against us; to bring the franchise to our brothers and sisters in the South, and gain our full say in the political life of our country with proper representation in government on all levels; to buy and rent homes everywhere unrestricted; to use the public facilities, restaurants, hotels, and the recreation facilities in town and country, we form the National Negro Labor Council (NNLC), an organization which unites all Negro workers with other suffering minorities and our allies among the white workers, and base ourselves on rank and file control regardless of age, sex, creed, political beliefs, or union affiliation, and pursue at all times a policy of militant struggle to improve our conditions.

We pledge ourselves to labor unitedly for the principles herein set forth, to perpetuate our councils and work concertedly with other organizations that seek improvement for Negro and other oppressed minorities.

We further pledge ourselves to work unitedly with the trade-unions to bring about greater cooperation between all sections of the Negro people and the trade-union movement; to bring the principles of trade-unionism to the Negro workers everywhere; to aid the trade-unions in the great unfinished task of organizing the South on the basis of fraternity, equality, and unity; to further unity between black and white workers everywhere.

Mr. Wood. Now, having read and gotten it into the records, will you answer the question asked you, which is, in what respect does it differ from the National Negro Congress?

Mr. Young. I take it this committee is in possession of information on the program of the National Negro Congress. You are now, as of my having read our preamble, in possession of information on the program of the National Negro Labor Council--

Mr. Wood. You are making a very fine assumption.

Mr. Young. I am sure you are competent to judge the question for yourself.

Mr. Wood. I am asking you for the difference.

Mr. Young. I refuse to answer the question on the basis of the fifth amendment.

Mr. Wood. Do you refuse to answer that question?

Mr. Young. That would apply to any question, that question and any other question that has within it reference to the National Negro Congress.

Mr. Wood. I want an answer. Do you refuse to answer the question asked you?

Mr. Young. Will you repeat what specific question you are talking about?

Mr. Wood. The question asked you.

What is the question? Read the question to him.

(The question was read by official court reporter.)

Mr. Young. As this committee is in possession of a copy--

Mr. Wood. Let's not assume things.

Mr. Young. I am trying to answer the question, if you will let me.

Mr. Wood. No, you are not. You are trying to evade my question.

Mr. Young. You will have to wait for my answer in order to determine whether I am evading or not. I haven't finished.

Mr. Wood. You are assuming what you don't know.

Mr. Young. You are assuming what I am going to say.

Mr. Wood. I want you to answer in what way the preamble you read, of the National Negro Labor Council, differs, if any, in respect to the National Negro Congress.

Mr. Young. I would inform you, also, the word is Negro.

Mr. Wood. I am sorry. If I made a different pronouncement of it, it is due to my inability to use the language any better than I do. I am trying to use it properly.

Mr. Young. It may be due to your southern background.

Mr. Wood. I am not ashamed of my southern background. For your information, out of the 112 Negro votes cast in the last election in the little village from which I come, I got 112 of them. That ought to be a complete answer of that. Now, will you answer the question?

Mr. Young. You are through with it now, is that it?

Mr. Wood. I don't know.

Mr. Young. I happen to know, in Georgia Negro people are prevented from voting by virtue of terror, intimidation, and lynchings. It is my contention you would not be in Congress today if it were not for the legal restrictions on voting on the part of my people.

Mr. Wood. I happen to know that is a deliberate false statement on your part.

Mr. Young. My statement is on the record.

Mr. Wood. Mine is, too.

Mr. Young. I will stand by my statement.

Mr. Jackson. I suggest that the witness answer the question directed by counsel.

Mr. Wood. Now, will you answer the question asked?

Mr. Young. If you will let me finish my answer, I will.

Mr. Wood. If you will answer the question, I will get a soap box and let you make a speech; if you will just answer the question.

Mr. Young. I will join you on a soap box. You have been doing pretty good in answering other questions. If you have a constitution of the National Negro

Congress, I will be glad to read your copy and point out to you what differences
exist between the two organizations.
Mr. Wood. Don't you know, without reading it?
Mr. Young. I have already answered it.
Mr. Wood. Please answer.
Mr. Young. I refuse to answer the question in connection with the Nation-
al Negro Congress, taking advantage of my rights under the fifth amendment.
Mr. Wood. Are you refusing to answer whether you know what it contains?
Mr. Young. I consider I have answered the question.
Mr. Wood. All right.
Mr. Tavenner. When did the National Negro Congress cease to function,
if it did?
Mr. Young. At the risk of being monotonous, I refuse to answer any ques-
tion referring to or having to do with the National Negro Congress, by reason
of the rights under the fifth amendment. However, I am prepared to discuss the
National Negro Labor Council.
Mr. Tavenner. Let me ask you, if the National Negro Labor Council is
merely a reactivation of the National Negro Congress?
Mr. Young. I will answer you this: The National Negro Labor Council is
an organization consisting of Negro trade-unions, in the main, and of white
trade-unions, also, who agree with our program, which was formed, as I told
you, in Cincinnati, October 27 and 28, of 1951.
Mr. Tavenner. Now, will you answer the question, please?
Mr. Young. The answer to the question is that the National Negro Labor
Council is an offshoot of no organization. It is a completely new organization,
formed with a new program, a program of bringing together, in the struggle for
Negro rights, the organized strength of the Negro people and the trade-union
movement; an organization which believes that in order to gain these rights,
it is necessary to maintain constant struggle; an organization primarily inter-
ested in, among other things, the fight for the ballot for the people in the
South, and that includes the State of Georgia, and the State of Virginia, where,
I understand, you are from, counsel.
Mr. Wood. Please give us credit for knowing we are from the southern
section of the country. I think this committee is familiar with it.
Mr. Young. I am, too, counsel.
Mr. Tavenner. In your answer, you referred to it not being an offshoot
of any other organization. My question is whether or not it is, in fact, a
reactivation of the National Negro Congress?
Mr. Young. I have indicated to you that, relying on my rights under the
fifth amendment, I refuse to answer any question concerning the National Negro
Congress.
Mr. Tavenner. Will you advise the committee to what extent, within your
knowledge, the Civil Rights Congress in this area has assisted the Communist
Party in attainment of any of its objectives?
Mr. Young. I have indicated to you, to this committee, I am no stool-
pigeon. I refuse to answer any question concerning organizations labeled as
subversive, relying on my rights under the fifth amendment.
Mr. Tavenner. Then, when you stated earlier in your testimony that you
would like to help this committee to examine into un-American activities, you
meant to put limitations upon that?
Mr. Young. I would say that the committee has put limitations upon an
investigation into un-American activities. This committee has failed to investigate the Moore slaying in--
Mr. Wood. Is that your reason for refusing to answer the questions asked
you?
Mr. Young. I am ready to point out to this committee, taking for granted
you may not know about some of the atrocities that have taken place against the
Negro people in this country--
Mr. Wood. I asked, if that is the reason you refuse to answer the questions?
Mr. Young. I merely submit that you investigate these un-American
activities.
Mr. Wood. At the moment, we are investigating un-American activities we
are asking you about and have been asking you about. Do you plan to answer them?
Mr. Young. I consider it an un-American activity to pry into a person's
private thoughts, to pry into a person's associates; I consider that an un-
American activity.

Mr. Wood. Is that your reason for not answering?

Mr. Young. I am unwilling to engage in un-American activities--

Mr. Wood. Is that your reason?

Mr. Young. My reason has been clearly stated; I rely upon the fifth amendment of the Constitution of the United States.

Mr. Tavenner. Have you been affiliated, in the past, with the Civil Rights Congress?

Mr. Young. I rely upon the fifth amendment of the Constitution of the United States, and refuse to answer that question.

Mr. Tavenner. The committee is informed that various petitions were prepared by the Civil Rights Congress, protesting the indictment of the 12 Communist leaders in New York City, and that you were one of the signers, a signer of one of the petitions. I am not interested, particularly, in whether you were or not. I am more interested in ascertaining the circumstances under which your signature, or that of any person, was obtained. Will you tell us that?

Mr. Young. Sir, I have explained to you my refusal to answer such questions. I think it would be quite foolish on my part, in view of the hysteria stirred up by this committee; in view of the many bills having to do with people's political association, etc., to indicate to you on any question any information which might amount to testifying against myself. Therefore, under the fifth amendment, I refuse to answer.

Mr. Potter. If there is any hysteria in this country, it is generated by people like yourself, and not by this committee.

Mr. Young. Congressman, neither me or none of my friends were out at this plant the other day brandishing a rope in the face of John Cherveny. I can assure you I have had no part in the hanging or bombing of Negroes in the South. I have not been responsible for firing a person from his job for what I think are his beliefs, or what somebody thinks he believes in, and things of that sort. That is the hysteria that has been swept up by this committee.

Mr. Potter. Today, there are 104,000 casualties in Korea testifying to this fact of hysteria you so blandly mention, which is a cold-blooded conspiracy, which is killing American boys, and, you, as members of the Communist Party of the United States, are just as much a part of the international conspiracy as the Communists in North Korea who are killing men there.

Mr. Young. I see you have on a decoration, and, I will inform you, I am also a veteran of the Armed Forces. I know you did your part. I want you to know I didn't have any part in sending anybody to Korea.

Mr. Jackson. Do you approve of the action of the United States in Korea?

Mr. Young. I refuse to allow this committee to pry into my personal and private opinions. I got some opinion on it, however.

Mr. Tavenner. Let me see if your opinions have been private in that respect. According to the Daily Worker of July 24, 1950, you signed a statement issued by the Council on African Affairs against the United States' policy in Korea, is that correct?[200]

Mr. Young. I refuse to answer any such question, relying upon my rights under the fifth amendment. What was the organization you mentioned?

Mr. Tavenner. Council on African Affairs.

Mr. Young. I would like for the record to show that organization has also been labeled subversive.

Mr. Jackson. Is that positively on the record?

Mr. Young. Very definitely it is.

Mr. Jackson. Let's make it very certainly a point, it has been labeled subversive, and there will be no doubt about it.

Mr. Wood. It might also, with equal propriety, be injected in the record that the Daily Worker has been labeled as subversive by the Attorney General of the United States.

Mr. Tavenner. May I ask the witness, that prior to January 24, 1950, did you know that the Council on African Affairs had been labeled a Communist organization by the Attorney General of the United States?

Mr. Young. I refuse to answer the question under the fifth amendment.

Mr. Tavenner. Have you attended Communist Party meetings?

Mr. Young. I refuse to answer that question under the fifth amendment.

Mr. Tavenner. I think, you have, from time to time, been interested in political meetings in this area and the area around Detroit, have you not?

Mr. Young. I am interested in political meetings.

Mr. Tavenner. Have you ever been a candidate for office?

Mr. Young.   In 1948, I ran for State senator on the Progressive Party ticket. At that time, I was also State director of the Progressive Party.

Mr. Jackson.   What was the verdict of the people in that election?

Mr. Young.   The verdict wasn't as good as your own. I wasn't elected, if that's what you mean.

Mr. Tavenner.   Did you confer with Pat Toohey, and did you receive support of his organization in your campaign? By organization, I mean, the Communist Party.

Mr. Young.   I have indicated I refuse to answer any such questions under the fifth amendment.

Mr. Tavenner.   Did you attend a banquet on May 17, 1941, given by the Communist Party of Michigan, to welcome Pat Toohey as the new secretary of the Communist Party of Michigan?

Mr. Young.   I refuse to answer any such questions under the fifth amendment.

Mr. Tavenner.   Did you attend a meeting in the Mirror Ballroom, 2940 Woodward Avenue, on January 18, 1942, sponsored by the Communist Party of Michigan, and referred to as the Lenin Memorial Meeting and Rally for Victory?

Mr. Young.   I refuse to answer any such questions under the fifth amendment.

Mr. Tavenner.   I would like to know if you performed any services for the Communist Party, and, if so, how it was obtained, how you were induced to give it, in connection with the appearance in Detroit of Benjamin J. Davis in 1948?

Mr. Young.   I refuse to answer any such question, under the privileges of the fifth amendment.

Mr. Tavenner.   Didn't you introduce him at a public meeting on July 27, 1948, at which time he spoke and made the statement "I am proud to be an American, a Negro, and a Communist?"

Mr. Young.   For the same reason, I refuse to answer.

Mr. Tavenner.   In speaking of un-American activities, which you said you would like to help the committee with, do you think it would be giving aid and comfort to the Communist Party, and assisting them in the attainment of its objectives, if people, with responsible positions in the community such as that which you held at that time, would actively support meetings at which known Communist members, such as Benjamin J. Davis were present, and where it was expected that statements of the character which I read to you would be made?

Mr. Young.   Are you asking me a suppositional question? If you are, and want me to suppose, I will. I think that any meeting in which the first Negro councilman ever elected to the office in the State of New York were to attend would be of interest to a great number of Negroes. It would be to the credit of any party if that Negro were elected under the label of that party. That is my supposition in answer to your question.

Mr. Tavenner.   Is that regardless of whether or not he was elected on the Communist Party ticket, as a part of the Communist Party movement, if you knew it to be such?

Mr. Young.   Well, supposing again, I would think that Negro people would be more interested in what a given candidate's program might happen to be, and what he was going to do to improve the conditions of Negro people, than any label tagged on to him by such a committee as yourselves and others.

Mr. Tavenner.   I am not speaking of the committee. Benjamin J. Davis was an open member of the Communist Party; elected on the Communist Party ticket. He didn't have to be labeled. He labeled himself. He said, definitely, in this meeting--

Mr. Young.   Personally, I would affirm any candidate for office by virtue of program on which he ran, and on that basis only; his program and his actions; these are the things which concern me as a voter.

Mr. Tavenner.   Therefore, if the Communist Party carried out its avowed objectives, its avowed program of working through mass organization, that is, by selecting groups of people and appealing to the particular items which that group is interested in, and organizing them as a Communist-front organization, because, that's what those organizations are, you would support such a thing, knowing that it is a Communist-front organization?

Mr. Young.   You can--

Mr. Tavenner.   Is that the sense and sum and substance of what you told us?

Mr. Young. You can draw the substance and sum you wish from my last answer, but, under the fifth amendment, I am not answering any question dealing with the Communist Party, and, I think, for pretty obvious reasons.

Mr. Tavenner. You state, you would sustain anyone who took a position which was favorable to the particular thing you were interested in?

Mr. Young. When I go in the ballot box, as of now, I have privacy; I vote as I see fit. Are you trying to invade the privacy of my ballot box?

Mr. Tavenner. Not at all.

Mr. Young. I don't see why you ask these questions.

Mr. Tavenner. It is a very important question.

Mr. Young. You asked me how I vote.

Mr. Tavenner. It is a very important matter to determine to what extent the Communists, through Communist-front organizations, are endeavoring to injure the economics of this area, the religion of this area, the social life of this area, and, in fact, the whole political structure as we know it in this country.

Mr. Young. Well, I leave that to you.

Mr. Tavenner. It is that that we are attempting to get at.

Mr. Young. I leave that to this committee to get at.

Mr. Tavenner. It is that we are asking you to help us with.

Mr. Young. I think I have indicated what my reaction to that is.

Mr. Tavenner. Did you attend a Communist Party meeting held at 2705 Joy Road, on March 18, 1950, in celebration of International Women's Day?

Mr. Young. I previously indicated my refusal to answer any questions of that nature on the privilege of the fifth amendment.

Mr. Tavenner. Did you attend a meeting of the Communist Party of Michigan on January 8, 1942, at which Pat Toohey, secretary of the Communist Party of Michigan, was a speaker?

Mr. Young. I refuse to answer for the same reason.

Mr. Tavenner. Were you acquainted with Pat Toohey personally?

Mr. Young. I refuse to answer for the same reason.

Mr. Tavenner. Mr. Chairman, I think that is all.

Mr. Jackson. I have several questions, Mr. Chairman. I assume, Mr. Young, that you believe in peace.

Mr. Young. Do you believe in peace?

Mr. Jackson. I do.

Mr. Young. I am for peace, too.

Mr. Jackson. Do you believe that it is possible, in the present conflict, between the Soviet Union and the United States, to work out a just and lasting peace at the conference table?

Mr. Young. I hope that it is.

Mr. Jackson. Do you feel that it is possible for the United States and the Soviet Union to coexist side by side in the same world?

Mr. Young. If you mean by that, do I hope that the United States and the Soviet Union will not go to war, that is the other side of the question.

Mr. Jackson. That is the obverse side. I certainly hope so. Do you believe in a more positive manner that it is possible for the Soviet Union and the United States to exist side by side in a peaceful world?

Mr. Young. I have indicated that I fervently hope that that is possible.

Mr. Jackson. I am sure that we are all in full agreement on that point. However, Mr. Stalin has said that it is inconceivable that the Soviet Union and the United States shall long exist side by side in the same world. I think that is one of the very many clear warnings that we have had as to the ultimate goal of communism. Implementation of that Communist policy is underway today on a dozen different fronts. Some of it is in the Armed Forces, some of it economic, some of it political, and some of it social. I have frequently expressed the opinion and I express it again, that I feel that anyone who takes up cudgels of the Communist Party today or lends any aid and assistance to the Communist Party in this country, in the light of what has developed over the course of the past 2 or 3 years, is in effect wielding a bayonet as efficiently as a Communist soldier in Korea is. Is there any portion of that with which you agree? [201]

Mr. Young. I will say that I am taking up the cudgel for the rights for full equality now and not 5 years from now, for my people. These are the cudgels that I am taking up. I don't know when you say "anybody" broadly whether you are inferring me or anything else.

Mr. Jackson. I am not inferring anything. I am asking your opinion on
that particular statement. As far as the war against fascism is concerned
there has been more sacrifice made by the people probably than by the majority
of the witnesses who have appeared before the committee and refused to answer
on the grounds of the fifth amendment. Congressman Potter has made a tremendous
sacrifice in the fight against fascism.
Mr. Young. The fight is still on.
Mr. Jackson. We have acknowledged that out in California. The people--
Mr. Young. Some of the victims of this committee--
Mr. Jackson. The people of your race have every privilege of the franchise. I do not think you can attack California or the California Member on
that basis.
Mr. Young. Can I say something on that?
Mr. Jackson. Yes.
Mr. Young. Our San Francisco council, and we are a national organization,
the National Negro Labor Council, just one month ago was successful in breaking
down the Jim Crow hiring practices of the T System Street Railway that exists
in San Francisco. That company prior to that time discriminated against Negroes
as bus drivers and also within the same month they were successful, after a
long fight, in breaking down the discrimination that Sears Roebuck, the company,
held against Negro saleswomen. You can't tell me that Jim Crow doesn't exist
in California. There is a whole lot wrong with California that has got to be
straightened out.
Mr. Jackson. You said that there is a whole lot wrong with all the world.
Mr. Young. I am interested in the United States and not the whole world.
Mr. Jackson. Let us not lose freedom--
Mr. Young. That is the point, Mr. Jackson, I am fighting for freedom
myself.
Mr. Jackson. So am I. Let us not lose individual freedom and human dignity by sacrificing it to an order of things which has filled concentration
camps to overflowing. If you think of the lot of the Negro who have in eighty-
some years come forward to a much better position--
Mr. Young. Mr. Jackson, we are not going to wait 80 more years, I will
tell you that.
Mr. Jackson. Neither are the Communists. They say they are going to
overthrow the Government by force and violence and effect all the changes
immediately.
Mr. Young. If you are telling me to wait 80 years, I will tell you I am
not prepared to wait and neither are the Negroes.
Mr. Jackson. Neither is the Communist Party.
Mr. Young. I am speaking for the Negro people and for myself. Are you
speaking for the Communist Party?
Mr. Jackson. I am speaking of the Communist Party.
Mr. Young. I thought you were speaking for the Communist Party.
Mr. Jackson. No. I think there are many in this room who are better
qualified to speak for the Communist Party than I am. Mr. Chairman, I have no
further questions.
Mr. Wood. Mr. Potter?
Mr. Potter. Mr. Young, I believe in your statement that you said that you
were in the service fighting fascism during the last war.
Mr. Young. That is right.
Mr. Potter. Then it is proper to assume that you are opposed to totalitarianism in any form, as I am.
Mr. Young. I fought and I was in the last war, Congressman, that is correct, as a Negro officer in the Air Corps. I was arrested and placed under
arrest and held in quarters for 3 days in your country because I sought to get
a cup of coffee in a United States Officers Club that was restricted for white
officers only. That is my experience in the United States Army.
Mr. Potter. Let me say this, I have the highest admiration, yes, the
highest admiration for the service that was performed by Negro soldiers during
the last war. They performed brilliantly.
Mr. Young. I am sure the Negro soldiers appreciate your admiration, Mr.
Potter.
Mr. Potter. At the same time, while I am just as much opposed to nazism
and fascism as you are, I am opposed to totalitarianism in any form. As you
well know the Communist International as dictated from Soviet Russia is probably

the most stringent form of totalitarian government in the world today. In case, and God forbid, that it ever happens, but in case the Soviet Union should attack the United States would you serve as readily to defend our country in case of such eventuality as you did during the last war?

Mr. Young. As I told you, Congressman, nobody has had to question the patriotism, the military valor of the Negro people. We have fought in every war.

Mr. Potter. I am not talking about the Negro people, I am talking about you.

Mr. Young. I am coming to me. I am a part of the Negro people. I fought in the last war and I would unhesitatingly take up arms against anybody that attacks this country. In the same manner I am now in process of fighting against what I consider to be attacks and discrimination against my people. I am fighting against un-American activities such as lynchings and denial of the vote. I am dedicated to that fight and I don't think I have to apologize or explain it to anybody, my position on that.

Mr. Potter. Mr. Young, you have many, many groups in this country that have the same purpose as what you are sponsoring here. Let me tell you this, the thing that you claim is your objective will not be accomplished by men like yourself.

Mr. Young. That is your opinion.

Mr. Potter. Absolutely that is my opinion and that is all.

Mr. Wood. Are there any further questions, Mr. Counsel?

Mr. Tavenner. I have one further question, Mr. Chairman. Have you at any time been chairman or in any other way connected with the Veterans' Affairs Committee of the Communist Party?

Mr. Young. I refuse to answer that or any similar question under my privileges under the fifth amendment.

Mr. Tavenner. I have no further questions.

Mr. Wood. Is there any reason why the witness should not be excused from further attendance before the committee?

Mr. Tavenner. No, sir.

Mr. Wood. Committee will stand in recess for 15 minutes and the witness is excused.

(The witness was excused.)

(A short recess was taken.)

Mr. Wood. Let us have order, please. Are you ready to proceed, Mr. Counsel?

Mr. Tavenner. Yes. I would like to call Mr. William R. Hood.

Mr. Wood. Will you raise your right hand and be sworn?

Mr. Hood. Yes.

Mr. Wood. Do you solemnly swear that the evidence you give this subcommittee will be the truth, the whole truth, and nothing but the truth, so help you God?

Mr. Hood. Yes.

TESTIMONY OF WILLIAM R. HOOD, ACCOMPANIED BY HIS COUNSEL, ERNEST GOODMAN

Mr. Wood. Are you represented by counsel, Mr. Hood?

Mr. Hood. I am.

Mr. Wood. Will counsel please identify himself for the record?

Mr. Goodman. I am Ernest Goodman of the Cadillac Tower, Detroit, Mich.

Mr. Tavenner. What is your name, please?

Mr. Hood. My name is William R. Hood.

Mr. Tavenner. When and where were you born, Mr. Hood?

Mr. Hood. I was born in 1910, but I categorically refuse to tell you where I was born. My father and mother are still in Georgia. I will write the name to the committee. My uncle was killed by a mob. I don't want them persecuted. I talked with my mother already and the hysteria created here in this Georgia city--with my father in business and my sister a school teacher in Georgia, I don't want them persecuted or to have reprisals as the result of my behavior in the city of Detroit.

Mr. Tavenner. How long have you lived in Detroit?

Mr. Hood. I came to Detroit in 1942.

Mr. Tavenner. How have you been employed?

Mr. Hood. I traveled for a life insurance company in the State of Georgia.

Mr. Tavenner. I meant here in the State of Michigan.

Mr. Hood. I worked at Chevrolet Gear & Axle, I think it was a short period in 1942 and I left because of discriminatory practices. They wouldn't promote or upgrade me. I was hired by the Ford Motor Car Co., January 26, 1943.

Mr. Tavenner. And you have been working there since?

Mr. Hood. I have been working for the Ford Motor Car Co. with the exception of the time I have been the representative and recording secretary of the largest union in the world, the UAW-CIO, Ford local 600.

Mr. Tavenner. During what period of time did you occupy that position?

Mr. Hood. I have occupied that position for 4 years and will be running for my fifth term in office this coming June.

Mr. Tavenner. I am sorry, I did not get the beginning of your service.

Mr. Hood. I was elected recording secretary of local 600 4 years ago. I hope I will be elected for the fifth time this June in spite of this committee.

Mr. Tavenner. The Daily Worker of September 1, 1951, carries an article on page 1 to the effect that you spoke in New York City on behalf of Louis Weinstock who had been indicted under the Smith Act. Is it correct that you did speak in behalf of Louis Weinstock at that time?

Mr. Hood. I refuse to answer about my appearance in New York in behalf of Mr. Weinstock under the privileges of the fifth amendment; however, I might tell you that I am very sympathetic toward minority people and other people that are kicked around in this Nation.

Mr. Tavenner. Were you sympathetic to Mr. Weinstock, who was charged, under the Smith Act, with advocating the use of force and violence in the overthrow of the Government of this country? [202]

Mr. Hood. I do not advocate the overthrow of the Government by force and violence. The methods and approaches used by the Government in trying to arrive at certain conclusions--I refuse to answer in respect to Mr. Weinstock on the basis of the privileges granted me under the fifth amendment.

Mr. Tavenner. Did Mr. Weinstock live in Detroit at any time?

Mr. Hood. I refuse to answer that question on the basis of the immunities which I have under the fifth amendment.

Mr. Tavenner. Did you know on September 12, 1951, that Louis Weinstock had been a functionary of the Communist Party for a number of years?

Mr. Hood. I refuse to answer any questions similar to that in respect to any individual's participation in anything, under the fifth amendment.

Mr. Tavenner. You spoke of having sympathy, as I understand it, for Weinstock?

Mr. Hood. I didn't say I had sympathy for Weinstock. I said I have sympathy for persecuted people in America and all over the world.

Mr. Tavenner. Did you consider that Weinstock was being persecuted?

Mr. Hood. I refuse to answer any question with respect to Weinstock under the immunities of the fifth amendment.

Mr. Tavenner. According to the Daily Worker of November 19, 1951, page 2, you were reported as being among the speakers at the Twentieth Anniversary National Conference of the American Committee for the Protection of the Foreign Born. Did you make such an address on that occasion?

Mr. Hood. I refuse to testify to this committee about any speeches I made other than those speeches that I made to my activity in local 600 as a functionary of the National Negro Labor Council for which I thought I was here, according to the press releases, anyway, yesterday.

Mr. Tavenner. Are you willing to tell the committee whether or not you were approached, and if so by whom, to assist in the meeting that I referred to, the American Committee for the Protection of the Foreign Born?

Mr. Hood. I think it logically follows that the question asked me now would be refused on the basis of my privileges and on the basis of your first question--on the basis of the privileges granted me under the Constitution of the United States and the fifth amendment.

Mr. Tavenner. Do you refuse to answer?

Mr. Hood. I refuse to answer and I so indicated in my remark. Perhaps you didn't hear me.

Mr. Tavenner. Will you tell the committee whether Abner W. Berry, to your knowledge, was active in the work of the American Committee for the Protection of the Foreign Born or at least that branch of it which was in the area of Detroit?

Mr. Hood. I refuse to answer. I could say I don't know but I refuse to answer on the basis of the privileges granted me under the fifth amendment.

Mr. Tavenner. Did I understand you to say to begin with that you did not know?

Mr. Hood. I am not going to use it--I don't know. I don't. I said under the fifth amendment.

Mr. Tavenner. Privately you are telling me you do not know but for the record you will not answer.

Mr. Hood. I say for the record that that question--I don't know what you are trying to lead it into. But I have certain privileges which I will clothe myself with on the basis of the experiences that I have had of this committee many of which are very, very penetrating to my heart, for example, calling a Negro in the Congress of the United States a black s--of-a-b--. I have nothing but utter contempt for a group like that.

Mr. Tavenner. Do you consider that that is in any way responsive to any question that I asked you? Are you not trying deliberately to go beyond the inquiry of this committee for the purpose of creating a scene? Is that your purpose?

Mr. Hood. I would like very much ˜for the committee to categorically understand that the line of questioning you have given me and my answers are certainly predicated on some of my experiences in America which I think this committee should be cognizant of and perfectly willing to do something about. There is something happening in America which evidently you do not know about which is un-American.

Mr. Tavenner. Then you are not willing to give this committee any information relating to the subject of this inquiry, which is communism in Detroit?

Mr. Hood. You ask me your questions and I will decide at that time whether I will answer.

Mr. Tavenner. I have asked you a question.

Mr. Hood. What is the question?

Mr. Tavenner. Did Abner Berry--

Mr. Hood. I refuse to answer the question.

Mr. Tavenner. Let me finish the question

Mr. Hood. You have already asked it and now my mind is refreshed.

Mr. Tavenner. Your mind is refreshed?

Mr. Hood. Yes.

Mr. Tavenner. What is your decision?

Mr. Hood. My decision is that on the question of Abner Berry with respect to some civil rights outfit in Detroit, I refuse to answer.

Mr. Potter. Do you know the gentleman?

Mr. Hood. I refuse to answer whether I know Abner Berry under my privileges, logically concluding that you will go into a million things.

Mr. Potter. When the question was first asked you, you said, on the side, "I don't know the man."

Mr. Hood. I didn't say anything of that nature. If you ask me whether I said it, I think I am intelligent enough to answer you.

Mr. Tavenner. Let's get the record clear, do you know him.

Mr. Hood. I refuse to answer for the privileges that I have. I told you I am no stool pigeon, and just like Mr. Young told you, if you know that I know him let the record show it.

Mr. Tavenner. Is that the basis for your answer?

Mr. Hood. My privileges under the fifth amendment.

Mr. Potter. But knowing this gentleman, do you feel that might tend to incriminate you?

Mr. Hood. I am clothed with certain privileges. I have the prerogative to call on them when I so desire under the amendment, which evidently the framers of the Constitution making this amendment certainly figured at some time under tyrannical and hysterical conditions a person would use them.

Mr. Potter. If you do not know this gentleman then certainly there will be nothing incriminating in answering that question.

Mr. Hood. The question of conclusions is left to me. I am here as the witness and not you.

Mr. Potter. You have been debating this question.

Mr. Hood. I refuse to answer. I am not debating and I so indicated in my previous statement that I made, Congressman Potter.

Mr. Potter. I will not argue. That is all right. I am a very tolerant man.

Mr. Hood. So am I tolerant. All in spite of what has been heaped on me.

Mr. Potter. There are many people who have had adversities.

Mr. Hood. Not as many as the Negro people in America.

Mr. Potter. I have nothing further.

Mr. Tavenner. According to the Michigan Worker, page 10, May 21, 1950, you were one of those who protested the prosecution of Eugene Dennis, according to our information. Is that correct?

Mr. Hood. I refuse to answer any questions with respect to Eugene Dennis.

Mr. Tavenner. Why?

Mr. Hood. Under the privileges of the fifth amendment, which I have afore-mentioned. If it is not monotonous I will tell you every time. I said "afore-mentioned" for the conservation of time.

Mr. Tavenner. You are reported having been a sponsor of the Mid-Century Conference for Peace held in Detroit in May 1950, is that correct?

Mr. Hood. I refuse to answer that question under the fifth amendment.

Mr. Tavenner. Let me explain, before you give your final answer, I am interested in knowing the circumstances under which your support of that matter was obtained if it was obtained. Does that change your answer?

Mr. Hood. I don't think it would, based upon my knowledge of this committee. I don't think it would change it, counsel.

Mr. Tavenner. As the recording secretary of the CIO, Local 600, UAW--I seem to have it backwards--were you required to sign a non-Communist affidavit?

Mr. Hood. I was, counsel.

Mr. Tavenner. Did you sign it?

Mr. Hood. I did, sir, for four consecutive years. I have been elected and I hope to sign it again. I hope I will be elected.

Mr. Tavenner. In view of that, may I ask whether at the time you signed the affidavit you were a member of the Communist Party?

Mr. Hood. I was not a member of the Communist Party.

Mr. Tavenner. Have you been a member at any time since the time you first signed that?

Mr. Hood. I have not been a member of the Communist Party from the time I first signed it.

Mr. Tavenner. The committee has information indicating that in 1947 you were issued a 1947 card, No. 68126 of the Communist Party.

Mr. Hood. It is a damned lie.

Mr. Tavenner. Have you ever been a member of the Communist Party?

Mr. Hood. I have already answered that question. As a Negro-American, based upon this committee's action, I refuse to testify about my past action in respect to the question that you asked me, under the fifth amendment. That is the answer.

Mr. Tavenner. I do not understand your answer. Have you ever been a member of the Communist Party?

Mr. Hood. I told you I refused as a Negro American particularly for reasons of my own. I refuse to answer that question under the fifth amendment. I refuse to answer.

Mr. Tavenner. When you say you refuse to answer for reasons of your own, to what are you referring? Are you referring to the fifth amendment or some other reason?

Mr. Hood. Counsel, will you please phrase your question again? Will you repeat the question?

Mr. Tavenner. Will you read the question?

(The question was read by the official court reporter.)

Mr. Hood. I am referring to the fifth amendment. I am not a lawyer but I said the fifth amendment. These are my own reasons.

Mr. Tavenner. Then if I understand your testimony correctly, you denied that you have been a member of the Communist Party at any time within the past 4 years, which is the period of time you have been the recording secretary of the UAW but you refuse to answer whether or not you have ever been a member of the Communist Party, is that your testimony?

Mr. Hood. I refuse to answer.

Mr. Jackson. I move that the witness be directed to answer the question.

Mr. Goodman. Just one moment, please.

Mr. Hood. I refuse to answer any question as to whether or not I have been a member of the Communist Party previous to 1947.

Mr. Wood. In view of the fact that the witness has testified that he was not a member of the Communist Party from 1947 to the present time, this Chair holds that the question as to whether or not he has ever been a member of the Communist Party is pertinent and directs the witness to answer the question.

Mr. Hood. I refuse to answer the question under the immunities of the fifth amendment.

Mr. Tavenner. Mr. Hood, according to the Daily Worker of October 23, 1951, page 3, you are said to have been a sponsor of a dinner at 13 Astor Place, New York City, to be given on October 26, 1951, for the defense of Dr. W. E. B. DuBois and sponsored by the trade-union committee to defend Dr. W. E. B. DuBois. If it is true that you were one of the sponsors of that dinner, I would like to know how your sponsorship was obtained.

Mr. Hood. I refuse to answer under the privileges of the fifth amendment.

Mr. Tavenner. The committee is also informed through notices in the Daily Worker of December 5, 1951, on page 2 and in the same paper of September 10, 1951, page 3, that you were scheduled as a speaker at a rally to be held in St. Nicholas Arena in New York City on September 10, 1951, for the repeal of the Smith Act. Do you recall whether or not you spoke on such occasion?

Mr. Hood. I refuse to answer under the fifth amendment.

Mr. Tavenner. Mr. Hood, the Washington, D.C., Evening Star of October 30, 1951, on page 7, carried a paid advertisement which was an open letter to J. Howard McGrath, Attorney General of the United States, protesting the jailing of four trustees of the bail fund of the Civil Rights Congress. Your name appears as one of the signers to that open letter. Will you tell the committee who solicited your signature and what interest was involved in soliciting your signature, if it was so obtained?[203]

Mr. Hood. I refuse to answer under the privileges of the fifth amendment.

Mr. Tavenner. Will you tell the committee what you know, if anything, regarding the bail fund plan for use of members of the Communist Party which existed within the Civil Rights Congress or any other group?

Mr. Hood. The bail right fund?

Mr. Tavenner. Yes, the bail fund.

Mr. Hood. What is that?

Mr. Tavenner. According to the paid advertisement from which it appears that you were a signer, a protest was made regarding the jailing of the trustees of the bail fund of the Civil Rights Congress. I am asking you now that you tell us what you know about the use of bail funds by the Civil Rights Congress. If I have not made it plain, I will break it down.

Mr. Hood. I think I understand your question.

Mr. Tavenner. I will break it down a little more if you would like.

Mr. Hood. There is no necessity for it. I refuse to answer it on the basis of the immunities of the fifth amendment.

Mr. Tavenner. I have no further questions, Mr. Chairman.

Mr. Jackson. I have no questions.

Mr. Potter. No questions.

Mr. Wood. The witness is excused from further attendance and a recess will be taken until 2 o'clock.

(The witness was excused.)

(Whereupon, at 12:30 p.m., the hearing was recessed until 2 p.m. this same day.

U.S. House, Committee on Un-American Activities. *Communism in the Detroit Area--Part I.* 82nd Cong. 2d sess. (Washington, D.C.: Government Printing Office, 1952), pp. 2878-98.

45.   LABOR UNIT SET UP FOR NEGRO RIGHTS

75 Anti-Communist Unions Form Committee to Improve
Lot of Individual Workers

Representatives of seventy-five anti-Communist trade unions formed a
National Negro labor committee yesterday to improve the lot of individual
Negroes and achieve the objectives of organized labor.

Meeting at the Theresa Hotel, Seventh Avenue and 125th Street, 350 delegates voted to expand an existing group in New York into a national organization to be known as the Negro Labor Committee, U.S.A. They adopted a constitution barring from membership "Communist or Communist-dominated trade
unions and all other anti-democratic groups."

The blessings of the nation's two big labor federations, the American
Federation of Labor and the Congress of Industrial Organizations, were given
to the new group through the appearance of James B. Carey, secretary of the
CIO, and Lewis G. Hines, representing William Green, president of the AFL.
Both pledged their organizations to the fight for Negro rights.

Mr. Carey assailed both Communists and white advocates for united action
against civil rights and outlined three objectives in the field of civil
liberties. They were economic and political equality and equality of opportunity. He said they could best be achieved "by organizing every last working
man and woman in our country into free labor unions."

Union Deplores Practice

Mr. Hines said that while some AFL unions still discriminated against
Negroes--a practice deplored by the leadership of the federation--great progress had been made, especially in the South, where he added, there were many
mixed locals.

Formation of the national Negro committee was regarded as a declaration
of war against the National Negro Labor Council, a leftist group, which met
last fall in Cincinnati. Mr. Carey termed the latter group "just another
front for the Communist party." The Voice of America recorded the proceedings
for broadcast over seas.

Discussing the role of labor in Negro workers' problems and democracy,
Frank R. Crosswaith, chairman of the committee, said the Negro could solve the
problems confronting him only "if and when organized labor recognizes its common interest with the Negro through education and organization with him to
meet and solve them."

A. Philip Randolph, president of the Brotherhood of Sleeping Car Porters,
AFL, called for the development of a "world congress of Negro workers and
peoples and their democratic allies to achieve greater unity and consciousness,
understanding, vision and statesmanship, to fight to throw off the yoke of
imperialistic colonialism on the one hand, and to avoid the dangerous quick-
sands of Russian world communism on the other."

Such a movement, he said, could "join with the International Confederation
of Free Trade Unions in helping to halt the march of the Communist-dominated
World Federation of Trade Unions, which seeks to win the working masses of
Africa and the West Indies, not for their economic, political and social well-
being and advancement, but to give strength and power to Russian Stalinism."

Delegates Adopt Resolutions

The delegates adopted resolutions on national policy, civil rights,
organization and the poll tax. The resolution dealing with national policy
reaffirmed "allegiance to democracy and liberty" and pledged "unswerving
opposition to any and all forces that challenge democracy and liberty."

On the question of civil rights, the delegates in favor of an effective
Federal anti-lynch law and resolved that "such a law should include the provision 'that whenever a Negro person or other citizen is lynched, the state
and county in which the lynching law'" occurs should pay to the kin of the
victim the sum of $50,000 to be taken from the Treasury of said state and that
dhe Department of Justice be strengthened to meet and deal with violators of
the law.

Other speakers included Dr. Channing Tobias, United States delegate to the Sixth Assembly of the United Nations; Willard Townsend, president of the United Transport Service, CIO; David Sullivan, president of Local 32-B, Building Service Employes International Union, AFL, and Charles S. Zimmerman, vice president of the International Ladies Garment Workers Union, AFL.[204]

New York Times, March 2, 1952.

46. HOOD STATEMENT ON "600" VICTORY

My re-election as recording secretary of Local 600, UAW-CIO, together with the re-election of my fellow-officers, Stellato, Rice and Grant, in the face of unprecedented attacks by the un-American Activities Committee with the open collusion of UAW President Walter P. Reuther, who attempted to seize our local by placing us under an administrator, must be viewed as a resounding endorsement by the Ford workers of our progressive program of unity and mili-tant action.

Local 600's resolute, consistent fight for Negro and white unity and our official support of the National Negro Labor Council were among the primary reasons the enemies of democracy felt it necessary to attack our local union. As president of the NNLC, I feel that my re-election in Local 600 was an expression of support of the NNLC. This, indeed, is the highest expression of labor unity.

With this overwhelming vote of confidence from my fellow workers and with a firm faith in the inevitable victory that shall be ours, I call upon all friends and supporters of the NNLC to join with us in making our Second Annual Convention in Cleveland, Ohio, on November 21, 22 and 23, a memorable highpoint in our surge along Freedom road.

Freedom, October 1952.

47. FREEDOM SALUTES: WILLIAM A. REED OF DETROIT

For many years Mr. William A. Reed has struggled with his efficient printing and accounting business on Warren and Bourbon Sts. in Detroit, Mich.

It is a small business. He employs five people: two printers and three office workers.

For a long time Mr. Reed has joined with other Negro printers in asking the Allied Printing Trades Council to unionize their shops, which would give them the right to use the union "bug" on their work and therefore increase the volume of their trade. They were consistently denied the label by the council on the basis of the lily-white policies of the printing trades.

Jim Crow in the printing trades has a two-sided disadvantage for Negroes. First of all young Negro printers are denied an important source of bona fide training, because this training can only be secured through apprenticeships in union shops.

Secondly, Negro small businessmen in the printing business are cut off from large contracts by the absence of the union bug from their work, and it is therefore difficult for them to meet union scale wages for their printers, on what Mr. Reed calls "Church ticket and calling card contracts."

With the cooperation of the Greater Detroit Negro Labor Council, Mr. Reed has re-applied to the Allied Printing Trades Council for membership. He and a representative of the Negro Labor Council met with President Clifford G. Sparkman, President of the Council and for the first time, the Council has indicated a willingness to go along with the application for membership . . . to go along with democracy.

Mr. Reed's admission will be an historic step toward breaking down the age-old discriminatory barriers against Negro printers in the union.

In estimating the importance of his fight, the crusading printer, himself, says: "Since every small business is directly dependent on the earnings of working people for his very existence, any notion on the part of the small businessman that his interests are different from those of labor is plain stupidity. Small business will feel the effects of a strike or layoff over-nite and it succeeds or fails as the fortunes of labor go up or down.

"I have operated a small business for more than twenty years and I think that every business would be helped if the employees of all small business would be given advantages of pay and working conditions comparable to those of industrial workers."

Freedom, November 1952.

48.   HAROLD WARD FREE--LABOR COUNCIL SPARKED CAMPAIGN

CHICAGO--The action of a Criminal Court jury in freeing Harold Ward, militant Negro trade unionist of the framed-up "murder" charges brought against him in the course of the recent International Harvester strike, is re-garded here as a major victory for the labor movement.

The all-white jury of 10 men and two women took an hour and 55 minutes to decide that Ward had not killed William Foster, a Negro strikebreaker, on October 3. In doing so, the jury justified the charge of the defense that Ward was on trial because, as financial secretary of the United Electrical-Farm Equipment Workers Local 108, he had been one of the outstanding leaders in maintaining unity between Negro and white workers in the bitterly-fought strike.

The freeing of Ward recalls the dramatic moment at the National Negro Labor Council Convention when his wife addressed a packed opening-night audience and told the delegates the kind of man her husband is. Mrs. Ruth Ward said:

"Harold is just about as guilty . . . as you or I are. He is guilty of some things. Guilty of murdering the peace of mind of the big bosses in Chicago. He has been a thorn in McCormick's side because he fights for the rank and file. . . . He is also guilty of fighting for peace. He went all the way across the sea, and that is terrible, they say. Every paper has tried him on that alone; he went to the Peace Conference. . . . So he is guilty of that . . . and he is guilty of something else, too. You know, this long bitter strike they had--he didn't work eight hours like he did at McCormick's. He worked 18, 20, 24 hours. He has gone as long as three days without sleep, fighting, fighting for the men in the strike--for the rank and file--and Harvester didn't like that either.

"He started with McCormick's in 1944; he started with the union in 1945. They all tie up together. He came home one day and I was just like the other wives--I didn't see why he didn't go on and take that foreman's job they offered him--it was nice and paid a little more money. But he didn't want that. It took him a long time to convince me, too; to show me that we have to work for everybody. Alone we don't get very far, and as Negroes we get even less far. So we have to work together just as Harold worked--for me, and his union."

Freedom, December 1952.

49.   KEY DELEGATES DISCUSS TOP CONVENTION ISSUES

If Labor Fails to Use Negro Potential, It Battles
"With an Arm Tied Behind Its Back"

By William R. Hood
(Recording Secretary, Local 600, United Auto Workers)

The entry of Negro workers on a large scale into the ranks of organized labor took place only a few years ago with the coming into being of the CIO.

The CIO thus served as a vehicle for creating a unity hitherto unknown in America: the unity of one million Negro industrial workers with their fellow white workers in industry. It was a bridgehead for the firm and fraternal bonds that today characterize the relationship of the Negro people to the labor movement.

Today, as the labor movement girds itself in anticipation of the anti-labor onslaught of the Eisenhower adminstration, it is a simple matter of self-preservation that makes it imperative for labor to look for support in the direction of the untapped reservoir of potential leadership and strength which its Negro membership has to offer.[205]

The failure to make use of this potential, projects labor into its battle for life with an arm tied behind its back.

This question, the utilization and bringing forward of Negro leadership, which has long been a political football in the union movement, must now be squarely faced by every honest and straight-thinking labor leader who has the over-all interest of our unions at heart.

The decision which is made at the 14th constitutional convention of the United Auto Workers, in Atlantic City this month on the elevation of a Negro unionist to elected office in our International Union may well determine whether or not the UAW-CIO will have the political stamina and moral fortitude to face up to the crisis that looms ahead.

Freedom, March 1953.

50. MILITANT VETERANS OF "600" APPEAL INTERNATIONAL RULE

When Walter Reuther placed an Administrator over Local 600 in March, 1952, five of the most militant leaders were removed from office and have been barred from seeking reelection.

The five are Dave Moore, Nelson Davis, John Gallo, Ed Locke and Paul Botin. Moore and Davis are Negroes who along with their three white union brothers bear the scars and wounds inflicted by the goons of the Ford Motor Company in the organizational drive in the giant Ford Rouge plant. They were removed by Reuther for being "members of, or subservient to" the Communist Party and doing "irreparable harm" to the UAW. They have appealed their cases to the National UAW Convention to be held in Atlantic City in March.

The two highest bodies of Local 600, the Executive Board and the General Council, have acted in the defense of the five militant leaders.

The entire Local 600 delegates will go to the UAW convention under mandate from the membership to fight and vote for the reinstatement of all five of its removed members.

Dave Moore and Nelson Davis along with other Negro leaders of Local 600 have not only given leadership to their Negro brothers and sisters, but to the white workers as well.

Here is their record:

Dave Moore was vice-president of the Gear and Axle Plant of Local 600 for four years, prior to his removal by Walter Reuther in March, 1952. He was a volunteer organizer in the union and was one of the six men who pulled the switches that shut down the Axle plant in the historic 1941 strike. As a result of this action he was fired and told by a foreman that he would never work at the Ford Motor Company again. However, after the victorious ten-day strike, the Gear and Axle workers rewarded Dave Moore for his stalwart leadership by electing him committeeman. Down through the years he has had many offices from committeeman to his last held position, the second highest in the unit, vice-president.

Nelson Davis has worked at the Ford Motor Company for 30 years and holds the distinction of being the first worker to wear a union button in the foundry. He was elected by the Foundry workers as district committeeman for three terms;

as bargaining committeeman for four terms, and vice-president of the General Council since the founding of the Local. When removed by Reuther, he was holding the office of vice-president and member of the General Council.

In a joint statement, Moore and Davis said: "If fighting against discriminatory policies of the Ford Motor Company and fighting for the rights of Negro men and women to be promoted to better jobs, if disagreeing with the International Union's lily-white executive board on issues affecting the good and welfare of members of Local 600 and the members of the UAW, constitute 'membership or subservience to the Communist Party,' then we say make the most of it."

Freedom, March 1953.

51. NEGRO LEADERSHIP--A KEY ISSUE

"Negro Up-Grading Benefits the Whole Union Movement"

By Layman Walker
(Recording Secretary, Loc. 742, UAW-CIO)

For many years we in the labor movement in the Detroit and Wayne County area, have waged a struggle for the advancement of Negro leadership in the local union bodies of the CIO.

It is now a matter of history that where the successful fight has been waged to advance Negro workers, the whole union movement has benefitted and been strengthened.

It is unfortunate that the examples set by many locals in the matter of Negro participation in top union leadership has not so far been emulated by the International UAW-CIO. This is a fact which offers no credit to our International Union but presents itself as a definite chink in our armour, and a weakness in the unity which our union must have in the critical period ahead.

I take my position now, as in the past for the very broadest application of democracy in the UAW, starting on the level of its top officers and extending into every rank and file committee of our great International Union.

We Must Make an All Out Drive for FEPC

By Joe Morgan

(President of the Frame and Cold-Header Unit of Loc. 600;
Natl. Vice-Pres. NNLC; Pres.,
Great Detroit NNLC.)

The recent mobilization at Lansing on the passage of a state FEPC bill was a tremendous success. This is only the beginning of mass mobilizations until such a bill is passed. We will show the state politicians that the question of Negro employment is not some political gimmick just to be tossed around at election time.

All UAW leaders must recognize that this will be labor's most critical year under a Big Business administration and therefore must make an all out drive for FEPC, giving concrete expression to this fact in life by electing a Negro to the executive board of the UAW at our rorthcoming convention.

This is the logic and meaning of our fight for FEPC, a fight that unites Negro and white workers in the common struggle to build a strong, united labor movement to weather the approaching storm.

Fight Cannot be Won With "Plans"

By James Watts
(FEPC Director, Ford Loc. 600)

These are the days that will try men's souls and will separate the men from the boys. The winning of the fight for survival of the CIO calls for

a rededication of the principles upon which it was founded. It is a fight
that cannot be won with "plans."

The strength of the Negro people, conditioned by 350 years of struggle,
is needed more than ever before if the CIO is going to pull through the big
struggle ahead. The first step must be the immediate elevation of a Negro to
post of Executive Vice-President. Second, the UAW in its forthcoming convention should face up to its responsibilities and elect a Negro to one of its
vice-presidencies. Third, CIO should immediately begin negotiations for the
return to its fold of the internationals expelled.

Freedom, March, 1953.

52. LABOR LOWERS BOOM ON JIM CROW; NNLC, KEY UNIONS HOLD ANTI-BIAS CONFERENCES

Each day brings added indications that important sections of the labor
movement are taking a new look at the divisive effects of anti-Negro discrimination and are making up their minds to enter the fight for equality with
new vigor.

Faced with the entrenched Big Business outlook of the Eisenhower administration and its millionaire cabinet, labor leaders who have not worried much
about FEPC in the past are beginning to realize that prejudice doesn't pay--
at least among workers.

Most important, the pressure of rank and file union members, FEPC shop
committees and local anti-discrimination bodies, and the militant initiative
of not-to-be-denied Negro workers, is beginning to bear fruit in the higher
echelons of labor's ranks.

Much credit for this development must go to the National Negro Labor
Council. Despite all efforts to defame and defile it, the Council has been a
prod to the sluggards and a goad upon the conscience of the complacent. It
has rendered valuable aid to the unions in their fight to catch up with the
soaring cost of living, and enjoys the enthusiastic support of increasing numbers of workers in basic industry.

The NNLC has just announced a new date for its 3rd Annual Convention:
December 3-5 at the Pershing Hotel on Chicago's Southside. At the center of
the convention deliberations will be a campaign against job discrimination
in the mammoth railroad industry. All unions, organizations and individuals
concerned with the question of democracy in employment should contact their
local Negro Labor Council or the NNLC national office at 410 E. Warren, Detroit,
Mich., and send delegates to this vital convention.

As we go to press the Brotherhood of Sleeping Car Porters has just concluded its triennial convention in Los Angeles with a strong blast against
McCarthyism, a plea for a world disarmament conference, and a call for a
national drive for jobs for Negroes as railroad switchmen, brakemen, conductors
and engineers. The incumbent slate of officers, headed by A. Philip Randolph,
were re-elected for a three-year term.

A new development on the jobs front are the two national anti-discrimination conferences being held by major international unions. The million-member
United Auto Workers, CIO, has just brought together in Detroit, 400 delegates
in a Fair Employment Practices conference to map out a drive to include a model
anti-discrimination clause in all contracts with the auto barons, and support
the NAACP crusade for "freedom by '63."

In Chicago on Oct. 30, 31, and Nov. 1, the United Packinghouse Workers,
CIO, will convene a conference of workers from its shops throughout the country
to heighten its efforts to eliminate Jim Crow hiring in the huge meat-packing
industry.

A new wind is blowing in the labor movement, a good wind. If it develops
hurricane proportions, as it should, it can go a long way toward blowing down
the temple of Old Jim Crow in the U.S.A.

Freedom, September 1953.

53. NAACP DEMANDS CURB ON RED AIMS

Convention Calls for Wide Action in World and Assails Communist-Ruled Unions

John N. Popham

DALLAS, Tex., July 3--The National Association for the Advancement of
Colored People called on the Federal Administration today to support nationalist movements among colonial peoples "because independence is the best
answer to Communist intrigue."

It also asked the Government to insist "as far as possible" that our
"allies and potential allies" abandon imperialist policies in order to release
armed forces from colonial revolts and thereby strengthen the free world's
military power for resisting aggression.

These demands were in a series of resolutions adopted at the final business session here of the association's forty-fifth annual convention. The
six-day meeting is being attended by about 700 delegates from thirty-six
states and the District of Columbia.

The convention will close tomorrow with a public rally at which the
principal speakers will be Dr. Ralph J. Bunche, United States member of the
United Nations Secretariat and Nobel Peace Prize winner, and Walter White,
executive secretary of the association.

Stand on Red-Ruled Unions

In a resolution on labor policies the association included a strong-
worded prohibition of cooperation by its members with Communist-controlled
unions and specifically denounced the National Negro Labor Council "because it
is completely Communist dominated."

The latter phases of the resolution brought heated debate, but the delegates rejected overwhelmingly all proposals to water down the language. A
foremost supporter of the anti-Communist declaration was William H. Oliver of
Detroit, co-director of the Fair Practices and Anti-discrimination Department
of the United Automobile Workers, CIO.

The resolution also appealed to unions that practice racial discrimination to end that practice and put strong anti-bias clauses in their contracts.
It urged Negro workers to use publicity and court action to combat such
practices anywhere in organized labor.

The resolution declared that "only a small and dwindling number of unions
was still guilty of racial discrimination. It asserted that the support of
the American labor movement for the association's civil rights campaign was
extremely important and could be in certain situations perhaps even decisive."

Warning on 'McCarthyism'[206]

In a resolution on civil liberties, the convention declared that "under
the banner of fighting communism, McCarthyism aims to lead the nation to
fascism." The resolution asserted that the role of the paid professional in-
former had become "increasingly odious" in court, grand jury and Congressional
proceedings.

The delegates urged President Eisenhower to "try to fill his campaign
pledge of opposition to the McCarran-Walter Act, which continues the inequities
of the national origin quota system."[207]

The convention spoke out for Federal and state legislative reforms to
help improve the conditions of migratory workers, supported a guaranteed annual
wage and asked that the minimum wage set in the Federal law be increased to
$1.25 an hour.

The association criticize the Atomic Energy Commission's installations for
alleged practicing of discrimination in the hiring and upgrading of Negro
workers. It called for support of an amendment to the Taft-Hartley Law proposed by Senators Irving M. Ives and Herbert H. Lehman of New York to make
discrimination in hiring an unfair labor practice.[208]

It was voted to hold next year's convention in Atlantic City and that
convention was urged to give top consideration to San Francisco as the place

for the 1956 convention.

New York Times, July 4, 1954.

54. NEGRO LABOR GROUP CALLED RED FRONT

WASHINGTON, Sept. 30.--A petition asking that the National Negro Labor
Council be required to register as a Communist-front organization was filed
with the Subversive Activities Control Board today by Herbert Brownell, Jr.,
the Attorney General.[209]
He asserted that the council whose headquarters are in Detroit, was under
the domination of Communists and operated primarily to support the objectives
of the party. Key party members, the Attorney General asserted, have been put
in chapters of the council throughout the country and they direct its activities and policies.
The Communist part has been ordered by the control board to register as
a Communist-action organization. It has pending in the Supreme Court an
appeal from that ruling.
The Subversive Activities Control Act of 1950 requires that organizations
found by the board to be Communist-action or Communist-front groups must register with the Attorney General. They must then file lists of officers and
members and submit accountings of financial receipts and disbursements.
The National Negro Labor Council has been on the list of subversive
organizations promulgated by the Attorney General. Mr. Brownell said in his
petition that it continued to receive financial and other support from the
Communist party.

New York Times, October 1, 1955.

PAUL ROBESON AND THE BLACK WORKER

55. SPEECH AT INTERNATIONAL FUR AND LEATHER WORKERS UNION CONVENTION

I am sure that I need not say that I thank you and that I am especially
proud to be here today.
I have been wandering back and forth across this America of ours trying
to help where I can. I got a telegram from Ben saying I would have to be here
and as a member of the Union, here I am. (Applause and cheers).[210]
It is a great privilege to be here on the day when two dear friends, and
two great fighters, Mr. Fast and Mr. Lee Pressman, are here.[211]
It was my privilege to be in Colorado not long ago with your attorney, Mr.
Pressman and what a magnificent job he did in the cause for freedom in that
part of America and I know that you have profited no end by listening to him
today.
Just a few things I am going to say. They have to do with things that I
think are very close to you and to me. Before that--unfortunately, Mr. Brown,
my accompanist, does not fly, and I was in Louisville a day or so ago, he had
to go on to California and I will catch up with him later. I am going to sing
a couple of songs, unaccompanied. I used to do that, too! (Mr. Robeson sang
"Water Boy," "Joe Hill.")
Since "Freedom Train" is going to reflect so much what Ben said about
what I feel and what you feel very much about, I would like to finish with that
and say a few words I have to say just before and then I will finish with
Langston Hughes' "Freedom Train."

As you know, I have given up the last year or so of my professional career
to go about in many parts of America and I have seen many things.

I have been, for example, in North Carolina where I stood on the very
soil on which my own father was a slave. My father came to New Jersey. I
was born not far from here, up around Trenton and Princeton. I know this part
of the world very well. My father was a wandering minister, going from one
small church to another, and I saw my cousins in North Carolina, sharecroppers,
tenant farmers trying to eke some kind of decent living from that land.

I was in the mountains of West Virginia a few weeks ago, just a couple
of weeks ago, and the things that I saw shocked me beyond words. I did not
know that we, the wealthy land that we are, we with our high standard of living
could allow thousands and thousands of workers to live like that.

I was in Pueblo, Colorado not long ago, with Mr. Pressman, and the next
morning we saw Spanish-Americans living practically under the ground in holes--
in Pueblo, Colorado.

In the South, in the cotton fields, across the whole South, in the fruitful fields of California, people from the Middle West of our country, practically living at the edge of subsistence.

Now why these things? These things should make us reflect upon the kind
of America that we have. Why should this be so?

The late President Roosevelt said that it was one-third of our nation
that was under-privileged. Perhaps you know more about that than I. As I go
about seeing things at their source, it seems it is possible more than two-
thirds, perhaps more than that, while the few control the great wealth and in
some way convince us that we have this very high standard of life.

I see too much poverty for us to boast.

Now as I was in Kansas City and saw what the police did--I was in the hall
a few days after the police had hit the workers over the heads, gone in and
torn up the union hall. I remember when on the Mesabi Range, I had a concert
there, I was on the picket line, and the scabs came out protected by the sheriff,
and they were bent over. I wanted to know why they were bent over and they
told me they had rifles in their hands and they were supposed to shoot if
necessary. They did shoot just the other night, yesterday, I understand, at
Waterloo, Iowa. I just came from there, too, speaking in the home state of
Mr. Wallace. Things happened in Charleston, South Carolina just the other day.[212]

These things mean there are forces in our life, I say they are the forces
of the few that are saying to the people as they aspire to a more decent life
not only shall we not give you more wages, not only shall you Negroes not have
any more civil rights, we will beat you down and see that you remain in a kind
of industrial serfdom as long as we have any kind of power.

These things, unfortunately, are not new in the struggle of mankind. I
often think how is it that we, the people, the great majority of the people,
struggling as we have for generation after generation forward to some better
life, how can it happen that everywhere in history a few seem to take the
power in their hands, confuse the people themselves and there they remain?

But that has been the history of the world or we might not be here because
who built this America of ours? The poor from England, the poor from Ireland,
the poor from Scotland and Wales, my own people brought as slaves to this land,
those who suffered in the old Poland, those who suffered in Czarist Russia,
those who suffered in the Balkans, in Asia, in Latin-America--we have built
this America. This has been built upon the very backs of ourselves and of our
forefathers.

And the Negro people of this land must realize today, as they face a new
kind of struggle, that they must have courage; they must have knowledge that
the very primary wealth of America is cotton, built upon the backs of our
fathers; that cotton taken to the textile mills of New England; and that we
don't have to ask for crumbs to be dropped from the few up top, but we have the
right and the responsibility to demand in a militant way a better life for ourselves and for the rest of those Americans and the peoples of the world who
still suffer and are oppressed. (Applause and cheers)

Now, this is the essence of the struggle that we fought under Roosevelt.
No one knows it better than your Union. I have gone about this land in many
places and everywhere do I see the Fur and Leather Workers in the vanguard of
progress.

I was in Cincinnati not long ago, in a real struggle. I was in the house

of Mr. Dickerson and there the whole core of progressive struggle was built
around our Union. So I know that we understand that somewhere things do get
confused now and then. The boys on top are pretty good at sowing the seeds
of confusion, but it is very simple if we remember our own struggle, how you
have grown and how you have built. And somewhere we had this great figure
of a Roosevelt who fought and called these people what they were, the people
who control our resources, the Economic Royalists, he called them. This
struggle went on, in our favor and in the favor of the Negro workers and the
Negro people throughout this land. And somewhere other forces came in and
have tried to undo all the great work that he built up.

But it does not rest in big worlds; it rests in very simple things. It
rests in the fact as to whether we sitting here, getting along pretty well,
whether other Americans doing very well, consider those who yet do not have
a decent life. Are they really people like ourselves?

This is the way I have tried to phrase it in the last weeks because as I
said to the people in Colorado, those of the progressive movement--how could
they sit there and allow people to live like these people did in Pueblo?

How can we dare face the world today knowing the suffering in many parts
of the world and stand and, for example, support and allow our government to
support a British Empire which supports a Smuts in South Africa, which has
millions of Africans and peoples from Asia in complete serfdom?

How can we stand and allow our government to suggest that we can think
more of the profits of a few people of Standard Oil of this very state, than
of the lives of one of the great peoples of the world, a people who gave us
the very basis of our ethics and our religion? Am I to say or to allow to say
a Forrestall, who went to Princeton about the same time I went to Rutgers--I
know a lot of these fellows on the board of Standard Oil--they say, "Roby,
why do you take the side you do?" They care nothing for the rights of the
ordinary laboring man. Let them starve, they say, just so we get the profits.
But I say to them, never, for example, shall my son go to a foreign land to
take up a gun to shoot a people that are close to him in the interests of any
kind of oil. (Applause and cheers)

So this is the basic thing, as I see it. Just people, millions and millions of them, aspiring people, very much the same all over the world. And if
we understand it in the South, if we understand that obviously nothing is perfect in this world, our struggle in America from the days of Jefferson down
through Lincoln and Roosevelt and through Wallace today has been somehow to
see that the many, the many can take some kind of real share of their labor,
that the few shall not keep on controlling our land, that there must be an
extension of this democracy to those who do not have it. And so this is so
all over the world.

Can't we understand what has happened in Hungary, in Yugoslavia, in China,
all over the world, where a few landlords owned all the land and told the
peasants, as they tell the Negroes in the South, they must remain in slavery?

They helped to defeat the fascism that kept them under heel because they
knew landlords sided with that fascism. We should understand today that when
the land comes to them and they get some share of it, like we got homestead
lands in the Middle-West--like the Negro people were promised forty acres and
a mule, they have not got it yet--somewhere, some day they will get some decent
share of that land in this land of ours.

But we must understand, having come from these different places in the
world that they have the same aspirations as we and that there are many ways
toward this freedom. We have our historic background; they have theirs. In
Scandinavia they do it one way; in England they do it another way. In Russia,
Yugoslavia and China they will do it their way. They have that privilege,
coming from their historic base. And we must understand and have respect for
the aspirations of other people and if our kind of life is so much better than
the rest of the world's, let's show it to the world, let's not try to beat the
backs of others. (Applause and cheers)

And from my own experience, coming up as I say, with a father who looked
in his time to the major parties to solve all the problems, well, he waited a
long while for the Republicans to do something. Perhaps he did not know that
the people who owned those plantations in the south, the people that own the
great industries, they have their interests served by these so-called major
parties.

I worked in a law office with a lot of them, one a Republican, one a

Democrat--they represent their interests. Like a man whom I knew in Seattle,
a so-called liberal today in Washington, checking everything to stop decent
housing, because he happened to represent the real estate interests. He cares
nothing where the veterans live, where people live who want decent homes; he
must fight for those kinds of profits.

And so it goes along, and these parties somewhere they have their interests
served.

And we must be very careful today, very careful as we succumb to a kind
of hysteria here and there because I ask you, what forces take our liberties
away? I ask you, in Binghamton, New York, for example, when I was there some
years ago, you said you must not say this in this town. Who were the men from
Cornell who were coming to speak on the same platform? They were the people who
owned Binghamton. Who are responsible for what happened in Kansas City? The
people who own the meat packing companies, who have the nerve to say to the
people of America, we, the few, are the American civilization.

They are not the American civilization! The people themselves are!
(Applause)

I talked to my manager some weeks ago and he said, "Paul, in your going
around defending labor, fighting for Wallace, you have no more concert career."
I said, "Tell me. I am interested. How did you figure that out?" He answered,
"Nobody will book you."

You know how that goes. All the little cities, you know how concerts are
built up, a very fine picture how the whole thing works. Twelve hundred
society bigwigs are the concert people in most of the towns. No ordinary
person can buy a ticket except by subscription, fifteen dollars, twenty dollars. A closed circle. So you go around America, doing concerts, singing to
about 1,200 or 2,000 people instead of tens of thousands and hundreds of
thousands. And the manager gets to think that this is America, this is American
culture.

I told him that he is just kidding. If I am not booked in Binghamton or
somewhere else, just hire the hall and I'll show him that there are a lot of
other people besides those 1,500. (Applause, cheers and delegates arose)

I shall finish with this reading of "The Freedom Train."

Proceedings of the Convention, May 20, 1948, pp. 201-04. FLWU Archives.

56.   ROBESON DARES TRUMAN TO ENFORCE FEPC

WASHINGTON--Paul Robeson last week marched at the head of a picket line
in front of the White House here and later, in a press conference, challenged
President Truman to make good on his civil rights promises and enforce his
FEPC order by protecting Negro workers from mass layoffs and discriminations
at the Bureau of Engraving and Printing.

When informed that President Truman had told reporters that he had not
noticed the three-week old picket line and, even if he had, would have no
comment, Robeson criticized the President and accused Mr. Truman of defaulting
on his civil rights pledges.

Accompanied by Charles P. Howard, Des Moine attorney who keynoted last
year's Progressive Party convention, Robeson came to Washington and spent two
afternoons marching in the picket line which has been maintained for three weeks
in front of the White House.

The marchers protested the jim-crow working conditions which have prevailed for many years in this Federal agency which comes directly under the
control of Secretary of Treasury John Snyder. These conditions have been
exposed by bureau workers before the House FEPC subcommittee and have been
called to the attention of Congress recently in speeches by Rep. Vito Marcantonio and Sen. William Langer in both houses of Congress. Resolutions demanding investigation of the discriminatory bureau conditions have been introduced in both houses. [213]

Some 1,800 war-service Negro women employees of the bureau now face loss
of their jobs while being denied the opportunity to qualify for permanent
status in their specialized fields, declared Mr. Robeson. He said: "If

President Truman is sincere about civil rights and about the FEPC order he
issued, he would do something about this."

Continuing, Mr. Robeson said: "Congress has not passed any civil rights
this year. But here is something which Truman and his cabinet officer, Snyder,
can do without waiting on Congress. They simply have to enforce the FEPC
order which the President issued, with much fanfare, a year ago."

Officials of the United Public Workers Union which is conducting the
picket line revealed that complaints filed with the Treasury's FEP board and
with the board established in the Civil Service Commission by appointment of
the President, have not been settled. Thomas Richardson, union official,
told reporters that Guy Moffett, chairman of the FEP board, had told the union
informally that it cannot direct a cabinet officer to do anything. Mr. Moffett said that the FEP board, under the President's order, is purely advisory
without effective enforcement powers.

Most of the Negro workers involved in the dispute served in specialized
jobs all through the war. Now, they are being displaced to make room for
white workers, say union officials. While the union supports the plan to
replace war service workers with permanent status employees, it contends that
in the bureau of engraving, Negro workers have been systematically denied any
opportunity to take examinations or to otherwise qualify for status. Replacement workers lack both the experience and training of these Negro workers, say
union officials.

Pittsburgh Courier, August 13, 1949.

57. REMARKS AT LONGSHORE, SHIPCLERKS, WALKING BOSSES & GATEMEN AND WATCHMEN'S CAUCUS

I want to thank you very much for allowing me to come in to say a word.
I am traveling about the country. I just came up from Dallas enroute to the
Northwest and I found that the Caucus was in session. Certainly, as a member
of the Union, knowing of the struggle that is around the corner, I wanted to
stop to say a word, to let you know that as a member of the Union, if there
is anything I can do, just let me know.

The struggle never seems to stop. It gets sharper and sharper. I pick
up the papers today and find that we and our Union have a real job to do.

I have been to Hawaii and have been in close touch with union matters.
I cannot tell you how proud I am to be a member of this Union. I go back to
the day when I was taken in. I have been a member of many unions.

I cannot tell you how proud I am to be with you. I have watched your
struggle, watched the consistent stand you have taken, and I know you are
going to continue to do that.

Taft-Hartley means death to the trade union movement. The two parties
have been playing around, and at every moment we see that Truman steps in and
uses every provision he can to do his part of the job. You have a real problem, I understand. It means that you are going to tell them, as you have told
them before, that you want no part whatsoever of this kind of legislation,
which not only would break the back of the labor movement but would set back
the whole struggle of the American people for generations. And I understand
that you are going to tell them that you want no part of voting on what the
employers have offered to you, that you will set the terms yourselves. That
I am very proud to see.

In traveling about the country it is quite clear that the struggle for
economic rights, the struggle for higher wages, the struggle for bread, the
struggle for housing, has become a part of a wider political struggle. They
have moved in to high places in government, and today the enemies of labor
control the working apparatus of the state. They have to be removed. There
has to be a basic change. I feel that this can only be done by seeing that
we put into power those who represent a political party which has the deep
interests of the people at heart. I am sure you understand that this cannot be
separated, that we must understand politically that Truman is in office through

one party, the Republicans are in through one party and are responsible for
Taft-Hartley, and that somewhere you have to see another group in there that
fights for the rights of labor and for the rights of the American people.

And so I travel about today not only as a member of the Union, not only
as an artist (I do concerts now and then), not only as a representative of the
Negro people, but I travel as one of the Progressive Party, fighting to put
Wallace in the presidential chair. Wallace is the man who might be there had
he not in 1944 said "Jim Crow must go," had he not fought so hard for the
rights of labor. He is the one public leader who has come out at once to say
that the hiring hall must remain and that these men must be fought to the
teeth; the people who are trying to break our backs.

And so I trust that you will realize the depth of that struggle, that you
will not separate them, that they cannot be separated, that they go hand in
hand, that the one way that this can be beaten is to give your energy, to give
your time, to give your money, to see that we can put representatives in Congress and a President in the White House and a Vice-President who will represent our interests.

It has been my great privilege since I have seen you last to have been
able to go to Hawaii for the Union; to have seen there working a real democratic way of life in the Union; workers from all over the world who have become a part of the American way of life, building a decent home and a decent
way of life for their children and for themselves in the Islands of Hawaii.

I managed to learn some of the sons of the people from the Philippines,
of the Japanese-Americans. I saw many Negroes there who have remained.

I want to thank the Union for what it is doing there. I hope pretty soon
to be down in the West Indies; I hope to drop by Cuba to see some of our fellows there.

And I want to repeat that I come today mainly as one in the Union, fighting its struggle, I shall be in the area for just two or three days. I shall
be back, I hope, soon again.

I am so proud to see the leadership that you have given to the whole labor
movement. I want to thank your courageous leader, Harry Bridges, for his
consistent stand.[214]

The final word is that as members of the ILWU, we have a tremendous responsibility. I cannot tell you how the labor movement throughout the country
looks to you as an example. And so there is added responsibility for you to
carry on the fight in the next few days, in the next few weeks, in the next
few months. . . .

"The issue is not the loyalty of the Negro people because that is not a
subject of debate. The real issue is whether the Negro people would permit
themselves to be divided by a group such as the Un-American Activities Committee in their fight for peace and human dignity. The committee's efforts
to make the loyalty of the Negro people an issue is an insult. How do they
dare to question our loyalty. I challenge the loyalty of the Un-American
Activities Committee.

"The truth is that the action of the committee is just one step from the
herding of black people into concentration camps. It is therefore very important that the Negro press step forward and defend, not me, but the Negro
people.

"We cannot forget that John S. Wood, chairman of the committee, once
called the Ku Klux Klan an American institution. Why, then, should Negroes
pick this type of committee to express their loyalty?

"Why did the committee merely question the loyalty of Negroes? How about
the Italians? Did Joe DiMaggio go down there to testify?[215]

"It should be clear that Robinson, by appearing before this committee,
has performed a profound political act that has aided those who would enslave
the Negro. He erred too in stating to this committee that the Negro didn't
need the help of the Communists. The Negro needs the help of all--Communist
or non-Communist. But it does not need the aid of a man who once called the
Ku Klux Klan an American institution.[216]

"My main concern is to get at this Un-American Activities Committee.
Again, I repeat I am willing to appear before the committee at any time.

"The statement I made before the Paris Peace Conference has been distorted.
I am not interested in war, but in peace, and here is what I said at that
conference:

"'It is unthinkable that the Negro people could be lured into any kind of war especially against the Soviet Union, where former colonial people have complete equality. The question is: Will the Negro be drawn into a war which can only extend their enslavement, or will they fight for peace?'

"If we were to go to war today, we'd be fighting for those who represent fascist Germany, the British Empire, and that one per cent of America that exploits the other ninety-nine per cent.

"I have no desire of being a 'Black Stalin.' All I want to do is to sing and act. These things I feel I will be able to do always. Negroes have a chance in this period to make greater gains than ever before. They must be militant, and they will succeed.

"Jackie Robinson told the committee about his willingness to fight for 'investment' in America. But it is not a question of going to war but a question of struggling for peace. When Jackie speaks of investment, he should remember that I too, have an investment in the United States. But I can't forget what could happen to my investment overnight under present conditions.

"The truth is that eighty-five concert engagements of mine have been cancelled of a total of eighty-five. But this does not worry me in the least since I can always find places to sing. Nor will it prevent me from earning a living, because long ago I prepared myself to sing in the various languages of the world, and as a result, I can now go to Alaska or Hong Kong and make a living singing there.

"But they can't scare me and they can't run me out of this country. I gave them a chance to throw me in jail. I refused to answer that certain question.

"Permit me to deny two reports. First, I did not write to Jackie Robinson asking him not to appear before the committee. Second, I did not say at Paris that colored people would not fight in a war against Russia. But when it became obvious to me that the statement I made had been purposely distorted, I said to myself, 'Okay, let it stand like that.' But now that organizations such as the House Un-American Activities Committee are attempting to use it to their advantage, I am taking the attitude, 'Let's put the statement back into context now.'"

Typescript, proceeding of the caucus, August 21, 1948, pp. 229-32. ILWU Archives.

58.   FORGE NEGRO-LABOR UNITY FOR PEACE AND JOBS

By Paul Robeson

I am profoundly happy to be here tonight.

No meeting held in America at this mid-century turning point in world history holds more significant promise for the bright future toward which humanity strives than this National Labor Conference for Negro Rights. For here are gathered together the basic forces--the Negro sons and daughters of labor and their white brothers and sisters--whose increasingly active intervention in national and world affairs is an essential requirement if we are to have a peaceful and democratic solution of the burning issues of our times.

Again we must recall the state of the world in which we live, and especially the America in which we live. Our history as Americans, Black and white, has been a long battle, so often unsuccessful, for the most basic rights of citizenship, for the most simple standards of living, the avoidance of starvation--for survival.

I have been up and down the land time and again, thanks in the main to you trade unionists gathered here tonight. You helped to arouse American communities to give to Peekskill, to protect the right of freedom of speech and assembly. And I have seen and daily see the unemployment, the poverty, the plight of our children, our youth, the backbreaking labor of our women-- and too long, too long have my people wept and mourned. We're tired of this denial of a decent existence. We demand some approximation of the American democracy we have helped to build.

Who Built This Land?

For who built this great land of ours? Who have been the guarantors of our historic democratic tradition of freedom and equality? Whose labor and whose life has produced the great cities, the industrial machine, the basic culture and the creature comforts of which our "Voice of America" spokesmen so proudly boast?[217]

It is well to remember that the America which we know has risen out of the toil of the many millions who have come here seeking freedom from all parts of the world:

The Irish and Scotch indentured servants who cleared the forests, built the colonial homesteads and were part of the productive backbone of our early days.

The millions of German immigrants of the mid-nineteenth century; the millions more from Eastern Europe whose sweat and sacrifice in the steel mills, the coal mines and the factories made possible the industrial revolution of the Eighties and Nineties; the brave Jewish people from all parts of Europe and the world who have so largely enriched our lives on this new continent; the workers from Mexico and from the East--Japan and the Philippines--whose labor has helped make the West and Southwest a rich and fruitful land.

And, through it all, from the earliest days--before Columbus--the Negro people, upon whose unpaid toil as slaves the basic wealth of this nation was built!

These are the forces that have made America great and preserved our democratic heritage.

They have arisen at each moment of crisis to play the decisive role in our national affairs.

The Strength of the Negro People

In the Civil War, hundreds of thousands of Negro soldiers who took arms in the Union cause won, not only their own freedom--the freedom of the Negro people--but, by smashing the institution of slave labor, provided the basis for the development of trade unions of free working men in America.

And so, even today, as this National Labor Conference for Negro Rights charts the course ahead for the whole Negro people and their sincere allies, it sounds a warning to American bigotry and reaction. For if fifteen million Negroes led by their staunchest sons and daughters of labor, and joined by the white working class, say that there shall be no more Jim Crow in America, then there shall be no more Jim Crow!

If fifteen million Negroes say, and mean it, no more anti-Semitism, then there shall be no more anti-Semitism!

If fifteen million Negroes, inspired by their true leaders in the labor movement, demand an end to the persecution of the foreign-born, then the persecution of the foreign-born will end!

If fifteen million Negroes in one voice demand an end to the jailing of the leaders of American progressive thought and culture and the leaders of the American working class, then their voice will be strong enough to empty the prisons of the victims of America's cold war.

If fifteen million Negroes are for peace, then there will be peace!

And behind these fifteen million are 180 million of our African brothers and sisters, 60 million of our kindred in the West Indies and Latin America-- for whom, as for us, war and the Point Four Program would mean a new imperialist slavery.

The Issues of Our Time

I know that you understand these problems--and especially the basic problem of peace. You have already outlined the issues in your sessions, and they are clear to liberty-loving men around the world.

Shall we have atom-bomb and hydrogen bomb and rocketship and bacteriological war, or shall we have peace in the world; the hellish destruction of the men, women and children, of whole civilian populations, or the peaceful construction of the good life everywhere?

This for all men is the over-riding issue of the day. From it all other

questions flow. Its solution, one way or the other, will decide the fate of
all other questions which concern the human family.

For the warmakers are also the fascist-minded; and the warmakers are also
the profit-hungry trusts who drive labor, impose Taft-Hartley laws and seek
to crush the unions.

Depending on how we succeed in the fight for peace, then, we shall find
the answers to the other two major questions of the day.

Shall we have fascist brute rule or democratic equality and friendship
among peoples and nations; the triumphant enshrinement of the "master race"
theories our soldiers died to destroy, or liberty and freedom for the American
people and their colonial allies throughout the world?

And finally, shall we have increased wealth for the already bloated monopolies in the midst of rising hunger, poverty and disease for the world's poor;
or shall the masses of toiling men and women enjoy the wealth and comforts
which their sweat and labor produce?

American Imperialism vs. the Colonial World

Yes, these are the issues.

They will be resolved in our time—and you may be sure that you have met,
not a moment too soon. Because in the five years since V-J Day the American
trusts and the government which they control have taken their stand more and
more openly on the side of a cold war which they are desperately trying to heat
up; on the side of the fascist and kingly trash which they seek to restore to
power all over Europe and Asia; on the side of the princes of economic privilege
whose every cent of unprecedented profits is wrung out of the toil-broken bodies
of the masses of men.

Mr. Truman and Mr. Acheson want us to believe that they seek peace in the
world. But the people's memory is not so short.[218]

How well and how bitterly do we recall that soon after Roosevelt died
American arms were being shipped to the Dutch—not for the protection of the
Four Freedoms, but to advance the claims of liberty—but for the suppression
of the brave Indonesian patriots in their fight for independence.

That was in 1946, and today—four years later—we have the announcement of
another program of arms shipments to destroy a movement for colonial independence
—this time arms for the French imperialists to use against the brave Viet-
Namese patriots in what the French progressive masses call the "dirty wars" in
Indo-China.

These two acts of the Truman Administration are significant landmarks of
our time!

They cry out to the world that our nation, born in a bloody battle for
freedom against imperialist tyranny, has itself become the first enemy of
freedom and the chief tyrant of the mid-century world. They warn more than
half the world's population who people the vast continents of Asia that, until
the course of our foreign policy is changed, they can no longer look to the
U.S. government for help in their strenuous struggles for a new and independent
life.

And, to be sure, they have already averted their gaze from us.

In every subject land, in every dependent area, the hundreds of millions
who strive for freedom have set their eyes upon a new star that rises in the
East—they have chosen as the model for their conduct the brave people and
stalwart leaders of the new People's Republic of China. And they say to our
atom-toting politicians, "Send your guns and tanks and planes to our oppressors,
if you will! We will take them away from them and put them to our own use!
We will be free in spite of you, if not with your help!

Africa in World Affairs

What special meaning does this challenge of the colonial world have for
American Negro workers and their allies?

We must not forget that each year 4,000 tons of uranium ore are extracted
from the Belgian Congo—the main source of United States supply. And that
Africa also provides more than half the world's gold and chrome, 80 per cent
of its cobalt, 90 per cent of its palm kernels, one-fifth of its manganese
and tin, one-third of its sisal fiber and 60 per cent of its cocoa—not to
mention untold riches yet unexplored.

And with this wealth, Africa produces also an immeasurable portion of the world's human misery and degradation.

But the African peoples are moving rapidly to change their miserable conditions. And 180 million natives on that great continent are an important part of the colonial tidal wave that is washing upon the shores of history and breaking through the ramparts of imperialist rule everywhere.

The Congo skilled worker extracting copper and tin from the rich mines of the land of his fathers may one day be faced with the same materials in the shape of guns provided his Belgian rulers by the Truman Administration under the Marshall Plan--but he is determined that the days of his virtual slave labor are numbered, and that the place for the Belgians to rule is in *Belgium and not in the Congo.*

And 25 million Nigerians-farmers, cattle raisers, miners, growers of half the world's cocoa--are determined that the land of *our* fathers (for the vast majority of American Negro slaves were brought here from Africa's West Coast) --shall belong to their fathers' sons and not to the freebooters and British imperialists supported by American dollars.

And twelve South African workers lie dead, shot in a peaceful demonstration by Laman's fascist-like police, as silent testimony to the fact that, for all their pass laws, for all their native compounds, for all their Hitler-inspired registration of natives and non-whites, the little clique that rules South Africa are baying at the moon. For it is later than they think in the procession of history, and that rich land must one day soon return to the natives on whose backs the proud skyscrapers of the Johannesburg rich were built.

How are we to explain this new vigor of the African independence movements? What is it that shakes a continent from Morocco to the Cape and causes the old rulers to tremble?

The core of the African nationalist movements, the heart of the resistance to continued oppression, the guiding intelligence of the independence aspirations of the Africans is invariably the organizations of the workers of the continent. Trade unions have arisen all over Africa and, as everywhere in modern times, they are the backbone of the people's struggle.

And what is true of Africa is even more strikingly true in the West Indies, in Cuba, Brazil and the rest of Latin America where 60 million Negroes are building strong trade unions and demanding a new day.

So it was a proud day in the history of the laboring men and women of the world when these African workers--railroad men, miners, mechanics, sharecroppers, craftsmen, factory workers--clasped grips with white, brown, yellow and other black workers' hands around the world and formed the World Federation of Trade Unions!

Abdoulaye Diallo, General Secretary of the Congress of Trade Unions of the Sudan, and a Vice-President of the WFTU, and Gabriele D'Arboussier, who was denied a visa to attend this conference, stand as signals to the world that the African worker recognizes, not only that his future lies in strong and militant trade unionism, but also in his fraternal solidarity with workers of all climes and colors whose friends are his friends and whose enemies are his also.

The Truman Plan for Africa

However much the official density of the top leadership of American labor may have prevented it from recognizing the real significance of the emergence of African labor, the American trusts and their hirelings in government have not been asleep. They have been steadily carrying forward their own plan for Africa, of which Truman's Point Four program is an essential though by no means the only part.

First, they say, we will spend the tax money of the American people to prop up the shaky empire builders of Europe who own and control most of Africa. And so the Marshall Plan sends billions to France, Italy, Belgium and Portugal.[21]

Second, they say, as a guarantee that the money is not wasted, we will send them arms under the Atlantic Pact so that they may put down any rising of the African peoples, or any demonstrations of sympathy for colonial freedom on the part of their own working classes.

Third, say the American banner-imperialists, with these guarantees, we will launch Point Four, which opens the door for investment of capital by American big business in African raw material and cheap labor.

Fourth, as an added guarantee that the investment of American monopoly--
already garnered as surplus profits from the labor of speeded-up American
workers--does not run the "risk" of any changes in government or "excessive"
demands for living wages by *African* workers, we will build our *own* bases in
Accra, Dakar and all over the African continent.

And fifth, should all these precautions fail: should the African people
eventually kick us and the British and the French and the Belgians and the
Itallians and Portugese rulers out of their continent, then, says the Point
Four program, we will compensate the American big business investors for their
losses--again out of the public treasury, the people's tax money.

Yes, this is the Truman plan for Africa, and the Africans don't like it
and are saying so louder and louder every day.

But it is only at the continent of Asia and Africa that the tentacles of
the American billionaires are aimed? Indeed not!

Ask the people of Greece whose partisans continue an uneven struggle for
democracy and independence as a consequence of the original Truman Doctrine!

Ask the Italian or French worker who, as a "beneficiary" of the Atlantic
Arms Pact and the Marshall Plan, sees the ships bring American tanks and guns
to his land while his children go hungry and ill-clad in the face of skyrocketing prices!

Ask the workers in Scandinavia and Britain who are weary of governments
incapable of meeting their needs because they are the slavish captives of the
American money-men who seek to dominate the world!

Ask the millions in Western Germany who see American influence placing
unrepentant fascists back into positions of power, before the stench of the
Dachaus and Buchenwalds--the Hitler crematoriums and mass murder camps--have
left the land.

Ask the proud citizens of the New Democracies of Eastern Europe and of
the Soviet Union who suffered most in World War II and whose every yearning for
peace and time to reconstruct their ravaged land is met by the arrogant ob-
struction of American diplomats!

They know and they will tell you without hesitation--these people who
are two-thirds of the world's population--that the seat of danger of aggressive
war and fascist oppression has shifted from the banks of the Rhine to the banks
of the Potomac, from the Reich-chancellery of Hitler to the Pentagon Building,
the State Department and the White House of the United States.

These peoples of the world look to us, the progressive forces in American
life, Black and white together, to stop our government's toboggan ride toward
war and destruction.

Do they look in vain? This conference answers, no!

The Task of Labor

Your tasks, then, are clear. The Negro trade unionists must increasingly
exert their influence in every aspect of the life of the Negro community. No
church, no fraternal, civic or social organization in our communities must be
permitted to continue without the benefit of the knowledge and experience which
you have gained through your struggles in the great American labor movement.
You are called upon to provide the spirit, the determination, the organizational
skill, the firm steel of unyielding militancy to the age-old strivings of the
Negro people for equality and freedom.

On the shoulders of the Negro trade unionists there is the tremendous
responsibility to rally the power of the whole trade-union movement, white and
Black, to the battle for the liberation of our people, the future of our women
and children. Anyone who fails in this does the Negro people a great disservice.

And to the white trade unionists presents--a special challenge. You must
fight in the ranks of labor for the full equality of your Negro brothers; for
their right to work at any job; to receive equal pay for equal work; for an end
to Jim Crow unions; for real fair employment practices within the unions as
well as in all other phases of the national life; for the elimination of the
rot of white supremacy notions which the employers use to poison the minds of
the white workers in order to pit them against their staunchest allies, the
Negro people--in short, for the unbreakable unity of the working people, Black
and white, without which there can be no free trade unions, no real prosperity,
no constitutional rights, no peace for anybody, whatever the color of his skin.

To accept Negro leadership of men and women and youth; to accept the fact that
the Negro workers have become a part of the vanguard of the whole American
working class. To fail the Negro people is to fail the whole American people.
     I know that you who have come from all parts of the nation will meet this
challenge. I have watched and participated in your militant struggles everywhere I have been these past years. Here in Chicago with the packinghouse
workers; with auto workers of Detroit; the seamen and longshoremen of the West
Coast; the tobacco workers of North Carolina; the miners of Pittsburgh and West
Virginia; and the steel workers of Illinois, Indiana, Ohio, Michigan and
Minnesota; the furriers, clerks and office workers of New York, Philadelphia
and numerous other big cities and small towns throughout the land.
     I have met you at the train stations and airports, extending the firm hand
of friendship. You have packed the meetings which followed Peekskill to overflowing, thus giving the answer to the bigots and the war-makers. I know you
well enough to know that, once the affairs of my people are in the hands of our
working men and women, our day of freedom is not far off. I am proud as an
artist to be one who comes from hardy Negro working people--and I know that you
can call on me at any time--South, North, East or West--all my energy is at your
call.
     So--as you move forward, you do so in the best traditions of American
democracy and in league with hundreds of millions throughout the world whose
problems are much the same as yours.
     These are peoples of all faiths, all lands, all colors, and all political
beliefs--united by the common thirst for freedom, security, and peace.
     Our American press and commentators and politicians would discourage these
basic human aspirations because Communists adhere to them as well as others.
Now I have seen the liberty-loving, peace-seeking partisans in many parts of
the world. And though many of them are not, it is also true that many are
Communists. They represent a new way of life in the world, a new way that has
won the allegiance of almost half the world's population. In the last war
they were the first to die in nation after nation. They were the heart of the
underground anti-fascist movements and city after city in Europe displays
monuments to their heroism. They need no apologies. They have been a solid
core of the struggle for freedom.
     Now, Mr. Truman and Mr. Acheson would have us believe that all the problems
of this nation, and the chief difficulties of the Negro people are caused by
these people who were the first anti-fascists.
     I, for one, cannot believe that the jailing of Eugene Dennis for the rea-
son that he contended that the House Un-American Activities Committee lacked
proper constitutional authority because it harbored as a member John Rankin
who holds office as a result of the disfranchisement of the Negro half of the
population of Mississippi and most of the white half as well--I cannot believe
that Dennis' jailing will help in the solution of the grievous problems of
Negro working men and women.
     Mr. Truman calls upon us to save the so-called Western democracies from
the "menace" of Communism.
     But ask the Negro ministers in Birmingham whose homes were bombed by the
Ku Klux Klan what is the greatest menace in their lives! Ask the Trenton Six
and the Martinsville Seven! Ask Willie McGee, languishing in a Mississippi
prison and doomed to die within the next month unless our angry voices save
him. Ask Haywood Patterson, somewhere in America, a fugitive from Alabama
barbarism for a crime he, nor any one of the Scottsboro boys, ever committed.
Ask the growing numbers of Negro unemployed in Chicago and Detroit. Ask the
fearsome lines of relief clients in Harlem. Ask the weeping mother whose son
is the latest victim of police brutality. Ask Maceo Snipes and Isaiah Nixon,
killed by mobs in Georgia because they tried to exercise the constitutional
right to vote. Ask any Negro worker receiving unequal pay for equal work,
denied promotion despite his skill and because of his skin, still the last
hired and the first fired. Ask fifteen million American Negroes, if you please,
"What is the greatest menace in your life?" and they will answer in a thunderous
voice, "Jim-Crow Justice! Mob Rule! Segregation! Job Discrimination!"--in short
white supremacy and all its vile works.
     Yes, we know who our friends are, and we know our enemies, too. Howard
Fast, author of the epic novel *Freedom Road* who went to jail this past Wednesday
for fighting against the restoration of fascism in Spain, is not our enemy. He
is a true friend of the Negro people. And George Marshall, Chairman of the

Civil Rights Congress, who went to jail last Friday and whose fight for the
life of Willie McGee of Mississippi is one of the great democratic sagas of
our time--he is not our enemy; he is a true friend of the Negro people. And
John Howard Lawson and Dalton Trumbo, Hollywood screen writers, who went to
jail the day before yesterday for maintaining their faith in the sacred
American doctrine of privacy of political belief--they too are friends of the
people.

Our enemies are the lynchers, the profiteers, the men who give FEPC the
run-around in the Senate, the atom-bomb maniacs and the war-makers.

One simple reason why I know that we shall win is that our friends are
so much more numerous than our enemies. They will have to build many, many
more jails--not only here but all over the world to hold the millions who are
determined never to give up the fight for freedom, decency, equality, abundance,
and peace.

I have just this past week returned from London where the Executive
Committee of the World Partisans for Peace met to further their crusade against
atomic destruction. And there, spokesmen of millions of men and women from
all parts of the globe--Europe, Asia, Africa, North and South America, Austra-
lia--pledged themselves anew that the Truman plan for the world shall not
prevail--that peace shall conquer war--that men shall live as brothers, not
as beasts.

These men and women of peace speak not merely for themselves, but for the
nameless millions whose pictures do not adorn the newspapers, who hold no
press conference, who are the mass of working humanity in every land.

Did I say nameless? Not any more! For one hundred million have already
signed their names in all lands to a simple and powerful pledge, drawn up at
Stockholm--a pledge which reads as follows:

We demand the unconditional prohibition of the atomic weapon as an instrument of aggression and mass extermination of people and the establishment of
strict international control over the fulfillment of this decision. . . . We
will regard as a war criminal that government which first uses the atomic
weapon against any country.

The Soviet Union and China are signing this pledge. People in all
nations of the world are signing it. Will you take this pledge now? (Audience
answers a loud "Yes!")

Your meeting tonight as men and women of American labor is in good time
because it places you in this great stream of peace-loving humanity, determined to win a world of real brotherhood. It will enable you, I hope, to place
the Negro trade unionists in the front ranks of a crusade to secure at least
a million signatures of Negro Americans to this Stockholm appeal for peace.

As the Black worker takes his place upon the stage of history--not for a
bit part, but to play his full role with dignity in the very center of the
action--a new day dawns in human affairs. The determination of the Negro
workers, supported by the whole Negro people, and joined with the mass of
progressive white working men and women, can save the labor movement, CIO and
AFL, from the betrayals of the Murrays and the Greens, the Careys, Rieves and
Dubinskys--and from the betrayals, too, of the Townsends, the Weavers and
Randolphs. This alliance can beat back the attacks against the living standards and the very lives of the Negro people. It can stop the drive toward
fascism. It can halt the chariot of war in its tracks.[220]

And it can help to bring to pass in America and in the world the dream
our fathers dreamed--of a land that's free, of a people growing in friendship,
in love, in cooperation and peace.

This is history's challenge to you. I know you will not fail.

Speech delivered at Chicago meeting of more than 900 delegates to the National
Labor Conference for Negro Rights, June 1950. Reprinted from the April 1976
issue of *Political Affairs*.

59. NATIONAL UNION OF MARINE COOKS AND STEWARDS CONVENTION

Just got back from the West Coast and an exciting visit with trade union
leaders and rank and filers who are charting a new course in American labor
history. The recent convention of the National Union of Marine Cooks and
Stewards set a standard in labor's struggle for the full rights and dignity
of the Negro people that other unions in our country might do well to emulate.

Revels Cayton, the dynamic union leader who is now an organizer for the
Distributive, Processing and Office Workers in New York, and George Murphy,
our general manager at FREEDOM, made the trip with me and we all had an exciting and fruitful time. "Rev" has his roots deep in the Coast where for many
years before coming to New York, he was the outstanding Negro labor leader in
a vast area that stretches from San Diego to Seattle. He was leader of the MCS,
and was closely associated with the struggles of the International Longshoremen's
and Warehousemen's Union--the men who keep the cargo moving on the docks and
in the huge warehouses of the coastal cities and whose president, Harry Bridges,
is one of the finest union leaders of our day.

For "Rev" it was like old home week as we sat with his old colleagues in
informal bull sessions which got to the heart of the problem the MCS and all
unions face; strengthening the bond of unity between its Negro and white
members.

The problem can be simply stated:

(1) The union faces the combined attacks of government agencies and
greedy waterfront employers because of its unrelenting fight for the economic
rights of its members and its progressive, pro-peace program.

(2) The union can only withstand these attacks if the membership stands
solid behind a militant, uncompromising leadership.

(3) This solid unity of the membership depends more than ever on a new
kind of fight against Jim Crow, not only in union affairs and contract negotiations, but in every aspect of American life.

For the Negro members know that their people are now suffering the most
brutal and calculated oppression in recent memory--legal lynching, police
brutality, arson, bombings, mob violence--all manner of insult and injury--
and they are looking to the union not only as the guarantor of their "pork
chops" but as a special defender of their rights and their very lives as well.

After one of those all-night sessions, I came away with the feeling that
the MCS will certainly settle this question in the right way. And the main
reason for this confidence is the splendid group of Negro leaders--men like
Joe Johnson, Charlie Nichols and Al Thibodeaux--who combine with their sterling
leadership in the general affairs of the union a constant battle to win the
entire membership for *actions,* not just words, around the vital problems that
face the hemmed-in, hard-pressed Negro communities of the nation. They are
important figures in labor circles who have refused to become so "integrated"
that they could forget their beginnings and their main strength--among the
masses of their people. We need more labor leaders like them, and like ILWU's
Bill Chester, throughout the land.

Of all my connections with working men and women, there is none of which
I am more proud than my honorary membership in MCS. I shall always cherish
fond memories of the convention in the Fillmore district of San Francisco, of
the wonderful audience of union men, their wives and friends, for whom I had
the honor to sing and speak.

But here again, the main drama of the convention was to be found not only
in the public mass meetings, but in the working sessions, committee meetings,
national council discussions, and caucuses which hammered out a fighting program, security, and equality. And I mean real equality, not just the paper
kind!

It would be hard for MCS to have any other kind of program and survive.
Fully 40 per cent of its membership is Negro and more than 60 per cent of the
convention delegates were colored members. The convention took place during
the last stirring days in the world-wide struggle to save the life of Willie
McGee. And it was a reassuring sign to see the men from the ships "hit the
deck" in the Golden Gate Commandery Hall, owned by Macedonia Baptist Church,
and vow vengeance against the lynchers.

Most important the key white leaders of the union, Hugh Bryson, president,

and Eddie Tangen, secretary-treasurer, recognized that their special responsibility was, not simply to ride the wave of indignation and red-hot
militancy of the Negroes, but, above all, to lead the white membership to an
understanding of its stake in the fight for Negro freedom.

For one thing is becoming clearer every day. If the Negro's struggle for
liberation is crushed under the hammer blows of American racists, the whole
labor movement will go down with it. The racist and the labor-hater have the
same face--big business. The industrialist and plantation owner who want to
return Negroes to slavery also want to return all labor to the sweatshop. And
if white workers want to keep their unions and their hard-won rights they'd
better move fast to see that Negro Americans gain their long-lost liberties.

That's the lesson of Hitler Germany which we must never forget and which
I never tire of telling American working men and women. The labor leaders who
stood aside in the early thirties and saw six million Jews set upon were soon,
themselves, in exile, in the good earth, or--if their knees were flexible
enough and their souls craven enough--in Hitler's phony "labor front."

And no sooner had Hitler crushed the natural opposition to his outlandish
campaign to "stop Communism," save "Western civilization," and preserve "Aryan
supremacy," than he plunged Germany and the world into the holocaust of World
War II.

Then it was not merely the Jews or the working class of Europe that suffered, but all mankind--men and women; tall and short; black, brown, yellow
and white; Mason, Pythian, and Elk; businessman, intellectual and professional
Catholic, Methodist, Presbyterian, and Baptist--hard shell and soft shell, too!

How well should this history of our times be remembered! Today's would-be
Hitlers are not in Germany; they are right here in the United States. They
would extend the Korean war (under the banner of Confederate flags!) to the
whole continent of Asia by refusing to make an honorable peace of equality with
the 475 million Chinese people. Whether by the MacArthur or the Truman plan,
it makes little difference--for they are both talking war, not peace; and the
proud people of Asia are still "hordes" of "coolies" and "gooks" in their sight.

They would turn Africa--emerging from the status of a slave continent--
into a blazing inferno in order to crush the independence movements on the West
Coast, the Sudan and South Africa, and in order to increase the fabulous wealth
which the Morgans, Firestones, Mellons, DuPonts and Rockefellers are extracting
from the inexpressible subjugation and misery of our African brothers and
sisters.

They would do all these things--if they could. To date they have been
stopped in their tracks by the steel-like will of Asia's millions, by the
determined liberation struggles of Africa's sons and daughters, by the stubborn
resistance of the people of Europe who suffered most from Hitler's maniacal
plan--and by the fact that they are not alone in possession of "the bomb."

More and more, however, the American war-minded madmen must feel the resistance of THEIR OWN COUNTRYMEN. They must be openly challenged and defeated,
lest our country go down the shameful road along which Hitler led Germany to
destruction and degradation.

There may be a few high-placed stooges in hand-me-down jobs who will try
to get the Negro people to go along with the program of our would-be world
conquerers. But they couldn't be found at the MCS convention. Instead there
were hard-working union men, talking and fighting for their people's rights
and for a decent life for all workingmen. They are emerging not only as union
leaders, but as the rightful stewards of the affairs of our entire people in
their community organizations. And one must mention the splendid women who are
fighting by the side of their men in MCS and ILWU.

The convention was a sign that the resistance to war, poverty and prejudice
is growing where it needs most to grow, among workingmen and women who have at
stake in this struggle their whole future and that of their children. The
focus of the struggle today is on whether we can force payment on the promises
which have been made to the Negro people for 87 years--and never kept. If we
don't cash in on them, then the American promissory note of the good life,
democratic government and human equality will be as phony as a nine dollar
bill to everybody else.

The MCS convention meant to me that the Negro people have some wonderful
allies in our job of seeing that there's some "promise-keeping" done--but
quick! It was sure good to be there!

"Here's My Story," *Freedom*, June 1951.

60. FORD LOCAL 600 PICNIC

I have been in Detroit many times during my work in America. But never
was there for quite such an occasion as the picnic Aug. 12 sponsored by the
foundry workers of Ford Local 600, UAW, CIO.

During the recent visit I recalled previous contacts with the auto city.
As an All-American football player just out of college, I played there with
Fritz Pollard of Akron. Great sections of the Negro community came out, just
as they turn out to see football and baseball stars there today. I had a
brother who lived in Detroit--died there--and it was the first time he had
seen me since I was a boy. I remember going around with him and later seeing
the fellows from the fraternity.[221]

When I began my concert career, I always insisted that my management
present me under the auspices of Miss Nellie Watts, the fine impresario in
Detroit. And often in those days I sang in the churches of the Negro community.

During the "Sojourner Truth" days I was there and spoke on many platforms
before and after the riots. On the opening night of *Othello* there were very
few rich folks in the audience. Nobody quite knew what had happened, but I saw
that the Ford workers, Negro and white, had most of the seats, and it was a
memorable opening.

In recent years, meetings and concerts for the Progressive Party, for our
paper, FREEDOM, and on behalf of Rev. Charles Hill's candidacy for the Common
Council have kept me in close touch with friends in Detroit's Paradise Valley.

But as I said, the union picnic was something else again. It took place
at Paris Park, about 20 miles outside the city limits. About 7,000 men, women,
and children attended and it was a real demonstration of the working people's
unity. Usually the various language groups in Detroit like to go off and have
their picnics by themselves, and the Negro people do the same. But here all
were joined together in an audience predominantly Negro but including large
sections of whites of various backgrounds: Irish, like Pat Rice, Local 600
vice-president; Scotch, Slavic, and especially Italian-Americans who had turned
out in great numbers to hear Vito Marcantonio.

Marcantonio made a tremendous contribution, I thought. Eloquent as usual,
he spoke in the workers' language and explained a good deal of what the present
situation means to them in terms of bread and butter. He demolished the phony
government "economic stabilization" program and showed that the way to win
security is to fight for peace.

I sang some songs and spoke a good deal about the struggles of the Negro
people. I was moved to pay tribute to the foundry workers who had sponsored
the picnic with the backing of the entire local.

Under the leadership of Nelson Davis, a veteran unionist who was the
organizer of the picnic, and others, the foundry workers have developed a unity
which is the core of the progressive militancy of the entire local. And this
unity is reflected among the general officers of the union: Carl Stellato,
president; Pat Rice, vice-president; Bill Hood, secretary, and W. G. Grant,
treasurer. These men know that they work together to defend the world's
largest local against the policies of UAW president Walter Reuther who, in his
support of the Truman war program, would tie the workers to wage freezes,
escalator clauses, and other gimmicks which lead to practical starvation and
depression.

One of the great lessons for me was what the picnic meant in terms of the
entire Negro community. I had a chance to go along with a number of the Negro
labor leaders from Local 600 and meet with a group of Negro ministers. We met
at the invitation of Rev. and Mrs. Ross and in their home. A number of clergymen were there including Rev. E. C. Williams and Rev. Charles H. Hill, who is
running for the Common Council and spoke eloquently at the picnic.

It was wonderful to see militant, progressive labor coming to these
religious leaders and saying, "We want to join with the ministry, leaders of
our people, in a common struggle for our folk." Well, the ministers said that
is what they had been wanting to hear for a long, long time.

And we had a luncheon with the business men. Mr. Reuben Ray, the head of
the Paradise Valley business men's organization, called the group together and
we discussed the necessity of small business and labor getting together. We
talked about the forthcoming national convention of the Negro labor councils
in Cincinnati and everybody agreed that our business community support this

project. Because it is clear that whatever helps the Negro worker and strengthens his position in industry and in the unions will also help the Negro businessman who depends on him for a livelihood. And most important of all, all sections of the Negro community, business, labor, church, professionals, have a
common struggle and goal--for full, equal citizenship and an end to Jim Crow
now.

We had a long talk with one of the leading physicians and he regretted
that we could not stay long enough to spend an evening with a group of the
professional men and women in his magnificent home. Here was a man with a
lively interest in social developments all over the world. He realized that
in our search for freedom we must profit from the experiences of other oppressed and formerly oppressed peoples in lands far away.

Well, there it is. For the first time in all these years of visits to
Detroit there were the real solid connections and possibilities of unity between all sections of the Negro people. And this was based on the strength
demonstrated by the Negro workers, united with their white brothers and sisters, at a memorable labor picnic.

Everybody concerned was interested in our paper FREEDOM, and promised to
help sell it and get subscriptions so that they may have a consistent voice
in molding the unity which is emerging.

"Here's My Story," *Freedom, September 1951.*

61. TOWARD A DEMOCRATIC EARTH WE HELPED TO BUILD

I just want to say a few words, I'm very happy to be here. I was talking
to your president, Bill Hood, a few minutes ago. He was saying how deeply he
felt that you the trade unionists of America--from the militant side of our
nation were saying to those who would stop us artists from appearing--you were
saying to them tonight, "Well, Paul's going to sing, he is going to sing
right here!" (Applause) So I want to thank you to begin with and say that of
course not only am I here as an artist, always that--but I am here as an artist
like many in the world today who give constantly of their talents and energies
to the struggles for freedom of the working masses of the world. (Applause)
And so I feel that I have sort of earned my honorary membership in the Trade
Union Councils.

Through the years I've been on your picket lines up and down the nation,
I've had many moving experiences. As I came in I saw an old friend from
Winston-Salem, Mrs. Velma Hopkins. I remember going down there into the deep
South, to help in their struggles. I remember a very sad last time going back
to say farewell to one of the great women of the labor movement, Miranda Smith.[222]
(Applause) For a time they said, "Well, maybe Paul had better not come into
the South," but I went in and came out all right. (Applause) And I say tonight as I've said many other times, I don't want any so-called Americans, or
un-Americans to tell me that I have not the right to go back to the North
Carolina (Loud applause) of my forefathers, that I have not the right to go
about America and about the earth saying that my people upon whose backs the
very wealth of this nation was built--that somewhere they must have their freedom. (Loud applause)

For that's all that I've been trying to do and say. And from many parts
of the world, you would be interested to know, I get letters daily--especially
from England. Just the other day one came saying, "Is it true, Paul, that you
can't sing, that there is danger when you sing? That you can't play in the
theater, that you can't be on the radio and television? You would be interested
to know that in every section of English opinion in the theater, in music, in
every field they have begun, as in the case of the Scottish miners, to say to
this government: "We want him over here to play 'Othello' again. We want to
hear him sing again, and we feel that something must be wrong where one who
fights as he has over here cannot sing in his own land." (Applause)

As I said when I was with you in Chicago a year ago, and as I have written
in the newspaper *Freedom* many times, somewhere we must see the necessity of
unity between all sections of labor in this land and throughout the world.

And especially today we must understand the deep struggle of the Negro people
in this land for these 300 years. Already you have shown me what I was talking
about in Chicago, because I am standing here tonight free with my shoulders back
because you have said, "Come to Cincinnati, Paul, and sing for us!" (Loud
applause) And so I can say to many Americans, "I've been to Cincinnati--to
the people of Cincinnati."

The Inquirer must remember one of my last visits here. I was the guest
of the City of Cincinnati. (Laughter) That's right, I sang in the ball park
for the city recreation fund.

Not long ago I stood in Cadillac Square for auto workers, black and white.
I stood on the packinghouse line in Chicago with the packinghouse workers and
I stand here tonight, therefore, saying let us find unity at this time against
those who are stepping upon your necks, who step upon the backs of labor and
who step especially upon the backs of the Negro people. (Applause) And let
us remember, we live in a time when hitherto colonial peoples all over the
world are winning their freedom. For a long time it was a pretty easy task
for England, for Belgium, for France, for our own imperialist nation--our own
imperialists who started out in earnest about the year of my birth. In the
year 1898 they went into Cuba, into Puerto Rico, into the Philippines. They
had gotten the idea of world domination. But now we see the seething of
millions and hundreds of millions of people in motion all over the world.
Still some evil people in our own land say there shall be no freedom. They
want to fasten a new colonialism on the masses of people.

We have a deep responsibility. Are we going to tell the Chinese people
to give back their freedom? They won't you know--no danger of that (Laughter)
(Applause) There are five hundred million of them, you know what I mean, five
hundred million--a lot of people. And they are moving along in India, hundreds
of millions who say to Nehru, "Stand your ground for the Indian people, don't
sell yourself to the imperialists wherever they may be, for you may not be
there if you do." (Laughter) And, then, there's the whole continent of Africa
(I'm proud to be the chairman of the Council on African Affairs). Every day
we receive word by cable. That continent is just seething all over the African
continent and they look to us here in Cincinnati, look to their allies in
America, to the struggling workers wherever they may be, to stop this government from going over to Africa and trying to put the people back into a kind
of serfdom and slavery when they are just about to emerge.[223]

England is calling upon us to save them in Egypt. I see in the paper
that our government may have to go to save the British Empire in Egypt. We
Negro people and the workers in America must understand that tomorrow the
English will be calling upon this government to come and save them in the Gold
Coast, to come and save them in Nigeria, to come and save them in a Federation
of the West Indies crying for their independence. What will we do then? Will
we go? I say, NO, not move a step! (Loud applause and hurrahs)

On the other hand we have the responsibility and we have the opportunity
to see that these things cannot happen, by doing what? By merging and fighting for our rights, Yes! Our day-to-day struggles for higher wages, for the
rights of labor wherever they may be, for upgrading, for full dignity. And
we also must understand that it will be very difficult to achieve these things
if we do not enter fully today into the struggle for peace to see that somewhere war does not destroy everybody. Under the guise of war measures they
can take away our rights with much more than a Taft-Hartley, much more than
the kind of terror that's going around today.

We've got to understand all these things in the background of the struggle
for freedom all over the world. And that's why of course, they want to im-
prison one of the great symbols of American unity, one of the great scholars
of our time whatever his color, one who has given his whole life to the concept and ideas of our true democratic faith. Today they would jail this great
man with whom it is my privilege to work day-by-day. Why would they take Dr.
DuBois? Because he fights for peace, because he fights for freedom, because
he fights for the full dignity and equality of his people to walk this earth in
freedom. (Applause) And they want to jail him because they know that if they
can shut him up talking about peace, then they can shut you up talking about
the freedom of the working people, then they can shut you up talking about the
freedom of the Negro people in America.

I just want to leave one more word, it's brought to my mind when I see
Mrs. Velma Hopkins and know that many people are here from the South. When

we talk about colonial struggles we sit here in certain parts in the North,
on the edge of the South here in Cincinnati. I traveled in '48 all over the
South. I stood in Memphis and saw the close struggles in many unions. I saw
white workers in the South come out on strike to see that Negro workers would
get equal pay. (Applause) I've seen great opportunities for strengthening
unity in this struggle. Let us not forget, therefore, that in talking about
the freedom of our people the core of it is there, where 10 million of our
folk are ground under day by day. They look to us, they look to us for full
understanding and when we talk about colonial and semi-colonial peoples let
us not forget that we in this land, are still, without question, a semi-colonial people. We are fighting against the idea of colonization too. Also in
relation to this, don't look at the oppression, look at that potential, that
great potential power. Our people know what it means to fight for freedom.
I walk on the streets every day and I tell you my people come up and say,
"Paul, stay in there, we know you're right, we know you're right." Somebody's
got to be there with the people, someone whom people can trust has got to be
there to lead them. The people know what's going on. It won't do for the
Sampsons, the Grangers, and the Schuylers to be shouting about how good it is
for Negroes in the United States today; that they're doing fine, you know.
No, they won't get away with that. Somewhere they're not doing fine, but we
got to see to it that they do do fine. (Applause)

     We talk about fighting for FEPC, fighting against poll tax or stopping
the filibuster. Do you know this Council can get behind all these drives.
They're shadow-boxing right now on the Senate floor, trying to get rid of
filibuster. Well, you can see that they do get rid of filibuster. Suppose
there was an anti-polltax, anti-lynch bill, you know what could happen down
in Mississippi and down in South Carolina, down in Georgia and Alabama and
those places? There could be other Senators sitting there, you know. (Audience
says "right" at that point, applause and laughter) There could be other representatives, you know, from those regions, as like in the days of Reconstruction. There were Negro representatives from those States; you know Mr.
Rankin couldn't get along with them. It would have to be some different kind
of a fellow to go along. (Laughter) So that the whole picture could change,
so that when one talks about struggles of Negro people, the struggle for
liberation, I see it not as isolating one Negro leader here, one Negro leader
there, one woman there, one man there. It's a concept of realizing that all
of us are struggling for our freedom; under the same pressures, looking for
freedom and some day if we are looking right, you'll see the whole thing
move--the whole thing--four million, five million, six million, seven million.
That's the kind of strength that our allies must see when something like the
labor councils are set up.

     To somewhere go into the Negro communities to win great sections, millions,
to the side of the common working class people for dignity and for a decent
life. I have--I can't tell you how proud I am to be with you tonight and to
wish you well. To forge this unity deep, so deep that nothing can ever just
even touch it a little bit let alone any chance of breaking it. I have great
confidence in these councils, in the working class movement of America, white
and black, to see that somewhere, in our time, this our time, we shall so labor
that our children and THEIR children shall work an American earth that we can
know and be proud is a democratic earth that WE have helped to build. (Applause,
ovation bursts into "We Shall Not Be Moved--Robeson is Our Leader, We Shall
Not be Moved")

Speech at convention of National Negro Labor Council, Cincinnati, Ohio,
October 27, 1951, *Daily World,* April 8, 1976.

                    62. THE NEGRO ARTIST LOOKS AHEAD

                            By Paul Robeson

     We are here today to work out ways and means of finding jobs for colored
actors and colored musicians, to see that the pictures and statues made by

colored painters and sculptors are sold, to see that the creations of Negro writers are made available to the vast American public. We are here to see that colored scientists and professionals are placed in leading schools and universities, to open opportunities for Negro technicians, to see that the way is open for colored lawyers to advance to workers who had come out on strike that Negro workers might get equal wages.

In the theater I felt this years ago and it would interest you to know that the opening night of *Othello* in New York, in Chicago, in San Francisco (I never told this to the Guild), I told Langner he could have just one third of the house for the elite. I played the opening night of *Othello* to the workers from Fur, from Maritime, from Local 65.

Just the other night I sang at the Rockland Palace in the Bronx, to this people's audience. We speak to them every night. To thousands. Somewhere, with the impetus coming from the arts, sciences and professions, there are literally millions of people in America who would come to hear us, the Negro artists. This can be very important. Marian Anderson, Roland Hayes, all of us started in the Baptist churches. I'm going right back there very soon. If you want to talk about audiences, I defy any opera singer to take those ball parks like Sister Tharpe or Mahalia Jackson. It is so in the Hungarian communities (I was singing to the Hungarian-Americans yesterday), the Russian-Americans, the Czech-Americans . . . all of them have their audiences stretching throughout this land.[224]

The progressive core of these audiences could provide a tremendous base for the future, a tremendous base for our common activity and a necessary base in the struggle for peace. These people must be won. We can win them through our cultural contributions. We could involve millions of people in the struggle for peace and for a decent world.

But, the final point. This cannot be done unless we as artists have the deepest respect for these people. When we say that we are people's artists, we must mean that. I mean it very deeply. Because, you know, the people created our art in the first place.

Haydn with his folk songs--the people made it up in the first place. The language of Shakespeare--this was the creation of the English-speaking people; the language of Pushkin, the creation of the Russian people, of the Russian peasants. That is where it came from--a little dressed up with some big words now and then which can be broken down into very simple images.

So, in the end, the culture with which we deal comes from the people. We have an obligation to take it back to the people, to make them understand that in fighting for their cultural heritage they fight for peace. They fight for their own rights, for the rights of the Negro people, for the rights of all in this great land. All of this is dependent so much upon our understanding the power of this people, the power of the Negro people, the power of the masses of America, of a world where we can all walk in complete dignity.

Masses and Mainstream (January 1952): 7-14.

63.   THE BATTLEGROUND IS HERE

Officers and Members of the Council--Friends:

It's good, so good, to be here--to enjoy once again the brotherhood and sisterhood of this great body of Negro working men and women, to share with you the dream of freedom, to plan with you for its achievenemt not in some distance but *now, today.*

I have been in many labor battles. It has seemed strange to some that, having attained some status and acclaim as an artist I should devote so much time and energy to the problems and struggles of working men and women.

To me, of course, it is not strange at all. I have simply tried never to forget the soil from which I spring.

Never to forget the rich but abused earth on the eastern coast of North Carolina where my father--not my grandfather--was a slave and where today many of my cousins and relatives still live in poverty and second-class citizenship.

Never to forget the days of my youth--struggling to get through school,
working in brick yards, in hotels, on docks and riverboats, battling prejudice
and proscription--inspired and guided forward by the simple yet grand dignity
of a father who was a real minister to the needs of his poor congregation in
small New Jersey churches, and an example of human goodness.

No, I can never forget 300-odd years of slavery and half-freedom; the
long weary and bitter years of degradation visited upon our mothers and sisters, the humiliation and Jim Crowing of a whole people. I will never forget
that the ultimate freedom--and the immediate progress of my people rest on
the sturdy backs and the unquenchable spirits of the coal miners, carpenters,
railroad workers, clerks, domestic workers, bricklayers, sharecroppers, steel
and auto workers, cooks, stewards and longshoremen, tenant farmers and tobacco
stemmers--the vast mass of Negro Americans from whom all talent and achievement
rise in the first place.

If it were not for the stirrings and the militant struggles among these
millions, a number of our so-called spokesmen with fancy jobs and appointments
would never be where they are. And I happen to know that some of them will
soon be looking around for something else to do. There's a change taking
place in the country, you know. My advice to some of this "top brass" leadership of ours would be: *You'd better get back with the Folks--if it's not
already too late.* I'm glad I never left them!

Yes, the faces and the tactics of the leaders may change every four years,
or two, or one, but the people go on forever. The people--beaten down today,
yet rising tomorrow; losing the road one minute but finding it the next; their
eyes always fixed on a star of true brotherhood, equality and dignity--*the
people* are the real guardians of our hopes and dreams.

That's why the mission of the Negro Labor Councils is an indispensable
one. You have set yourself the task of organizing the will-to-freedom of the
mass of our people--the workers in factory and farm--and hurling it against
the walls of oppression. In this great program you deserve--and I know you
will fight to win the support and cooperation of all other sections of Negro
life.

I was reading a book the other day in which the author used a phrase
which has stuck in my memory. He said, "We are living in the rapids of history" and you and I know how right he is. You and I know that for millions
all over this globe it's not going to be as long as it has been.

Yes, we are living "in the rapids of history" and a lot of folks are
afraid of being dashed on the rocks. But not us!

No, not us--and not 200 million Africans who have let the world know that
they are about to take back their native land and make it the world's garden
spot, which it can be.

In Kenya, Old John Bull has sent in his troops and tanks, and has said
Mau Mau has got to go. But Jomo Kenyatta, the leader of Kenya African Union,
with whom I sat many times in London, has answered back. He says, "Yes, someone has got to go, but in Kenya it sure won't be 6 million black Kenyans. I
think you know who'll be leaving and soon."[225]

And, in South Africa there'll be some changes made too. FREEDOM is a
hard won thing. And, any time seven thousand Africans and Indians fill the
jails of that unhappy land for sitting in "White Only" waiting rooms, for
tearing down jim crow signs like those which are seen everywhere in our South,
you know those folks are ready for FREEDOM. They are willing to pay the price.

The struggle in Africa has a special meaning to the National Negro Labor
Council and to every worker in this land, white as well as Negro. Today, it
was announced that the new Secretary of Defense will be Charles E. Wilson,
President of the General Motors Corporation. General Motors simply happens to
be one of the biggest investors in South Africa, along with Standard Oil,
Socony Vacuum, Kennecott Copper, the Ford Motor Company, and other giant
corporations.

You see, they are not satisfied in Alabama and Utah, auto workers in
Detroit and Atlanta, oil workers in Texas and New Jersey. They want super
duper profits at ten cents an hour wages, which they can get away with only if
the British Empire, in one case, or the Malan Fascists, in another, can keep
their iron heels on the black backs of our African brothers and sisters.

Now, I said more than three years ago that it would be unthinkable to me
that Negro youth from the United States should go thousands of miles away to
fight against their friends and on behalf of their enemies. You remember that

a great howl was raised in the land. And I remember, only the other day, in
the heat of the election campaign, that a group of Negro political figures
pledged *in advance* that our people would be prepared to fight any war any
time that the rulers of this nation should decide.

Well, I ask you again, should Negro youth take a gun in hand and join
with British soldiers in shooting down the brave people of Kenya?

I talked just the other day with Professor Z. K. Mathews, of South Africa,
a leader of the African National Congress, who is now in this country as
visiting professor at Union Theological Seminary in New York.

Professor Mathews' son is one of those arrested in Capetown for his defiance of unjust laws. I ask you, shall I send my son to South Africa to shoot
down Professor Mathews' son on behalf of Charles E. Wilson's General Motors
Corporation?

I say again, the proper battlefield for our youth and for all fighters
for a decent life, is here; in Alabama, Mississippi, and Georgia; is here,
in Cleveland, Chicago, and San Francisco; is in every city and at every
whistle stop in this land where the walls of Jim Crow still stand and need
somebody to tear them down.

Excerpts from an Address to the Annual Convention of the National Negro Labor
Council, November 21, 1952, at Cleveland, Ohio, Paul Robeson Archives, Berlin,
German Democratic Republic.

64. THE UAW SHOULD SET THE PACE

As a great organization of American workers, the United Auto Workers,
prepares for its convention in Atlantic City this month, my mind goes back
to many of the bitter labor battles which have made the union movement strong
and won some measure of security and dignity for millions of working men and
women.

Most precious of recollections is Cadillac Square, Detroit. It was my
privilege to stand there and sing to thousands of auto workers, massed in a
historic demonstration, as the CIO took over Ford's.

These struggles have given me great strength and confidence, and added
much to my understanding. I shall always consider it a major factor in the
course which I have taken that on returning to America from abroad in the
early days of the CIO, I plunged into the magnificent struggles of labor.

I had been prepared for this by my experiences abroad. In the Spanish
trenches I saw workers give their lives in a struggle to soften fascism and
maintain a popular democracy, only to be betrayed by U.S. big business interests who supported the butcher Franco--and still support him with the
official sanction of the U.S. government! Previously, in England, I had
held long sessions with leaders of the Labor Party, and had traveled all over
the British Isles, visiting with the Welsh miners, railwaymen, dock workers
and textile workers--sharing their griefs and little triumphs, learning their
songs, basking in the warmth of their generous friendship and hospitality.

I had learned, during these years, an important lesson: that the problems
of workers the world over are much the same and that eventually, they must all
find similar answers.

From the U.S. scene of the late Thirties and early Forties another lesson
became crystal clear: as the union movement grew in strength and numbers,
the fight for equal rights progressed apace. The organizing drives needed a
strong phalanx of support from the whole Negro community--the church, civic,
fraternal and social organizations--in short, all organized expressions of 15
million oppressed citizens. (It is not idle to recall these days how many
organizing committees, faced with goon squads, city officials who were flunkies
of Big Business, and a solid anti-union press, found sanctuary and their only
meeting places in the confines of the Negro church!)

And thousands of white workers began to understand for the first time that
in order to warrant the confidence placed in the labor movement by practically
the entire people, they had to fight to overcome the crimes that had been committed against Negro workers for generations. They couldn't fall for the old
"divide and rule" trick and succeed in their battles with the employers.

The union had to be for all workers or there would be--no union.

This was the spirit of the early days of CIO and it sorely needs reviving today. For labor faces a pitched battle, and the same sturdy alliance which brought CIO into being must be re-established and strengthened to preserve and extend its gains.

But the latest word is that Secretary of Labor Durkin is going to leave all decisions regarding Taft-Hartley up to Eisenhower--which means up to the billionaires who advise the president.

So far as Negroes are concerned there was a great Republican hue and cry before the elections that the General would treat everyone fairly, regardless of creed or color. But now there are anguished howls in our press because the White House has announced the appointment of secretaries, under-secretaries, assistant secretaries, ambassadors, bureau chief--and all the lush political plums are being allotted with not a Negro among them. The president has not even seen fit to continue the Truman practice of appointing a Negro to the United Nations delegation!

Yes, all signs point to the fact that labor's needs and Negro rights will be expendable in the new administration unless a popular, fighting movement of great proportions develops throughout the land.

Of course, labor wants more than Taft-Hartley repeal, though that is the key. It wants and needs a better social security system, wage increases now, a real housing program, a national health insurance plan, an end to the re-strictions on the right of free speech, and, most important, peace.

And Negroes' goals, of course, extend far beyond a few political appoint-ments. We want full equality--in work and play, in voting rights and school opportunities, in seeking private advancement and holding public office.

These are some of the reasons the UAW convention is so important. It can set the pace for the rest of labor. It can put new cement in the Negro-labor alliance by recognizing the rightful demands of its Negro members for long overdue places in its top councils of leadership; by stepping up the fight against job discrimination and for FEPC; by taking a forthright position on all questions affecting our struggle for equality in the nation; and, most important, by issuing a clarion call and taking steps to implement it, for a united labor drive to really organize the South.

That's a big order. But nothing less will do if the labor movement is to live up to its responsibilities to its own membership and to the nation. Know-ing thousands of rank and file members and a good section of the forward-looking leadership of this great union, I am confident they will not fail.

"Here's My Story," *Freedom,* March 1953.

65. FIGHT WE MUST

It is always an occasion of great importance to me to take part in the activities of the National Negro Labor Council. My mind goes back to your great conventions--Chicago last year; Cleveland in 1952; the founding conven-tion in Cincinnati in '51; and even before that the great gathering of trade unionists in Chicago in June of 1950 which gave birth to the idea of a mili-tant, mass organization of the Negro workers fighting courageously for their economic needs and for the rights of their entire people.

You said that this organization was called for because there was a crying need for somebody to pay consistent attention to the job problems of the breadwinners of our people. Somebody had to give *top priority* to the ques-tions of discrimination in employment, FEPC, growing joblessness, and the shameful spectacle--in this nation which boasts of leading the so-called "Free World"--of not only single plants, but whole industries which eliminate Negroes either altogether or from the skilled, better-paying jobs. It was time, you said, not only to talk about being the last hired and first fired--but to do something about it.

And who could do this job for the Negro workers better than Negro working men and women themselves? The answer was obvious then, and is just as obvious now: "Who would be free, *himself* must strike the blow."

Of course, you never sought to do the job alone. You knew that the initiative had to be yours, but you knew just as surely that your crusade had to involve thousands and eventually millions of others if it was going to succeed. And so you proclaimed a doctrine in Cincinnati that got right down to the heart of the matter, and that brought the delegates right up on their feet. You said, to paraphrase a slogan which has been the rule of your organizational existence, "We do not need or ask *anybody's permission* to fight for our own livelihood, our own security, our own lives, but we seek *everybody's cooperation.*"

You sought first of all the cooperation of the labor movement with its 15 million Negro and white workers in AFL, CIO and independent unions. And of equal importance, you sought the support and cooperation of the long-established organizations of Negro life--the church, our fraternal bodies, the NAACP, the Urban League and our business institutions.

And, realizing that cooperation is a two-way street, you offered the resources of your organization in support of those who were engaged on other fronts of the battle against Jim Crow. You could be counted on to join the mounting fight against segregation in education, housing, health, reaction-- in all phases of American life.

But all the while you have kept your big guns turned on the fundamental issue--jobs and economic security for our people. You have realized that it's on the production line that the whole ugly practice of segregation and discrimination bears its most bitter fruit; and that in the end the battle to lick Jim Crow in production will largely determine its fate everywhere else.

When the Dixiecrats decree that Negro and white children shall not go to school together they are preparing the ground for the day when they will not be allowed to work on the same machine together. When they decree that Negroes must ride in a hot, grimy railroad car--half baggage and half coach--while whites ride in air-conditioned comfort, they are setting the stage for public acceptance of the fact that Negroes can be porters and waiters--servants--on the railroads, but not engineers, conductors, trainmen and clerks.

Oh, yes, it's at the point of production and at the pay-window of the American economy that Jim Crow pays off for those who love it most. It pays off in $4.5 billion every year in super-profits for the monopolies, sweated out of the toil-worn bodies of Negro workers.

That is why, though I manage to keep busy with many responsibilities, I always feel a special urgency to do what I can to advance the program of the National Negro Labor Council. That is why I have said before, and repeat today, that whenever you call upon me for service I will be there, shoulder to shoulder with you, the finest sons and daughters of the Negro people and of the entire working population of this land.

That is precisely what I meant when, in 1947 at a concert in St. Louis, I announced that I would put aside my formal concert career for the time being to enter the day-to-day struggles of my people and the working masses of this country. I meant the struggle for our daily bread--such battles as I had been part of on the picket lines on the Mesabi iron ore range, with the auto workers in Cadillac Square, the gallant tobacco workers in Winston-Salem, the longshoremen, cooks and stewards in San Francisco, the furriers, electrical workers and a host of others.

No, of course. I'm not the only one who has recognized your importance and your potential. Among the first to pay tribute to you, in their own way, have been the traditional enemies of our people and of American democracy. They've complimented you by leveling against the NNLC and its leaders the most vicious and unprincipled attack.

Because you fight all-out for the rights of Negro workers they say you somehow endanger the nation's security. That's a lie.

Because you proclaim your solidarity with African and Asian workers and call for the independence of all colonial peoples they say you somehow betray our national interests. That's a lie.

Because you preach the truth--that the Negro's well-being is served by peace, not war, by building schools, homes, and roads, not guns, tanks and bombs--they say you lack patriotism. And that's a lie.

They would like to hound you out of business if possible--discredit your leaders, make you register with the so-called Subversive Activities Control Board, stop you from publishing literature, holding meetings, arousing the nation in support of your program.

They'd like to shut you up while Talmadge defies the Supreme Court on
segregated education and spouts his arrogance over nationwide radio and TV
hookups, and while a new rash of hate groups, including the recently formed
National Association for the Advancement of *White* People, flood the mails
with filthy "white supremacy" propaganda.

But here you are meeting today—a fighting, democratic organization,
determined that "just like the tree that's planted by the water, you shall
not be moved."

And while I know that nobody in this room has ever had any doubt but that
you'd be here, I think this is a fitting moment to say that the NNLC—despite
all the attacks, including a few from leaders of our own people who should
know better—despite the difficult times we've had, always with insufficient
money and often with little encouragement—despite all this the NNLC is needed
today more than ever, and our best days lie just ahead of us.

I think I know how great the need is. For I live in Harlem, and as I sit
in the parish house of my brother's church Mother AME Zion, and as I walk up
and down the avenues or visit with friends, the signs of hard times are everywhere. In New York State the production index has dropped 10 per cent in the
past year and unemployment insurance claims have steadily risen.

Even in so-called "good times" the vast majority of Negro workers live at
a bare subsistence level. Our family income is still—after all the economic
"progress" of the World War II period—just one-half the family income of
white workers. And when the firing starts Negroes—by statistical count—lose
their jobs twice as fast as anybody else.

What's true of New York is doubly true of the major industrial centers in
Pennsylvania, the Middle West and the West Coast. The president of the United
Steelworkers of America recently announced at their convention that one out of
every three steelworkers in the nation is either out of work or working part-
time. And it's difficult to pick up a newspaper without reading that a couple
of auto plants have merged and "merged" a few thousand workers out of jobs; or
that another company has "retooled" thousands more onto the breadlines.

It's enough that the Eisenhower administration started out by giving away
our national wealth in tideland oil, public power and tax concessions to the
monopolies, but when they start *taking away* our jobs and telling us that the
pain in our stomachs is not really hunger but imagination, then it's really
time for something drastic to be done.

I'm glad that you raised your voice with that of the labor movement, and
I know that you are unique in Negro life, in putting forward a comprehensive
anti-depression program to stem the downward trend of the economy and provide
jobs for the unemployed.

It seems to me that instead of giving the AFL a political lecture, as he
did at their convention, Secretary of Labor Mitchell ought to be forced to
say where he stands on the AFL proposal for a billion dollar appropriation for
building public schools as a part of the implementation of the Supreme Court
ruling against segregation.

And when it comes to housing—why we could use the 300,000 housing units
authorized annually in the administration bill among Negroes alone and we'd
still be in a terrible fix for a decent place to live.

Another way to fortify our economy against depression would be to open
the doors to two-way worldwide trade, which means specifically trade with
China, the Eastern European democracies, and the Soviet Union. But, oh no,
says our government, we don't like their politics. Well, I'm not here to say
we must like the politics of these nations, for that's not necessary for
normal commercial relations. But isn't it true that our government fosters
trade with fascist Spain and with Malan's South Africa. So if politics is to
be the yardstick in international trade it means that the U.S. government is
saying to 15,000,000 Negroes that it approves the politics of the most oppressive, racist dictatorship on the face of the globe today.

Of course, the embargo on trade with China, dictated by McCarthy, Knowland
and the China Lobby, is having an opposite effect from that intended. They
think that by embargoing China they will starve the government out and eventually
get the discredited Chiang Kai Shek off the little island of Taiwan (Formosa)
and back into business as an American puppet on the mainland.[226]

But China's trade and economy and well-being are constantly expanding.
Trade delegations are constantly going to and from Britain and many other Western nations, excluding only the United States among the great powers. And the

ones to feel the brunt of the policy are the American workers who, instead
of walking the streets in search of work, could be making the tractors, farm
implements, tools and structural steel which New China needs and is ready
to buy.

Of course, a comprehensive program for the economic welfare of Negroes
depends not only on fighting to hold on to what we have and to prevent unemployment. If that were the extent of our program we'd always remain at the
bottom rung of the ladder.

We must always be breaking new ground. And you couldn't have picked a
better place to break it than on the nation's railroads. Railroad men have
always played a big part in the life and legend of our people. John Henry
would certainly be proud to know that you are launching a campaign to guarantee that hiring will be color blind on the railroads which he and his fellow
workers built.

This campaign should stir Negro life and the nation as few crusades in
the past. Every Negro leader who has worked for awhile carrying bags or
waiting table while preparing for his career ought to lend the weight of his
prestige to your efforts. For instance, Dr. Ralph Bunche once worked on the
railroad to help pay his way through school. Now, as long as Negroes are
barred from the skilled trades in the industry the implication is plain that
the man who holds the highest position of any American in the United Nations
is unfit to collect tickets, or yell *All Aboard* or turn the throttle on an
American railroad--because he is a Negro.

I hope that Dr. Bunche and many other outstanding Negroes who at one
time labored in the dirty end of railroading will consider this an insult to
them personally as well as to their entire people and will throw their weight
behind the Council in this campaign.

But not only are there those who once worked on the roads. There are the
thousands of Negroes who work there now. They enjoy a highly respected position in our communities throughout the nation. Their activities touch on the
lives of the millions of our people. They are to be found in every church,
lodge, club and society. It is here that we must take our message, spread
our pamphlets and other literature, secure signatures for the petition to Vice
President Nixon and the Contract Compliance Committee. If this campaign is
taken to the bed rock of Negro life, to the heart of our organizational activities, there is no question in my mind but that we'll stir this nation, place
the railroad magnates on the spot where they belong, and wind up with some
Negroes driving trains as well as sweeping them, selling tickets as well as
buying them, giving orders as well as taking them.[227]

Fight we must, on this front and on many others if we are to restore and
expand this democracy of ours. I know we'll win and I intend to keep on
fighting until we do.

Speech at meeting of the National Council of the National Negro Labor Council,
Hotel Theresa, New York City, September 25, 1954, Paul Robeson Archives,
Berlin, German Democratic Republic.

THE AFL-CIO MERGER PROPOSED

66. LABOR LEADERS EXPRESS VIEWS ON THE PROPOSED MERGER

The hottest issue affecting the Negro in organized labor is the AFL's "invitation" for the CIO to return to the folds of the "House of Labor."

What makes the issue so hot is that the invitation was actually an ultimatum.

At its 70th convention in San Francisco in September, the AFL voted to extend the "invitation" to the CIO, its 36 national unions and 6,000,000 members to rejoin the senior federation from which it split off in 1935, but on the AFL's terms "or be raided."

"We'll give them (the CIO) a few months to make up their minds to come back into the AFL," one AFL national vice president is quoted as saying. "If they don't we'll go out and smash them."

The issue is of primary importance to Negro workers because under the CIO's non-discrimination policy they have made great gains as against the AFL's craft union closed shop policy where Negroes are barred from certain unions and in other instances are forced to join segregated locals.

Any change now or in the future, they fear, might affect their status as full-fledged union members.

The CIO's flat rejection of the offer was a bit of consolation, especially when Philip Murray, CIO president, made it clear that the CIO had no intention of being either swallowed up or carved up by the AFL craft union philosophy.

Murray's rejection of the AFL offer is also an outright challenge to the AFL.

It could, therefore, clear the way for a showdown of a 16-year rivalry between the two powerful labor federations that could result in bitter labor warfare, wild-cat strikes, full-fledged jurisdictional battles, industrial dislocations, even bloodshed and murder.

This could happen in 26 CIO unions which are in direct rivalry with the 109 AFL unions.

What would happen to the Negro workers involved in these battles, the CIO Negro members are asking. Will AFL segregated unions be pitted against mixed, non-segregated CIO unions? Would race hatred and prejudice flare up again?

Should the CIO be swallowed up by the AFL, either by force or merger, what would actually happen to the Negro now in the CIO? Will he be forced into the AFL's present pattern of the segregated craft union? Will he lose his CIO seniority and be deprived of the opportunity of training and advancement now guaranteed by the CIO? Will the AFL craft union-closed shop practice (the practice of insisting upon its own members being employed before other workers are considered) be rammed down their throats without any recourse?

To get the answers to these questions, the Defender took them to Philip Murray, CIO president; William Green, AFL president; Walter P. Reuther, president of the United Auto Workers and CIO vice president; Willard Townsend, president of the United Transport Service Employees union and CIO executive board member; A. Philip Randolph, president of the Brotherhood of Sleeping Car Porters, AFL; and Julius Thomas, industrial secretary of the National Urban League.

Philip Murray

Q.--Suppose there is a merger agreement which would involve the transfer of certain workers from a CIO union to an AFL union, would the CIO consent to such transfer if that AFL union has discriminatory practices?

A.--MURRAY--Absolutely not. We would absolutely not accept or work out any agreement with anybody that practices discrimination.

Q.--Would you, as president of the CIO, go on record as making an iron-clad commitment to the Negro and other minority members of the CIO that they would suffer no change in their status as full and equal members as a result of any merger agreement the CIO might make with the AFL?

A.--The only people I would not make that commitment to are the Communists. We do not intend in any discussions that may be had with the AFL or with any other group to forfeit the rights and privileges of any organization affiliated

with the CIO or any of its members. We want all of our members protected.
Q.--In an all powerful federation, would you favor the power lying in a
strong central body or with individual unions as now exist?
A.--With the unions, a strong central body would create a dictatorship.

William E. Green

The following two questions were asked in a telegram to the AFL president,
William E. Green.
(1) Should such a merger become effective, would Negro members in certain
CIO unions be subjected to transfer to other AFL unions which are regarded as
segregated?
(2) Would you go on record as assuring the Negro and other minority CIO
members that they would suffer no change in their status as full and equal
members of the AFL?
(3) In an all-powerful federation would you favor a strong central control policy or would the unions still be autonomous?
A.--GREEN--Our invitation to representatives of CIO means a meeting of
representatives of both organizations should be held for purpose of establishing organic unity. It does not provide that CIO organization shall be absorbed
and blended into AFL. However, all Negro workers who wish to become affiliated
with AFL may do so with uncompromising assurance that they will be extended
equal rights and will suffer no change in their status as full and equal members. AFL international unions affiliated with AFL would maintain their autonomous authority and exercise freedom of action on part of all members.

Walter R. Reuther

Q.--In the event of a merger agreement, will the CIO leaders make any
effort to protect the Negro members who might be swallowed by AFL segregated
unions?
A.--REUTHER--We are not willing to work out organic unity with the AFL on any
basis that would compromise the basic principles on which the CIO was founded.
One of these principles involves the acceptance into membership, with all
rights and privileges, workers without regard to race, creed, color or sex.
We would insist upon a clear understanding that these people would be
fully protected and applied as the basis for the united labor movement.

Willard Townsend

Should there be a death struggle between the CIO and AFL, what do you
think would happen to the Negroes now in the CIO?
A.--TOWNSEND--Such a struggle would never take place. The AFL has neither
the courage nor finance to launch an out-and-out fight against us.
Q.--If the AFL segregated unions are pitted against mixed, non-segregated
CIO unions with a much larger percentage of white members, do you think race
hatred and prejudice would flare up?
A.--That is actually going on now and has been going on while we were
organizing.
Q.--Are you in favor of the merger?
A.--No. Should there ever be a merger, the Negro would lose out. There
is still too much discrimination in the AFL for any merger to ever wipe it out.

Julius Thomas [228]

Q.--What do you think of a merger between the AFL and the CIO?
A.--THOMAS--I am against any merger of the CIO and AFL if it means the
return to any craft union concept of labor union organization. Union membership should not be a prerequisite to employment. I am not anti-union in any
form, but I am positively against any union which insists upon a closed shop.
It is my feeling that the Negro will be on the CIO side if it came to a
showdown. The AFL has long practiced and advocated separate segregated locals.
As far as I know the AFL has not done a thing about segregation and discrimination in its folds. Some of the locals still won't have or even consider a
Negro for membership. The AFL has not made even a feeble attempt to establish

a clear-cut policy in this respect.

Chicago Defender, November 24, 1951.

67. MEANY VOWS FIGHT ON BIAS WHEN LABOR'S RANKS UNITE[229]

AFL Head's Pledge Gets Backing of Reuther's Aide at Conference

By Stanley Levey

ATLANTIC CITY, Feb. 26--George Meany, president of the American Federation of
Labor, said today that the merged labor movement would not tolerate racial or
religious discrimination.

Mr. Meany, who will head the unified group to be formed by a merger of the
AFL and the Congress of Industrial Organizations, addressed the first session
of a two-day national trade union conference called by the Jewish Labor Committee. The committee represents 500,000 Jewish union members.

Acknowledging that bigotry and discrimination would not soon disappear,
Mr. Meany asserted that a "good trade union movement" could not exist except in
"an atmosphere of freedom." He called upon labor and the public to wage an
unremitting fight to "clean up the remaining small-minded spots."

Mr. Meany said the Bill of Rights was of great importance to trade unions,
and he developed the argument that the worker who remained unorganized because
of his race or religion posed a serious economic threat to organized wage earners.

As president of the merged labor federation Mr. Meany will be the leader of
more than 15,000,000 unionists. The new group which is expected to come into
being before the end of the year will have machinery, probably a civil rights
department--to fight discrimination within the ranks of labor, he said.

This theme also was taken up by Arthur J. Goldberg, general counsel of the
CIO Representing Walter Reuther, CIO president. Mr. Goldberg said a "united
labor movement can do much, much more than any of us have been able to do separately to win these battles."

Mr. Goldberg also seized the opportunity--without naming names--to assail
Michael J. Quill, president of the Transport Workers Union, CIO, for his opposition to merger. Mr. Quill has taken the position that the CIO should receive advance assurances against racketeering, raiding and racial discrimination before merging.

"I am aware," Mr. Goldberg said, "of some demagogue attacks upon this unity
agreement--attacks which question the good faith of the CIO, attacks which specifically mention the subject of civil rights and pretend that the labor movement
will retreat in this field because of the merger.

"Of course the record of unions in America is not perfect. The record of
the CIO is not perfect, though I would be proud to measure it alongside the
record of any other organization. Let me say to you that I know the leaders
of the AFL are just as sincere as are the leaders of the CIO in their desire to
eliminate any vestige of discrimination anywhere in the union movement of
America."

Mr. Meany hailed the Supreme Court decision on desegregation in public
schools as a "milestone in civil rights." And he urged that the states seeking
to avoid the law by "legal and technical device," be deprived of any Federal
aid to education. Mr. Meany disclosed that he had received a letter recently
from a member of the South Carolina State Senate urging him to "mind your own
business" on desegregation.

"I wrote him a courteous reply," Mr. Meany said, "more courteous than the
one he sent me. I told him public education was the AFL's business and had
been for seventy-five years."

The labor leader outlined what he called the "positive side" of the merger.
Instead of thinking about the evils to be eliminated, he said, we should have
in mind the objectives to be sought. These include, he said, "better housing,
better schools, an ever-rising standard of living, an ever better share of the
wealth, increased political activity and understanding, improved civil rights
and increased activity in the international field."

During the day's panel discussions both Charles Zimmerman, chairman of the conference, and Jacob T. Zukerman, president of the Workmen's Circle, a Jewish fraternal organization, attacked the committee in charge of celebrating the 300th anniversary of the Jewish community in New York.

The conference will close tomorrow with workshop meetings and a report on future activities.

New York Times, February 27, 1955.

NOTES AND INDEX

NOTES

1   For background on Norman Thomas, see Vol. VI, note 52.

2   For background on A. Philip Randolph, see Vol. V, note 111.

3   George Baldanzie (1907-1972) was born in Black Diamond, Pennsylvania.
He began working in local coal mines, but moved to Paterson, New Jersey
where he secured employment in a textile mill. He helped found and became
the first president of the Federation of Dyers (1933-1936), affiliated
with the United Textile Workers of America. Baldanzie became a leading
advocate in UTW for affiliation with the Congress of Industrial Organizations. He was elected president of the UTW-Textile Workers Organizing
Committee in 1938, and when it was reorganized into the Textile Workers
Union, he served as executive vice-president from 1939 to 1952. Baldanzie
also served on the CIO executive board. In 1952 he ran for the TWU presidency but lost, and was stripped of his offices.
    For background on Frank Crosswaith, see Vol. VI, pp. 215-16, 506,
note 135.
    For background on Howard Kester, see Vol. VI, note 142.
    Leo Krzycki (1881-1966), a native of Milwaukee, Wisconsin, became a
lithographer, and eventually rose to the office of general vice-president
(1904-1908). He was elected to several city offices on the Socialist
ticket before becoming an organizer for the Amalgamated Clothing Workers
of America in 1920, and then vice-president in 1922. In 1936, John L.
Lewis appointed Krzycki a CIO organizer in the rubber industry.
    John C. Lawson (1900-   ) was born in Aberdeen, Scotland, immigrated
to Vermont, and entered the stone quarries of Graniteville. For fifteen
years he served as local president of the United Stone and Allied Products
Workers of America before election to the union's executive board from
1930 to 1945. He was appointed USA-PWA international organizer in 1934,
and was elected secretary-treasurer.
    For background on Henry L. Mitchell, see Vol. VI, note 142.

4   For background on William Green, see Vol. VI, note 52. For background
on John L. Lewis, see Vol. VI, note 68 and note 126.

5   Warren Homer Martin (1902-1968) graduated from William Jewell College
in Missouri in 1928, and attended the Kansas City Baptist Theological
Seminary. He served as a pastor in 1931, but quit to take a job at a
Chevrolet plant in 1932. When he became local president of the AFL
affiliated United Automobile Workers in 1934, Martin was discharged so
he moved to Detroit. There he organized a UAW local and became its
president in 1936. He led the UAW into the CIO, but lost control of the
local in 1939, then led a small group of UAW members back to the AFL.
Martin left the union movement and became active in the Democratic Party
of Michigan. In 1961 he moved to Los Angeles where he died.
    Roy Wilkins (1901-1981) was born in St. Louis, Missouri, and graduated
from the University of Minnesota in 1923. He worked for the Kansas City
Call until 1931 when he became the assistant executive-secretary of the
NAACP. In 1934, Wilkins was appointed editor of The Crisis. When Walter
White (see note 16) died in 1955, Wilkins became executive-secretary of
the NAACP, a position he held until his retirement in 1977. As the head
of the NAACP, Wilkins served during the years of the modern civil rights
struggle, and he was a key leader in that effort. He received many honors
for his public service including the Presidential Medal of Freedom (1969).
    For the background on Benjamin J. Davis, Jr., see Vol. VI, note 123.

6   Henry Johnson's reminiscence was recorded by a Works Progress Admini-
ministration worker in 1937, and the transcript is in the WPA's "Negro
in Illinois" survey deposited at the George Cleveland Hall Branch of the
Chicago Public Library. Johnson was born in Siblo, Texas, and his father
was a logger, plasterer, and farmer who had been a member of the International Workers of the World. Henry Johnson followed a parapetetic life
living in numerous cities. He also worked at a number of jobs including
plasterer, bricklayer, singer, and union organizer. He even found time

to graduate from City College of New York (1934). In 1932, he began work as an organizer for the International Workers' Order, an organization founded by the Communist Party. He enlisted in the CIO drive to organize Chicago's steel industry in 1936, and in 1937 became an organizer for the CIO in meatpacking. Johnson also was active in the National Negro Congress who "loaned" him to the Steel Workers Organizing Committee (CIO) to organize in the mills of Gary, Indiana, in early 1937. By 1938, Johnson was assistant national director of the Packinghouse Organizing Committee.

7   The Scottsboro Case revealed the worst aspect of race relations in twentieth-century America. On March 31, 1931, nine black youths were indicted at Scottsboro, Alabama, for the alleged rape of two white women, Ruby Bates and Victoria Price. Eight of the boys (one escaped) were tried, convicted, and sentenced to death, although both women proved dubious plaintiffs and one later recanted her testimony. The trial became a cause célèbre for those who believed that the charges against the youths had not been proven, and that their convictions stemmed from racial prejudice. Defense efforts won the boys a retrial in which the death penalties were commuted, but sentences still ranged up to ninety-nine years. Eventually, all were freed. The ninth youth, who remained a fugitive for many years, finally surfaced in New York City and received a pardon in 1977.

8   Edward E. Cox (1880-1952) was born in Camilla, Georgia, graduated from Mercer University's law school in 1902, and served in the United States Congress from 1925 until his death.

9   The Farmer-Labor Party was formed in 1920 by members of the Progressive Party, and chiefly in the Midwest. Its membership was composed of farmers and laborers, as its name implied, who advocated public ownership of utilities, the establishment of government banks, farm relief measures, and progressive labor legislation. In 1924, it joined Robert La Follette's Progressive Party.

10   For background on Henry Ford, see Vol. VI, note 78.
The "Memorial Day Massacre" occurred on May 30, 1937. The Steel Workers Organizing Committee failed to gain recognition from Little Steel, composed of Republic Steel, Bethlehem, Inland and Youngstown Sheet and Tube, and 70,000 steel workers walked out on strike. Little Steel was led by Tom M. Girdler, president of Republic Steel. The bitterness of the 1937 strike was highlighted at Republic's South Chicago plant on May 30, when families of strikers were strolling across a field toward a meeting and were attacked by police. During the assault, ten strikers were shot (seven in the back) thirty were wounded and sixty required medical attention from the beatings they received.
"The Hearsts" refers to the Hearst family, whose fortune was founded in a newspaper chain. The Hearsts were ardently anti-labor.

11   For background James Weldon Johnson, see Vol. V, note 99.

12   The reference to Samuel Johnson's comment comes from James Boswell's recollection of a woman who, in referring to Johnson's dictionary, once asked the famous author "how he came to define *Pastern* the *knee* of a horse; instead of making an elaborate defence, as she expected, he at once answered, 'Ignorance, Madam, pure ignorance.'" See Boswell's *Life of Johnson*, G. B. Hill and L. F. Powell (eds.), 6 Vols. (Oxford, 1934-50), I, pp. 293.

13   "I.R.T." refers to the Inter-Regional Transit Authority.

14   Michael Joseph Quill (1905-1966) was born in Ireland, and immigrated to the United States in 1926. One of the founders of the Transport Workers Union of America (1934), Quill was elected president in 1935. He led the union into the CIO in 1937, and joined its executive board. Quill was active in New York City politics, serving several times as a city

councilman from the Bronx. A member of the American Labor Party. Quill resigned during the late 1940's, and led a reorganization of the New York CIO Council which eliminated Communist influence. In 1950, he became a CIO vice-president. Early in his career Quill was a Communist, but toward the end he became militantly anti-Communist.

15   For background on the Reverend Adam Clayton Powell, Sr., see Vol. VI, note 52.

16   Vito Marcantonio (1902-1954) was born in New York and graduated from New York University in 1925 with a degree in law. He was elected as a Republican to the United States Congress in 1935, but failed to gain reelection. From 1939 to 1951, however, he served in Congress as a member of the American Labor Party. In 1949, Marcantonio ran for mayor of New York, but lost, and served as president of International Labor Defense.

     Walter F. White (1893-1955) was born in Atlanta, Georgia. While his family was spared in the race riot of 1906, he always remembered the scenes of brutality against blacks. After graduation from Atlanta University, White did postgraduate work in economics and sociology at the College of the City of New York. After becoming assistant secretary of the NAACP, White played a leading role in investigating lynchings. When James Weldon Johnson (see Vol. V, n 99) resigned his post as executive-secretary of the NAACP in 1930, White replaced him, and remained in the post until his death.

17   The New Negro Alliance of Washington, D.C. was founded during the Great Depression to combat employment discrimination against blacks by white-owned businesses in the ghetto. Its motto was "Buy Where You Work--Buy Where You Clerk," and its primary weapon was the boycott. The Alliance's most noteworthy campaign in Washington was against Peoples Drug Store.

18   The Norris-La Guardia Act (1932) was the first attempt to erect safeguards against the misuse of the injunction in labor disputes. By forbidding injunctions which would sustain "yellow dog" contracts or prevent boycotts and picketing, the act was a major gain for organized labor.

19   Abram L. Harris (1899-1963), a native of Richmond, Virginia, graduated from Virginia Union University in 1922, and received an M.A. from the University of Pittsburgh in 1924. In 1931, he earned a Ph.D. in economics from Columbia University. Harris was an instructor at West Virginia State College before he went to the Minneapolis Urban League in 1925. He became a professor of economics at Howard University, head of the department in 1931, and spent the remainder of his career at Howard. His writings include, *The Black Worker* (with Sterling Spero) published in 1931, *The Negro as Capitalist* (1936), and *Economics and Social Reform* (1958).

20   For background on Booker T. Washington, see Vol. IV, note 8.

21   For background on W. E. B. Du Bois, see Vol. IV, note 136.

22   Alain Leroy Locke (1886-1954), was a native Philadelphian who attended Harvard University, where he was elected to Phi Beta Kappa. After graduation in 1907, he received a Rhodes Scholarship for two years of study at Oxford University. Returning to America in 1912, Locke became a professor at Howard University, and earned the Ph.D. from Harvard in 1918. Locke became chairman of the department of philosophy at Howard, where he remained until his retirement in 1953. Among his numerous works are *The New Negro* (1925), his most well-known contribution.

23   See Abram L. Harris, *The Negro As Capitalist; A Study of Banking and Business Among American Negroes* (Philadelphia, 1936).

24   For background on William Pickens, see Vol. V, note 64.

25   For background on Matthew Woll, see Vol. VI, note 72. For John P. Frey, see Vol. V, note 31.

26   A poll tax is levied upon a person rather than property, and although usually small, it is regressive in that it bears no relationship to ability to pay. Many southern states requirèd payment of a poll tax as a prerequisite to voting in order to discourage Negroes from exercising the franchise. In 1964 the Twenty-Fourth Amendment to the Constitution prohibited the poll tax in federal elections.

27   For background on Earl Browder, see Vol. VI, note 116.

28   Walter T. Hardin was born in Tennessee, moved to Johnstown, Pennsylvania, and joined the Industrial Workers of the World. He was active in the 1919 steel strike in Johnstown through the Amalgamated Association of Iron, Steel, and Tin Workers. Hardin became a Communist, and in 1929 moved to Pontiac, Michigan. During the 1930's, he was an organizer for the Auto Workers Union (Communist), and was a leader of the hunger marches and anti-eviction demonstrations in that city. Subsequently, he quit the party, and in 1937 became an organizer for the United Auto Workers-CIO.

29   "Fred Thomas" refers to Rolland J. Thomas (1900-1967). Born in East Palestine, Ohio, Thomas was forced to drop out of Wooster College to find employment. In 1923, he went to work for Fisher Body in Detroit, and in 1929 for Chrysler, also in Detroit. In 1930, Thomas was elected president of Local 7 of the United Automobile Workers. The following year he was elected UAW vice-president, and in 1939 was elected international president. During World War II, he served on several national boards, including the War Labor Board, and became a CIO vice-president. In 1946, Walter Reuther (see note 190) defeated Thomas for the UAW presidency, but Thomas was elected first vice-president. Following the AFL-CIO merger, he became an assistant to its president, George Meany (see note 229).

30   "Martin" refers to Warren Homer Martin (see note 5). "Hoover" refers to Herbert Hoover (see note 90). "Girdler" refers to Tom M. Girdler (see note 10).

31   Horace R. Cayton and George S. Mitchell, *Black Workers and the New Unions* (Chapel Hill, N.C., 1939).

32   For Paul Robeson, see pages 492, 587-612.

33   Willard S. Townsend (1895-1957) was born in Cincinnati, Ohio. An Afro-American, Townsend received a B.A. in Chemistry from the University of Toronto, and an LLB from the Blackstone College of Law in Chicago. He worked variously as a redcap, a dining-car waiter, a teacher, and again as a redcap in the 1930's. In 1936, he founded the AFL Labor Auxiliary of Redcaps in Chicago, and became its first president. He organized an independent Brotherhood of Redcaps in Chicago (1938), which was given an international charter by the CIO in 1942, and he became a member of the CIO executive board that year. In 1940, he was elected vice-president of the National Urban League. After the AFL-CIO merger in 1955, he was elected a vice-president and executive council member. Townsend also authored *What the Negro Wants* (1944), and *Full Employment and the Negro Workers* (1945).

34   Philip Murray (1886-1952) was born in Scotland, and entered the coal mines at age ten. After immigrating to the United States in 1902, and settling in western Pennsylvania, Murray became active in the United Mine Workers of America. He rose through the ranks to become a vice-president in 1919. Active in the CIO organizing drives of the late 1930s, he was appointed chairman of the Steel Workers Organizing Committee (1936-1942), and elected president of the CIO in 1940. Because of differences with John L. Lewis, Murray was expelled from the UMWA in 1942. He led strikes against the steel industry in 1946, 1949, and 1952.

Murray also served on numerous public commissions, and was a member of
the NAACP executive committee.

35   The "Green-Woll-Hutcheson Clique" refers to key figures in the AFL
leadership: William Green, president of the AFL (see Vol VI, note 52);
Matthew Woll of the AFL executive council, and one of the most conservative craft unionists (see Vol. VI, note 72); William L. Hutcheson (1874-
1953), long-time president of the United Brotherhood of Carpenters (1915-
1951), and opponent of CIO industrial unionism.

36   Adam Clayton Powell, Jr., was a minister, civil rights leader, and
controversial congressman from New York City. Born in New Haven, Connecticut, November 29, 1908, Powell graduated from Colgate University in 1930,
and became assistant pastor of his father's church in Harlem, where the
elder Powell had gathered the largest religious congregation in America.
When Harlem became a congressional district in 1944, Powell ran for office
as an independent and was elected to consecutive terms until 1967. He had
numerous legislative successes, especially in the field of equal employment opportunity. However, he often irritated members of Congress less
supportive of civil rights by his constant use of the so-called "Powell
amendment," a rider designed to make government color-blind when dispens-
ing government funds. In March 1967, the House of Representatives
stripped him of his seat because of a number of dubious practices, which
included making a European "junket" at government expense, ignoring a
court order, and a fifteen-year legal battle with the Internal Revenue
Service. The Supreme Court later declared the House action illegal and,
after a final losing bid for office in 1970, Powell retired to the
Bahamas, where he died of cancer on April 4, 1972.

37   "Green, Frey, and Wharton" are references to leading figures in the AFL:
William Green, president of the AFL (see Vol. VI, note 52), John P. Frey
(see Vol. V, note 31), and Arthur O. Wharton (1873-1944) who served as
president of the International Association of Machinists from 1926 to
1939. He was known as the AFL's "archpriest of craft exclusivism."

38   For background on William Z. Foster, see Vol. V, note 114.

39   For background on James W. Ford, see Vol. VI, note 115.

40   Benjamin Careathers, a black Communist who led hunger marchers that won
public relief for the unemployed, personally enrolled nearly 2,000 steel
workers in the Pittsburgh area, most of them blacks. He won public
praise from Philip Murray for unionizing the Jones-Laughlin steel mill
at Aliquippa.

41   William N. Jones, managing editor of the Baltimore *Afro-American,* one
of the leading Negro weeklies in the United States, was nominated as
William Z. Foster's vice-presidential running-mate on the 1932 Communist
Party ticket.
         For background on Lester Granger, see Vol. VI, note 115.

42   William J. Walls (b. 1885) received an A.B. degree from Livingstone
College in 1908, and a B.D. degree in 1913. A native of North Carolina,
between 1920 and 1924 he served as editor of the Charlotte *Star of Zion.*
He also became a bishop in the African Methodist Episcopal Zion Church,
and chairman of its board of publications. Bishop Walls was a member of
the President's American Clergymen's Committee, and served on the executive
board of the National Council of Churches of Christ in the United States.

43   For background on Robert L. Vann, see Vol. VI, note 59.

44   For background on T. Arnold Hill, see Vol. V, note 135.

45   For the definitive account of the campaign to make lynching a federal
crime, see Robert L. Zangrando, *The NAACP Crusade Against Lynching, 1909-
1950* (Philadelphia: Temple University Press, 1980).

46   For background on George S. Schuyler, see Vol. VI, note 7.

47   David J. McDonald (1902-   ), of Pittsburgh, Pennsylvania, entered the
steel mills at age fifteen. He became a secretary to Philip Murray (see
note 34) of the United Mine Workers. In 1936, Murray appointed him
secretary-treasurer of the Steel Workers Organizing Committee, and continued in that capacity after the United Steelworkers of America was
founded in 1942. He became president of USWA following Murray's death
in 1952, and in 1955 was elected a vice-president in the newly merged
AFL-CIO. In the 1960s, McDonald was criticized for being "soft" with
management, and in 1965 was unseated by I. W. Able.

48   For background on Brookwood Labor College, located at Katanah, New York,
see Vol. VI, note 129.

49   John Mitchell, Jr. (b. 1863) was born a slave in Henrico County, Virginia. In 1883-84 he worked as a reporter for the black newspaper, *The
Richmond Planet,* before assuming the position of editor and transformed
it into the leading black journal in the state.

50   Louis H. Redding, a Wilmington, Delaware attorney, was educated at
Brown University before receiving a law degree from Harvard University.
Redding was active in the NAACP, and in 1950 won *Parker V. University of
Delaware,* which obtained admission of blacks as undergraduates at the
University of Delaware. In 1954, he successfully argued the Delaware
cases on public school desegregation before the U.S. Supreme Court, which
were part of *Brown v. Board of Education,* invalidating racial segregation
in public education.

51   For the most authoritative analysis of blacks and the strike at Ford
Motor Company, see August Meier and Elliott Rudwick, *Black Detroit and
the Rise of the UAW* (New York, 1979).

52   George "Edmonds" refers to Edmunds, a black organizer for the United
Mine Workers of America. Between about 1910 and the early 1930s, Edmunds
served as an international representative of the UMWA. He was called
from retirement by CIO head, John L. Lewis, to work as an organizer for
the Steel Workers Organizing Committee.

53   See George W. Lee, *Beale Street: Where the Blues Began* (College Park,
Maryland, 1969, originally 1934).

54   Arthur W. Mitchell (1883-1968) was born in Chambers County Alabama,
attended Tuskegee Institute, Columbia University, and Harvard University.
An Afro-American, Mitchell taught school in Alabama and founded Armstrong
Agricultural School in West Butler, Alabama. In 1927, he began practicing
law in Washington, D.C., but moved his practice to Chicago in 1929. He
was a delegate to the Democratic Convention of 1936 and 1940, and was the
first black American to address a national convention. From 1935 to 1943
he served as a Democrat in the United States Congress.

55   Romare Bearden (1914-   ) was born in North Carolina, and graduated
from New York University. One of America's primier artists, Bearden
painted and then changed to a medium of collage and painting. He is
famous for his rendition of black ghetto life. Bearden first gained widespread recognition during the World War II Era with his mural of Negro
aspirations.

56   "Men like Gary, Schwab and Carnegie" refers to three of the most powerful steel magnates in the United States: Elbert H. Gary, and Charles M.
Schwab, both of whom were associated with the United States Steel Corporation, and Andrew Carnegie, who sold his own steel mills to U.S. Steel.

57   Noel Beddow was an attorney, and the chief compliance officer for the
National Recovery Administration in Alabama. He was appointed executive-
secretary of the Steel Workers Organizing Committee.

58   Luther Patrick (1894-1957) was born in Morgan County, Alabama, attended
        Louisiana State University, Purdue University, and in 1918 received a law
        degree from the University of Alabama. The author of numerous books of
        poetry, Patrick also worked as a radio commentator before entering politics.
        From 1937 to 1943 he served in the United States Congress as a Democratic
        representative of Alabama.

59   The American Liberty League (1934-1940) opposed what it regarded as the
        excesses of President Roosevelt's New Deal programs, particularly those
        related to labor. Among the leaders of this bipartisan organization were
        Jouett Shouse, John W. Davis, and Alfred E. Smith. Financial support
        came from wealthy industrialists, and although the League spent one mil-
        lion in a campaign against Roosevelt, his overwhelming election in 1936
        destroyed the organization.

60   Martin Dies served in Congress as a Texas Democrat from 1931 to 1945,
        and again from 1953 to 1959. Dies headed the House Un-American Activities
        Committee, which was formed as a temporary investigative committee in
        1938 to advance the career of the Texas congressman who served as its
        chairman. Dies was particularly active in his investigation of communist
        activity in the union movement. Like his more famous clone, Joseph
        McCarthy, Dies employed character assassination as a means for emphasizing
        his own "patriotism."

61   William A. Mitch (1881-   ), the son of an Ohio coal miner, entered the
        pits in 1894. He became involved in union work early, and served the
        United Mine Workers of America as a traveling auditor, then as secretary-
        treasurer of District 11 (Indiana) from 1915 to 1931. In 1933, Mitch
        reorganized District 20 (Alabama), along with William Dalrymple, and black
        UMWA organizer Walter Jones. He led a srike for union recognition in
        Alabama in 1934, and succeeded in gaining the dues check-off among ninety
        per cent of the operators. He served as president of District 20 from
        1933 until 1946, and as president of the Alabama State Federation of Labor
        from 1933 to 1937. In 1936, Mitch was appointed director of the southern
        region of the Steel Workers Organizing Committee, and then president of
        the Alabama State Industrial Union Council.

62   "Mellons and Rockefellers and Morgans" refers to three of America's most
        powerful financiers: Andrew W. Mellon, John D. Rockefeller, and John P.
        Morgan.

63   Joseph E. Curran (1906-   ) was born in New York, and in 1922 began
        his career as a seaman. He joined the International Seamen's Union in
        1935, and led a wildcat strike aboard the *S. S. California*. When the men
        were discharged, a protracted strike on the east coast led to the forma-
        tion of the National Maritime Union, a rival of the ISU. Curran was
        elected president of the NMU in 1937, and became a CIO vice-president in
        1941. After the AFL-CIO merger in 1955, Curran also served as a vice-
        president of the organization and as a member of the executive board.
        He retired as president of the NMU in 1973.

64   "Faruseth" is a misspelling of Andrew Furuseth.
        The Morro Castle disaster of September 1934, was a mysterious tragedy
        at sea which took 135 lives. The cruise ship *Morro Castle* was homebound
        fromHavana, Cuba, to New York. On September 7, the captain died of a
        heart failure, and shortly thereafter a fire of unknown origin was dis-
        covered. The acting captain, William Warms, failed to order a slower
        speed and heavy winds fanned the flames. An SOS was not ordered until
        the radio cabin was engulfed in flames. What followed was a demonstration
        of poorly trained seamen and officers. Fortunately, the ship was only
        six miles from the New Jersey coast. Convictions of the ship's officers
        for negligence eventually were overturned in a higher court.

65   Sir William Schwenck Gilbert (1836-1911) and Sir Arthur Seymour Sullivan
        (1842-1900) were a writer-musical composer team who created numerous light
        operas, including "H.M.S. Pinafore" (1878), "The Pirates of Penzance"

(1879), "The Mikado" (1885). They are known as the "Savoy Operas" because most of them were produced at the Savoy Theatre in London.

66   See Upton Sinclair, *The Jungle*, (New York, 1905).

67   Lillian Gaskins was a black woman of Harlem who was active in organizing
the dressmakers, and who served as a delegate on the International Ladies'
Garment Workers' Union executive board.
For background on Ashley Totten, see Vol. VI, note 43.

68   For background on William Pickens, see Vol. V, note 64.
Max Yergan (1894-) was born in Raleigh, North Carolina, graduated
from Shaw University (1914), and in 1916 entered service with the international Young Men's Christian Association. His work took him abroad to
India, South America, and the Middle East. Most of his service was in
Africa, however, and from 1937 to 1948, Yergan served as director of
the Council on African Affairs. During this period he also served a term
as president of the National Negro Congress. He received numerous awards
for social service, including the Harmon Award (1928) for his work in
South Africa, and the Spingarn Medal (1933), also for service in South
Africa.

69   Ferdinand C. Smith was a black Communist from Jamaica who helped found
the National Maritime Union, and became its first secretary and vice-
president. He was branded an "undesirable alien" by the Truman administration during the "red baiting" of the early 1950s. In August 1951,
he chose to leave the United States and return to his native land of
Jamaica.

70   For background on Frederick Douglass, see Vol. I, notes 8, 12 and 21;
on Nat Turner, see Vol. I, note 2; on Denmark Vesey, see Vol. I, note 2;
on Soujourner Truth, see Vol. II, note 86.
Gabriel Prosser planned a slave revolt in Virginia to be launched on
August 30, 1800. Over 1,000 slaves amassed about six miles from Richmond
for the march on the city, but a violent storm scattered the rebels, and
Governor James Monroe quickly sent in 600 troops. Scores of slaves were
arrested, and thirty-five were executed, including Gabriel Prosser himself.
Harriet Tubman, fugitive slave and abolitionist, became a legendary
figure on the Underground Railroad. Born to slave parents in Maryland,
probably in 1821, she made her escape to freedom about 1849, by following
the north star. Throughout the 1850s, she made repeated journeys into
slave territory to lead other fugitives, including her parents, to freedom. Undoubtedly, one reason for the phenomenal success of her reported
300 journeys into slave states was the enforced rule of death to any
slave who turned back. Her exploits were known to most of the leading
abolitionists, including John Brown who sought her counsel for the
Harper's Ferry raid in 1859. When the Civil War began, she served as an
army cook and nurse, and became a spy and guide for Union forays into
Maryland and Virginia. After the war, she managed a home for indigent
and aged Negroes until her death on March 10, 1913. Harriet Tubman was
buried with full military honors.

71   The "Townsend Plan" was introduced by Francis Everett Townsend (1867-
1960), a Long Beach, California, physician. It called for a $200 per month
pension to all persons over sixty. The funds were to be raised through a
sales tax, issued in script which had to be spent within a month.
Townsend's plan and organizational efforts resulted in a pressure group
estimated at nearly thirty million. After passage of the Social Security
Act (1935) the Townsend Plan lost its appeal.

72   Benito Mussolini (1883-1945) a former socialist and editor of *Avanti*,
turned Fascist in the 1920s and rose to become Dictator of Italy on
December 31, 1923. Siding with Adolph Hitler during World War II, he fell
from power as the Nazis withdrew from Italy. On July 25, 1943, he resigned
and was placed under arrest. On April 28, 1945, Mussolini was executed
by Italian anti-Fascist forces.

For background on Angelo Herndon, see Vol. VI, pp. 384, 490–503.

73   For background on Marcus Garvey, the "provisional president" of the Universal Negro Improvement Association, see Vol. VI, note 32.

74   Equal Rights probably refers to the National Equal Rights League, background on which may be found in Vol. VI, note 112. For the American Negro Labor Congress, see Vol. VI, pp. 436–45. For the referred to "Sanhedrin," see Vol. VI, note 18.

75   For background on Walter Winchell and Walter Lippman, see Vol. VI, note 113.

76   The National Movement for the Establishment of a Forty-Ninth State was an ideological offshoot of the black nationalist movement led by Marcus Garvey. Instead of a new state in Africa, however, it contemplated the creation of a separate (49th) state for Negroes within the United States. For Marcus Garvey, see Vol. VI, note 32.

77   Thomas Kennedy (1887–1963), son of a Pennsylvania coal miner, started work in the mines at twelve. He became the secretary-treasurer of his United Mine Workers local, and began a steady ascent in the organization. From 1910 to 1925, he served as District president in the anthracite fields, as UMWA international secretary-treasurer from 1925 to 1947, and then as international vice-president, 1947–1960. When John L. Lewis retired, Kennedy became president, but old and ill, he left the office in the hands of Tony Boyle. Kennedy served on many national boards, and was elected lieutenant-governor of Pennsylvania in 1934. He made a bid for the Democratic gubernatorial nomination in 1938, but was defeated.

78   Hugo L. Black (1886–1971) became a prominent Birmingham, Alabama, lawyer, and then served in the U.S. Senate (1927–1937), where he fought against big-business combinations and led the fight for passage of the Fair Labor Standards Act. President Franklin Roosevelt appointed him to the Supreme Court in 1937, where he continued to support strong social welfare and civil liberties legislation.

79   For background on Bishop Richard Allen, see Vol. I, note 2.

80   Charles H. Wesley (1891–   ), a native of Louisville, Kentucky, graduated from Fisk University before receiving his M.A. from Yale University in 1913. Subsequently, Wesley earned a Ph.D. from Harvard University (1925) and a D.D. from Wilberforce University (1928). He joined the Howard University history department in 1914 and served as its chairman from 1921 to 1942. He also served as executive director and as president of the Association for the Study of Negro Life and History. Wesley is the author of numerous books including *Negro Labor in the United States, 1850-1925*.
      Crystal Bird Fauset (d. March 28, 1965) was elected to the Pennsylvania House of Representatives in 1938. She was the first black woman elected to a state legislature in the United States.

81   For background on Mayor Fiorello La Guardia, see Vol. VI, note 52.

82   For the Thirteenth Amendment to the Constitution, see Vol. I, note 14. The Fourteenth Amendment became law in 1868. By far the most detailed of the three Civil War Amendments, it established Negro citizenship and denied the states the right to abridge citizenship privileges of blacks without "due process of the law." It was this clause which provided the basis on which the modern civil rights movement was founded.

83   For background on Richard B. Moore, see Vol. VI, note 60.

84   Rex Ingram, stage and film actor, played such roles as "De Lawd" in the film *The Green Pastures* (1936), and the Genie of the Lamp in *The Thief of Bagdad* (1940). Ingram was one of the few established black actors of the thirties and forties who could command a significant salary for his work.

85   Loren Miller's father was born a slave and eventually moved to Pender,
Nebraska, where Loren was born in 1903. He attended the University of
Kansas and Howard University, and received a law degree from Washburn
Law School. Miller practiced law in Los Angeles, and published the
California Eagle. A vice-president of the NAACP, he argued numerous
racial discrimination cases before the U.S. Supreme Court. See Loren
Miller, *The Petitioners: The Story of the Supreme Court of the United
States and the Negro* (New York, 1966).

86   Sterling A. Brown (1901-   ) was born in Washington, D.C. He graduated
from Williams College (1922) and received an M.A. from Harvard in 1923.
He taught at several universities and was professor of English at Howard
University. A prolific poet and author, his books include *Southern Road*
(1932), *The Negro in American Fiction* (1938), and *The Negro Caravan* (1941).

87   Ben Gold (1898-   ) was born in Russia and immigrated to the United
States in 1910. He joined the International Fur Workers Union in 1913
and was elected to the Furriers' Joint Board in 1919. For joining the
Communist faction in the union he was suspended from the union in 1924,
but was soon reinstated. From 1925 to 1929, he served as Manager of the
New York Furriers' Joint Board. After leading the general strike in 1926
he was expelled from the IFWU for being a Communist. He served as president of the Communist-organized Needle Trade Workers Industrial Union
after 1928, and in 1937 after the two unions merged, Gold was elected
president. In 1950, Gold resigned from the Communist Party, but was
indicted in 1954, nevertheless, and he gave up his position in the furriers' union.

88   Robert M. La Follette, Jr. (1895-1953) was born in Madison, Wisconsin,
and attended the University of Wisconsin. From 1919 to 1925 he was his
father's private secretary, served as vice-president of the Robert M.
La Follette (his father) and Burton K. Wheeler presidential campaign of
1924, and in 1925 was elected to the United States Senate to fill the
vacancy caused by the death of his father. He was reelected in 1928 and
served in the Senate until 1947.

89   John Brophy (1883-1963) was born in England, the son of a coal miner.
He immigrated with his family to Pennsylvania in 1892. At age twelve he
entered the mines, joined the United Mine Workers of America in 1899, and
became the union's leading advocate for nationalization of the coal industry. He became president of District 2 (Central Pennsylvania), and
when John L. Lewis abandoned the miners' strike of 1922, Brophy continued
the strike against the orders of Lewis. Along with other anti-Lewis
forces, he formed the Save the Union Committee which unsuccessfully supported Brophy against Lewis in the presidential election of 1926. After
a reconciliation with Lewis, Brophy was appointed UMWA organizer, 1933-
1935, and then national director of the CIO, 1935-1939. For a number of
years he organized steel and auto workers, and in 1951 became director of
the CIO's department of industrial union councils. Brophy retired in
1961.

90   "Chief G-Man Hoover" refers to John Edgar Hoover (1895-1972). He was
born in Washington, D.C., and graduated from George Washington University
in 1916. In 1924, he became the director of the Federal Bureau of Investigation, a position he retained until his death.

91   John Allen was a very effective black organizer for the STFU. He was
driven off the plantation where he was working in Eastern Arkansas. For
a time he worked in Missouri, and then went to Mississippi. In this
piece Allen escaped, but later on, in Mississippi, he was not so fortunate. His body was found in the Coldwater River, "shot to pieces." H. L.
Mitchell to Ronald L. Lewis, June 23, 1982.

92   Joseph T. Robinson (1872-1937), was born in Arkansas, attended the
University of Arkansas, and became a lawyer. He served in the state
legislature for several years before being elected to the United States

Congress from 1903 to 1913. In 1913 he was elected governor, but soon was sent to the United States Senate to fill a vacancy. Robinson served as a Democratic Senator until his death in 1937. In 1938, he was the vice-presidential candidate with Alfred E. Smith of New York, and under President Franklin Roosevelt he worked for New Deal legislation.

93   J. E. Clayton was a graduate of Prairie View Agricultural College for Negroes in Texas. He was a minister and taught in the segregated schools of Texas. After World War I, he acted as an agent for several railroad companies for selling right-of-way land to black farmers. Consequently, he was widely known and respected by whites and blacks throughout the western states. He was more than a fast talking promoter, however, for he worked assiduously for a better life for southern blacks, and that is what brought him to be an organizer for the STFU. Apparently, Clayton was a spellbinding speaker with powerful connections. He was an early supporter of Lyndon B. Johnson, and confident of Texas senator Tom Connally, and at the founding of the United Nations following World War II, Clayton acquired credentials to represent labor at the meeting. H. L. Mitchell to Ronald L. Lewis, September 4, 22, 1982. See also, H. L. Mitchell, *Mean Things Happening in This Land* (Montclair, N.J., 1979), pp. 183-84.

94   Frank O. Lowden (1861-1943) was born in Minnesota, graduated from the State University of Iowa, and Union College of Law in Chicago. He married the daughter of industrialist George Pullman, and himself acquired a fortune as the director of various corporations. He served as United States congressman from Illinois from 1906 to 1911, and in 1916, was elected governor of Illinois. He made a strong stand against the pacifists and socialists during World War I, and in the "Red Scare" of 1919-1920. When Lowden and General Leonard Wood tied for the Republican presidential nomination, Warren G. Harding won the nod.

95   Gunnar Myrdal, *An American Dilemma* (New York, 1944), p. 475.

96   Sidney Hillman (1887-1946) was born in Russia, but immigrated to the United States in 1907 and entered the garment industry. He led a group opposed to the United Garment Workers Union, and became the first president of the new Amalgamated Clothing Workers of America. He served on several New Deal labor advisory boards. One of the early supporters of the CIO, Hillman was elected first vice-president in 1937, and served as chairman of the Textile Workers Organizing Committee. During World War II he was associated director general of the Office of Production Management, and served as a member of the War Production Board.

97   For background on Emmett J. Scott, see Vol. V, p. 228.

98   For Eugene Talmadge, see note 103.

99   Earl B. Dickerson was born in Canton, Mississippi, in 1891. After receiving his B.A. degree at the University of Illinois (1914), he earned a law degree from the University of Chicago (1920). He served as an alderman in Chicago, was appointed to the President's Committee on Fair Employment Practice (1941-43), and served as a director and president of the National Lawyers Guild.

100   Revels Cayton was a black official of the National Union of Marine Cooks and Stewards. He served as business agent for the union on the West Coast and as a trustee of the Marine Federation.

101   Gerald L. K. Smith (1898-1976) was born and raised in Wisconsin, attended Valparaiso and Butler Universities in Indiana, and at age 19, became a minister in the Disciples of Christ Church. In 1928, he was invited to lead a church in Shreveport, Louisiana. There, he met Huey Long and worked as a social reformer and union organizer. When Long was elected governor, Smith became his aide. Following Long's assassination in 1935, Smith was forced to leave Louisiana, and became a political conservative.

He became an ardent opponent of President Roosevelt's New Deal, and was
an associate of Father Coughlin. In 1942, Smith founded his racist, pro-
fascist paper *The Cross and the Flag,* which was listed by the U.S. Attorney General as seditious. He also organized the America First Party,
which ran him for President in 1944. Following World War II, he founded
the Christian National Crusade to further his dream of a "White, Christian
America by the deportation of Jews, and by shipping blacks to Africa.
For background on Father Charles E. Coughlin, see Vol. VI, note 93.

102   Frank Porter Graham (1886-1972) was educated at the University of North
Carolina, and at Columbia, Chicago, and London Universities. He returned
to his alma mater and served as professor of history from 1915 to 1930,
when he assumed the presidency of the University of North Carolina. He
held that position until 1949 when he was appointed to the U.S. Senate.
Graham failed to gain the nomination of his party in 1950. A liberal
activist, Graham was interested in education, race relations, civil
liberties, and peace. President Truman appointed him to the Committee on
Civil Rights in 1946.

103   Eugene Talmadge (1884-1946), a native of Georgia, graduated from the
University of Georgia law school and practiced law. A flamboyant politician after the demagogical mold, Talmadge served three terms as Georgia's
commissioner of agriculture, and was elected to four terms as governor
(1932, 1934, 1940, 1946). He used the Ku Klux Klan as a mechanism for
achieving and retaining political power, and he used that power to keep
blacks locked into their caste status, and to break strikes in the textile
industry. "Cracker" was a term applied to poor southern whites, but came
to connote a white racist.

104   The "Pepper Poll tax bill" refers to the effort of Claude D. Pepper
(1900-   ), a Democratic U.S. Senator from Florida, to end the use of
poll taxes as a requirement for voting. A liberal New Deal Democrat,
Pepper was constantly at odds with other southern members of Congress
and the Senate.

105   Rayford W. Logan (1897-   ) was born in Washington, D.C. He graduated
from Williams College in 1917, and earned M.A. (1932) and Ph.D. (1936)
degrees from Harvard University. Logan taught at Virginia Union University and Atlanta University before taking a position at Howard University
as professor of history and dean of the graduate school. He authored
many articles and books, including *The Negro in the United States* (1957).
       Layle Lane was a black socialist school teacher, and pioneer in New York
teacher unionism.

106   John E. Rankin (1882-1960) received a law degree from the University of
Mississippi in 1910, and entered state Democratic politics. He served in
the United States Congress from 1921 to 1953.
       Theodore G. Bilbo (1877-1947) attended Peabody College, Vanderbilt
University law school, and the University of Michigan. He taught in the
high schools of Mississippi for several years before he was admitted to
the bar in 1908. He entered politics and served in the State senate
(1908-1912), as lieutenant governor (1912-1916), and as governor (1916-
1920, 1928-1932). In 1934 he was elected to the United States Senate
where he served until his death.
       For background on Eugene Talmadge, see note 103.
       For background on Edward E. Cox, see note 8.
       Ellison D. ("Cotton Ed") Smith (1866-1944) of South Carolina, graduated
from Wofford College in 1889, and served in the State legislature (1896-
1900). He was engaged in the cotton business, and was one of the principa
figures in the organization of the Southern Cotton Association in 1905.
He served as a general organizer in the cotton protective movement (1905-
1908). In 1908, he was first elected as a Democrat to the United States
Senate where he continued to serve until his death.
       Allen J. Ellender (b. 1890), a native of Louisiana, received a law
degree from Tulane University in 1913, and served in a variety of politica
positions in the state, including house floor leader (1928-1932) and
speaker (1932-1936). In 1936, he was elected to the United States Senate,

and continued to hold that position until the mid-seventies.

Thomas T. Connally (1877-1963) graduated from Baylor University (1896), and received a law degree from the University of Texas in 1898. After serving in numerous elective posts in Texas, he was elected to the United States Congress in 1917 and served until 1929. In 1928, Connally was elected to the United States Senate, and served in that capacity until 1953 when he retired to a private legal practice.

Hatton W. Sumners (1875-1962) of Texas, was admitted to the bar in 1897, and practiced law in Dallas until 1913 when he began a long career in the United States Congress, serving until 1947.

For background on Martin Dies, see note 60.

Joe Starnes (1895-1962), a native of Alabama, taught school and served in World War I before taking a law degree from the University of Alabama in 1921. He practiced law and served in state political offices until 1935 when he became a congressman, and served until 1945.

Carter Glass (1858-1946), of Lynchburg, Virginia, was a reporter, city editor, and then owner of the *Lynchburg Daily News* and of the *Daily Advance*. He served in various state offices, and in 1902 became a member of Congress, serving until 1918 when he was appointed Secretary of the Treasury by President Woodrow Wilson. He resigned in 1920 to become a United States Senator, a position he held until his death.

Howard W. Smith (1883-   ) graduated from the University of Virginia law school in 1903, and for many years served in the state courts. From 1931 until 1967 he served in each succeeding Congress.

For background on Patrick Henry, see Vol. IV, note 82.

For background on Crispus Attucks, see Vol. VI, note 85.

107   "VE-Day," refers to May 8, 1945, Victory-in-Europe Day. It followed the unconditional surrender of the German armies on May 7, making the end of World War II in Europe.

108   James F. Byrnes (1879-1972) was born in Charleston, South Carolina, read law, and became a lawyer in 1903. He practiced law, and published the Aiken (S.C.) *Journal and Review*. Byrnes entered politics and served in the United States Congress from 1911 to 1925. He was an unsuccessful candidate for the Senate in 1924, but was elected in 1930, and reelected in 1936. President Franklin Roosevelt appointed him to the Supreme Court in 1941, but in October 1942, Byrnes resigned to head the War Mobilization Board (1943-1945). President Harry Truman appointed him Secretary of State in 1945, and he served until 1947. From 1950 to 1955, Byrnes served as governor of South Carolina.

109   "VJ-Day" refers to August 15, 1945, Victory-in-Japan Day. It followed the unconditional surrender of Japan on August 14, marking the end of World War II in the Pacific.

110   Harvey W. Brown (1883-1956) became a machinist apprentice in 1900, and joined the International Association of Machinists. He served in various offices of the IAM, including Wilkes-Barre local agent (1911-1915), international organizer (1915-1916), and IAM vice-president in 1921. In 1938 and 1939, Brown served as acting president of the IAM, and then president, 1940-1948. He also was elected as AFL vice-president in 1941. Brown withdrew the IAM from the AFL because of jurisdictional disputes with the carpenters and operating engineers. In 1948, the IAM was forced to remove the racial exclusion clause from the ritual. Possessed of a bellicose style of leadership, Brown was constantly embroiled in conflict within the union and without.

111   David Sarnoff, president of the Radio Corporation of America, and a Jew, "balanced" the first group appointed to the Fair Employment Practices Committee in 1941. The first committee was made up of: Mark Ethridge, publisher of the *Louisville Courier Journal*, Chairman; Philip Murray, president of the CIO; William Green, president of the AFL; Milton P. W. Webster, black vice-president of the Brotherhood of Sleeping Car Porters; Earl B. Dickerson, Negro attorney and member of the Chicago City Council; and David Sarnoff.

112   Will W. Alexander 1884-1956), a Methodist minister, became an expert
on southern race relations and a leading southern spokesman for liberal
racial policies. In 1917, he helped create the Commission on Interracial
Cooperation and served as its director until 1944. Alexander also helped
to establish Dillard University and served as its president from 1931 to
1935. As vice-president of the Rosenwald Fund he assisted many promising
young blacks by providing fellowships for advanced study. As assistant
administrator of the Resettlement Administration and as administrator of
the Farm Security Administration, he helped to shape New Deal farm tenan-
cy legislation and policy. During World War II he served as a consultant
to several federal agencies on race relations.

113   Boris Shiskin was an economist and legislative consultant of the AFL
who protected the organization's interests on the Fair Employment Committee.

114   William H. Baldwin, Jr., was president of the Long Island Railroad, an
important figure in the Pennsylvania Railroad and the Southern Railroad
systems, and Booker T. Washington's closest white friend. Although he
did not live to witness the event, Baldwin was one of the whites who
assisted in founding the National Urban League. Like other Progressives,
he believed that it was the duty of the middle and upper classes to lead
the way toward development of the social institutions which would personal
development of individuals in modern society. It was the duty of these
classes to remove the needless barriers to Negro advancement as well.
Nevertheless, Baldwin believed that Anglo-Saxon standards were the bench-
mark to which the downtrodden blacks and immigrants should measure their
progress.

115   Wendell Lewis Willkie (1892-1944) graduated from Indiana University in
1913, and entered the legal profession. In 1933, he became president of
the Commonwealth and Southern Corporation with headquarters in New York.
Although he was a Democrat, Willkie's business and political connections
enabled him to win the Republican presidential nomination in 1940. Willkie
was not an isolationist, however. He supported President Roosevelt's
foreign policy, and outlined his own internationalist views in his book,
One World (1943). Nevertheless, he did oppose New Deal domestic legislation as too extravagant.

116   Monsignor Francis Joseph Haas (1889-1953) was born in Racine, Wisconsin,
was ordained a priest in the Roman Catholic Church in 1913, and earned a
Ph.D. in sociology (1922) at the Catholic University of America. In Milwaukee, he taught sociology at Marquette University, and in 1931 became
dean of the school of social service at Catholic University. Haas was
appointed a consultant to the National Recovery Administration and to the
Works Progress Administration after 1933 on the labor question. In 1943,
he became first chairman of the United States Committee on Fair Employment
Practices, and also was named bishop of Grand Rapids, Michigan. He wrote
extensively on social problems.

117   For background on the Missouri Compromise, see Vol. IV, note 81.

118   Dorie Miller (1919-1943) was born near Waco, Texas, the son of a sharecropper. He enlisted in the U.S. Navy and was serving as a messman aboard
ill-fated *Arizona* when the ship was sunk by Japanese aircraft during the
attack on Pearl Harbor, December 7, 1941. During the battle Miller manned
a machine gun and brought down four Japanese planes, for which he received
the Navy Cross. Miller was killed in action aboard the *Liscome Bay* in
December 1943.

119   Wayne L. Morse (1900-1974) was born in Madison, Wisconsin, and graduated
from the University of Wisconsin before taking law degrees at Minnesota
and Columbia Universities. From 1931 to 1944, he served as dean of the
law school at the University of Oregon, and became a leading authority
on labor arbitration. Morse served in the United States Senate from 1943
to 1969, during which time he was a fiercely independent legislator,

but supported labor legislation and opposed the Taft-Hartley Act (1947). His opposition to the war in Vietnam contributed to his defeat for re-election in 1968.

120   Mary T. Norton (1875-1959) was born in New Jersey and graduated from Packard Business College in New York (1896). Active in local Democratic circles, she was elected to the state Democratic committee in 1921, and was a delegate to numerous national conventions of the Democratic Party between 1924 and 1948. From 1925 to 1951 she served in the United States House of Representatives. In Congress she chaired the House Committee on Labor.

121   Malcolm Ross was named to chair the Fair Employment Practices Committee in 1943 when Monsignor Francis J. Haas (see note 116) resigned to become a bishop. Ross was Haas's deputy. During the late 1920s, and throughout the depression years of the thirties, Ross investigated the problems of the poor and wrote about them extensively. See for example, *Machine Age in the Hills* (New York, 1933).

122   Plummer B. Young, Sr. (b. 1884) was born in Littleton, North Carolina. In 1911, he founded the Guide Publishing Company, which became the black newspaper, *Norfolk Journal and Guide* (Norfolk, Virginia). Young was active in the politics of Virginia as a leading conservative black spokesman.

123   Sam T. Rayburn (1882-1961) graduated from East Texas Normal College (1903), studied law at the University of Texas, and became a lawyer in 1908. He was elected to the State house of representatives (1907-1913), and then to the United States House of Representatives from 1913 until his death. He was elected Speaker of the House in 1940, and retained that position for the duration of his career.

124   See Herbert R. Northrup, "Organized Labor and Negro Workers," *Journal of Political Economy*, 51 (June 1943): 206-21.

125   "P.T.C." refers to the Philadelphia Regional Transportation Company.

126   "TWU" refers to the Transport Workers Union.

127   The "P.R.T." Employers Union refers to the company union of the Philadelphia Regional Transportation Company.

128   Francis B. Biddle (1886-1968) was born into a prominent Philadelphia family, graduated from Harvard University (1909) and Harvard Law School (1911) before becoming a prominent corporation lawyer. He served occasionally as a special United States Attorney from 1922 to 1926, as chairman of the National Labor Relations Board in 1934-1935, and as council for the Tennessee Valley Authority in 1938. He was drawn to the New Deal, and President Roosevelt appointed him judge of the U.S. Court of Appeals in Philadelphia (1939), U.S. Solicitor General (1940), and U.S. Attorney General (1941). Following his resignation in 1945, he served on the international war crimes tribunal at Nuremburg, Germany, and in 1951 he was appointed to the Permanent Court of Arbitration at The Hague.

129   This list includes two of the greatest boxers of all time. Joe ("Brown Bomber") Louis (1914-1981) was born in Alabama and began boxing as an amateur. He won the heavyweight Golden Gloves title and, thereafter, turned professional. In 1937, he won the heavyweight crown by a knockout from Jimmy Braddock. During World War II, Louis volunteered for service in the Army. Louiw held the title until 1949 when he retired. He attempted an unsuccessful comeback, and retired in 1951.
        Ray ("Sugar Ray") Robinson (1921-   ) was born Walker Smith in Detroit, Michigan. Moving to New York when he was twelve, Sugar Ray entered amateur boxing as a teenager. Having won all 89 of his amateur bouts, and the 1939 Golden Gloves featherweight championship, Robinson turned professional in 1940. He was drafted into the Army during World War II

and toured Army bases with Joe Louis. He won the welterweight champion-
ship in 1946, and in 1951 took the middleweight crown. He is considered
one of the greatest all-round fighters in the history of the sport.

130   Ernest Calloway was a black coal miner and United Mine Workers of
America organizer in West Virginia and Kentucky. He was "on loan" to
the CIO as a SWOC organizer.

131   Dr. James J. McClendon presided over the Detroit NAACP during the late
1930s and early 1940s when the United Automobile Workers-CIO launched its
struggle to gain control over the workers at Ford Motor Company. Not
until 1939 did McClendon show the slightest interest in organized labor.
By then, however, sentiment on the NAACP board, and in the black community,
was tilting away from unquestioning support of Henry Ford, who for years
practiced a benevolent paternalism toward black workers to forestall
unionism. McClendon remained publically uncommitted until 1941, when,
with the support of the national executive director of the NAACP, Walter
White, he succumbed to pressures and came out for the UAW-CIO over the
UAW-AFL affiliate.

132   For background on Secretary of Labor Francis Perkins, see Vol. note 23.

133   Louis E. Martin was a graduate of the University of Michigan. In 1936,
he became the editor of the Michigan *Chronicle,* a weekly subsidiary of
the Chicago *Defender.* Martin became a staunch supporter of the United
Automobile Workers-CIO, to the chagrin of numerous black community leaders, and the Ford Motor Company.

134   Shelton Tappes, a black Ford employee who strongly supported the United
Automobile Workers-CIO, became chairman of the committee which was responsible for working out the first Ford contract, and which included an
anti-discrimination clause. Tappes became an important spokesman in the
black community of Detroit because of his union position. An active member of the left-wing in Local 600, Tappes, nevertheless, steadfastly
refused to join the Communist Party. This position eventually cost him
his position as recording-secretary.
       Veal Clough was a Ford foundry worker and plant committeeman for the
UAW-CIO. He was fired for his union activity, and became an organizer
for the UAW-CIO.

135   Van Amberg Bittner (1885-1949), the son of a Pennsylvania coal miner,
began working in the mines at age eleven, and at sixteen was elected
president of his United Mine Workers local. In 1908, he was elected vice-
president of District 5, and then president. He became a UMWA international representative, and because of his work in West Virginia, was
elected District 17 president. From 1933 to 1942 he served on the
Appalachian Coal Conference. Bittner became an organizer for the CIO in
the steel industry during the late 1930s. He resigned all union offices
after conflicts with John L. Lewis, and served as a labor advisor on
several governmental boards during World War II. After the war, Bittner
became director of the CIO's Southern Organization Drive.

136   Robert F. Wagner (1877-1953) was born in Germany, and immigrated with
his parents to New York in 1885. He graduated from the College of the
City of New York in 1898, and New York Law School in 1900. From 1905 to
1918, he served in the state legislature, and in other state positions,
including the New York Supreme Court from 1919 to 1926. Wagner served in
the United States Senate from 1926 to 1949.

137   The "Double V"" campaign of the *Pittsburgh Courier,* a major black newspaper, refers to the paper's campaign for a victory against the Nazis
abroad, and a victory against racism at home.

138   Horace R. Cayton (1903-   ) was born in Seattle, Washington. His
mother was the daughter of Hiram Revels, one of the two blacks elected to
the United States Senate during Reconstruction. He spent four years at
sea as a youth, and traveled widely. Afterward he graduated from the

University of Washington (1932), and became a research assistant in
sociology under Robert Park. Two years later he was appointed special
assistant to the U.S. Secretary of Interior. After a year of teaching
at Fisk University, Cayton became co-director of a research project
dealing with Chicago blacks (1936-1939), which became the embryo for his
major work, *Black Metropolis* (1945), co-authored with John Gibbs St.
Clair Drake, Jr. In 1939, he published with George S. Mitchell, *Black
Workers and the New Unions,* a model study of blacks and the union movement. Cayton also published his autobiography, *Long Old Road* (1965).

139   James Leary came up through the mines of Butte, Montana, to become
recording secretary of the Butte local of the International Union of
Mine, Mill and Smelter Workers (which grew out of the radical Western
Federation of Miners). In 1940, he won election as international secre-
tary-treasurer, and thereafter was in the forefront of the right-wing in
IUMMSW to purge the union of communist influence. This meant he fought
a running battle with his old friend, and president Reid Robinson.
Leary made an unsuccessful bid for the union presidency in 1946.

140   Oscar Noble (1914-   ) was born in Jacksonville, Florida, and moved
to Pontiac with his family during World War I. By age 21, Noble was a
machine operator for the Pontiac Motor Company. Because of his natural
ability to communicate, and gain the trust of both black and white workers,
Noble joined the UAW staff in 1937. He played an active role in organizing Pontiac, and in lining up support for the union in the black community. He represented Plant 6, where most of the workers were white,
on the bargaining committee.
     Victor Reuther (1912-   ), with his brother Walter Reuther (see note
190), played a pivotal role in organizing the United Automobile Workers
during the late 1930s. During World War II, he served as a representative
of labor on the War Manpower Commission. In 1946, he became the UAW's
education director, and in 1951 was appointed to head the CIO's European
office. From 1953 to 1955, he served as an administrative assistant to
the president of the CIO.

141   For background on the Trade Union Unity League (TUEL), see Vol. VI,
note 117.

142   Alfred McClung Lee and Norman D. Humphrey, *Race Riot* (New York, 1943).

143   Judge Ira W. Jayne was a devoted white contributor to the NAACP who also
recruited numerous other prominent whites into the Detroit branch.
     Herbert H. Lehman (1878-1963) was born in New York, graduated from
Williams College (1899), and became a partner in Lehman Bros., an investment firm. He was elected lieutenant governor of New York (1929-1932),
and then Governor (1933-1942). Lehman also served in several federal
capacities during World War II. After an unsuccessful bid for a Senate
seat in 1946, Lehman was elected as a Democrat to fill the unexpired term
of Senator Robert Wagner in 1949. He was reelected to a full term in
1950.

144   John J. Delaney (1878-1948) was born in New York, attended Manhattan
College, and graduated from the Brooklyn Law School of St. Lawrence
University in 1914. He was elected as a Democrat to fill an unexpired
term in the United State House of Representatives (1918-1919), but declined the renomination in order to pursue his business interests. He
was returned to Congress in 1931, however, and reelected to succeeding
congresses until his death.

145   The reference to "John" being shot on the picket line with Fanny Sellins
is probably an error. Sellins, a grandmother and widow who was an experienced organizer for the United Mine Workers in the tradition of
"Mother Jones," was on the picket line at a mine near Natrona, located on
the Allegheny River outside of Pittsburgh. Accounts differ, but she was
shot to death by a company guard. Dying with her from similar causes was
a coal miner named Joseph Strezelecki.

146   The "Four Freedoms" were enunciated by President Franklin D. Roosevelt in his annual message to Congress on January 6, 1941. They were: Lend-Lease for Americas allies; Freedom of Speech and expression; Freedom of Worship; Freedom from fear. These were "essential human freedoms" upon which the world should be organized.

147   For background on the "New Negro," see Vol. VI, note 84.

148   Gunnar Myrdal, *An American Dilemma,* (New York, 1944), p. 402.

149   "Unwelcome ghost of a dusky Banquo" refers to Banquo in Shakespeare's *Hamlet* who returns to haunt his friend's conscience in the way A. Philip Randolph returned to haunt the annual AFL conventions. For background on Randolph, see Vol. V, note 111.

150   For background on Milton P. Webster, see Vol. VI, note 44.

151   The Crosser-Dill Act (1934), or the Railway Labor Act, created a smaller mediation board than had existed, and established a thirty-six member Adjustment Board with members from labor and management. It gave employees the right to organize and bargain collectively.

152   For background on Rienzi B. Lemus, see Vol. VI, note 71.

153   John T. Clark (b. 1883) was born in Louisville, Kentucky, and graduated from Ohio State University in 1906. After teaching at a high school for several years, he became a field secretary for the National Urban League in New York (1916-1917). Thereafter, he served as executive secretary of the NUL in Pittsburgh (1917-1926), and then St. Louis (1926-1949). Also, he was elected 3rd vice-president of the National Conference of Social Work in 1940.

154   For background on Benjamin Tillman, see Vol. III, note 60.

155   John R. Commons, *Institutional Economics* (Madison, Wisc., 1934), was one of numerous books published by the eminent professor from the University of Wisconsin. In this book, Commons (1862-1944) helped change the focus of economics by aligning the discipline more closely with the social sciences. He was one of the founders of the modern field of labor history and labor studies.

156   For background on John Fitzpatrick, see Vol. VI, note 52.

157   For background on Cyril Briggs, see Vol. VI, note 106.

158   For background on Thomas J. Curtis, see Vol. VI, note 52.

159   Morris Feinstone (1878-1943), a native of Poland, immigrated to England and rose in the Woodcarver's union to become its president in 1895. He immigrated to the United States in 1910, settled in New York, and in 1926 became executive secretary of the United Hebrew Trades. Feinstone represented the UHT on the executive board of the Central Trades and Labor Council of Greater New York. Also, he was vice-chairman of the Jewish Labor Committee, publisher of the *Jewish Labor Forward*, and served on the boards of the Rand School and the *New Leader*. Feinstone was a leading advocate of the American Labor party.

160   For background on Bennie Smith, see Vol. VI, pp. 244-46 and index.

161   Daniel J. Tobin (1875-1955) was born in Ireland, and immigrated to the United States in 1890. He settled in Boston and began work as a teamster, joined the International Brotherhood of Teamsters, and rose to become its president in 1907. Tobin retained that position until 1952, and was elected a vice-president of the AFL from 1933 to 1952. In 1940, he served as an administrative assistant to President Franklin Roosevelt in 1940, and served on numerous government and labor organization boards.

162   For background on William D. Mahon, see Vol. IV, note 32.

163   Charles J. Mac Gowan (1887-1960), a native of Scotland, immigrated with
his family to Canada before moving to the United States in 1913. He served
an apprenticeship as a boilermaker, and after 1917 served the International
Brotherhood of Boilermakers in many capacities. In 1936, he was elected
vice-president of the IBB, and in 1944, was elected to the presidency.
Mac Gowan was elected a vice-president of the AFL in 1947, and in 1955,
of the AFL-CIO, a position he held until his death.

164   For background on Frank Duffy, see Vol. V, note 32.

165   Joseph P. Ryan (1884-1963) began work on the New York docks in 1912,
and became a full-time union professional in 1916. He was elected president of the Atlantic Coast District of the International Longshoremen's
Association in 1918, the same year he was elected vice-president of the
ILA. In 1927, Ryan was elected president of the ILA. He served as a
vice-president of the New York Federation of Labor between 1926 and 1946,
and as president of the Central Labor Council of Greater New York from
1928 to 1938. Ryan was elected president of the ILA for life in 1943,
but resigned from the ILA in 1953 after expulsion from the AFL on charges
of corruption. He was convicted of corruption in 1955, and received a
fine and a suspended jail sentence. The ILA became alienated from the
union movement during his years in office because of its domination by
gangsters, and because of Ryan's obsessive anti-communism.

166   "Mr. Morrison" refers to Frank Morrison. For background, see Vol. IV,
note 33.

167   Walter F. George (1878-1957) was born in Webster County, Georgia,
graduated from Mercer University with a law degree in 1901, and became a
judge of the state's superior court, and then court of appeals, from
1912 to 1917. He served on the Georgia supreme court from 1917 to 1922,
when he was elected to the United States Senate. Subsequently, George
was elected to the Senate until 1957. From 1955 to 1957 he served as
President pro tempre of the Senate, and was President Dwight Eisenhower's
special ambassador to the North Atlantic Treaty Organization.

168   Albert Thomas (1898-1966) was born in Nacogdoches, Texas, graduated
from Rice Institute (1920), and received a law degree from the University
of Texas (1926). After serving in several local public offices, he was
elected as a Democrat to the United States Congress from 1937 to 1966.

169   For background on the Kellogg-Briand Pact, see Vol. VI, note 51.

170   Haile Selassié (1892-1975), the Emperor of Ethiopia from 1930 to 1974,
assumed power in a coup, and changed his name from Tafari Makonnen to
Haile Selassie I. As absolute monarch, he outlawed slavery, and instituted other reforms. He was forced into exile in 1935 when the Italian
fascist dictator, Benito Mussolini, conquered Ethiopia. During World
War II, Ethiopia was liberated and Haile Selassie regained his throne.
Opposition to his rule increased, and in 1974 the army finally succeeded
in seizing control.

171   The white primary was one means by which blacks were disfranchised in
the South. Until 1940, state Democratic organizations, rather than the
states, determined voter eligibility at the polls. Thus, by limiting
party membership to whites only, blacks were effectively disfranchised.
After 1940, the system began to crumble, and by 1953 federal courts
ruled the white primary unconstitutional.

172   Richard J. Gray (1887-1966) was born in Albany, New York, where he
became a bricklayer, and subsequently was elected local president (1927)
of the Bricklayers, Masons and Plasterers International Union. Gray
rose in the organization to become international treasurer of the BMPIU
(1928-1936), and international secretary (1936-1946). An opponent of

industrial unionism, his intransigence further strained relations between the AFL and the Committee on Industrial Organization during the late 1930s. Gray became president of the building and construction trades union department of the AFL in 1946, but after the AFL-CIO merger in 1955, his abrasiveness with CIO leaders, along with his support of the McCarthy anti-Communist witchhunts, forced his resignation in 1960.

173   Alfred E. Smith (1873-1944) was a native of New York, where he entered politics at an early age, and rose through the ranks. He served in numerous local and state offices. While serving as president of the New York Board of Aldermen, he ran for governor (1918) and won. Smith was so popular that he was reelected three times. In 1928, Smith became the first Irish Catholic ever to receive the nomination of a major party to run for the presidency. He lost the race to Herbert Hoover, at least partly, because he was opposed to prohibition and was an urban "boss."

174   For his involvement in the Munich "Beer Hall Putch" of November 8-11, 1923, Adolph Hitler was arrested and imprisoned. The ill-advised attempt to overthrow the Bavarian government by the young leader of the growing National Socialist Party was easily crushed. While serving his term in prison, Hitler wrote *Mein Kampf,* a book which outlined his career, theories, and his program for revitalizing Germany.

175   For background on the Know-Nothing Party, see Vol. I, note 52.

176   Alexander Pushkin (1799-1837) was the first Russian poet to criticize the social order under Czarist rule. See, for example, *Boris Godunov* (1825), and *Kapitanskaia Dochka* (1832).
        Alexander Dumas (1802-1870), the French novelist, and playwright, is best known for his novels *The Three Musketeers* (1844), *The Count of Monte Cristo* (1844-1845), and *The Black Tulip* (1945).
        Both artists were to some degree Negroid in ancestry.

177   Hirohito (1901-   ) became emperor of Japan in 1926, succeeding his father Yoshihito. Apparently he opposed his nation's drift into World War II, but was powerless to oppose it. He is credited with influencing the decision to surrender to the Allies in 1945, which ended the war. The Constitution of 1946 stripped the emporer of all but his ceremonial powers.

178   For Crispus Attucks, see Vol. VI, note 85; for Wendell Phillips, see Vol. I, note 67; for Charles Sumner, see Vol. II, note 39.

179   Gustave M. Bugniazet (1878-1960), of New York, became an electrician, and served as local business manager of the International Brotherhood of Electrical Workers. He moved to Philadelphia, and was elected international vice-president in 1911, serving until 1925. Bugniazet served the union in various other capacities as well, and in 1925 became international secretary. He was elected a vice-president of the AFL in 1930, and held that position until 1946. He served on numerous AFL boards and committees, and was a member of the AFL committee which attempted to resolve the differences between the AFL and the CIO (1936-1937). In addition to acting as secretary of the IBEW benefit fund, Bugniazet edited *The Journal of Electrical Workers and Operators.*

180   Samuel Langhorne Clemens (Mark Twain), was born in 1835 in Hannibal, Missouri. He worked on Mississippi River boats for a number of years, and became a pilot. After the Civil War, success as a newspaper reporter led him into a lucrative career as a lecturer and novelist. His most famous are classics, *Tom Sawyer* (1876), *Life on the Mississippi* (1883), and *Huckleberry Finn* (1884). He died in 1910.
        The "dictator down in Washington, Mr. Vinson," refers to Frederick M. Vinson. See note 201.

181   Harry S. Truman (1884-1972), 33rd President of the United States (1945-1953), was born in Missouri, served in World War I, and ran a haberdashery.

He attended Kansas City School of Law (1923–1925), and entered Kansas
politics. Truman served as a county judge from 1926 to 1934, when he was
elected to the United States Senate (1935–1944). In 1944, he ran as
Franklin Roosevelt's vice-president, and when President Roosevelt died in
April 1945, Truman succeeded to the presidency. During the post-war years,
he instituted the Truman Doctrine and the Marshall Plan to deter the spread
of communism, and to facilitate the European economic recovery. Truman
was elected to a full term in 1948, even though he was opposed by southerners because of his civil rights program. Truman vetoed the Taft-Hartley
Act of 1947, but Congress overrode his veto. He declined to seek renomination in 1952, and retired from public life.

182   Jacob S. Potofsky (1894-   ) immigrated with his family from Russia to
the United States in 1905, and settled in Chicago. He entered work in a
men's clothing factory became active in the union movement and rose
through various local offices of the Amalgamated Clothing Workers of
America to become assistant general secretary-treasurer of the ACWA (1916–
1934). Having moved to New York, he became assistant president of the
ACWA in 1934, and became one of the original members of the CIO executive
board. From 1940 to 1946, Potofsky served as general secretary-treasurer
of the ACWA, and in 1946 was elected president of the union, an office he
held until 1972 when he retired. Potofsky served on numerous public boards,
including the Labor Management and Manpower Policy Committee of the Office
of Defense Mobilization.

183   Felix H. Knight (1876–1952) a native of Missouri, became a railroad
carman, and joined the St. Louis local of the Brotherhood of Railway
Carmen of America in 1902. After serving in numerous union offices, he was
appointed assistant general president of the BRCA in 1913, and held that
position until 1934. Knight was appointed general president of the union
in 1934, and was elected to the office the following year. In 1936, he
was elected an AFL vice-president. Knight resigned his union positions
when he retired in 1947.

184   George M. Harrison (1895–1968) was born in Missouri, and went to work
at various jobs for the Missouri Pacific Railroad from 1909 to 1917, when
he became chairman of the St. Louis local of the Brotherhood of Railway
and Steamship Clerks. From 1922 to 1925, Harrison served as a vice-president of the BRC, and in 1928 was elected grand president of the union.
He held that position until 1963, when he became chief executive officer,
and then president emeritus in 1965. During World War II, Knight served
on several important government boards, including the National Youth
Administration, the National Defense Mediation Board, and the President's
Council of Economic Advisors.

185   Robert Byron (1880–1959), a native of Scotland, immigrated to Springfield,
Illinois parents in 1888. He began his career as a sheet metal worker in
1897, and served in various local offices of the Sheet Metal Workers'
International Association until 1908, when he became an international representative for the SMWIA. In this capacity he traveled widely, and in
1939 became international president, a post he held until his death.
Byron also was vice-president of the AFL's building and metal trades
departments.
       Patrick V. McNamara (1894–1966) attended Fore River Apprentice School
in Massachusetts from 1912 to 1916, and learned the trade of pipefitter.
After moving to Detroit, he joined the United Association of Journeymen
and Apprentices of the Plumbing and Pipe Fitting Industry of the United
States and Canada, and was elected president of UA local 636 (Detroit).
McNamara held that position until 1954, as well as other local positions,
such as vice-president of the Detroit Federation of Labor (1939–1945),
and was a member of the Detroit Common Council (1946). In 1954, he was
elected as a Democrat to the United States Senate, where he was a co-
sponsor of the Labor-Management Reporting and Disclosing Act of 1959.

186   Clarence M. Mitchell (1911-   ), a native of Baltimore, Maryland,
graduated from Lincoln University and the University of Maryland Law School.

He served as the Director of the NAACP Washington Bureau from 1950 to
1978. He received the Spingarn Medal in 1969, and the Presidential Medal
of Freedom in 1980.

187   Charles Hamilton Houston (1895-1950) a Washington, D.C. lawyer who was
one of the principal architects of the NAACP legal approach against racial
discrimination. He devised the legal strategy for *Brown v. Board of Education of Topeka, Kansas* (1954) which led to the desegragation of public
education. He was also responsible for upgrading Howard University's
law school to one of national recognition.

188   "The Steele and Tunstall Cases" refers to *Steele v. Louisville & Nashville Railroad* (1944), *and Tunstall v. Locomotive Firemen* (1944). Both
cases involved discrimination against black railroad workers and represented important benchmarks in the law against racial discrimination.
Unfortunately, by the end of World War II blacks were nearly eliminated
from all but the menial jobs in the railroad industry.

189   For the case of James Tillman against the railroad brotherhoods and
the Frisco Railroad, see p. 543. A similar case involving the same line
was settled by the U.S. Supreme Court in *Brotherhood of Railway Trainmen
v. Howard* (1952).

190   Walter P. Reuther (1907-1970) was born in Wheeling, West Virginia, and
attended Wayne State University for three years. He moved to Detroit in
1926 after being discharged from Wheeling Steel Corp. for union activities.
He worked for Ford Motor Co., became a foreman in 1931, but again was discharged for union activism. He and his brother Victor (see note 140) em-
barked on a three-year world tour (1933-1935), and on his return became
an organizer for the United Automobile Workers. He became local 175
president in 1935, and was elected to the union's executive board in 1936.
Reuther rose in the union to become first vice-president of the UAW in
1942, and was elected president of the UAW in 1946. That year he was
elected a vice-president of the CIO, and became president of the CIO in
1951. After the AFL-CIO merger he served as president of its industrial
union department. In 1968, however, he led the UAW out of the AFL-CIO.
He was killed in a plane crash in 1970.

191   Felix Frankfurter (1882-1965) was born in Vienna, Austria, and immigrated to the United States in 1894. He graduated from Harvard Law
School in 1906, and after eight years in the profession, became a professor of law at Harvard (1914-39). During World War I he chaired the
War Labor Policies Board. A liberal on issues of civil rights and labor
questions, he helped establish the American Civil Liberties Union. President Franklin Roosevelt appointed him to the Supreme Court where he served
from 1939 to 1962. His writings include *The Case of Sacco and Vanzetti*
(1927), *The Labor Injunction* (1930), and *Law and Politics* (1939).
        William O. Douglas (1898-1980), was a professor of law at Yale Univer-
sity from 1928 to 1934. He was appointed to the Security and Exchange
Commission in 1934, and became its chairman from 1937 to 1939. President
Franklin Roosevelt appointed him to the Supreme Court in 1939, where he
remained until he retired in 1975. A consistent liberal, he set forth his
judicial ideas in *We the Judges* (1955), and *The Right of the People* (1958).
        Robert H. Jackson (1892-1954), an ardent New Deal supporter, was ap-
pointed U.S. Solicitor General (1938), U.S. Attorney General (1940), and
to the Supreme Court (1941). He authored two books, *The Supreme Court
in the American System of Government* (1955), and *The Struggle for
Judicial Supremacy* (1940).
        Harold H. Burton (1888-1964) was born in Jamaica Plain, Massachusetts,
graduated from Bowdoin College (1909), and received an LL.B. from Harvard
University in 1912. He moved to Ohio and was admitted to the bar in 1912
and practiced law in Cleveland. He served in numerous city and state
offices, including Mayor of Cleveland (1935-1940), until 1941 when he
was elected to the United States Senate. In 1945, Burton was appointed
to the United States Supreme Court, and served until he retired in 1958.

Tom C. Clark (1899-1988) was born in Dallas, Texas, received A.B. (1921) and LL.D. (1922) degrees from the University of Texas, and entered legal practice. He rose up through several public offices, and in 1943 became Assistant Attorney General of the United States in charge of the anti-trust division, and then the criminal division (1943-1945), Department of Justice. In 1945 he was appointed United States Attorney General, serving until 1949, when he was appointed to the Supreme Court (1949-1967).

192   Frederic Moore Vinson (1890-1953) was born in Kentucky. He served in Congress from 1923 to 1938, with the exception of one term. For a short period he served as a judge on the U.S. Court of Appeals for the District of Columbia, directed various federal agencies during World War II, and from 1945 to 1946 was President Franklin Roosevelt's Secretary of the Treasury. Roosevelt appointed him Chief Justice of the Supreme Court in 1946.

Stanley F. Reed (1884-1980) was born in Mason County, Kentucky, re-ceived an A.B. degree from Kentucky Wesleyan College (1902), and an A.B. degree from Yale University in 1906. After studying law at the University of Virginia, Reed became a member of the Kentucky bar in 1910 and prac-ticed in Maysville. From 1935 to 1938 he served as United States Soli-citor General and represented the U.S. before the Supreme Court. In 1938 he was appointed to the Supreme Court a position he held until his retirement in 1957.

Sherman Minton (1890-1965) was born in Georgetown, Indiana, received an LL.B. degree from Indiana University in 1915, and an LL.M. degree from Yale University in 1916. He practiced law in Indiana until 1935, when he was elected to the United States Senate (1935-1941). In 1941, Minton was appointed U.S. Circuit Judge (7th Circuit), a position he held until 1949, when he was appointed to the United States Supreme Court. He re-tired in 1956.

193   Joseph C. Waddy (1911-   ) was born in Virginia, and graduated from Lincoln University (1935) and Howard University Law School (1938). He practiced law in Washington, D.C. until 1962, when he was appointed judge on the municipal court. Waddy was a partner with Charles Houston (see note 187), and was active in several civil rights organizations.

194   For background on Ida B. Wells-Barnett, see Vol. V, notes 15 and 16.

195   Arthur J. Goldberg (1908-   ), a native of Chicago, received a law degree as editor of the *Illinois Law Review* (1929-1930). During the 1930s, Goldberg practiced law, and then became professor of law at John Marshall Law School (1939-1948). In 1948, Goldberg became general council for the CIO and the United Steelworkers of America, and played a major role in the negotiations which led to the AFL-CIO merger. President John Kennedy appointed Goldberg U.S. Secretary of Labor in 1961, and served until 1962 when he was appointed to the U.S. Supreme Court. In 1965 he was appointed U.S. Ambassador to the United Nations, returned to private prac-tice in 1968, and made an unsuccessful run for governor of New York in 1970.

196   Maurice E. Travis (1910-   ) was a business agent for the United Steel-workers of America in California until 1944, when he was purged for being a Communist. He then became an international representative for the Inter-national Union of Mine, Mill and Smelter Workers, and executive assistant to its president. In 1946 Travis was chosen vice-president, and that same year became president. His ascent caused friction between the left and right wings in IUMMSW, and he resigned the presidency in 1947. Charges that the union was dominated by Communists led to its expulsion from the CIO in 1950, even though Travis had resigned publically from the party in 1949. He was indicted in 1956 because of his Communist connections, and shortly thereafter retired from union work. In 1967 the case was dis-missed.

197   Asbury Howard was regional director of the International Mine, Mill and

Smelter Workers in Alabama and Mississippi, clerk of the Starlight Baptist Church in Bessemer, Alabama, president of the Bessemer branch of the NAACP, and president of the Bessemer Voters League, whose mission was to get blacks registered and to the polls on election day.

198   Paul Lawrence Dunbar (1872-1906) was born and attended high school in Dayton, Ohio. After graduation in 1891, he became an elevator operator and wrote poetry in his spare time. His first book of poetry *Oak and Ivy* (1893), was published at his own expense, as was his second. The best poems of these first two books were published in a third, *Lyrics of Lowly Life* (1896), which was a success. Dunbar was the first black American poet since Phillis Wheatley to win acclaim. Also, he was the first to use Negro dialect in the formal structure of his art. He died in 1906 from tuberculosis.

For background on the Negro poet James Langston Hughes, see Vol. VI, note 124.

199   Members of the United States House Committee on Un-American Activities represented here are:

John S. Wood (1885-1968), a native of Georgia, was a law graduate of Mercer University, and rose through state politics to become a United States Congressman from 1931 to 1935. After a decade of private practice, Wood was reelected to Congress from 1945 to 1953.

Charles E. Potter (1916-   ), a native of Michigan, graduated from Eastern Michigan University in 1938, and enlisted when World War II began. As a result of a serious wound he lost his legs. In 1947, he was elected as a Republican and served until 1952, when Potter was elected to the United States Senate. He remained in the Senate until 1959 when he failed to be reelected.

Henry M. Jackson (1912-   ) was born in Everett, Washington, attended Stanford University, and received a law degree from the University of Washington in 1935. In 1941, Jackson was elected to the United States House of Representatives where he served until 1953, when he was elected to the United States Senate. As of 1982, he still served in the Senate.

200   The Council on African Affairs was founded in 1937. Paul Robeson was co-founder and served as its chairman. Until 1955, the Council was the most significant American organization advocating African liberation from colonial rule. Its program called for assistance to the African masses; dissemination of accurate information about Africa; influencing governmental policies toward Africa which would promote liberation; to oppose imperialism; to stop the shipment of American arms to European powers for use in Africa; to strengthen the alliance between African and American progressives.

201   "Mr. Stalin" refers to Joseph V. Stalin who assumed power in the Soviet Union following the death of Lenin in 1924. His struggle for power lasted until 1926, when Stalin overcame the leftist opposition led by Leon Trotsky. Stalin ruled the Soviet Union until his death on March 5, 1953.

202   The Alien Registration Act (1940), also known as the Smith Act, strengthened the law governing the admission and deportation of aliens. Designed to check subversive activities, it made the advocacy of violent overthrow of the government illegal. Thus, any member of the Communist Party was guilty by association. Nevertheless, the Supreme Court upheld the law's constitutionality in 1951.

203   James H. McGrath (1903-1966), a native of Rhode Island, graduated from Providence College in 1936, and received a law degree from Boston University in 1948. He rose through the ranks of the Democratic Party, and was elected governor of Rhode Island from 1940 to 1945, when he was appointed United States Solicitor General. He resigned this post when he made a successful bid for the United States Senate in 1946. He resigned from the Senate to become President Harry Truman's Attorney General in 1949, a position he held until 1952.

204   Channing H. Tobias (1882-1961) was born in Augusta, Georgia, and
attended Paine College. He also attended Drew Theological Seminary and
the University of Pennsylvania. An ordained minister, he returned to
Paine College in 1911 and taught Biblical studies. He spent many years
working with the Y.M.C.A., and in 1943 joined the board of directors of
the NAACP, serving as chairman from 1953 to 1960. With Walter White
(see note 16) he helped organize the campaign "Free By '63." Tobias also
served as director of the Phelps-Stokes Foundation (1946), and President
Harry S. Truman appointed him to the Committee on Civil Rights (1954).
        Charles S. Zimmerman (1896-   ) immigrated from Russia to the United
States in 1913, and secured work in a New York garment factory. He
joined the International Ladies' Garment Workers' Union in 1916, and
served in various local union offices. During the 1920s, he was a member of the Communist Party, for which he was expelled from ILGWU in 1925,
but was reinstated in 1931. Zimmerman was elected a ILGWU vice-president
in 1934. He also served as head of the Trade Union Council of the American Labor Party, as a member of the National Council for a Permanent Fair
Employment Practices Commission, and as a chairman of the AFL-CIO civil
rights committee. When he retired in 1972, Zimmerman was general manager
of the ILGWU Dress Joint Council and New York Dress Joint Board.

205   Dwight David Eisenhower (1890-1969), 34th President of the United States
(1953-1961), was born in Denison, Texas, graduated from the United States
Military Academy (1915), and rose to become Supreme Commander of the
Allied Expeditionary Forces in Western Europe during World War II. After
the war, he became president of Columbia University (1948), and in 1951
served as Supreme Commander of NATO until 1952 when he resigned to run
for the presidency. He defeated Adlai E. Stevenson in 1952, and defeated
Stevenson again in 1956.

206   "McCarthyism" was the term applied to the hysterical search for communists who presumably had infiltrated the highest levels of the United
States government. Joseph R. McCarthy (1908-1956), a senator from
Wisconsin after 1947, publically charged that there 205 communists in the
State Department alone. McCarthy became chairman of the Senate investigating sub-committee, and in 1953 conducted televised hearings in which
he accused high officials of conspiracy. President Eisenhower denounced
him in 1954, and the Senate voted to censure McCarthy's conduct.

207   The McCarran-Walter Act of 1952 codified United States immigration laws,
retaining most of the earlier provisions of the 1924 act on maximum quotas
for various nationalities. It did remove the ban against immigration of
Asian and Pacific people, however.

208   Irving M. Ives (1896-1962), a native of New York, graduated from Hamilton College (1920), and after World War I entered the banking business
(1920-1930). From 1930 to 1946, he served in the New York State Assembly,
and in 1944-1945 as chairman of the New York State Temporary Commission
Against Discrimination. He was elected as a Republican to the United
States Senate in 1946, and again in 1952. In 1954, he made an unsuccessful bid for election as governor of New York.

209   Herbert Brownell, Jr. (1904-   ) was born in Peru, Nebraska, received
a B.A. from the University of Nebraska in 1924, and an LL.B. degree from
Yale University in 1927. He entered the practice of law in New York, and
served several terms in the state assembly. Brownell managed Thomas
Dewey's gubernatorial campaign in 1942, and his presidential bids in 1944,
and 1948. He became United States Attorney General in President Eisenhower's cabinet, serving from 1953 to 1958.

210   "Ben" refers to Benjamin Gold. See note 87.

211   Howard [Melvin] Fast (1914-   ) is a writer of historical fiction, some
of which relates to the labor movement. See, for example, *Power* (1963)
and *Clarkson* (1947). Fast was a member of the Communist Party from 1943

to 1956, during which time he won the Stalin International Peace Prize
(1953). Lee Pressman (1906-   ) was educated at Cornell and Harvard
before his admission to the New York bar in 1929. Specializing in labor
law, he became general counsel for the Steelworkers Organizing Committee
in 1936 and then general counsel for the United Steelworkers of America.
A member of the Communist Party, he was forced to resign his union position during the Cold War and was called to testify before the House Un-
American Activities Committee in 1950. He left the labor movement to
enter private practice in 1948.

212   Henry A. Wallace (1888-1965) was born into a family already distinguished
for government service. His father, Henry C. Wallace, was President
Harding's Secretary of Agriculture, although he died in office. Upon
graduation from Iowa State College (1910), Henry A. Wallace joined the
family periodical, *Wallace's Farmer,* the leading agricultural newspaper
in the nation. He became an authority on farm economics, and developed
several strains of hybrid corn. Wallace became President Franklin
Roosevelt's Secretary of Agriculture (1933-1940), and was elected vice-
president (1941-1945). He served President Truman briefly as Secretary
of Commerce (1945). In 1948, Wallace ran for the presidency on the
Progressive Party ticket.

213   John W. Snyder (1895-   ), a native of Arkansas, attended Vanderbilt
University before enlisting for World War I. He entered the banking
business after the war, and became an assistant to the Reconstruction
Finance Corporation from 1937 to 1943. In 1945, Snyder was appointed
Federal Loan Administrator, and that same year promoted to director of
war mobilization and reconversion. He joined President Truman's cabinet
as Secretary of the Treasury in 1946, and served until 1953.
       William Langer (1886-1959) was born in North Dakota, graduated from
law school at the University of North Dakota (1906), and from Columbia
University (1910). He became the attorney general of North Dakota (1916-
1920), and in 1932 was elected governor, but was removed from office by
the state supreme court. Nevertheless, Langer was reelected governor
in 1937 before being elected to the United States Senate in 1940, and
continued to serve in that office until his death.

214   Harry A. R. Bridges (1901-   ), a native of Australia, became a seaman
and then immigrated to the United States in 1920. He became an organizer
for the Industrial Workers of the World in 1921. After he gained work
as a longshoreman in San Francisco in 1922, Bridges began organizing for
the International Longshoremen's Association and between 1933 and 1935
helped edit *The Waterfront Worker.* He led the longshore strike of 1934,
and organized the International Longshoremen's and Warehousemen's Union,
composed of Pacific Coast ILA locals, which he then led into the CIO in
1937. In 1939 he began a ten-year battle with the U.S. government to
prevent his deportation. Finally, in 1949 he was convicted of perjury
for swearing that he was not a member of the Communist Party, and was
sentenced to a prison term, but in 1955 a higher court overturned the
lower court decision.

215   Joseph DiMaggio (1914-   ) was a professional baseball player who
spent most of his illustrious career with the New York Yankees.

216   Jack ("Jackie") Roosevelt Robinson (1919-1972) became the first black
professional baseball player to sign a major league contract when he was
signed by the Brooklyn Dodgers in 1946. He attended junior college and
then the University of California--Los Angeles before taking a commission
in the Army during World War II. Following an outstanding career in
baseball, Robinson enjoyed further success as a businessman, and as a
sports commentator and columnist.

217   "Voice of America," an international short-wave radio broadcast established by Congress in 1948, is known primarily for its programs beamed
behind the "iron curtain." In 1953, it became part of the U.S. Information Agency, and it continues to broadcast news of the "free world." In
effect, it is a propaganda vehicle operated by the U.S. government.

218   "Mr. Acheson" refers to Dean G. Acheson (1893-1971). He was born in
Middletown, Connecticut, received a B.A. from Yale in 1915, and an LL.B.
from Harvard in 1918. Acheson became a private secretary to Supreme Court
Justice Louis Brandeis, and then in 1921 joined a law firm. President
Franklin Roosevelt appointed him Undersecretary of the Treasury in 1933,
and served as Assistant Secretary of State from 1941 to 1945. From 1945
to 1947, Acheson served as Undersecretary of State, and in 1949 President
Harry Truman appointed him Secretary of State, a position he held until
1953. His most important contributions were the formation of the North
Atlantic Treaty Organization, implementation of the president's Point-
Four Program, and engineering the United Nations' intervention on behalf
of South Korea. Among his books are *Power and Diplomacy* (1958), and
Present at the Creation (1969).

219   The "Marshall Plan," formally the European Recovery Program, was inaugurated in 1947 to foster economic recovery for those countries outside
the Soviet orbit which were affected by the ravage of World War II.
Secretary of State George C. Marshall, for whom it was named, managed the
economic assistance program which cost the United States $12.5 billion
dollars. The program ceased to function in 1956.

220   The "betrayals of the Murrays and Greens, the Careys, Rieves and Dubin-
skys . . . the Townsends, the Weavers and Randolphs" refers to: Philip
Murray (see note 34); William Green (see Vol. VI, note 52); James B. Carey
(1911-1973), president of the United Electrical, Radio and Machine Workers
of America (1935-1965), one of the most progressive unions in the movement
on issues of race; Emil Rieves (1892-   ), president of the Textile
Workers Union of America (1939-1956), and then chairman of the TWU executive council (1956-1960); David Dubinsky (see Vol. VI, note 136);
Willard S. Townsend (see note 33); Robert C. Weaver (see Vol. VI, note
25); A. Philip Randolph (see Vol. V, note 111).

221   Fritz Pollard, Jr. (1915-   ) was the son of Frederick Pollard, an
all-American football player. By winning the hurdles at the 1936 Olympics,
Fritz became North Dakota's first black athlete to achieve fame. He was
also an outstanding football player.

222   Miranda Smith was a Negro leader of all-black local 22, Food, Tobacco,
Agricultural and Allied Workers Union-CIO, in Winston-Salem, North Carolina. She was active in the 1943 strike against R. J. Reynolds Tobacco
Company. Smith was a Communist and was forced onto the sidelines during
the post-war purges, but local 22 continued to exist. In 1949, Smith was
FTA Southern Regional Director, and, as a member of the union's national
executive board, occupied the highest position any black woman had held
to that time in the labor movement.

223   Jawaharlal Nehru was a founder of the Indian nationalist movement to
gain independence from Great Britain, which was achieved in August 1947.
Nehru became prime minister and established a position of neutrality
between the capitalist and Communist nations during the Cold War Era
following World War II. Nehru died suddenly on May 27, 1964.

224   Mahalia Jackson (1911-1972) was born in New Orleans, Louisiana, and in
the 1930s gradually emerged as the "Queen of Gospel Singers." She was
invited to sing at the White House by presidents Eisenhower and Kennedy.
    Rosetta ("Sister") Tharpe (1910-   ) was a jazz singer and musician
born in Cotton Plant, Arkansas. In her early years Sister Tharpe sang in
gospel choirs before turning to jazz. She performed with such notables
as Cab Calloway and Lucky Millinder, and made numerous recordings for
Decca.

225   "Old John Bull" is a perjorative reference to Great Britain which controlled the colony of Kenya, Africa, where a secret anti-white (i.e.
British) organization known as Mau Mau began the struggle for independence
in the early 1950s. Its leader, Jomo Kenyatta, an English educated Kenyan
of significant accomplishments, was imprisoned for nine years. Kenyatta
was released in August 1961, and in June 1963, he was sworn in as independ-

ent, Kenya's first prime minister.

226   McCarthy refers to Senator Joseph McCarthy of Wisconsin (see note 206).
      William F. Knowland (1908-   ) graduated from the University of Cali-
fornia at Berkeley in 1929, and engaged in newspaper publishing in Oakland, California. He rose through the state Republican Party, holding
numerous political posts, and in 1945 was appointed to the United States
Senate to fill a vacancy. He was elected to a full term in 1946, and
was reelected in 1952. From 1953 to 1955, he was Senate majority leader,
and from 1955 to 1959 Senate minority leader. In 1958, he waged an unsuccessful bid to become governof of California, and retired to private
life.
      Chiang K'ai-shek (1887-1975) led the Chinese Nationalist government
from 1928 until his death. Except for the period of the Sino-Japanese
War from 1937 to 1945, Chiang was engaged in constant warfare with the
Communists, who finally defeated him in 1949 and forced him to move the
Nationalist government from the mainland to the island of Taiwan.

227   "Vice president Nixon" refers to Richard M. Nixon (1913-   ). Born in
California, Nixon graduated from Whittier College in 1934, and from Duke
University Law School in 1937. After serving in the Navy during the war,
he was elected to Congress in 1946, and was reelected in 1948. In 1950,
he was elected to the United States Senate, where he served until 1953
when he became President Dwight Eisenhower's vice-president. Nixon served
in that capacity until 1961, and in 1960 made an unsuccessful bid for the
Presidency. He also was an unsuccessful candidate for governor of California in 1962. In 1968, however, he waged a successful campaign for President, and was reelected in 1972. His involvement in the Watergate Affair
forced his resignation, however.

228   Julius A. Thomas was the director of the National Urban League's
industrial-relations department.

229   George Meany (1894-1980), of New York, became a plumber in 1910, and
in 1922 was elected business agent for New York Local 463 of the United
Association of Plumbers and Steam Fitters. In 1932, Meany was elected a
vice-president of the New York State Federation of Labor, and president
from 1934 to 1939. He was elected AFL secretary-treasurer in 1939, and
became the first director of Labor's League for Political Education
(1948). Upon the death of William Green in 1952, Meany was appointed and
then won election as president of the AFL. After the AFL-CIO merger in
1955, he was elected president of the new organization, a position he
held until his death. An ardent anti-Communist during the 1950s, Meany
gained firm control over the AFL-CIO by crushing all opposition, and
exerted a powerful influence within the councils of the Democratic Party.